Oil Paintings in Public Ownership in Staffordshire

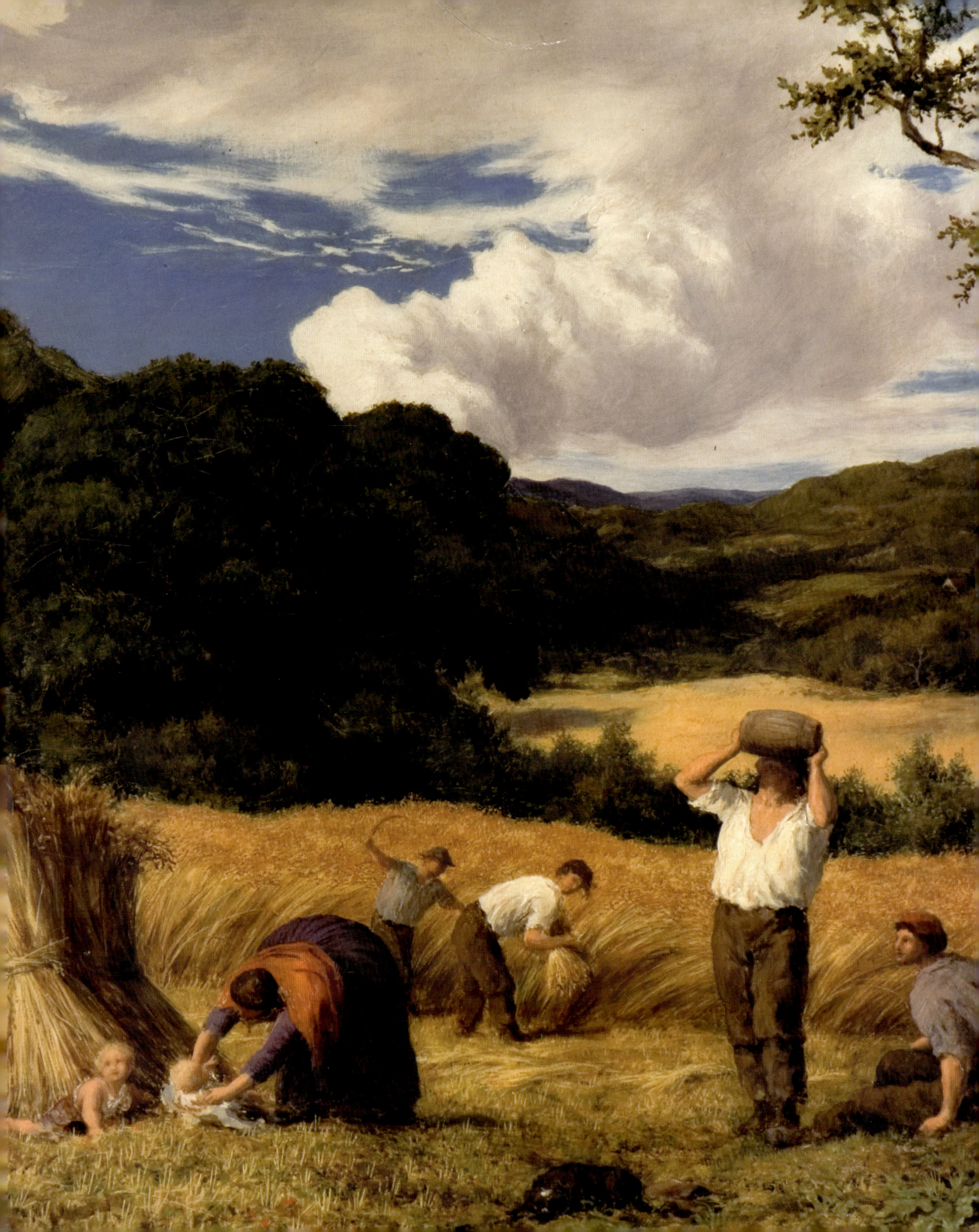

Oil Paintings in Public Ownership in Staffordshire

The Public Catalogue Foundation

Andrew Ellis, Director
Sonia Roe, Editor
Catherine Goodwin, Catalogue Coordinator
Robert Glowacki, Todd-White Art Photography

First published in 2007 by the Public Catalogue Foundation, St Vincent House, 30 Orange Street, London, WC2H 7HH

ISBN 1-904931-34-0 (hardback)
ISBN 1-904931-33-2 (paperback)

Staffordshire photography: Robert Glowacki, Todd-White Art Photography

Designed by Jeffery Design, London

Distributed by the Public Catalogue Foundation, St Vincent House, 30 Orange Street, London, WC2H 7HH
Telephone 020 7747 5936

Printed and bound in the UK by Butler & Tanner Ltd, Frome, Somerset

Cover image:

Bevan, Tony b.1951
The Meeting (detail), 1992
Wolverhampton Art Gallery (see p. 244)

Image opposite title page:

Linnell, William 1826–1906
Cornfield in Surrey (detail), 1860
Wolverhampton Art Gallery, (p. 295)

Back cover images (from top to bottom):

Tift, Andrew, b.1968
The Black-Country Steelworkers, 1992
The New Art Gallery Walsall, (see p.218)

Clarkson, Jack 1906–1986
Potteries View with Canal
Borough Museum & Art Gallery, (see p. 31)

Maclise, Daniel 1806–1870
Phoebe and Silvius in the Forest of Arden, from Shakespeare's 'As You Like It', 1853
The New Art Gallery Walsall (see p. 211)

Contents

* Biddulph Library is managed by Staffordshire County Council and Ingestre Hall Residential Arts Centre and Sandwell Museum Service Collection are administered by Sandwell Metropolitan Borough Council.

Following page: Caravaggio, Michelangelo Merisi da (after), 1571–1610, *St Anthony Abbot* (detail), The Potteries Museum & Art Gallery (p. 107)

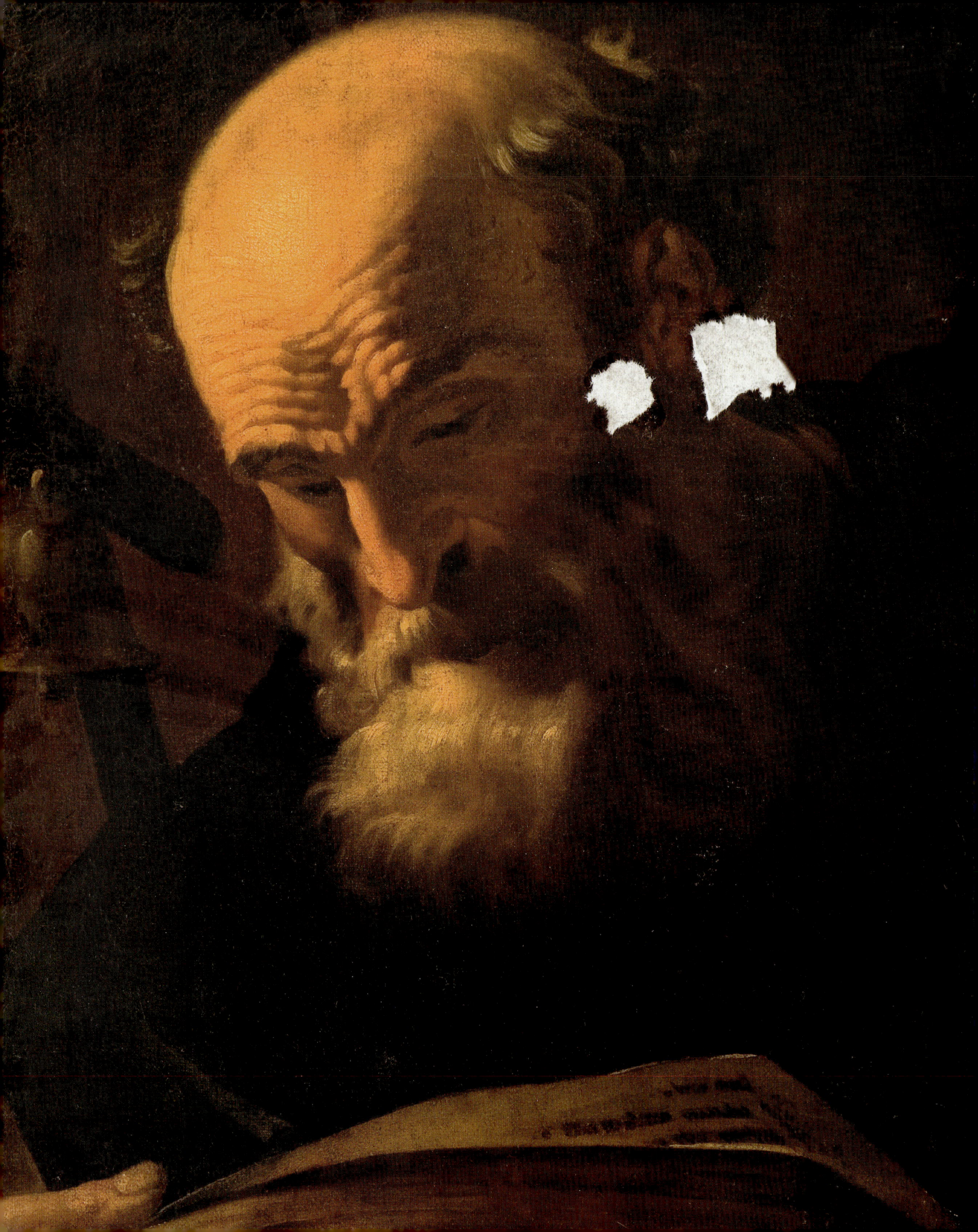

Foreword

Teaching in Ghana, shortly after Nkrumah had fallen I witnessed the first post-fall election. 'How do you feel about it?' I eagerly asked my university colleagues. 'Same thing different,' was their cynical refrain. I have a similar, but uncynical, reaction to this catalogue.

What is different is the size of Staffordshire – or its perceived size. For a man from Stoke, Wolverhampton seems to be as close as Rhyl is to Rangoon. That did not make fundraising easy. We made it, though, and our efforts were well repaid.

For, what is the same is that in yet another English county here is yet another breathtaking collection of paintings.

For portrait lovers, the small Staffordshire County Council collection offers a fascinating range, from the sixteenth century, running through Dicksee and Herkomer, Palin and Birley, to the present day. The Potteries museum in Stoke has an extraordinary wealth of essentially British Art in its stores: Ayrton, Clausen, Coldstream, Gilman and Ginner – through the alphabet to Carel Weight. There is a large collection of work by John Currie with a wonderful portrait of Mark Gertler who (like Currie) tragically took his own life. Wyndham Lewis, Nevinson, Dessau, a magnificent Lowry – they are all there. Then nip across to Wolverhampton Art Gallery for a staggering shipwreck by Francis Danby, a luscious swagger portrait of a Lady in Red by Alfred Egerton Cooper (a local man) or a magnificent prize bull by the reclusive Edmond Bristow. Compare that with the other prize bull paintings by Bretland, Brown, Verboeckhoven and Gauci in this catalogue and you may agree that, there is a fascinating book to be written on eighteenth and nineteenth century cattle portraits.

The lesson from all this becomes clearer and clearer. I try to visit the collections (and their stacks) covered in our catalogues before publication. Even so, I find increasingly that until I see the completed catalogue, I will have woefully underestimated the quality and range of work in the collections visited. So it happened in our recent Hampshire catalogue (with the Portsmouth Collection). It has happened to me again in Staffordshire with the Potteries collection. I am sure I am not alone in this reaction.

With this, our sixteenth catalogue in the series, no one can possibly doubt any longer the startling strength of the collection of oil paintings in public ownership in this country. The Foundation must urgently complete this series, not least to enable all those responsible to see and understand what we own and to work out how to care for it in future.

We are therefore, and as always, most grateful to those that have made this volume possible. Our leading financial supporters for this catalogue are the Charles Hayward Foundation and the Renaissance West Midlands Museum Hub. Renaissance West Midlands has generously committed to supporting all five of our proposed West Midlands catalogues. We are extremely grateful to the Hub and in particular to Jane Arthur.

On the ground in Staffordshire the work on the catalogue has been coordinated brilliantly by Katey Goodwin and the photography has been carried out by Robert Glowacki. A very big thank you to them both. Finally, allow me to extend the appreciation of the Public Catalogue Foundation to all the collections that have participated (in all cases) with such great enthusiasm.

Fred Hohler, Chairman

The Public Catalogue Foundation

The Public Catalogue Foundation is a registered charity. It is publishing a series of illustrated catalogues of all oil paintings in public ownership in the United Kingdom.

The rationale for this project is that whilst the United Kingdom holds in its public galleries and civic buildings arguably the greatest collection of oil paintings in the world, an alarming four in five of these are not on view. Furthermore, few collections have a complete photographic record of their paintings let alone a comprehensive illustrated catalogue. In short, what is publicly owned is not publicly accessible.

The Public Catalogue Foundation has three aims. First, it intends to create a complete record of the nation's collection of oil, tempera and acrylic paintings in public ownership. Second, it intends to make this accessible to the public through a series of affordable catalogues which will later go online. Finally, it aims to raise funds for the conservation and restoration of paintings in participating collections through the sale of catalogues by these collections.

Collections benefit substantially from the work of the Foundation not least from the digital images that are given to them for free following photography and the increased recognition that the catalogues bring. These substantial benefits come at no financial cost to the collections. The Foundation is funded by a combination of support from individuals, companies, the public sector and charitable trusts.

Financial Supporters

The Public Catalogue Foundation would like to express its profound appreciation to the following organisations and individuals who have made the publication of this catalogue possible and to our Master Patron who has led our fundraising campaign in this county.

Donations of £10,000 or more

The Charles Hayward Foundation
David E. D. Johnson
Renaissance West Midlands

Donations of £5,000 or more

The 29th May 1961 Charitable Trust
Aurelius Charitable Trust
The John S. Cohen Foundation
Stavros Niarchos Foundation

Donations of £1,000 or more

National Gallery Trust
P. F. Charitable Trust
The Pilgrim Trust
The Bernard Sunley Charitable Foundation
The Welton Foundation

Other Donations

Sir Patrick Cormack
Lord Stafford
Peter H. S. Kelley

National Supporters

The Bulldog Trust
The John S. Cohen Foundation
Marc Fitch Fund
National Gallery Trust
P. F. Charitable Trust
The Pilgrim Trust
Stavros Niarchos Foundation
The Bernard Sunley Charitable Foundation
Garfield Weston Foundation

National Sponsor

Christie's

Acknowledgements

The Public Catalogue Foundation would like to thank the individual artists and copyright holders for their permission to reproduce for free the paintings in this catalogue. Exhaustive efforts have been made to locate the copyright owners of all the images included within this catalogue and to meet their requirements. Copyright credit lines for copyright owners who have been traced are listed in the Further Information section.

The Public Catalogue Foundation would like to express its great appreciation to the following organisations for their kind assistance in the preparation of this catalogue:

Bridgeman Art Library
Flowers East
Marlborough Fine Art
National Association of Decorative & Fine Arts Societies (NADFAS)
National Gallery, London
National Portrait Gallery, London
Royal Academy of Arts, London
Tate

The participating collections included in this catalogue would like to express their appreciation to the following individuals and organisations who have contributed so generously to the county's collections and who in many cases continue to do so:

Mr H. Bagnall
Mrs Kate P. Bantock
Dr Barnett-Stross
Frank Brangwyn
British Steel plc
Mrs M. C. Cartwright
Paresh C. Chakraborty
Miss P. Chetwynd
Ralph Nicholas Chubb
Contemporary Art Society
Stanley Cope
The Cuthbert family
Miss Mary Jean Elliot
Kathleen Epstein
Charles James Fox
Friends of Wolverhampton Art Gallery
John Gallimore
Mrs Gleaves
Lady Holden
W. J. (Reverend) Holgate
Mr Philip Horsman
Thomas Jones
Miss Joule
Miss Julia Kearns
Miss A. C. Layng
Mr Paul Lutz
Mr Gerald P. Mander
Mrs Doris Melland
Mrs S. Morris
The National Art Collections Fund (The Art Fund)
William Mainwaring Palin
George Phoenix
Miss F. M. Rees
Mrs P. R. Richardson
Dr John Russell
Chris William Sheldon
Noel Spencer
Peter Stanyer
Mr William Thompson
Mrs Thornhill
H. J. Thrustan
Anthony Twentyman
Victoria & Albert Museum Purchase Grant Fund
War Artists Advisory Committee
Wedgwood Company
Dr W. D. Wilkins
William Woodall
Herbert W. Wright

Catalogue Scope and Organisation

Medium and Support
The principal focus of this series is oil paintings. However, tempera and acrylic are also included as well as mixed media, where oil is the predominant constituent. Paintings on all forms of support (e.g. canvas, panel, etc.) are included as long as the support is portable. The principal exclusions are miniatures, hatchments or other purely heraldic paintings and wall paintings *in situ*.

Public Ownership
Public ownership has been taken to mean any paintings that are directly owned by the public purse, made accessible to the public by means of public subsidy or generally perceived to be in public ownership. The term 'public' refers to both central government and local government. Paintings held by national museums, local authority museums, English Heritage and independent museums, where there is at least some form of public subsidy, are included. Paintings held in civic buildings such as local government offices, town halls, guildhalls, public libraries, universities, hospitals, crematoria, fire stations and police stations are also included. Paintings held in central government buildings as part of the Government Art Collection and MoD collections are not included in the county-by-county series but should be included later in the series on a national basis.

Geographical Boundaries of Catalogues
The geographical boundary of each county is the 'ceremonial county' boundary. This county definition includes all unitary authorities. Counties that have a particularly large number of paintings are divided between two or more catalogues on a geographical basis.

Criteria for Inclusion
As long as paintings meet the requirements above, all paintings are included irrespective of their condition and perceived quality. However, painting reproductions can only be included with the agreement of the participating collections and, where appropriate, the relevant copyright owner. It is rare that a collection forbids the inclusion of its paintings. Where this is the case and it is possible to obtain a list of paintings, this list is given in the Paintings Without Reproductions section. Where copyright consent is refused, the paintings are also listed in the Paintings Without Reproductions section. All paintings in collections' stacks and stores are included, as well as those on display. Paintings which have been lent to other institutions, whether for short-term exhibition or long-term loan, are listed under the owner collection. In addition, paintings on long-term loan are also included under the borrowing institution when they are likely to remain there for at least another five years from the date of publication of this catalogue. Information relating to owners and borrowers is listed in the Further Information section.

Layout
Collections are grouped together under their home town. These locations are listed in alphabetical order. In some cases collections that are spread over a number of locations are included under a single owner collection. A number of collections, principally the larger ones, are preceded by curatorial forewords. Within each collection paintings are listed in order of artist surname. Where there is more than one painting by the same artist, the paintings are listed chronologically, according to their execution date.

The few paintings that are not accompanied by photographs are listed in the Paintings Without Reproductions section.

There is additional reference material in the Further Information section at the back of the catalogue. This gives the full names of artists, titles and media if it has not been possible to include these in full in the main section. It also provides acquisition credit lines and information about loans in and out, as well as copyright and photographic credits for each painting. Finally, there is an index of artists' surnames.

Key to Painting Information

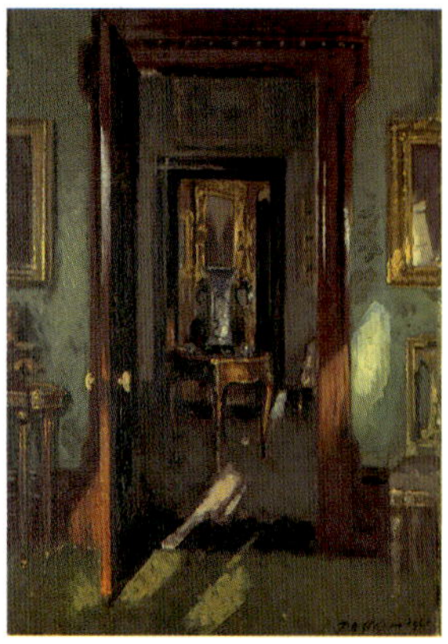

Almost all paintings are reproduced in the catalogue. Where this is not the case they are listed in the Paintings Without Reproductions section. Where paintings are missing or have been stolen, the best possible photograph on record has been reproduced. In some cases this may be black and white. Paintings that have been stolen are highlighted with a red border. Some paintings are shown with conservation tissue attached to parts of the painting surface.

Adam, Patrick William 1854–1929
Interior, Rutland Lodge: Vista through Open Doors 1920
oil on canvas 67.3 × 45.7
LEEAG.PA.1925.0671.LACF

Artist name This is shown as surname first. Where the artist is listed on the Getty Union List of Artist Names (ULAN), ULAN's preferred presentation of the name is always given. In a number of cases the name may not be a firm attribution and this is made clear. Where the artist name is not known, a school may be given instead. Where the school is not known, the painter name is listed as *unknown artist.* If the artist name is too long for the space, as much of the name is given as possible followed by (...). This indicates the full name is given at the rear of the catalogue in the Further Information section.

Painting title A painting followed by *(?)* indicates that the title is in doubt. Where the alternative title to the painting is considered to be better known than the original, the alternative title is given in parentheses. Where the collection has not given a painting a title, the publisher does so instead and marks this with an asterisk. If the title is too long for the space, as much of the title is given as possible followed by *(...)* and the full title is given in the Further Information section.

Execution date In some cases the precise year of execution may not be known for certain. Instead an approximate date will be given or no date at all.

Artist dates Where known, the years of birth and death of the artist are given. In some cases one or both dates may not be known with certainty, and this is marked. No date indicates that even an approximate date is not known. Where only the period in which the artist was active is known, these dates are given and preceded with the word *active.*

Medium and support Where the precise material used in the support is known, this is given.

Dimensions All measurements refer to the unframed painting and are given in cm with up to one decimal point. In all cases the height is shown before the width. An (E) is indicated where a painting has not been measured and its size has been calculated by sight only. If the painting is circular, the single dimension is the diameter. If the painting is oval, the dimensions are height and width.

Collection inventory number In the case of paintings owned by museums, this number will always be the accession number. In all other cases it will be a unique inventory number of the owner institution. (P) indicates that a painting is a private loan. Details can be found in the Further Information section. Accession numbers preceded by 'PCF' indicate that the collection did not have an accession number at the time of catalogue production and therefore the number given has been temporarily allocated by the Public Catalogue Foundation. The symbol indicates that the reproduction is based on a Bridgeman Art Library transparency (go to www.bridgeman.co.uk) or that Bridgeman administers the copyright for that artist.

Facing page: Zoffany, Johann (attributed to), 1733–1810, *Bennet Langton Contemplating the Nolleken's Bust of Johnson* (detail), c.1785, Samuel Johnson Birthplace Museum, (p. 25)

THE PAINTINGS

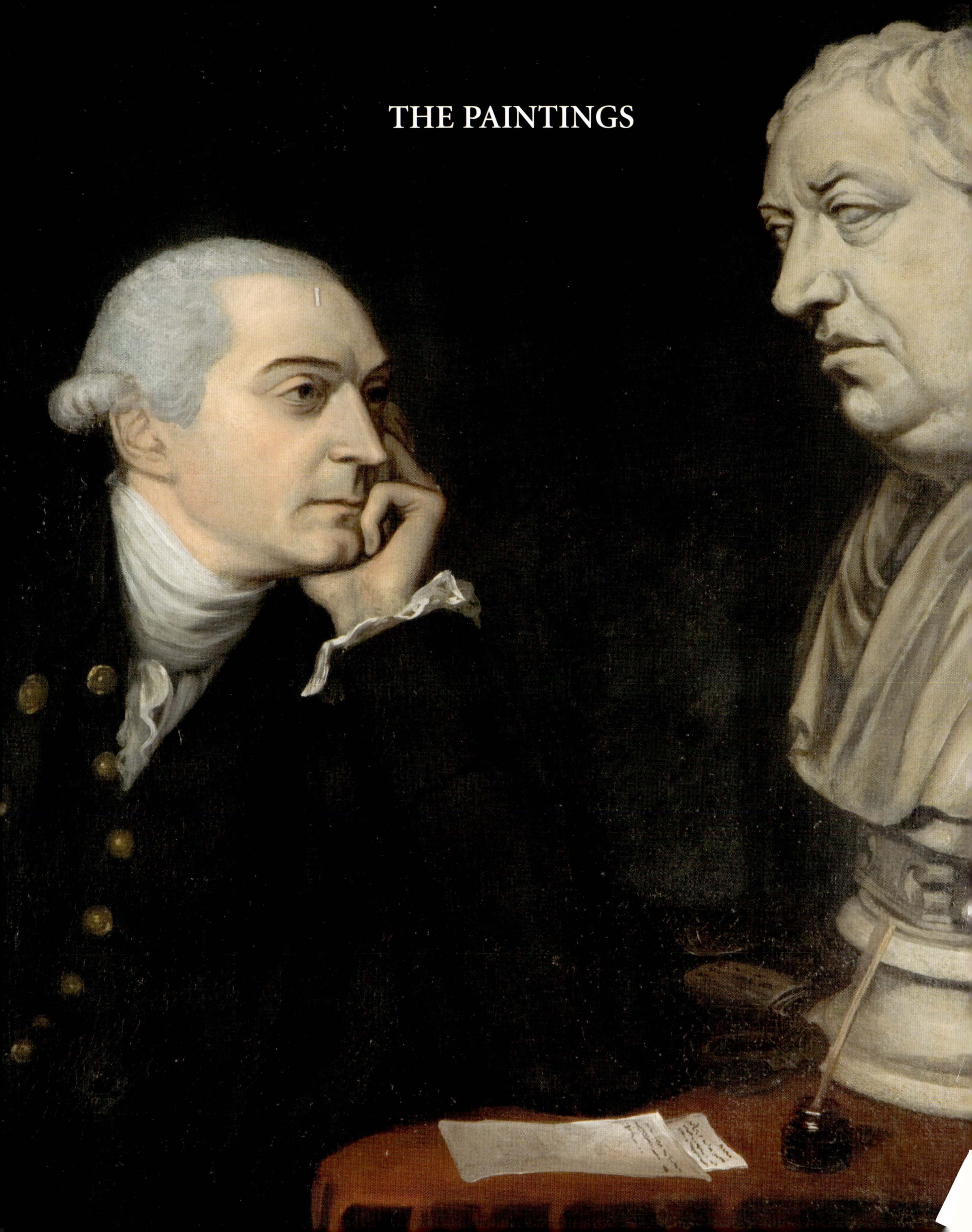

East Staffordshire Borough Council

East Staffordshire Borough Council's collection includes oil paintings, watercolours and prints with views of the Staffordshire and Derbyshire landscape and portraits of local dignitaries. Some of the paintings and prints are on display in Council buildings around Burton-upon-Trent.

Caroline Owen, Exhibition Co-ordinator

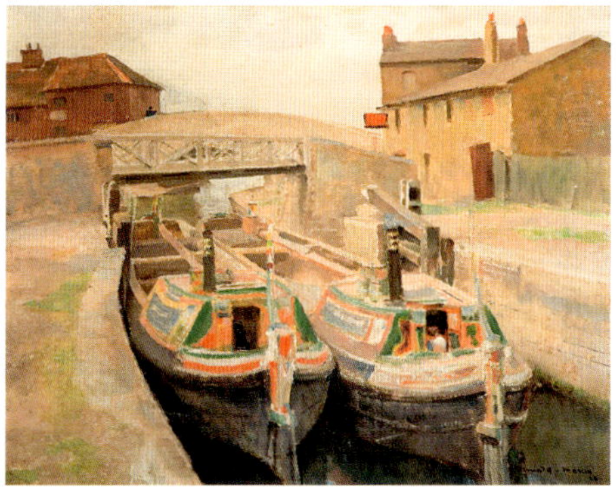

Mason, Arnold 1885–1963
Barges
oil on canvas 37 x 44.5
1967/A

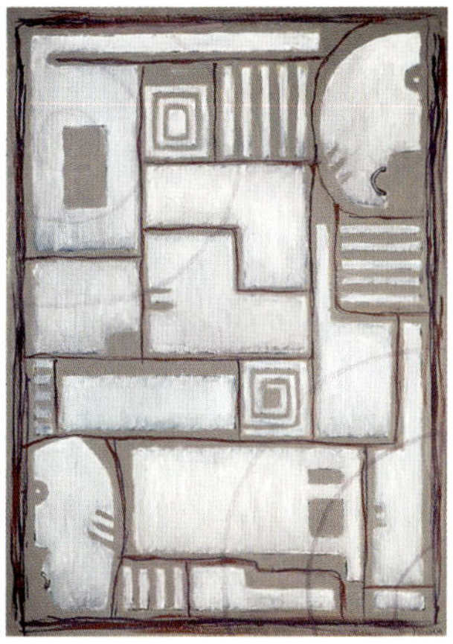

Stent, M.
*Blue and Grey Squares** 2004
oil on board 81 x 56
PCF1

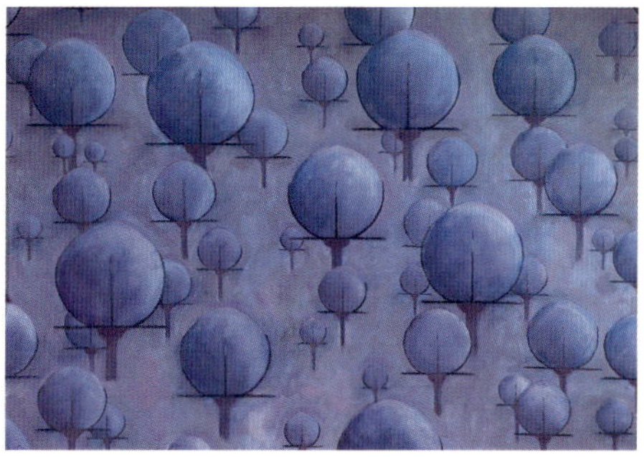

Stent, M.
*Blue Circles** 2004
oil on board 55.5 x 80
PCF2

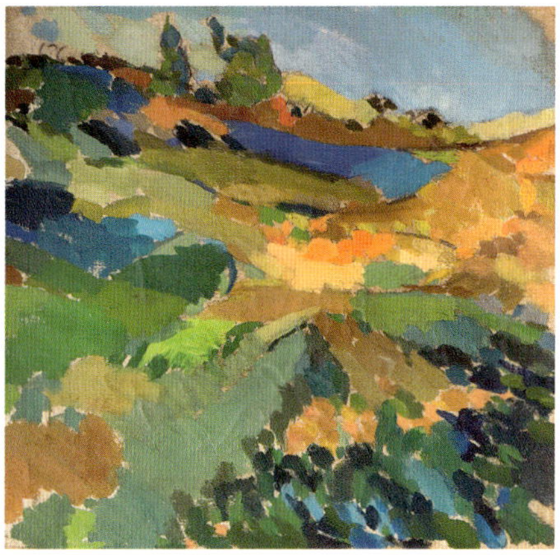

Sutton, Philip b.1928
Landscape, June 1956 1956
oil on canvas 40 x 40
PCF3

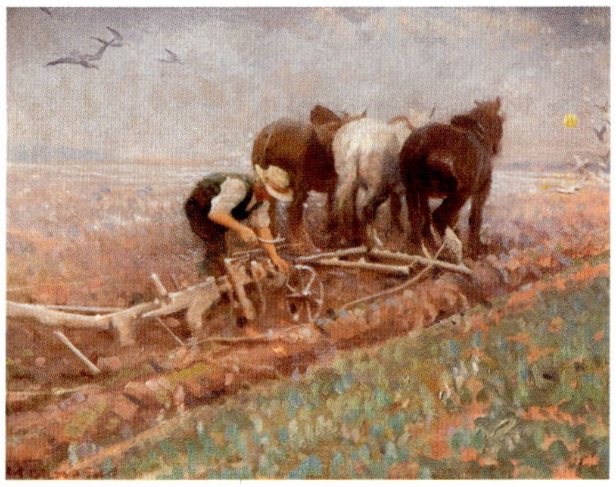

Townsend, E.
Evening
oil on board 30 x 38
314/36

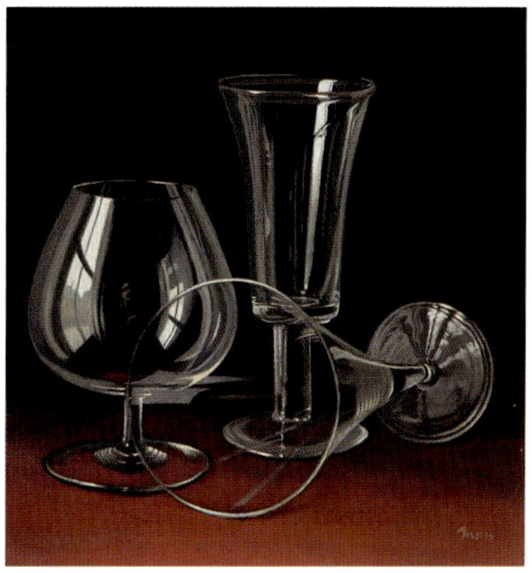

Tuson, J.
Three Goblets
oil on board 32 x 30
PCF4

Museum of Cannock Chase

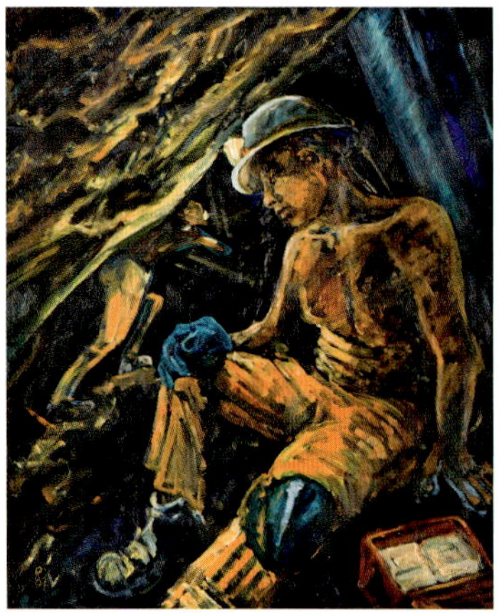

Clare, Pat b.1938
The Last Snapping 1994
oil on board 73.5 x 60.5
2004.0082.00001

Churnet Valley Railway

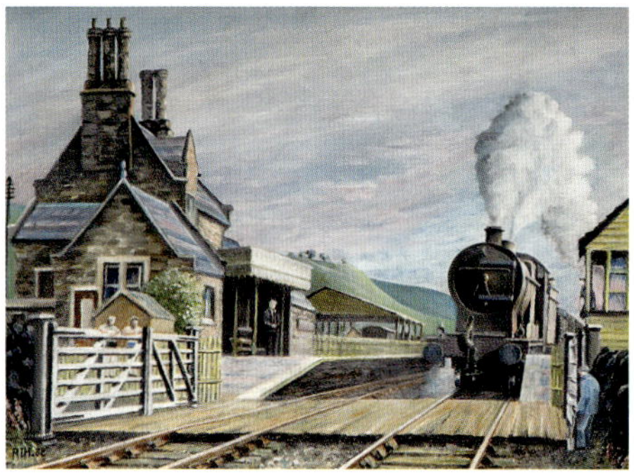

R. C. H.
Train at Cheddleton Station 1988
oil on board 38 x 49.5
PCF3

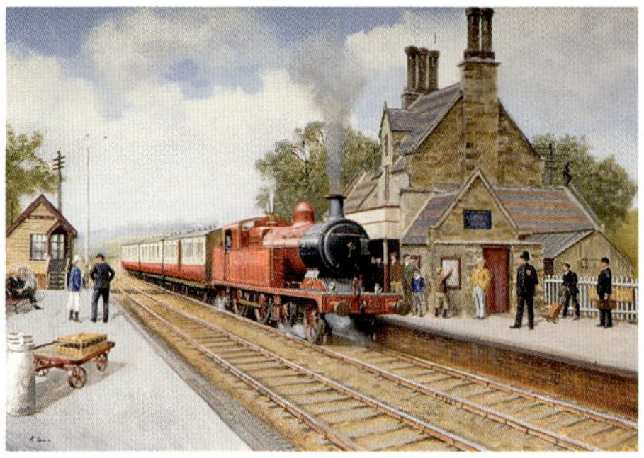

Simm, Richard b.1926
Train at Cheddleton Station
oil on canvas 39 x 54.5
PCF4

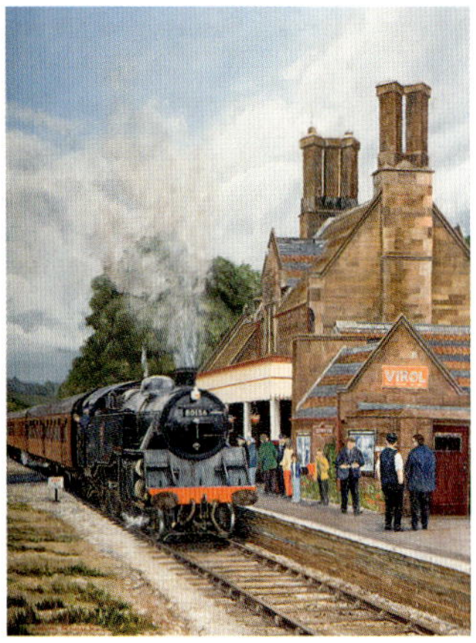

Skidmore, Michael b.1943
Class '4MT' Standard Tank 80136 at Cheddleton Station on the Churnet Valley Railway 2001
oil on board 60 x 45
PCF2

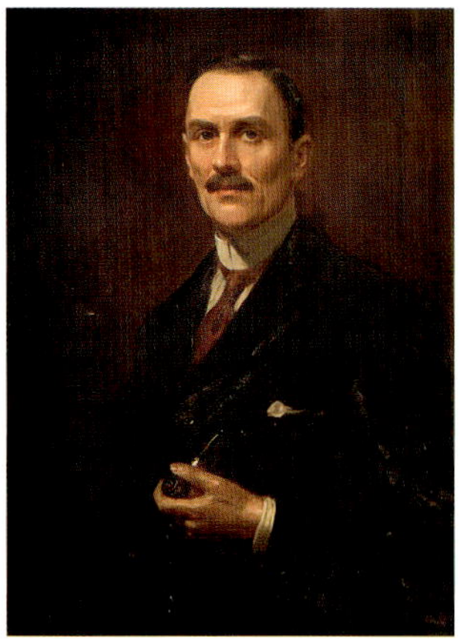

unknown artist
F. A. L. Barnwell, Last General Manager of the North Staffordshire Railway Company (1919–1923) 1920
oil on canvas 89 x 68
PCF1

Ingestre Hall Residential Arts Centre

Ingestre Hall was the ancestral home of the Earls of Shrewsbury. Built by Sir Walter Chetwynd in 1613, the Jacobean mansion house is now run as a residential arts centre. The collection of portraits features members of the Chetwynd and Talbot families from the sixteenth to the twentieth century. The hall and collection are in the ownership of Sandwell Metropolitan Borough Council.

John Thomson, Sandwell Metropolitan Borough Council

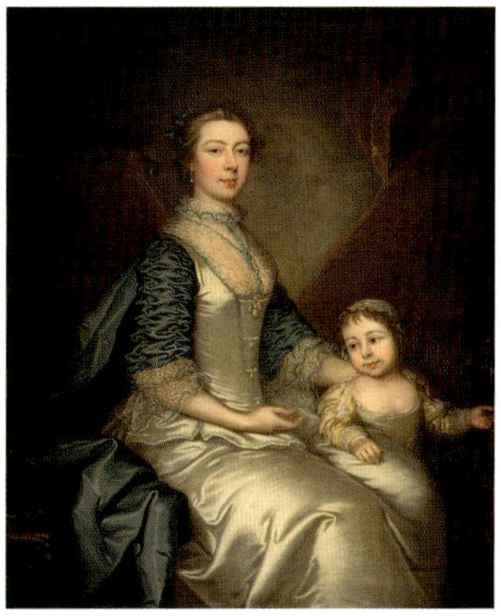

Bardwell, Thomas 1704–1767
Catherine Talbot of Ingestre and Hillingdon (1722–1785) 1752
oil on canvas 135 x 100
PCF1

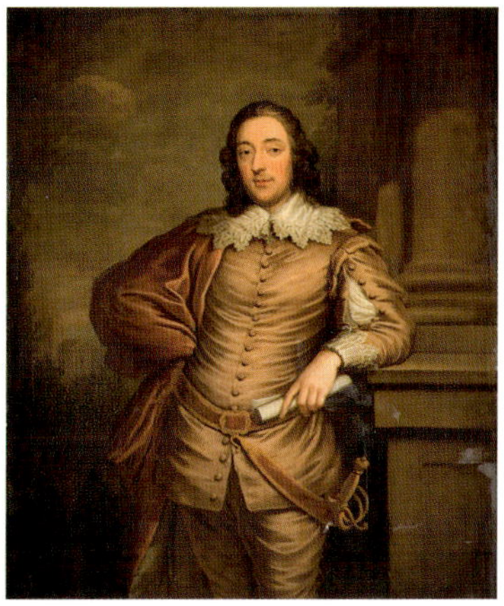

Bardwell, Thomas 1704–1767
The Honourable John Talbot, MP, of Lincoln's Inn Fields (1711–1756) 1753
oil on canvas 200 x 110
PCF2

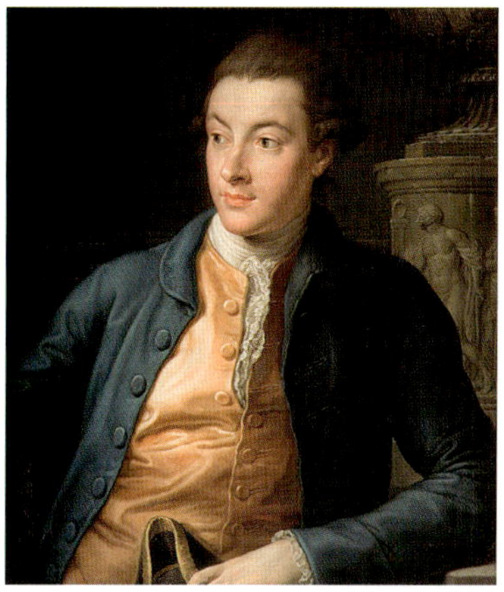

Batoni, Pompeo 1708–1787
John Chetwynd, 1st Earl Talbot (1750–1793) 1773
oil on canvas 90 x 70
PCF3

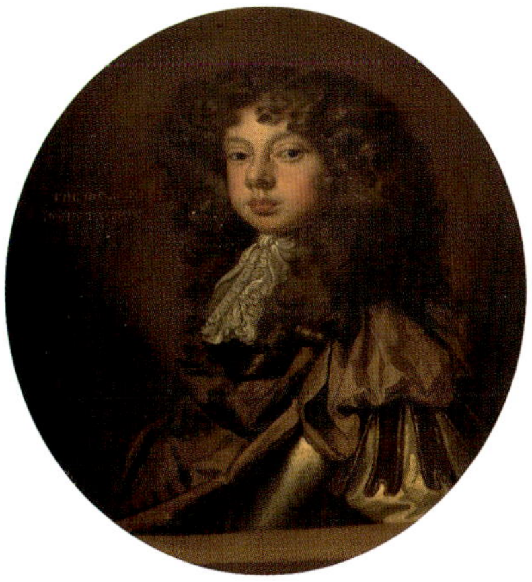

Beale, Mary 1633–1699
The Honourable John Talbot, Younger Brother of Charles, Duke and 12th Earl of Shrewsbury (1664–1685/1686)
oil on canvas 70 x 50
PCF5

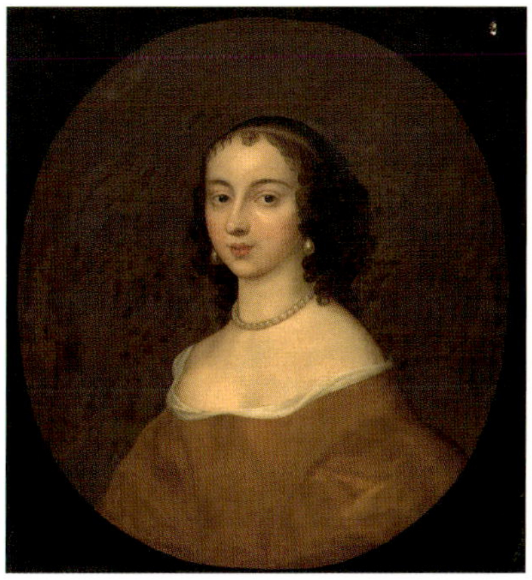

Beale, Mary (attributed to) 1633–1699
Anna Maria, Countess of Shrewsbury (1642–1702) 1659
oil on canvas 70 x 55
PCF4

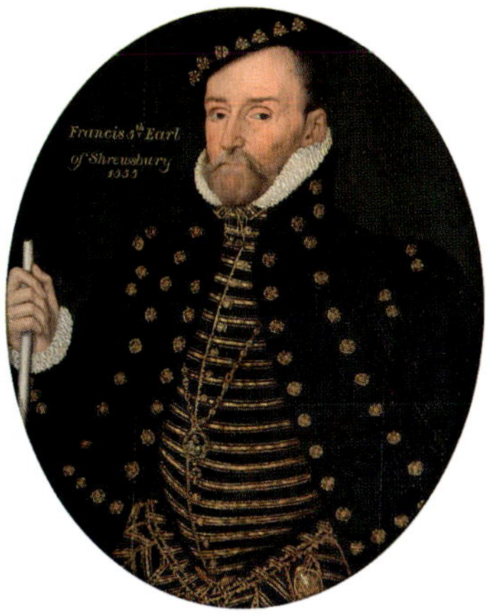

British (English) School
Francis Talbot, 5th Earl of Shrewsbury, KG (1500–1560) 1555
oil on canvas 71 x 57
PCF6

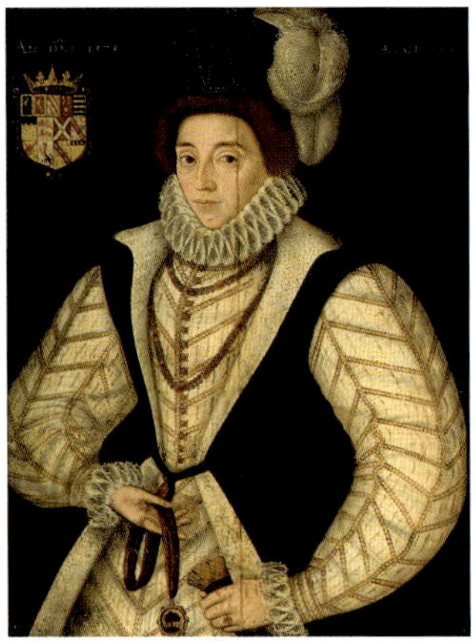

British (English) School
Elizabeth, Countess of Shrewsbury (c.1525–1608) 1575
oil on canvas 70 x 50
PCF7

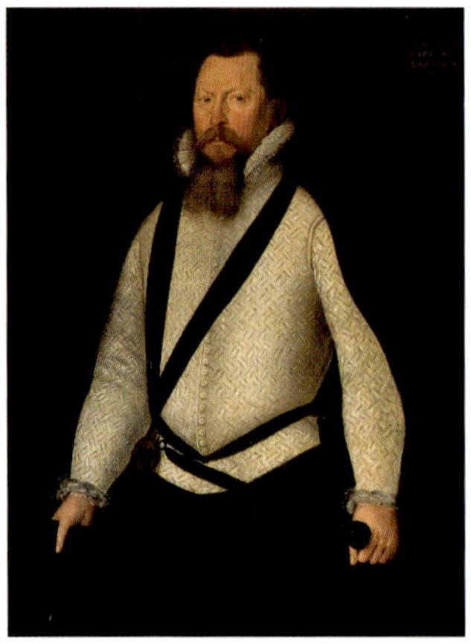

British (English) School
George Talbot, 6th Earl of Shrewsbury and Waterford (1528–1590) 1580
oil on canvas 110 x 90 (E)
PCF8

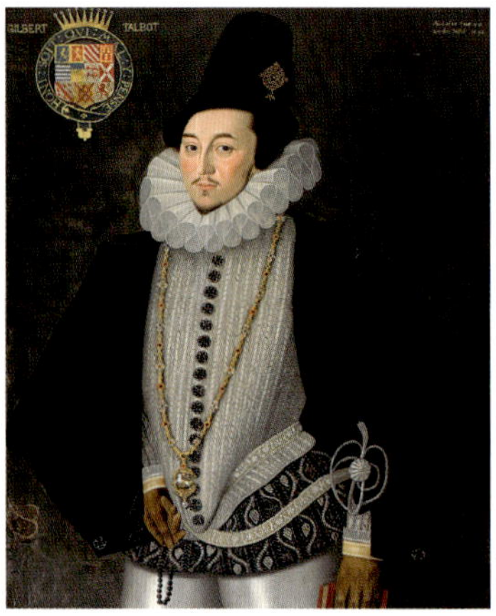

British (English) School
Gilbert Talbot, 7th Earl of Shrewsbury (1552–1616) 1592
oil on canvas 110 x 90 (E)
PCF9

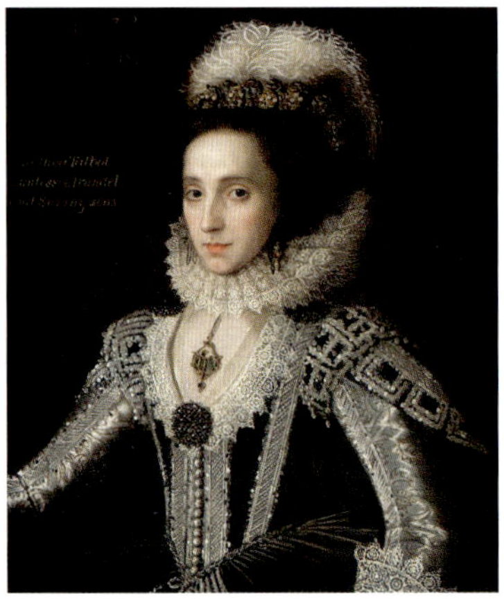

British (English) School
Alathea Talbot, Countess of Arundel and Surrey (c.1590–1654) 1619
oil on canvas 100 x 75 (E)
PCF10

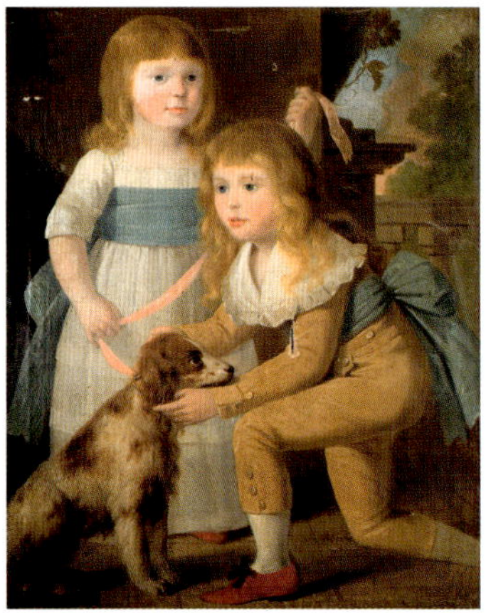

British (English) School
John Talbot, 16th Earl of Shrewsbury and Waterford (1791–1852), and Charles Talbot
oil on canvas 90 x 70
PCF11

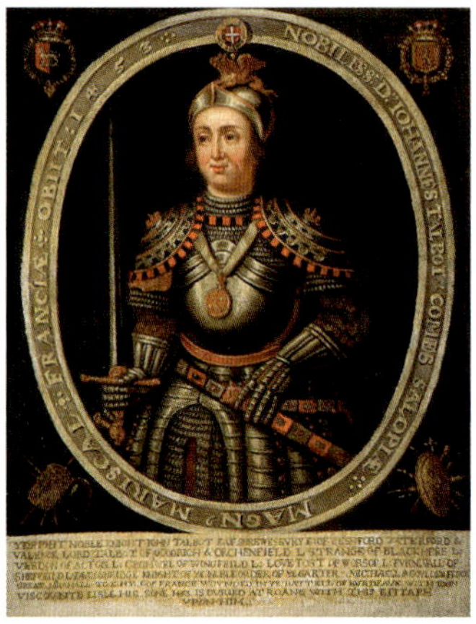

Cecill, Thomas (copy after)
active 1625–1640
Sir John Talbot, 1st Earl of Shrewsbury and Waterford (1383–1453) 19th C
oil on canvas 50 x 38
PCF12

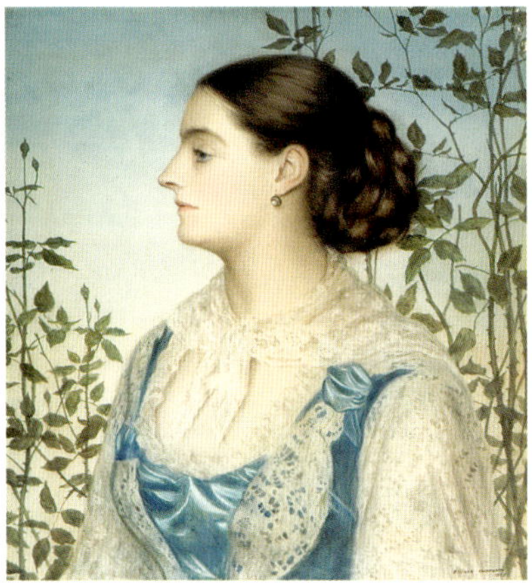

Clifford, Edward 1844–1907
Anna Theresa, Countess of Shrewsbury (1836–1912) 1875
oil on canvas 60 x 40
PCF13

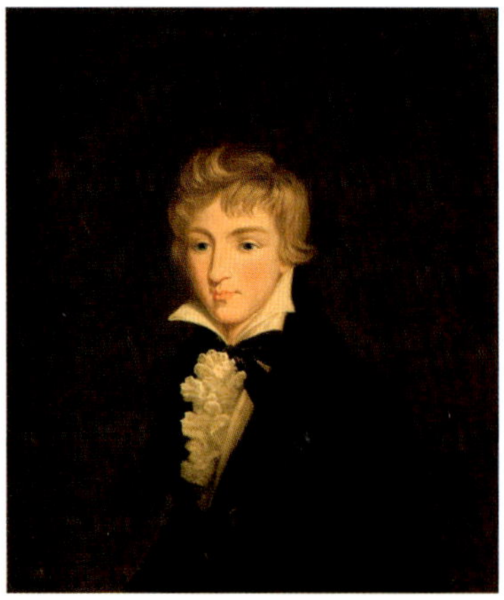

Clover, Joseph 1779–1853
Lord James Beresford, 4th Son of Henry de la Poer (1816–1841) 1825
oil on canvas 100 x 80 (E)
PCF14

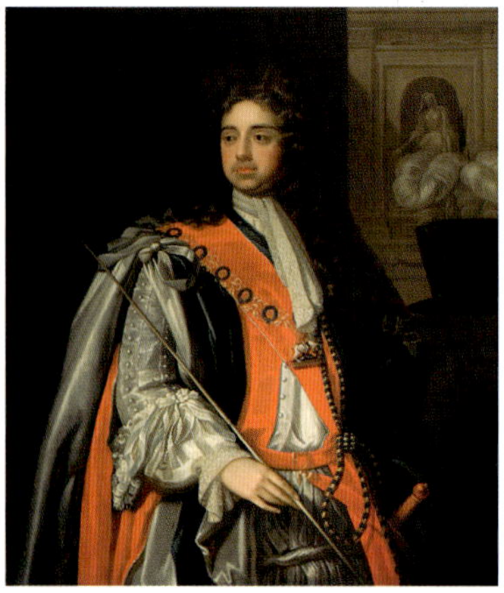

Dahl, Michael I 1656/1659–1743
Charles Talbot, Duke and 12th Earl of Shrewsbury (1660–1718)
oil on canvas 140 x 100
PCF15

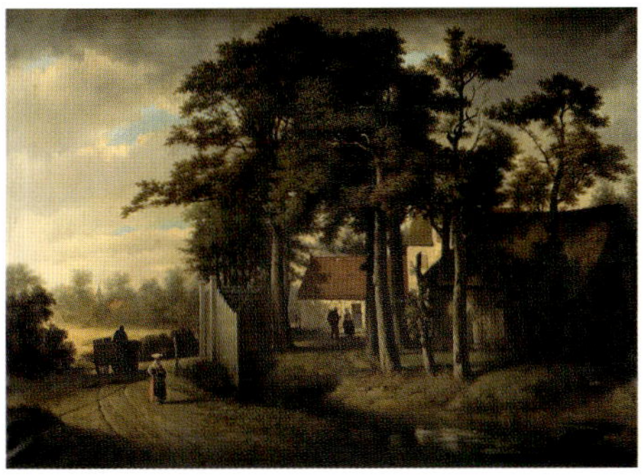

Dutch School
A Country Scene
oil on canvas 97 x 130
PCF16

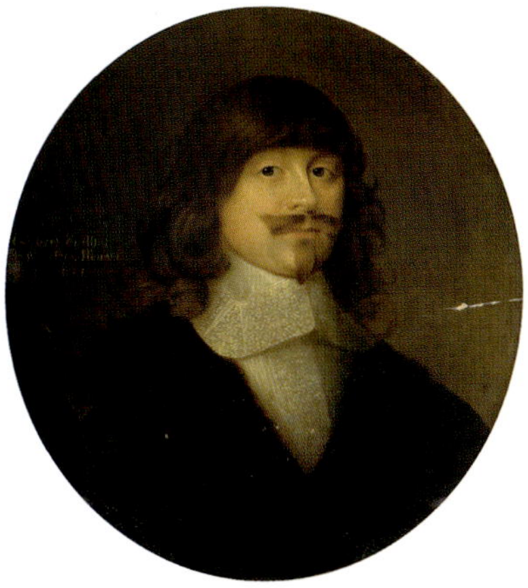

Dyck, Anthony van (school of) 1599–1641
Sir Gilbert Talbot, Knight of Salwarp (1606–1695)
oil on canvas 75 x 50
PCF17

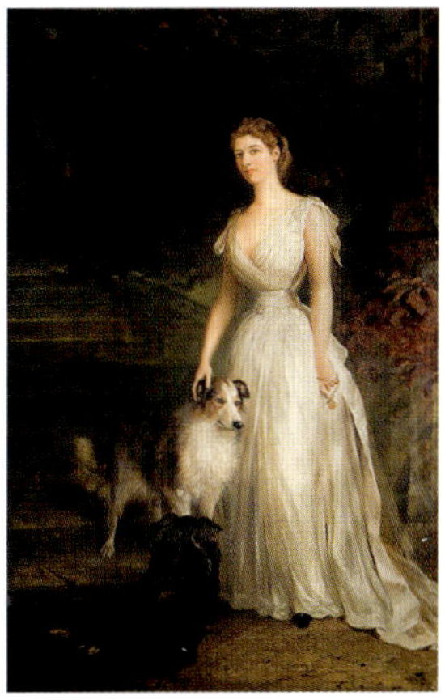

Grant, Henry active 1868–1895
Ellen Mary, Countess of Shrewsbury 1894
oil on canvas 230 x 147
PCF18

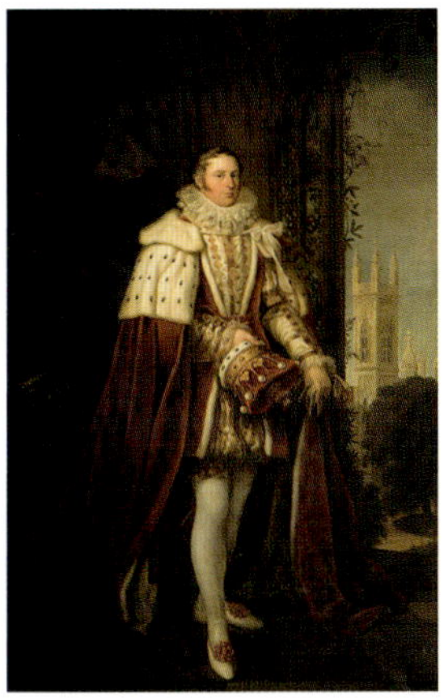

Hamburger, Johann Konrad 1809–1871
John Talbot, 16th Earl of Shrewsbury and Waterford (1791–1852) 1832
oil on canvas 250 x 160
PCF19

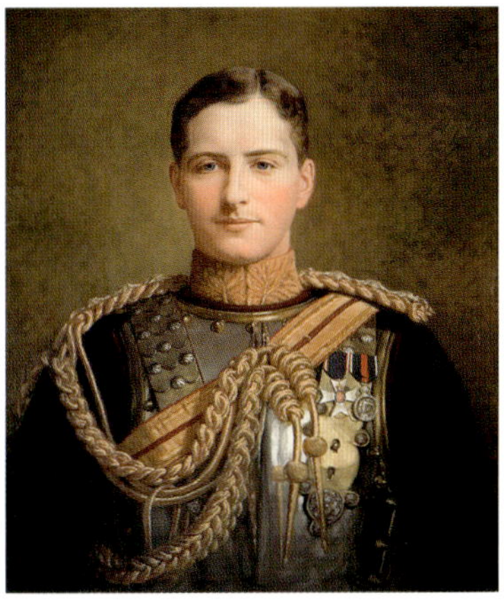

Hardy, Dorofield active 1882–1927
Charles John Alton Chetwynd, Viscount Ingestre, MVO (1882–1915) 1915
oil on canvas 75 x 60
PCF20

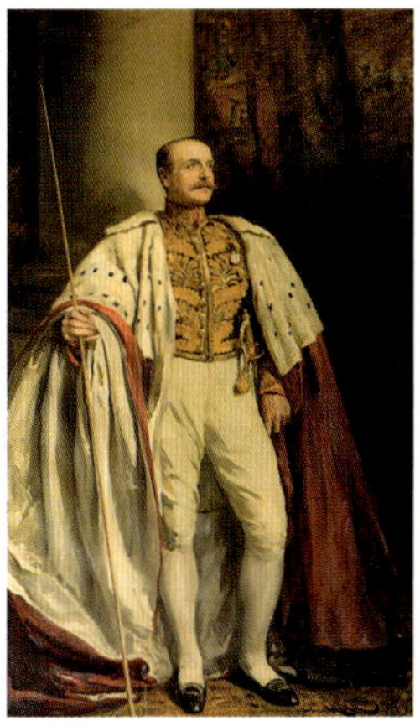

Herkomer, Hubert von 1849–1914
Charles Henry John, 20th Earl of Shrewsbury and Waterford, KCVO (1877–1921) 1903
oil on canvas 210 x 140
PCF21

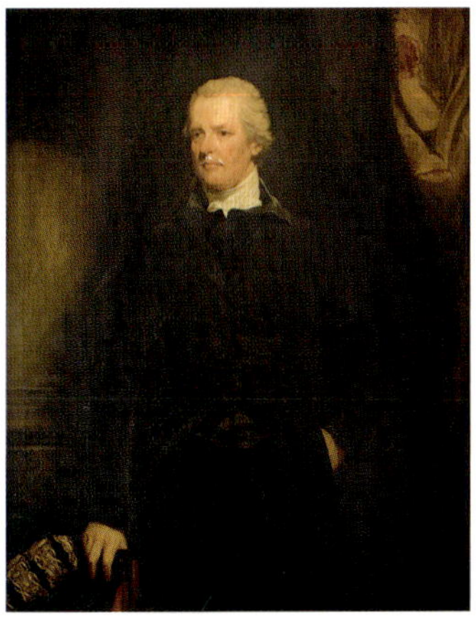

Hoppner, John 1758–1810
William Pitt, PC (1759–1806)
oil on canvas 140 x 110
PCF22

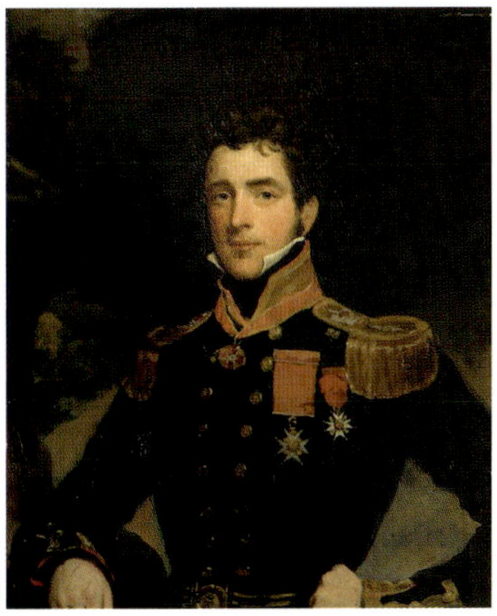

Jackson, John 1778–1831
Henry John, Viscount Ingestre (1803–1868)
oil on canvas 90 x 60
PCF23

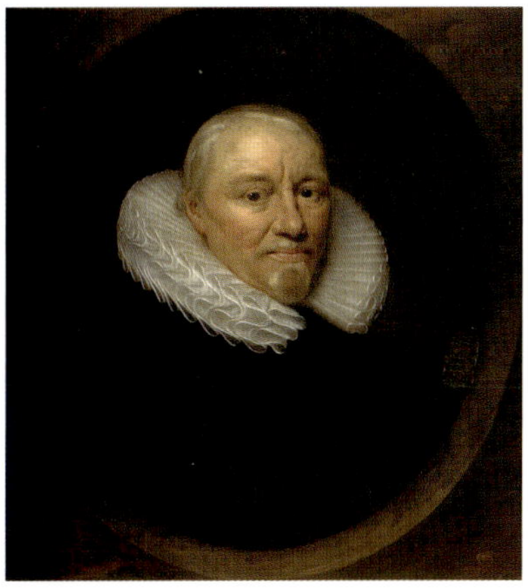

Janssens van Ceulen, Cornelis 1593–1661
John Talbot of Grafton (1542–1611)
oil on canvas 70 x 60 (E)
PCF24

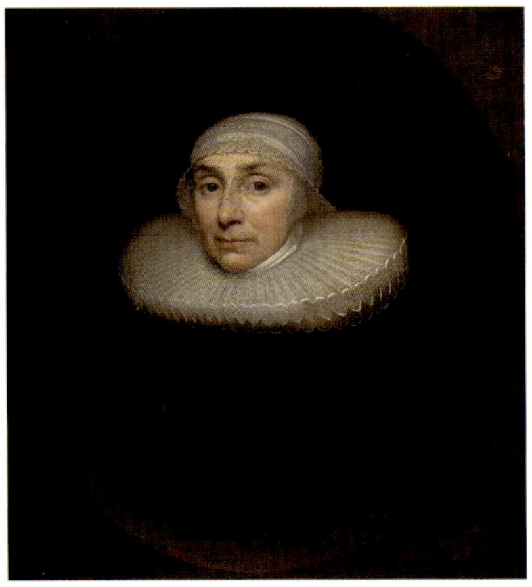

Janssens van Ceulen, Cornelis 1593–1661
Margaret Talbot, Second Wife of John Talbot (d.1620)
oil on canvas 70 x 60 (E)
PCF25

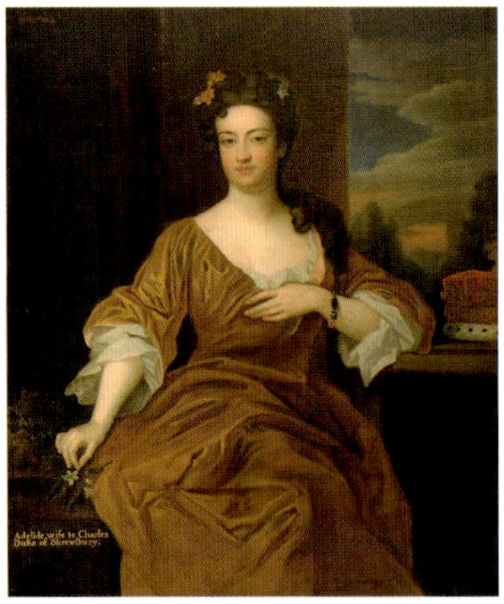

Kneller, Godfrey (school of) 1646–1723
Adelhida, Duchess of Shrewsbury (1665–1726)
oil on canvas 135 x 103
PCF26

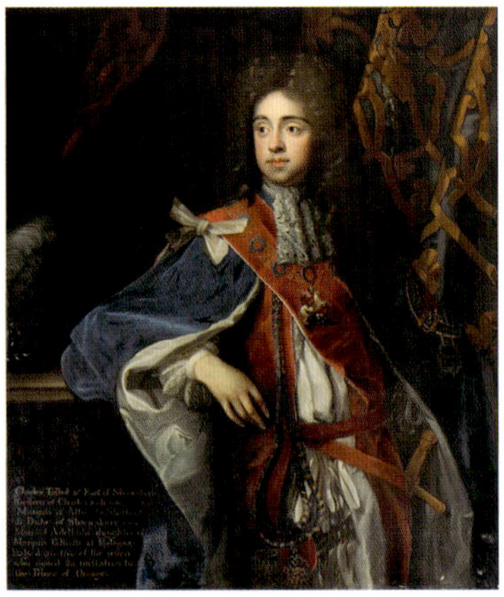

Kneller, Godfrey (school of) 1646–1723
Charles Talbot, Duke and 12th Earl of Shrewsbury (1660–1718)
oil on canvas 140 x 100
PCF27

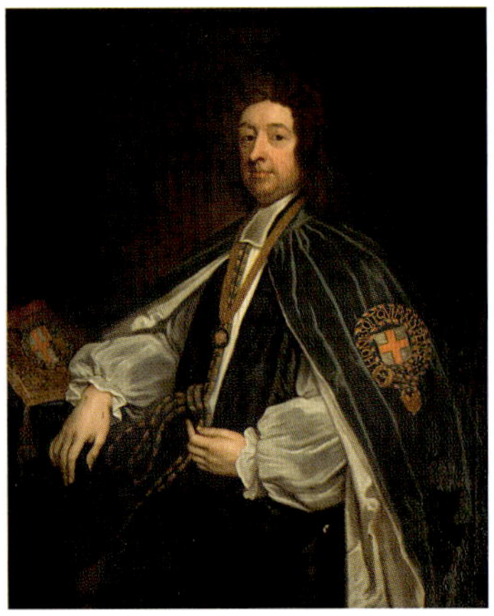

Kneller, Godfrey (school of) 1646–1723
Right Reverend William Talbot, Bishop of Durham (c.1658–1730)
oil on canvas 140 x 100
PCF28

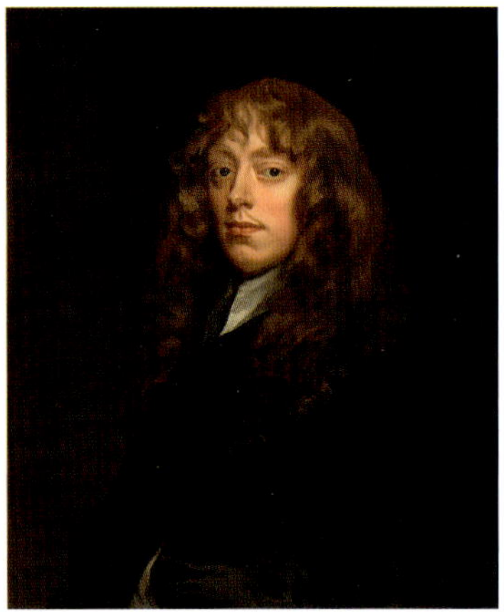

Lely, Peter 1618–1680
Sir Walter Chetwynd, MP of Ingestre (1634/1635–1693)
oil on canvas 70 x 50
PCF29

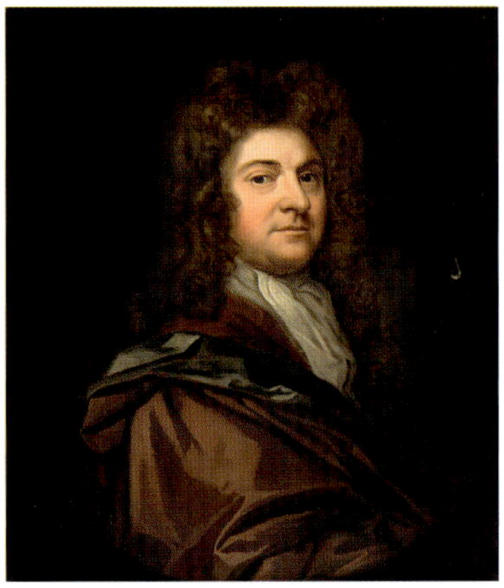

Medina, John Baptist de 1659–1710
John Chetwynd, MP (d.1702)
oil on canvas 80 x 50
PCF30

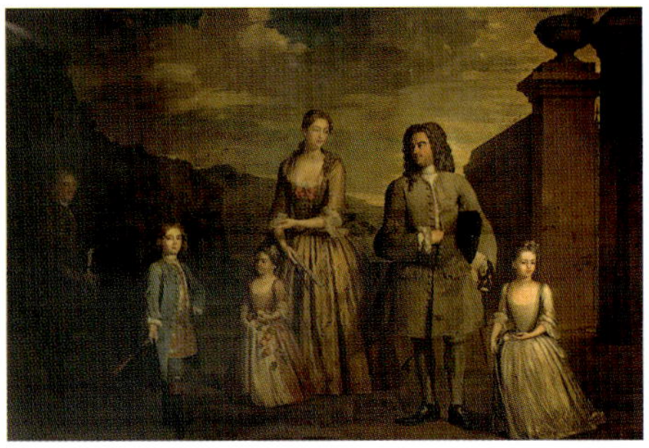

Myn, Herman van der 1684–1781
John Chetwynd, 2nd Viscount Chetwynd and Family 1732
oil on canvas 250 x 390
PCF31

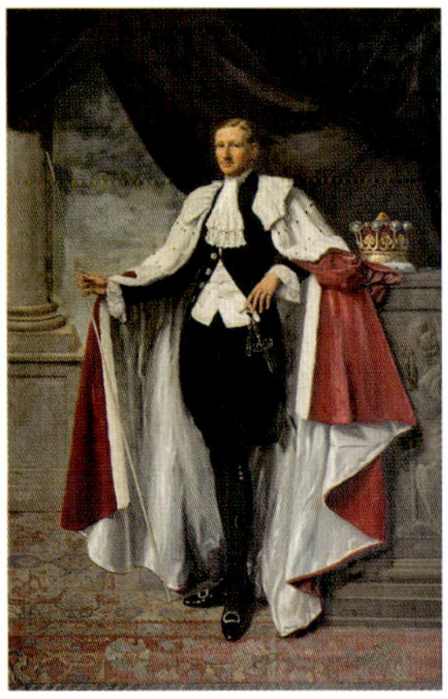

Orde, Cuthbert Julian 1888–1968
John George Charles Henry Alton Alexander Chetwynd, 21st Earl of Shrewsbury and Waterford (1914–1980) 1937
oil on canvas 250 x 160
PCF32

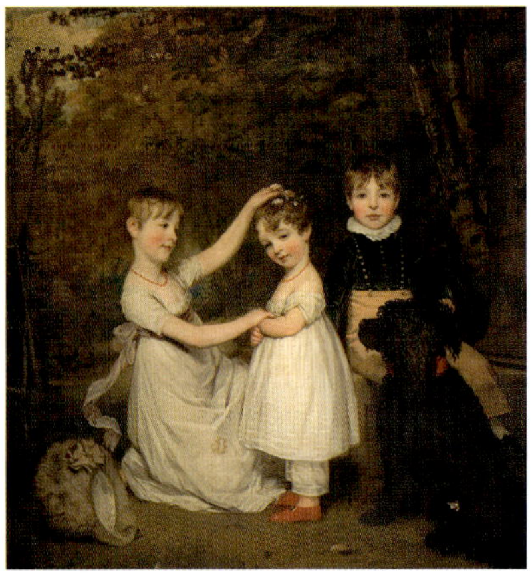

Phillips, Thomas 1770–1845
The Children of the 2nd Earl Talbot 1807
oil on canvas 200 x 180 (E)
PCF33

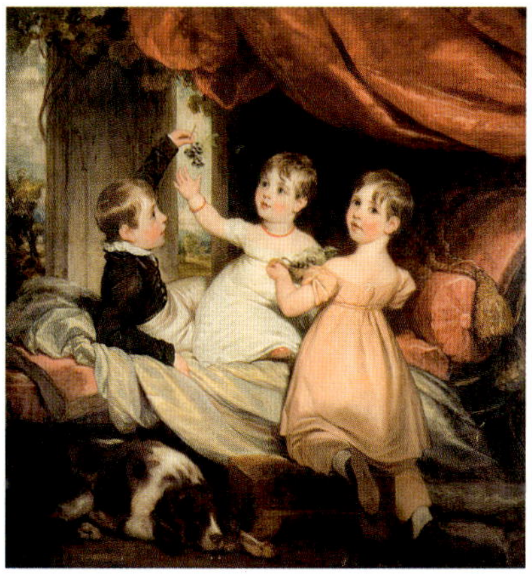

Phillips, Thomas 1770–1845
The Children of the 2nd Earl Talbot 1811
oil on canvas 145 x 145
PCF34

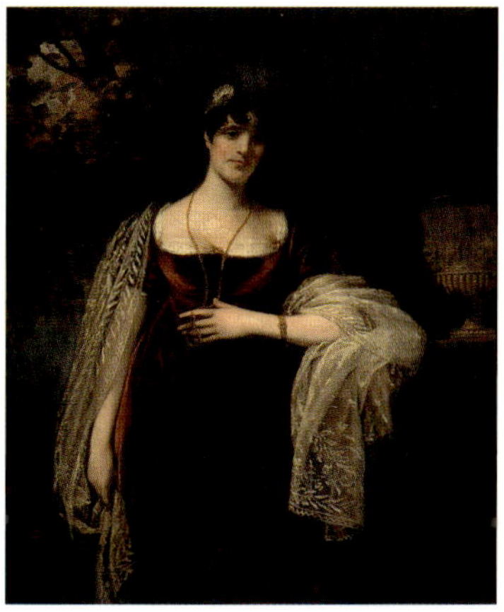

Phillips, Thomas 1770–1845
Frances Thomasine, Countess Talbot, Wife of the 2nd Earl Talbot (1778–1819)
oil on canvas 130 x 100
PCF35

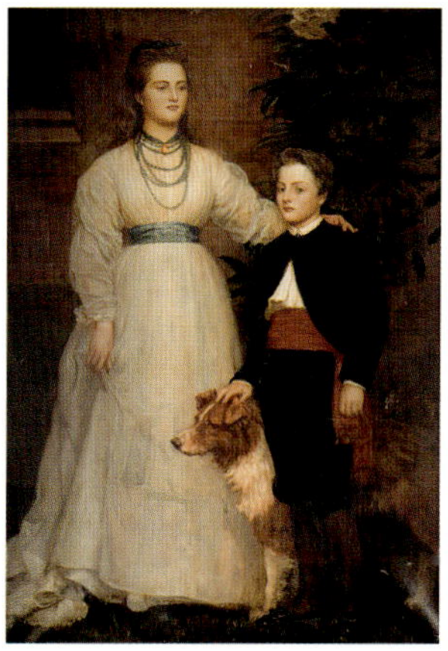

Prinsep, Valentine Cameron 1838–1904
Theresa Susey Helen Talbot, Later Marchioness of Londonderry and Charles Henry John, Viscount Ingestre (1860–1921)
oil on canvas 250 x 120
PCF36

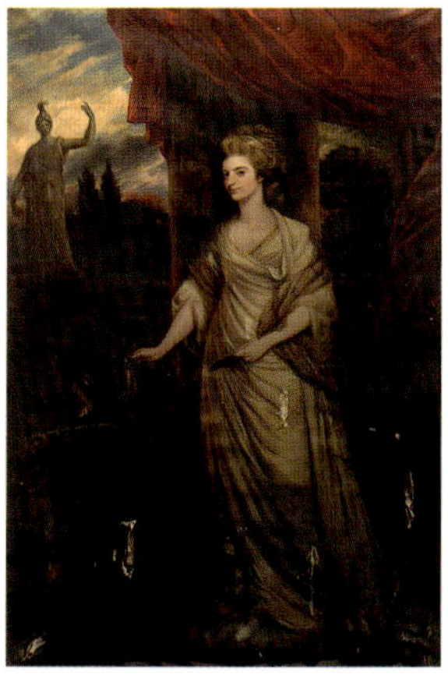

Reynolds, Joshua (copy after) 1723–1792
Charlotte, Countess Talbot (1754–1804)
oil on canvas 250 x 160
PCF38

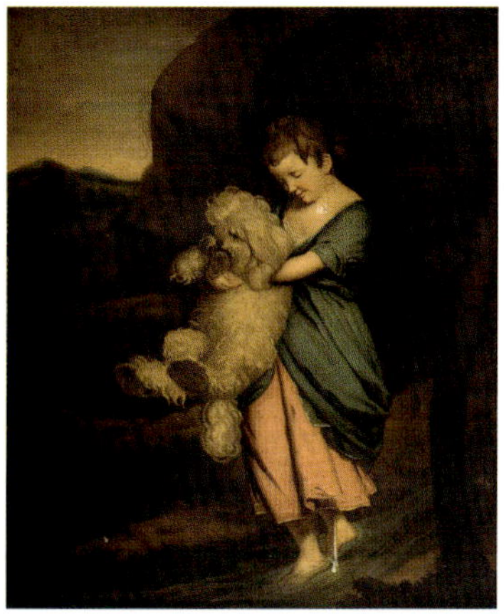

Reynolds, Joshua (copy of) 1723–1792
Crossing the Brook
oil on canvas 70 x 50
PCF37

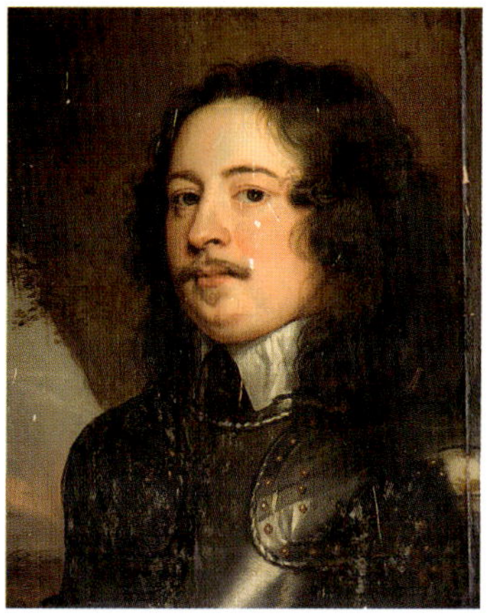

Russell, Theodore (attributed to) 1614–1689
Sir Gilbert Talbot, Knight of Salwarp (1606–1695)
oil on canvas 38 x 30
PCF39

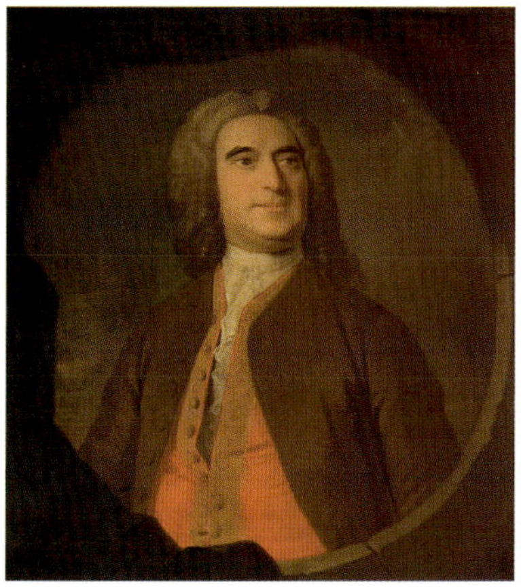

Slaughter, Stephen 1697–1765
John Chetwynd, 2nd Viscount Chetwynd (c.1680–1767)
oil on canvas 80 x 50
PCF40

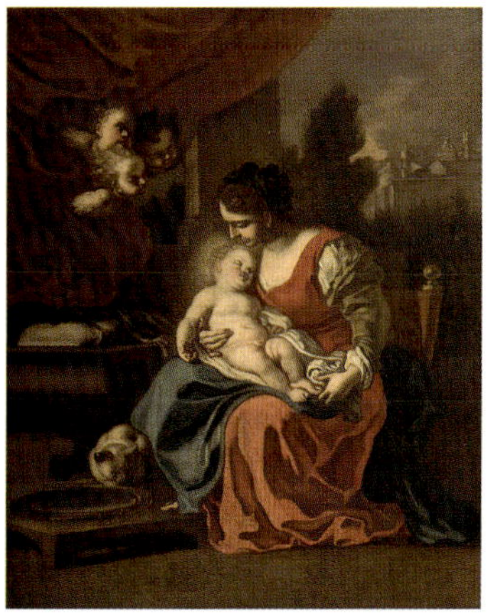

Solimena, Francesco (style of) 1657–1747
The Virgin with the Infant Christ
oil on canvas 50 x 30
PCF41

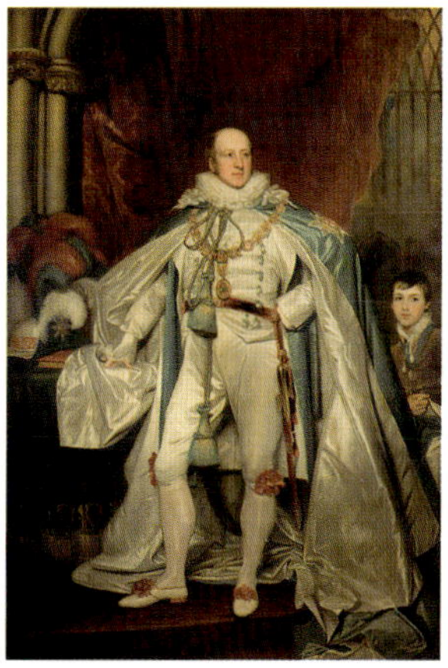

Thompson, Thomas Clement c.1780–1857
Charles Chetwynd, 2nd Earl Talbot (1777–1849)
oil on canvas 275 x 140
PCF43

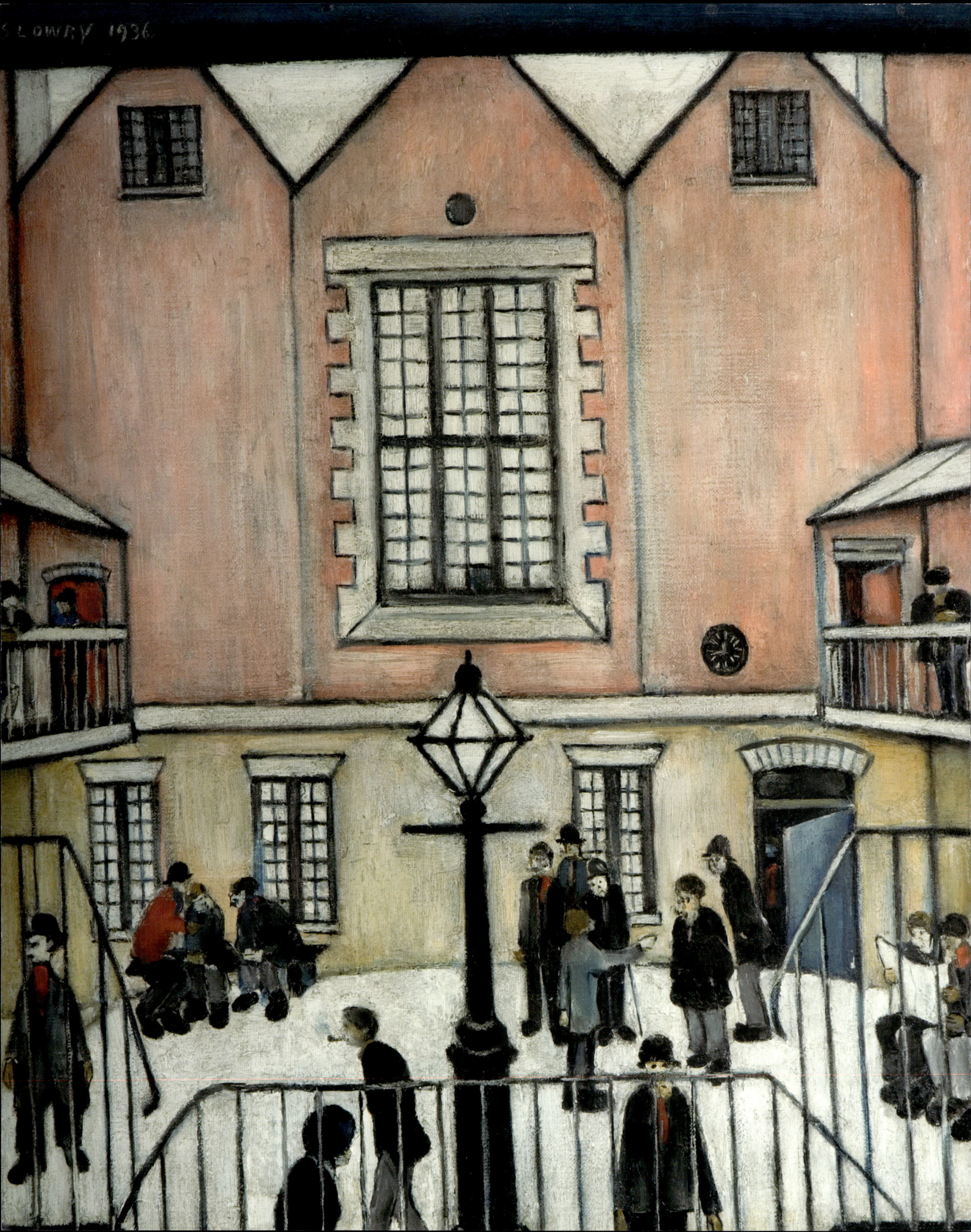
S LOWRY 1936

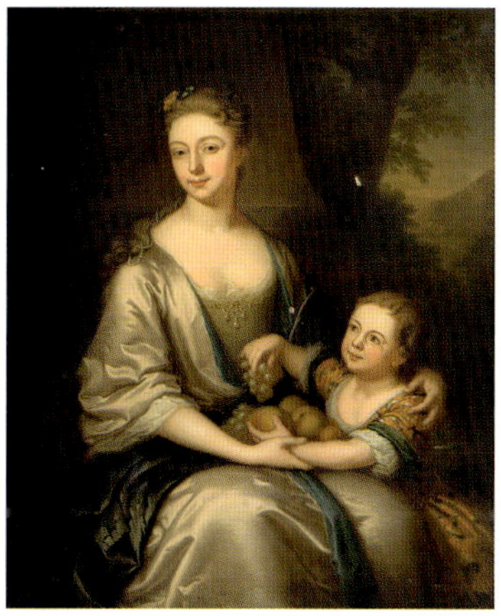

unknown artist early 18th C
Esther, Viscountess Chetwynd, Wife of John, 2nd Viscount Chetwynd, and Her Son, John Chetwynd (1699–1741)
oil on canvas 150 x 97
PCF53

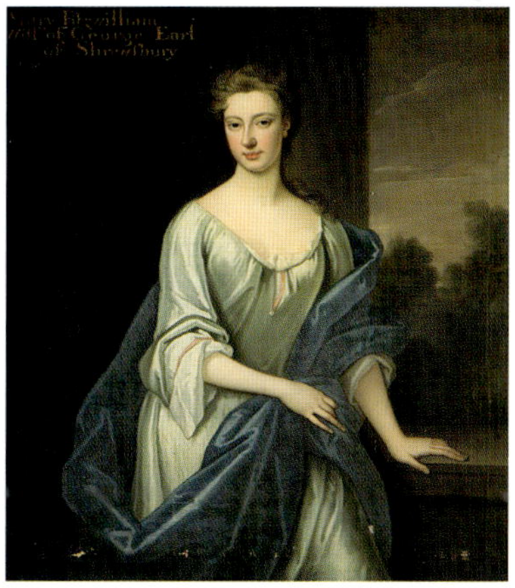

unknown artist early 18th C
The Honourable Mrs Mary Talbot, Wife of George Talbot of Heythrop (1698–1752)
oil on canvas 135 x 103
PCF52

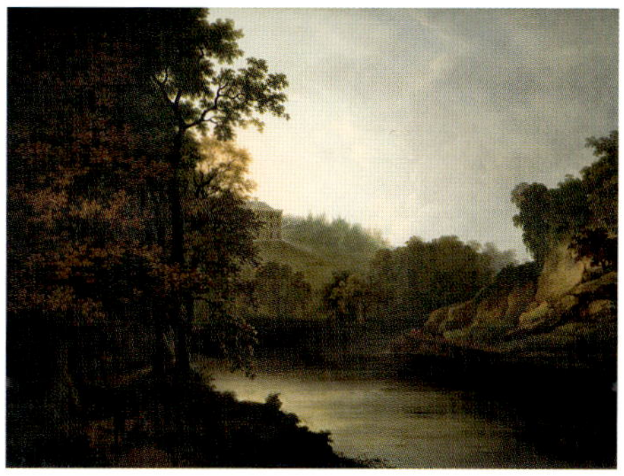

unknown artist
A View of Beau Park 1810
oil on canvas 75 x 120
PCF44

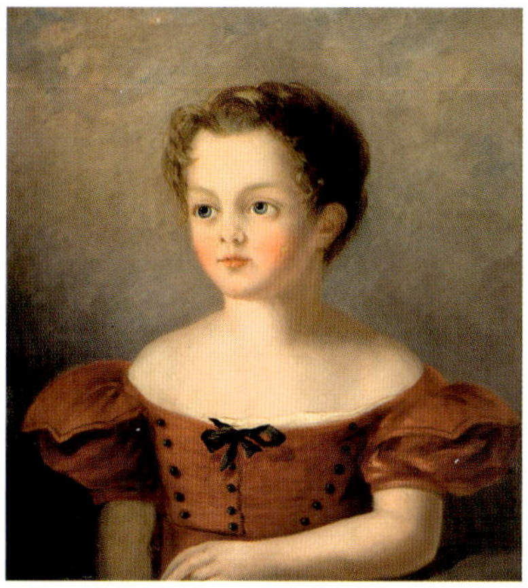

unknown artist early 19th C
Charles John Chetwynd-Talbot, 19th Earl of Shrewsbury (1830–1877)
oil on canvas 47 x 41
PCF55

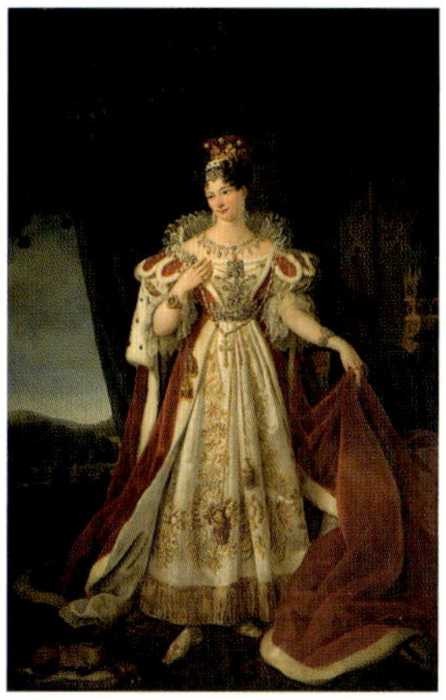

unknown artist early 19th C
Maria Theresa, Countess of Shrewsbury (1795–1856)
oil on canvas 250 x 160
PCF54

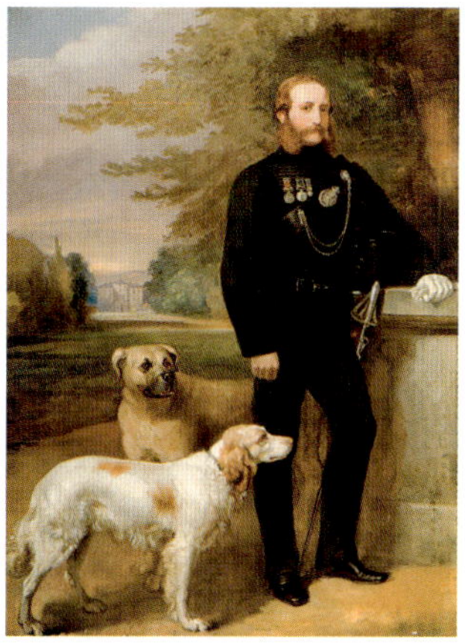

unknown artist mid-19th C
Captain Charles Arthur Talbot, Grandson of the 2nd Earl Talbot (1834–1869)
oil on canvas 250 x 140
PCF56

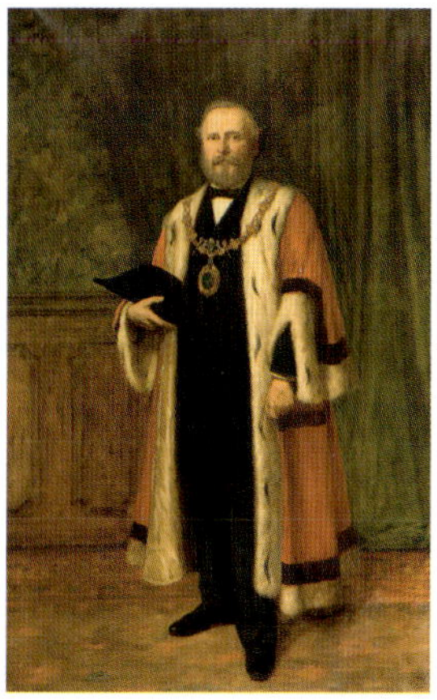

unknown artist
Alderman Reuben Farley, JP
oil on canvas 210 x 140
PCF60

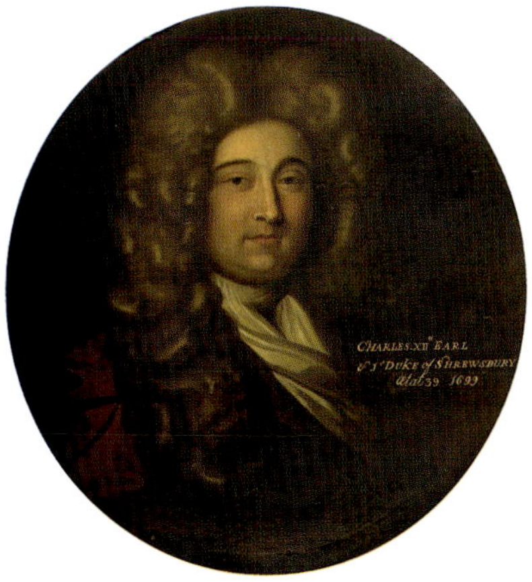

unknown artist
Charles, 12th Earl & 1st Duke of Shrewsbury, 1699
oil on canvas 70 x 50
PCF48

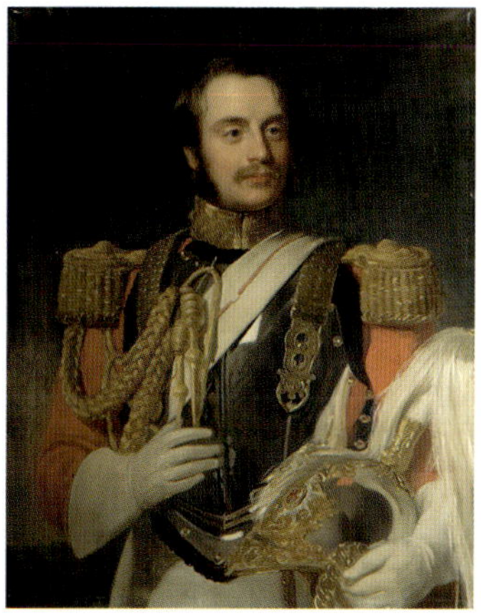

unknown artist
Charles John Chetwynd-Talbot, Viscount Ingestre (1830–1877)
oil on canvas 90 x 60
PCF50

Facing page: Lowry, Laurence Stephen, 1887–1976, *The Courtyard* (detail), 1936, The Potteries Museum & Art Gallery (p. 138)

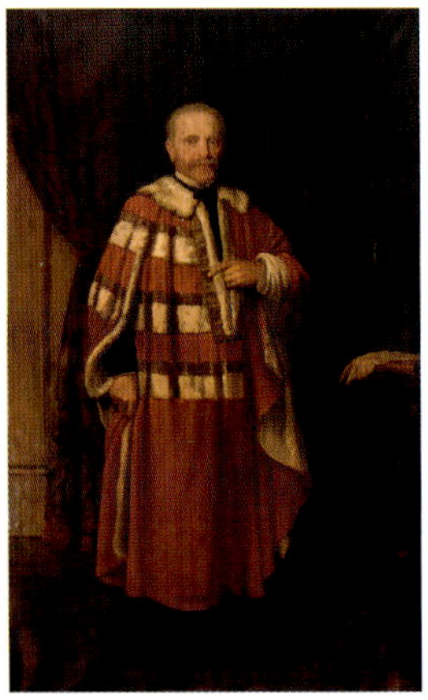

unknown artist
Earl of Dartmouth
oil on canvas 210 x 140
PCF61

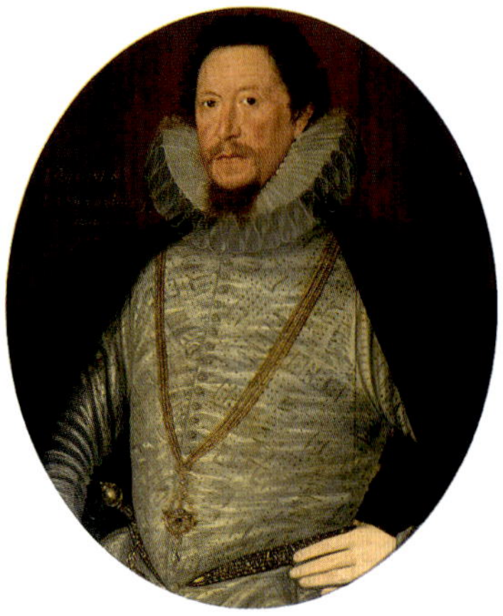

unknown artist
Edward Talbot, 8th Earl of Shrewsbury (1561–1618)
oil on canvas 71 x 57
PCF46

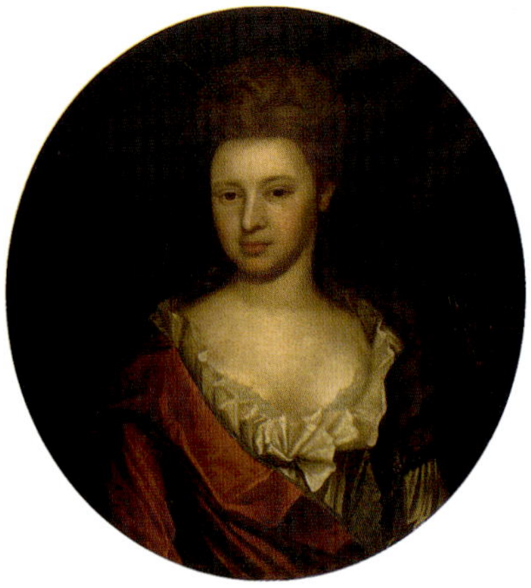

unknown artist
Esther, Mrs Chetwynd (1699–1741)
oil on canvas 70 x 50
PCF47

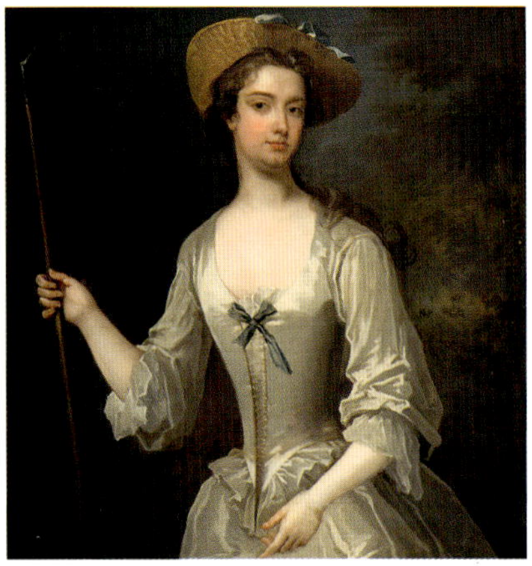

unknown artist
Honourable Mrs Catherine Talbot, Later Wife of Honourable John Talbot (1722–1785)
oil on canvas 110 x 100
PCF49

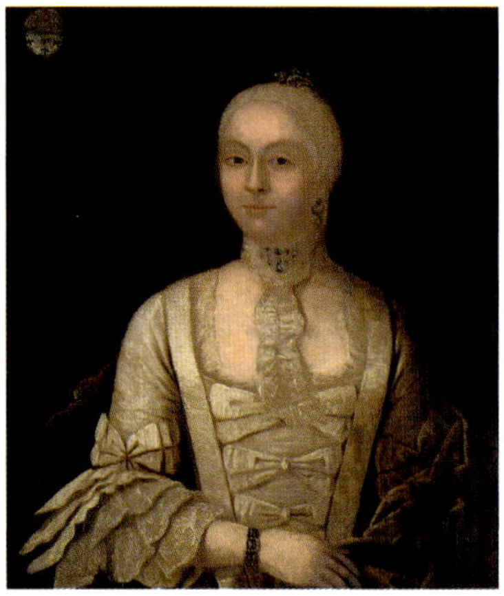

unknown artist
Portrait of a Lady
oil on canvas 80 x 62
PCF45

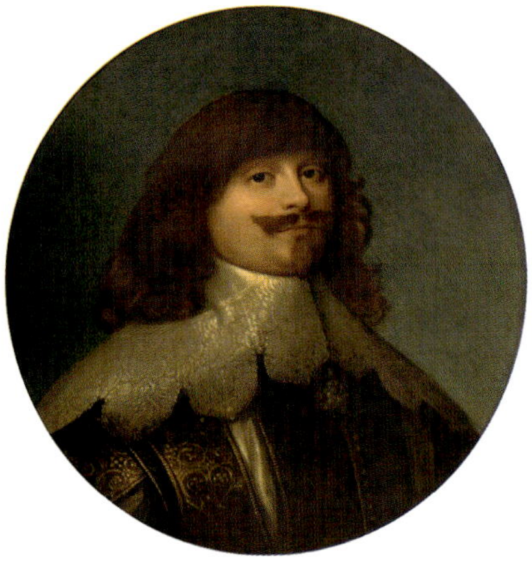

unknown artist
Sir Gilbert Talbot, Knight of Salwarp (1606–1695)
oil on canvas 70 x 50
PCF57

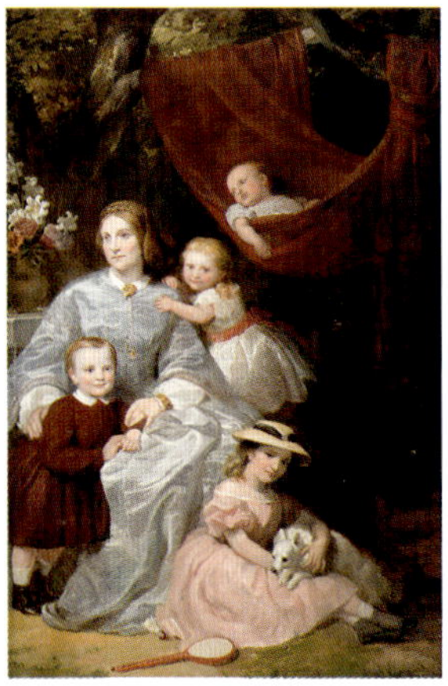

unknown artist
The Family of Captain Charles Arthur Talbot
oil on canvas 250 x 140
PCF51

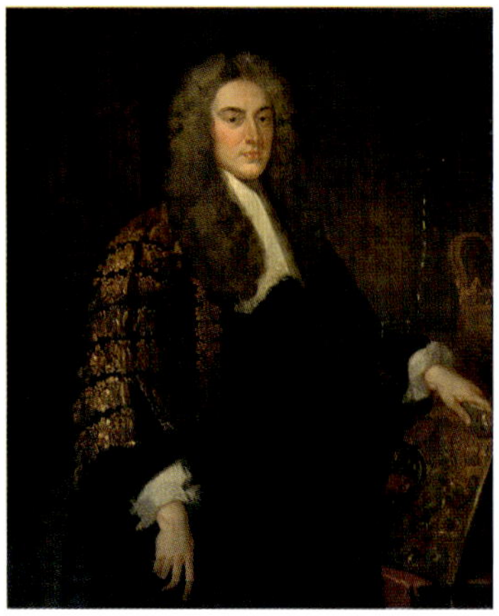

Vanderbank, John c.1694–1739
Charles Talbot, 1st Lord Talbot (1685–1737)
oil on canvas 140 x 100
PCF58

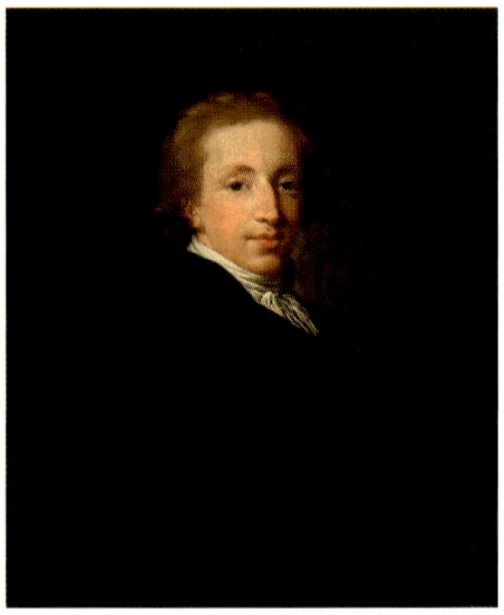

Vigée-LeBrun, Elisabeth Louise 1755–1842
Charles Chetwynd, 2nd Earl Talbot (1777–1849) 1798
oil on canvas 90 x 60
PCF59

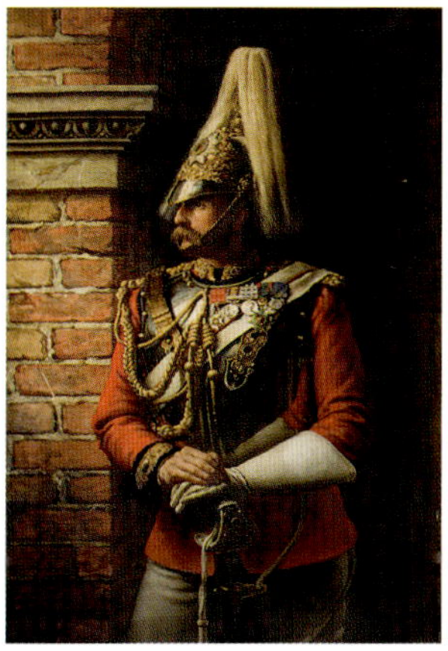

Wortley, Archibald J. Stuart 1849–1905
Sir Reginald Arthur James Talbot, KCB, 3rd Son of the 18th Earl of Shrewsbury (1841–1929)
oil on canvas 200 x 97
PCF42

Leek Town Council

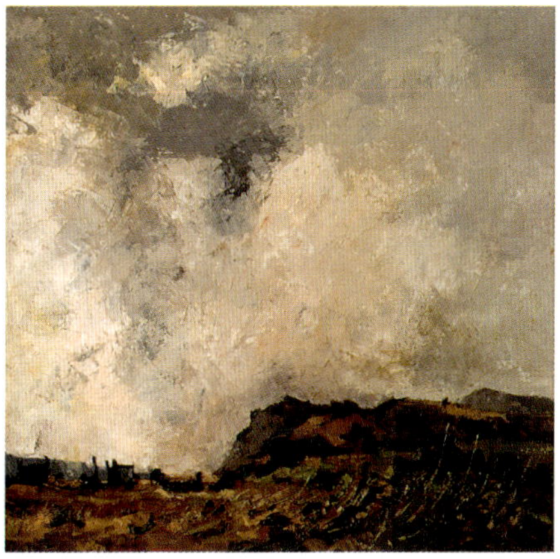

Dawson, Robert 1926–1997
Rain Storm over the Roaches
oil on board 90 x 90 (E)
PCF1

Staffordshire Moorlands District Council

On the 11th September 1882 the foundation stone of the Nicholson Institute was laid by Mrs J. Nicholson and on the 16th October 1884 the building opened. The building cost £20,000 and was paid for by Joshua Nicholson who became head of the firm Brough, Nicholson & Hall in 1884. The building boasted a free library with a reference section and newsroom, a museum and art gallery and a place where art classes and lectures could be held. Oscar Wilde delivered a lecture in 1885 on 'Dress' here and works by Poussin, Canaletto, Da Vinci and Ruysdael graced the walls of this building, on loan from the South Kensington Museum (now the Victoria & Albert Museum).

In 1900 the buildings for the Leek School of Art, Science and Technology were opened and art education in the service of industry was consolidated in Leek. The collection of artworks and curiosities, which the Nicholson Institute housed, were built up as gifts from local businessmen and residents. These were housed in the original Art Club Room. Examples of donations include a collection of silk moths presented by Henry Davenport and Thomas Wardle and paintings such as Richard Jack's *The Swedish Dyehouse* which were bought by the Library Committee and the Urban District Council. By 1890 exhibits were being turned away due to lack of space.

In 1998 the decision was made to carefully store all the Collection within the Staffordshire Moorlands District Council buildings, as the Nicholson Institute could no longer be maintained as an operating museum space (the Council cannot accept any donations at present). The Nicholson Institute building is still an important architectural feature within the historic market town of Leek and houses the town's library services and Leek College. Until 2005, the main gallery in the Institute was used as a venue for local exhibiting artists and meeting groups, such as the Staffordshire Society of Artists. The gallery has also been a venue for the annual Leek Arts Festival Open Exhibition.

Staffordshire Moorlands District Council currently house the Nicholson Collection in storage, as the building no longer acts as a functioning museum space. There are plans in progress to make the Collection more accessible to the public and to reinstate the gallery as an arts exhibition venue for the town and district. The Council's arts development team is currently working in partnership with other organisations, such as the Public Catalogue Foundation, Staffordshire Arts & Museums Service, Staffordshire County Council's Library Services and The Potteries Museum & Art Gallery to achieve this. It is hoped that the Collection will be made accessible again through the use of eight specially commissioned cases, the development of internet resources and outreach projects.

Any enquiries about the items within the Collection, or plans for the future use of the gallery, can be made via Staffordshire Moorlands District Council, Arts Development Service (www.staffsmoorlands.gov.uk).

Deborah Nicklin, Arts Development Officer

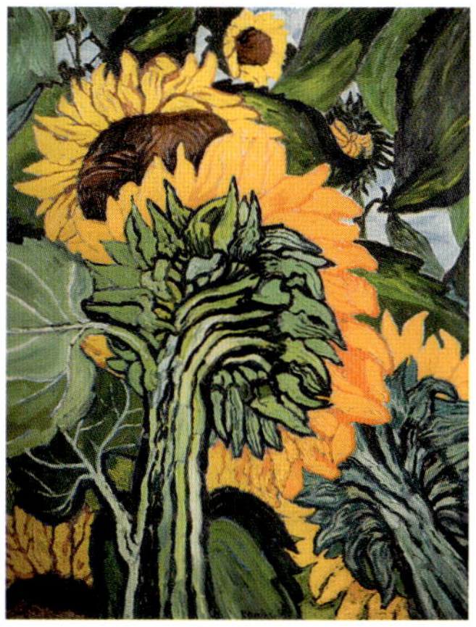

Bratby, John Randall 1928–1992
Sunflowers
oil on canvas 120 x 90.5
LEKAG:1994.56

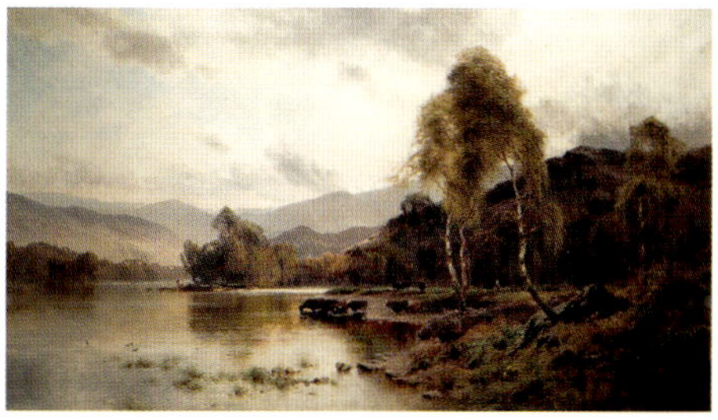

Breanski, Alfred de 1852–1928
Silvery September
oil on canvas 75 x 126
LEKAG:1994.4

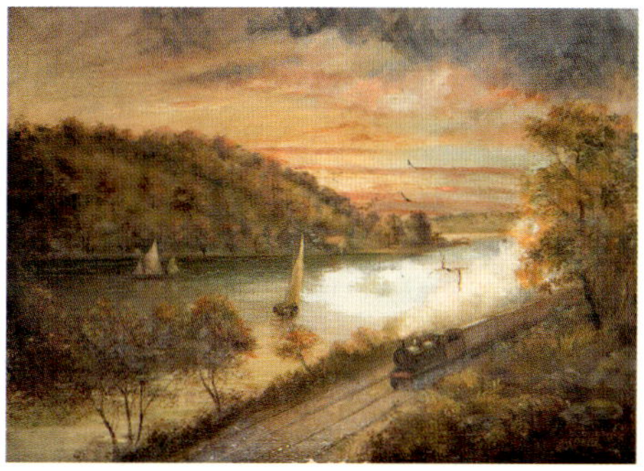

Campling, H. R. active 1882–1904
Rudyard Lake 1900
oil on canvas 53 x 71
LEKAG:1994.11

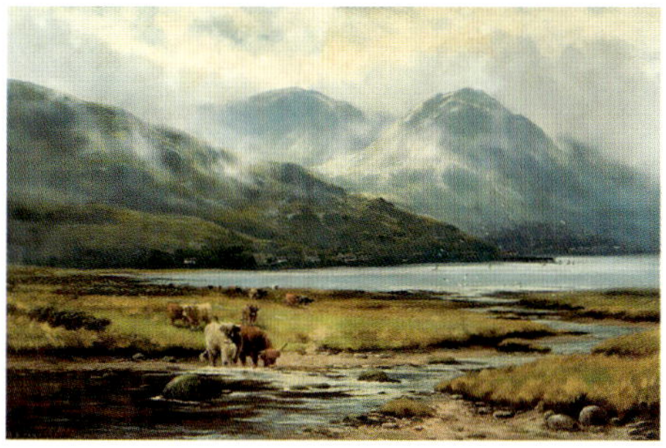

Cubley, Henry Hadfield 1848–1934
Morning Mists, Arrochar 1915
oil on canvas 90 x 136 (E)
LEKAG:1994.7

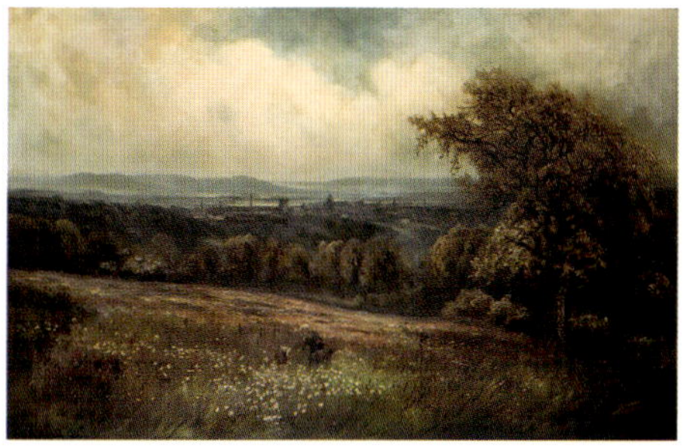

Cubley, Henry Hadfield 1848–1934
Leek from Ladderedge 1918
oil on canvas 90 x 136 (E)
LEKAG:1991.1

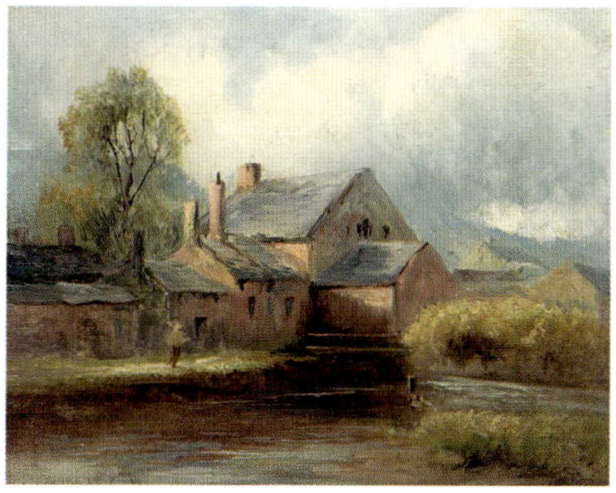

Cubley, Henry Hadfield 1848–1934
The Old Mill
oil on board 32 x 40.5
LEKAG:1994.25

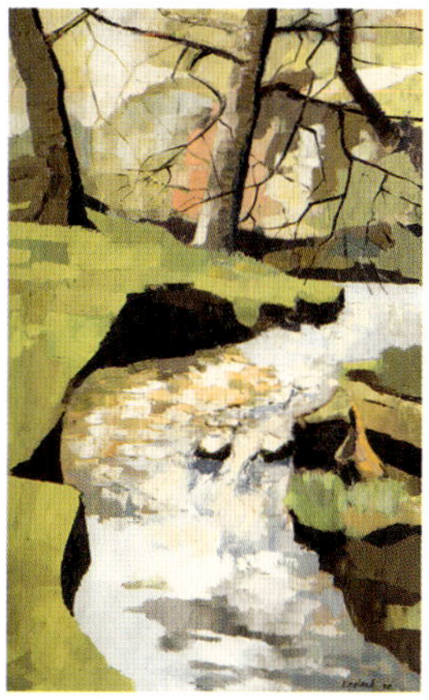

England, Frederick John b.1939
Rudyard Stream 1970
oil on canvas 112.5 x 68.5
LEKAG:1994.13

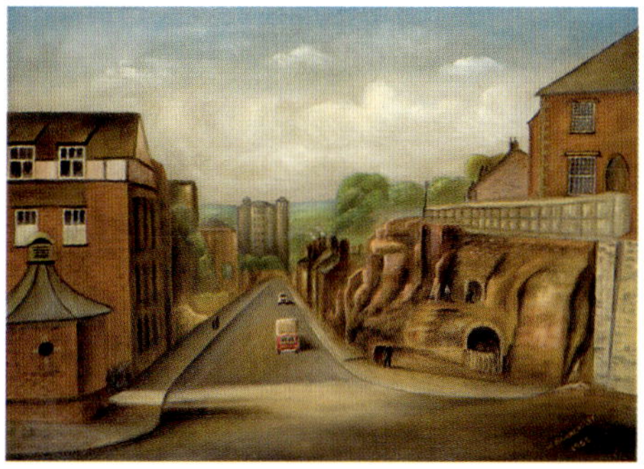

Hammersley, W.
Mill Street, Leek 1963
oil on board 44 x 60
LEKAG:1994.44

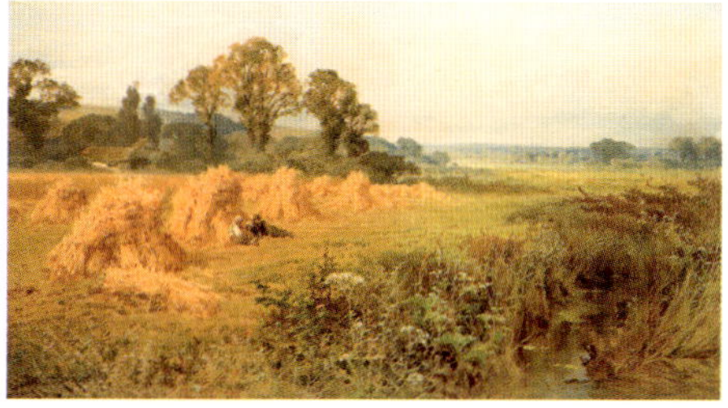

Hooper, John Horace c.1850–c.1899
Near Guildford
oil on canvas 60 x 105.5
LEKAG:1994.10

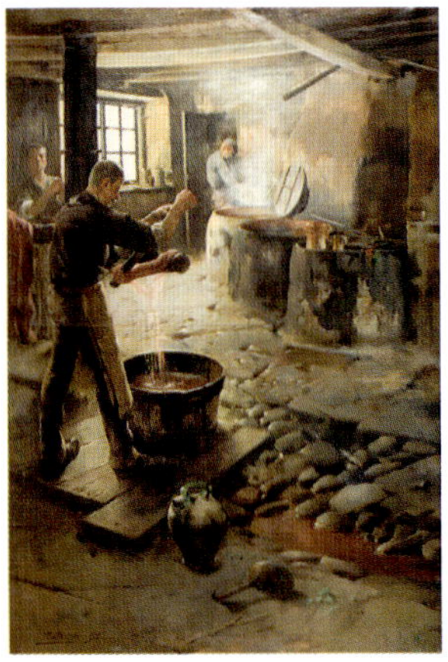

Jack, Richard 1866–1952
The Swedish Dyehouse 1893
oil on canvas 183 x 119
LEKAG:1994.17

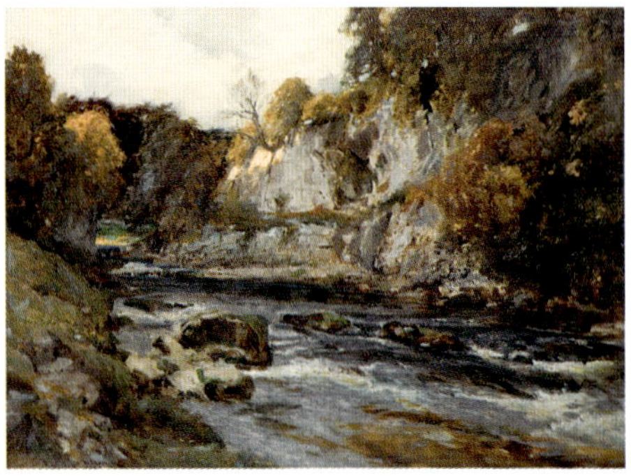

Jack, Richard 1866–1952
Loup Scar, Wharfedale
oil on canvas 79 x 101
LEKAG:1994.3

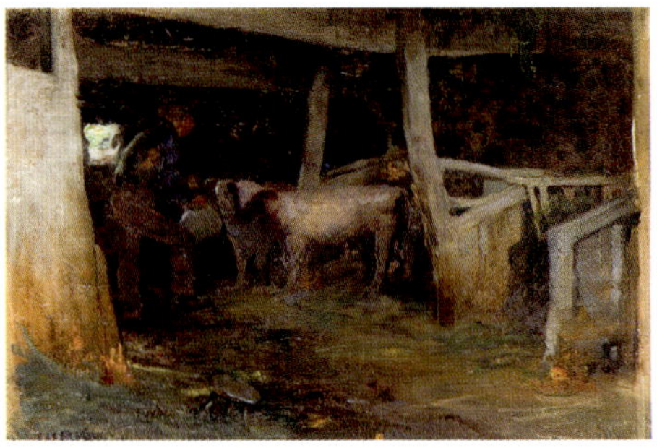

Kean, William R.
Feeding the Calves
oil on canvas 32.5 x 47
LEKAG:1994.35

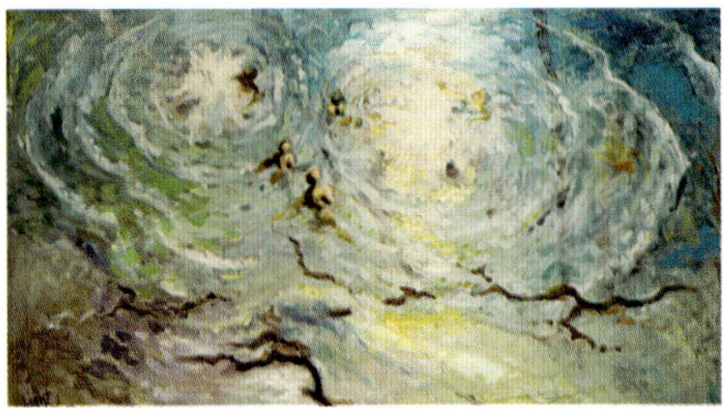

Light, David G. b.1959
Malaccan Beach
oil on canvas 61 x 104
LEKAG:1994.14

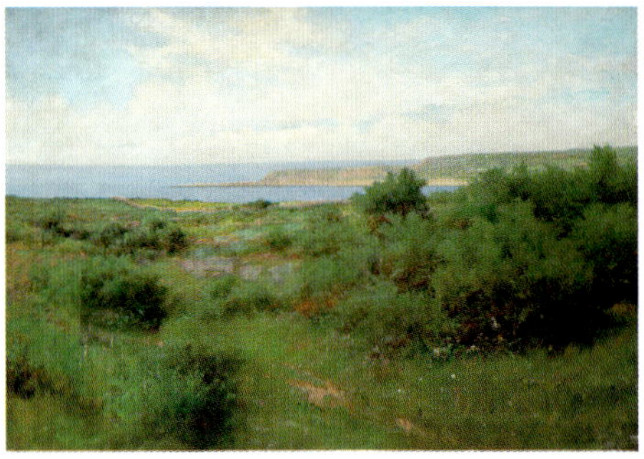

Newey, Harry Foster 1858–1933
Oxwich Moor
oil on canvas 55 x 75
LEKAG:1994.8

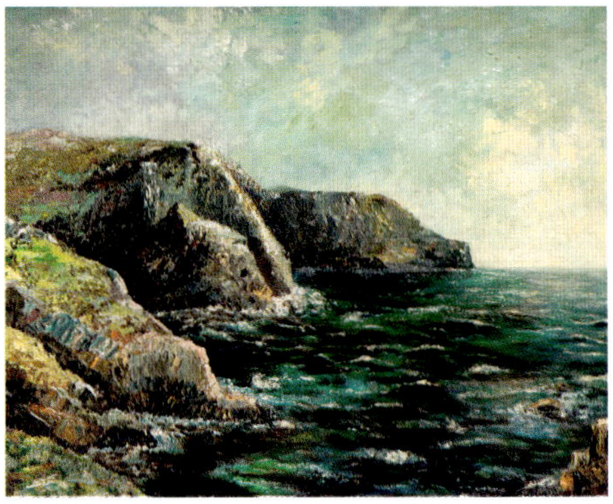

Nierinck, Dorothy M.
Welsh Coast
oil on board 57 x 69
LEKAG:1994.65

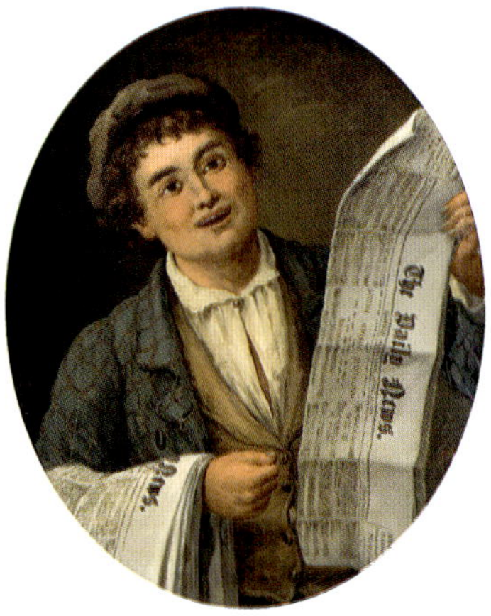

O'Neill, A.
Newsboy
oil on canvas 63 x 51
LEKAG:1994.80

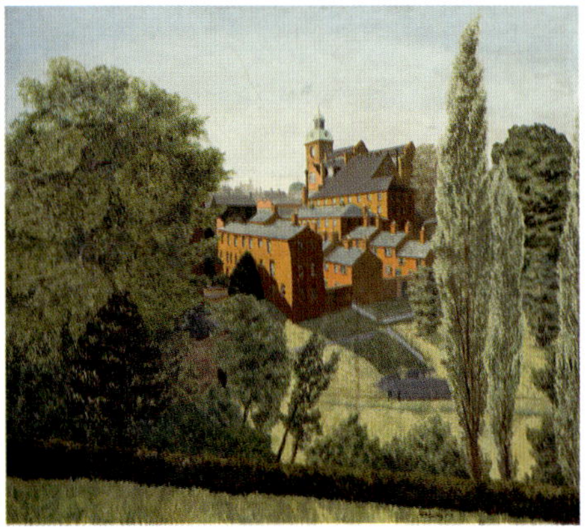

Oversby, M. D.
Brough Park and the Nicholson Institute, Leek 1960
oil on canvas 100 x 121
LEKAG:1994.16

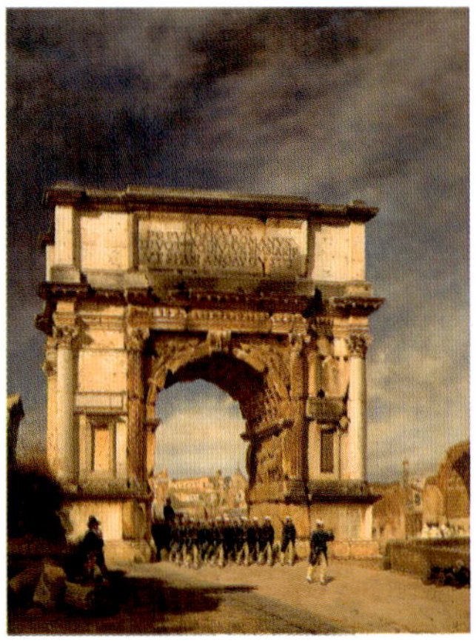

unknown artist
Arch of Titus, Rome 1835
oil on canvas 99 x 72
LEKAG:1994.5

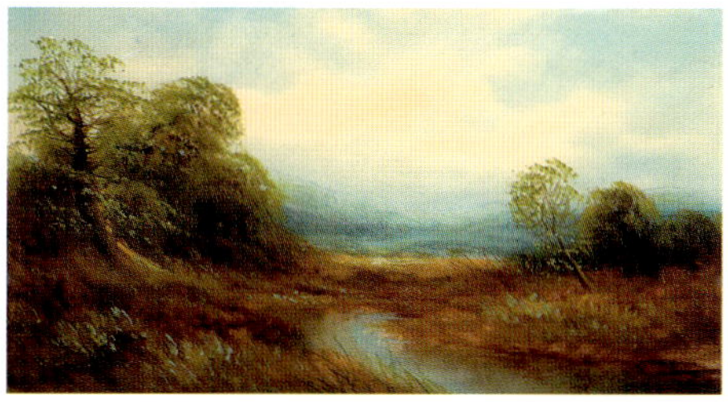

unknown artist
Landscape Scene and Mountains
oil on board 25 x 45
LEKAG:1994.39

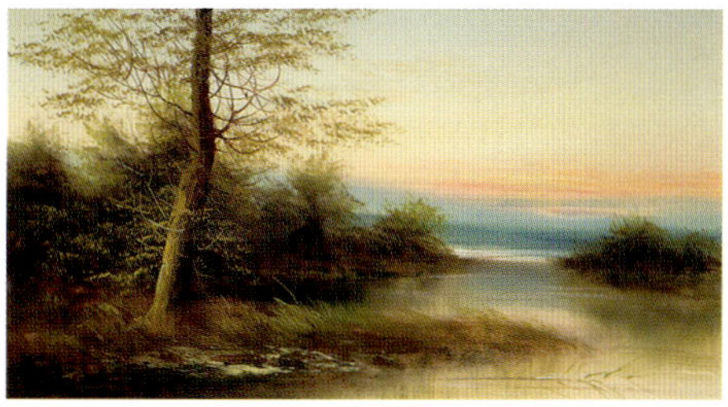

unknown artist
Landscape Scene at the Edge of the River
oil on board 25.5 x 45
LEKAG:1994.38

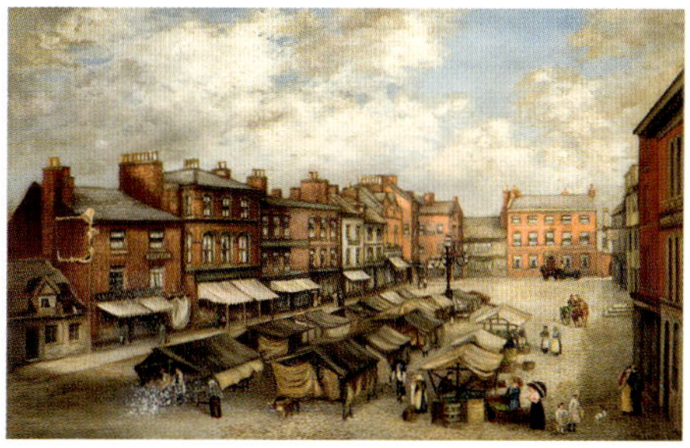

unknown artist
Market Square
oil on canvas 59.5 x 89.5
LEKAG:1994.64

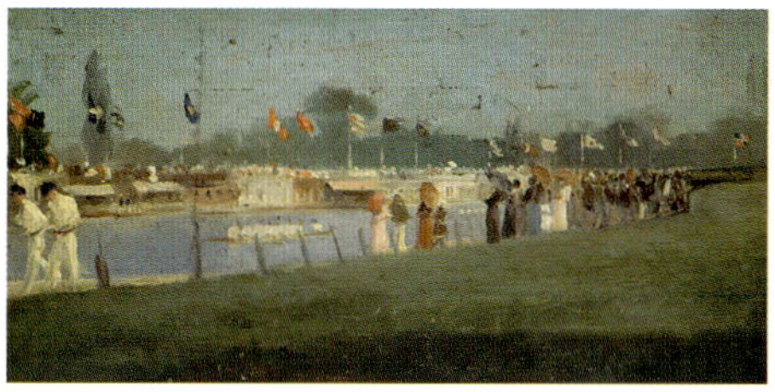

Whistler, J. M. N.
Henley Regatta
oil on panel 17.5 x 32.5
LEKAG:1994.57

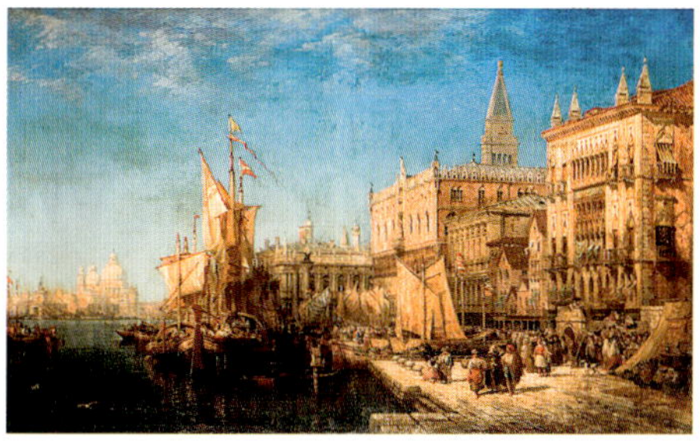

Wyld, William 1806–1889
Venice
oil on canvas 128 x 201
LEKAG:1991.2

Erasmus Darwin House

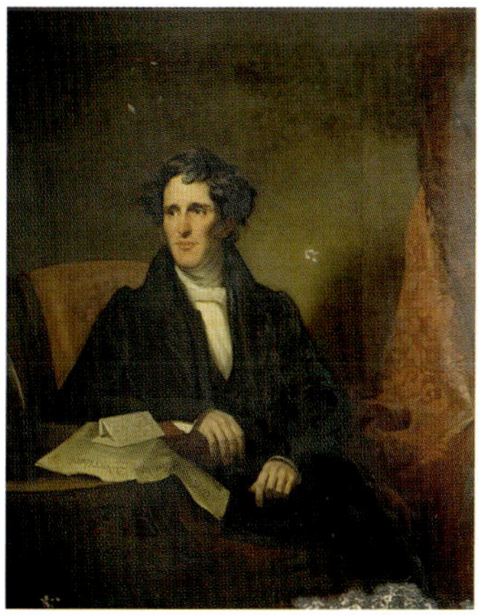

British (English) School early 19th C
Reverend Chancellor James Thomas Law (1790–1876)
oil on canvas 144.8 x 111.8
EDH 43.10

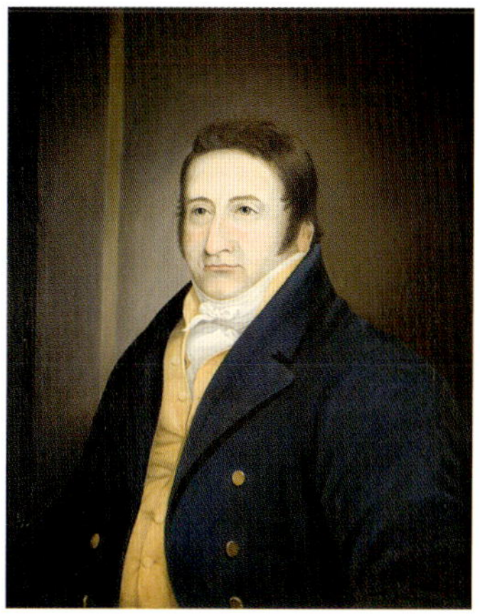

British (English) School early 19th C
William Green (?)
oil on canvas 48.3 x 38.1
EDH 43.9

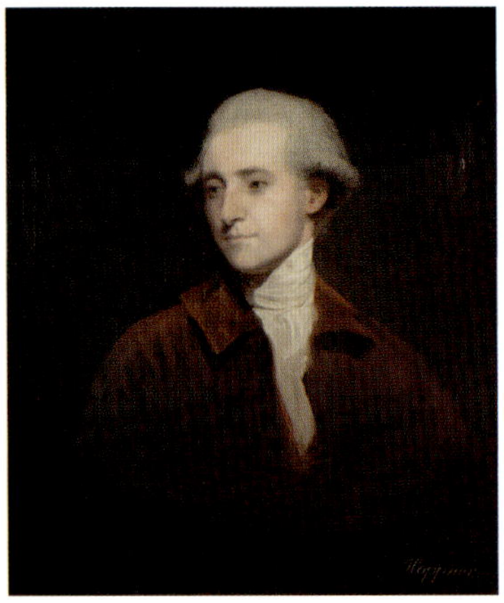

Hoppner, John 1758–1810
George Canning (1770–1827) (?)
oil on canvas 76.2 x 63.5
EDH 43.11

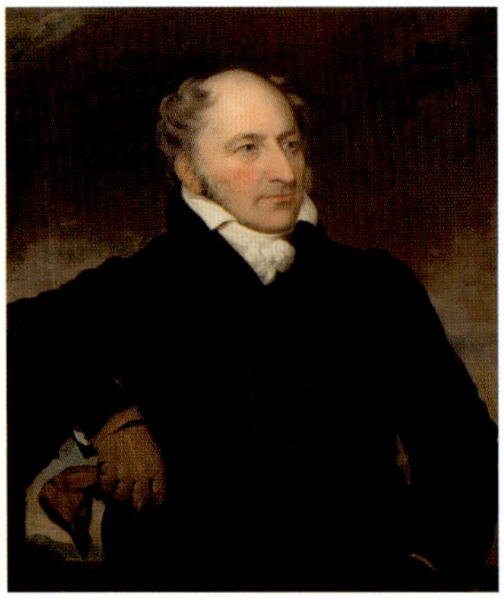

unknown artist early 19th C
Dr Robert Levett of Lichfield (d.1782)
oil on canvas 87.6 x 71.1
EDH 43.13

Lichfield District Council

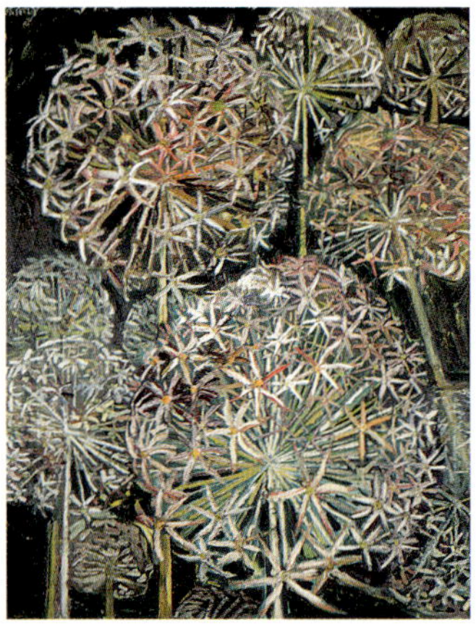

Bratby, John Randall 1928–1992
Flowers of Summer 1966
oil on canvas 113 x 87
1983.145.51

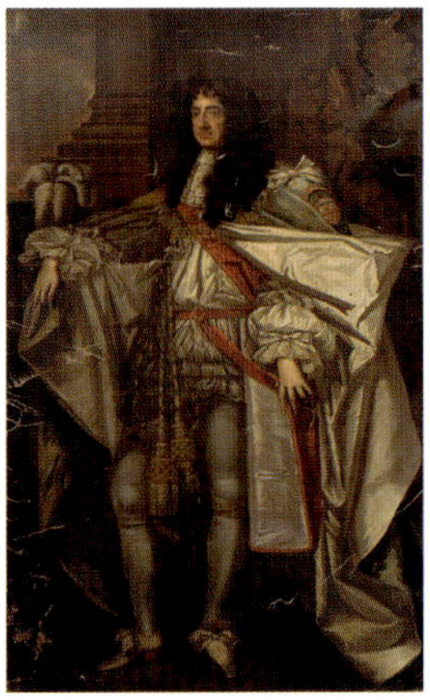

British (English) School
Charles II (1630–1685)
oil on canvas 228.5 x 133.5
1985.1.13

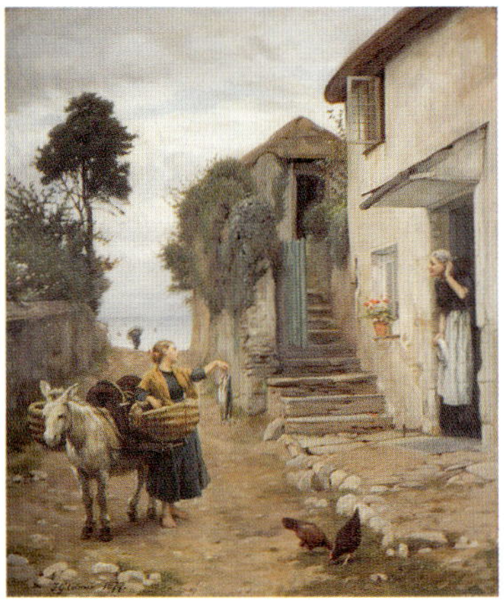

Cotman, Frederick George 1850–1920
The First Otter
oil on canvas 53 x 44.5
LDC.04

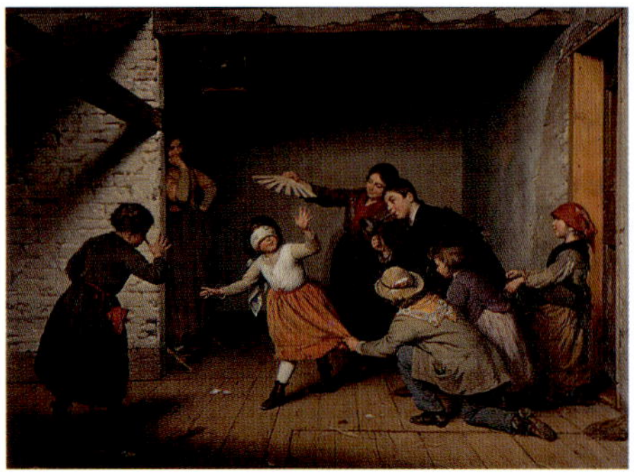

Paoletti, Antonio Ermolao 1834–1912
Blind Man's Bluff
oil on canvas 43 x 58.5
LDC.03

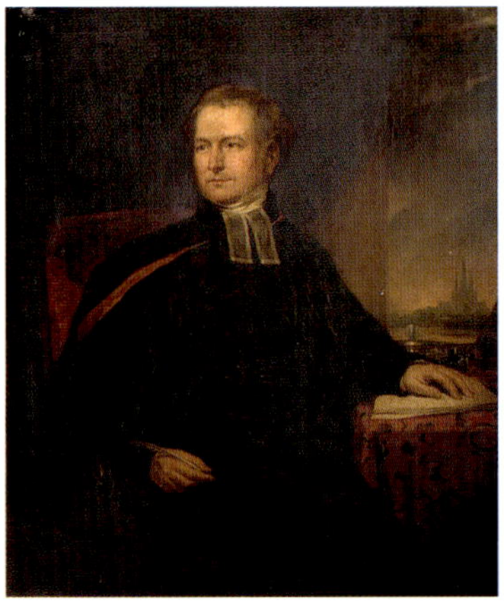

Pickersgill, Henry William (style of)
1782–1875
Canon Bailye (1783–1830) c.1850
oil on canvas 127 x 101.5
1985.1.7

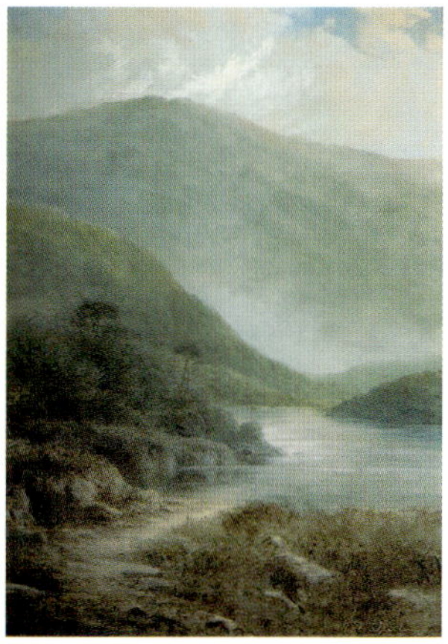

Preston, William
Extensive Lake and Mountains
oil on canvas 73.5 x 48
LDC.05

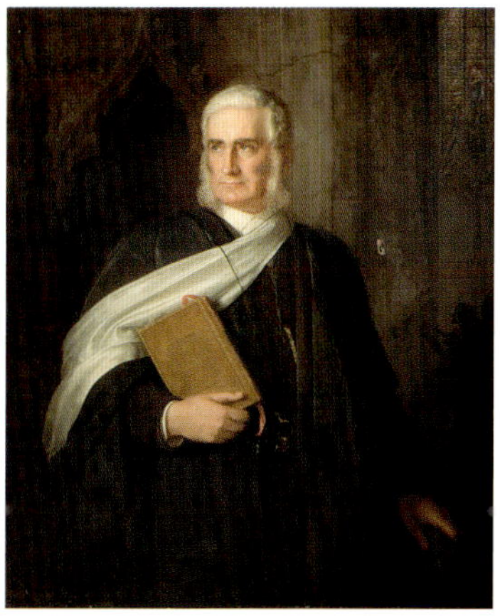

Schmitt, Guido Philipp 1834–1922
Reverend John Gylby Lonsdale (1818–1907) 1878
oil on canvas 127 x 101.5
1985.1.2

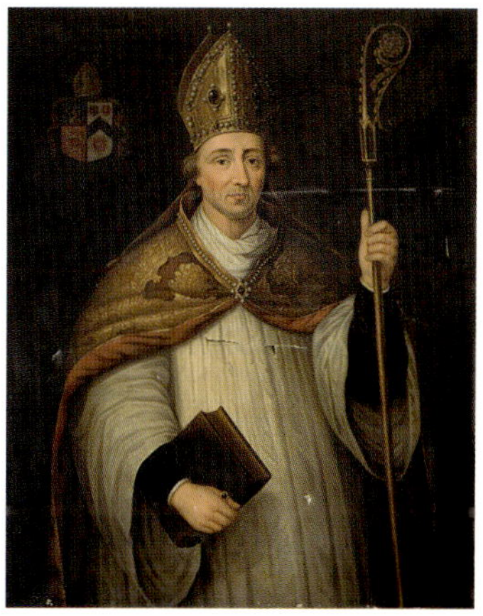

Smith
Gulielmus Smyth, Bishop of Lincoln 1836
oil on canvas 122 x 96.5
LDC.01

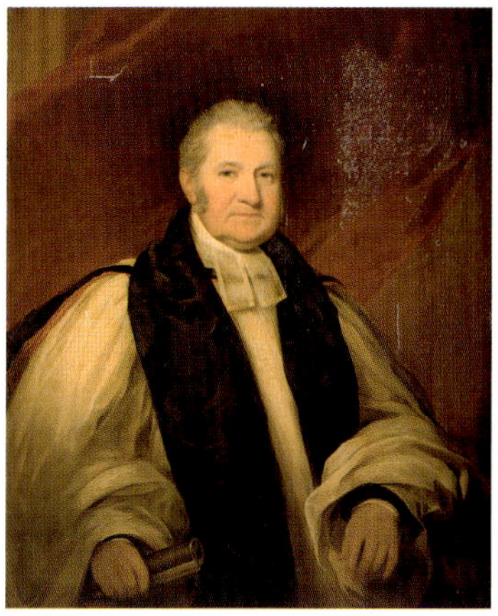

unknown artist 19th C
Reverend Chancellor Law
oil on canvas 104 x 84
1985.1.1

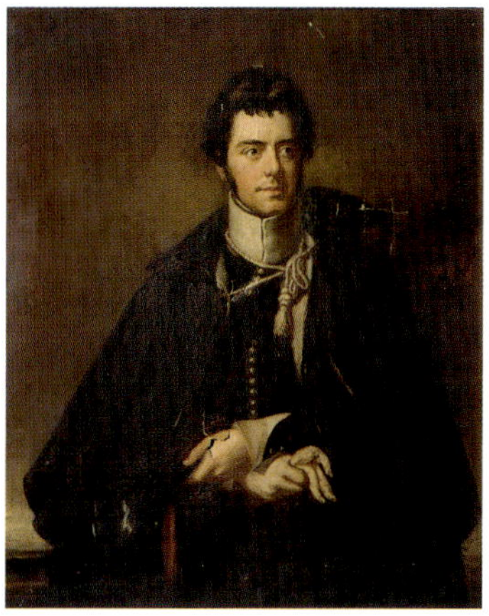

unknown artist mid-19th C
Mr John Mott (1787–1869)
oil on canvas 127 x 101.5
1985.1.6

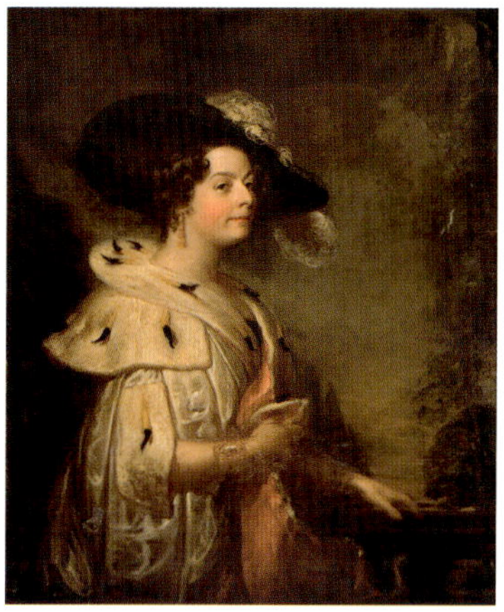

unknown artist mid-19th C
Mrs Henrietta Mott
oil on canvas 127 x 101.5
1985.1.5

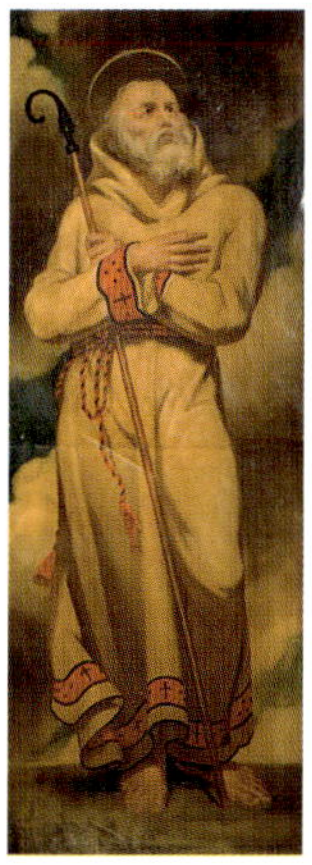

unknown artist
Biblical Figure
oil on canvas 168 x 58
1983.138.1

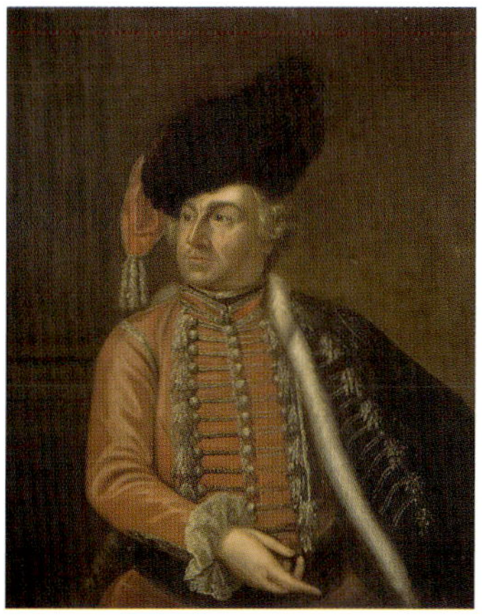

unknown artist
David Garrick (1717–1779)
oil on canvas 122 x 91
1983.147.1

Lichfield Heritage Centre

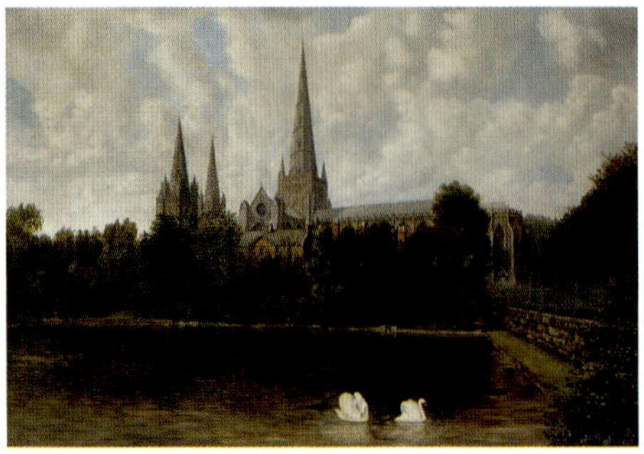

Smith, H. J. b.1876
View of Lichfield Cathedral 1892–1896
oil on canvas 75 x 150
HE38

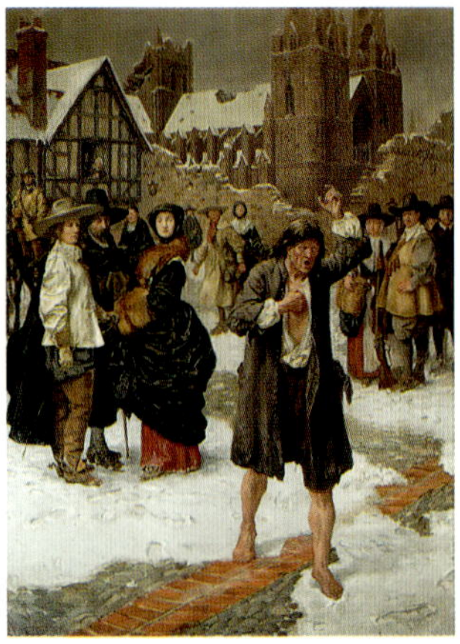

Spence, Robert 1871–1964
Woe to the Bloody City of Lichfield
oil on canvas 300 x 170 (E)
HE70

Samuel Johnson Birthplace Museum

Samuel Johnson's Birthplace in Lichfield has been a personal museum dedicated to Samuel Johnson since 1901. It has been preserved as a public memorial to the genius of the late Dr Samuel Johnson and as a place of historic interest. The museum collections have been built up since 1901. The Collection comprises personalia, pictures, furniture, manuscripts and books. Three significant donations form the major part of the book collection; the Hay Hunter, the Wood and the Blum Libraries. The book collection consists of the works of Johnson and his contemporaries, books owned by Johnson and his friends, as well as biographies and critical studies of Johnson and his contemporaries.

Samuel Johnson's Birthplace also has letters and manuscripts relating to key figures such as Samuel Johnson, James Boswell, Anna Seward, Hester Piozzi, Joshua Reynolds and Sarah Siddons. In addition there are many documents associated with the history of Lichfield.

The Birthplace Museum has a number of interesting oil paintings and pastels of Johnson as well as watercolour paintings of local views. There are also engravings of Johnson, his contemporaries and associated views. Significant items of furniture include Johnson's portable desk, Boswell's bookcase and Johnson's armchair. The Collection also contains important personal items belonging to Johnson.

Annette French, Curator

Facing page: Italian School, *The Madonna and Child* (detail), c.1400, The New Art Gallery Walsall, (p. 208)

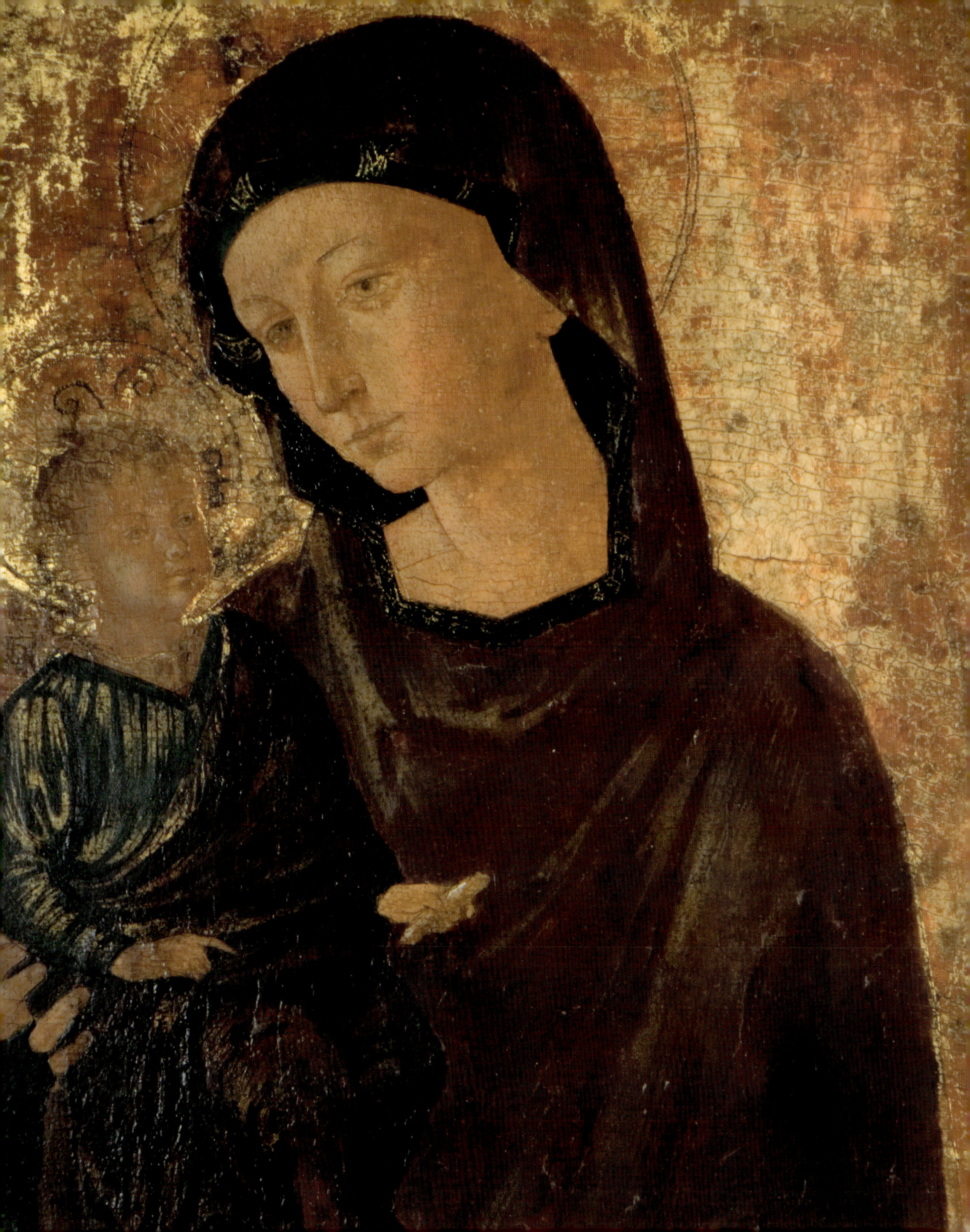

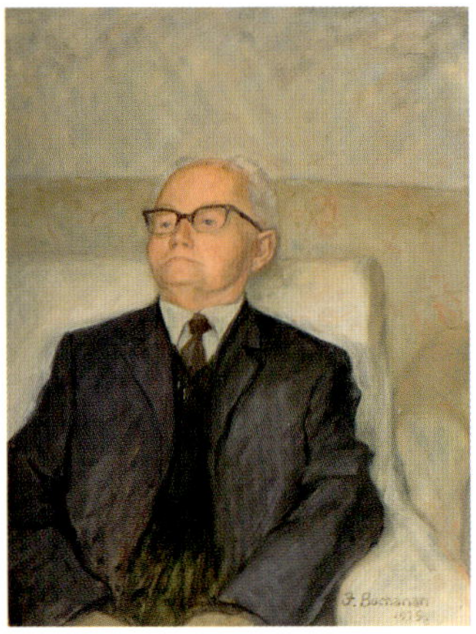

Buchanan, J.
Albert Sperrin (1903–1987) 1979
oil on canvas 53 x 42.5
2000.281

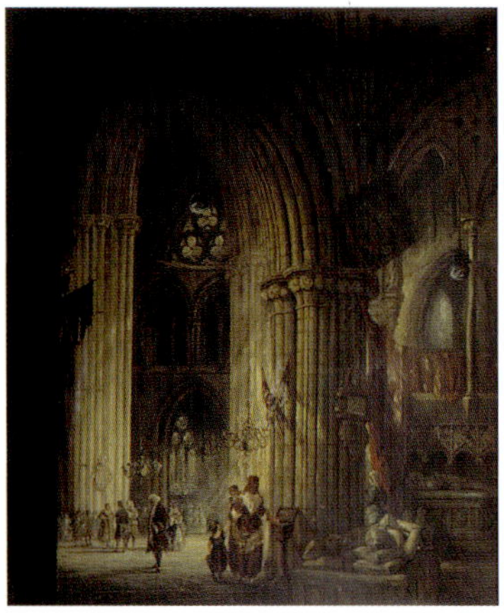

Fulleylove, John 1845–1908
Dr Johnson in Lichfield Cathedral 1891
oil on canvas 75 x 68
2000.212

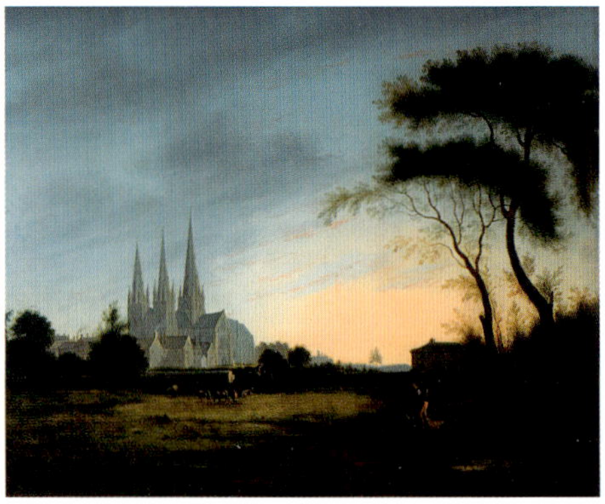

Glover, John (circle of) 1767–1849
Lichfield Cathedral from Sandford Street
oil on canvas 58.5 x 75
2001.1346

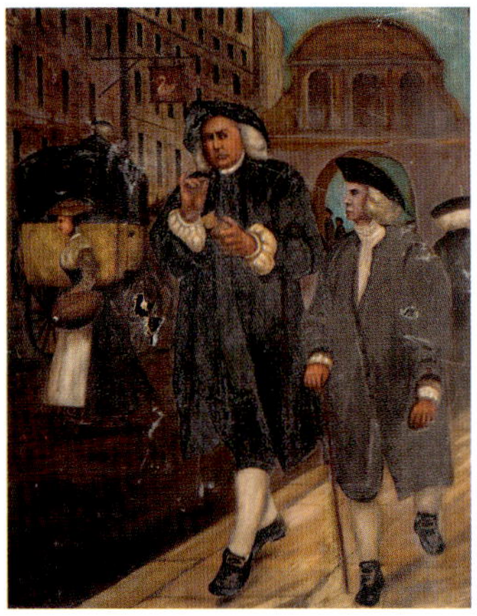

Holgate, W. J. (Reverend) c.1842–c.1920
Johnson and Oliver Goldsmith Walking down Fleet Street, London c.1920
oil on canvas 91.5 x 71.5
2000.170

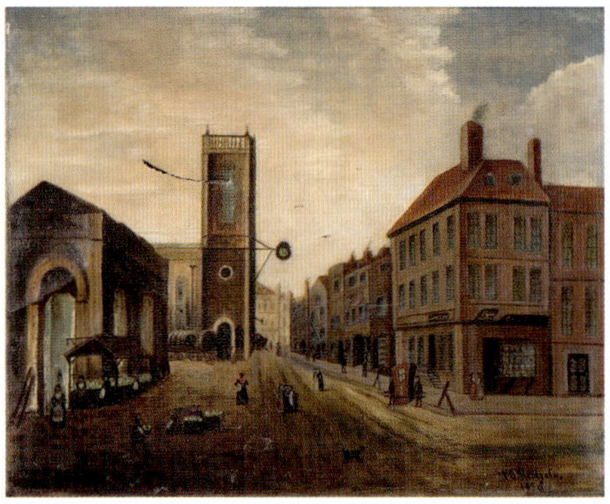

Holgate, W. J. (Reverend) c.1842–c.1920
Lichfield Market Place during the Days of Dr Johnson c.1920
oil on canvas 63.5 x 75.5
2000.169

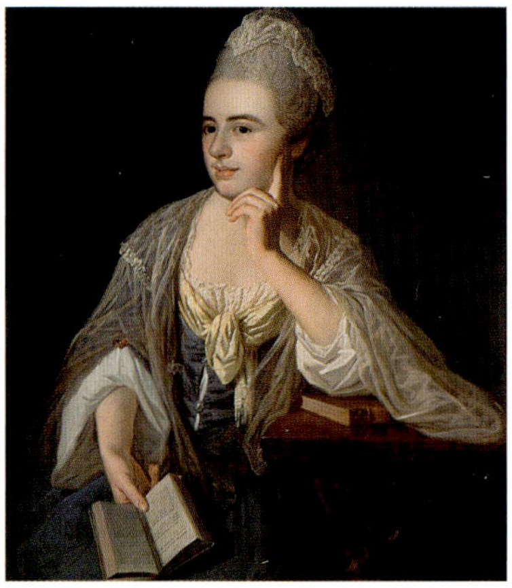

Millar, James 1735–1805
Mrs Esther Day
oil on canvas 99 x 87
2001.532

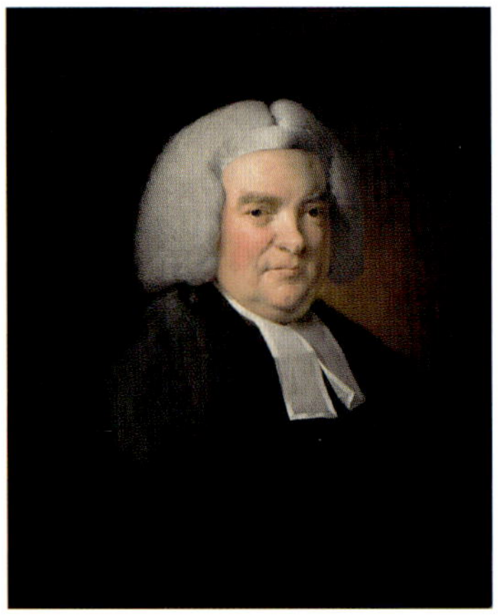

Opie, John 1761–1807
Reverend Dr John Taylor c.1785
oil on canvas 90 x 76.5
2001.1345 (P)

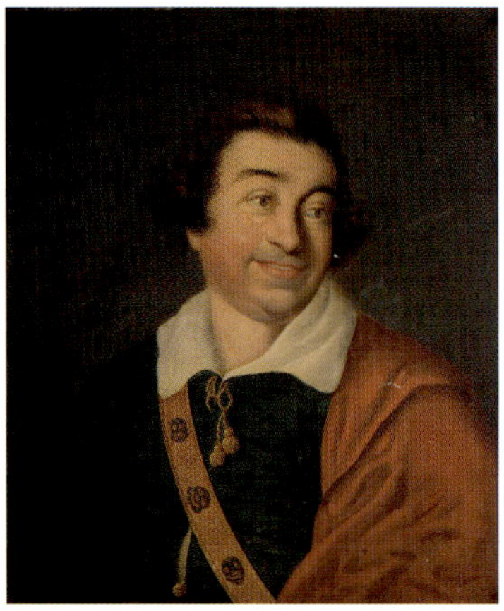

Pether, William 1731–1819
David Garrick (1717–1779) 1776
oil on canvas 77 x 66.5
2000.340

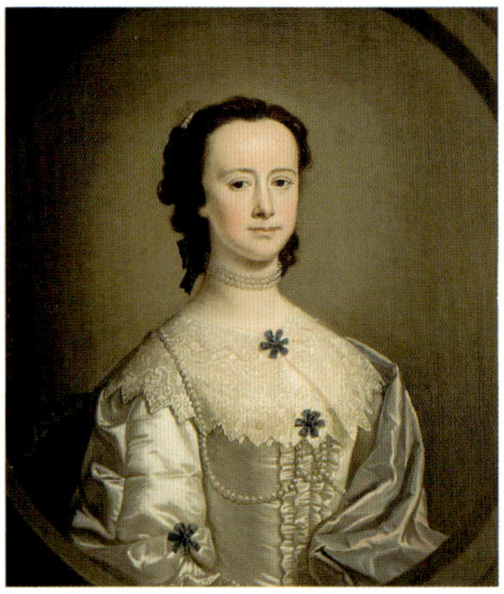

Pickering, Henry active 1740–c.1771
Elizabeth Hunter, later Mrs Thomas Seward (d.1780) 1755
oil on canvas 89.5 x 77
2001.443

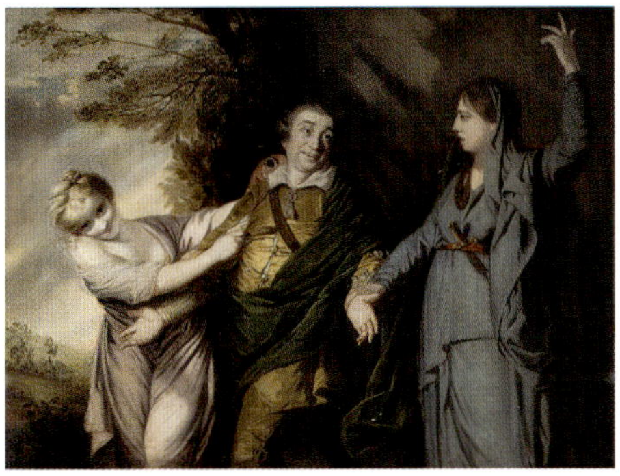

Reynolds, Joshua (after) 1723–1792
David Garrick between Tragedy and Comedy late 18th C
oil on canvas 80 x 100.5
2000.276

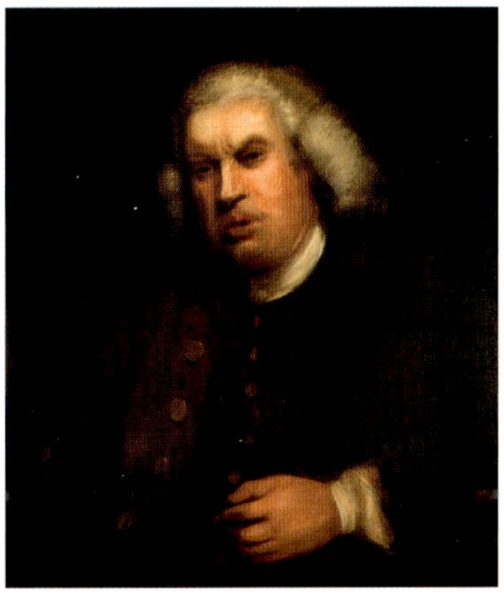

Reynolds, Joshua (after) 1723–1792
Samuel Johnson (1709–1784) 19th C
oil on canvas 90 x 78
2001.523

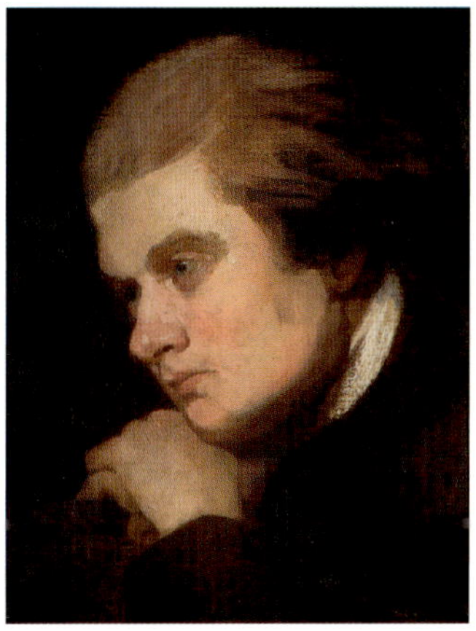

Reynolds, Joshua (attributed to) 1723–1792
Johnson as a Young Man (1709–1784)
oil on canvas 58 x 49
2001.178

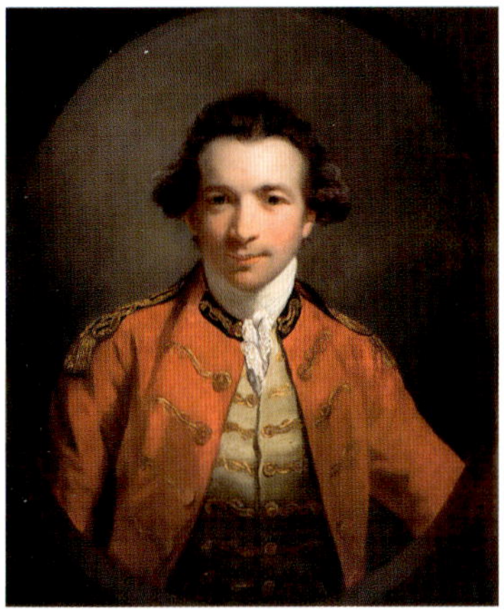

Reynolds, Joshua (school of) 1723–1792
Sir Thomas Mills (sometimes known as Major André) (d.1793) 1772–1778
oil on canvas 93 x 80
2001.116

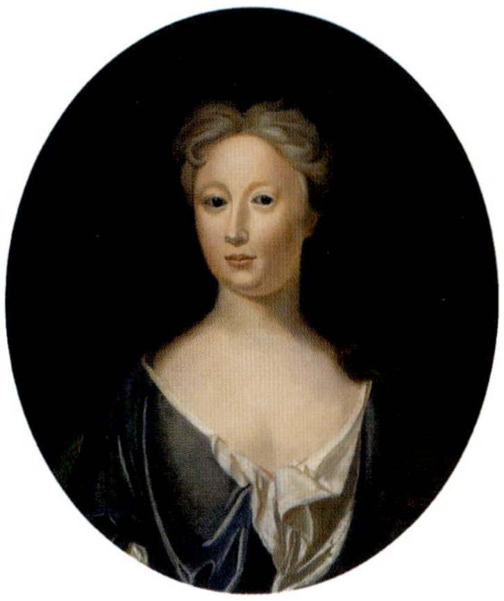

Sanders, John M.
Mrs Samuel Johnson (1689–1752) c.1980s
oil on canvas 84.5 x 73
2001.177

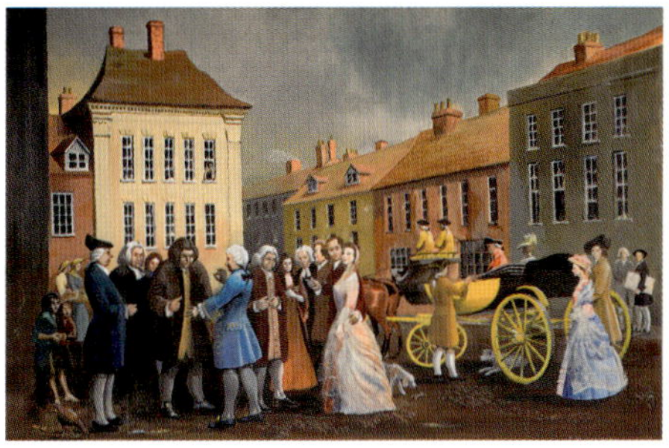

Sanders, John M.
Lichfield Market Square with Carriage
oil on canvas 63 x 93.5
2000.346

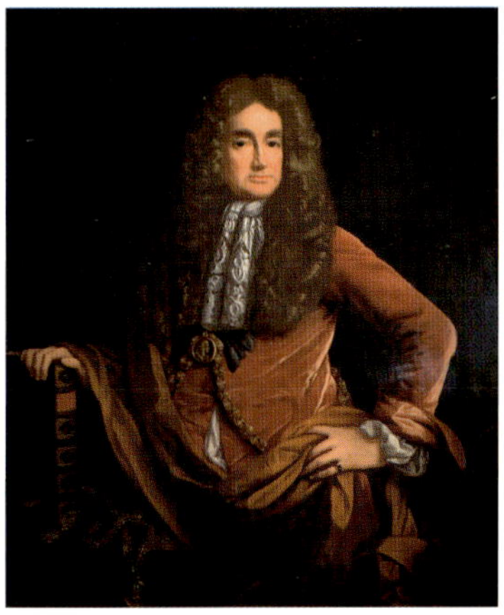

Smith, J.
Elias Ashmole (1617–1692) (after John Riley) 1836
oil on canvas 160 x 123 (E)
2001.531

unknown artist late 17th–early 18th C
A Member of the Dyott Family
oil on canvas 160 x 123 (E)
2001.533

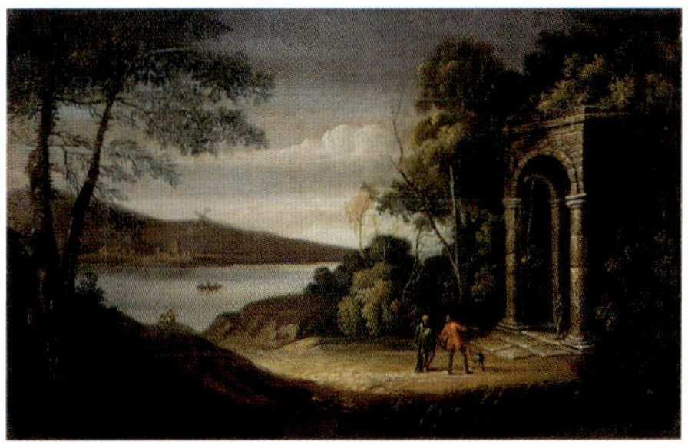

unknown artist early 18th C
Landscape in a Classical Manner
oil on canvas 28 x 37.5
2000.78

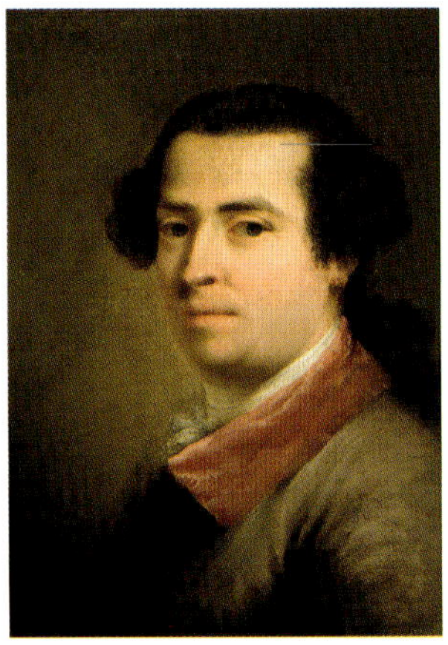

unknown artist 18th C
David Garrick (1717–1779) as a Young Man
oil on canvas 58.5 x 49.5
2001.183

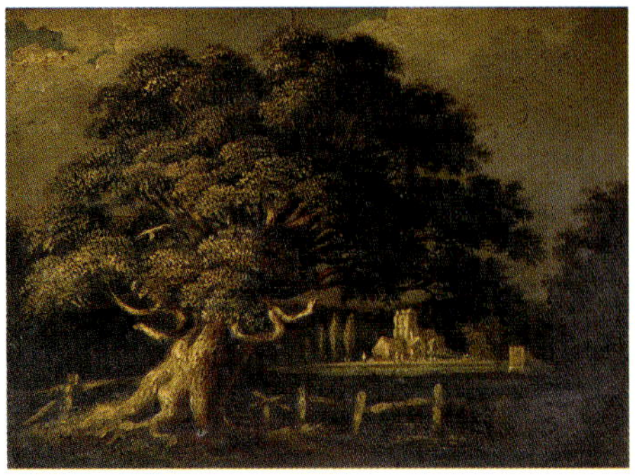

unknown artist late 18th–early 19th C
Johnson's Willow
oil on canvas 31.5 x 37.5
2000.280

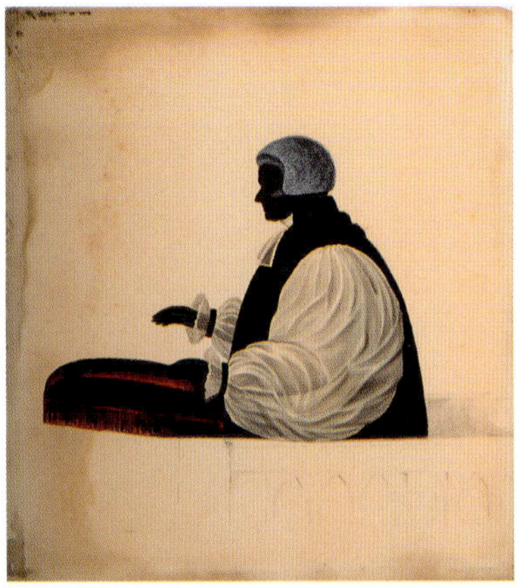

unknown artist early 19th C
Bishop Ryder (1777–1836)
oil on cardboard 22 x 19
2000.235

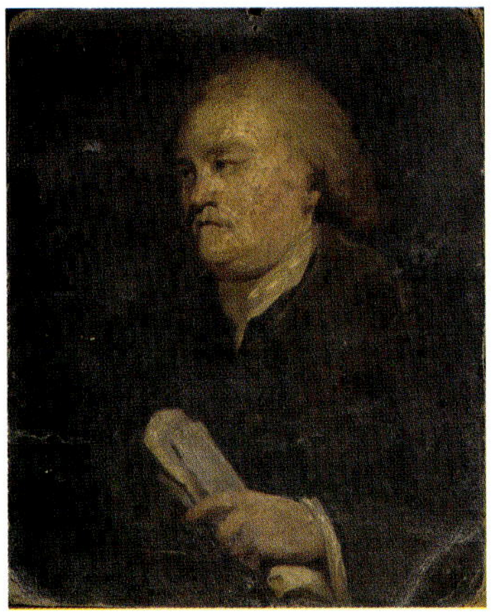

unknown artist 19th C
Dr Johnson without His Wig (1709–1784)
oil on cardboard 31 x 24
2000.103

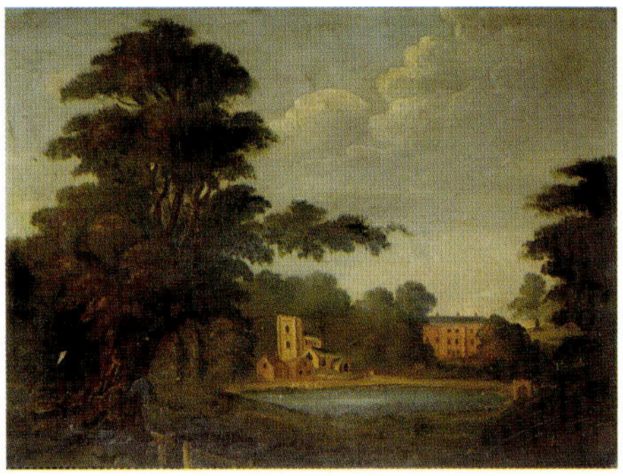

unknown artist 19th C
Johnson's Willow, St Chad's Church and Stowe House
oil on panel 27 x 32
2000.163

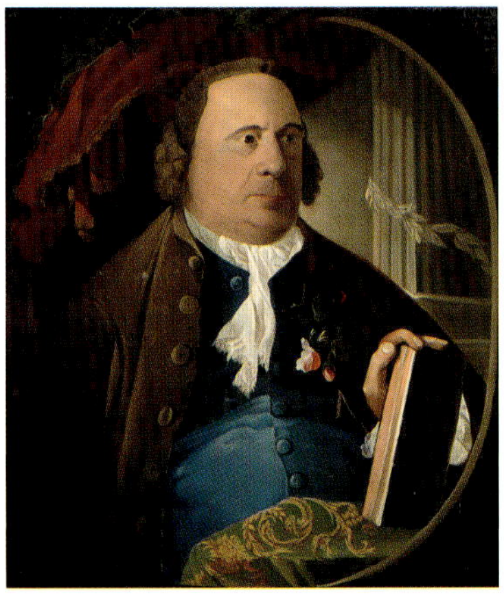

unknown artist
Samuel Johnson (1709–1784)
oil on canvas 77.5 x 64.5
2000.216

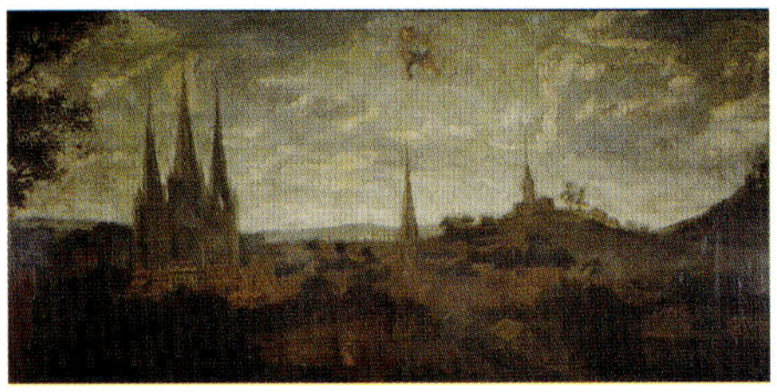

unknown artist
South-West Prospect View of Lichfield
oil on canvas 105 x 190
2001.445

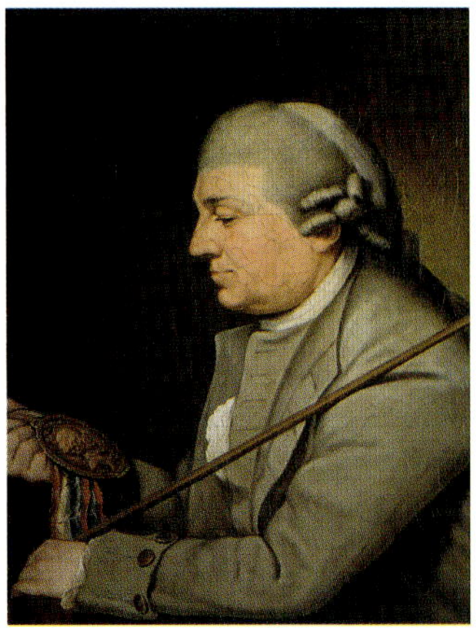

Vandergucht, Benjamin (copy of) 1753–1794
David Garrick in His Regalia as Steward of Stratford Jubilee, 1769 18th C
oil on canvas 96.5 x 83.5
2001.137

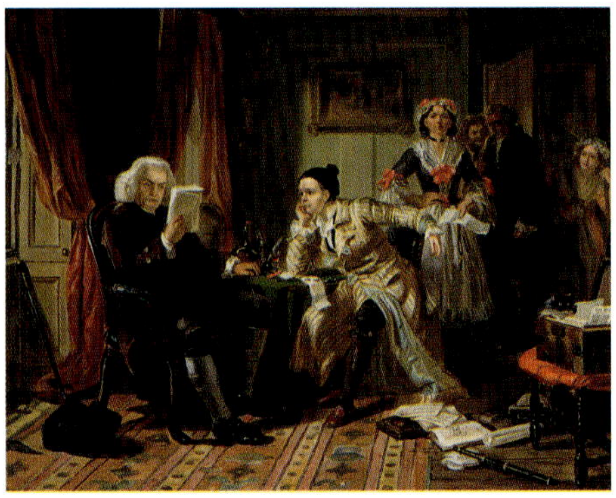

Ward, Edward Matthew 1816–1879
Johnson Reading the Manuscript of 'The Vicar of Wakefield'
oil on canvas 43.5 x 54.5
2001.161

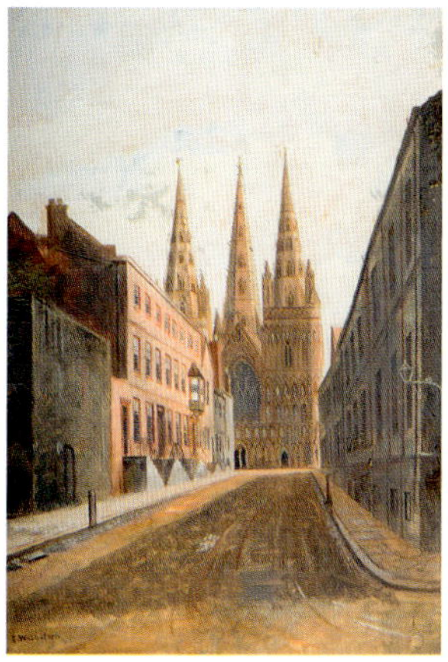

Willis-Pryce, George 1866–1949
West Front of Lichfield Cathedral
oil on canvas 51 x 38
2001.33

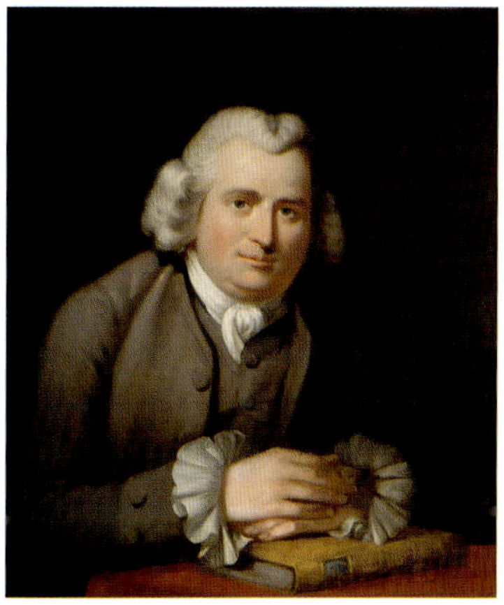

Wright, Joseph (after) 1756–1793
Erasmus Darwin (1731–1802) late 18th–early 19th C
oil on canvas 90.5 x 78
2001.119

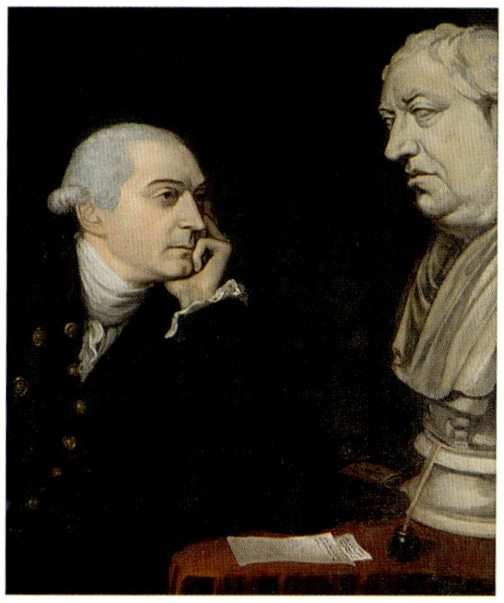

Zoffany, Johann (attributed to) 1733–1810
Bennet Langton Contemplating the Nolleken's Bust of Johnson c.1785
oil on canvas 93 x 79
2001.135

The Staffordshire Regiment Museum

The Staffordshire Regiment Museum's Collection tells the story of the Regiment and its forbears from its formation in Lichfield in 1705. It includes uniforms, equipment, medals (including 8 of the Regiment's 13 Victoria Crosses), badges, paintings and regimental memorabilia. There are special sections covering militia and volunteers, the Zulu War, both World Wars and the Gulf War. There is a children's hands-on area and outside there are armoured vehicles, two Anderson Shelters and a long section of a First World War trench. The Regimental archive and library are onsite and may be viewed by appointment.

Dr Erik Blakeley, Curator

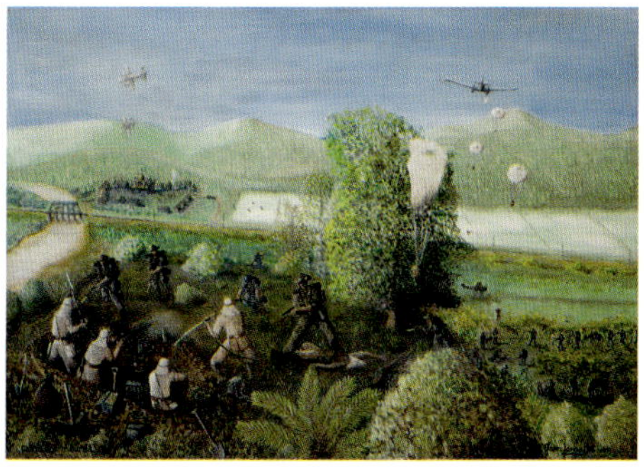

Lancaster, J.
Lieutenant George Albert Cairns, VC (1913–1944), in Action in Burma (1944) 1991
oil on board 90 x 122
7441

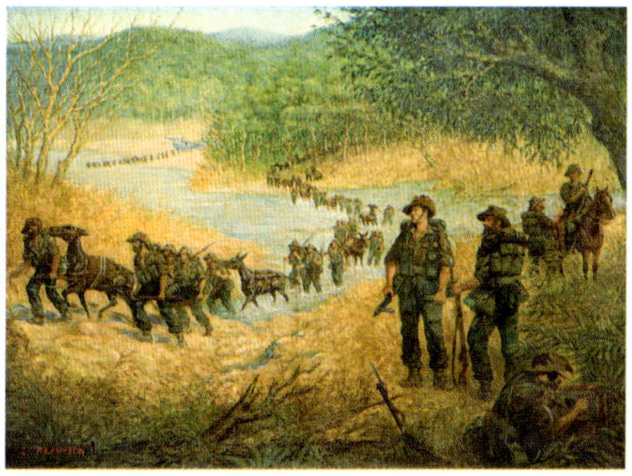

Lawson, Cecil active 1907–after 1944
1st South Staffords on the March in Burma, 1944 after 1944
oil on canvas 60 x 96 (E)
832

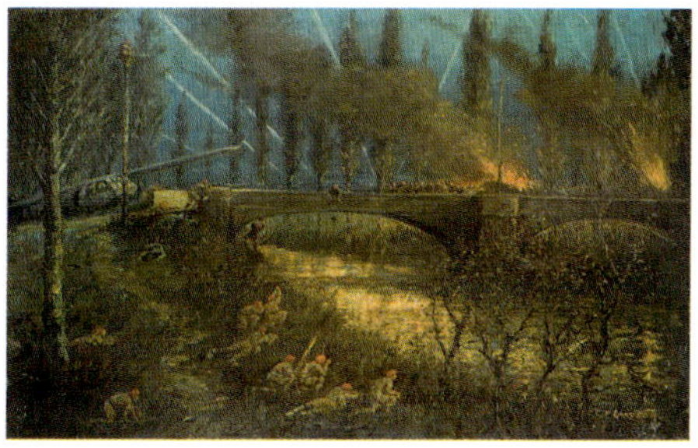

Lawson, Cecil active 1907–after 1944
Capture of Ponte Grande, Syracuse, 1943
oil on canvas 60 x 96 (E)
2079

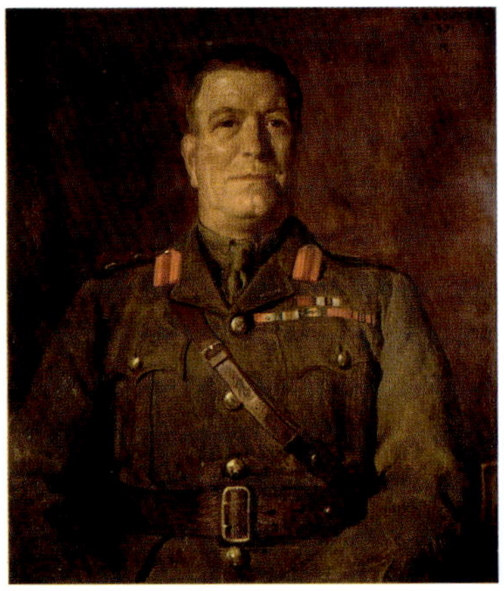

Souter, John Balloch 1890–1972
Lieutenant Colonel J. C. Chaytor 1931
oil on canvas 75 x 62.5
7241

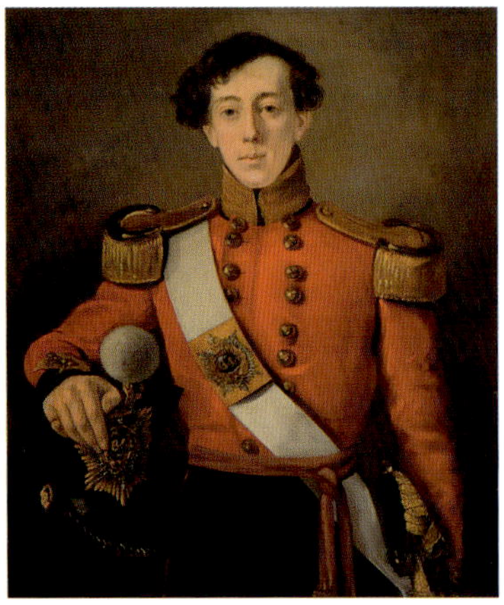

unknown artist
Officer of the 64th Foot c.1835
oil on canvas 60 x 50
249

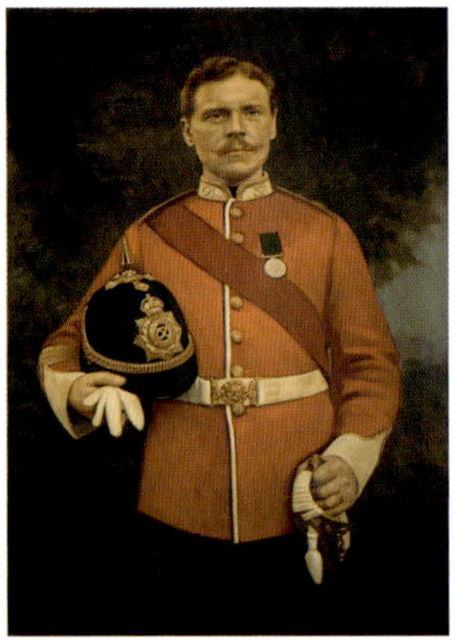

unknown artist
QMS C. Laban, 5th South Staffords 1911
oil on canvas 74 x 48.5
5043

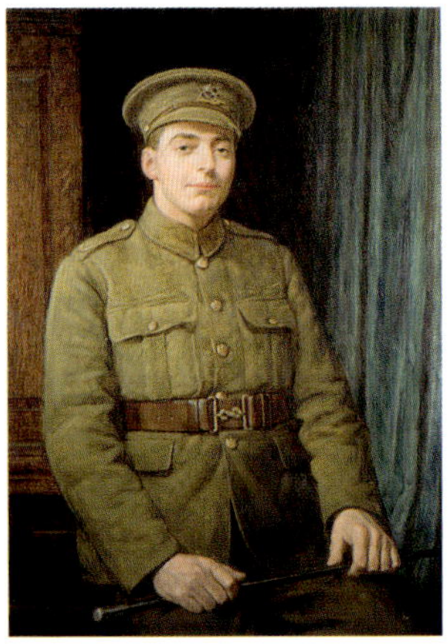

unknown artist
A South Staffords Soldier
oil on canvas 74 x 55
7468

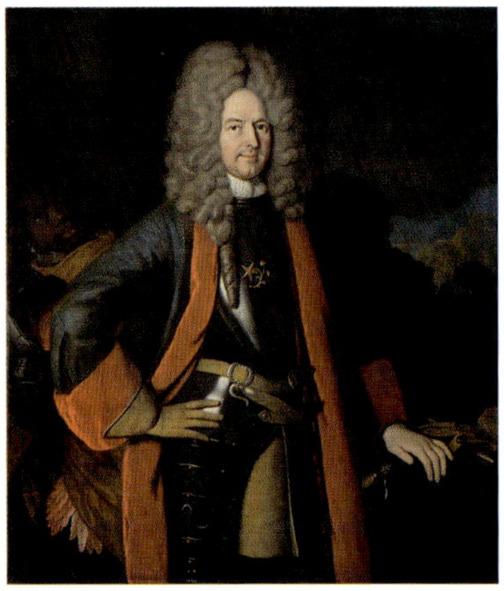

unknown artist
Colonel Luke Lillingston
oil on canvas 81 x 68
897

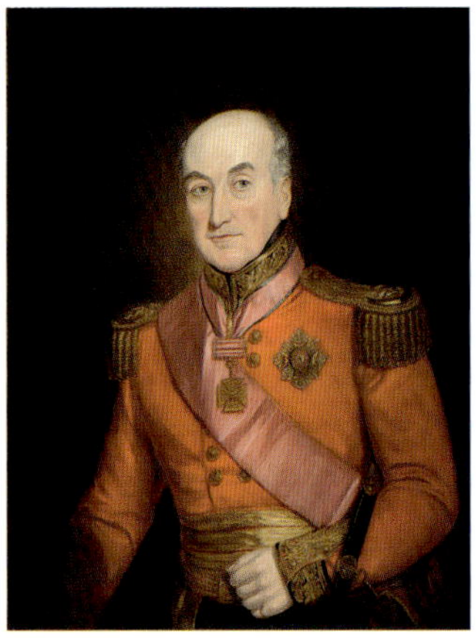

unknown artist
Lieutenant General Sir William Pringle
oil on canvas 90 x 70
5561

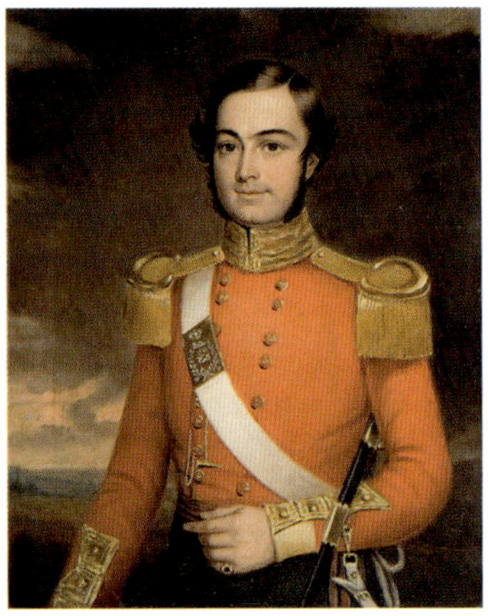

unknown artist
Lieutenant General Thorne, Officer of the 80th Foot (1849–1850)
oil on canvas 52 x 41.5
900

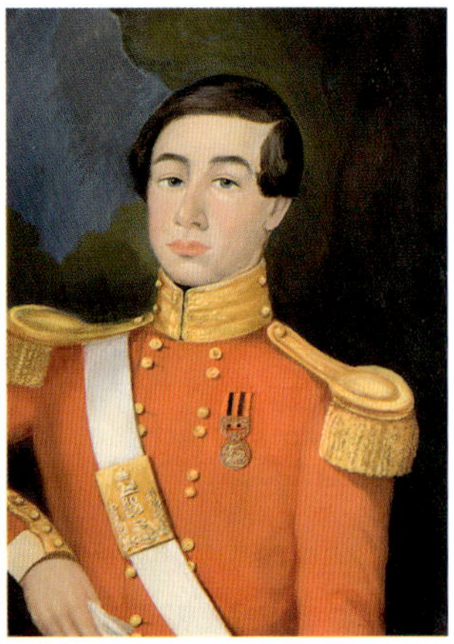

unknown artist
Lieutenant Thomas Quill
oil on board 34.5 x 24
5099

Borough Museum & Art Gallery

Newcastle-under-Lyme Borough Museum and Art Gallery's fine art collection represents over 100 years of collecting. For the main part the collection is characterised by local scenes and local artists alongside more regionally and nationally recognised artists. Being cheek by jowl with The Potteries Museum & Art Gallery our collection also includes a number of ceramic works.

The Collection is based on a core of around 120 works donated to the Borough by Mr Joseph Mayer in the 1880s. Mayer was a native of Newcastle-under-Lyme and made his fortune as a goldsmith in Liverpool. He used his money to purchase art and antiquities. His donation to Newcastle-under-Lyme consisted of oil paintings, watercolours and engravings. It was Mayer's intention that they would afford 'a good variety of study for [art] pupils'. Amongst the paintings he donated is *The Mock Mayor* by Robert William Buss. This painting was commissioned by Mayer and depicts the burlesque which took place on Newcastle's market cross when the townsfolk took it upon themselves to elect a Mayor of their own choosing and not one selected by the corporation.

A number of paintings in the Collection were bequeathed to the Borough in the early 1900s by Mr John Gallimore. Gallimore, also a native of the town, was a builder by trade and served the Borough as Alderman, Mayor and Justice of the Peace. His bequest include some of the finest works in the Museum and Art Gallery's collections, namely *Una* by George Percy Jacomb-Hood (based on a scene from Spenser's *Fairie Queene*) and the genre painting *Thirsty* by Jameson Middleton.

The Collection was originally housed at Hobbergate Art Gallery, which was established in 1973. A town museum was already in existence (founded in 1943) in two rooms in the town centre. In 1987 the Hobbergate Art Gallery closed and the fine art and museum collections were united under one roof when the Borough Council acquired The Firs, a large Victorian villa, which is now known as the Borough Museum and Art Gallery. In advance of the move the fine art collection was rationalised and a number of works were sold and some of the remaining paintings were conserved.

The acquisition policy states that the focus of collecting is on work by local artists and of local scenes. During the last two decades a number of paintings have been acquired, including scenes of Newcastle-under-Lyme by Henry Lark I Pratt (1805–1873).

The Collection currently includes 76 oil paintings but totals in excess of 300 works, most of which are watercolours (excluded from this catalogue entry). The works cover topographical scenes, portraits, still lifes and work by former pottery artists such as William Mussill (1828–1906). The Museum and Art Gallery now actively collects work by contemporary local artists and commissioned six local artists to each produce a work to commemorate the Millennium.

Due to lack of suitable gallery space the museum can only show a small number of its fine art collections on a permanent basis. The works that are displayed are either hung on the museum staircase or in room settings. Annual in-house exhibitions are held to show the reserve collections and there are plans to improve access via the museum's website. Inclusion in this catalogue provides us with a unique opportunity for the collection to be more widely seen and appreciated, for which we are grateful.

Delyth Copp, Museum and Arts Officer

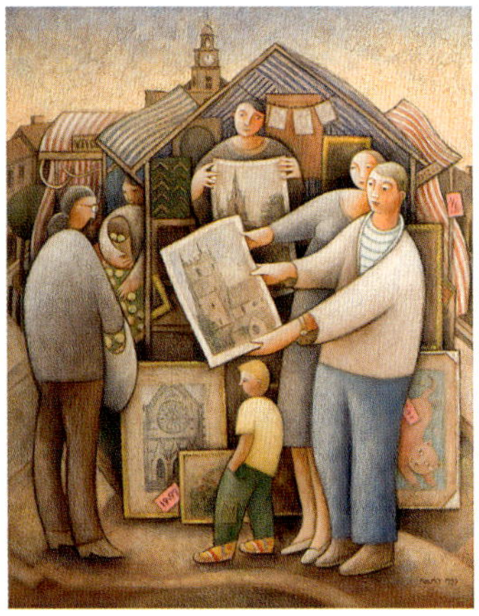

Borsky, Jiri b.1945
Newcastle Market 1999
oil on board 67 x 51
PAC 297.99

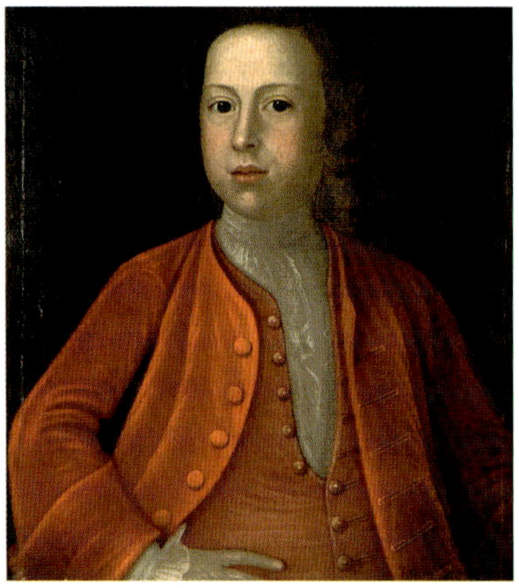

British (English) School
Nathaniel Beard (1696–1772), Mayor of Newcastle-under-Lyme c.1730
oil on canvas 62.5 x 55
PAC 182-88

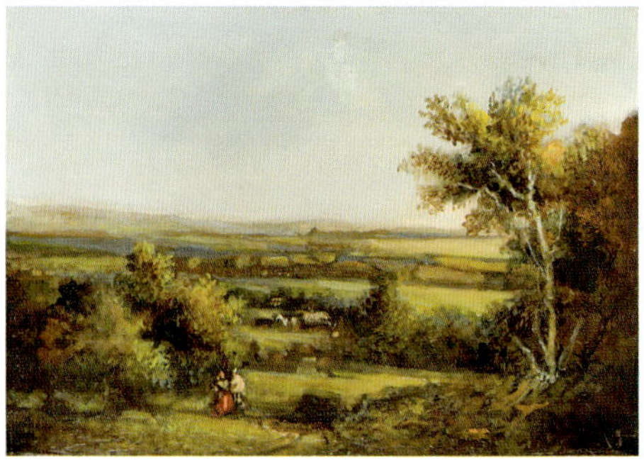

British (English) School
View of Newcastle from Keele Bank 1875
oil on canvas 45 x 62
PAC 275-88

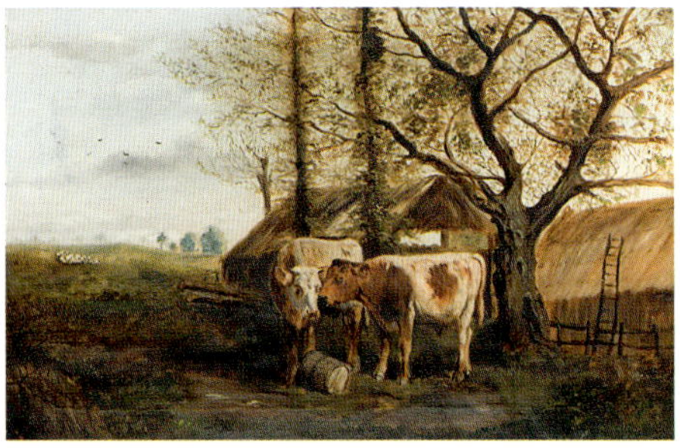

British (English) School
Cattle by a Barn 1884
oil on canvas 64 x 95
PAC 251-88

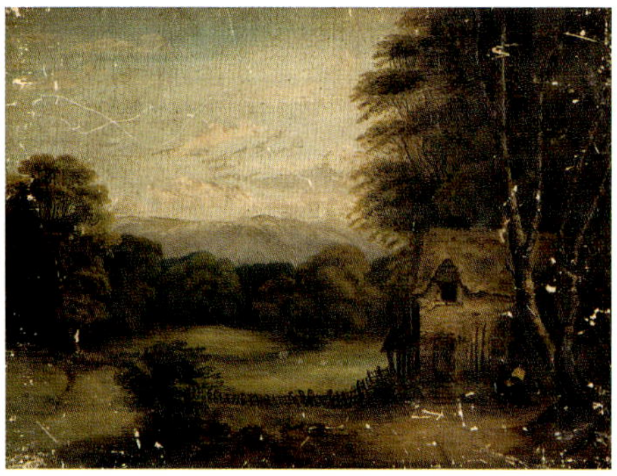

British (English) School 19th C
Figure by Cottage in Landscape
oil on canvas 33.5 x 43.5
PAC 243-88

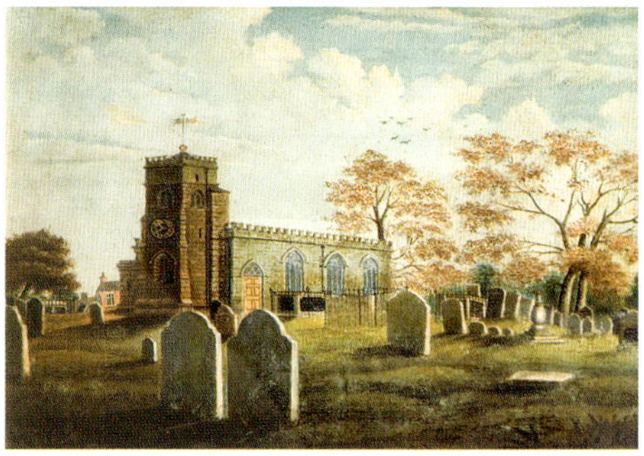

British (English) School 19th C
Keele Church, Staffordshire
oil on board 32.5 x 41
PAC 185-88

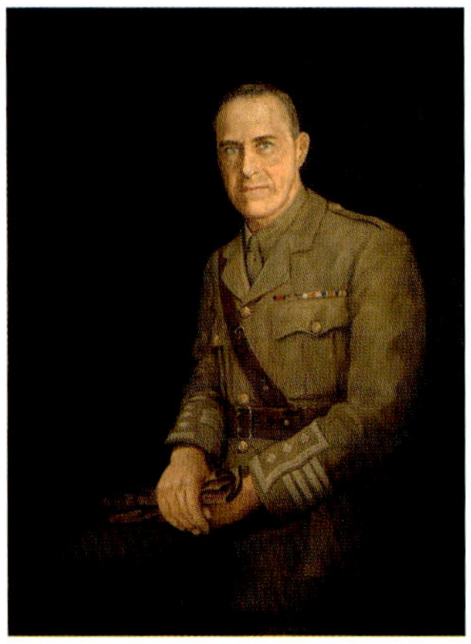

British (English) School 20th C
Colonel Josiah Wedgwood (1872–1943)
oil on canvas 114 x 84
PAC 183-88

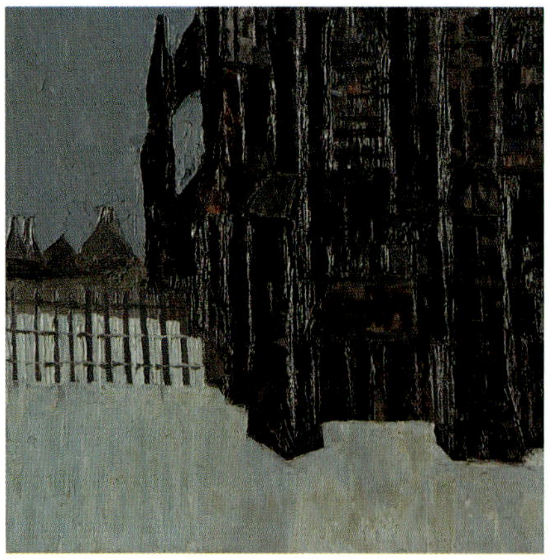

British (English) School 20th C
Longton Church
oil on canvas 61 x 61
PAC 177-88

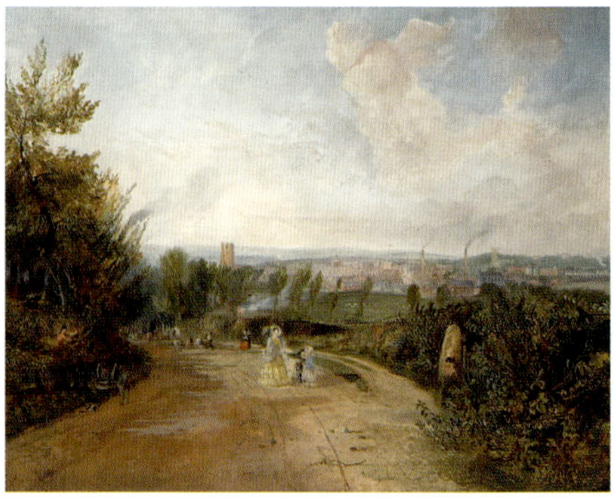

Brooks, Adriana J.
Newcastle, from Clayton Fields 1850
oil on board 49 x 59
PAC 168-88

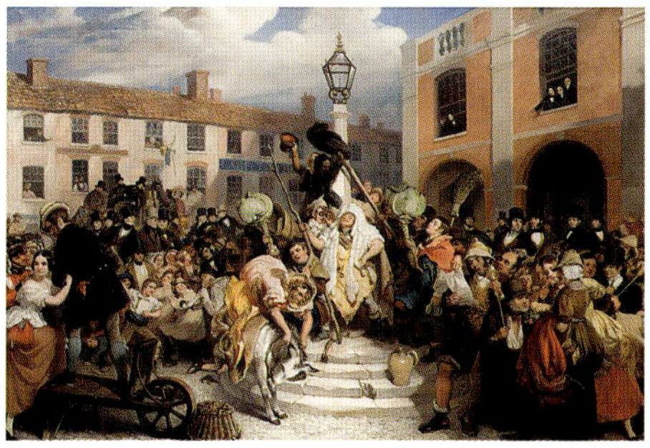

Buss, Robert William 1804–1875
The Mock Mayor 1844
oil on paper 119 x 169
PAC 150-88

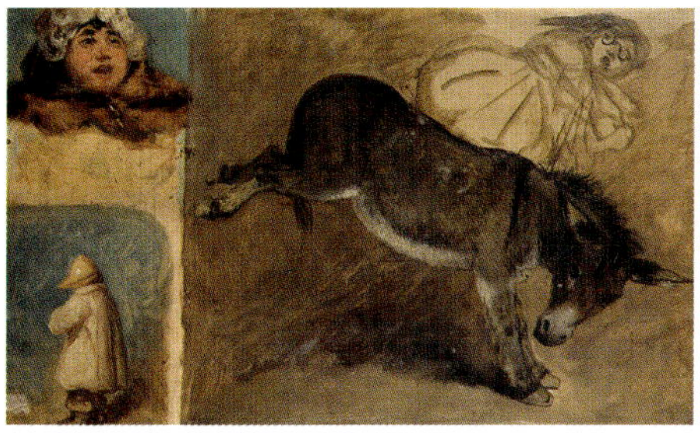

Buss, Robert William 1804–1875
Cartoon for 'The Mock Mayor'
oil on board 23.5 x 38
PAC 169-88

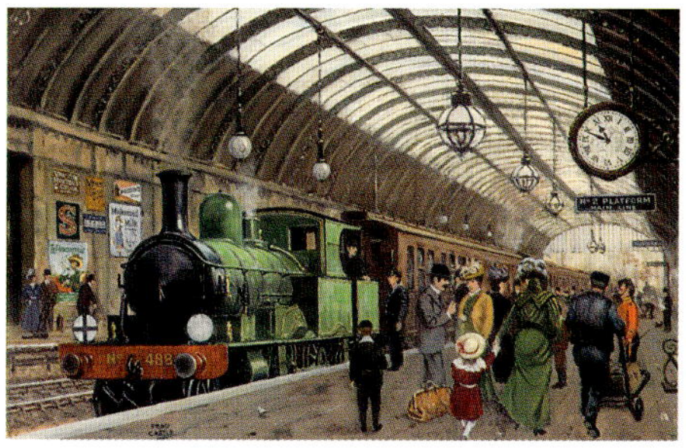

Castle, Fred 1912–1996
Is this the Age of the Train? 1983
oil on board 50 x 70
PAC 156-88

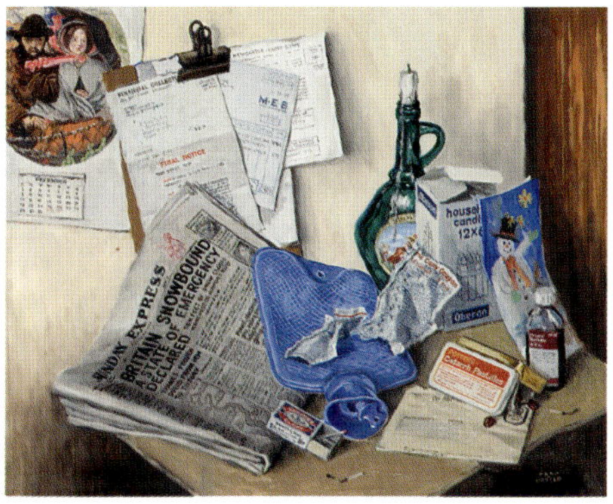

Castle, Fred 1912–1996
Winter c.1983
oil on board 50 x 60
PAC 174-88

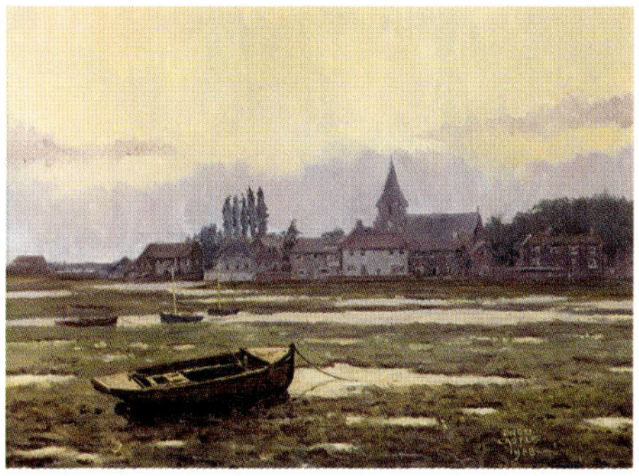

Castle, Fred 1912–1996
Bosham 1988
oil on board 34 x 44
PAC 211-88

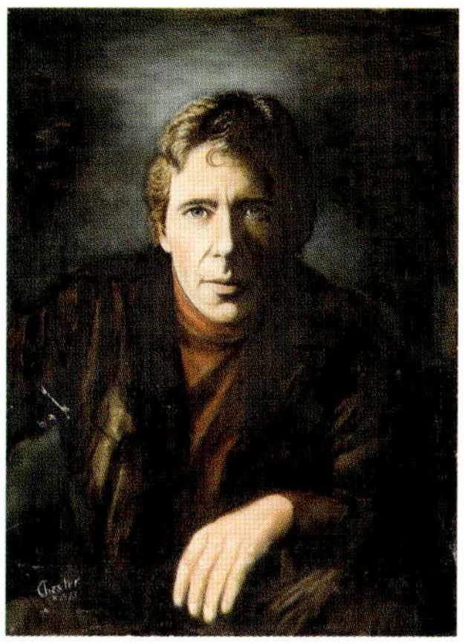

Chester, Charlie
Lord Snowdon (b.1930) 1973
oil on canvas 56 x 40.5
PAC 239-88

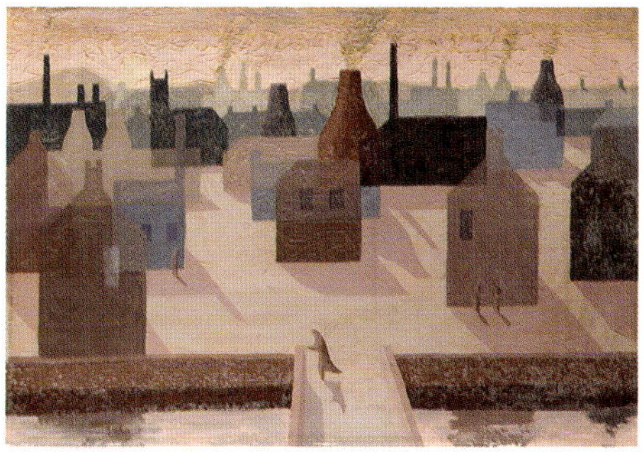

Clarkson, Jack 1906–1986
Sunset over Potteries Landscape 1963
acrylic on board 36 x 46
PAC 191-88

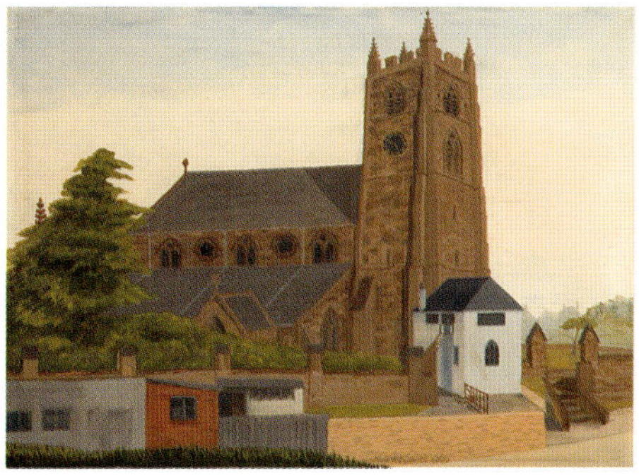

Clarkson, Jack 1906–1986
St Giles' Church 1965
acrylic on board 38 x 51
PAC 189-88

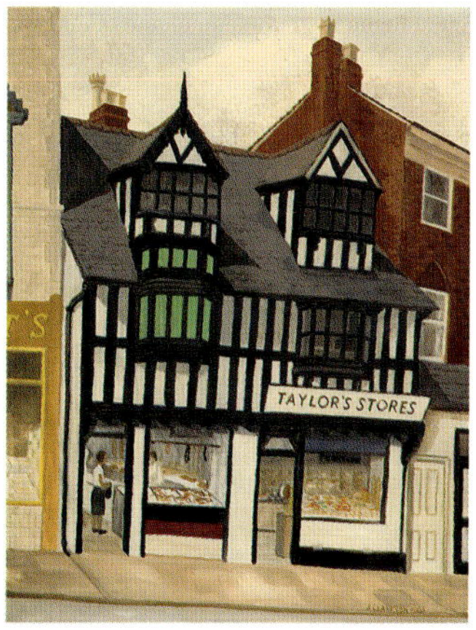

Clarkson, Jack 1906–1986
Taylor's Stores 1965
acrylic on board 51 x 38
PAC 188-88

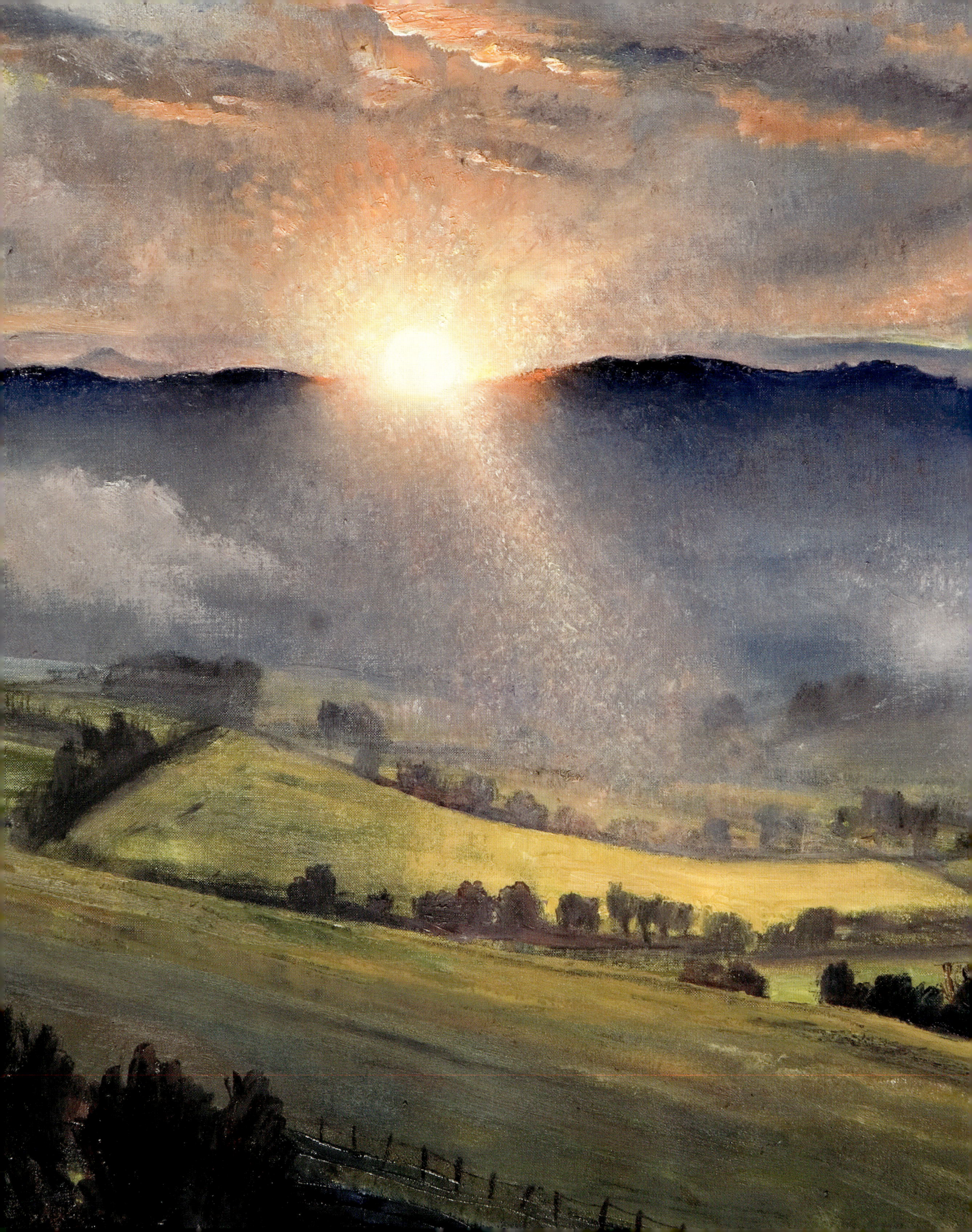

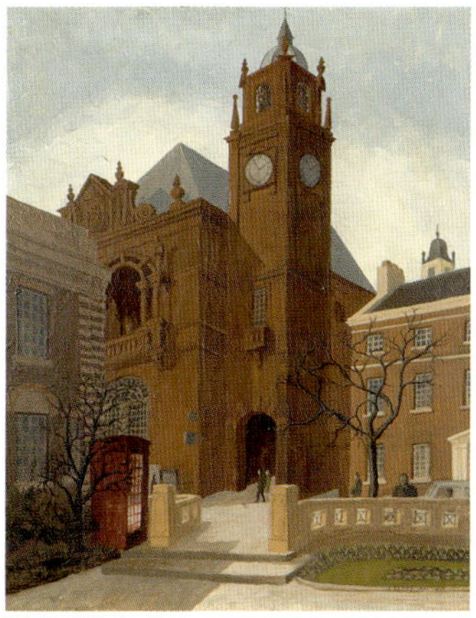

Clarkson, Jack 1906–1986
Municipal Hall, Newcastle-under-Lyme
oil on board 58.5 x 44.5
PAC 176-88

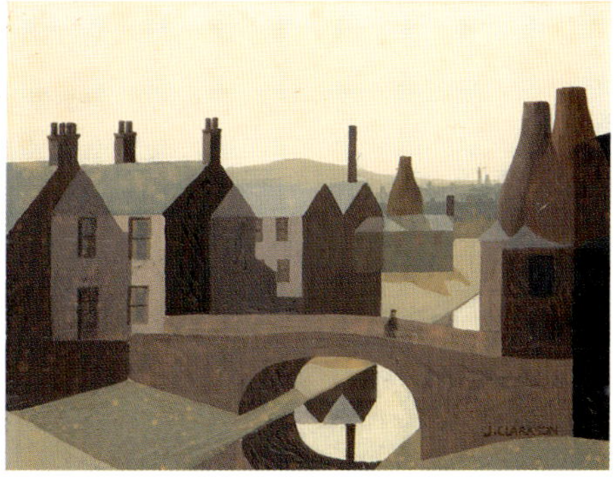

Clarkson, Jack 1906–1986
Potteries View with Canal
acrylic on board 20 x 25
PAC 190-88

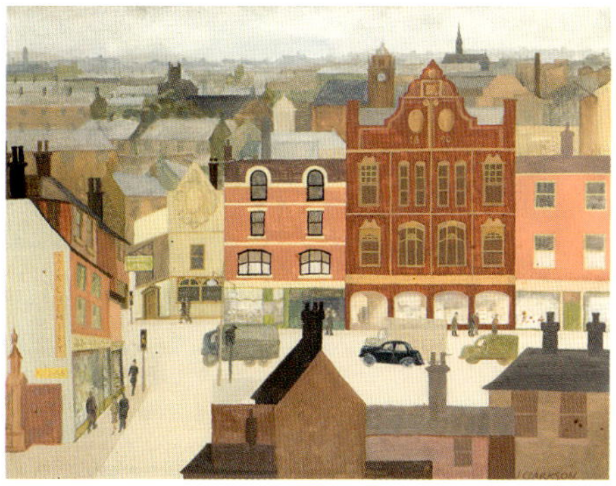

Clarkson, Jack 1906–1986
Red Lion Square
oil on board 48.5 x 60
PAC 258-88

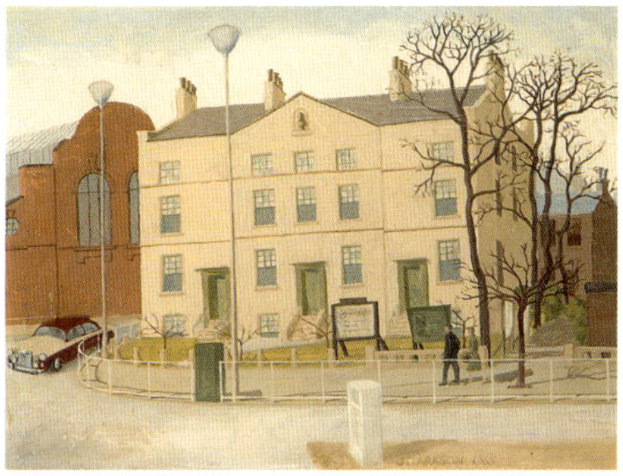

Clarkson, Jack 1906–1986
The Old Borough Treasurers, Nelson Place
oil on canvas 35 x 43
PAC 259-88

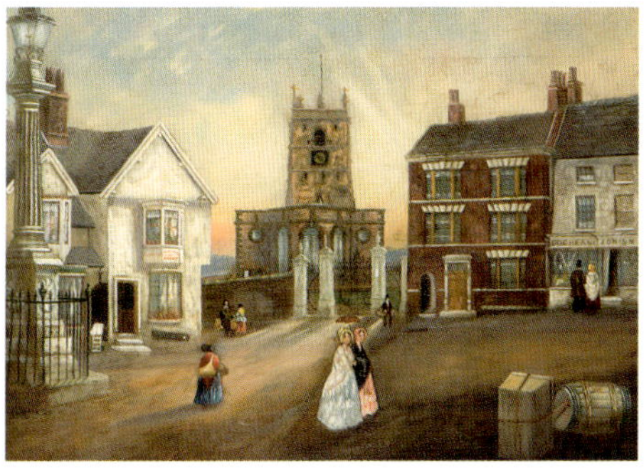

Colley, R. M.
Red Lion Square 1848
oil on canvas 45 x 60
PAC 162-88

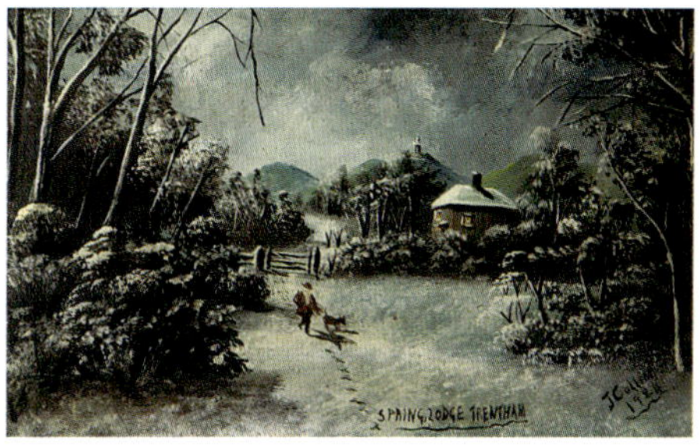

Collinge, J.
Spring Lodge, Trentham 1924
oil on board 36 x 48.5
PAC 268-88

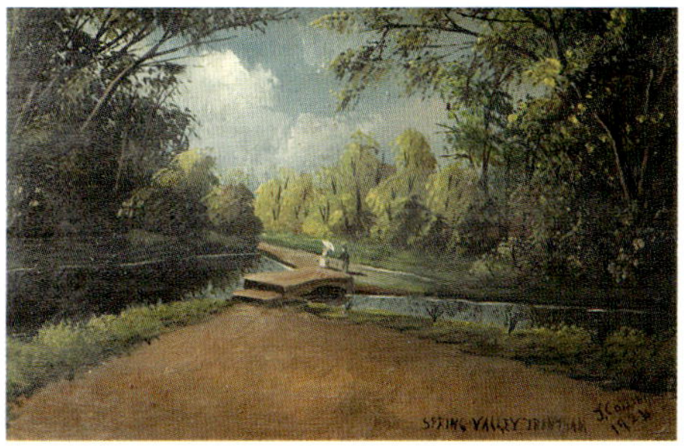

Collinge, J.
Spring Valley, Trentham 1924
oil on board 36 x 48.5
PAC 269-88

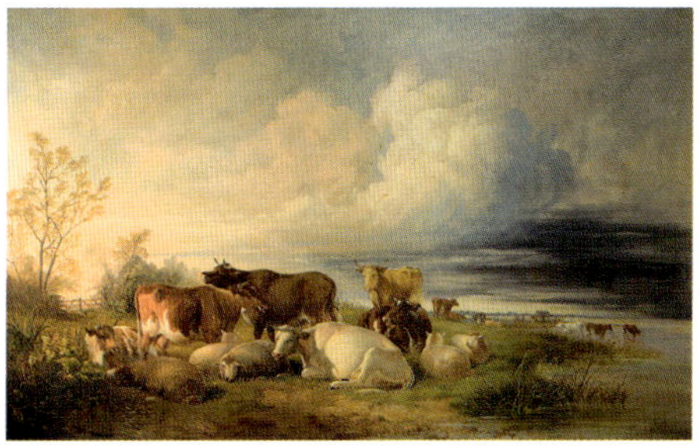

Cooper, Thomas Sidney 1803–1902
Cattle and Sheep at Rest in a Meadow 1876
oil on canvas 76 x 122
PAC 180-88

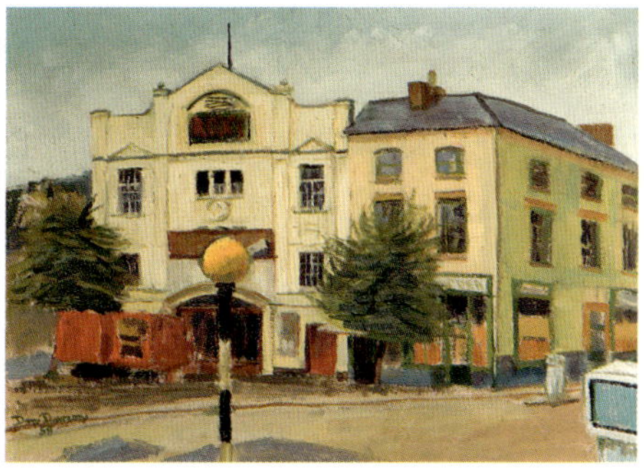

Dawson, Dan
Roxy Cinema, Nelson Place 1958
oil on canvas 45.5 x 61
PAC 266-88

Facing page: Knight, Laura, 1877–1970, *Sundown* (detail), 1940–1947, Wolverhampton Art Gallery, (p. 291)

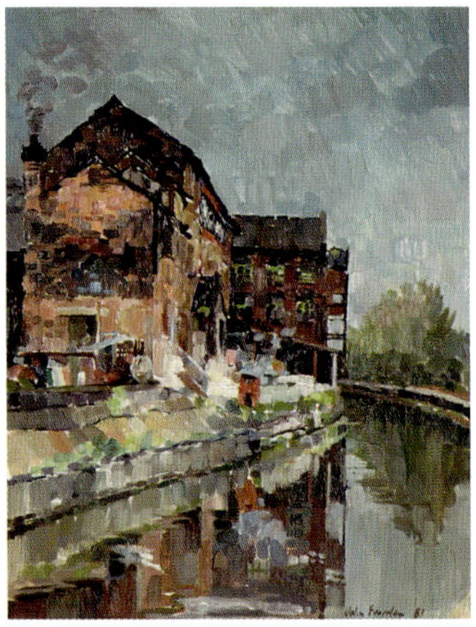

Everden, John
Canal Side Buildings, Middleport 1981
oil on board 44 x 34
PAC 166-88

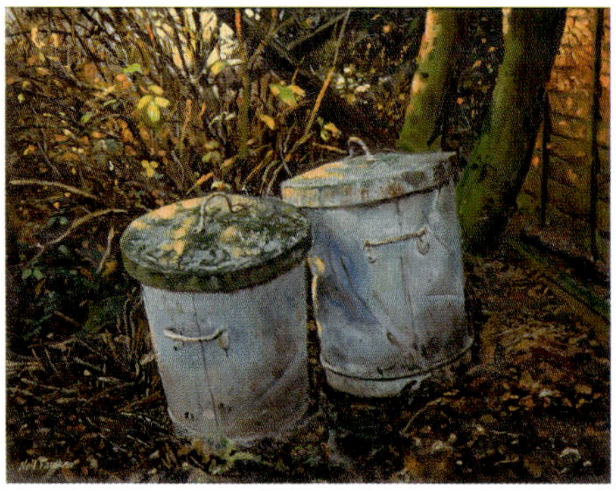

Faulkner, Neil b.1952
Parkwood Avenue 1992
oil on canvas 40 x 50
PAC 273-88

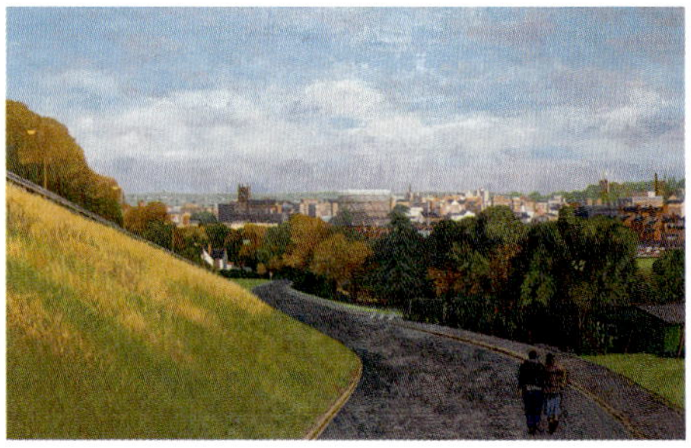

Fletcher, Doreen b.1952
View from Clayton Fields, Newcastle-under-Lyme 1989
oil on canvas 65 x 90.5
PAC 213-88

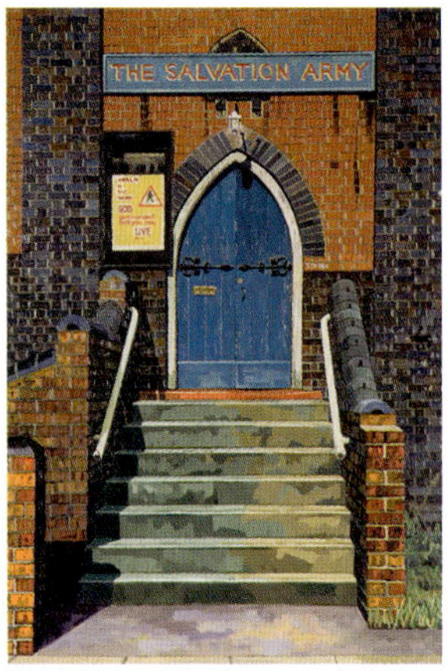

Fletcher, Doreen b.1952
Salvation Army Building
oil on canvas 75 x 50
PAC 170-88

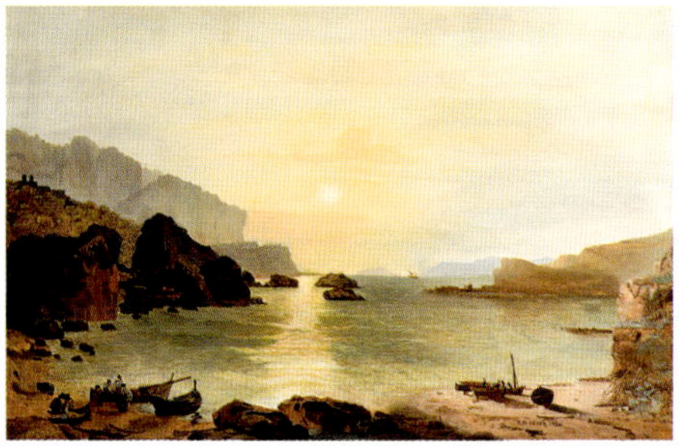

Fryer, E. M.
Isle of Capri 1936
oil on canvas 40 x 61
PAC 265-88

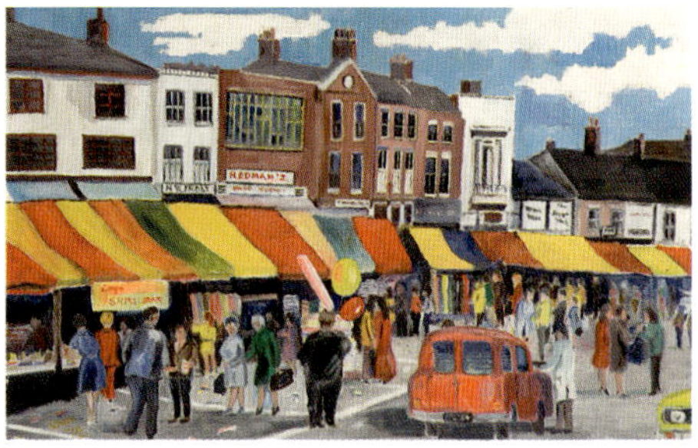

Griffiths, J. W.
Newcastle Market 1972
oil on board 58.5 x 84
PAC 249-88

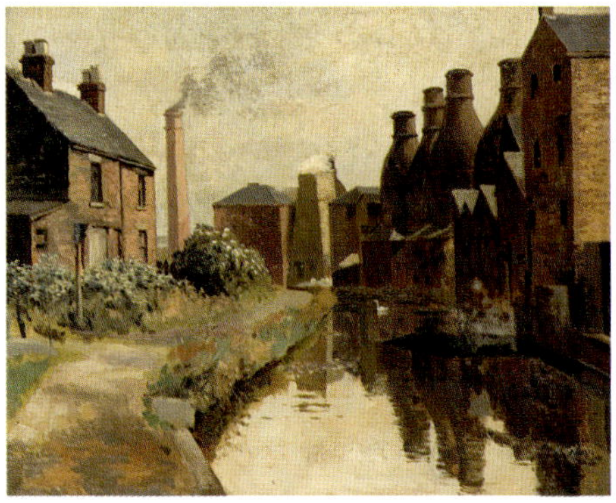

Harper, W. K.
Wood's Pottery, Longport 1950
oil on canvas 51 x 61
PAC 160-88

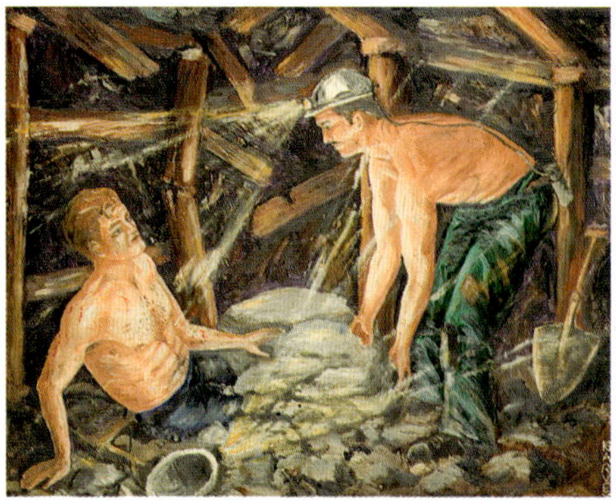

Harvey
Coal Miners
oil on board 49 x 59

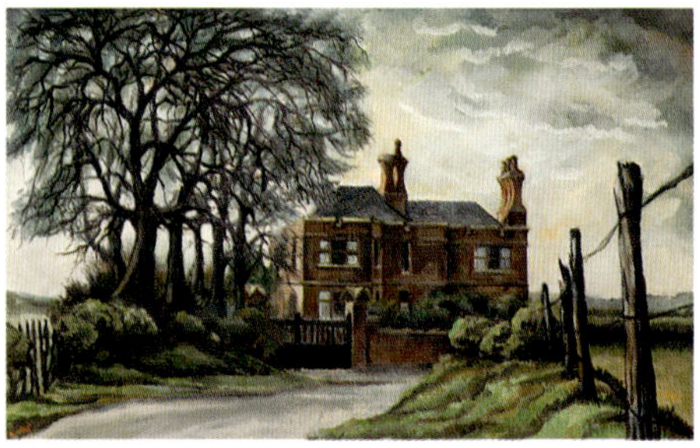

Hinks, Thomas
Lodge House, Caverswall 1973
oil on canvas 48 x 74
PAC 178-88

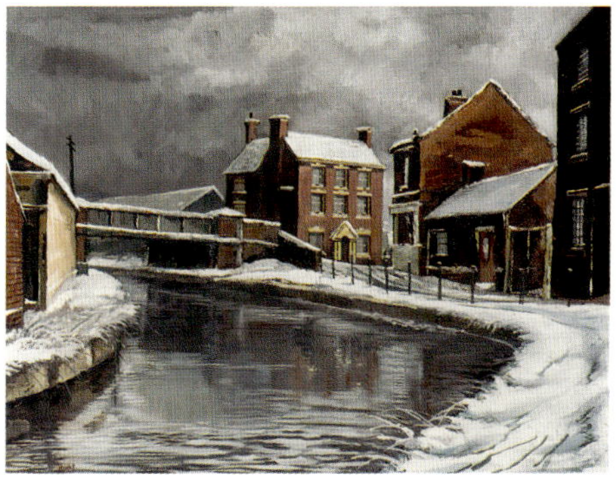

Hinks, Thomas
Longport Bridge
oil on board 60 x 75
PAC 173-88

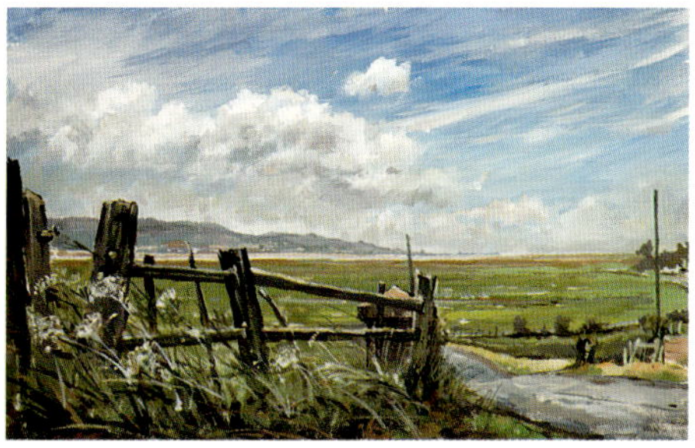

Hinks, Thomas
The Dee Estuary
acrylic on board 38 x 55
PAC 171-88

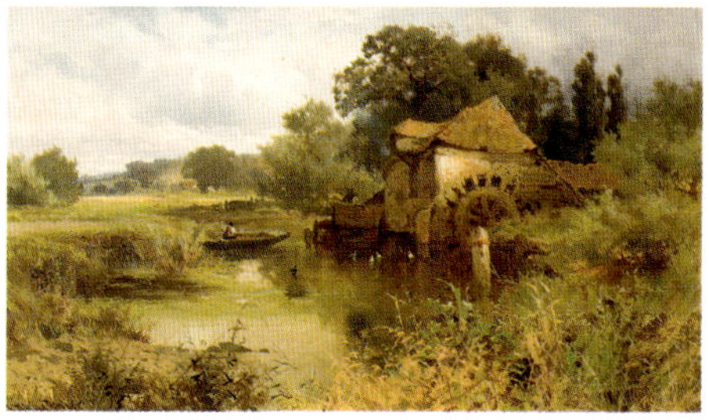

Hooper, John Horace c.1850–c.1899
The Mill
oil on canvas 57 x 103
PAC 181-88

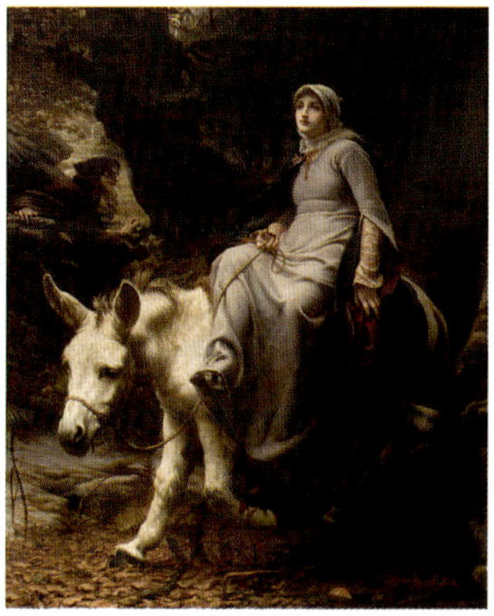

Jacomb-Hood, George Percy 1857–1930
Una
oil on paper 138 x 105
PAC 152-88

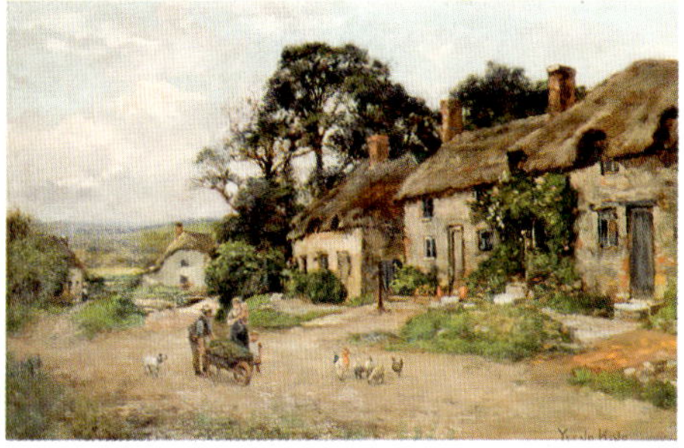

King, Yeend 1855–1924
Figures by a Country Cottage
oil on board 35 x 53
PAC 165-88

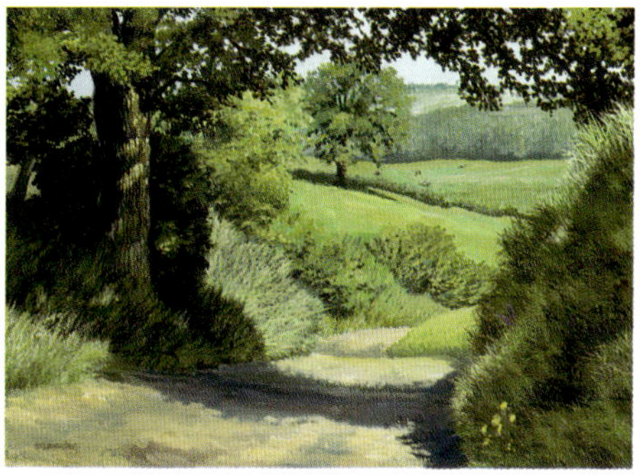

Lancaster, Gordon
Well Bank, Betley
oil on board 43 x 53.5
PAC 216-88

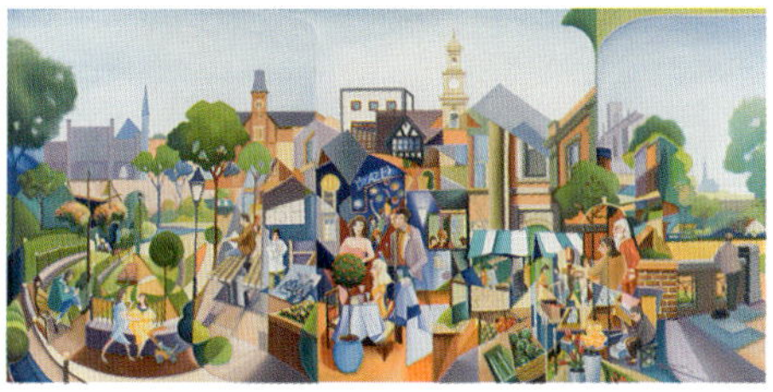

Lloyd, Tim b.1959
A Town on Millennium's Eve 1999
oil on canvas 50 x 100
PAC 299-00

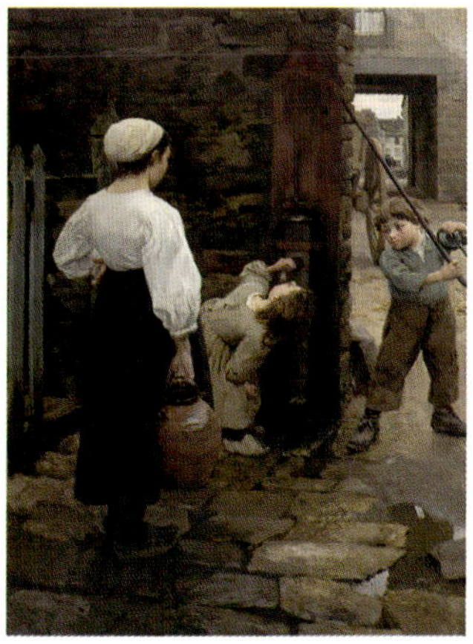

Middleton, Jameson
Thirsty 1883
oil on canvas 180 x 100
PAC 153-88

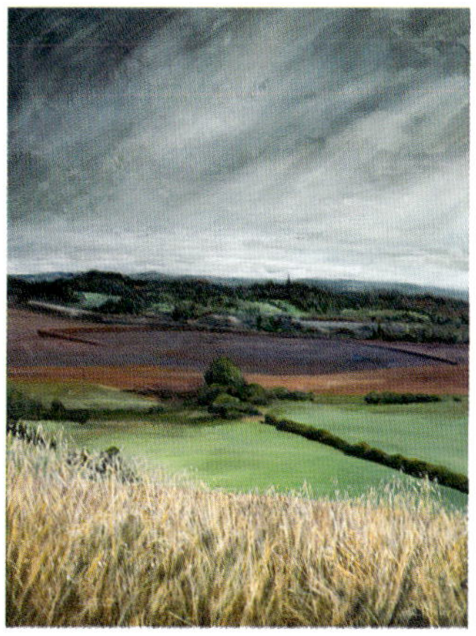

Miller, Lesley b.1946
View of Newcastle from Alsager's Bank 1999
acrylic on canvas 60 x 45
PAC 302-00

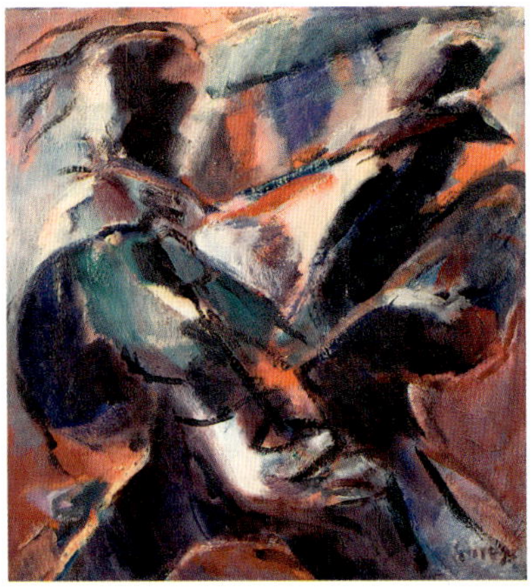

Moore, David R. b.1941
Lonnie and Sutch at the Frog Inn, Newcastle
oil on canvas 100 x 90
PAC 270-88

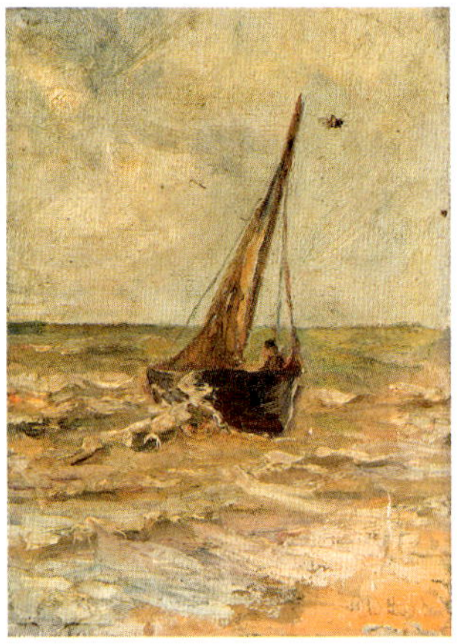

Mottain
'La Roche'
oil on canvas 30 x 21.5
PAC 242-88

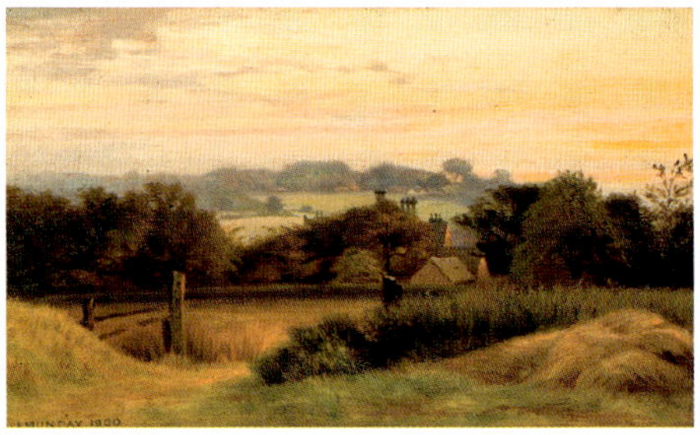

Munday, John active 1890–1903
View of Maer Hall 1900
oil on canvas 30 x 40
PAC 284-97

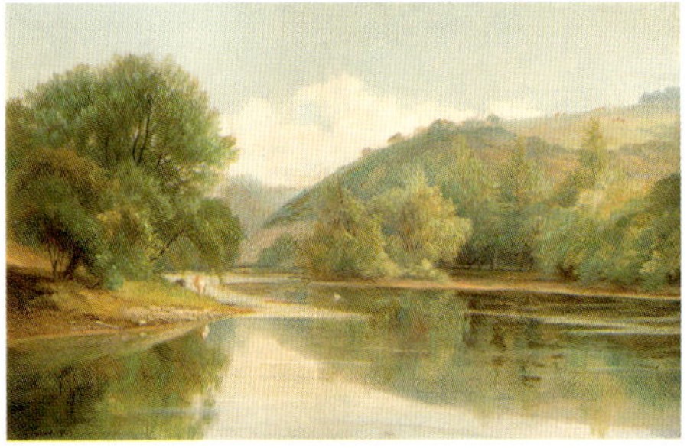

Munday, John active 1890–1903
Clough Hall Lake, Kidsgrove 1903
oil on canvas 34 x 52
PAC 218A-88

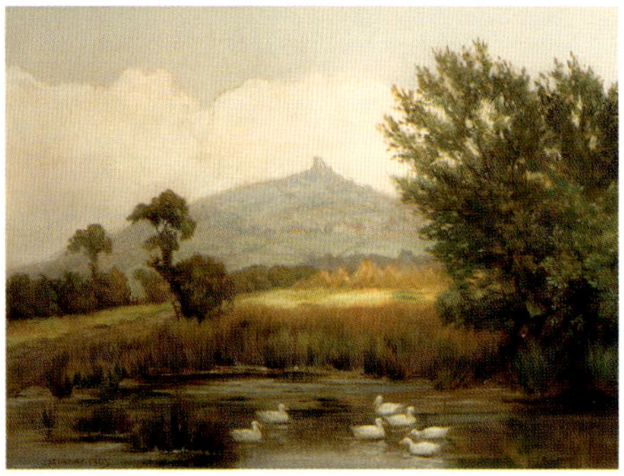

Munday, John active 1890–1903
Mow Cop from Moss House Farm, near Hall Green 1903
oil on canvas 51 x 69 (E)
PAC 218-88

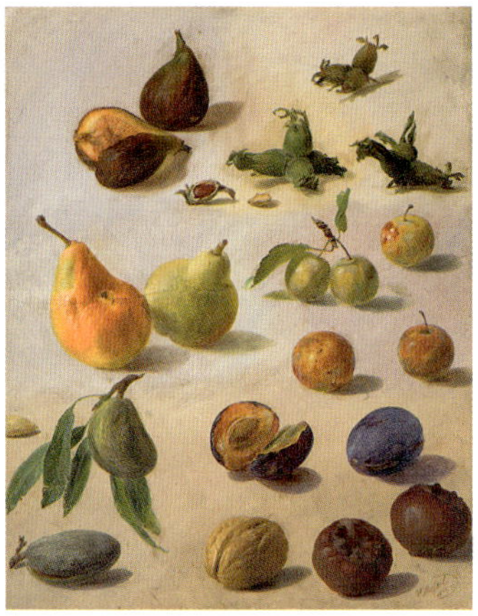

Mussill, William 1828–1906
Study of Fruit and Nuts 1857
oil on paper 41.5 x 32
PAC 127-88

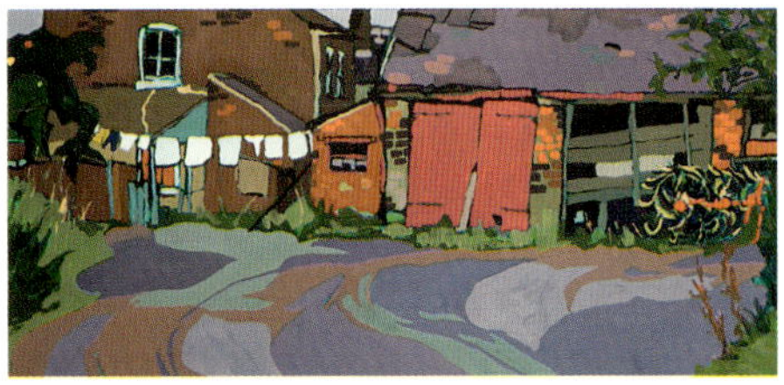

Newlove, Margery G.
Bullerthorpe Farm
acrylic on board 29.5 x 60
PAC 172-88

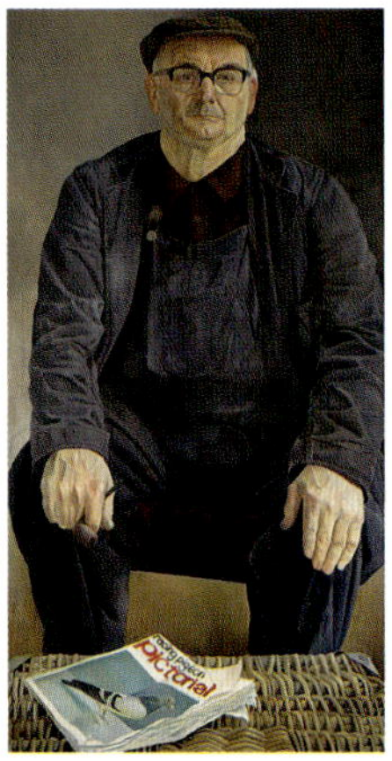

Owen, Susan M. active 1974–1977
The Pigeon Fancier 1974
oil on canvas 164 x 82
PAC 154-88

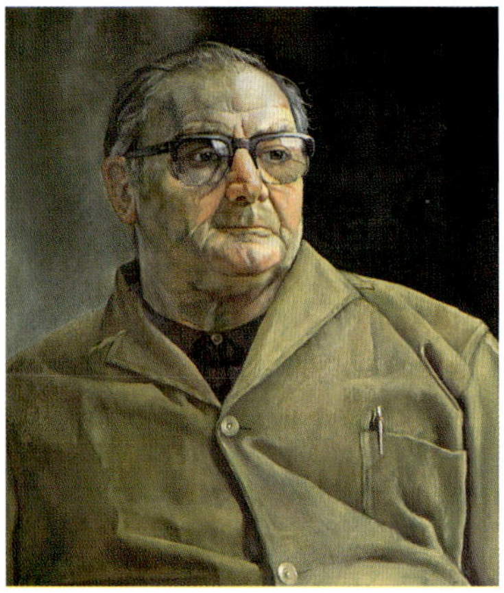

Owen, Susan M. active 1974–1977
Portrait of the School Caretaker 1977
oil on canvas 65.5 x 56
PAC 159-88

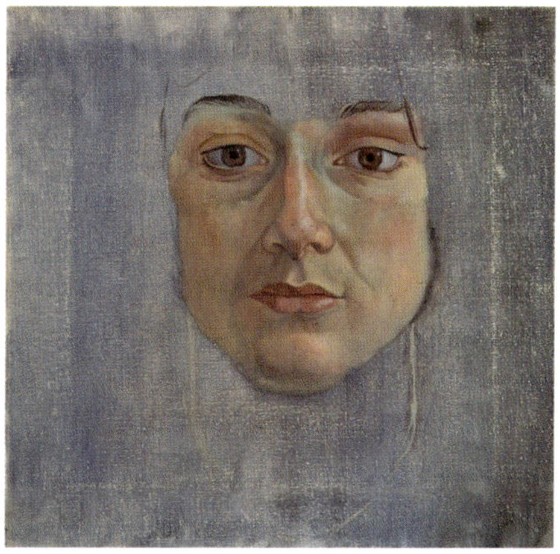

Owen, Susan M. active 1974–1977
Unfinished Oil Sketch of a Young Woman's Face
oil on canvas 35.5 x 35.5
PAC 155-88

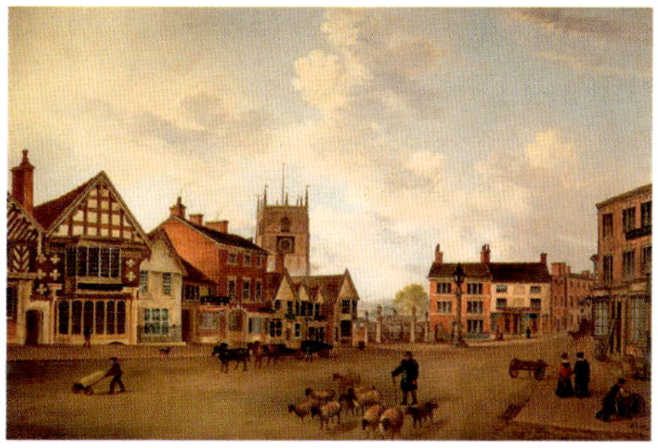

Pratt, Henry Lark I 1805–1873
Red Lion Square 1854
oil on board 38 x 57
PAC 164-88

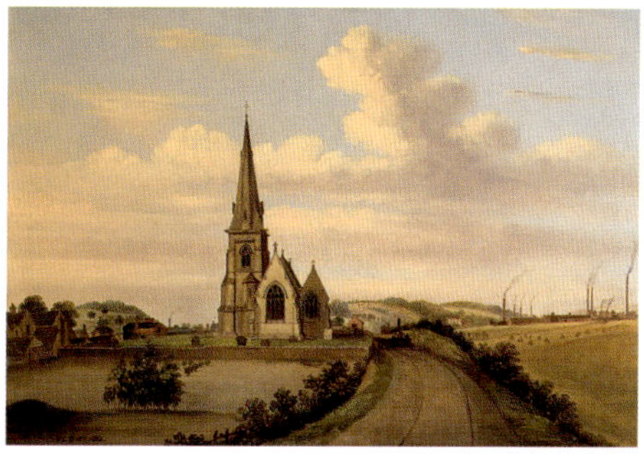

Pratt, Henry Lark I 1805–1873
Looking West of St Luke's Church, Silverdale 1861
oil on canvas 40 x 50
PAC 304-01

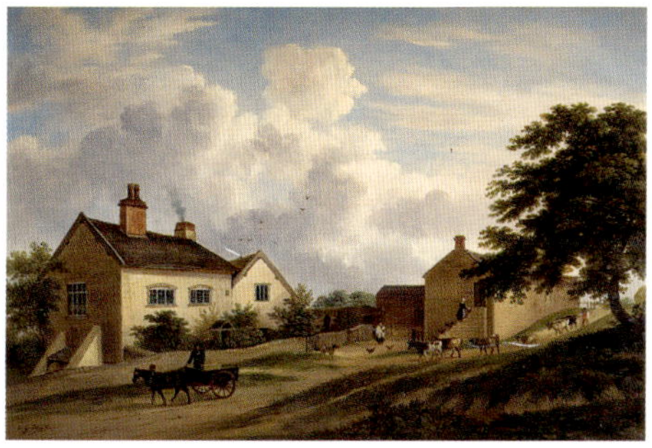

Pratt, Henry Lark I 1805–1873
Old Farmstead in Trentham Road 1861
oil on canvas 40 x 50
PAC 305-01

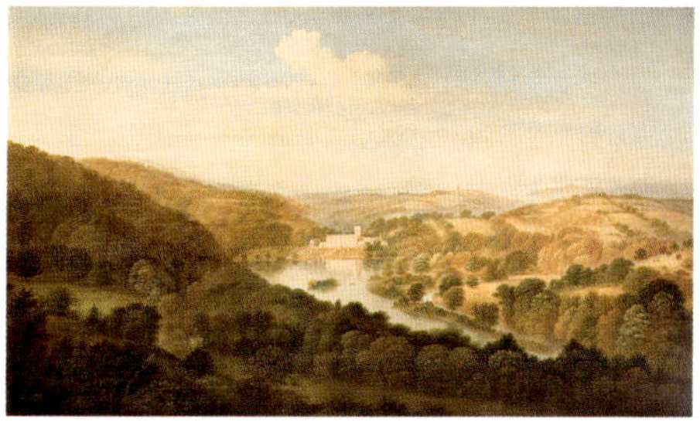

Pratt, Henry Lark I 1805–1873
Trentham Hall 1862
oil on board 40 x 77
PAC 152-88

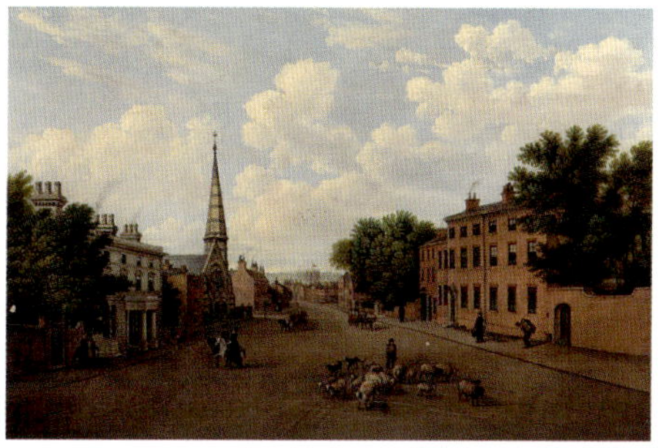

Pratt, Henry Lark I 1805–1873
King Street, Newcastle-under-Lyme 1865
oil on board 51 x 73.5
PAC 161-88

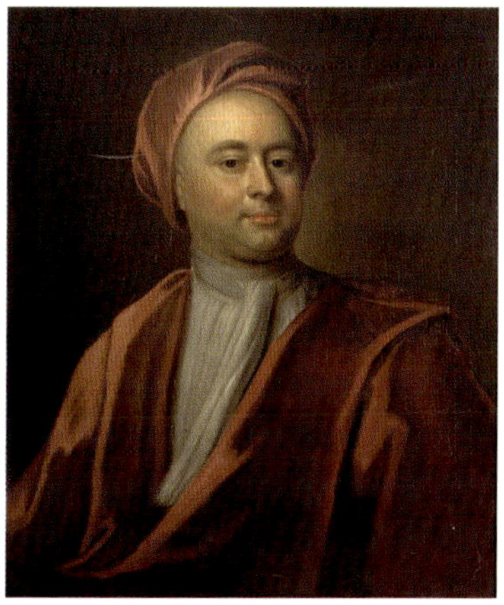

Richardson, Jonathan the elder 1665–1745
Elijah Fenton (1683–1730)
oil on canvas 74.5 x 62.5
PAC 163-88

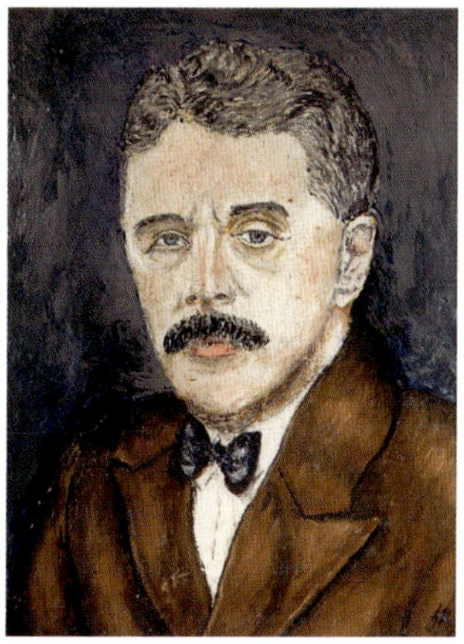

Ridgway, J.
Arnold Bennett (1867–1931) 1978
oil on board 14.3 x 10.3
PAC 240-88

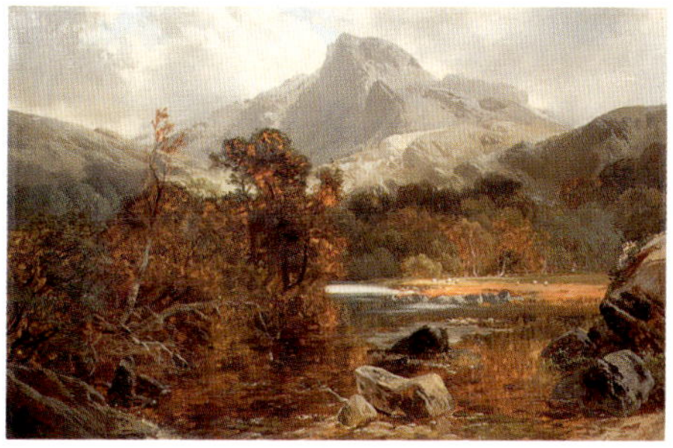

Roe, Clarence 1850–1909
Snowdonia
oil on canvas 71 x 101.5
PAC 244-88

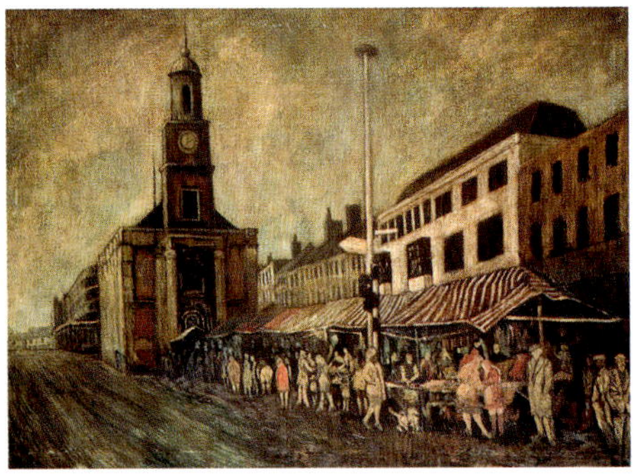

Rose, Donald
Guildhall and Market Stalls 1975
oil on canvas 95 x 126
PAC 184-88

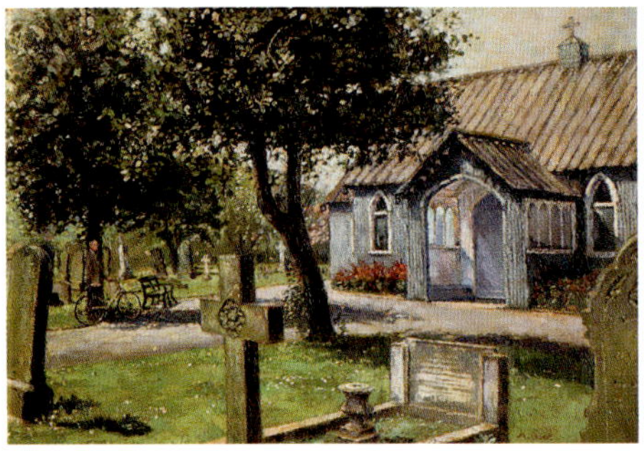

Scott, Alan
The Chapel in Silverdale Cemetery 1999
oil on canvas 29 x 40
PAC 300-00

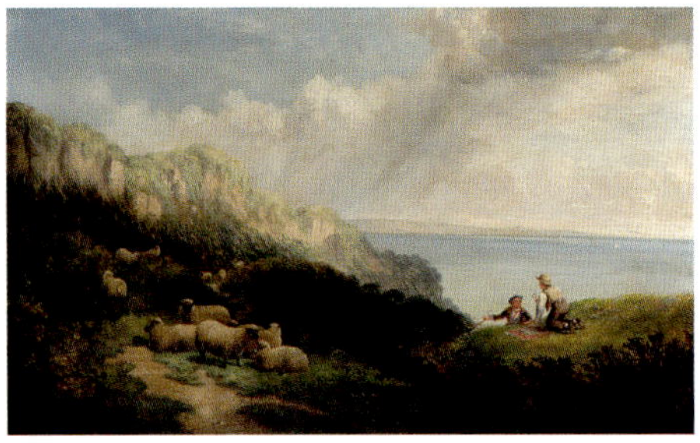

Stanton, George Clark 1832–1894
Shepherd Boys with their Flock
oil on canvas 48 x 73.5
PAC 157-88

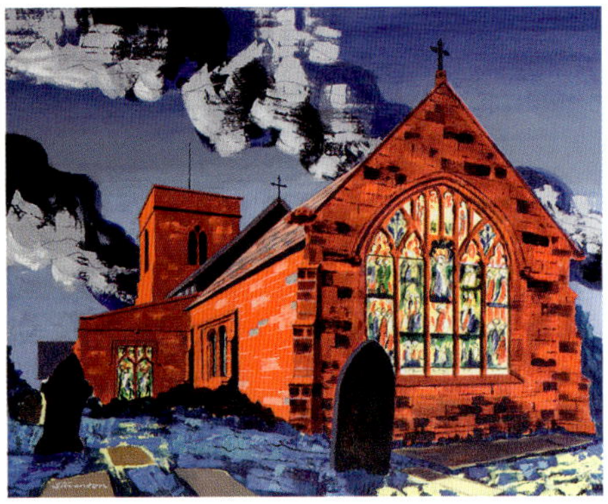

Stevenson, Stewart b.1935
Betley Church
acrylic on canvas 74.5 x 90
PAC 301.00

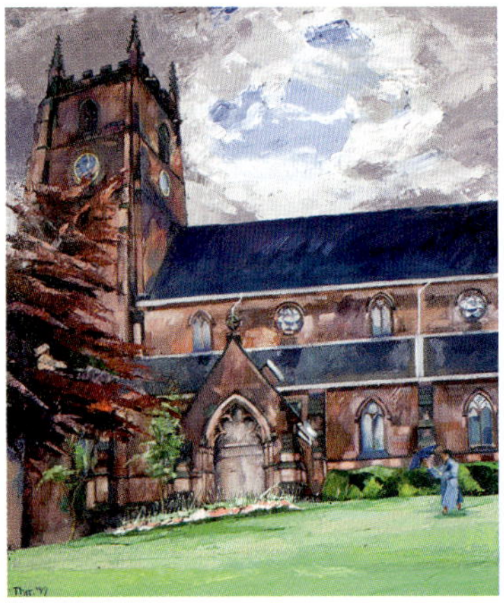

Thirlwall, John b.1943
After the Storm, St Giles 1999
oil on canvas 100 x 84
PAC 303.00

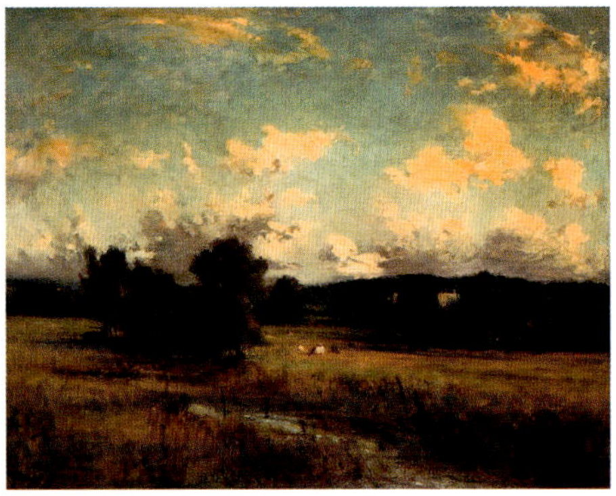

Toft, J. Alfonso 1866–1964
Cattle in Landscape, Trentham, Stoke-on-Trent
oil on canvas 90 x 110
PAC 179-88

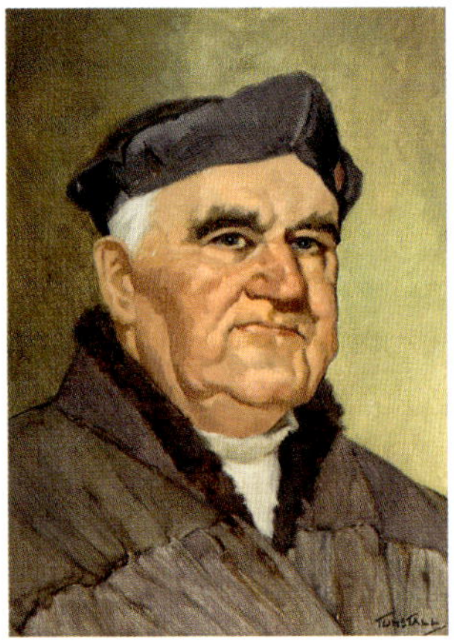

Tunstall, Eric 1897–1987
The Advocate 1959
oil on board 40 x 29
PAC 167-88

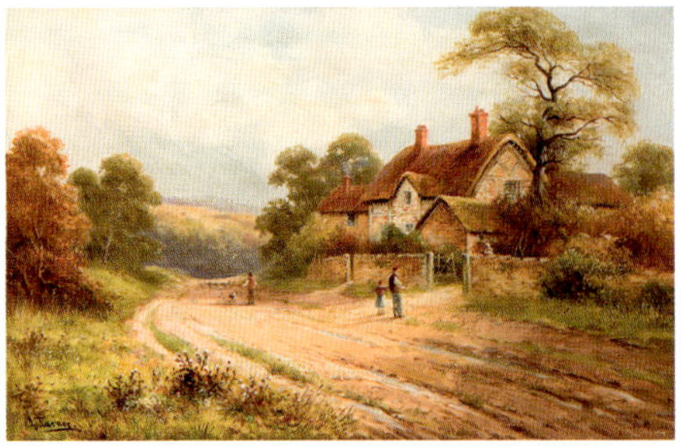

Turner, George II 1843–1910
Country Lane with Cottage
oil on canvas 40 x 61
PAC 187-88

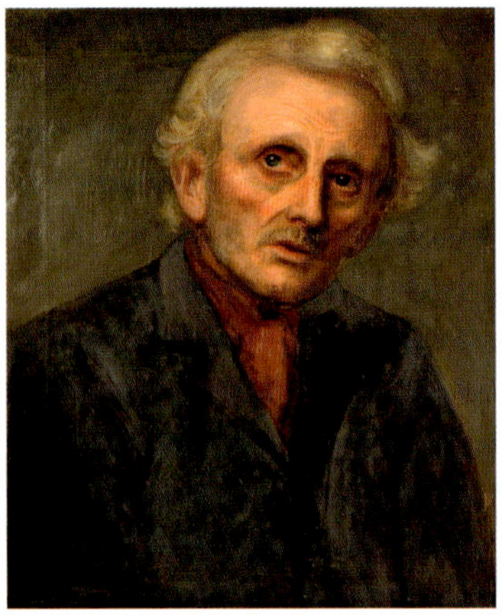

unknown artist
Old Joe, the Newcastle Match Seller c.1920
oil on canvas 52 x 42
PAC 175-88

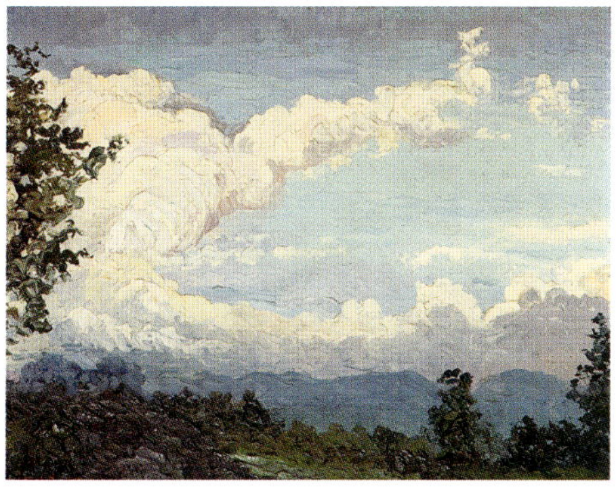

Wade, George A. active 1950–1960
Cloud Study 1950
oil on board 42 x 52.5
PAC 186-88

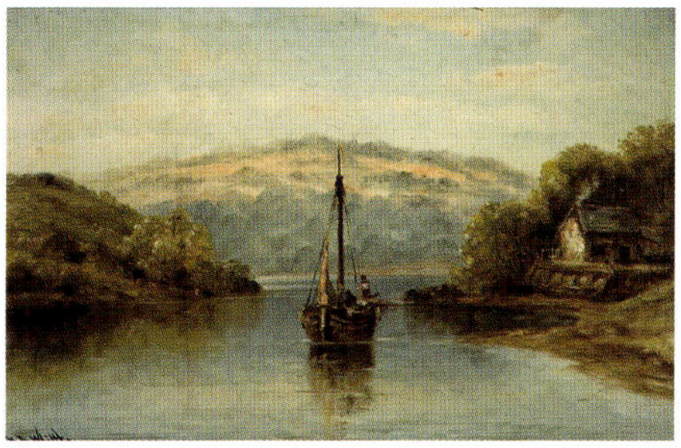

Whittle, Harry Armstrong active 1867–1876
Fishing Boat in a Mountainous River Landscape with Cottages
oil on board 44 x 59.5
PAC 252-88

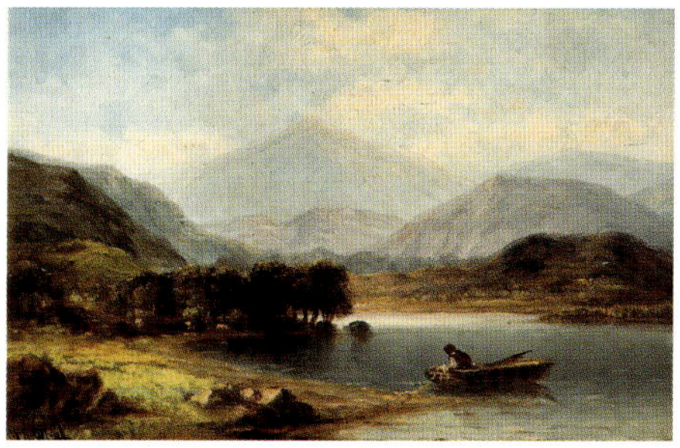

Whittle, Harry Armstrong active 1867–1876
Rowing Boat at the Bank
oil on board 44 x 59.5
PAC 253-88

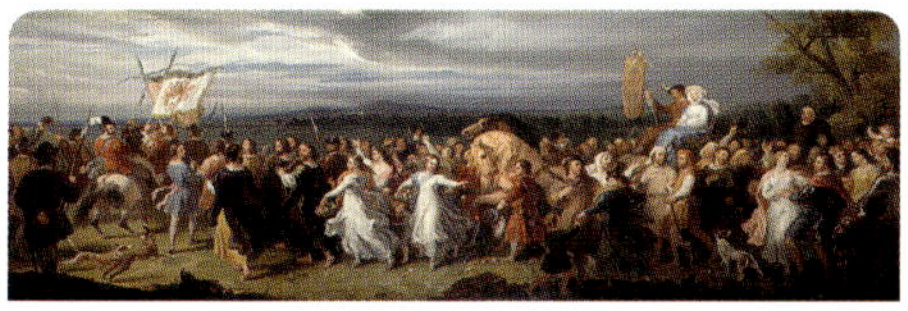

Wright, John Massey 1777–1866
Claiming the Wichnor Flitch 1817
oil on panel 45 x 128
PAC 151-88

Keele University

Keele University was established in 1949, the first British university to be created in the aftermath of the Second World War. From the outset, the University's ethos was liberal and progressive with equal emphasis placed on the arts and sciences for all undergraduates.

There was considerable local support for the creation of the University and its development. It was from this spirit of generosity that the art collection was formed with the donation in the early 1960s of a major collection of British art by Sir Barnett Stross. He was MP for Stoke-on-Trent and an eminent radiologist with a professional concern for the lung diseases suffered by workers in the local pottery, metal and coal mining industries.

The collection that he and his wife had assembled during the 1930s–1950s included works from many established artists working in Britain, such as Michael Ayrton, Jacob Kramer and Duncan Grant. Rowley Smart was clearly one of his favourite artists. It was this collection that laid the foundation for Keele's art collection. During the early 1960s, a significant number of works were acquired from artists working at the University as Gulbenkian Fellows, which introduced abstract works to the collection.

The University's collecting policy aims to continue the practice of these early years by collecting work by British artists of the twentieth and twenty-first centuries. For practical reasons it is not possible to provide long-term display space for the works, but many are on display in public spaces on campus and they are shown in the art gallery temporary exhibition programme. Items from the collection can be viewed by appointment for research purposes.

John Rhodes, Arts Development Officer

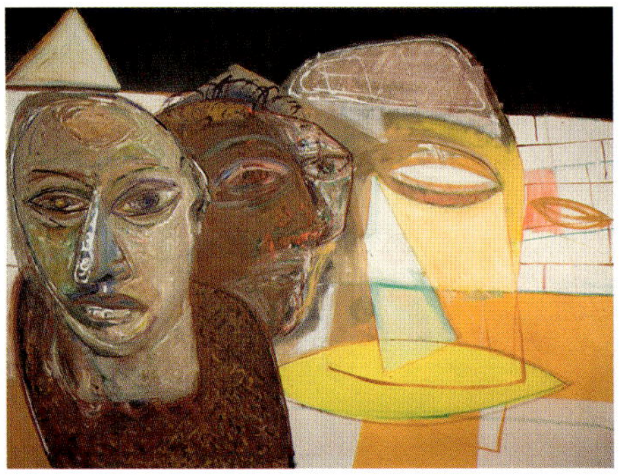

Abrahams, Peter b.1958
Carbon Horizon
oil on canvas 122 x 152
2007/03

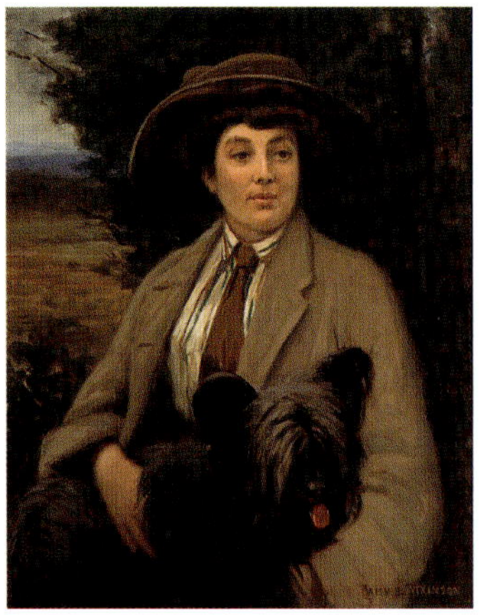

Atkinson, Amy B. 1859–1916
Lady with a Dog
oil on canvas 90 x 70
1998/02

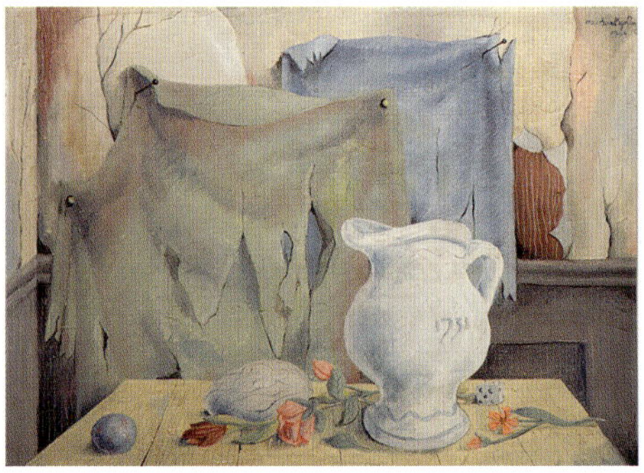

Ayrton, Michael 1921–1975
The White Jug 1940
oil on canvas 39.5 x 49.5
1997/054

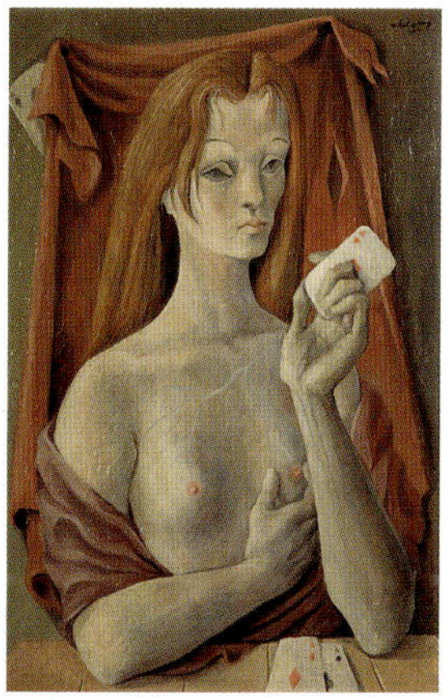

Ayrton, Michael 1921–1975
The Fortune Teller 1941
oil on canvas 49.5 x 33.5
1997/022

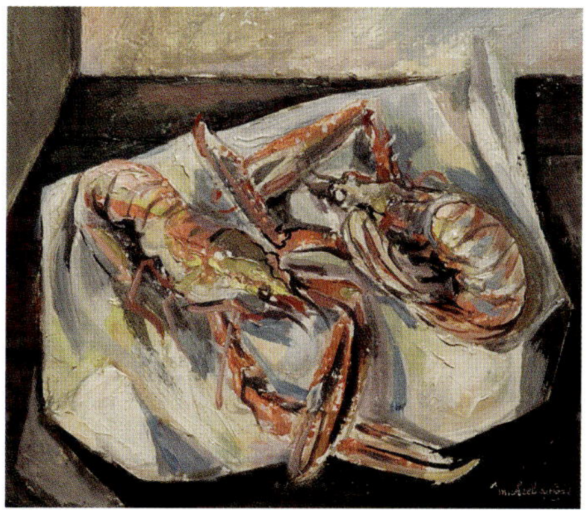

Ayrton, Michael 1921–1975
Crayfish 1943
oil on board 23.5 x 26
1997/012

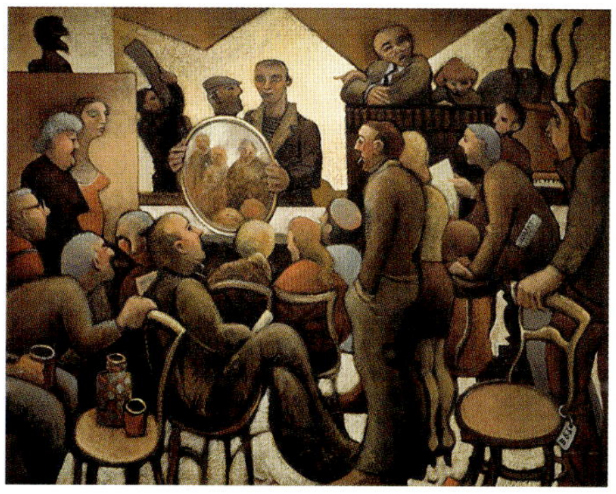

Borsky, Jiri b.1945
The Auction 1983
acrylic on canvas 85 x 105
lib.1

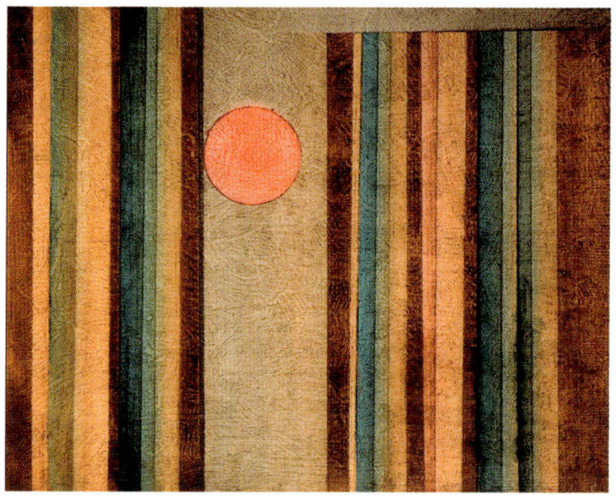

Brody, E. M.
Stripes and Circles
oil on board 33 x 40
1997/036

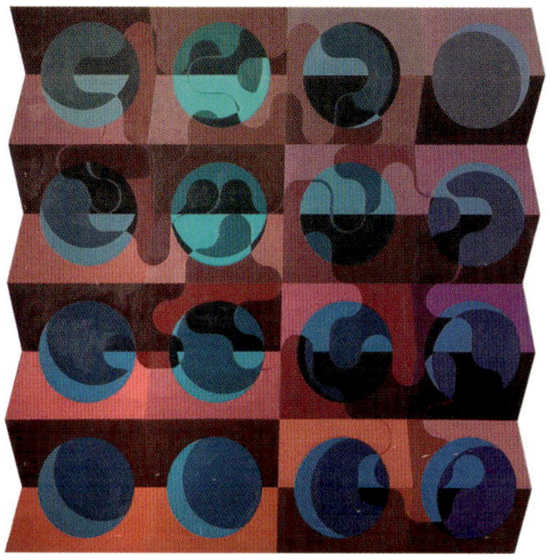

Clarke, Paul Montem b.1915
*Abstract Circles**
oil on canvas 96 x 96
1997/117

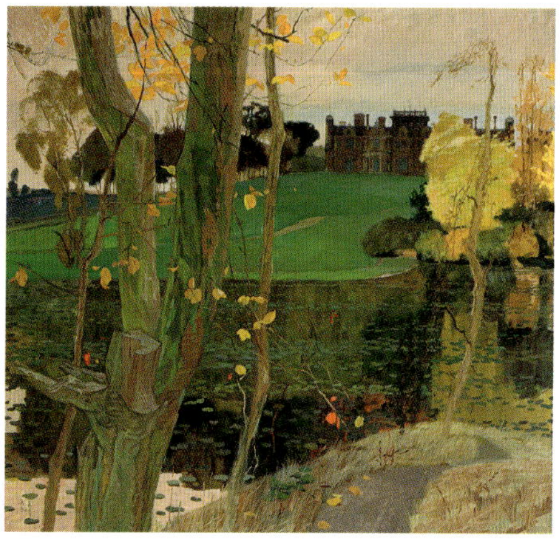

Dai, Shi-he active 1989–1990
Keele Hall 1989
oil on canvas 197 x 197
1998/01

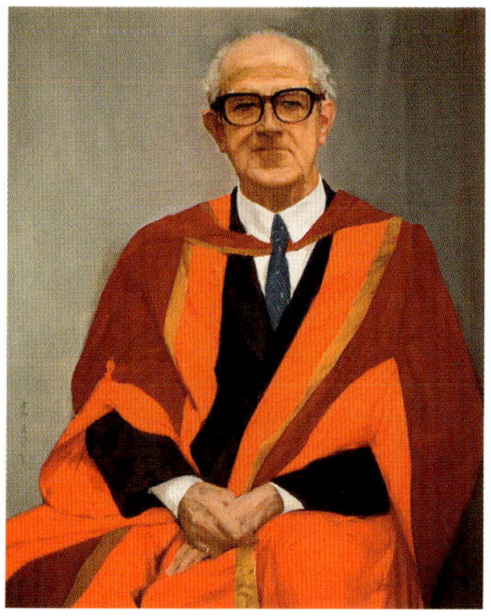

Dai, Shi-he active 1989–1990
Professor William Campbell Stewart 1990
oil on canvas 73.5 x 58.5
1998/07

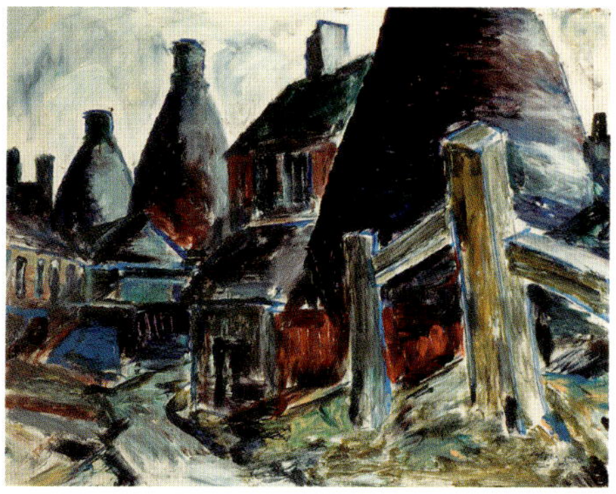

Emery, Alston active 1973–c.1992
Longton Ovens 1973
oil on board 58 x 74
1997/083

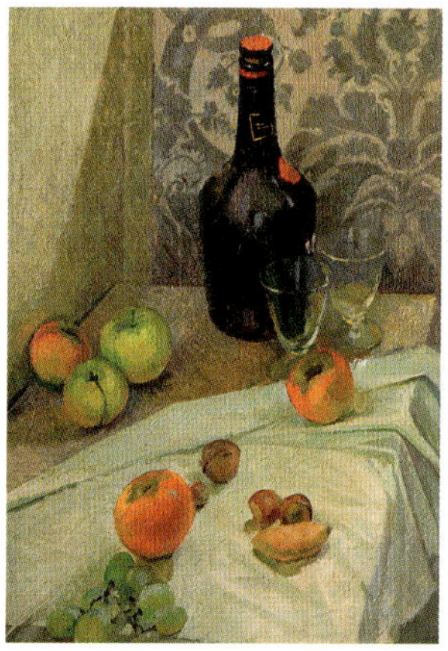

Folkes, Peter L. b.1923
Still Life 1956
oil on canvas 44.5 x 34
1997/107

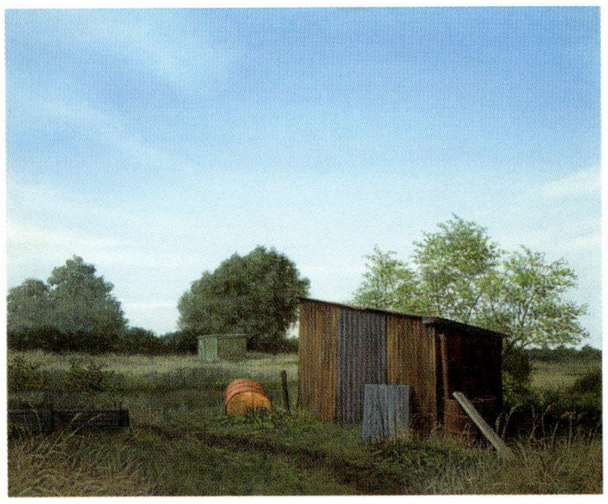

Gleeson, David Paul b.1956
Staffordshire Sheds, Castlefields 1991
oil on board 35 x 39
2006/06

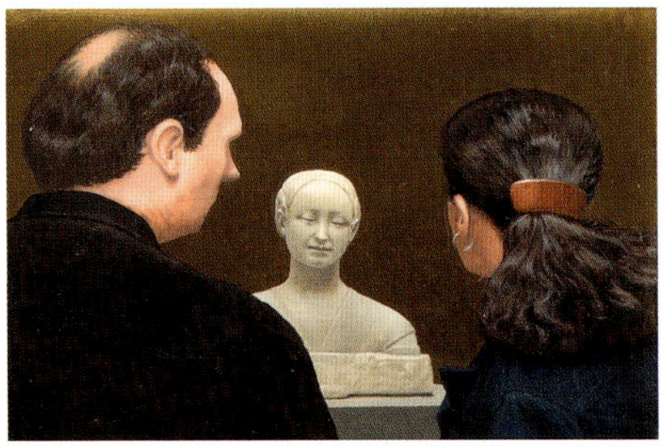

Gleeson, David Paul b.1956
In the Victoria & Albert LIV 2001
acrylic on board 14 x 17.5
2006/07

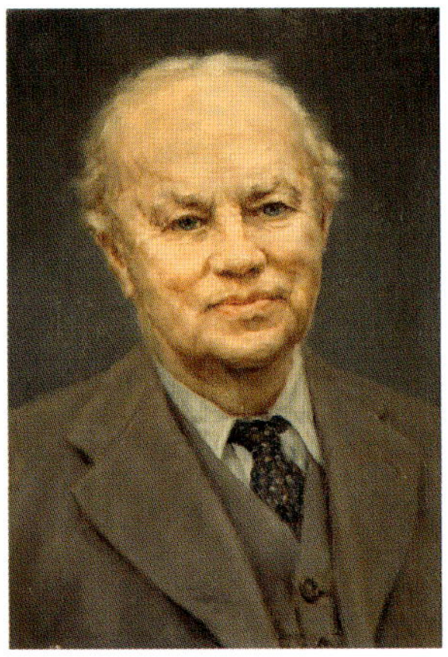

Goodwin, Robin L. H.
Lord Lindsay of Birker (1879–1952) 1953
oil on wood 34 x 24
1998/03

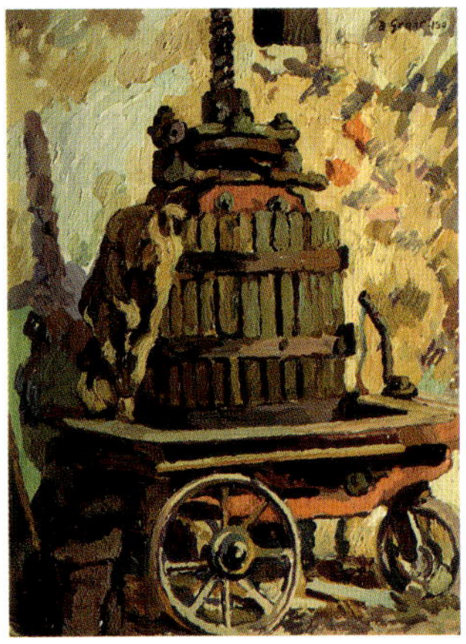

Grant, Duncan 1885–1978
The Wine Press 1930
oil on canvas 44.5 x 36
1998/18

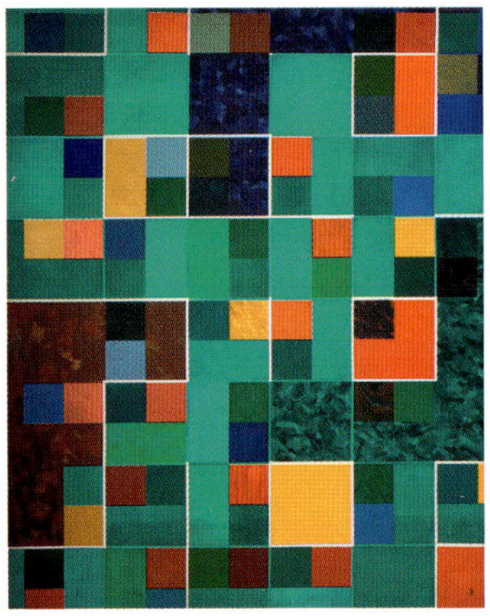

Harding, Tony b.1946
*Squares** 1976
oil on canvas 150 x 118.5
2003/01

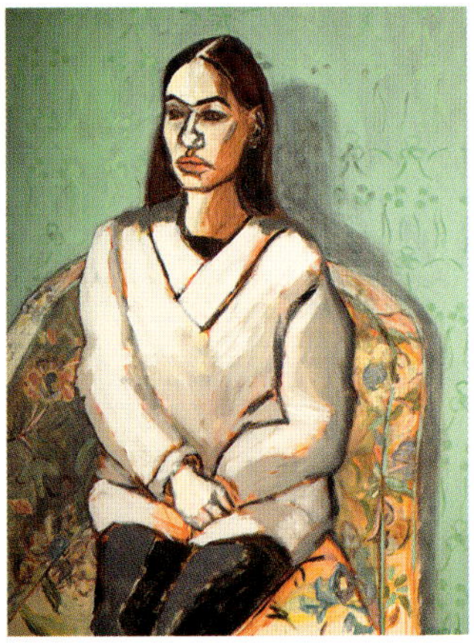

Held, Julie b.1958
Stephanie Hurst 1989
oil on canvas 101.5 x 76
2006/37

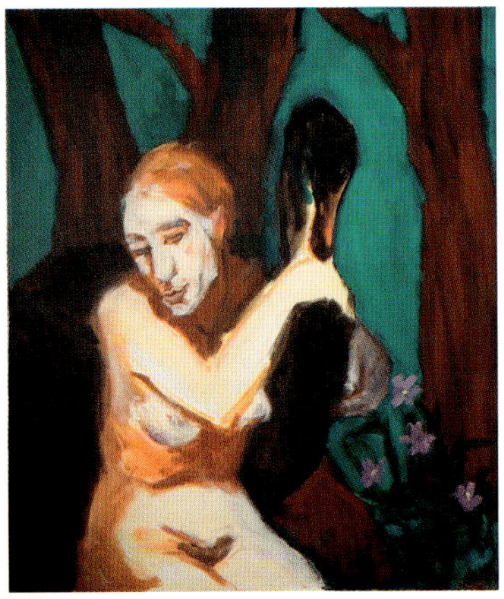

Held, Julie b.1958
Woman with Swan I 1989
oil on canvas 76.5 x 66 (E)
2006/35

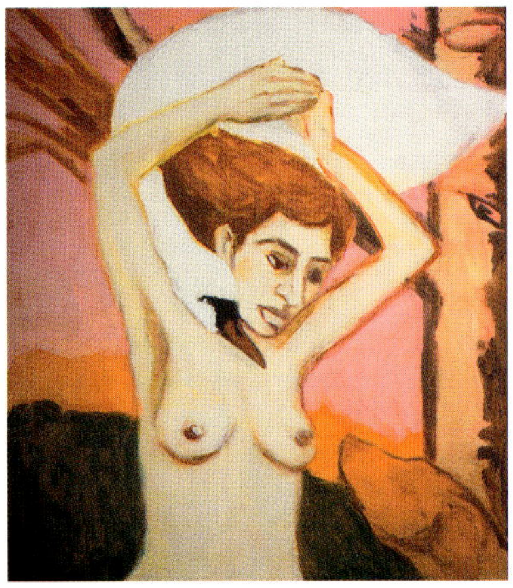

Held, Julie b.1958
Woman with Swan II 1989
oil on canvas 76.5 x 66 (E)
2006/36

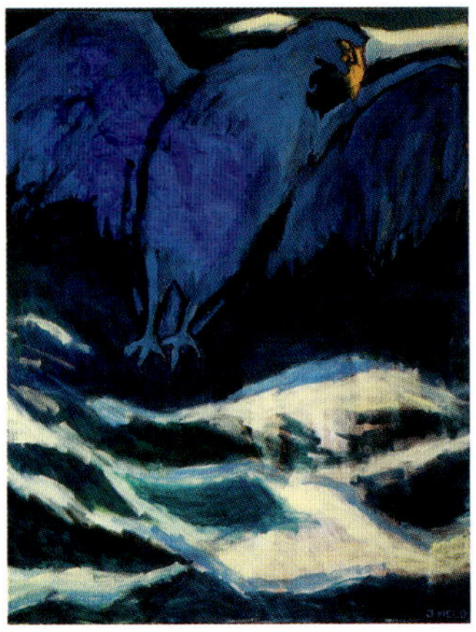

Held, Julie b.1958
Ceyx 1991
oil on canvas 122 x 91.5
1998/19

Facing page: Coldstream, William Menzies, 1908–1987, *At the Zoo* (detail), 1930, The Potteries Museum & Art Gallery (p. 115)

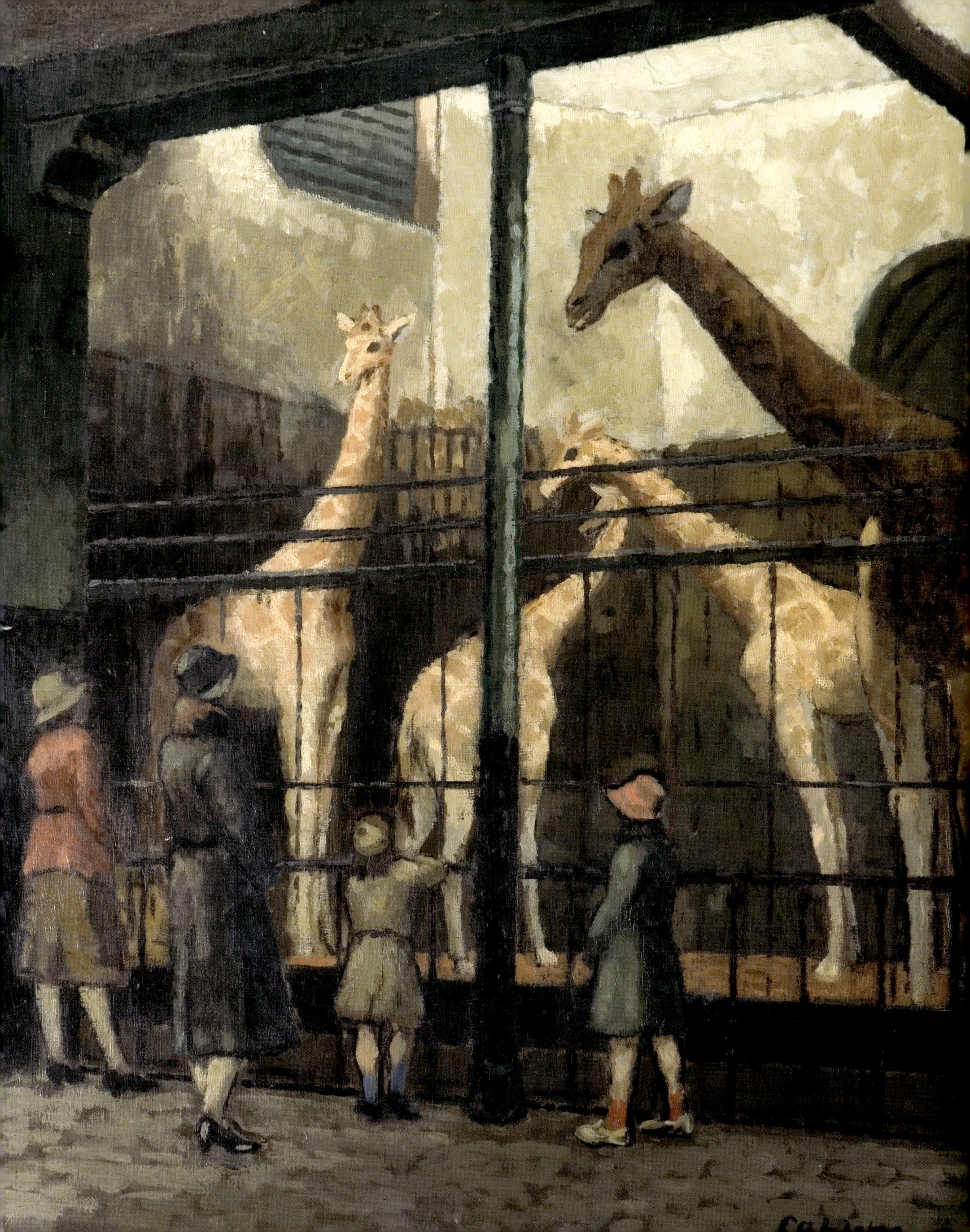

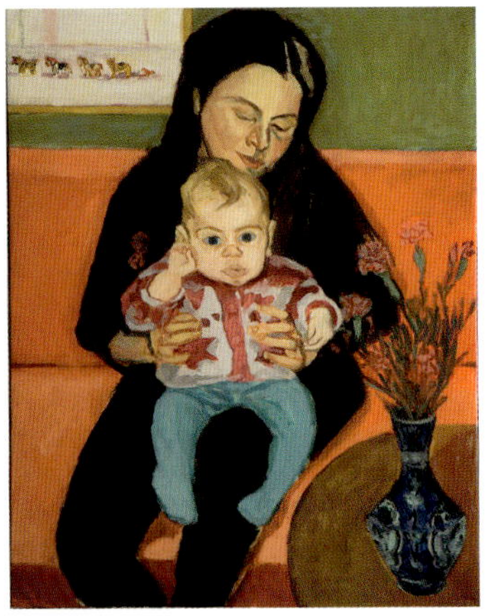

Held, Julie b.1958
Anna and Bonnie
oil on canvas 102 x 76
1998/20

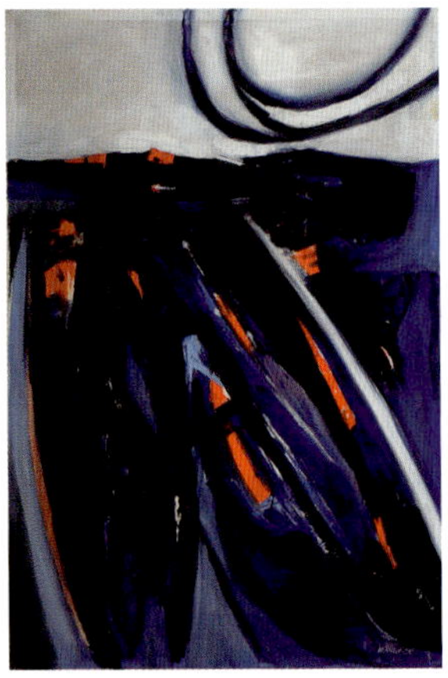

Henderson, Ian active 1966–1967
Lancashire 1966
oil on canvas 121.5 x 91
1998/45

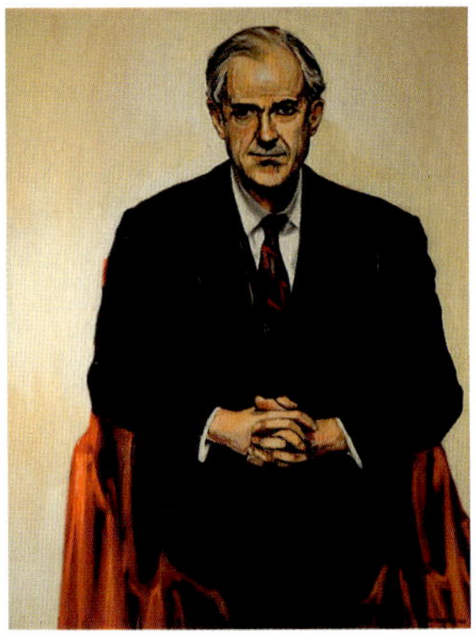

Henderson, Ian active 1966–1967
Professor Harold Taylor, Vice-Chancellor 1967
oil on canvas 118.5 x 98
1998/08

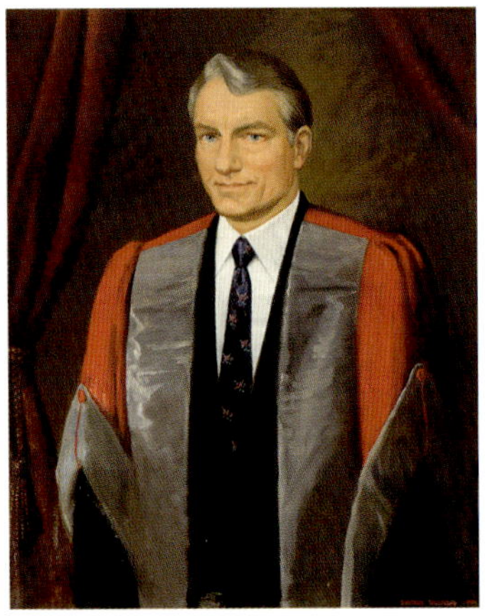

Ionschaev, Suulvan
Dr David Harrison, Vice-Chancellor 1991
oil on canvas 75.5 x 58
1998/09

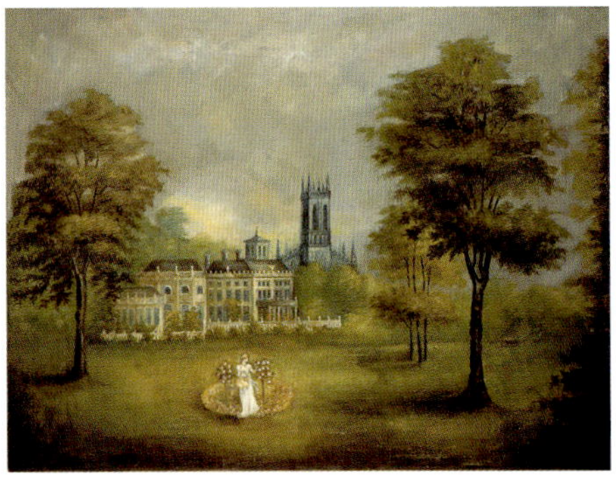

Jones, J.
The Residence of Charles Meigh Esquire
oil on board 71 x 90.5
1997/093

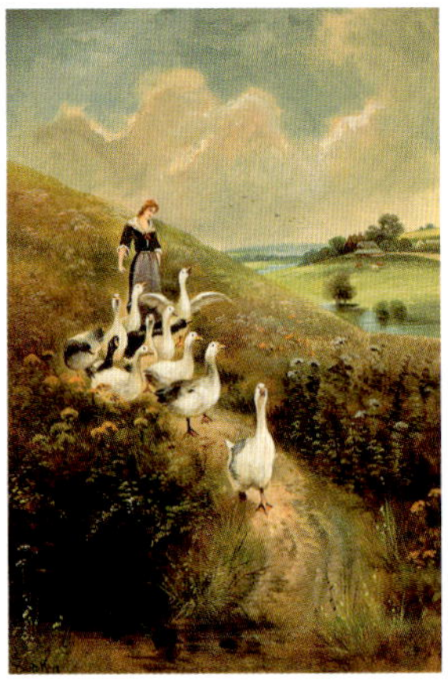

King, Yeend 1855–1924
Goose Girl
oil on canvas 50 x 34.5
1997/040

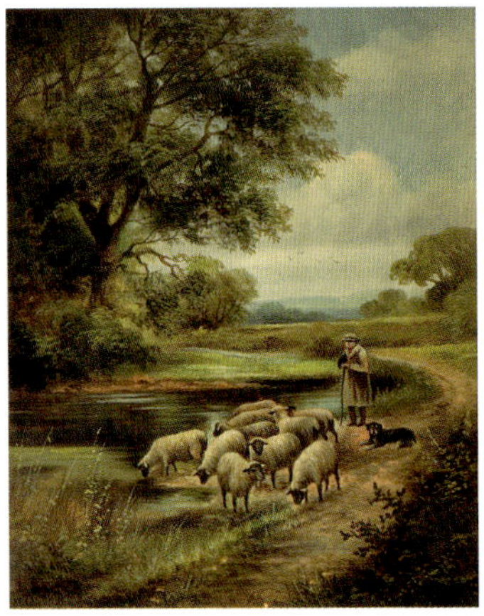

King, Yeend 1855–1924
Shepherd with His Flock
oil on canvas 49.5 x 34
1998/25

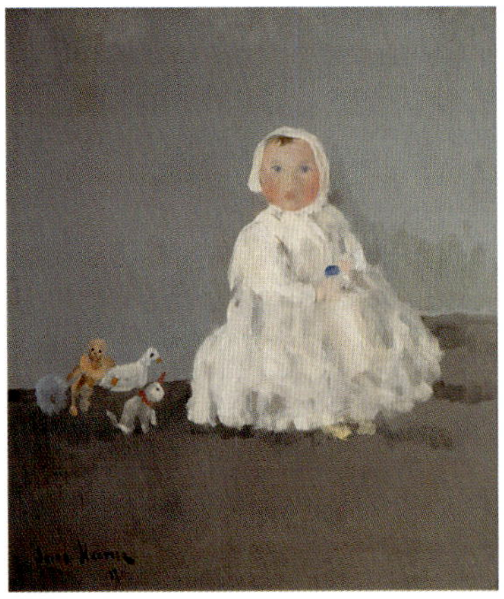

Kramer, Jacob 1892–1962
Child c.1937
oil on canvas 75.5 x 63
1997/085

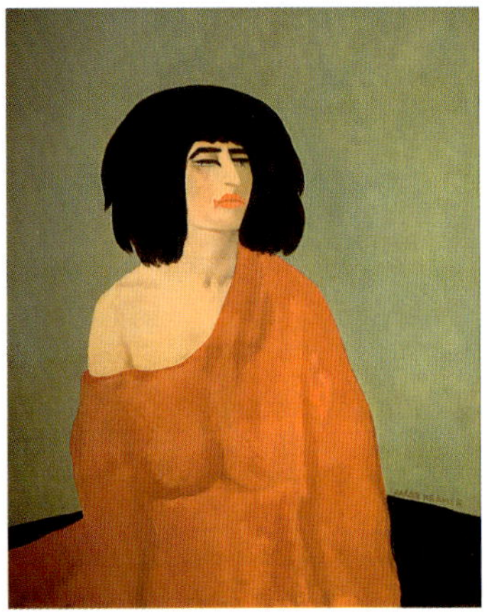

Kramer, Jacob 1892–1962
Rohalla
oil on canvas 76 x 63
1997/084

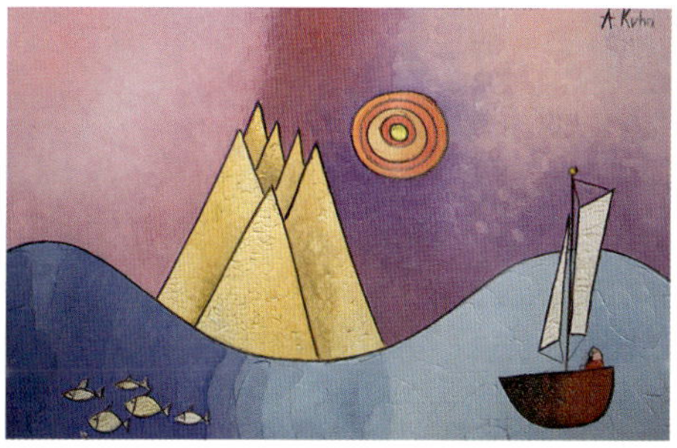

Kuhn, Andrzej b.1930
Explorer
oil on board 62.5 x 90
1997/111

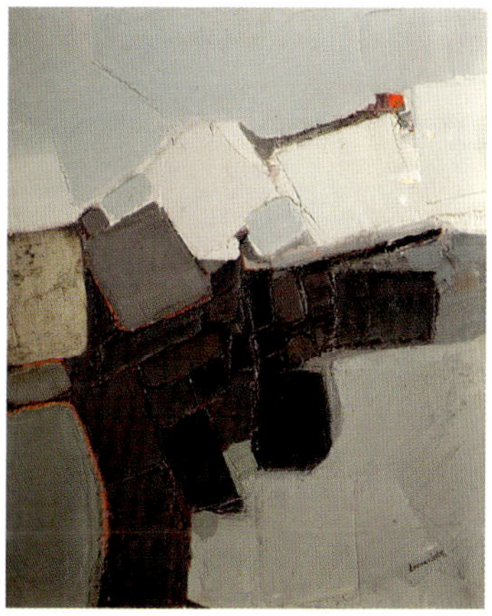

Leeson, Laurence b.1930
Peninsula I 1962
oil on board 75.5 x 63
1997/058

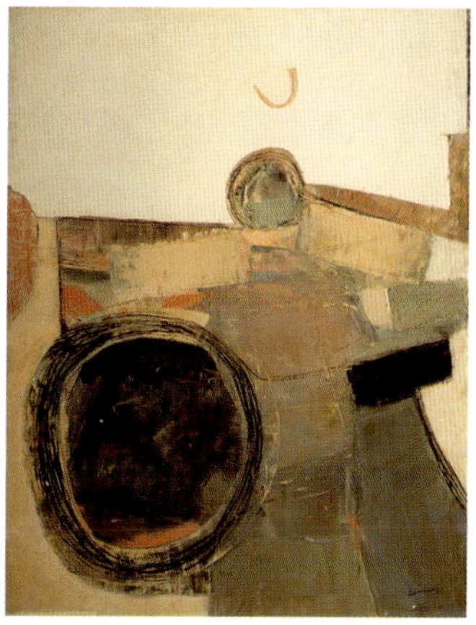

Leeson, Laurence b.1930
Diminishing Circle 1963
oil on canvas 126 x 101
1997/097

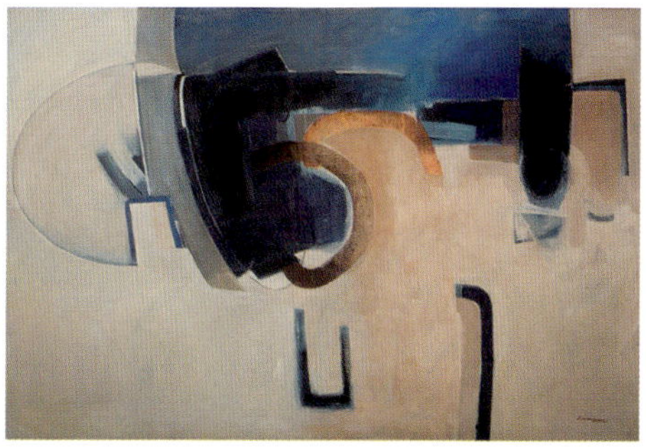

Leeson, Laurence b.1930
Parts 1965
oil on canvas 91.5 x 122
1997/098

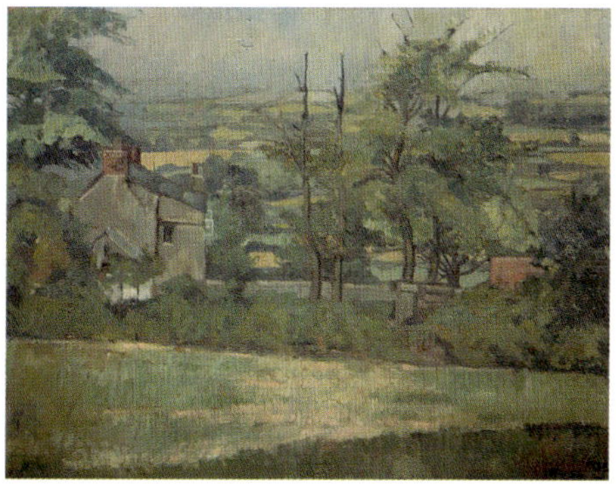

Lovatt, Enos b.1937
Landscape 1955
oil on canvas 60 x 75
2006/33

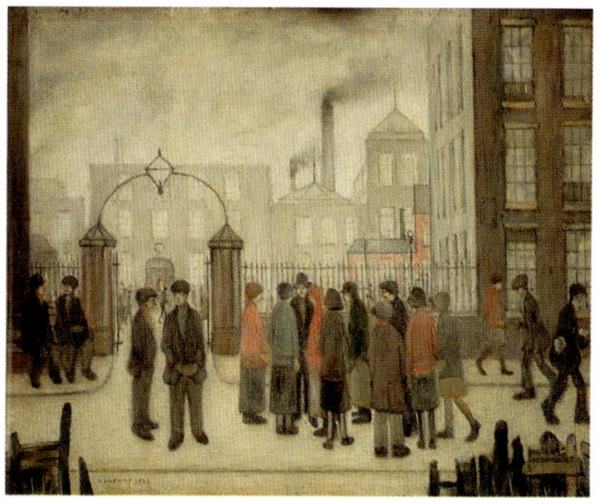

Lowry, Laurence Stephen 1887–1976
The Mill Gates 1928
oil on canvas 39 x 49.5
1998/17

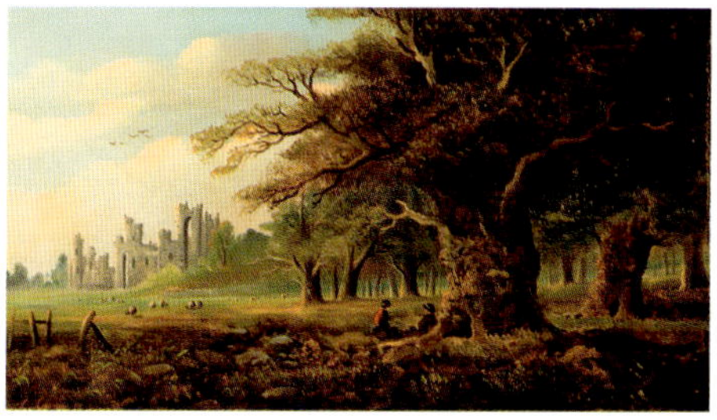

Lyons, L.
Castle in a Landscape
oil on canvas 30.5 x 50.5
1997/086

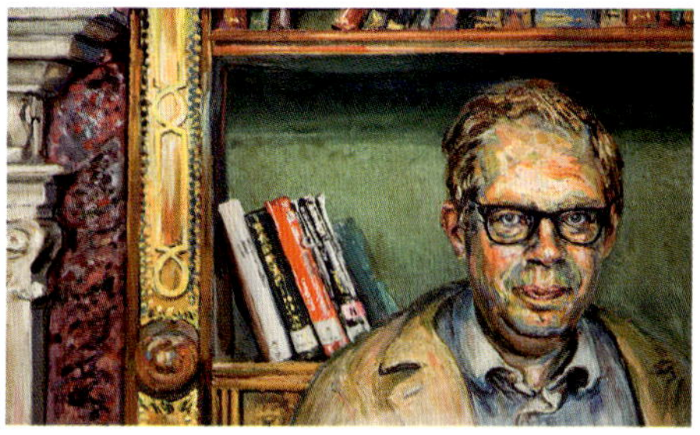

Naylor, Ian b.1964
Dr Michael B. Akehurst 1990s
oil on board 61 x 93
lib.2

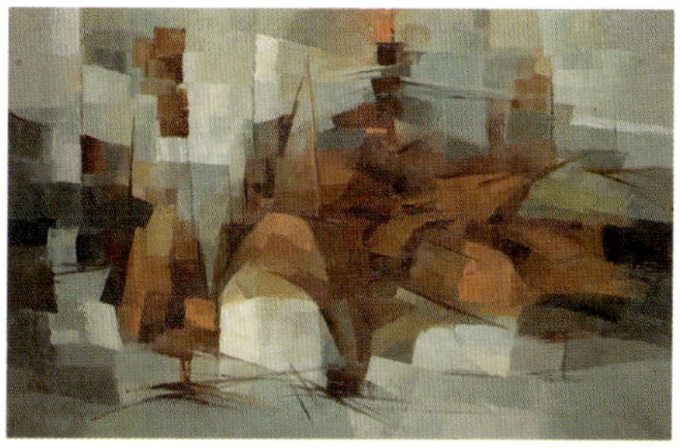

Pass, Donald b.1930
The Cedars
oil on canvas 64 x 89
2007/01

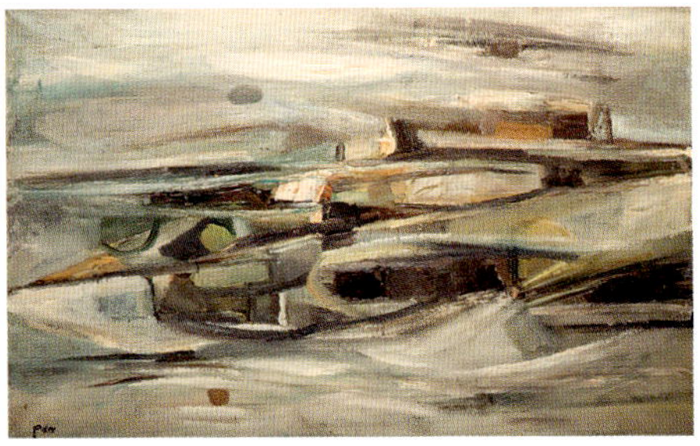

Pass, Donald b.1930
The Wave
oil on canvas 61.5 x 90
1997/087

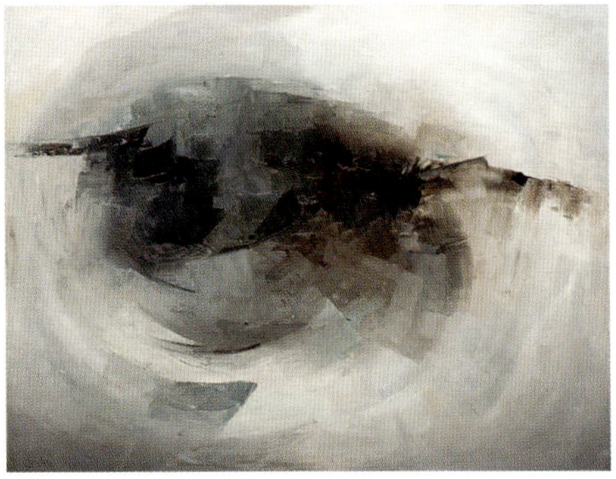

Pass, Donald b.1930
White Landscape
oil on canvas 76.5 x 91
1997/088

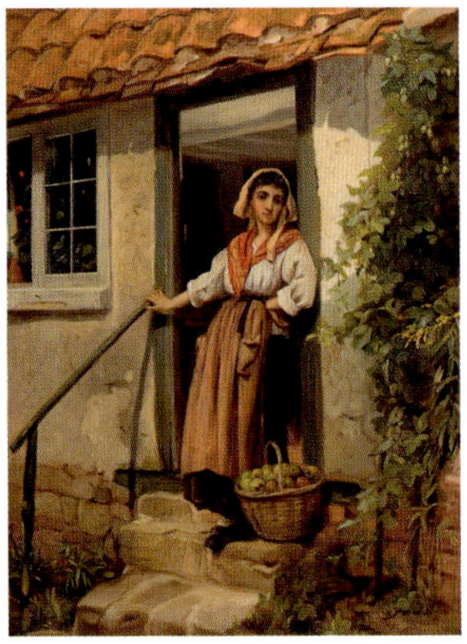

Pelham, Thomas Kent active 1860–1892
At the Cottage Door
oil on canvas 89.5 x 69
1997/092

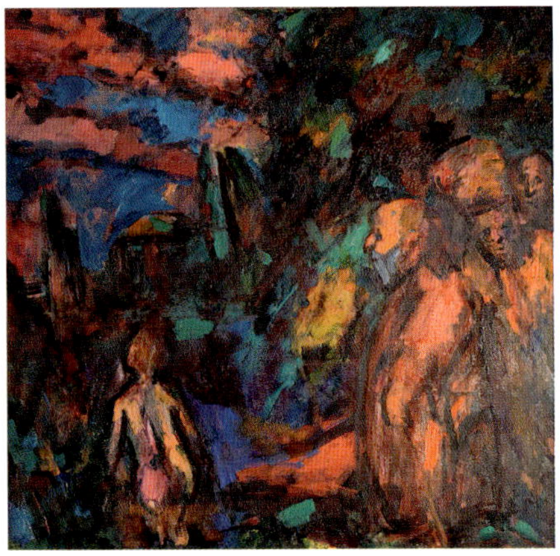

Praag, Arnold van b.1926
Susannah and the Elders I
oil on canvas 101 x 101
2007/02

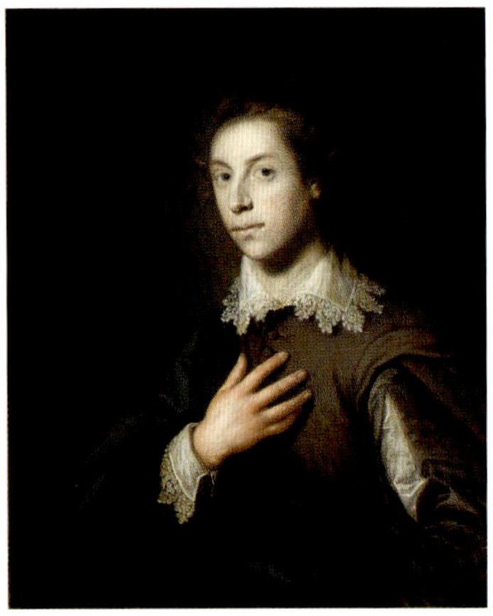

Reynolds, Joshua (attributed to) 1723–1792
John Sneyd
oil on canvas 63 x 53
1998/42

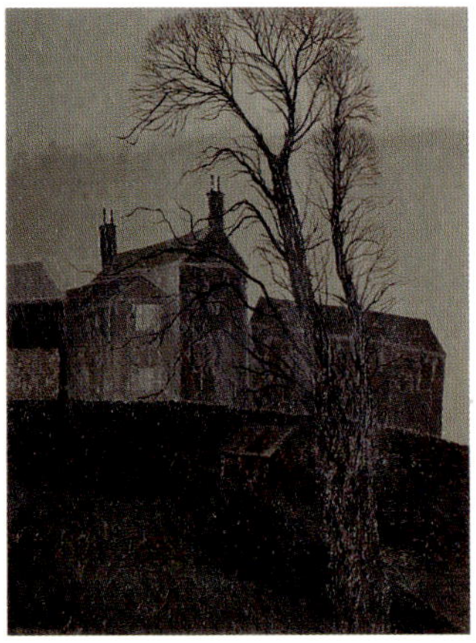

Simcock, Jack b.1929
Trees and Houses 1960
oil on board 74.5 x 59
1997/057

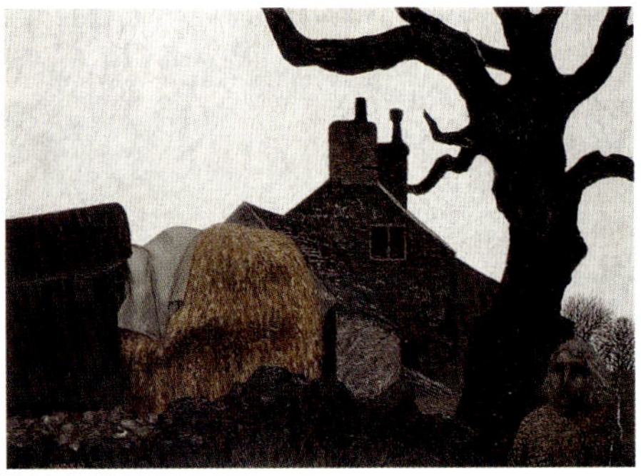

Simcock, Jack b.1929
Farm 1962
oil on board 74.5 x 100
1997/099

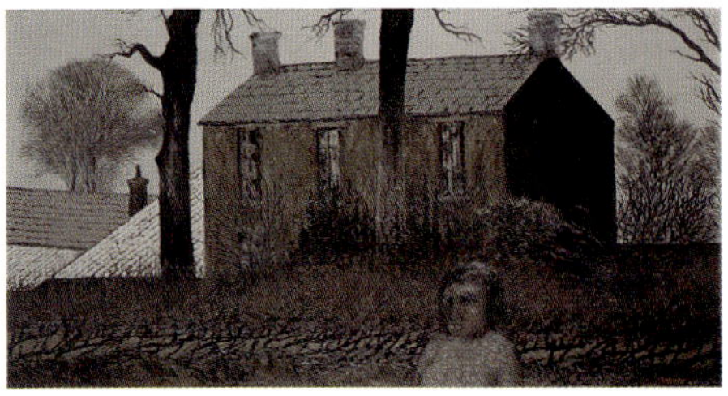

Simcock, Jack b.1929
The Old House 1964
oil on board 60 x 105.5
1997/116

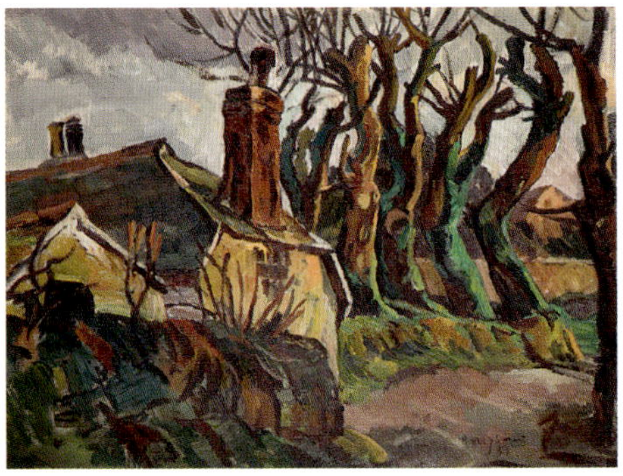

Smart, Rowley 1887–1934
The Four Witches 1933
oil on canvas 48 x 63
1997/080

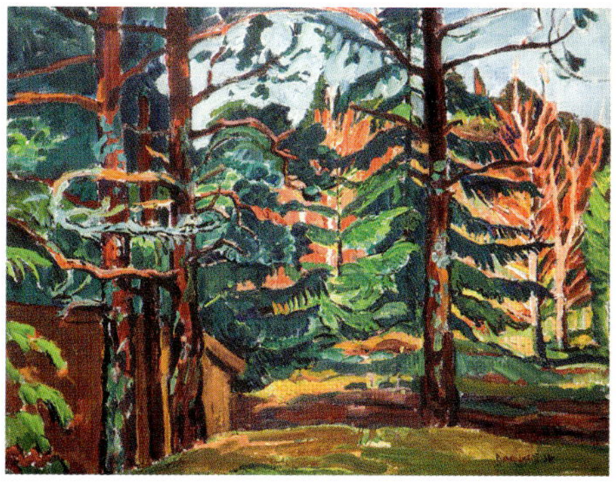

Smart, Rowley 1887–1934
Swedish Landscape 1934
oil on canvas 50 x 60
1997/071

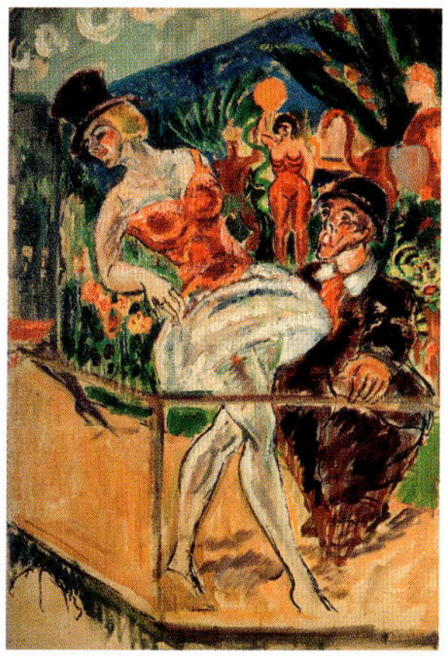

Smart, Rowley 1887–1934
Circus
oil on canvas 60 x 40
1997/076

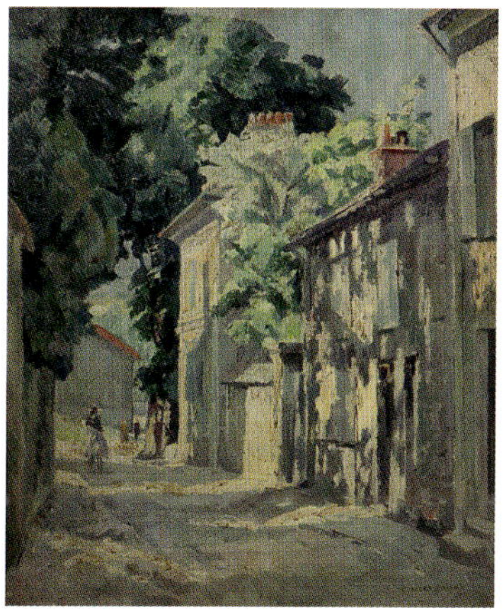

Smart, Rowley 1887–1934
Giverny
oil on canvas 58 x 47.5
1997/072

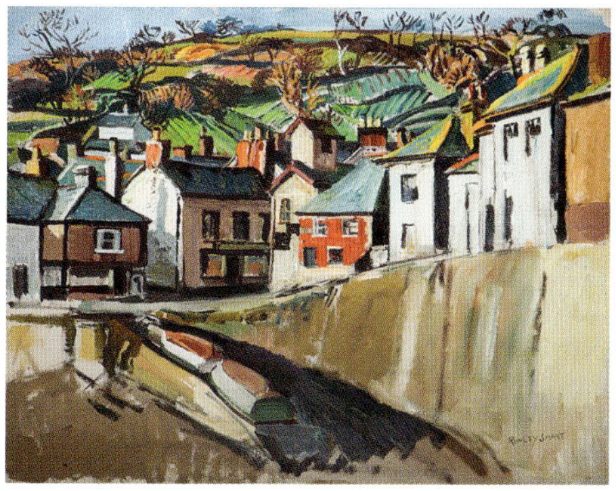

Smart, Rowley 1887–1934
Mousehole
oil on canvas 53 x 63
1998/33

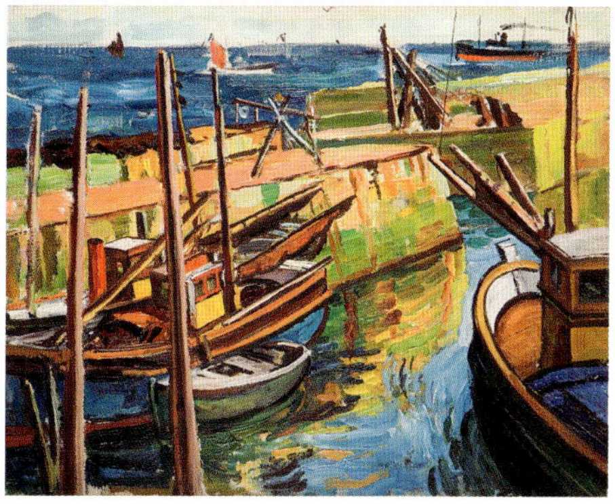

Smart, Rowley 1887–1934
Mousehole, the Harbour
oil on canvas 40 x 60
1997/002

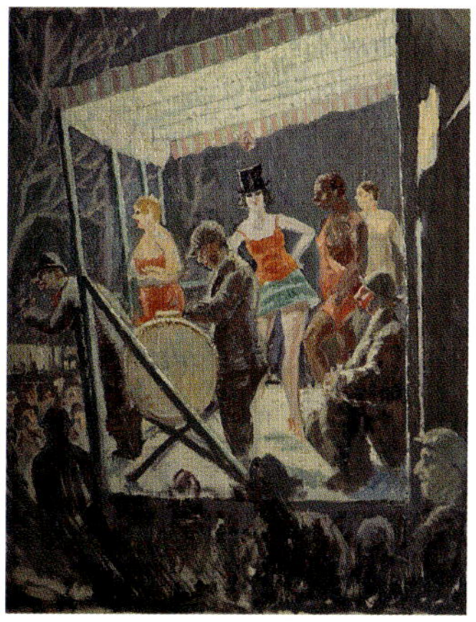

Smart, Rowley 1887–1934
Nocturne
oil on canvas 64 x 53.5
1997/075

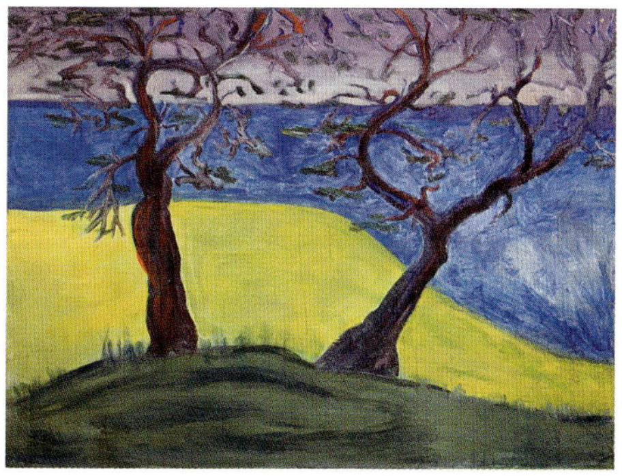

Smyth, Leslie
Corfu 1977
oil on canvas 105.5 x 120
2006/34

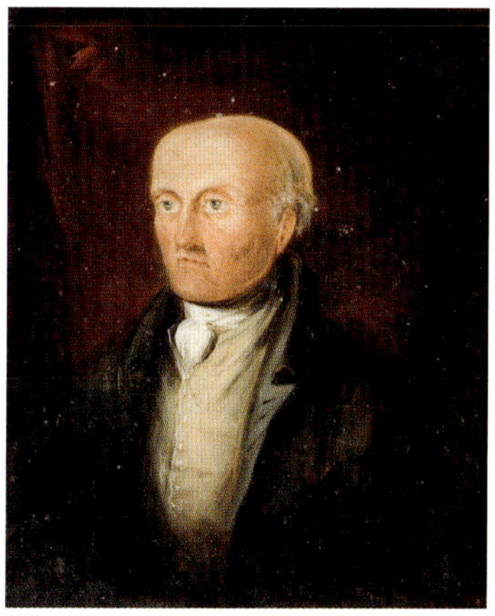

Sneyd, Charlotte Augusta 1800–1882
Colonel Walter Sneyd c.1820
oil on board 19 x 15
lib.Sneyd

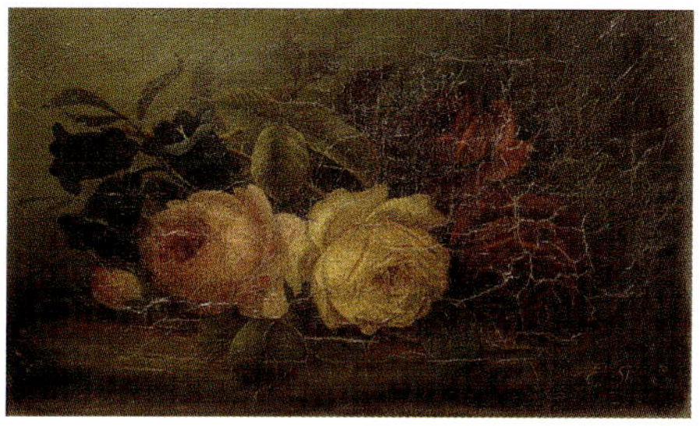

Steele, Edwin 1803–1871
Roses
oil on canvas 19.5 x 29
1997/096

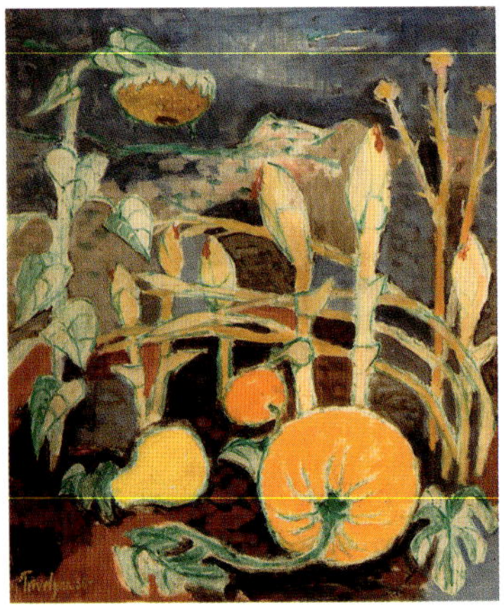

Trevelyan, Julian 1910–1989
Italian Field 1956
oil on canvas 59.5 x 49.5
1997/079

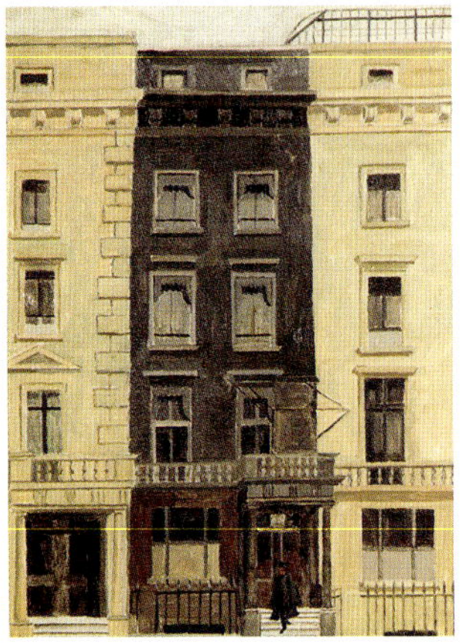

unknown artist
Le Play House, Belgrave Road, London
1920–1939
oil on canvas 35.5 x 25.5
lib.3

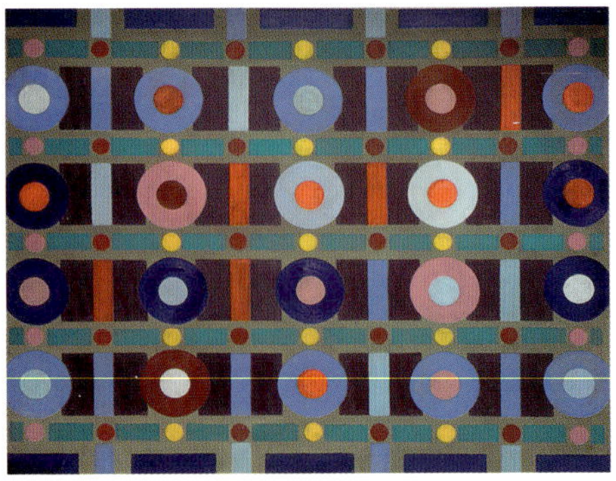

unknown artist
*Circles**
oil on canvas 98 x 122
2006/39

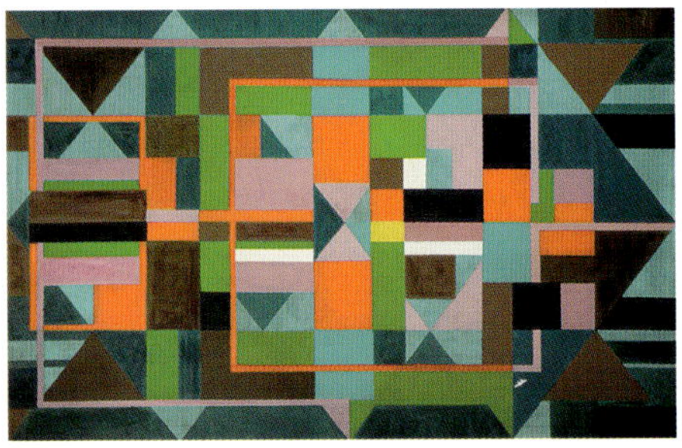

unknown artist
*Geometric Shapes**
oil on canvas 86 x 122
2006/38

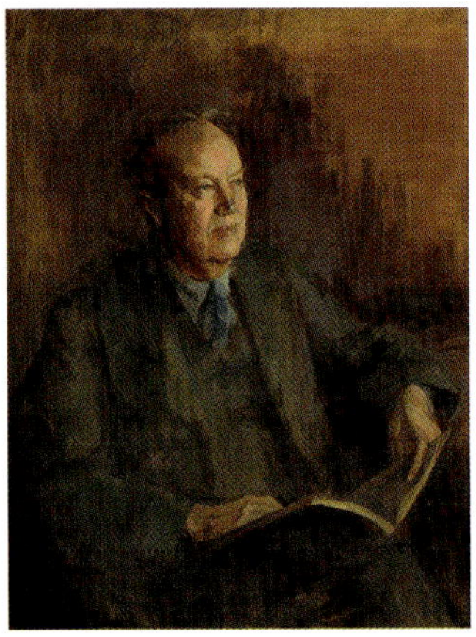

unknown artist
Lord Lindsay of Birker (1879–1952)
oil on canvas 101.5 x 81
1997/089

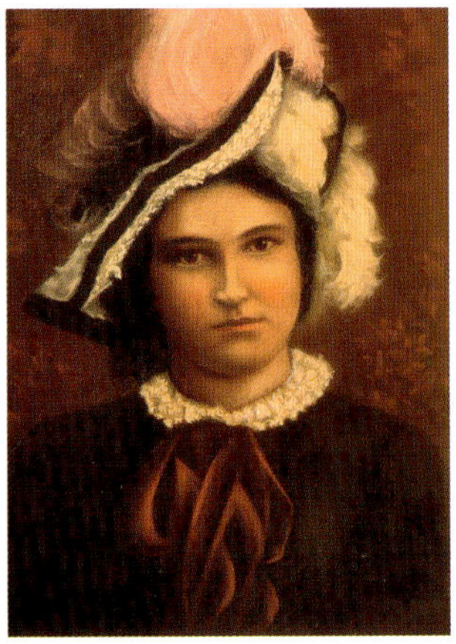

unknown artist
Portrait of a Girl
oil on canvas 30 x 20
1997/035

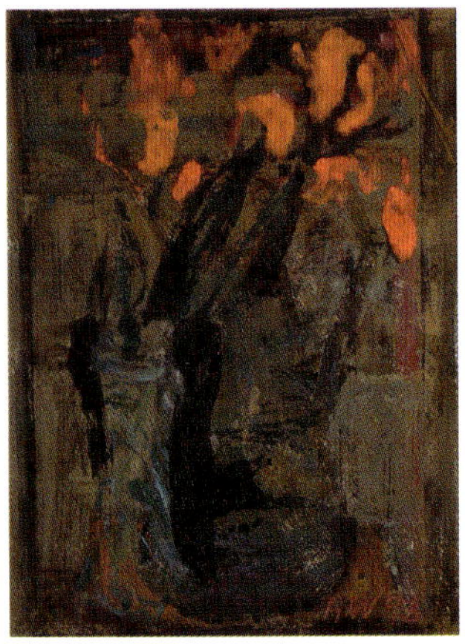

Wild, Tony b.1941
Gladioli 1992
oil on paper 80 x 57.5
1998/21

Sandwell Metropolitan Borough Council

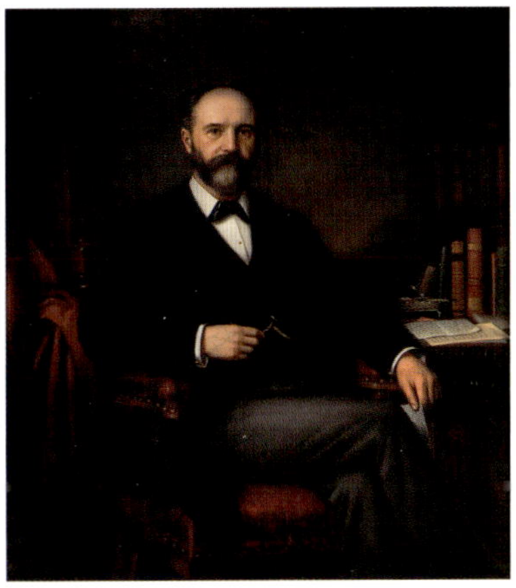

Gibbs, J.
Daniel Hipkins 1900
oil on canvas 160 x 140 (E)
PCF1

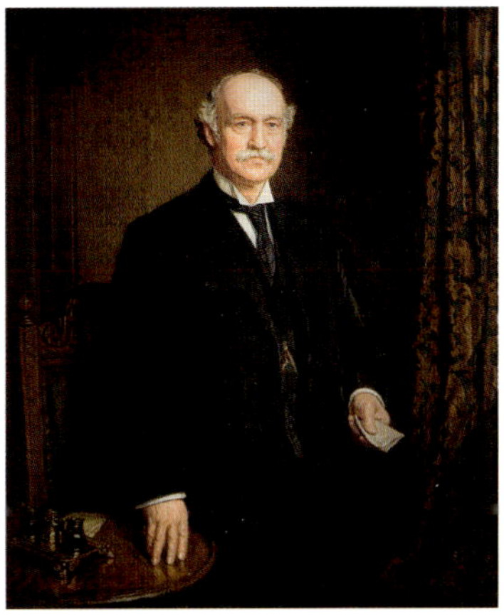

Munns, John Bernard 1869–1942
Thomas E. Saller, JP, CC 1924
oil on canvas 130 x 110
PCF3

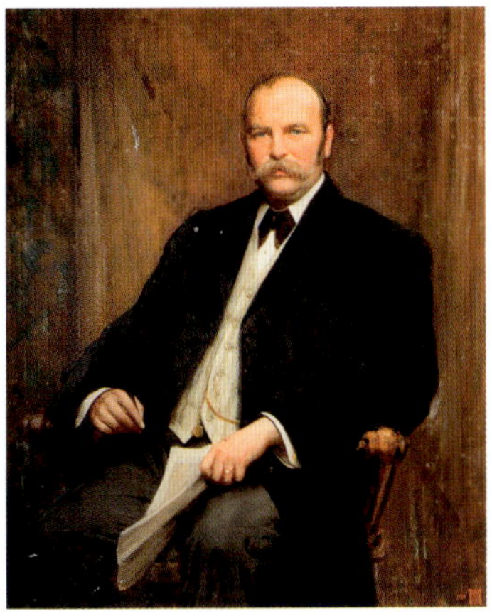

unknown artist
Portrait of a Gentleman 1919
oil on canvas 125 x 100
PCF4

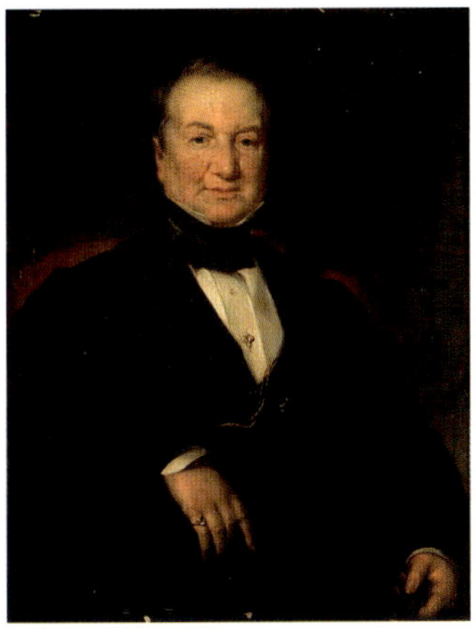

unknown artist
Joseph Hall (1789–1862)
oil on canvas 89 x 67
PCF5

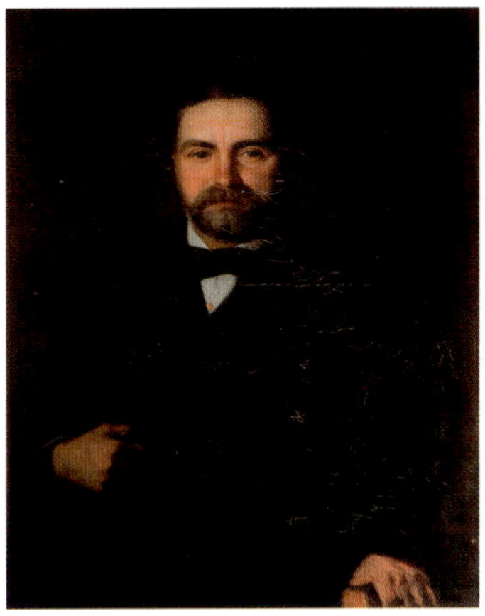

unknown artist
Portrait of a Gentleman
oil on canvas 90 x 70 (E)
PCF2

Sandwell Museums Service Collection

Sandwell Museums Service incorporates six sites located within the geographical area administered by Sandwell Metropolitan Borough Council. The sites are Wednesbury Museum & Art Gallery, Haden Hill House, Oak House Museum, Sandwell Council House, Bishop Asbury's Cottage, Galton Valley Canal Heritage Centre and Tipton Heritage Centre.

The Sandwell Museum Service Collection primarily contains works painted during the mid-Victorian period. Subject matter includes English and Dutch landscapes and portraits of dignitaries associated with the contemporary administrative boundaries of Sandwell Metropolitan Borough Council. The Collection is primarily displayed at Wednesbury Museum & Art Gallery, although works from the Collection are used to enhance displays at other service sites.

Wednesbury Museum & Art Gallery was opened in 1891. It was built to display a large collection of works owned by Edwin Richards and his wife

Mary. The Richards lived in Wednesbury and owned an axel manufacturing company. They were prolific collectors of art and especially favoured landscapes. In her will, Mary Richards donated their substantial collection to the town of Wednesbury and provided £2,000 to commence the construction of a public gallery. The remainder of the building costs were financed by public subscription.

Upon completion of the gallery, Wednesbury Borough Council established an art gallery committee. This committee produced two catalogues of the collection (dated 1910 and 1930) and purchased additional works for the collection. By 1930, there were 355 works in the collection, including 25 works by the landscape artist James Webb.

During the Second World War, the art collection was placed in storage at subterranean caves in Kinver, Staffordshire. The gallery building was used as council offices. After the war, the paintings were returned but not all were placed back on display in the gallery.

In 1948, Wednesbury Borough Council decided to sell the fine art collection, including works from the Mary Richards' bequest. Today only 54 paintings remain from the original collection. In the postwar era, Wednesbury Borough Council started collecting portraits of council members and mayors. The Collection now holds 172 oil paintings.

Wednesbury Museum & Art Gallery continued to be used as council offices and a community centre until 1973 when the decision to re-open the gallery was taken by the newly created Sandwell Metropolitan Borough Council. The Collection has changed relatively little since 1973. Works are still added to the Collection, but the cost of collecting fine art places severe restrictions upon further development of the Collection.

Emma Cook, Collections Manager

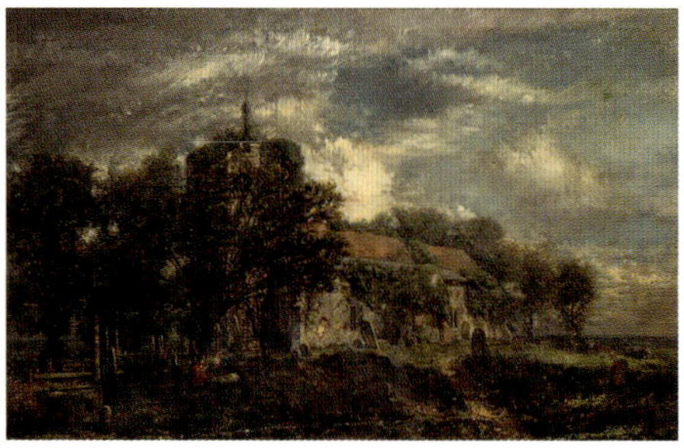

Anthony, Henry Mark 1817–1886
A Country Churchyard
oil on canvas 57.5 x 89
1891.1, P.12

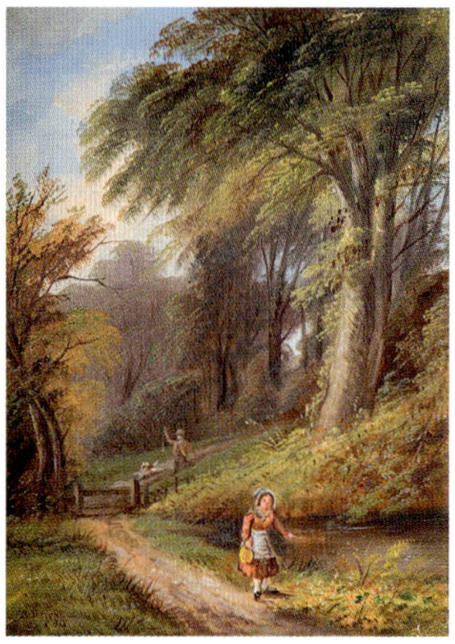

Bagley, Samuel D. active 1886–1898
Coming out of the Wood 1898
oil on canvas 39.5 x 25.5
1973.1, P.202

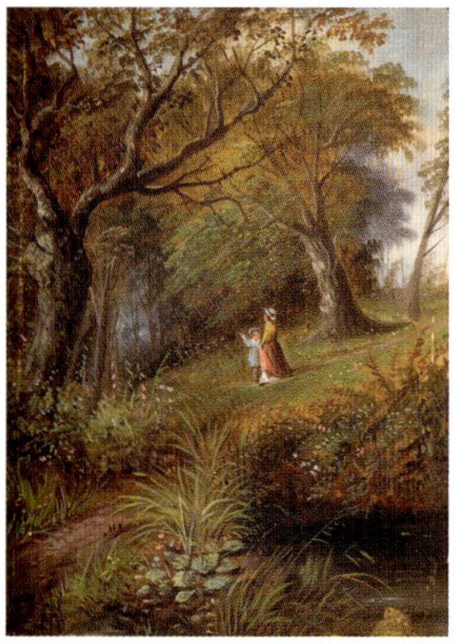

Bagley, Samuel D. active 1886–1898
The Path through the Wood
oil on canvas 39.5 x 25.5
1973.2, p.203

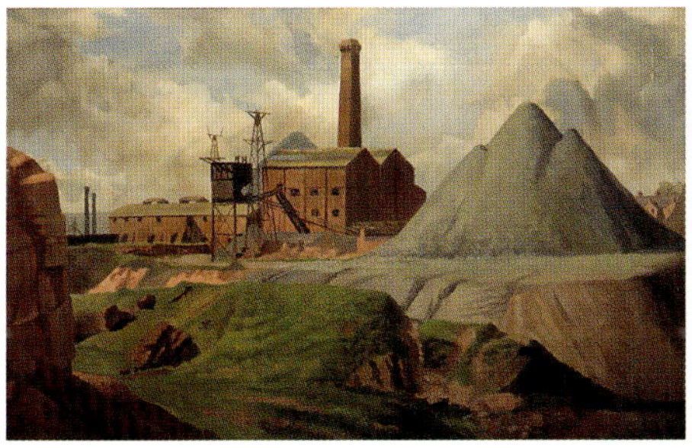

Baker, John L. b.1922
Coal Mine 1949
oil on canvas 51 x 76
B.432, P.177

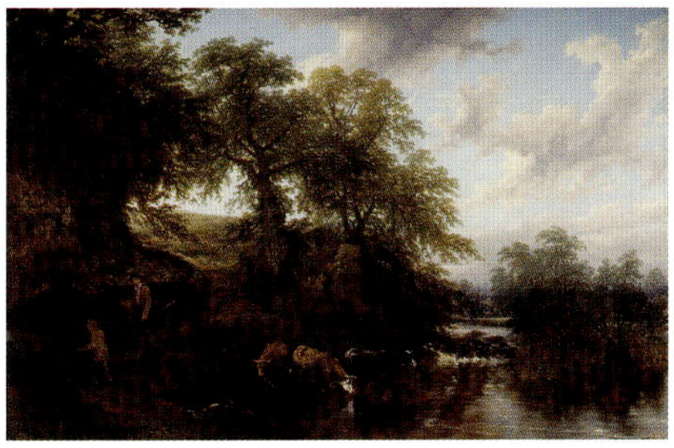

Baker, Thomas 1809–1869
River Avon, near Warwick 1848
oil on canvas 51.1 x 76.2
1891.2, P.159

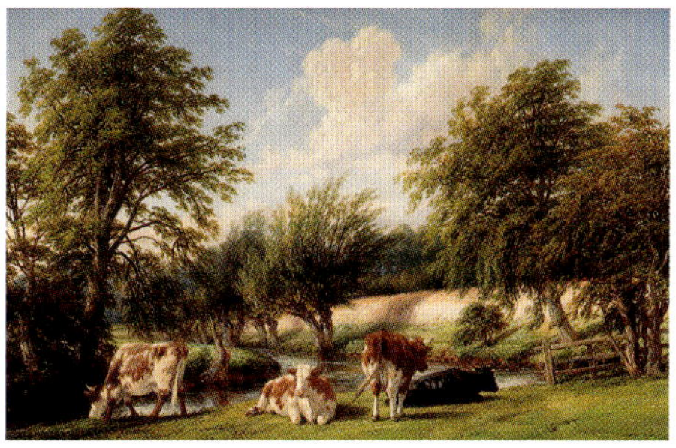

Baker, Thomas 1809–1869
At the River's Brink 1864
oil on canvas 33 x 48.3
1891.3, P.152

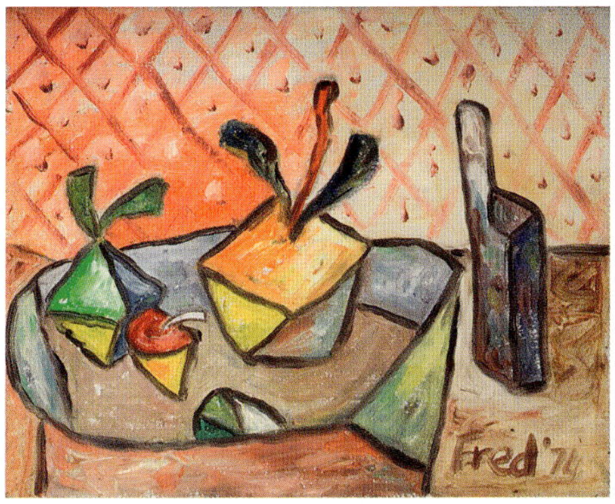

Barnfield, Fred b.1935
Still Life 1974
oil on canvas 25.5 x 30.5
1974.53, P.231

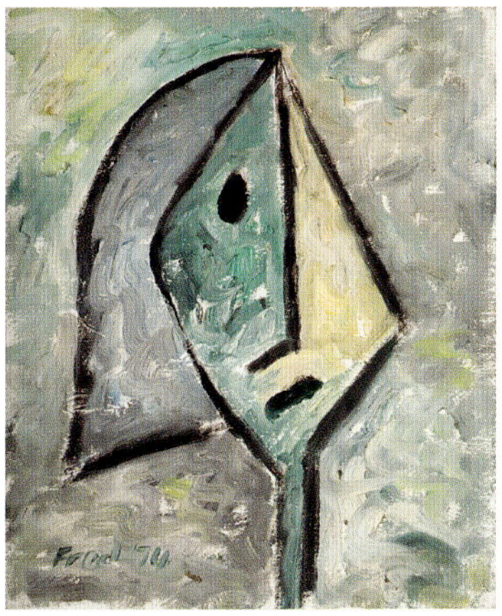

Barnfield, Fred b.1935
Woman 1974
oil on canvas 38 x 30.5
1974.54, P.232

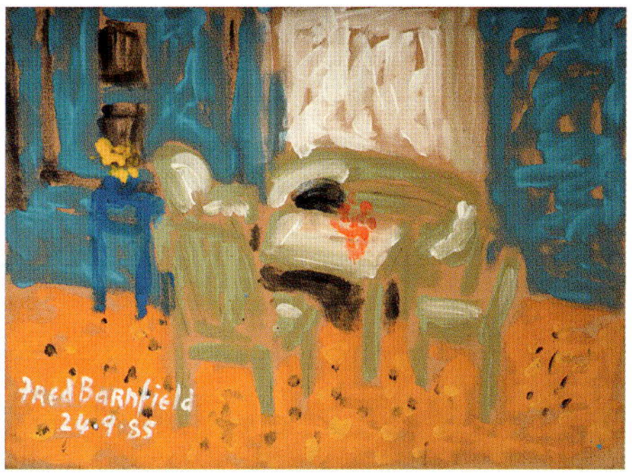

Barnfield, Fred b.1935
Domestic Interior 1985
oil on canvas 45.5 x 59.5
P.97

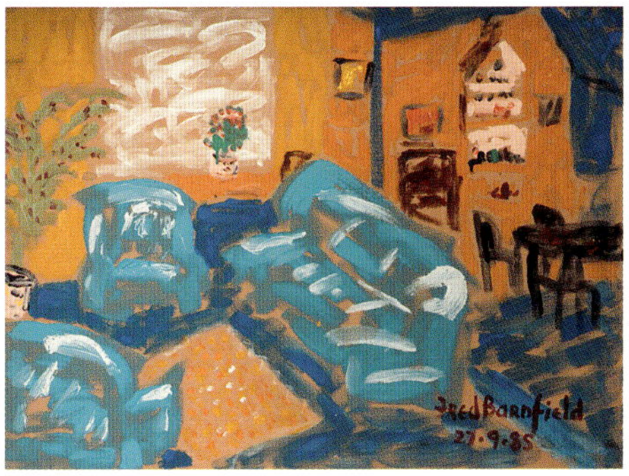

Barnfield, Fred b.1935
Domestic Interior 1985
oil on canvas 77 x 100.5
P.179

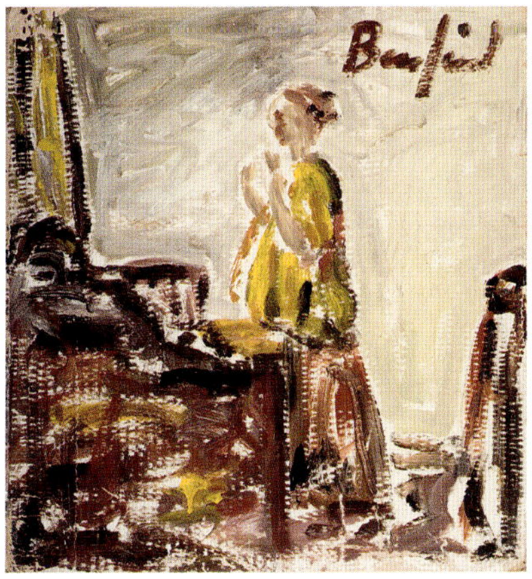

Barnfield, Fred b.1935
Standing Female
oil on cardboard 58.5 x 53.5
P.331

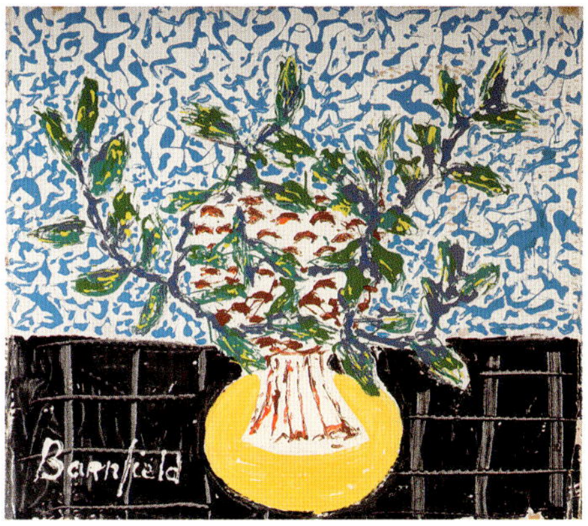

Barnfield, Fred b.1935
Still Life
oil on cardboard 58.5 x 65
P.330

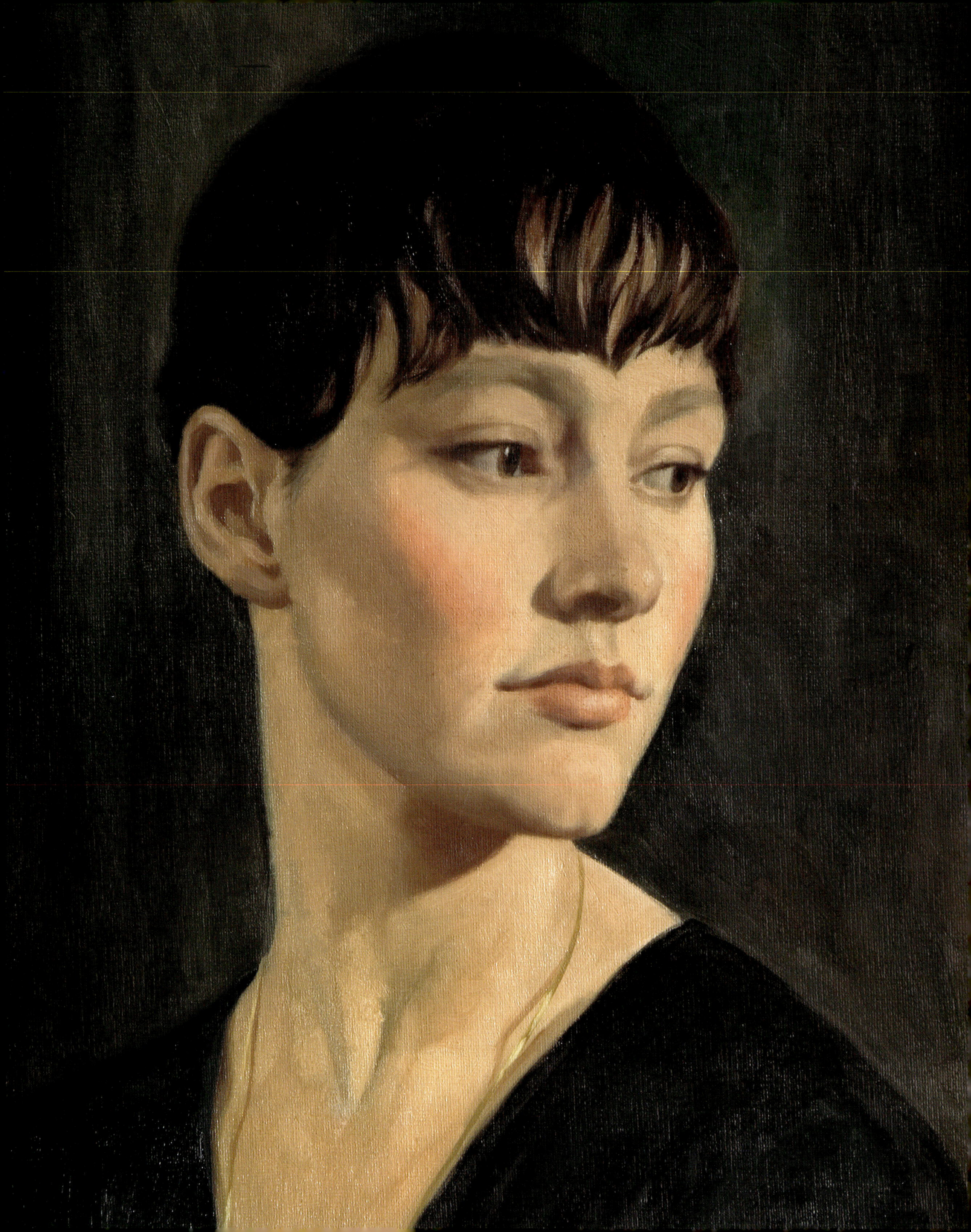

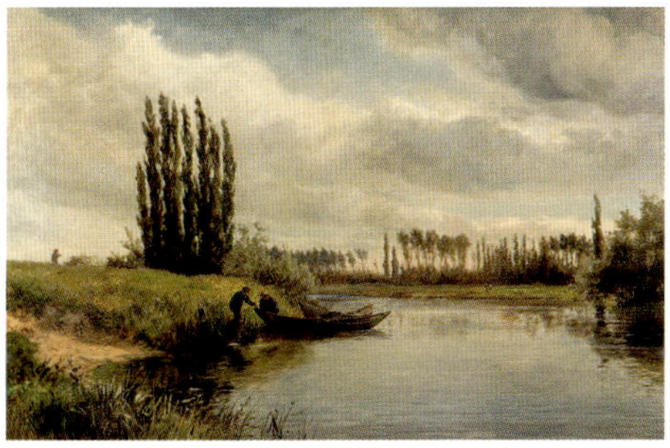

Bates, David c.1840–1921
Joinville on the River Marne 1875
oil on canvas 40.5 x 61
1891.4, P.293

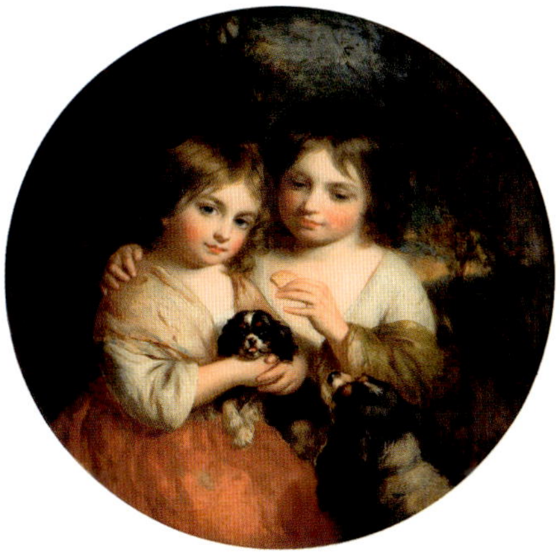

Baxter, Charles 1809–1878
The Sisters 1864
oil on canvas 36 x 37
1891.5, P.7

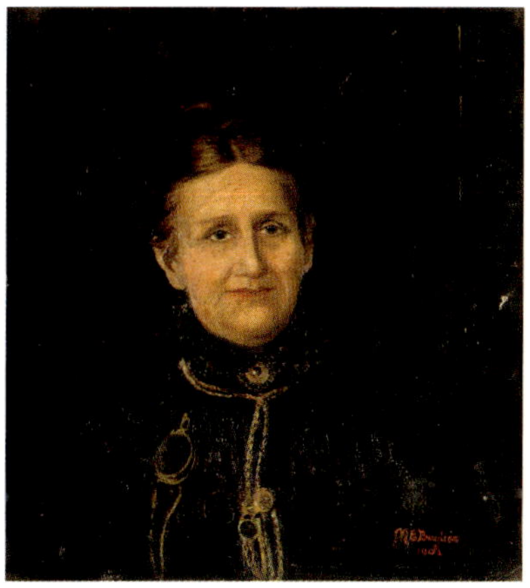

Bayliss, Margaret E. active 1902–1938
Mrs Issac Griffiths 1902
oil on canvas 51 x 45.5
1926.1, P.52

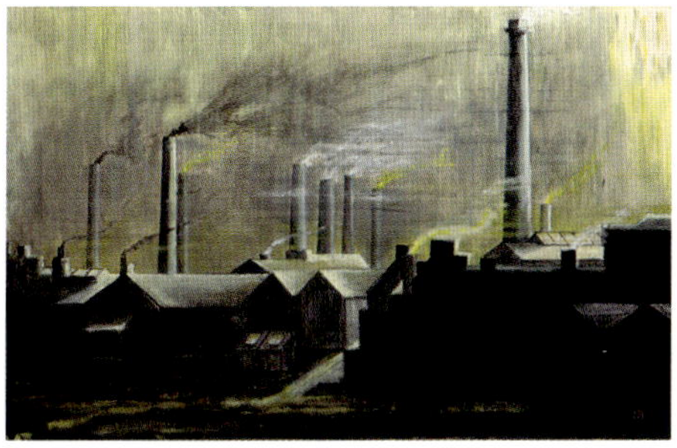

Biddle, Norman 1932–2000
Pollution Pre-War
oil on canvas 46.5 x 69
E12-05

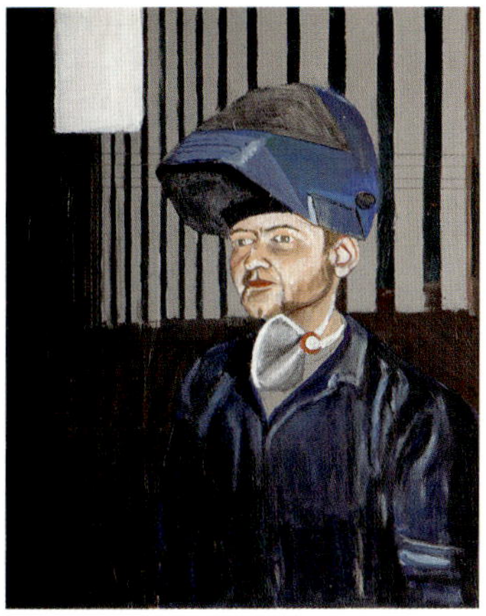

Biddle, Norman 1932–2000
Portrait
oil on board 39.5 x 30
E12-05

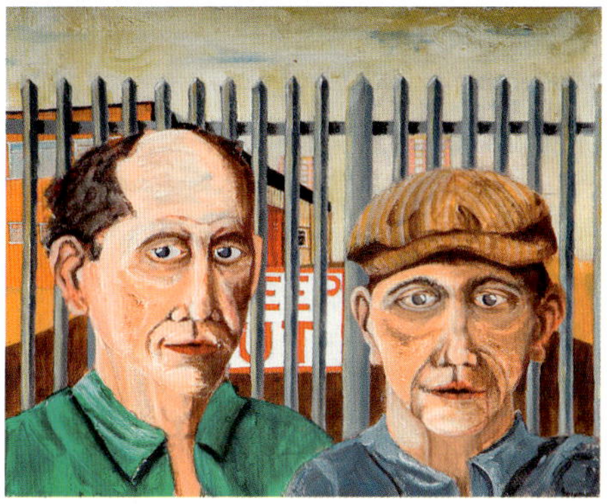

Biddle, Norman 1932–2000
Portrait of Two Faces
oil on canvas 38 x 47
E12-05

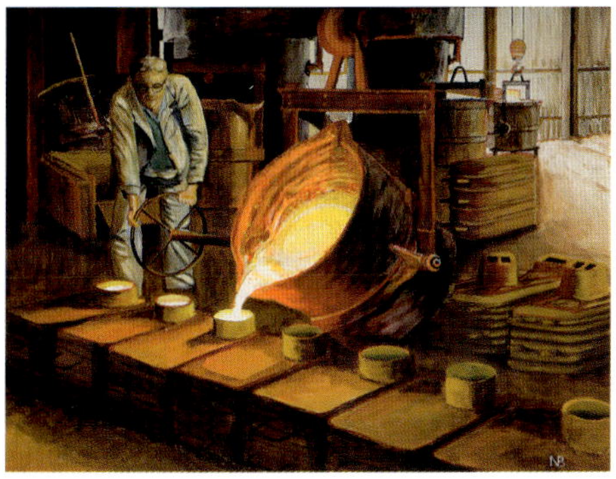

Biddle, Norman 1932–2000
Pouring Metal into Moulds
oil on board 72.5 x 88
E12-05

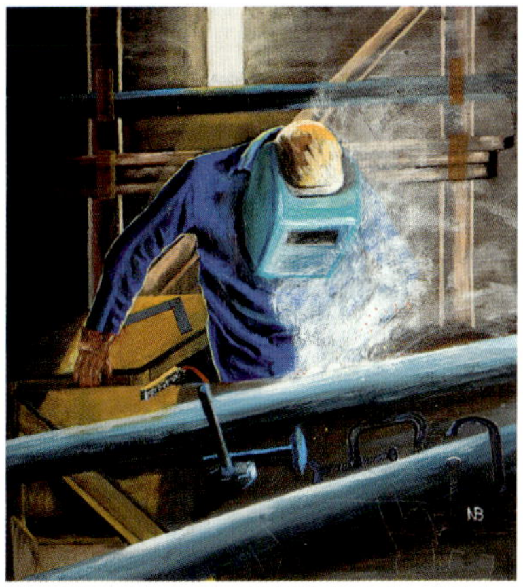

Biddle, Norman 1932–2000
Welding in Operation
oil on board 61 x 54
E12-05

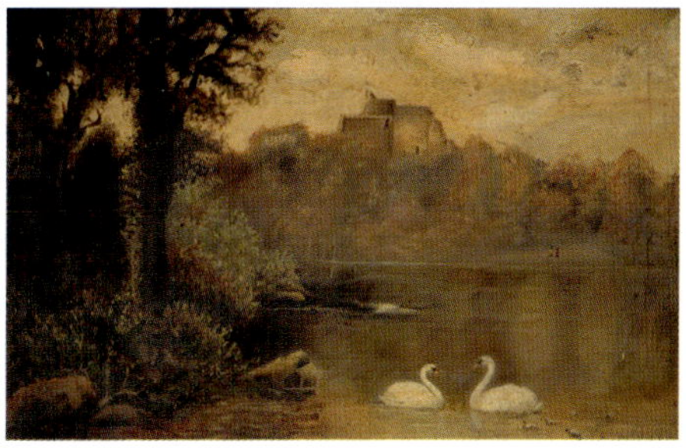

Billingsley, James active 1881–1932
Landscape with Lake 1909
oil on canvas 30.5 x 45.5
1973.4, P.184

Facing page: Tunstall, Eric, 1897–1987, *The Dancer* (detail), The Potteries Museum & Art Gallery (p. 168)

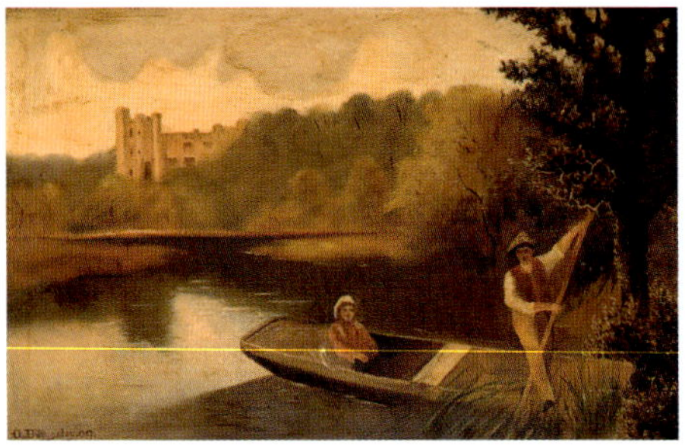

Billingsley, James active 1881–1932
River Scene with Punt 1909
oil on board 30.5 x 45.5
1973.3, P.185

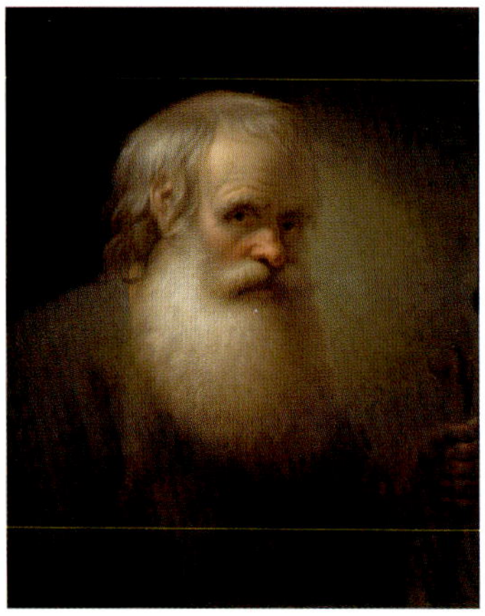

Bird, Edward (attributed to) 1772–1819
Old Bearded Man
oil on canvas 69 x 56.5
1891.6, P.93

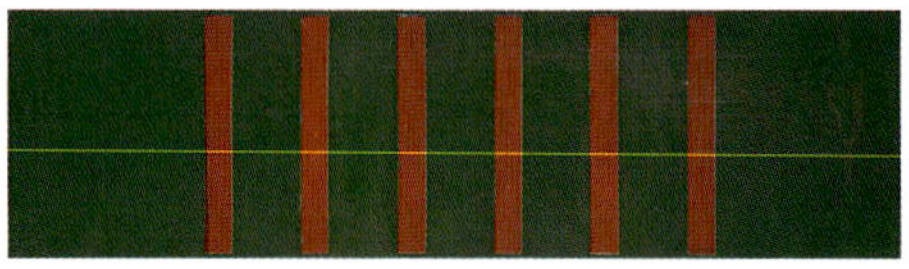

Burch, I. G.
Red Stripes on Green 1981
oil on canvas 17.8 x 61
1982.7, P.218

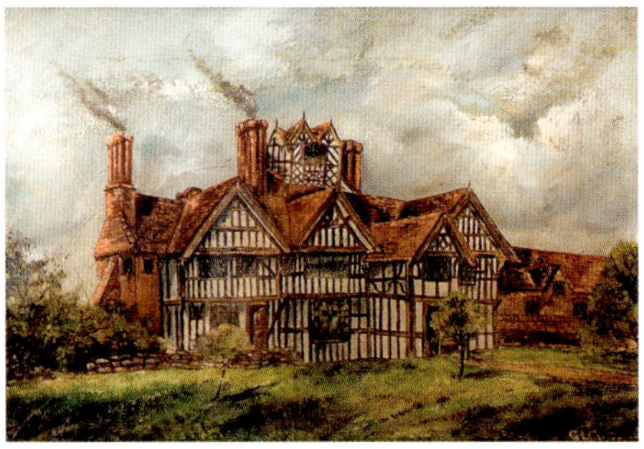

Cartwright, G. L.
Oak House
oil on canvas 29 x 40.5
1986.29, P.118

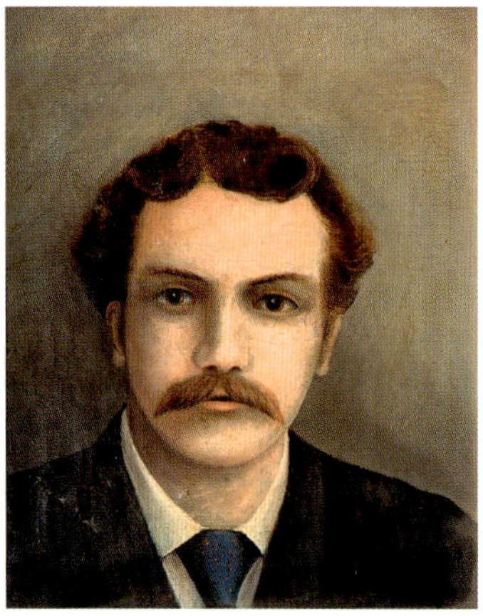

Challis, Henry 1867–1962
Self Portrait c.1890
oil on canvas 25.5 x 20.5
1987.169, P.129

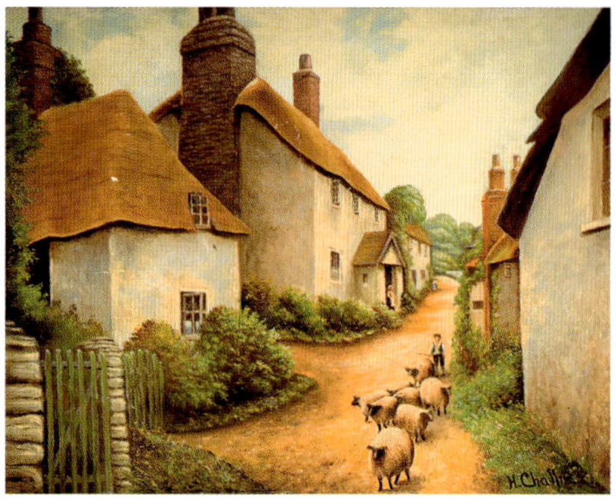

Challis, Henry 1867–1962
Buckland Village
oil on board 58.5 x 71
1987.130, P.130

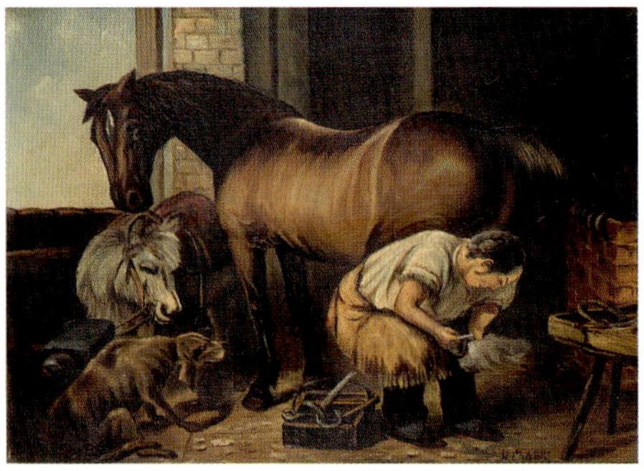

Challis, Henry 1867–1962
Shoeing the Horse
oil on canvas 30.5 x 40.5
1987.168, P.61

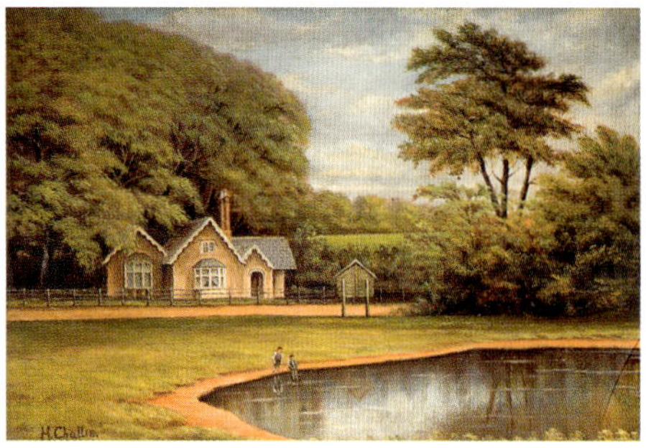

Challis, Henry 1867–1962
The Lodge, Warley Woods
oil on board 44 x 57
1976.29, P.149

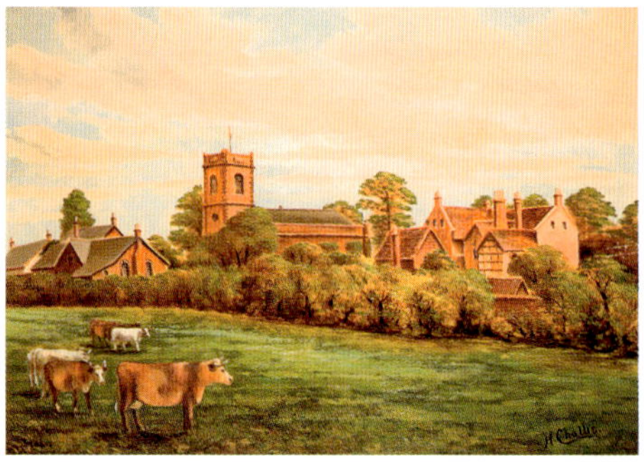

Challis, Henry 1867–1962
The Old Church and Vicarage, Smethwick
oil on canvas 38 x 52
P.148, 1976.30

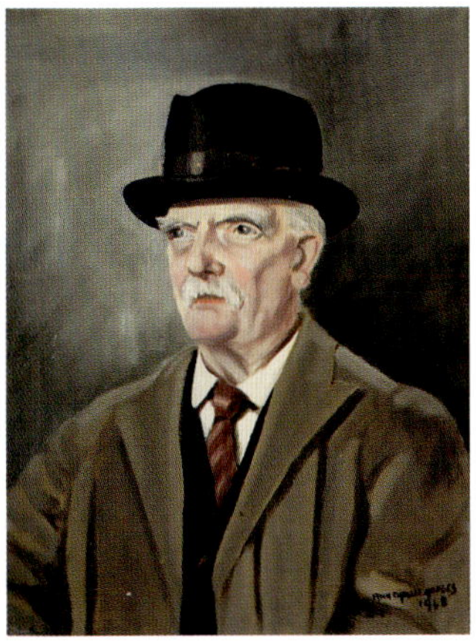

Challis Hodges, Ann
Henry Challis (1867–1962) 1948
oil on board 68.5 x 50.5
P.151

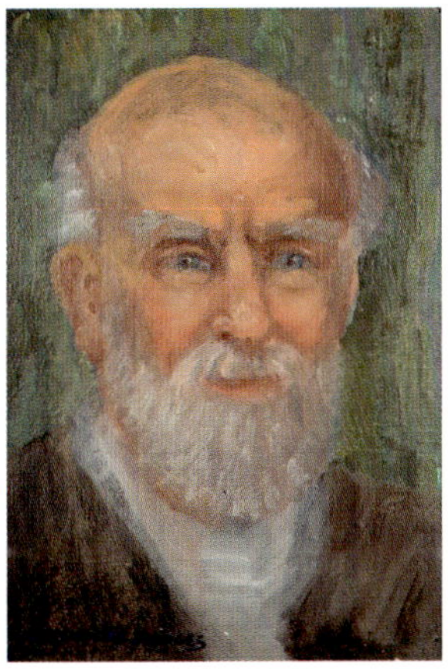

Challis Hodges, Ann
Henry Challis (1867–1962), in His 95th Year
oil on board 40.5 x 26.5
1976.31, P.131

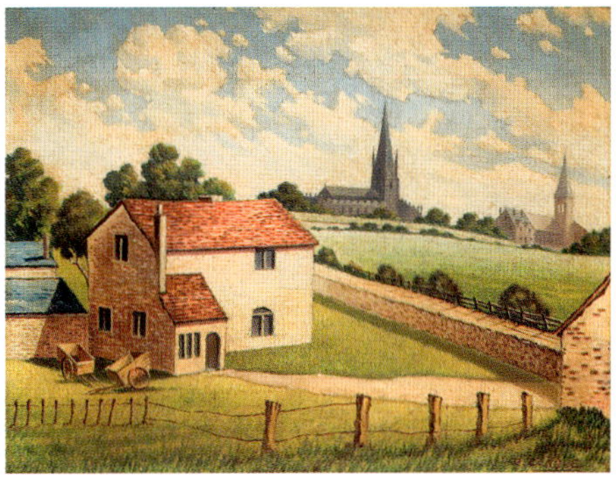

Clarke, D.
Wednesbury Manor House
oil on card 21 x 25.5
B.428, P.219

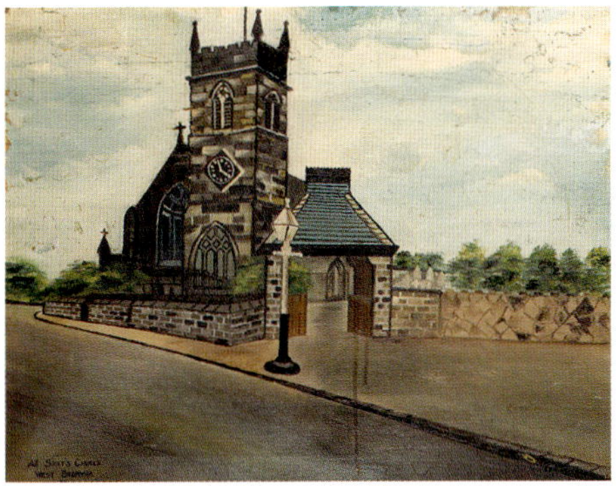

Clemson, Joe
All Saints' Church, West Bromwich 1950
oil on canvas 44 x 55
E136–01

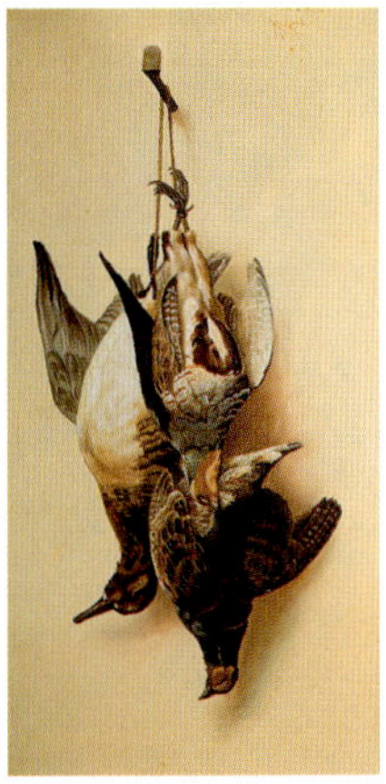

Cockin, Alice active 1890–1900
Brace of Pheasants
oil on canvas 61 x 30.5
P.342

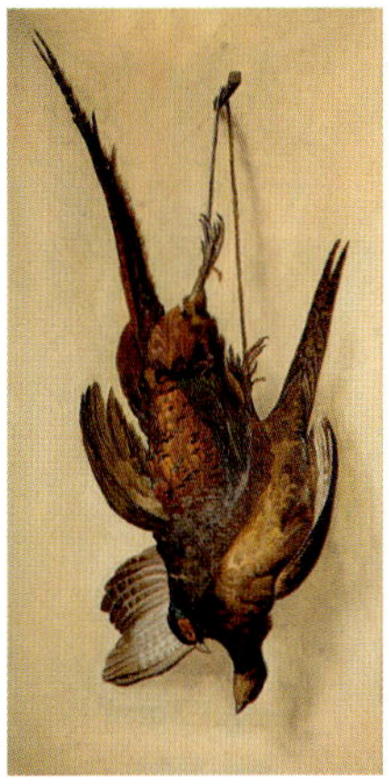

Cockin, Alice active 1890–1900
Brace of Pheasants
oil on canvas 61 x 30.5
P.343

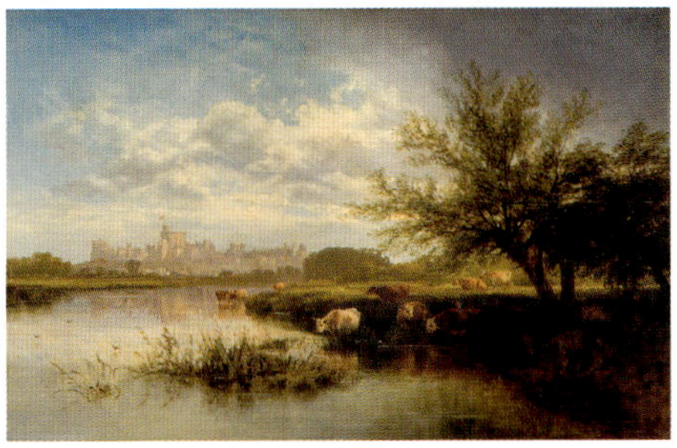

Cole, George 1810–1883
Windsor Castle from the Thames 1876
oil on canvas 51 x 73.5
1891.7, P.157

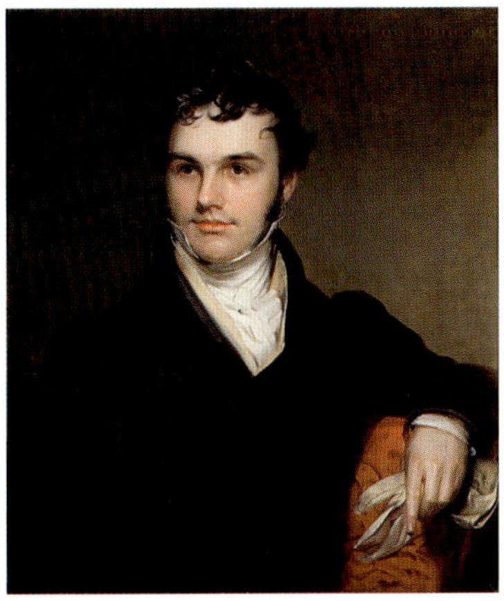

Coleman, Edward 1795–1867
Regency Gentleman 1826
oil on canvas 77.5 x 65
P.346

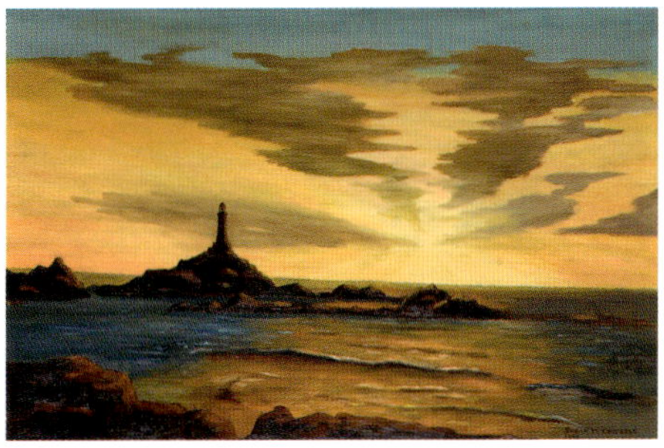

Cotterill, Susan M.
Lighthouse 1977
oil on board 51 x 76
P.192

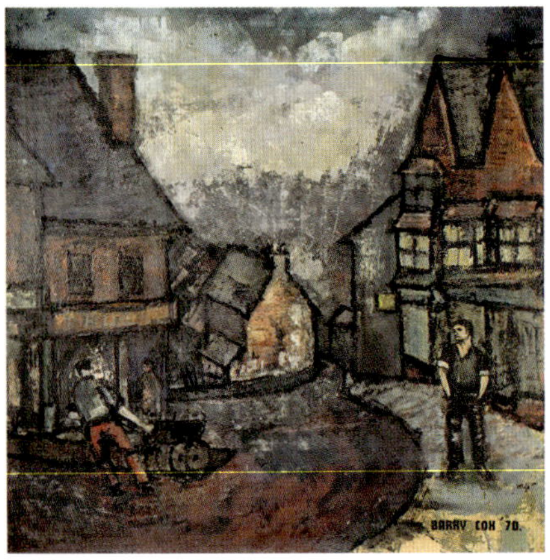

Cox, Barry
Glassworks 1970
oil on canvas 118.1 x 116.8
P.339

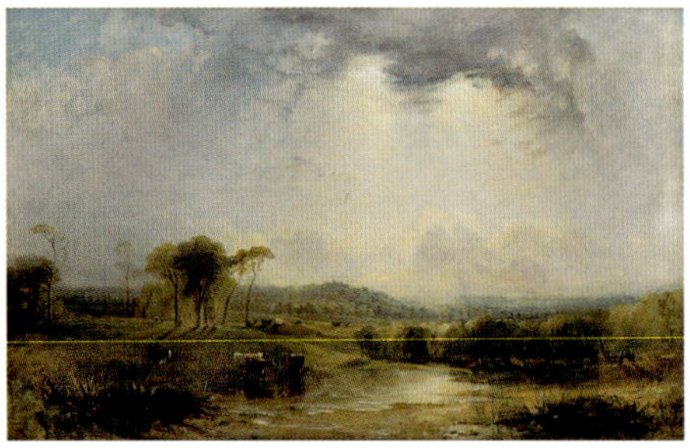

Creswick, Thomas 1811–1869
Landscape with Harrow in the Distance
oil on canvas 50.8 x 76.2
1891.8, P.13

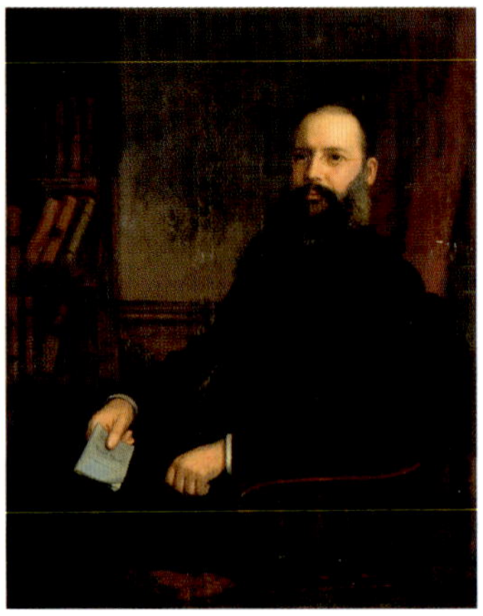

Crump, Joseph
Reverend J. H. Crump c.1892
oil on canvas 112 x 86.5
1987.106, P.105

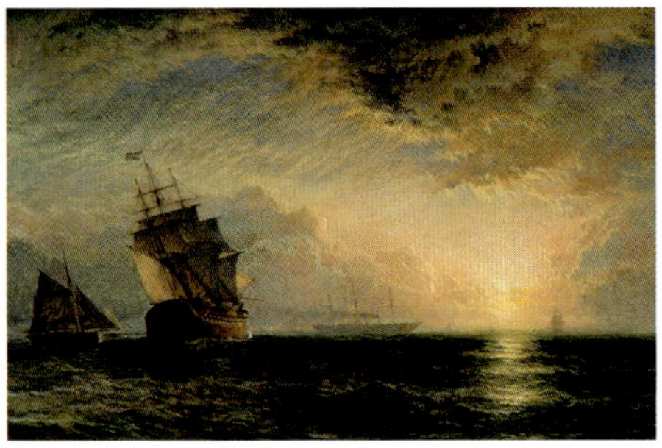

Dawson, Henry 1811–1878
Seascape 1871–1872
oil on canvas 51 x 76
1891.10, P.16

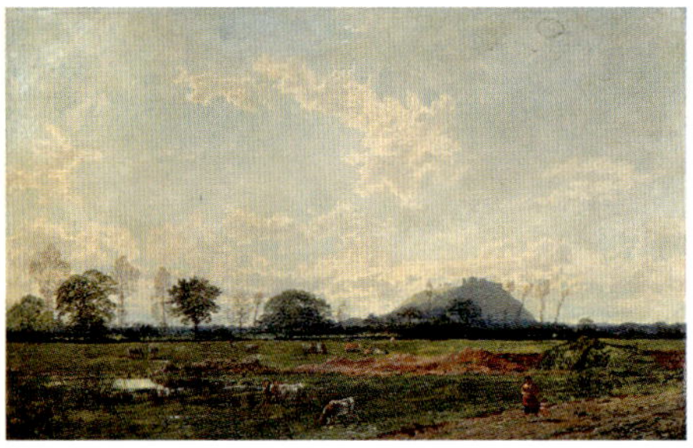

Dawson, Henry 1811–1878
Brent Knoll
oil on canvas 30.5 x 45.5
1891.17, P.235

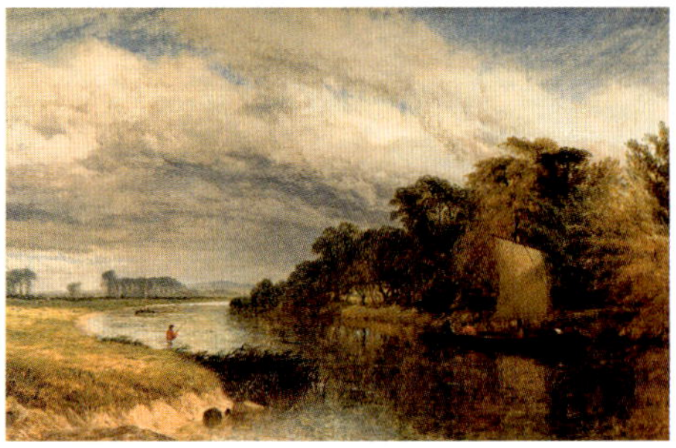

Dawson, Henry 1811–1878
On the River Trent
oil on canvas 52 x 77.5
1891.1, P.18

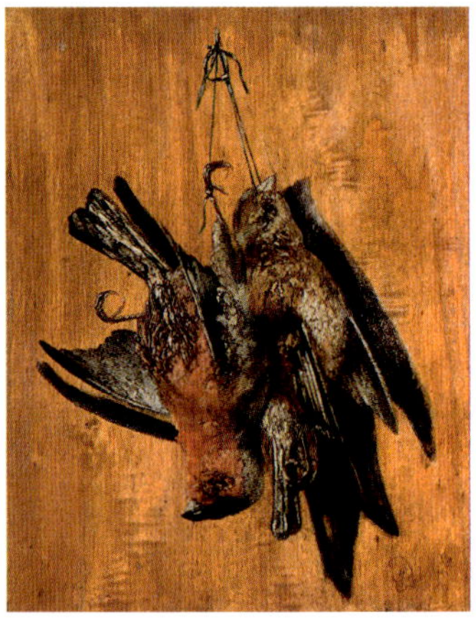

Dupré, E.
Study of Dead Songbird (81)
oil on board 25.5 x 19.5 (E)
1891.11, P.210

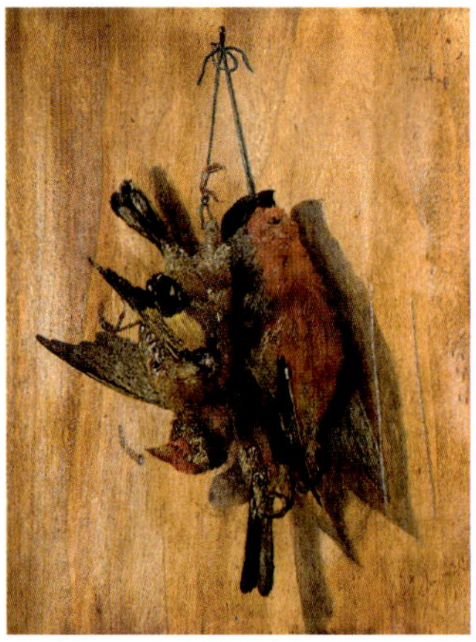

Dupré, E.
Study of Dead Songbird (82)
oil on board 25.5 x 19.5 (E)
1891.12, P.211

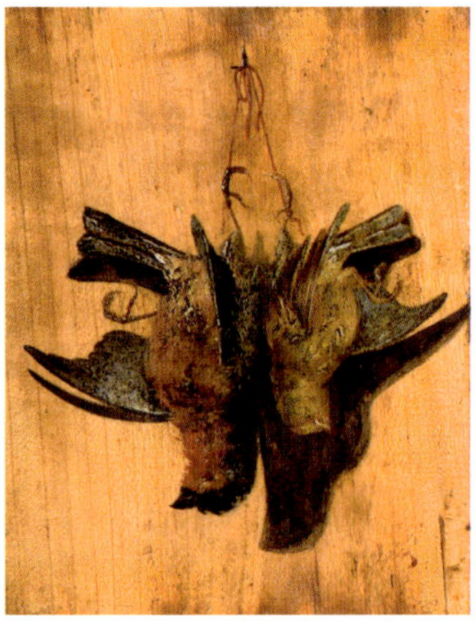

Dupré, E.
Study of Dead Songbird (83)
oil on board 25.5 x 19.5 (E)
1891.13, P.212

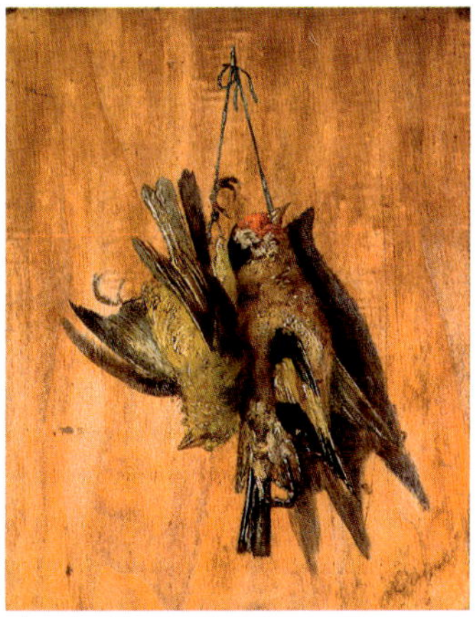

Dupré, E.
Study of Dead Songbird (84)
oil on board 25.5 x 19.5 (E)
1891.14, P.213

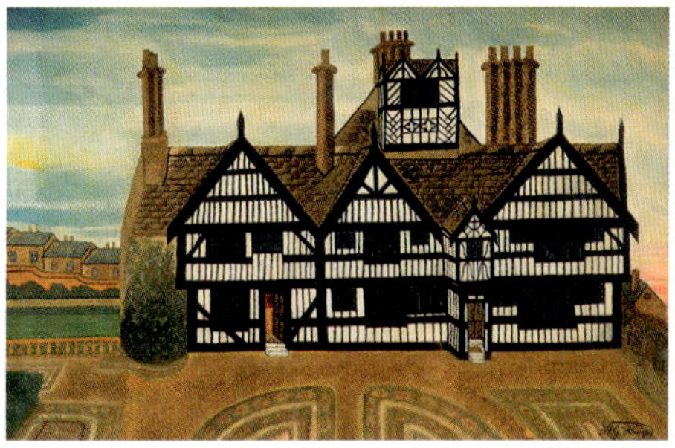

Frazer, H. G.
The Old Oak House Museum, September 1912 1912
oil on paper 30 x 45.5
P.125

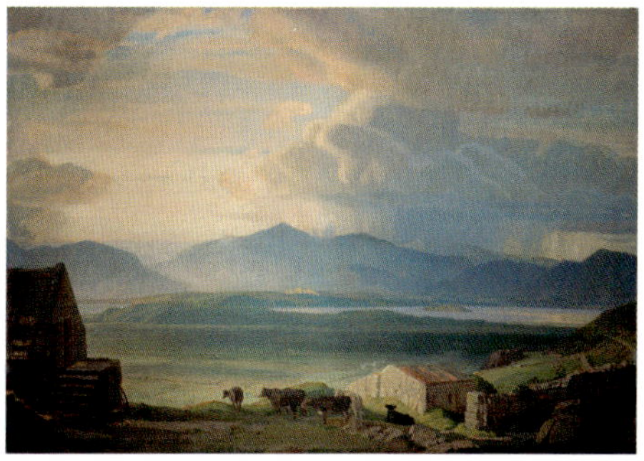

Gere, Charles March 1869–1957
The Snowdon Range 1937
oil on canvas 124.5 x 172.5
1973.5, P.62

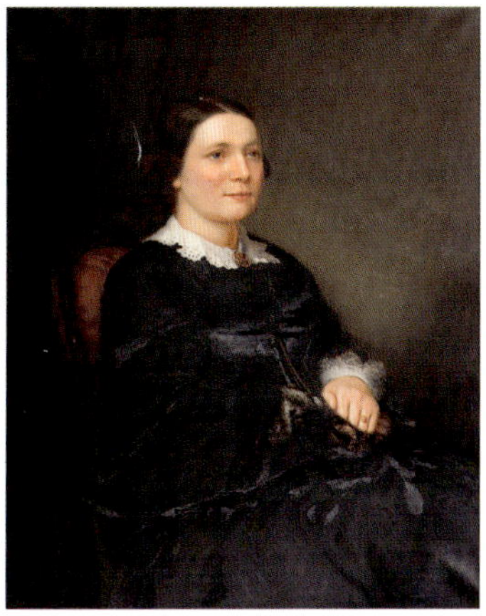

Gibbs, Joseph active 1852–1907
Mary Ann Richards (1820–1894) 1891
oil on canvas 91.5 x 71
1891.15, P.31

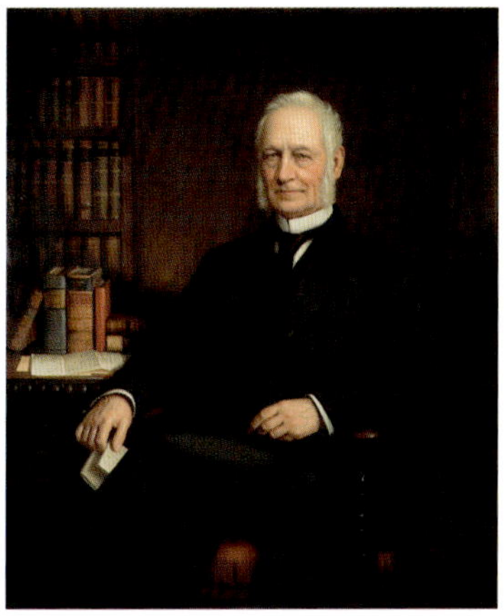

Gibbs, Joseph active 1852–1907
Sir James Timmins Chance 1902
oil on canvas 127 x 101.5
1987.107, P.169

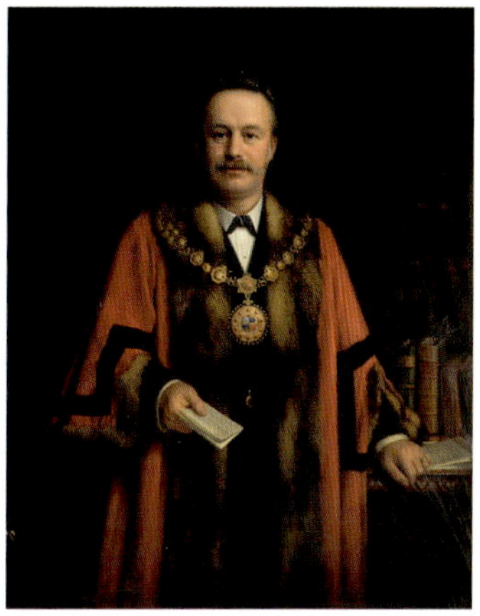

Gibbs, Joseph active 1852–1907
Alderman George Bowden, Mayor of Smethwick (1903–1905) 1904
oil on canvas 112 x 86.5
1987.112, P.189

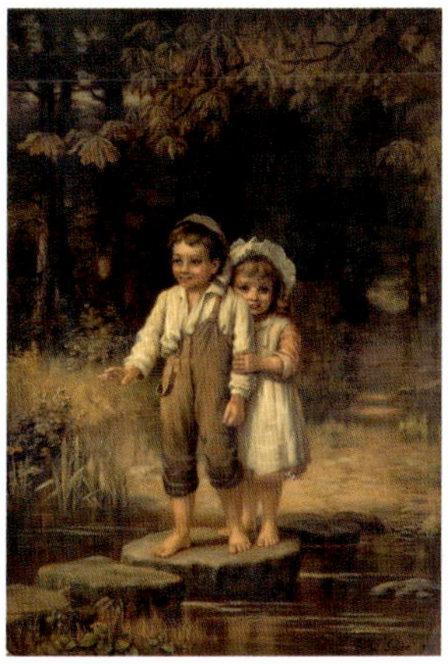

Gibbs, Joseph active 1852–1907
Stepping Stones (The Nearest Way Home) 1907
oil on canvas 91.5 x 61
1979.3, P.198

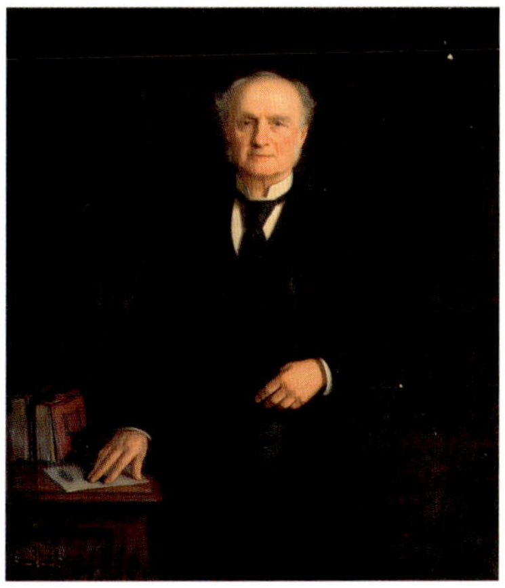

Gibbs, Joseph active 1852–1907
Frederick Talbot, Headmaster of Chance's School, Smethwick (1845–1892)
oil on canvas 127 x 101.5
1987.108, P.91

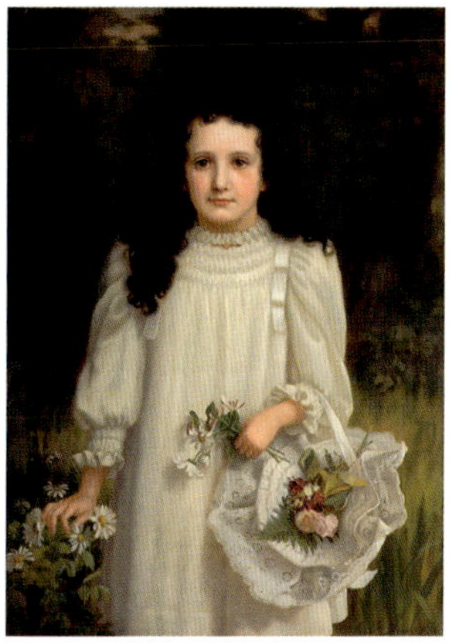

Gibbs, Joseph active 1852–1907
Muriel Dorothy Windle
oil on canvas 86.5 x 61
1979.1, P.94

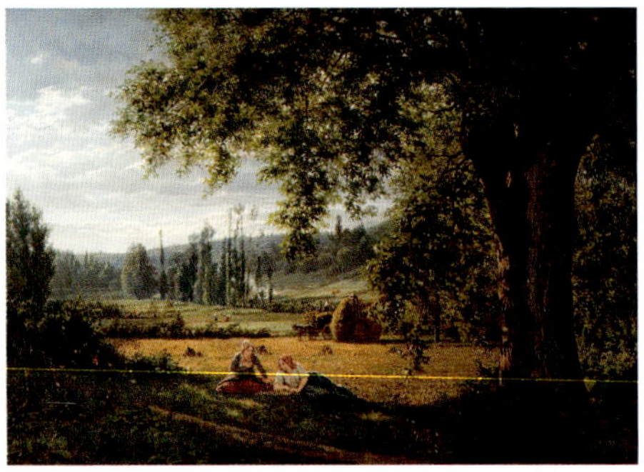

Gibot, E.
Wooded Landscape, Normandy
oil on canvas 65.5 x 89
1922.1, P.95

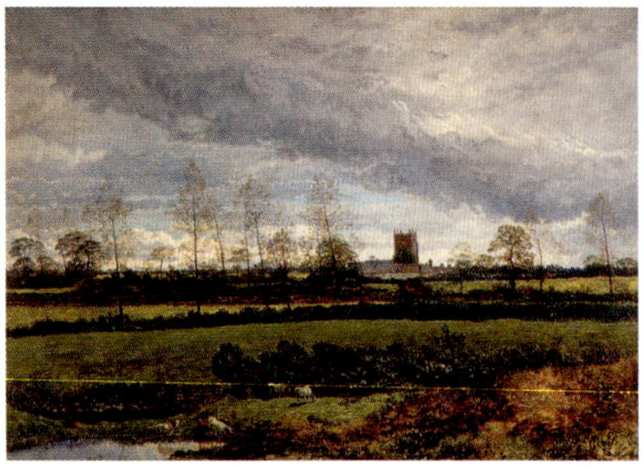

Hargitt, Edward 1835–1895
East Brent Church, Brent Knoll 1880
oil on canvas 30.5 x 45.5
1891.16, P.108

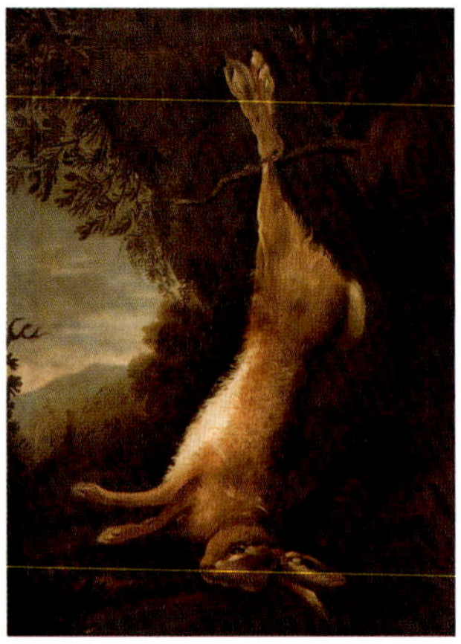

Harper, John 1759–1841
Dead Hare in Landscape
oil on canvas 75 x 58.5
1891.48, P.119

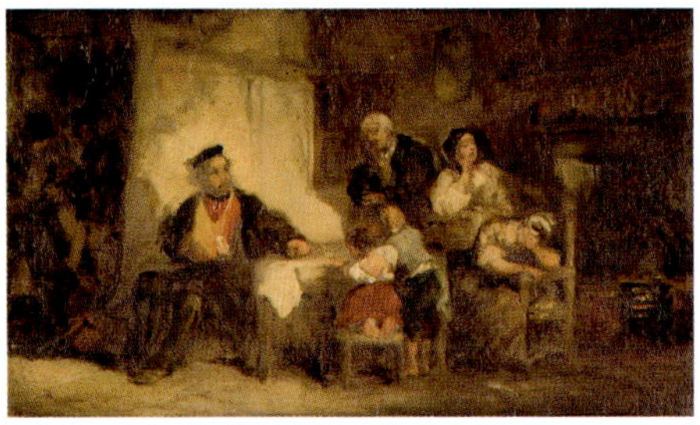

Harvey, George 1806–1876
Interior, a Sad Scene
oil on canvas 18 x 30.5
1984, P.20

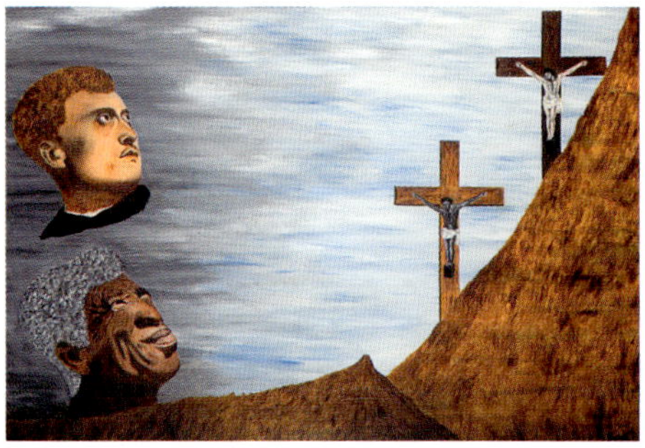

Hems
The Same Faith 1963
oil on board 53.5 x 76
P.76

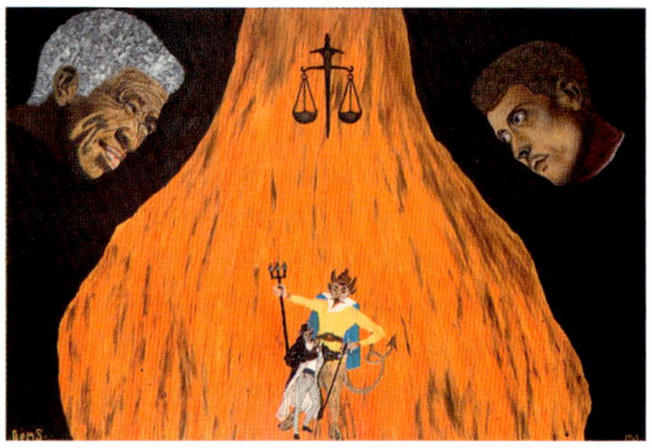

Hems
The Same Temptation 1963
oil on board 53.5 x 76
P.77

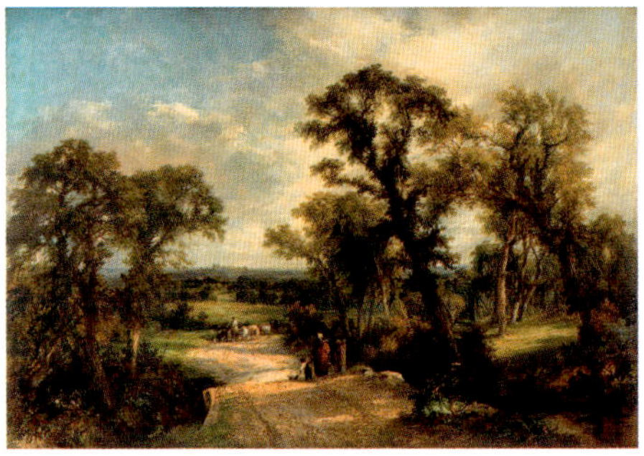

Henshaw, Frederick Henry 1807–1891
Windsor Castle from the Great Park (Morning)
oil on canvas 127 x 183
1891.18, P.25

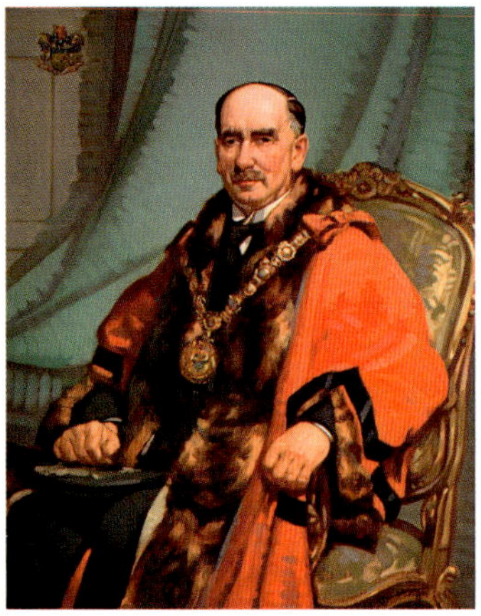

Hodges, Merrett active c.1895–1961
Alderman Arthur Thomas Morris, JP, Mayor of Smethwick (1927–1929) 1930
oil on canvas 102.9 x 76.2
1987.125, P.68

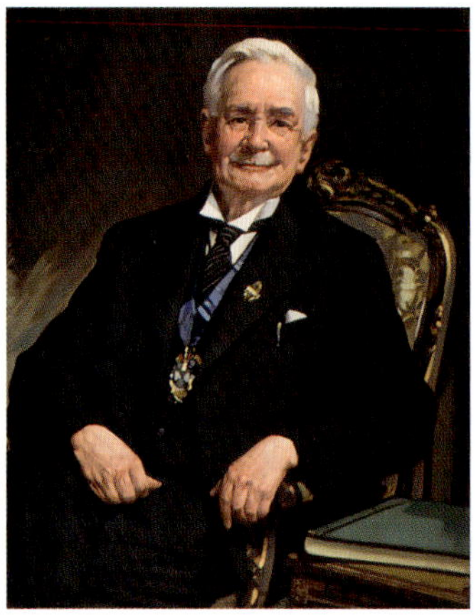

Hodges, Merrett active c.1895–1961
Councillor George Henry Griffin, Mayor of Oldbury (1939–1940)
oil on canvas 91.5 x 71
P.82

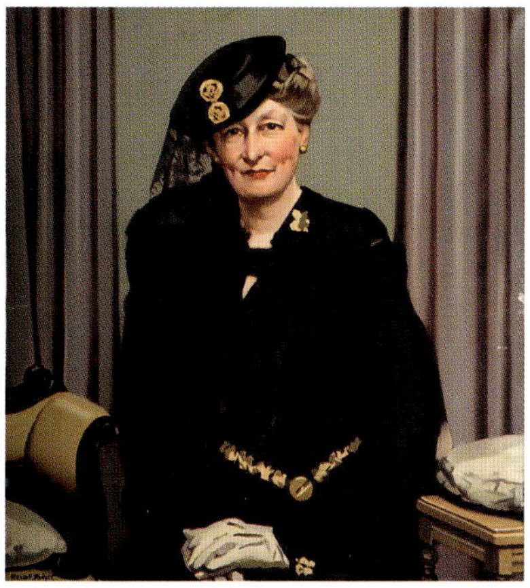

Hodges, Merrett active c.1895–1961
Lady in Black
oil on canvas 81.5 x 71
P.128

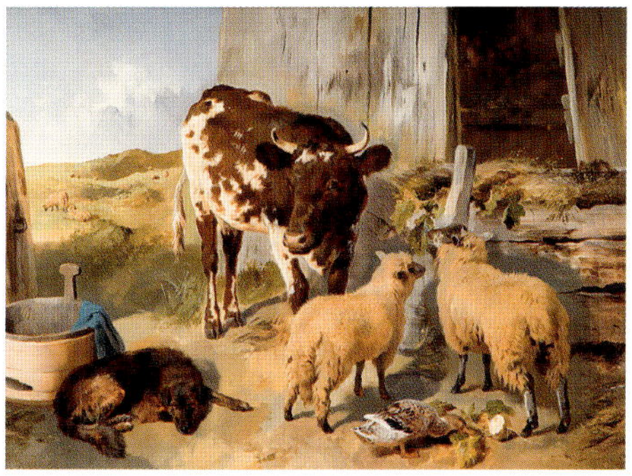

Horlor, George W. active 1849–1891
A Corner of the Farmyard 1856
oil on canvas 45.1 x 61
1891.19, P.107

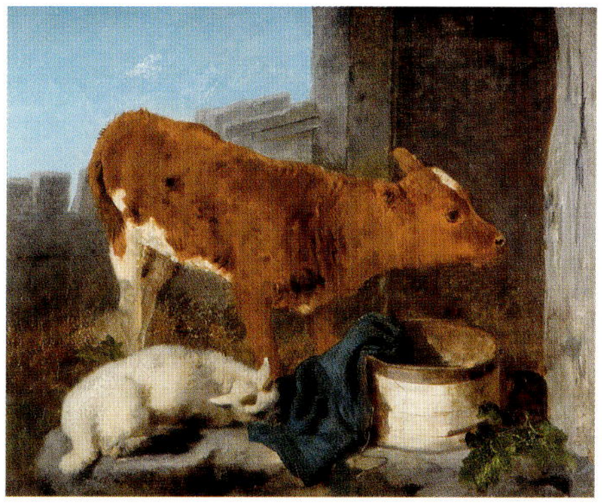

Horlor, George W. active 1849–1891
Calves Feeding 1867
oil on canvas 51 x 61
P.127

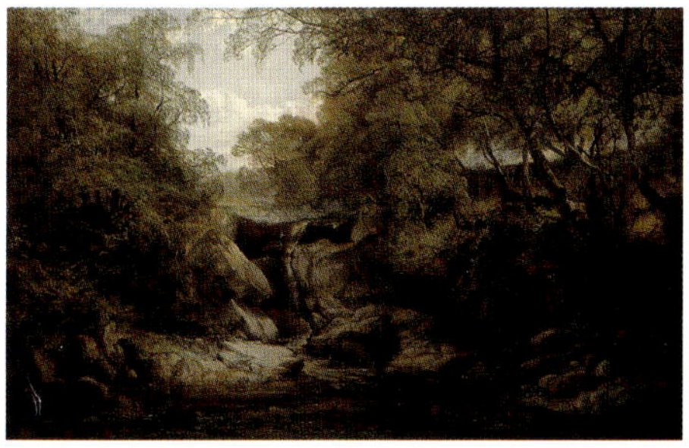

Hulme, Frederick William 1816–1884
Waterfall 1870
oil on canvas 61 x 91.5
1987.128, P.51

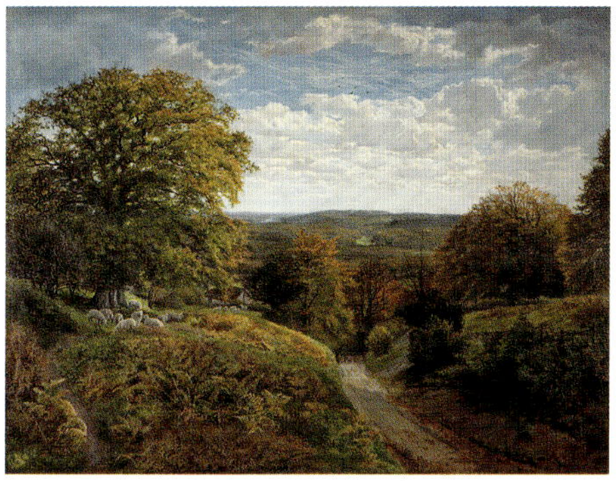

Hulme, Frederick William 1816–1884
A Surrey Landscape
oil on canvas 101.5 x 127
P.298

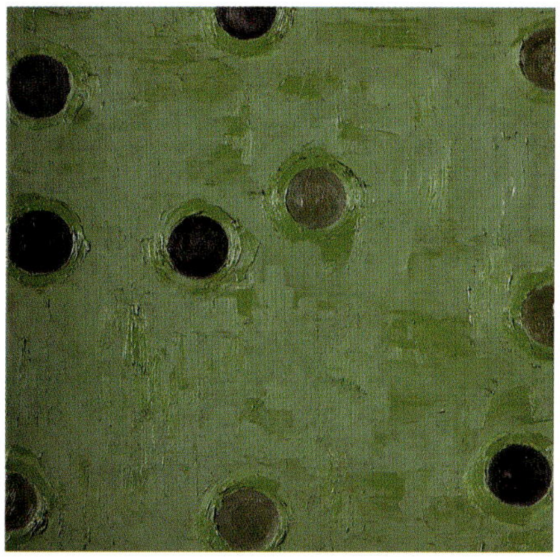

Irish, David
Abstract Spots on Dark Background 1980
oil on canvas 45.5 x 45.5
1982.10, P.208

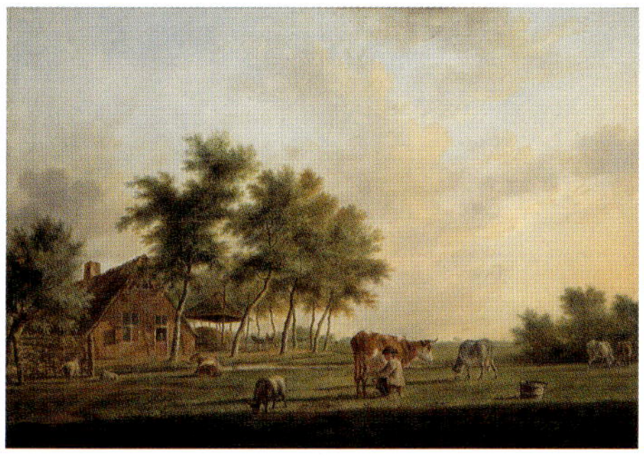

Jansens, I.
Landscape with Cattle
oil on canvas 42.5 x 52.5
1902.1, P.294

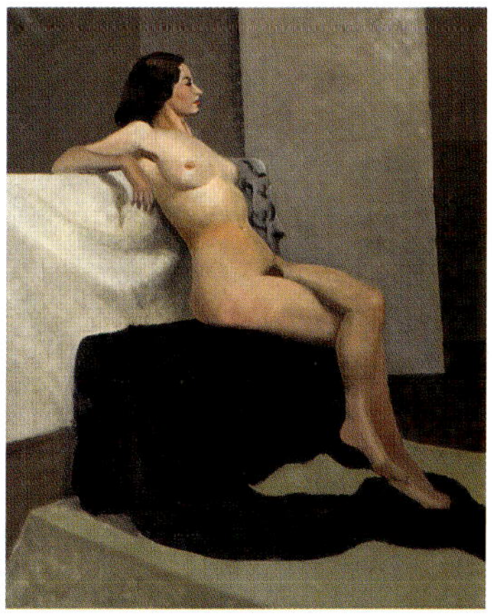

Jones, Frank Edwin 1919–1944
Nude Study
oil on canvas 92.5 x 72.5
E09 1999, P.321

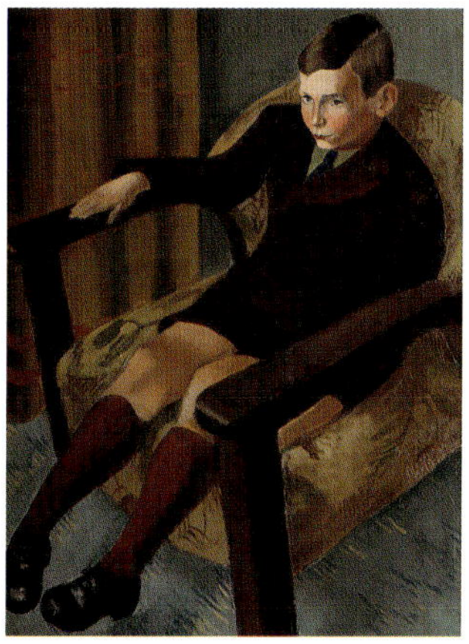

Jones, Frank Edwin 1919–1944
Portrait of a Boy
oil on canvas 62 x 45.5
E09 1999, P.322

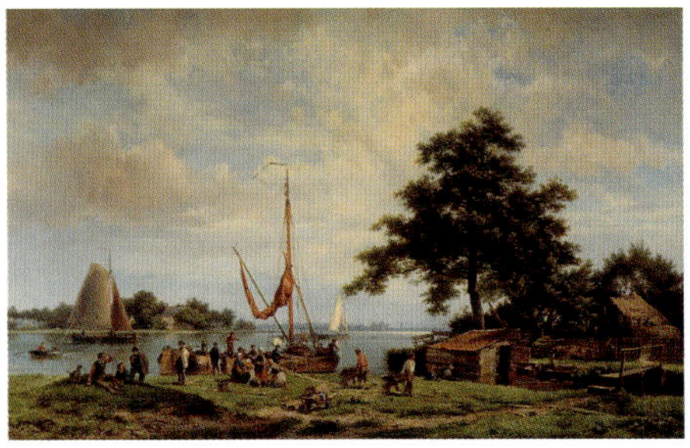

Koekkoek, Hermanus the elder 1815–1882
Loading Boats 1866
oil on canvas 58.5 x 93
1891.21, P.33

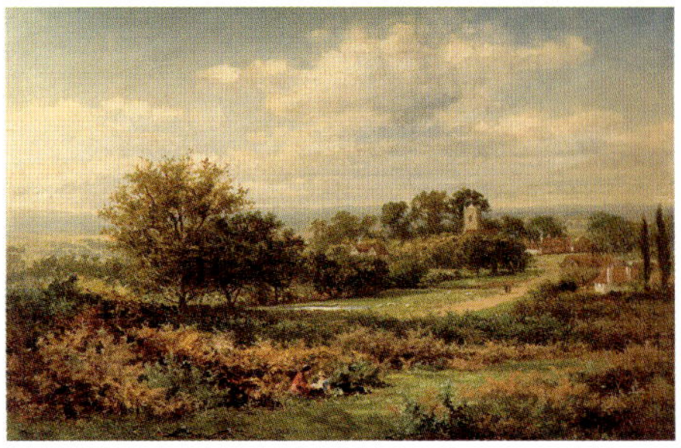

Leader, Benjamin Williams 1831–1923
Near Line Park, Kent 1873
oil on canvas 40.5 x 61
1891.22, P.19

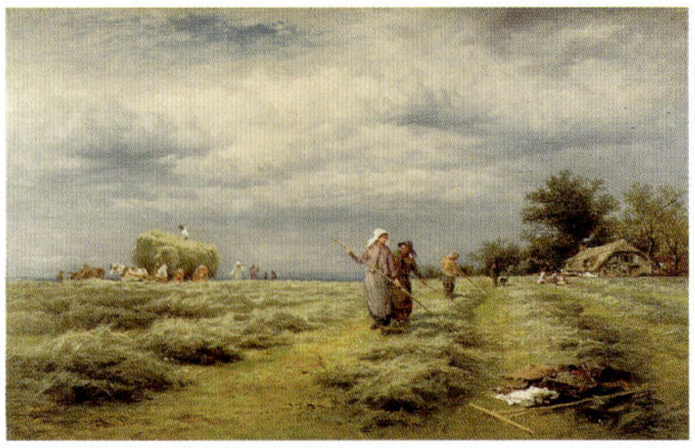

Leader, Benjamin Williams 1831–1923
Haymaking 1876
oil on canvas 76 x 137
1891.23, P.21

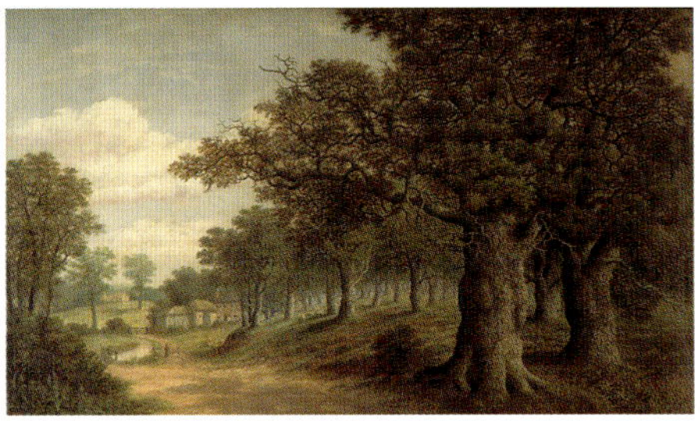

Leaver, Charles 1824–1888
On the Edge of the Forest 1887
oil on canvas 85.1 x 142.2
B426, P.104

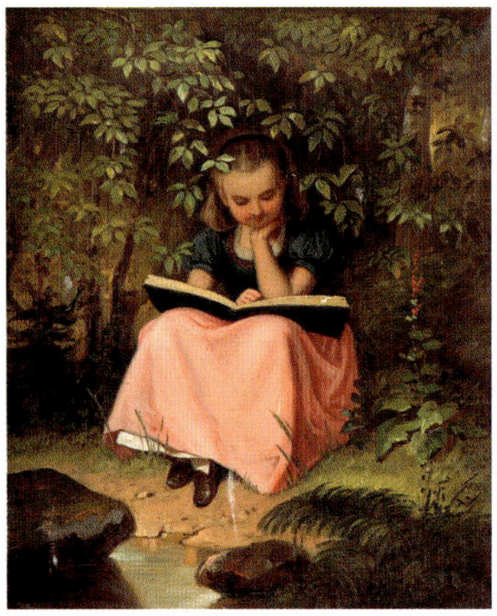

Leidler, R. H.
The Reading Lesson
oil on canvas 33 x 27
1973.6, P.183

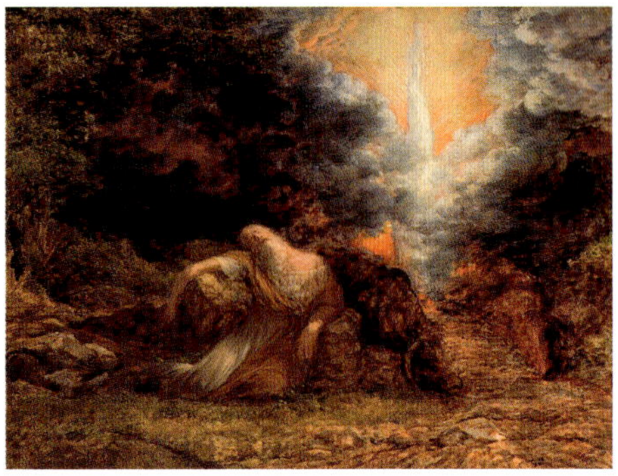

Linnell, John 1792–1882
Abraham's Vision 1853
oil on canvas 71 x 91.5
1891.24, P.6

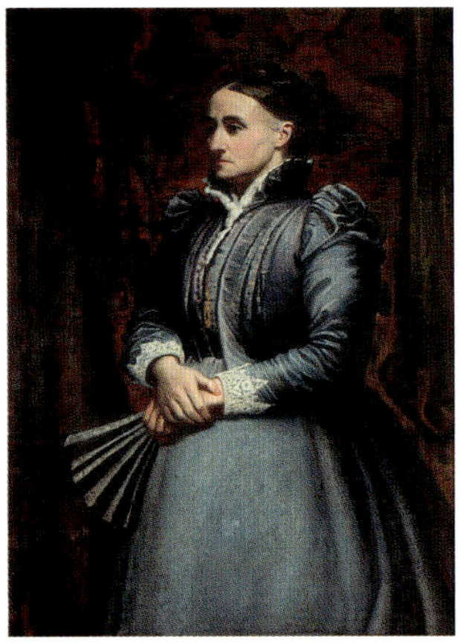

Lones, Thomas Sutton active 1889–1897
Mrs Jabez Lones, First Mayoress of Smethwick (1899–1901) 1893
oil on canvas 134.5 x 89
1987.105, P.197

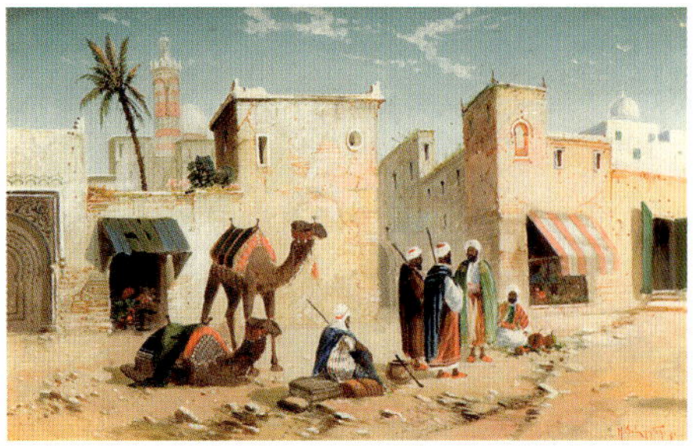

Lynton, Henry Stanton active 1886–1904
Arabian Village Scene 1891
oil on canvas 40.5 x 61 (E)
1973.7, P.167

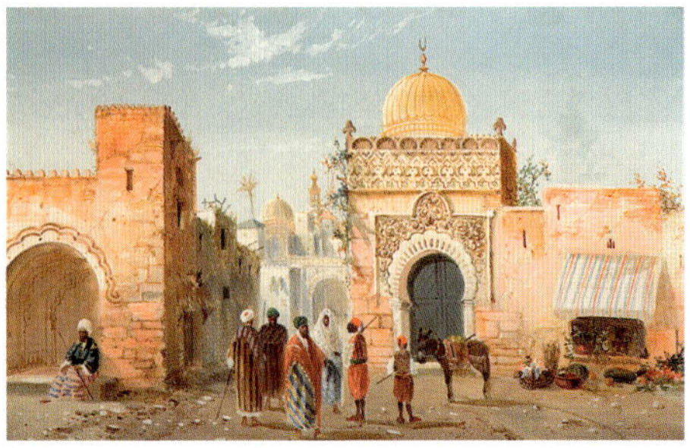

Lynton, Henry Stanton active 1886–1904
Arabian Village Scene 1891
oil on canvas 40.5 x 61 (E)
1973.8, P.166

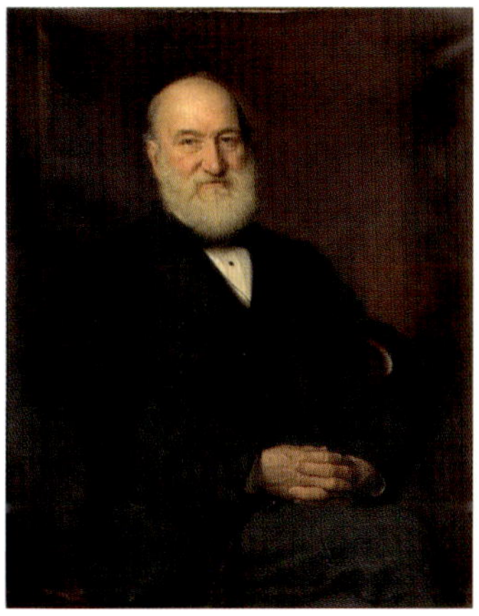

H. T. M.
Portrait of a Man with a Beard
oil on canvas 112 x 86.5
P.66

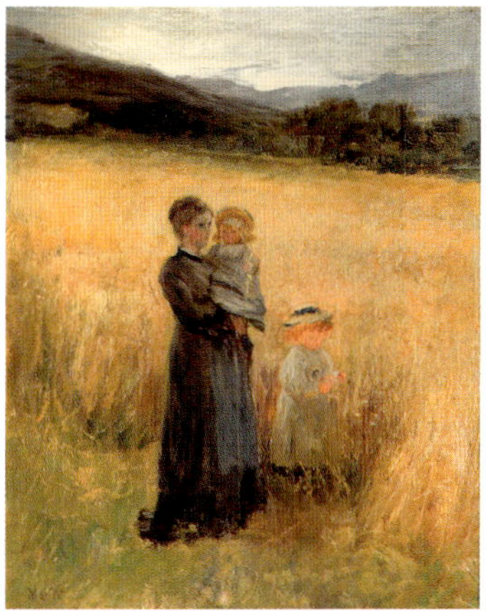

MacWhirter, John 1839–1911
Cornfield with Figures
oil on canvas 39.5 x 28
1891.25, P.8

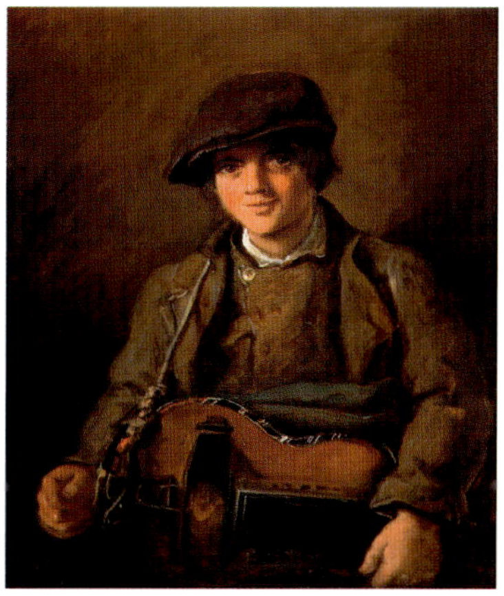

Millais, John Everett (attributed to)
1829–1896
Hurdy Gurdy Boy 1843
oil on canvas 61 x 51
1910.1, P.17

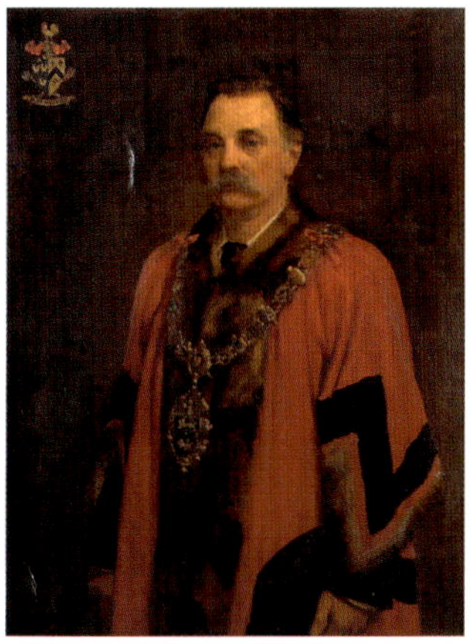

Miller, Philip Homan 1845–1928
Alderman Wilson Lloyd, Mayor of the Wednesbury Corporation (1888–1890) 1897
oil on canvas 54.5 x 40
P.116

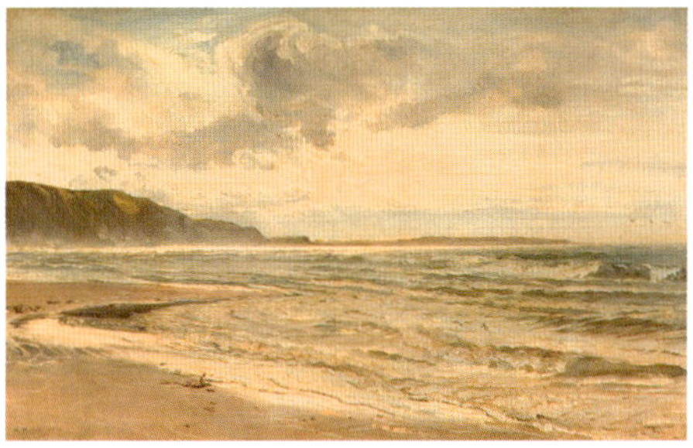

Moore, Henry 1831–1895
Grey Morning on the Beach 1868
oil on canvas 42 x 66
1891.26, P.164

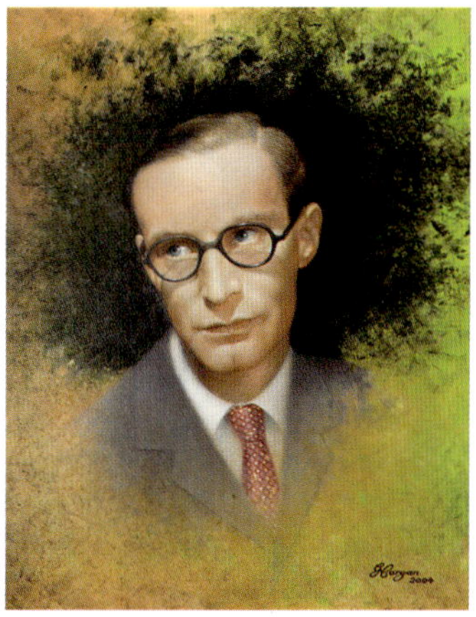

Morgan, Gary b.1962
Richard Wattis (1912–1975) 2004
oil on canvas 90 x 75
E24-04

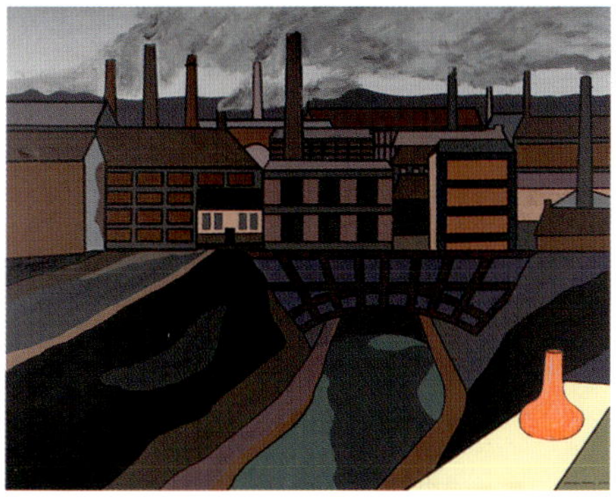

Morris, Stephen b.1935
The Ruskin Connection 2000
oil on canvas 87 x 97
E76-02

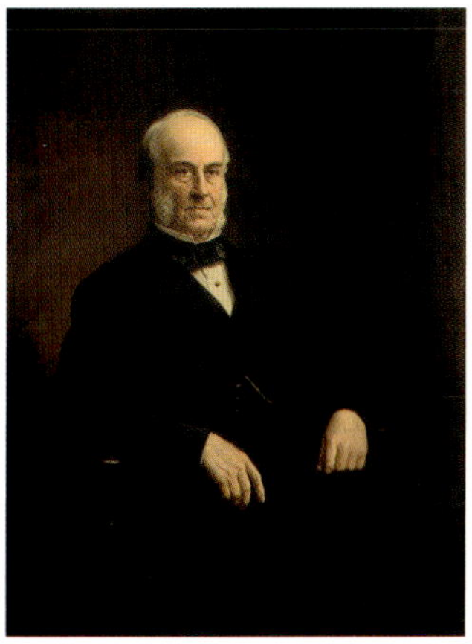

Munns, Henry Turner 1832–1898
Joseph Smith (d.1884) 1883
oil on canvas 127 x 101.5
P.207, WAG-4-1997

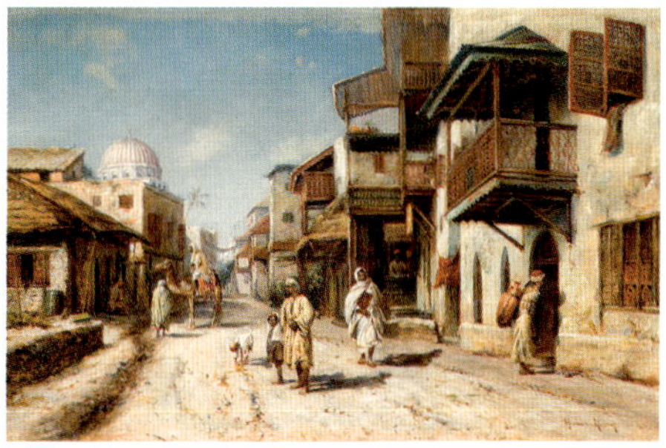

Norman, Horace
Street in Mombasa
oil on canvas 49 x 71.5
1987.129, P.187

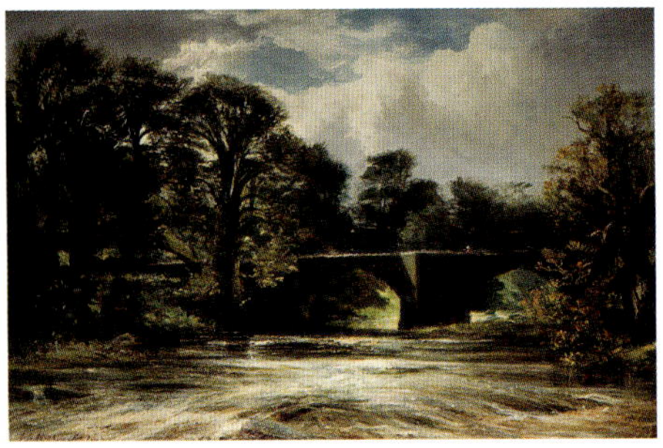

Oswald, John Henry active 1874–1899
River Scene, Autumn on the Esk 1874
oil on canvas 68 x 98.5
1891.27, P.122

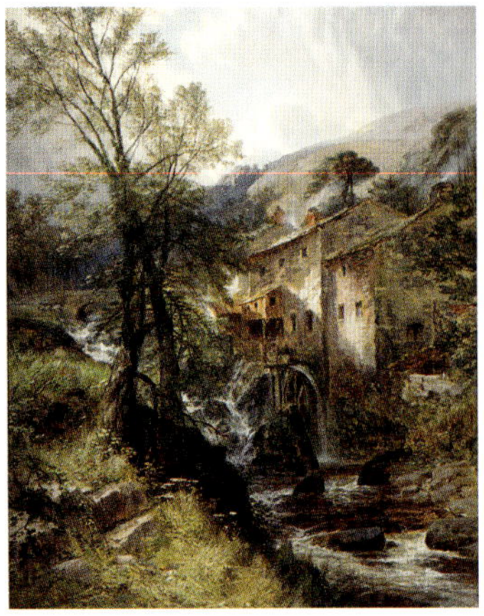

Pettitt, Edwin Alfred 1840–1912
Watermill, near Lynton, Devon 1874
oil on canvas 91.5 x 71
1891.28, P.160

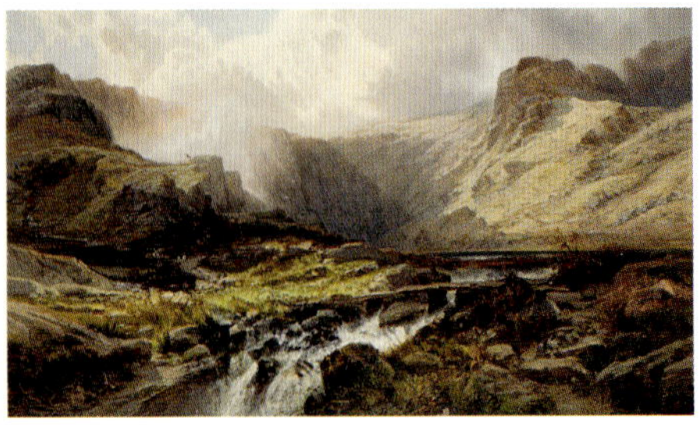

Pettitt, Edwin Alfred 1840–1912
Idwal from Ben Glog
oil on canvas 51.5 x 92
1891.29, P.9

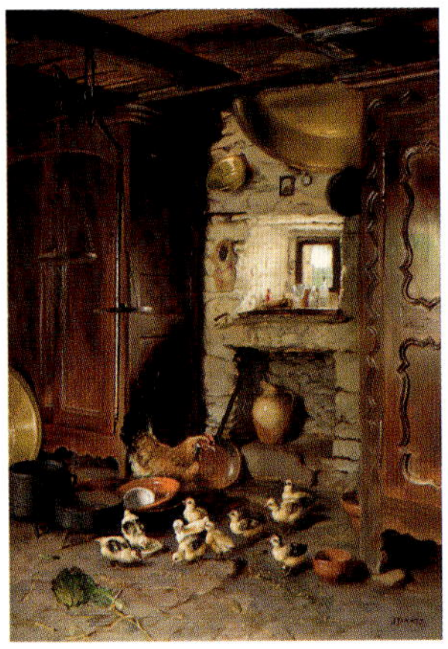

Pratt, Jonathan 1835–1911
Interior, French Farmhouse
oil on canvas 45.5 x 32
1948.1, P.295

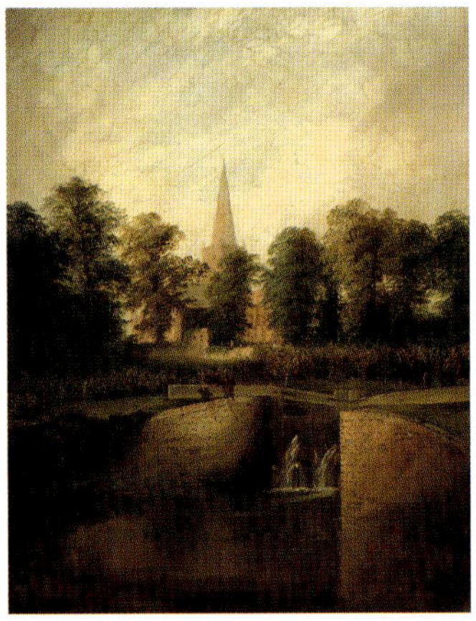

Richards, W.
Holy Trinity Church, Stratford-upon-Avon
1879
oil on canvas 92.5 x 72.5
1973.12, P.165

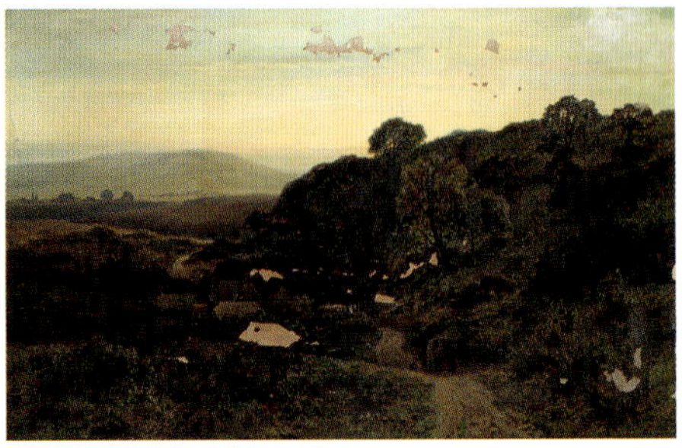

Rivers, Leopold 1852–1905
O'er Hill and Dale
oil on canvas 61 x 91.5
1987.114, P.67

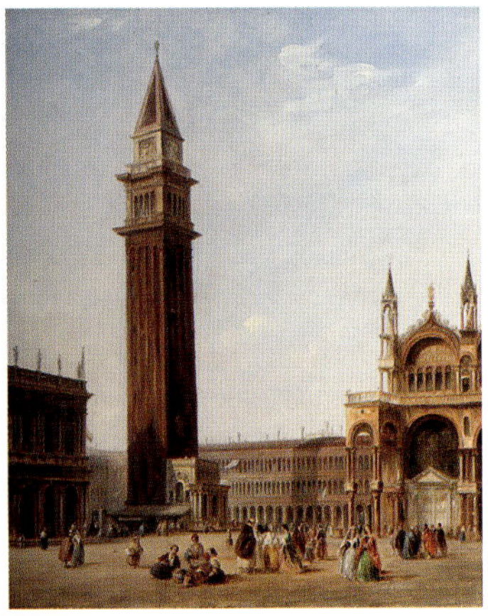

Roberts, David 1796–1864
St Mark's, Venice
oil on canvas 61 x 50.5 (E)
1922.3, P.29

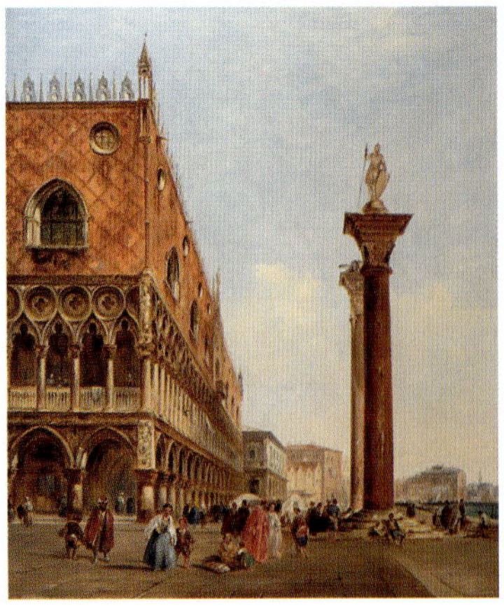

Roberts, David 1796–1864
The Doge's Palace, Venice
oil on canvas 61 x 50.5 (E)
1922.2, P.34

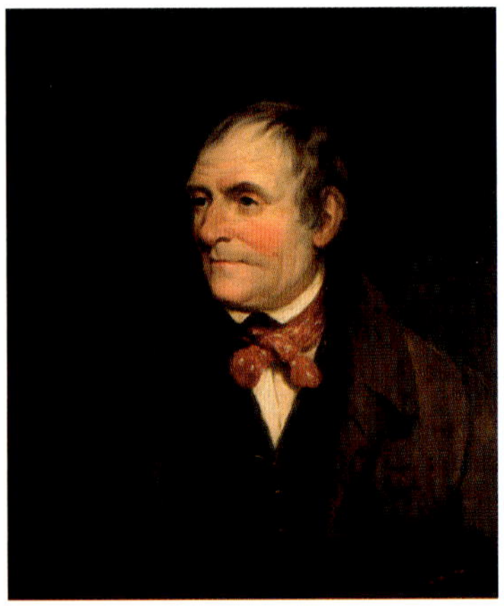

Roden, William Thomas 1817–1892
A Wednesbury Cocker
oil on canvas 89 x 50.5
1892.1, P.168

Facing page: Stokes, Marianne, 1855–1927, *Madonna and Child* (detail), Wolverhampton Art Gallery, (p. 324)

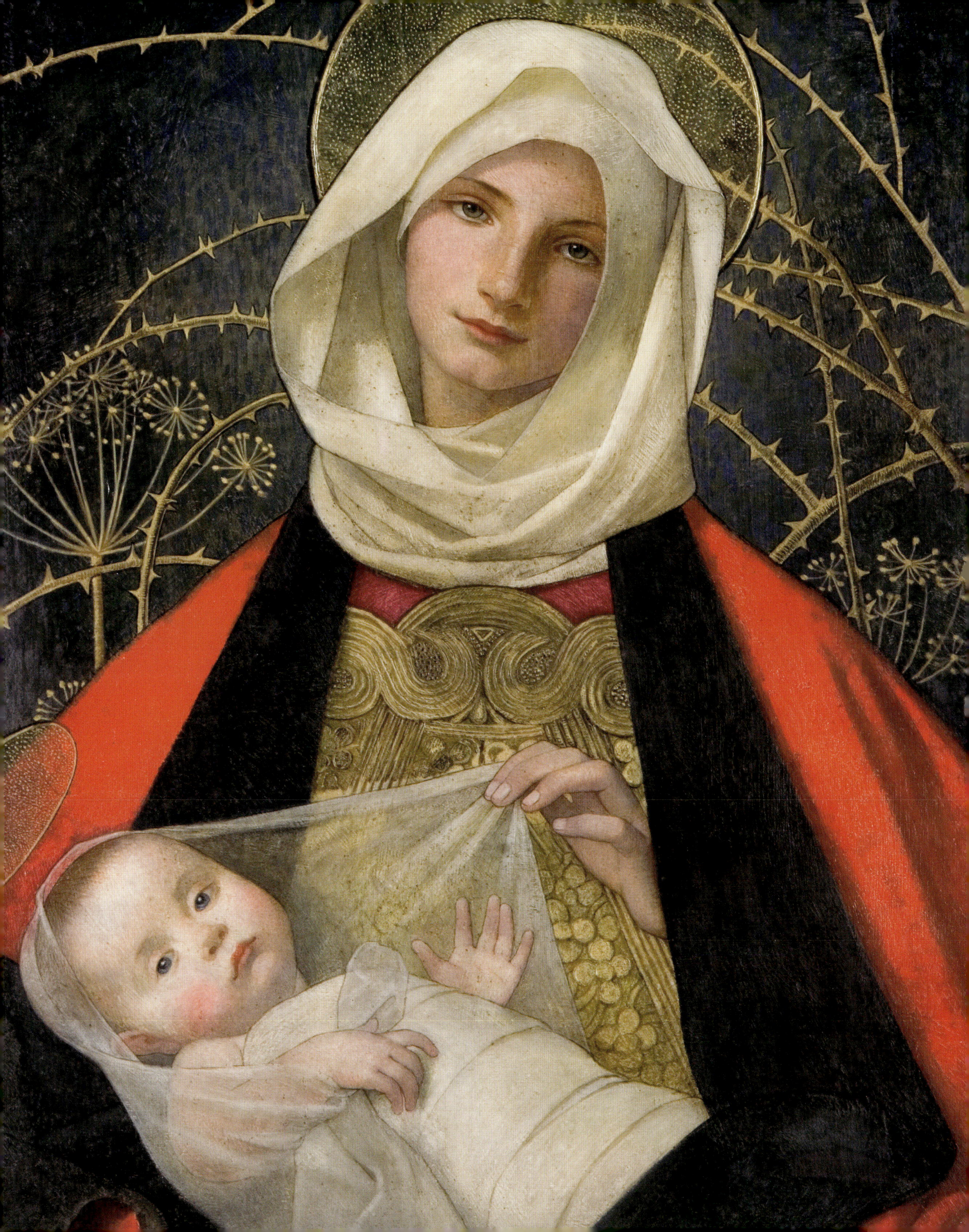

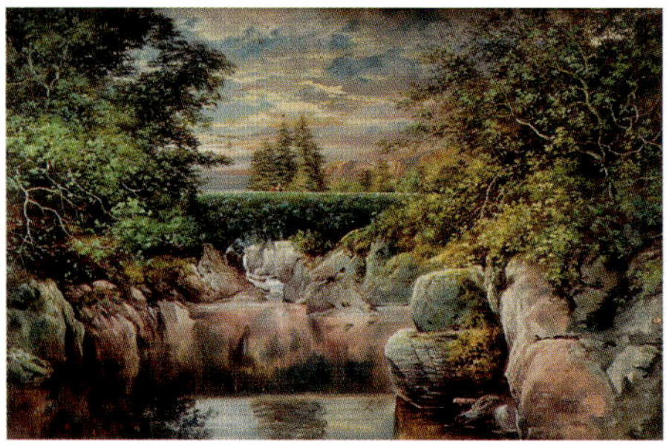

Salter, Edward active 1880–1888
The Waterfall 1888
oil on canvas 50.5 x 76
P.188

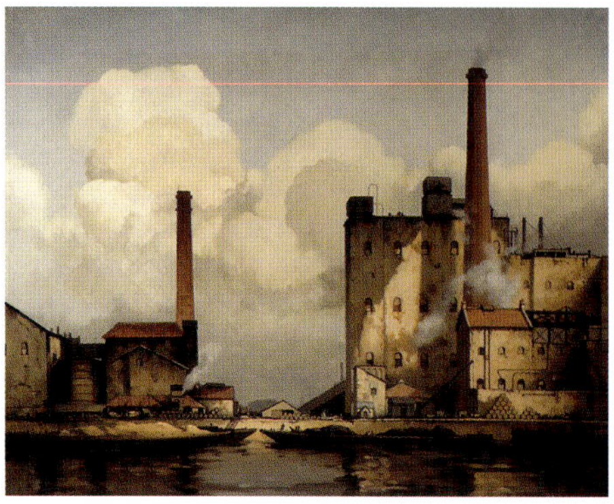

Smith, David Murray 1865–1952
The Thames at Hammersmith 1930
oil on canvas 63.5 x 76
1935.1, P.195

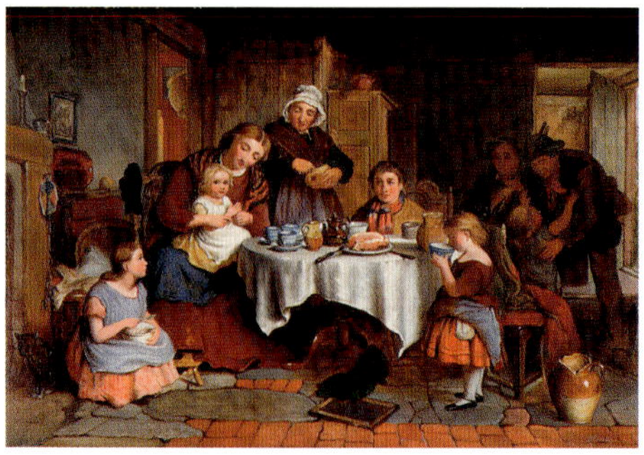

Smith, George 1829–1901
Saying Grace, Cottage Interior 1874
oil on canvas 25.5 x 35.5
1891.30, P.299

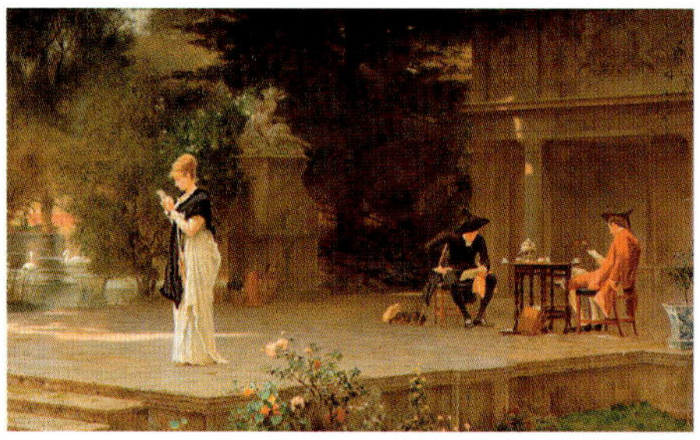

Stone, Marcus C. 1840–1921
The Post Bag
oil on canvas 51.5 x 82
1891.31, P.15

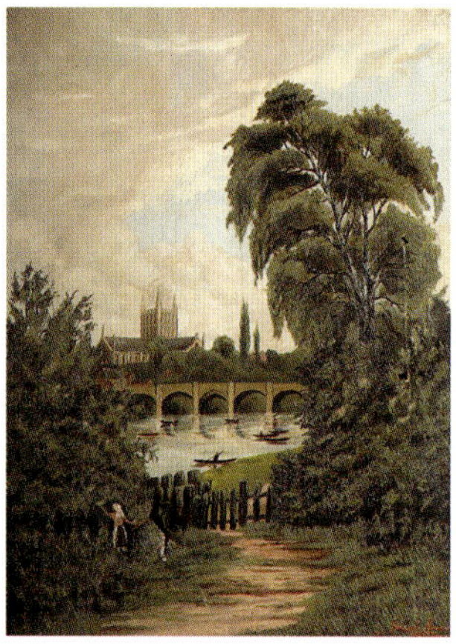

Swain, Joseph 1859–1923
Hereford Catherdral 1897
oil on board 59.5 x 41.5
1987.210, P.73

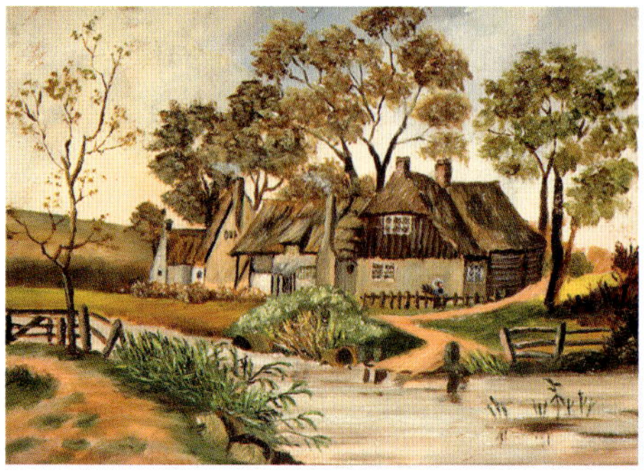

Swain, Joseph 1859–1923
Warley Hall Farm 1900
oil on board 18.5 x 24
1987.212, P.86

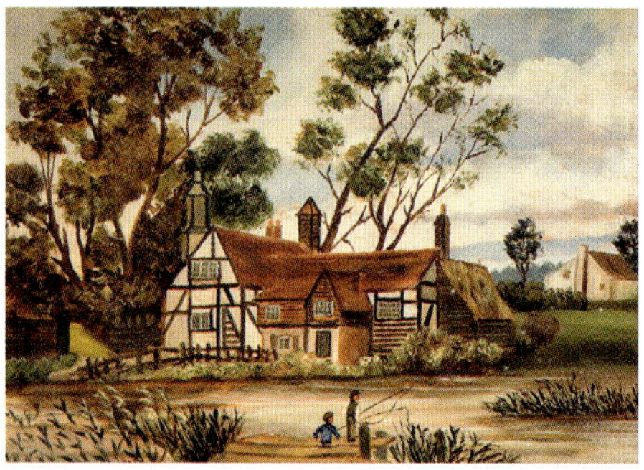

Swain, Joseph 1859–1923
Perry Hill Farm
oil on board 18.5 x 25
1987.211, P.85

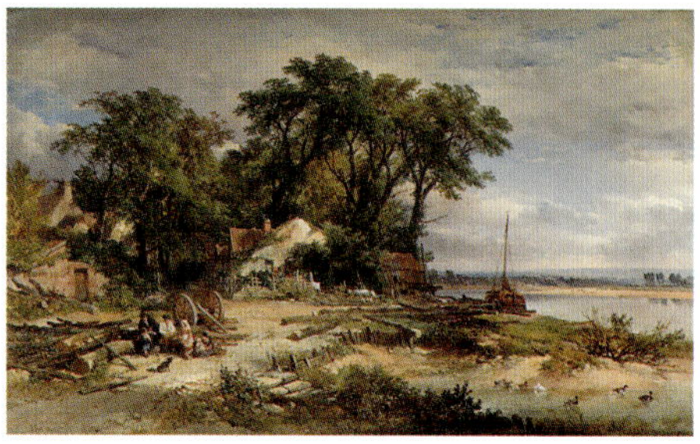

Syer, John 1815–1885
Scene on the River Avon 1854
oil on canvas 106.5 x 167.5
1891.32, P.26

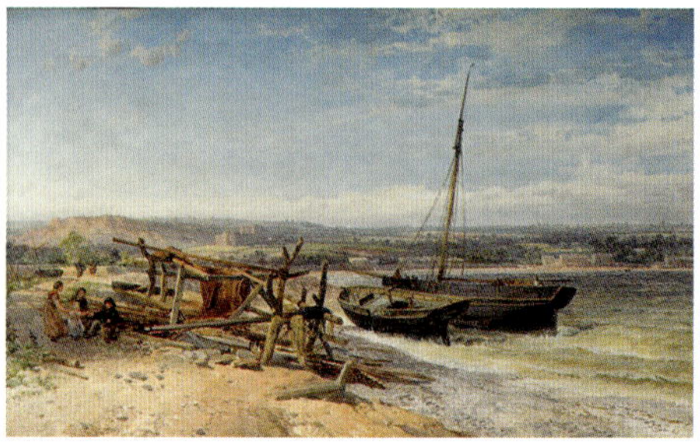

Syer, John 1815–1885
Estuary Scene
oil on canvas 48.5 x 76
1891.33, P.10

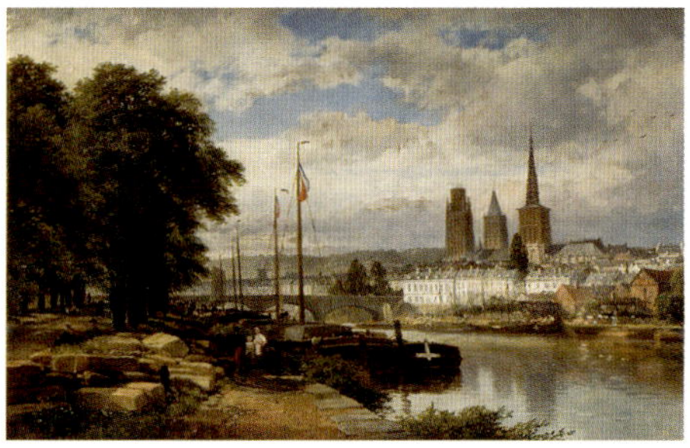

Syer, John 1815–1885
River Scene, Rouen
oil on canvas 84 x 127
1891.34, P.22

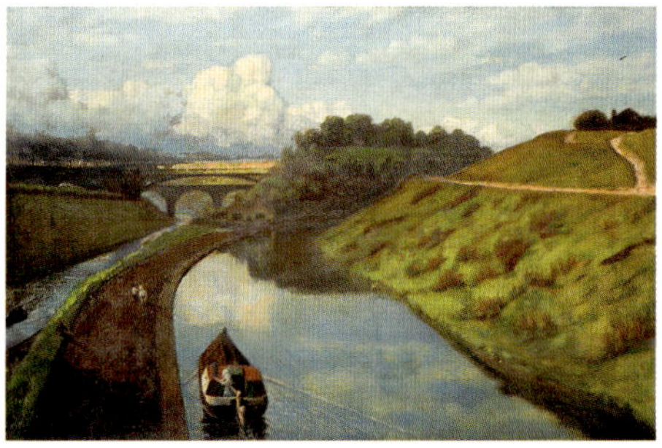

Taylor, Edward Richard 1838–1912
Galton Bridge 1905
oil on canvas 61 x 91.5
1987.115, P.154

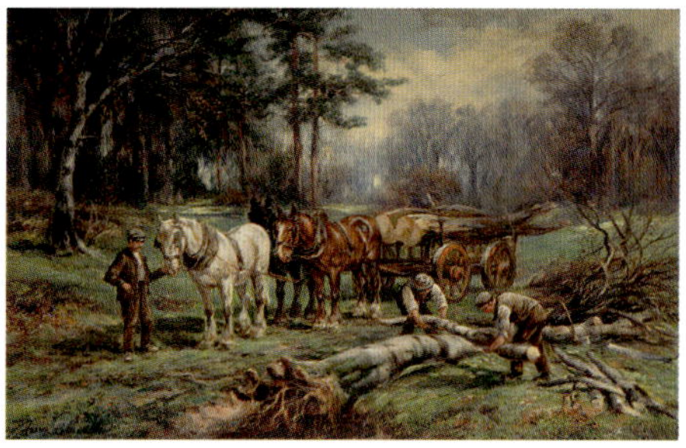

Thomas, Frank
Warley Woods, Loading Timber
oil on canvas 40.5 x 61
1987.237, P.70

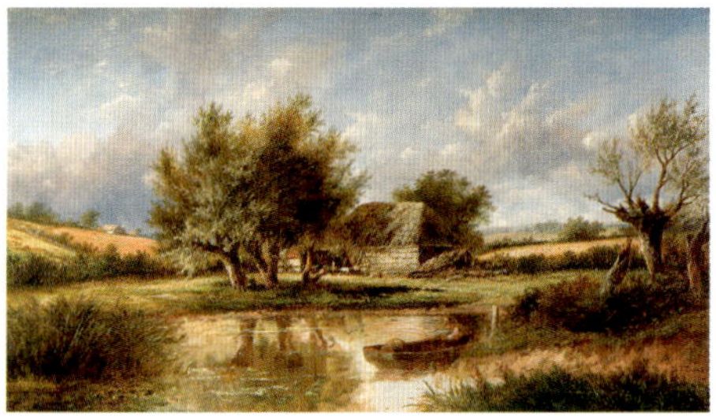

Thors, Joseph c.1834–1898
Punt Fishing
oil on canvas 76 x 127
1891.35, P.24

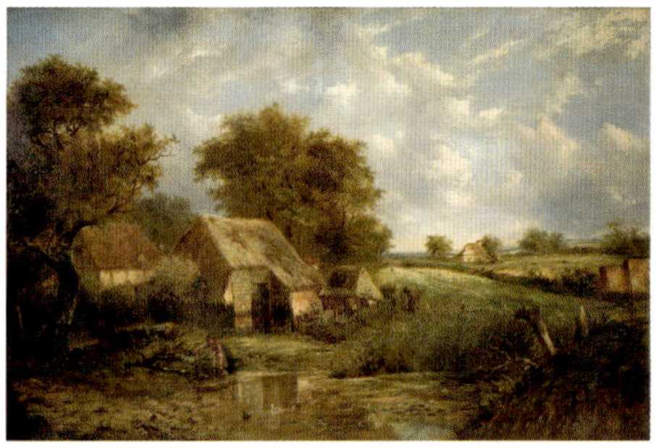

Thors, Joseph c.1834–1898
The Homestead
oil on canvas 101.5 x 152.5
1891.36, P.23

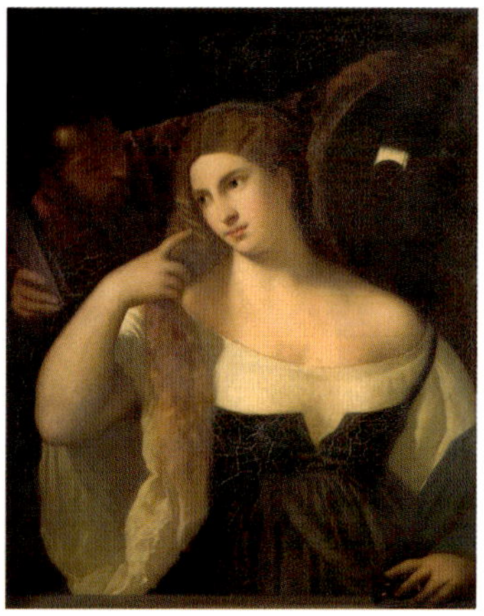

Titian (copy after) c.1488–1576
Laura De Dianti, Young Woman at Her Toilet
oil on canvas 99 x 78.5
1917.1, P.69

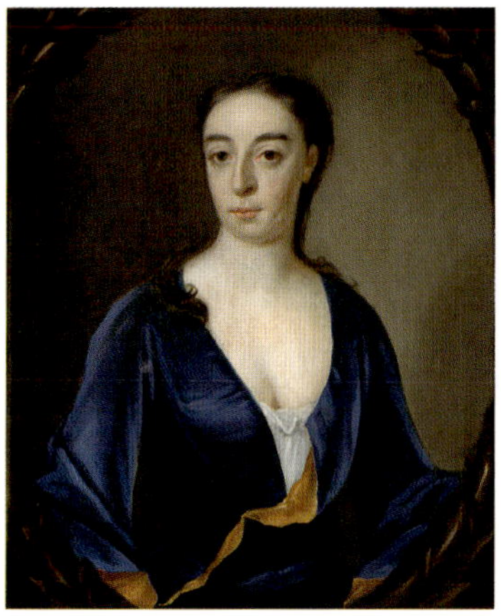

unknown artist
Mary Rotton, Wife of Thomas Haden 1730s
oil on canvas 93 x 78
3218 (B)

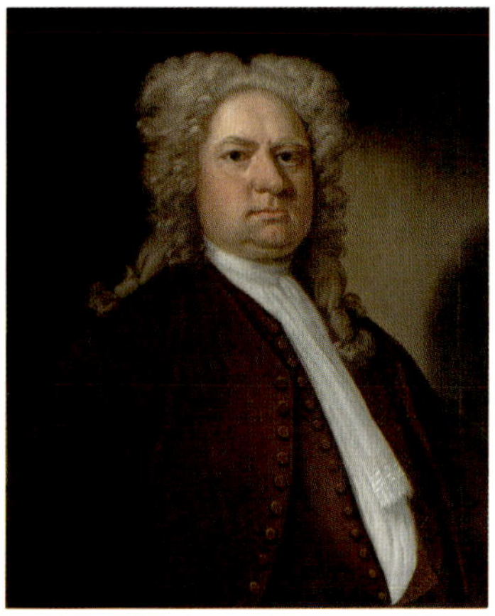

unknown artist
Thomas Haden (1684–1756) 1730s
oil on canvas 90.5 x 78
3218 (A)

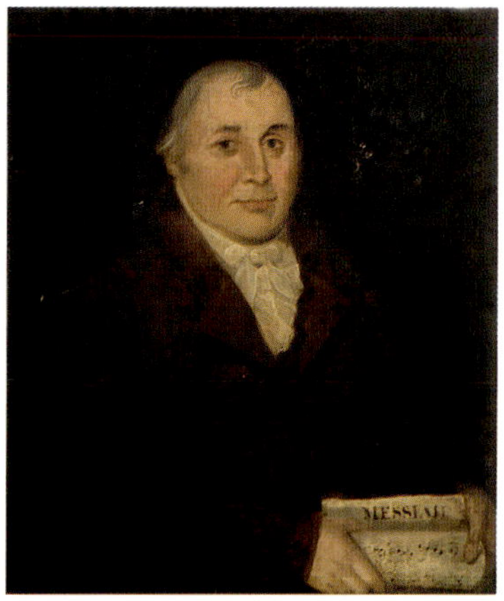

unknown artist 18th C
Edward Fisher (1751–1810)
oil on canvas 76 x 63.5
1984.6, P.171

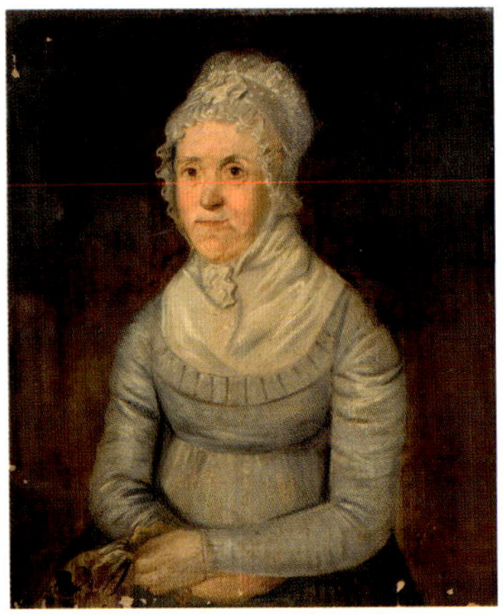

unknown artist 18th C
Mary Bissell, (1751–1824), Wife of Edward Fisher
oil on canvas 76 x 63.5
1984.5, P.172

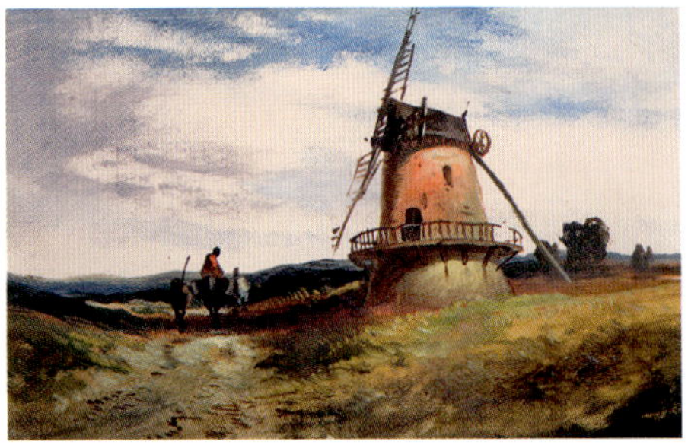

unknown artist
Smethwick Windmill 1868
oil on paper 31 x 37.5
1987.132, P.89

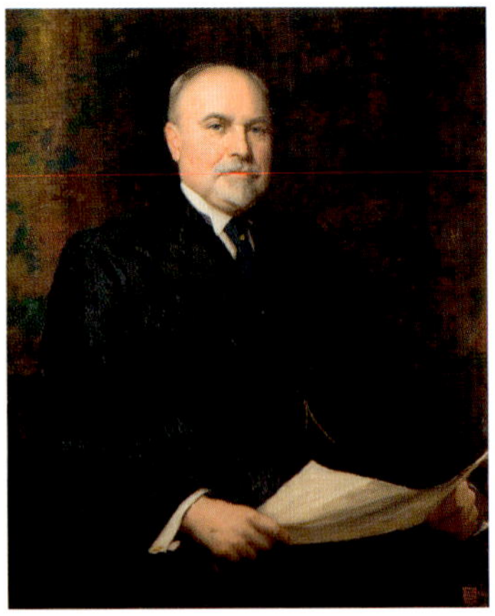

unknown artist
John Whyman, JP 1911
oil on canvas 96.5 x 76
1987.127, P.106

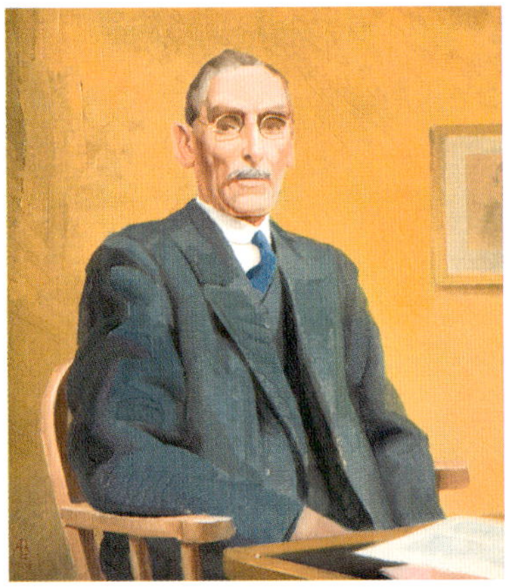

unknown artist
Portrait of Gentleman with Glasses 1936
oil on canvas 40.5 x 35.5
P.228

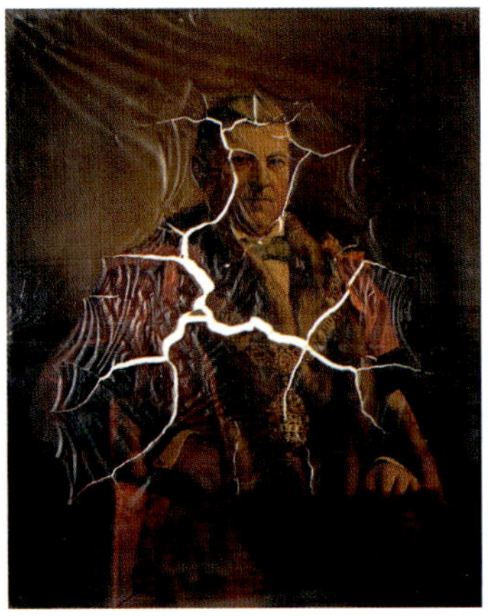

unknown artist
Alderman Henry Lloyd
oil on canvas 51 x 40.5
P.117

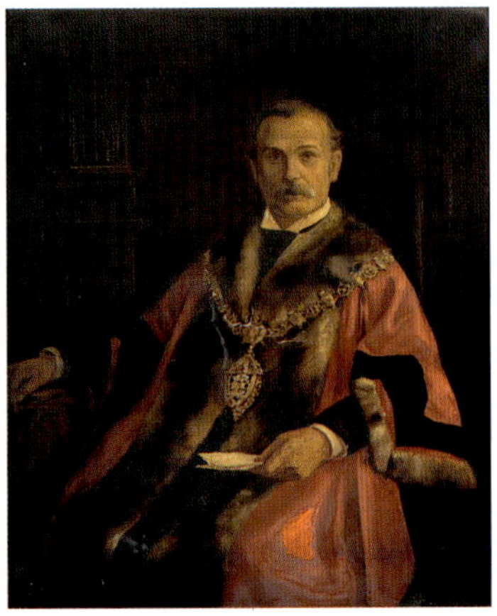

unknown artist
Alderman Iaian Oldbury, JP, Mayor (1896–1898 & 1902–1905)
oil on canvas 49.5 x 39.5
P.115

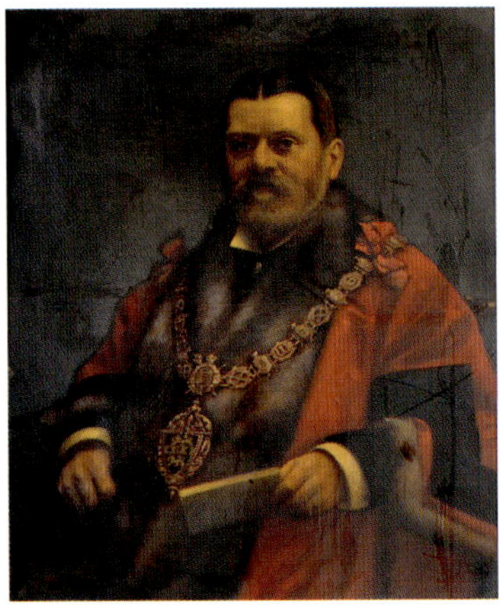

unknown artist
Alderman Issac Griffiths, JP, Wednesbury Corporation Mayor (1908–1909)
oil on canvas 61 x 51
P.111

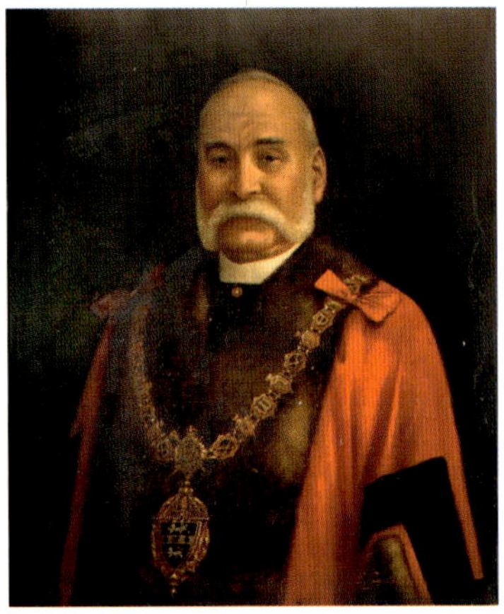

unknown artist
Alderman John Ashley Kilvert, JP (1833–1920)
oil on canvas 59.5 x 49.5
PCF1

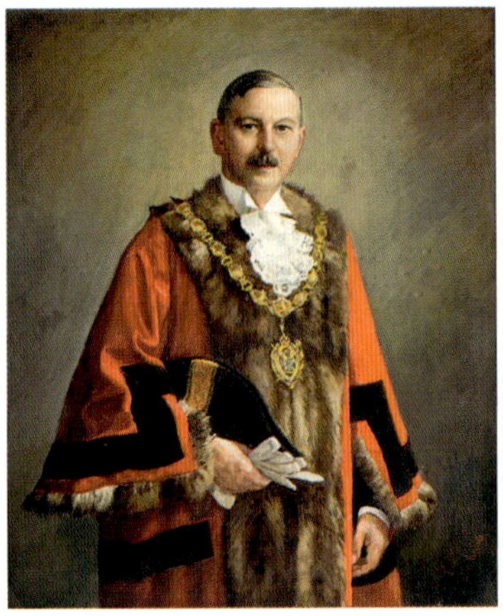

unknown artist
Alderman K. H. Wilson, JP, Charter Mayor, Oldbury (1935–1936)
oil on canvas 61 x 50
1987.24, P.92

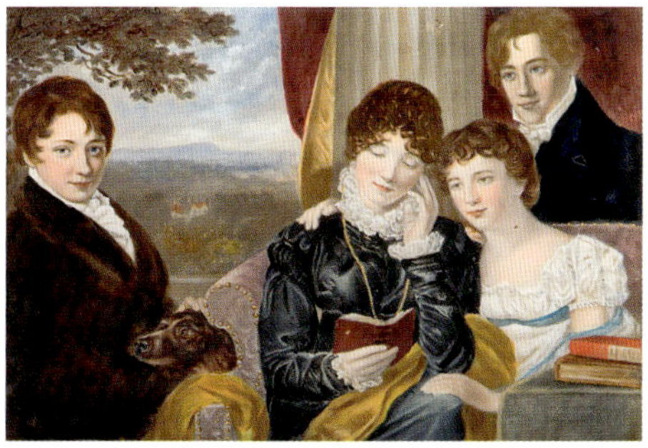

unknown artist
Alfred Barrs, Frederick Barrs, Emmeline Barrs and Annie Elizabeth Haden
oil on board 20 x 28
518

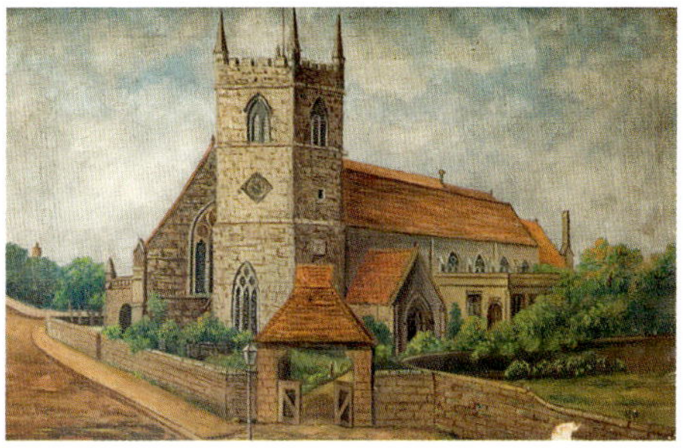

unknown artist
All Saints' Church, West Bromwich
oil on board 21 x 30.5
1974.50, P.194

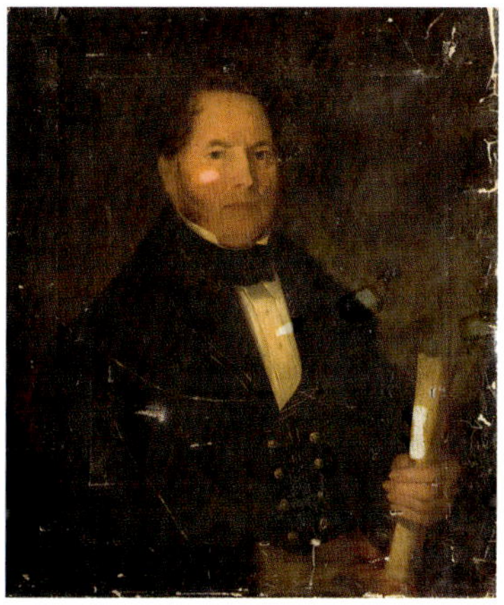

unknown artist
Barber Wilkes
oil on canvas 77.5 x 64
1984.13, P.300

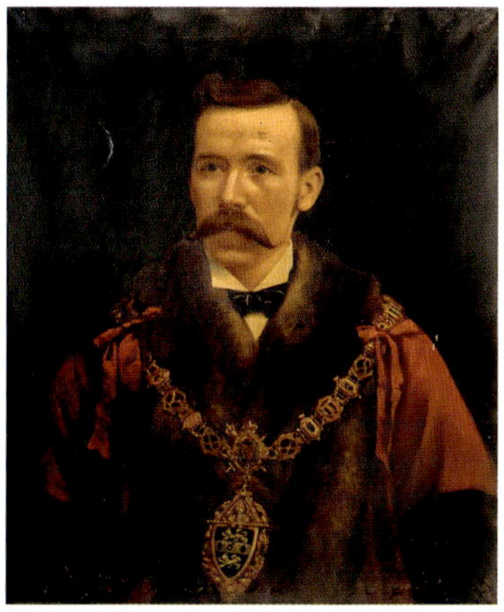

unknown artist
C. D. Joynson, JP, Mayor of Wednesbury (1898–1900)
oil on canvas 61 x 51
P.110

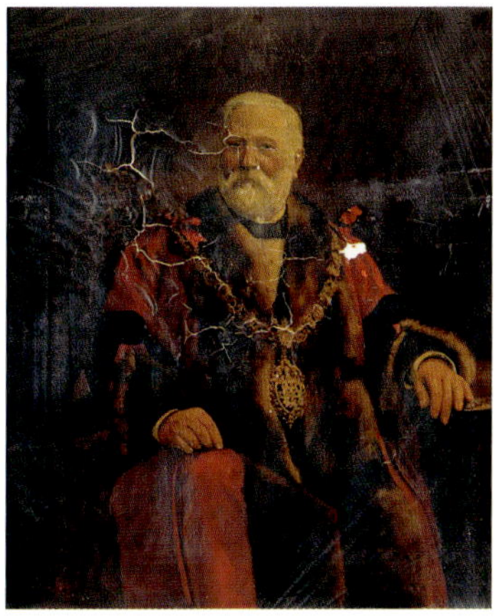

unknown artist
Councillor John Knowles, JP, Mayor of Wednesbury (1894–1896)
oil on canvas 51 x 40.5
P.114

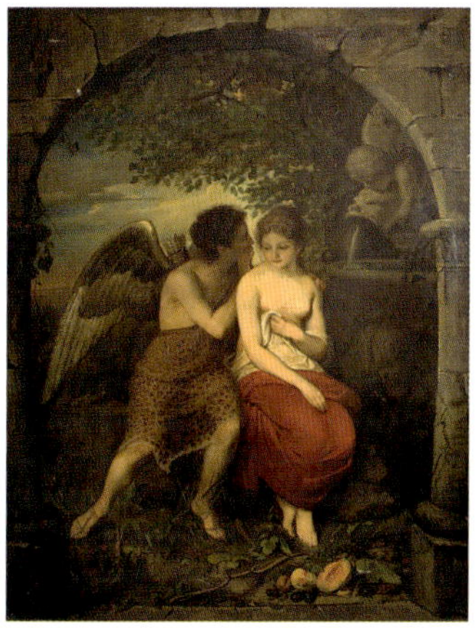

unknown artist
Cupid and Psyche
oil on canvas 244 x 185.5
1973.11, P.60

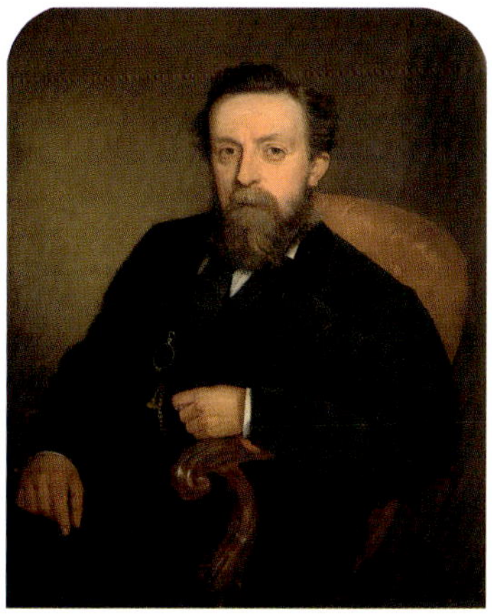

unknown artist
George Collins, Chairman of Smethwick Library
oil on canvas 91.5 x 71
1987.113, P.156

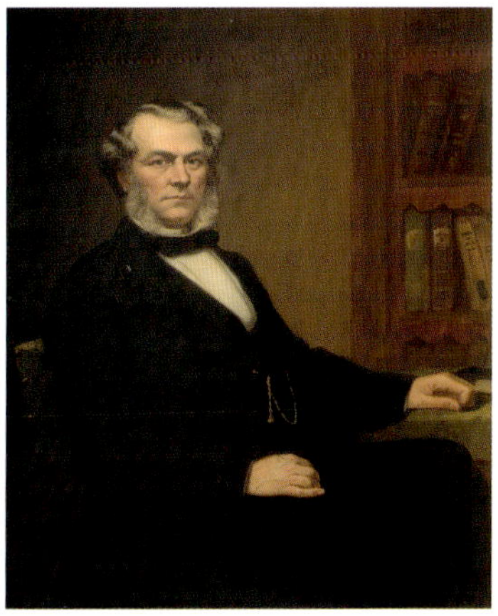

unknown artist
John James Russell
oil on canvas 127 x 101.5
P.49, WAG-4-1997

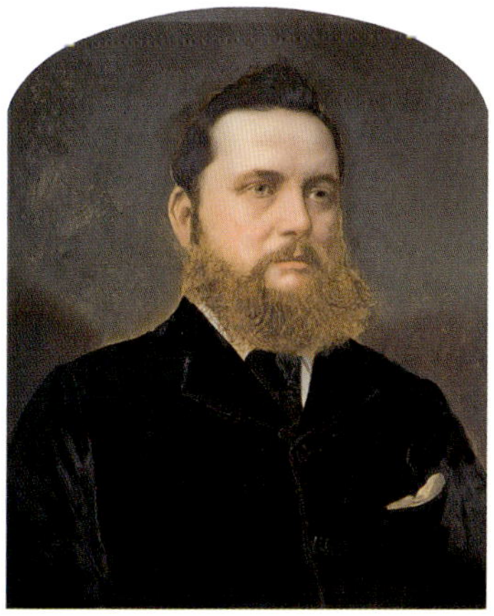

unknown artist
Portrait of a Gentleman
oil on canvas 37.5 x 30
1973.13, P.63

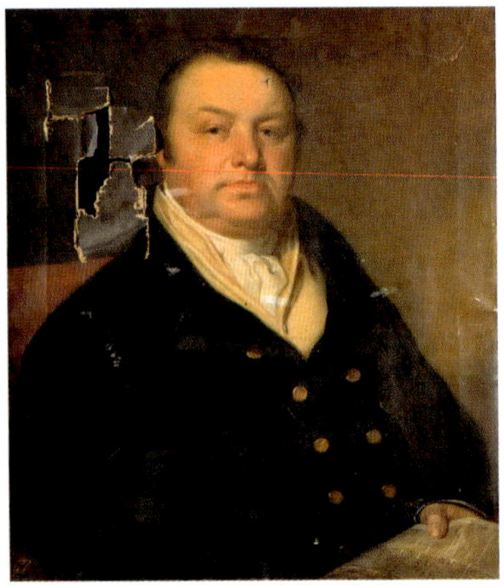

unknown artist
Portrait of a Gentleman (member of the Jesson family)
oil on canvas 77 x 64
1984.11

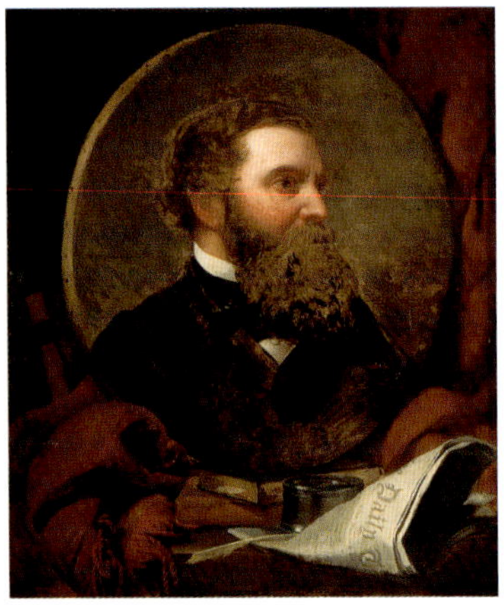

unknown artist
Portrait of a Gentleman with a Beard
oil on canvas 76.5 x 64
P.243

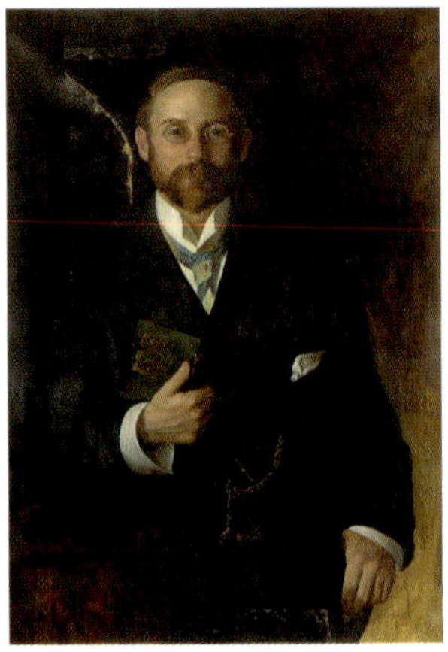

unknown artist
Portrait of a Man in Glasses with a Beard
oil on canvas 87 x 58.5
P.155

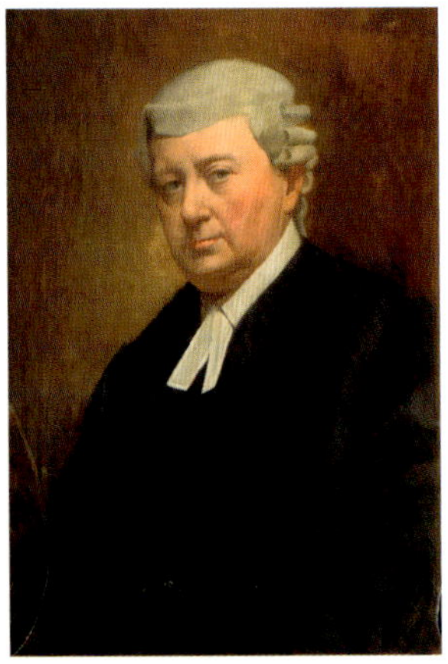

unknown artist
Portrait of a Man with a Wig
oil on canvas 76 x 50
P.50

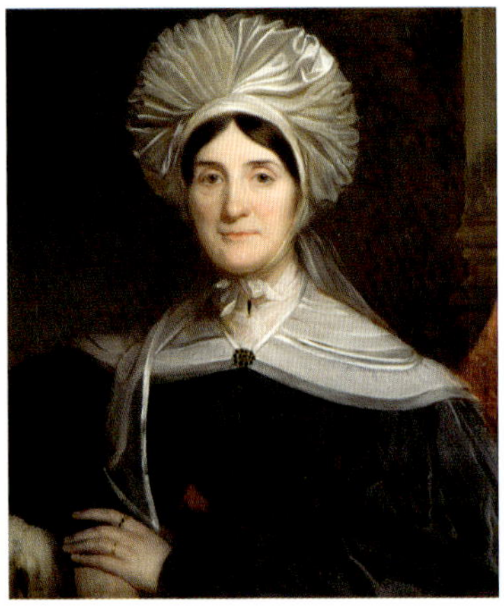

unknown artist
Portrait of a Woman in a Bonnet
oil on canvas 76 x 63.5
1984.12, P.301

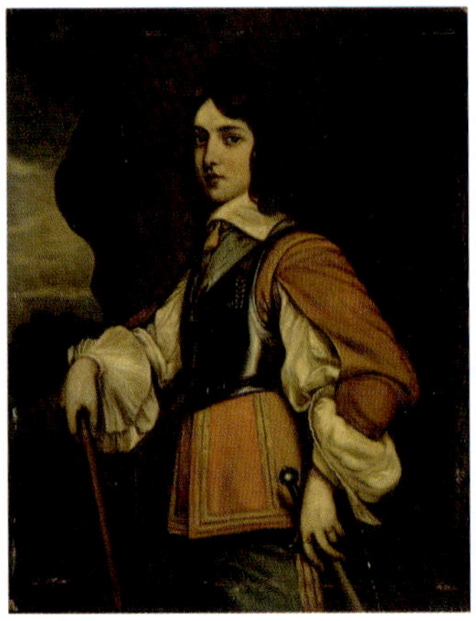

unknown artist
Portrait of a Young Cavalier
oil on board 26.5 x 19.5
P.312

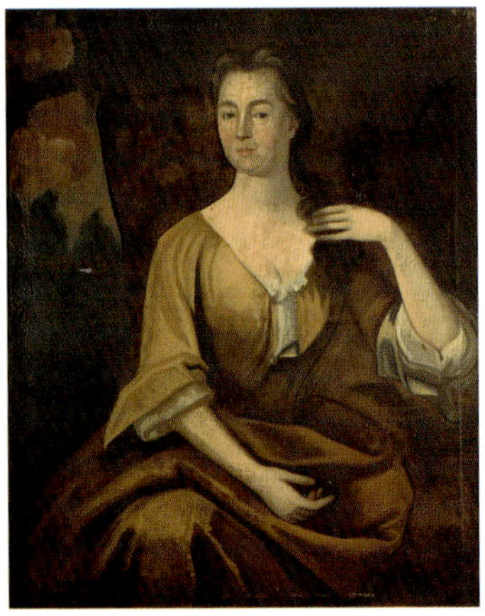

unknown artist
Portrait of a Young Lady
oil on canvas 127 x 98.5
P.340

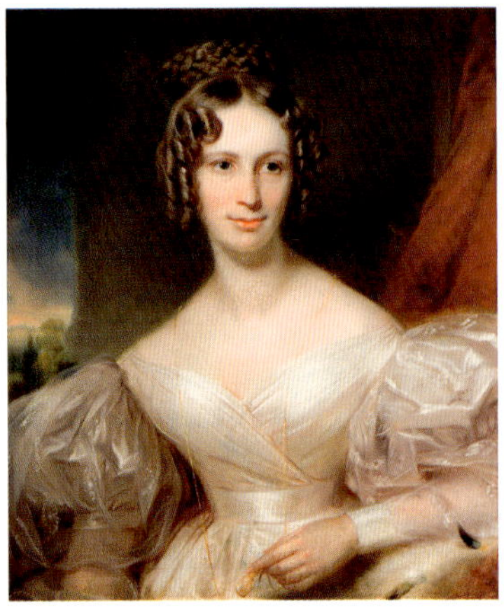

unknown artist
Portrait of a Young Woman
oil on canvas 76 x 63.5
P.170

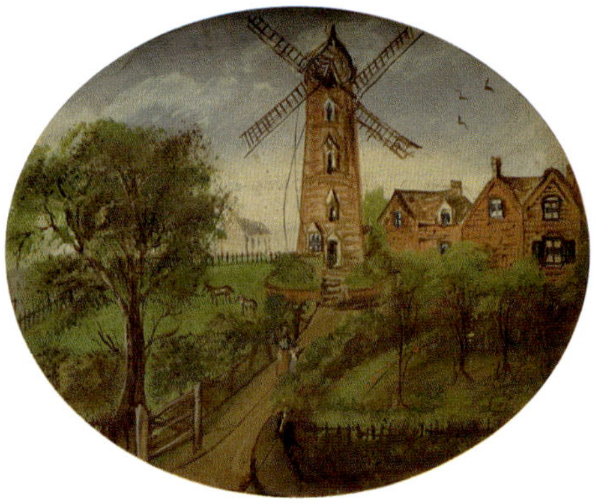

unknown artist
Smethwick Windmill
oil on canvas 18 x 26.5
1987.165, P.89

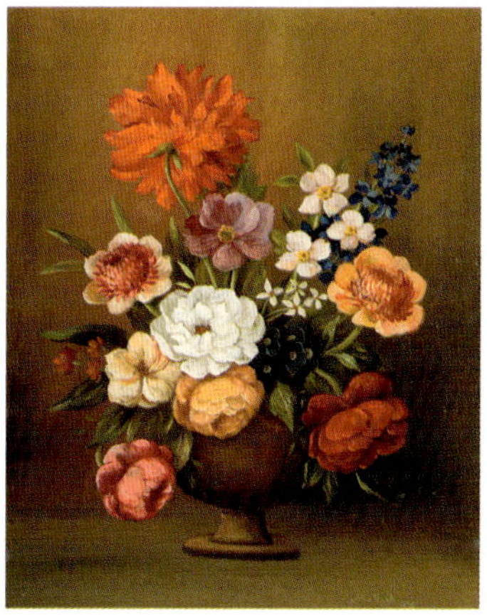

unknown artist
Still Life, Vase of Flowers
oil on canvas 51 x 41.5
P.334

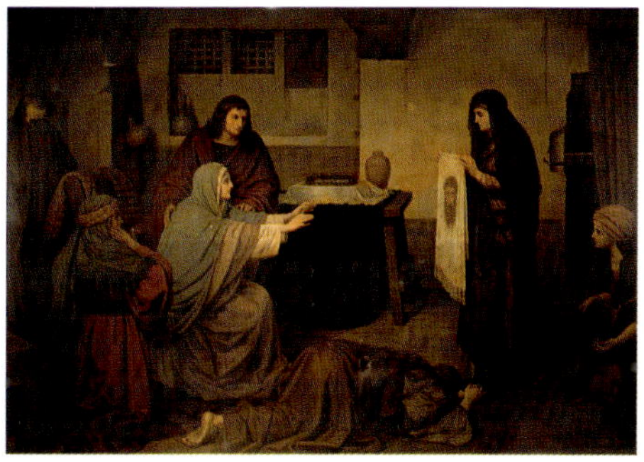

unknown artist
The Night of Good Friday
oil on canvas 160 x 221
1918.1, P.163

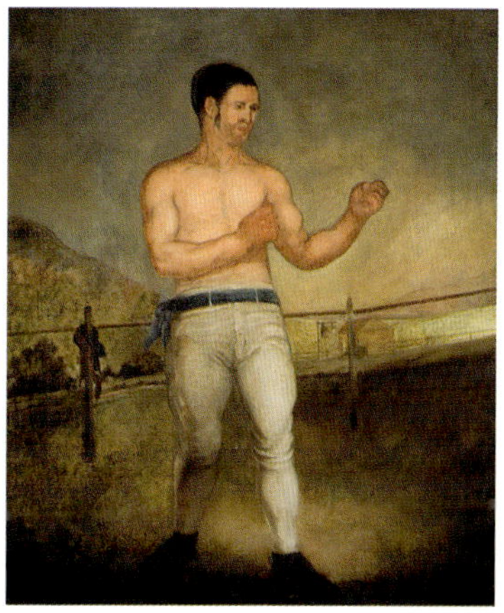

unknown artist
The Tipton Slasher
oil on canvas 81 x 61
E52-03

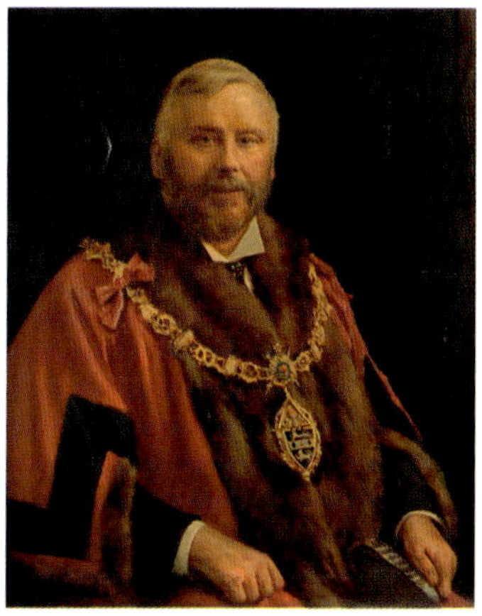

unknown artist
Wednesbury Alderman Mayor Hunt
oil on canvas 51 x 40.5
P.78

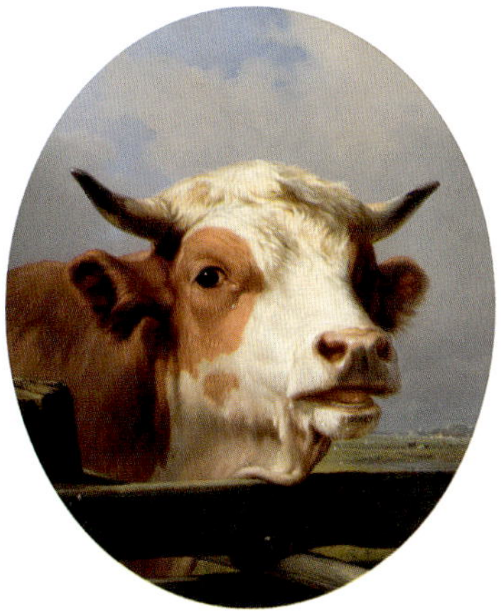

Verboeckhoven, Eugène 1799–1881
Bull's Head 1857
oil on canvas 104 x 83
1891.37, P.14

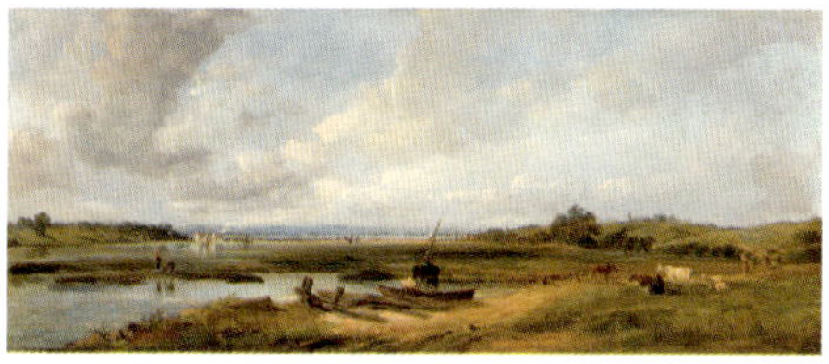

Vickers, Alfred 1786–1868
Dutch Landscape
oil on canvas 32 x 74
1891.39, P.236

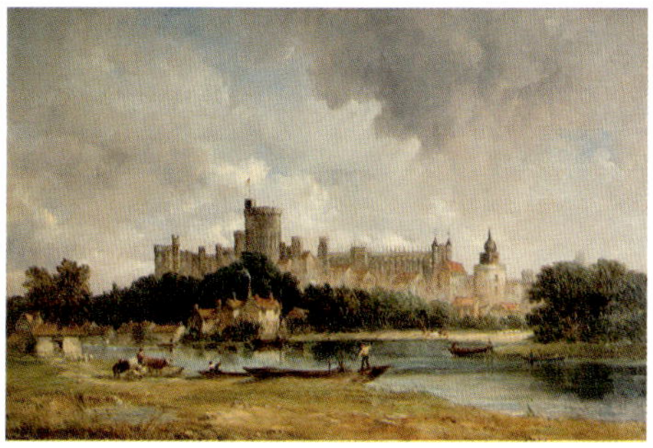

Vickers, Alfred 1786–1868
Windsor Castle from the Thames
oil on canvas 65 x 95.5
1891.38, P.30

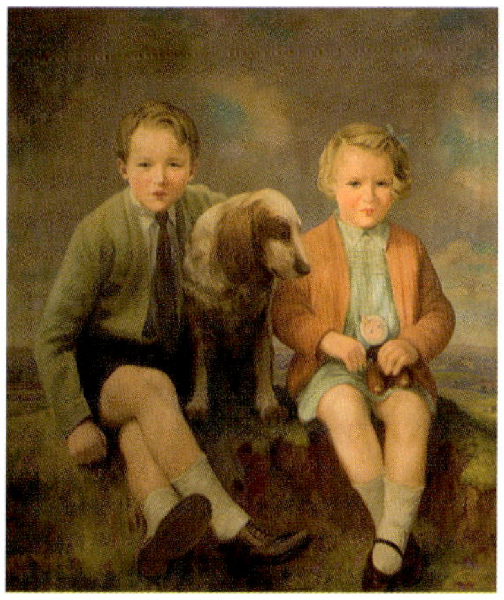

Waldron West, E.
Kenneth Anthony and Gillian West 1949
oil on canvas 100 x 86
P.324, 3218

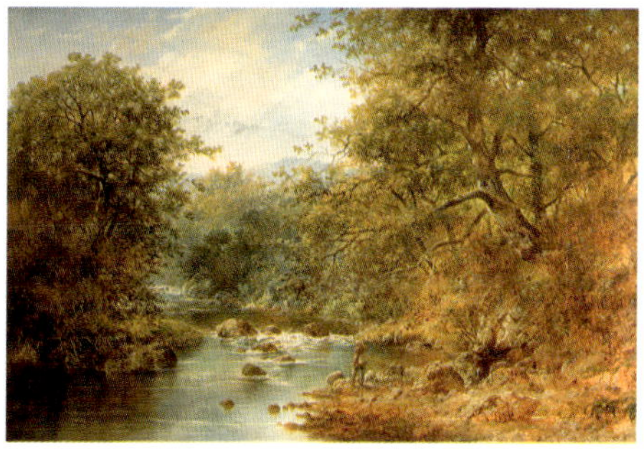

Ward, James Charles active 1830–1878
Angler's Nook 1869
oil on canvas 106.5 x 152.5
1891.40, P.3

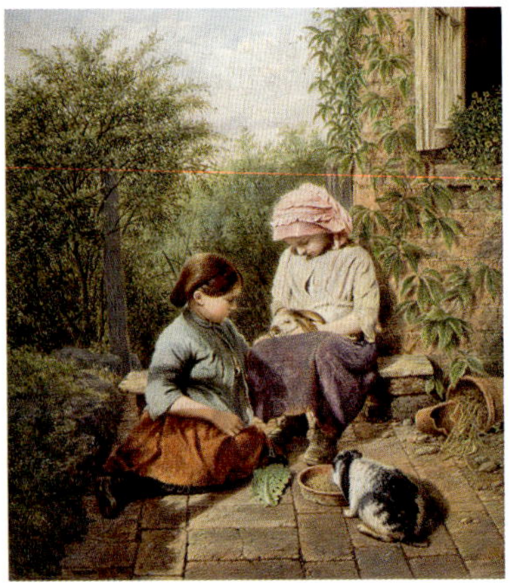

Ward, William H. active 1850–1899
Pet Rabbits 1875
oil on canvas 35.5 x 30.5
1891.42, P.35

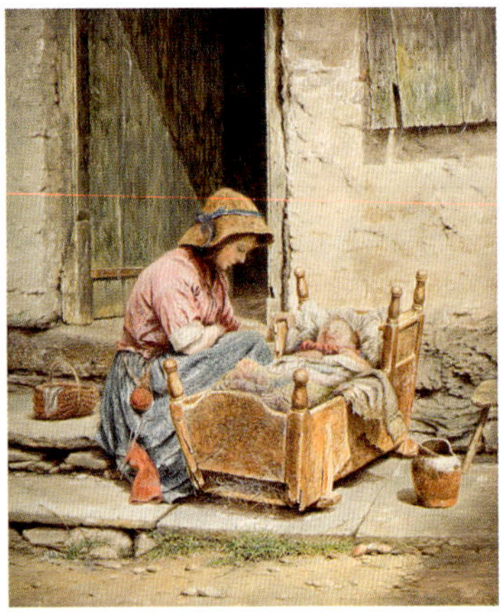

Ward, William H. active 1850–1899
Minding Baby 1895
oil on canvas 30.5 x 25.5
1891.41, P.28

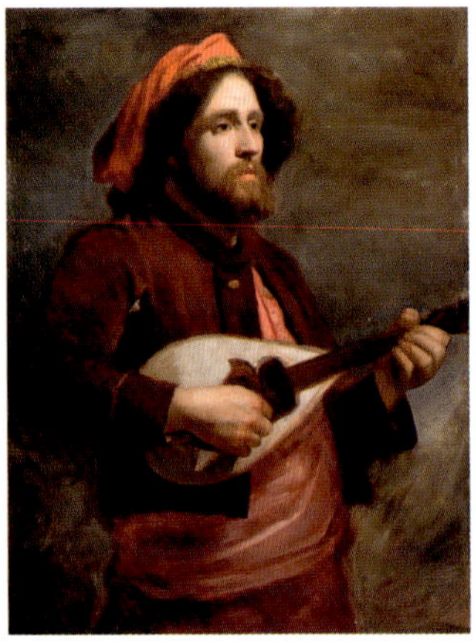

Watts, George Frederick 1817–1904
The Wandering Minstrel
oil on canvas 76 x 51
1910.2, P.11

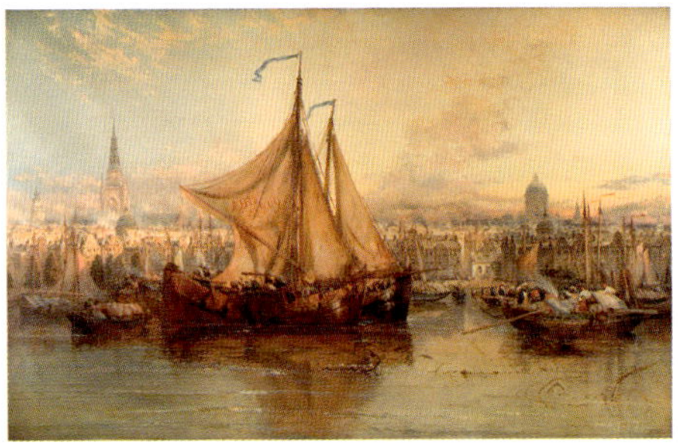

Webb, James c.1825–1895
The Harbour, Amsterdam 1876
oil on canvas 122 x 188.5
1891.44, P.158

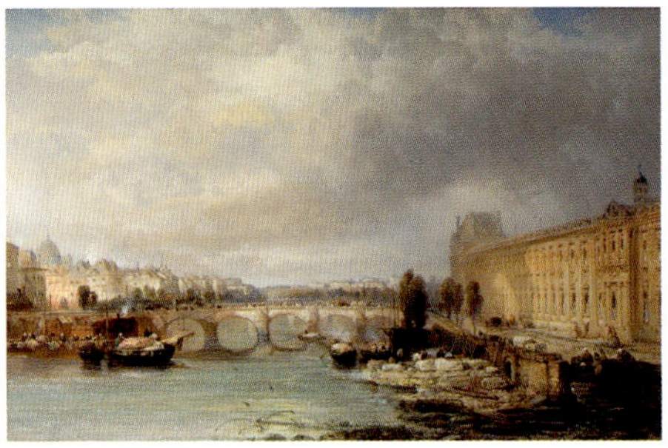

Webb, James c.1825–1895
Paris 1878–1879
oil on canvas 51 x 76
1891.45, P.4

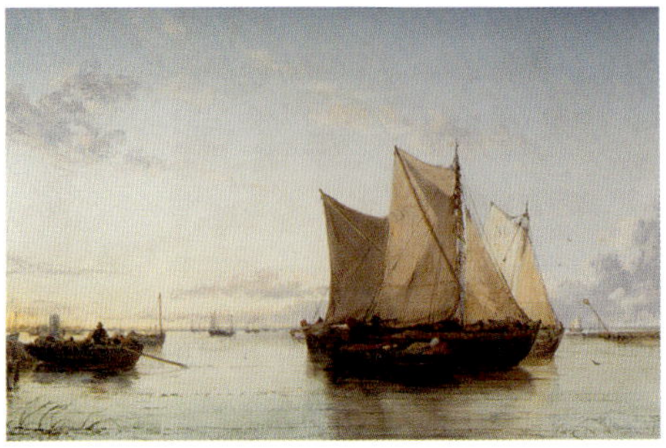

Webb, James c.1825–1895
A Quiet Evening
oil on canvas 51 x 76
1891.43, P.2

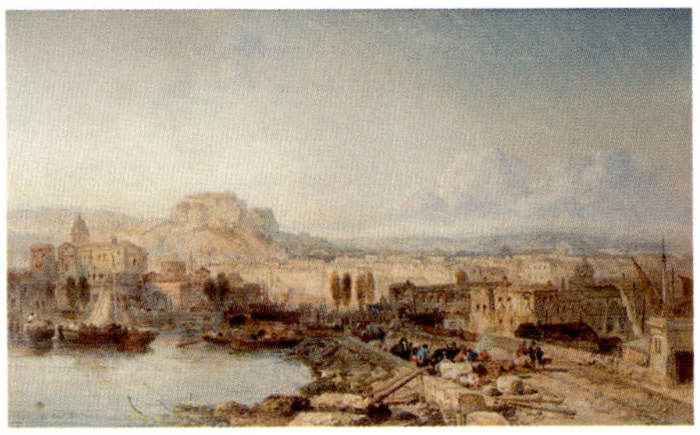

Webb, James c.1825–1895
Naples
oil on canvas 51 x 76
1891.46, P.5

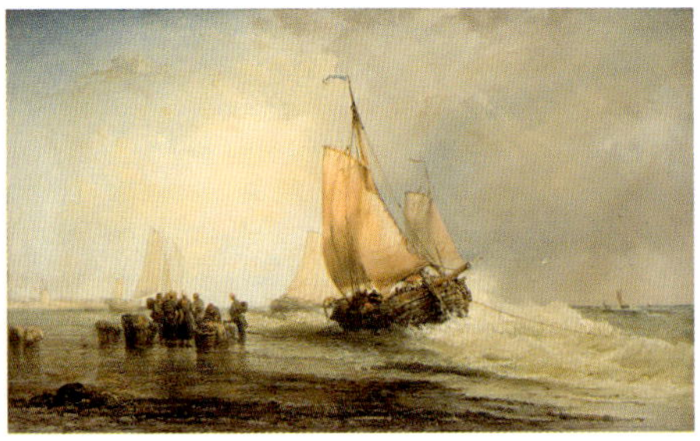

Webb, James c.1825–1895
On the Dutch Coast
oil on canvas 61 x 96.5
1958.1, P.1

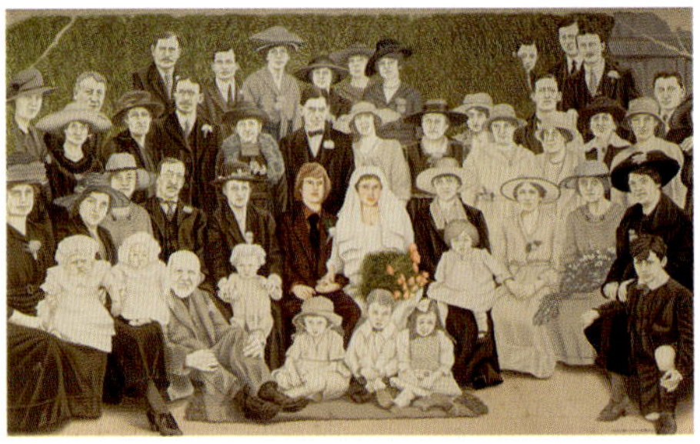

Wedgbury, David b.1937
The Wedding 1978
oil on canvas 56 x 86.5
P.47

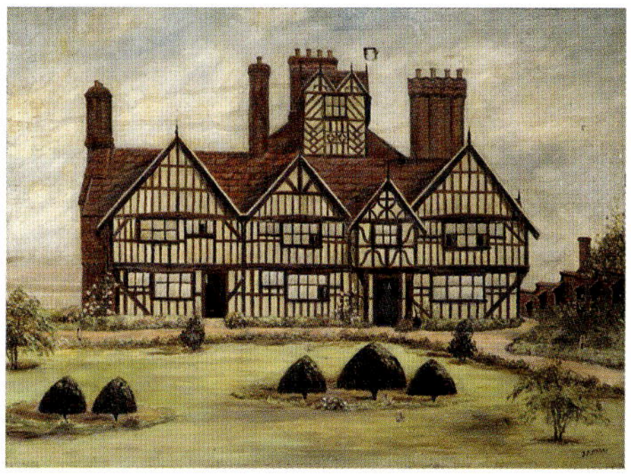

White, J. A.
Oak House
oil on canvas 45.5 x 61
P.227

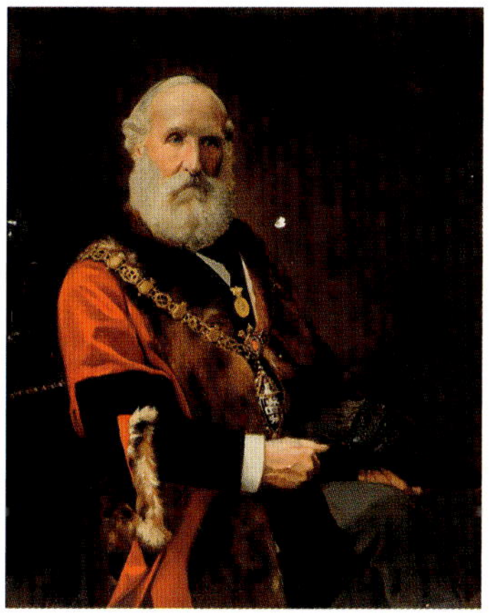

Whitlock Brothers
Alderman Richard Williams (d.1909), JP, Honorary Freeman of the Borough of Wednesbury Corporation (1899)
oil on canvas 50.5 x 40.5
P.113

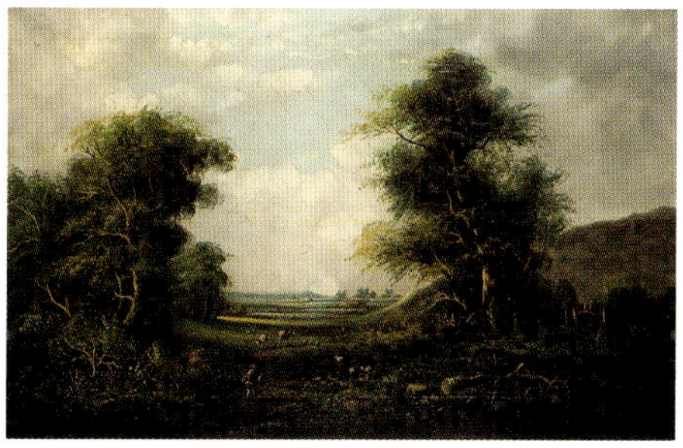

Williams, H. A.
Landscape
oil on canvas 61.5 x 91
1973.9, P.190

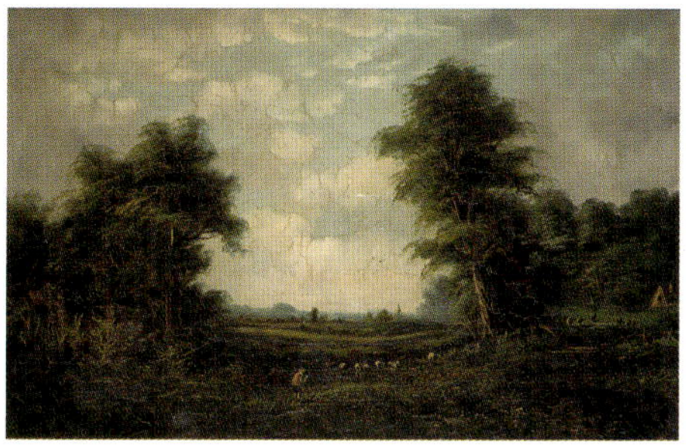

Williams, H. A.
Landscape
oil on canvas 61.5 x 92
1973.10, P.206

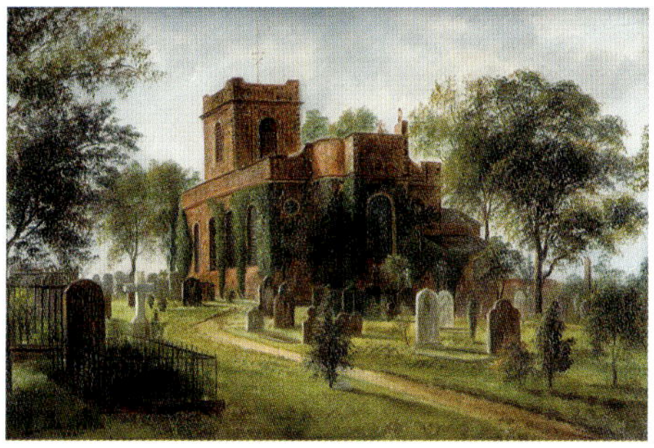

Willis-Pryce, George 1866–1949
Old Church 1944
oil on canvas 28 x 40.5
1987.166, P.79

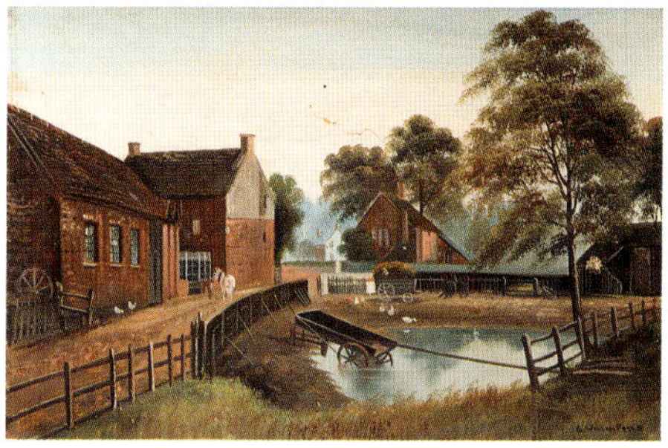

Willis-Pryce, George 1866–1949
Old Chapel Farm
oil on canvas 28 x 40.5
1987.167, P.124

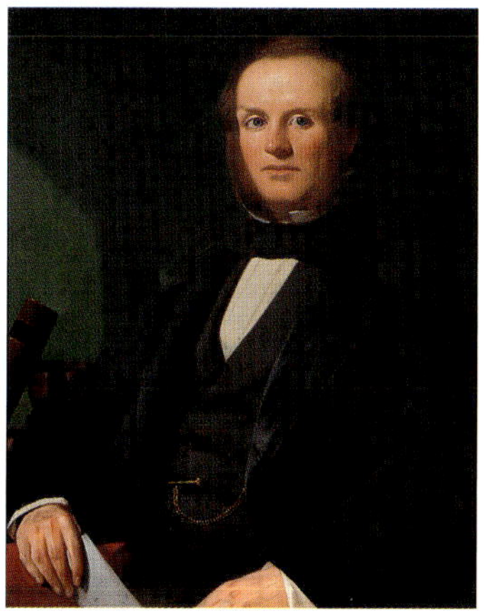

Wivell, Abraham II (attributed to)
active 1840–1865
Edwin Richards
oil on canvas 91.5 x 71
1891.47, P.32

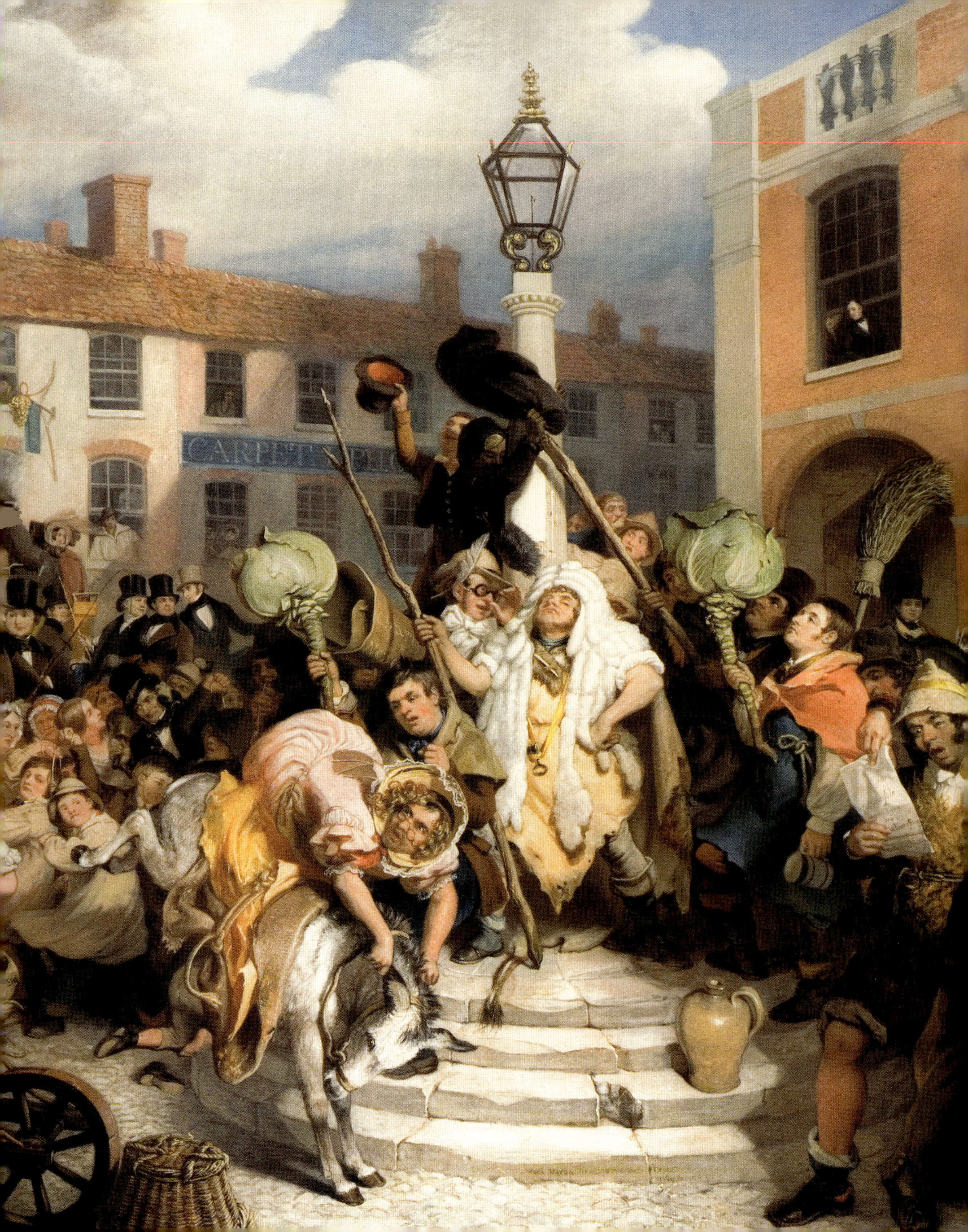
CARPET

Museum of the Staffordshire Yeomanry

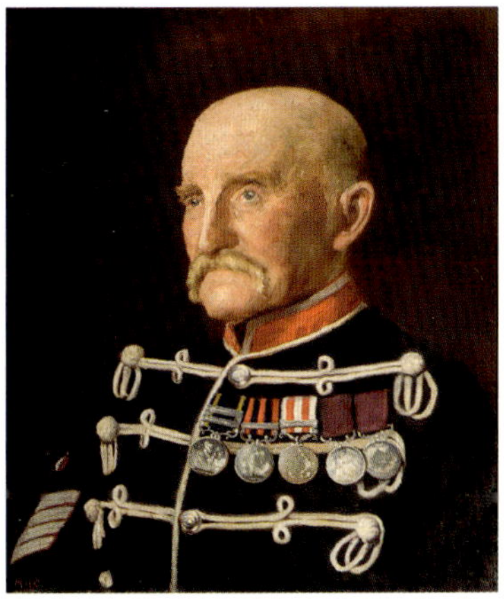

M. H. C.
John Stafford (1829–1932)
oil on canvas 75 x 50
PCF1

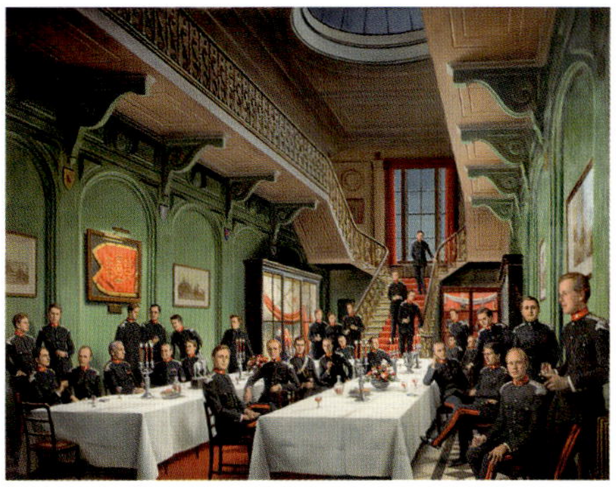

Sancha, Carlos Luis 1920–2001
Officers of the Yeomanry at Dinner c.1965
oil on canvas 90 x 116
PCF2

Stafford Borough Council

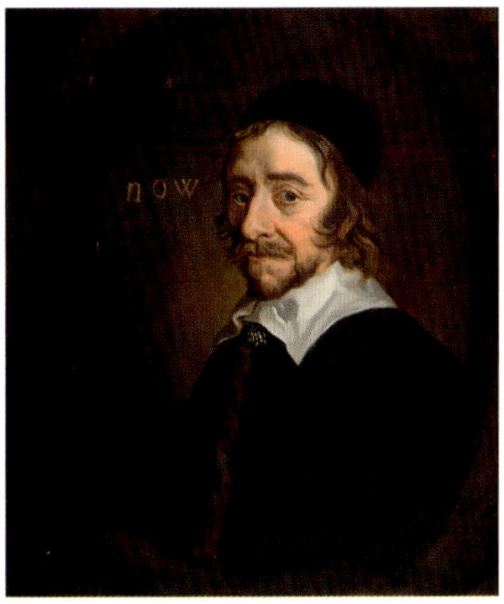

Aris, Joyce active 1940s
John Bradshaw, MP for Stafford (1602–1659) (after John Riley)
oil on canvas 72 x 59
PCF4

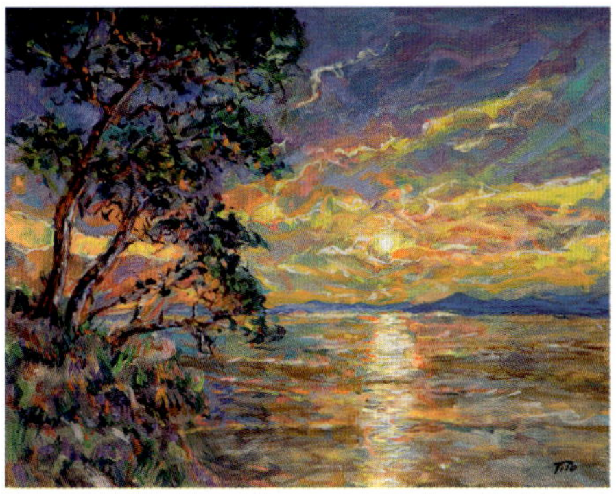

Figueras, Tito
Sunset over the Sea
oil on canvas 33.5 x 41.5
PCF2

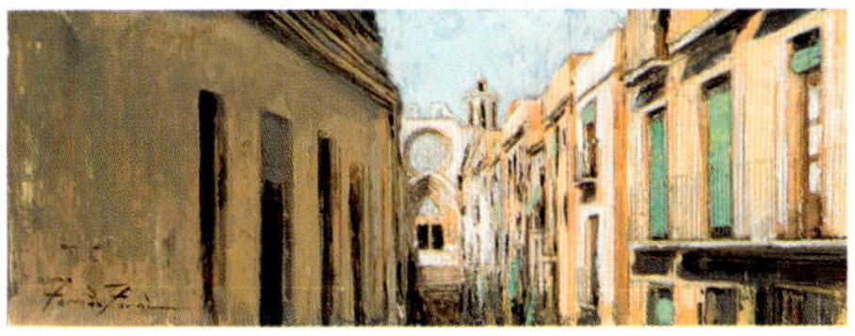

Torné, Tomás
Tarragona 2001
oil on canvas 25 x 65
PCF3

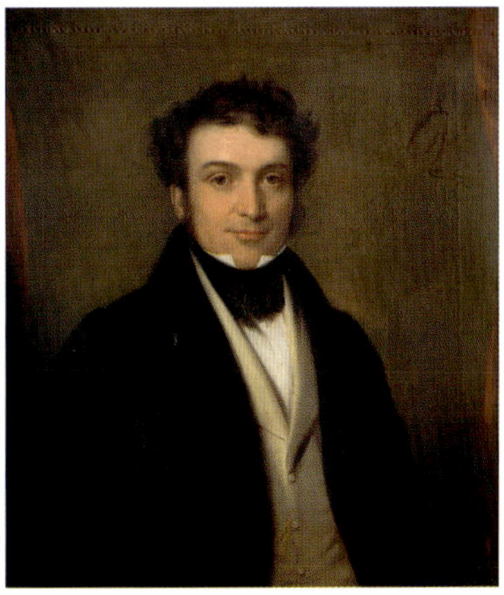

unknown artist
Alderman Thomas Sidney (1805–1889)
oil on canvas 74 x 62
PCF5

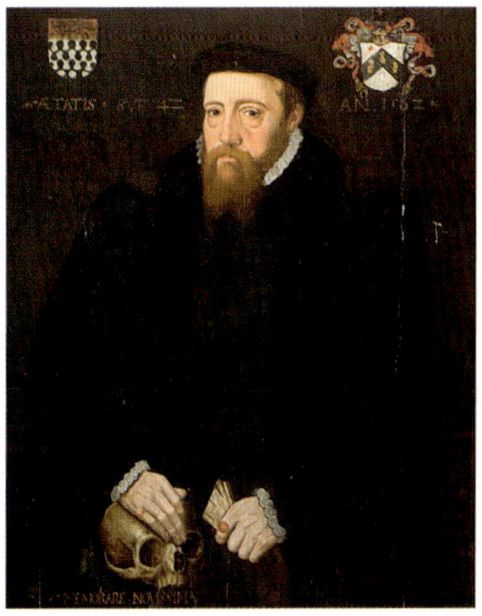

unknown artist
Matthew Craddock (1520–1592)
oil on board 76.5 x 62.5
PCF1

Facing page: Buss, Robert William, 1804–1875, *The Mock Mayor* (detail), 1844, Borough Museum & Art Gallery, (p. 29)

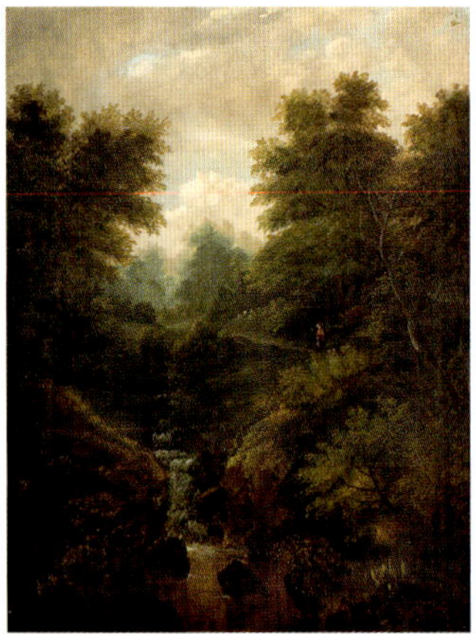

unknown artist
Woodland Landscape
oil on canvas 90 x 70
PCF6

Staffordshire Arts and Museums Service

Staffordshire County Council's fine and decorative art collections have been acquired over the past 70 years. The fine art collection now contains over 700 prints, drawings, watercolours, maps and oil paintings. These reflect the landmarks, landscape and people of Staffordshire, and include locally and nationally known artists. In addition there are around 300 items in the decorative art collection, which is particularly strong in the field of contemporary craft jewellery.

Many of the works in oil were collected by Stafford Museum & Art Gallery, which originally opened as the Wragge Museum in 1878. By 1934 Stafford Museum had moved to purpose-built premises at The Green and had a dedicated art gallery. The collections were eventually transferred from the care of Stafford Borough Council to Staffordshire County Council in the 1980s. In 1992 the Art Gallery was relocated to the Shire Hall in the centre of the town, where it remains today. Meanwhile, the County Council had opened the Staffordshire County Museum in 1964, using the former servants' block at Shugborough Hall, just outside Stafford. Although it did not specifically develop an art collection, the County Museum acquired a number of oil paintings, including portraits of Staffordshire families and livestock paintings, as part of its social and agricultural history collections. These include portraits of the Whitby family, owners of the Shugborough Estate in the early seventeenth century, and of the Joule family, a brewing dynasty from Stone. This background is reflected in the nature of the oil paintings held by Staffordshire Arts & Museum Service. Typically, for a local authority collection, there are portraits of civic dignitaries, Members of Parliament and Justices of the Peace. There are also a large number of works by amateur artists of local landmarks and views. These are often of limited artistic merit but enormous local and social historical value.

Of the local artists represented in the collections, a few are worth mentioning in more detail. Thomas Peploe Wood (1817–1845) was born in Great Haywood, Staffordshire and was a prolific watercolourist and draftsman. A large number of watercolours of Staffordshire buildings were commissioned from him by the antiquarian William Salt, which now form an important part of the Staffordshire Views Collection held at the William Salt Library in Stafford. As well as a large number of preparatory sketches, Staffordshire Arts and Museum Service is fortunate to hold a number of his relatively rare oils, including the genre pieces *Cattle Piece* and *Gypsy Scene*, in addition to two views of the landscape around Ilam in the north of the county.

John Prescott Knight (1803–1881) was born in Stafford, the son of Edward Knight Prescott, an actor. He was well known as a painter of portraits and genre scenes and although now relatively obscure, is the only Stafford-born artist with a national reputation. The Collection contains a number of portraits of his family, as well as one of his genre pieces, *Smugglers Alarmed*.

Believed to have been born in Stafford in 1750, Michael Keeling (d.1820) was an accomplished portrait painter and is represented by three portraits, including one of his last commissions, a portrait of William Horton, founder of Stafford's shoe trade.

Mabel Frances Layng (1881–1937) although born in Macclesfield, Cheshire, was brought up in Stafford, where her father was headmaster of King Edward VI Grammar School between 1884 and 1901. She was a pupil of Sir Frank Brangwyn and is represented here by one work in oils, *The Omnibus*. Staffordshire Arts and Museum Service also cares for 16 watercolours by this obscure artist, who deserves to be better known.

Since the 1980s, selective acquisition of new work has continued, focusing on contemporary work by artists who are associated with Staffordshire, and additional works by local artists already represented. A series of public art commissions using the County Museum's social history collection as inspiration has been particularly fruitful, most notably Lisa Milroy's series of charcoal drawings and oil paintings of Stafford-made shoes. Other contemporary artists represented by works in oil or acrylic include Brendan Neiland, Peter Markey and David Gleeson.

Although the Shire Hall Gallery in Stafford is a temporary exhibition venue and does not have permanent gallery space, the County Art Collection is featured in at least one exhibition a year, and many works are integrated in the permanent display spaces at the County Museum, Servants' Quarters and Park Farm on the Shugborough Estate. The Public Catalogue Foundation has provided a wonderful opportunity to make our paintings more widely known, and we are pleased to have had a chance to be involved in this worthwhile project.

Chris Copp, Museums Officer

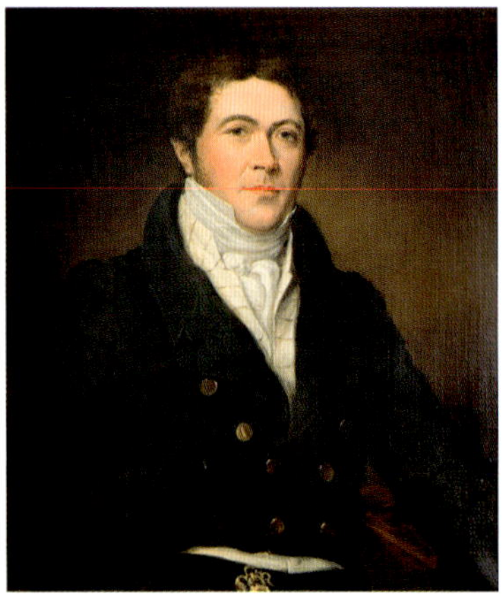

Arrowsmith, Thomas 1772–c.1829
John Joule (1783–1858) 1825
oil on canvas 76 x 63.5
STFMS : 74.014.0003

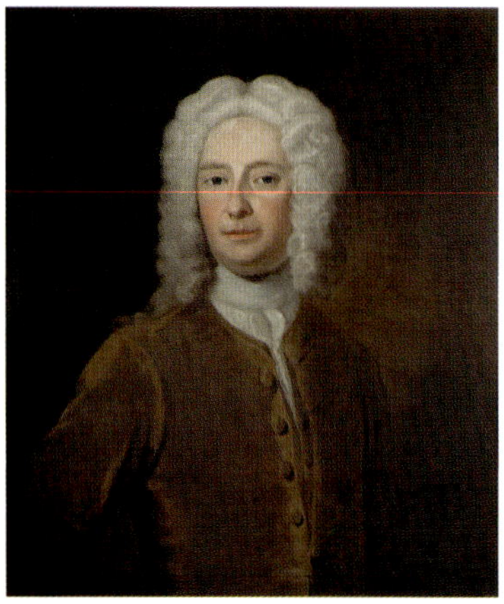

Bardwell, Thomas 1704–1767
A Member of the Whitby Family 1750s
oil on canvas 95.7 x 83.6
STFMS : 65.038.0005

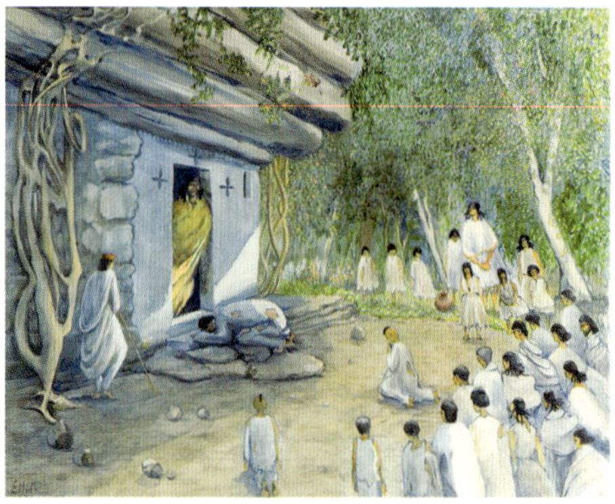

Barnardo, Eilidh 1911–1994
On a Journey, 1968–1969 c.1969
oil on canvas 63.5 x 76
STFMS : G98.003.0003

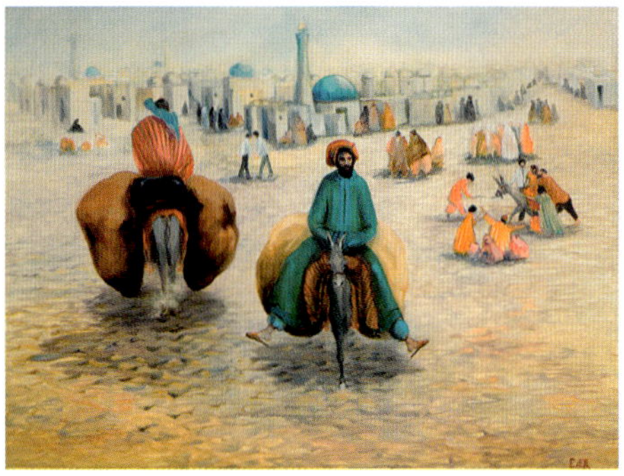

Barnardo, Eilidh 1911–1994
Ride into Khiva, Turkmenistan, Eastern USSR c.1970
oil on canvas 51 x 66
STFMS : G98.003.0005

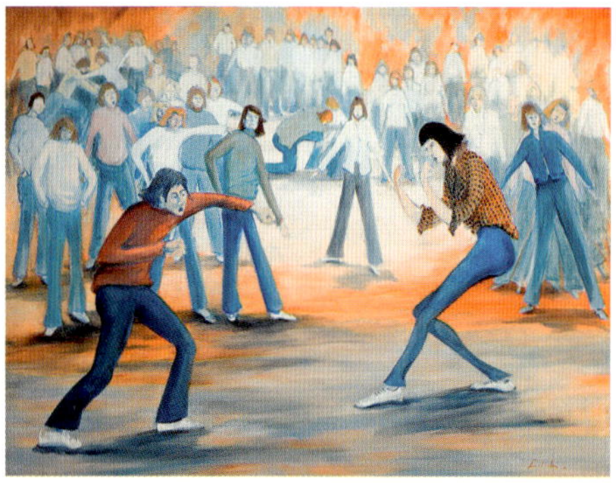

Barnardo, Eilidh 1911–1994
Spoiling for a Fight c.1986
oil on canvas 101 x 127
STFM : G98.003.0001

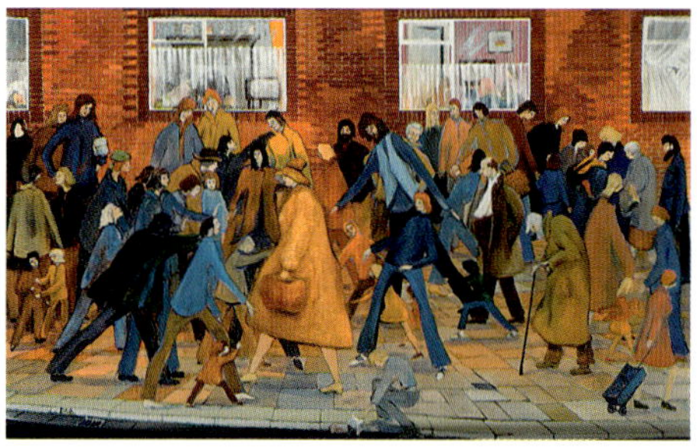

Barnardo, Eilidh 1911–1994
Crowded Pavement c.1990
oil on canvas 74 x 106
STFMS : G98.003.0004

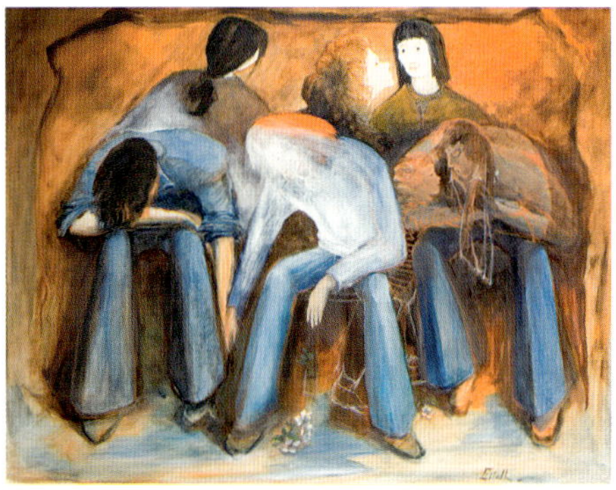

Barnardo, Eilidh 1911–1994
Youthful Despair No.2 c.1990
oil on canvas 101.5 x 126.5
STFMS : G98.003.0002

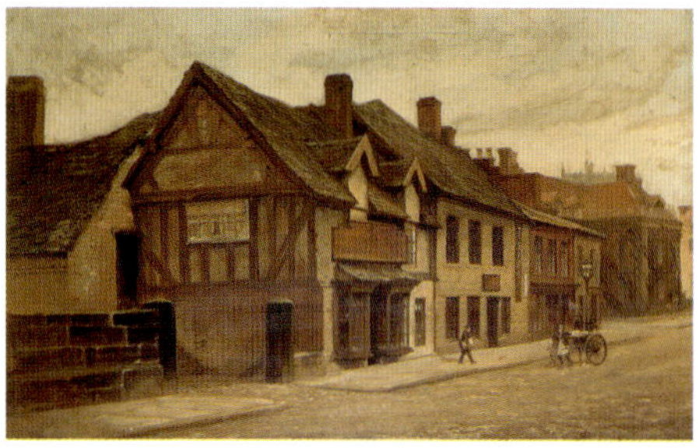

Bracewell, J. H.
Greengate Street from the Bridge and the Old Pork Pie Shop c.1900
oil on canvas 29.5 x 44.5
STFMS : G94.163.0001

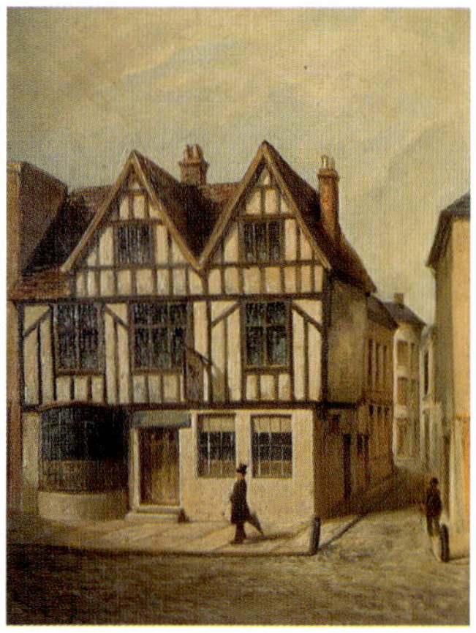

Bracewell, J. H.
The Roebuck Inn, Stafford c.1900
oil on canvas 29 x 22
STFMS : G94.133.0001

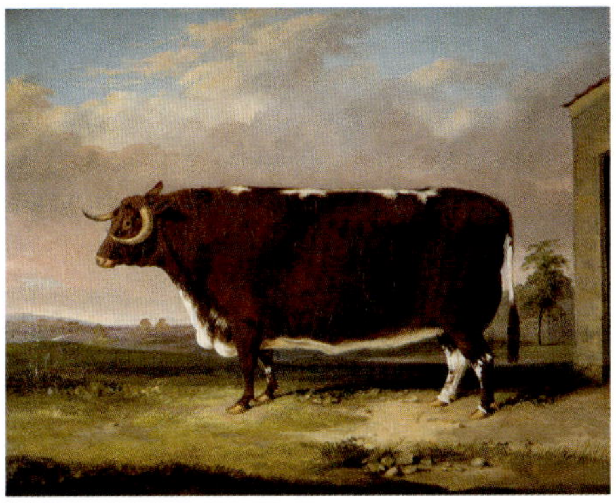

Bretland, Thomas W. 1802–1874
Longhorn Cow 1864
oil on canvas 61.5 x 75
STFMS : 95.050.0003

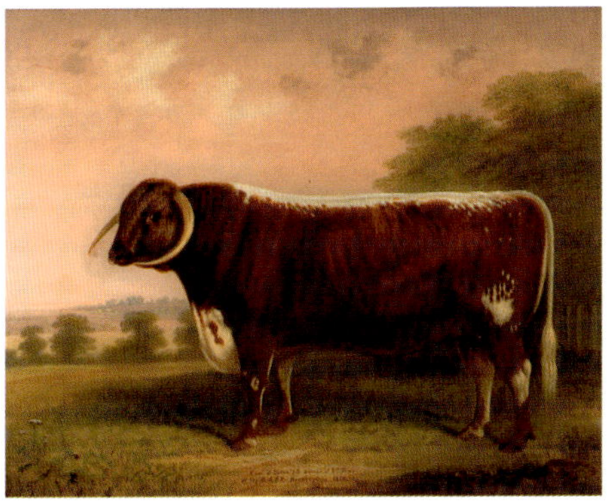

Brown, Edward 1823–1877
'Earl of Upton' 1876
oil on canvas 50 x 70 (E)
STFMS : 95.050.0001

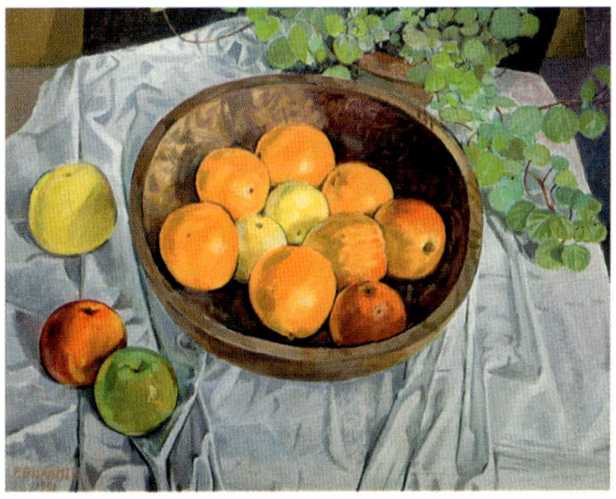

Burnhill, Peter b.c.1930
Wooden Bowl with Fruit 1991
oil on canvas 46.5 x 56.7
STFMS : G92.001.0001

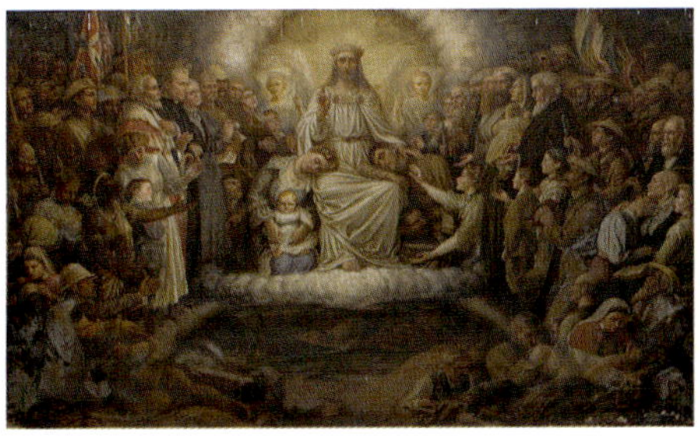

Camm, Thomas William 1839–1912
Christus Consolator 1901–1912
oil on canvas 244 x 305
STFMS : 65.083.0001

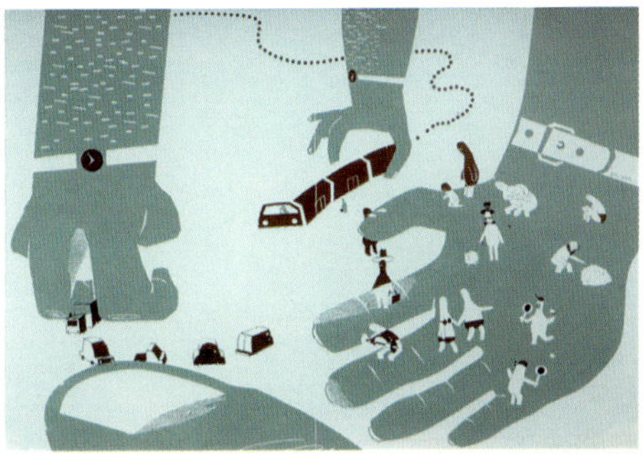

Carter, Graham b.1975
Lovely Big Hands 2005
acrylic on silkscreen print 38.2 x 53.8
STFMS : G2005.005.0004

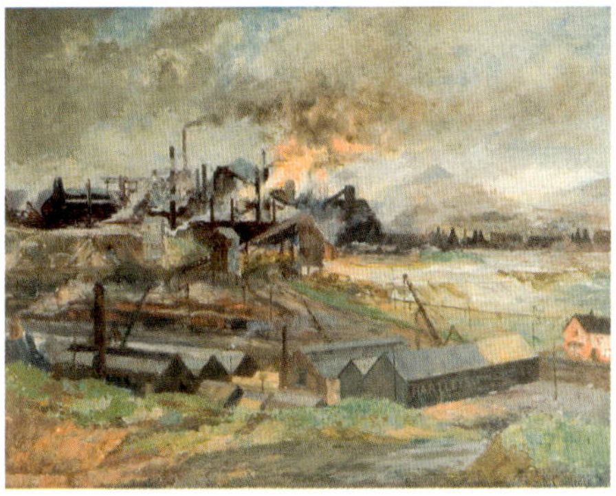

Cartledge, William 1891–1976
Shelton Bar and Messrs Josiah Wedgwood and Sons Ltd 1949
oil on canvas 61 x 74
STFMS : G95.021.0001

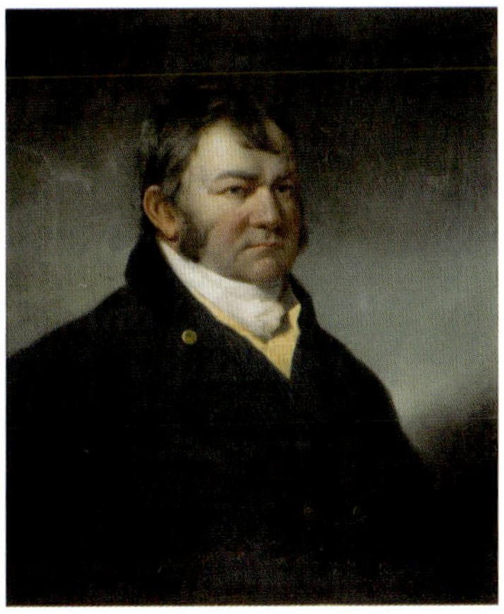

Chandler, John Westbrooke
1764–1804/1805
William Horton (1750–1832) 1803–1804
oil on canvas 73.5 x 60
STFMS : G94.137.0001

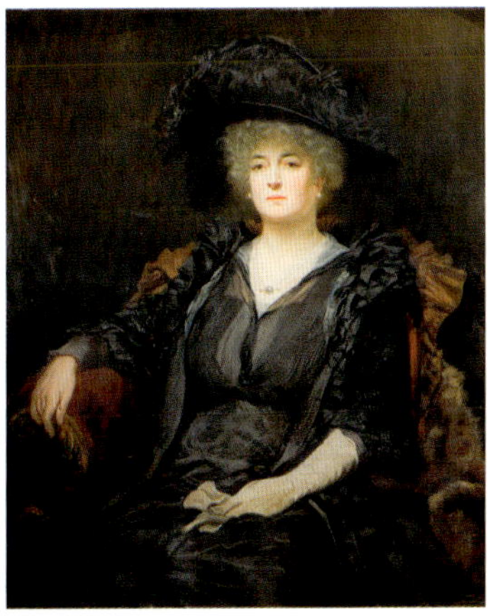

Charlton, John 1849–1917
Florence Parker-Jervis (d.1938) 1915
oil on canvas 120 x 90
STFMS : 66.082.0001

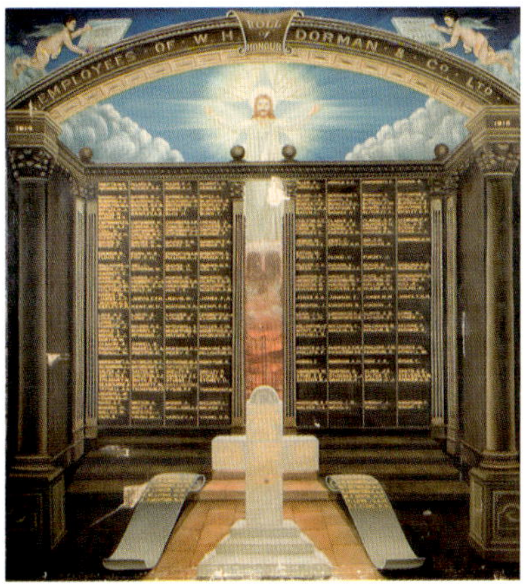

Clewlow, Harry active 1919–1939
Roll of Honour for W. H. Dorman, 1914–1918 c.1919
oil on canvas 147 x 131
STFMS : 2002.013.002

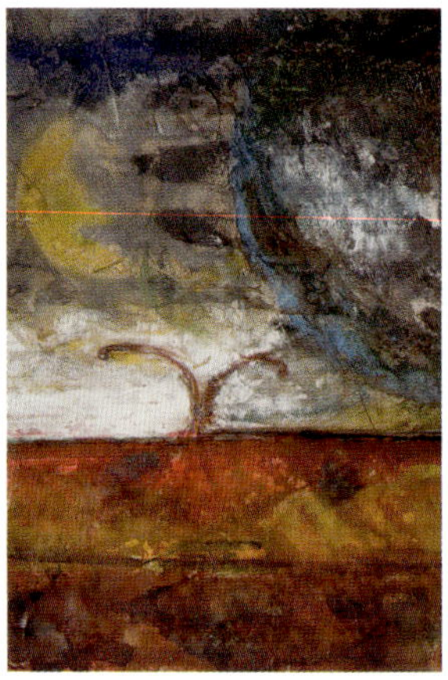

Cooper, Lucien b.c.1960
Primary 1991
acrylic & tempera on paper 64 x 54
STFMS : G94.003.0001

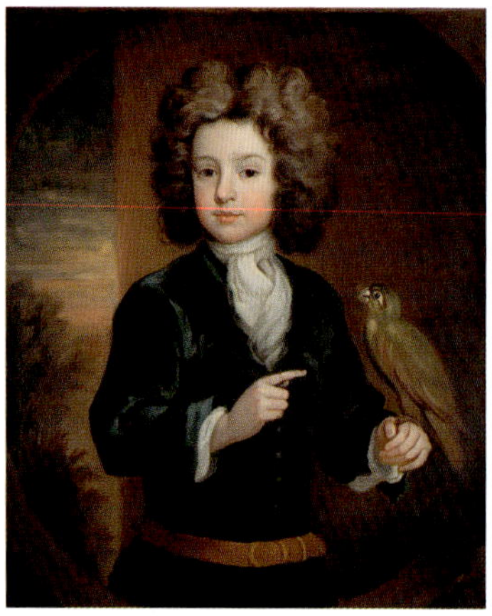

Dahl, Michael I 1656/1659–1743
Thomas Whitby
oil on canvas 94 x 80.7
STFMS : 65.038.0004

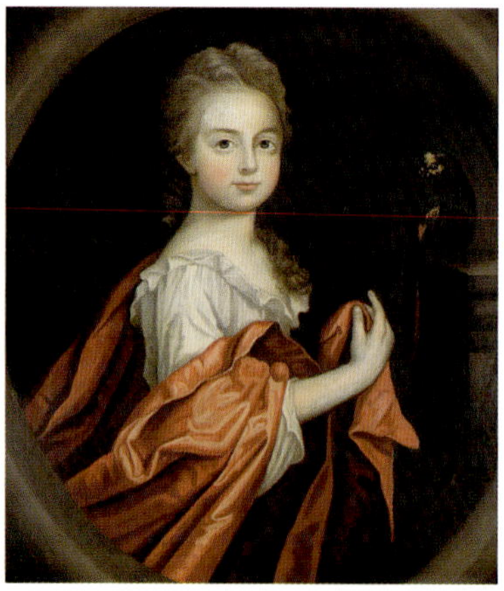

Dahl, Michael I 1656/1659–1743
Thomas Whitby's Sister
oil on canvas 93.2 x 81.5
STFMS : 65.038.0003

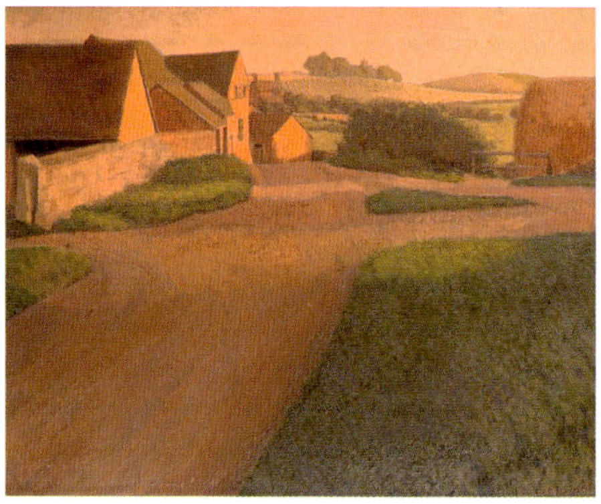

Davies, E. J.
St Thomas's Farm, near Stafford c.1950
oil on canvas 56.8 x 67
STFMS : G95.011.0001

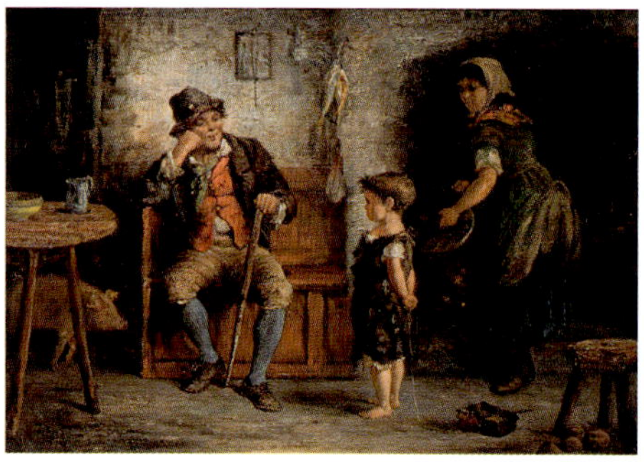

Drummond, Julian 1824–1906
Cottage Interior 1879
oil on canvas 49.5 x 67.3
STFMS : G95.183.0001

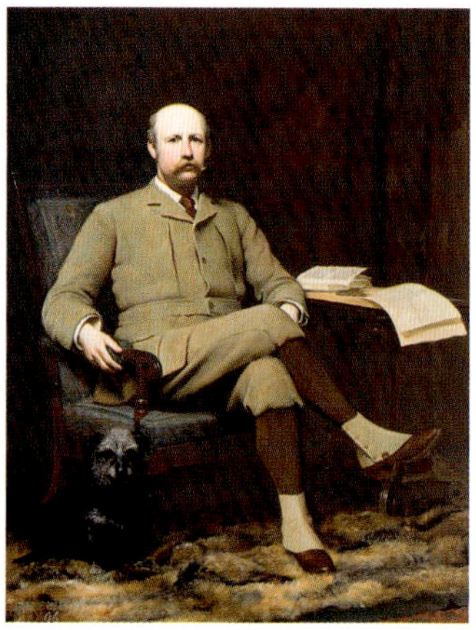

Dutton, John Frederick Harrison
active 1890–1918
Mr E. R. Twemlow 1896
oil on canvas 217 x 172
STFMS : 68.102.0001

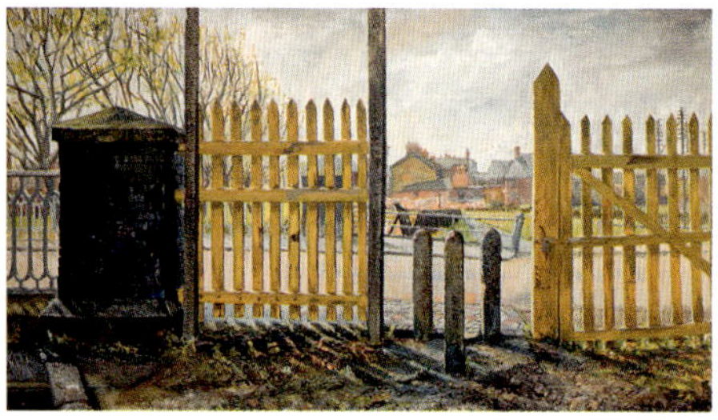

Dutton, Martin J.
Stafford Landscape c.1955
oil on board 41.5 x 70
STFMS : G94.156.0001

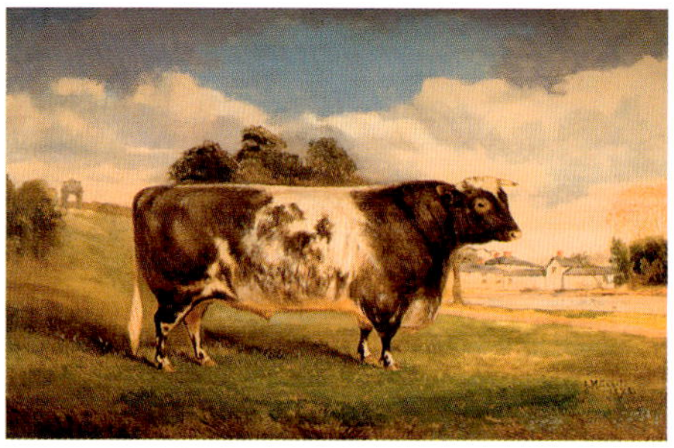

Gauci, A. M. active 1848–1884
'Sir Arthur' 1873
oil on canvas 50 x 68
STFMS : 88.089.0001

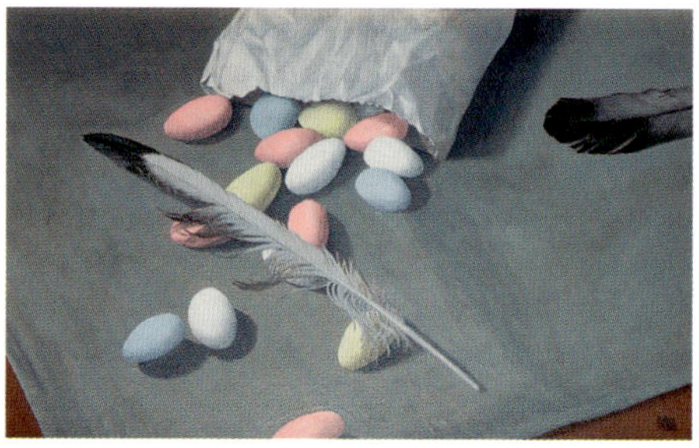

Gleeson, David Paul b.1956
Feathers and Sugared Almonds 1986
acrylic on board 32 x 42.5
STFMS : G94.328.0001

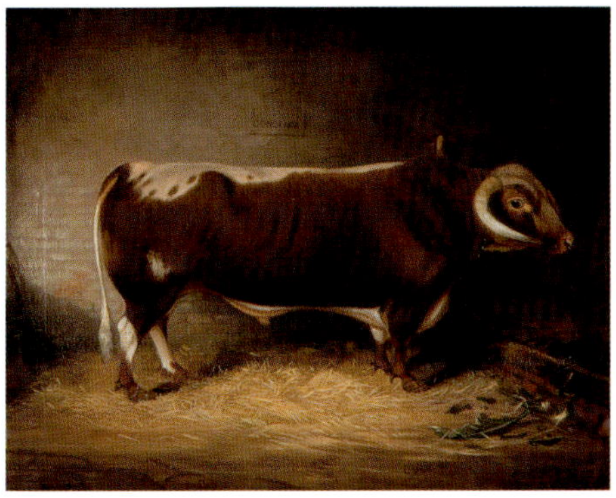

Gregory, G. active 1836–1848
'Conqueror' 1848
oil on canvas 61.5 x 75
STFMS : 95.050.0002

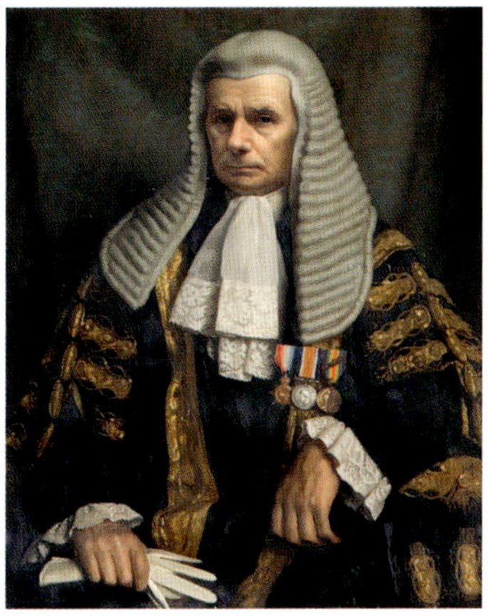

Halliday, Edward Irvine 1902–1984
Lord Justice Wrottesley 1950
oil on canvas 104 x 70
SHG.Ct1.1

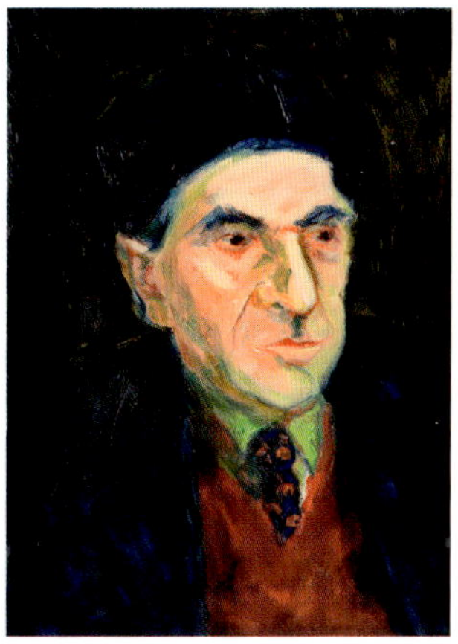

Held, Julie b.1958
Portrait of a Man 1997
oil on canvas 43 x 30
STFMS : G98.001.0001

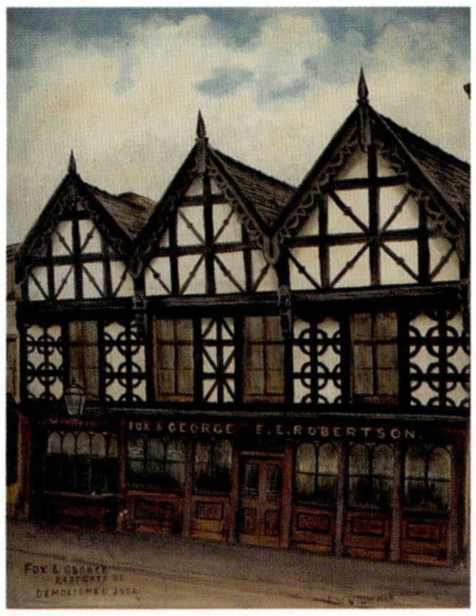

Hickman, F. W.
Fox and George, Eastgate Street, Stafford, Demolished 1904 c.1904
oil on board 44.3 x 34
STFMS : G95.012.0001

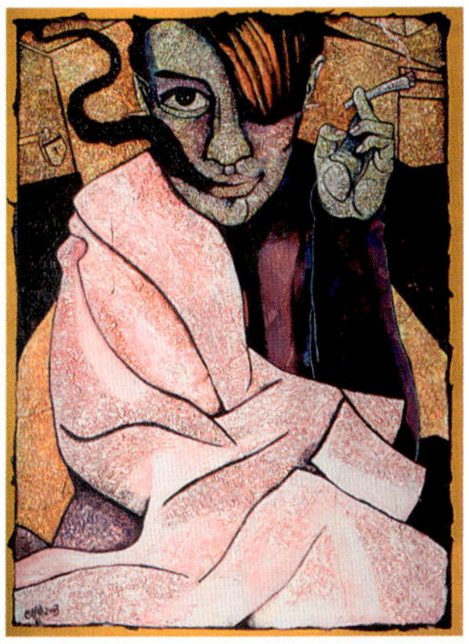

Hill, Paul b.1959
Whacky Backy 2003
acrylic on board 85 x 59
STFMS : G2004.001.0001

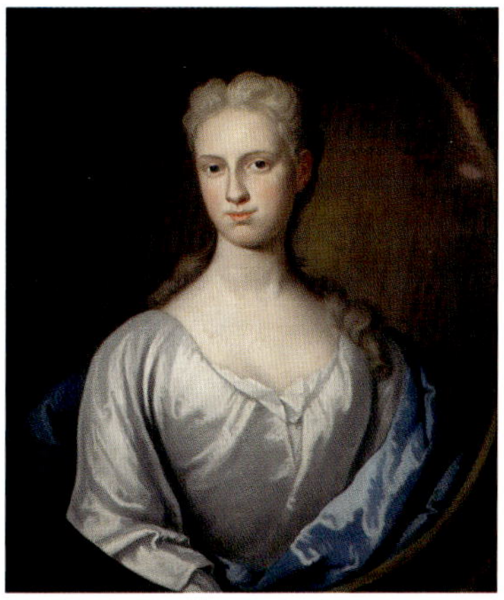

Hudson, Thomas 1701–1779
Mrs R. Whitby 1750s
oil on canvas 96.3 x 83.4
STFMS : 65.038.0001

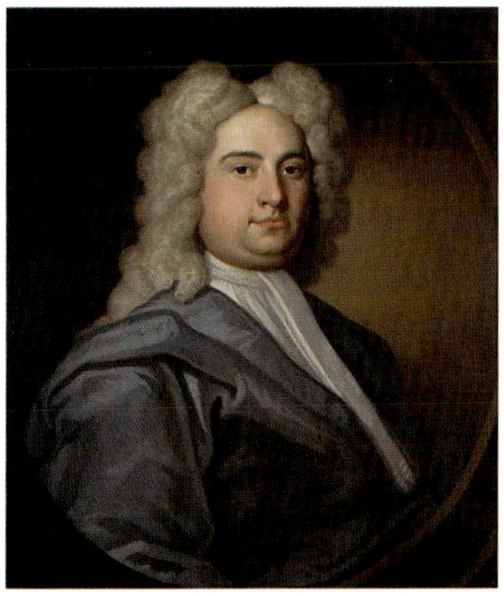

Hudson, Thomas 1701–1779
Richard Whitby 1750s
oil on canvas 95.1 x 82.5
STFMS : 65.038.0002

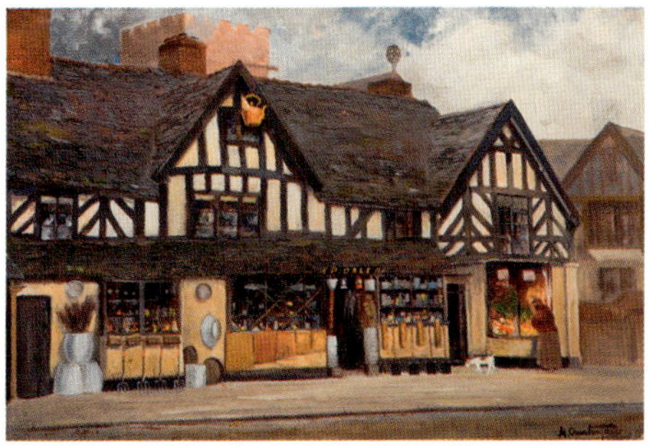

Jones, Horace Overton active 1894–1924
Dale's Shop, Stafford 1917
oil on canvas 35 x 49.5
STFMS : G94.146.0001

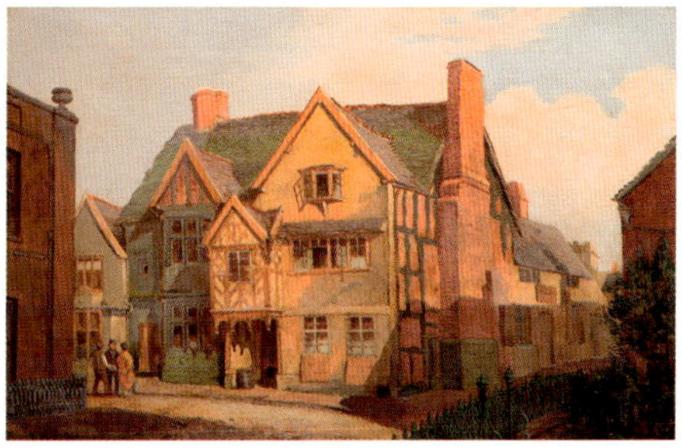

Jones, T. W.
The Noah's Ark Inn, Crabbery Street, Stafford c.1900
oil on canvas 36 x 53.8
STFMS : G94.130.0001

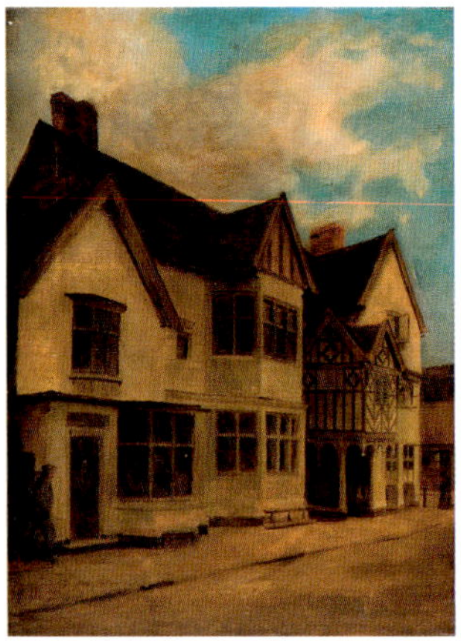

Jones, T. W.
The Noah's Ark Inn, Crabbery Street, Stafford c.1900
oil on canvas 35 x 24
STFMS : G94.131.0001

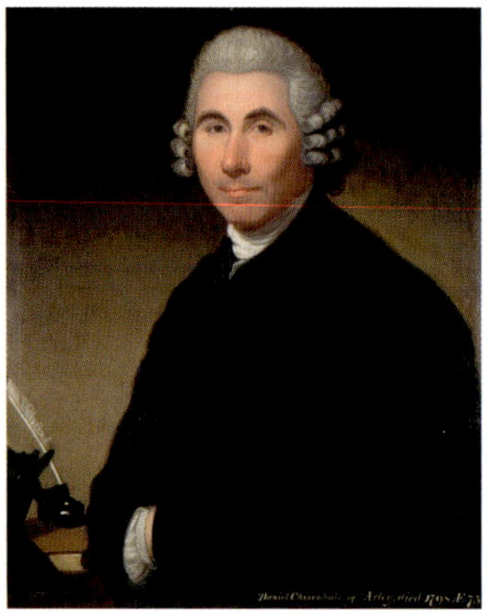

Keeling, Michael 1750–1820
Daniel Chisenhale of Arley (1725–1798) 1774
oil on canvas 74 x 63
STFMS : G94.138.0001

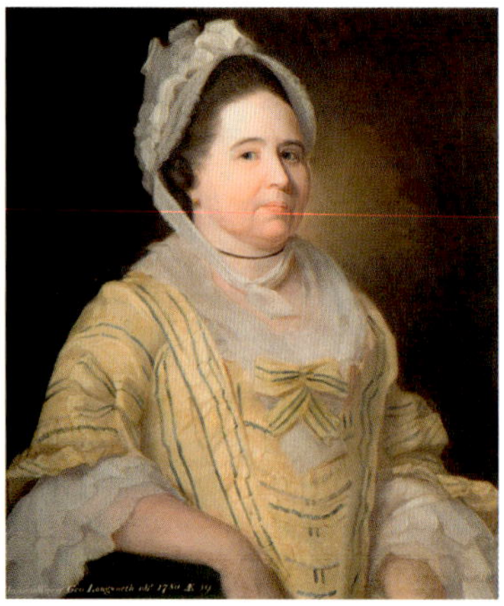

Keeling, Michael 1750–1820
Hannah Longworth (1721–1780) 1774
oil on canvas 76 x 61
STFMS : G95.025.0001

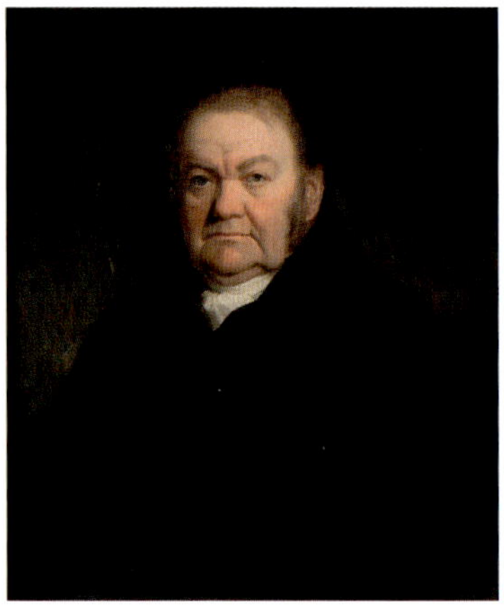

Keeling, Michael 1750–1820
William Horton (1750–1832) 1820
oil on canvas 74 x 61
STFMS : G95.029.0001

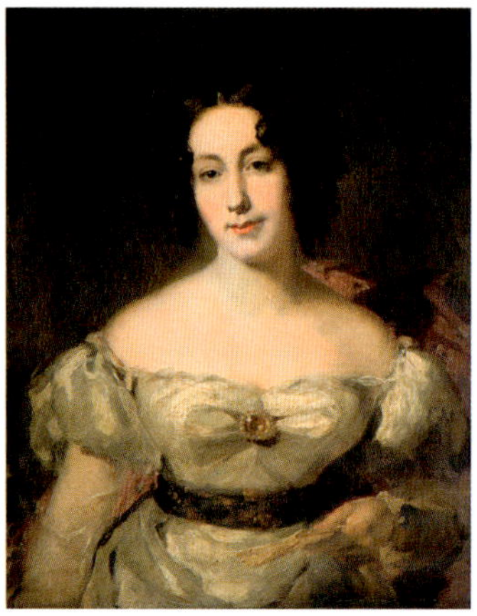

Knight, John Prescott 1803–1881
Clarissa Isabella Hague (1798/1799–1869) 1825–1830
oil on canvas 74 x 57.5
STFMS : G94.139.0001

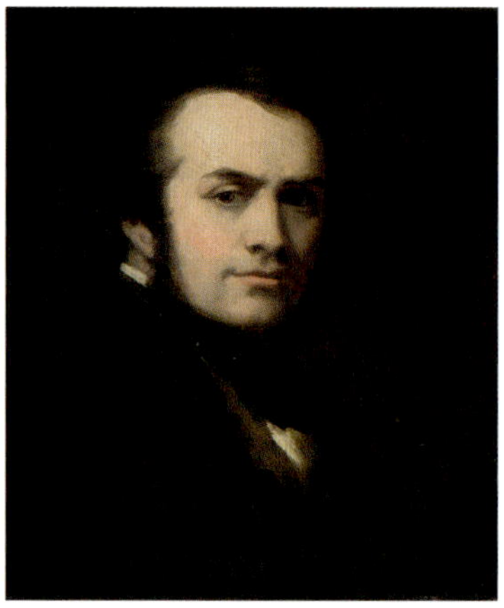

Knight, John Prescott 1803–1881
Self Portrait in a Brown Study c.1829
oil on canvas 55 x 45.5
STFMS : G94.143.0001

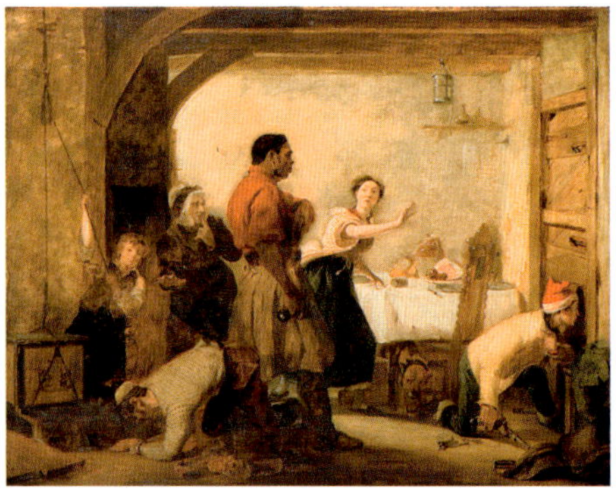

Knight, John Prescott 1803–1881
Smugglers Alarmed c.1830
oil on canvas 60 x 75
STFMS : G94.142.0001

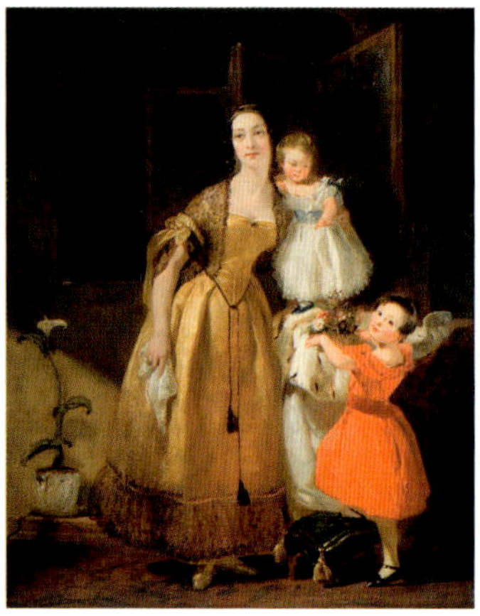

Knight, John Prescott 1803–1881
Mrs John Prescott Knight and Her Children c.1837
oil on canvas 91 x 70.5
STFMS : G95.024.0001

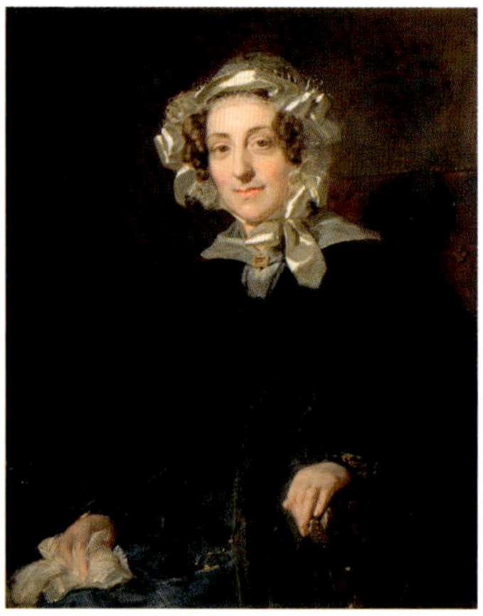

Knight, John Prescott 1803–1881
Portrait of a Lady 1838–1840
oil on canvas 90 x 70
STFMS : G95.023.0001

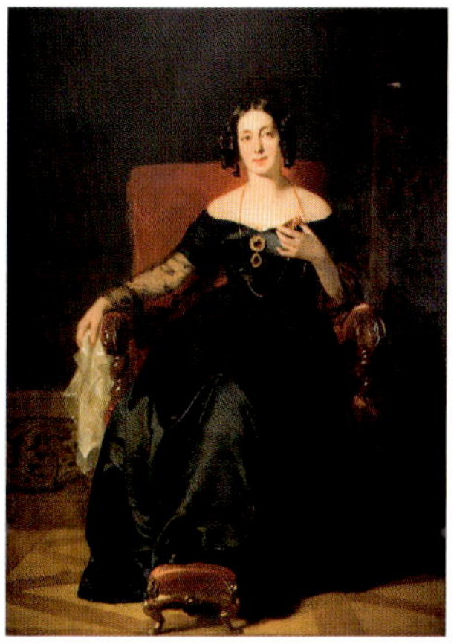

Knight, John Prescott 1803–1881
Clarissa Isabella Knight (1798/1799–1869)
1842–1843
oil on canvas 169 x 121
STFMS : G97.009.0001

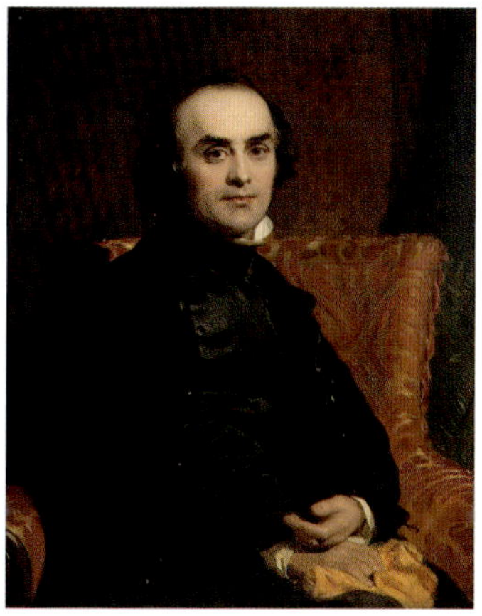

Knight, John Prescott 1803–1881
Self Portrait 1844–1845
oil on canvas 88.5 x 69
STFMS : G95.030.0001

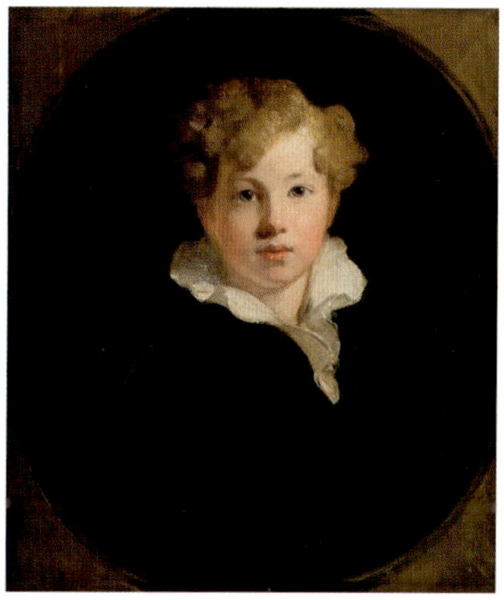

Knight, John Prescott 1803–1881
Miles Julian Prescott Knight (1835–1871)
c.1845
oil on canvas 59 x 49
STFMS : G94.140.0001

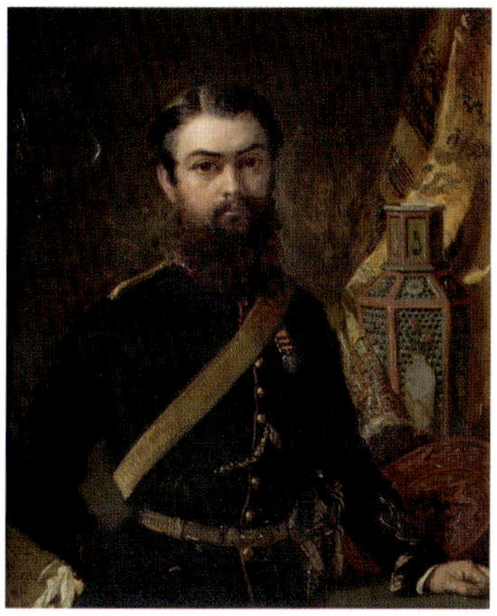

Knight, John Prescott 1803–1881
A. S. Prescott (1832–1917) 1861
oil on canvas 59.5 x 47.5
STFMS : G94.144.0001

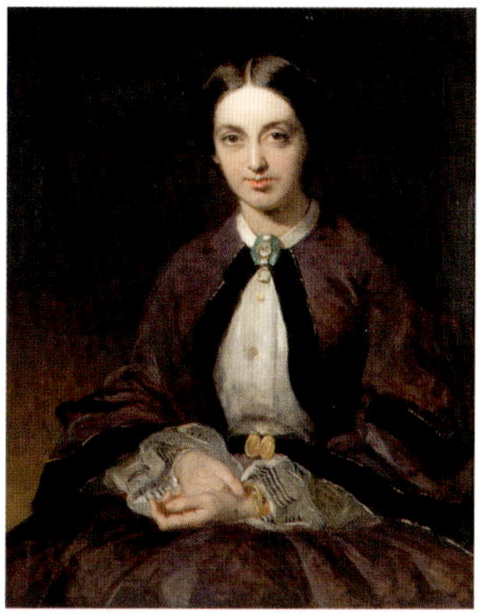

Knight, John Prescott 1803–1881
Clare (Miss Clara) (1838–1869) 1861–1863
oil on canvas 92.5 x 71
STFMS : G94.141.0001

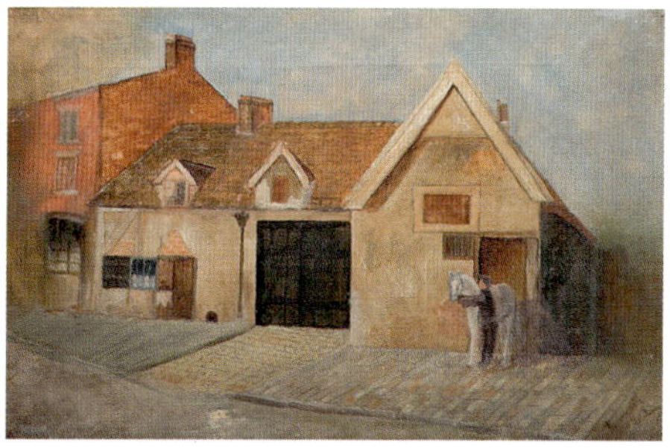

Lawton, G.
Izaak Walton's Birthplace, Stafford 1903
oil on canvas 20.6 x 30.5
STFMS : 86.024.0417

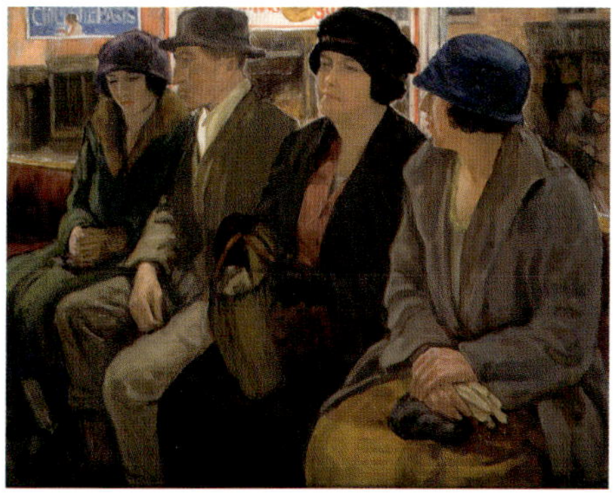

Layng, Mabel Frances 1881–1937
The Omnibus 1920s
oil on canvas 62.5 x 75
STFMS : G94.052.0001

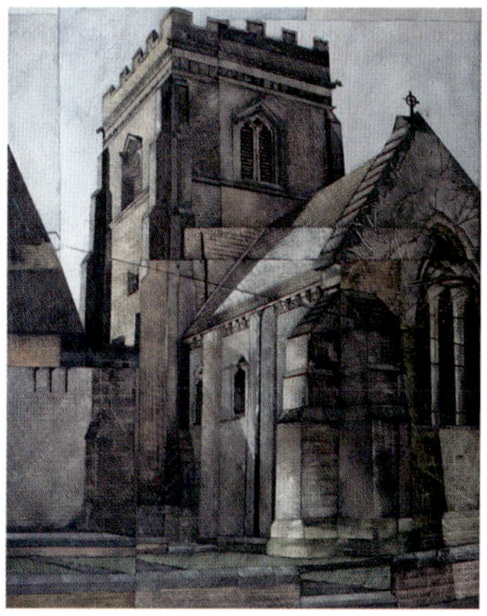

Lippett, Mark b.1975
Spring Sun 2004
acrylic on board 92 x 75
STFMS : G2004.004.0001

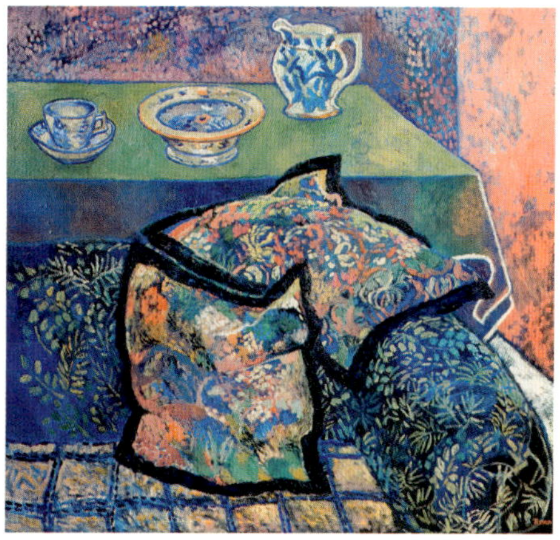

Lord, Tessa
Jug and Cushions 1992
oil on canvas 89 x 90
STFMS : G94.005.0001

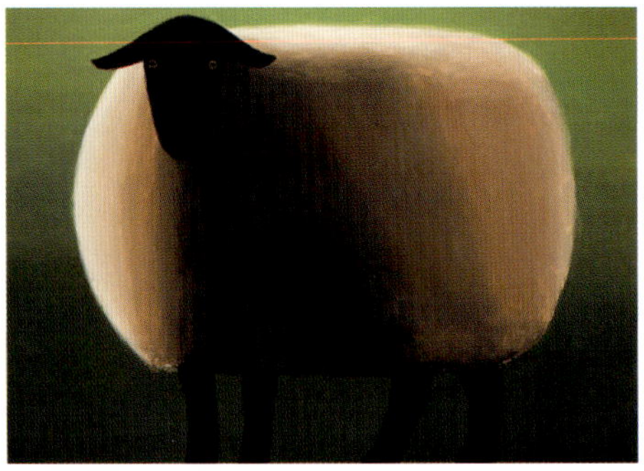

Markey, Peter b.1930
Black-Faced Sheep 1991
oil on board 90 x 120
STFMS : G94.026.0001

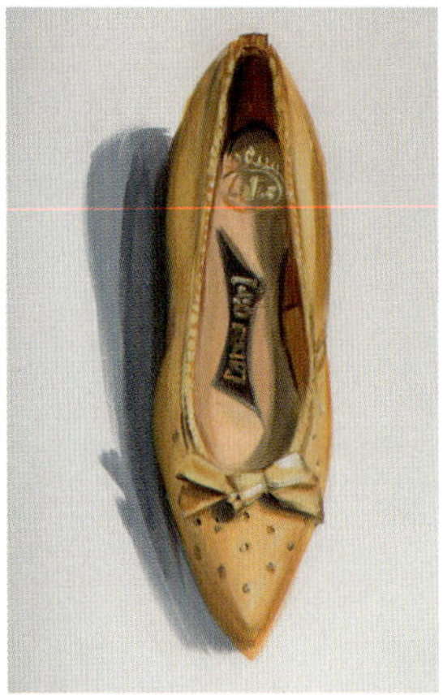

Milroy, Lisa b.1959
Lotus 'Career Girl' Shoe 2002
oil on canvas 57.9 x 37.4
STFMS : G2002.003.0005

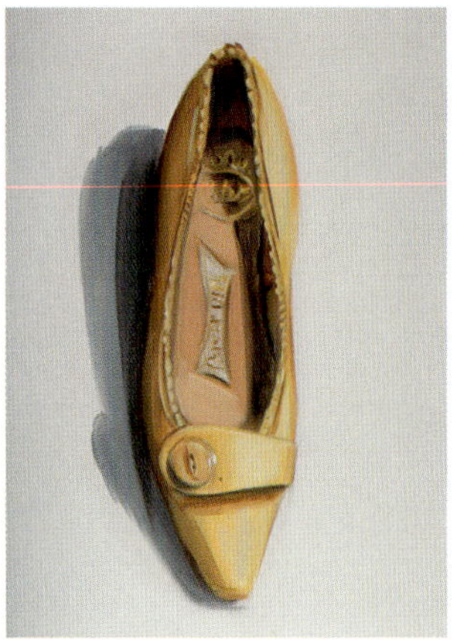

Milroy, Lisa b.1959
Lotus 'Career Girl‘ Shoe 2002
oil on canvas 59 x 41.2
STFMS : G2002.003.0009

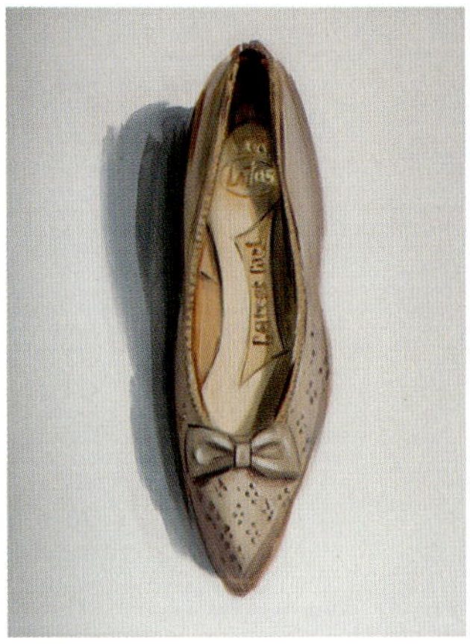

Milroy, Lisa b.1959
Lotus 'Career Girl' Shoe 2002
oil on canvas 60.5 x 45
STFMS : G2002.003.0011

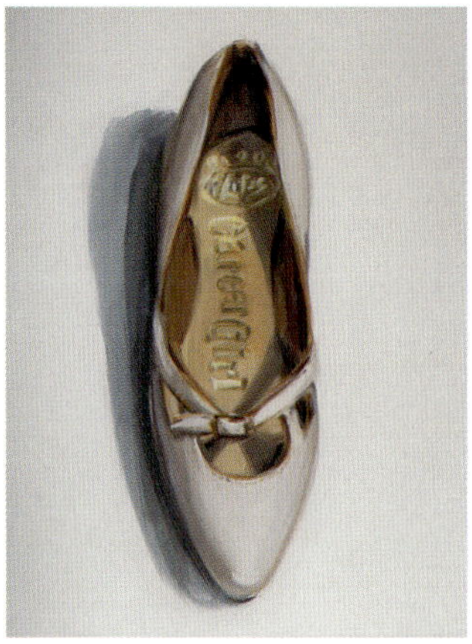

Milroy, Lisa b.1959
Lotus 'Career Girl' Shoe 2002
oil on canvas 57 x 42.5
STFMS : G2002.003.0012

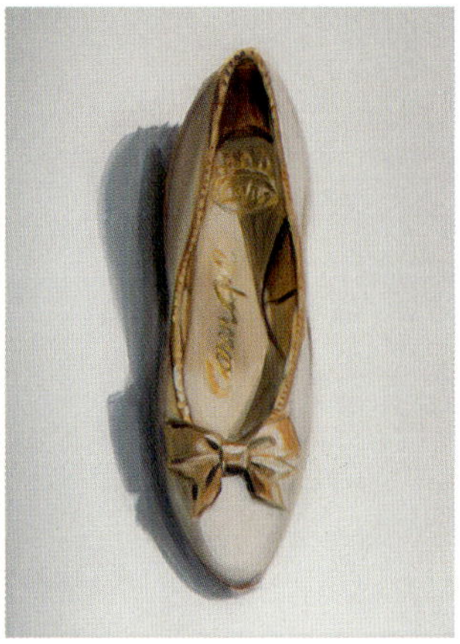

Milroy, Lisa b.1959
Lotus 'Career Girl' Shoe 2002
oil on canvas 59.3 x 43
STFMS : G2002.003.0013

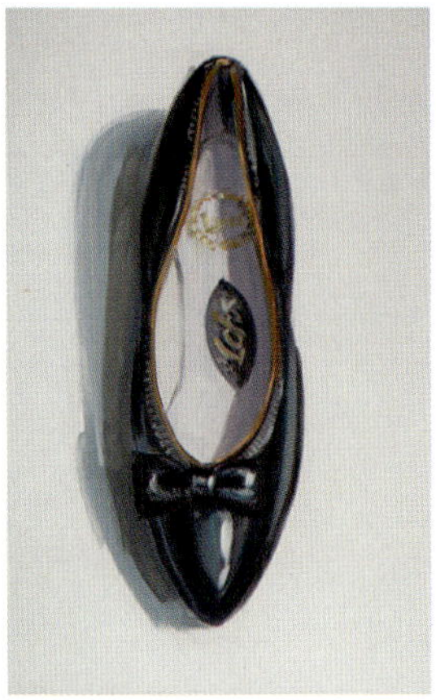

Milroy, Lisa b.1959
Lotus Shoe 2002
oil on canvas 57 x 37
STFMS : G2002.003.0006

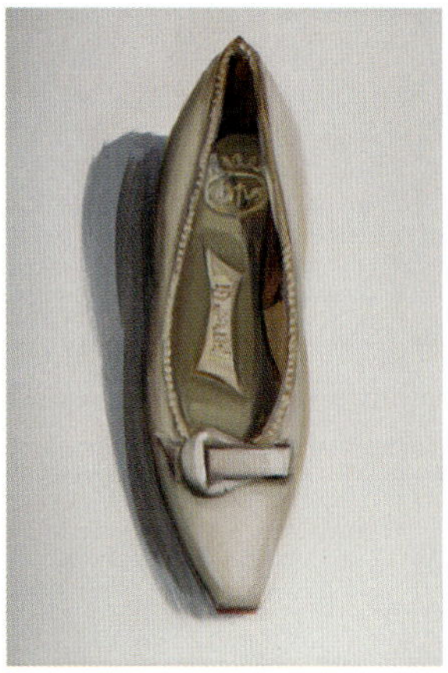

Milroy, Lisa b.1959
Lotus Shoe 2002
oil on canvas 59 x 40.6
STFMS : G2002.003.0007

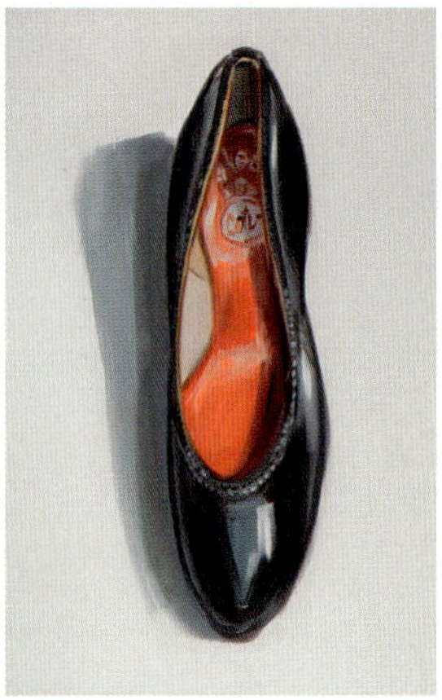

Milroy, Lisa b.1959
Lotus Shoe 2002
oil on canvas 57 x 37
STFMS : G2002.003.0008

Facing page: Currie, John, 1883–1914, *The Supper* (detail), 1912–1914, The Potteries Museum & Art Gallery (p. 117)

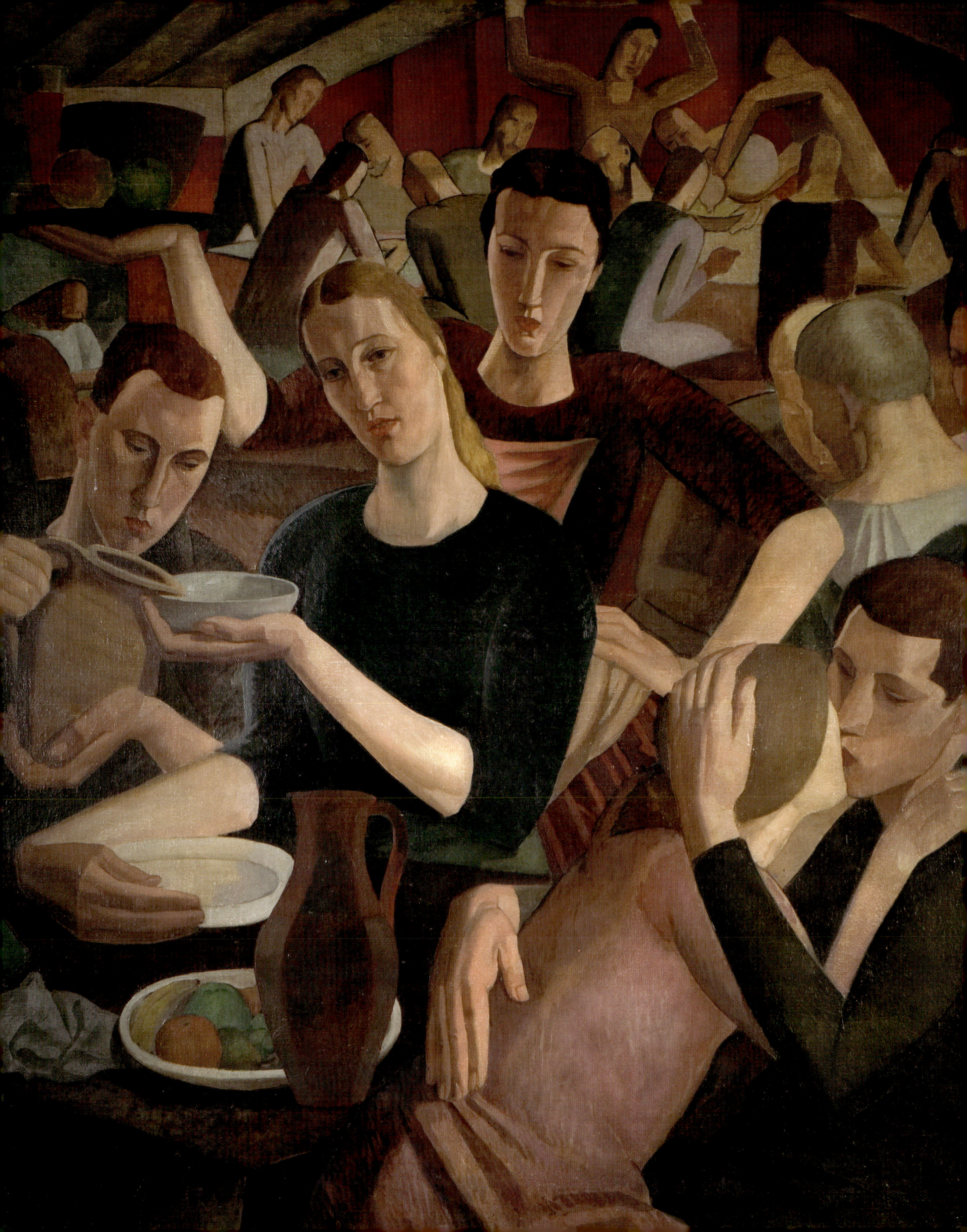

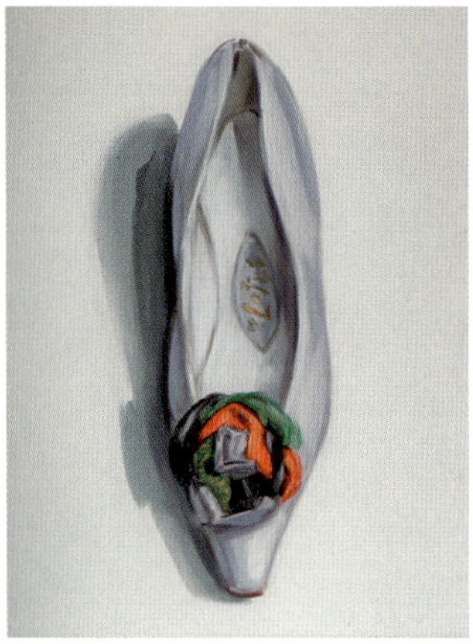

Milroy, Lisa b.1959
Lotus Shoe 2002
oil on canvas 58 x 43.6
STFMS : G2002.003.0010

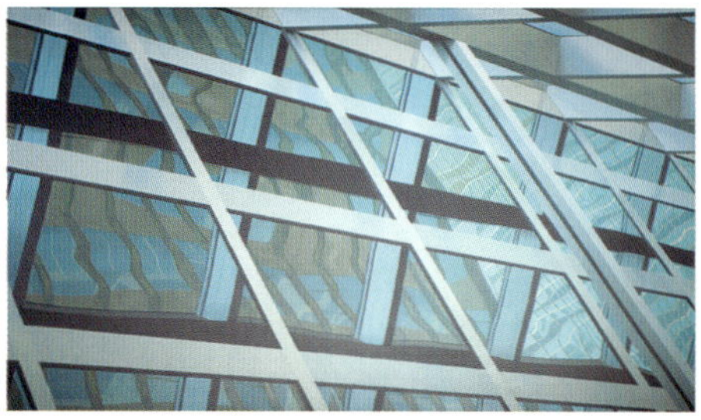

Neiland, Brendan b.1941
Awning 1979
acrylic on canvas 142 x 238
STFMS : G94.050.0001

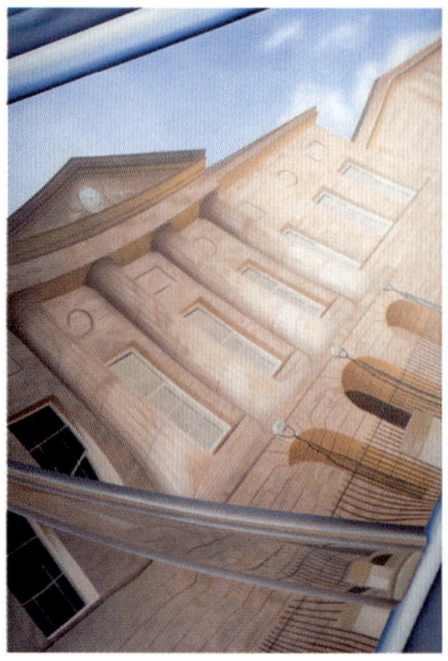

Neiland, Brendan b.1941
Shire Hall 1993
acrylic on canvas 175 x 118
STFMS : G98.003.0001

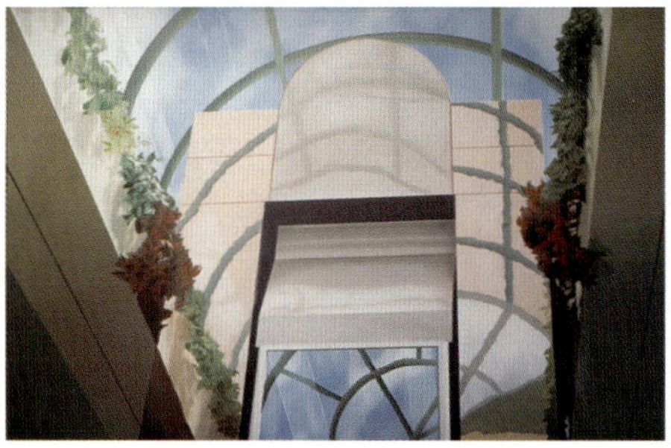

Neiland, Brendan b.1941
Shire Hall Atrium 1993
acrylic on canvas 118 x 175
STFMS : G98.002.0001

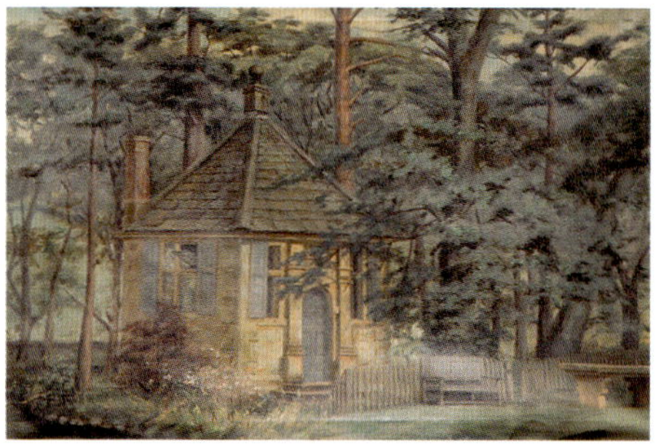

Nuttall, M. P.
Fishing Lodge, Beresford Dale 1905
oil on canvas 39 x 56
STFMS : G97.016.0001

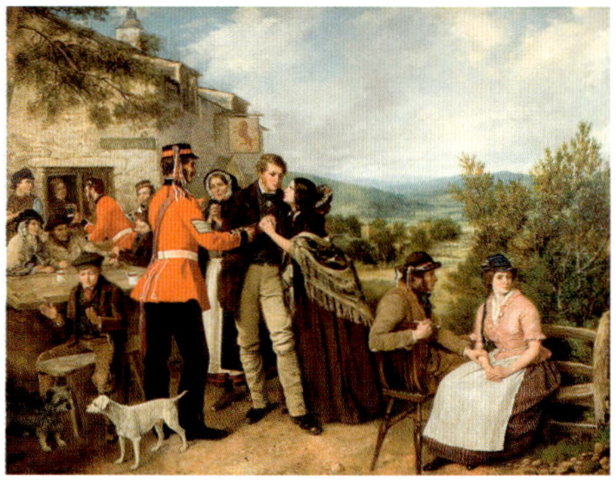

O'Neil, Henry Nelson (attributed to)
1817–1880
The Recruiting Sergeant (The King's Shilling) 1855–1865
oil on canvas 127 x 152.5
STFMS : G94.159.0001

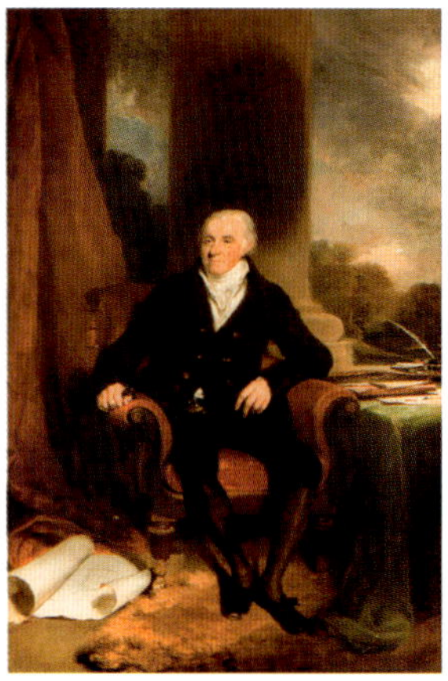

Owen, William 1769–1825
John Sparrow (1736–1821), Chairman of Quarter Sessions (1792–1816) 1800–1820
oil on canvas 190 x 145 (E)
SHG.Ct2.1

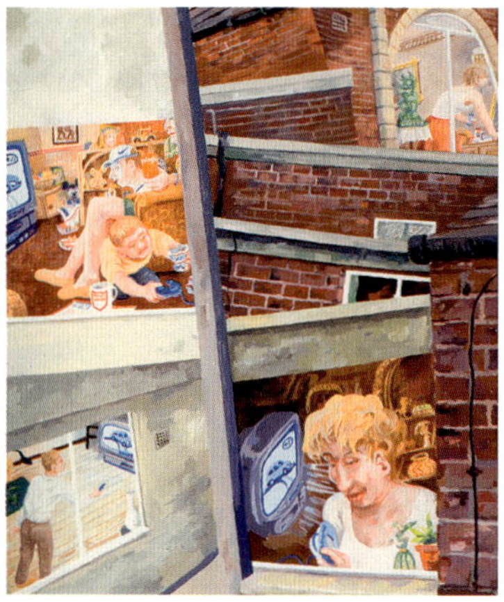

Phillips, Tony b.1952
Homes 2003
acrylic on canvas 71.5 x 59.3
STFMS : G2004.002.0001

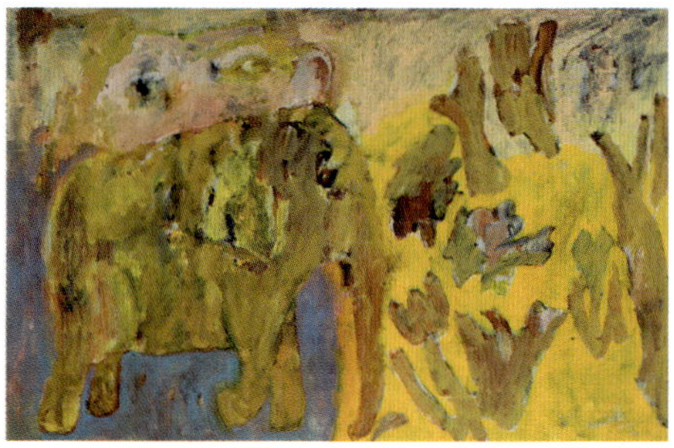

Reed, Graeme John Robert b.1964
Elephant 1993
oil on card 64 x 94
STFMS : G94.009.0001

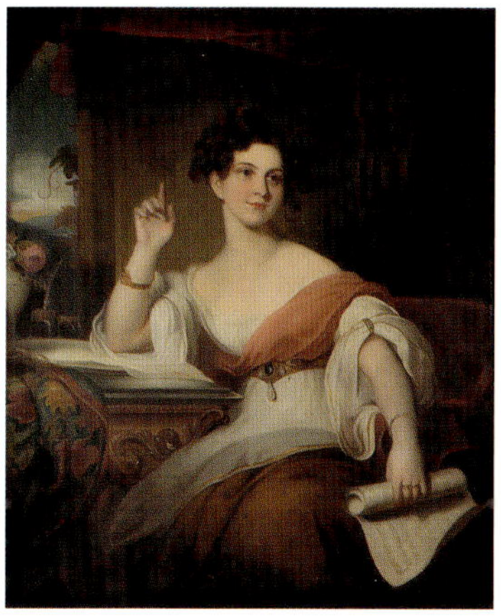

Scott, John 1802–1885
Mary Anne Jervis, Lady Forester (c.1803–1893) 1834
oil on canvas 142.7 x 118.6
STFMS : 66.188.0001

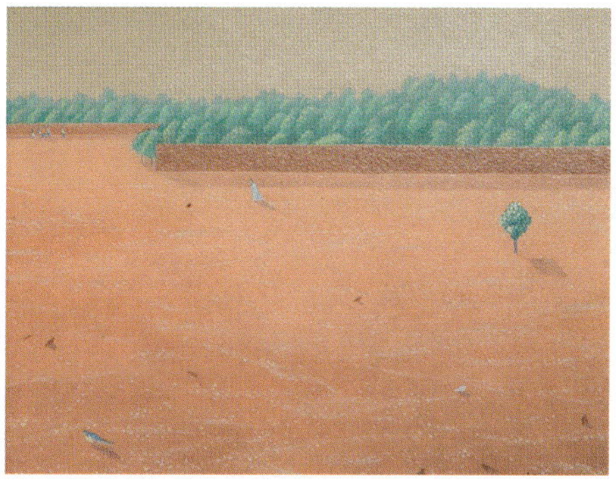

Shaw, David Carson b.1942
Walking in the Heat 1987
oil on board 13 x 16.5
STFMS : G90.002.0001

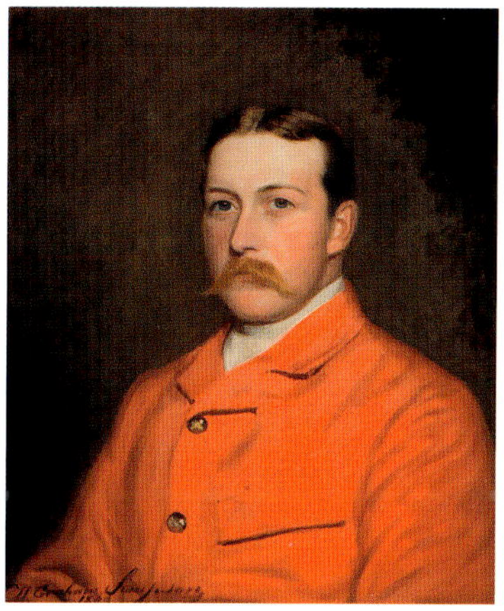

Simpson, W. Graham active 1880–1898
Hubert de Gotham Parker-Jervis (1859–1894) 1880
oil on canvas 75 x 60
STFMS : 66.082.0002

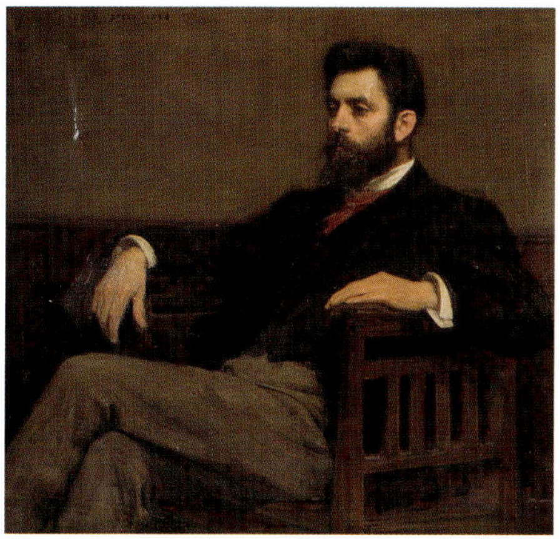

Speed, Harold 1872–1957
Sir Walter Essex (1857–1941) 1896
oil on canvas 99 x 107
STFMS : G97.008.0001

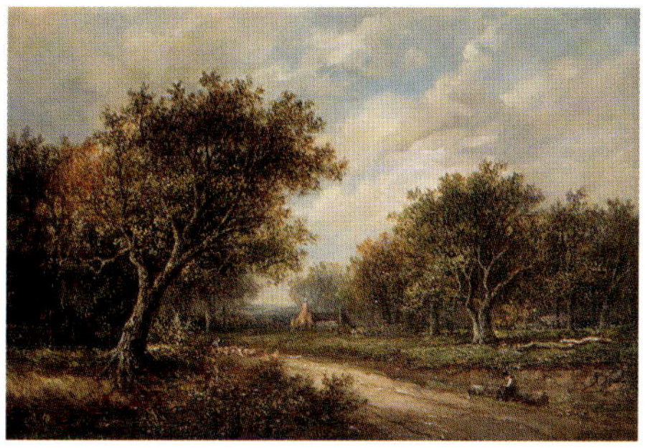

Thors, Joseph c.1834–1898
Road near Warwick c.1870
oil on canvas 25 x 35
STFMS : G95.017.0001

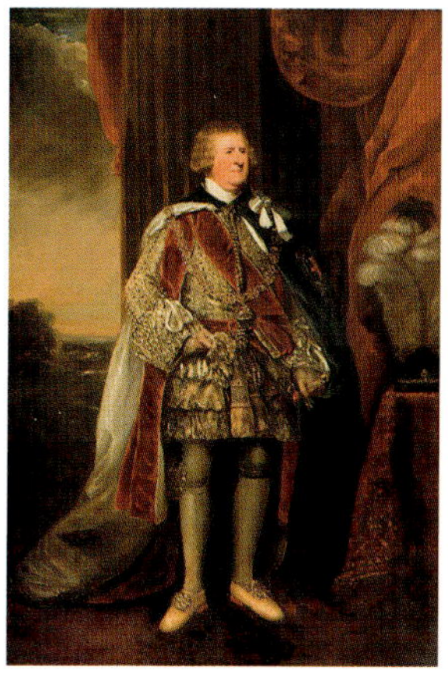

unknown artist
George Granville, 2nd Marquis of Stafford, 1st Duke of Sutherland (1758–1833) 1800–1830
oil on canvas 240 x 105 (E)
SHG.Ct1.2

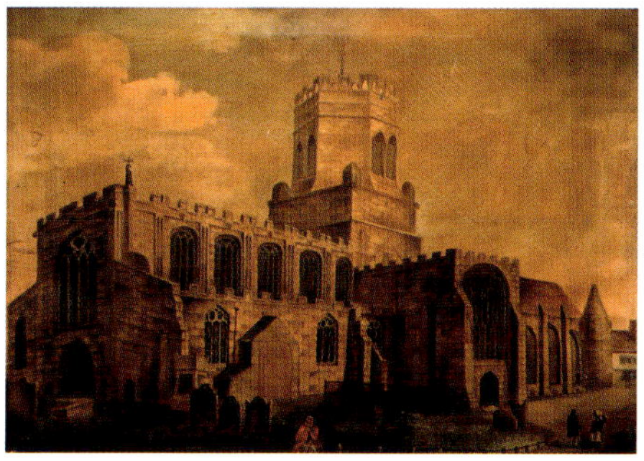

unknown artist
St Mary's Church, Stafford 1800–1840
oil on canvas 56 x 74.5
STFMS : G94.155.0001

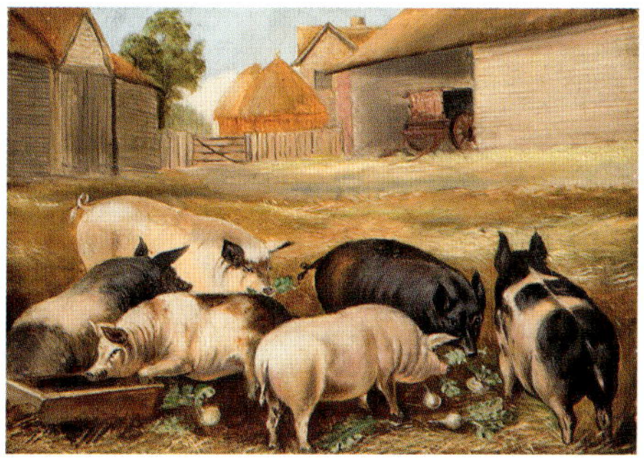

unknown artist
The Pretty Pigs c.1850
oil on board 21.5 x 29.8
STFMS : G2006.003.0001

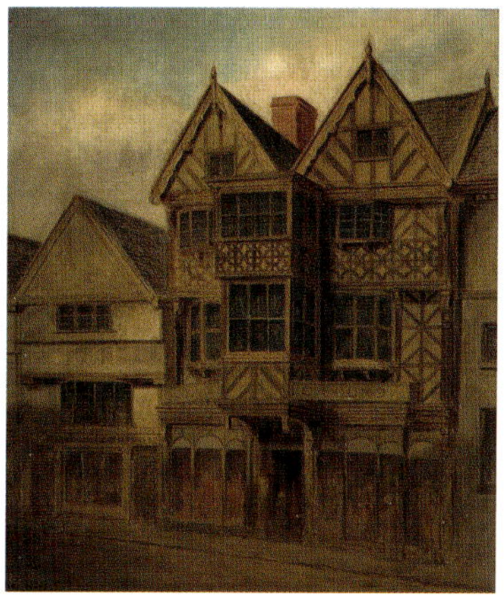

unknown artist
Elizabethan House, Gaolgate, Stafford c.1880
oil on canvas 29 x 24.5
STFMS : G94.134.0001

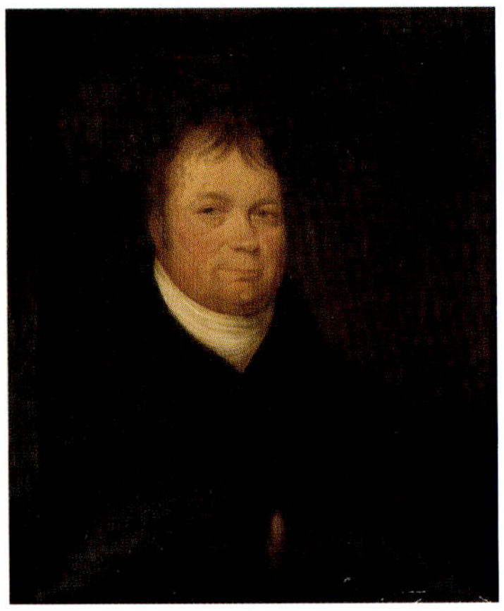

unknown artist early 19th C
Francis Joule, Maltster (1755–1837)
oil on canvas 76 x 63
STFMS : 74.014.0001

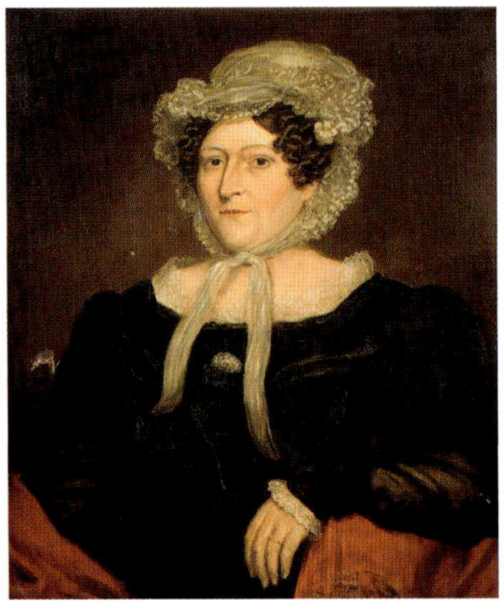

unknown artist early 19th C
Mary Joule (d.1828)
oil on canvas 75 x 63
STFMS : 74.014.0004

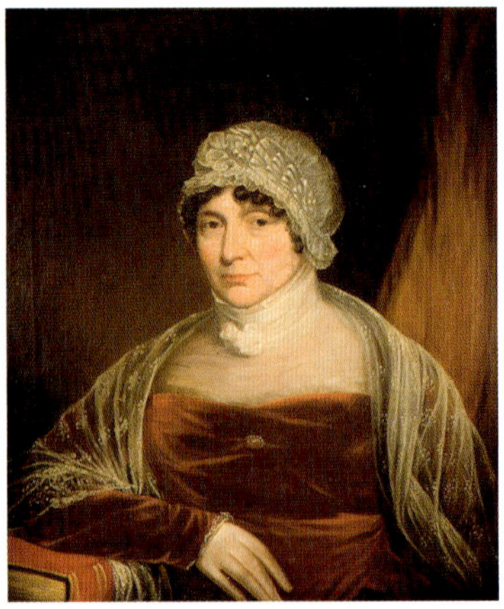

unknown artist early 19th C
Mrs Smith, Mother of Mary Joule
oil on canvas 79 x 61
STFMS : 74.014.0006

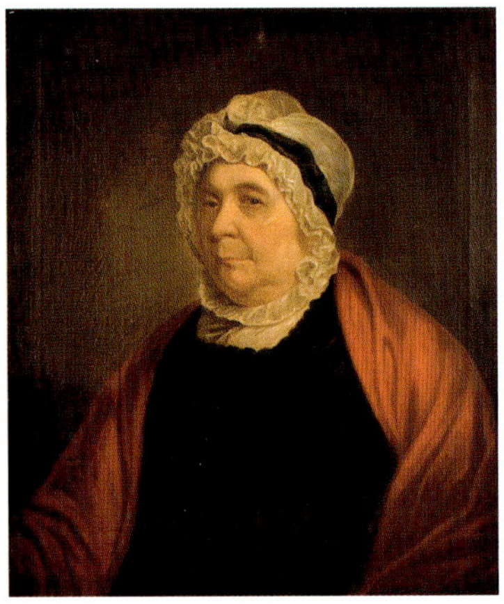

unknown artist early 19th C
Sarah Joule (d.1828)
oil on canvas 75 x 63
STFMS : 74.014.0002

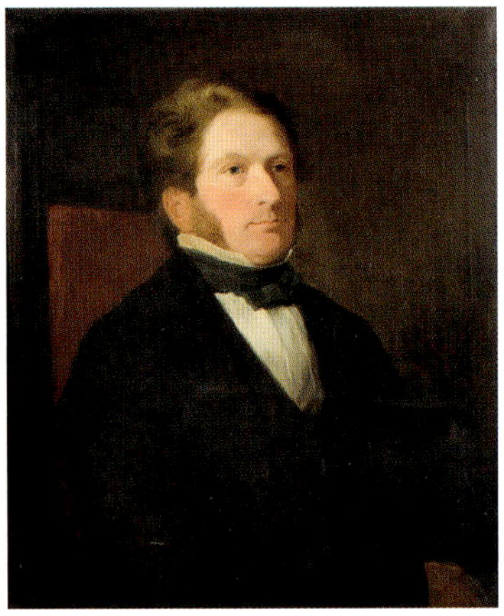

unknown artist mid-19th C
John Smith Joule (1806–1879)
oil on canvas 76 x 63.5
STFMS : 74.014.0005

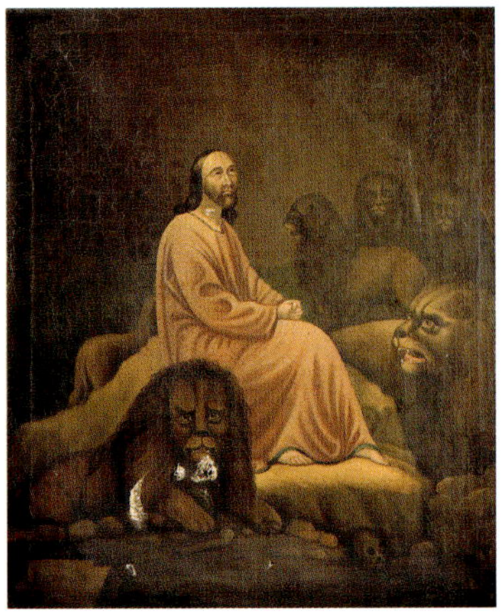

unknown artist 19th C
Daniel and the Lions
oil on canvas 94.9 x 80.8
STFMS : 64.066.0002

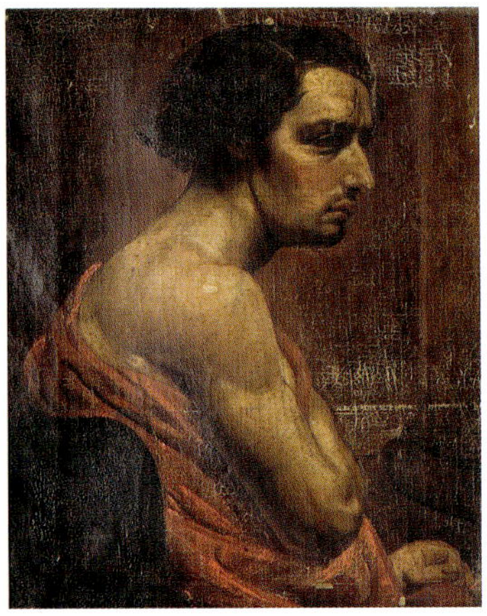

unknown artist 19th C
Portrait of a Young Man in a Toga
oil on canvas 30 x 20
STFMS : G97.013.0001

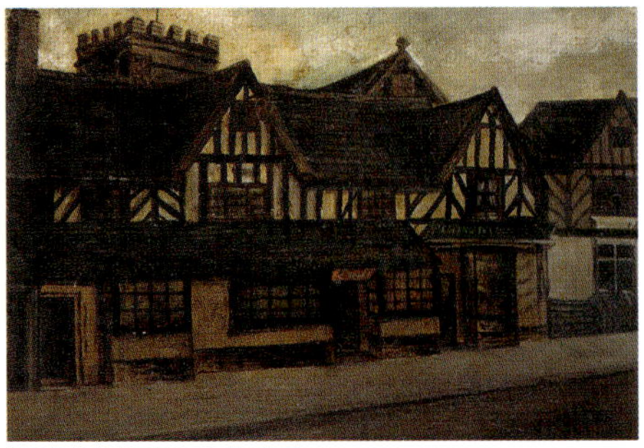

unknown artist
Dale's Shop, Stafford c.1930
oil on canvas 24.4 x 34
STFMS : G94.132.0001

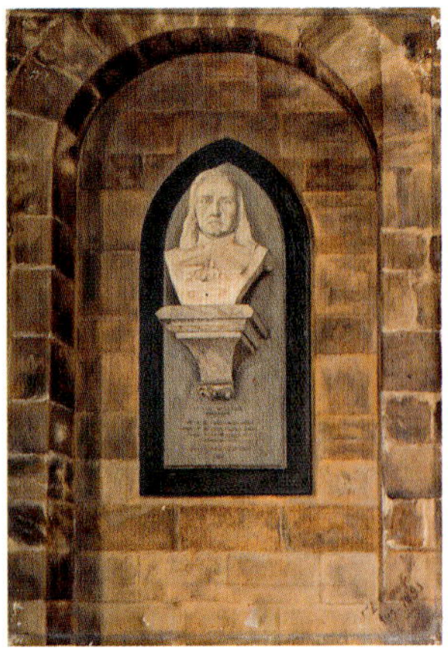

unknown artist early 20th C
Bust of Izaak Walton
oil on board 31.9 x 22.5
STFMS : 86.024.0436

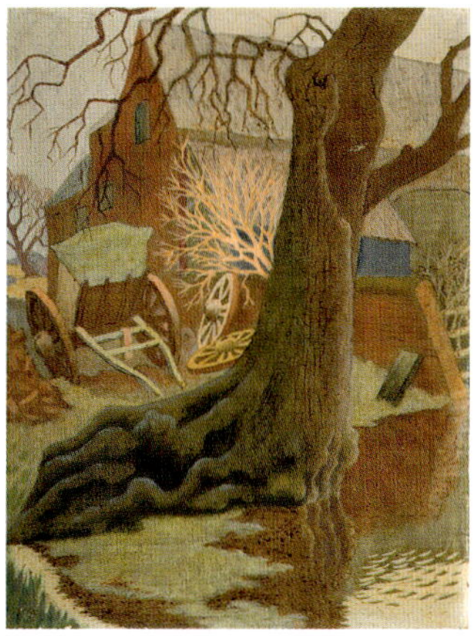

Weake, D. B.
Farmyard, Shirley 1950s
oil on board 37.5 x 27
STFMS : G94.135.0001

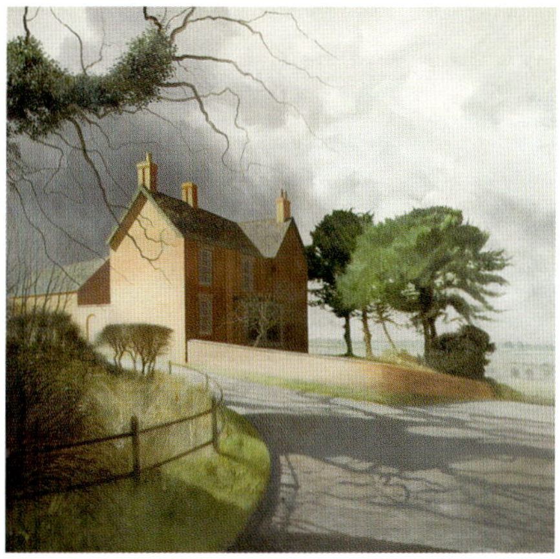

Wilson, Douglas b.1936
High Offley
oil on board 120.5 x 120.5 (E)
STFMS : G95.001.0001

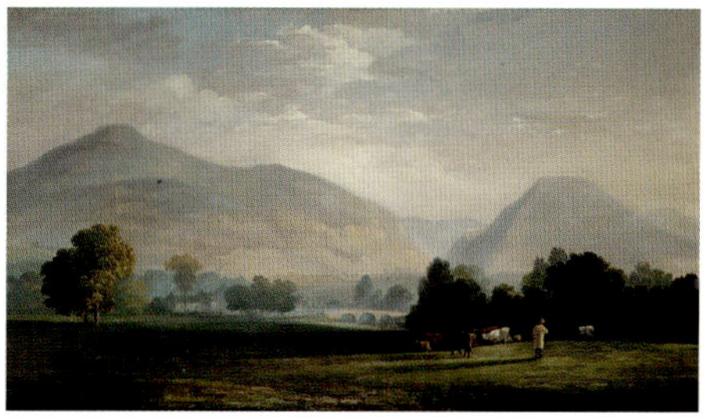

Wood, Thomas Peploe 1817–1845
The Bridge at Ilam 1836
oil on canvas 38 x 62
STFMS : G95.002.0001

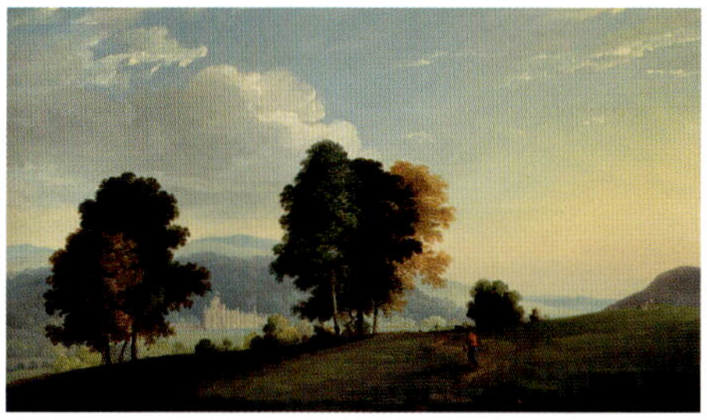

Wood, Thomas Peploe 1817–1845
Ilam Hall c.1840
oil on canvas 38 x 61.5
STFMS : G95.003.0001

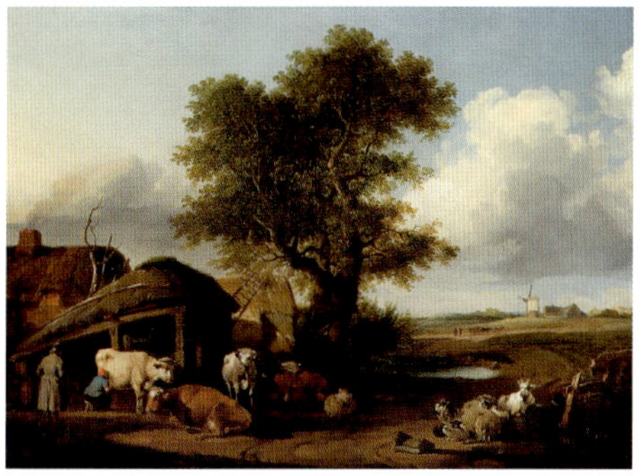

Wood, Thomas Peploe 1817–1845
Cattle Piece 1843
oil on canvas 63.5 x 83
STFMS : G95.007.0001

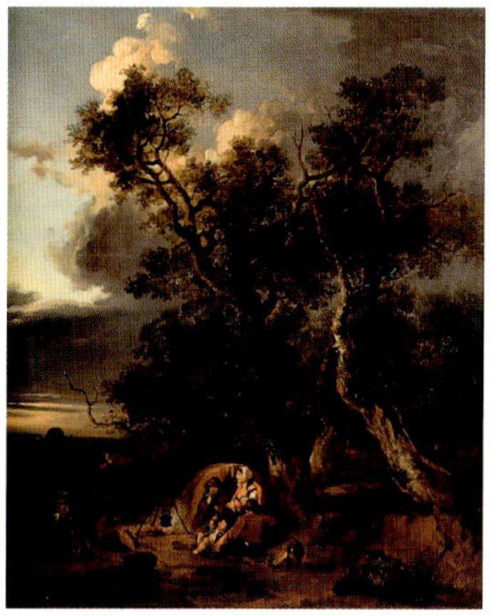

Wood, Thomas Peploe 1817–1845
Gypsy Scene 1843
oil on canvas 73 x 59
STFMS : G95.006.0001

Staffordshire County Council

Over the last century, Staffordshire County Council has amassed a large collection of paintings and prints. The majority of them were collected before 1932, when the first inventory was compiled by the then Clerk, Eustace Joy. Many of the prints and pictures were purchased through the County Council's Picture Fund established as a separate fund for this purpose.

It is a collection peculiar to Staffordshire itself, the basis of acquisition having been the county, its people, its topography and its places of beauty and interest. The oil paintings in the County Council's Collection are all portraits of local dignitaries and aristocrats, with the earliest, of Sir Richard Bagot, dating from the late sixteenth century. There is also a significant collection of early printed maps of Staffordshire. The majority of the oil paintings and maps are on display in the County Council buildings in Stafford.

Nigel Pursey, Chief Executive

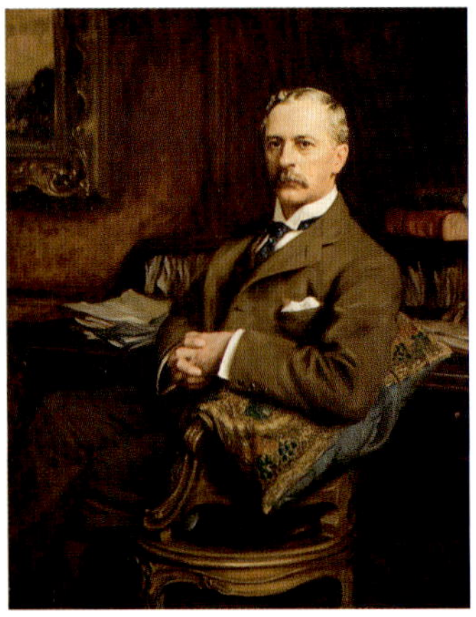

Bennett, Frank Moss 1874–1952
Thomas Francis Anson, Baron Soberton, Viscount Anson of Shugborough and Orgreave, Earl of Lichfield (1856–1918) 1920
oil on canvas 120.5 x 88.5 (E)
PCF 15

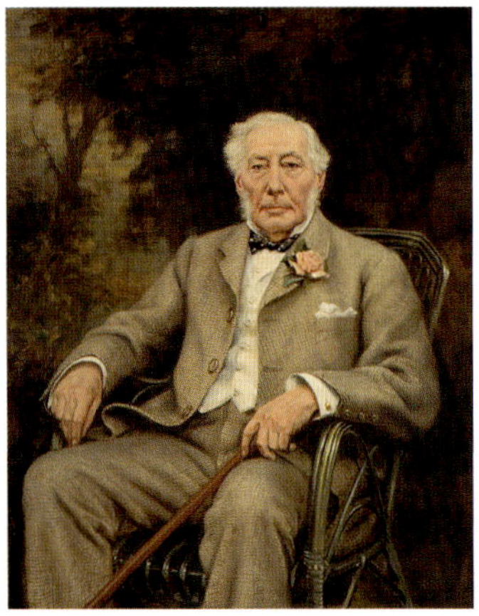

Bennett, Frank Moss 1874–1952
Frank James, DL, JP (1821–1924) 1921
oil on canvas 122 x 91.5
PCF 23

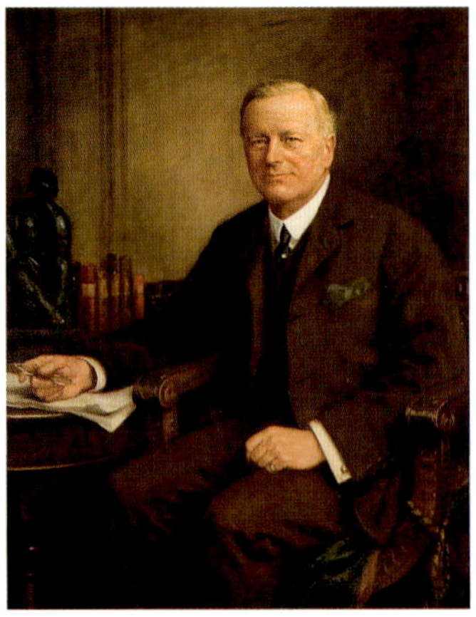

Bennett, Frank Moss 1874–1952
Sir Gilbert Henry Claughton, Bt (1856–1921)
1921
oil on canvas 108 x 86
PCF 17

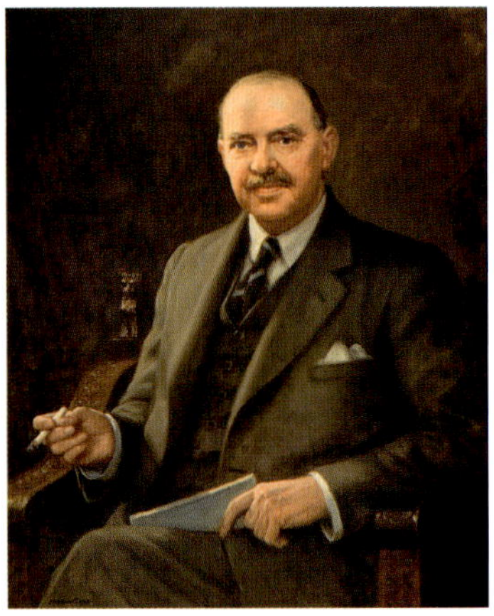

Bennett, Frank Moss 1874–1952
Lieutenant-Colonel William Edward Harrison (d.1937), OBE 1933
oil on canvas 91.5 x 71
PCF 20

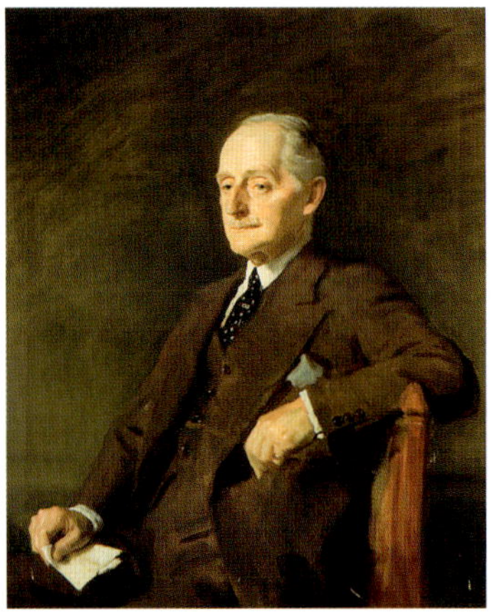

Birley, Oswald Hornby Joseph 1880–1952
Lieutenant-Colonel George Augustus Anson (b.1857), CBE 1930
oil on canvas 102 x 82.5
PCF 14

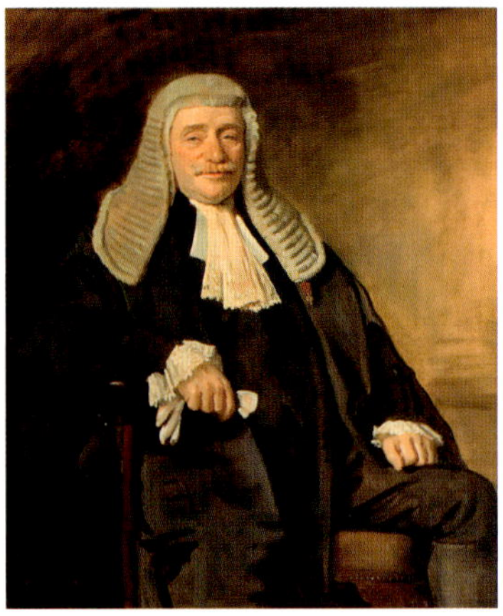

Birley, Oswald Hornby Joseph 1880–1952
Sir John Edwin Mitchell (1863–1931), OBE 1930
oil on canvas 127 x 100
PCF 24

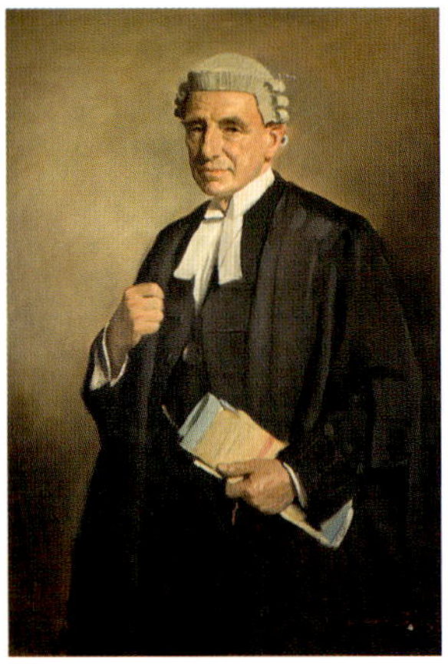

Birley, Oswald Hornby Joseph 1880–1952
Roy Eustace Joy, MA 1933
oil on canvas 126 x 84
PCF 11

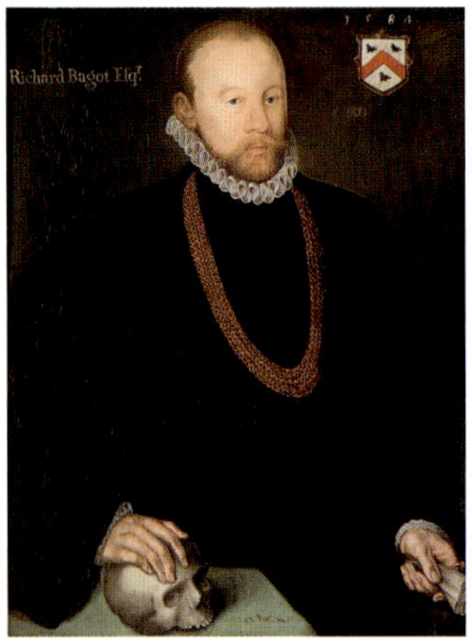

British (English) School
Sir Richard Bagot (c.1530–1597) 1584
oil on panel 91.5 x 71
PCF 27

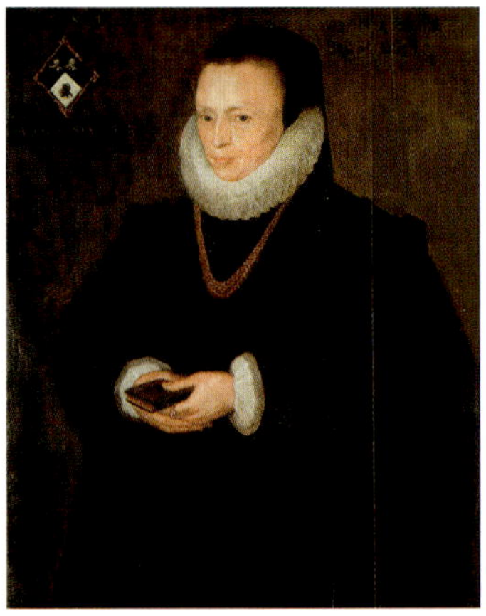

British (English) School
Mary Saunders (d.1608), Lady Bagot
1584
oil on wood 91.5 x 71
PCF 29

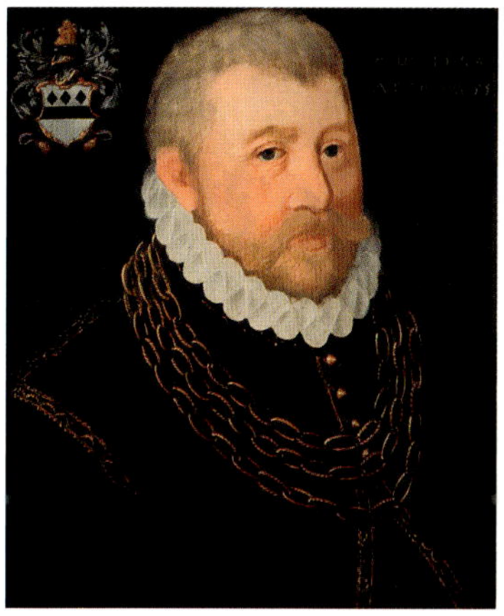

British (English) School
Sir Walter Aston of Tixall (1584–1639)
c.1635–1640
oil on panel 55 x 45
PCF 28

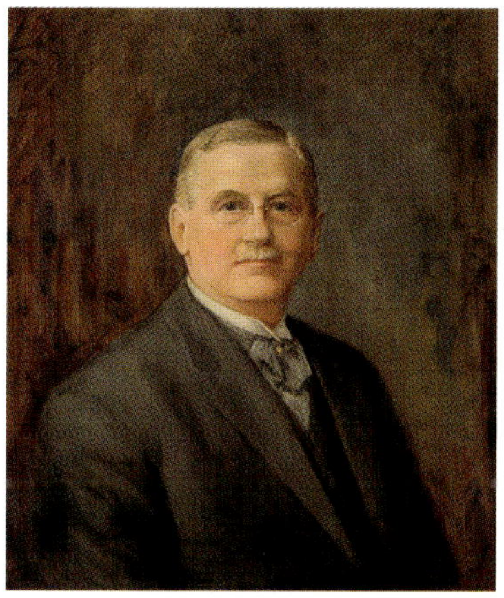

British (English) School
Sir Julian Osborn Whitehouse (d.1942), JP for Staffordshire (1926–1942) c.1945–1946
oil on canvas 75 x 62
PCF 21

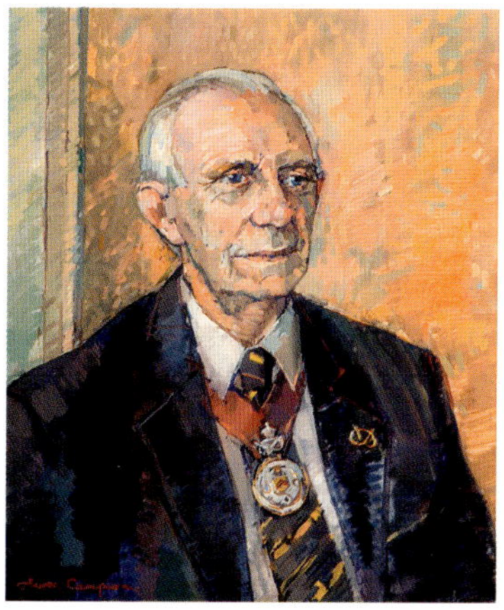

Campion, Oliver 1928–2000
F. A. Cholerton, CBE, M Univ (Keele) (d.2004), Chairman of Staffordshire County Council (1981–1989) 1989
oil on canvas 61 x 50
PCF 1

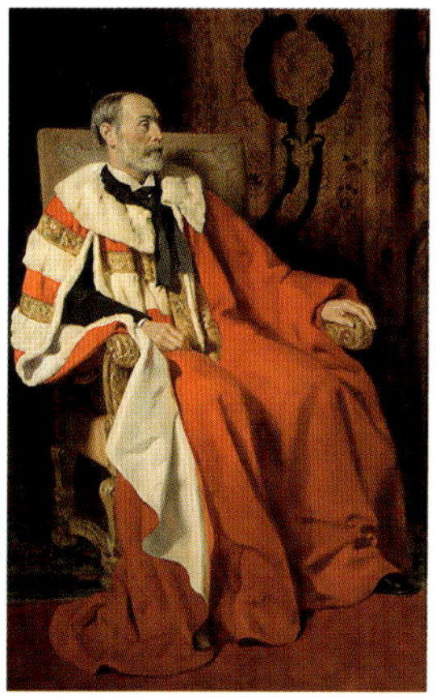

Collier, John 1850–1934
Edward George Percy Littleton, 3rd Baron Hatherton (1842–1930) 1913
oil on canvas 183 x 119
PCF 18

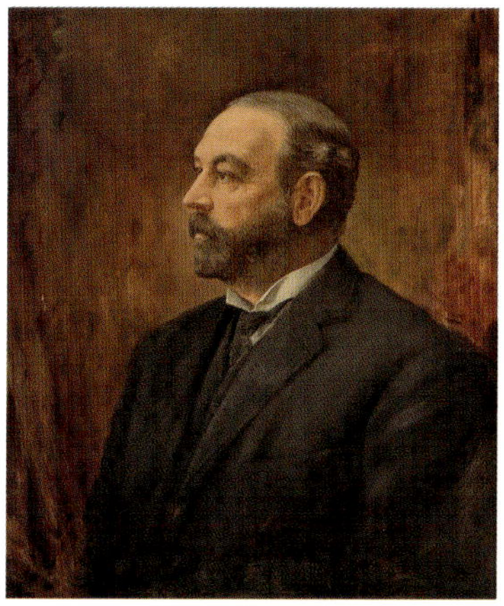

Collings, Keturah b.1862
Robert George Paterson, OBE 1940s
oil on canvas 76 x 63.5
PCF 22

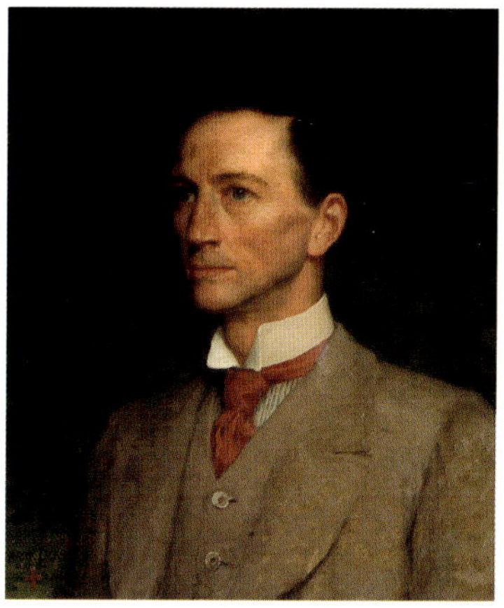

Dicksee, Frank 1853–1928
Godfrey Rathbone Benson, Baron Charnwood (1864–1945) 1919
oil on canvas 61 x 51
PCF 16

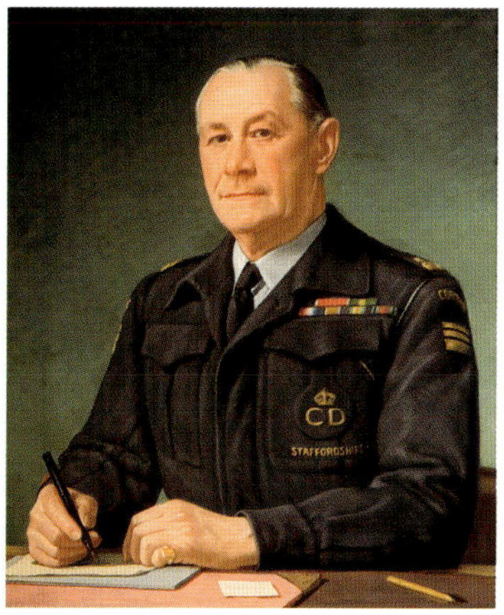

Dodd, Francis 1874–1949
Colonel Sir William John Kent, CBE, TD, DL, JR c.1945
oil on canvas 75 x 62
PCF 10

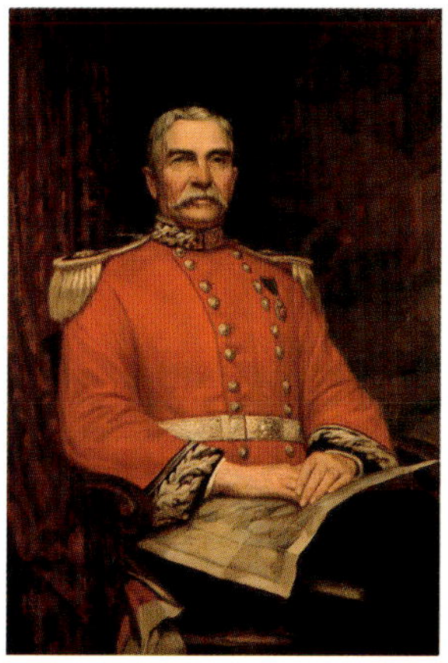

Harper, Edward Steel II 1878–1951
Lieutenant-Colonel Joseph Henry Wilkinson, DL, JP, VD (1845–1931) 1921
oil on canvas 126 x 84
PCF 12

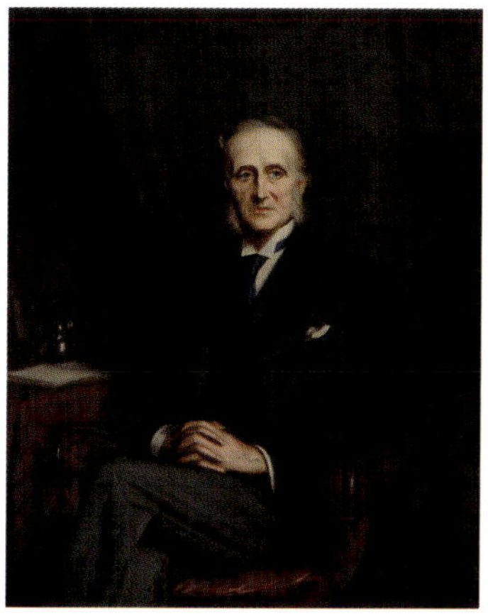

Herkomer, Hubert von 1849–1914
Dudley Francis Stuart Ryder, 4th Baron Harrowby, Viscount Sandon, 4rd Earl of Harrowby (1831–1900) 1900
oil on canvas 124.5 x 100
PCF 3

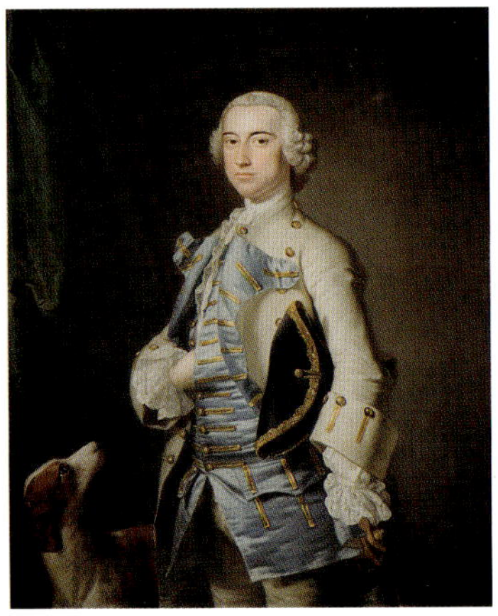

Hudson, Thomas 1701–1779
Jeremiah Smith of Brewood, High Sheriff of Staffordshire 1762
oil on canvas 124.5 x 100
PCF 2

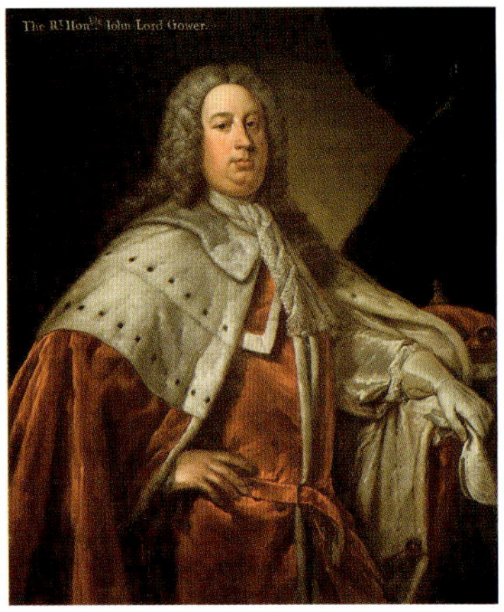

Hudson, Thomas (attributed to) 1701–1779
John Leveson Gower, 2nd Baron and 1st Earl Gower, Viscount Trentham (1694–1754) c.1750
oil on canvas 127 x 101.5
PCF 9

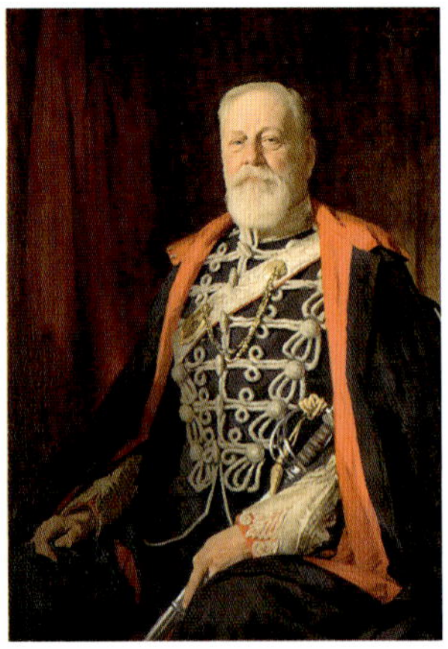

Llewellyn, William Samuel Henry 1858–1941
Sir Reginald Hardy, 2nd Bt, of Dunstall Park (1848–1938) c.1893
oil on canvas 124.5 x 84
PCF 26

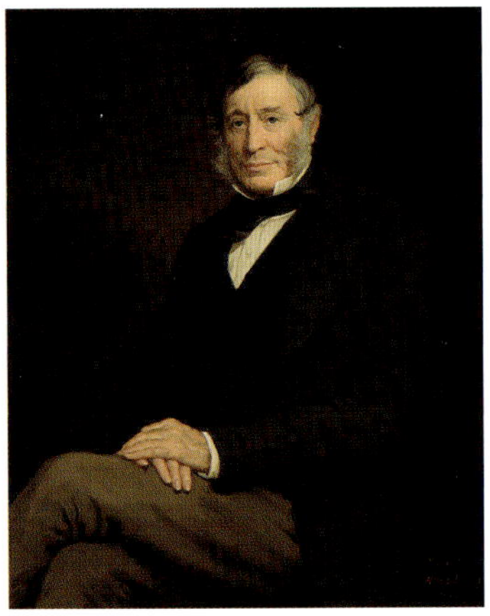

Ouless, Walter William 1848–1933
Thomas Fletcher Twemlow of Betley (1816–1894) 1925
oil on canvas 114 x 85
PCF 25

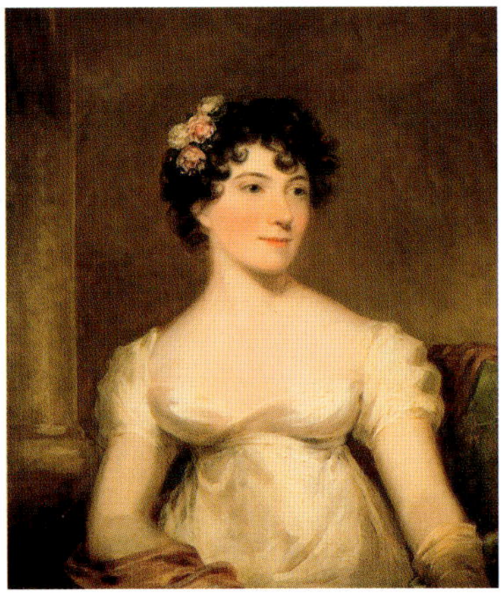

Owen, William 1769–1825
Charlotte Sparrow c.1815–1820
oil on canvas 74 x 63.5
PCF 6

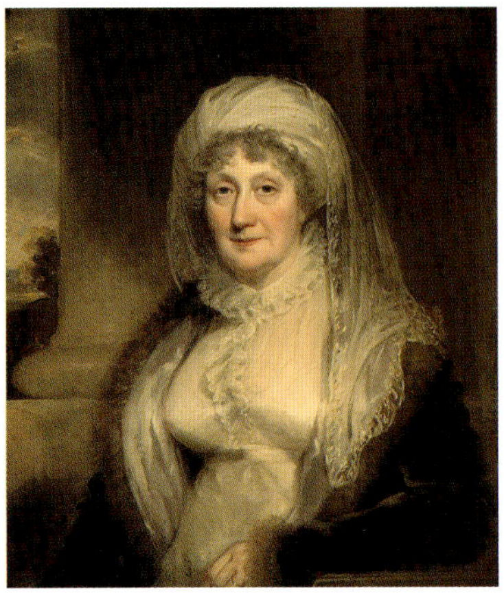

Owen, William 1769–1825
Elizabeth Sparrow of Bishton Hall c.1815–1820
oil on canvas 73.5 x 64
PCF 5

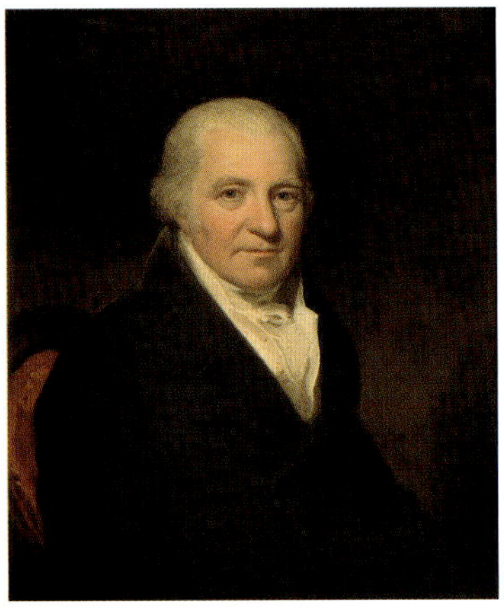

Owen, William 1769–1825
John Sparrow of Bishton Hall (1736–1821) c.1815–1820
oil on canvas 73.5 x 63.5
PCF 4

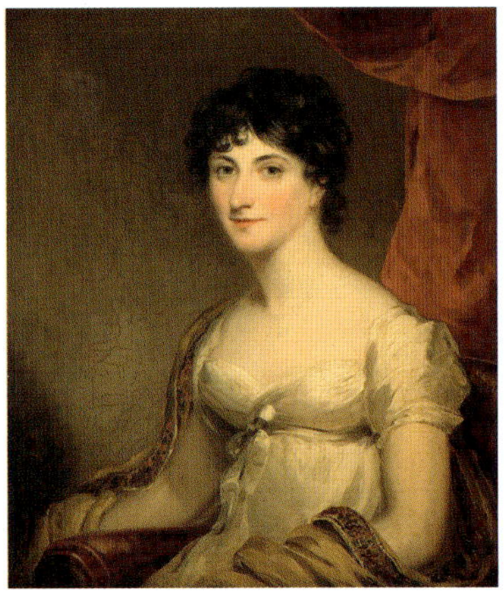

Owen, William 1769–1825
Lady Hannah Chetwynd c.1815–1820
oil on canvas 74 x 63.5
PCF 7

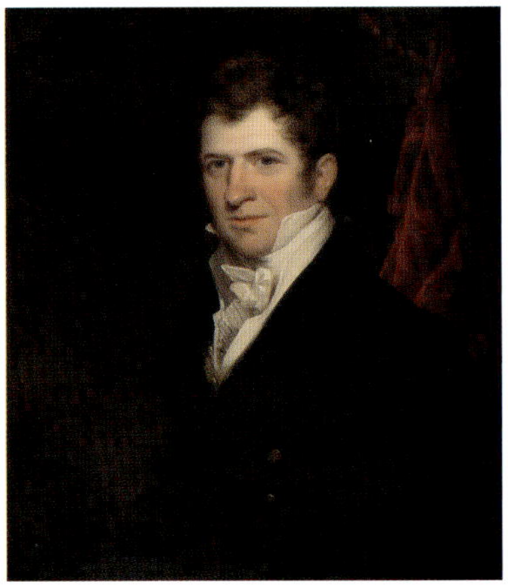

Owen, William (attributed to) 1769–1825
Sir George Chetwynd, 2nd Bt, of Grendon and Brocton (1783–1850)
oil on canvas 73.5 x 63.5
PCF 8

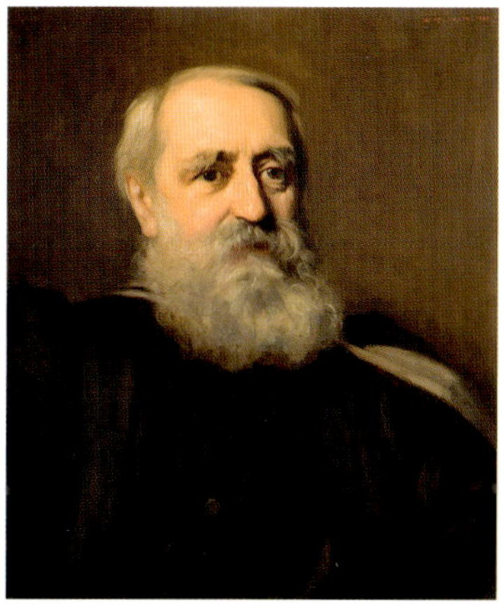

Palin, William Mainwaring 1862–1947
Francis Elliott Kitchener, MA, JP (1838–1915) 1912
oil on canvas 61 x 51
PCF 13

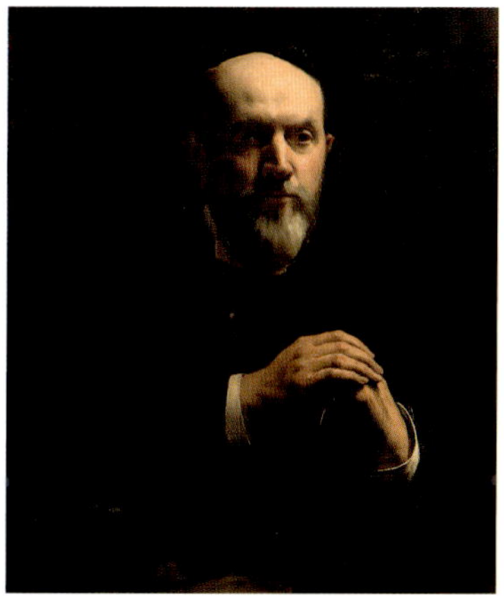

Palin, William Mainwaring 1862–1947
John Wilcox Edge (1844–1923) 1923
oil on canvas 76 x 63.5
PCF 32

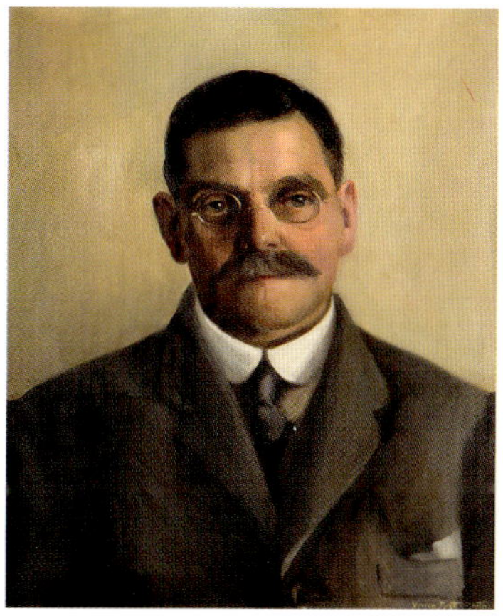

Smith, Vivian Brett
Portrait of a Gentleman c.1920
oil on canvas 58.5 x 48
PCF 34

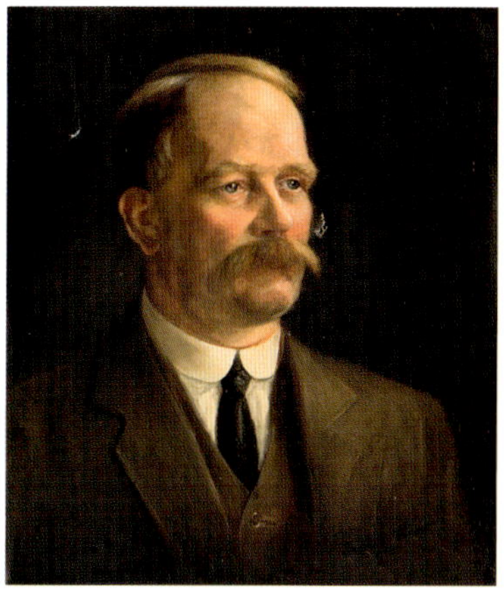

Trent, Irene E.
John T. Homer, CBE, DL c.1920
oil on canvas 60 x 50
PCF 33

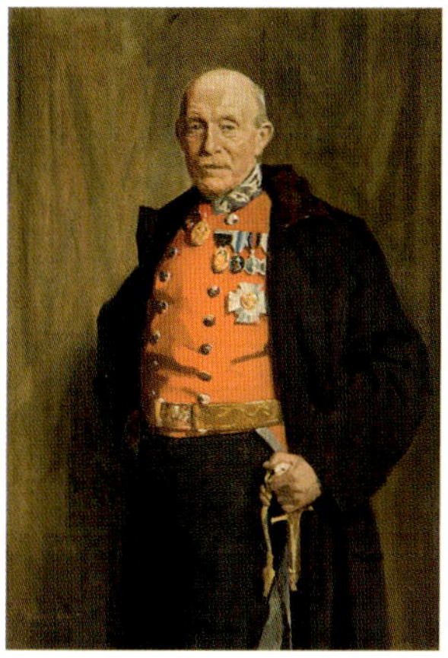

Watt, George Fiddes 1873–1960
William Heneage Legge, 6th Earl and 8th Baron of Dartmouth (1851–1936)
oil on canvas 122 x 81
PCF 19

Staffordshire Police Museum

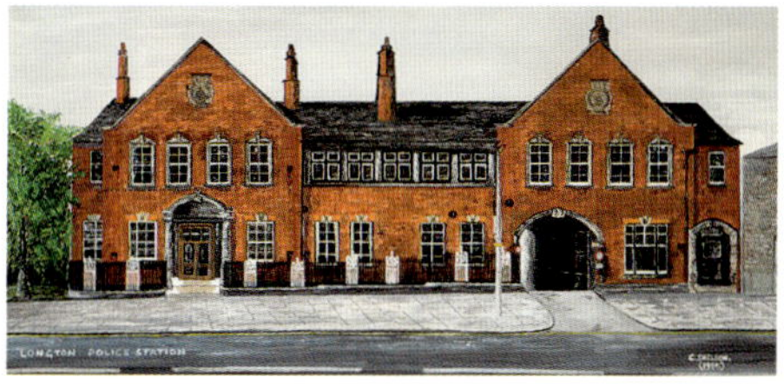

Sheldon, Chris William b.1948
Longton Police Station 1988
oil on board 29 x 59
PCF9

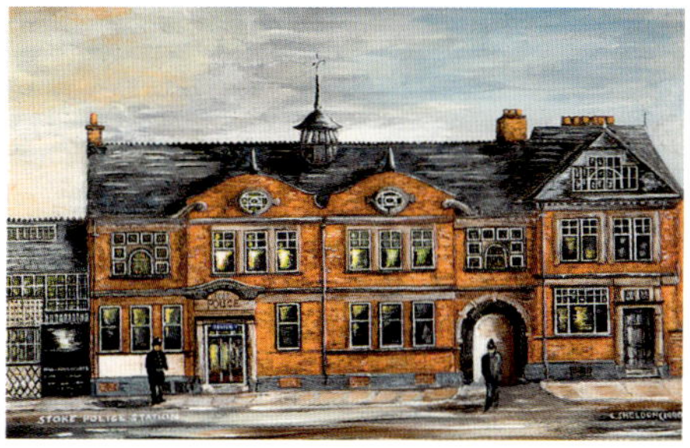

Sheldon, Chris William b.1948
Stoke Police Station 1990
oil on board 26.5 x 40.5
PCF7

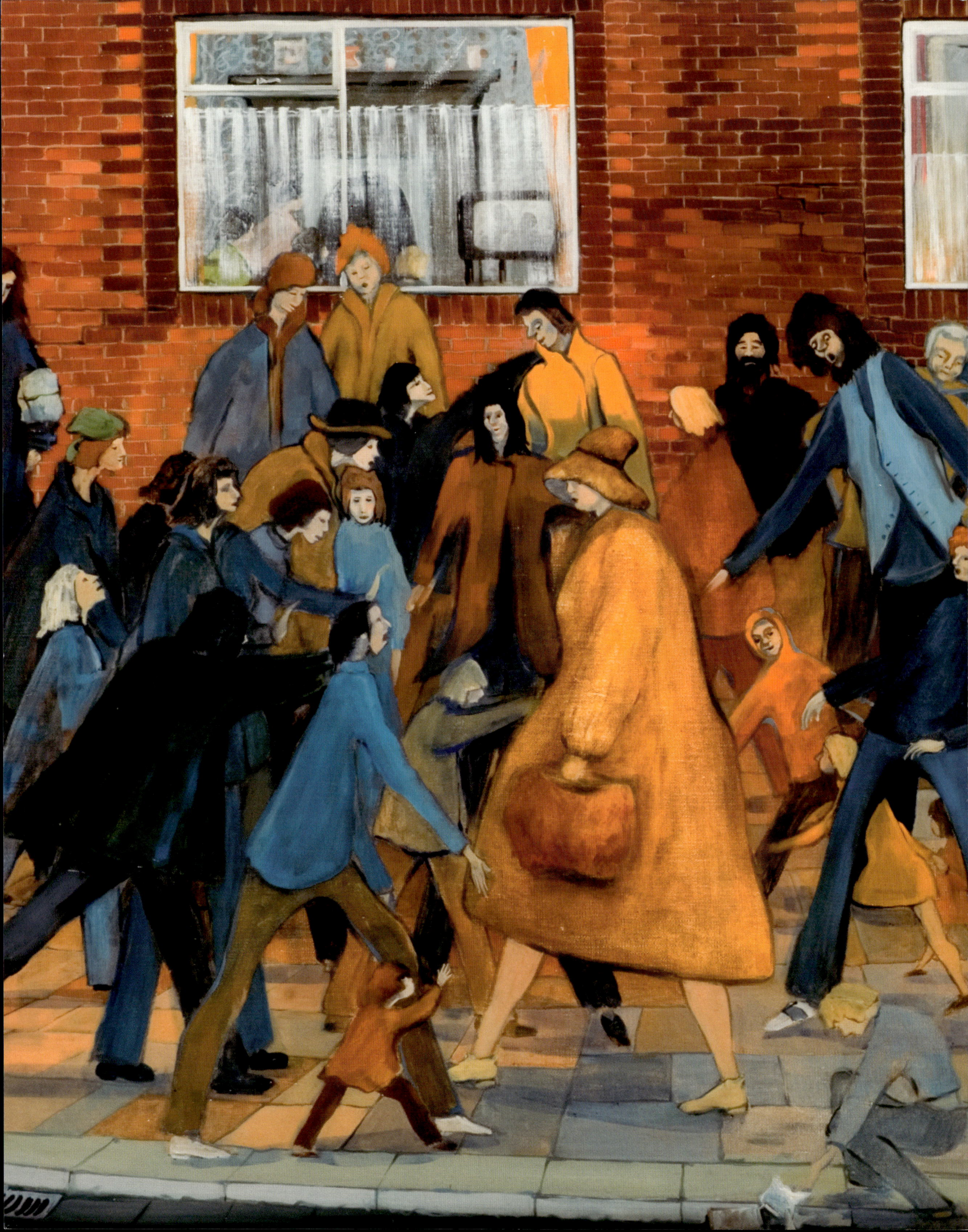

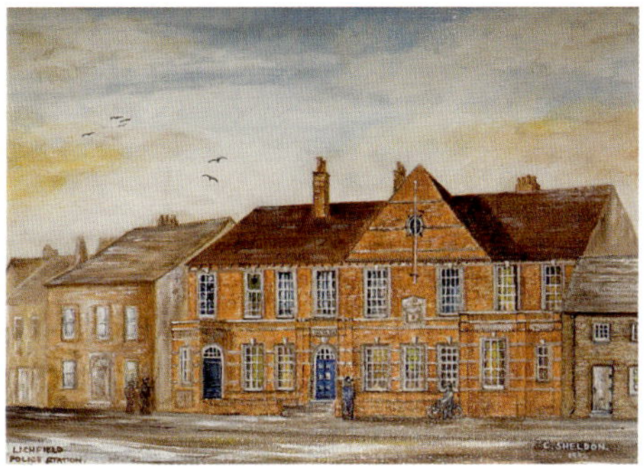

Sheldon, Chris William b.1948
Lichfield Police Station 1992
oil on board 27 x 36
PCF14

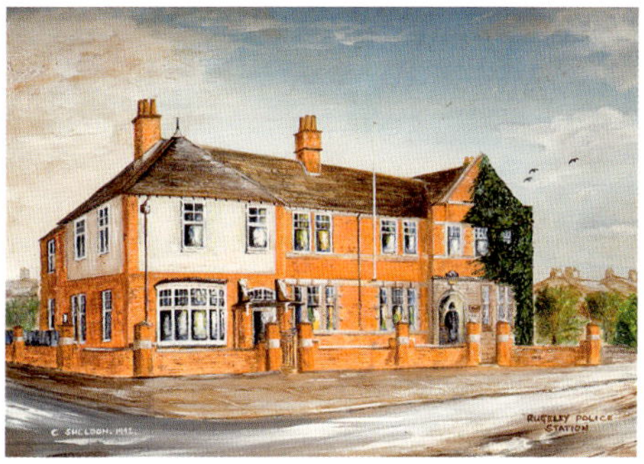

Sheldon, Chris William b.1948
Rugeley Police Station 1992
oil on board 29.5 x 39.5
PCF8

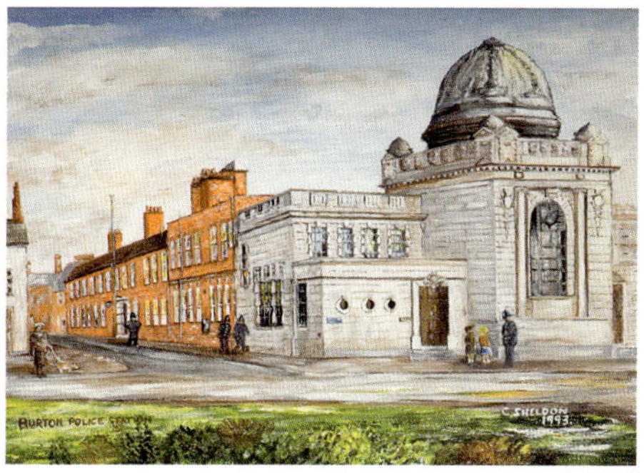

Sheldon, Chris William b.1948
Burton-on-Trent Police Station 1993
oil on board 29.5 x 39.5
PCF10

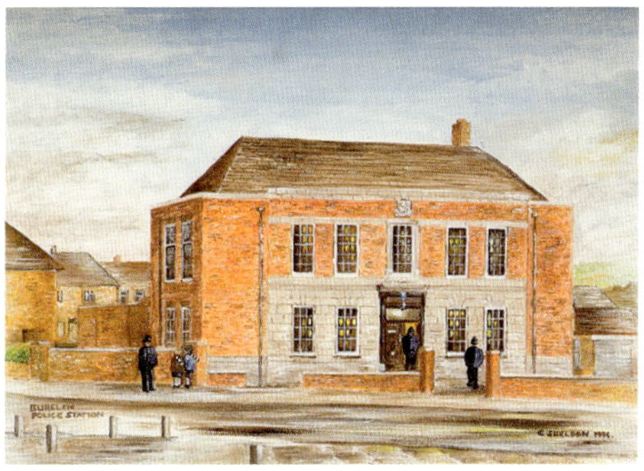

Sheldon, Chris William b.1948
Burslem Police Station 1994
oil on board 29.5 x 39.5
PCF12

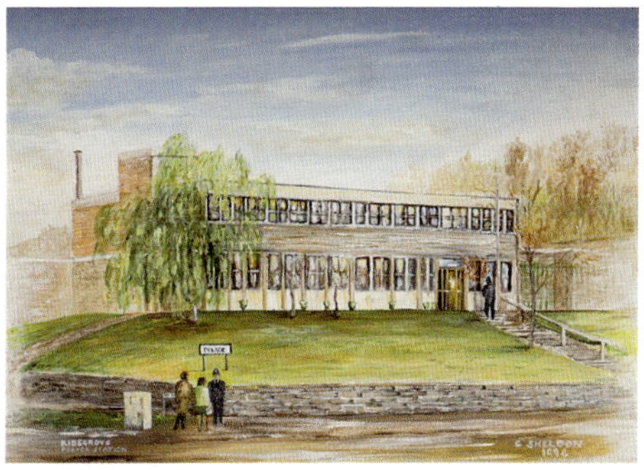

Sheldon, Chris William b.1948
Kidsgrove Police Station 1994
oil on board 29.5 x 39.5
PCF13

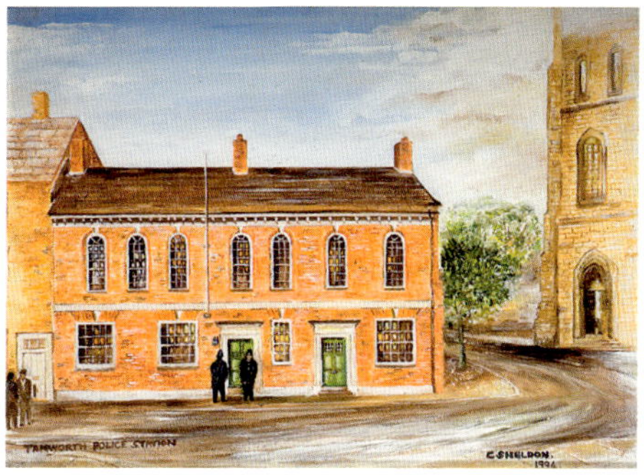

Sheldon, Chris William b.1948
Tamworth Police Station 1994
oil on board 29.5 x 39.5
PCF6

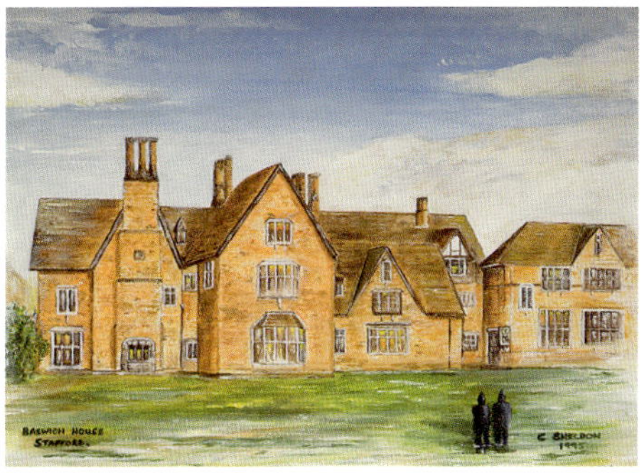

Sheldon, Chris William b.1948
Baswich House, Stafford 1995
oil on board 29.5 x 39.5
PCF11

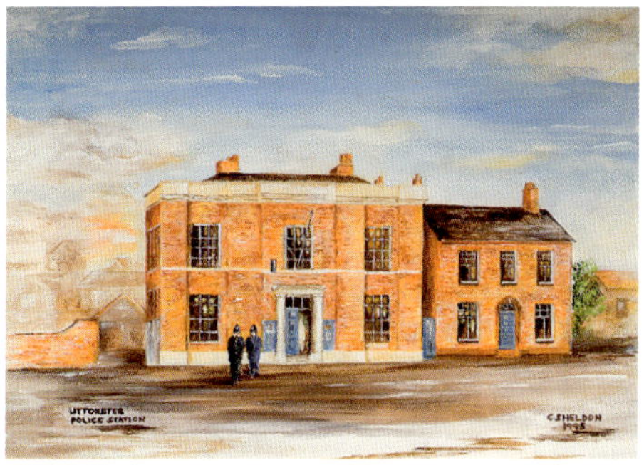

Sheldon, Chris William b.1948
Uttoxeter Police Station 1995
oil on board 29.5 x 39.5
PCF5

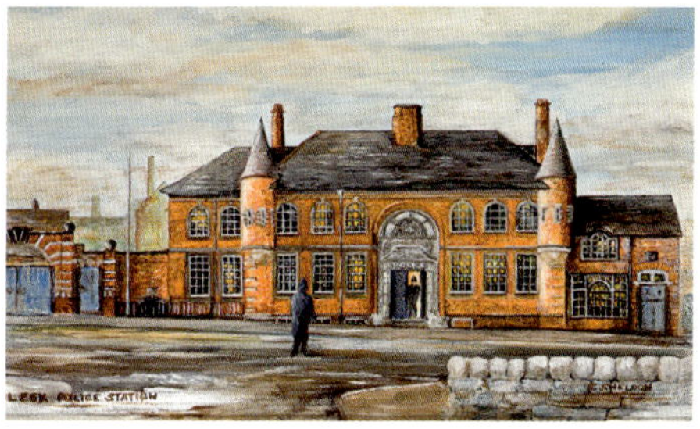

Sheldon, Chris William b.1948
Leek Police Station
oil on board 24.5 x 39.5
PCF4

Facing page: Barnardo, Eilidh, 1911–1994, *Crowded Pavement* (detail), c.1990, Staffordshire Arts and Museums Service (p. 74)

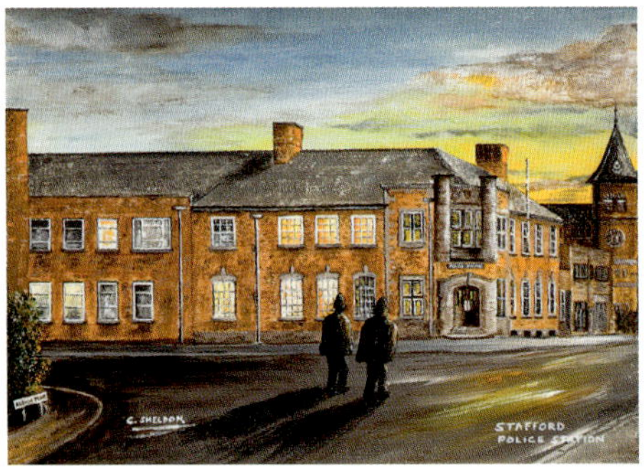

Sheldon, Chris William b.1948
Stafford Police Station
oil on board 29 x 39
PCF15

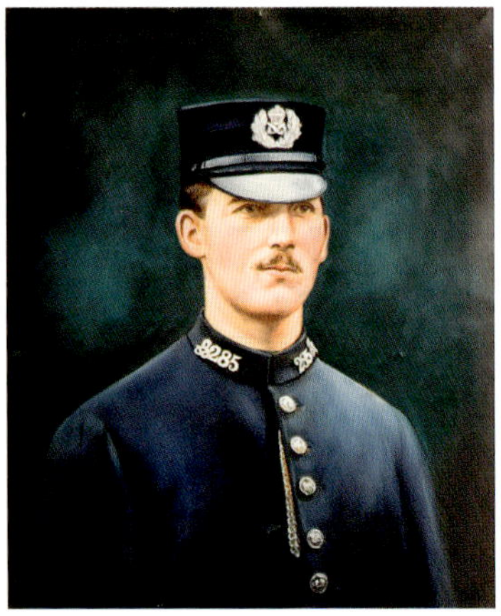

unknown artist
Portrait of a Staffordshire Policeman
oil on paper 49 x 39
SPM.030

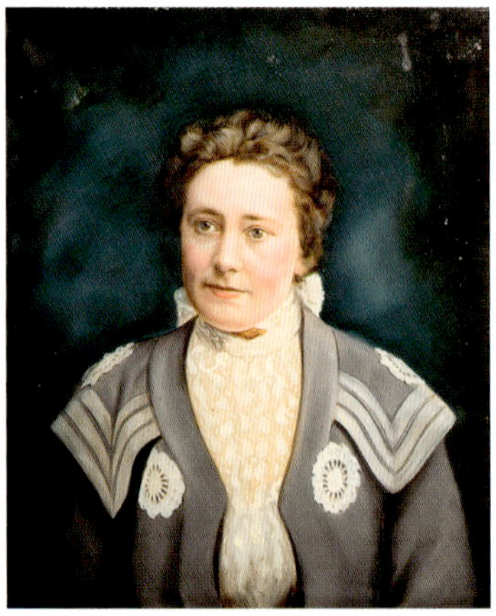

unknown artist
Portrait of a Staffordshire Policeman's Wife
oil on paper 49 x 39
SPM.031

Spode Museum Trust

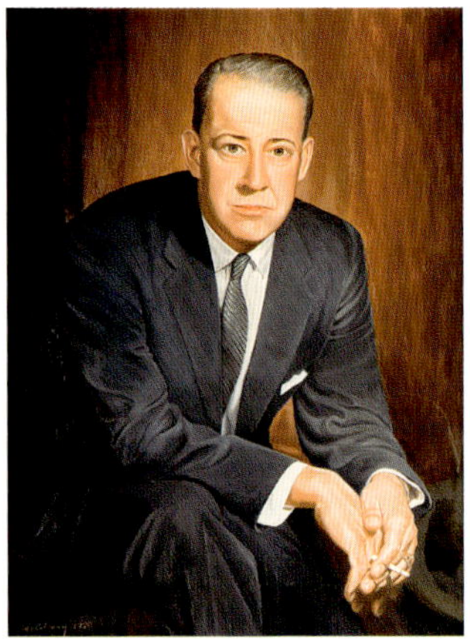

Holdway, Harold 1913–2002
William Wendel, Chairman of Carborundum International 1970
oil on board 59 x 44.5
WTC 2006.6

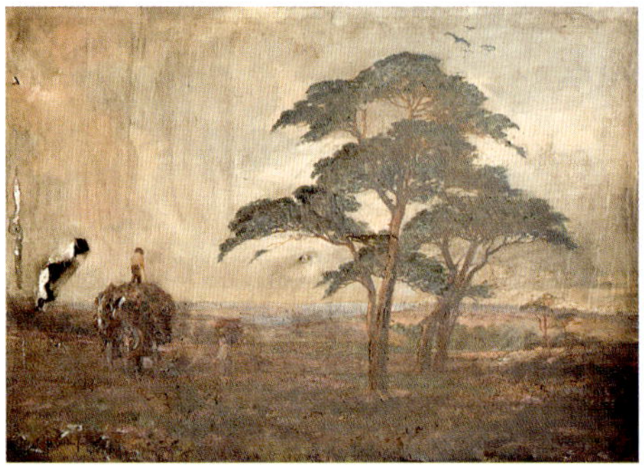

Jones, Horace Overton active 1894–1924
At Rhosneigr, Anglesey 1924
oil on canvas 90 x 121
WTC 2006.5

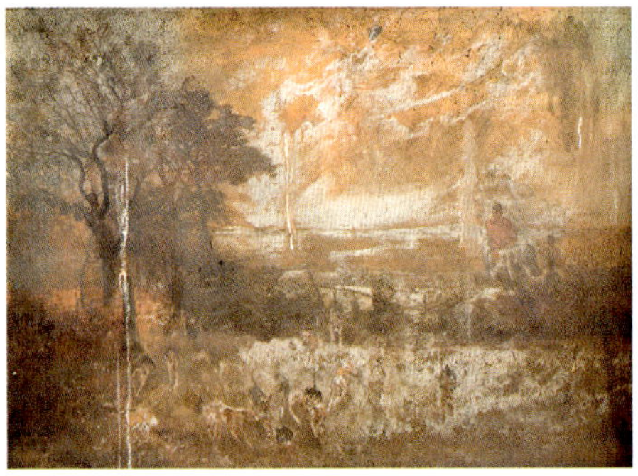

Jones, Horace Overton (attributed to)
active 1894–1924
Hunting with Hounds
oil on canvas 90 x 121
WTC 2006.4

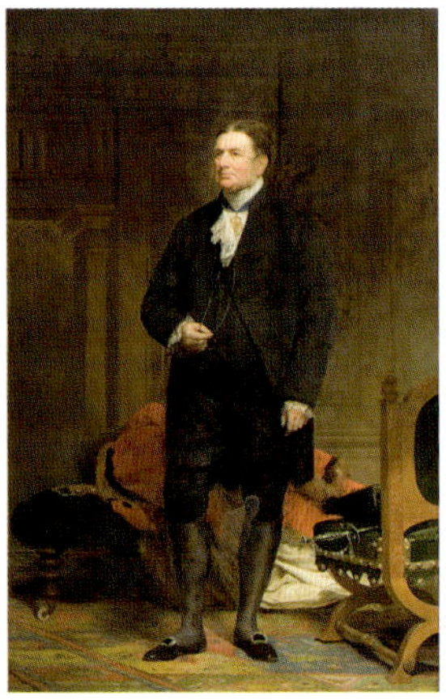

unknown artist
The Right Worshipful W. T. Copeland (1797–1868), Alderman, President 1861
oil on canvas 238 x 147
WTC 2006.3

The Potteries Museum & Art Gallery

The North Staffordshire Potteries is the only area in the United Kingdom to be identified with one industry, ceramics. The production of ceramics has shaped the landscape of Stoke-on-Trent and surrounding area and informed its economic heritage and material culture. The influence of the ceramic and associated industries on the Potteries is reflected in the collections held in the City's museums and art gallery. The evolution of The Potteries Museum & Art Gallery is convoluted as it has been through many changes in its history.

Stoke-on-Trent comprises six towns: Tunstall, Burslem, Hanley, Stoke-upon-Trent, Fenton and Longton. During the early nineteenth and twentieth centuries collections developed in each of the six towns. In 1910 the administration of the towns and their museums was brought under the control of one authority, Stoke-on-Trent (which achieved the status of city in 1925). The focus of the early museums was to improve the standard of design in the pottery industry, primarily through the collection of ceramic material. Over more recent years collections of fine and decorative arts, natural history, archaeology and social history have also developed through donations, bequests and purchases. With the outbreak of the Second World War the museums closed, with the exception of Hanley Museum & Art Gallery.

In 1956 the first local authority museum was opened in Stoke-on-Trent. It was the first phase in a project to re-house and display the previously disparate collections. Over the past 25 years the Museum has undergone extensive development work and in 1981 the second phase of the City Museum & Art Gallery was opened by HRH The Prince of Wales. In 1982 it won the Museum of the Year Award.

Stoke-on-Trent Museums Service currently consists of The Potteries Museum & Art Gallery, Gladstone Pottery Museum, Eturia Industrial Museum and Ford Green Hall. The Potteries Museum & Art Gallery (previously The City Museum & Art Gallery) is the principle repository for the collections. The Museum is widely known for housing the world's finest collection of Staffordshire ceramics, as well as holding the most comprehensive collection of British twentieth-century studio ceramics.

The Museum's Fine Art Collection initially began when Dr John Russell gave his collection of Impressionistic paintings to the city, on condition that it built an art gallery. In 1927 the Russell Art Gallery opened in two rooms adjoining Hanley Museum. The opening of the gallery enabled Hanley to become a key centre for temporary exhibitions in the Potteries. A priority for the Museum was the ability to support and interpret contemporary artists, a philosophy which still exists.

One of the strengths of the Fine Art Collection lies in early twentieth-century British art production. This includes works by the Slade School artists, Scottish Colourists, Walter Sickert of the Camden Town School, Duncan Grant of the Bloomsbury Group, a small sample of British Surrealists from Conroy Maddox to Eileen Agar and work by the war artists; in particular Paul Nash. One of the most popular oil paintings in the collection, and with which the Museum is most heavily identified, is *The Family* by Bernard Fleetwood-Walker. The Collection also contains works by local artists as diverse as James Holland and Arthur Berry, as well as pottery designers turned artists such as

Margret Marks and Gordon Mitchell Forsyth. The local landscape is captured in many of the works by artists both living in the area and those who have passed through, depicting scenes from the eighteenth century to the present day, for example John Constable and Julian Trevelyan.

In addition to the oil paintings, the Museum holds a vast collection of prints. These provide a greater historical and international context for the works in oil. The print collection covers European and Japanese printmakers from the sixteenth century to the present day. A notable example is the complete series of Francisco de Goya's *Los Proverbios*. Other examples are by Manet, Toulouse-Lautrec and Degas, nineteenth-century Japanese woodcuts and twentieth-century British prints by Sir Henry Moore, Dame Laura Knight, Eric Gill and James Whistler.

The Museum's Fine Art Collection has largely grown through donations although some works have been purchased by the gallery itself or with assistance from the Arts Council, The Friends of The Potteries Museum & Art Gallery and the Contemporary Art Society. Through the Contemporary Art Society Special Collection Scheme the Museum has been able to acquire works that challenge traditional divisions between art and craft, collecting works by Grayson Perry, Gavin Turk and Jacqui Poncelet. The Collection has developed in a less than coherent fashion which has left the Collection somewhat disjointed. However, a more unified approach to collecting is evolving which will focus on enriching the works already held in the Collection and developing the presence of contemporary works. Early twentieth century art production forms the backbone of the Collection, which largely depicts landscape images such as *On the Edge of Dartmoor* by Gerald Moira and various works by Adrian Allinson.

For the future, the Museum is keen to establish and develop partnerships with other museums and institutions regionally, nationally, and internationally and increase opportunities for supporting the creativity of artists and communities to take the collections forward and develop a proactive approach to contemporary collecting. This will result in a collection of contextual material to work alongside the existing permanent collection.

Specifically for the Fine Art Collection, the aim is to acquire art in all media relating to the history and future development of Stoke-on-Trent, reflecting the changing face of the landscape. Over recent years collecting in this area has been less active, but the Museum will be seeking opportunities to reinvigorate collecting. Acquiring work by key local artists who are not currently represented, as well as work by artists and designers with links to the pottery industry, will be central to developing the Collection.

Jean Milton, Collections Officer, Arts

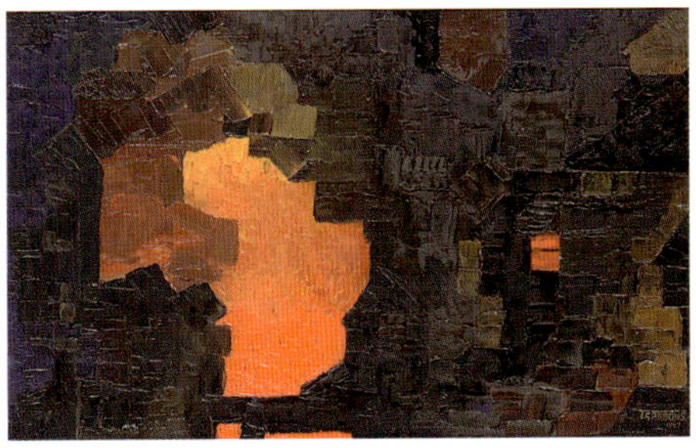

Abbotts, T. G.
Steel Town 1967
oil on panel 48.5 x 75
1967.FA.21

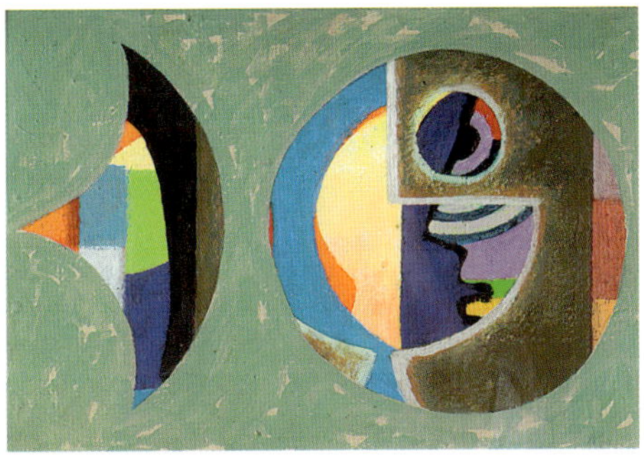

Agar, Eileen 1899–1991
The New Planet 1963
acrylic on canvas 26 x 36
1999.FA.2

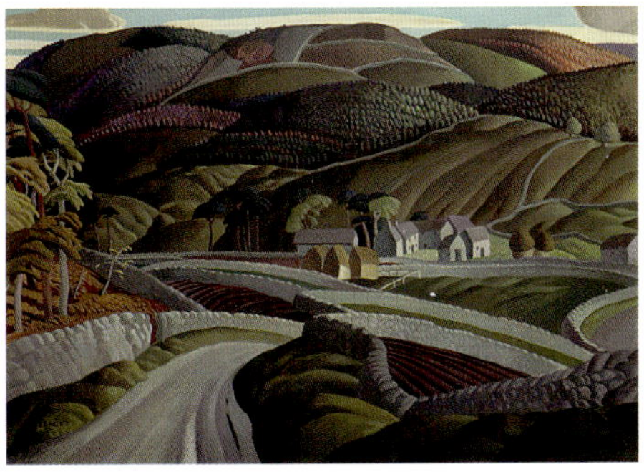

Allen, Harry Epworth 1894–1958
A Derbyshire Farmstead
tempera on paper 36.5 x 50
1934.FA.70

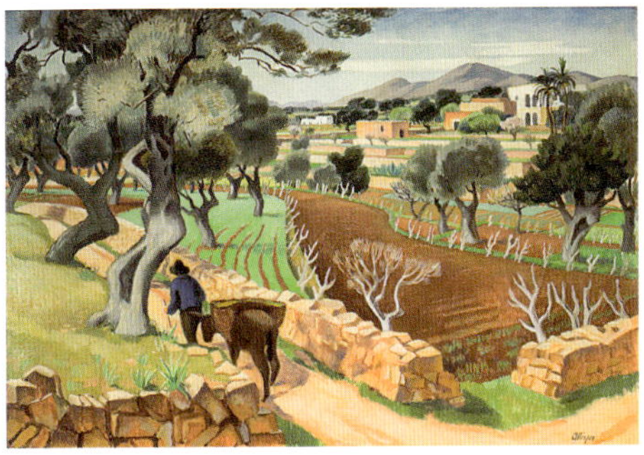

Allinson, Adrian Paul 1890–1959
Ibiza
oil on canvas 63 x 90
1937.FA.291

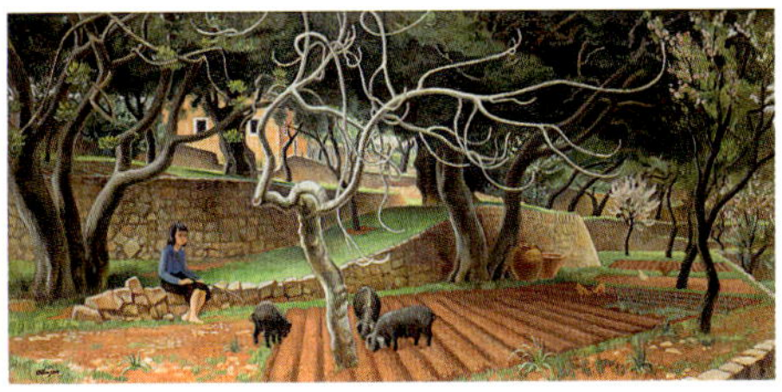

Allinson, Adrian Paul 1890–1959
Ibizan Orchard
oil on canvas 67 x 136
1962.FA.37

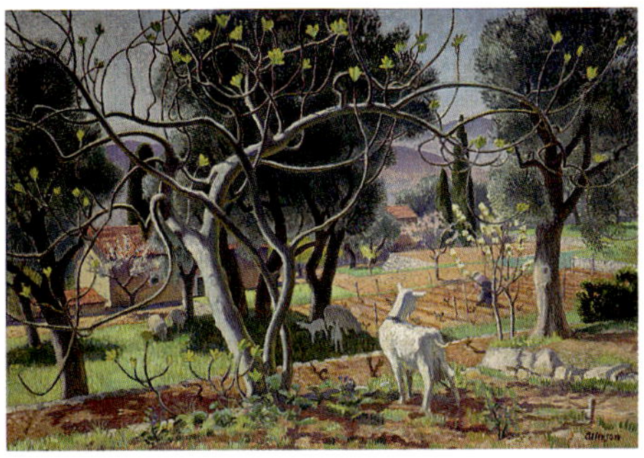

Allinson, Adrian Paul 1890–1959
The Fig Tree
oil on panel 60 x 85
1986.FA.6

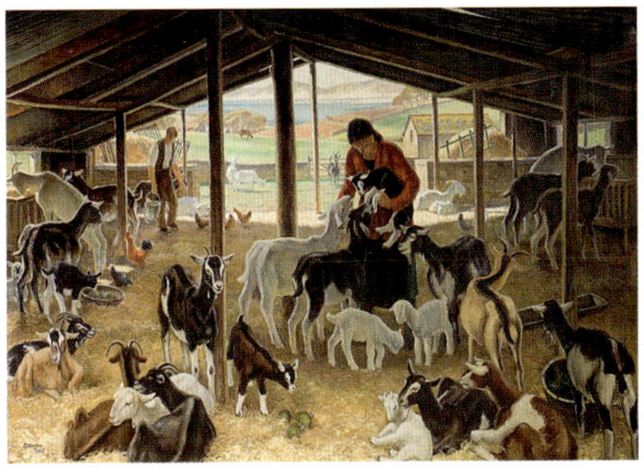

Allinson, Adrian Paul 1890–1959
The Goat Farm
oil on canvas 112 x 174
1967.FA.33

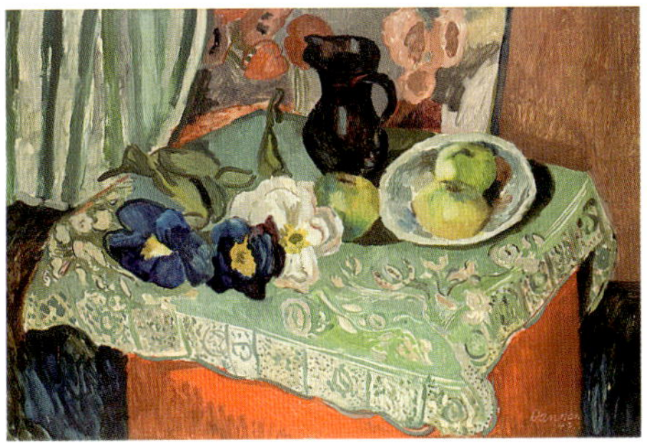

Annan, Dorothy 1908–1983
Still Life with Flowers 1943
oil on canvas 54.5 x 78.5
1947.FA.761

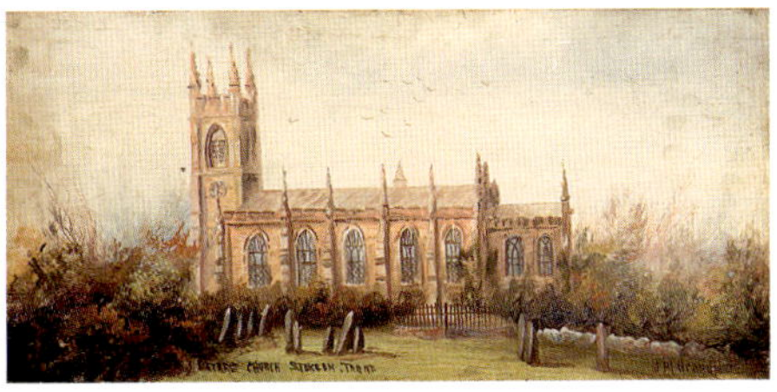

Arandale, J. M.
St Peter's Church, Stoke-on-Trent
oil on canvas 29.9 x 61
1961.FA.85

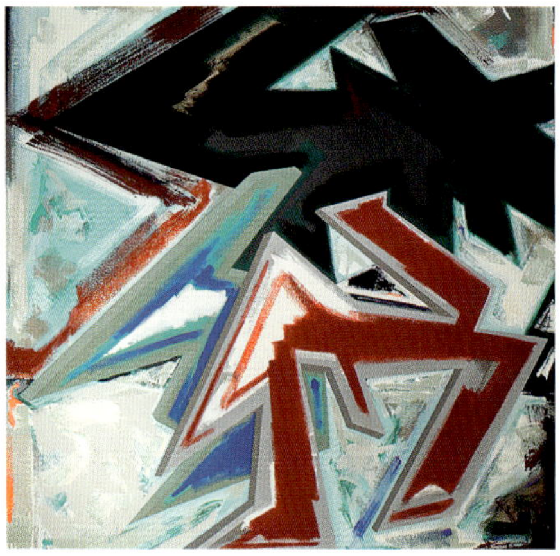

Ashbaugh, Dennis John b.1946
It Looks Grim 1980
oil on canvas 182 x 182
1983.FA.2

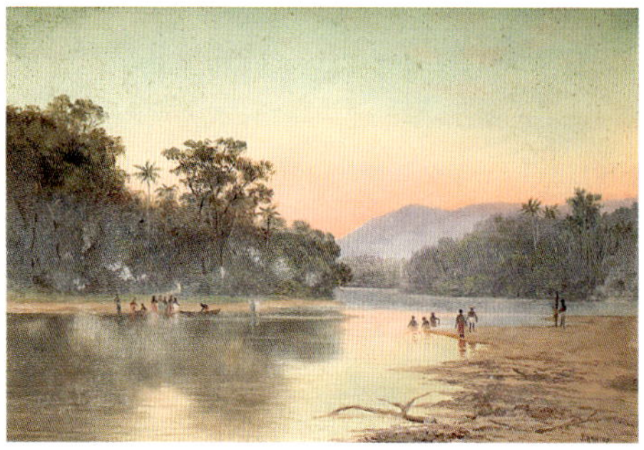

Ashton, James 1859–1935
Mount Kandy, Colombo
oil on paper 24.3 x 34
1961.FA.130

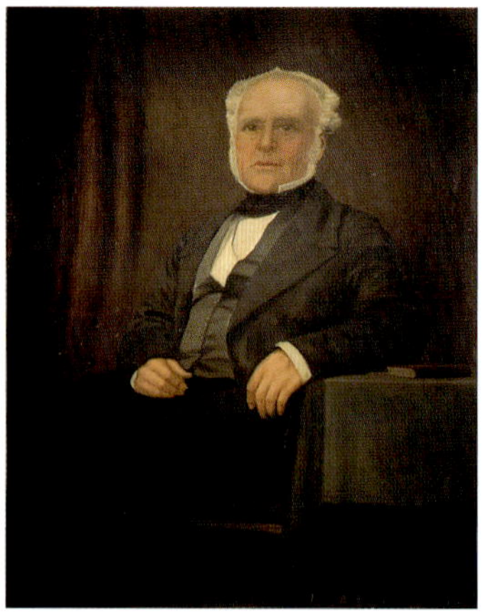

Ashwell, B. C.
James Clover
oil on canvas 105 x 79
PCF1

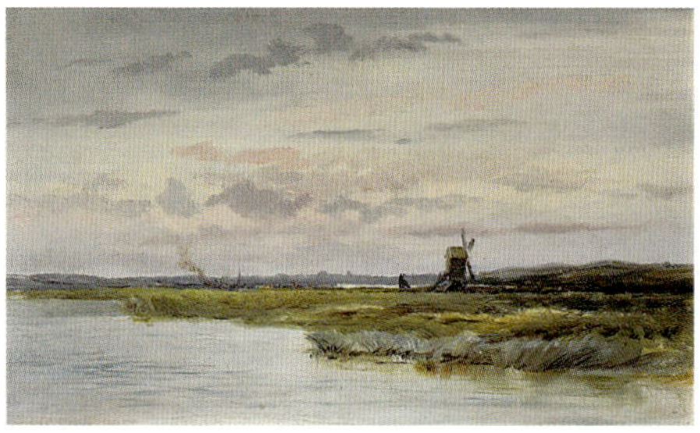

Aumonier, James 1832–1911
At Barking
oil on panel 19.5 x 32
1954.FA.191

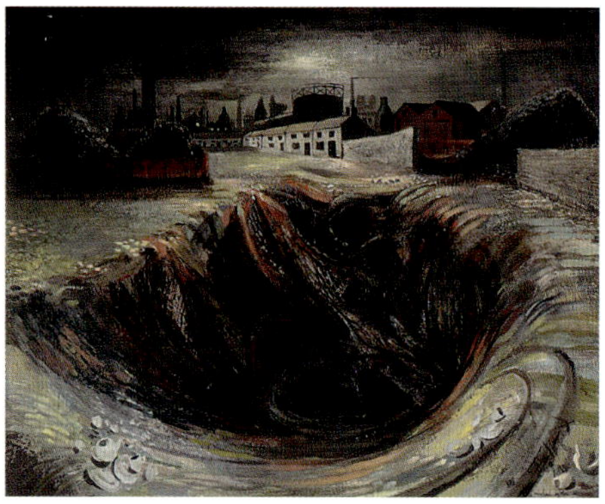

Ayrton, Michael 1921–1975
The Tip, Hanley 1946
oil on panel 49.5 x 59.5
1982.FA.38

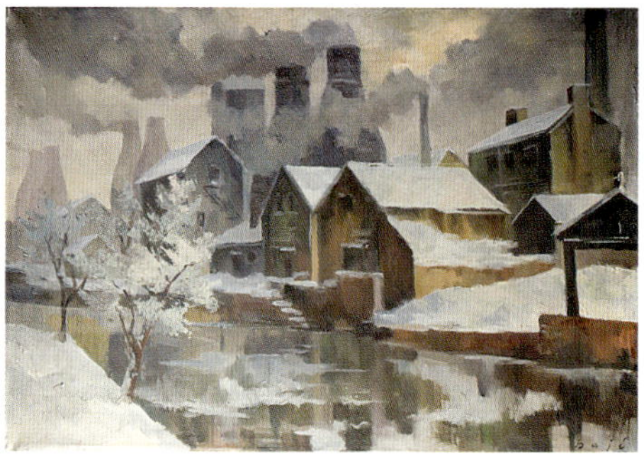

Bajo, D. Y.
Smoke and Snow
oil on canvas 57.2 x 78.7
1950.FA.17

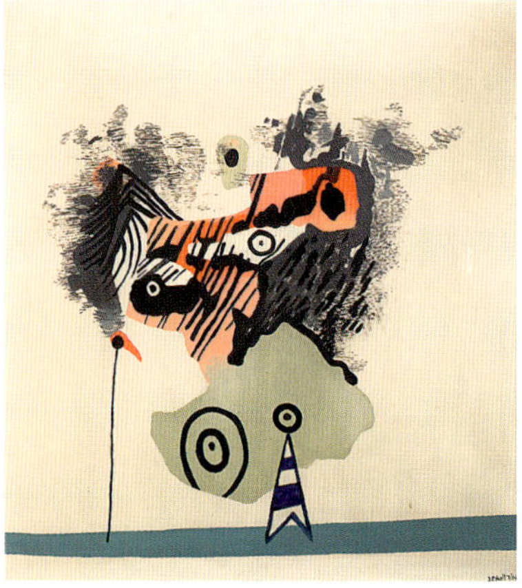

Ball, J. Pat
Composition 1966
oil on canvas 70 x 63
1967.FA.14

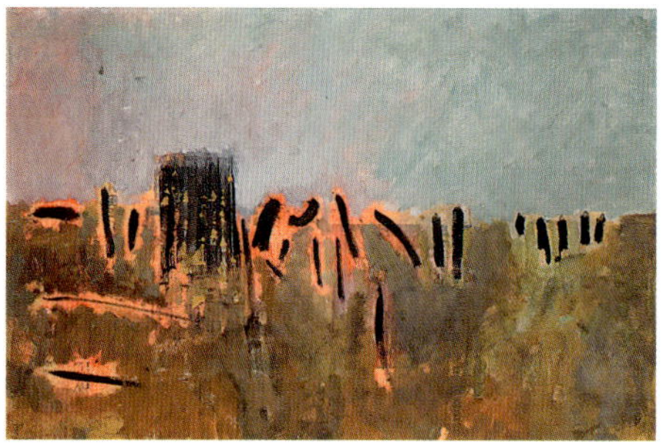

Ball, J. Pat
Wet Afternoon
oil on board 79 x 117
1969.FA.5A

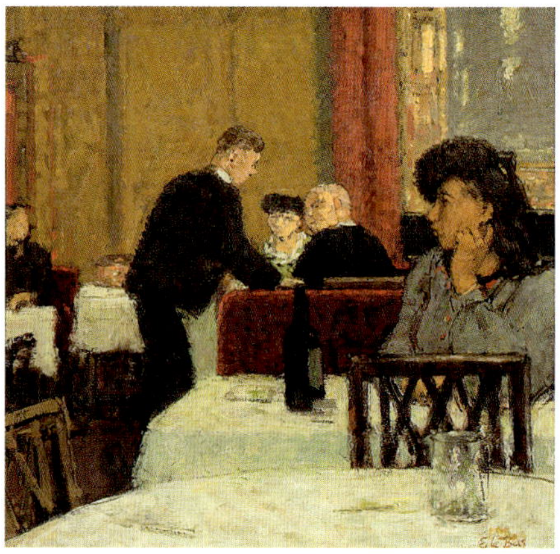

Bas, Edward le 1904–1966
Café Royale
oil on canvas 54 x 56
1950.FA.118

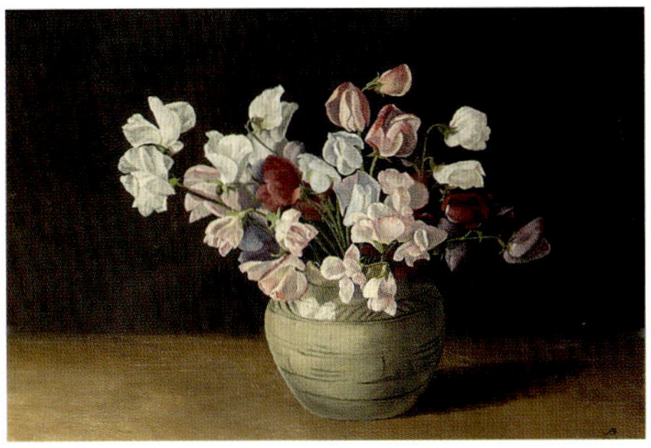

Bennett, Charles Howson active 1912–1913
Sweetpeas in an Earthenware Bowl 1912
oil on canvas 33 x 48
1958.FA.78

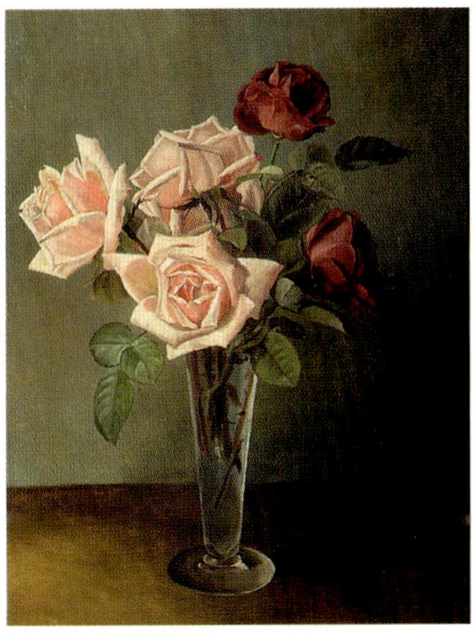

Bennett, Charles Howson active 1912–1913
Roses in a Glass Vase 1913
oil on canvas 38.5 x 29
1958.FA.75

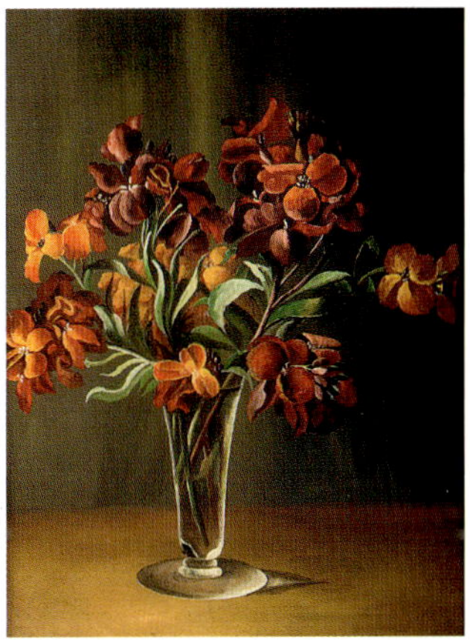

Bennett, Charles Howson active 1912–1913
Bronze Wallflowers in a Glass Vase
oil on canvas 39 x 28
1958.FA.77

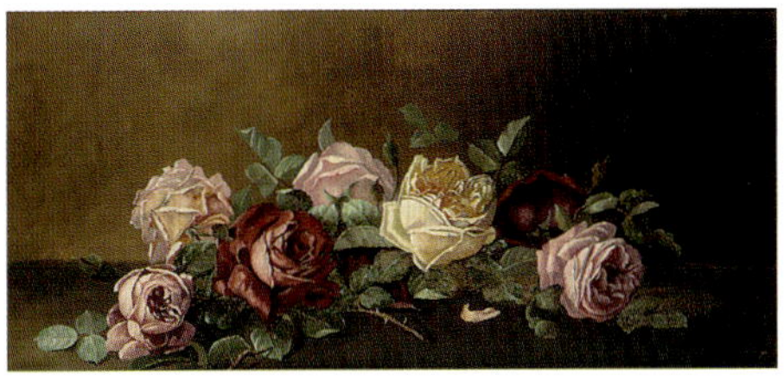

Bennett, Charles Howson active 1912–1913
Pink, Yellow and Red Roses
oil on canvas 28.5 x 59
1958.FA.76

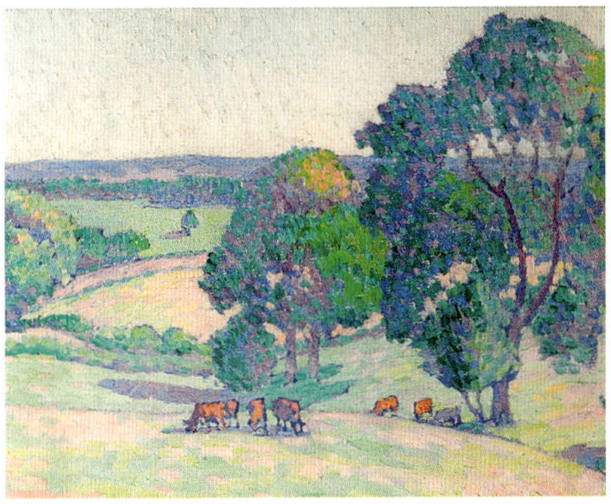

Bevan, Robert Polhill 1865–1925
The Ash Tree
oil on canvas 43 x 53
1953.FA.7

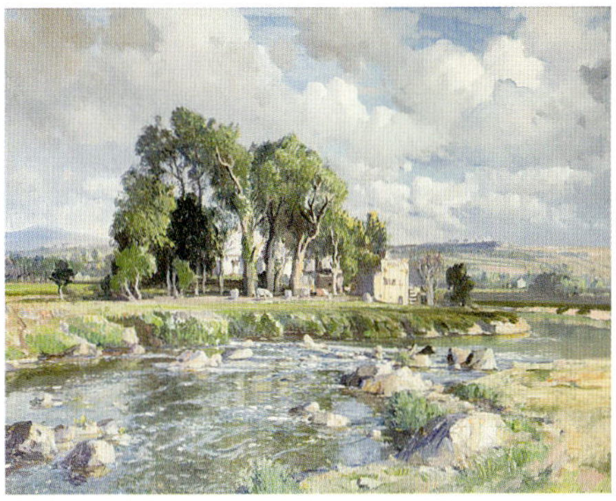

Birch, Samuel John Lamorna 1869–1955
Fresh Winds on a May Day, Isla River, Aberdeenshire
oil on canvas 60 x 65
1931.FA.25

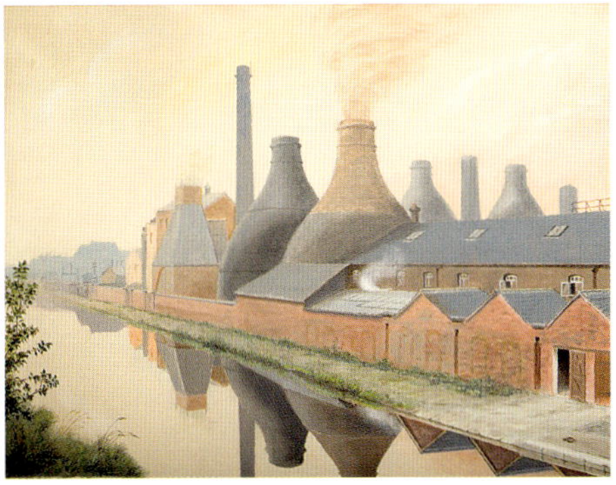

Birchall, Harold H.
Reflections, Etruria Vale 1949
oil on canvas 40 x 51
1950.FA.42

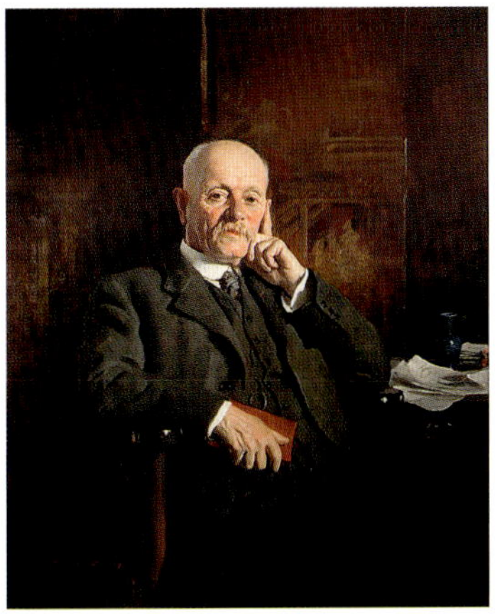

Birley, Oswald Hornby Joseph 1880–1952
Bernard Moore (1850–1935) 1924
oil on canvas 125 x 100
PCF2

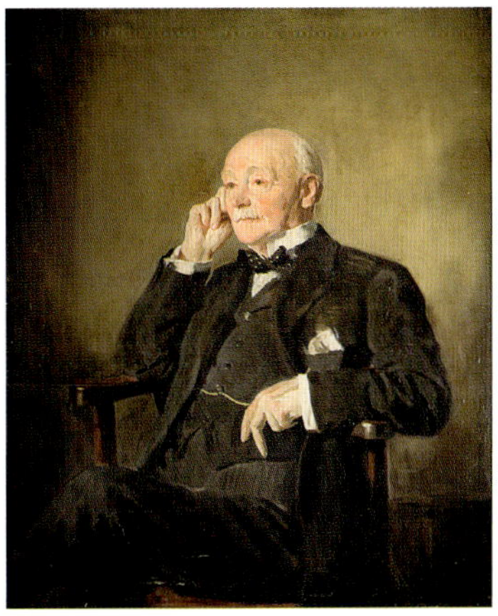

Birley, Oswald Hornby Joseph 1880–1952
A. P. Llewellyn
oil on canvas 108 x 86.5
PCF3

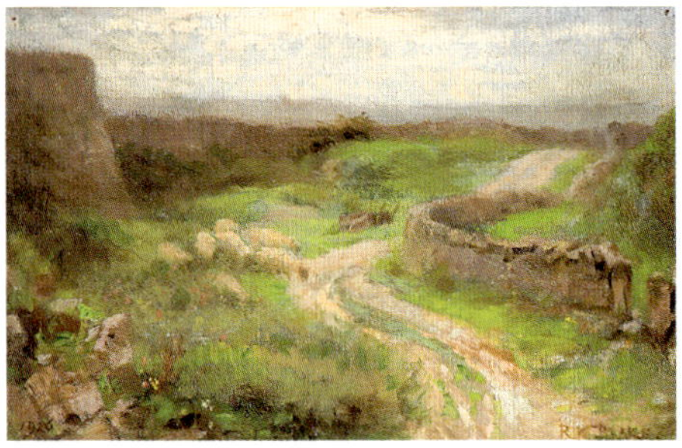

Blake, Rosa K. active 1926–1962
Wetton Quarry 1926
oil on canvas 19 x 29 (E)
1962.FA.30

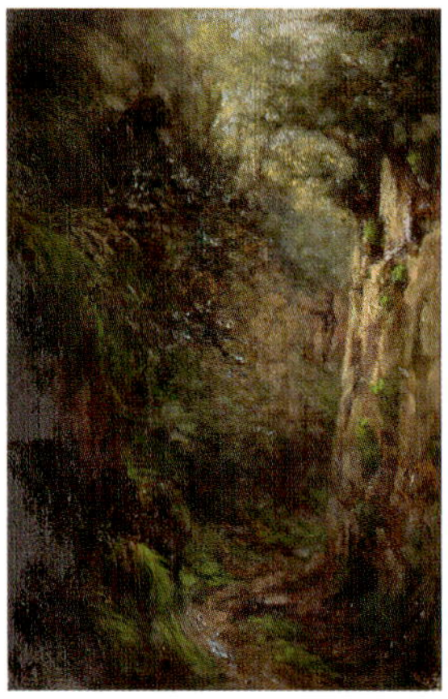

Blake, Rosa K. active 1926–1962
Ludchurch 1938
oil on canvas 29 x 19 (E)
1960.FA.113

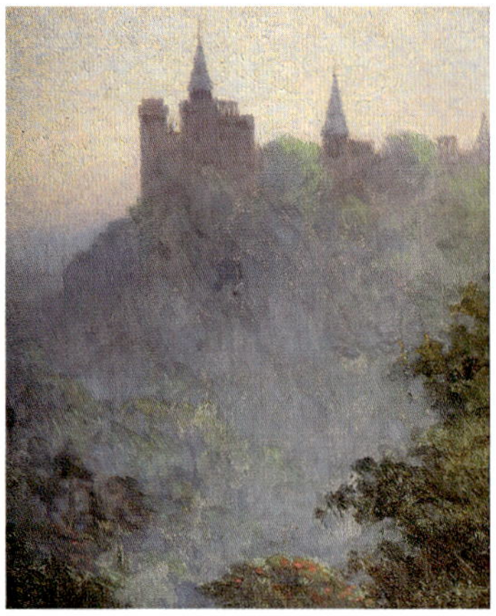

Blake, Rosa K. active 1926–1962
Alton Castle
oil on canvas 28 x 23
1962.FA.29

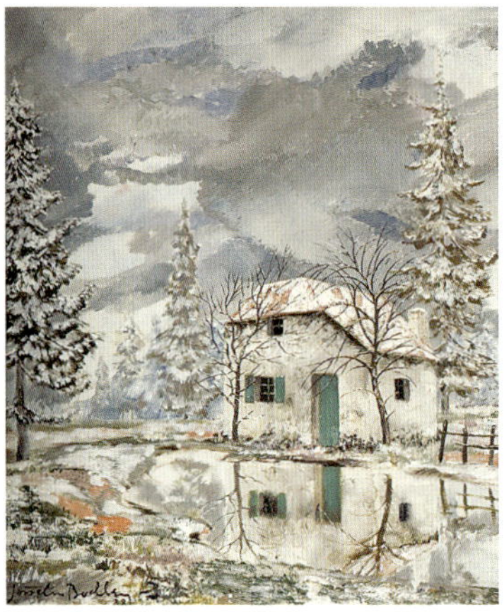

Bodley, Josselin 1893–1974
Frost 1938
oil on canvas 45 x 37
1964.FA.65A

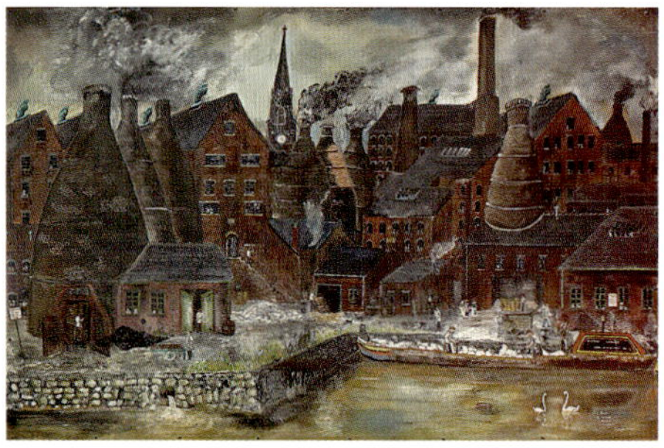

Boote, R., Mollart D., Mountford J. & Stewart A.
Potteries
oil on panel 122 x 183
1960.FA.38

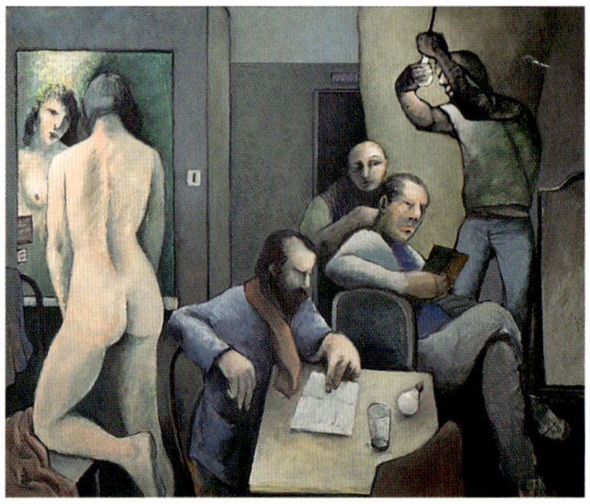

Borsky, Jiri b.1945
Actors in a Dressing Room 1980
oil on canvas 122 x 143
1980.FA.32

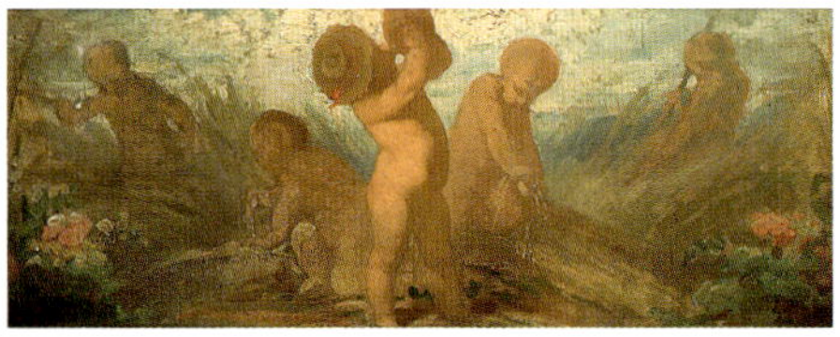

Boullemier, Antonin c.1840–1900
Infant Bacchantes
oil on canvas 18 x 44
1954.FA.92.2

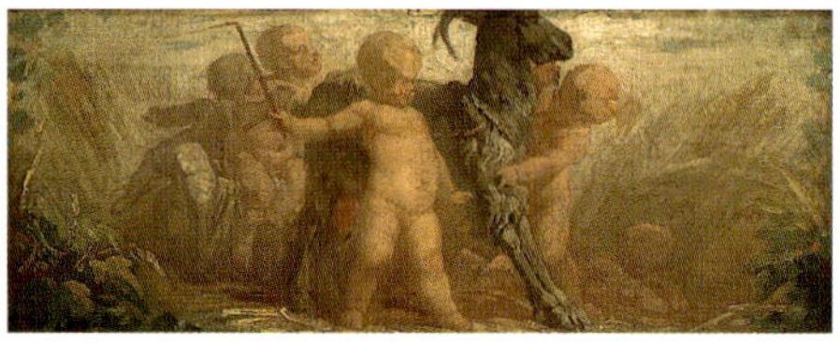

Boullemier, Antonin c.1840–1900
Infant Bacchantes
oil on canvas 18 x 44
1954.FA.92.4

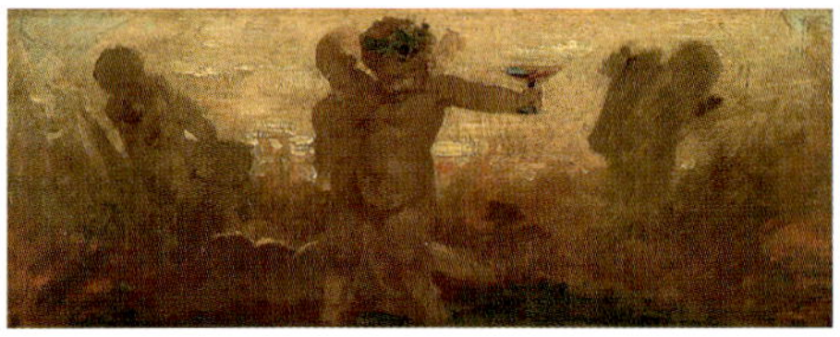

Boullemier, Antonin c.1840–1900
Infant Bacchantes Drinking
oil on canvas 18 x 44
1954.FA.92.3

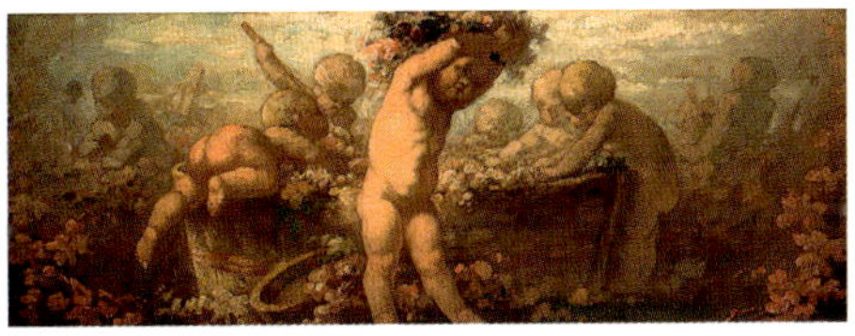

Boullemier, Antonin c.1840–1900
Putti with Flowers
oil on canvas 18 x 44
1954.FA.92.1

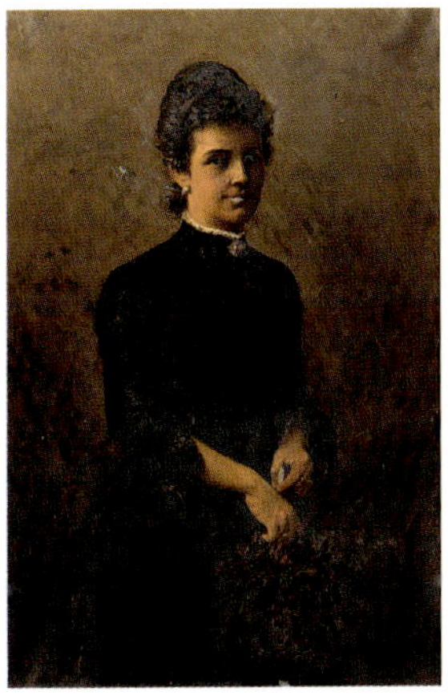

Boullemier, Antonin c.1840–1900
The Late Mrs. W. Sherratt of Handle House, Stoke-on-Trent
oil on canvas 106 x 68
1961.FA.128

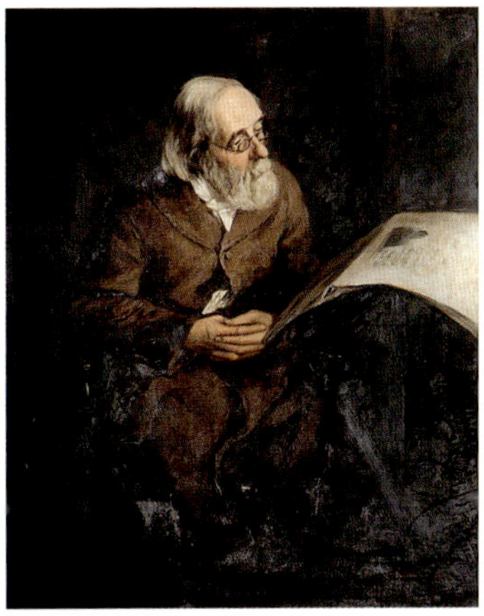

Boullemier, Lucien 1877–1948
George Howson (1818–1896) 1897
oil on canvas 125 x 99
1986.FA.26

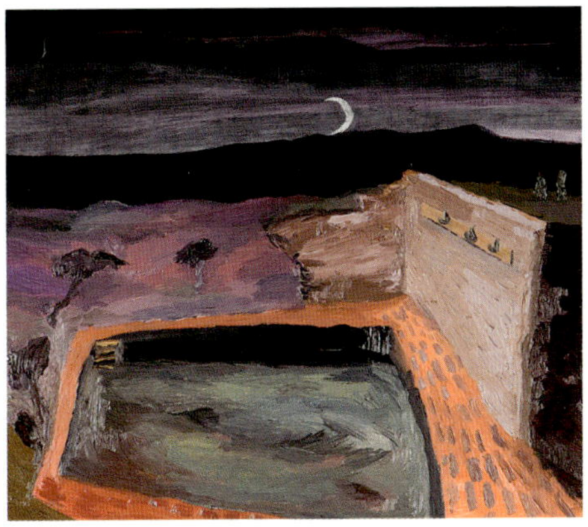

Bowers, Kelvin b.1946
Swimming Pool (Coat Hooks and Crescent Moon)
oil on panel 34 x 38
1991.FA.2

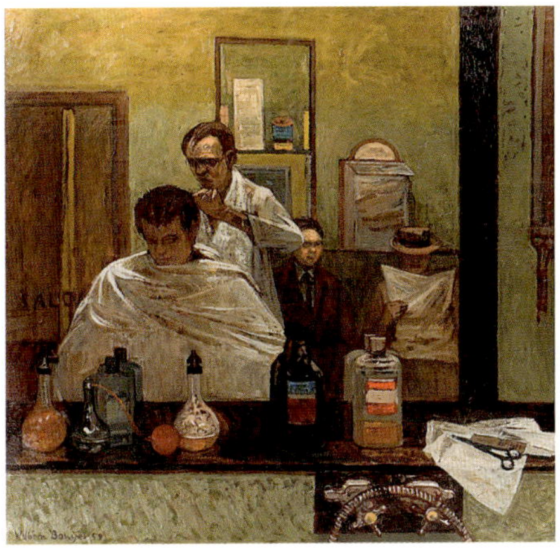

Bowyer, William b.1926
Short Back and Sides 1958
oil on canvas 110 x 111
1958.FA.52

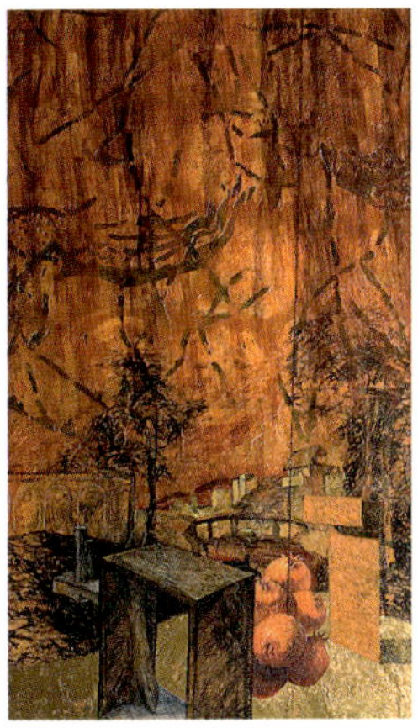

Boyd, Stephen b.1959
The Tempest (after Giorgione)
oil, encaustic & gold leaf on canvas 214 x 168
1990.FA.7

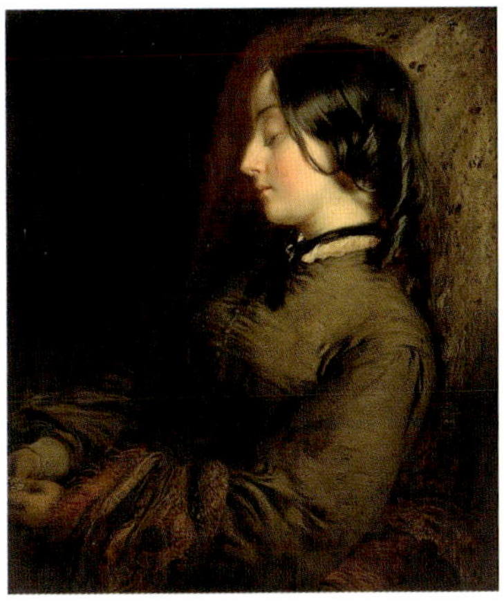

Bradley, William 1801–1857
Portrait of a Seated Woman Sleeping
oil on canvas 74 x 61
1946.FA.749

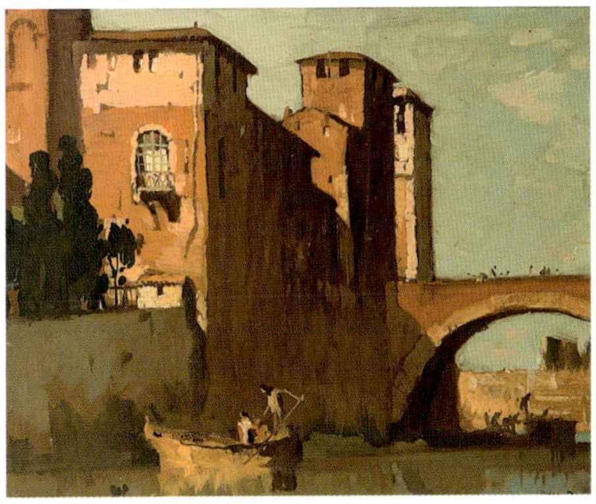

Brangwyn, Frank 1867–1956
Rome
oil on panel 44 x 51
1937.FA.249

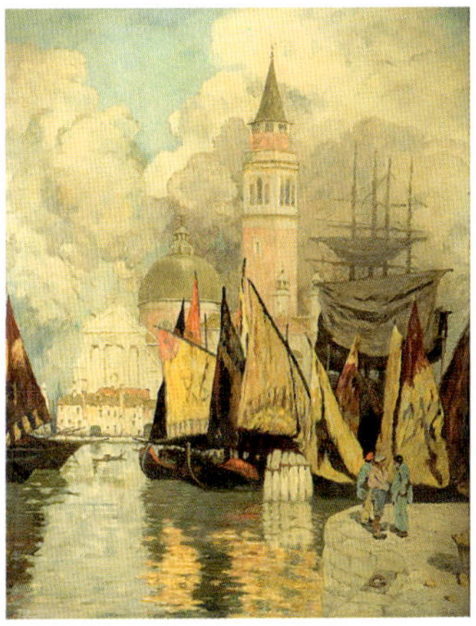

Brangwyn, Frank 1867–1956
San Giorgio, Venice
oil on canvas 90 x 69.5
1963.FA.35

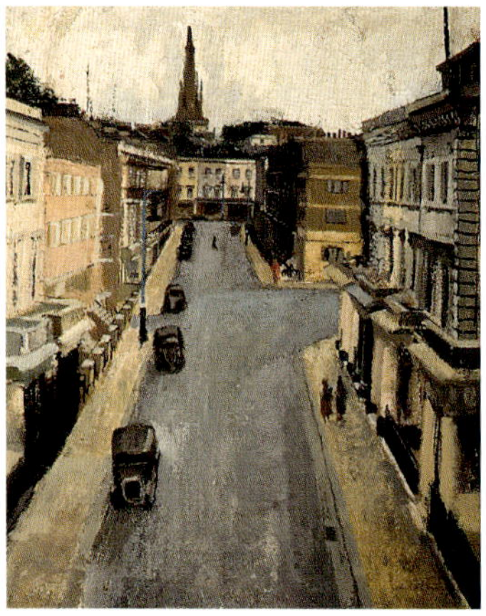

Bridgeman, Ann b.1934
Pimlico
oil on canvas 69 x 54
1958.FA.65

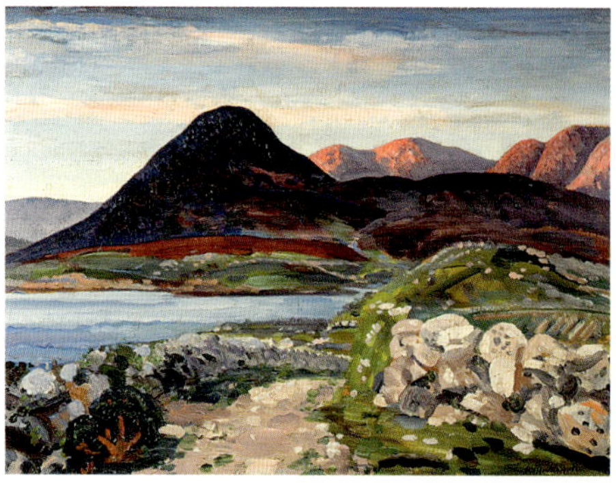

Brockhurst, Gerald Leslie 1890–1978
Ballynakill, Connemara
oil on panel 44 x 59
1947.FA.835

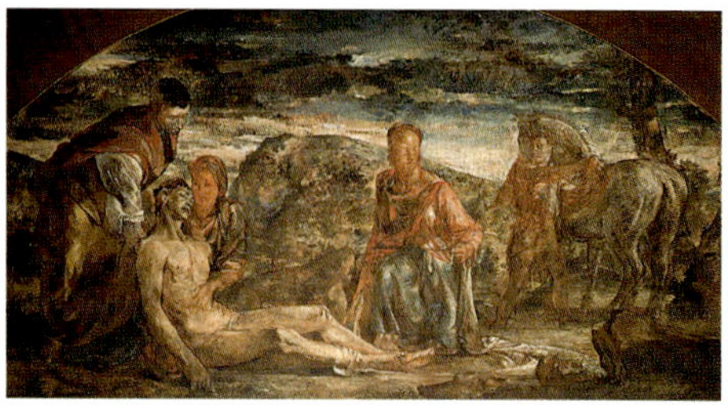

Brooker, Peter Alfred 1900–1965
The Dead Christ 1927
oil on panel 107 x 195
1962.FA.28

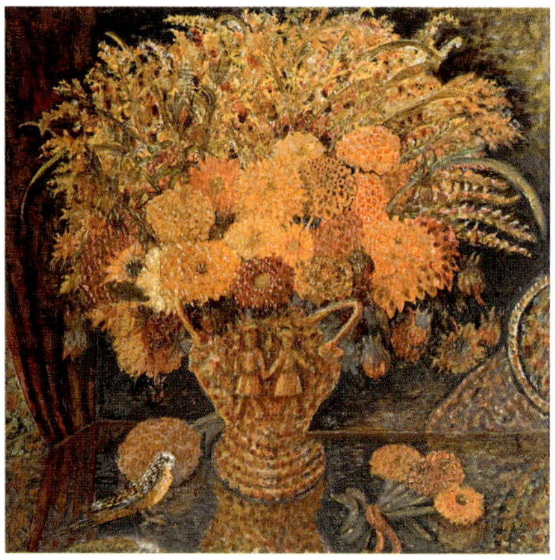

Brown, Charles William 1882–1961
Flowers in a Vase 1952
oil on board 55 x 61 (E)
1983.FA.1.1440

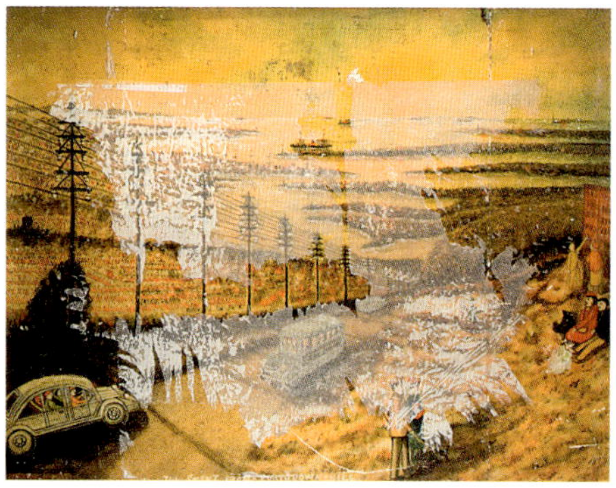

Brown, Charles William 1882–1961
The Solent from Portsdown Hill 1953
oil on board 61 x 76
1983.FA.1.1431

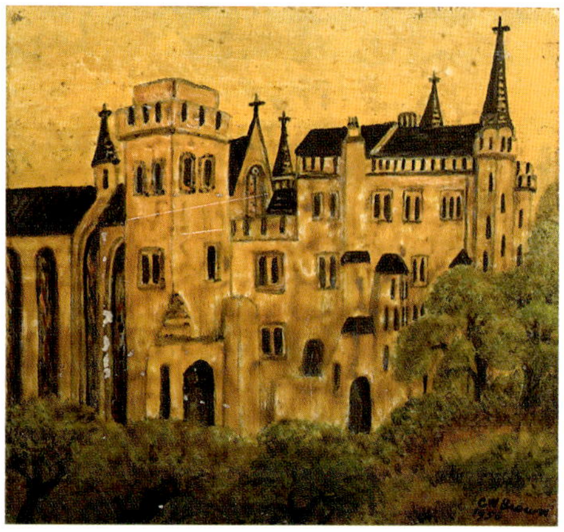

Brown, Charles William 1882–1961
Alton Towers 1956
oil on panel 29.5 x 30.5 (E)
1983.FA.1.1104

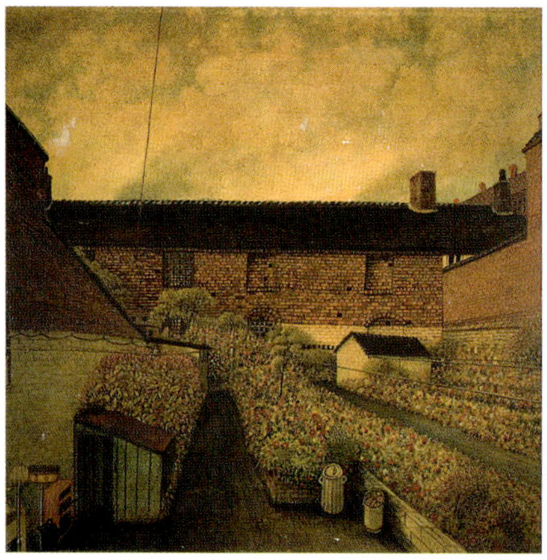

Brown, Charles William 1882–1961
Back Gardens 1956
oil on board 90 x 90
1983.FA.1.1463

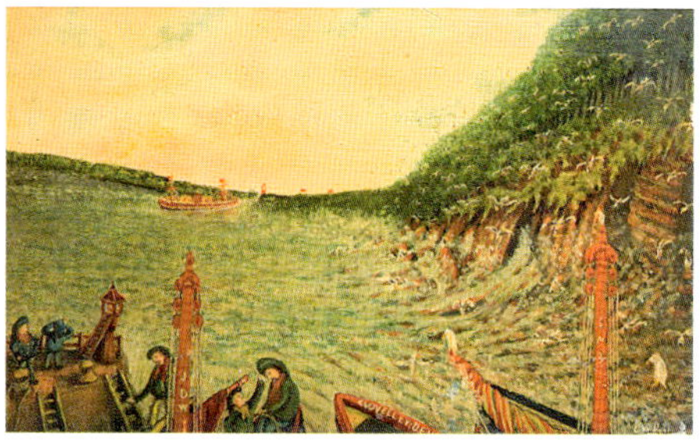

Brown, Charles William 1882–1961
Clovelly, Devon 1956
oil on board 26.5 x 42
1983.FA.1.1437

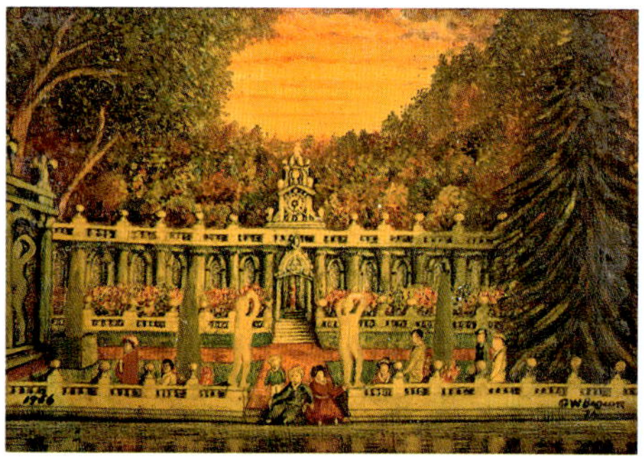

Brown, Charles William 1882–1961
Garden 1956
oil on panel 25.5 x 35.5
1983.FA.1.1119

Facing page: Harvey, Harold C., 1874–1941, *The Little Maiden* (detail), 1934, Wolverhampton Art Gallery, (p. 279)

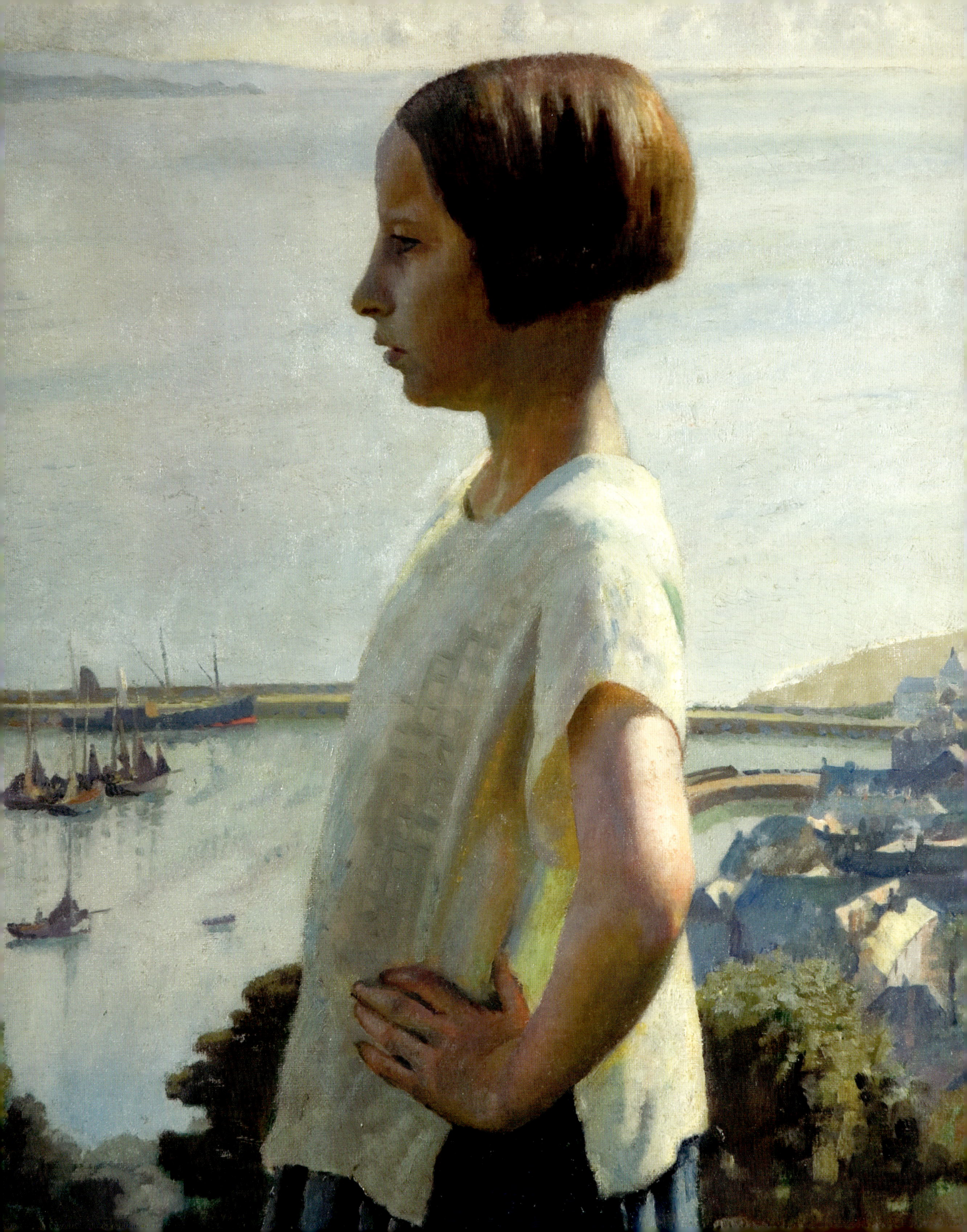

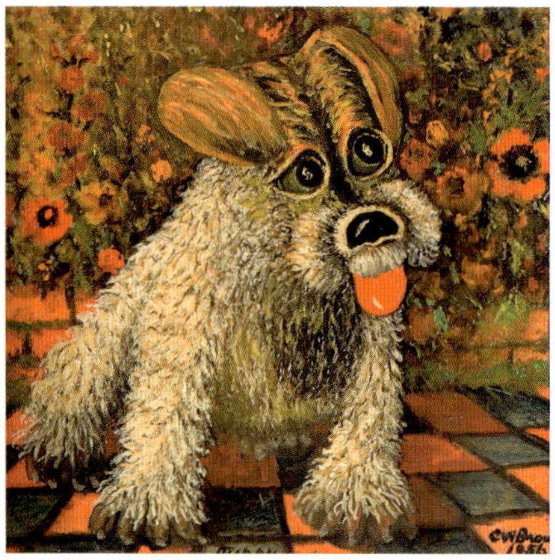

Brown, Charles William 1882–1961
Puppy 1956
oil on board 29.5 x 29.5
1983.FA.1.546

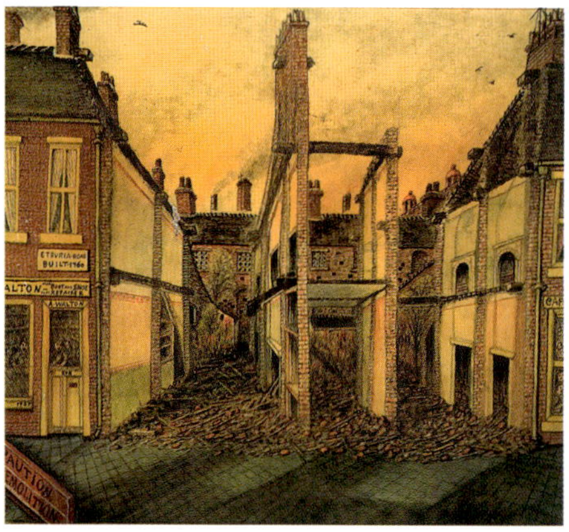

Brown, Charles William 1882–1961
Demolition 1957
oil on board 61 x 64
1983.FA.1.1445

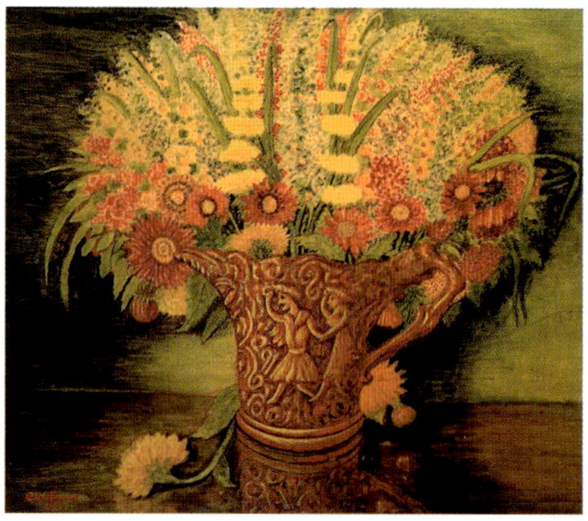

Brown, Charles William 1882–1961
Flowers in a Jug 1957
oil on board 55.5 x 61.5
1983.FA.1.1442

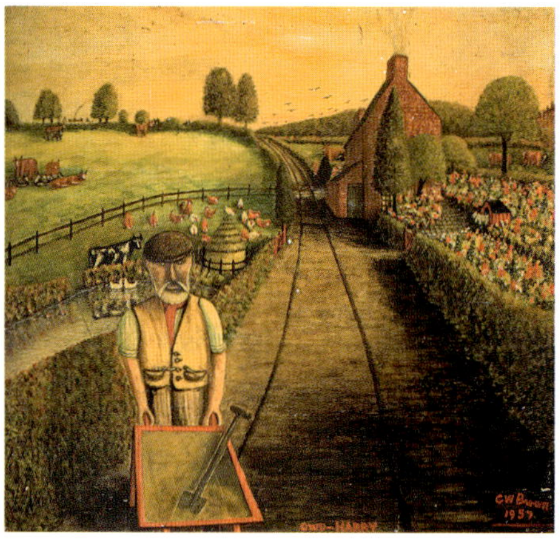

Brown, Charles William 1882–1961
'Owd Harry' 1957
oil on board 61 x 61
1983.FA.1.545

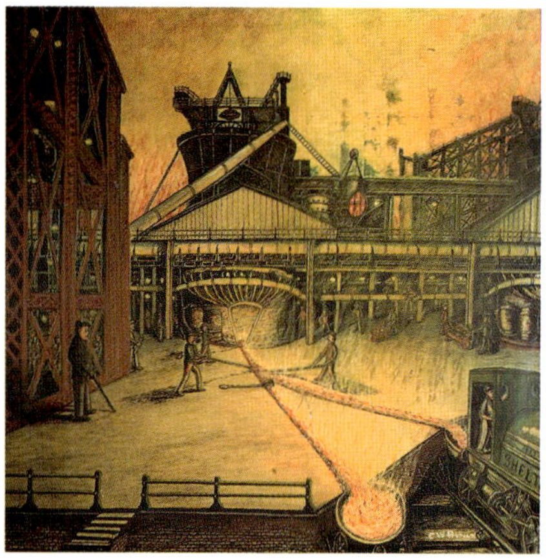

Brown, Charles William 1882–1961
Tapping a Blast Furnace 1957
oil on board 60 x 60
1983.FA.1.1457

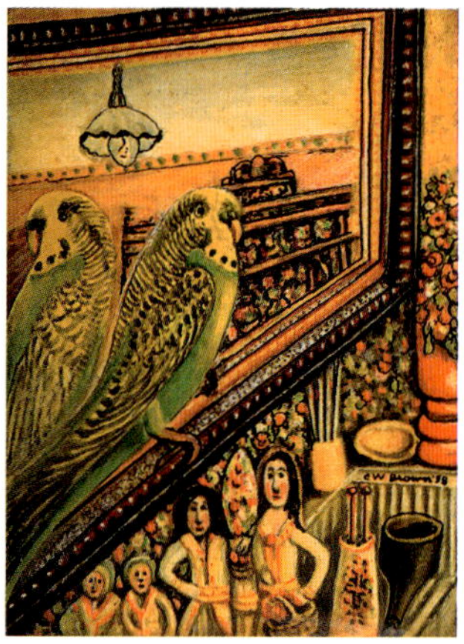

Brown, Charles William 1882–1961
Interior 1958
oil on panel 25 x 17.5
1983.FA.1.1106

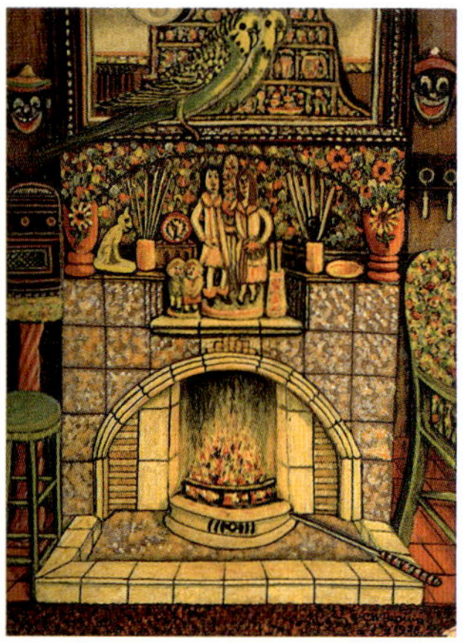

Brown, Charles William 1882–1961
Interior 1958
oil on panel 35.5 x 25.5
1983.FA.1.1333

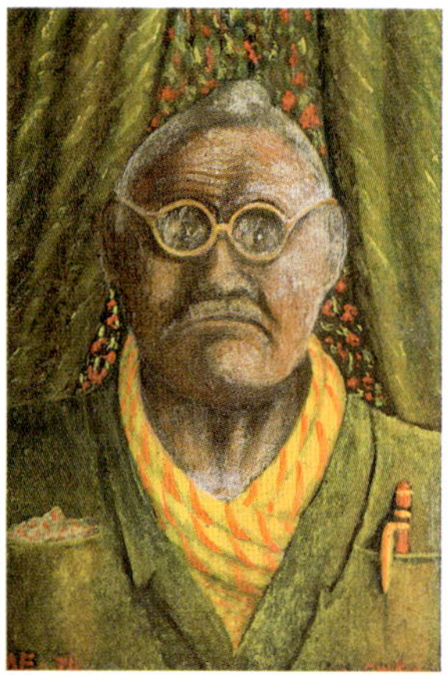

Brown, Charles William 1882–1961
Me, 76 1958
oil on board 24.5 x 16.5
1983.FA.1.549

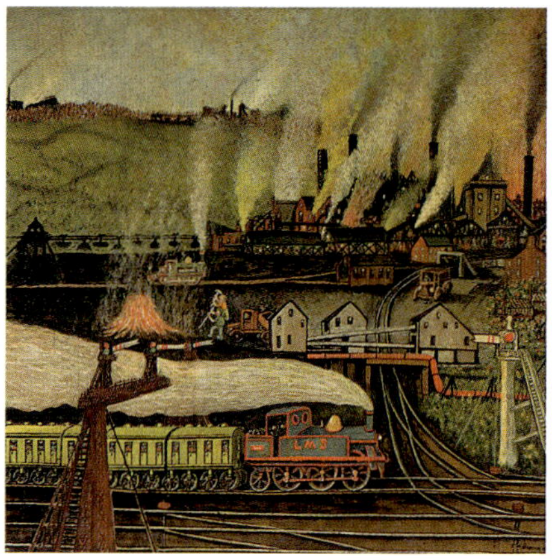

Brown, Charles William 1882–1961
Mixed Industry, Shelton 1958
oil on board 60 x 60
1983.FA.1.1369

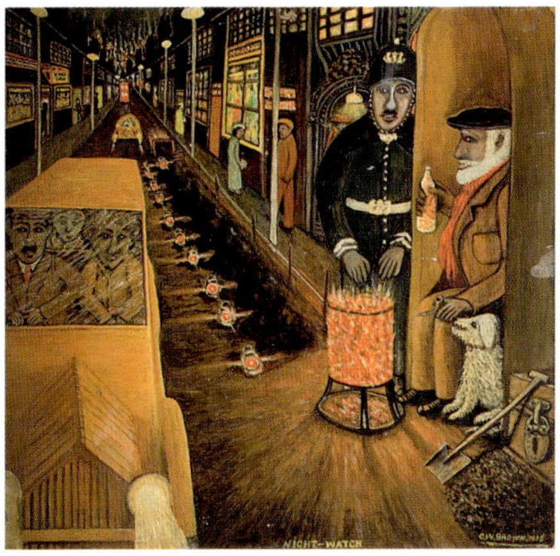

Brown, Charles William 1882–1961
Night Watch 1958
oil on board 61 x 61
PCF4

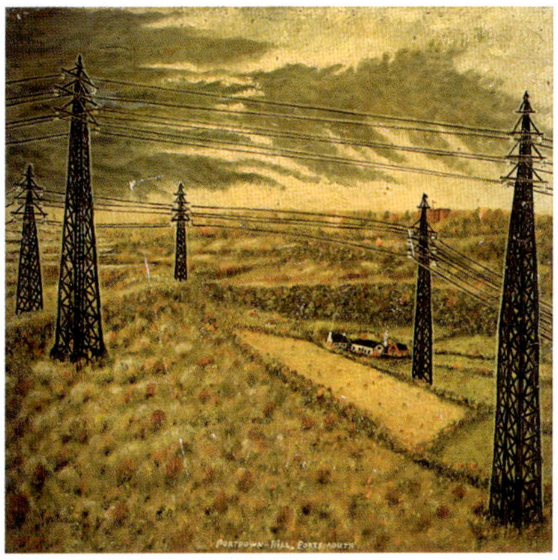

Brown, Charles William 1882–1961
Port-Down Hill, Portsmouth 1958
oil on board 61 x 61
PCF5

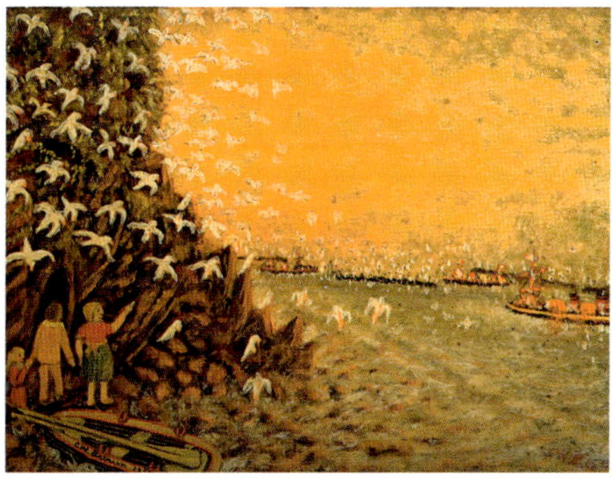

Brown, Charles William 1882–1961
Rocks and Sea 1958
oil on panel 22.5 x 29
1983.FA.1.1118

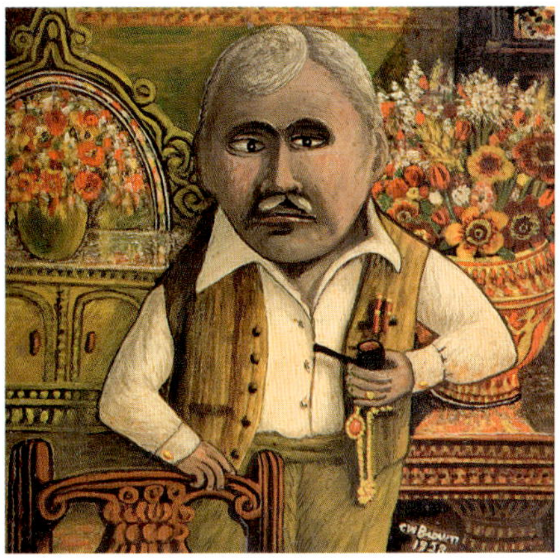

Brown, Charles William 1882–1961
Self Portrait 1958
oil on board 30.5 x 30.5
1983.FA.1.1334

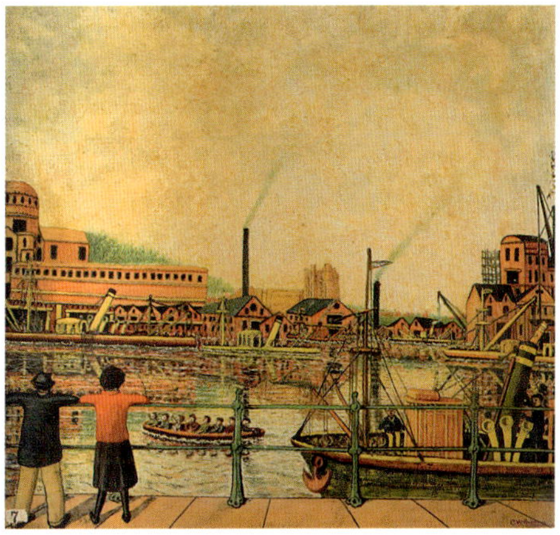

Brown, Charles William 1882–1961
View of Portsmouth Harbour 1958
oil on board 61 x 61
1983.FA.1.544

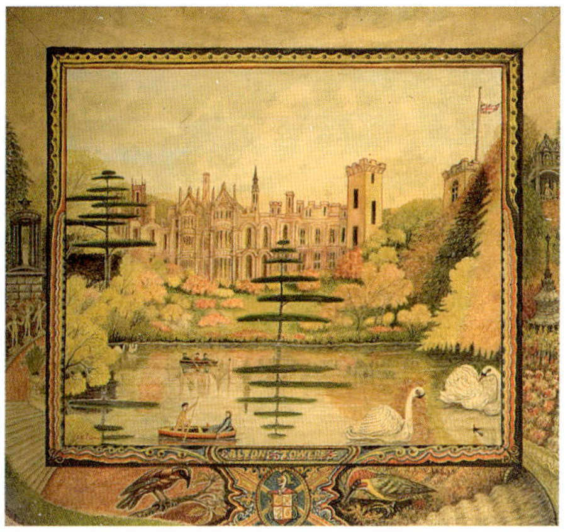

Brown, Charles William 1882–1961
Alton Towers
oil on board 78.5 x 83
1983.FA.1.1433

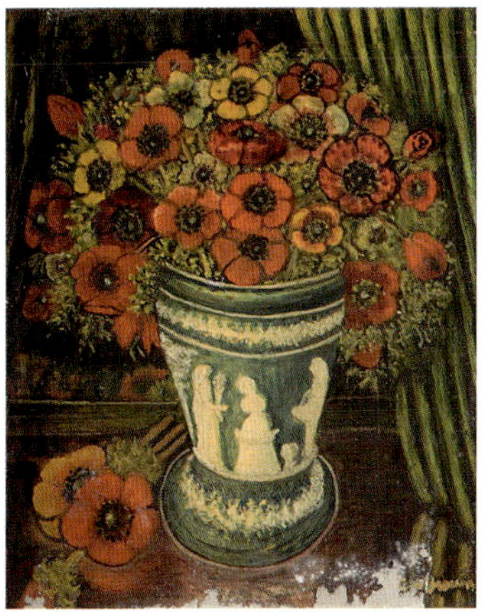

Brown, Charles William 1882–1961
Anemones
oil on panel 29 x 22.5
1983.FA.1.1109

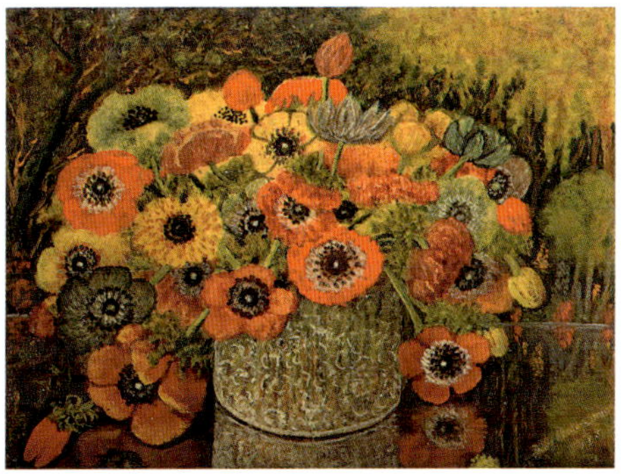

Brown, Charles William 1882–1961
Anemones
oil on panel 22.5 x 29.5
1983.FA.1.1153

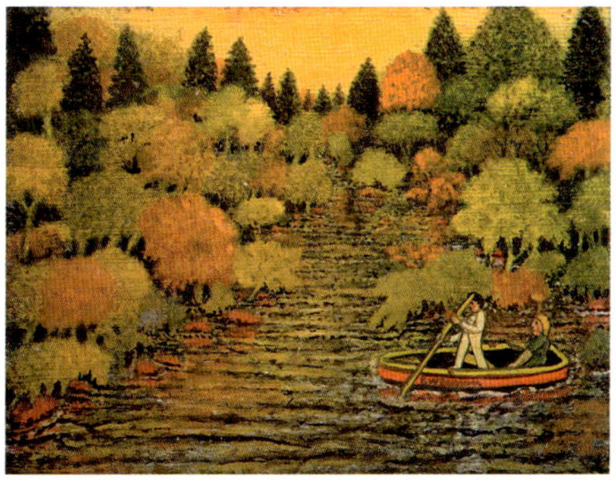

Brown, Charles William 1882–1961
Boating
oil on panel 23 x 29
1983.FA.1.1110

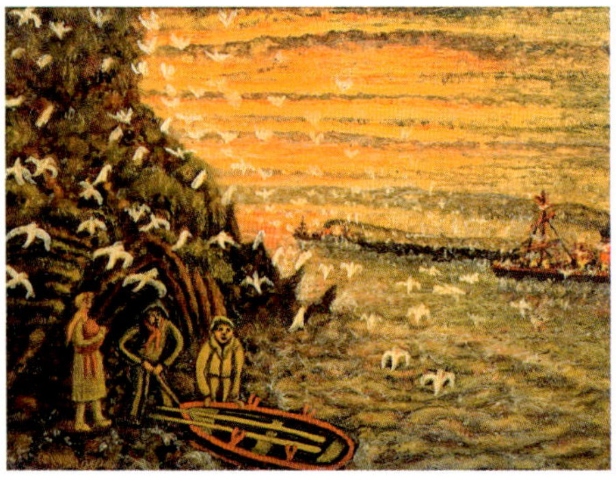

Brown, Charles William 1882–1961
Cliffs, Sea and Gulls
oil on panel 23 x 29
1983.FA.1.1105

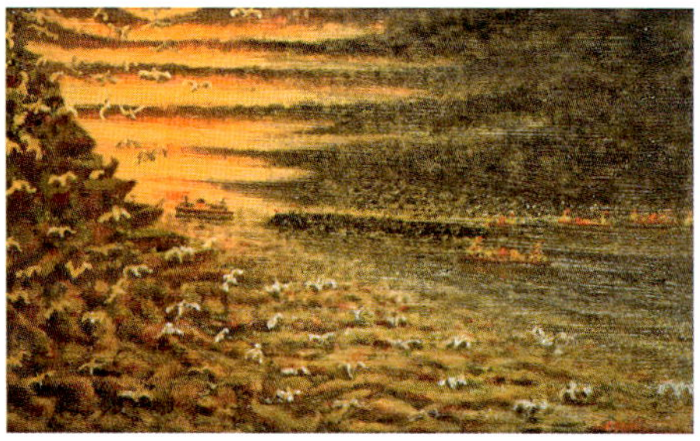

Brown, Charles William 1882–1961
Cliffs, Sea and Gulls
oil on board 25 x 40
1983.FA.1.1444

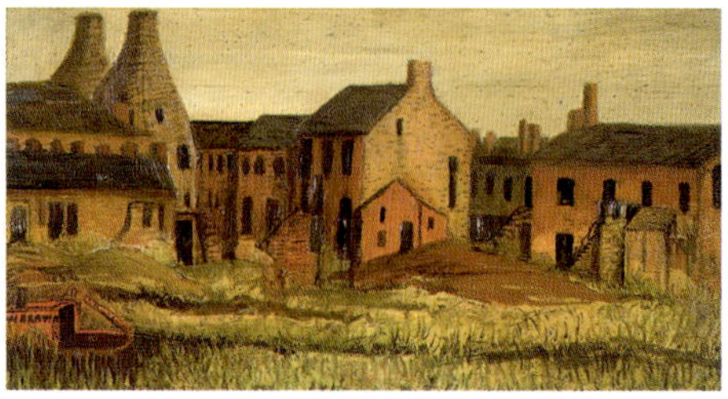

Brown, Charles William 1882–1961
Desolation
oil on board 38 x 71
1983.FA.1.1455

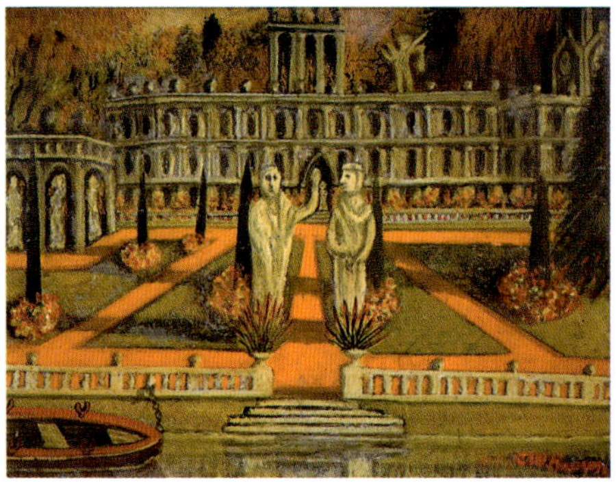

Brown, Charles William 1882–1961
Garden
oil on panel 23 x 29
1983.FA.1.1108

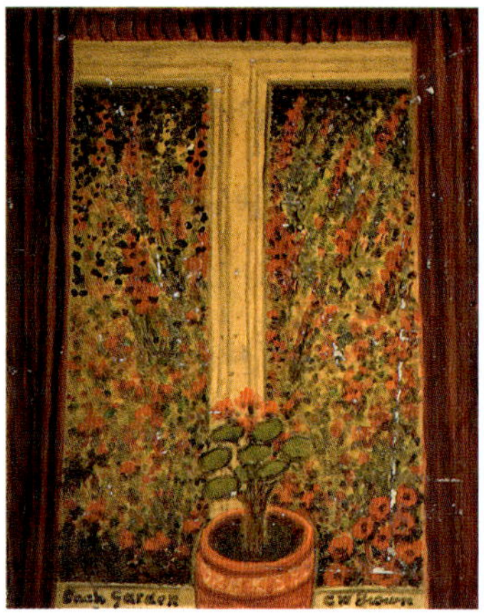

Brown, Charles William 1882–1961
Garden
oil on panel 29 x 23
1983.FA.1.1151

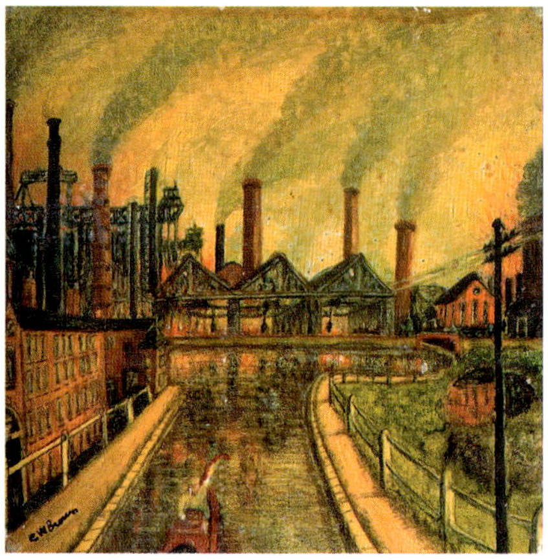

Brown, Charles William 1882–1961
Industrial Scene
oil on panel 31 x 29.5
1983.FA.1.1103

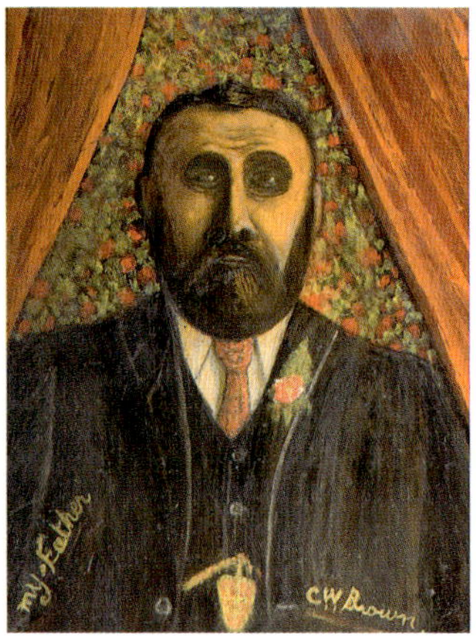

Brown, Charles William 1882–1961
My Father
oil on panel 26.5 x 20
1983.FA.1.1107

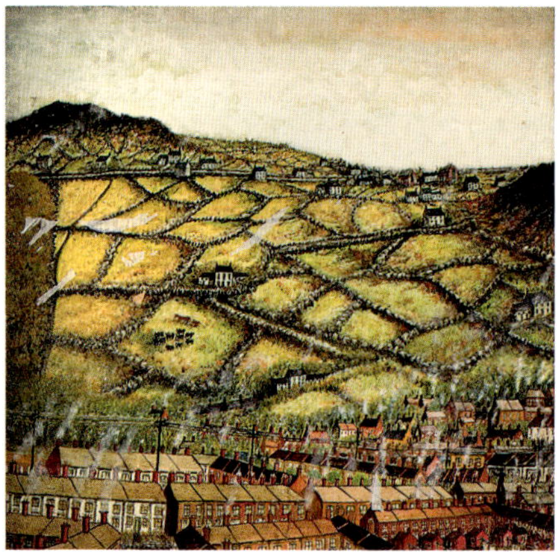

Brown, Charles William 1882–1961
North Staffordshire Landscape
oil on board 61 x 61
PCF6

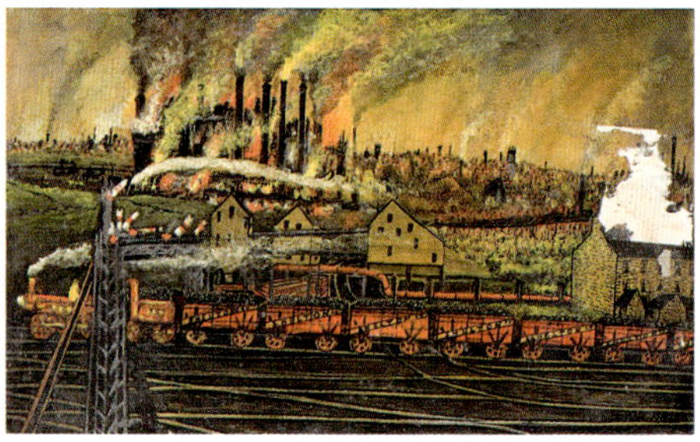

Brown, Charles William 1882–1961
Shelton
oil on panel 30 x 47
1983.FA.1.1115

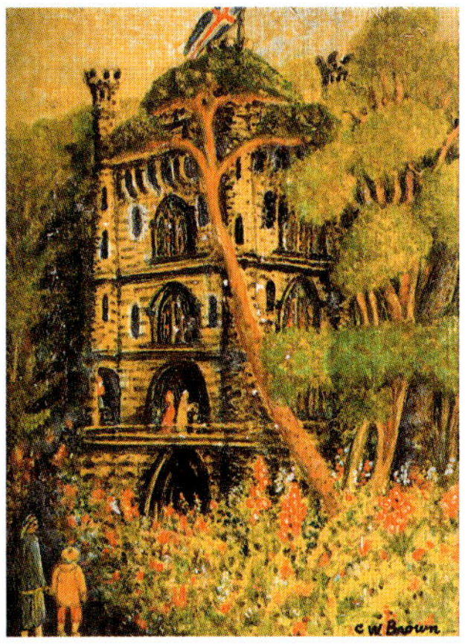

Brown, Charles William 1882–1961
Tower
oil on panel 36 x 25.5
1983.FA.1.1113

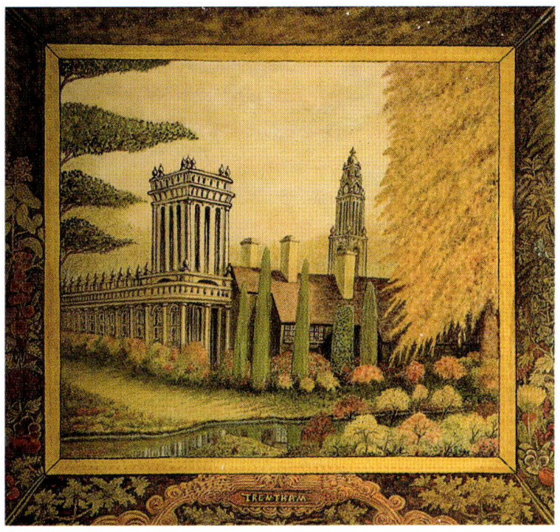

Brown, Charles William 1882–1961
Trentham
oil on board 81 x 84
1983.FA.1.1434

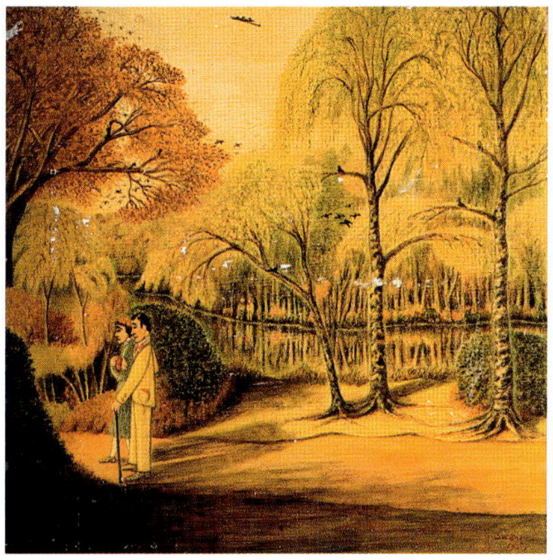

Brown, Charles William 1882–1961
Walking in the Park
oil on board 61 x 61
PCF7

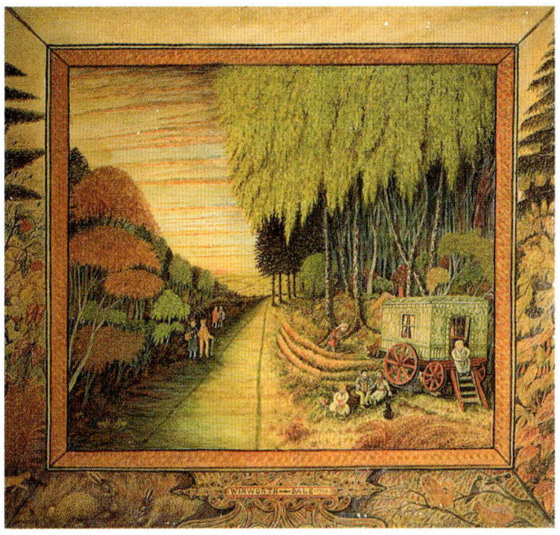

Brown, Charles William 1882–1961
Winworth Dale, Tean
oil on board 78.5 x 83
1983.FA.1.1432

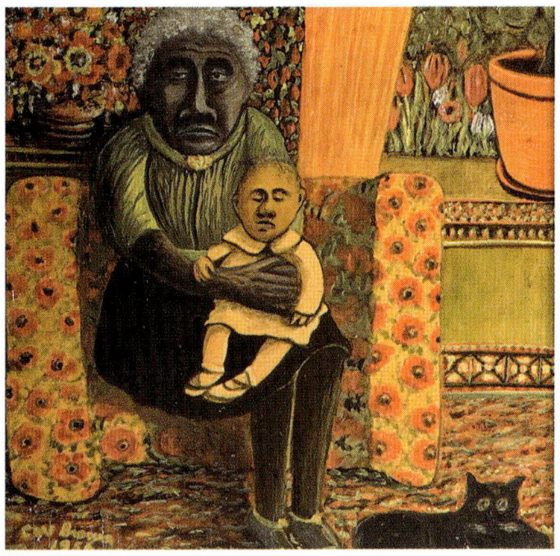

Brown, Charles William 1882–1961
Woman and Child
oil on board 29 x 29
1989.FA.26

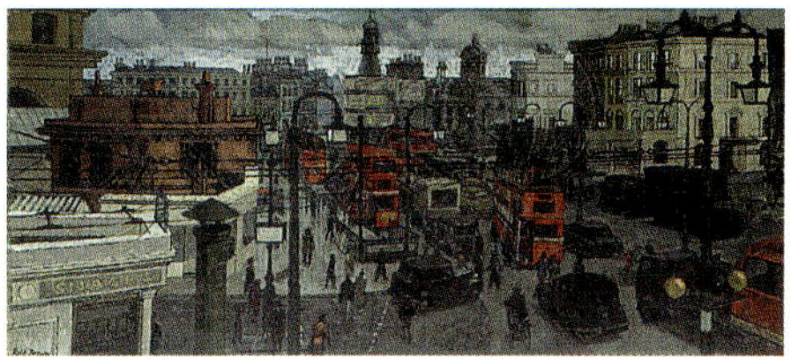

Brown, Robert b.1927
King's Cross
oil on board 45.5 x 101
1956.FA.33

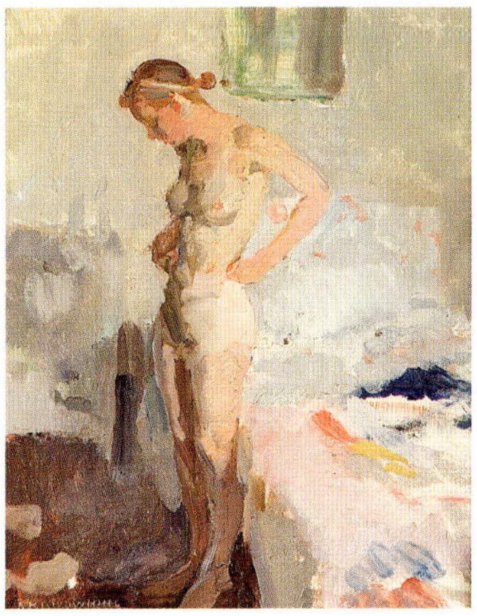

Browning, Amy Katherine 1881–1978
Early Morning
oil on canvas 44 x 35
1945.FA.700

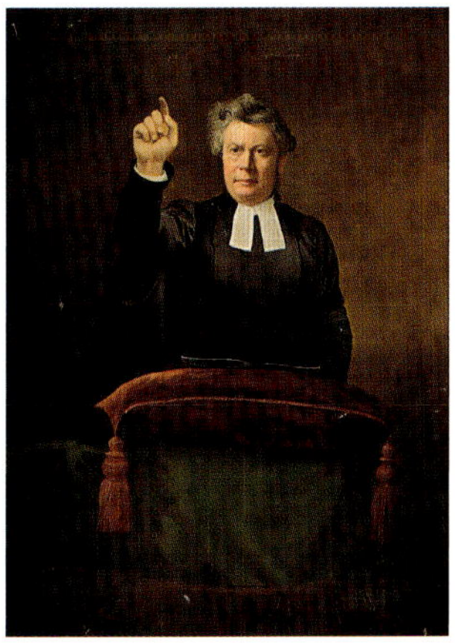

Buckley
The Vicar of Sneyd 1858
oil on canvas 170 x 110
1970.FA.1

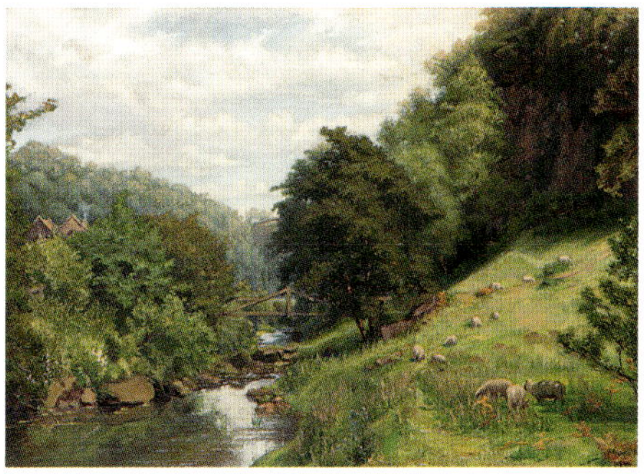

Budd, Herbert Ashwin 1881–1950
View on the Churnet 1903
oil on canvas 44 x 60
1954.FA.97

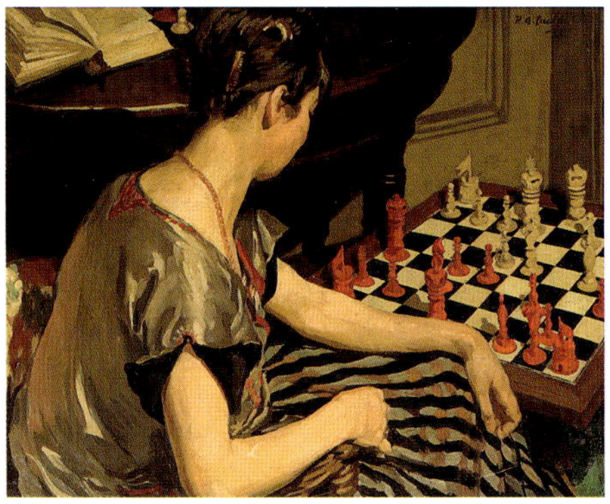

Budd, Herbert Ashwin 1881–1950
The Chess Board 1927
oil on canvas 61.5 x 74.5
1951.FA.25

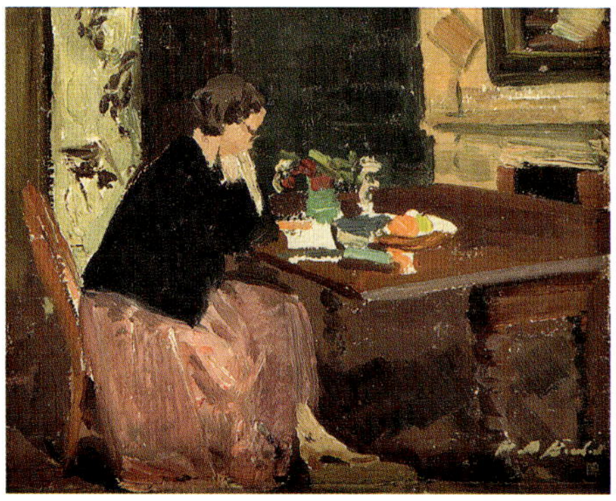

Budd, Herbert Ashwin 1881–1950
Interior
oil on panel 22.5 x 28
1951.FA.24

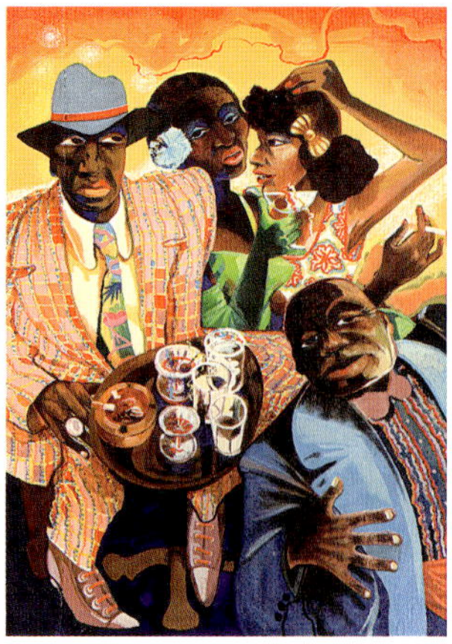

Burnett, June b.1936
Zoot 58
oil on canvas 149 x 104
1990.FA.6

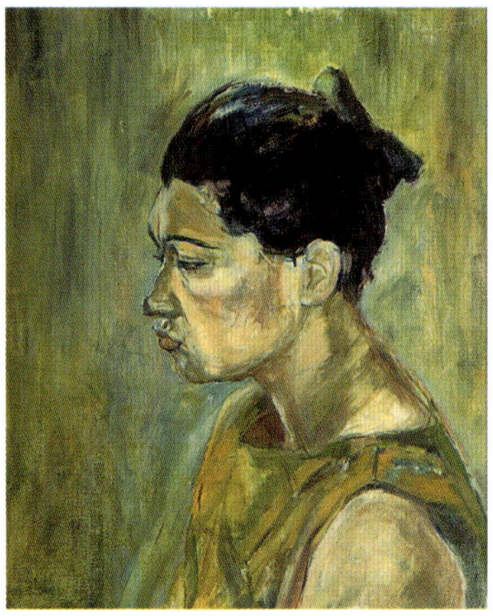

Burnley, Heather b.1937
Portrait
oil on canvas 51 x 41
1968.FA.76

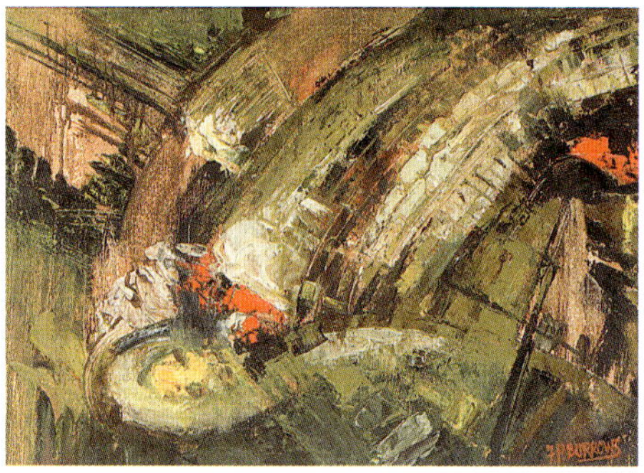

Burrows, Roy b.1922
Abstraction from Log
oil on board 36.5 x 50
1968.FA.4

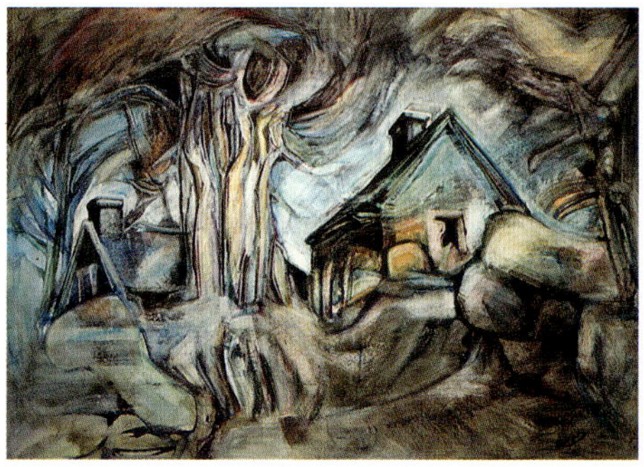

Burrows, Roy b.1922
Cowlyd Hafod
oil & acrylic on panel 84 x 115
1973.FA.4A

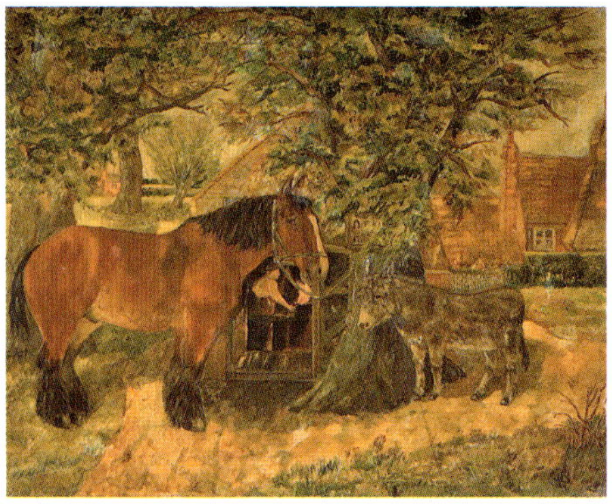

Butler, Charles J.
The Vagabond, Beare Green Common 1920
oil on canvas 50 x 61
PCF8

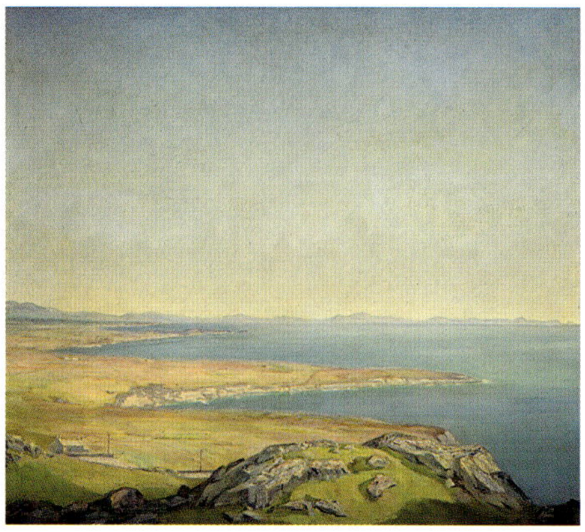

Buttle, George Allen 1870–1925
The Three Bays
oil on canvas 62 x 68
1954.FA.90

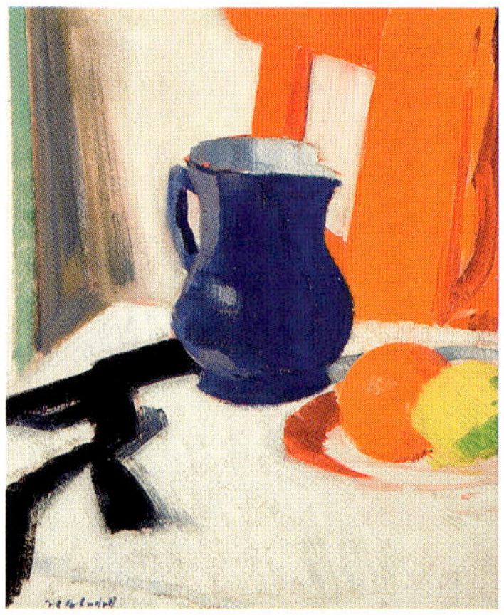

Cadell, Francis Campbell Boileau
1883–1937
Blue and Orange 1940
oil on panel 42.5 x 35
1958.FA.108

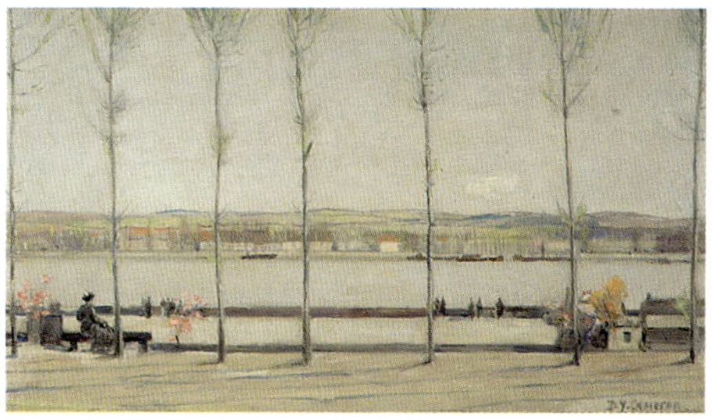

Cameron, David Young 1865–1945
Caudebec
oil on canvas 38.5 x 63.5
1945.FA.699

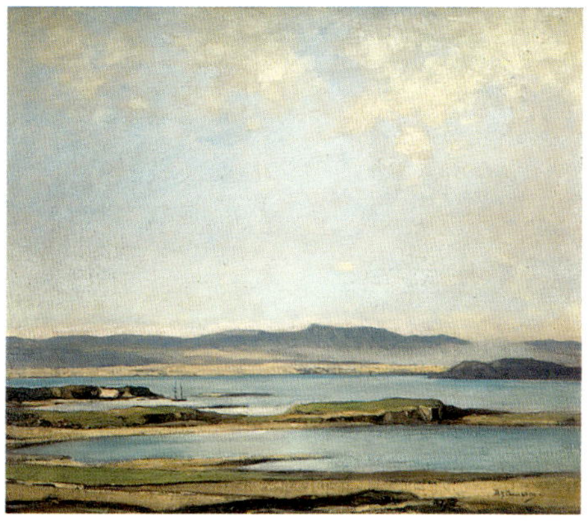

Cameron, David Young 1865–1945
Dunstaffnage
oil on canvas 43.5 x 49
1947.FA.771

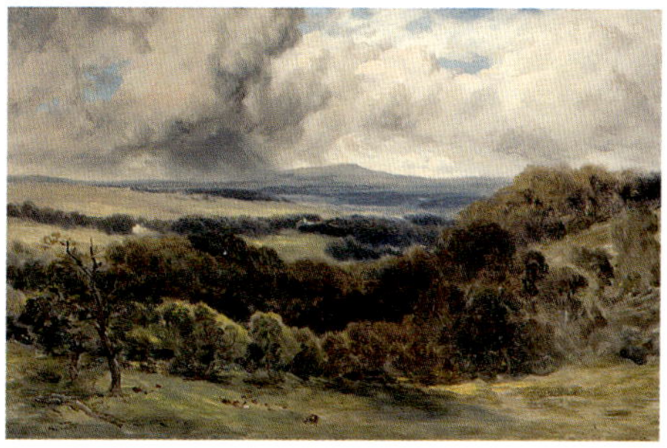

Cameron, David Young 1865–1945
Over the Hills, near Glasgow
oil on canvas 40 x 59.5
1963.FA.82

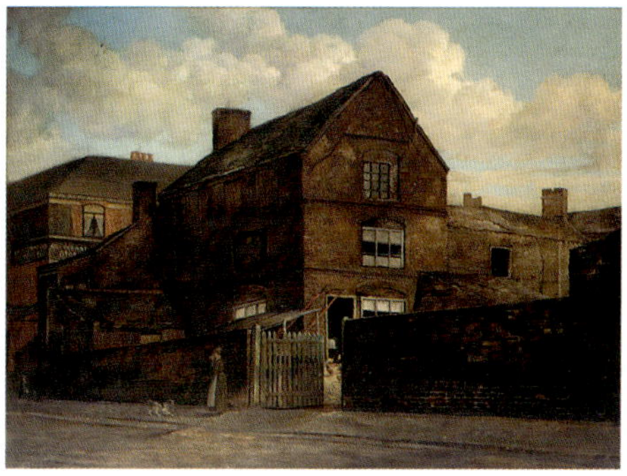

Capey, John
Tunstall Manor Court Leet 1909
oil on canvas 70 x 90
1954.FA.91

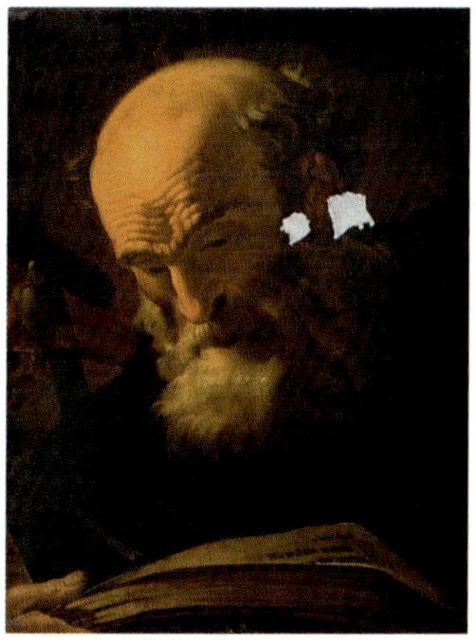

Caravaggio, Michelangelo Merisi da (after)
1571–1610
St Anthony Abbot
oil on canvas 64 x 46
1954.FA.203

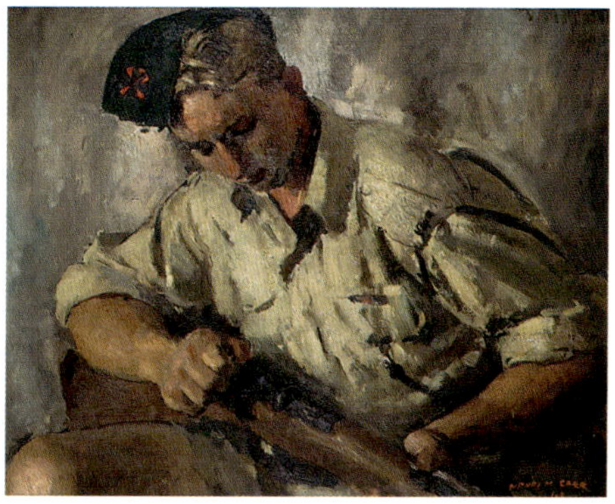

Carr, Henry Marvell 1894–1970
B. R. Hill, HH, First Battalion, KRRC, 6852209, RFN (Soldier Cleaning His Rifle) 1943
oil on canvas 50 x 60
1947.FA.778

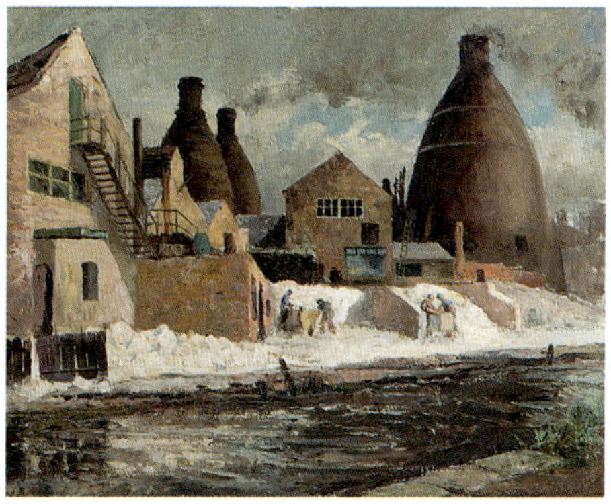

Cartledge, William 1891–1976
Ridgways, Bedford Works, Shelton
oil on canvas 63 x 74.5
1950.FA.10

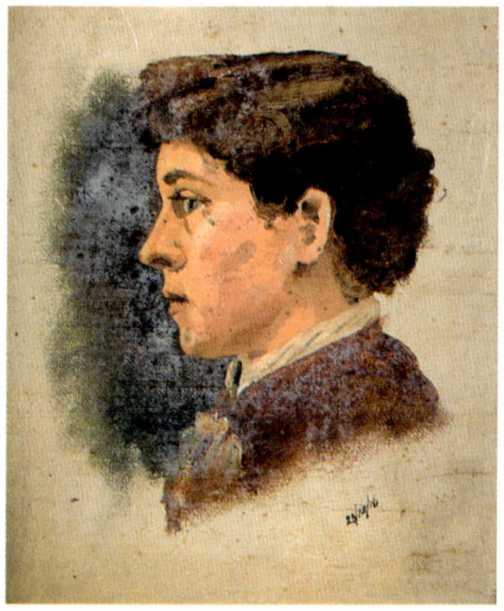

Cartlidge, George 1868–1961
Portrait of a Lady 1886
oil on canvas 20 x 16.5
1996.FA.164

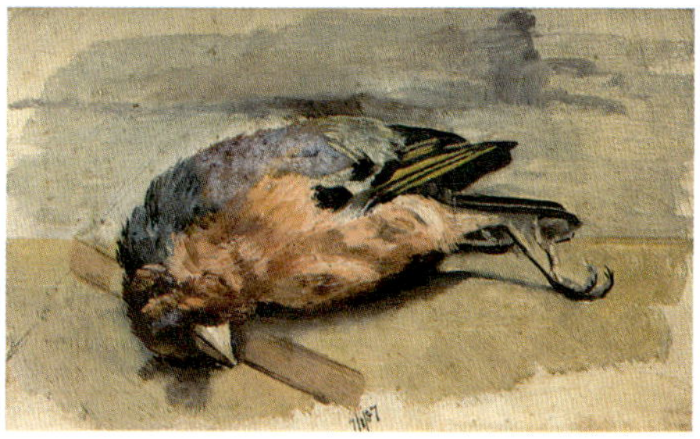

Cartlidge, George 1868–1961
Study of a Dead Chaffinch 1887
oil on canvas 10.5 x 17
1996.FA.141

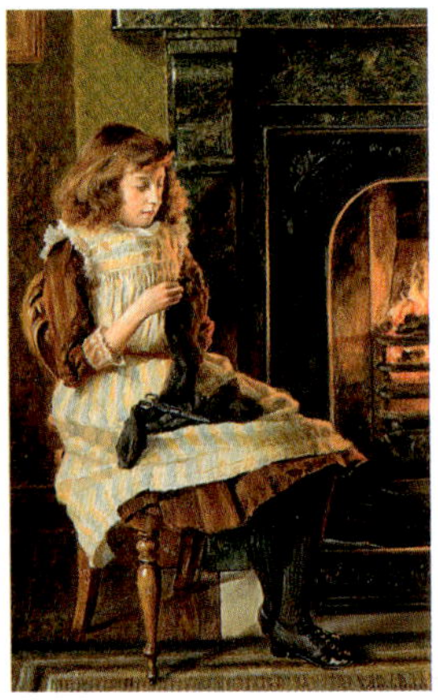

Cartlidge, George 1868–1961
Miss Mary Cartlidge 1890
oil on panel 26 x 16
1996.FA.53

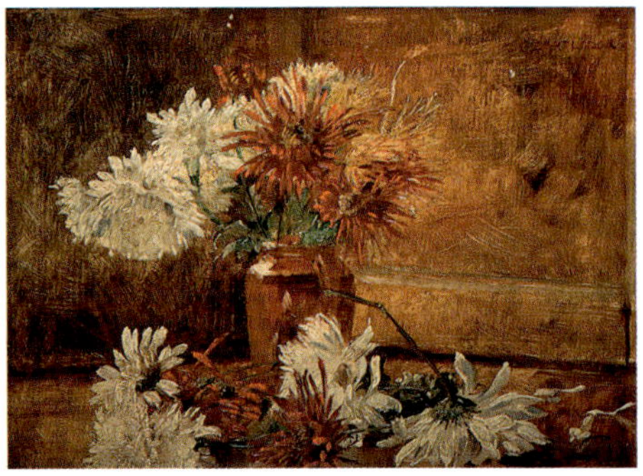

Cartlidge, George 1868–1961
Still Life, Chrysanthemums 1891
oil on panel 22 x 29.5
1996.FA.25

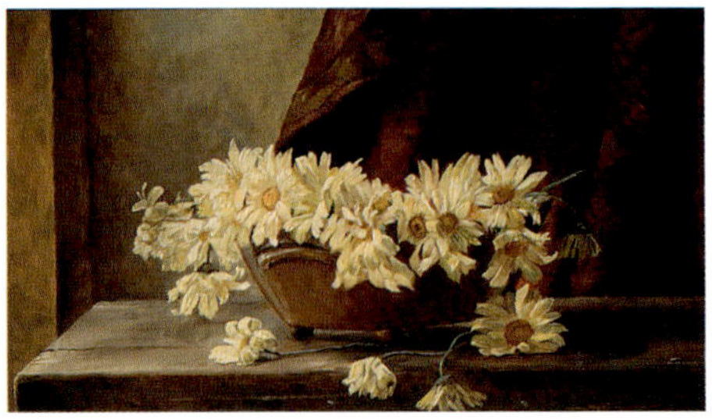

Cartlidge, George 1868–1961
Marguerites 1892
oil on canvas 28.5 x 49
1996.FA.70

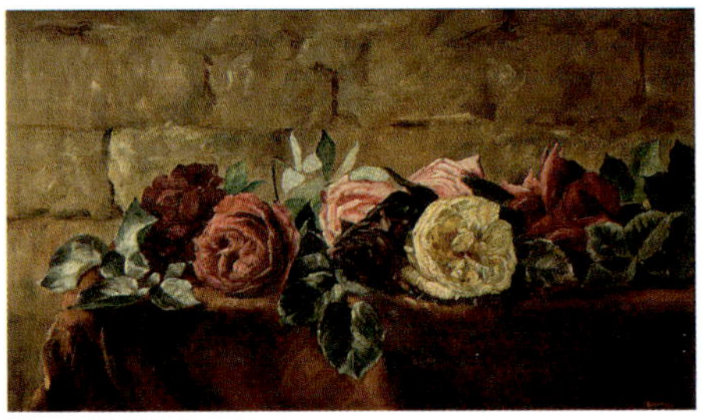

Cartlidge, George 1868–1961
Roses 1892
oil on canvas 28.5 x 48.5
1996.FA.79

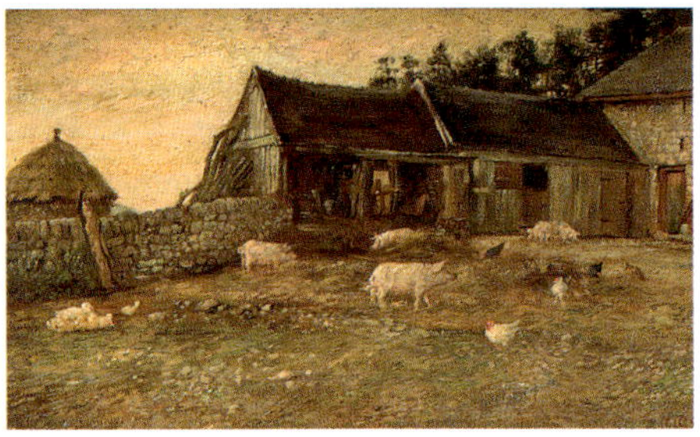

Cartlidge, George 1868–1961
Farmyard Evening, Hale House, Horton c.1892
oil on panel 20.5 x 33.5
1996.FA.50

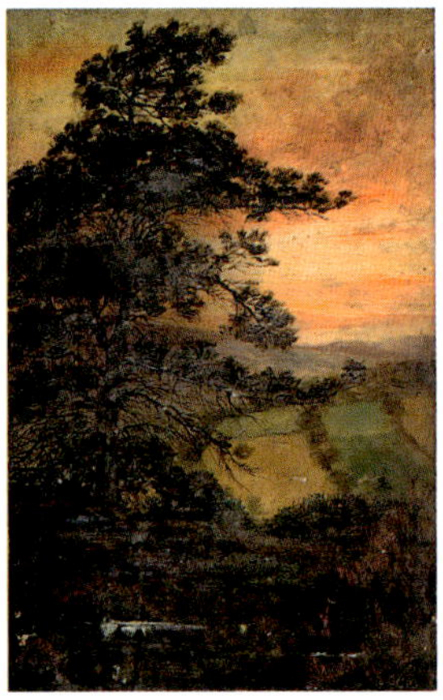

Cartlidge, George 1868–1961
Landscape with a Tree at Sunset 1893
oil on canvas 39 x 29.5
1996.FA.165

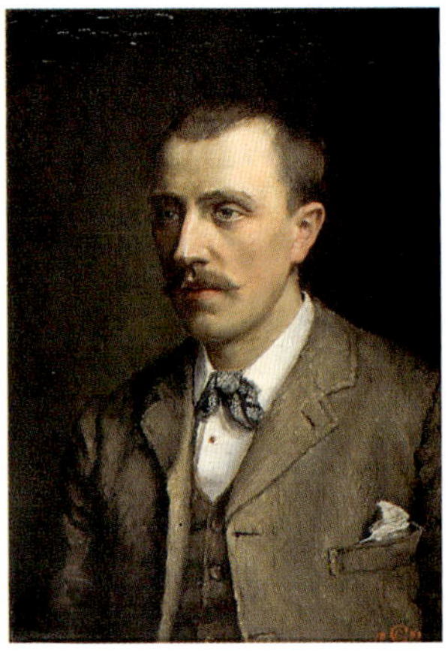

Cartlidge, George 1868–1961
Self Portrait 1893
oil on canvas 23.5 x 16
1996.FA.43

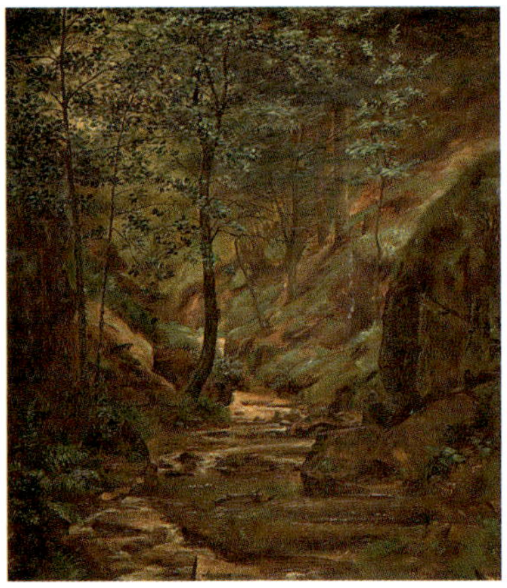

Cartlidge, George 1868–1961
Woodland Scene 1893
oil on canvas 60 x 50
1996.FA.69

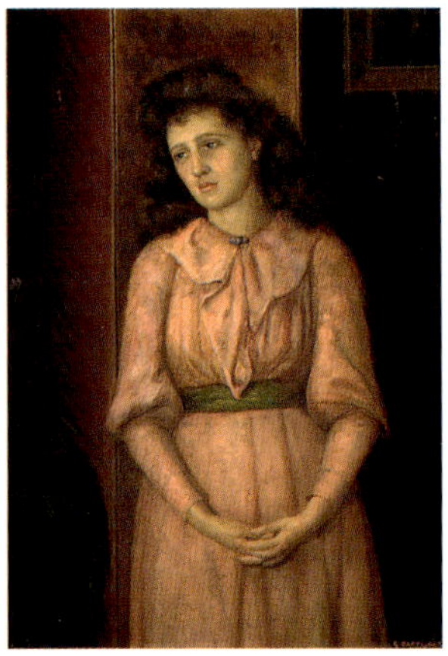

Cartlidge, George 1868–1961
Miss Mary Cartlidge 1895
oil on panel 43.5 x 29
1996.FA.30

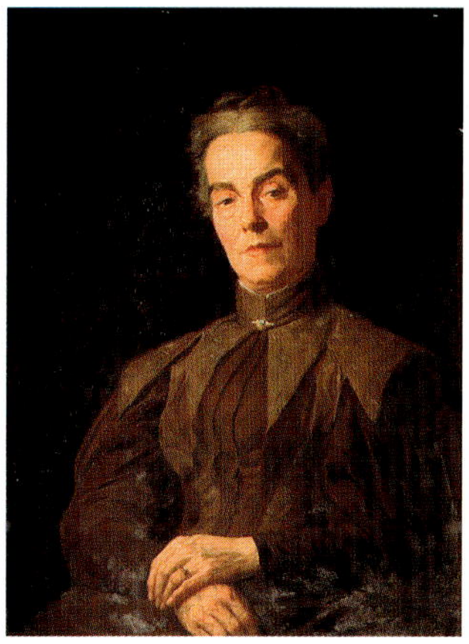

Cartlidge, George 1868–1961
Miss Annie Sneyd Falkner (Mrs Willets) 1896
oil on canvas 49 x 29.5
1996.FA.54

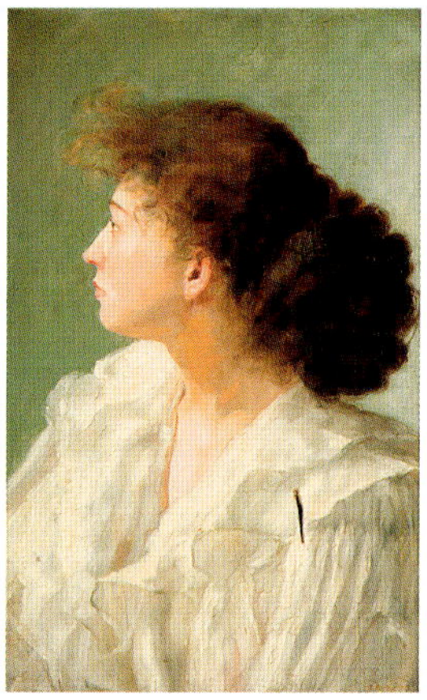

Cartlidge, George 1868–1961
Mrs Alfred Leese, Aunt to George Cartlidge 1896
oil on canvas 87 x 67
1996.FA.67

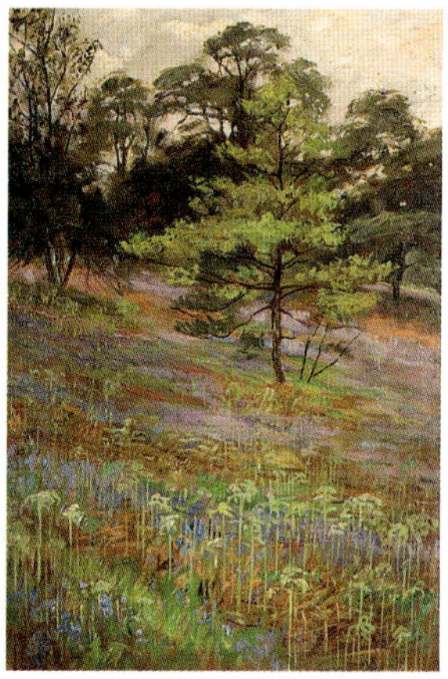

Cartlidge, George 1868–1961
Bluebells, Cliff Park, Rudyard 1899
oil on panel 29 x 19.5
1996.FA.76

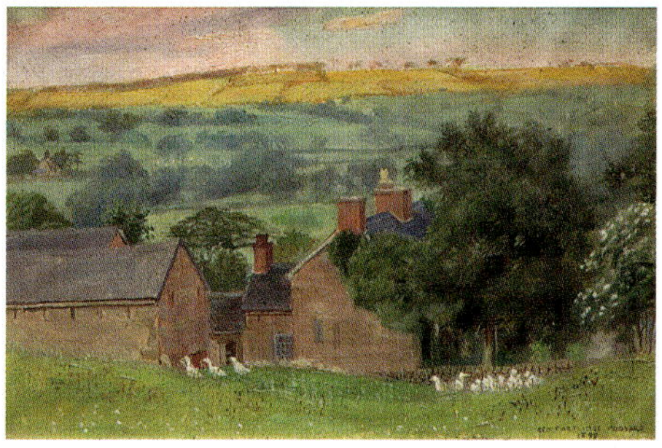

Cartlidge, George 1868–1961
Geeson Hill, Rudyard 1899
oil on panel 12.5 x 19
1996.FA.45

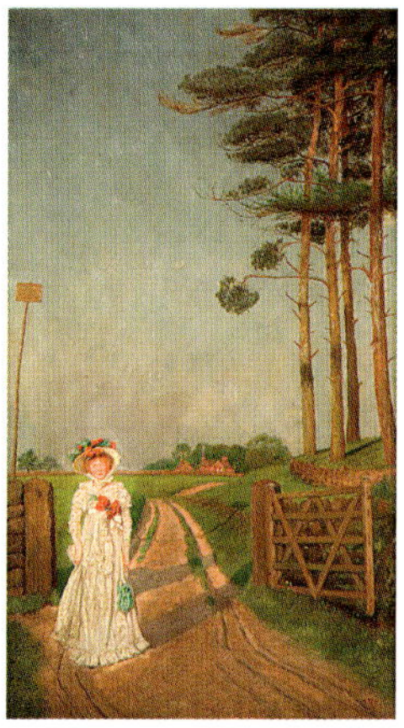

Cartlidge, George 1868–1961
The Cart Road 1900
oil on canvas 78 x 48
1996.FA.75

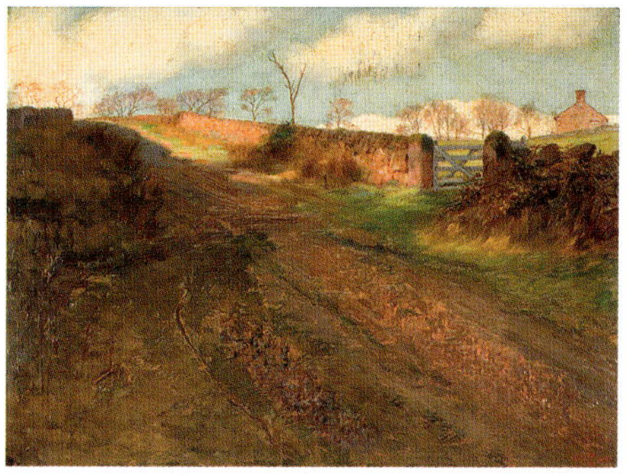

Cartlidge, George 1868–1961
Winter Sunshine, Cliff Park, Rudyard 1900
oil on card 22 x 30
1996.FA.29

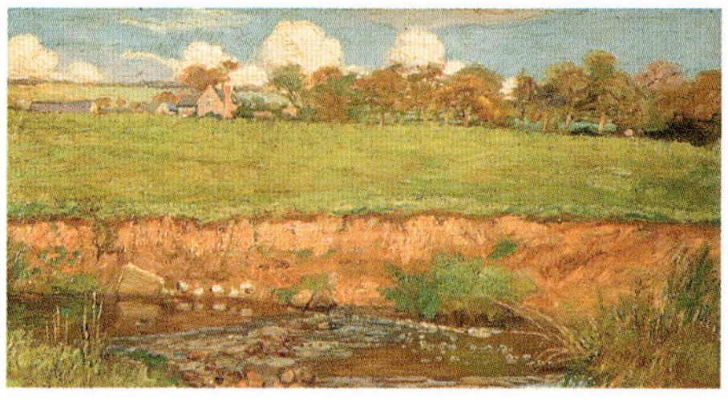

Cartlidge, George 1868–1961
Boot Hall, Horton, from the Brook 1901
oil on card 16 x 31
1996.FA.27

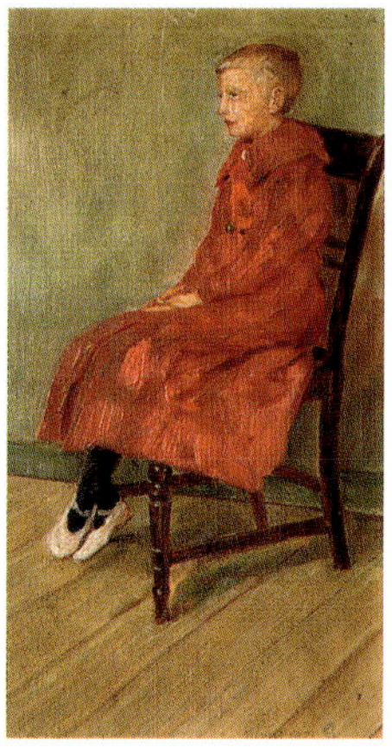

Cartlidge, George 1868–1961
Boy in Red 1901
oil on linen paper 26 x 13
1996.FA.34

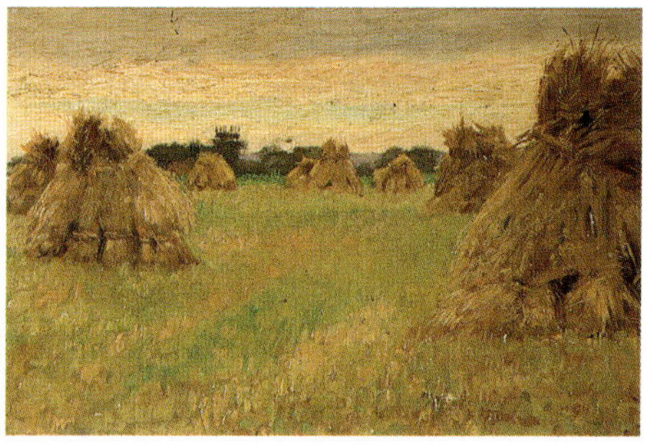

Cartlidge, George 1868–1961
Oat Kivers, Horton 1901
oil on canvas 24 x 28
1996.FA.77

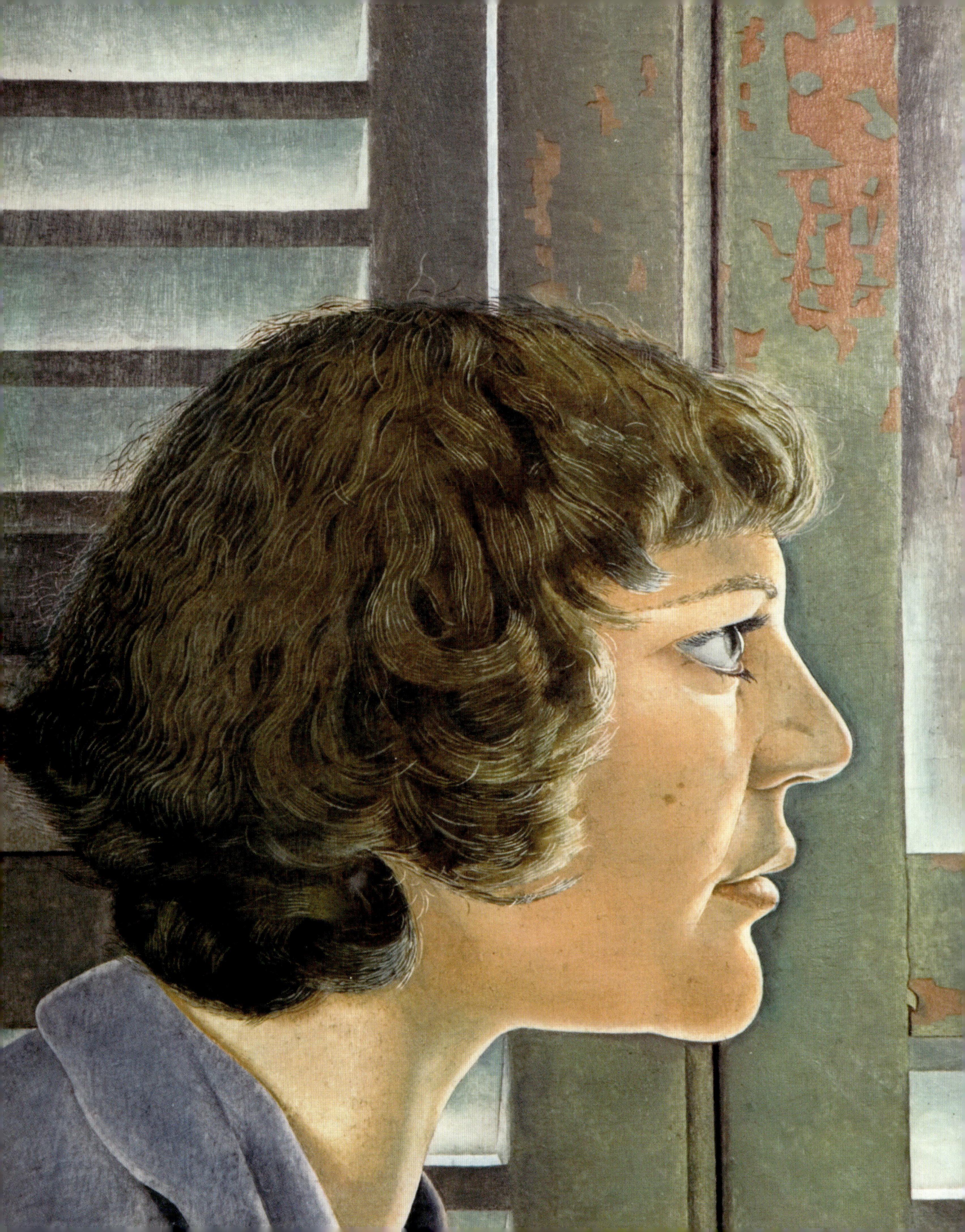

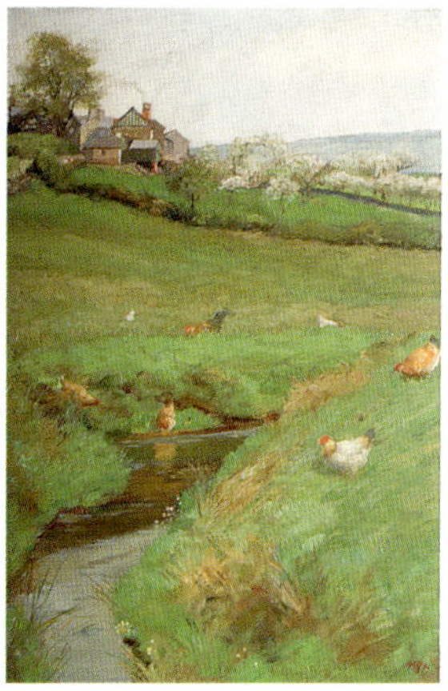

Cartlidge, George 1868–1961
Springtime, Haracles Hall Field, Rudyard 1901
oil on panel 29 x 18.5
1996.FA.78

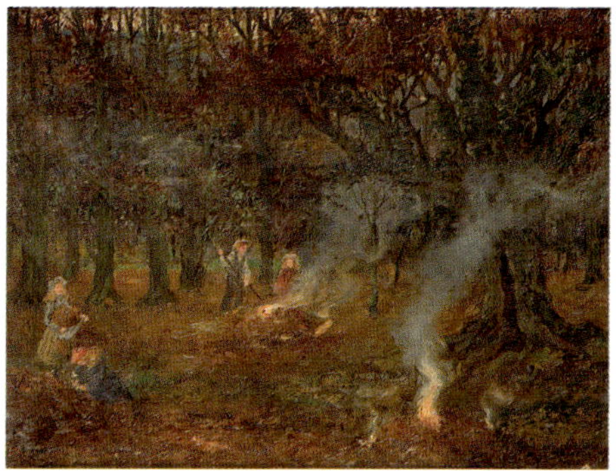

Cartlidge, George 1868–1961
Burning Autumn Leaves 1902
oil on canvas 27 x 35
1996.FA.42

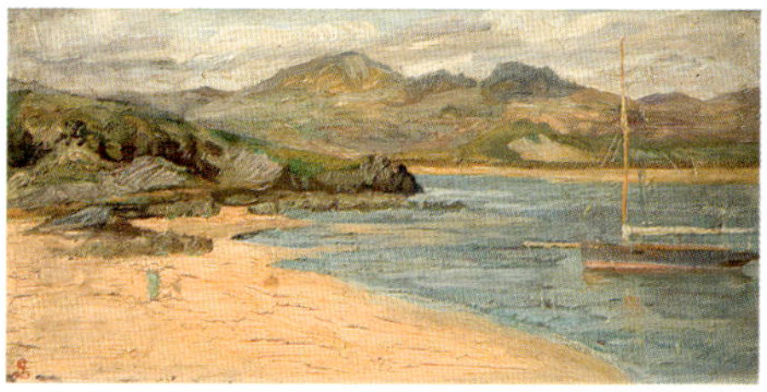

Cartlidge, George 1868–1961
Borth-y-Gest, North Wales 1903
oil on panel 15.5 x 31.5
1996.FA.47

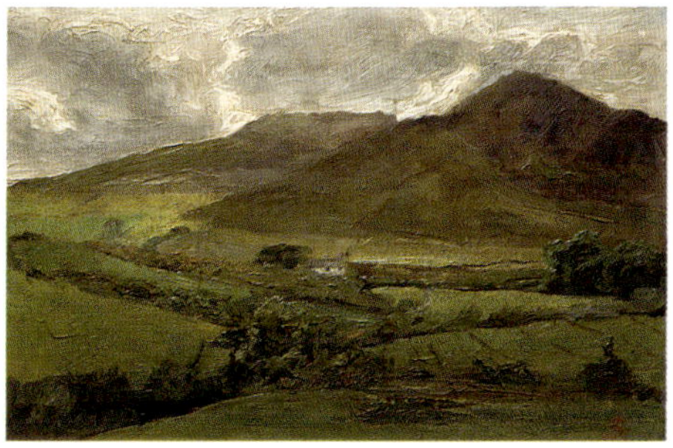

Cartlidge, George 1868–1961
Moorland Landscape 1903
oil on card 23 x 31.5
1996.FA.51

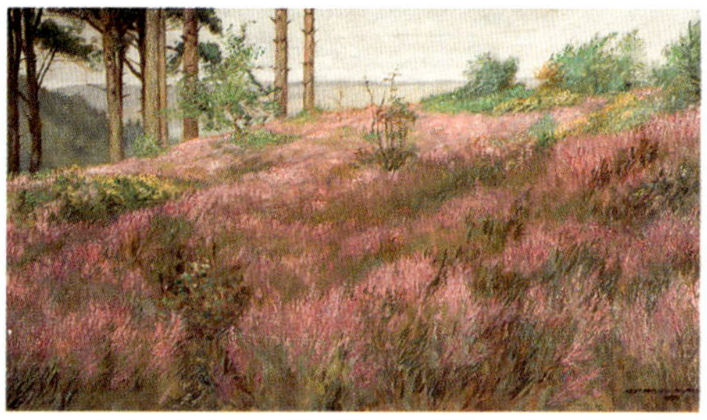

Cartlidge, George 1868–1961
In September, a Staffordshire Hilltop 1909
oil on canvas 28.5 x 50
1996.FA.28

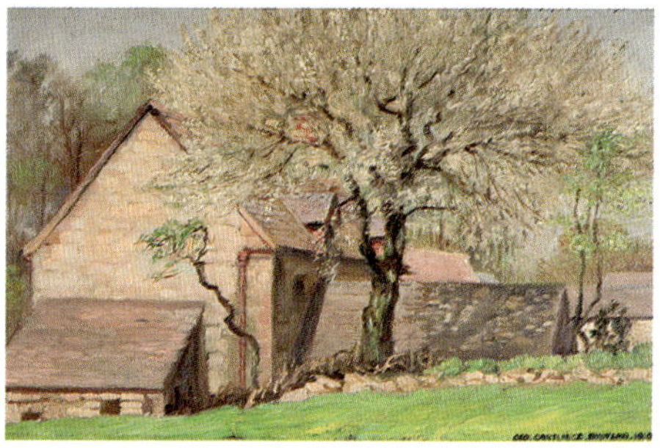

Cartlidge, George 1868–1961
A Cherry Tree in May, New House in Horton 1919
oil on canvas 14 x 21.5
1996.FA.246

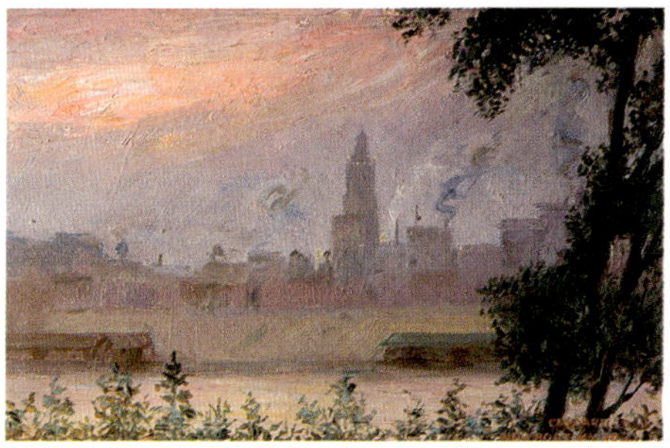

Cartlidge, George 1868–1961
Alhambra Tile Works, Newport, Kentucky, USA 1921
oil on paper 13 x 21
1996.FA.46

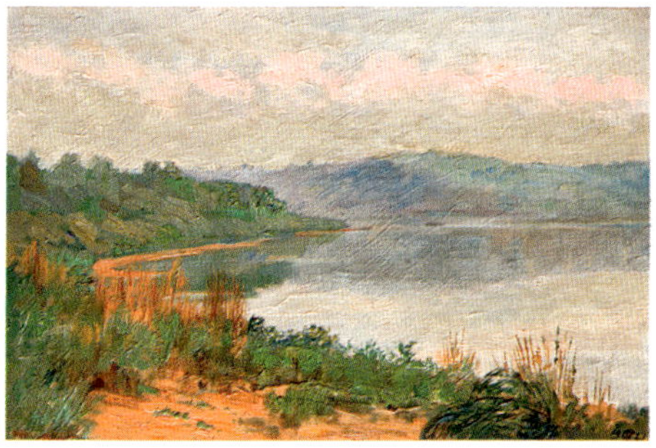

Cartlidge, George 1868–1961
Ohio River, Newport, Kentucky, USA 1921
oil on panel 23.5 x 30.5
1996.FA.39

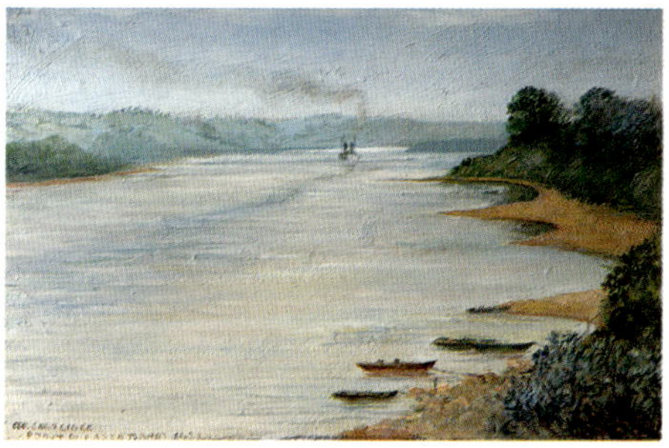

Cartlidge, George 1868–1961
Point Pleasant, Ohio, USA 1921
oil on paper 14 x 21.5
1996.FA.24

Facing page: Freud, Lucian, b.1922, *Kitty* (detail), 1948–1949, The New Art Gallery Walsall, (p. 202)

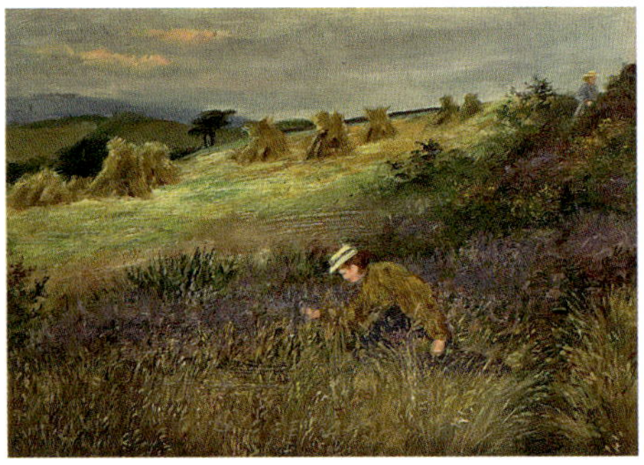

Cartlidge, George 1868–1961
Field to Daisy House, Horton c.1935
oil on panel 22 x 28
1996.FA.32

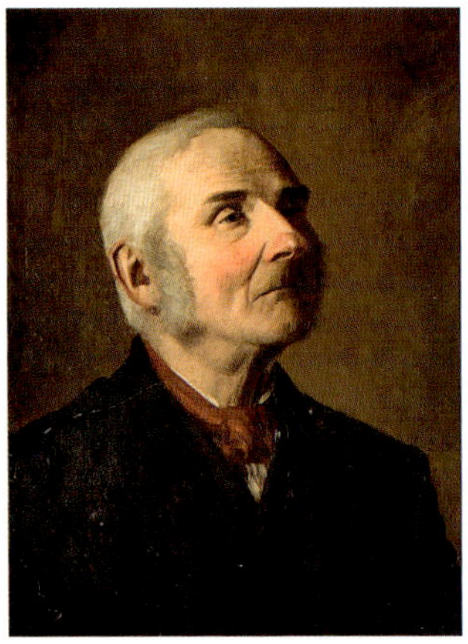

Cartlidge, George 1868–1961
A Model from Art School (Portrait of an Old Man)
oil on canvas 53 x 39
1996.FA.68

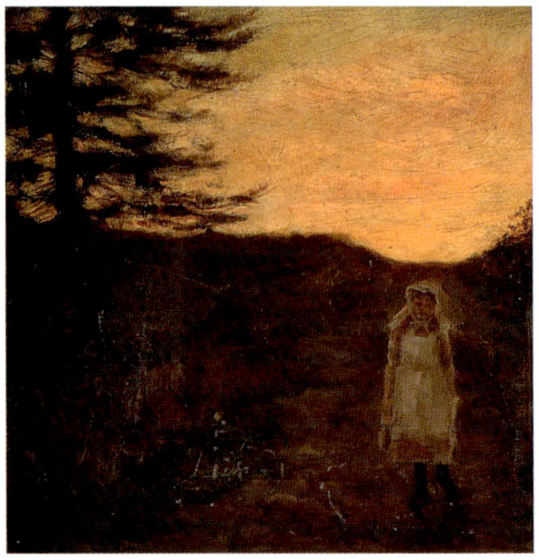

Cartlidge, George 1868–1961
A Moorland Road, Bradshaw
oil on panel 24 x 22.5
1996.FA.59

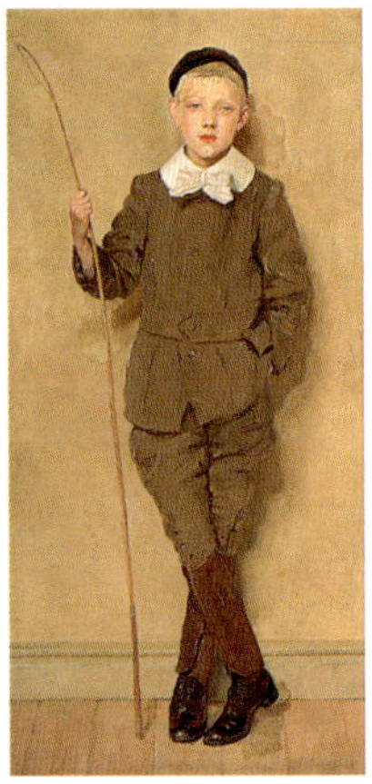

Cartlidge, George 1868–1961
George Falkner Cartlidge
oil on canvas 60 x 29.5
1996.FA.73

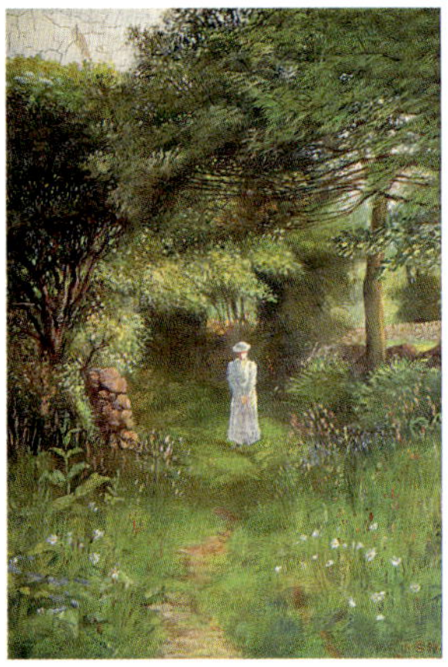

Cartlidge, George 1868–1961
Landscape, Silver Birch Trees and Rocks
oil on board 29 x 19
1996.FA.62

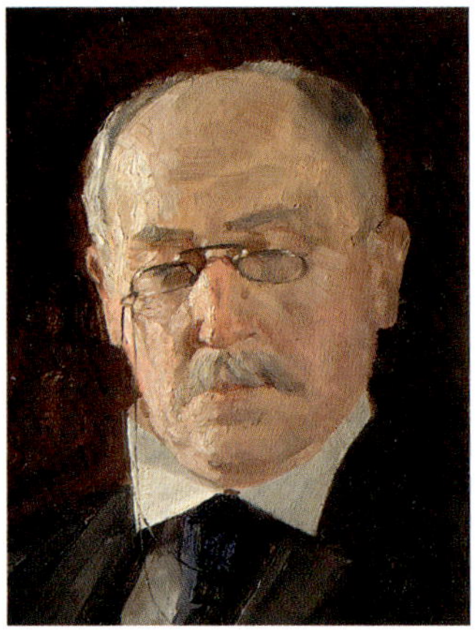

Cartlidge, George 1868–1961
Lewis George Cartlidge
oil on panel 28 x 21.5
1996.FA.44

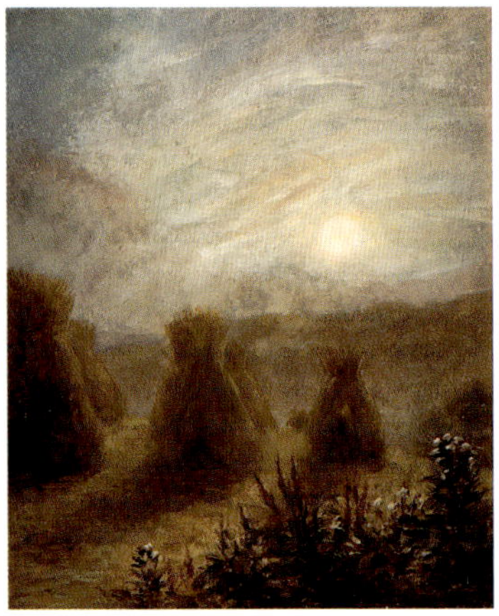

Cartlidge, George 1868–1961
Moon Rising over a Field of Corn Stooks
oil on panel 28 x 24.5
1996.FA.40

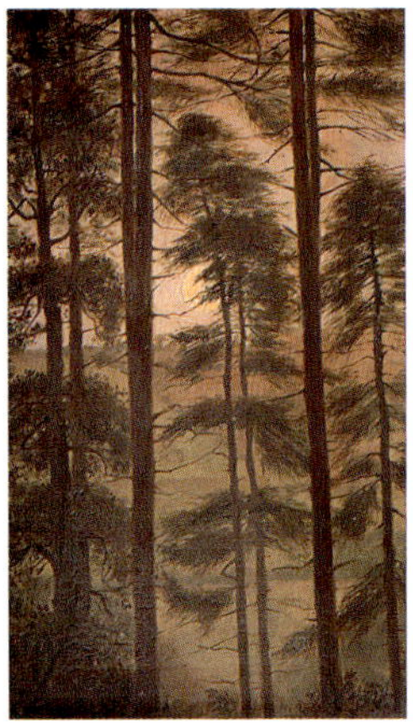

Cartlidge, George 1868–1961
Moon through Fir Trees, Rudyard
oil on canvas 50 x 29
1996.FA.72

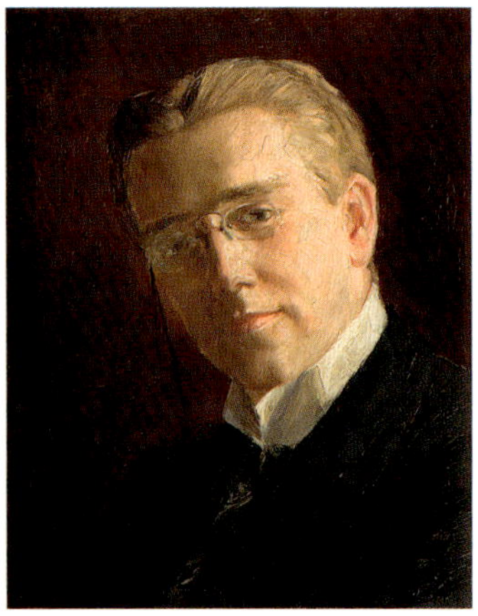

Cartlidge, George 1868–1961
N. Benjamin Beaumont Barlow
oil on panel 28 x 24
1996.FA.41

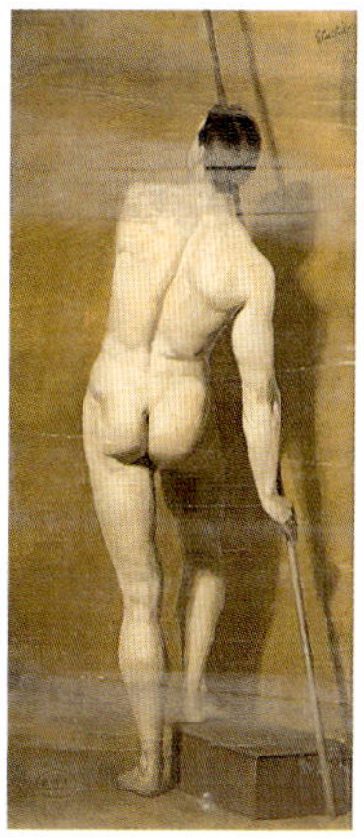

Cartlidge, George 1868–1961
Study of a Male Nude with Javelin
oil on canvas 45.5 x 19
1996.FA.166

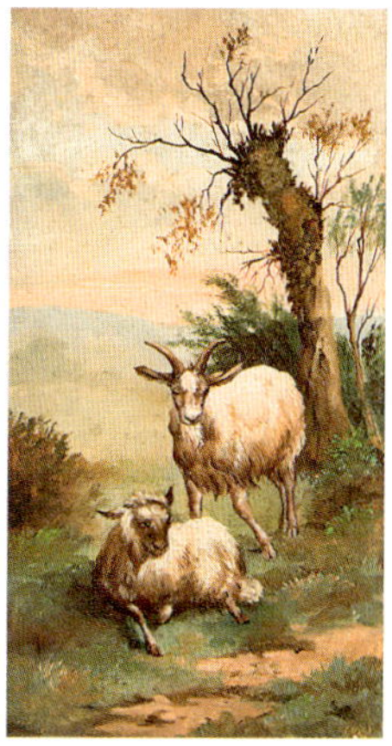

Cartlidge, George 1868–1961
Two Goats in a Field by a Tree
oil on card 21 x 10.5
1996.FA.149

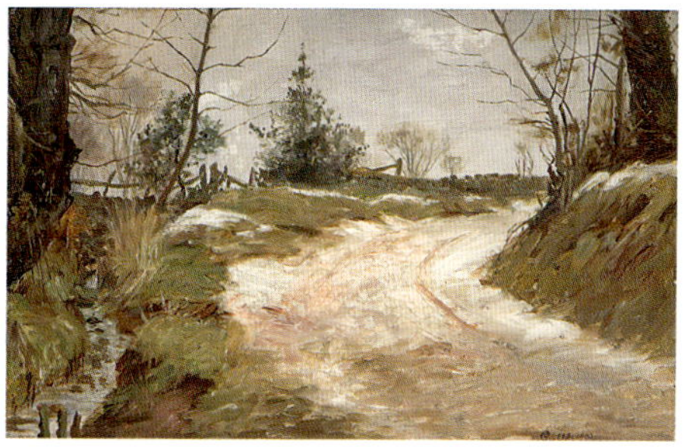

Cartlidge, George 1868–1961
Winter Scene, Heath House Road, Rudyard
oil on panel 19 x 29.5
1996.FA.74

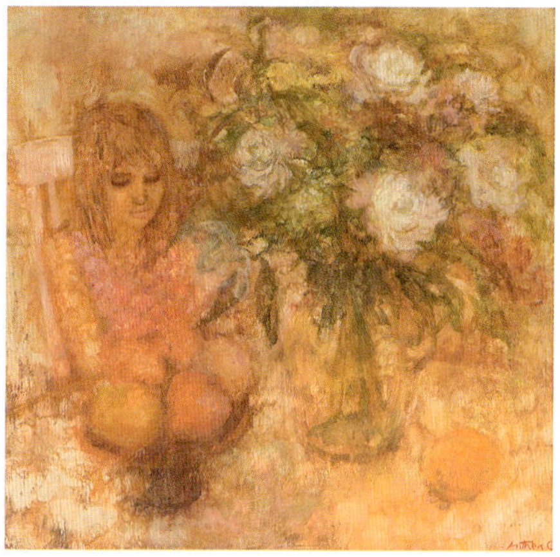

Chapman, Anthea b.1933
Flowers on the Table c.1967
oil on canvas 75 x 75
1967.FA.37

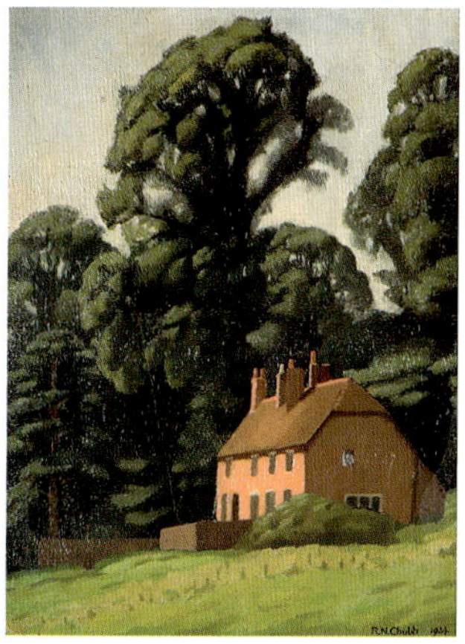

Chubb, Ralph Nicholas 1892–1960
The Red Farm 1924
oil on canvas 31 x 23
1959.FA.40

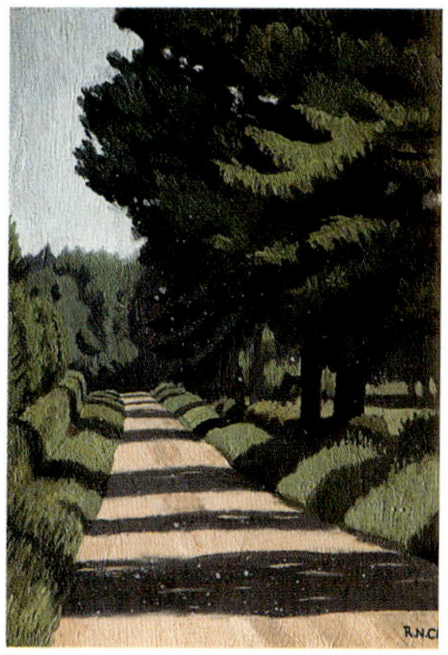

Chubb, Ralph Nicholas 1892–1960
The Country Lane
oil on canvas 31 x 22.5
1959.FA.39

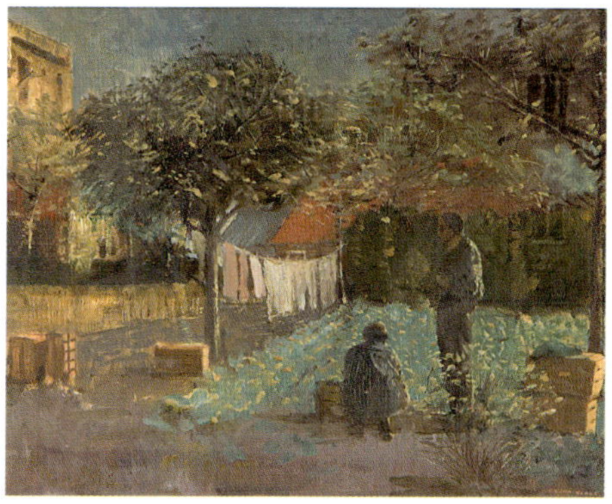

Clark, Cosmo 1897–1967
Evening Light in a Spanish Garden
oil on canvas 49 x 60
1966.FA.7A

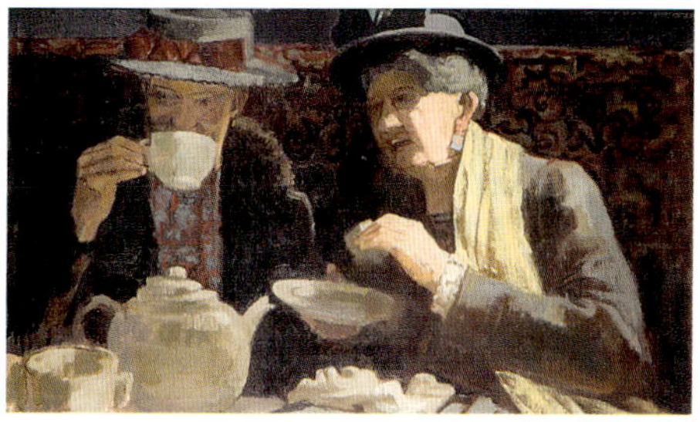

Clarke, Paul Montem b.1915
The Merry Wives 1949
oil on canvas 37 x 59
1957.FA.40

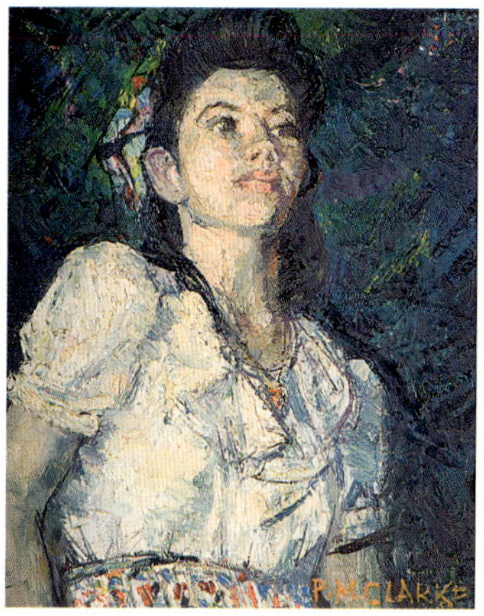

Clarke, Paul Montem b.1915
Portrait of a Malay Girl, Mary 1958
oil on paper 49 x 38.5
1958.FA.109

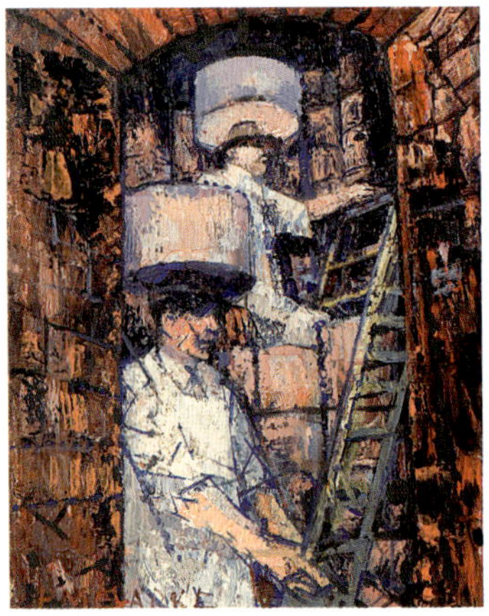

Clarke, Paul Montem b.1915
In the Bottle Oven
oil on card 48 x 38
1960.FA.111

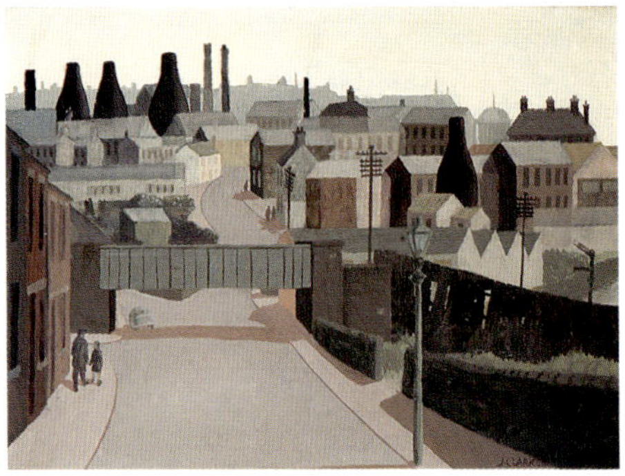

Clarkson, Jack 1906–1986
Century Street, Hanley
acrylic on panel 34 x 45
1986.FA.32

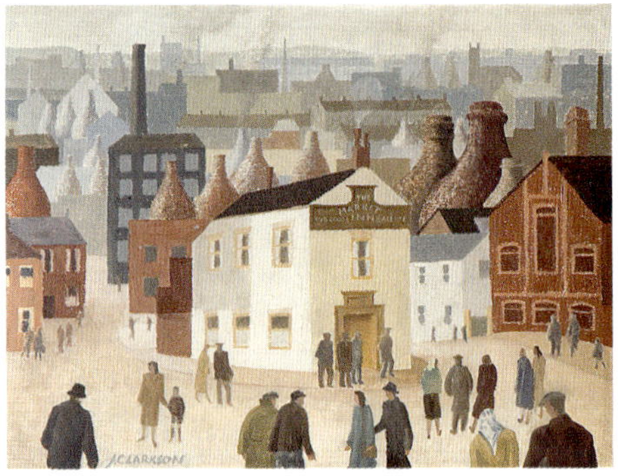

Clarkson, Jack 1906–1986
Market Inn
oil on panel 34 x 44
1950.FA.12

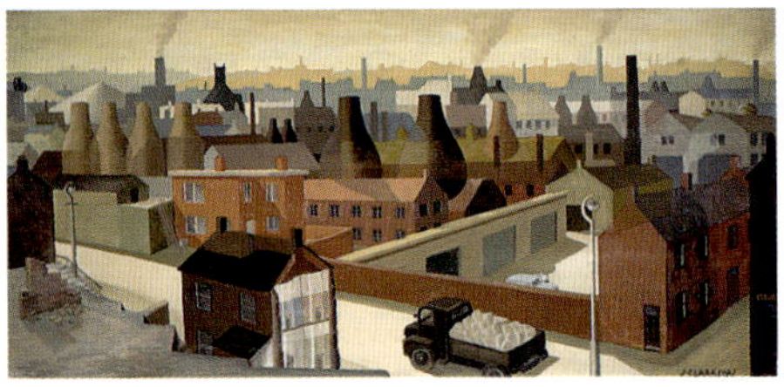

Clarkson, Jack 1906–1986
View of Hanley
oil on panel 58 x 120
1986.FA.33

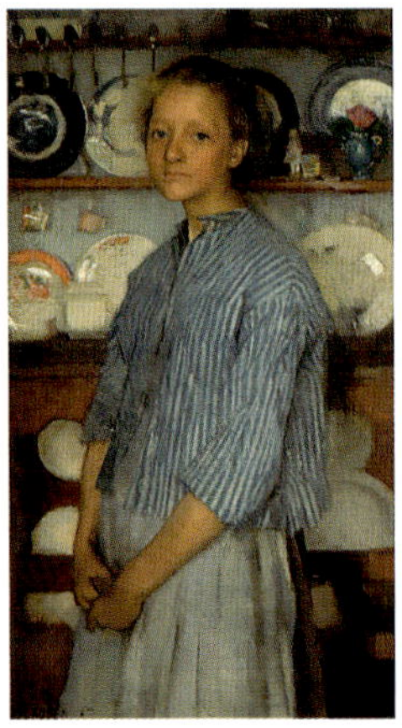

Clausen, George 1852–1944
Normandy Peasant 1887
oil on canvas 51.5 x 28
1949.FA.891

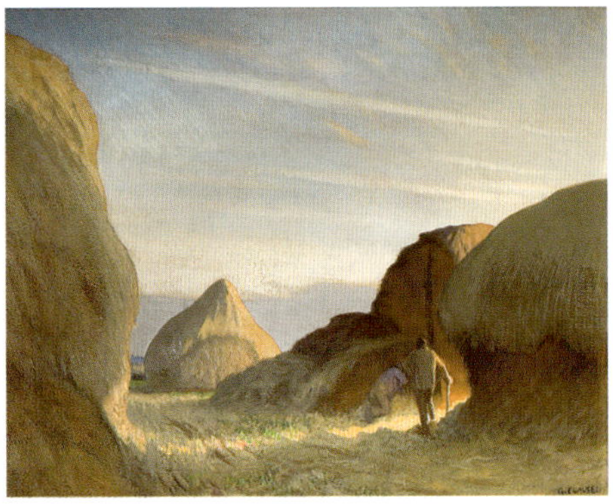

Clausen, George 1852–1944
Rickyard, Morning 1923
oil on canvas 52.5 x 60
1947.FA.773

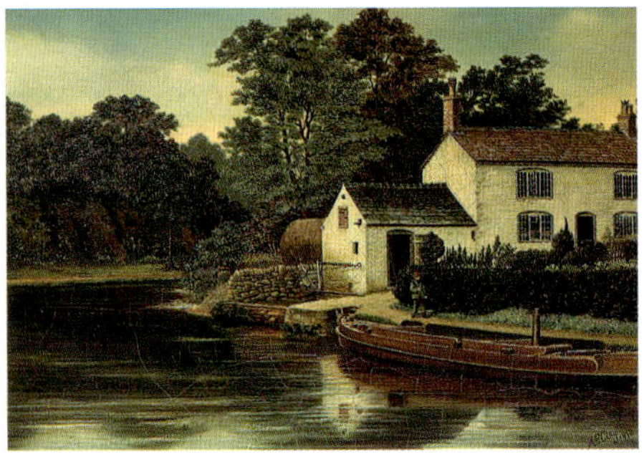

Clay, A. P.
Canal Scene, House and Narrowboat 1918
oil on board 23.5 x 33.5
1973.FA.7A

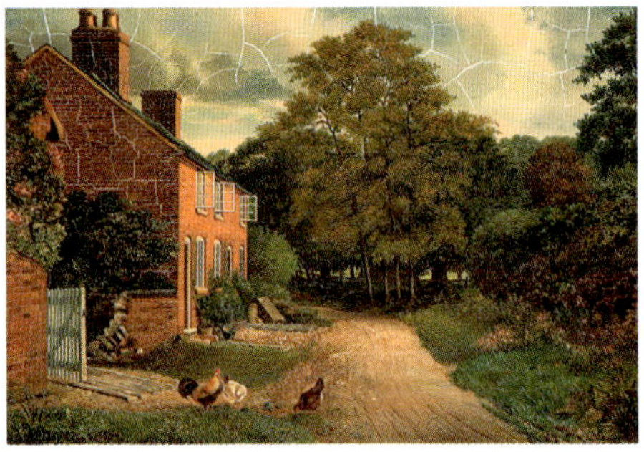

Clay, A. P.
Rural Scene 1918
oil on canvas 23 x 33.5
1973.FA.6A

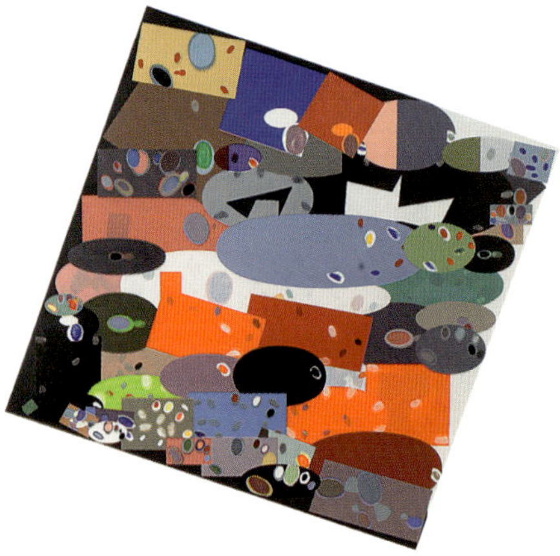

Cohen, Bernard b.1933
Somersault 1974–1975
acrylic on canvas 91.5 x 91.5
1979.FA.13

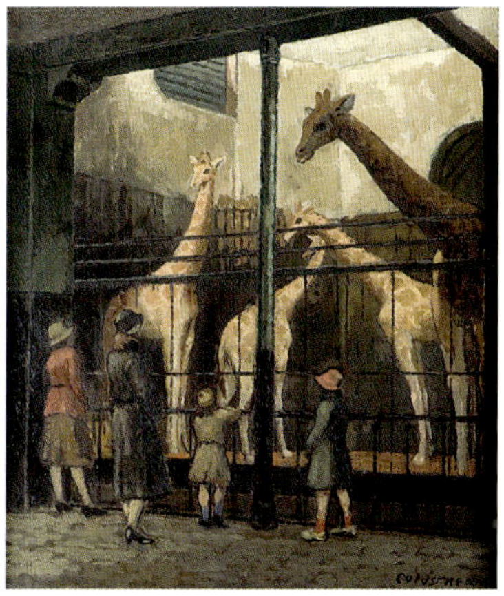

Coldstream, William Menzies 1908–1987
At the Zoo 1930
oil on canvas 38 x 29
1931.FA.26

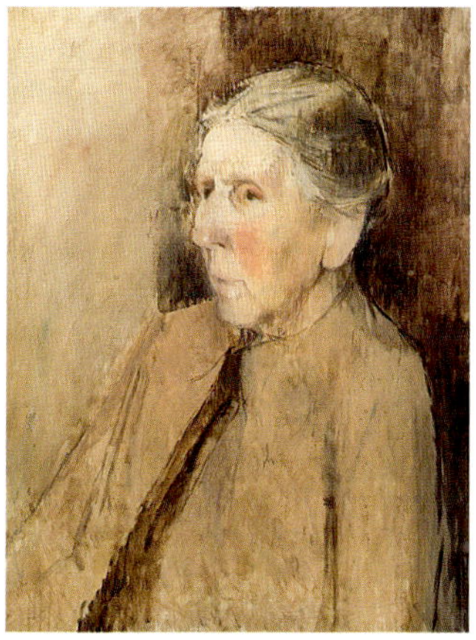

Coldstream, William Menzies 1908–1987
Mrs Auden 1936–1937
oil on canvas 74 x 55
1947.FA.767

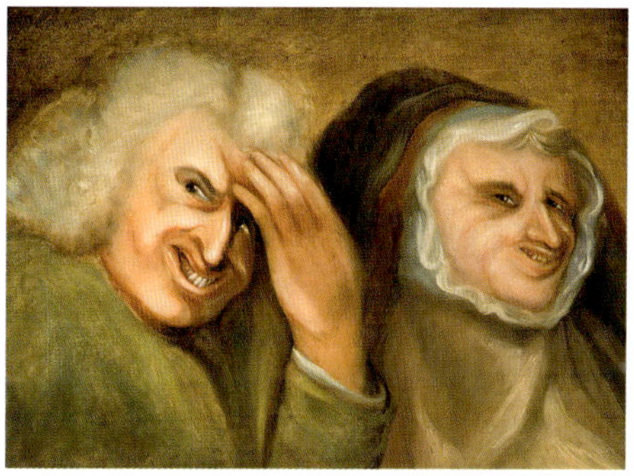

Collier, John 1708–1786
Tim Bobbin and His Wife
oil on canvas 47.5 x 63
1963.FA.150

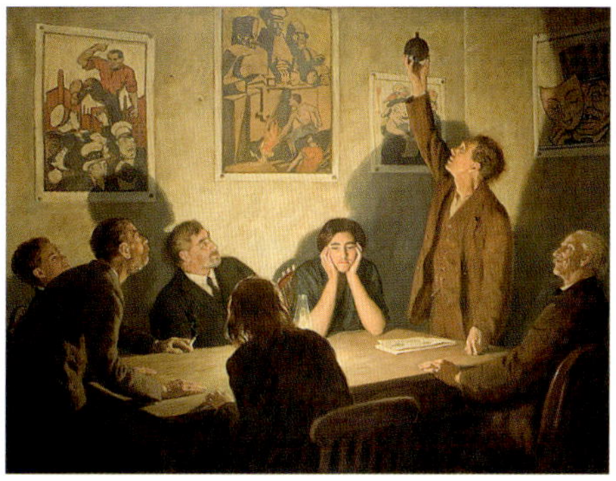

Collier, John 1850–1934
Brotherhood of Man
oil on canvas 110.5 x 140
1936.FA.210

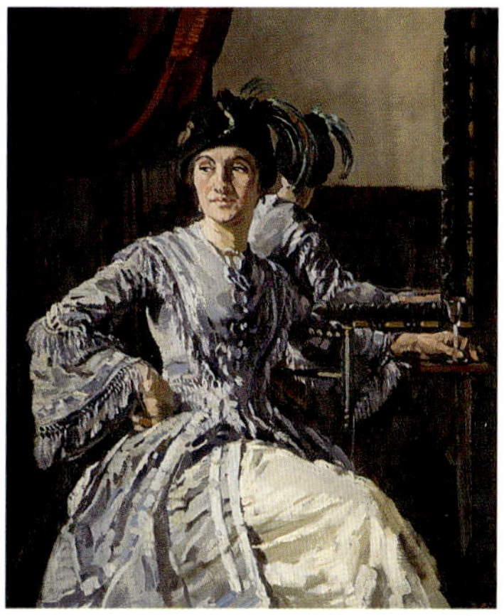

Connard, Philip 1875–1958
The Lilac Dress
oil on canvas 67 x 55
1954.FA.89

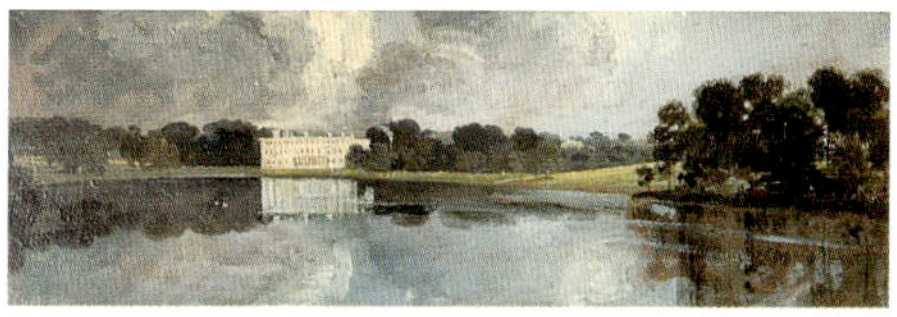

Constable, John 1776–1837
Trentham Hall c.1801
oil on canvas 10 x 31
1984.FA.8

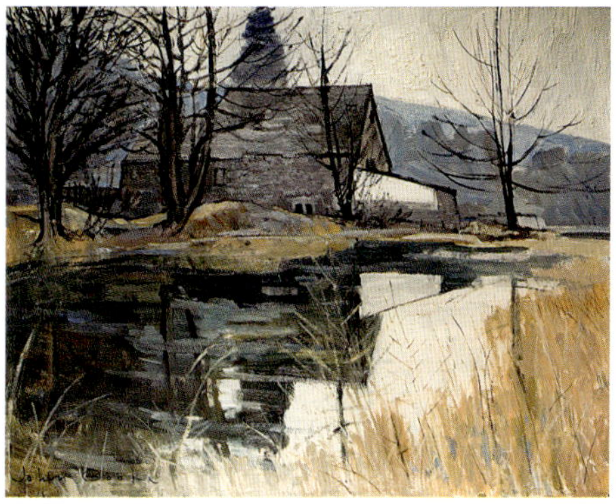

Cooke, John b.1929
Lathkill Dale 1971
oil on board 63 x 73
1973.FA.12A

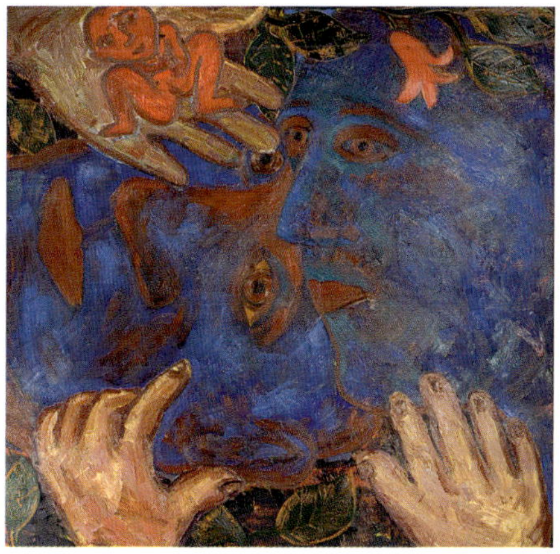

Cooper, Eileen b.1953
Out of the Wild 1985
oil on canvas 157 x 157
1989.FA.12

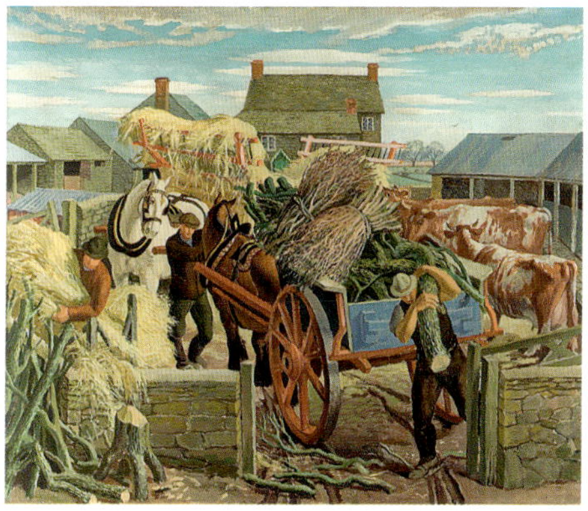

Cooper, Gerald 1898–1975
Winter
oil on canvas 74.5 x 88
1935.FA.180

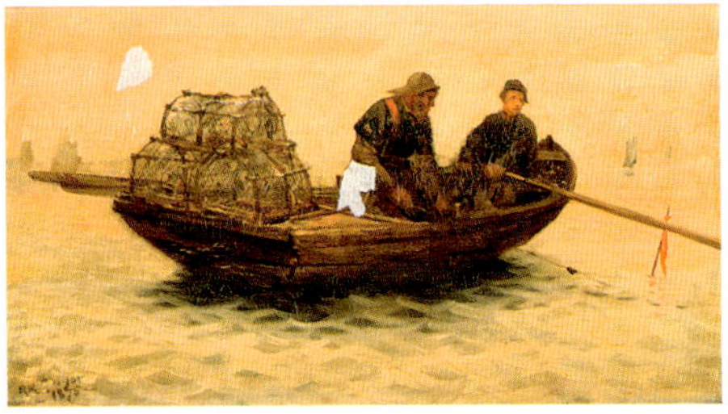

Cope, J.
Guildford
oil on canvas 30 x 50
1954.FA.132

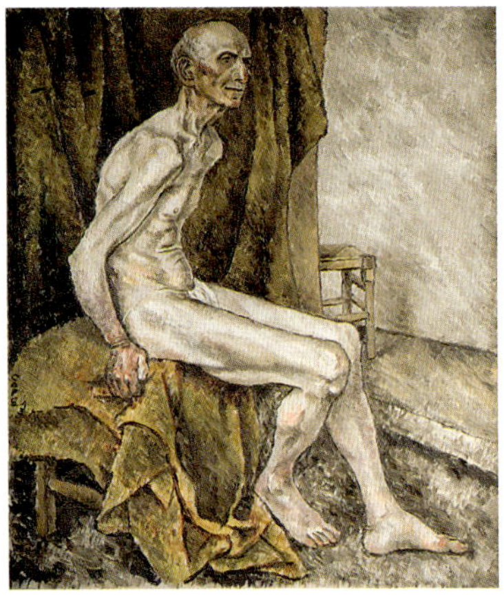

Cope, Norman d.1943
Nude Old Man 1943
oil on canvas 76 x 61
1972.FA.15A

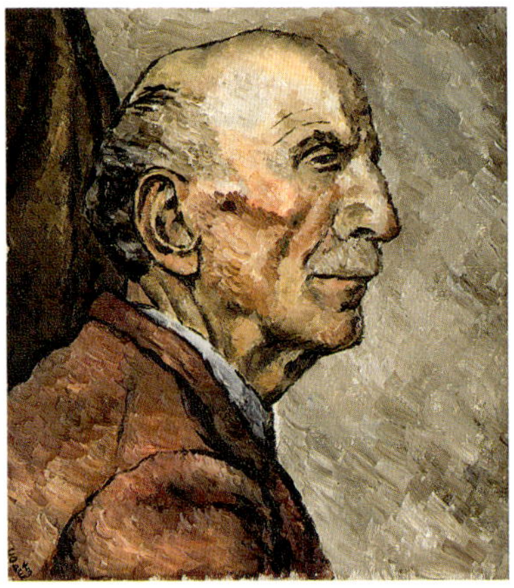

Cope, Norman d.1943
Portrait of an Old Man
oil on canvas 29 x 21
1972.FA.13A

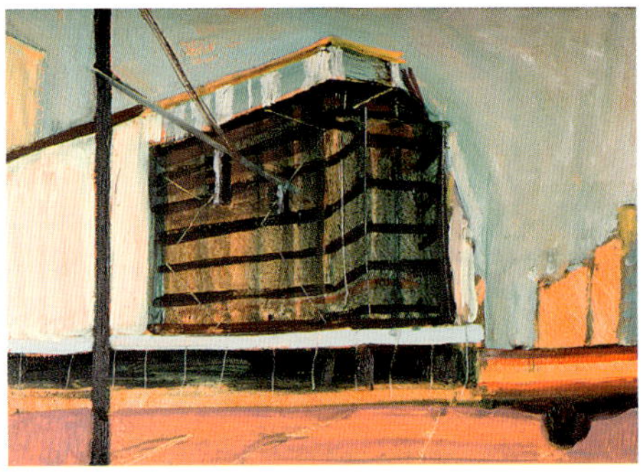

Coverley, Tracey b.1970
From Charlie's Point
oil on panel 21 x 28.5
1991.FA.3

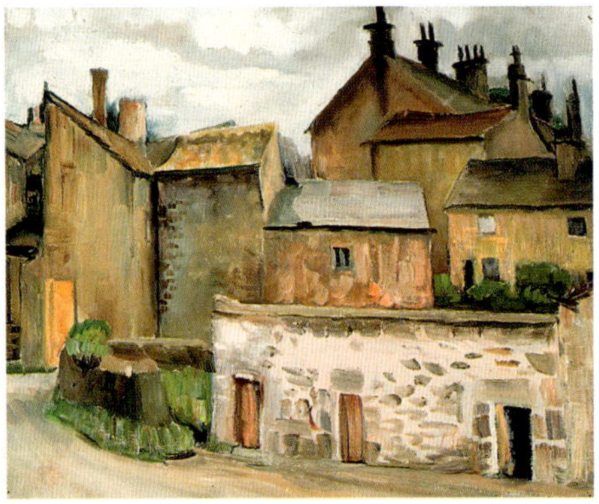

Coxon, Raymond James 1896–1997
Hebden Bridge, Yorkshire
oil on canvas 36 x 44
1942.FA.532

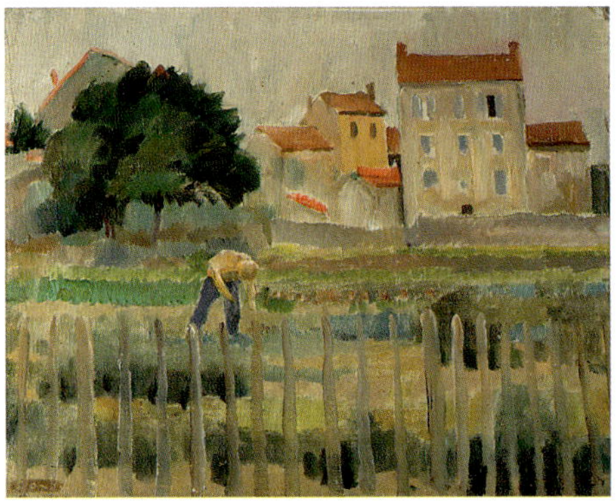

Coxon, Raymond James 1896–1997
Kitchen Garden
oil on canvas 36 x 45
1942.FA.531

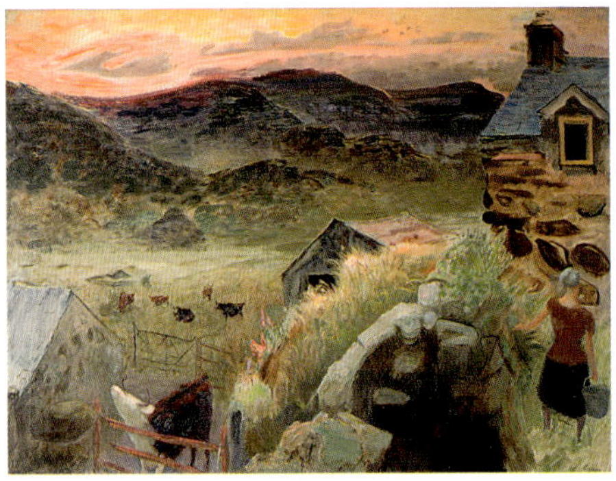

Coxon, Raymond James 1896–1997
Portmadoc
oil on canvas 69 x 90
1987.FA.42

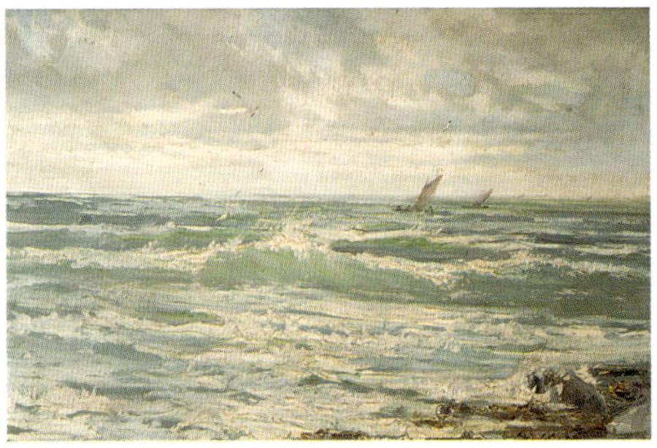

Cubley, Henry Hadfield 1848–1934
The Incoming Tide 1918
oil on canvas 42 x 61.5
1950.FA.34

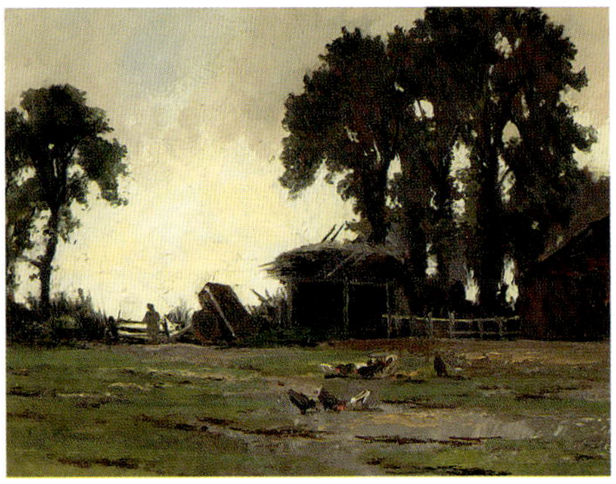

Cubley, Henry Hadfield 1848–1934
Farmyard
oil on board 21 x 27
PCF9

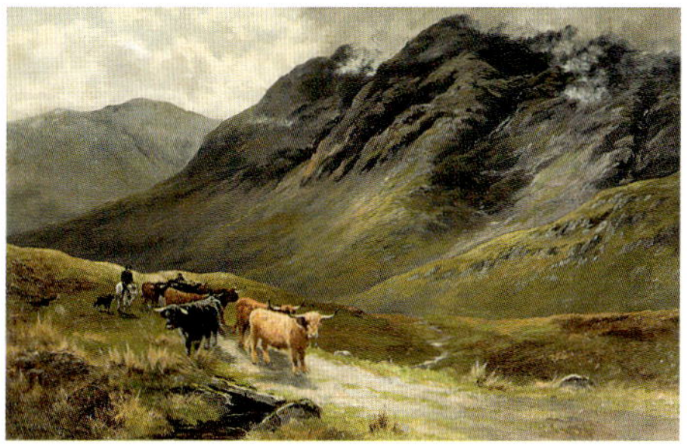

Cubley, Henry Hadfield 1848–1934
Highland Castle
oil on canvas 59.5 x 90
PCF10

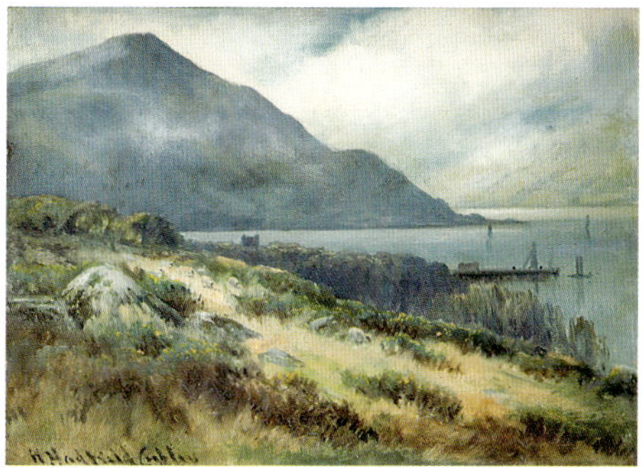

Cubley, Henry Hadfield 1848–1934
Landscape with Pier and Lake
oil on board 36.5 x 49
PCF11

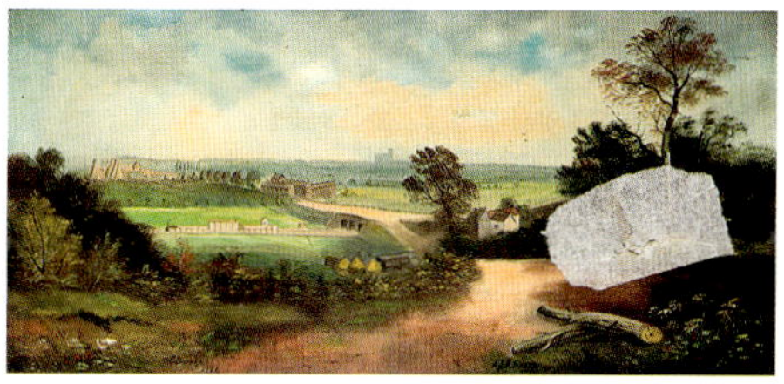

Cubley, Henry Hadfield 1848–1934
Landscape with Sheep
oil on board 20.5 x 41
PCF12

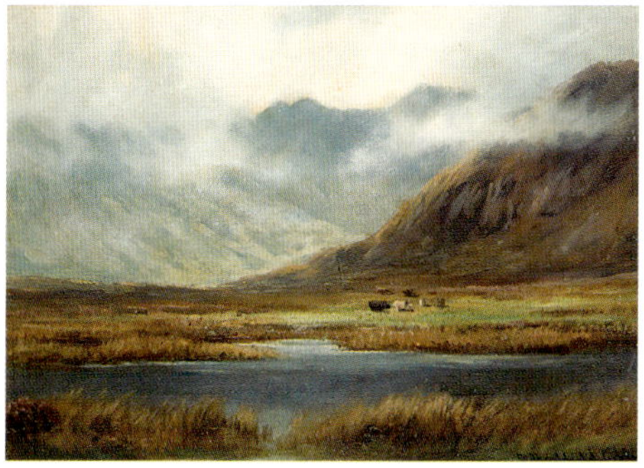

Cubley, Henry Hadfield 1848–1934
Mountain and Lake
oil on board 36 x 49
PCF13

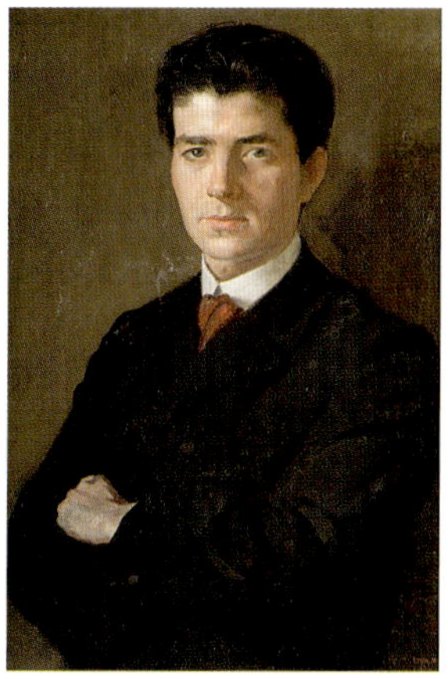

Currie, John 1883–1914
Self Portrait 1905
oil on canvas 73 x 48.5
1998.FA.11

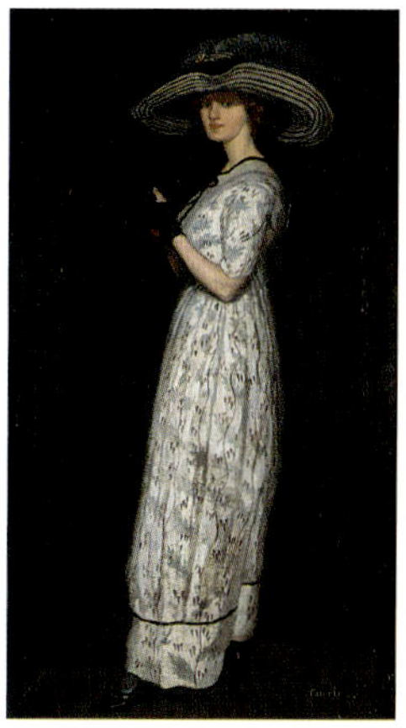

Currie, John 1883–1914
The Glad Eye, Dressed for Promenade c.1907
oil on canvas 100 x 55.5
1963.FA.59

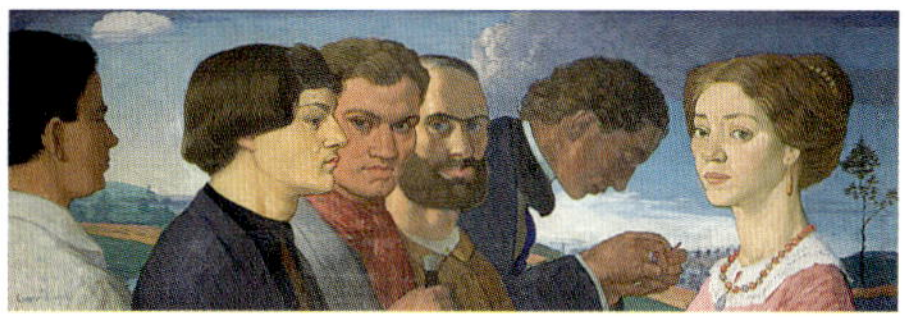

Currie, John 1883–1914
Some Later Primitives and Madame Tisceron 1912
tempera on canvas 46 x 127
1957.FA.18

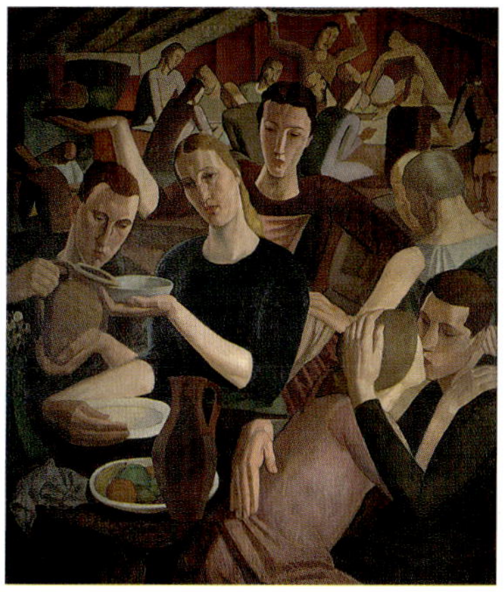

Currie, John 1883–1914
The Supper 1912–1914
oil on canvas 144 x 122
1945.FA.673

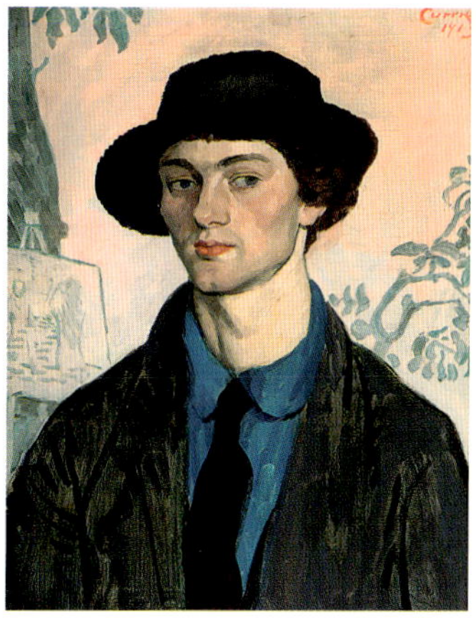

Currie, John 1883–1914
Mark Gertler (1891–1939) 1913
oil on canvas 57.5 x 44.5
1935.FA.83

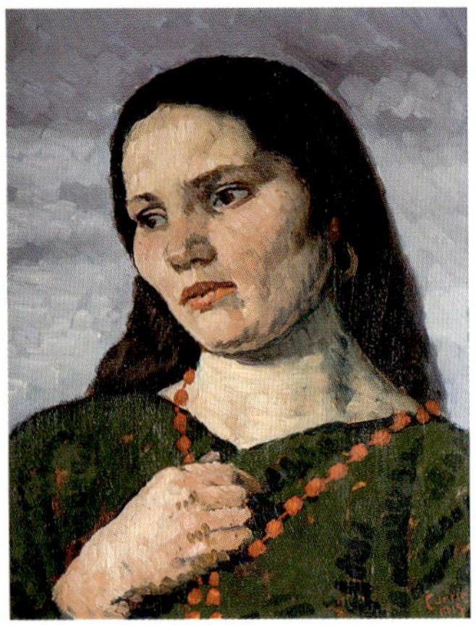

Currie, John 1883–1914
The Red Necklace 1913
oil on panel 39 x 31
1957.FA.58

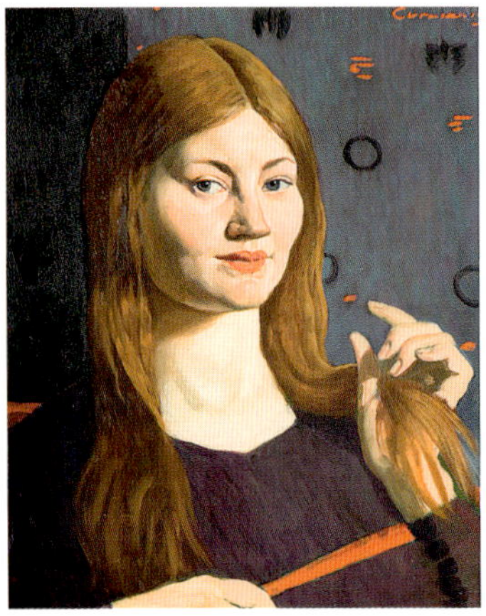

Currie, John 1883–1914
The Witch 1913
oil on panel 49 x 39
1953.FA.16

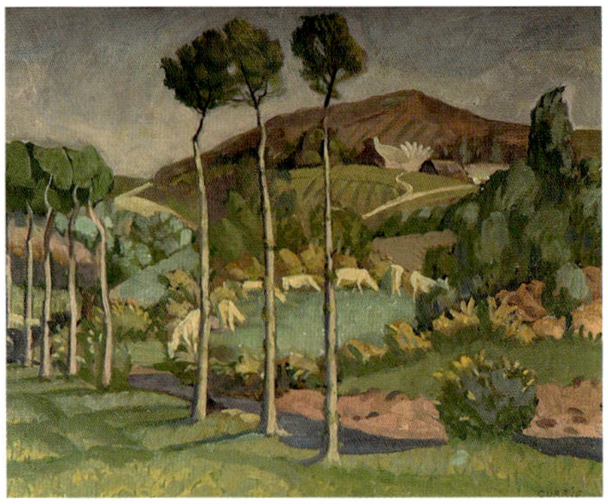

Currie, John 1883–1914
Normandy Landscape 1914
oil on panel 49 x 59
1952.FA.10

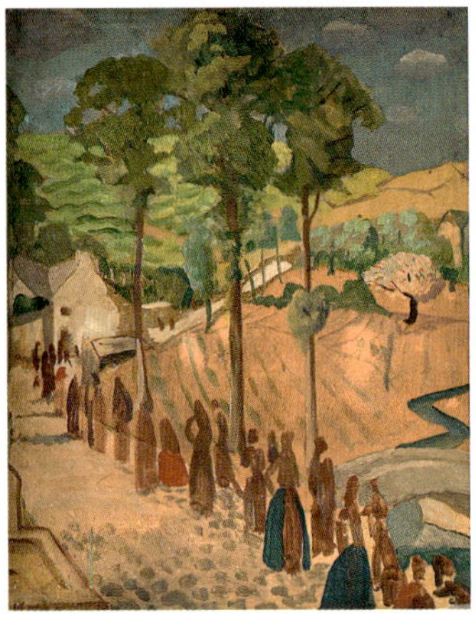

Currie, John 1883–1914
The Procession 1914
oil on panel 65.5 x 51.5
1958.FA.2

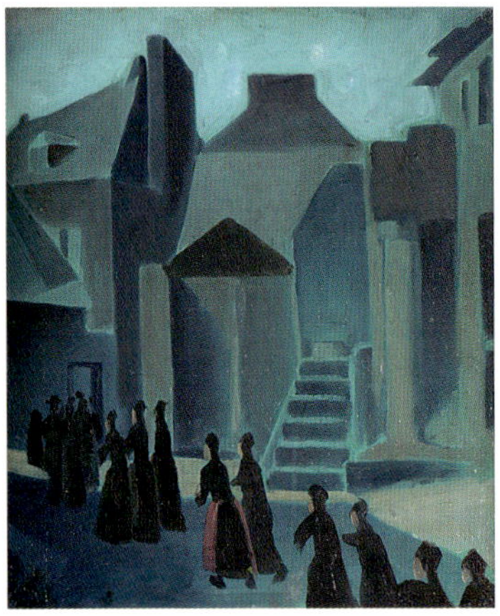

Currie, John 1883–1914
Study for 'Woman's Pay' c.1914
oil on canvas 60 x 49.5
1958.FA.5

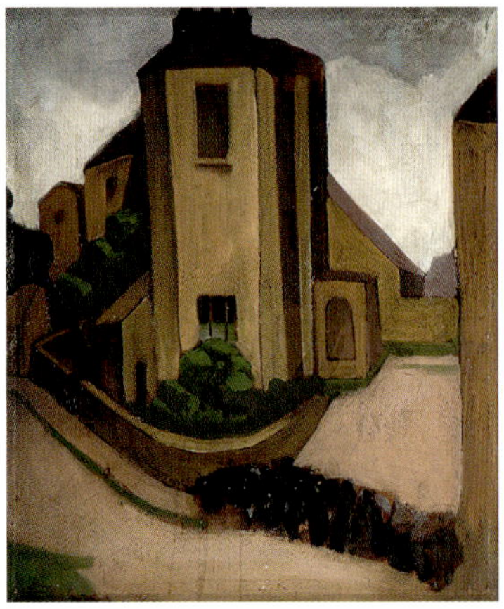

Currie, John 1883–1914
The House c.1914
oil on panel 60 x 49.5
1958.FA.3

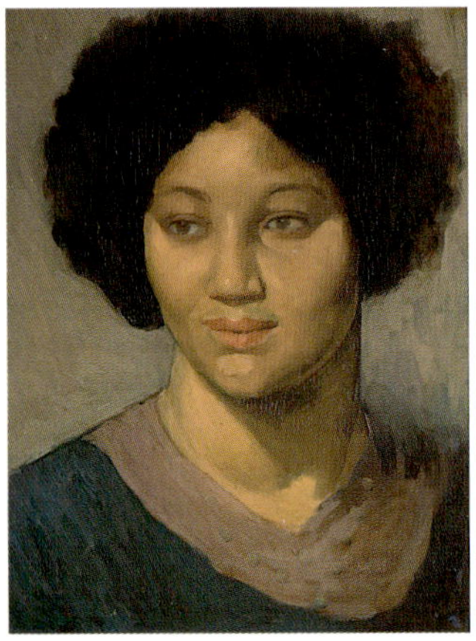

Currie, John 1883–1914
A Girl from Afar
oil on panel 44 x 33
1963.FA.21

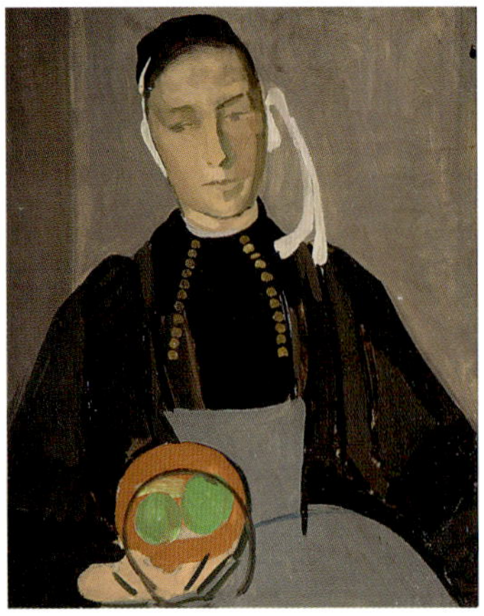

Currie, John 1883–1914
Breton Woman with Apples
oil on panel 63 x 51
1958.FA.23

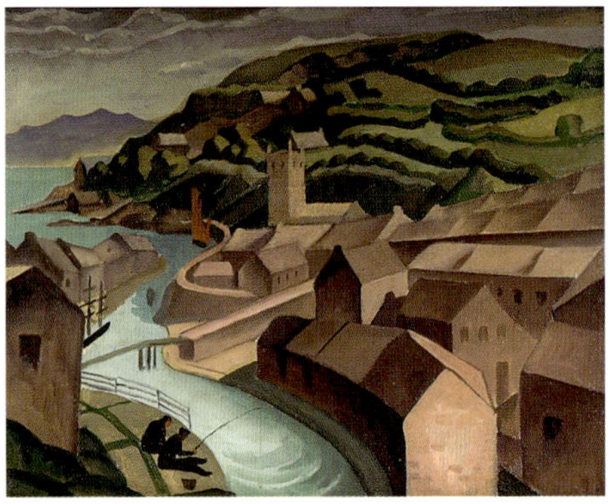

Currie, John 1883–1914
Dartmouth
oil on canvas 50 x 60.5
1952.FA.12

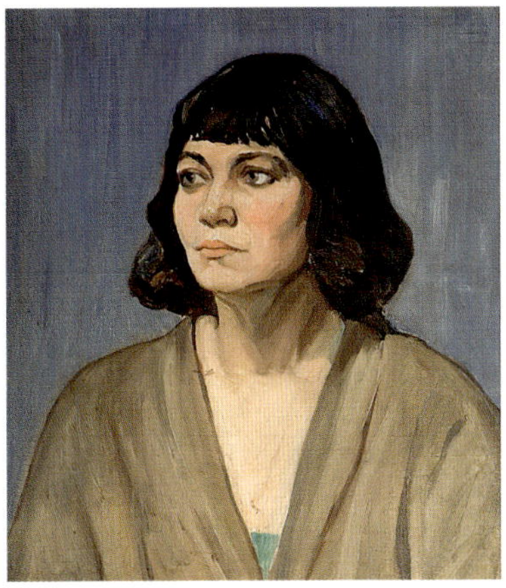

Currie, John 1883–1914
Female Portrait
oil on canvas 54 x 48
1952.FA.55

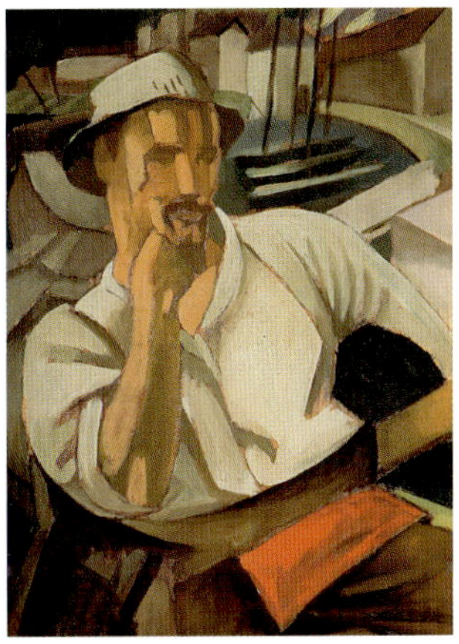

Currie, John 1883–1914
Fisherman
oil on panel 39.5 x 29
1958.FA.1

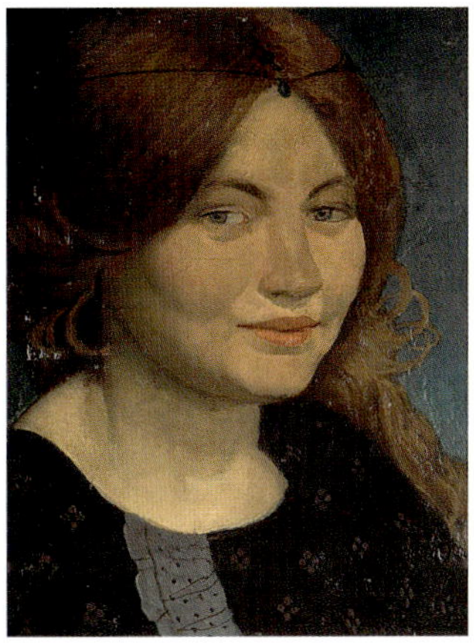

Currie, John 1883–1914
Head of a Girl
oil on canvas 31.5 x 23.5
1956.FA.4

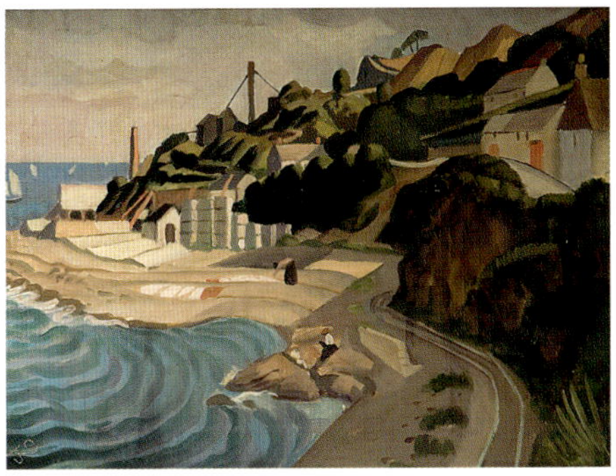

Currie, John 1883–1914
Newlyn, Looking towards Mousehole
oil on canvas 50 x 65
1952.FA.11

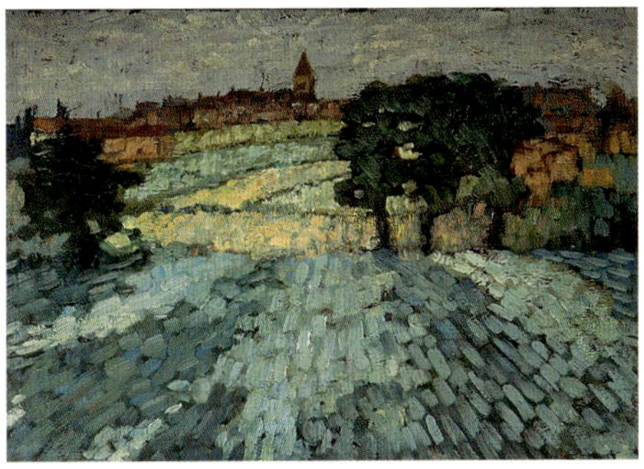

Currie, John 1883–1914
Penkhull
oil on canvas 24 x 34
1950.FA.114

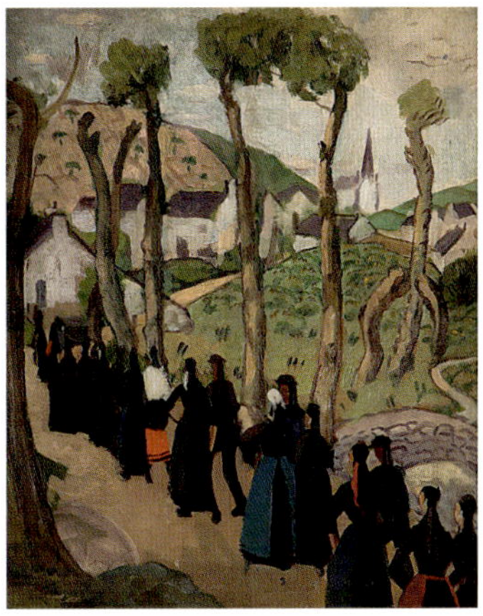

Currie, John 1883–1914
The Procession
oil on panel 63 x 51
1958.FA.23.1

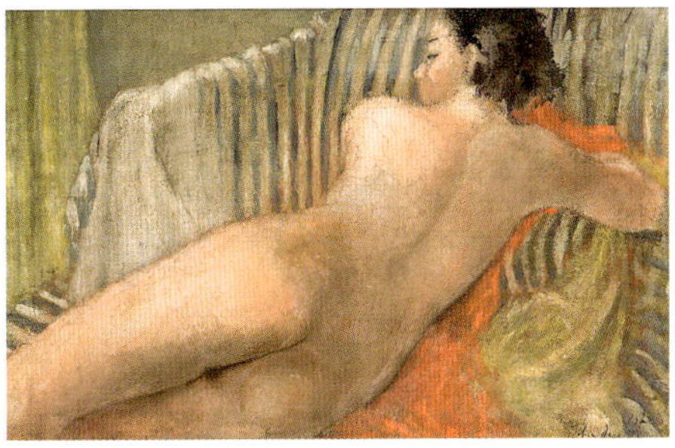

Darwin, Robin 1910–1974
Nude
oil on canvas 49 x 75
1947.FA.769

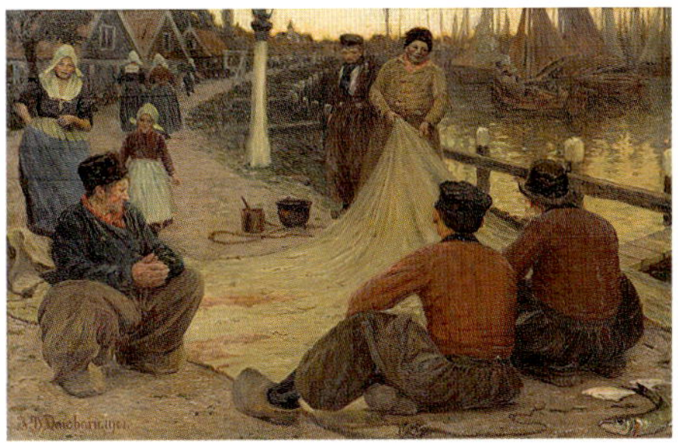

Dawbarn, Joseph Yelverton 1856–1943
Fishing Village on the Zuider Zee 1901
oil on canvas 59 x 89
1963.FA.81

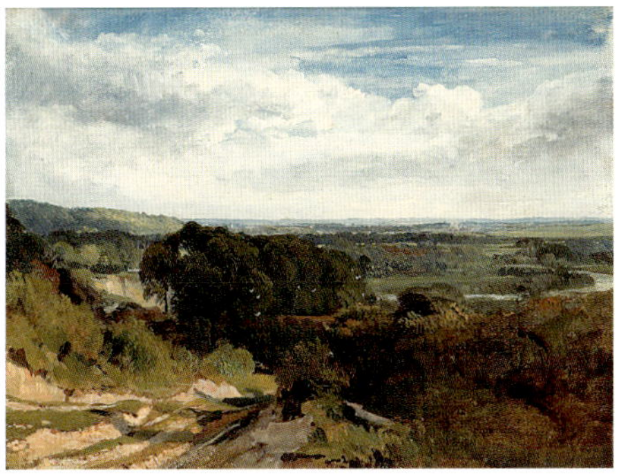

De Wint, Peter 1784–1849
Cliveden-on-Thames c.1810–1812
oil on panel 43 x 57
1940.FA.425

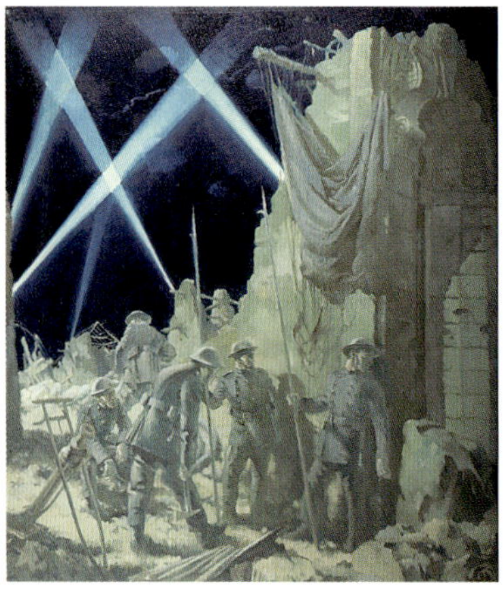

Dessau, Paul Lucien 1909–1999
Invasion 1942
oil on canvas 90.5 x 70.5
1942.FA.568

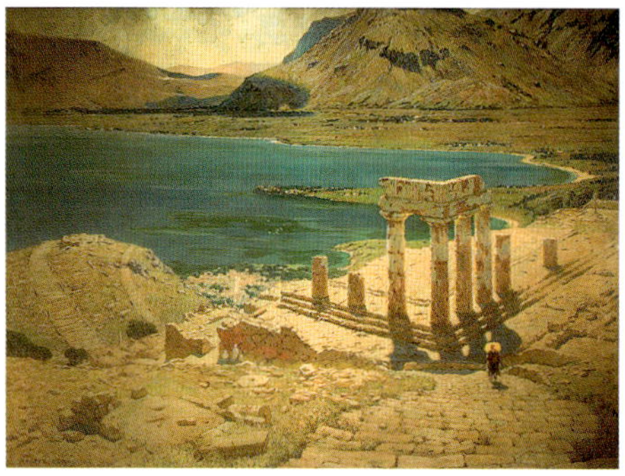

Donne, Walter J. 1867–1930
Temple of the Sun 1914
oil on canvas 144 x 184
1935.FA.199

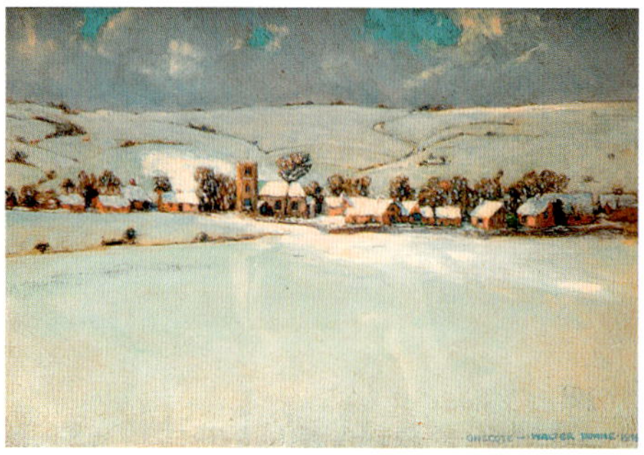

Donne, Walter J. 1867–1930
Onecote 1919
oil on board 23.5 x 34.5
1952.FA.50b

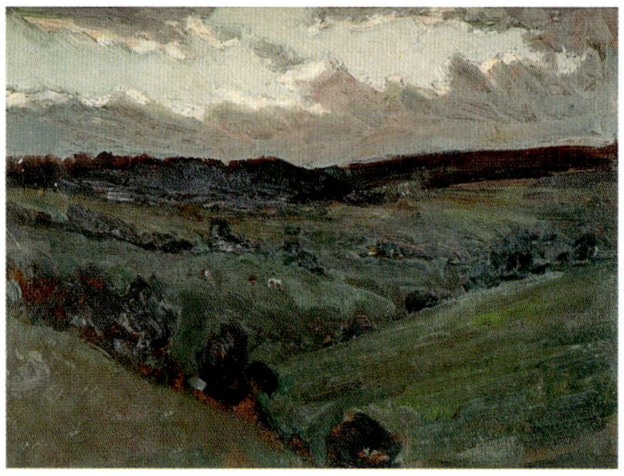

Donne, Walter J. 1867–1930
A Moorland Landscape, Staffordshire
oil on board 24 x 34
1952.FA.50a

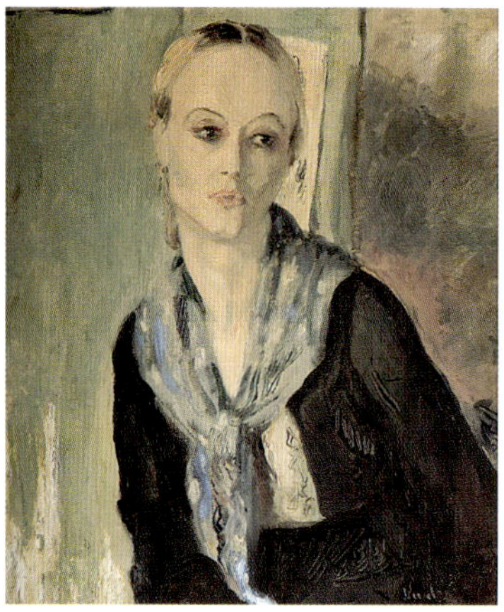

Dunlop, Ronald Ossory 1894–1973
Eileen 1912
oil on canvas 59 x 39
1933.FA.43

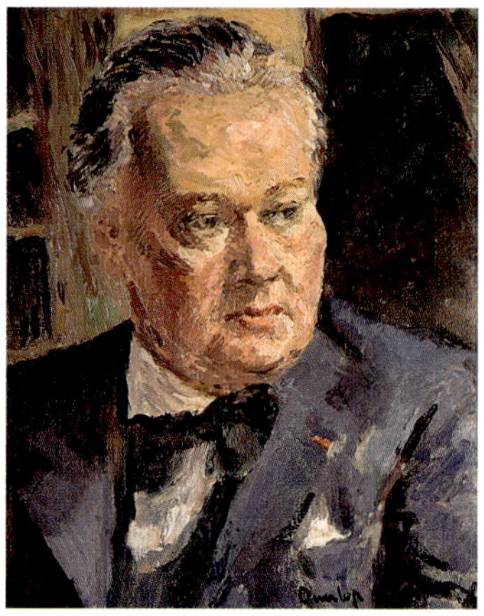

Dunlop, Ronald Ossory 1894–1973
C. R. W. Nevinson (1889–1946)
oil on canvas 49.5 x 39.5
1948.FA.849

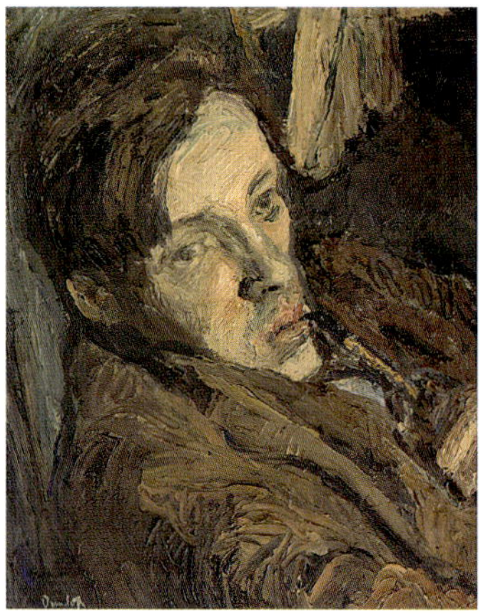

Dunlop, Ronald Ossory 1894–1973
The Poet
oil on canvas 49.5 x 39.5
1933.FA.44

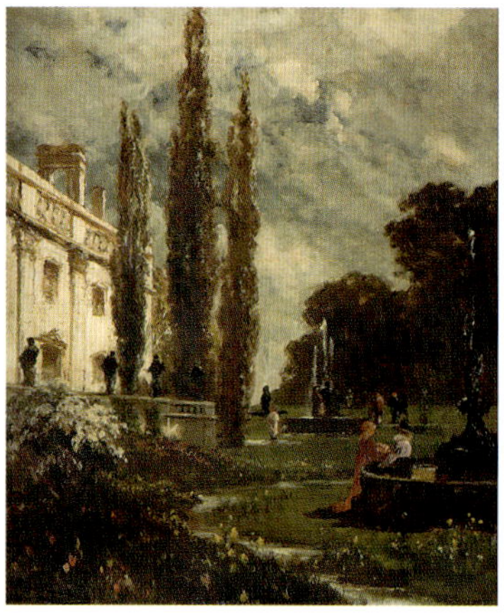

Ellis, Edwin 1841–1895
House and Gardens
oil on canvas 74 x 62
1929.FA.49

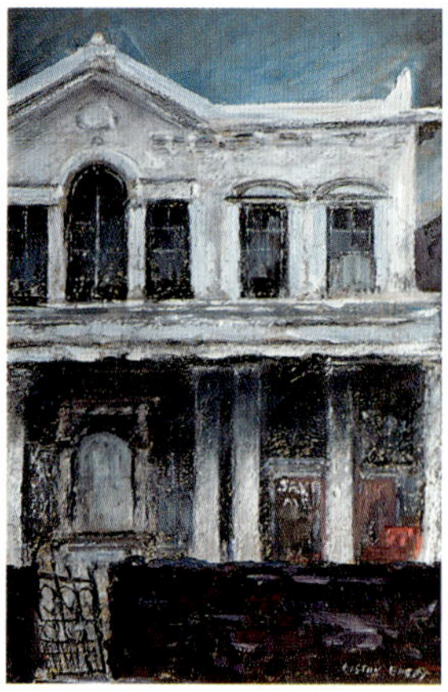

Emery, Alston active 1973–c.1992
Bethesda Chapel c.1992
oil on panel 53 x 34
1995.FA.5

Facing page: Stubbs, George, 1724–1806, *Wedgwood Family* (detail), 1780, Wedgwood Museum, (p. 182)

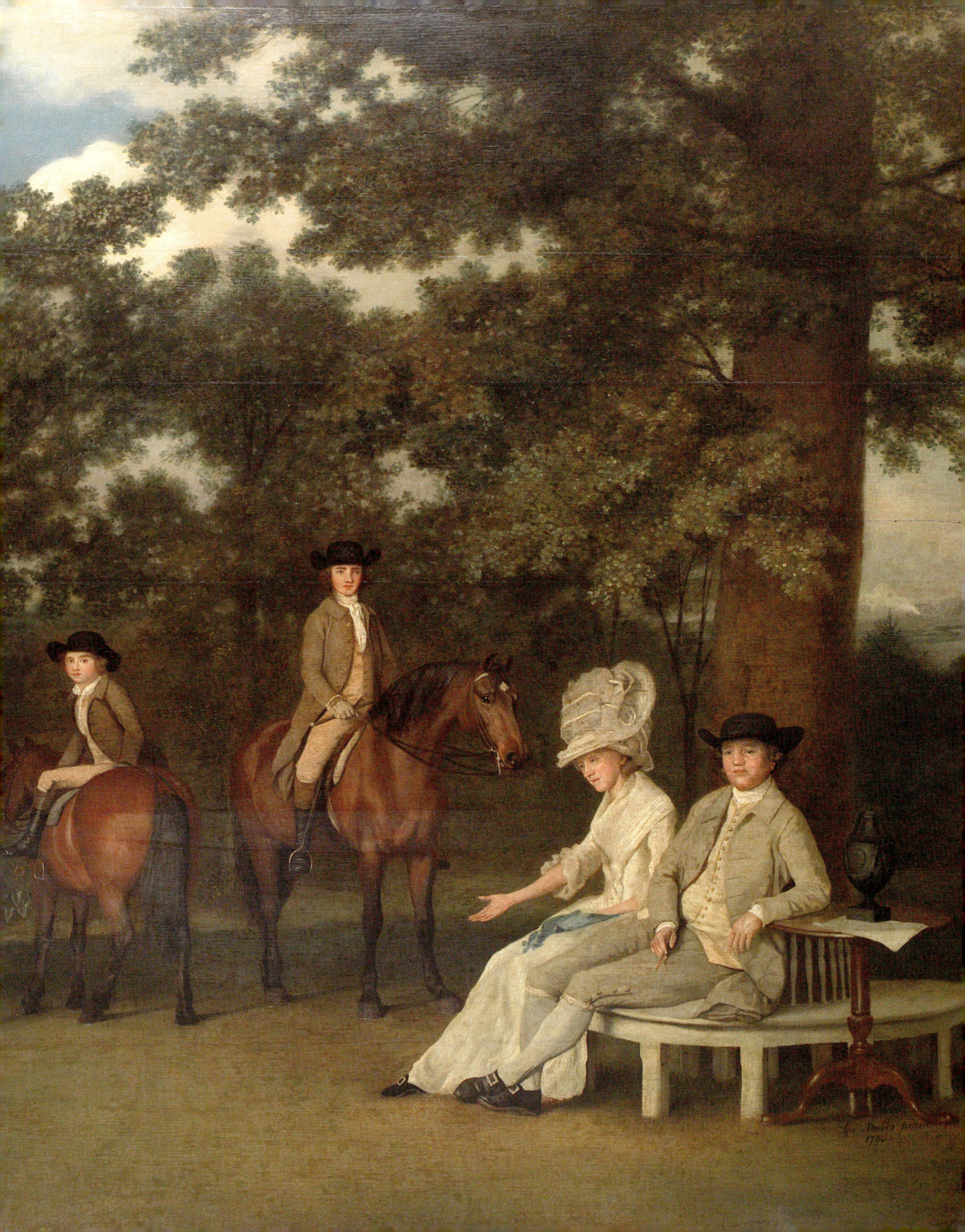
1780

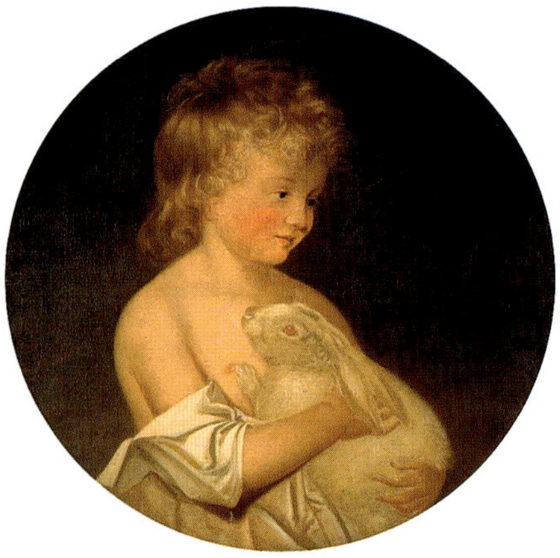

Emery, John 1777–1822
Boy with Rabbit
oil on canvas 50
1991.FA.9

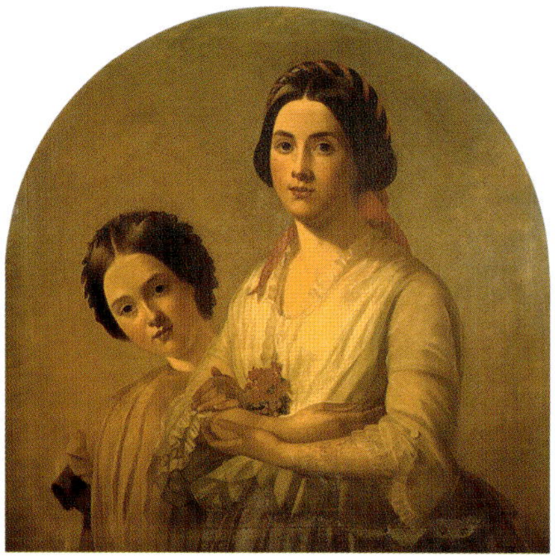

Emery, John 1777–1822
Marianne and Anne
oil on canvas 90 x 90
PCF14

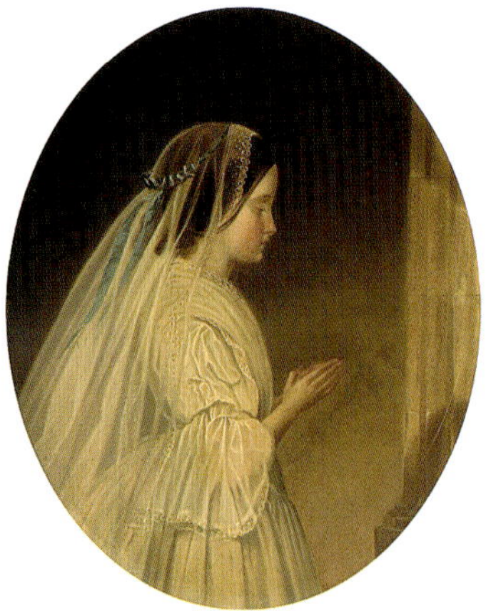

Emery, John 1777–1822
Marianne in Confirmation Dress
oil on canvas 43 x 34
PCF15

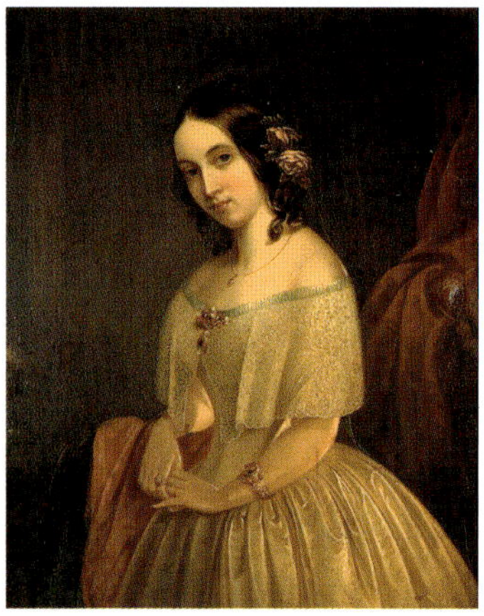

Emery, John 1777–1822
Portrait of a Young Lady
oil on canvas 43.5 x 34.5
PCF16

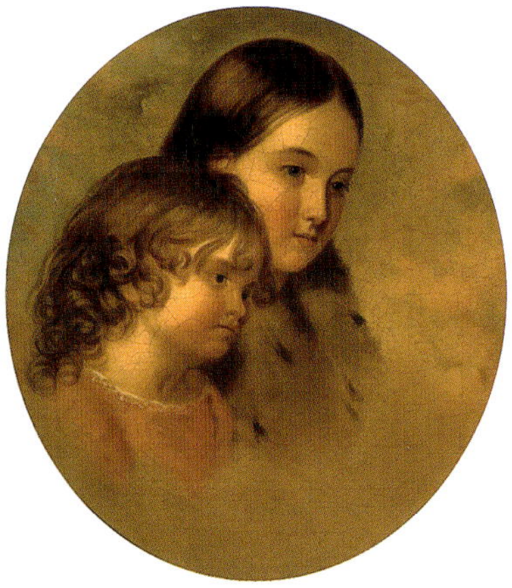

Emery, John 1777–1822
Portrait of the Artist's Daughters
oil on canvas 39 x 35
PCF17

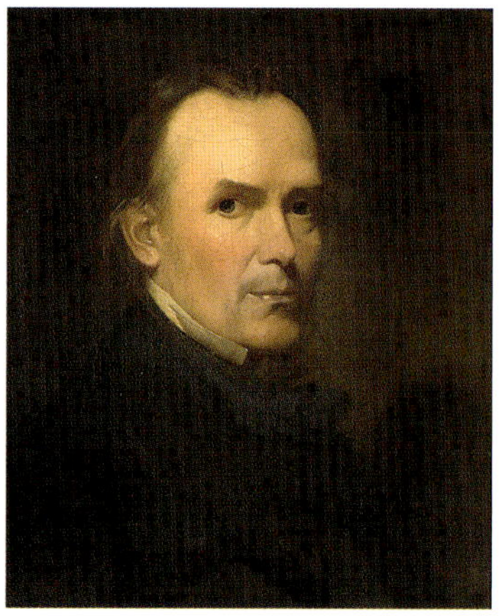

Emery, John 1777–1822
Self Portrait
oil on canvas 51 x 42
PCF18

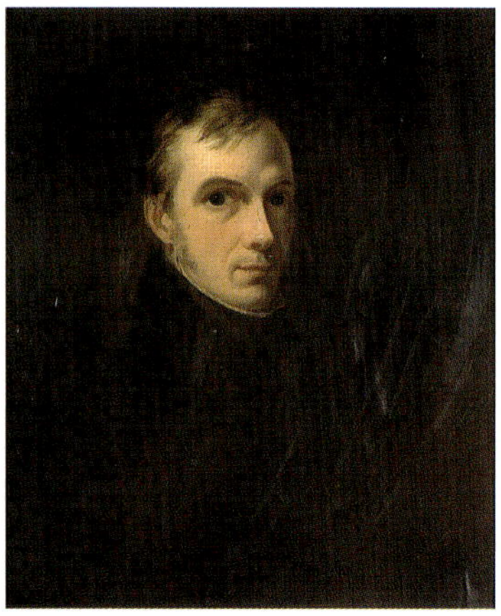

Emery, John 1777–1822
Self Portrait
oil on canvas 30 x 25
PCF19

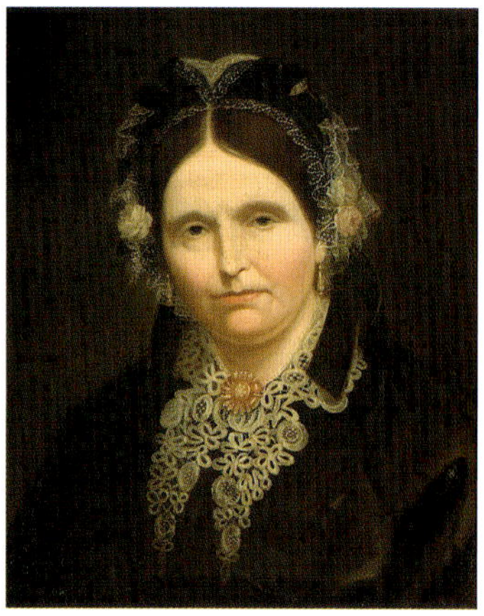

Emery, John 1777–1822
Susannah Toft
oil on canvas 51 x 42
PCF20

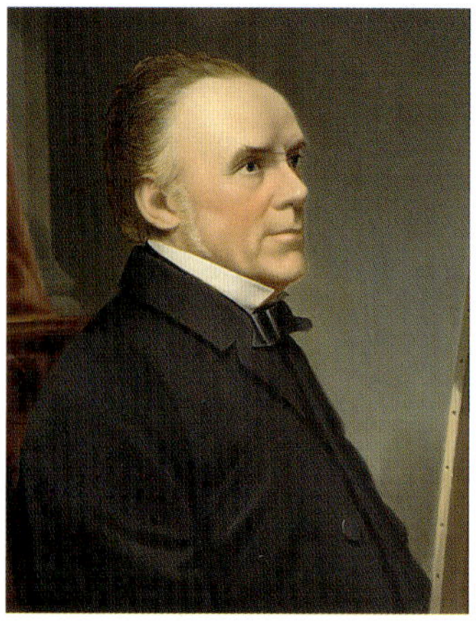

Emery, John (after) 1777–1822
Self Portrait
oil on paper 38.5 x 29.5
1991.FA.8

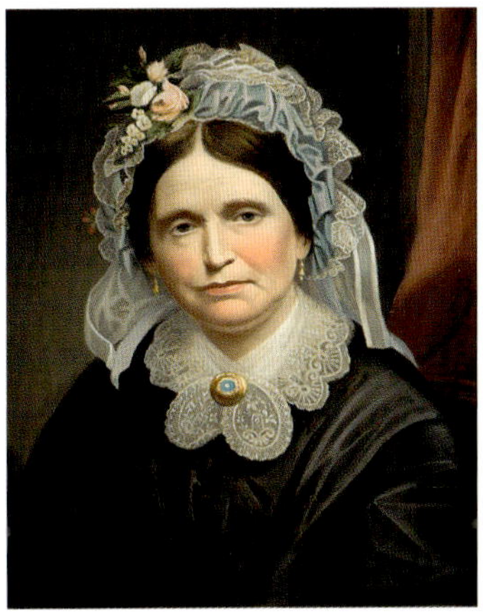

Emery, John (after) 1777–1822
Susannah Toft
oil on paper 39 x 29
1991.FA.7

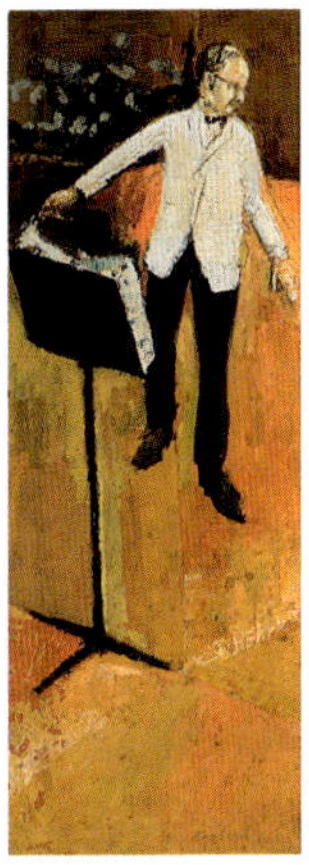

England, Frederick John b.1939
Joseph Rosenstock at Lewisham Station 1966
oil on panel 70 x 24
1967.FA.22

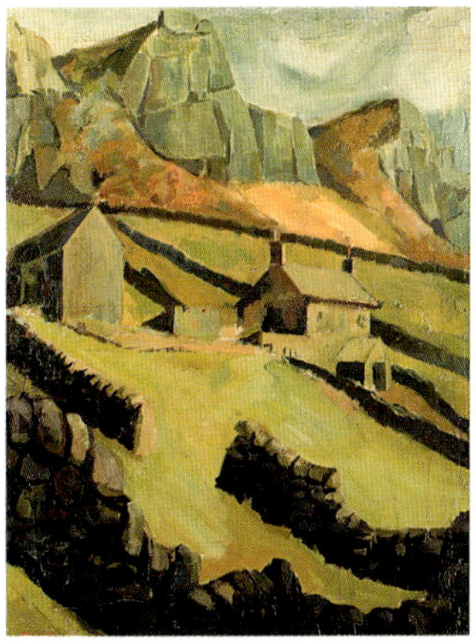

England, Frederick John b.1939
Below Five Clouds, the Roaches
oil on panel 101 x 76.5
1963.FA.62

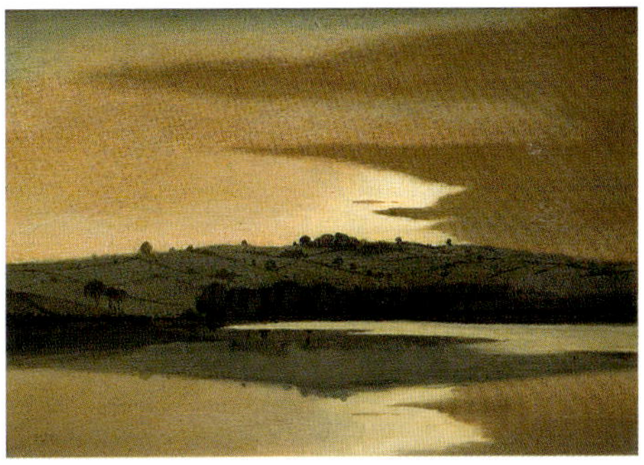

Errill, Frederick F.
April Moonrise 1948
oil on panel 34 x 47
1964.FA.30A

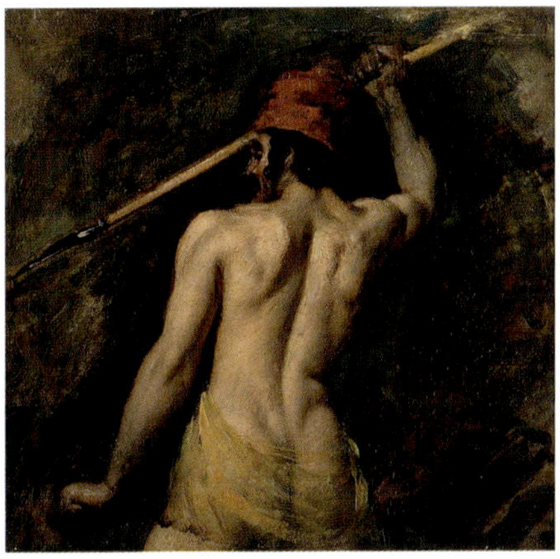

Etty, William 1787–1849
A Greek Slave c.1812
oil on paper 43 x 43
1954.FA.188

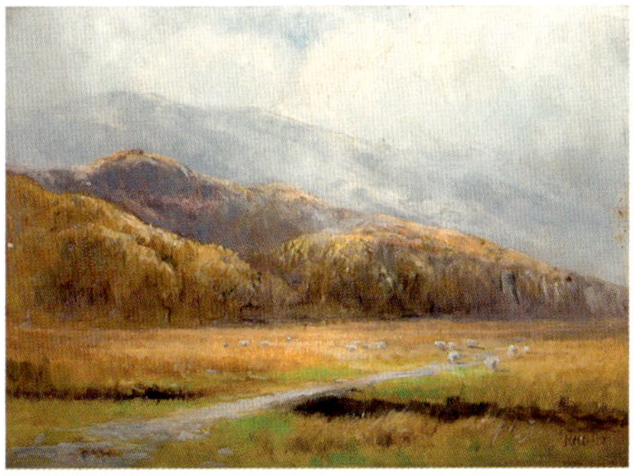

Evans, E. J. B. active c.1900–1920
Etruria 1903
oil on canvas 24.5 x 49.5
PCF21

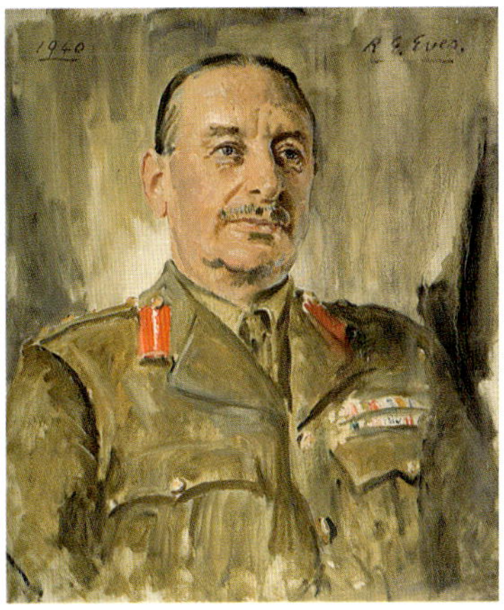

Eves, Reginald Grenville 1876–1941
Colonel Henry Edward Medlicott (1882–1948) 1940
oil on canvas 60 x 50
1947.FA.779

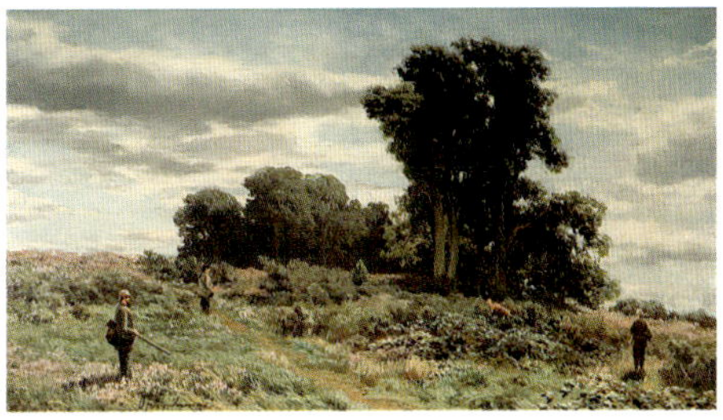

Farquharson, David 1839–1907
Forest of Meikleour, Perthshire
oil on canvas 34 x 59
1972.FA.1A

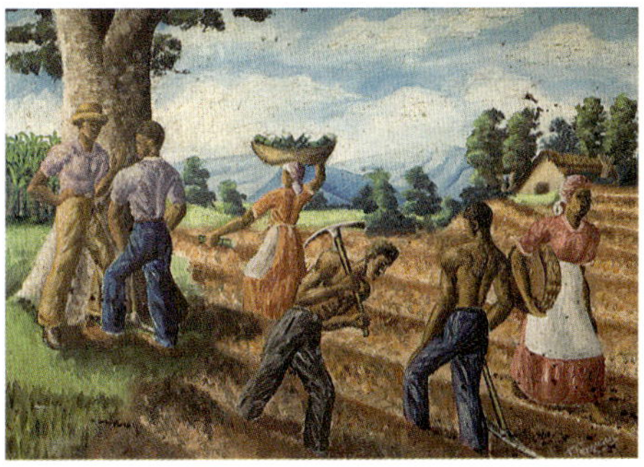

Ferguson, V. active 1940s
Food Production, Jamaica
oil on canvas 41.5 x 56
1947.FA.783

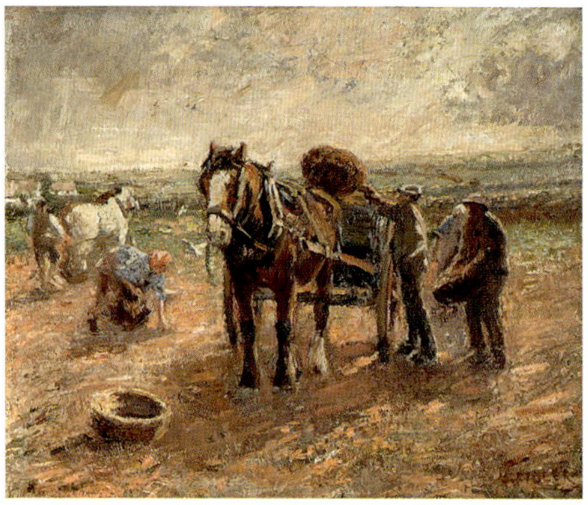

Fidler, Harry 1856–1935
Clearing the Potato Field
oil on canvas 75 x 90
1935.FA.79

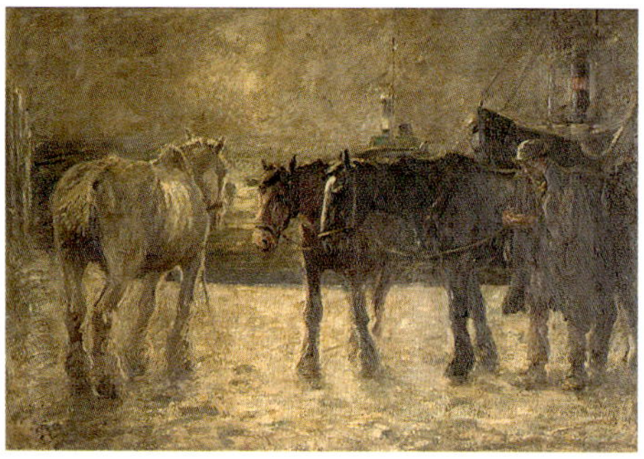

Fidler, Harry 1856–1935
The Last Journey
oil on canvas 126 x 183
1935.FA.84

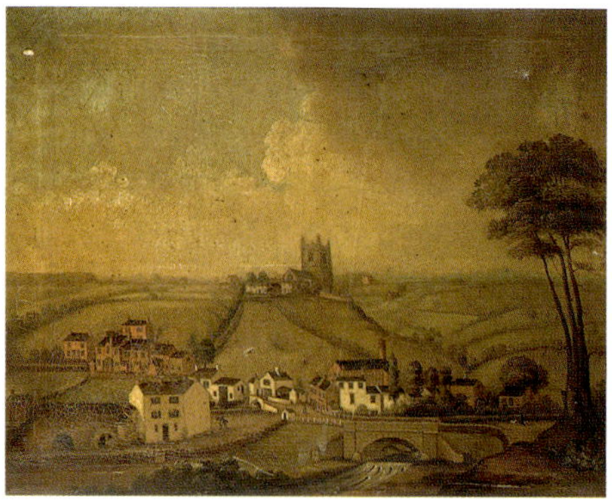

Findler, L.
Cheddleton c.1871
oil on canvas 61.5 x 74
1954.FA.25

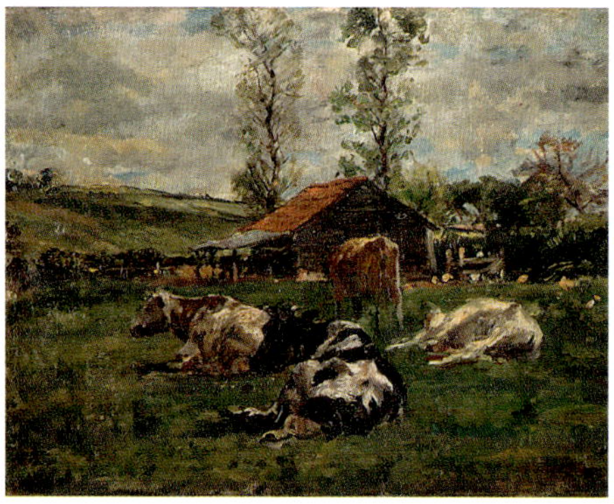

Fisher, Mark 1841–1923
Cows Grazing
oil on canvas 32 x 38
1955.FA.5

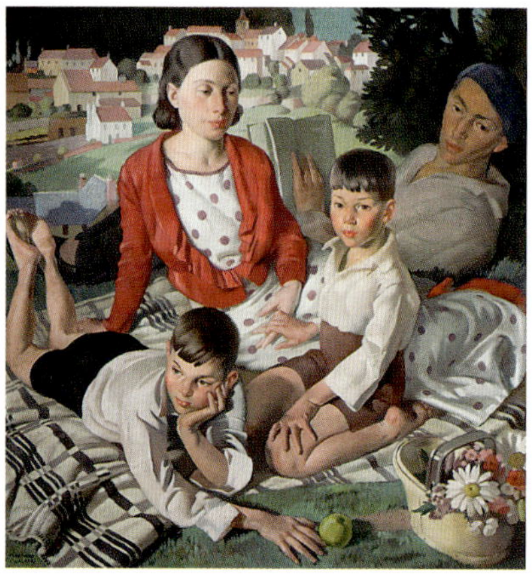

Fleetwood-Walker, Bernard 1893–1965
The Family
oil on canvas 100 x 92
1932.FA.4

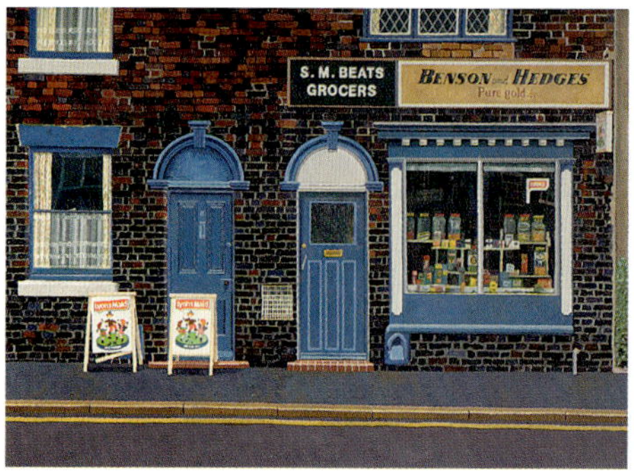

Fletcher, Doreen b.1952
Beats Grocers 1979
oil on canvas 70.5 x 101.5
1982.FA.5

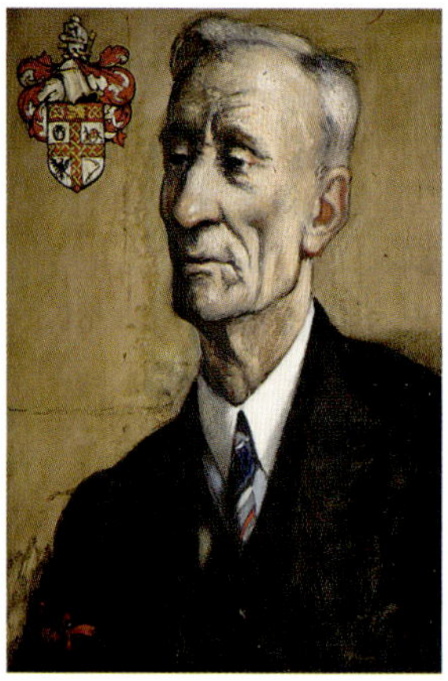

Forsyth, Gordon Mitchell 1879–1952
Jim Mason (1879–1952) 1944
oil on panel 54.5 x 40
1957.FA.22

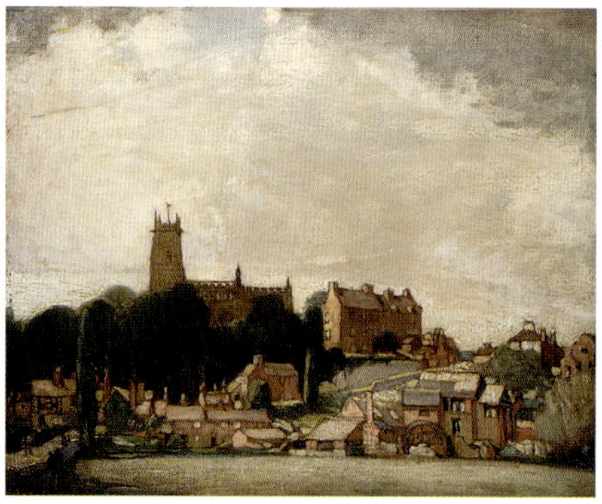

Forsyth, Gordon Mitchell 1879–1952
Market Drayton, Shropshire
oil on canvas 55 x 65
1941.FA.494

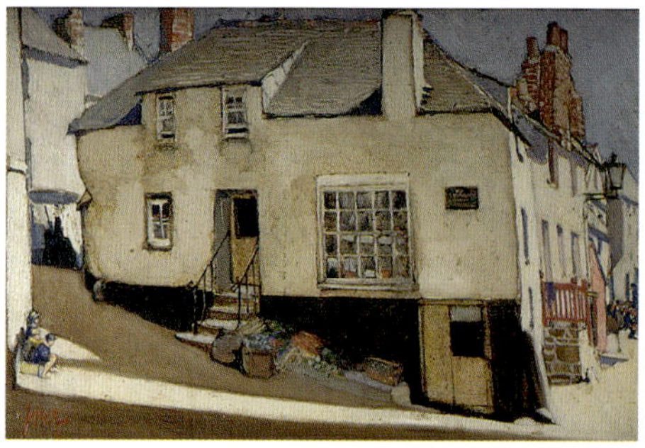

Forsyth, Gordon Mitchell 1879–1952
Old Houses, St Ives
oil on canvas 39 x 49.5
1924.FA.2

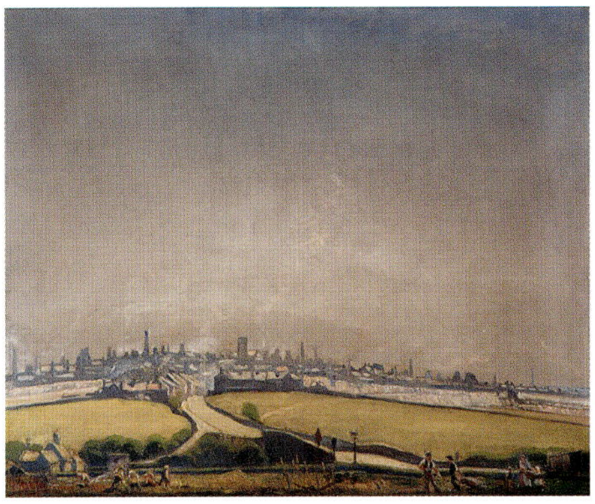

Forsyth, Gordon Mitchell 1879–1952
The Sytch, Burslem
oil on canvas 55 x 65
1954.FA.88

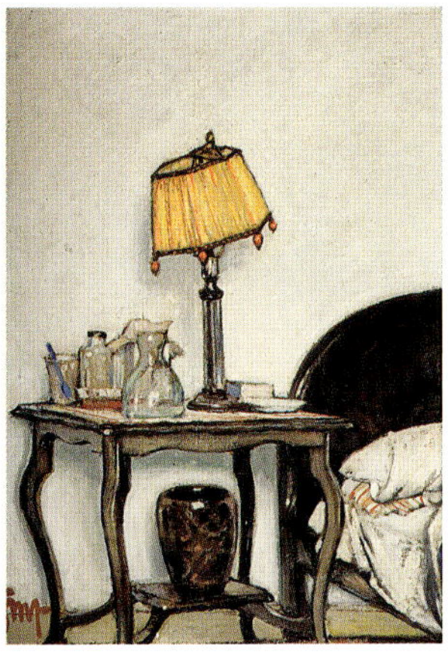

Forsyth, Gordon Mitchell 1879–1952
The Yellow Lamp
oil on canvas 48.5 x 33
1972.FA.7

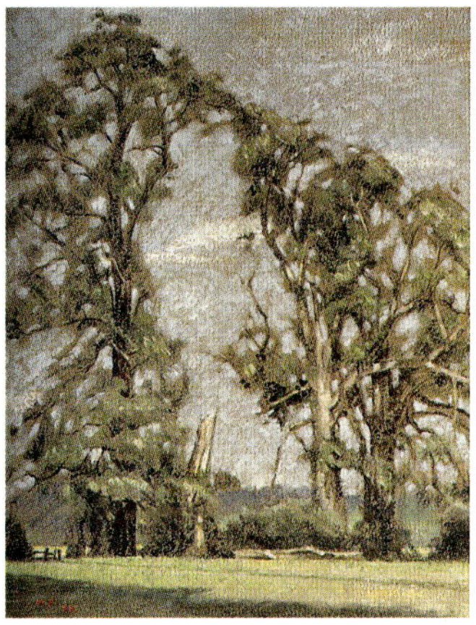

Forsyth, Moira 1905–1991
Trees at Sellack, Wye Valley 1939
tempera on panel 37 x 27
1964.FA.15A

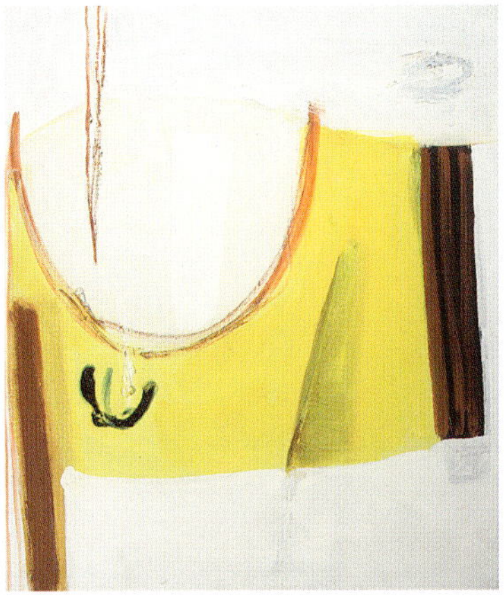

Frost, Terry 1915–2003
Yellow and Ochre 1959
oil on canvas 74 x 61.5
1986.FA.17

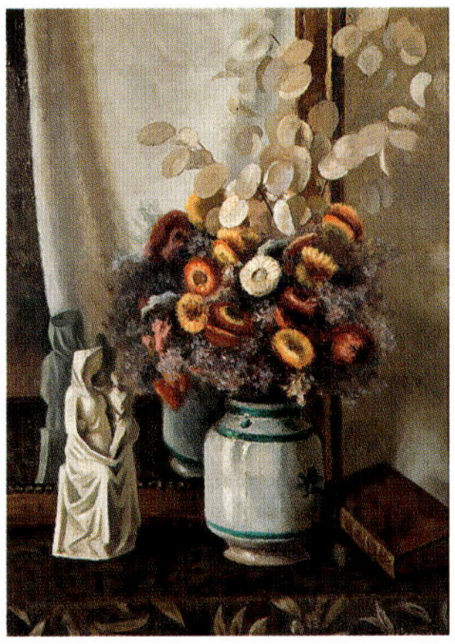

Fry, Roger Eliot 1866–1934
Immortelles
oil on panel 54 x 39
1953.FA.62

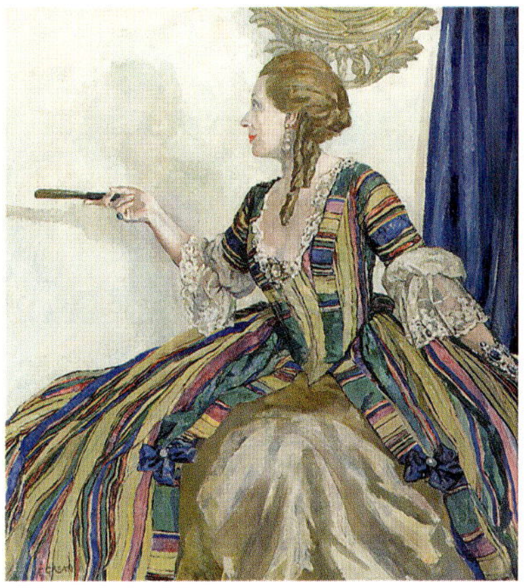

Gabain, Ethel 1883–1950
Miss Edith Evans in a Restoration Comedy
oil on canvas 101.5 x 91.5
1935.FA.182

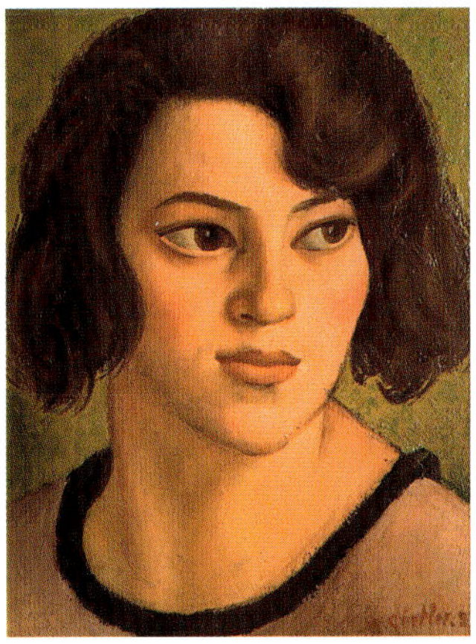

Gertler, Mark 1892–1939
Head of a Basque Shepherdess 1922
oil on panel 33 x 24
1935.FA.198

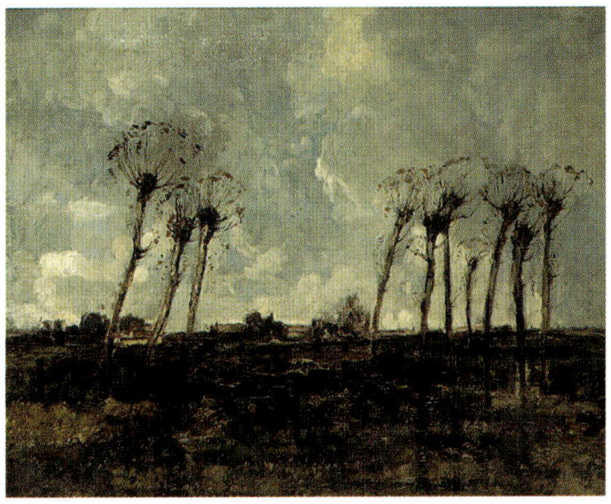

Gibson, William Alfred 1866–1931
On the Riviera
oil on canvas 50 x 60
1947.FA.772

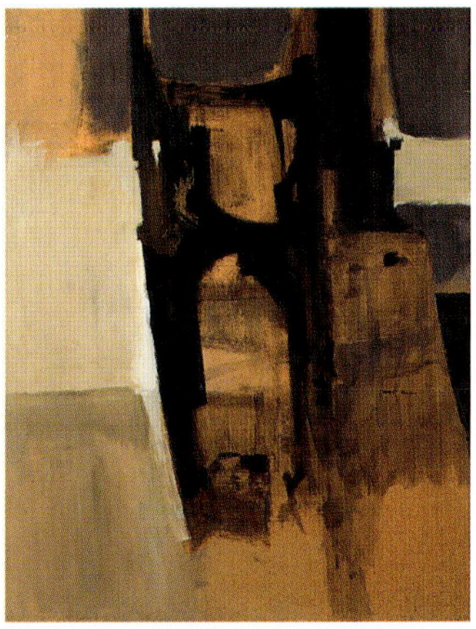

Giles, Anthony E. b.1925
Tinscape
oil on panel 101 x 77
1966.FA.6

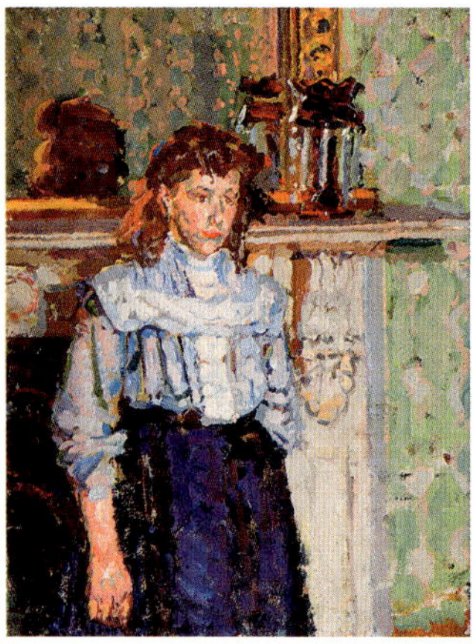

Gilman, Harold 1876–1919
Interior with a Girl by a Mantelpiece c.1912
oil on canvas 40.5 x 30.5
1979.FA.11

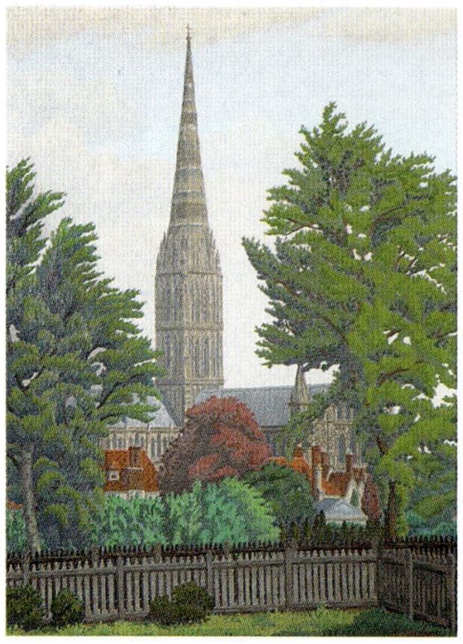

Ginner, Charles 1878–1952
Salisbury Cathedral
oil on canvas 66.5 x 50
1937.FA.282

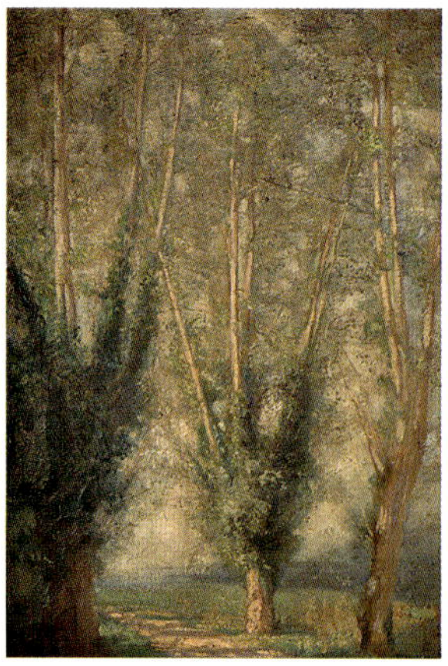

Gleaves, Percy 1882–1944
Three Trees 1908
oil on canvas 60 x 40
1970.FA.21

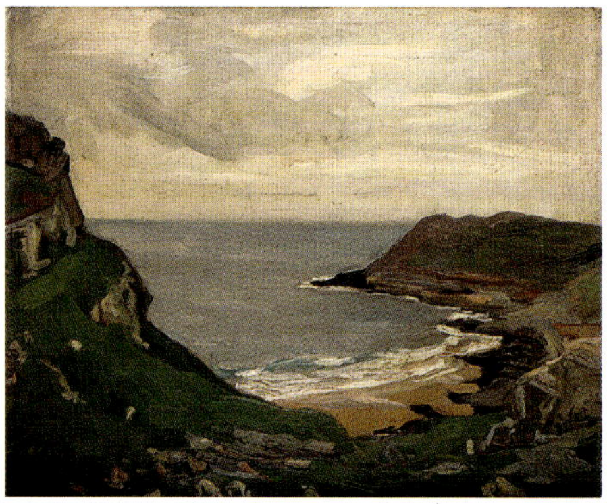

Gleaves, Percy 1882–1944
Coastal Scene
oil on canvas 31 x 37.5
1970.FA.5A

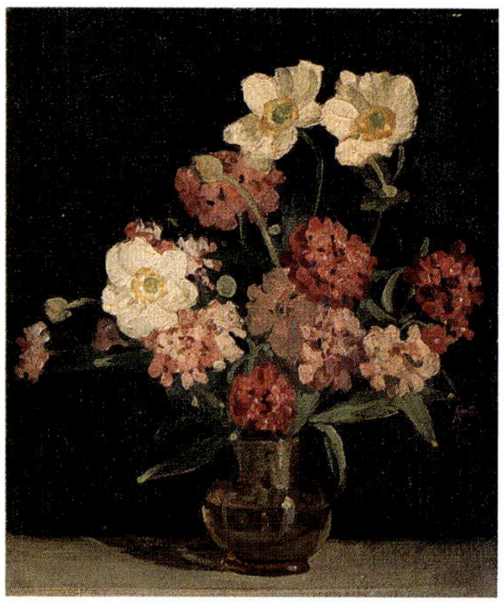

Gleaves, Percy 1882–1944
Japanese Anemones and Zinnias in a Glass Vase
oil on canvas 26 x 21
1970.FA.6

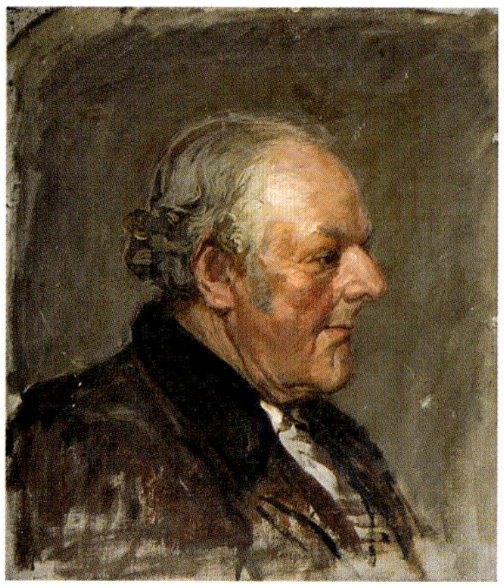

Gleaves, Percy 1882–1944
Portrait of an Old Man
oil on canvas 54.5 x 47
1970.FA.203A

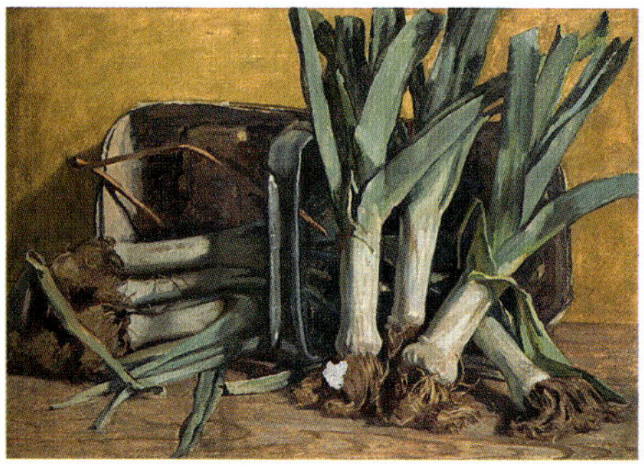

Gleaves, Percy 1882–1944
Still Life of Leeks against a Basket
oil on canvas 46 x 63
1970.FA.204A

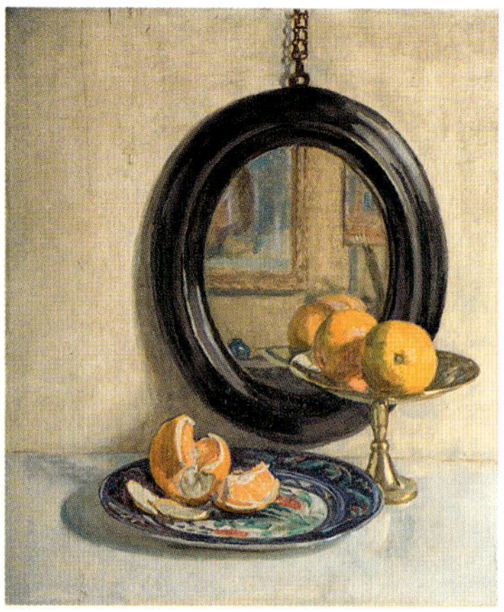

Gleaves, Percy 1882–1944
Still Life of Oranges in front of a Mirror
oil on canvas 57 x 47
1970.FA.222A

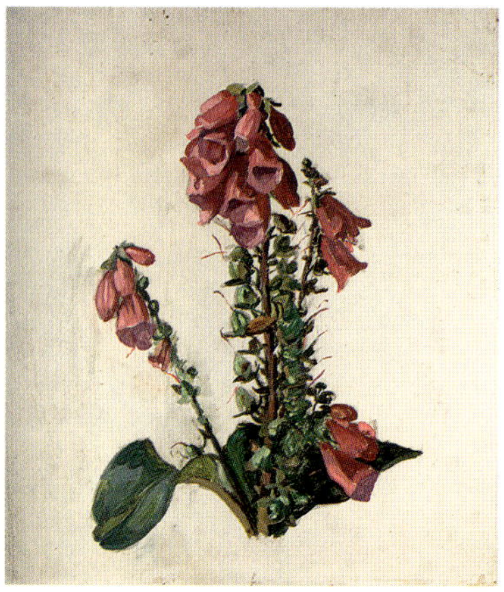

Gleaves, Percy 1882–1944
Study of Foxgloves
oil on paper 38 x 32.5
1970.FA.223A

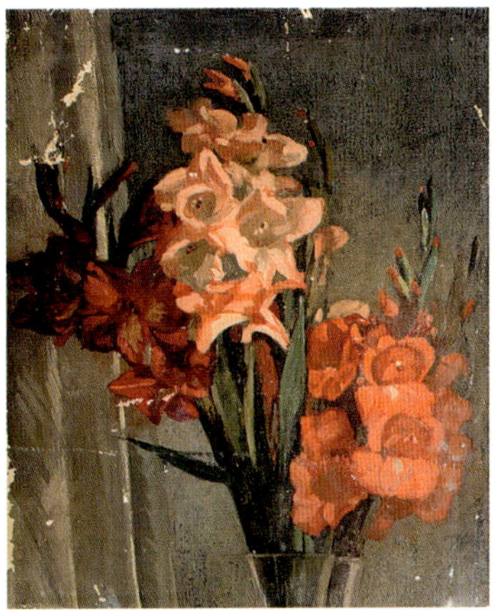

Gleaves, Percy 1882–1944
Study of Gladioli
oil on canvas 43 x 34
1970.FA.4A

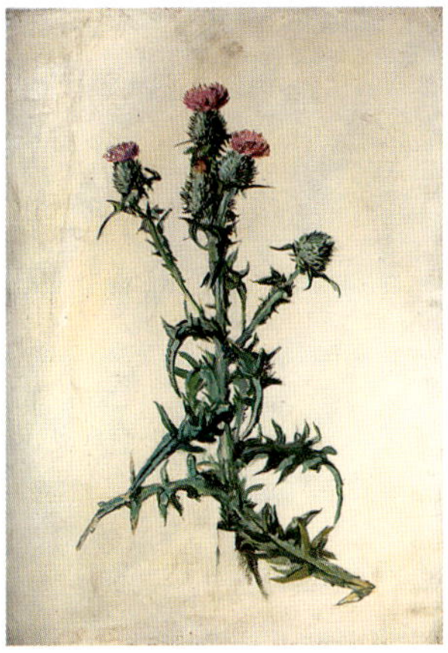

Gleaves, Percy 1882–1944
Study of Thistles
oil on paper 56 x 38
1970.FA.224A

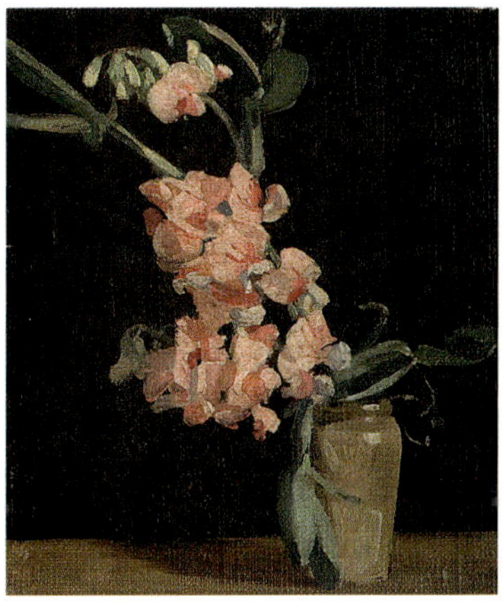

Gleaves, Percy 1882–1944
Sweet Peas in a Green Vase
oil on canvas 26 x 21
1970.FA.7

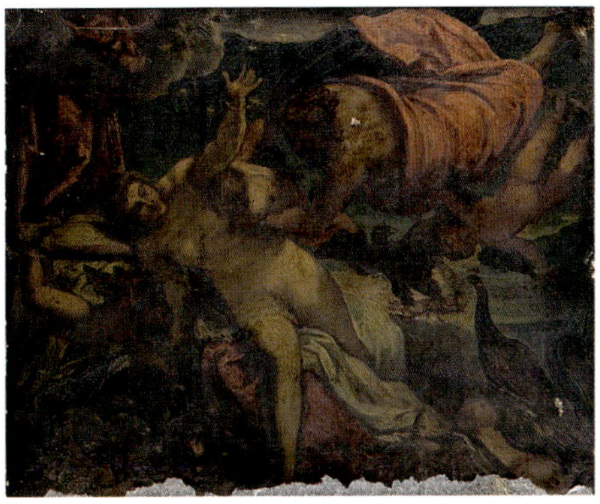

Gleaves, Percy 1882–1944
The Origin of the Milky Way (after Jacopo Tintoretto)
oil on canvas 41 x 46
PCF22

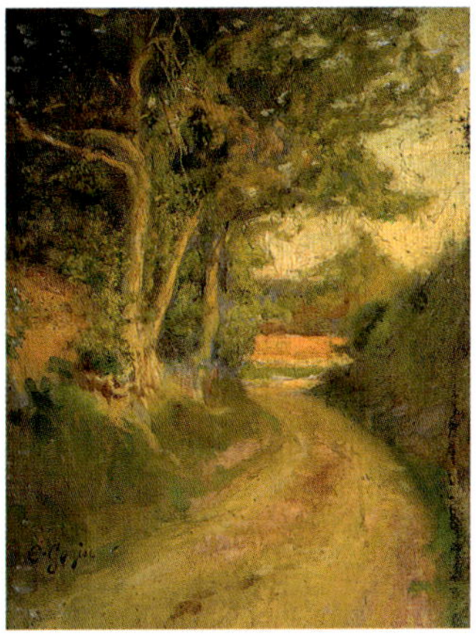

Gogin, Charles 1844–1931
A Sussex Lane
oil on board 44 x 33.5
1945.FA.563

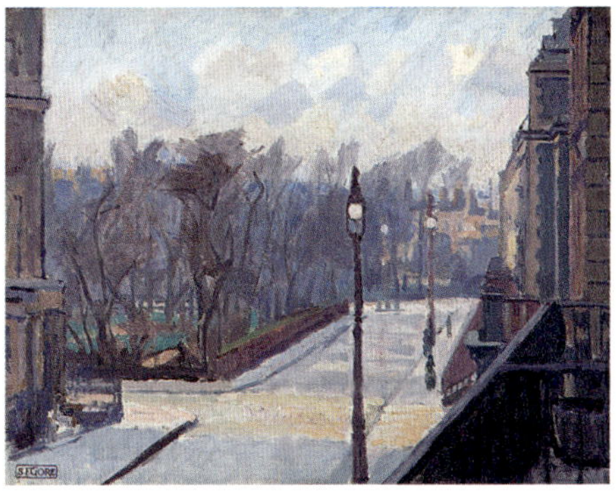

Gore, Spencer 1878–1914
Harrington Square from No.2 Houghton Place 1913
oil on canvas 40 x 51
1983.FA.5

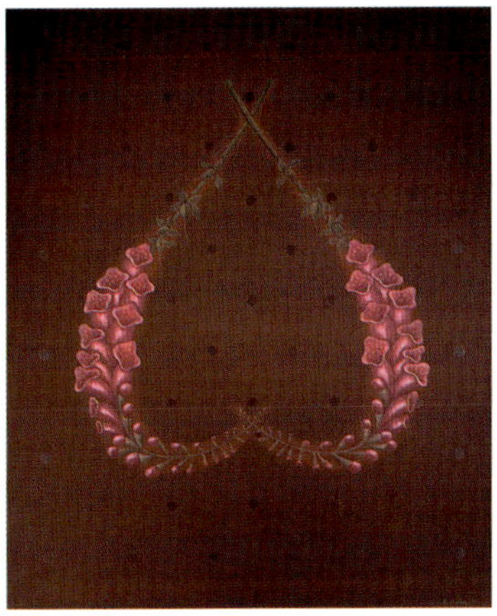

Gosling, Paul
Medicine 1991
acrylic on canvas 149.5 x 120
1991.FA.1

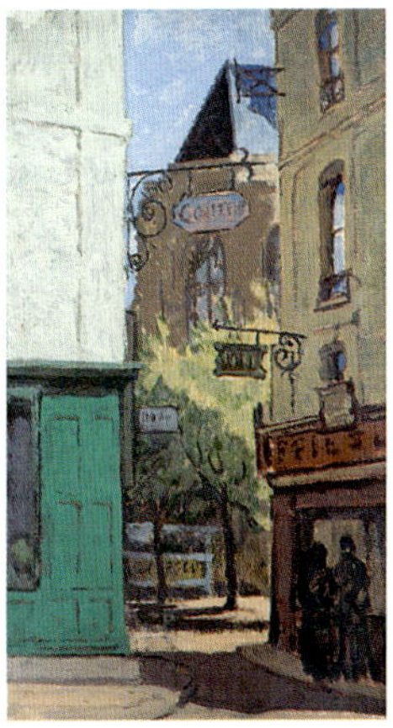

Gosse, Laura Sylvia 1881–1968
St Rémy
oil on canvas 39 x 32
1935.FA.82

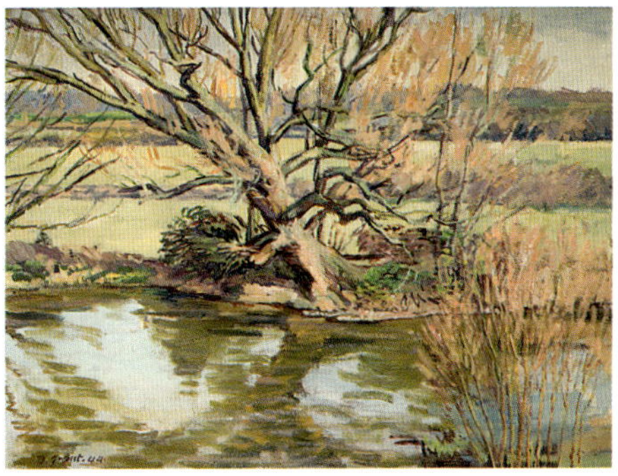

Grant, Duncan 1885–1978
Flatford-on-Avon 1944
oil on canvas 49.5 x 65.5
1948.FA.848

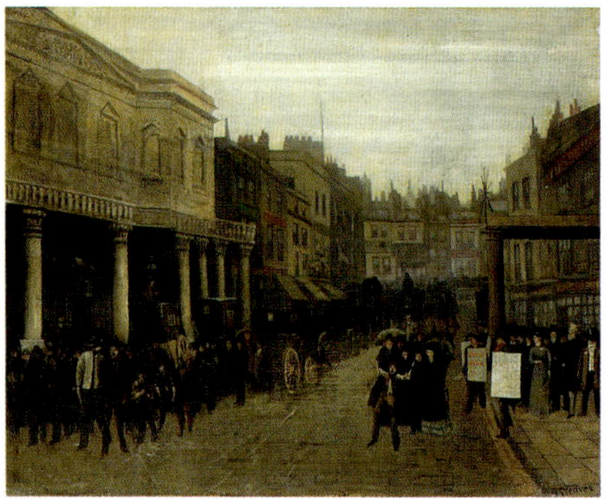

Greaves, Walter 1846–1930
The Haymarket
oil on canvas 51 x 61
1953.FA.6

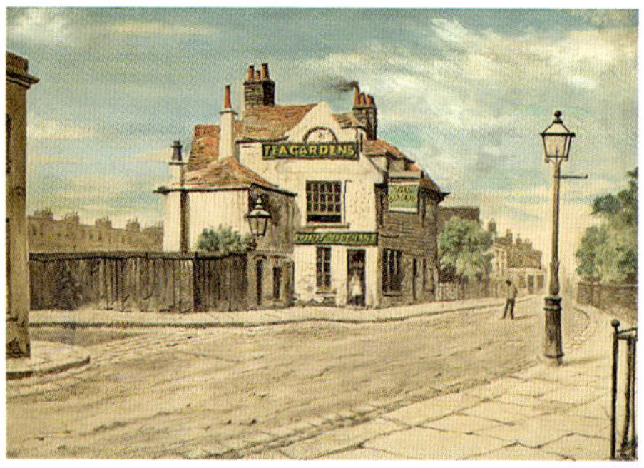

Greaves, Walter 1846–1930
The Street Singer
oil on canvas 44.5 x 60
1938.FA.322

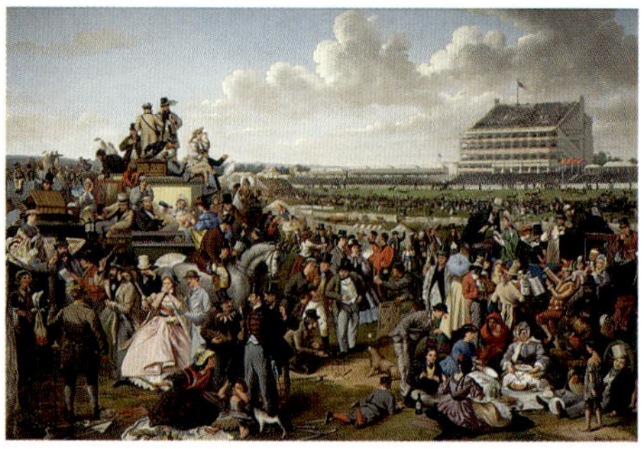

Green, Aaron 1820–1898
Epsom Downs, 1863 1871
oil on canvas 84 x 120
1958.FA.48

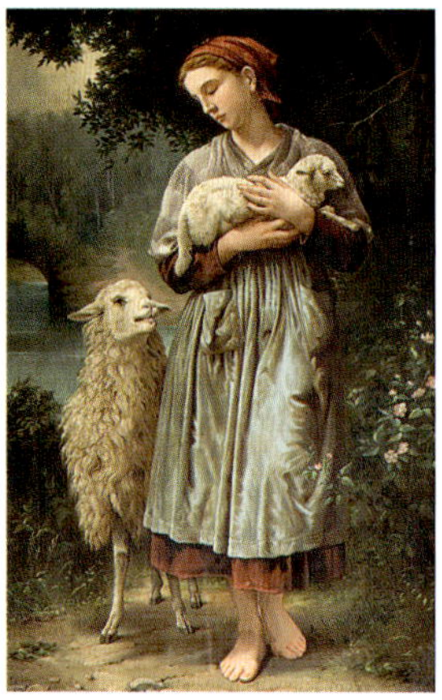

Green, Aaron 1820–1898
Girl with a Lamb 1879
oil on canvas 63 x 39
1958.FA.25

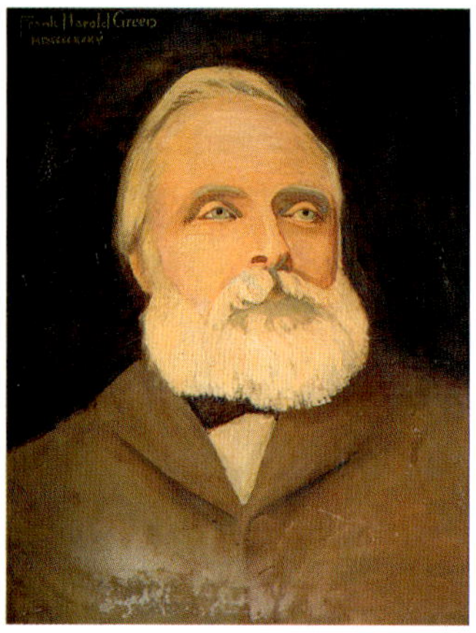

Green, Frank Harold
Spencer Green (1839–1903) 1935
oil on canvas 54.5 x 42
2001.C.654

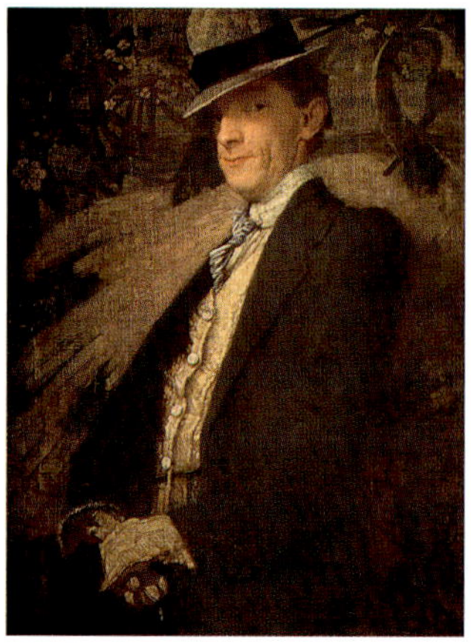

Greenwood, Orlando 1892–1989
The Card 1909
oil on canvas 77 x 57
1957.FA.50

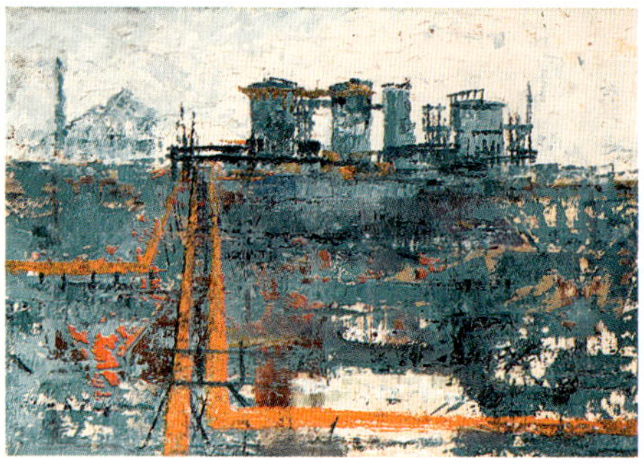

Grundy, Robert B.
New Industry
oil on panel 41 x 55
1960.FA.41

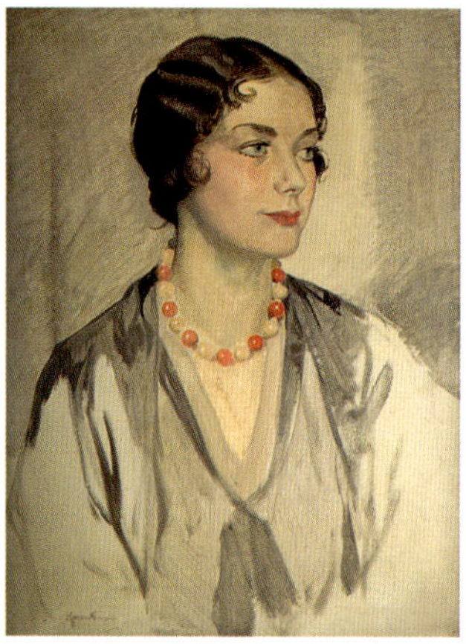

Gunn, Herbert James 1893–1964
Michie
oil on canvas 60 x 44
1942.FA.547

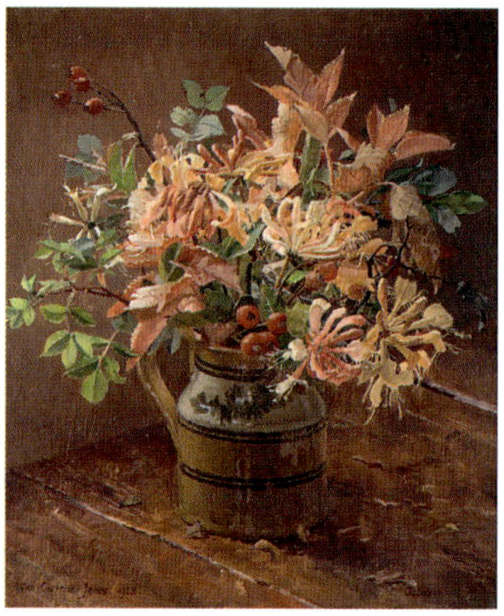

Gwynne-Jones, Allan 1892–1982
Honeysuckle 1928
oil on panel 39 x 33
1953.FA.29

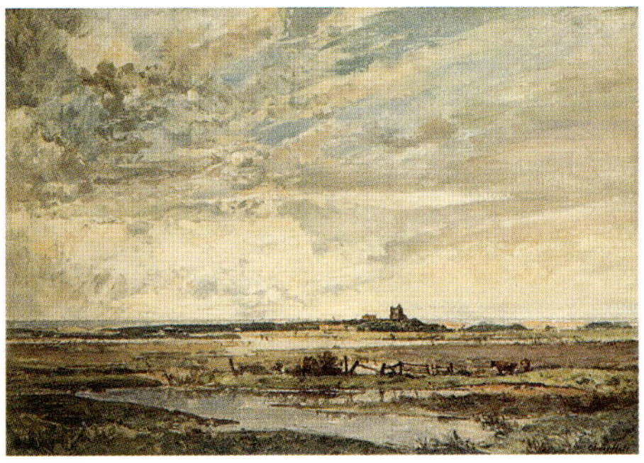

Hall, Oliver 1869–1957
Marshland on the Norfolk Coast
oil on canvas 54 x 74
1932.FA.6

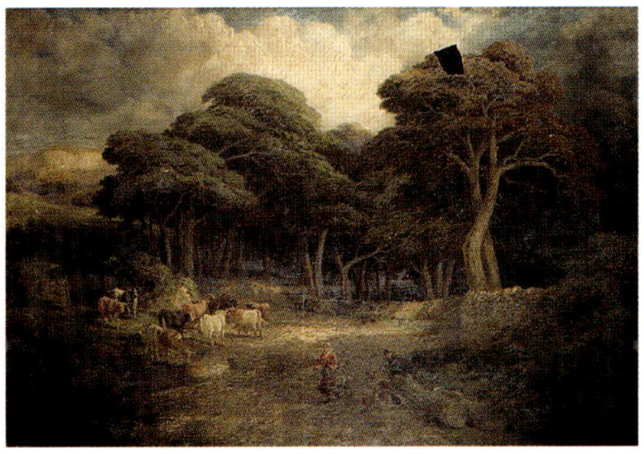

Hargitt, Edward 1835–1895
Landscape with Cattle and Women Feeding Hens 1891
oil on canvas 118 x 150
1954.FA.147

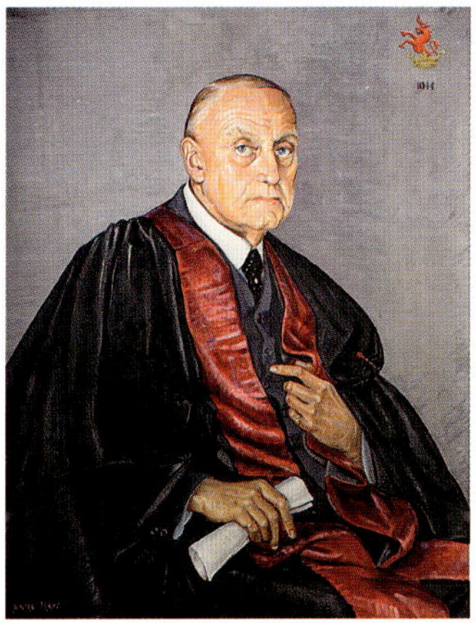

Hart, Anna active 1944–1945
Mr Eric Young 1944
oil on canvas 110 x 75
1945.FA.687

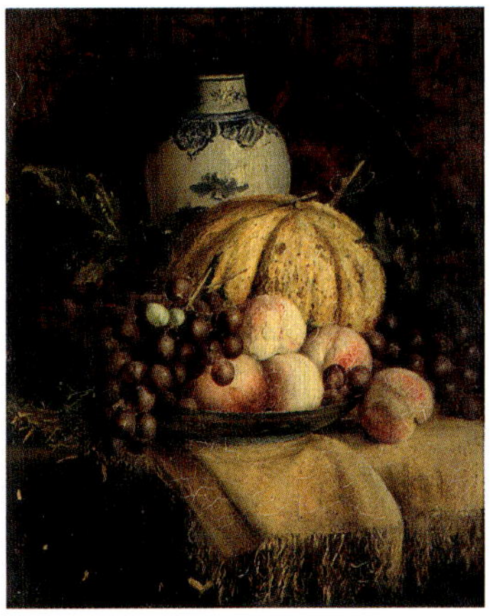

Hastling, Annie E. b.1845
Still Life 1875
oil on canvas 49.5 x 38.5
1954.FA.129

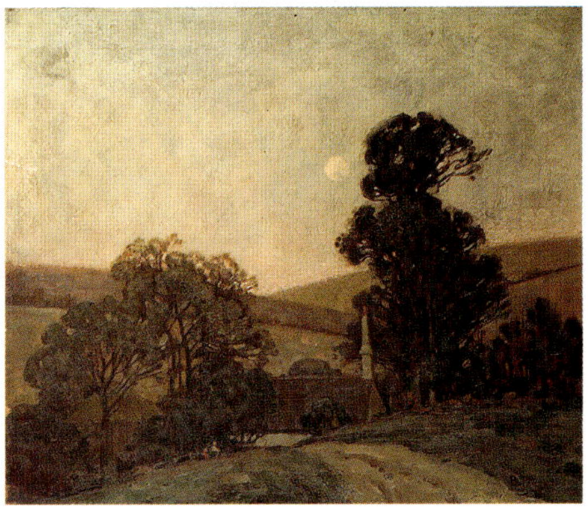

Haughton, Benjamin 1865–1924
A Cornish Homestead
oil on canvas 35 x 40
1937.FA.272

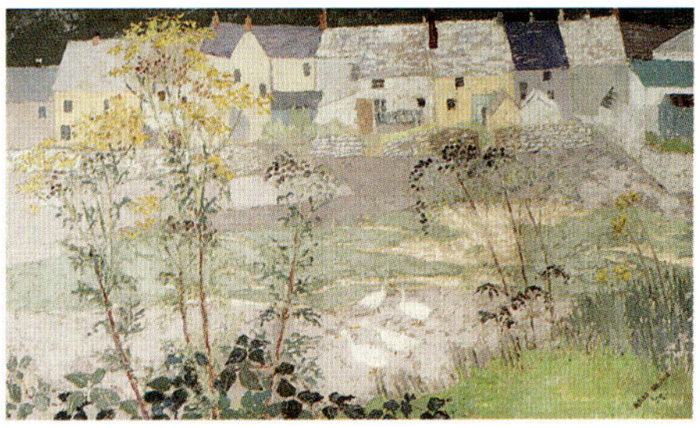

Heath, Nancy Lilian 1922–1995
Cottages, Old Fishguard 1959
oil on board 46 x 67
1959.FA.63

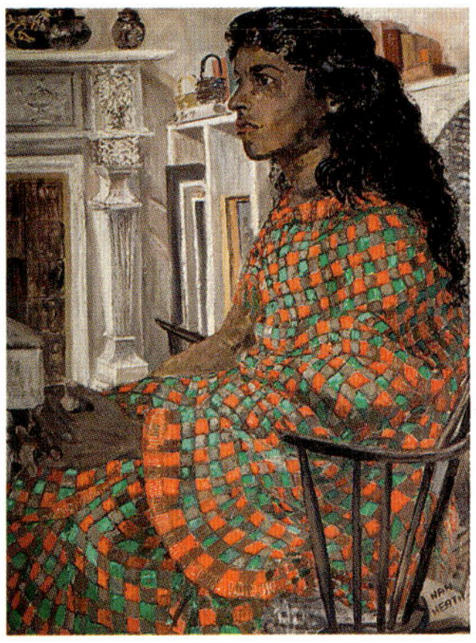

Heath, Nancy Lilian 1922–1995
Sheila
oil on canvas 90 x 67
1968.FA.1A

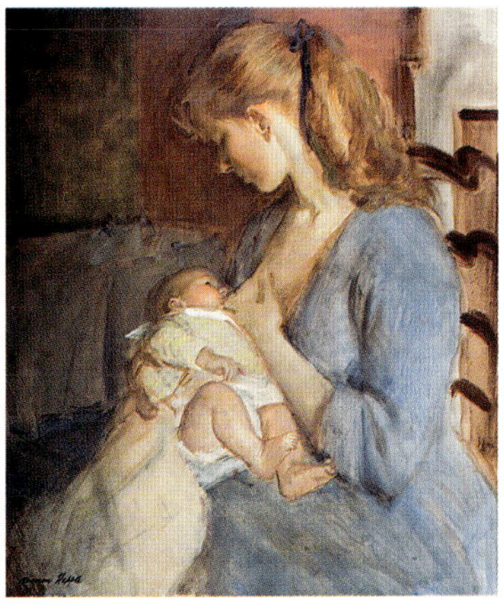

Hepple, Norman 1908–1994
Mother and Child
oil on canvas 60 x 50
1950.FA.44

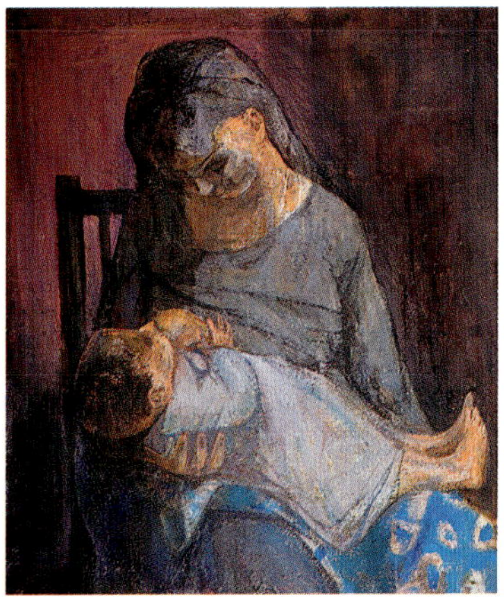

Herald, Albert b.1925
Mother and Child
oil on canvas 75 x 63
1960.FA.1

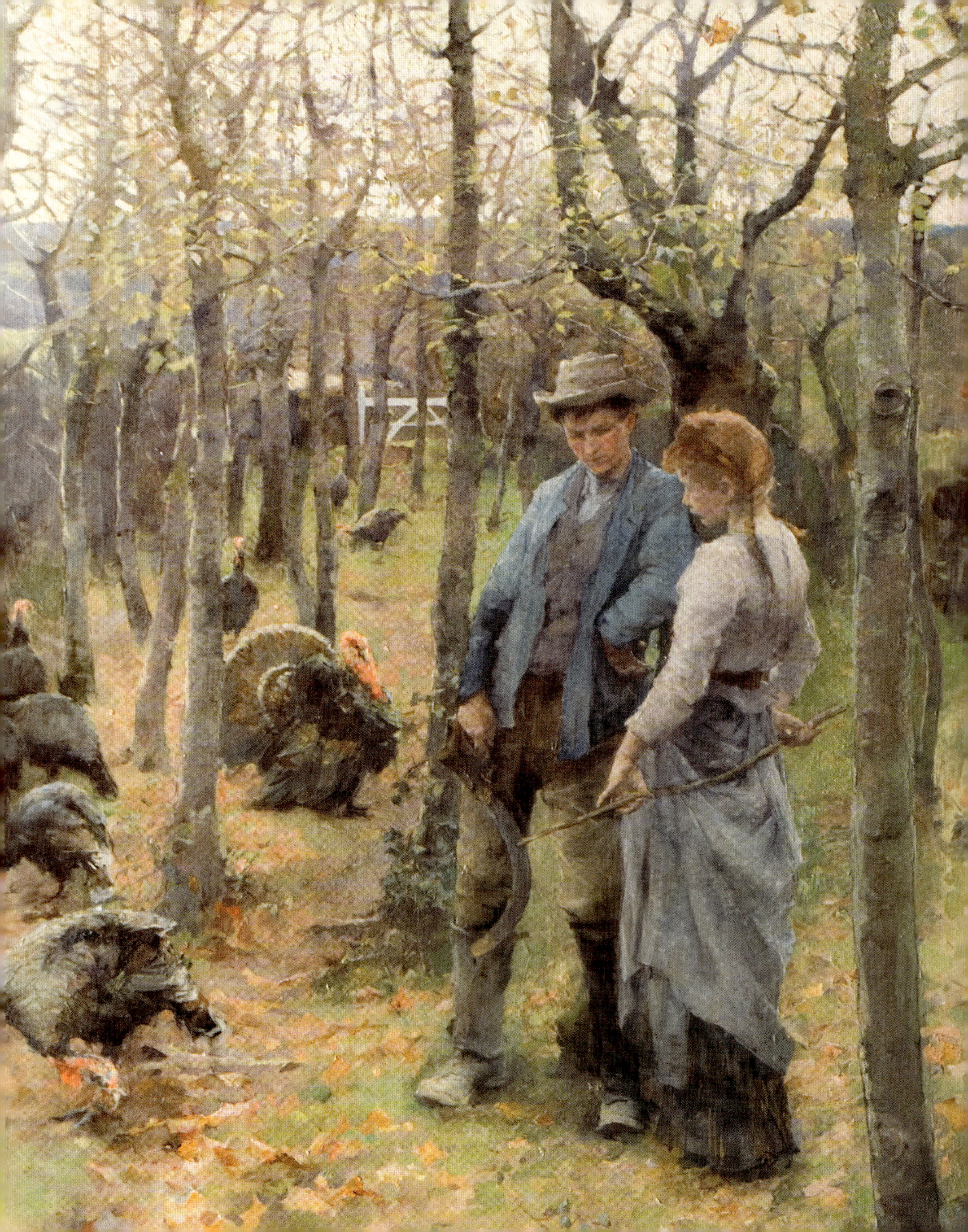

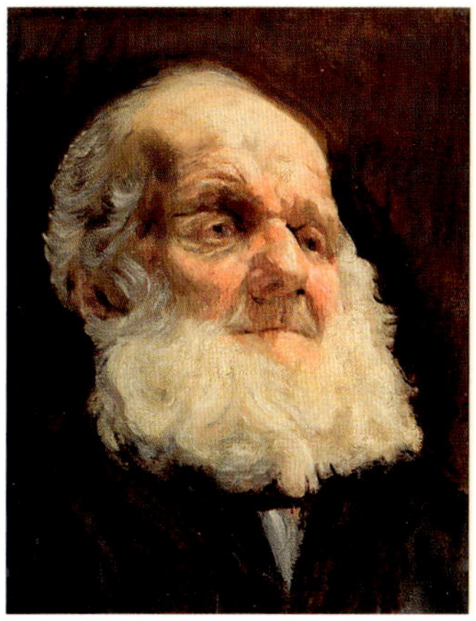

Herkomer, Hubert von 1849–1914
Head of an Old Man
oil on canvas 38.5 x 29.5
1958.FA.53

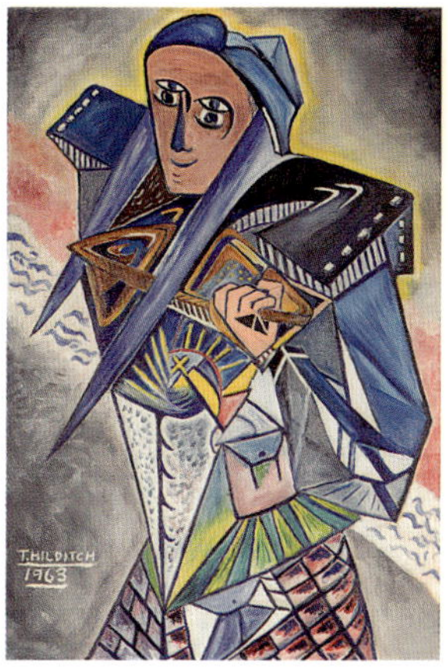

Hilditch, Tom 1933–1985
Walking Man 1963
oil on canvas 75 x 50
1988.FA.8

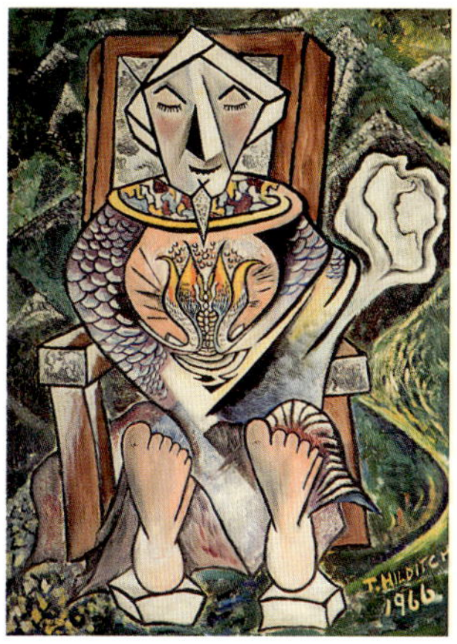

Hilditch, Tom 1933–1985
Seated Man 1966
oil on canvas 73.5 x 52
1988.FA.9

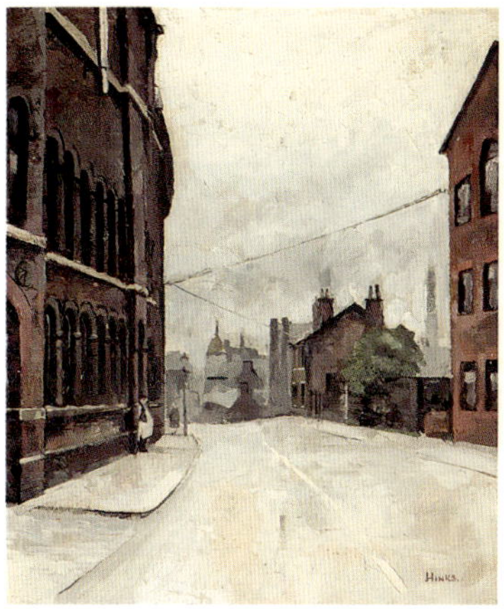

Hinks, Thomas
Sutherland Road, Longton
oil on canvas 58 x 47.5
1962.FA.77

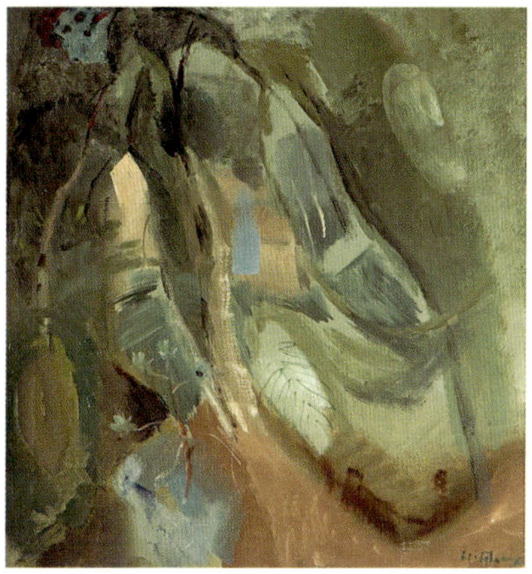

Hitchens, Ivon 1893–1979
House with Blue Door, among Trees 1942
oil on canvas 59 x 54
1988.FA.10

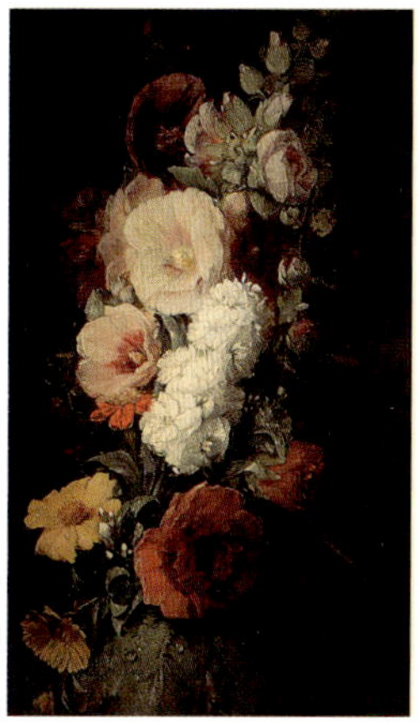

Holland, James 1800–1870
Flowers from Nature c.1828
oil on panel 47.5 x 27.5
1950.FA.49

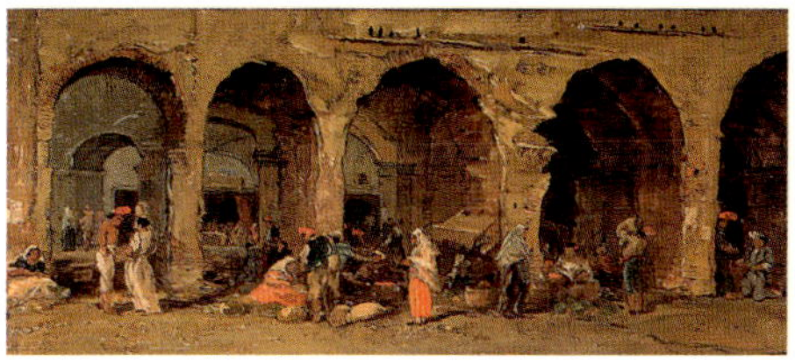

Holland, James 1800–1870
The Fish Market 1835
oil on panel 16 x 35
1954.FA.108

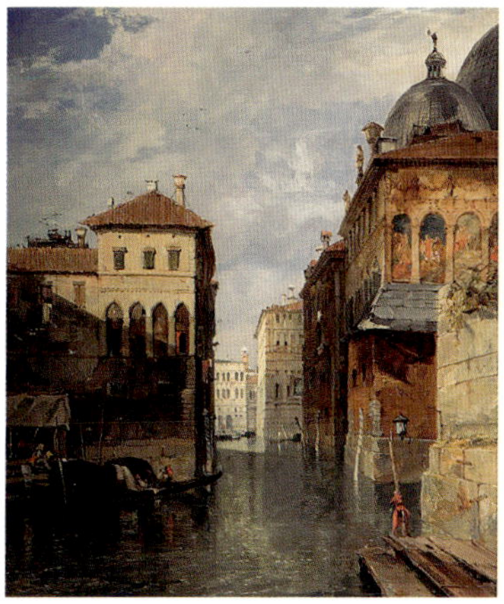

Holland, James 1800–1870
Venice 1839
oil on canvas 59 x 49.5
1939.FA.339

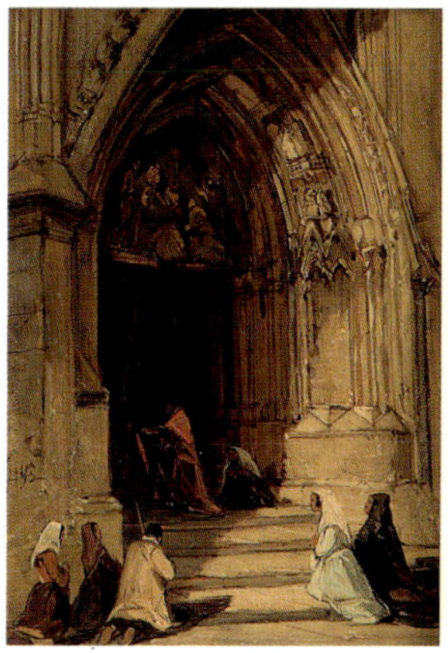

Holland, James 1800–1870
North Door, Notre Dame, Paris 1845
oil on panel 25 x 17
1955.FA.3

Facing page: Forbes, Elizabeth Adela Stanhope, 1859–1912, *The Edge of the Woods* (detail), 1894, Wolverhampton Art Gallery, (p. 272)

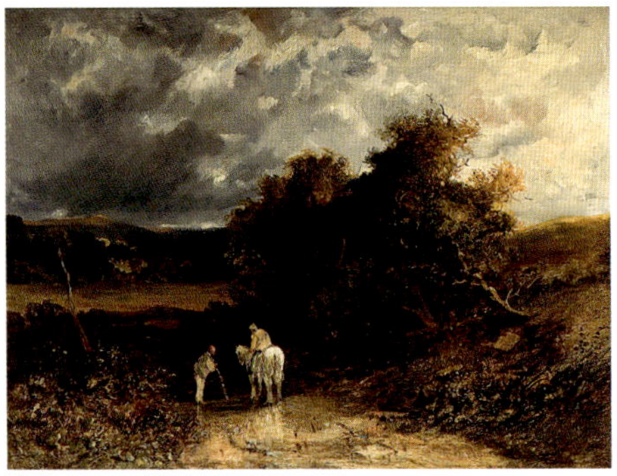

Holland, James 1800–1870
Countrymen with a White Horse 1847
oil on canvas 47 x 61
1965.FA.47

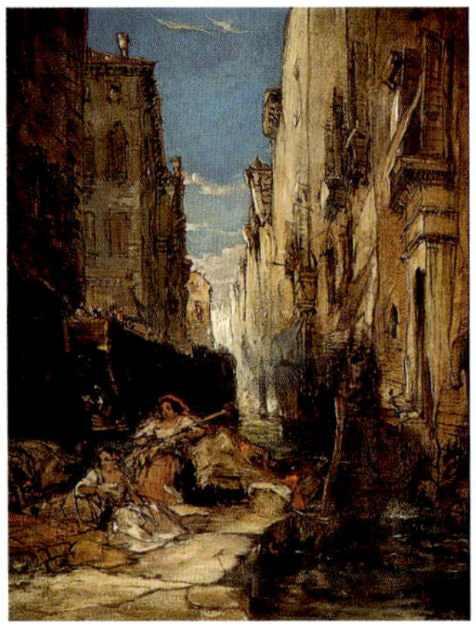

Holland, James 1800–1870
Venice c.1851
oil on panel 34.5 x 26
1951.FA.33

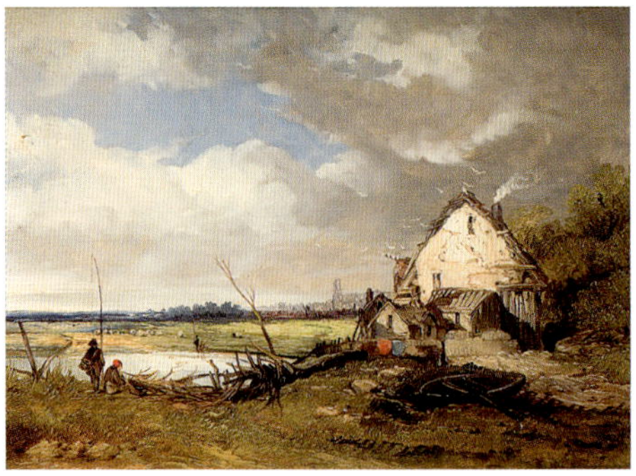

Holland, James 1800–1870
Anglers by a Cottage on a River Bank
oil on canvas 29 x 39
1946.FA.746

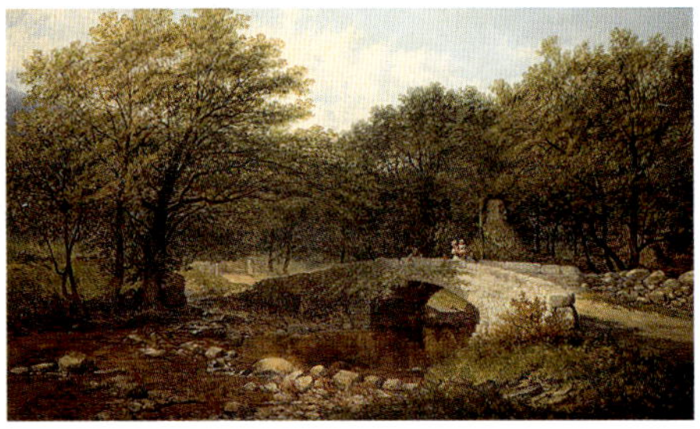

Holland, James 1800–1870
Bridge and Trees
oil on canvas 66 x 105
1950.FA.102

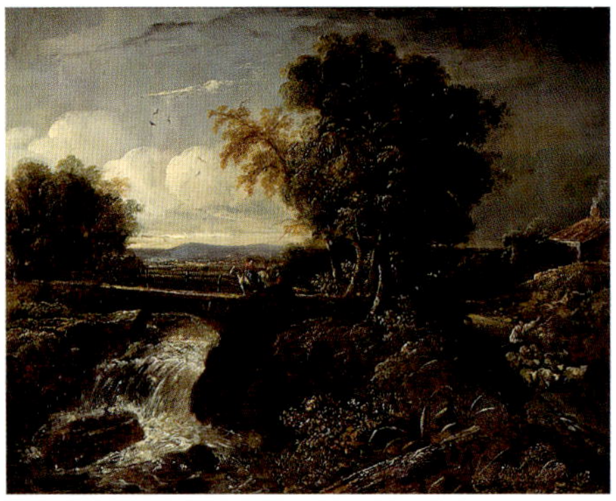

Holland, James 1800–1870
Bridge and Waterfall Scene
oil on panel 28 x 36
1950.FA.103

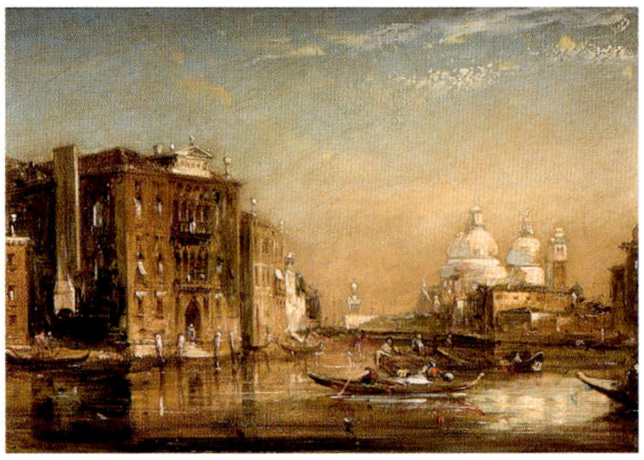

Holland, James 1800–1870
Canal Scene, Venice
oil on canvas 24.5 x 34.5
1963.FA.83

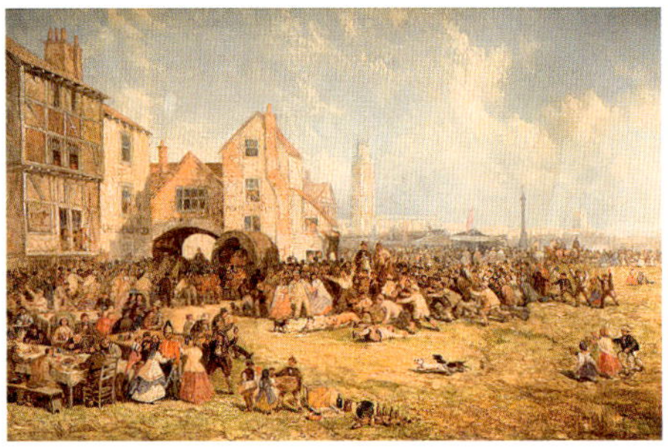

Holland, James 1800–1870
Catching the Pig at Boston Fair
oil on canvas 35 x 52.5
1949.FA.890

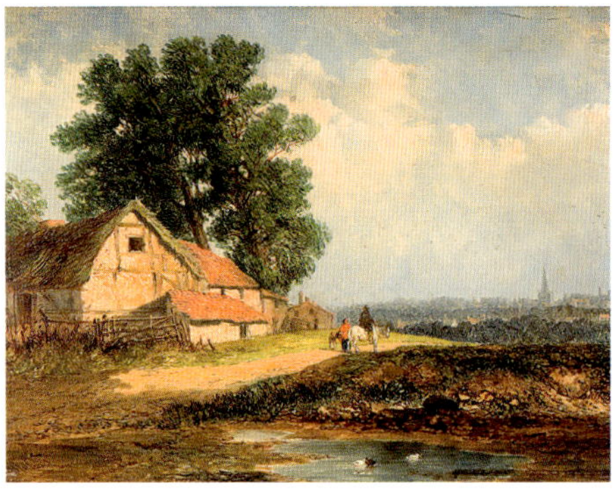

Holland, James 1800–1870
Distant View of Birmingham
oil on panel 28.5 x 36.5
1950.FA.99

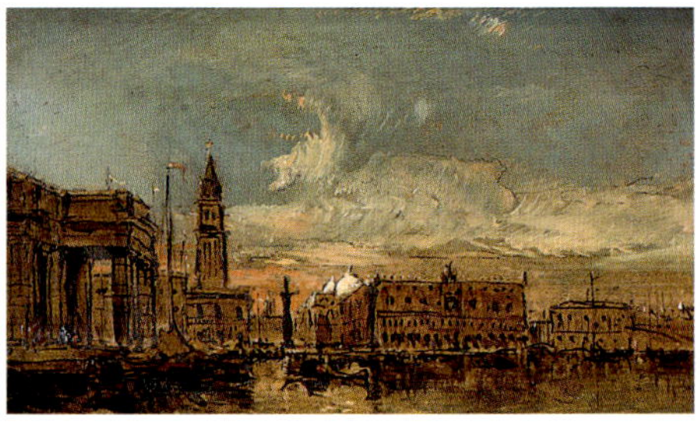

Holland, James 1800–1870
Grand Canal, Venice
oil on panel 17.5 x 28.5
1954.FA.107

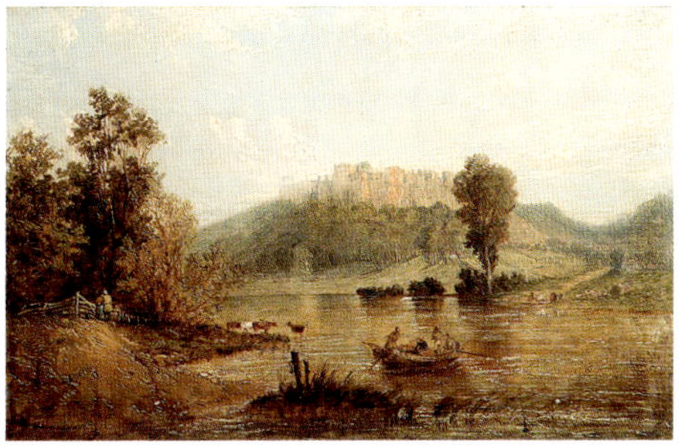

Holland, James 1800–1870
Lake and Castle Scene
oil on canvas 31 x 46
1948.FA.878.2

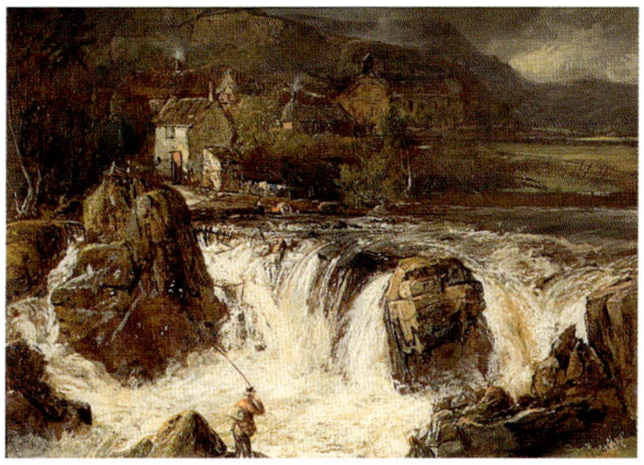

Holland, James 1800–1870
Llangollen
oil on panel 25 x 34
1946.FA.724

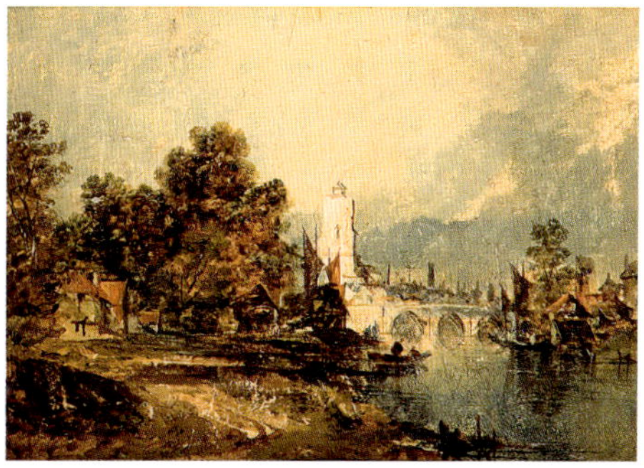

Holland, James 1800–1870
On the Rhône
oil on canvas 29 x 39.5
PCF23

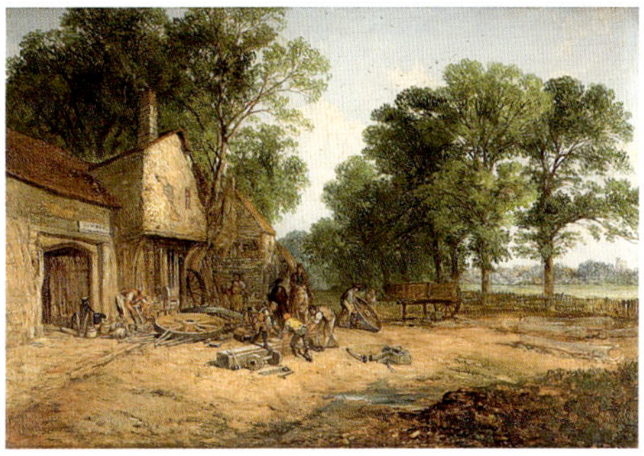

Holland, James 1800–1870
The Wheelwright's Shop
oil on canvas 48 x 68.5
1956.FA.35

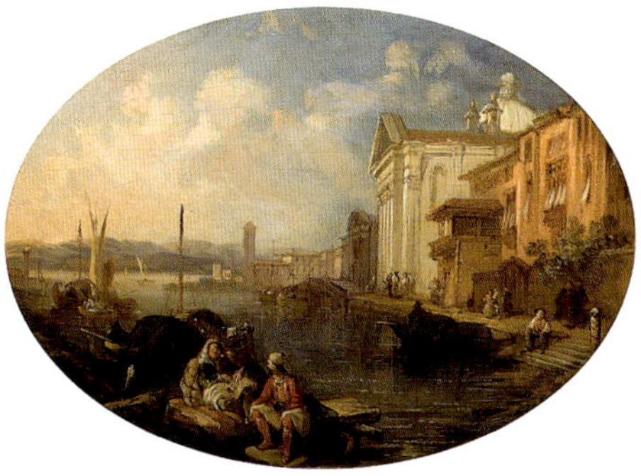

Holland, James 1800–1870
Venice
oil on panel 15 x 20
1950.FA.37

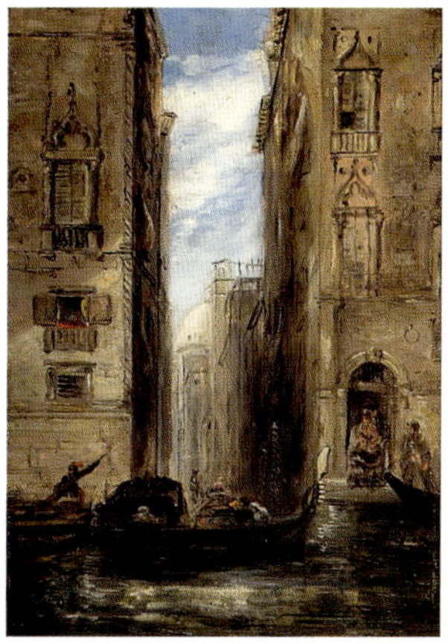

Holland, James 1800–1870
Venice, Narrow Canal
oil on panel 24 x 17
1950.FA.38

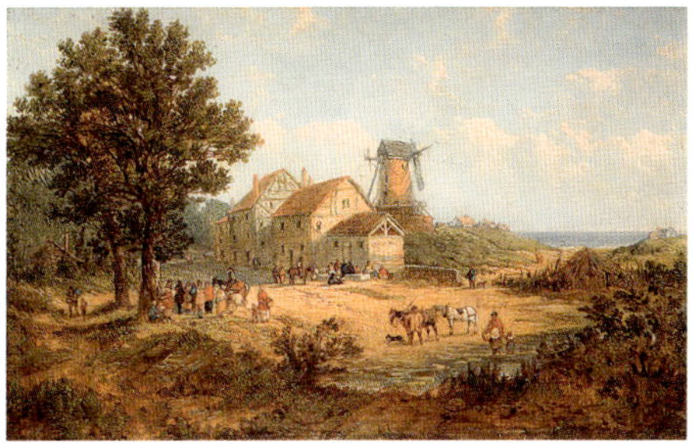

Holland, James 1800–1870
Windmill
oil on canvas 29.5 x 45
1948.FA.878.1

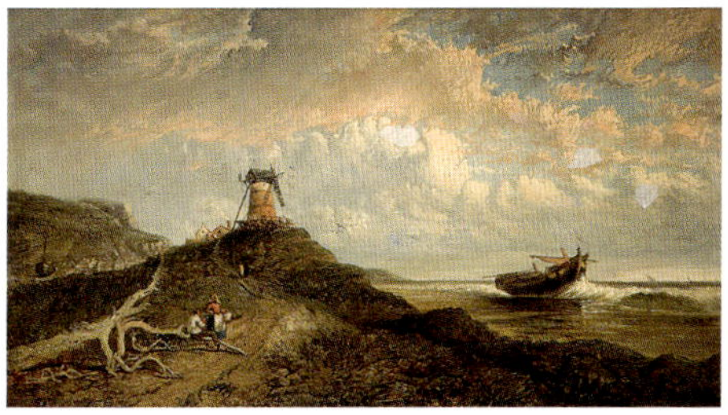

Holland, James 1800–1870
Windmill and the Sea
oil on canvas 44 x 75
1950.FA.101

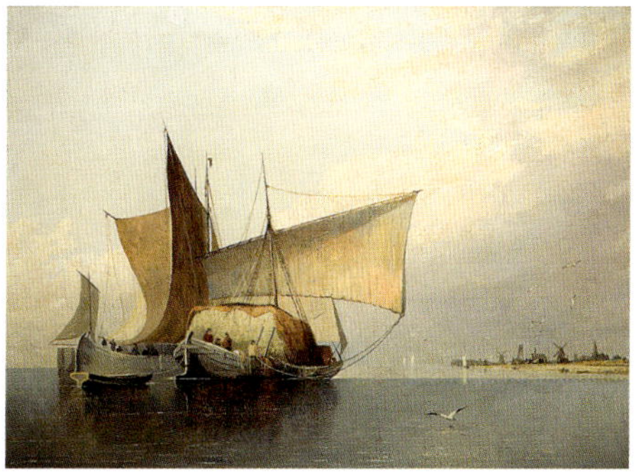

Holland, James 1800–1870
Yacht Scene
oil on canvas 80 x 105
1951.FA.32

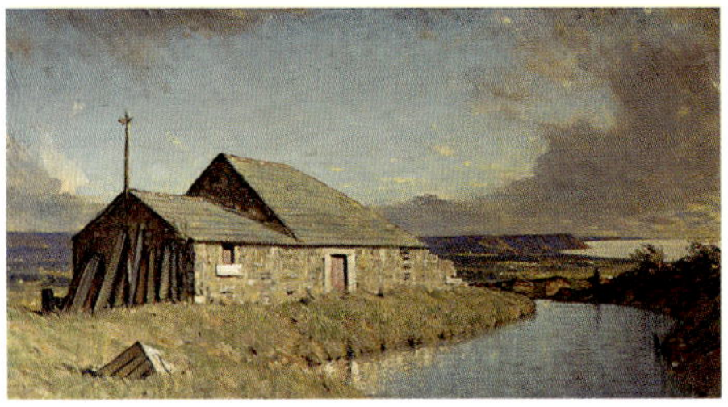

Holmes, Charles John 1868–1936
Bude Canal 1915
oil on canvas 43.5 x 79
1947.FA.770

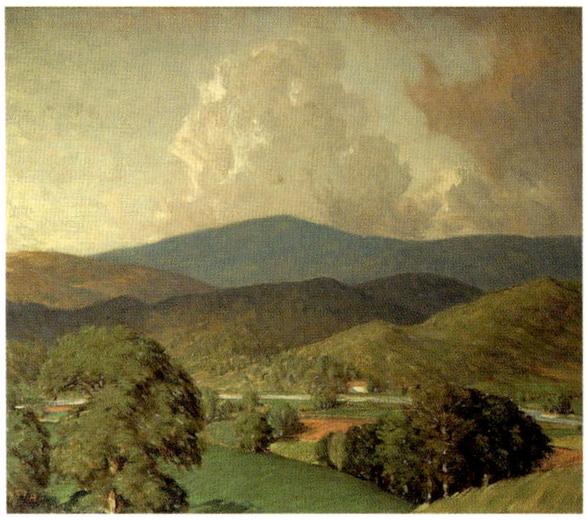

Holmes, Charles John 1868–1936
The Eden, near Lazonby 1926
oil on canvas 66 x 74
1928.FA.31

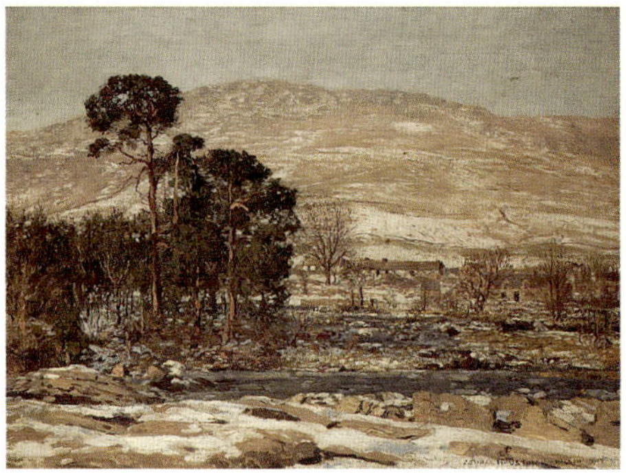

Houston, George 1869–1947
Killin 1917
oil on canvas 67 x 89
1926.FA.7

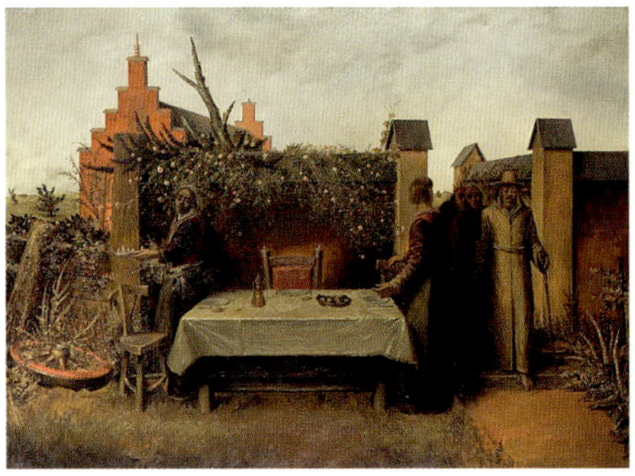

Houthuesen, Albert Anthony 1903–1979
The Supper at Emmaus 1927
oil on canvas 89 x 120
1962.FA.26

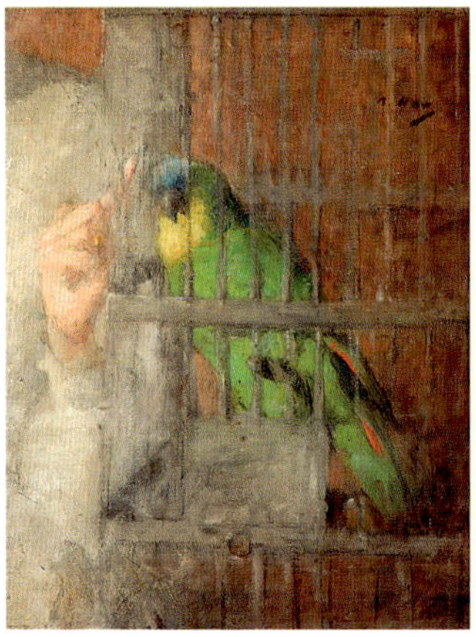

How, Julia Beatrice 1867–1932
Etude, le perroquet
oil on canvas 44 x 34
1936.FA.225

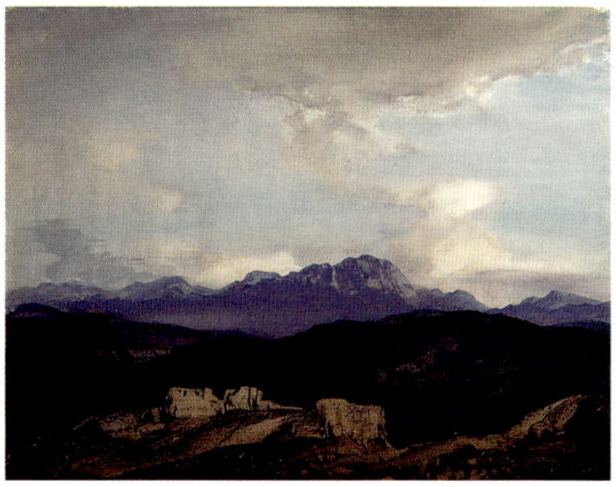

Hunt, Cecil Arthur 1873–1965
Atlas Mountains, near Constantine
tempera on paper 46 x 58
1933.FA.28

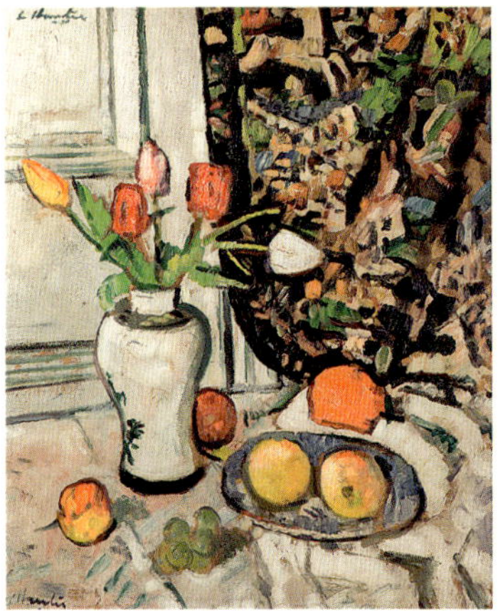

Hunter, George Leslie 1877–1931
Still Life
oil on panel 66 x 54
1946.FA.730

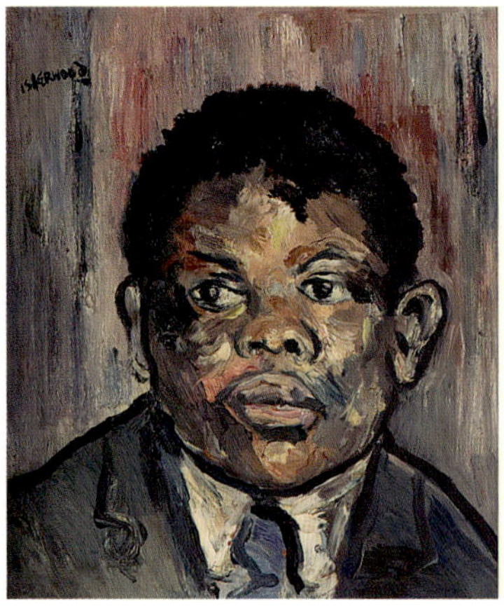

Isherwood, James Lawrence 1917–1988
Head of a Nigerian
oil on panel 34 x 29
1958.FA.37

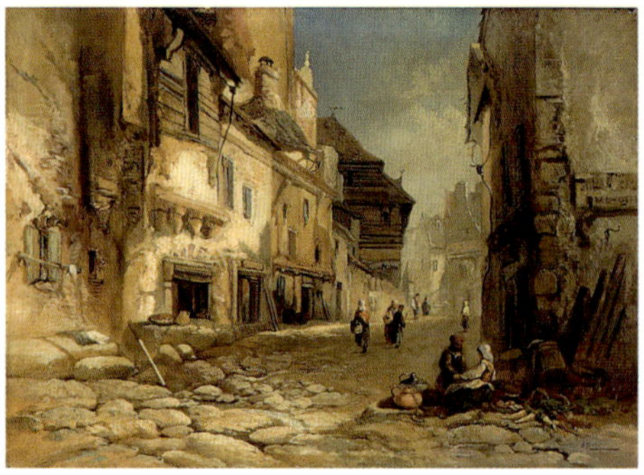

Jackson, G.
View of a Cobbled Street with Peasants 1854
oil on canvas 40 x 54
1957.FA.52

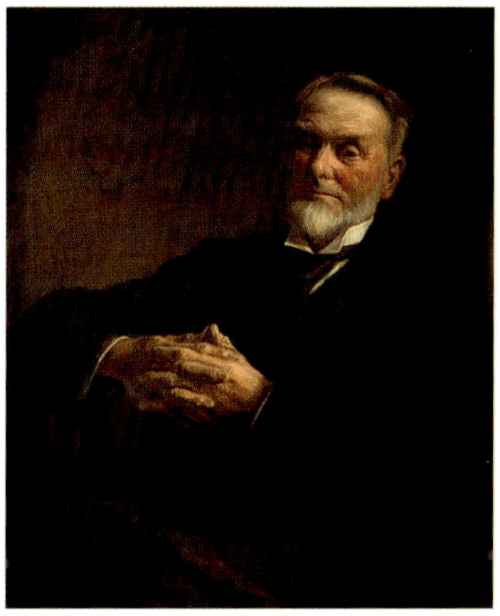

Jackson, Gerald Goddard b.1878
William Douglas-Phillips 1912
oil on canvas 84 x 67.5
PCF24

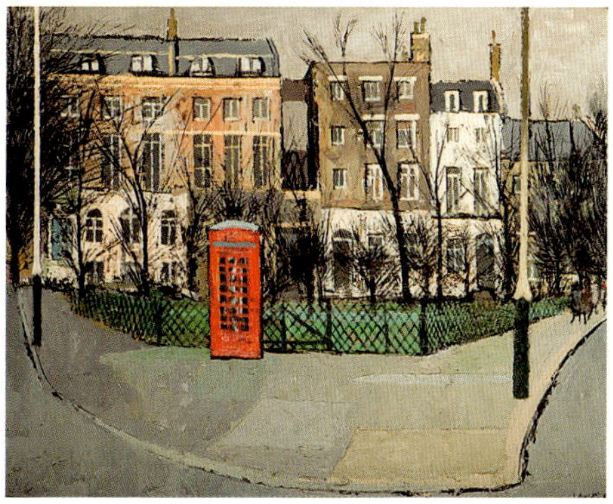

Johnson, Charles G. 1902–1983
The Green, Kennington Road 1961
oil on board 62 x 74
1961.FA.127

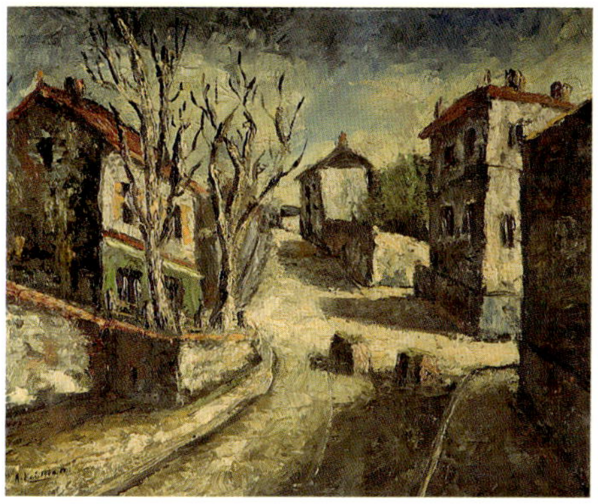

Kelman, A.
Street Scene
oil on canvas 44 x 52
1957.FA.53

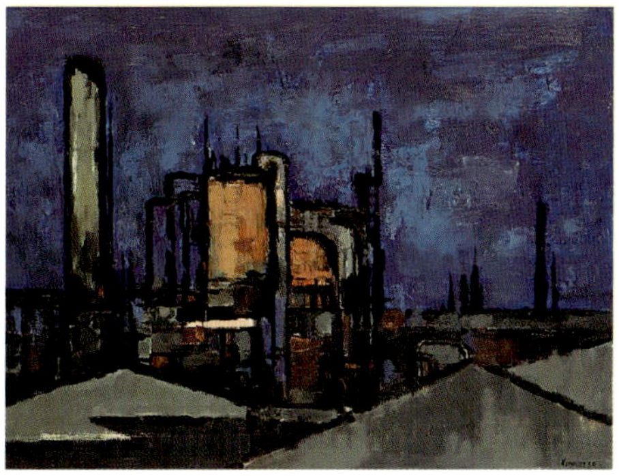

Kennerley, George b.1912
Industrial Landscape 1959
oil on canvas 69 x 89
1959.FA.44

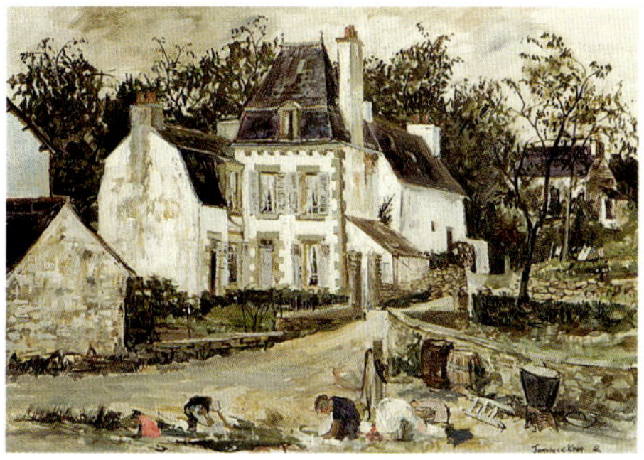

King, Jeremy b.1933
La Forêt, Fouesnant 1966
oil on canvas 57 x 79
1967.FA.36

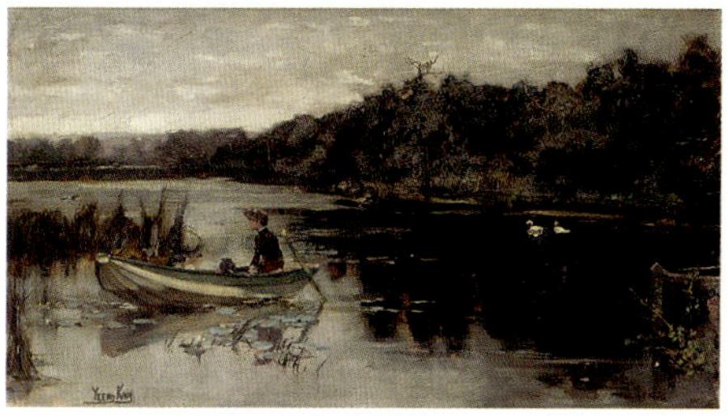

King, Yeend 1855–1924
On the Upper Thames
oil on panel 23 x 39
1954.FA.122

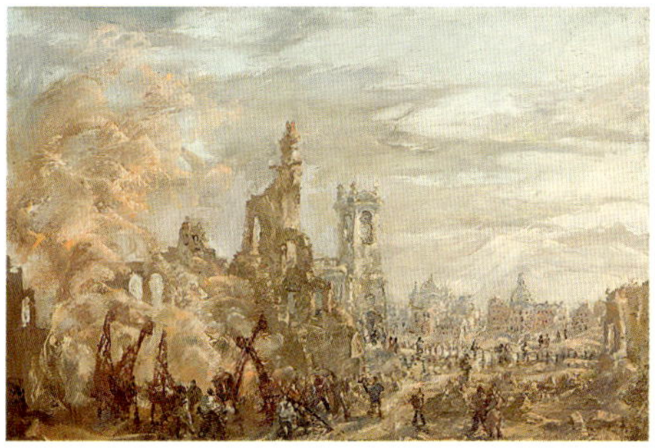

Kirk, Eve 1900–1969
The Red Chimney: A Bombed Part of London
oil on board 36 x 54
1956.FA.9

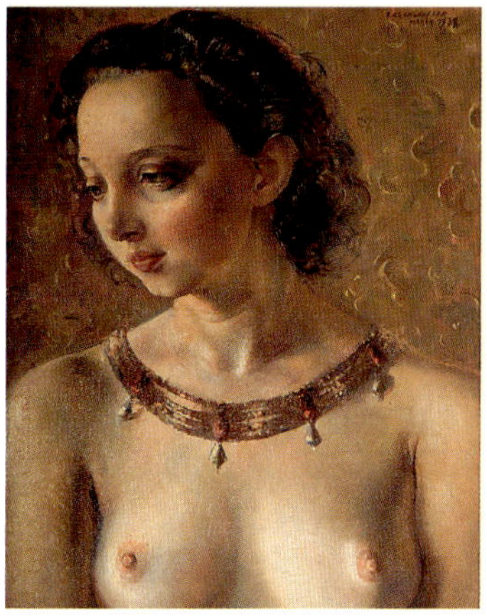

Klinghoffer, Clara 1900–1970
The Oriental Necklace 1938
oil on panel 39 x 31
1938.FA.327.1

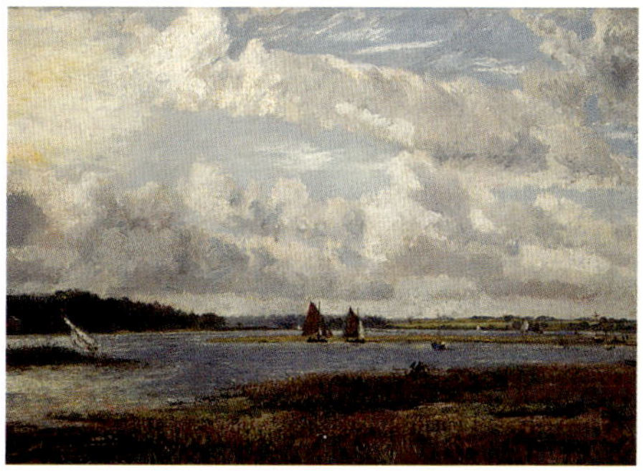

Knight, John William Buxton
1842/1843–1908
Near Harwich 1896
oil on canvas 58 x 69
1955.FA.6

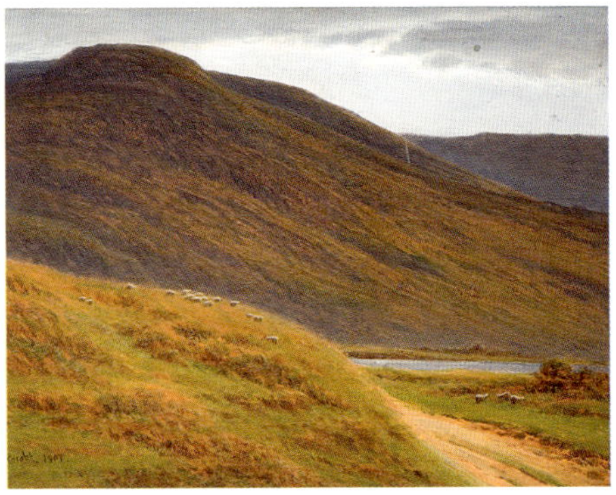

Knight, John William Buxton
1842/1843–1908
Moorland Landscape 1907
oil on board 48 x 60
1947.FA.830m

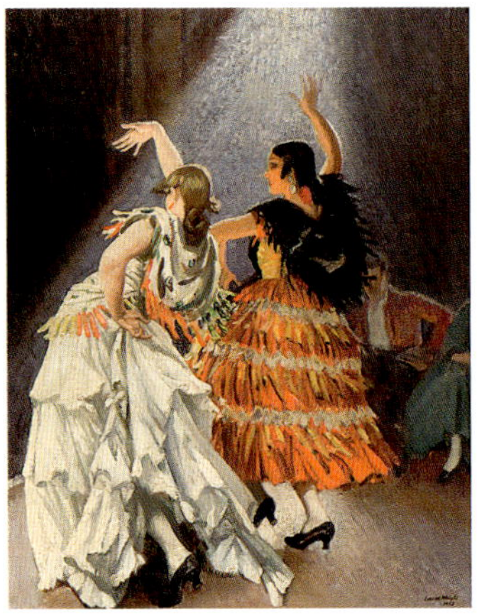

Knight, Laura 1877–1970
The Rehearsal 1923
oil on canvas 89.5 x 69.5
1967.FA.34

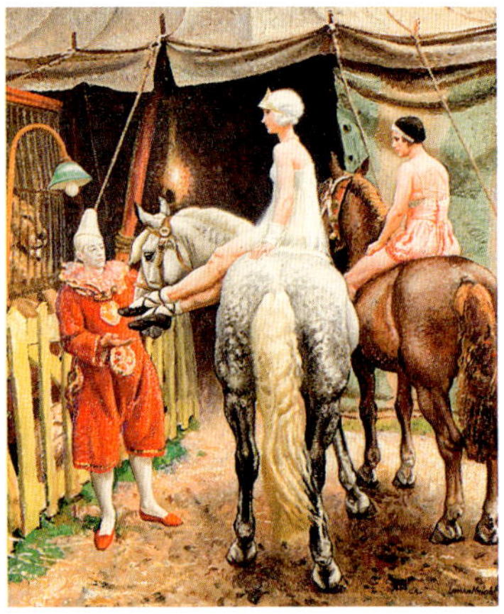

Knight, Laura 1877–1970
The Rosinbacks
oil on canvas 78 x 63.5
1932.FA.3

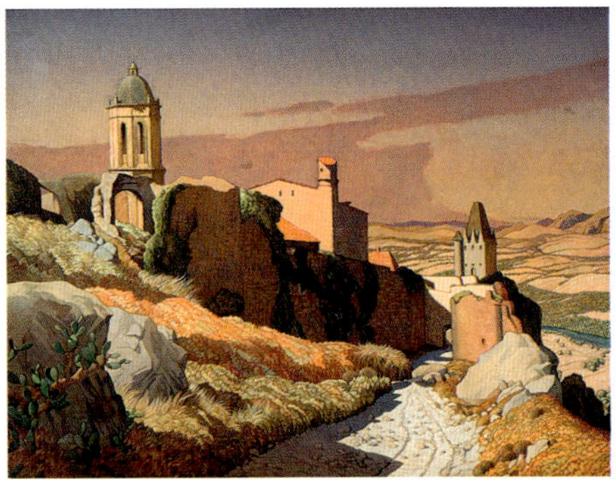

Kortright, Reginald Guy b.1877
The Priest's Walk
oil on canvas 68 x 90
1933.FA.30

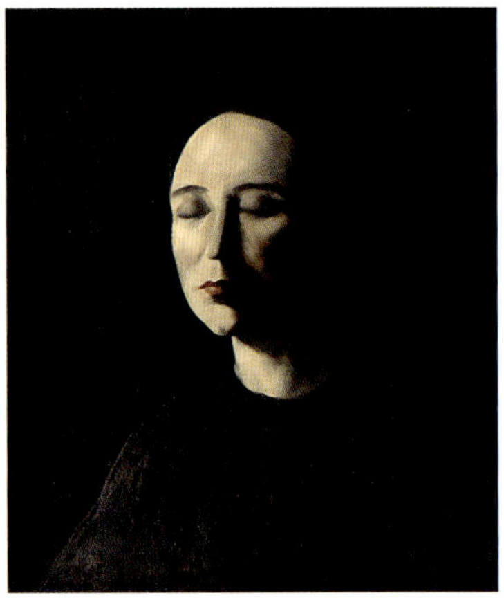

Kramer, Jacob 1892–1962
Dolores
oil on canvas 75 x 62
1935.FA.89

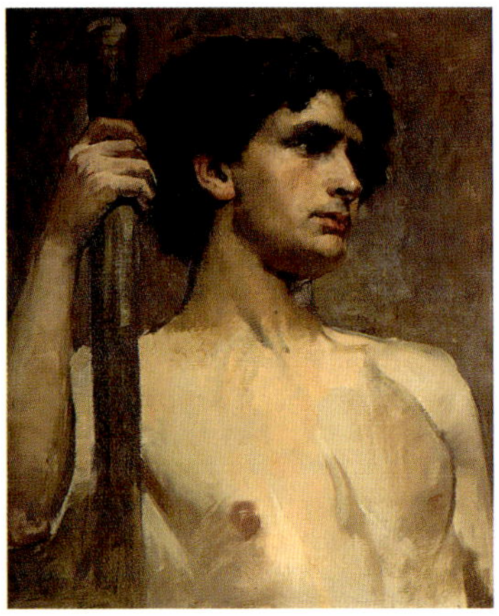

La Thangue, Henry Herbert 1859–1929
Nude Study
oil on canvas 53 x 43
1944.FA.631

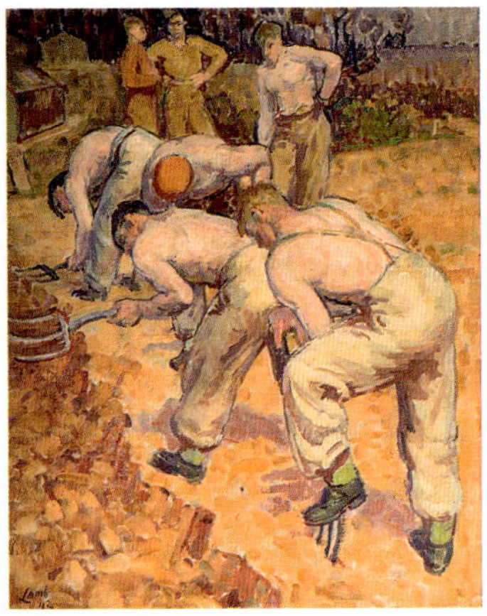

Lamb, Henry 1883–1960
Fatigue, Canadian Forces 1942
oil on canvas 49.5 x 39
1947.FA.780

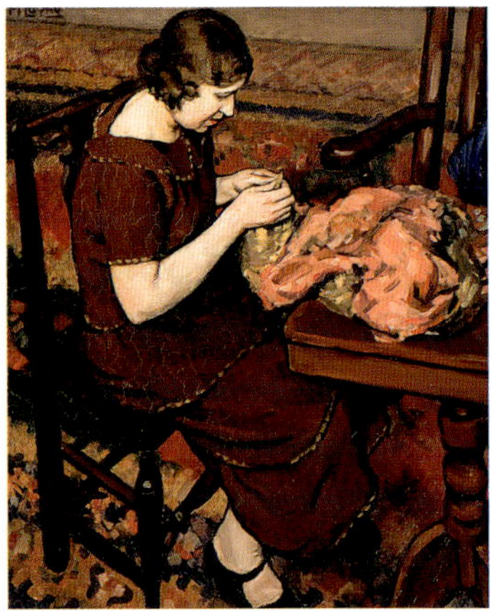

Layng, Mabel Frances 1881–1937
The Sewing Girl
oil on canvas 75 x 62
1938.FA.305

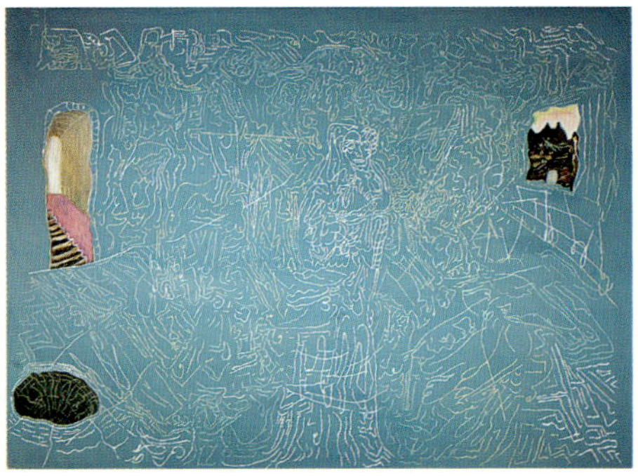

Leapman, David b.1959
Treeman 1987
acrylic on canvas 165 x 186
1992.FA.7

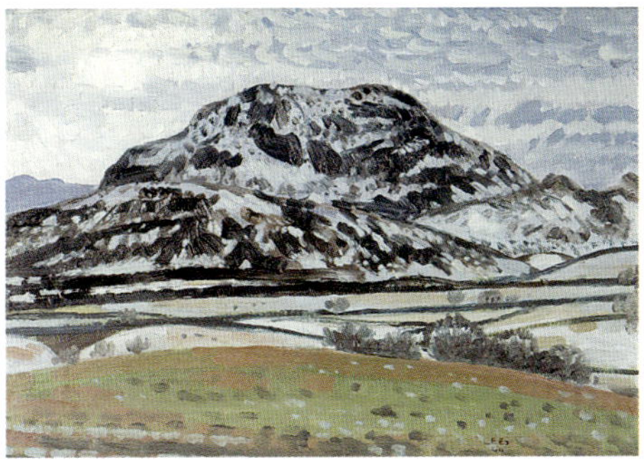

Lees, Derwent 1885–1931
Arenig Fawr 1911
oil on panel 24.5 x 35
1924.FA.29

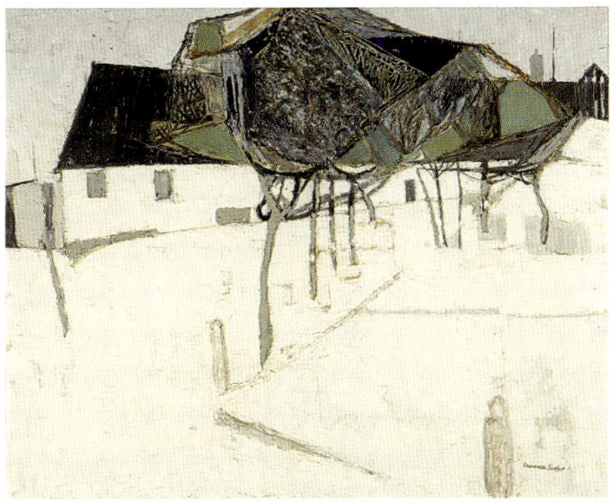

Leeson, Laurence b.1930
The Orchard No.2 1959
mixed media on panel 49 x 60
1974.FA.2

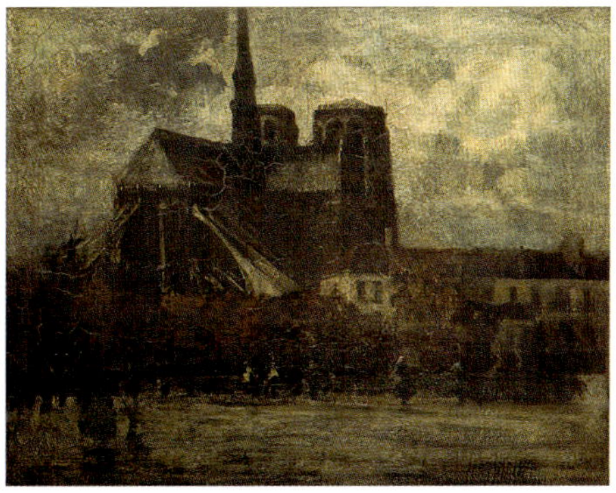

Lessore, Jules 1849–1892
Notre Dame de Paris
oil on canvas 31 x 40
1947.FA.763

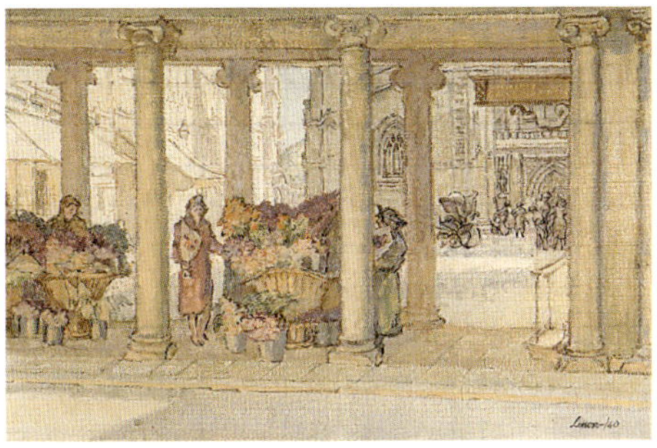

Lessore, Thérèse 1884–1945
The Pump Room, Bath 1940
oil on canvas 53.5 x 80
1945.FA.672

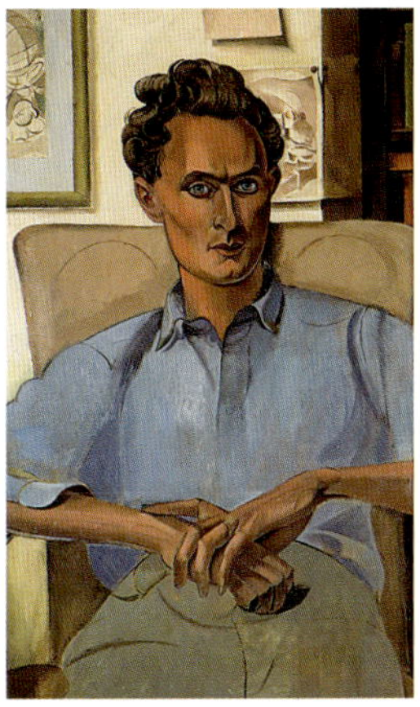

Lewis, Wyndham 1882–1957
Stephen Spender (1909–1995) 1938
oil on canvas 99 x 58
1939.FA.347

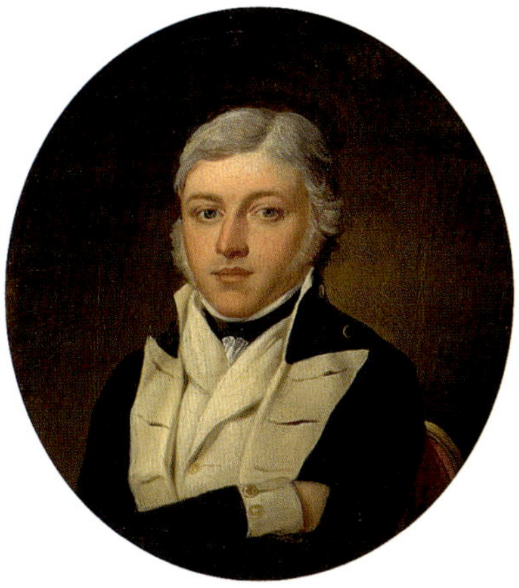

Livesay, Richard 1750–c.1826
Rear Admiral Clement Sneyd (1773–1854)
oil on canvas 24 x 22
1952.FA.16

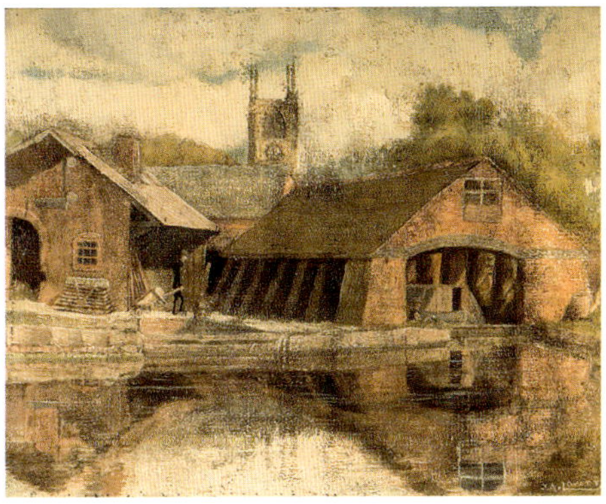

Lovatt, James Alfred 1873–1952
The Barge Builder's Yard, Stone
oil on canvas 24 x 30
1945.FA.686

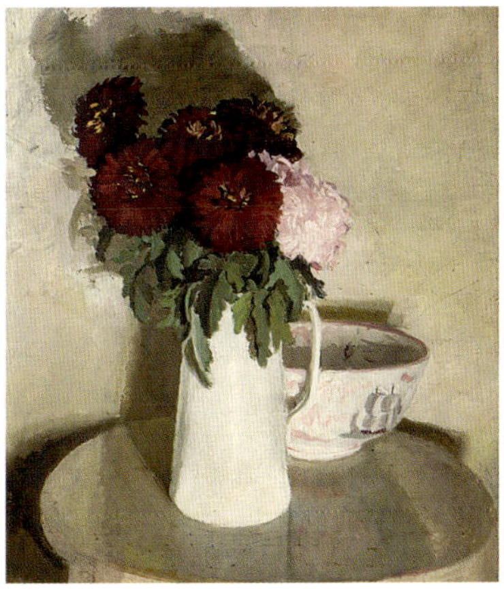

Low, Diana 1911–1975
Sunderland Bowl with Flowers
oil on canvas 63 x 34
1950.FA.117

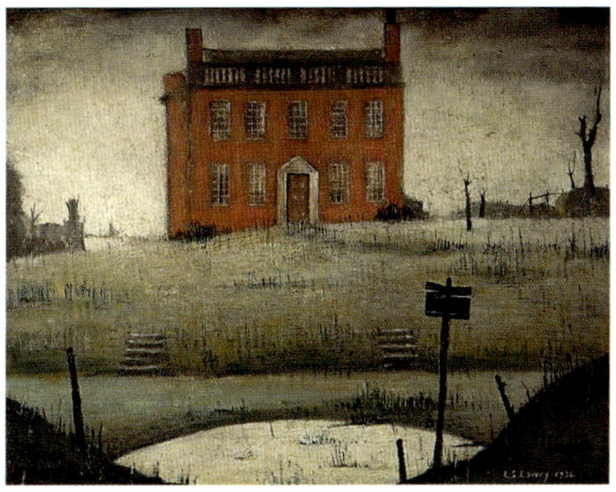

Lowry, Laurence Stephen 1887–1976
The Empty House 1934
oil on wood 41.5 x 52
1942.FA.566

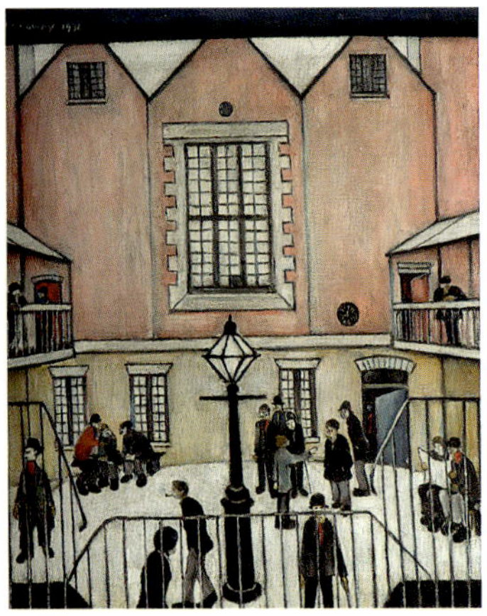

Lowry, Laurence Stephen 1887–1976
The Courtyard 1936
oil on canvas 51 x 40.5
1989.FA.27

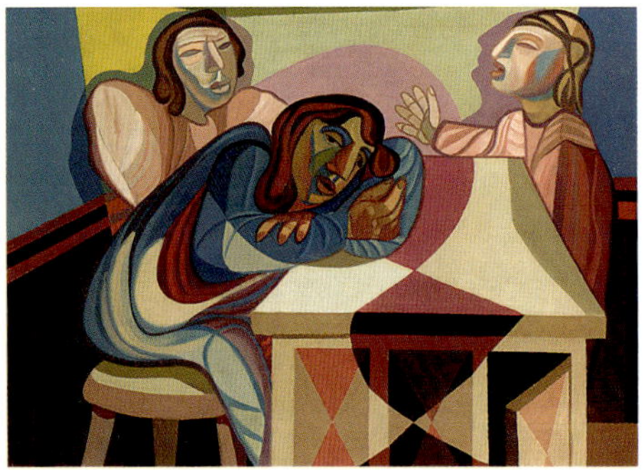

Macbryde, Robert 1913–1966
The Supper at Emmaus 1958
oil on canvas 73.5 x 99
1980.FA.33

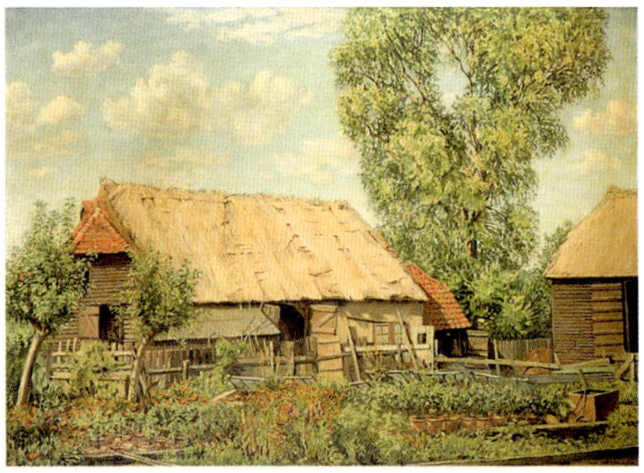

Maclaren, Helen b.1898
Old Barn in Hertfordshire 1934
oil on canvas 74 x 100
1937.FA.294

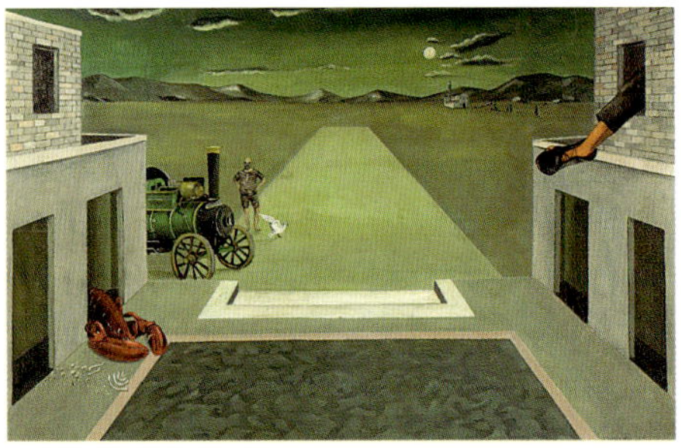

Maddox, Conroy 1912–2005
The Late Sleeper 1973
oil on canvas 55.5 x 86
1996.FA.249

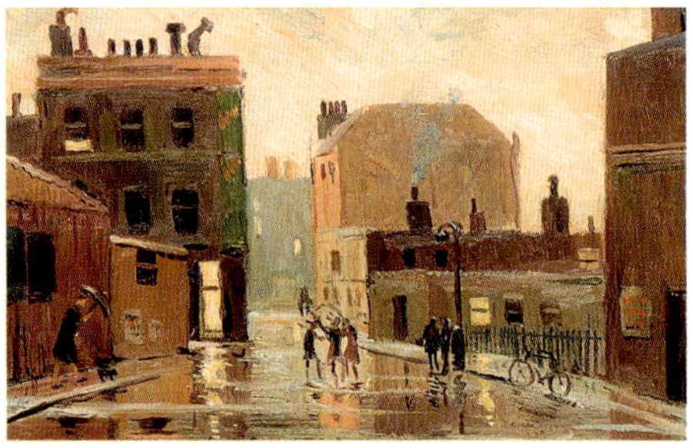

Makinson, Trevor b.1926
Camden Town Street 1948
oil on canvas 19 x 29
1948.FA.885

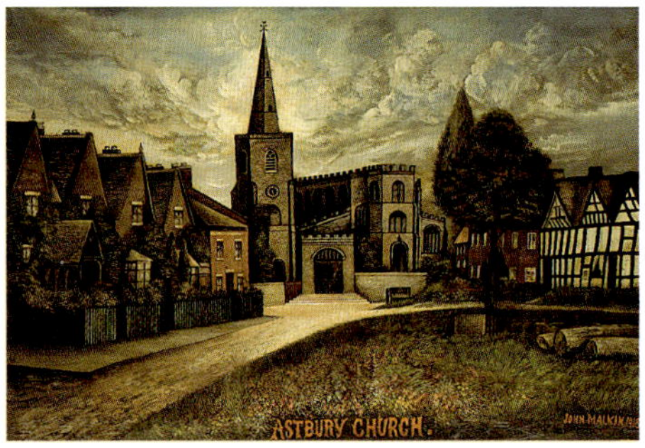

Malkin, John
Astbury Church 1918
oil on canvas 80 x 115
1960.FA.43

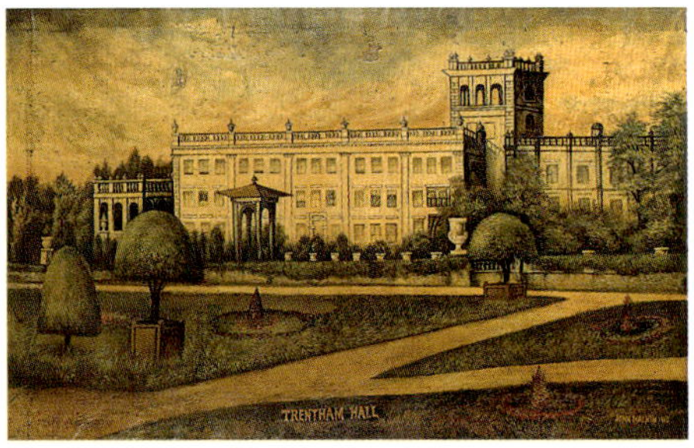

Malkin, John
Trentham Hall 1918
oil on canvas 72 x 112
1944.FA.6

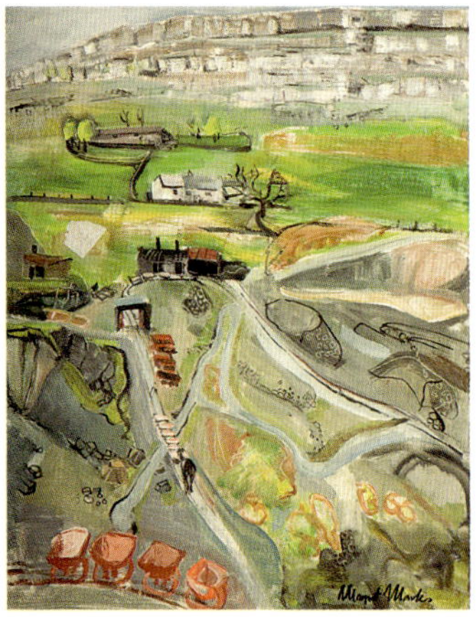

Marks, Margret 1899–1990
Quarry, Cauldon Low c.1955
oil on canvas 62.5 x 50
1997.FA.8

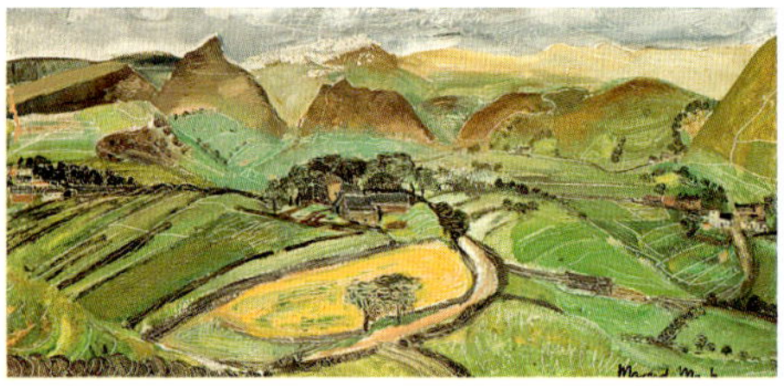

Marks, Margret 1899–1990
Yellow Field, Earlsterndale, Derbyshire c.1955
oil on canvas 28.5 x 59
1997.FA.7

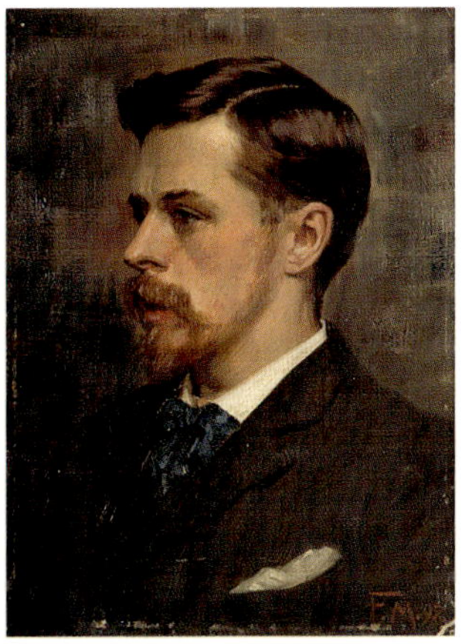

Marriott, Frederick 1860–1941
Frank Clayton Bennett 1898
oil on board 35.8 x 25.6
1967.FA.31

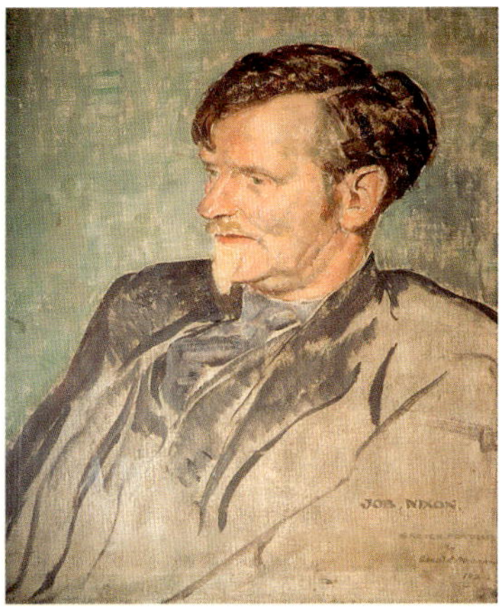

Mason, Arnold 1885–1963
Job Nixon (1891–1938) 1932
oil on canvas 59 x 49
1936.FA.224

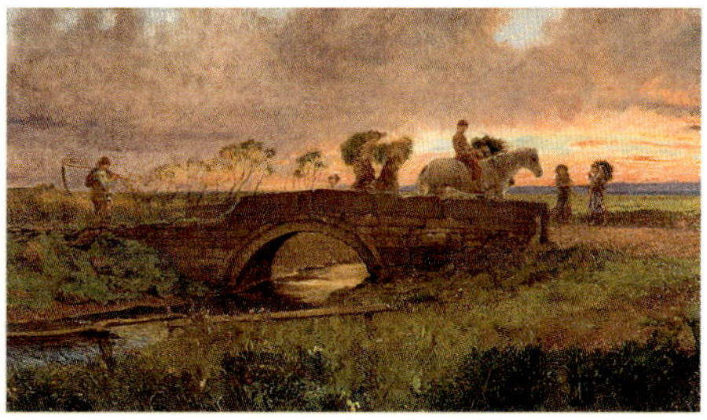

Mason, George Heming 1818–1872
Evening, near Southport c.1868
oil on canvas 32 x 55
1994.FA.2

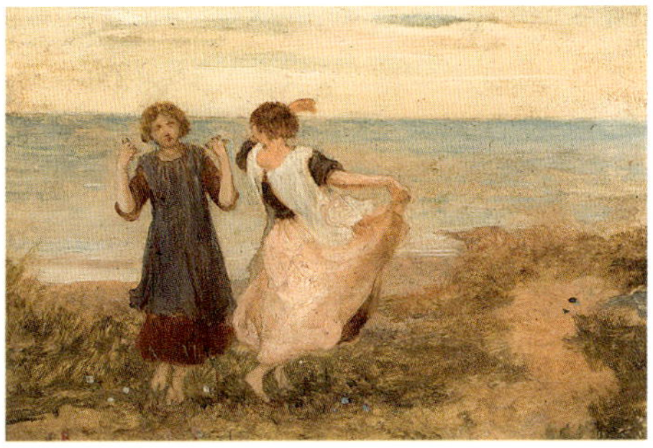

Mason, George Heming 1818–1872
Sketch for 'Girls Dancing, a Pastoral Symphony' 1869
oil on board 13 x 18
1935.FA.85

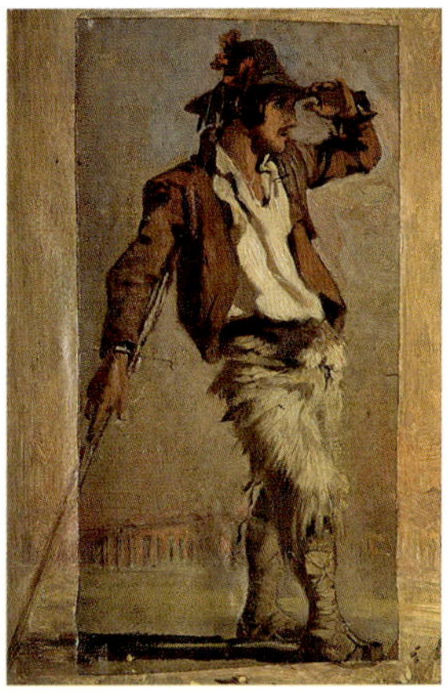

Mason, George Heming 1818–1872
Goatherd of the Campagna
oil on paper 25 x 16
1954.FA.100

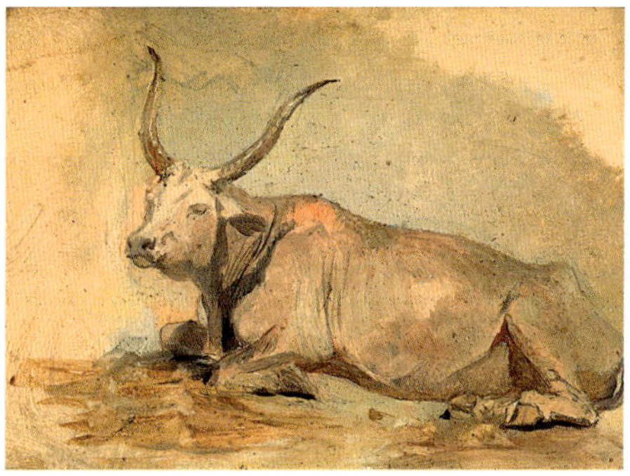

Mason, George Heming 1818–1872
Roman Ox (Lying down)
oil on paper 10 x 13.5
1992.FA.1

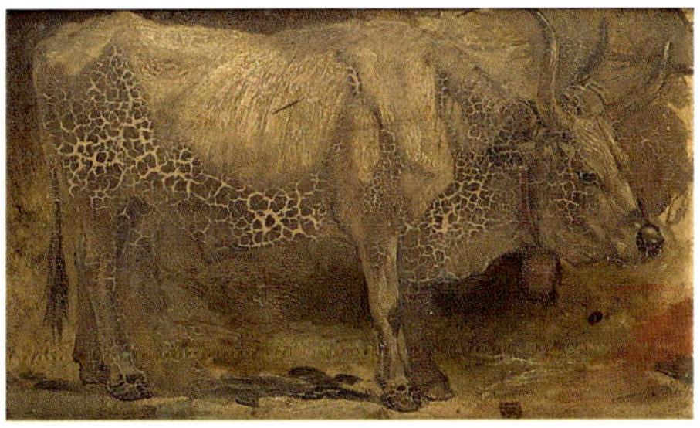

Mason, George Heming 1818–1872
Roman Ox (Standing)
oil on panel 11 x 18.5
1992.FA.2

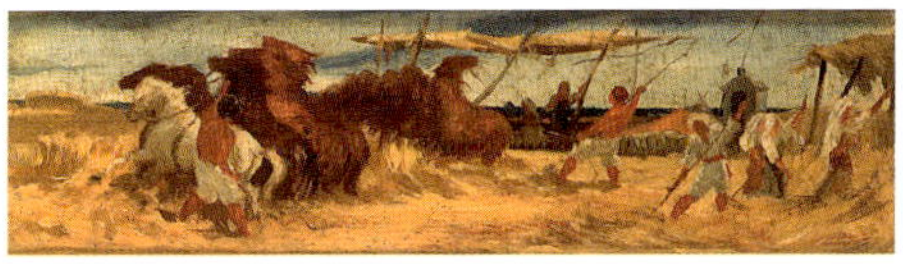

Mason, George Heming 1818–1872
Threshing Corn
oil on panel 7 x 24
1935.FA.86

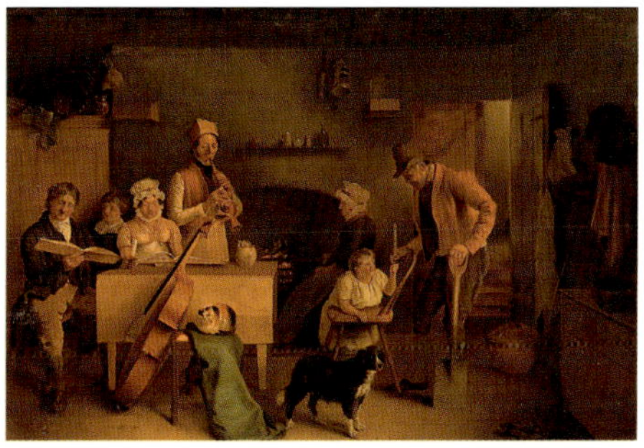

Mason, George Heming (attributed to)
1818–1872
Cottage Interior
oil on panel 46 x 66
1955.FA.13

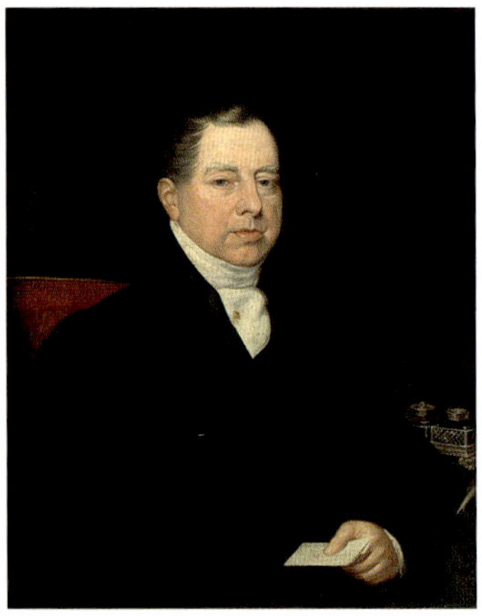

McCall, William b.c.1786
Josiah Spode II (1754–1827) before 1821
oil on canvas 90 x 69
1954.FA.184

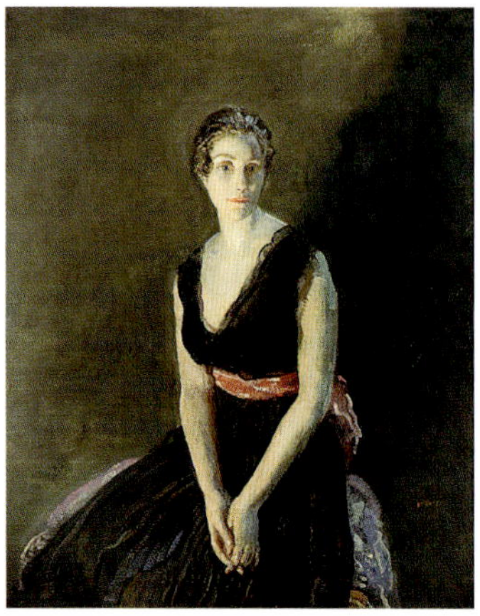

McEvoy, Ambrose 1878–1927
Mrs Lydia Russell
oil on canvas 114 x 100
1961.FA.126

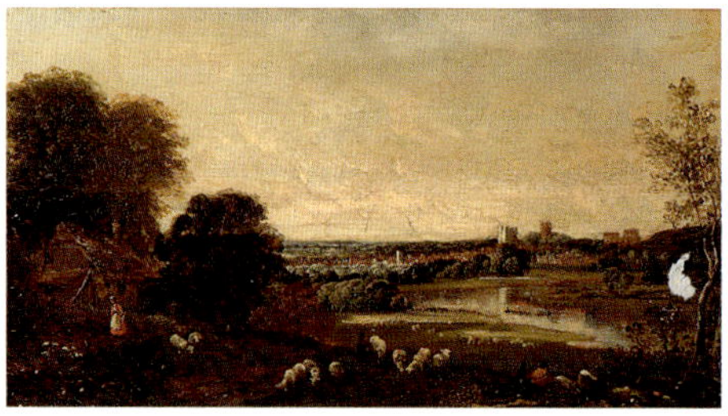

McGregor, Robert 1848–1922
Crab Fishers
oil on canvas 23 x 40
1954.FA.123

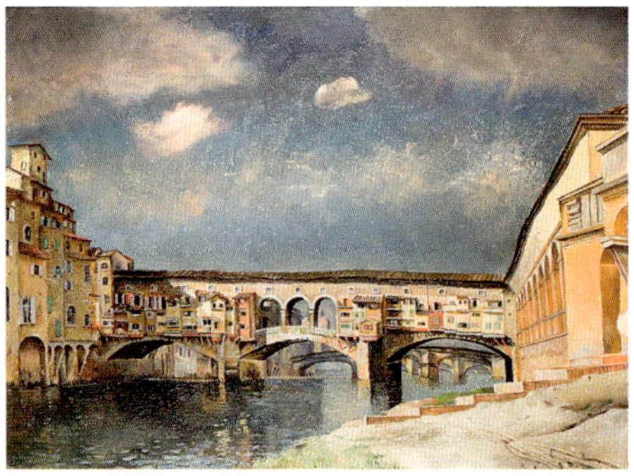

McKinnon, Sine 1901–1996
Ponte Vecchio, Florence
oil on panel 42 x 55
1935.FA.90

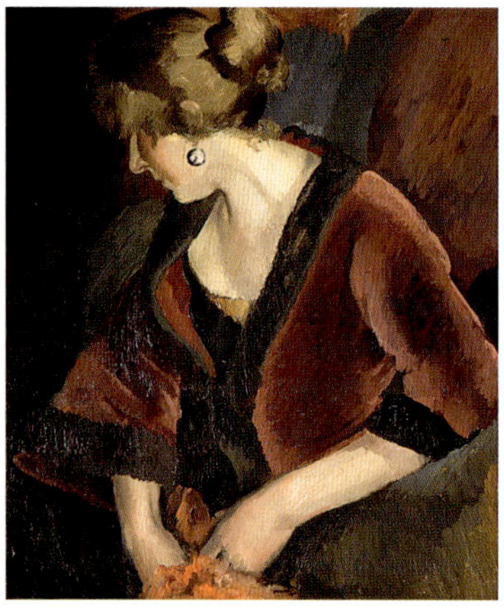

Meninsky, Bernard 1891–1950
Lady in Red 1922
oil on canvas 75 x 62
1952.FA.52

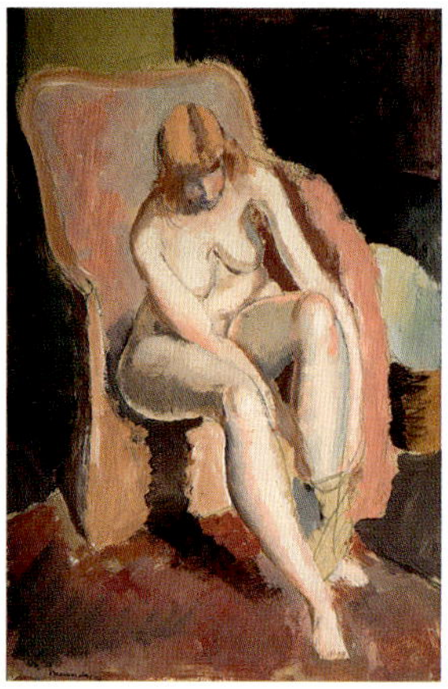

Meninsky, Bernard 1891–1950
Seated Nude 1924
oil on panel 40 x 29
1947.FA.768

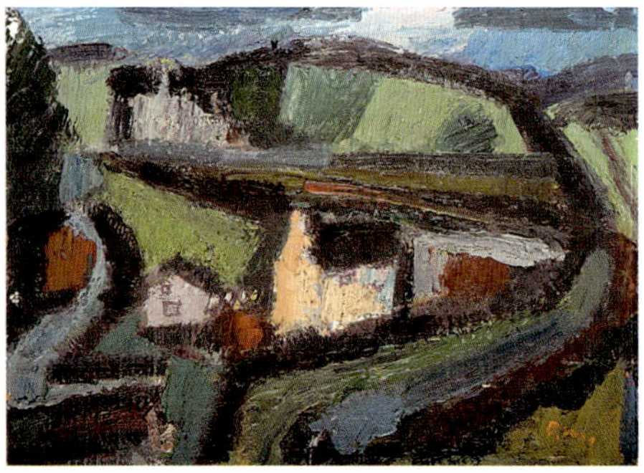

Milward, Frith 1906–1982
Hindlow, Derbyshire
oil on board 40.6 x 52.1
1969.FA.10A

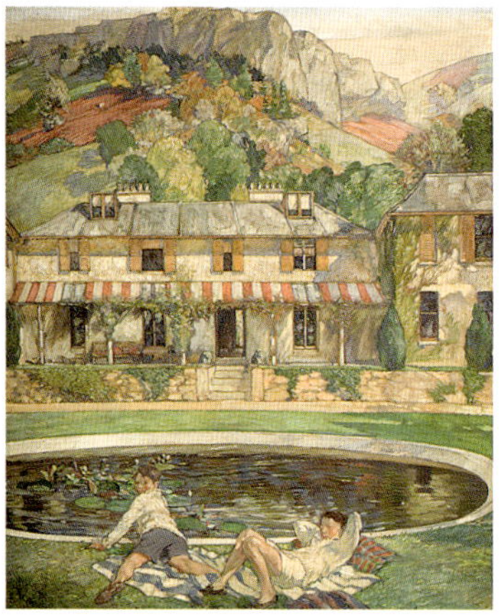

Moira, Gerald 1867–1959
On the Edge of Dartmoor
oil on canvas 172 x 140
1942.545

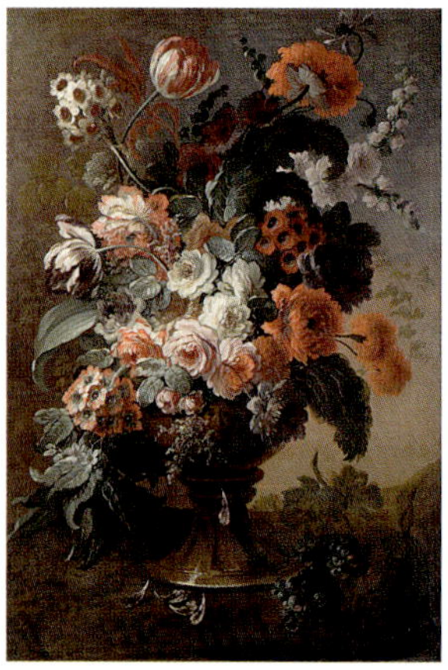

Monnoyer, Jean-Baptiste 1636–1699
Still Life of Flowers
oil on canvas 121 x 80
1980.FA.30

Facing page: Bratby, John Randall, 1928–1992, *Flowers of Summer* (detail), 1966, Lichfield District Council, (p. 18)

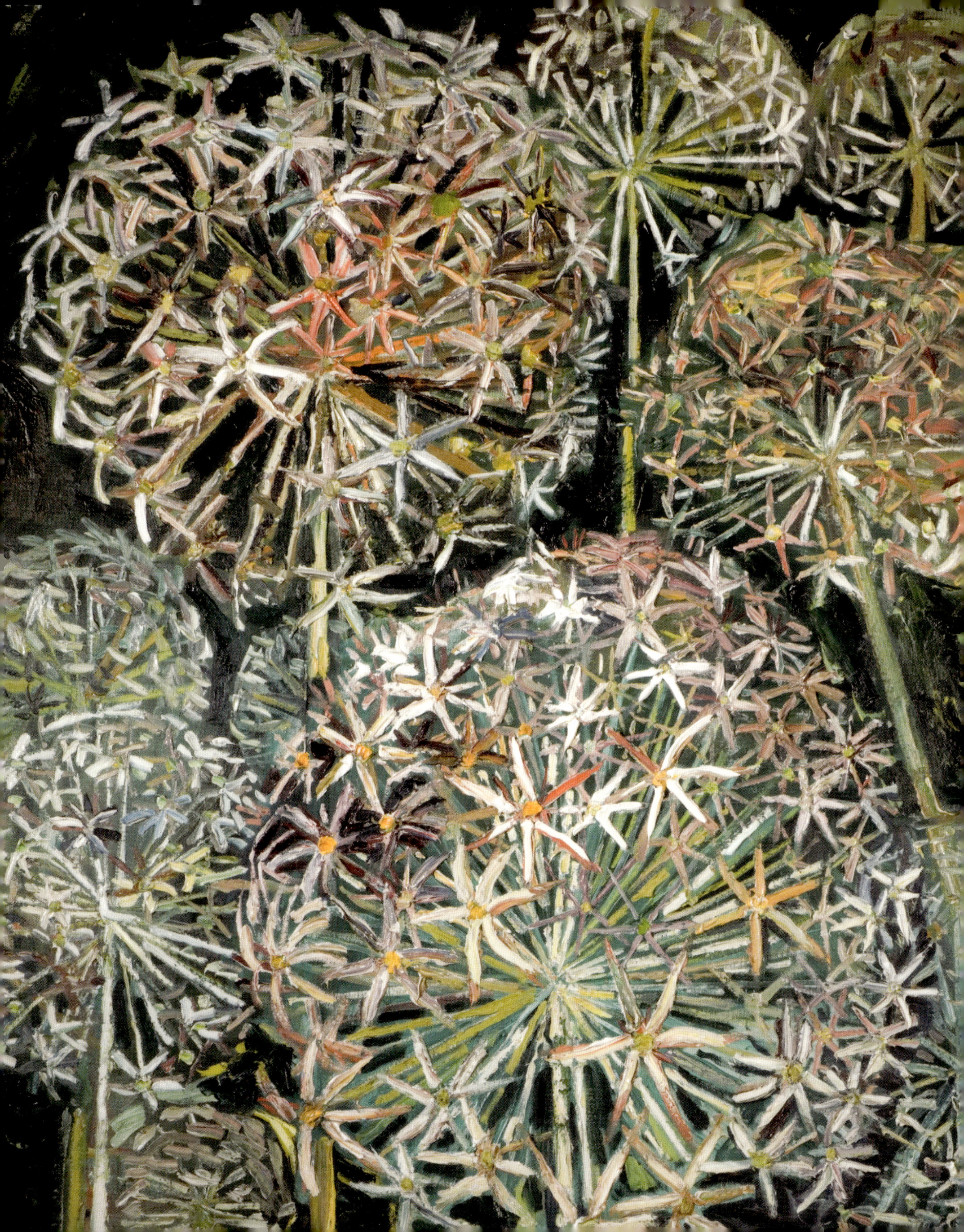

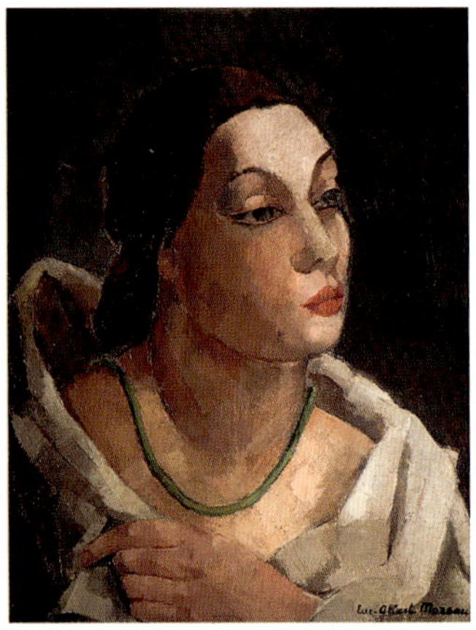

Moreau, Luc-Albert 1882–1948
Head of a Woman
oil on canvas 62 x 53.5
1985.FA.17

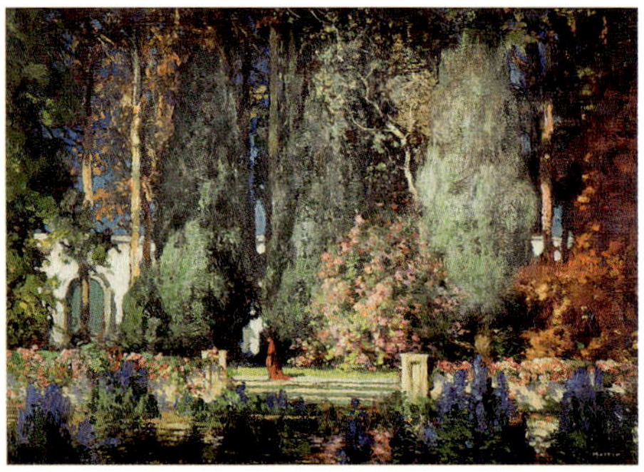

Mostyn, Thomas Edward 1864–1930
The Cardinal's Garden
oil on canvas 49 x 67
PCF25

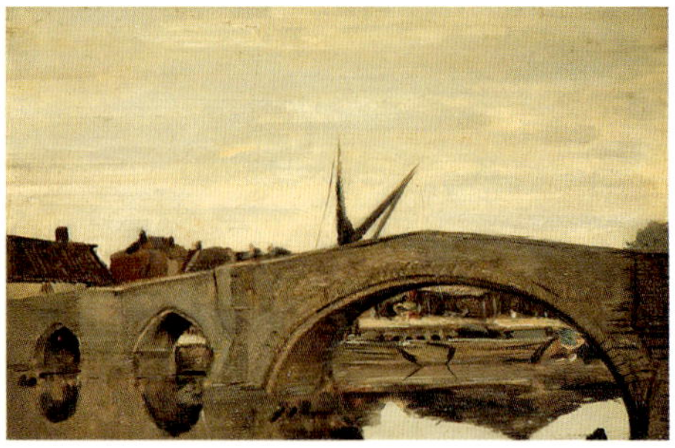

Muirhead, David 1867–1930
The Bridge at Aylesford 1924
oil on board 34.5 x 39.5
1928.FA.2

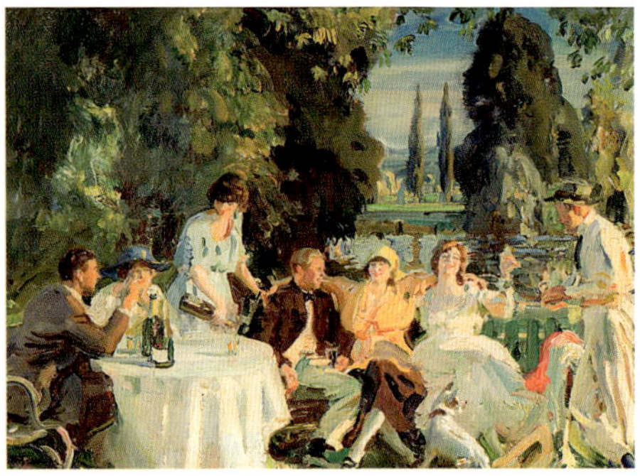

Munnings, Alfred James 1878–1959
Tagg's Island 1919
oil on canvas 48 x 65
1927.FA.10

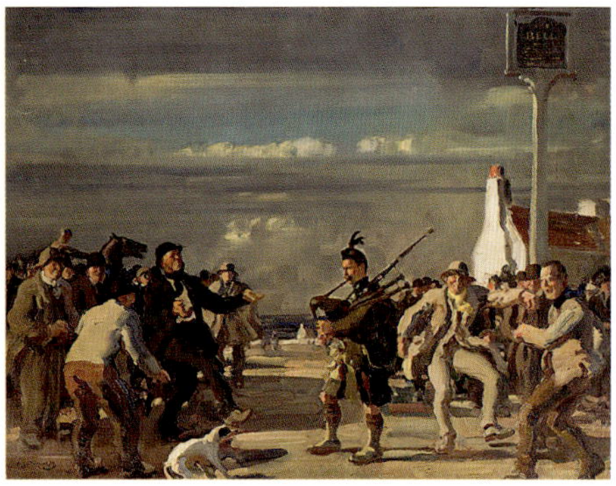

Munnings, Alfred James 1878–1959
A Piper
oil on canvas 79 x 100
1927.FA.9

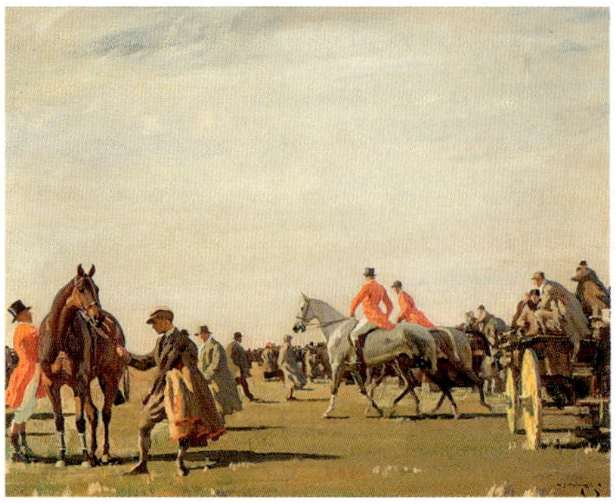

Munnings, Alfred James 1878–1959
Point-to-Point
oil on canvas 72.4 x 90.2
1927.FA.8

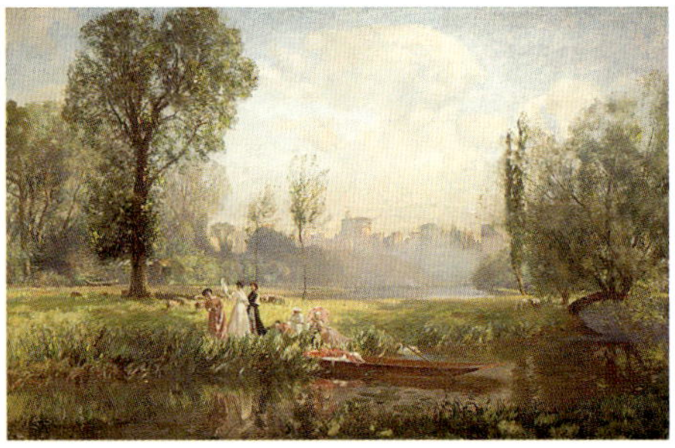

Murray, David 1849–1933
Windsor Castle 1897
oil on canvas 121 x 182
1939.FA.340

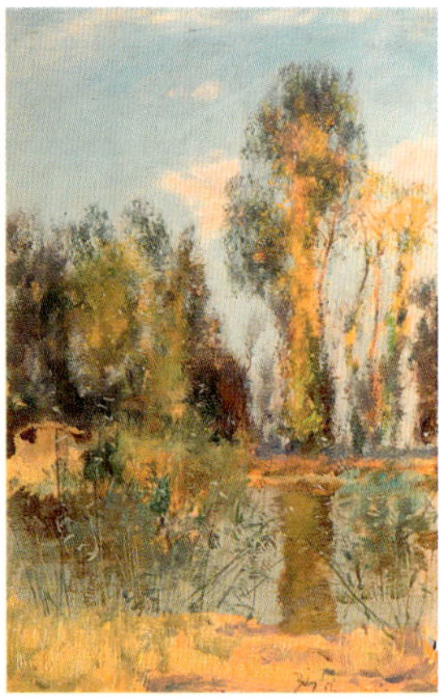

Murray, David 1849–1933
Study
oil on canvas 19.5 x 13.5
1935.FA.87

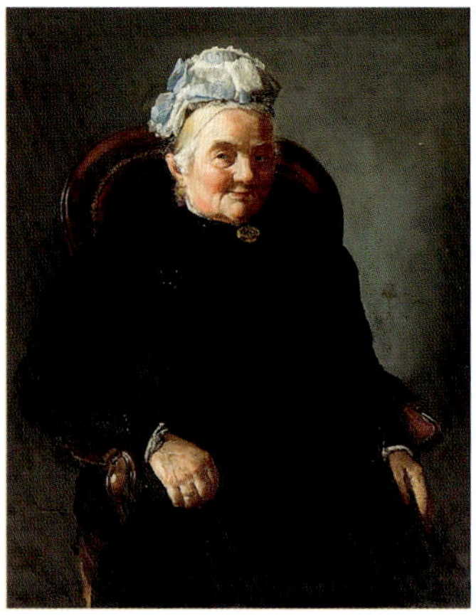

Mussill, Wenzel d.1906
Portrait of the Artist's Housekeeper
oil on canvas 95.5 x 72
1935.FA.81

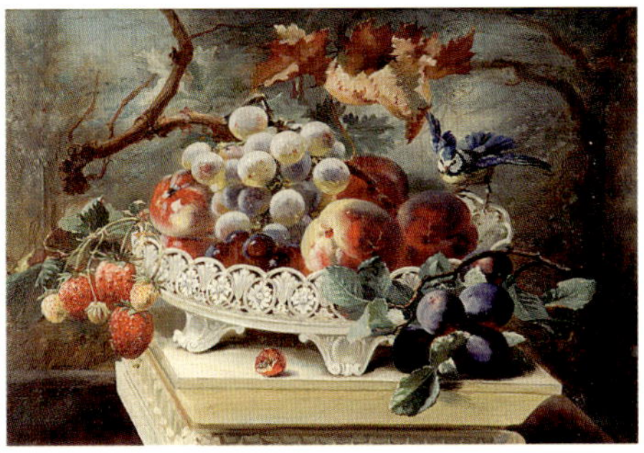

Mussill, William 1828–1906
Still Life of Fruit with Blue Tit
oil on canvas 35 x 50
PCF26

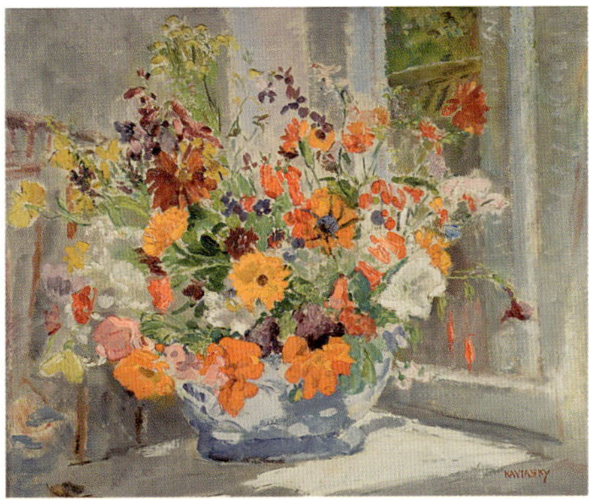

Naviasky, Philip 1894–1982
Flower Piece
oil on canvas 60 x 73
1935.FA.209

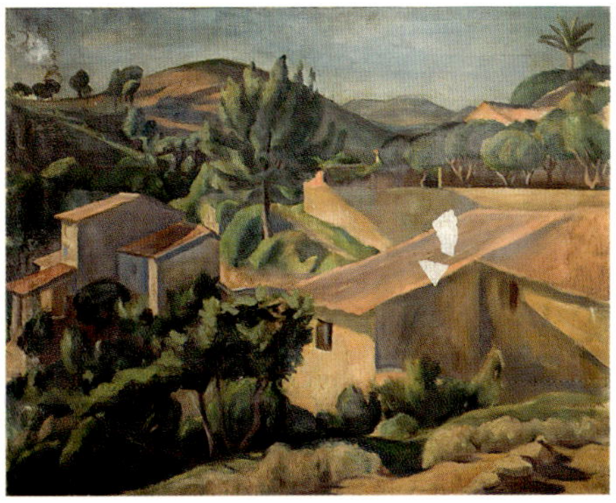

Nelson, Geoffrey C. active 1914–1931
The South of France c.1928
oil on canvas 60 x 72
1962.FA.27

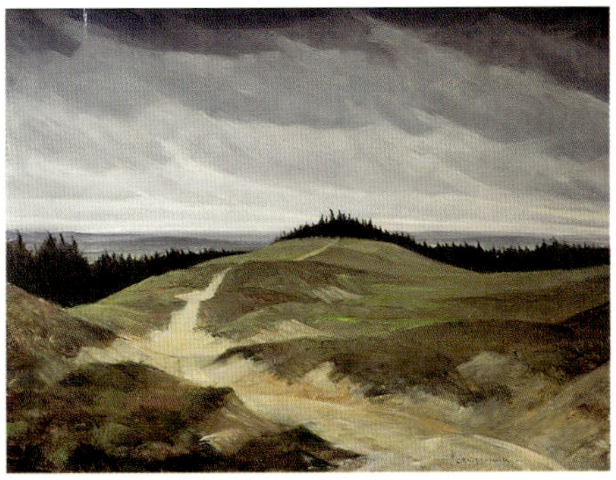

Nevinson, Christopher 1889–1946
Sandy Path before 1919
oil on canvas 70.5 x 90.5
1945.FA.698

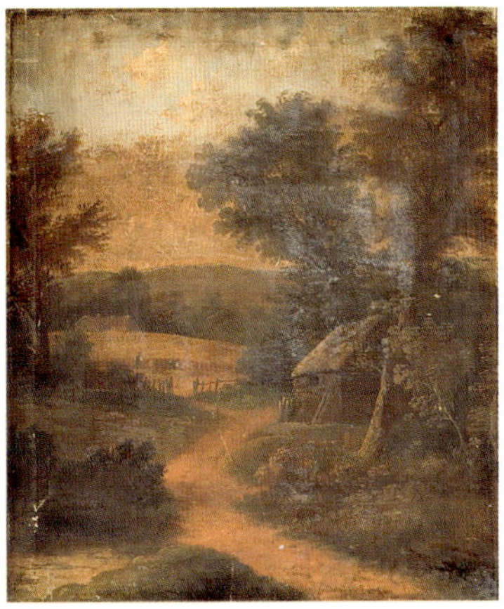

Newey, Harry Foster 1858–1933
Harvesting Scene
oil on canvas 60 x 51
1954.FA.211.a

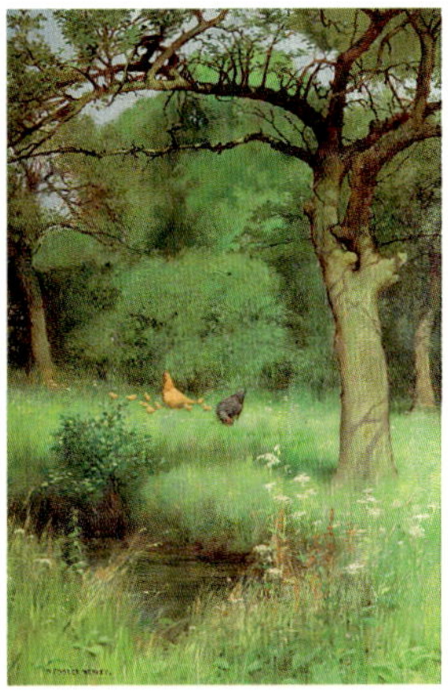

Newey, Harry Foster 1858–1933
In an Old Orchard
oil on canvas 44 x 30
1954.FA.124

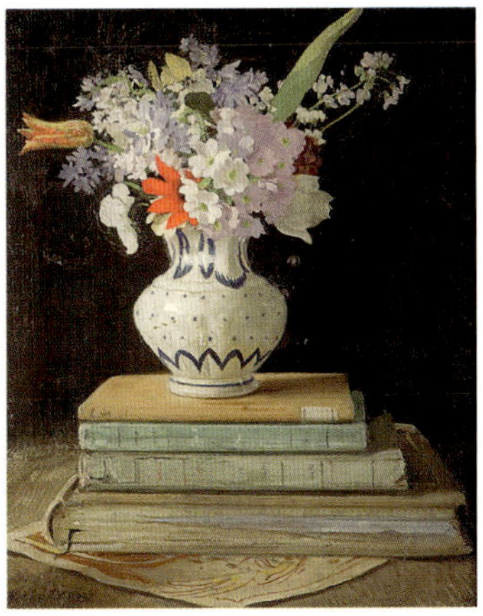

Nicholson, William 1872–1949
Flower Piece with Books 1927
oil on canvas 49 x 38
1928.FA.3

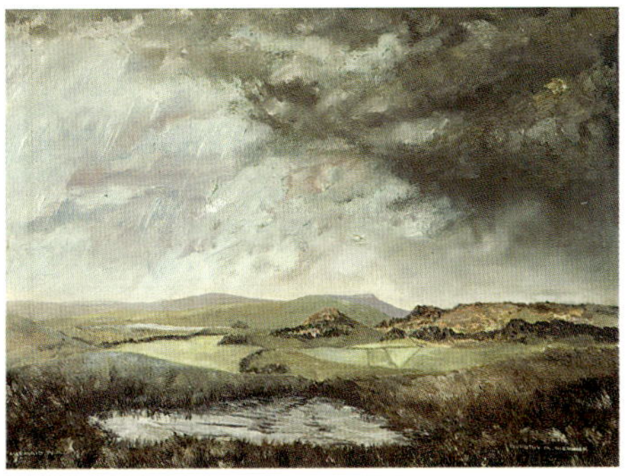

Nierinck, Dorothy M.
The Mermaid Pool
oil on canvas 48 x 65
1967.FA.20

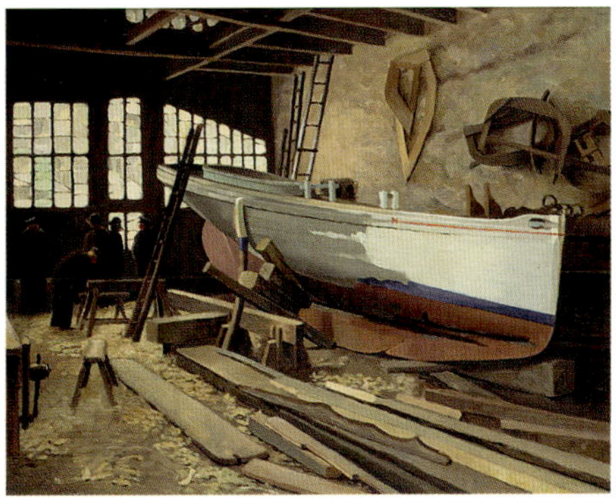

Ninnes, Bernard 1899–1971
In for Repairs c.1932
oil on canvas 49 x 60
1932.FA.12

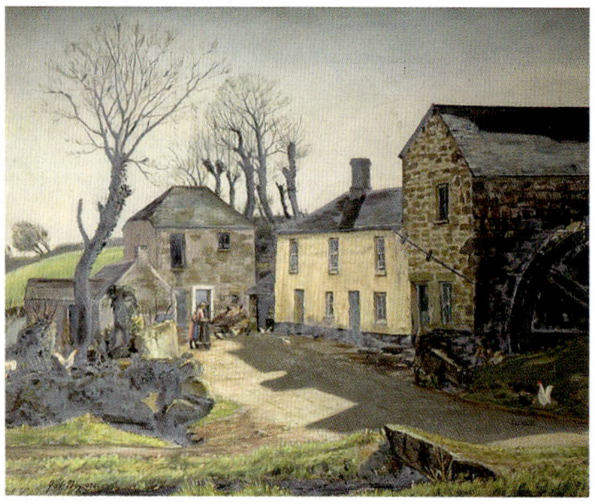

Nixon, Job 1891–1938
Near Lamorna 1932
oil on canvas 49 x 59
1946.FA.735

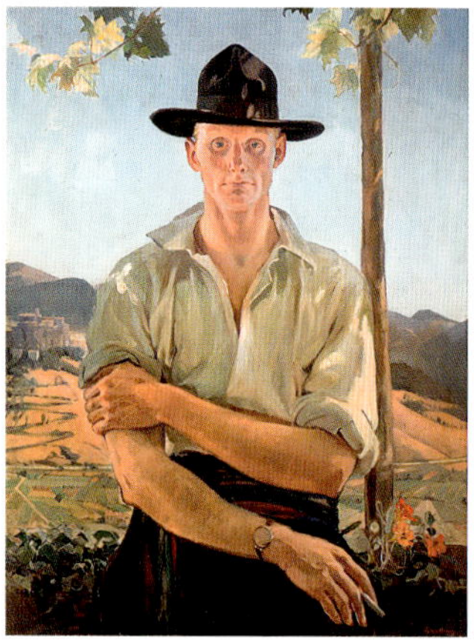

Nixon, Job 1891–1938
Portrait of a Man
oil on canvas 98.5 x 73
PCF63

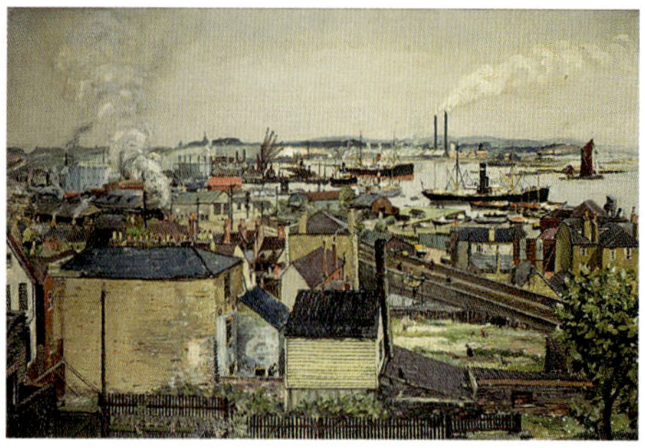

Nixon, Job 1891–1938
Rochester
oil on canvas 48 x 70
1942.FA.536

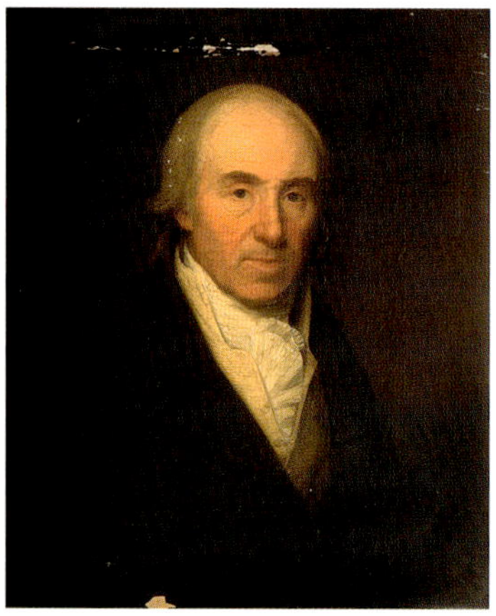

Northcote, James 1746–1831
Elijah Mayer (1765–1813)
oil on canvas 66 x 54.5
1954.FA.185

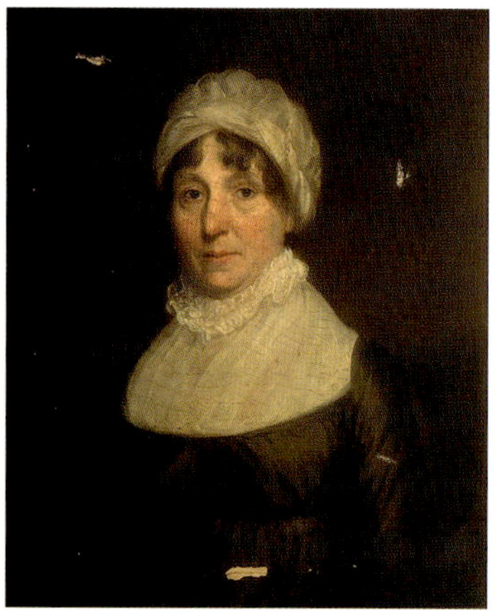

Northcote, James 1746–1831
Mrs Mayer
oil on canvas 66 x 54.5
1954.FA.185a

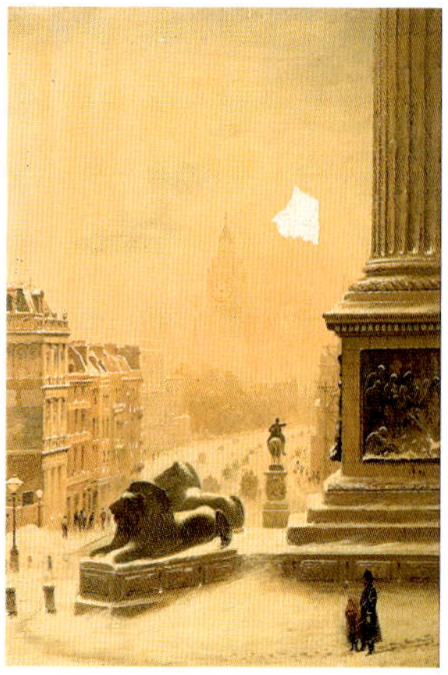

O'Connor, John 1830–1899
View from the National Gallery 1881
oil on canvas 46.5 x 31
1954.FA.128

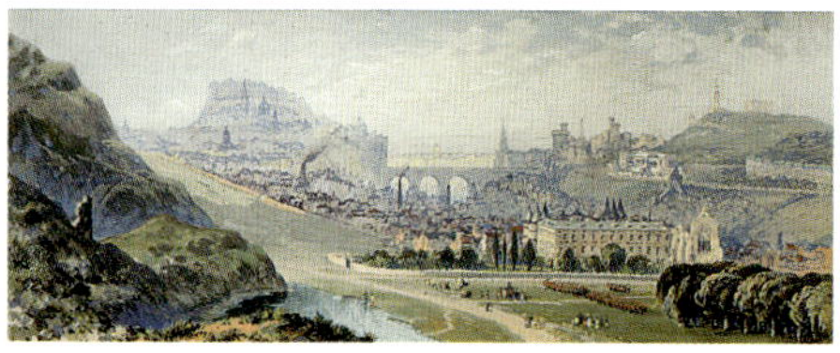

O'Connor, John 1830–1899
Edinburgh from St Anthony's Chapel
oil on board 35.5 x 88
1954.FA.183

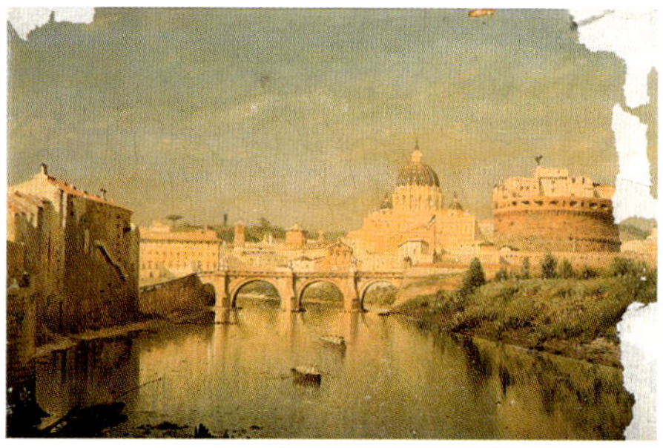

O'Connor, John 1830–1899
Rome, The Bridge of Sant'Angelo
oil on canvas 31 x 45
PCF27

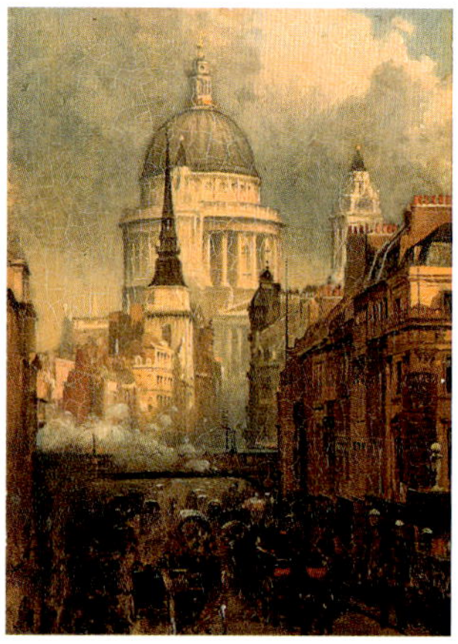

O'Connor, John 1830–1899
St Paul's from Ludgate Hill
oil on canvas 35 x 25
1954.FA.130

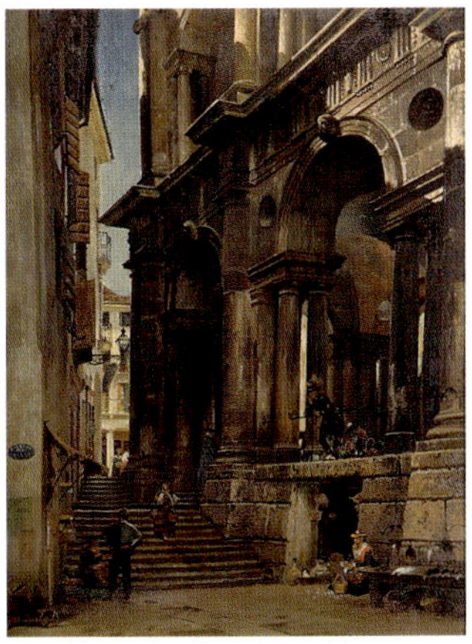

O'Connor, John 1830–1899
The Town Hall of Vicenza
oil on canvas 49 x 37
PCF28

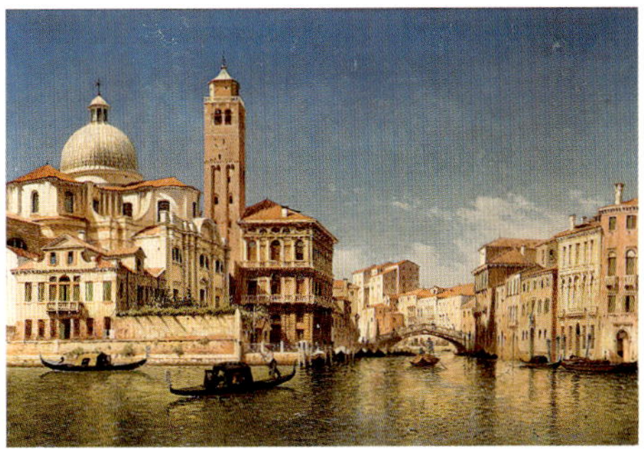

O'Connor, John 1830–1899
Venetian Scene
oil on canvas 32 x 46
PCF29

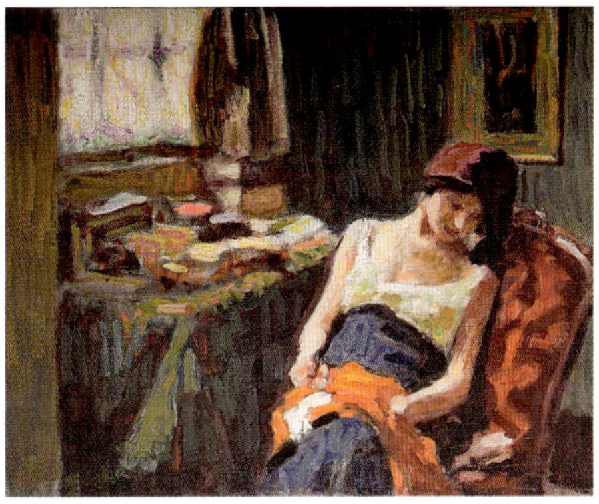

O'Conor, Roderic 1860–1940
Interior
oil on canvas 49 x 59
1956.FA.34

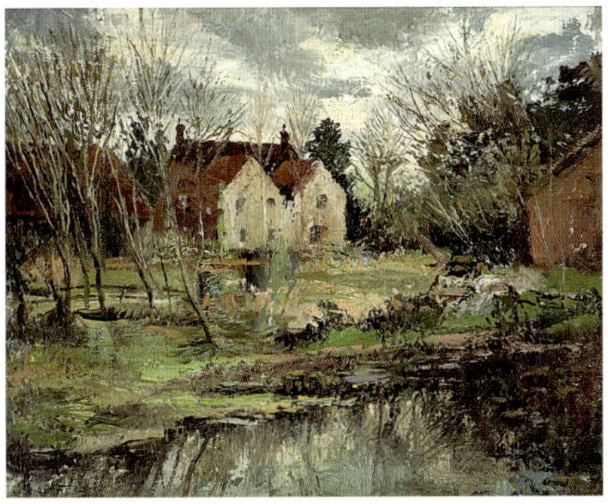

Ormrod, Frank 1897–1988
Garden and Pond c.1949
oil on board 49 x 60
1950.FA.116

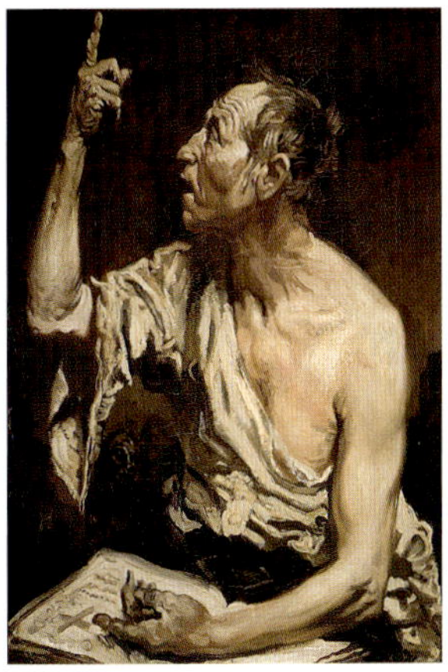

Orpen, William 1878–1931
St Patrick
oil on canvas 100 x 77.5
1936.FA.244

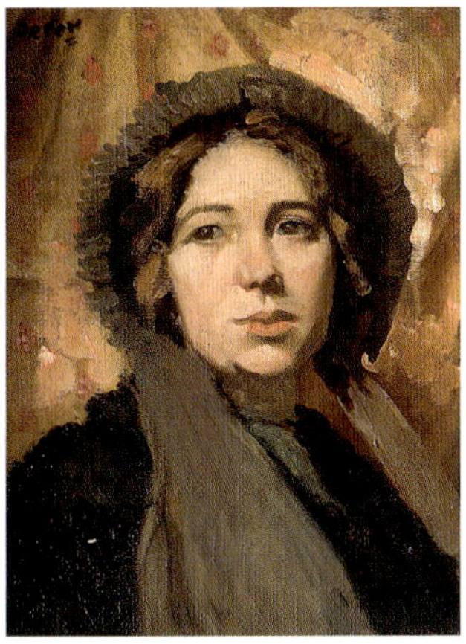

Orpen, William 1878–1931
The New Bonnet
oil on canvas 44 x 34
1967.FA.19

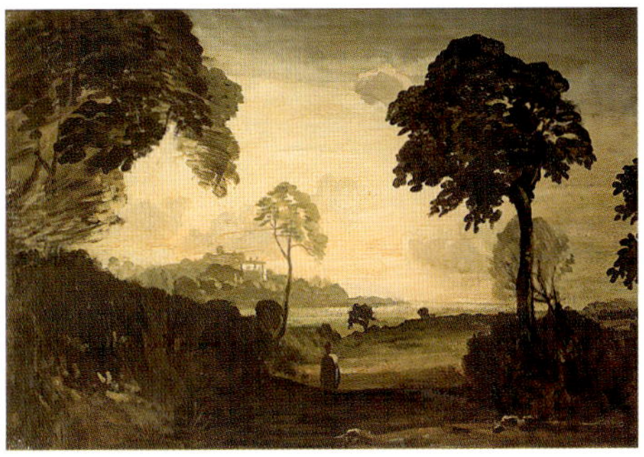

Padwick, Philip Hugh 1876–1958
Landscape with Trees
oil on canvas 60 x 90
1959.FA.13

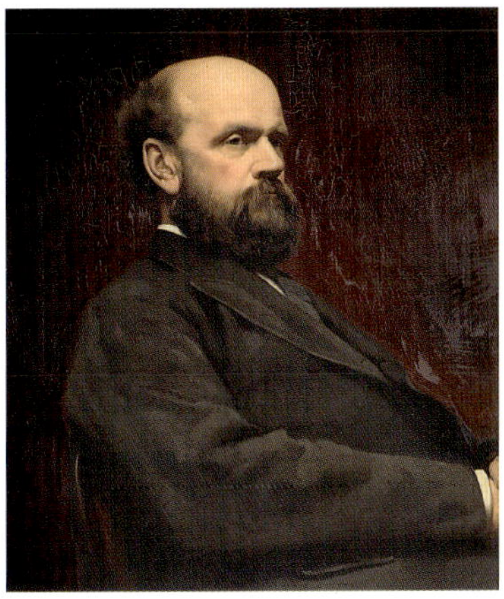

Palin, William Mainwaring 1862–1947
William Millett Edge 1888
oil on canvas 74.5 x 62
1954.FA.146

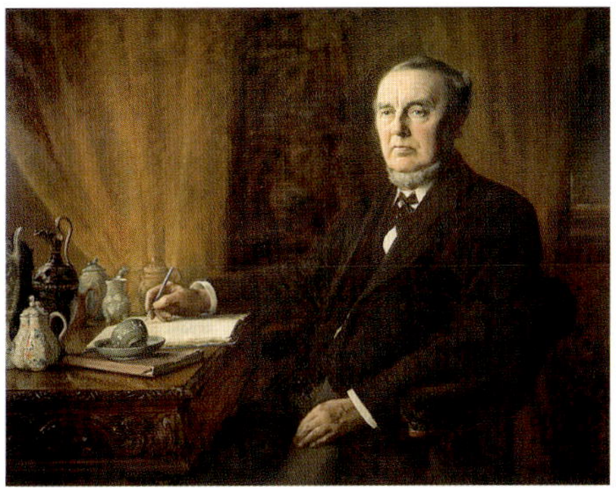

Palin, William Mainwaring 1862–1947
Thomas Hulme, JP (1830–1905) c.1894
oil on canvas 100 x 125
1954.FA.140

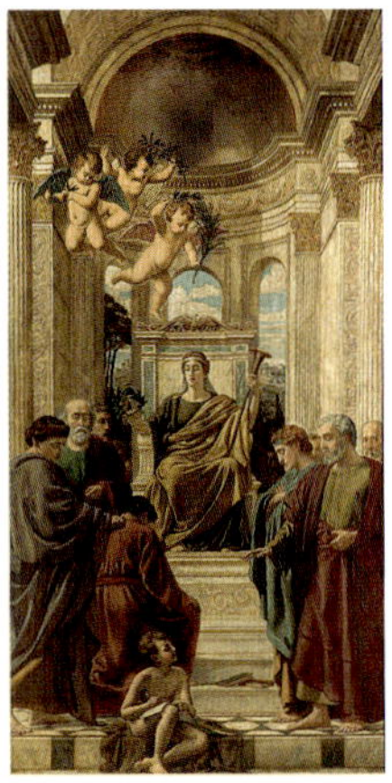

Palin, William Mainwaring 1862–1947
The Temple of Fame 1895
oil on canvas 165 x 83
1935.FA.187

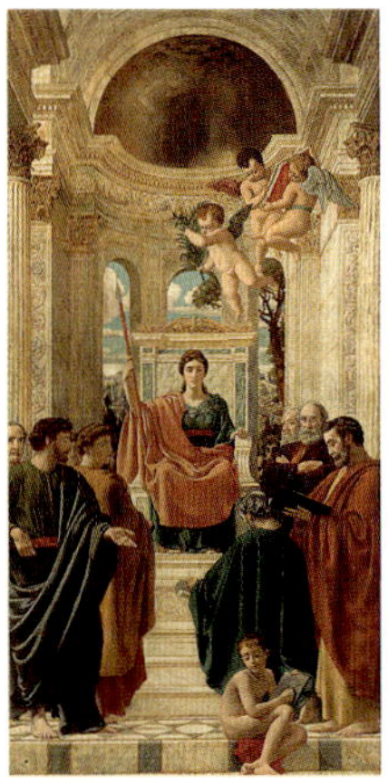

Palin, William Mainwaring 1862–1947
The Temple of Minerva
oil on canvas 163 x 81
1935.FA.188

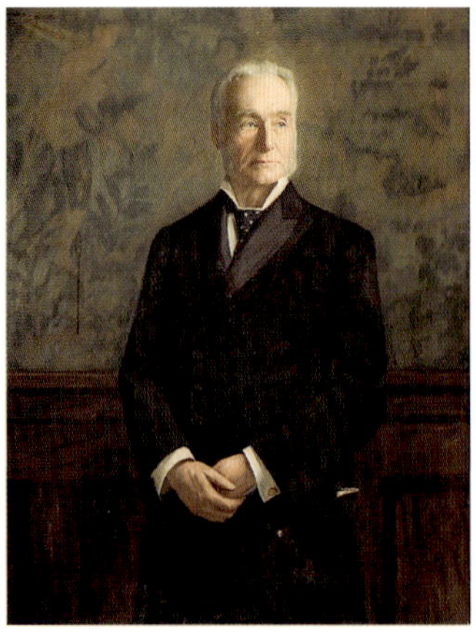

Palin, William Mainwaring 1862–1947
John Alcock, JP
oil on canvas 125 x 100
1954.FA.136

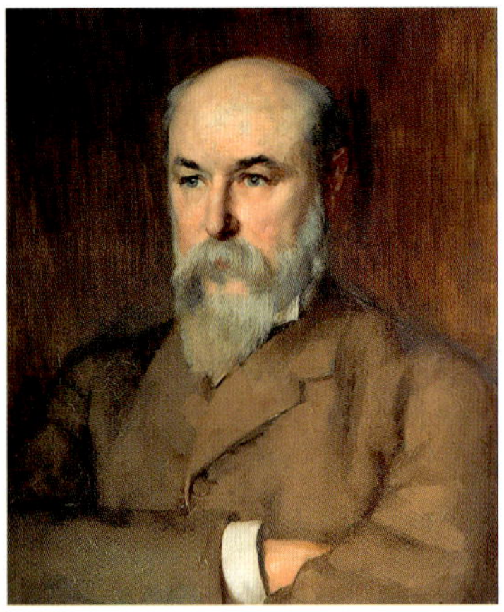

Palin, William Mainwaring 1862–1947
William Woodall, MP (1832–1901)
oil on canvas 60 x 50
1954.FA.187

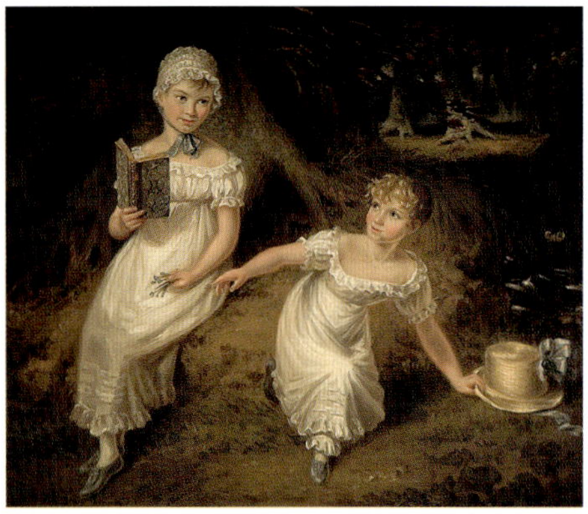

Parry, David Henry 1793–1826
The Misses Heywoods 1817
oil on canvas 44 x 51
1972.FA.3

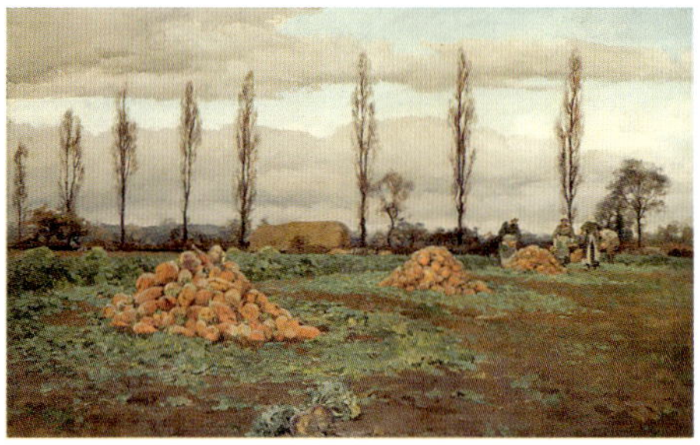

Parsons, Alfred William 1847–1920
The Swede Harvest
oil on canvas 39 x 59
1963.FA.84

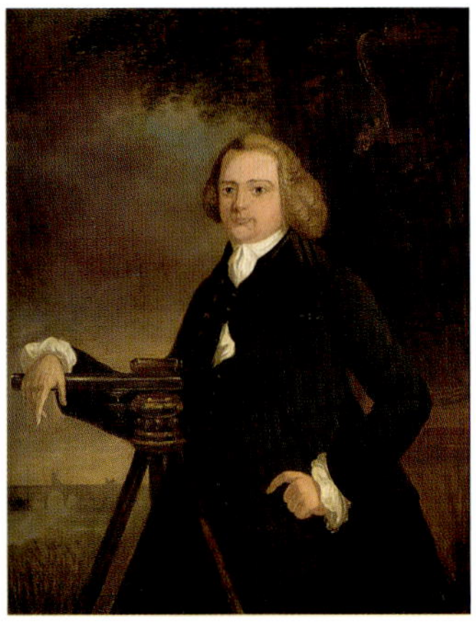

Parsons, Francis d.1804
James Brindley (1716–1772)
oil on canvas 73 x 56.5
1954.FA.186

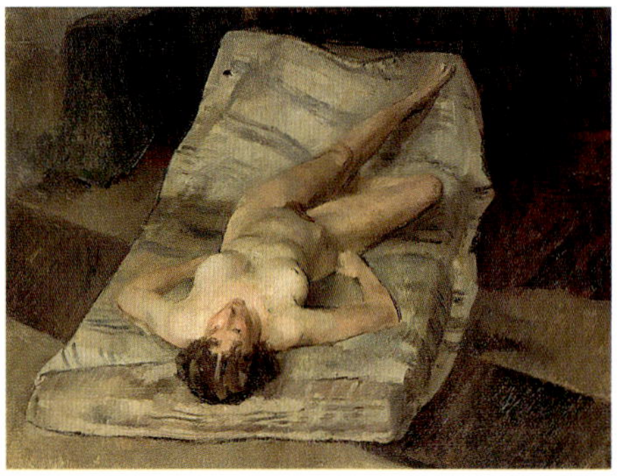

Pass, Donald b.1930
Nude Study 1953
oil on canvas 40 x 50
1954.FA.36

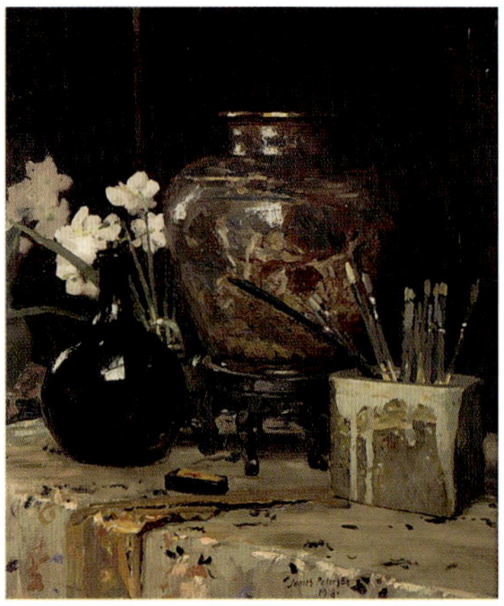

Paterson, James 1854–1932
Still Life: Persian, Japanese, Dutch 1918
oil on canvas 58.5 x 48
1947.FA.836

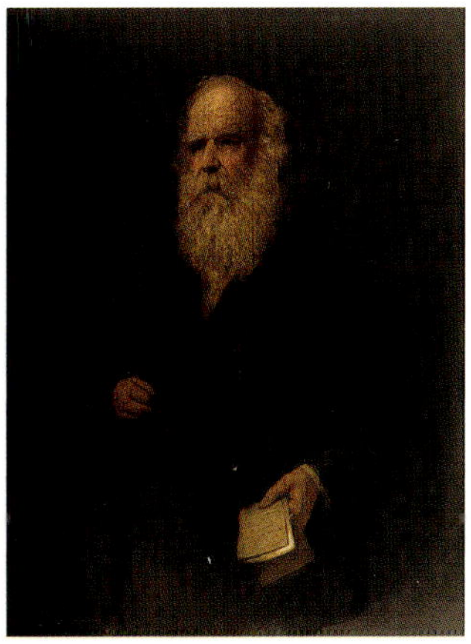

Peake, John Nash 1837–1905
Sir Smith Child (1808–1896) c.1890
oil on canvas 74.5 x 63.5
1982.FA.3

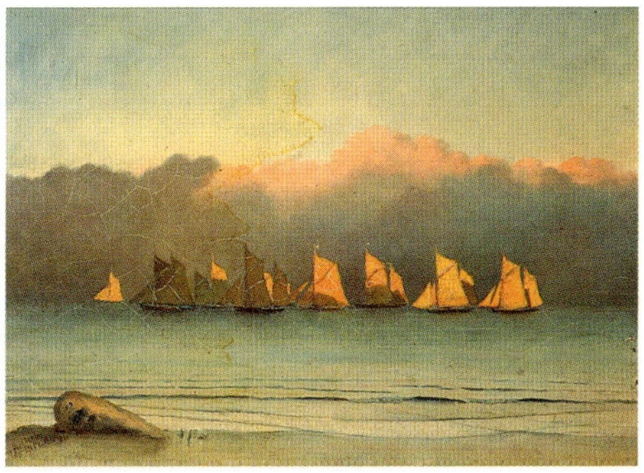

Peake, John Nash 1837–1905
Fishing Fleet, Tenby 1896
oil on canvas 29 x 38
1954.FA.96

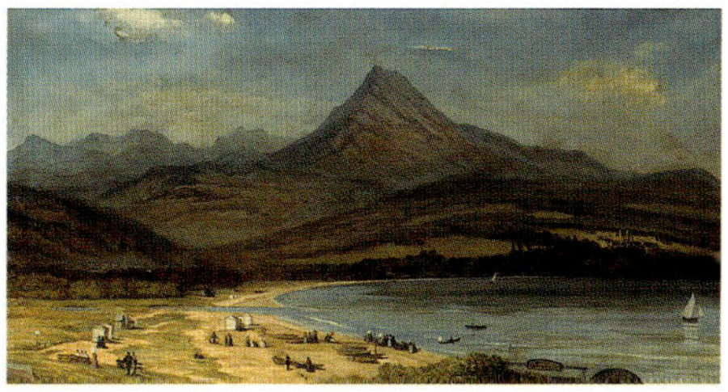

Peake, John Nash 1837–1905
The Isle of Arran 1899
oil on canvas 48 x 89
1960.FA.2

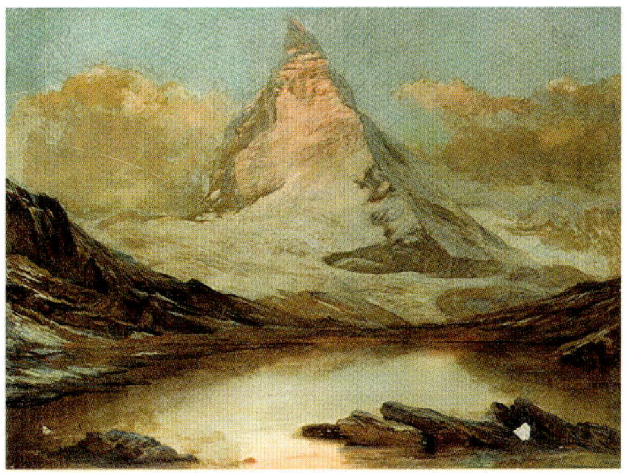

Peake, John Nash 1837–1905
The Matterhorn 1899
oil on board 86 x 112
1954.FA.200

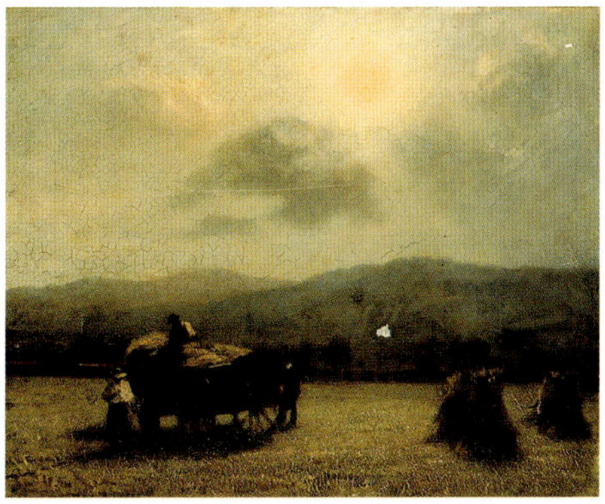

Peake, John Nash 1837–1905
The Last Load
oil on canvas 51 x 61
1954.FA.126

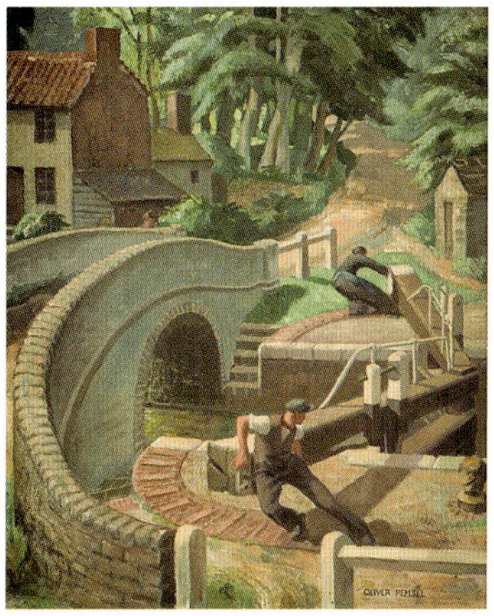

Pemsel, Oliver 1910–1989
The Lock Gates c.1935
oil on canvas 65.5 x 54
1935.FA.181

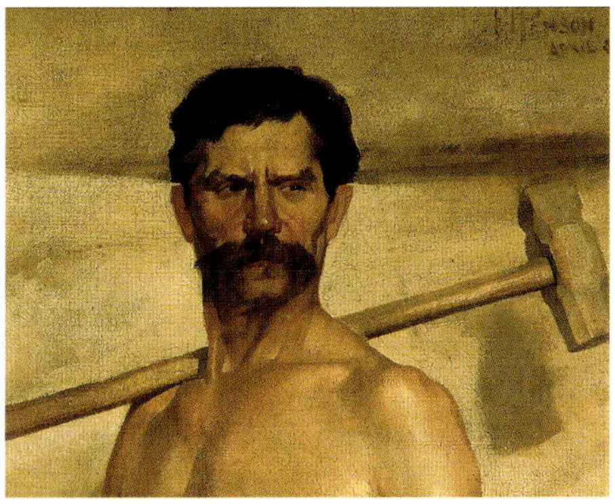

Penson, Frederick Thomas 1866–1951
Cornish Miner 1885
oil on canvas 23 x 28
1949.FA.892

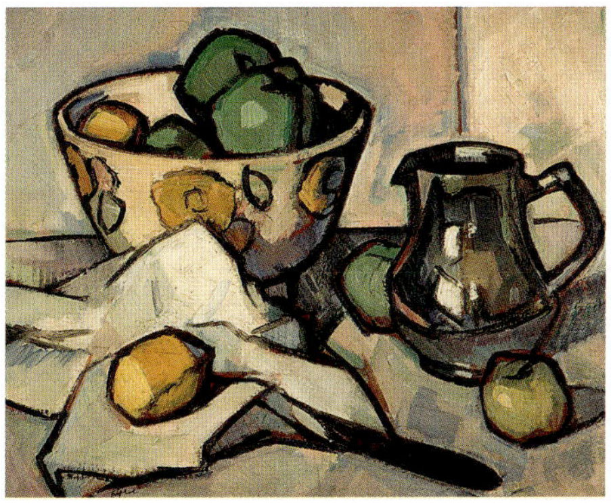

Peploe, Samuel John 1871–1935
Still Life
oil on canvas 43 x 53.5
1960.FA.123

Peppercorn, Arthur Douglas 1847–1926
Quiet Waters
oil on canvas 30 x 44
1972.FA.2A

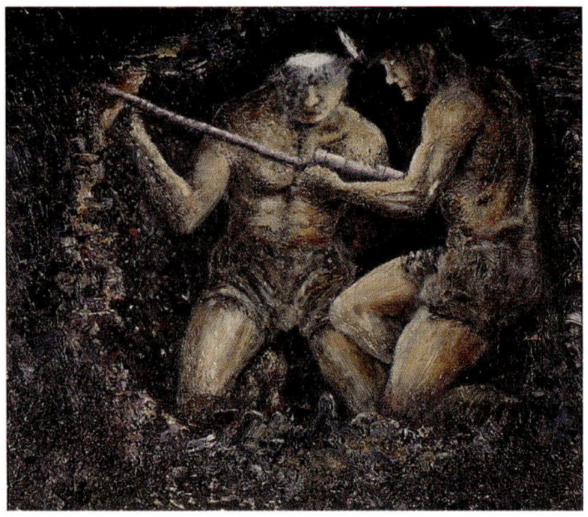

Phillips, Norman 1920–1988
Borer and Mate
oil on panel 59 x 66.5
1994.FA.1

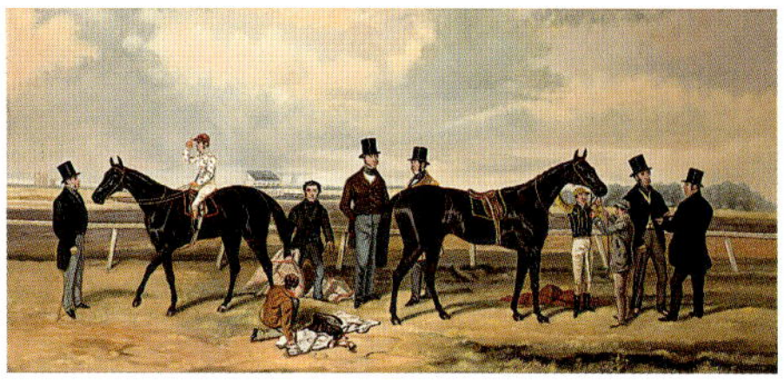

Phipps, J. active 1838–1861
York Racecourse
oil on canvas 54.5 x 112
1954.FA.35

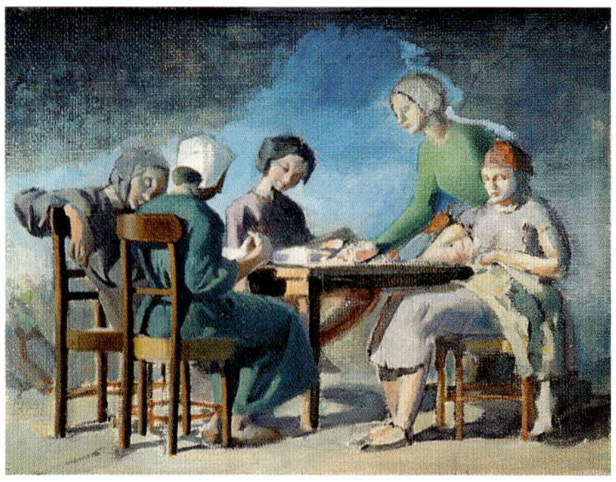

Pickering, W. E.
Five Women Working by a Table
oil on panel 37 x 47
1953.FA.13

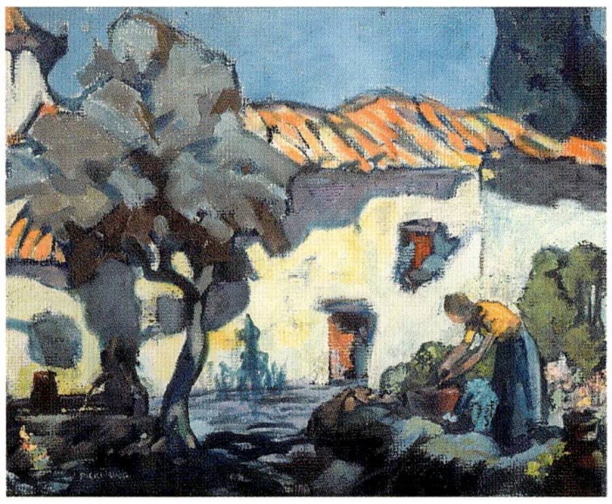

Pickering, W. E.
Spanish Scene
oil on board 35 x 42.5
1953.FA.14

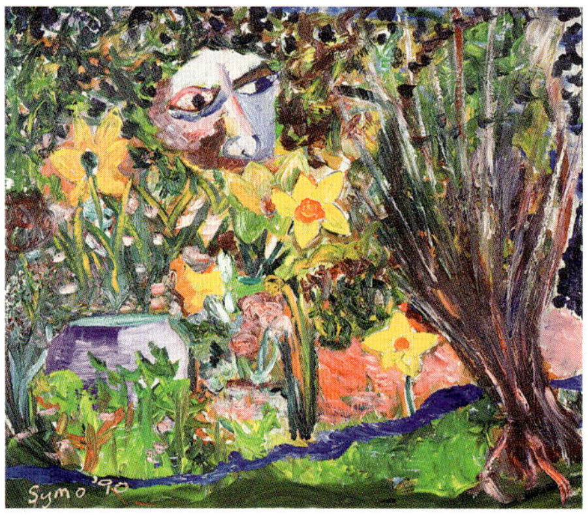

Plant, Simon b.1954
The Tare 1990
acrylic on panel 69 x 80
1990.FA.2

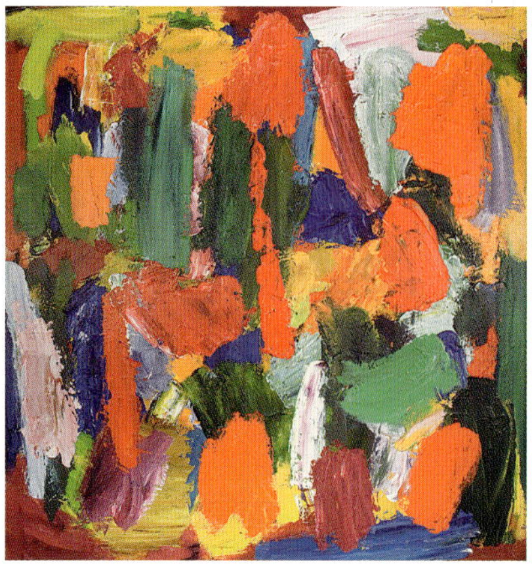

Pollock, Fred b.1937
Firefly Summer 1991
acrylic on canvas 170 x 157
1996.FA.251

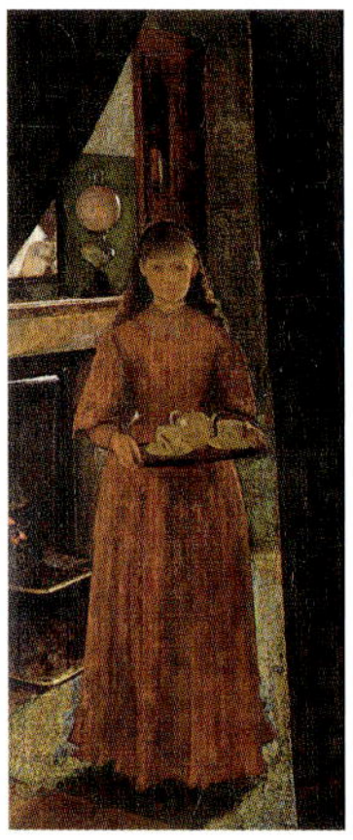

Potter, Frank Huddlestone 1845–1887
Morning Tea
oil on panel 71 x 30
1958.FA.54

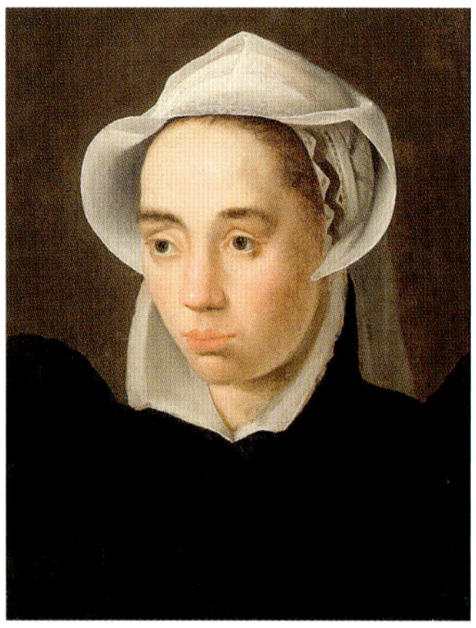

Pourbus, Frans the younger 1569–1622
Woman in a White Cap
oil on panel 40 x 31
1957.FA.15

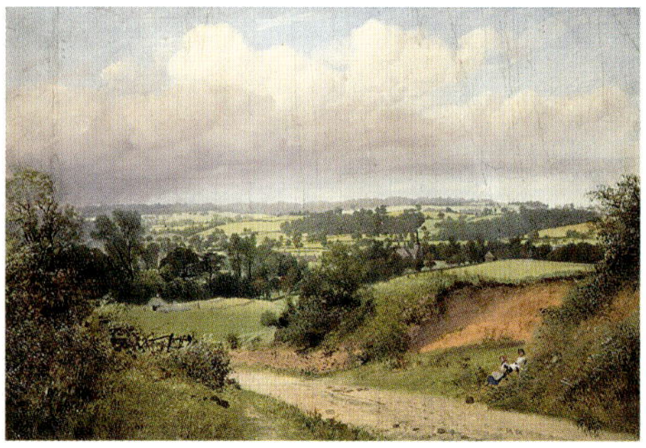

Pratt, Henry Lark I 1805–1873
Trent Vale from Penkhull 1846
oil on board 30 x 45
1954.FA.93

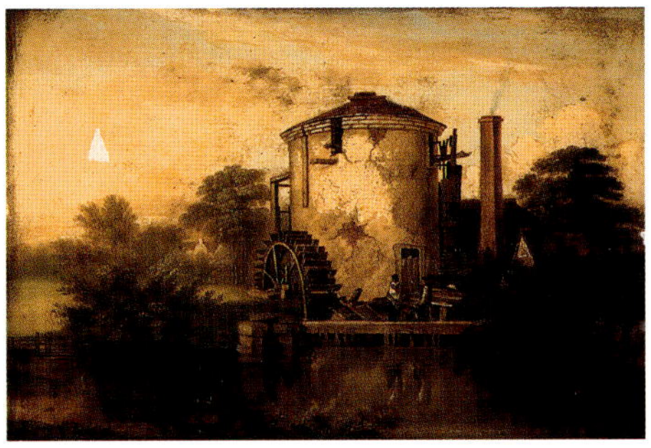

Pratt, Henry Lark I 1805–1873
Boothen Mill, Stoke
oil on panel 41 x 60
1954.FA.193

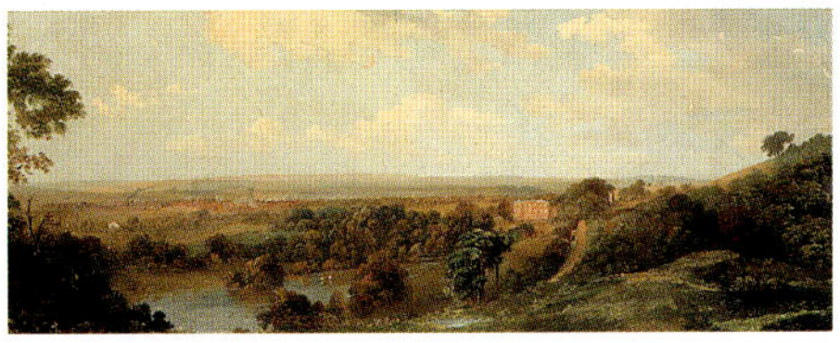

Pratt, Henry Lark I 1805–1873
Etruria Hall
oil on board 33.5 x 82
1954.FA.142

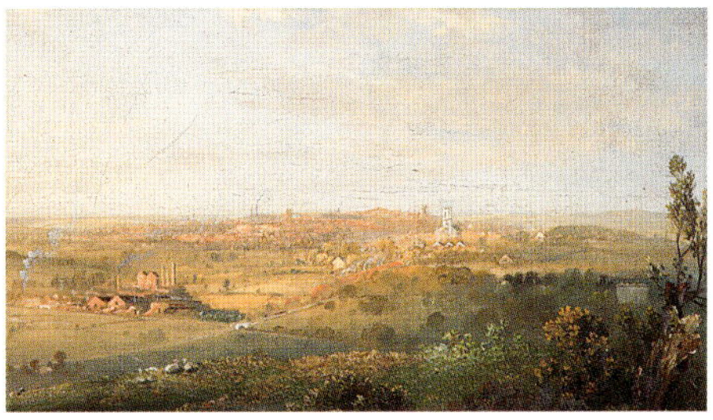

Pratt, Henry Lark I 1805–1873
Local Landscape
oil on panel 34 x 57
1954.FA.149

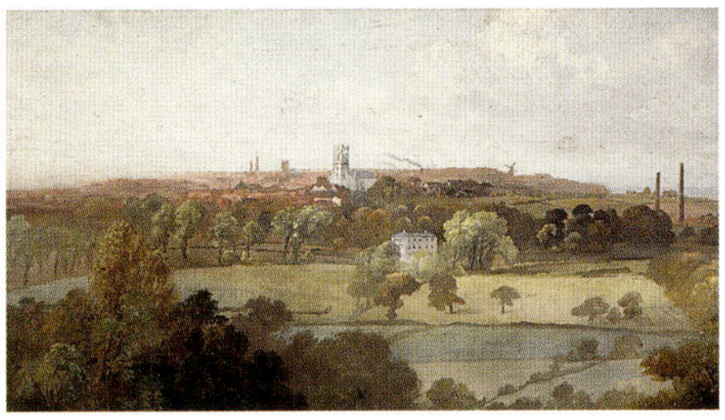

Pratt, Henry Lark I 1805–1873
Local Landscape
oil on panel 32.2 x 53.5
1954.FA.155

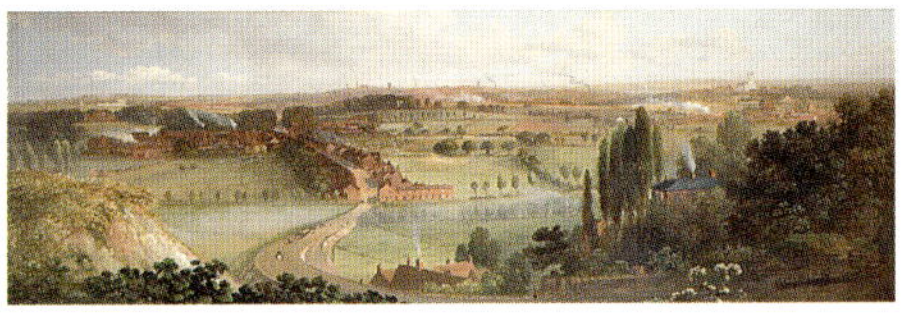

Pratt, Henry Lark I 1805–1873
Local Landscape
oil on panel 45 x 132
1954.FA.156

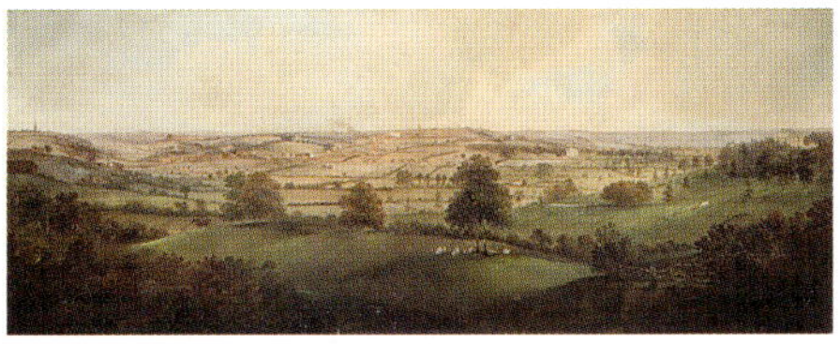

Pratt, Henry Lark I 1805–1873
Potteries Landscape
oil on panel 54 x 136
PCF30

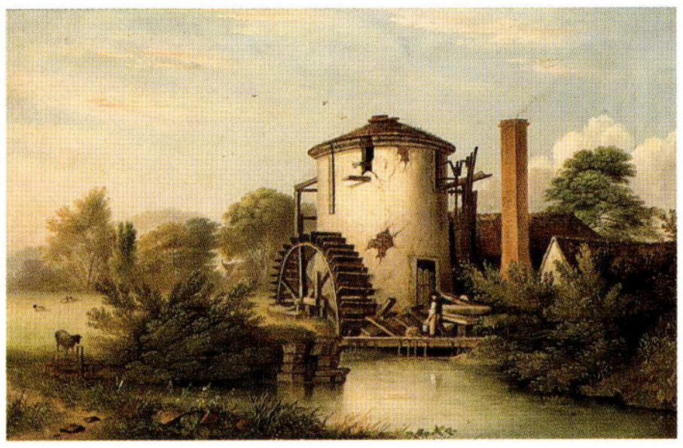

Pratt, Henry Lark I 1805–1873
Strongford Mill, near Trentham
oil on canvas 41 x 62
1954.FA.12

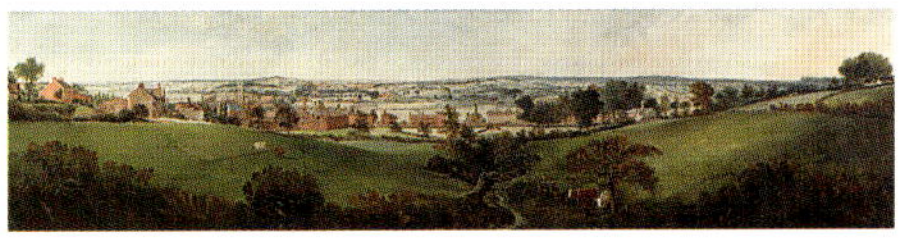

Pratt, Henry Lark I 1805–1873
View from Basford Bank
oil on panel 67 x 270
1954.FA.148

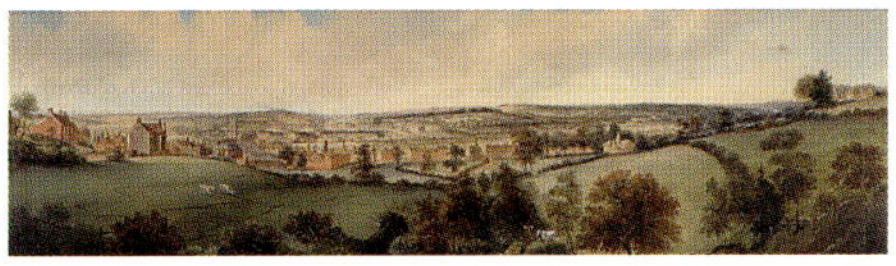

Pratt, Henry Lark I 1805–1873
View of Stoke from Penkhull
oil on canvas 40 x 165
1985.FA.18

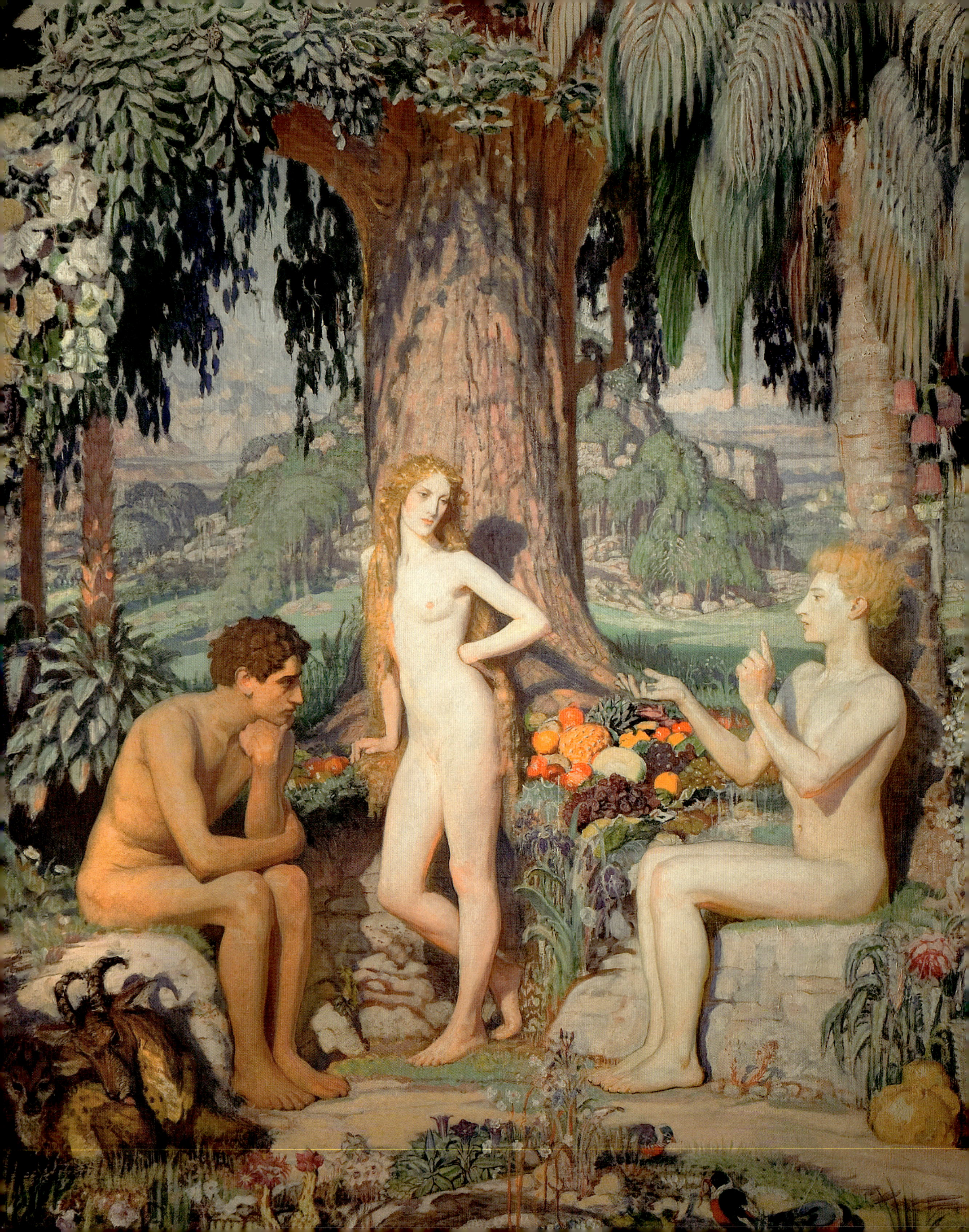

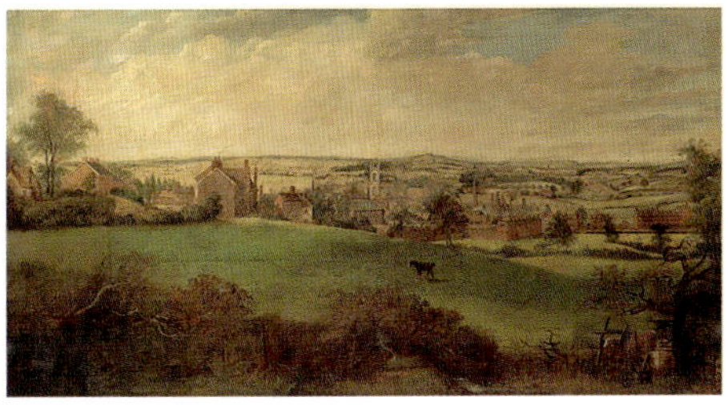

Pratt, Henry Lark I (attributed to)
1805–1873
View of Stoke from Penkhull
oil on canvas 78 x 140
1985.FA.181

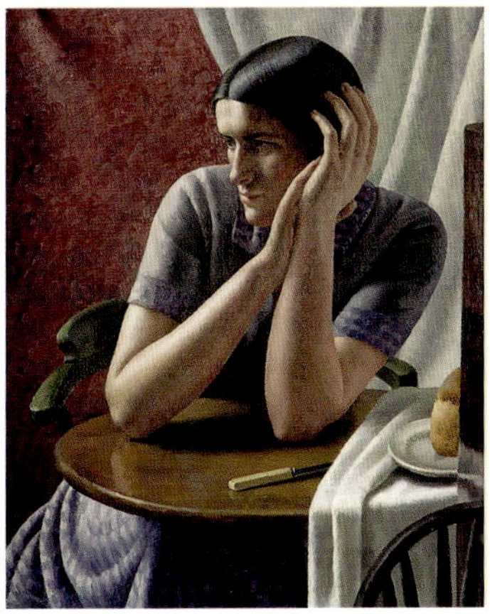

Procter, Dod 1892–1972
Clara
oil on canvas 74.5 x 59
1928.FA.1

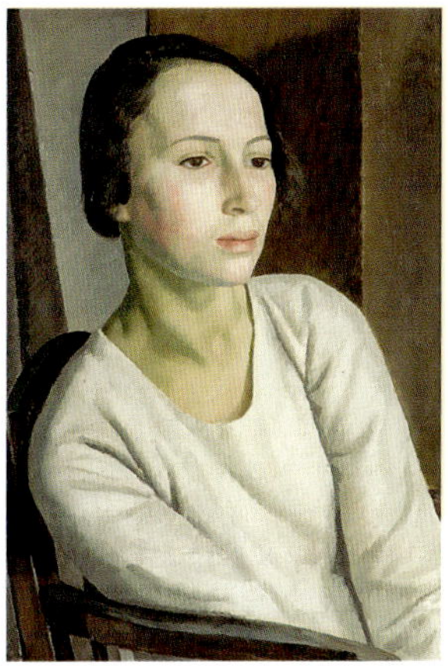

Procter, Dod 1892–1972
Girl in White
oil on panel 52 x 36
1926.FA.38

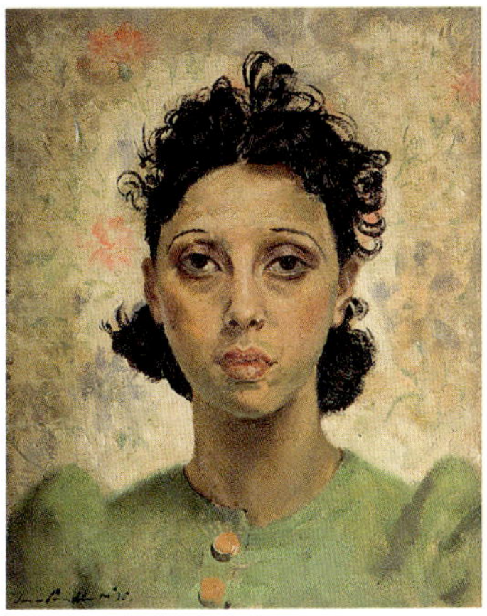

Proudfoot, James 1908–1971
Dark Girl 1935
oil on canvas 50 x 40
1937.FA.350

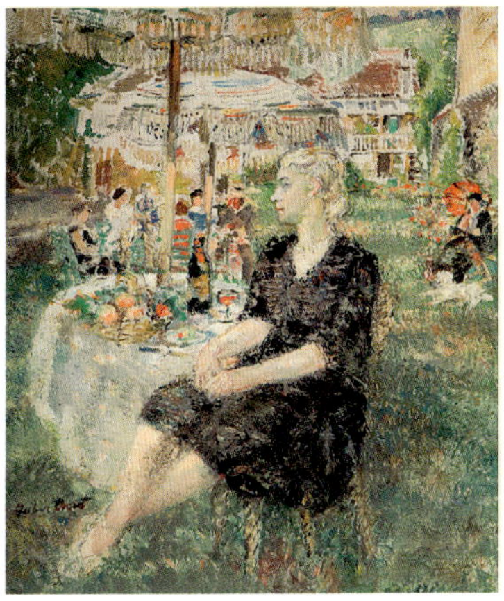

Prout, Margaret Fisher 1875–1963
La patronne
oil on panel 59 x 49
1963.FA.91

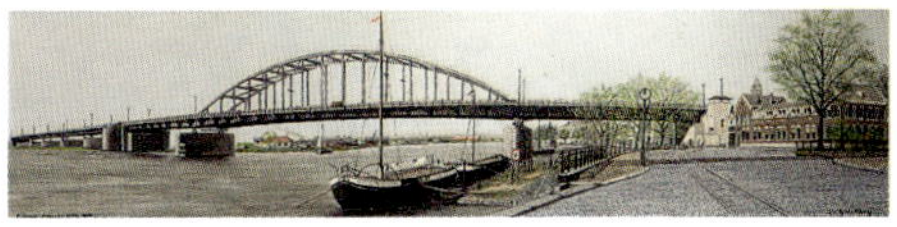

Raay, G. W.
Rynsburg Arnhem Vor, 1944
oil on canvas 28 x 118
PCF31

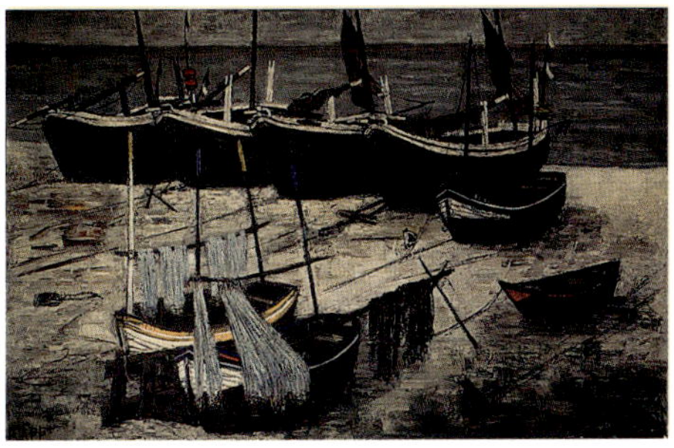

Rapp, Ginette 1928–1998
Yport c.1954
oil on canvas 114 x 194
1965.FA.10

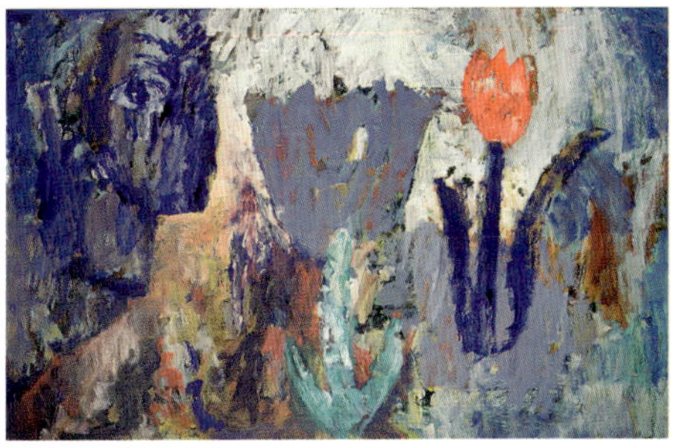

Reed, Graeme John Robert b.1964
Looking Closely at the Flowers
oil on paper 65 x 97
1993.FA.16

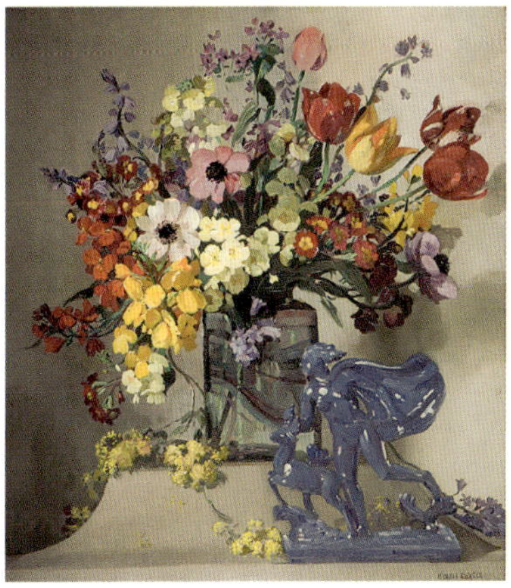

Richter, Herbert Davis 1874–1955
Diana c.1932
oil on canvas 73.5 x 61.5
1932.FA.5

Facing page: Watson, George Spencer, 1869–1934, *The Creation* (detail), 1921, Wolverhampton Art Gallery, (p. 335)

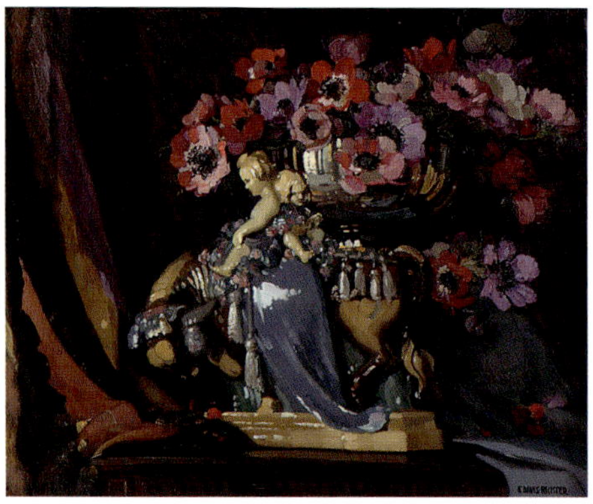

Richter, Herbert Davis 1874–1955
The Flower Show
oil on canvas 61.5 x 74.5
PCF32

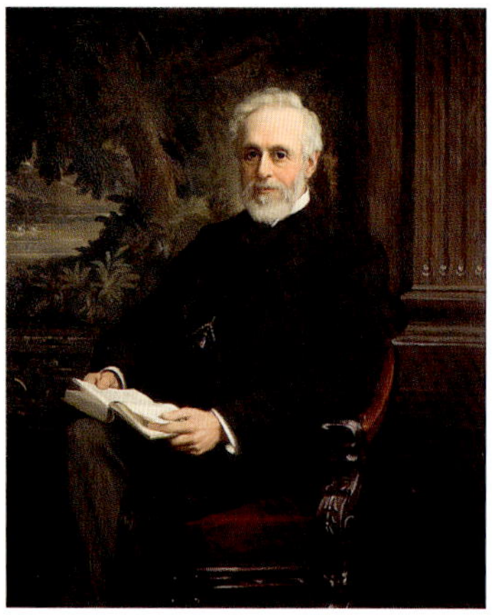

Roberts, Ellis William 1860–1930
Sir Henry Doulton (1820–1897) 1898
oil on canvas 125 x 100
1954.FA.141

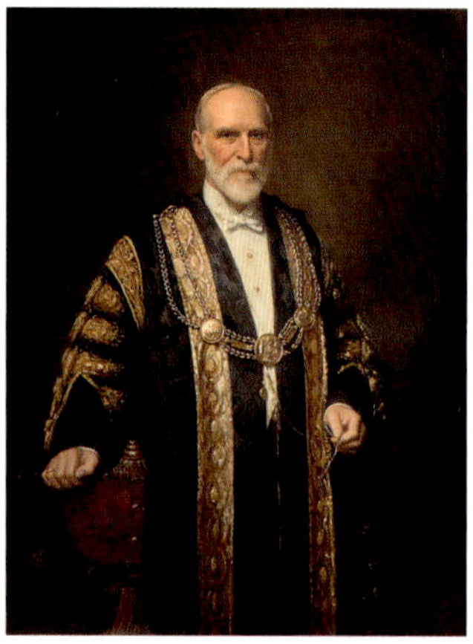

Roberts, Ellis William 1860–1930
George Bennion 1912
oil on canvas 140 x 100
PCF33

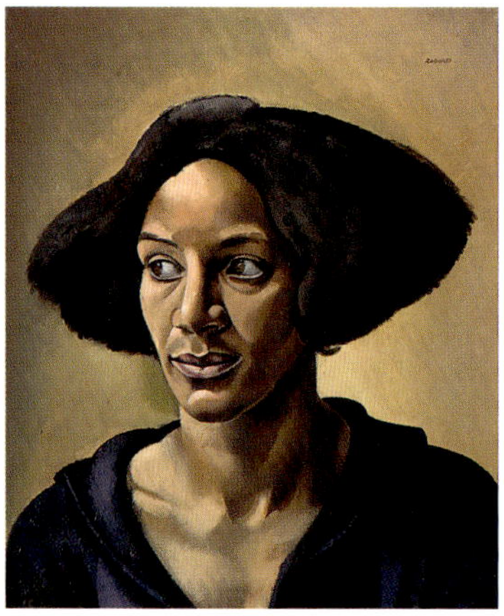

Roberts, William Patrick 1895–1980
Portrait of a Negress
oil on canvas 59 x 48.5
1938.FA.306

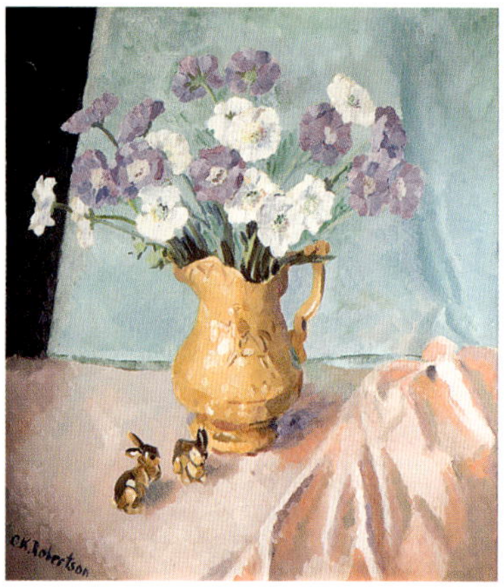

Robertson, Constance 1895–1964
Scabious
oil on panel 65 x 56
1935.FA.200

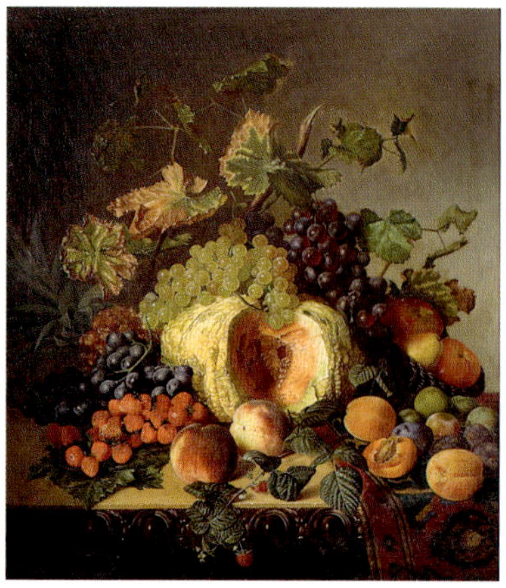

Robinson, John Charles 1824–1913
Still Life with Fruit 1861
oil on canvas 80 x 62
1945.FA.711

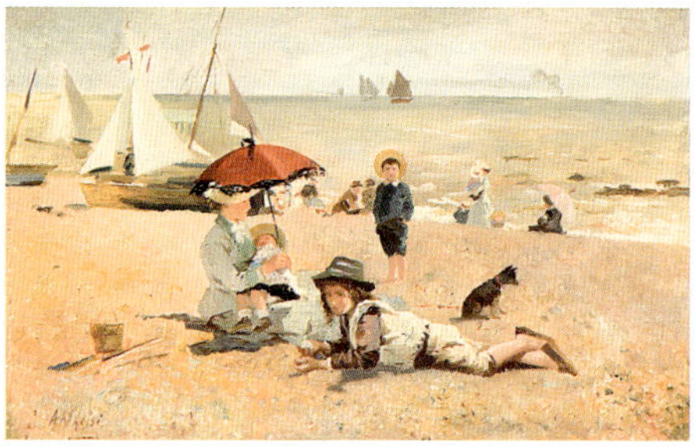

Roisi, A. M.
Rest by the Sea
oil on panel 33 x 52
1954.FA.95

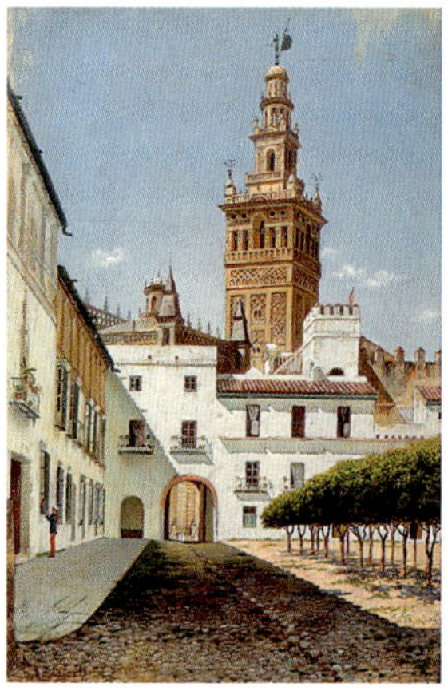

Roldan, Eduardo b.1926
La Giralda, Seville
oil on board 22 x 14.5
PCF34

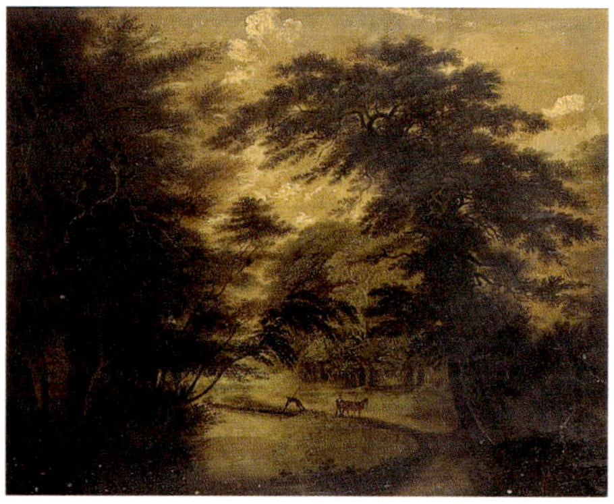

Rush
Wooded Scene with Two Figures and a Horse
oil on canvas 30 x 35
1954.FA.190

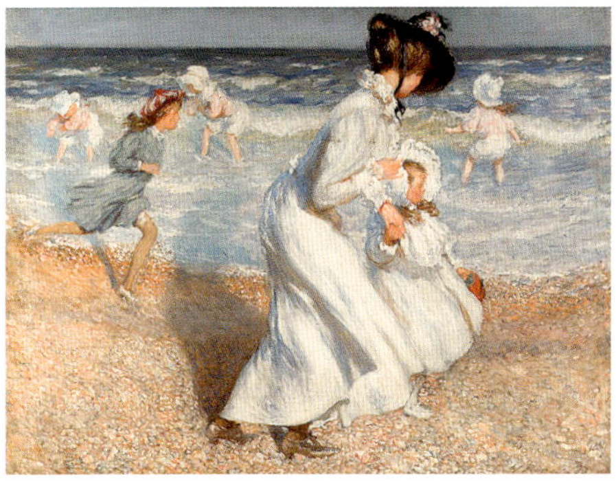

Russell, Walter Westley 1867–1949
Boulogne Sands 1922
oil on canvas 70 x 90
1950.FA.48

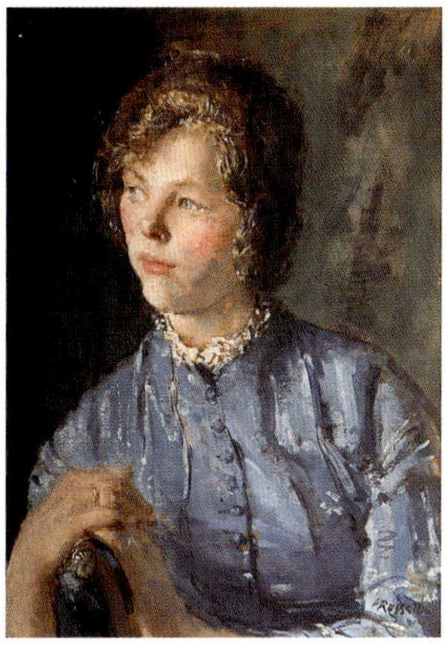

Russell, Walter Westley 1867–1949
Lydia
oil on panel 35 x 25
1950.FA.46

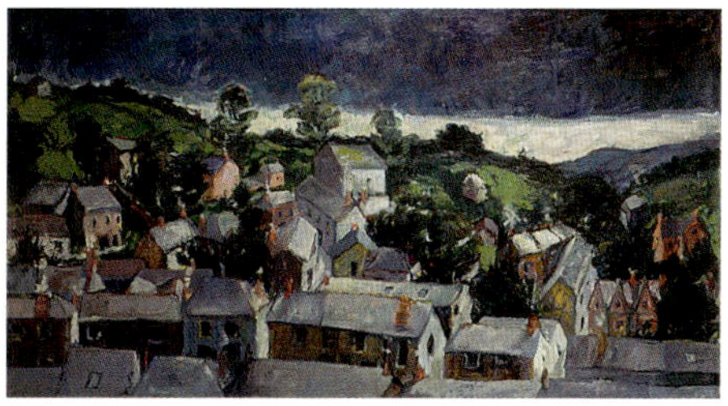

Ryan, Adrian 1920–1998
Dawn, Newlyn, Cornwall c.1952
oil on canvas 69.5 x 126
1959.FA.45

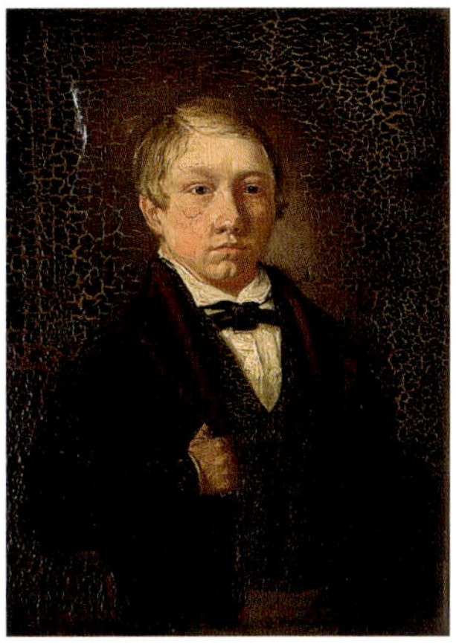

Ryles, Frederick Rieland 1831–1908
Self Portrait c.1840
oil on panel 18 x 13
1985.FA.15

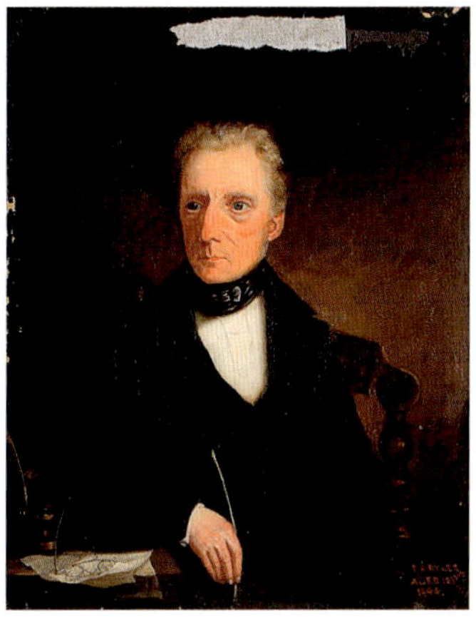

Ryles, Frederick Rieland 1831–1908
Simeon Shaw (1785–1859) 1844
oil on canvas 46 x 36
1985.FA.3

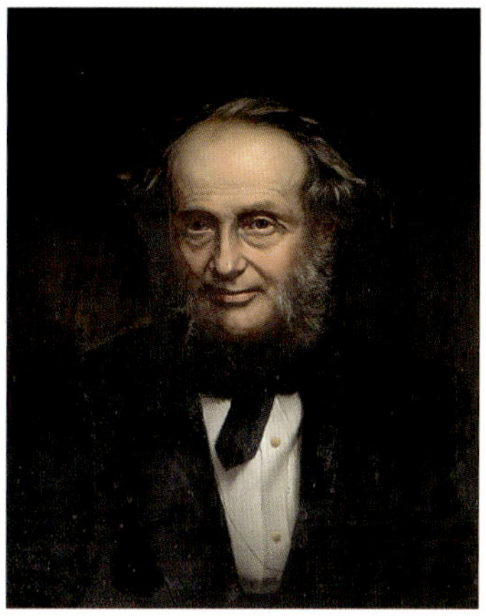

Ryles, Frederick Rieland 1831–1908
Thomas Pinder (d.1867)
oil on canvas 59 x 46
1954.FA.133

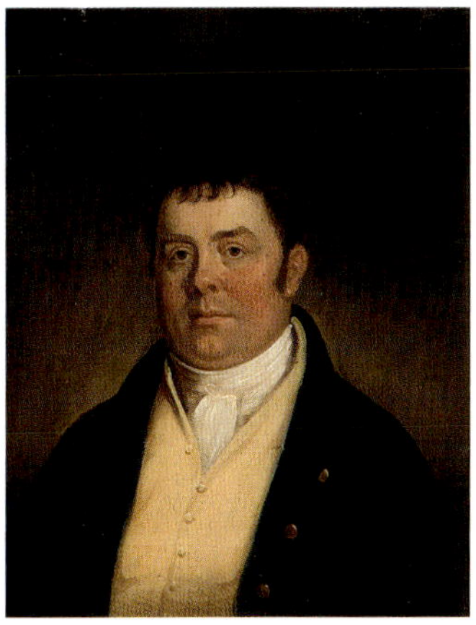

Ryles, Thomas 1825–1903
Job Ridgway (1759–1814)
oil on board 29 x 24
1953.FA.15

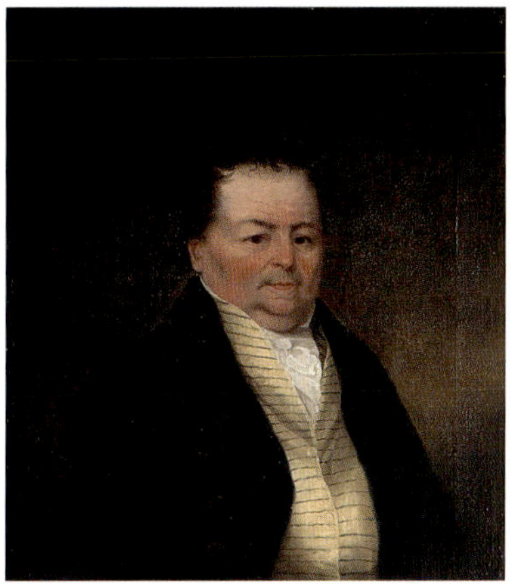

Ryles, Thomas (attributed to) 1825–1903
William Hackwood (d.1849) c.1900
oil on canvas 34 x 29.5
1951.FA.76

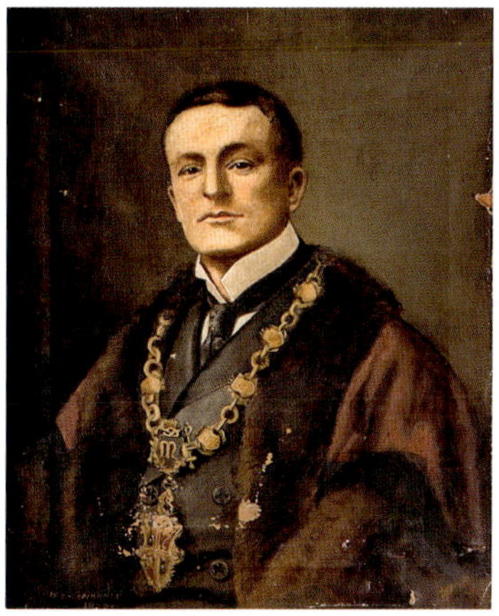

Sambrook, Elliott
Alderman William Bratt, JP, Electoral Mayor of Burslem, November 1898 1899
oil on canvas 54 x 43
1964.FA.893a

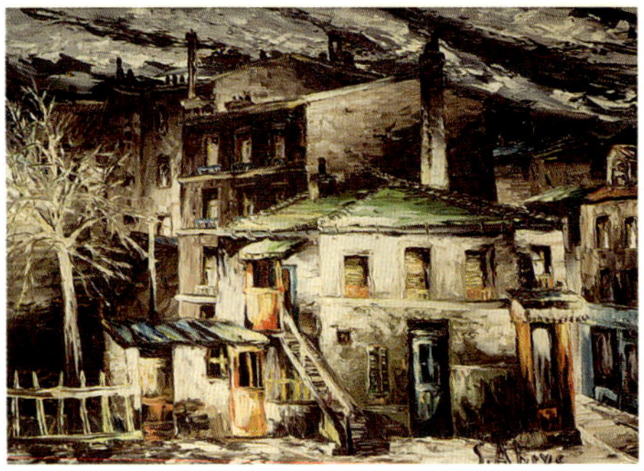

Schwarz-Abrys, Léon 1905–1990
Porte de Montreuil, Paris
oil on board 58 x 79
1958.FA.4

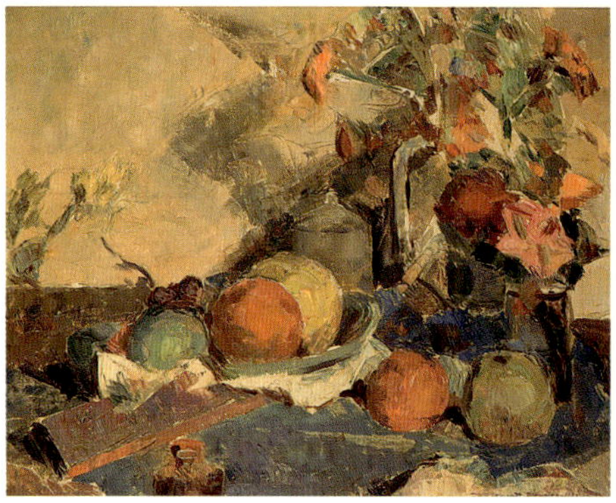

Seabrooke, Elliott 1886–1950
The Blue Cloth 1932
oil on canvas 47.5 x 58.5
1958.FA.61

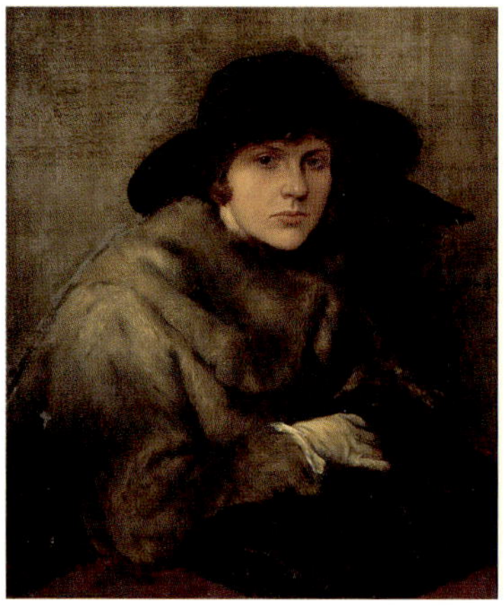

Shannon, Charles Haslewood 1863–1937
Lady in Grey Fur
oil on canvas 74 x 62
1950.FA.112

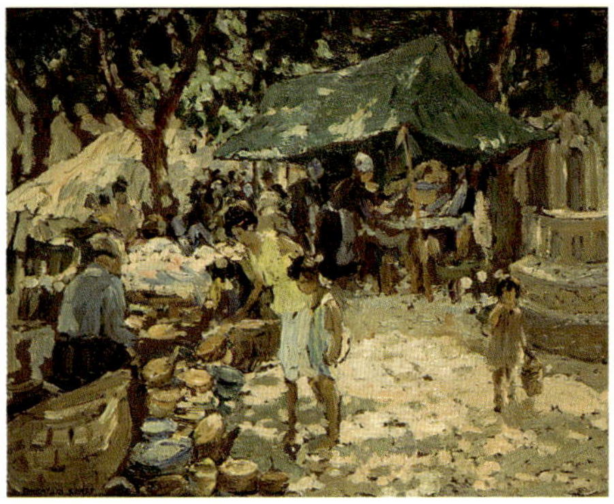

Sharp, Dorothea 1874–1955
The Market, Cassis
oil on canvas 48.5 x 59
1973.FA.17A(i)

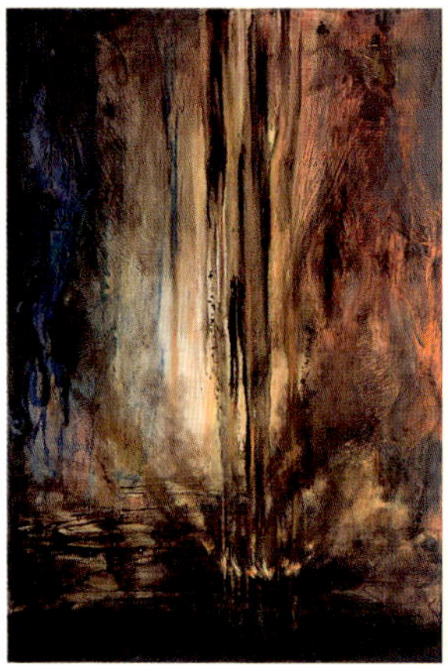

Shave, Terry b.1952
Fire Ring Series No.15
oil on canvas 182.5 x 122
1990.FA.9

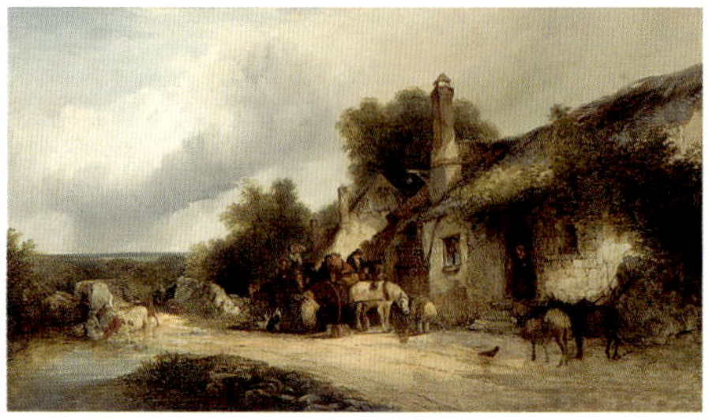

Shayer, William 1788–1879
The Blue Ball, North Devon
oil on canvas 73.5 x 124
1954.FA.139

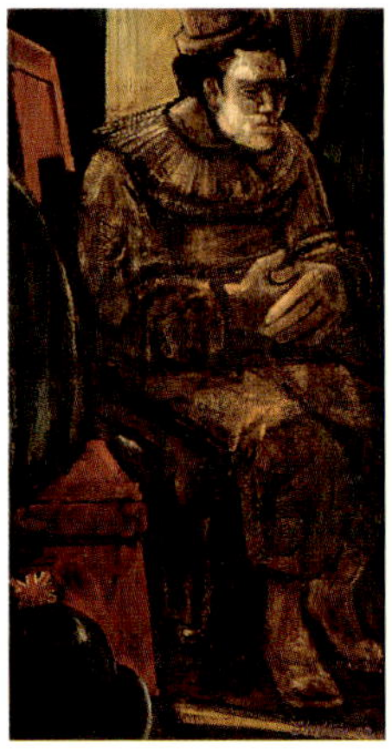

Shelton, John b.1923
Clown Resting 1962
oil on panel 82 x 42.5
1987.FA.37

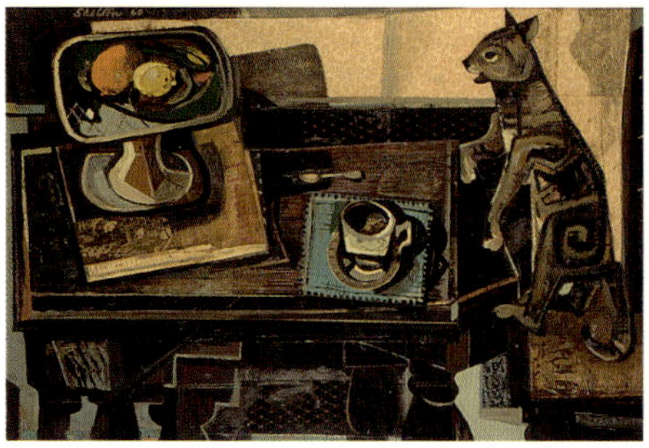

Shelton, John b.1923
Cat on a Table
mixed media on panel 66 x 94
1989.FA.22

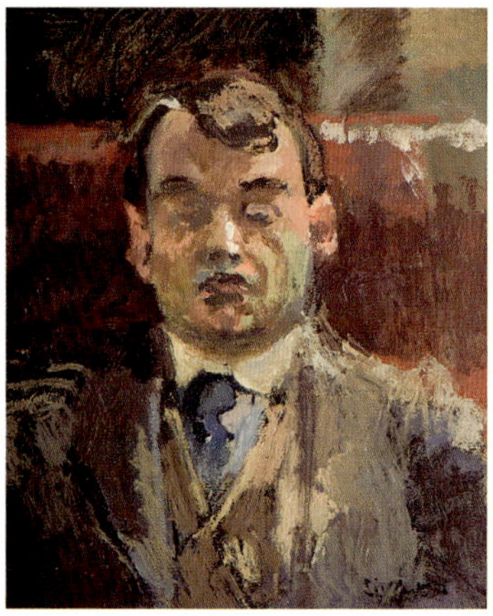

Sickert, Walter Richard 1860–1942
Maurice Asselin (1882–1947) 1915–1916
oil on canvas 49.5 x 39
1941.FA.493

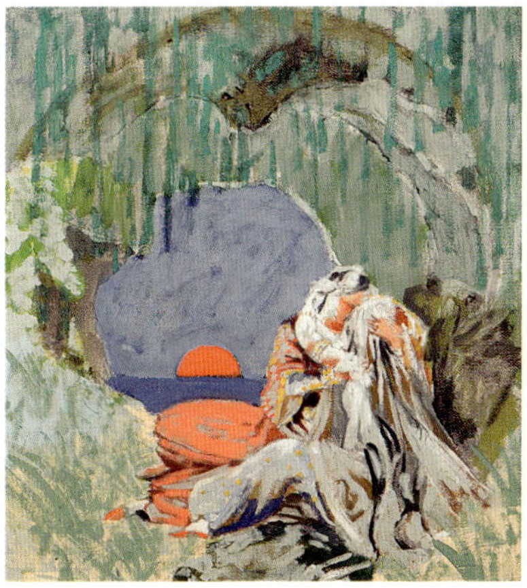

Sickert, Walter Richard 1860–1942
Don Juan and Haidee (Idyll) (after Gilbert) c.1934
oil on canvas 55 x 49.5
1965.FA.37A

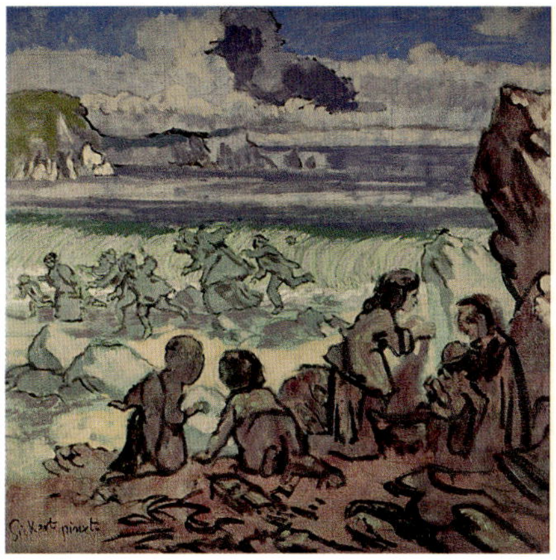

Sickert, Walter Richard 1860–1942
The Wave
oil on canvas 73 x 73
1956.FA.3

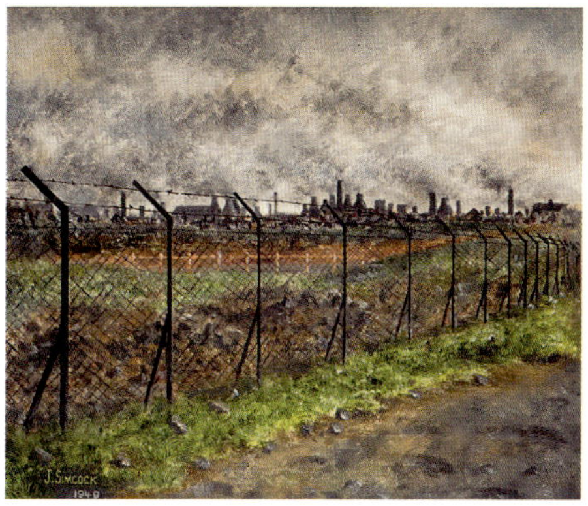

Simcock, Jack b.1929
From a Back Lane 1949
oil on paper 25.5 x 30
1950.FA.7

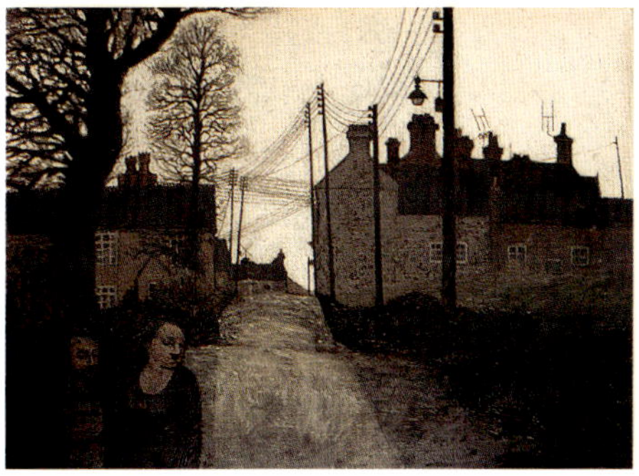

Simcock, Jack b.1929
The Rose and Crown 1956
oil on panel 73 x 99
1957.FA.28

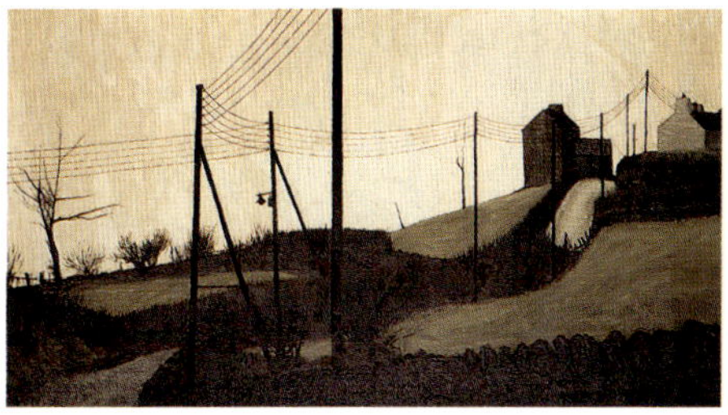

Simcock, Jack b.1929
Biddulph Moor 1957
oil on board 52.5 x 90
1957.FA.27

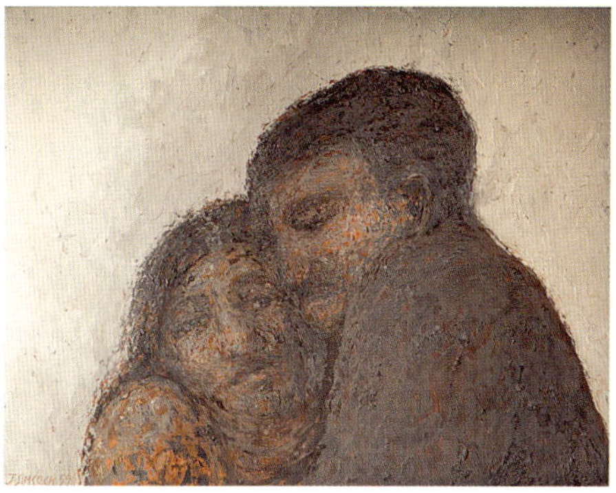

Simcock, Jack b.1929
Two Figures 1959
oil on panel 37 x 47
1987.FA.35

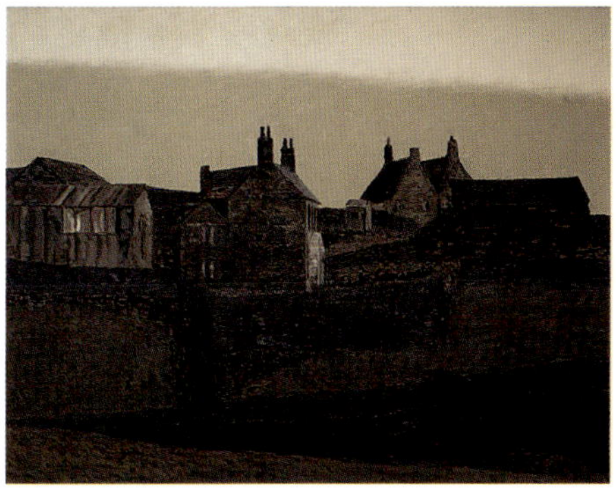

Simcock, Jack b.1929
Manor Farm 1960
oil on panel 60 x 74
1960.FA.122

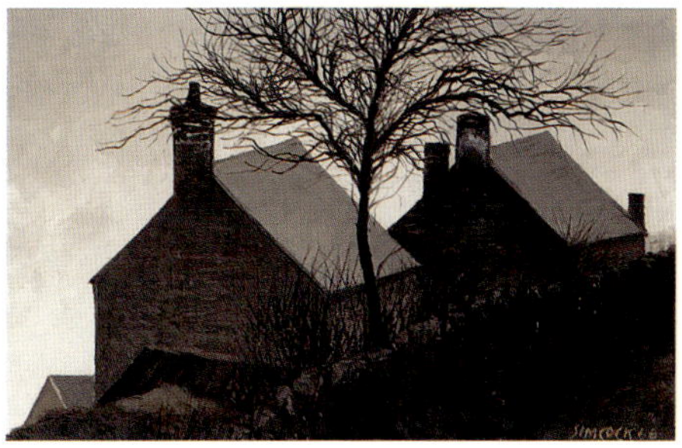

Simcock, Jack b.1929
Houses 1966
oil on panel 17 x 28
1977.FA.66

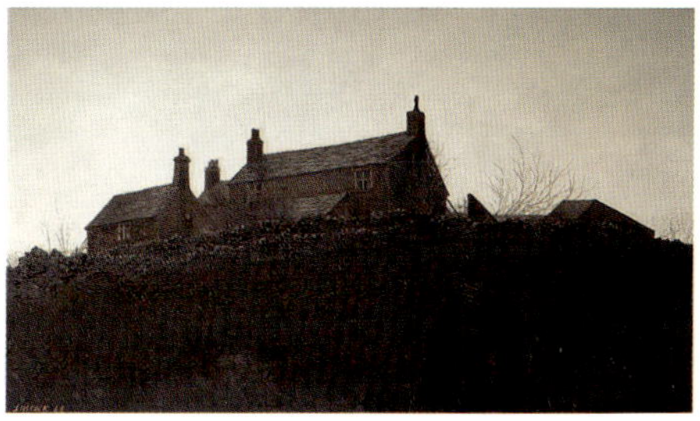

Simcock, Jack b.1929
Cottages and Head 1968
oil on board 43 x 64
1973.FA.11a

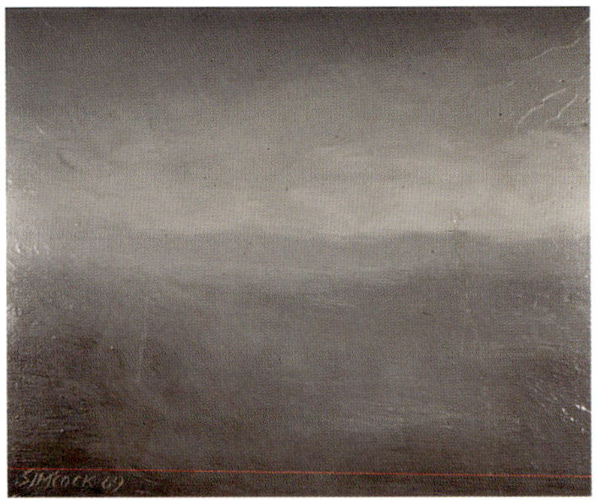

Simcock, Jack b.1929
Landscape 1969
oil on panel 13 x 16
1977.FA.69

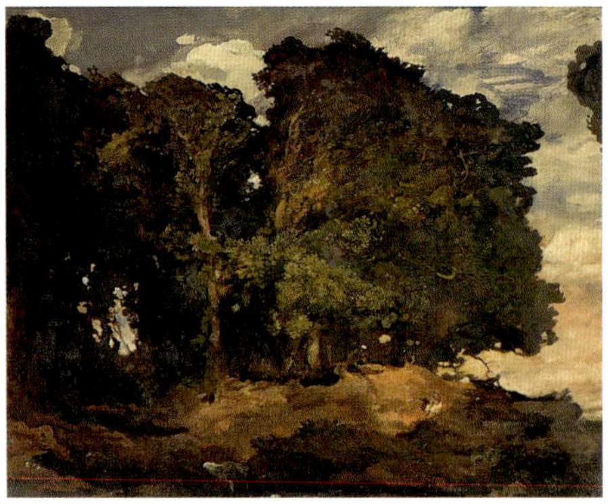

Sims, Charles 1873–1928
Country Scene, Forest Trees
oil on canvas 61 x 76
1927.FA.11

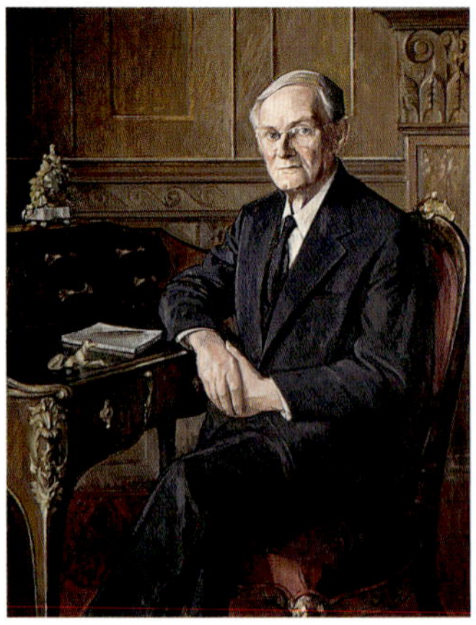

Skinner, John b.1953
Ernest James Dalzell Warrillow, MBE, FSA, Photographer and Historian (1909–2000) 1977
oil on panel 79 x 59
1978.FA.6

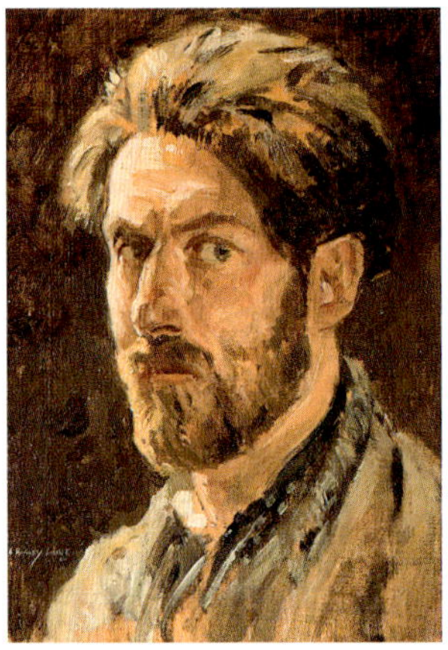

Smart, Rowley 1887–1934
Self Portrait 1922
oil on panel 34 x 23.5
1956.FA.32

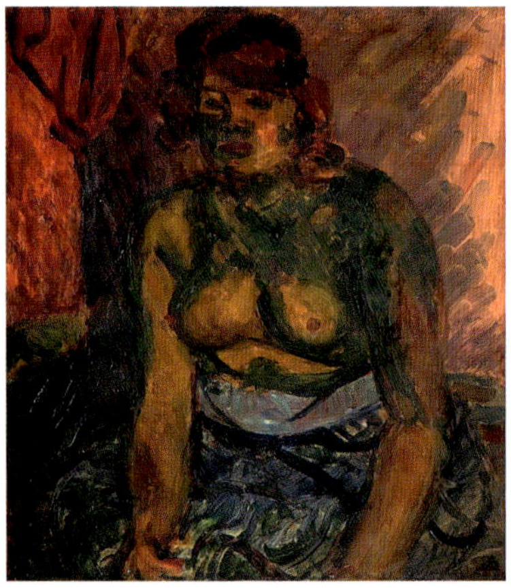

Smith, Matthew Arnold Bracy 1879–1959
Seated Nude 1923
oil on canvas 63.5 x 54
1979.FA.12

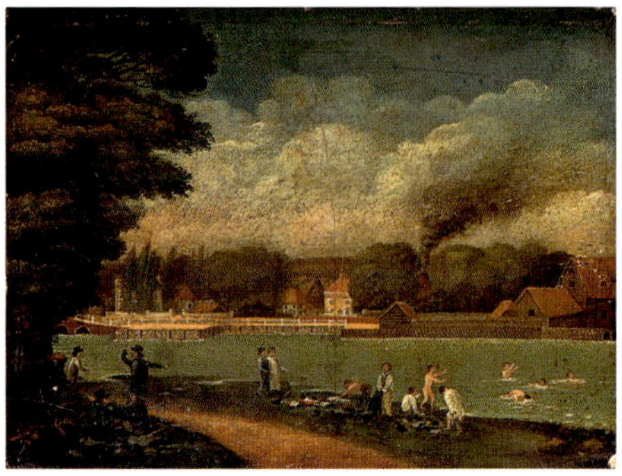

Smith, T.
View of Pottery, Fareham
oil on panel 11.4 x 15.9
1942.FA.592

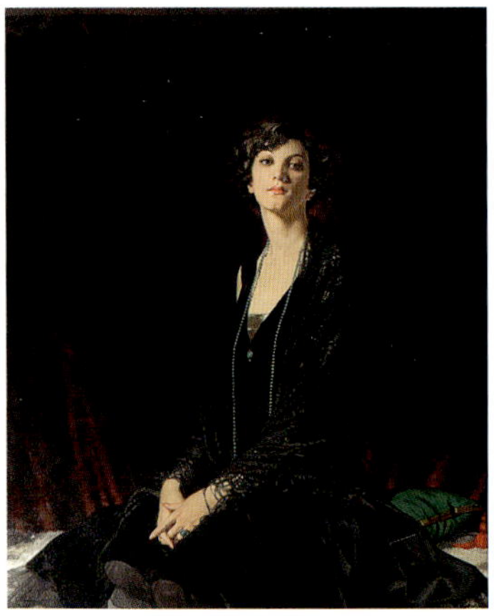

Somerville, Howard 1873–1952
Norah
oil on canvas 124.5 x 100
1956.FA.52

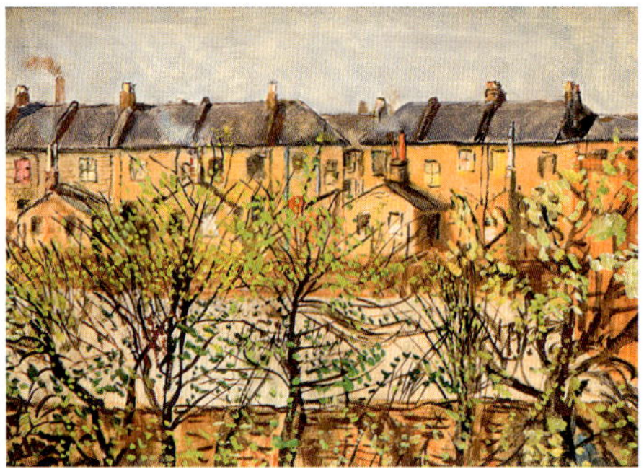

Spear, Ruskin 1911–1990
Spring in Hammersmith
oil on panel 40 x 52
1950.FA.100

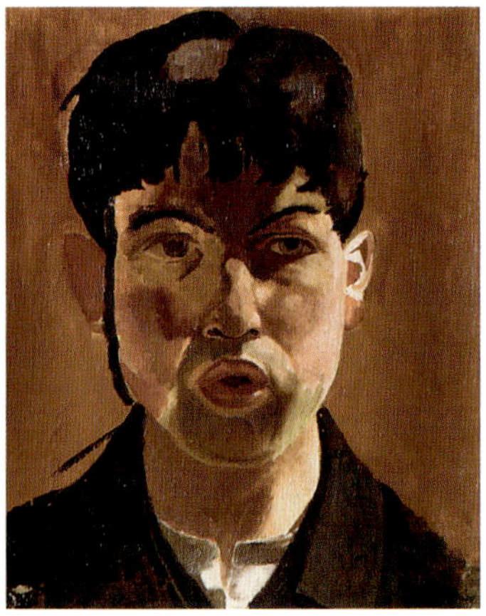

Spencer, Gilbert 1893–1979
Self Portrait 1914
oil on canvas 50 x 39.5
1952.FA.51

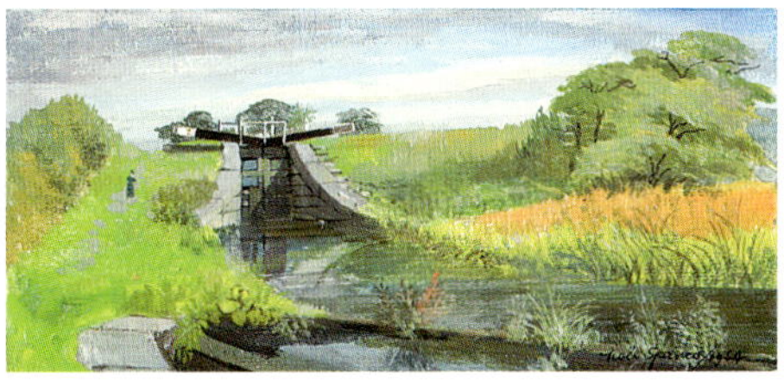

Spencer, Noël 1900–1986
Landscape with Lock Gates 1964
tempera on panel 12.5 x 26.5
1980.FA.19

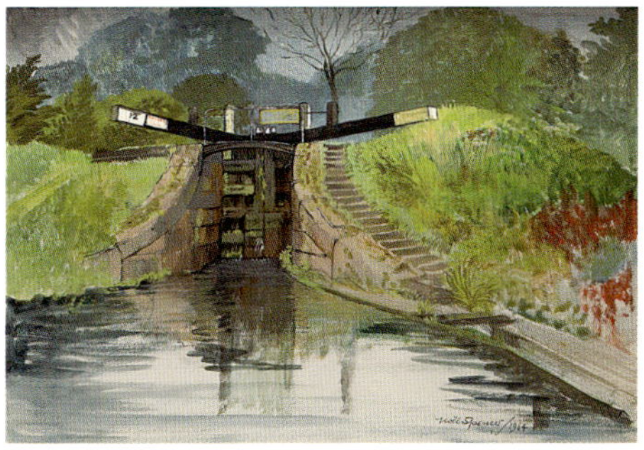

Spencer, Noël 1900–1986
Landscape with Lock Gates 1964
tempera on panel 26.5 x 38
1980.FA.22

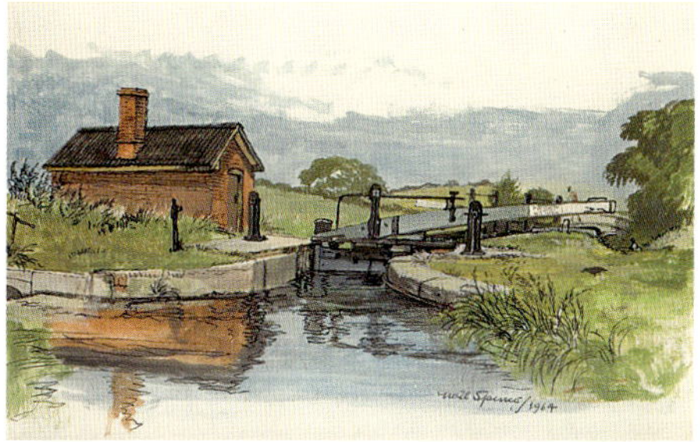

Spencer, Noël 1900–1986
Landscape with Lock Gates and Building 1964
tempera, pen & ink on paper 20.5 x 28
1980.FA.21

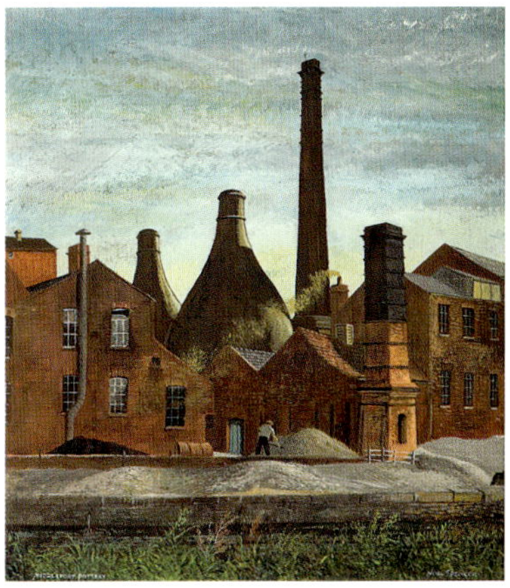

Spencer, Noël 1900–1986
Middleport Pottery 1964
tempera on paper 42 x 39
1980.FA.15

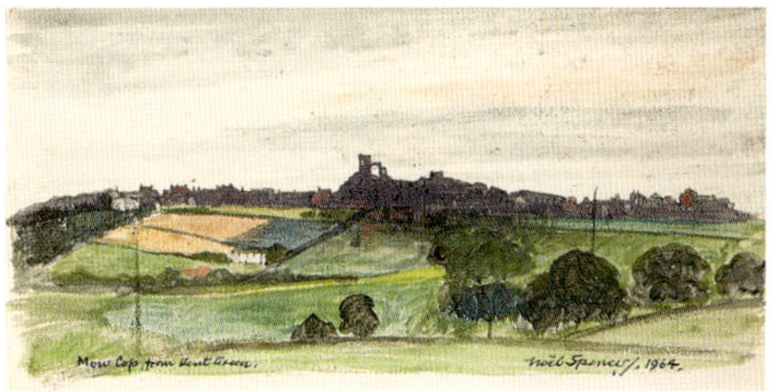

Spencer, Noël 1900–1986
Mow Cop from Kent Green 1964
tempera on panel 14 x 26.5
1980.FA.20

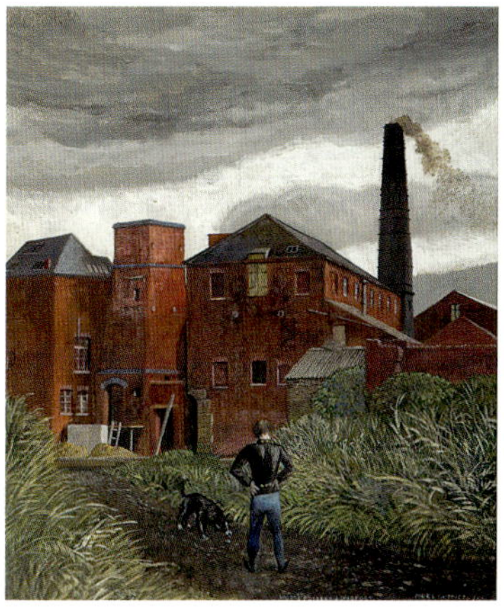

Spencer, Noël 1900–1986
Wood's Pottery, Longport 1964
tempera on paper 44 x 37
1980.FA.16

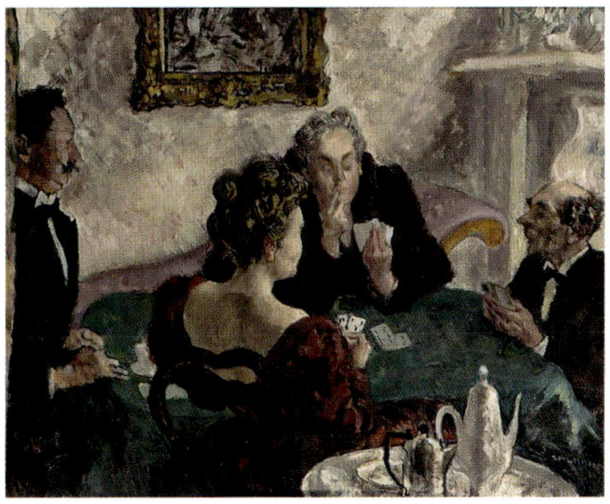

Spurrier, Steven 1878–1961
The Card Game c.1948
oil on canvas 49 x 60
1948.FA.879

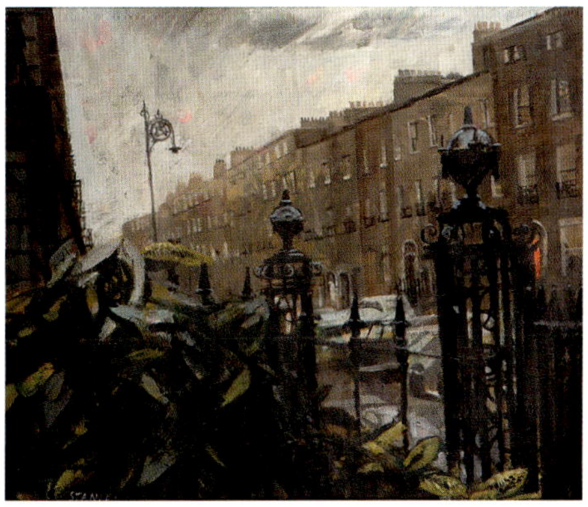

Stanley, Jacqueline b.1928
Warrington Square, Dublin
oil on panel 43.5 x 49
1969.FA.6A

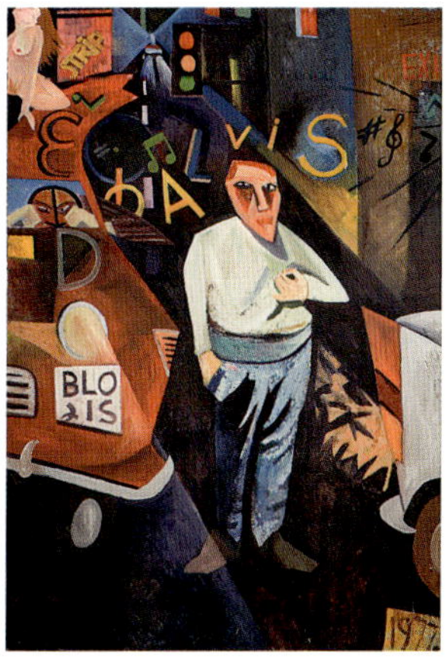

Stanyer, Peter b.1952
Lenny Hackett 1977
oil on panel 182 x 121.5
1979.FA.8

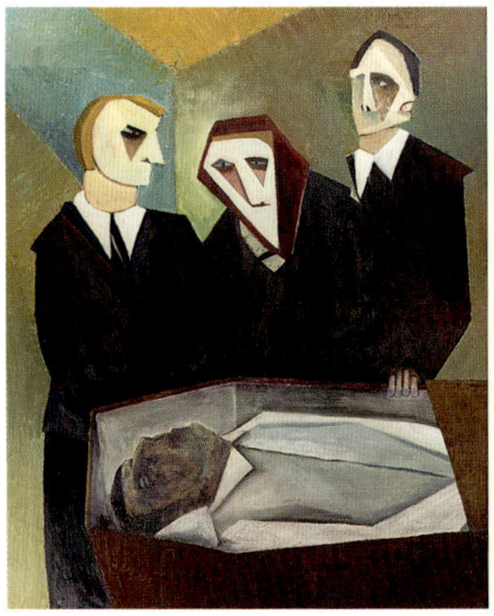

Stanyer, Peter b.1952
The Chapel of Rest, the Death of My Father
oil on panel 112 x 90
1979.FA.9

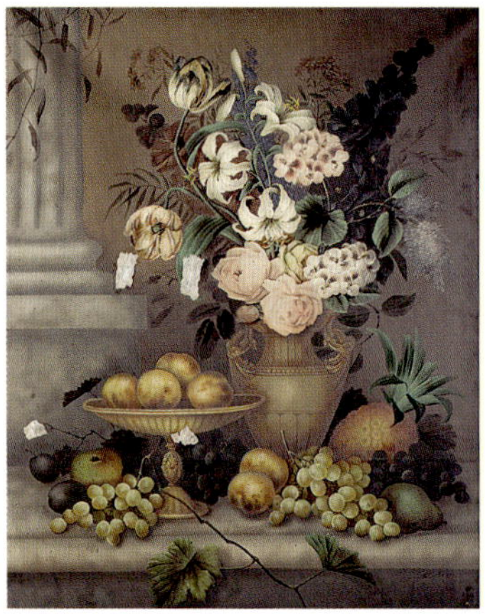

Steele, Edwin 1837–1898
Still Life of Flowers and Fruit 1896
oil on canvas 91 x 71
1950.FA.97

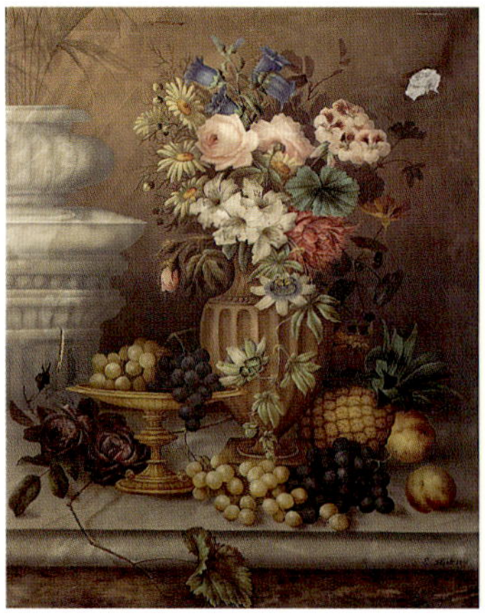

Steele, Edwin 1837–1898
Still Life of Flowers and Fruit 1896
oil on canvas 90 x 70
1950.FA.98

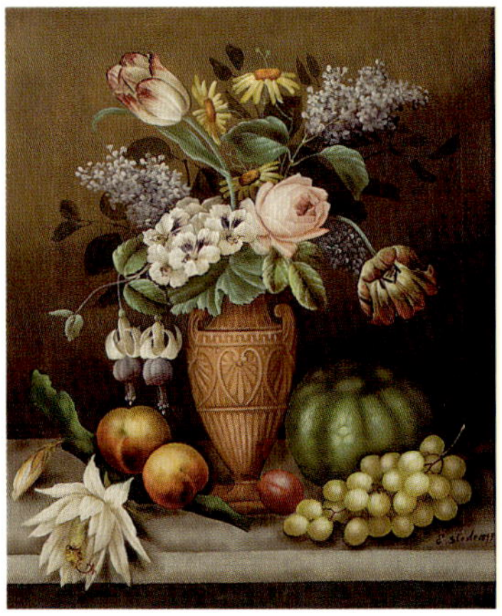

Steele, Edwin 1837–1898
Still Life of Flowers and Fruit 1899
oil on canvas 60 x 49.5
1962.FA.34

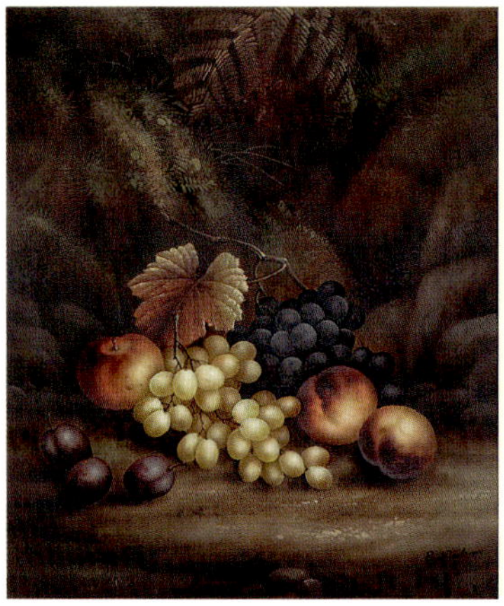

Steele, Edwin 1837–1898
Still Life of Fruit 1899
oil on canvas 57 x 48
1962.FA.32

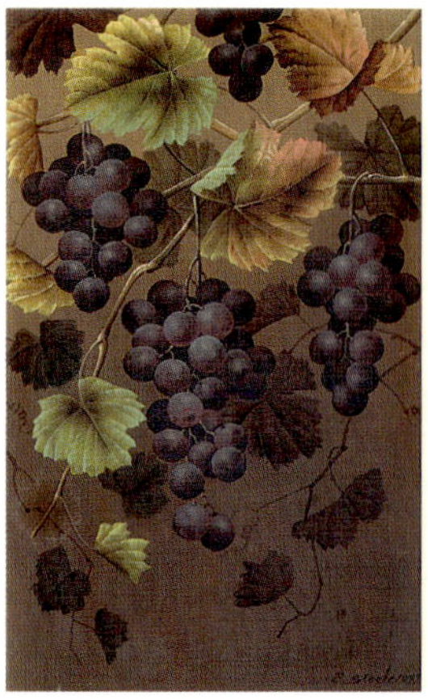

Steele, Edwin 1837–1898
Still Life of Fruit 1899
oil on canvas 46.5 x 28
1962.FA.33

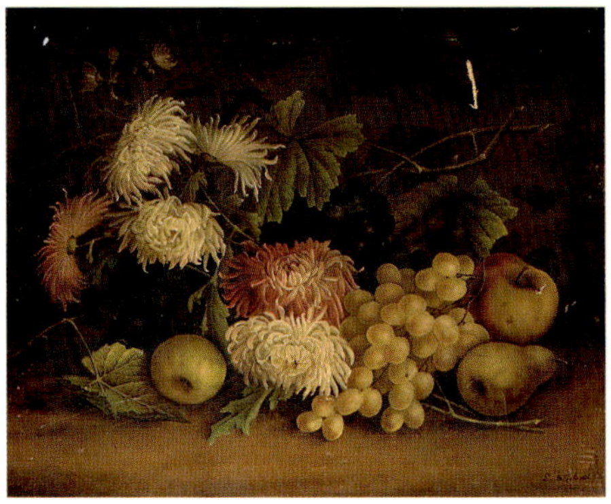

Steele, Edwin 1837–1898
Still Life of Flowers and Fruit 1901
oil on canvas 51 x 61
1958.FA.100

Steele, Edwin 1837–1898
Still Life of Flowers and Bird's Nest
oil on panel 28 x 38
1950.FA.95

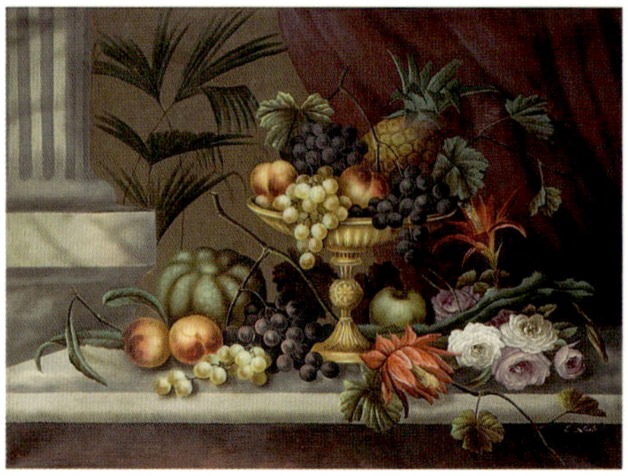

Steele, Edwin 1837–1898
Still Life of Flowers and Fruit
oil on canvas 68 x 88
1950.FA.96

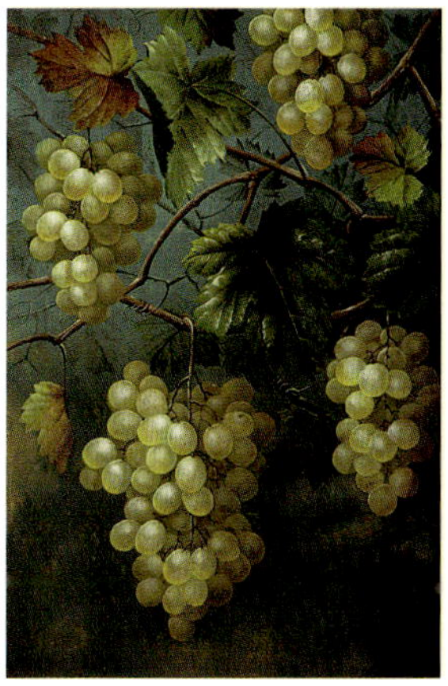

Steele, Edwin 1837–1898
Still Life of Grapes and Vine
oil on canvas 48 x 32
1954.FA.125

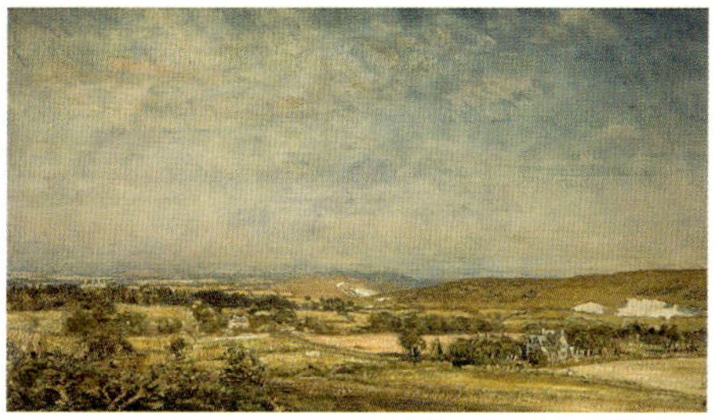

Steer, Philip Wilson 1860–1942
Freshwater Bay 1919
oil on canvas 43 x 74.5
1950.FA.110

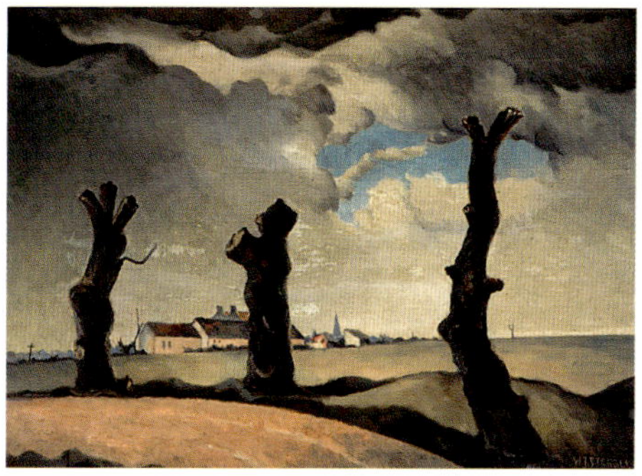

Steggles, Walter James 1908–1997
Three Trees
oil on panel 22 x 31
1945.FA.659

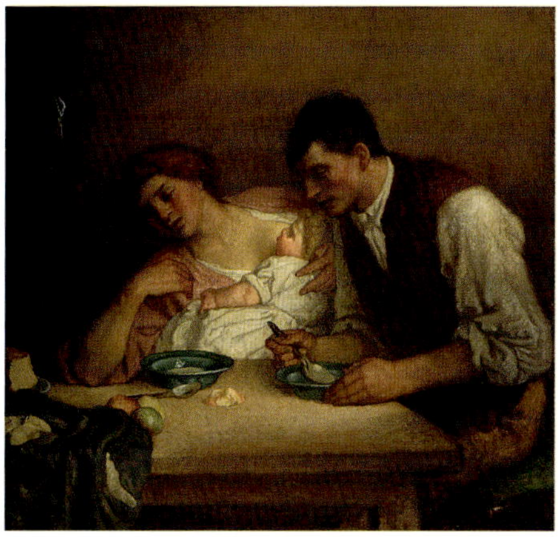

Strang, William 1859–1921
Supper Time 1905
oil on canvas 109 x 115
1924.FA.28

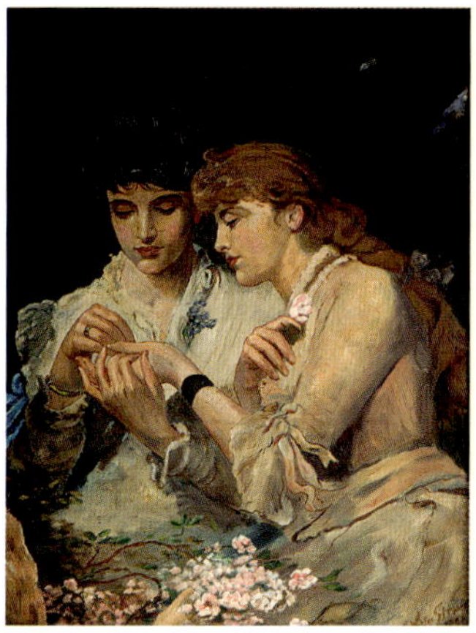

Strange, A. Victor
A Thorn amidst Roses
oil on canvas 56 x 43
1954.FA.111

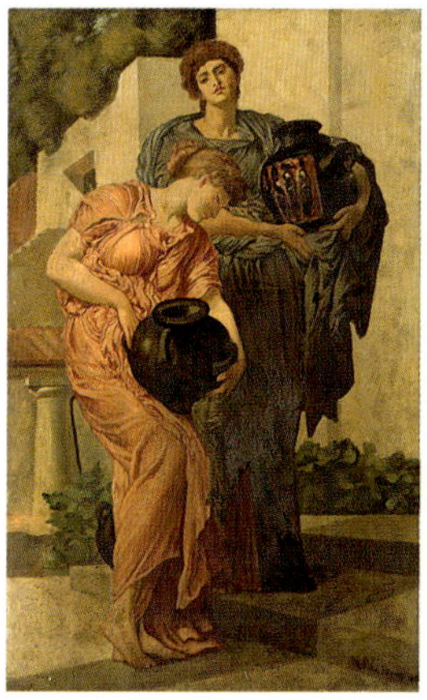

Strange, A. Victor
Classical Scene
oil on canvas 92 x 56
PCF35

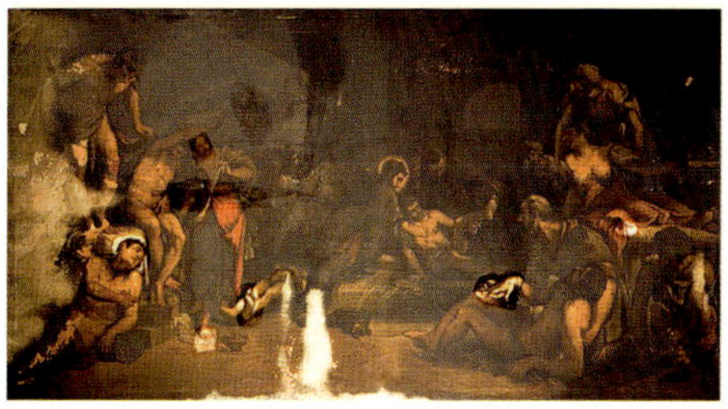

Strange, A. Victor
St Roch Curing the Plague (after Jacopo Tintoretto)
oil on canvas 90 x 162
1954.FA.202

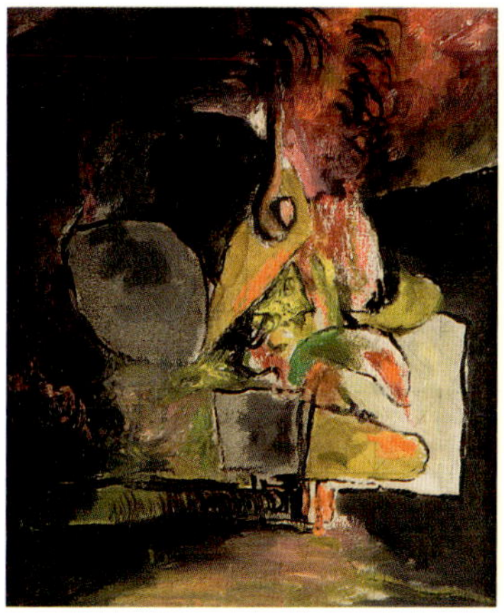

Sutherland, Graham Vivian 1903–1980
Foundry, Ladle Feeding Furnace c.1941
oil on canvas 32 x 26
1947.FA.782

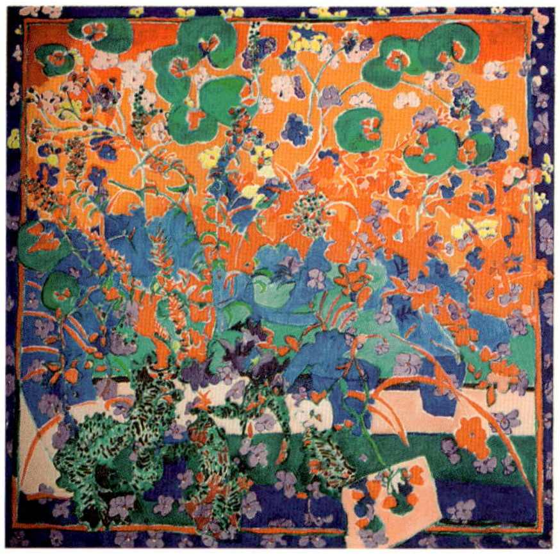

Sutton, Philip b.1928
'Shall I compare thee to a summer's day?' 1988
oil on canvas 128 x 128
PCF36

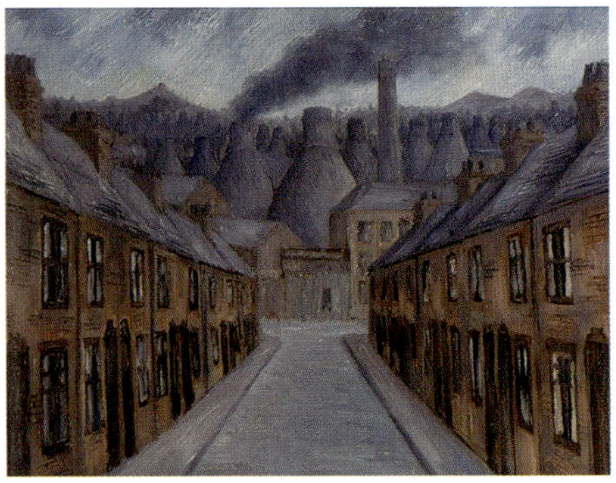

Tait, Jessie b.1928
Home and Factory
oil on canvas 33.5 x 44
1950.FA.11

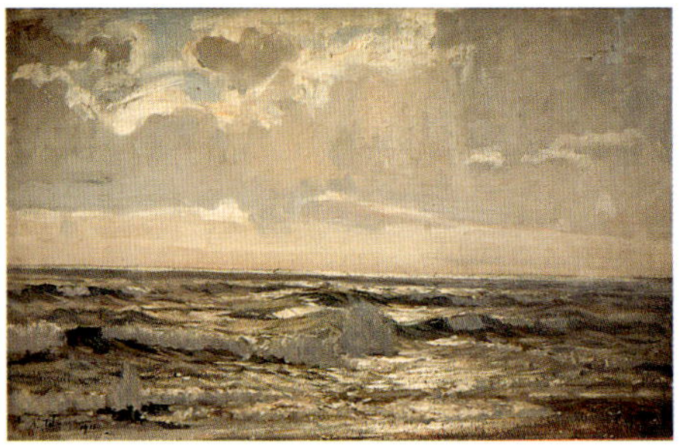

Talmage, Algernon Mayow 1871–1939
Break in the Storm 1917
oil on canvas 82 x 120
1938.FA.338

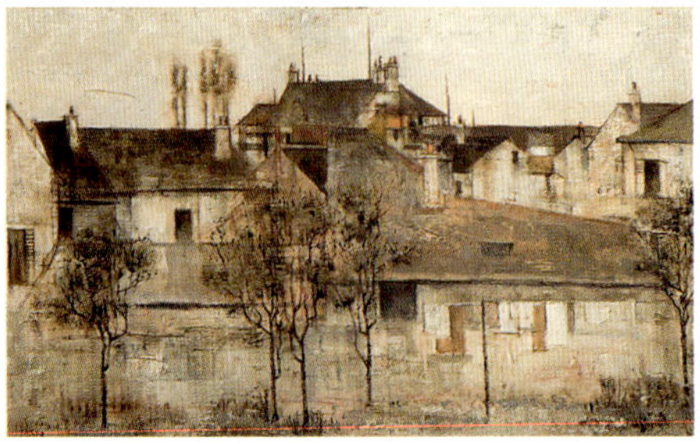

Taylor, James Spence b.1921
Les toits
oil on panel 58 x 89
1956.FA.5

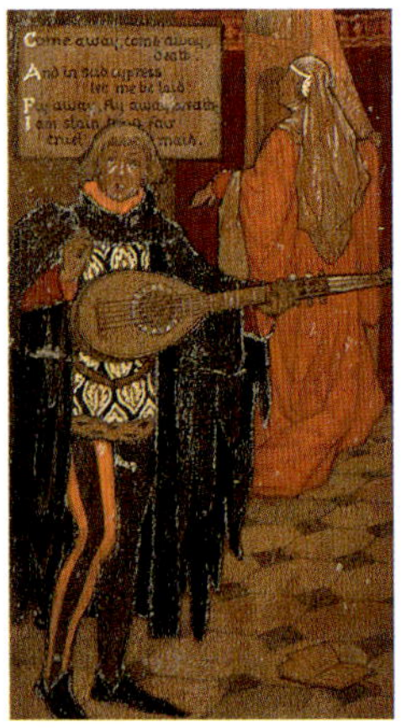

Theaker, Harry George 1873–1954
Minstrel
oil on board 23 x 13
PCF37

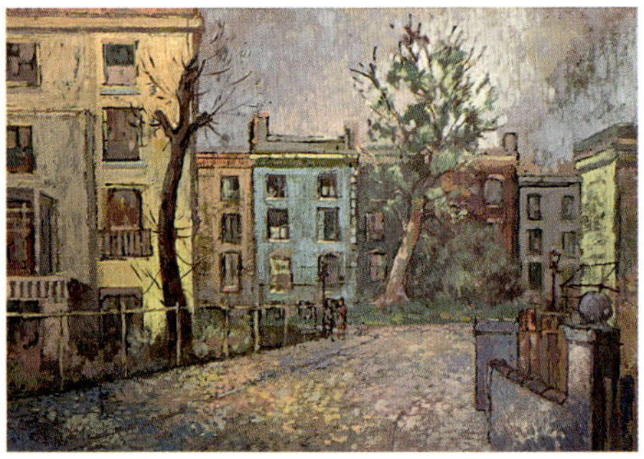

Thompson, Philip
Bayswater
oil on canvas 70 x 98
1956.FA.51

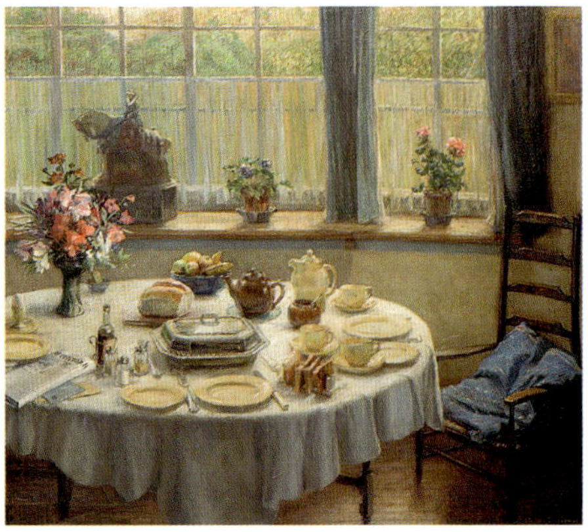

Thorogood, Stanley 1873–1953
Breakfast Is Ready c.1919
oil on canvas 51 x 56
1993.FA.1

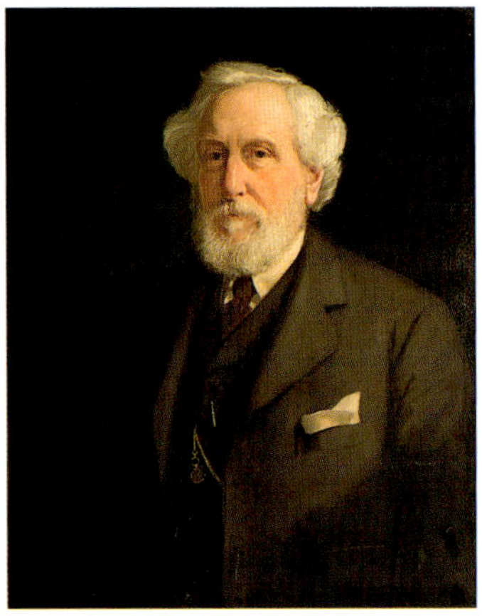

Tickner, H.
Dr Spunton 1919
oil on canvas 76 x 63
PCF38

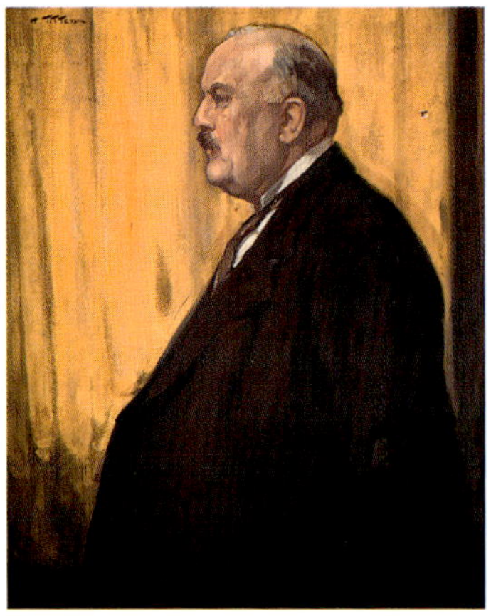

Tittensor, Harry 1887–1942
Alderman John Hughes
oil on canvas 86.5 x 52
1950.FA.115

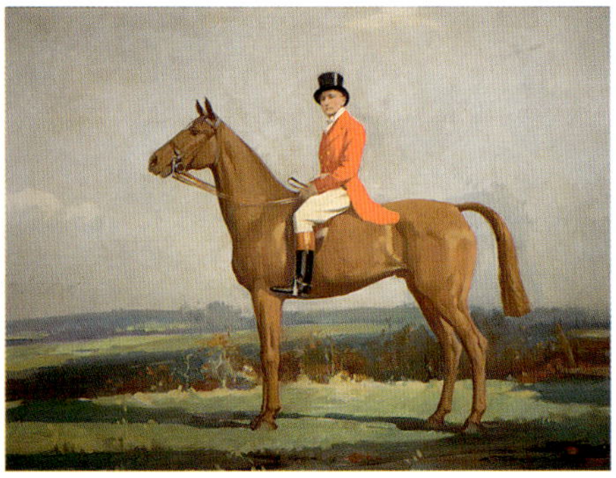

Tittensor, Harry 1887–1942
Man on a Horse
oil on canvas 84 x 111
PCF39

Facing page: Borsky, Jiri, b.1945, *The Auction* (detail), 1983, University of Keele Art Collection, (p. 39)

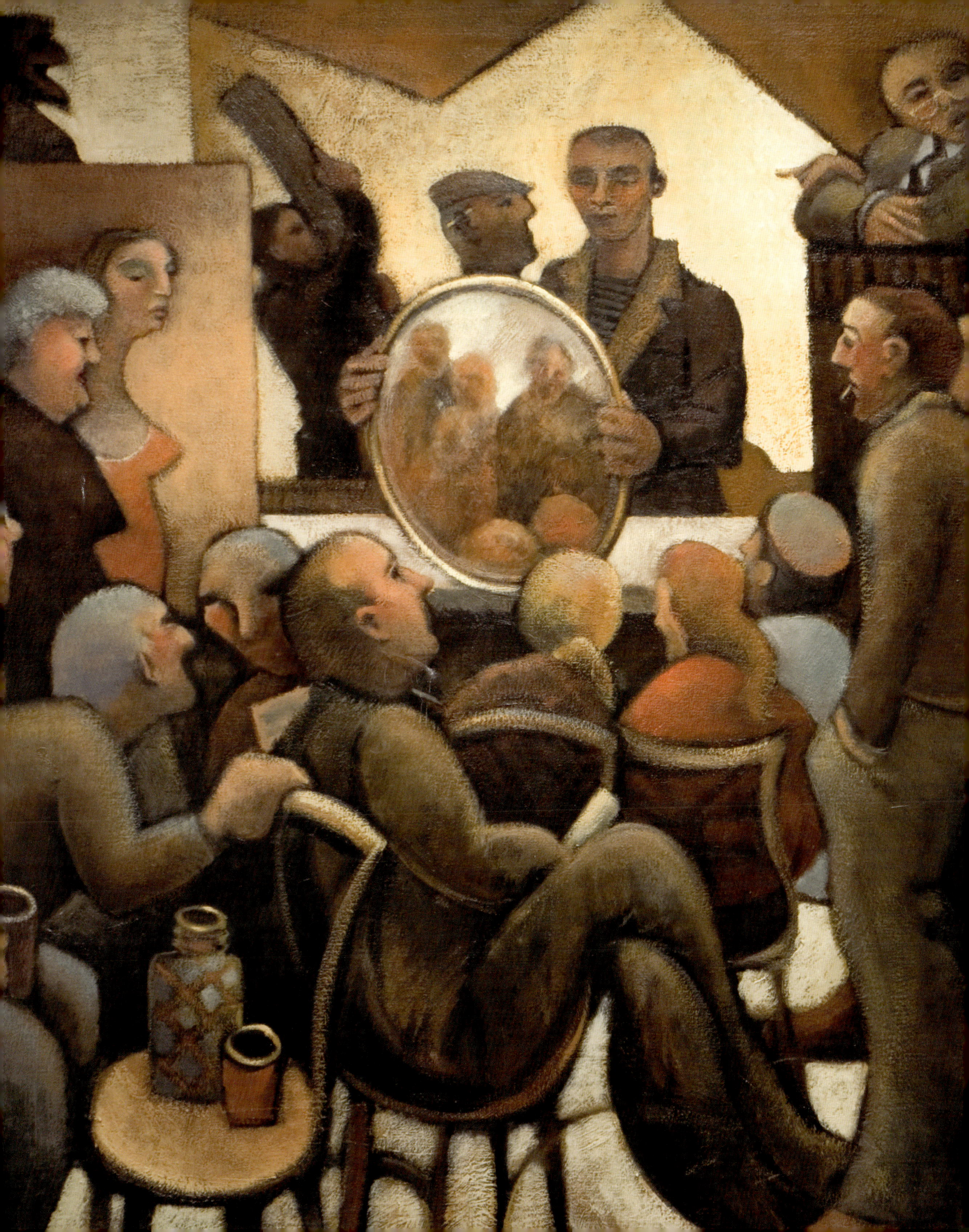

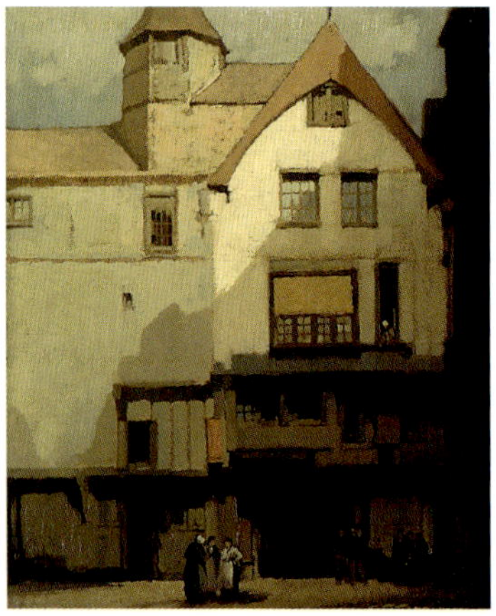

Tittensor, Harry 1887–1942
Place des Alpes
oil on canvas 57 x 46
1941.FA.495

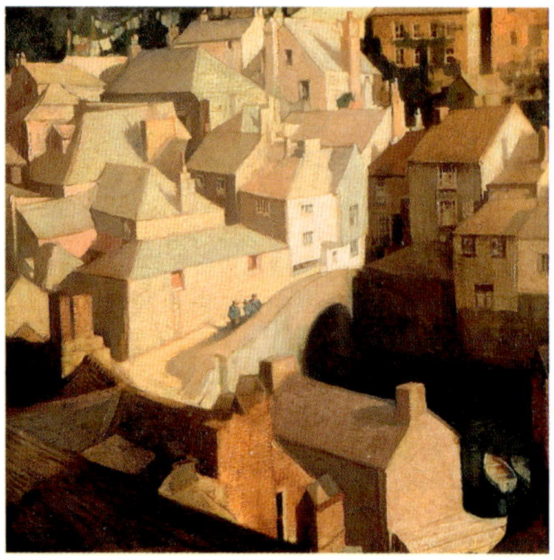

Tittensor, Harry 1887–1942
Polperro
oil on canvas 53 x 53
1963.FA.122

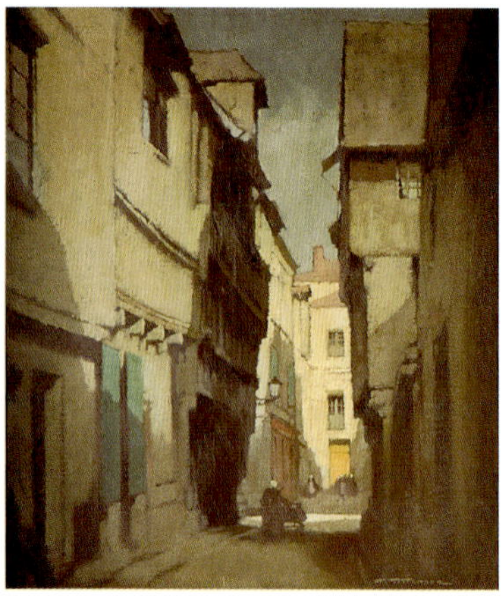

Tittensor, Harry 1887–1942
Rue de la Paix, Lisieux
oil on panel 57 x 47
1942.FA.567

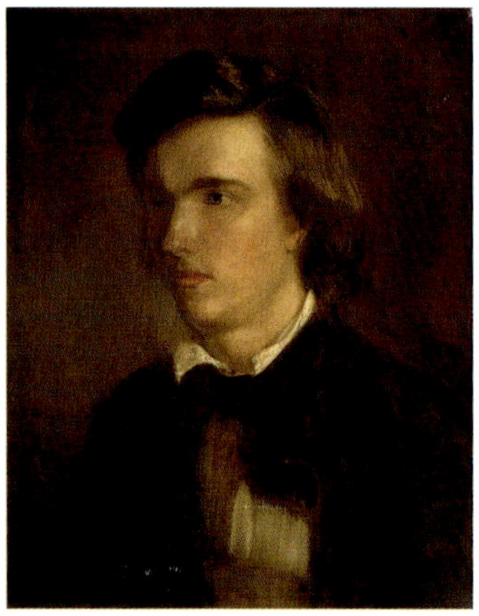

Toft, Charles 1831–1909
Self Portrait c.1858
oil on canvas 51.5 x 42
1959.FA.35

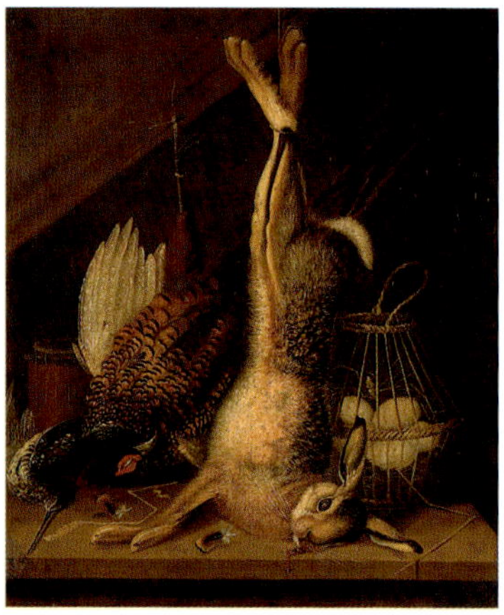

Toft, Charles 1831–1909
Still Life, Dead Game
oil on canvas 73.5 x 61
1961.FA.129

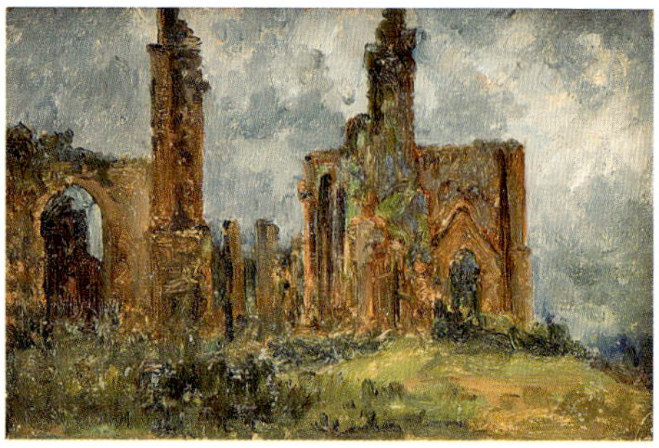

Toft, J. Alfonso 1866–1964
Finchale Priory 1912
oil on card 16 x 24.3
1967.FA.12A.2

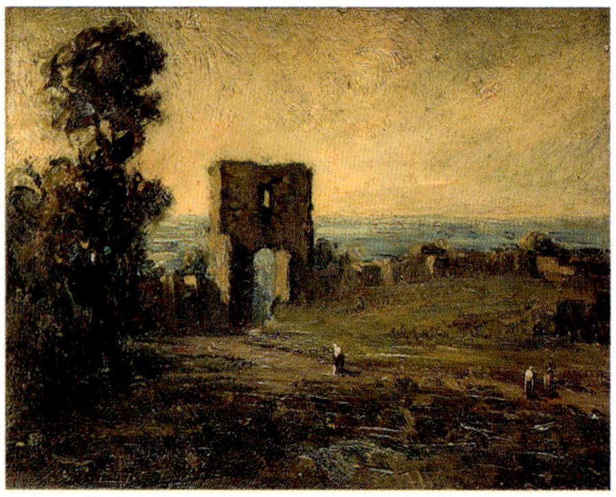

Toft, J. Alfonso 1866–1964
A Castle Gate and Wall
oil on panel 21.5 x 27
1967.FA.12A.4

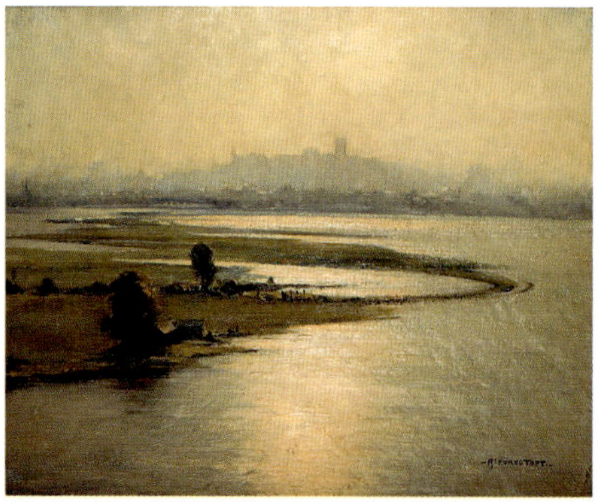

Toft, J. Alfonso 1866–1964
Alnwick Castle
oil on canvas 51 x 61
1964.FA.879A

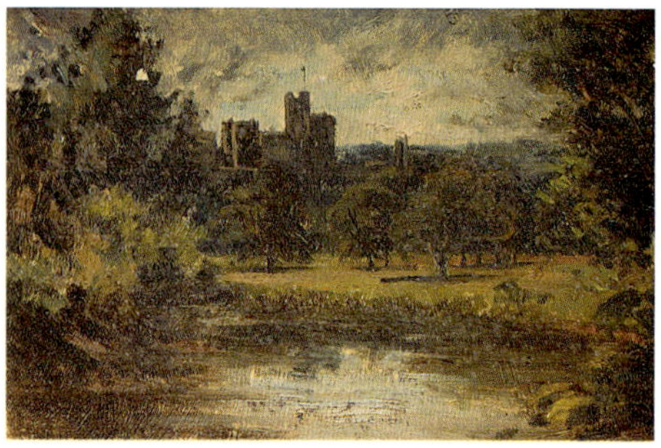

Toft, J. Alfonso 1866–1964
Alnwick Castle
oil on panel 15.8 x 24
1967.FA.12A.17

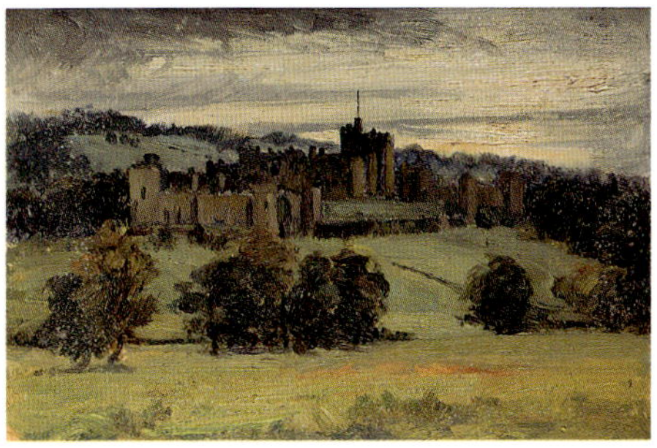

Toft, J. Alfonso 1866–1964
Alnwick Castle
oil on panel 16 x 24
1967.FA.12A.18

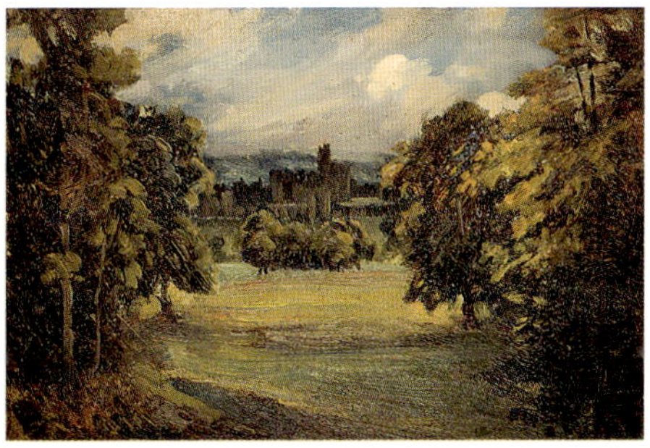

Toft, J. Alfonso 1866–1964
Alnwick Castle
oil on panel 16 x 24
1967.FA.12A.41

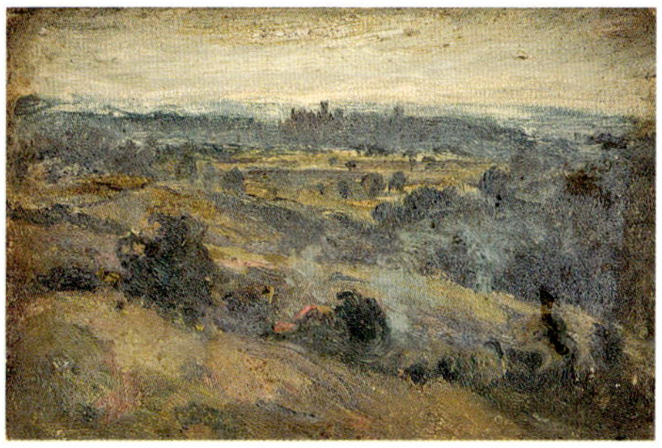

Toft, J. Alfonso 1866–1964
Alton Towers
oil on card 15.3 x 23.5
1967.FA.12A.43

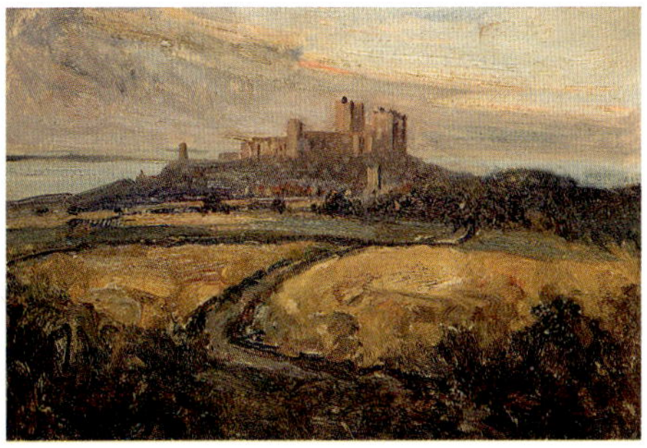

Toft, J. Alfonso 1866–1964
Bamburgh Castle
oil on panel 16 x 24 (E)
1967.FA.12A.42

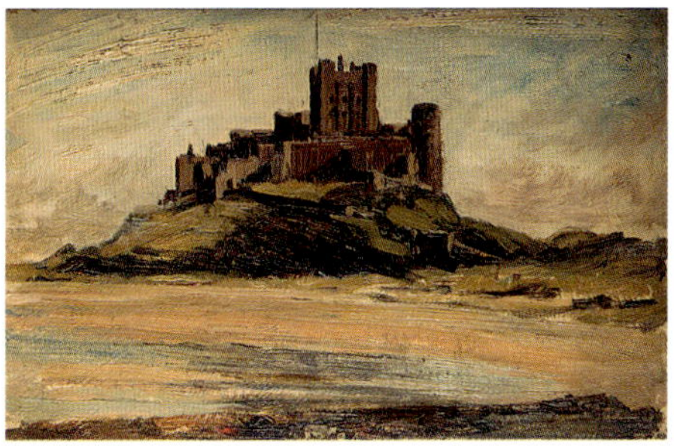

Toft, J. Alfonso 1866–1964
Bamburgh Castle
oil on panel 16 x 24 (E)
1967.FA.12A.47

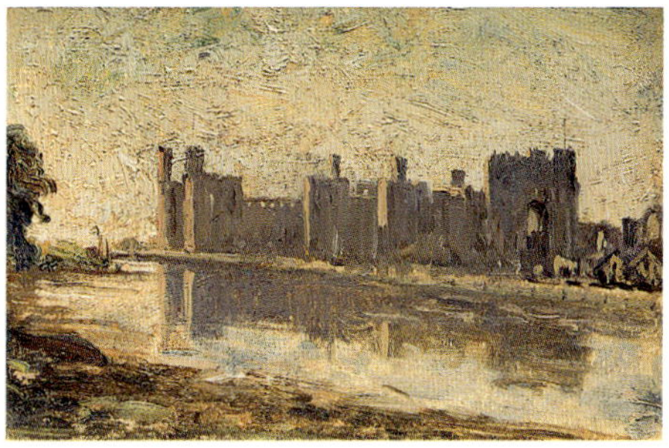

Toft, J. Alfonso 1866–1964
Caernarvon Castle
oil on panel 15.5 x 24
1967.FA.12A.38

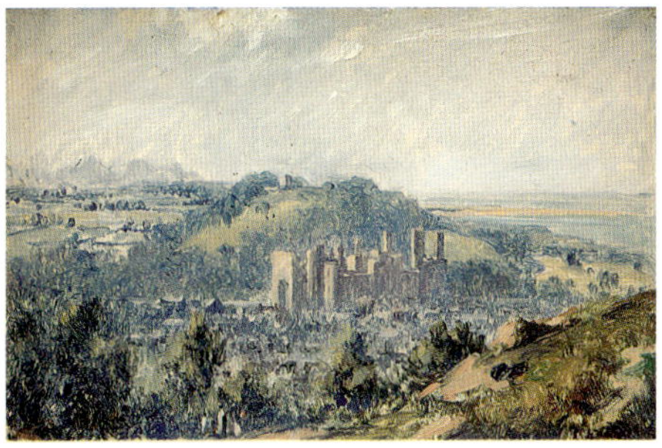

Toft, J. Alfonso 1866–1964
Caernarvon Castle from Twit Hill
oil on panel 15.5 x 24
1967.FA.12A.37

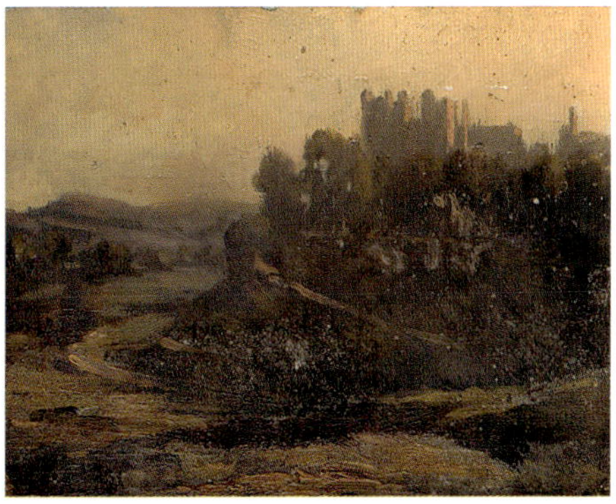

Toft, J. Alfonso 1866–1964
Castle on a Hill
oil on card 20.3 x 25.5
1967.FA.12A.49

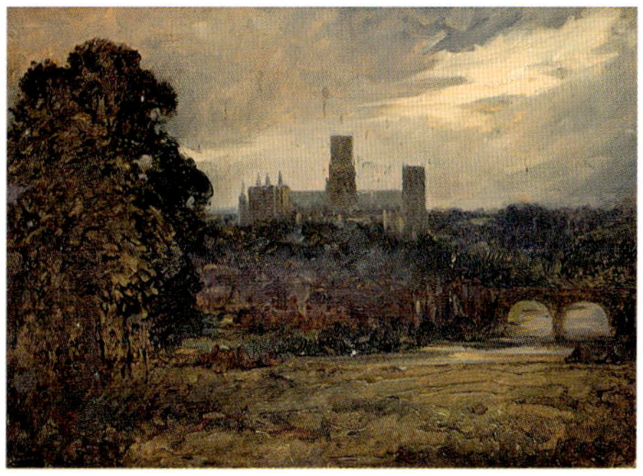

Toft, J. Alfonso 1866–1964
Castle, River and Viaduct
oil on panel 26.5 x 35.5
1967.FA.12A.15

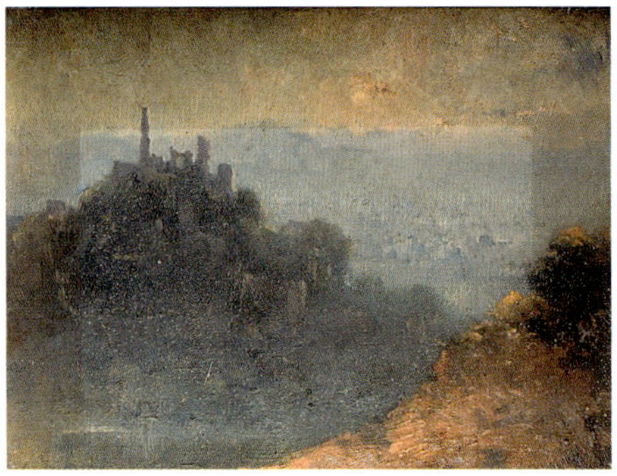

Toft, J. Alfonso 1866–1964
Castle Ruins in Mist
oil on card 25 x 33
1967.FA.12A.9

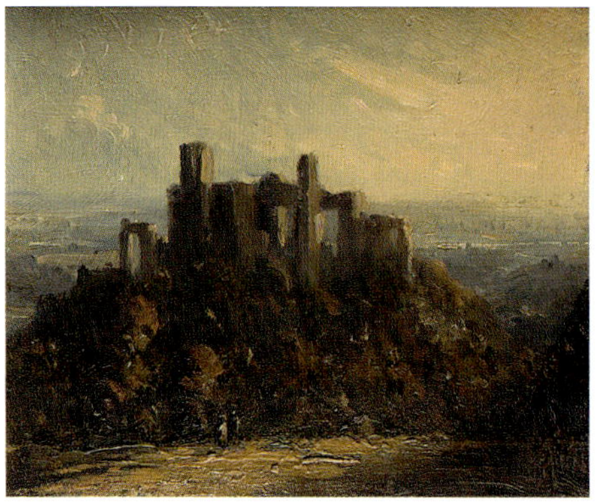

Toft, J. Alfonso 1866–1964
Castle Ruins on a Mound
oil on panel 23.5 x 28
1967.FA.12A.6

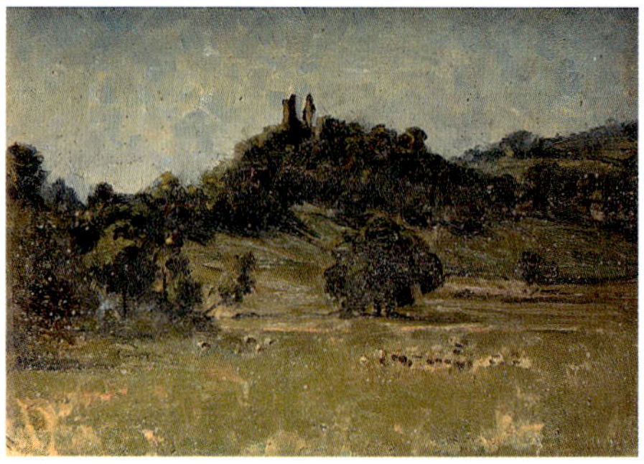

Toft, J. Alfonso 1866–1964
Castle Ruins on a Mound (possibly Wigmore Castle)
oil on card 25.4 x 35.4
1967.FA.12A.8

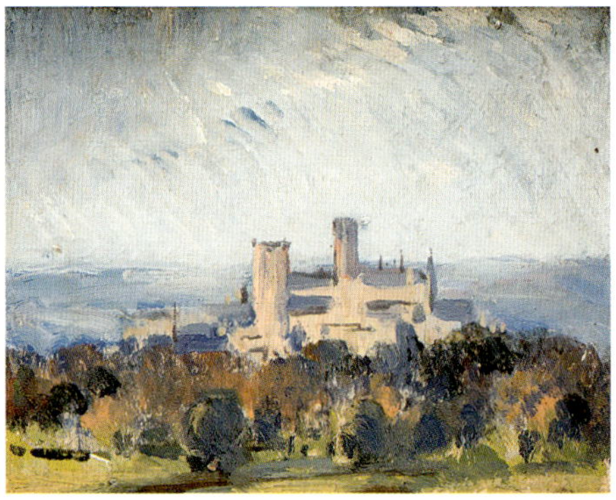

Toft, J. Alfonso 1866–1964
Castle Scene
oil on panel 12.8 x 21.5
1967.FA.12A.48

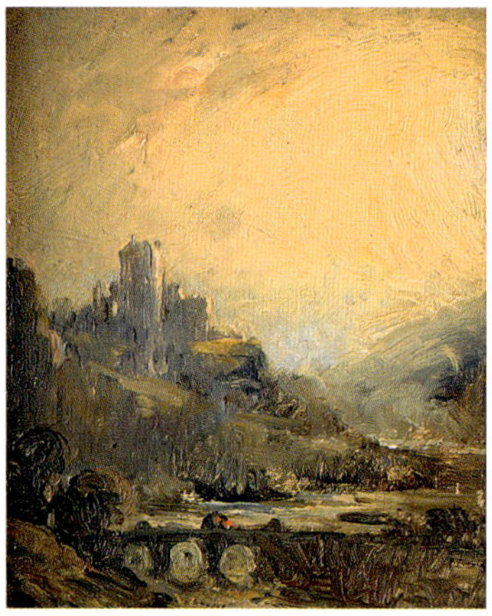

Toft, J. Alfonso 1866–1964
Castle with Yellow Sky
oil on card 22 x 17.6
1967.FA.12A.33

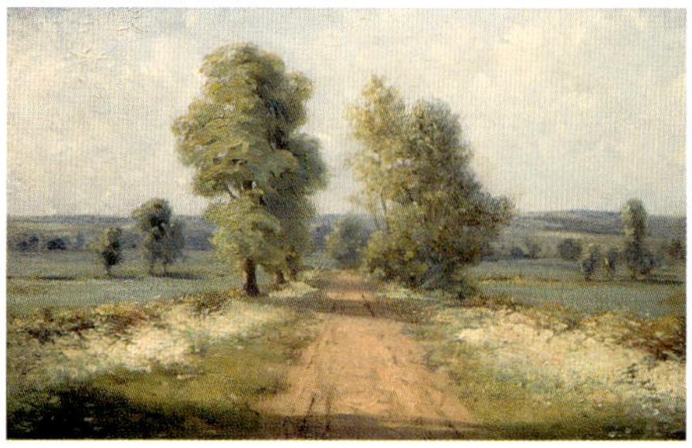

Toft, J. Alfonso 1866–1964
Country Lane
oil on canvas 45 x 60
1964.FA.878

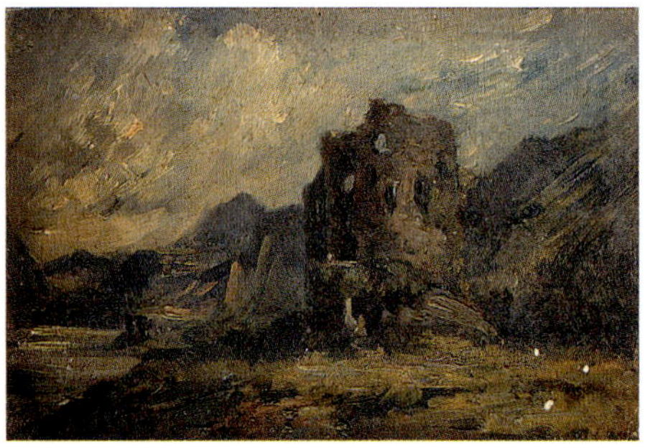

Toft, J. Alfonso 1866–1964
Dolbadarn Castle
oil on panel 17 x 25
1967.FA.12A.20

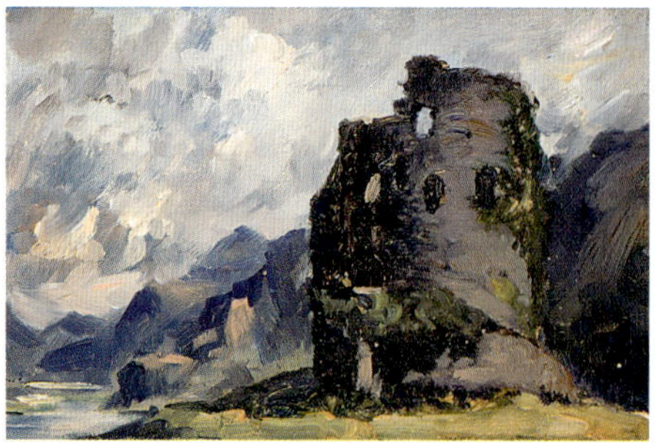

Toft, J. Alfonso 1866–1964
Dolbadarn Castle and Lake
oil on panel 15.5 x 24 (E)
1967.FA.12A.35

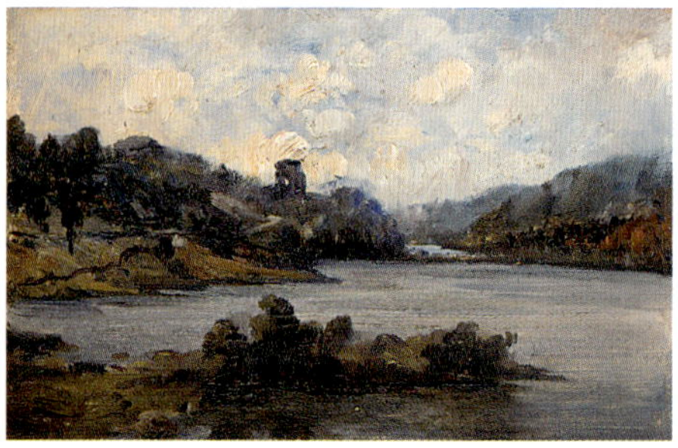

Toft, J. Alfonso 1866–1964
Dolbadarn Castle and Lake
oil on panel 15.5 x 24 (E)
1967.FA.12A.36

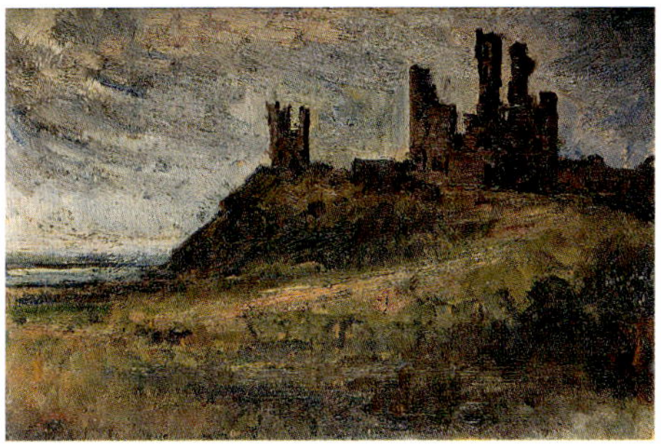

Toft, J. Alfonso 1866–1964
Dunstanburgh Castle
oil on card 16 x 24
1967.FA.12A.25

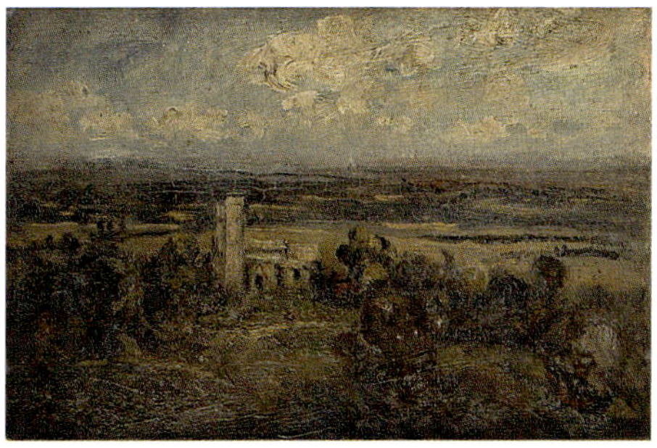

Toft, J. Alfonso 1866–1964
Ellesborough, Buckinghamshire
oil on card 16 x 23.8
1967.FA.12A.21

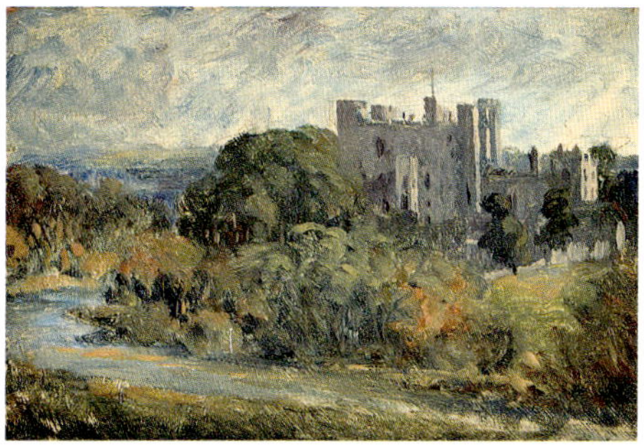

Toft, J. Alfonso 1866–1964
Haughton Castle
oil on panel 16 x 24
1967.FA.12A.29

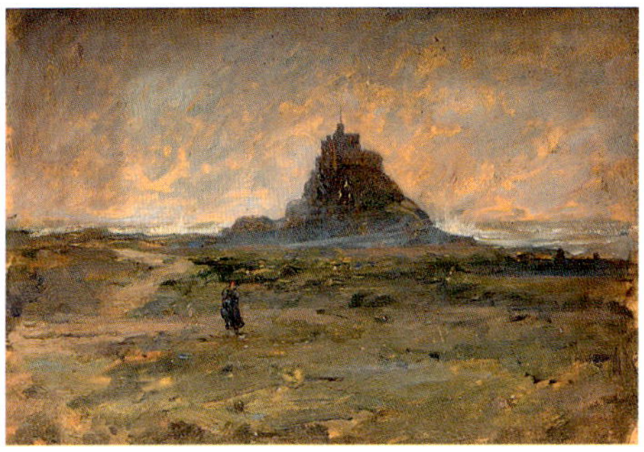

Toft, J. Alfonso 1866–1964
Holy Island
oil on panel 26 x 35.5
1967.FA.12A.16

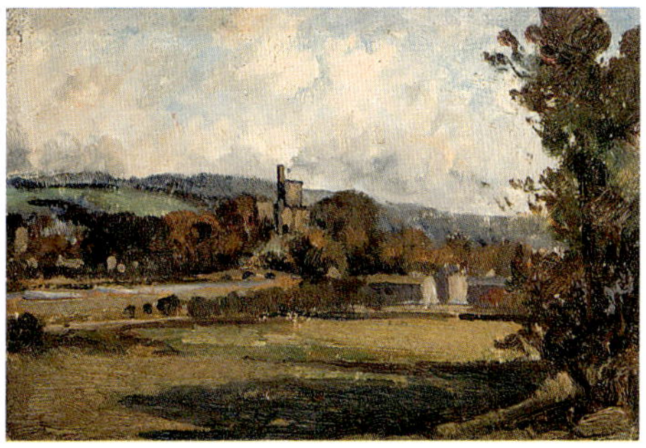

Toft, J. Alfonso 1866–1964
Hornby, near Lancaster
oil on panel 16 x 23.8 (E)
1967.FA.12A.39

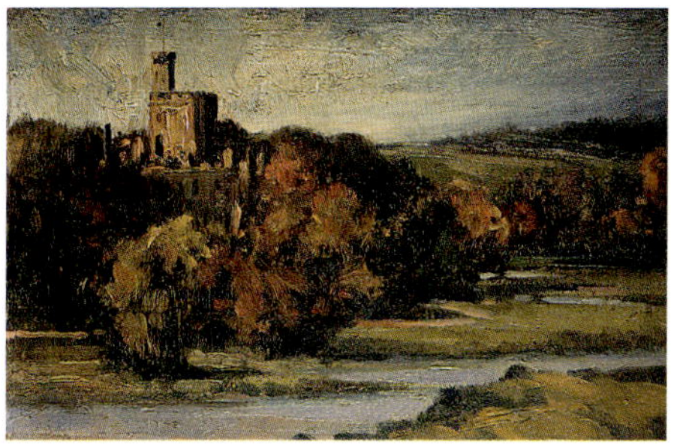

Toft, J. Alfonso 1866–1964
Hornby Castle, near Lancaster
oil on panel 16 x 23.8 (E)
1967.FA.12A.45

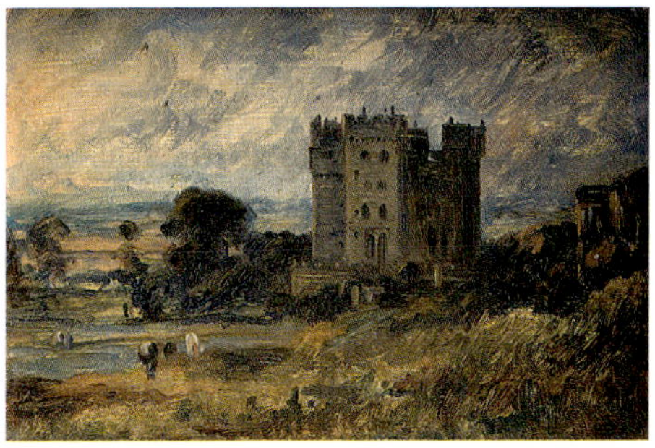

Toft, J. Alfonso 1866–1964
Hylton Castle, near Durham
oil on card 16 x 23.6
1967.FA.12A.10

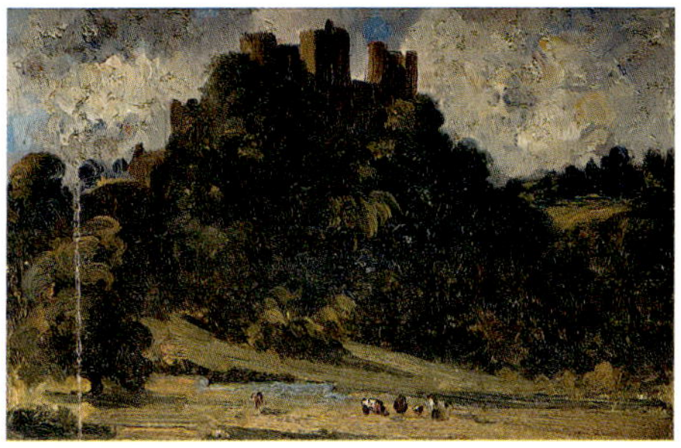

Toft, J. Alfonso 1866–1964
Keep on a Mound, with River and Cows
oil on card 15.3 x 23.7
1967.FA.12A.19

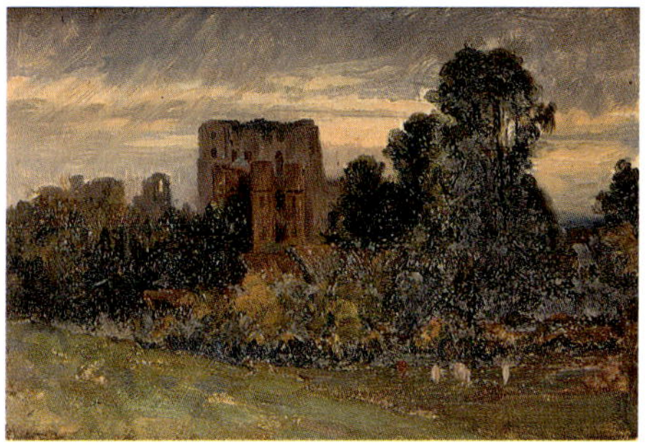

Toft, J. Alfonso 1866–1964
Kenilworth Castle
oil on card 16 x 23.5 (E)
1967.FA.12A.23

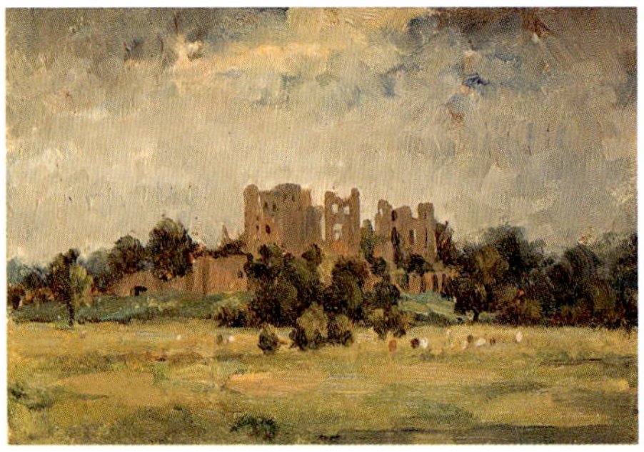

Toft, J. Alfonso 1866–1964
Kenilworth Castle
oil on card 16 x 23.5 (E)
1967.FA.12A.26

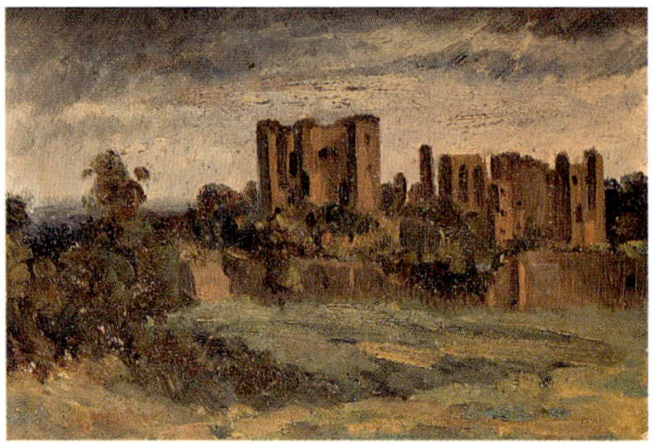

Toft, J. Alfonso 1866–1964
Kenilworth Castle
oil on card 16 x 23.5 (E)
1967.FA.12A.40

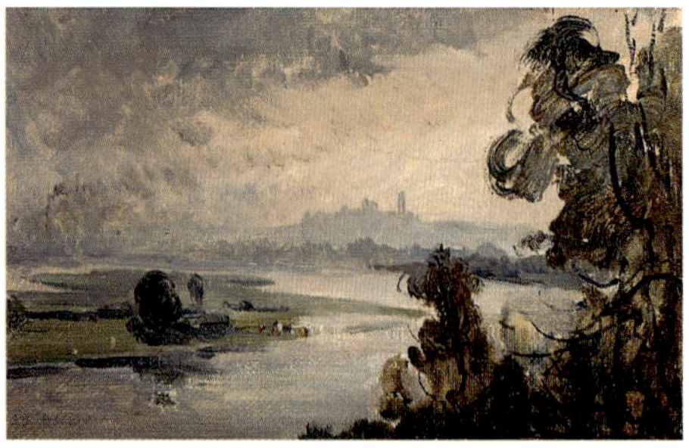

Toft, J. Alfonso 1866–1964
Lancaster from the Aqueduct over River Lune
oil on card 15 x 23.7
1967.FA.12A.44

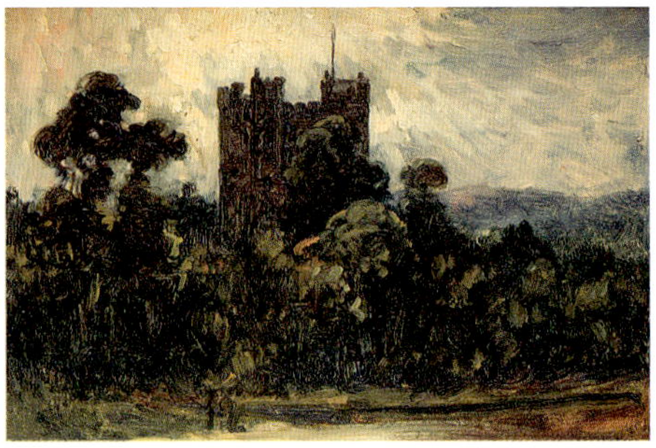

Toft, J. Alfonso 1866–1964
Langley Castle
oil on card 16 x 24
1967.FA.12A.11

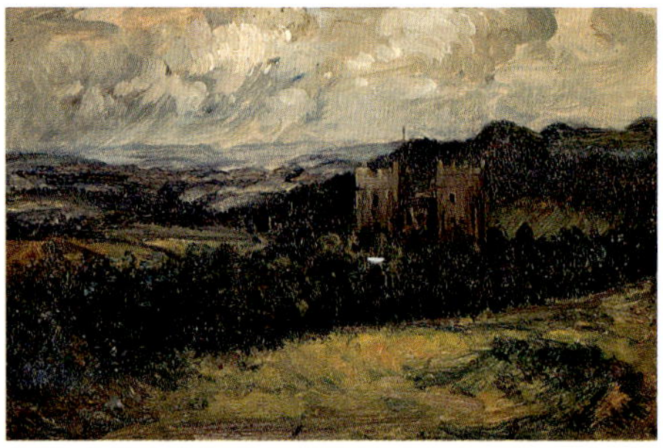

Toft, J. Alfonso 1866–1964
Langley Castle, North Tyne
oil on panel 15.8 x 24
1967.FA.12A.34

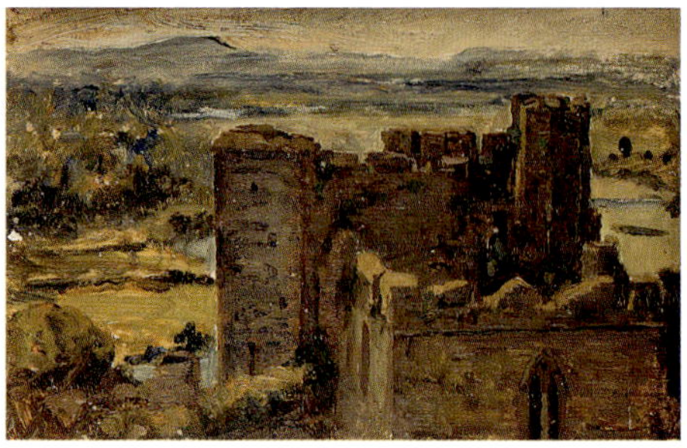

Toft, J. Alfonso 1866–1964
Ludlow Castle
oil on panel 15.5 x 23.8
1967.FA.12A.22

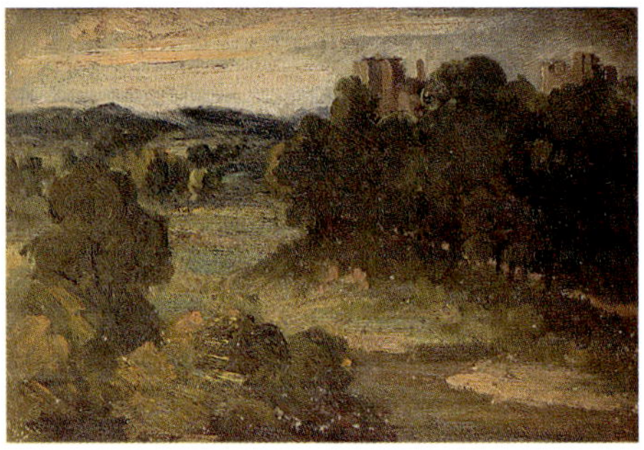

Toft, J. Alfonso 1866–1964
Ludlow Castle
oil on card 16.3 x 24
1967.FA.12A.30

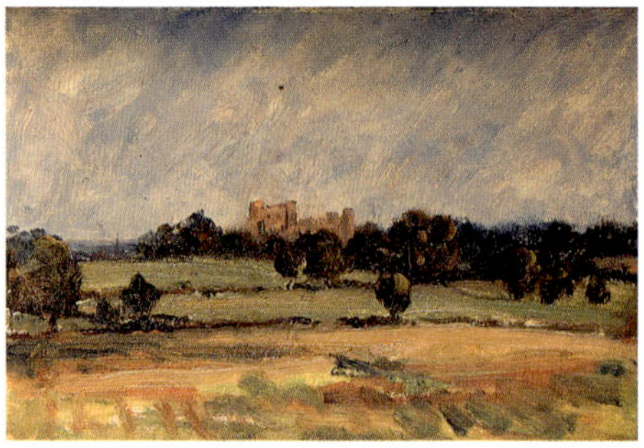

Toft, J. Alfonso 1866–1964
Ludlow Castle
oil on card 16 x 23.5
1967.FA.12A.31

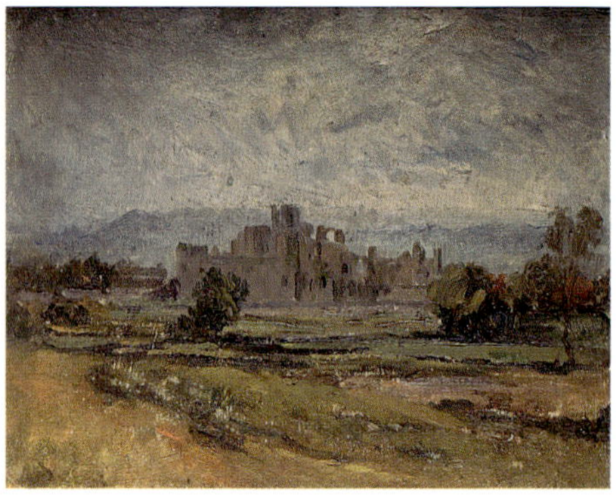

Toft, J. Alfonso 1866–1964
Middleham Castle
oil on card 21.5 x 27
1967.FA.12A.5

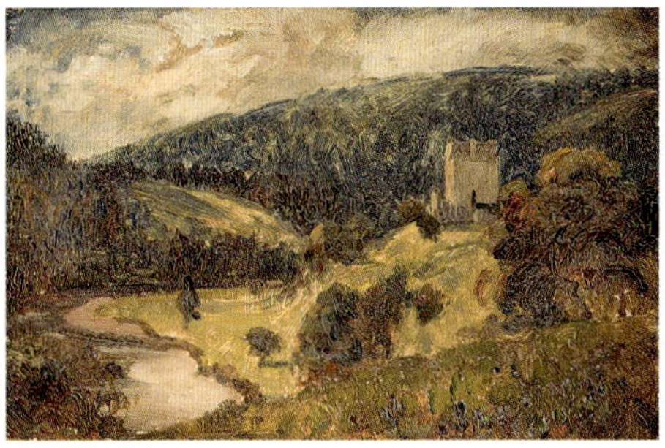

Toft, J. Alfonso 1866–1964
Neidpath Castle
oil on panel 16 x 24
1967.FA.12A.46

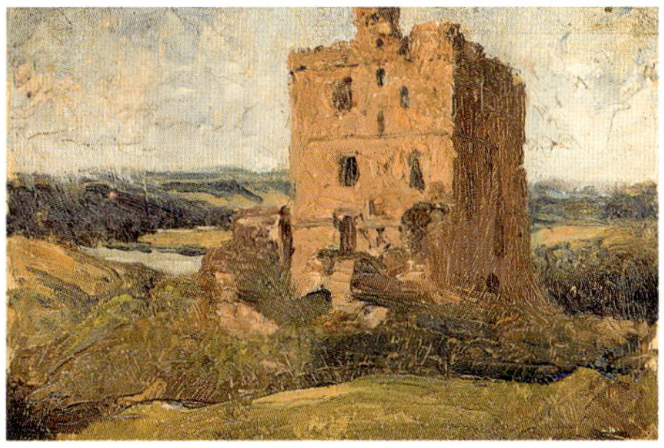

Toft, J. Alfonso 1866–1964
Norham Castle
oil on panel 16 x 24 (E)
1967.FA.12A.1

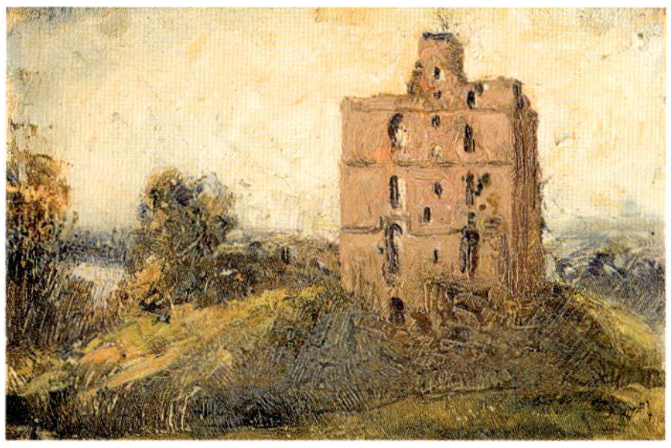

Toft, J. Alfonso 1866–1964
Norham Castle
oil on card 16 x 24 (E)
1967.FA.12A.24

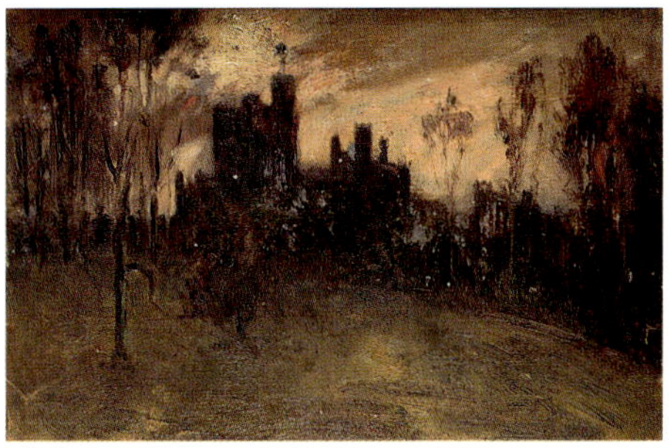

Toft, J. Alfonso 1866–1964
Powis Castle
oil on panel 15.8 x 24
1967.FA.12A.32

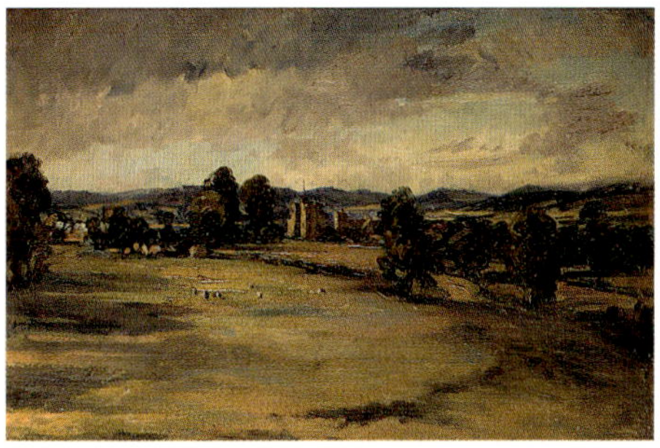

Toft, J. Alfonso 1866–1964
Stokesay Castle
oil on card 25.4 x 35.3
1967.FA.12A.7

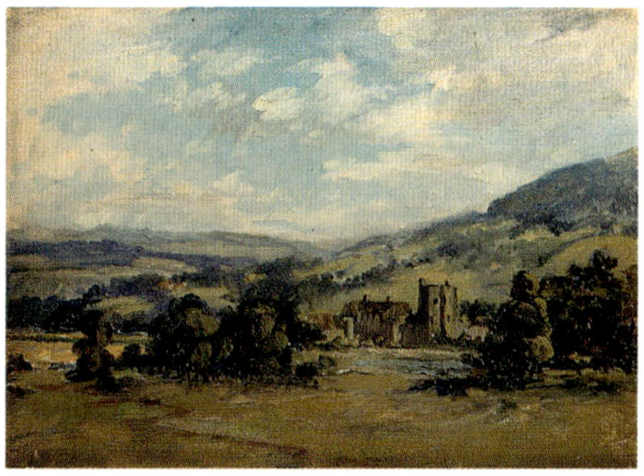

Toft, J. Alfonso 1866–1964
Stokesay Castle
oil on card 25.3 x 34.8
1967.FA.12A.14

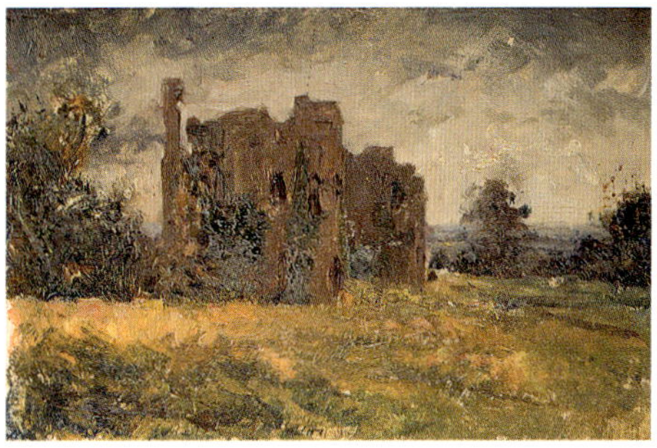

Toft, J. Alfonso 1866–1964
Turzel Castle
oil on panel 16 x 24 (E)
1967.FA.12A.13

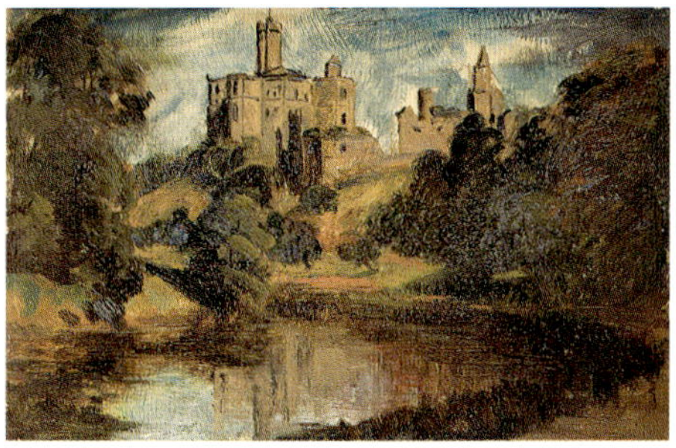

Toft, J. Alfonso 1866–1964
Warkworth Castle
oil on panel 16 x 24 (E)
1967.FA.12A.3

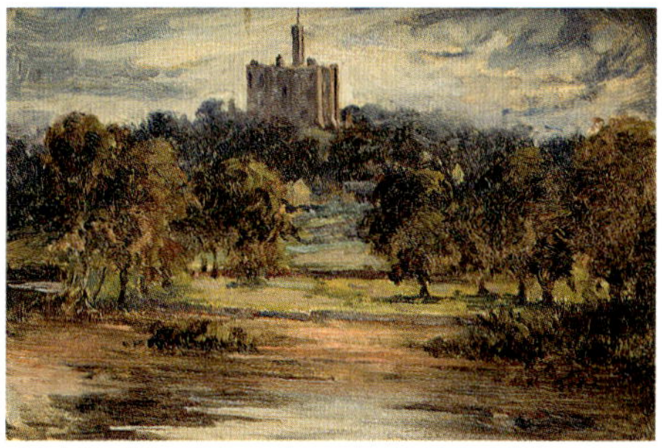

Toft, J. Alfonso 1866–1964
Warkworth Castle
oil on panel 15.8 x 24
1967.FA.12A.12

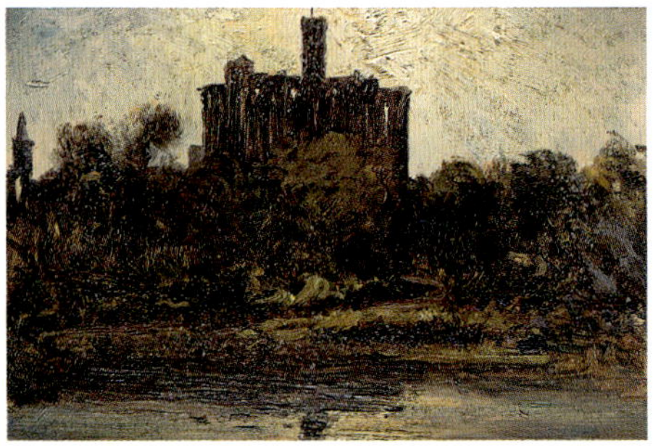

Toft, J. Alfonso 1866–1964
Warkworth Castle
oil on panel 15.7 x 24
1967.FA.12A.28

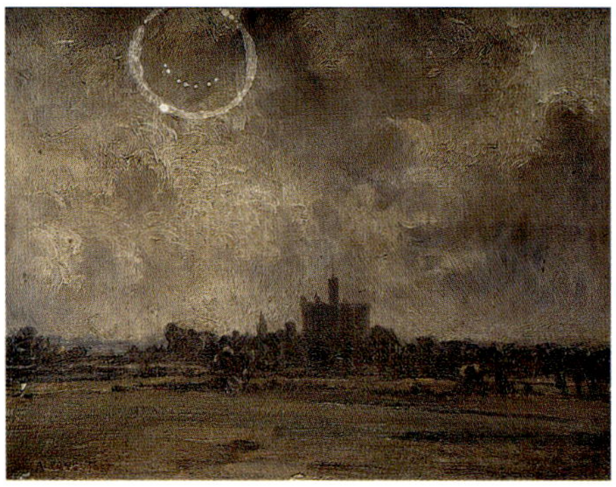

Toft, J. Alfonso 1866–1964
Warkworth Castle
oil on canvas 20.5 x 25.8
1967.FA.12A.50

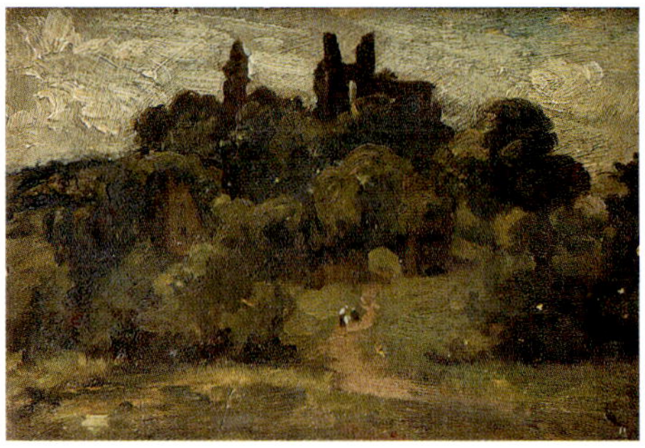

Toft, J. Alfonso 1866–1964
Wigmore Castle
oil on panel 16 x 24 (E)
1967.FA.12A.27

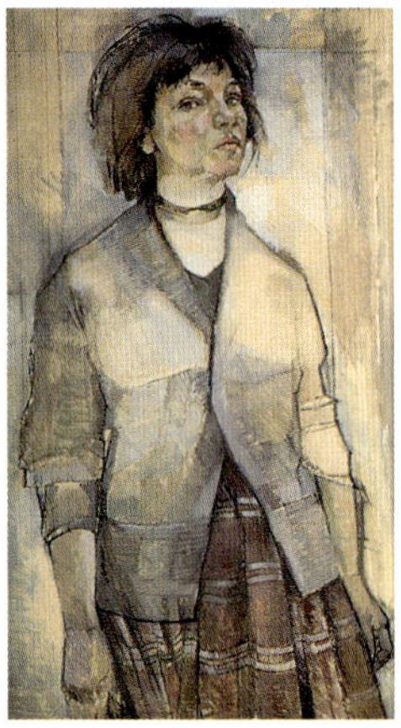

Tolansky, Ottilie 1912–1977
Self Portrait
oil on canvas 88 x 49
1964.FA.887A

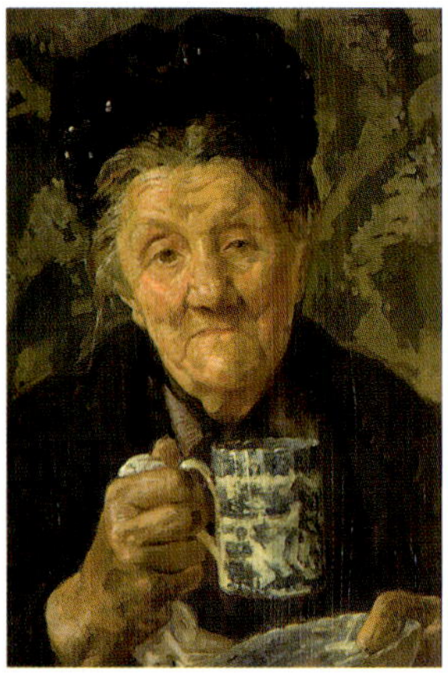

Tomlinson, Reginald R. 1885–1978
The Old Mug 1931
oil on panel 39 x 29
1935.FA.92

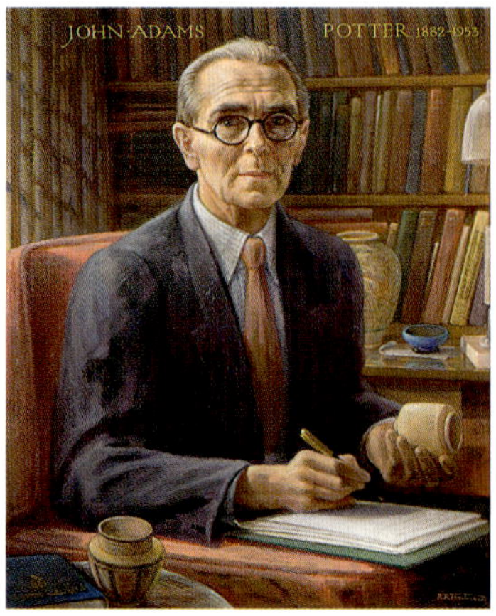

Tomlinson, Reginald R. 1885–1978
John Adams, Potter 1957
oil on canvas 90 x 70
1962.FA.7

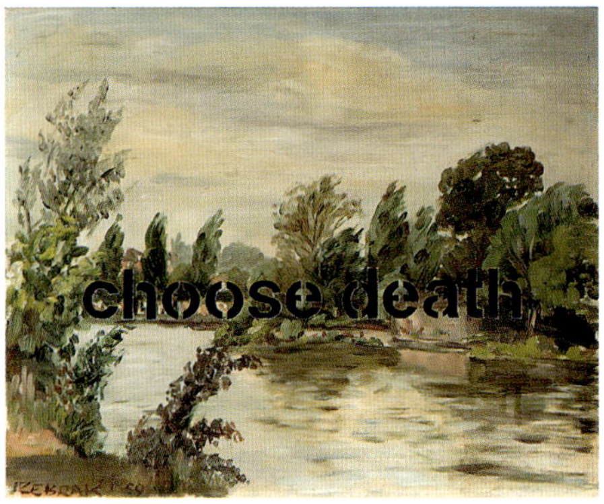

Toren, Amikam b.1945
Untitled: Armchair Painting 1995
oil on canvas 51 x 61
2006.FA.9

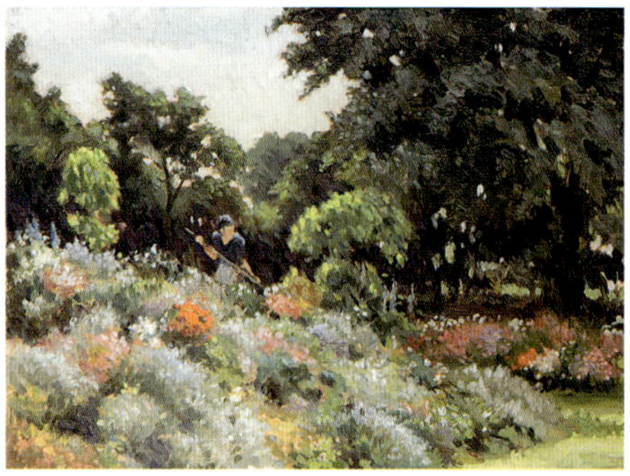

Tunstall, Eric 1897–1987
Mabel Gardening
oil on paper 33 x 44
1958.FA.66

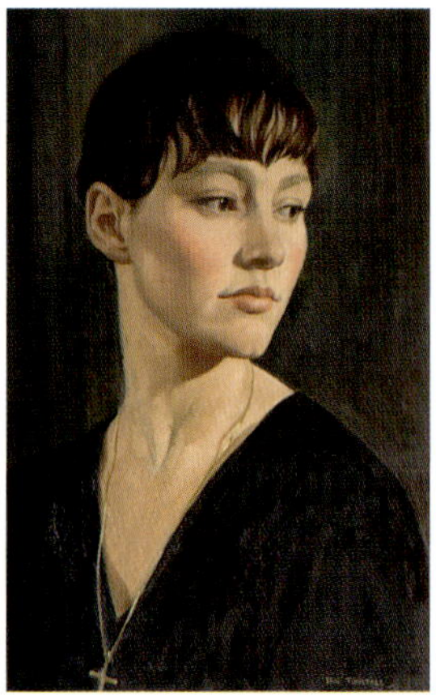

Tunstall, Eric 1897–1987
The Dancer
oil on canvas 47 x 32
1959.FA.64

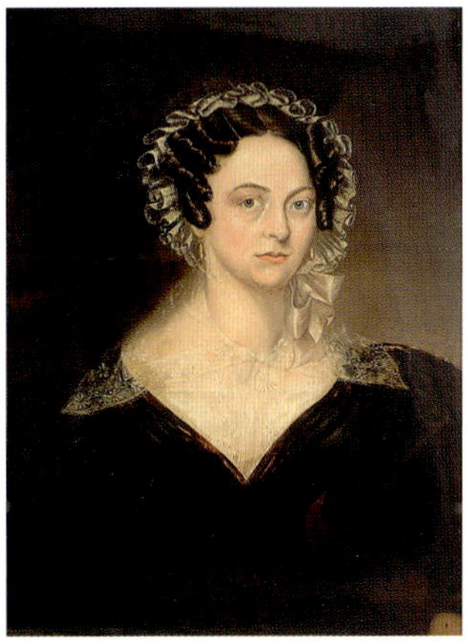

unknown artist
Portrait of a Woman 1800–1825
oil on canvas 72 x 52.5
1953.FA.40.2

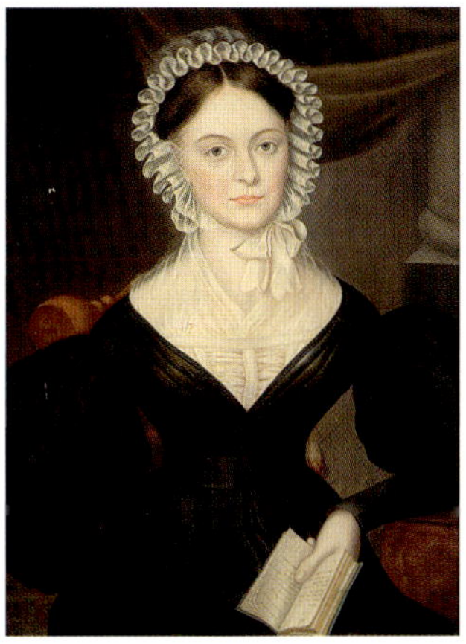

unknown artist
Woman Wearing White Cap, Black Dress and Holding a Book 1800–1825
oil on canvas 72.5 x 52
1953.FA.40.1

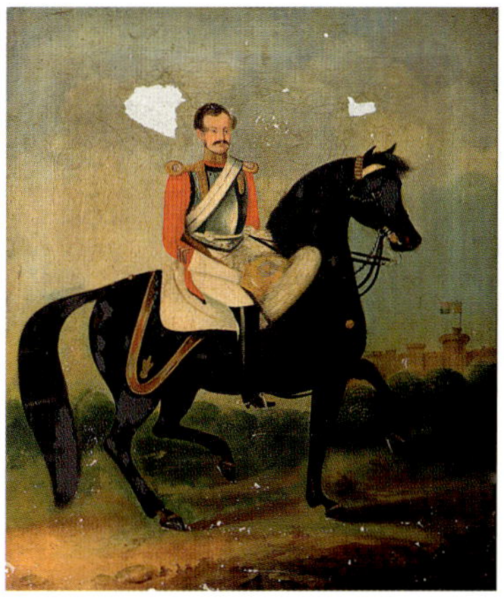

unknown artist
William Allen of Stoke in Full Dress Uniform of the Life Guards c.1825
oil on canvas 60 x 50
1958.FA.51

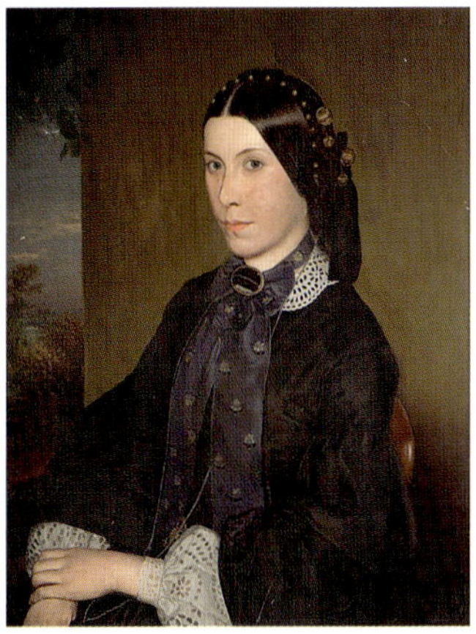

unknown artist
Lady of Keele 1860–1870
oil on canvas 75 x 62
1942.FA.533

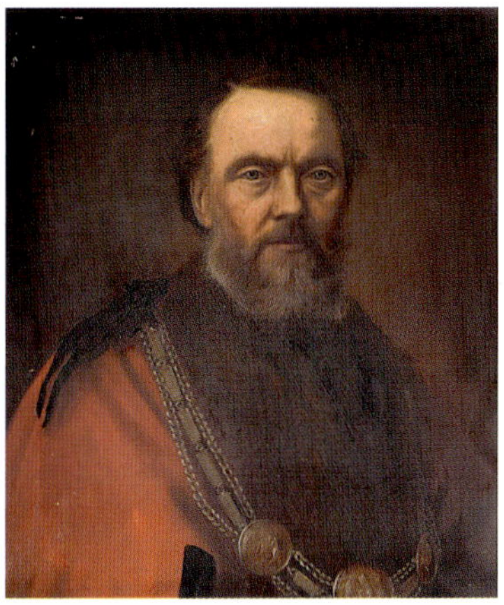

unknown artist
William Cooper, Mayor of Longton c.1878
oil on canvas 60 x 49
1960.FA.45

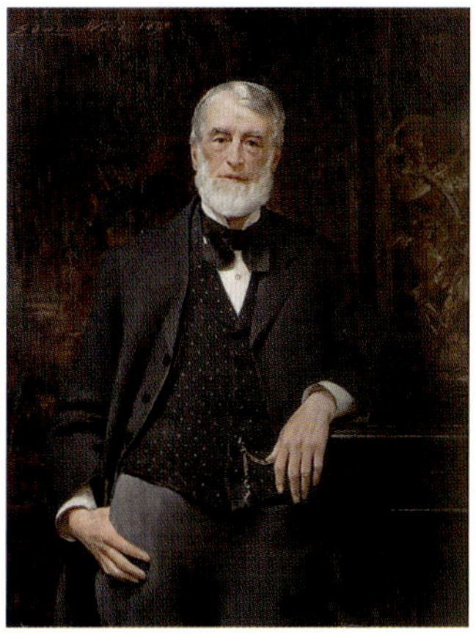

unknown artist
Alderman George Ridgway (1822–1899)
c.1898
oil on canvas 100 x 80
PCF40

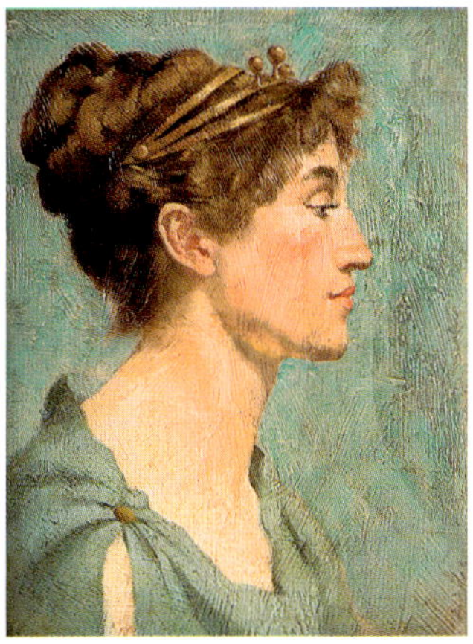

unknown artist
Study of a Head 1901
oil on canvas 23.5 x 19
PCF41

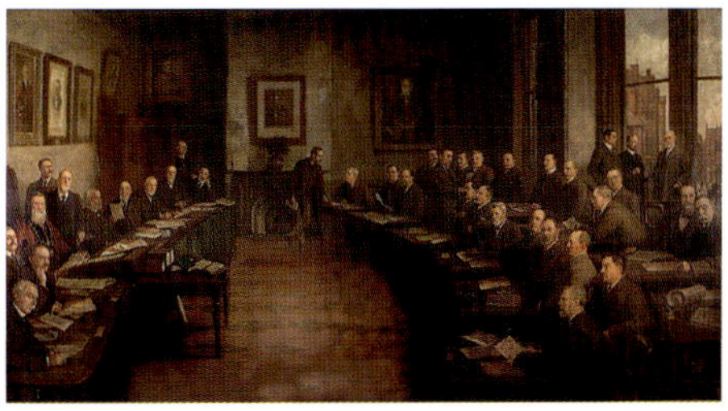

unknown artist
Council Chambers, Hanley Town Hall
1906–1907
oil on canvas 175 x 270
PCF42

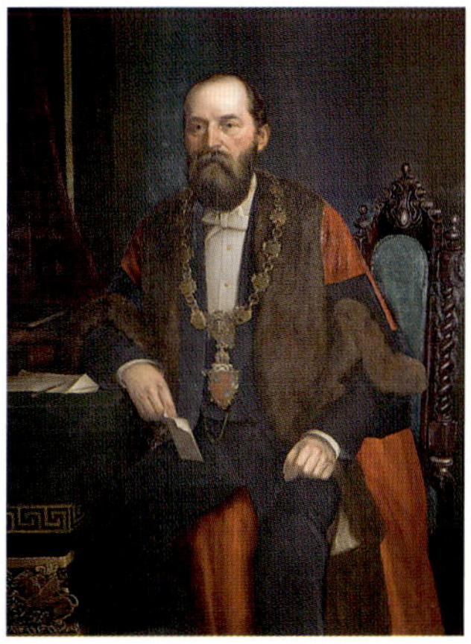

unknown artist
Alderman Francis Thomas Wood
oil on canvas 127 x 93
1982.FA.6

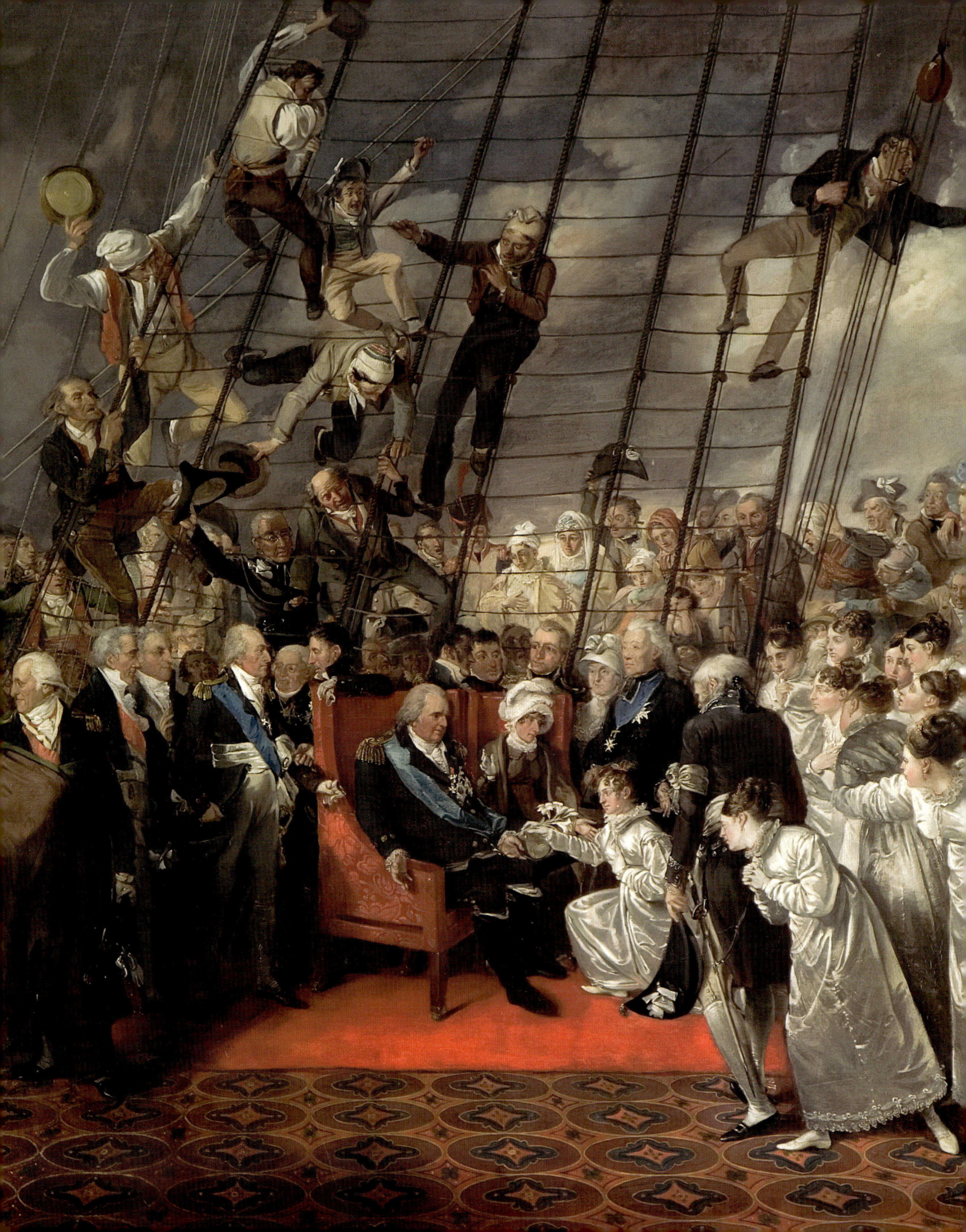

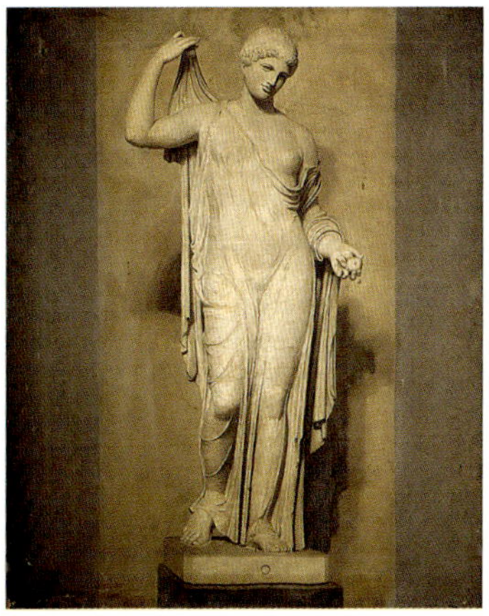

unknown artist
*Aphrodite Victorious**
oil on canvas 86.5 x 52
PCF46

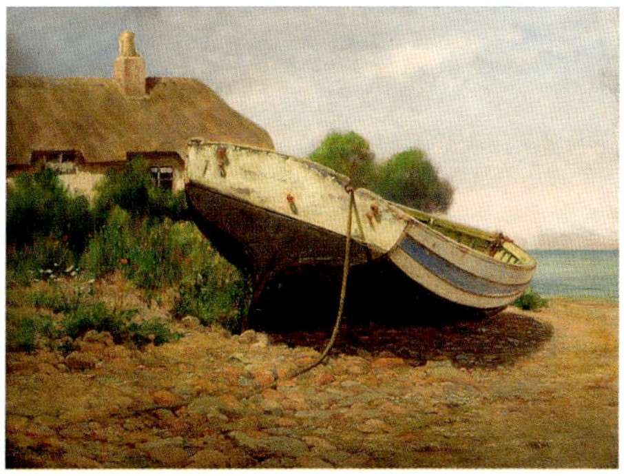

unknown artist
Boat and Cottage
oil on canvas 36 x 46
1954.FA.158

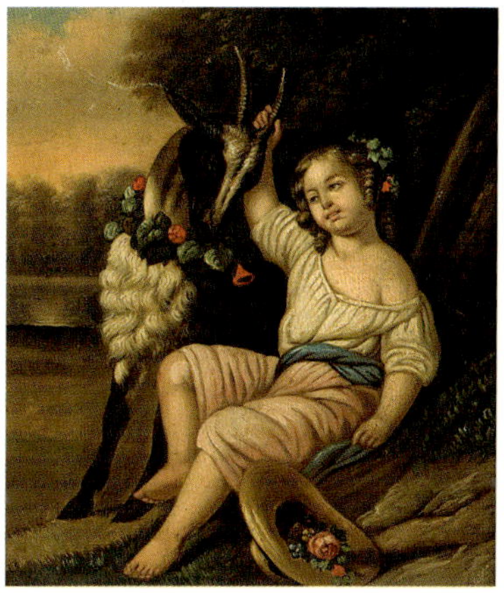

unknown artist
Boy Seated beside a Goat
oil on canvas 24 x 21
1963.FA.76

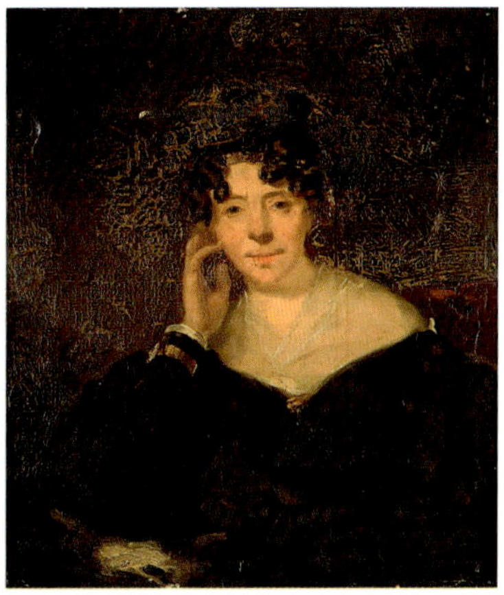

unknown artist
Elizabeth Heming (Mrs George Miles Mason)
oil on canvas 76 x 63
1989.FA.19

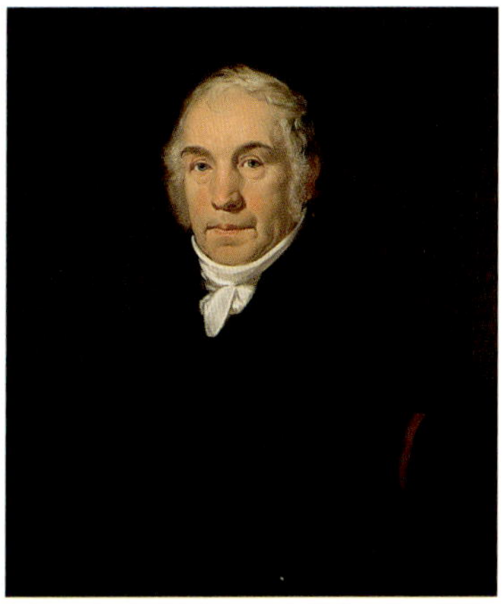

unknown artist
Enoch Wood (1759–1840)
oil on canvas 73 x 61.5
1954.FA.216

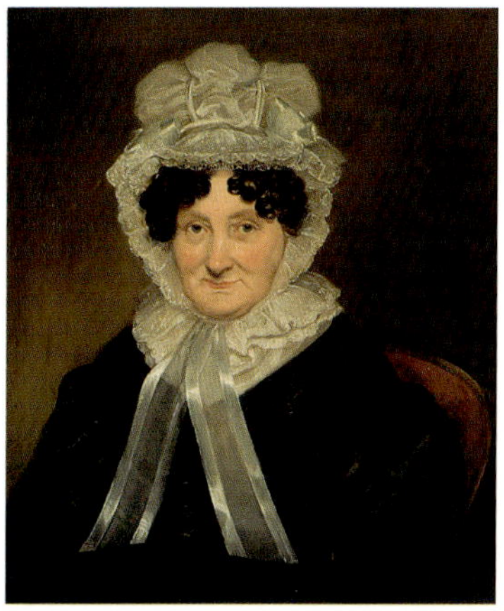

unknown artist
Mrs Enoch Wood (1758–1841)
oil on canvas 73 x 61.5
1954.FA.217

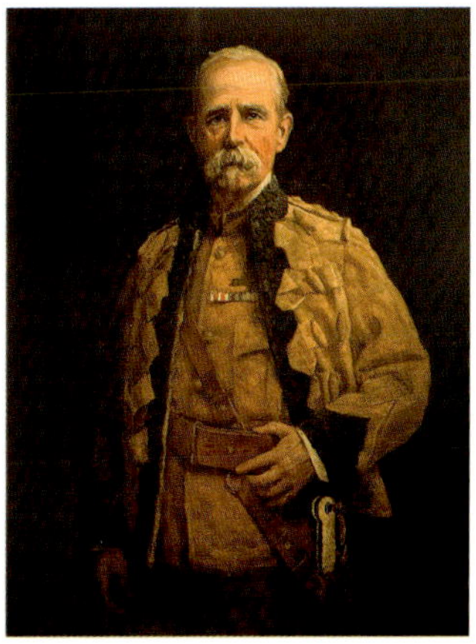

unknown artist
Field Marshall the Right Honourable Lord Roberts, VC, GCB, CGSI
oil on canvas 125 x 103
PCF43

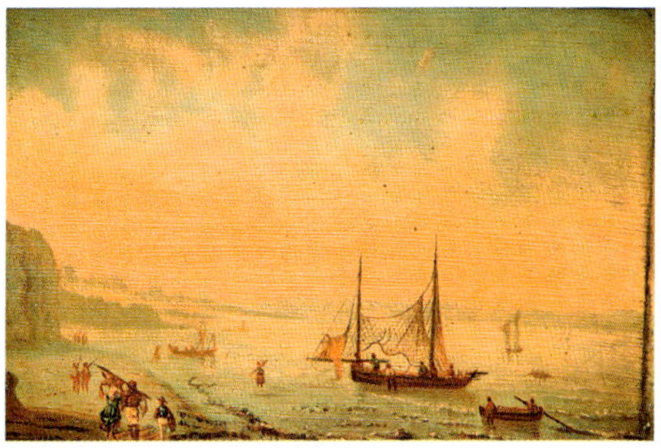

unknown artist
Fishing Boats
oil on tin 16.5 x 24.5
1961.FA.70

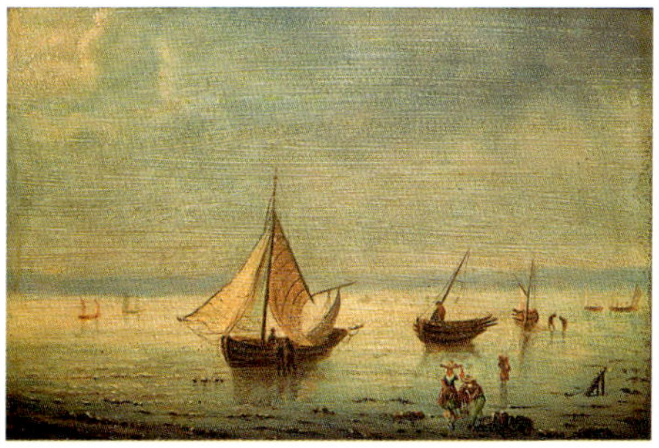

unknown artist
Fishing Boats
oil on tin 17 x 25
1961.FA.71

Facing page: Bird, Edward, 1772–1819, *The Arrival of King Louis XVIII of France at Calais* (detail), Wolverhampton Art Gallery, (p. 245)

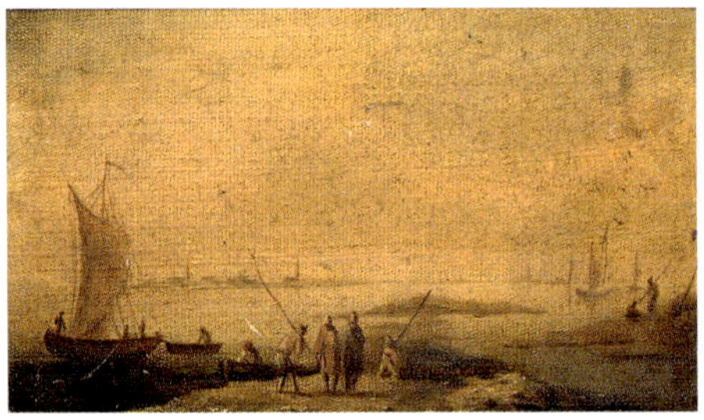

unknown artist
*Fishing Boats**
oil on canvas 14 x 24
PCF44

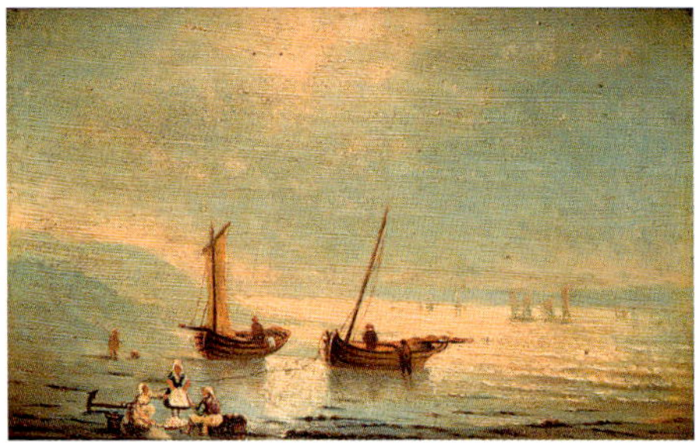

unknown artist
Fishing Boats and a Group of Women
oil on tin 16.5 x 24.5
1961.FA.69

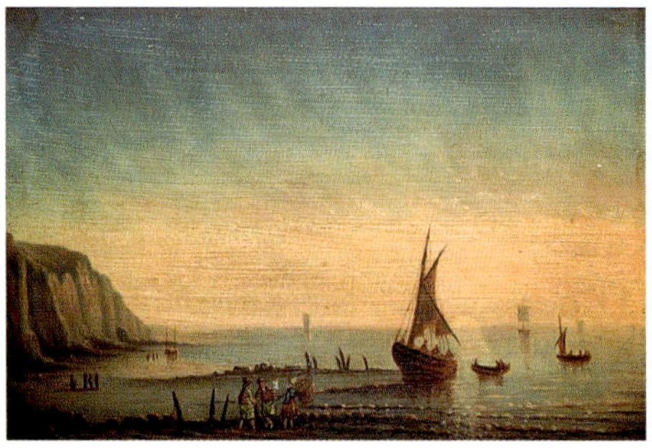

unknown artist
Fishing Boats in a Bay with a Group of Fishermen
oil on tin 17.5 x 24.5
1961.FA.68

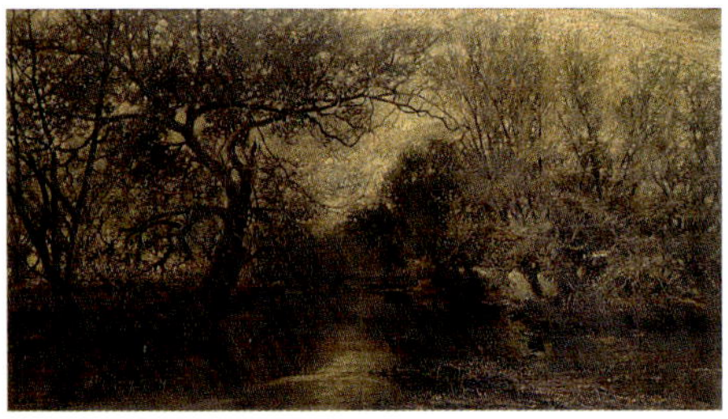

unknown artist
*Forest Scene**
oil on canvas 60 x 104
PCF45

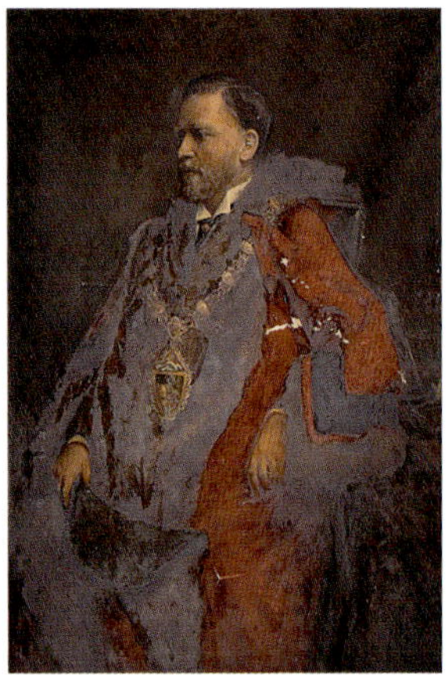

unknown artist
J. A. Kirkham, Mayor of Stoke
oil on canvas 121 x 90
PCF47

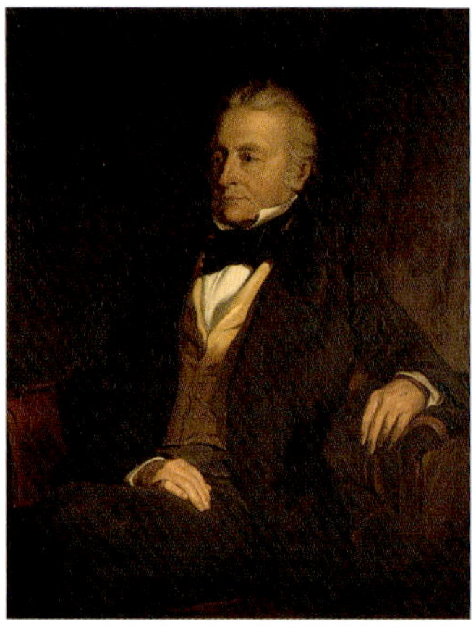

unknown artist
John Davenport (1765–1848)
oil on canvas 74 x 55
1954.FA.218

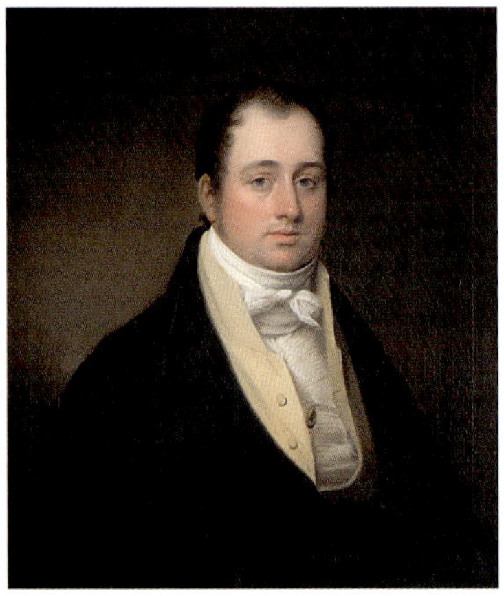

unknown artist
John Wood II (1778–1848)
oil on canvas 76 x 63
1966.FA.2A

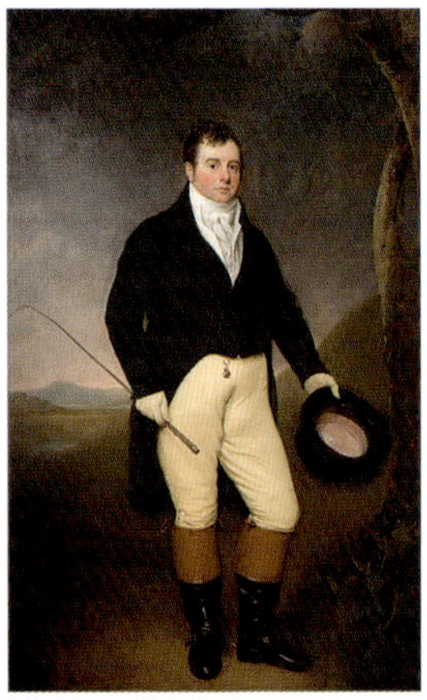

unknown artist
Josiah Spode II (1755–1827) in Hunting Costume
oil on canvas 227 x 136
1954.FA.152

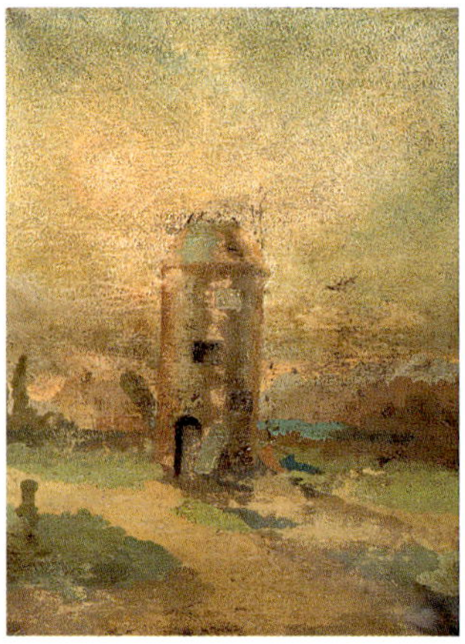

unknown artist
Josiah Wedgwood's Old Mill on the Jenkins
oil on canvas 26 x 19
1952.FA.57.1

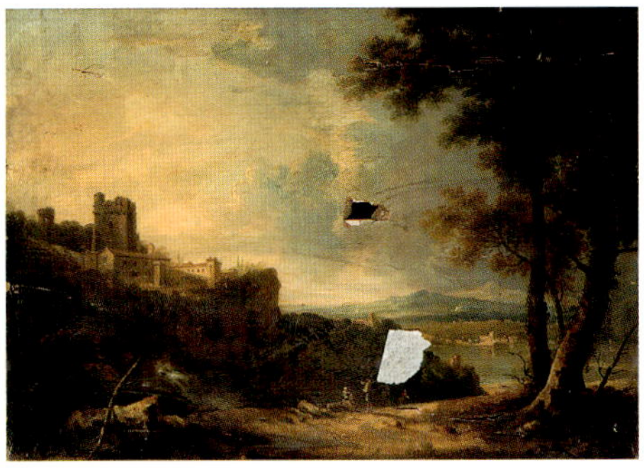

unknown artist
Landscape with Castle Ruins
oil on canvas 71 x 91
PCF48

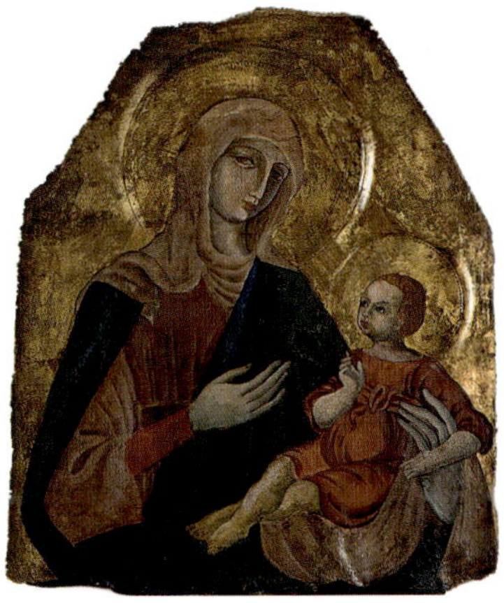

unknown artist
Madonna and Child
oil on board 46.5 x 37.5
1975.FA.13

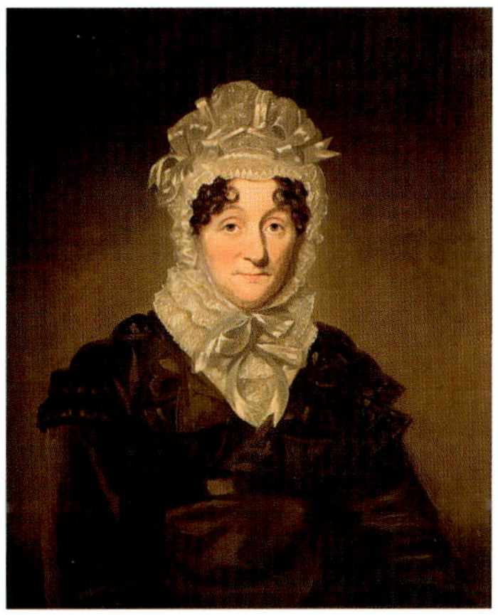

unknown artist
Mary Baddely, née Wedgwood (1764–1824)
oil on canvas 76 x 64
1966.FA.1

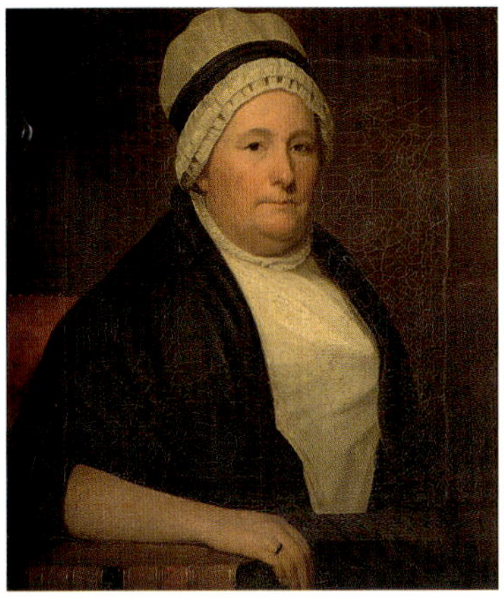

unknown artist
Mary Wood, née Price, of Brownhills (1742–1825)
oil on canvas 74 x 62
1966.FA.3A

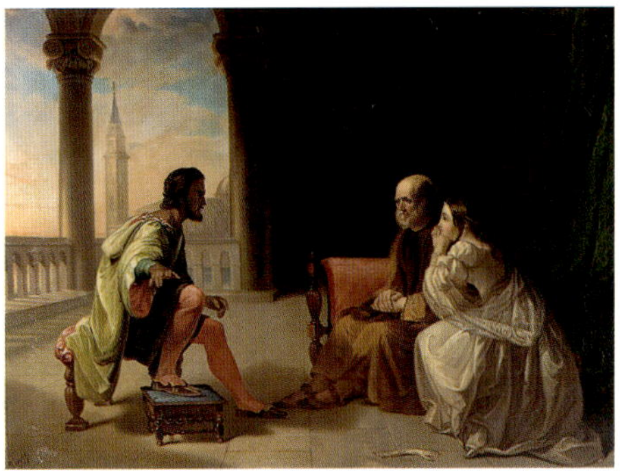

unknown artist
*Meeting in Venice** 1879
oil on canvas 71 x 91
PCF49

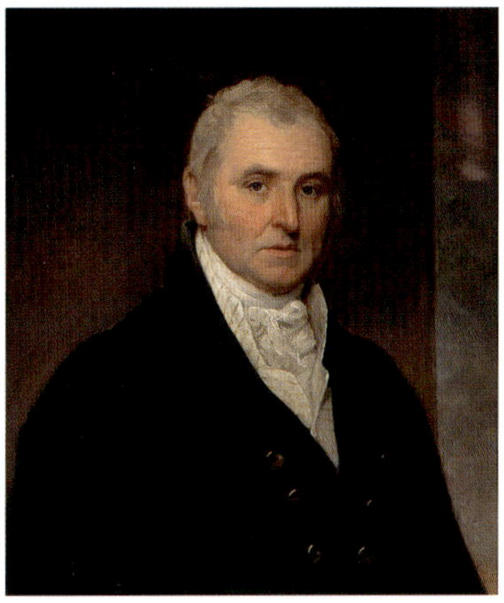

unknown artist
Miles Mason (1752–1822), Potter
oil on canvas 73 x 61.5
1989.FA.17

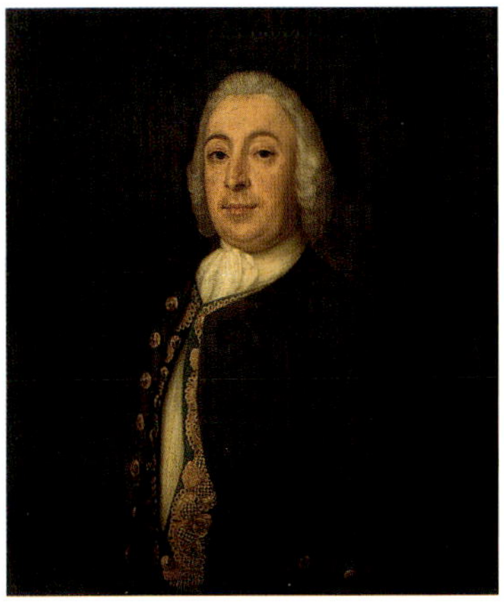

unknown artist
*Portrait of a Gentleman**
oil on canvas 74 x 62
PCF50

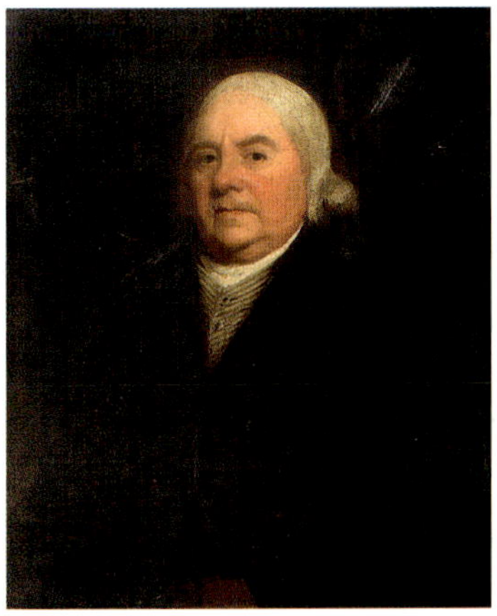

unknown artist
*Portrait of a Gentleman**
oil on canvas 74.5 x 61
PCF51

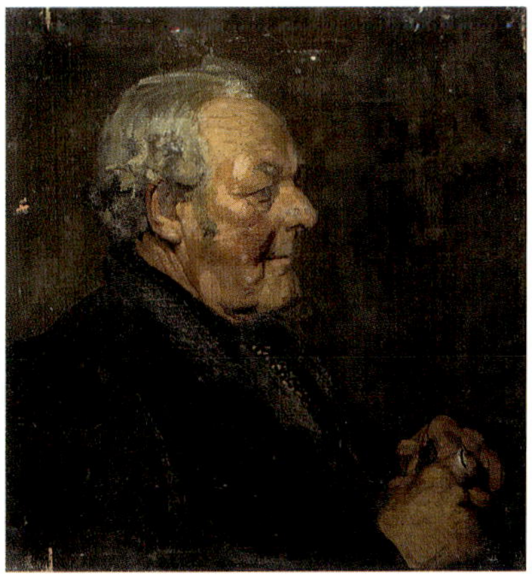

unknown artist
*Portrait of a Gentleman**
oil on canvas 55 x 51
PCF52

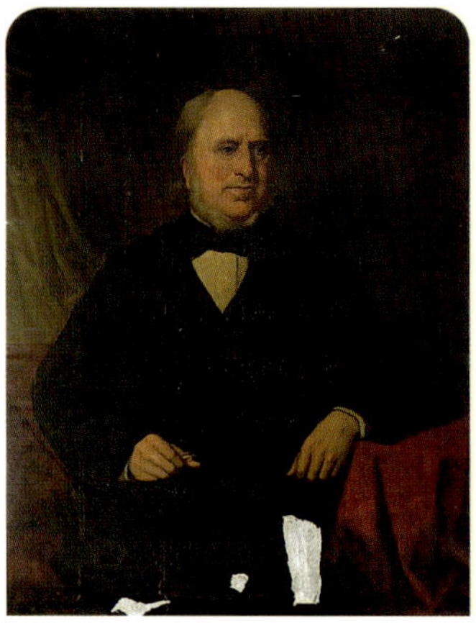

unknown artist
*Portrait of a Gentleman**
oil on canvas 109 x 84
PCF53

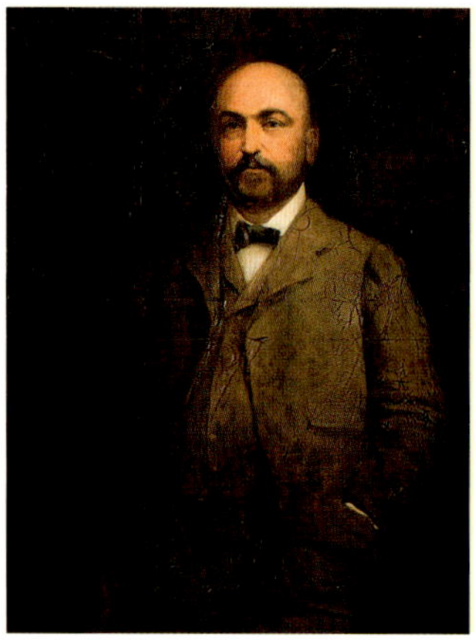

unknown artist
*Portrait of a Gentleman**
oil on canvas 129 x 100
PCF54

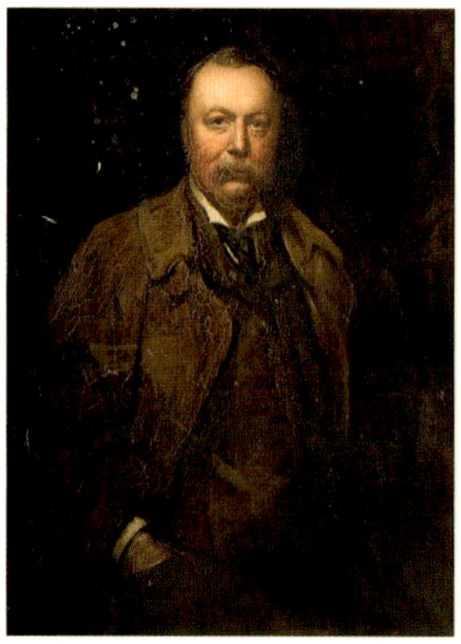

unknown artist
*Portrait of a Gentleman**
oil on canvas 129 x 100
PCF55

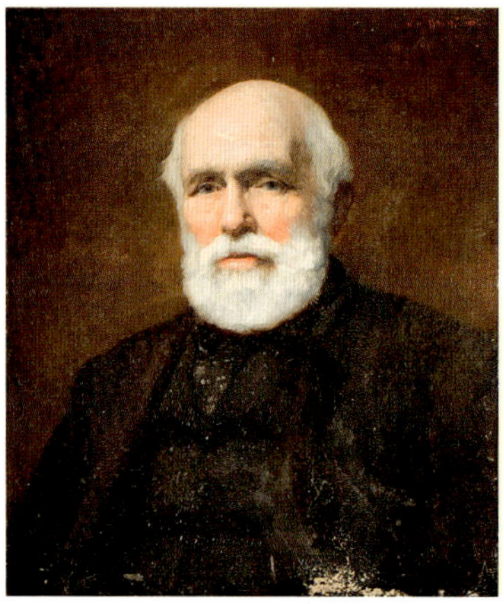

unknown artist
*Portrait of a Gentleman**
oil on canvas 61 x 51
PCF56

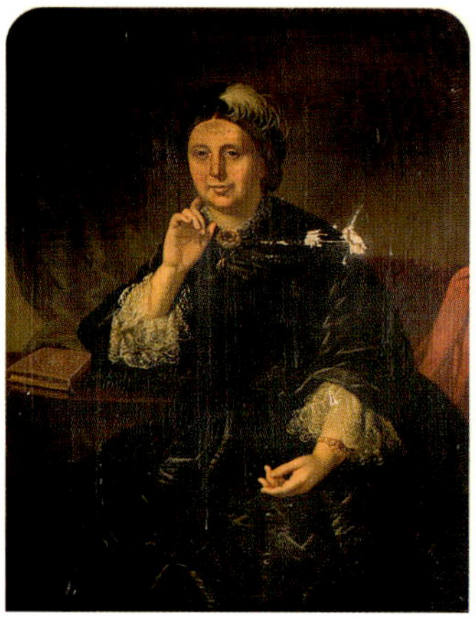

unknown artist
*Portrait of a Lady**
oil on canvas 110 x 85
PCF57

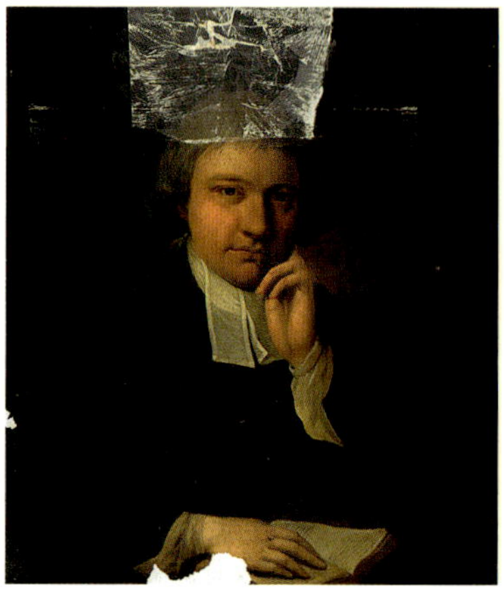

unknown artist
*Portrait of a Reverend**
oil on canvas 71.5 x 60
PCF58

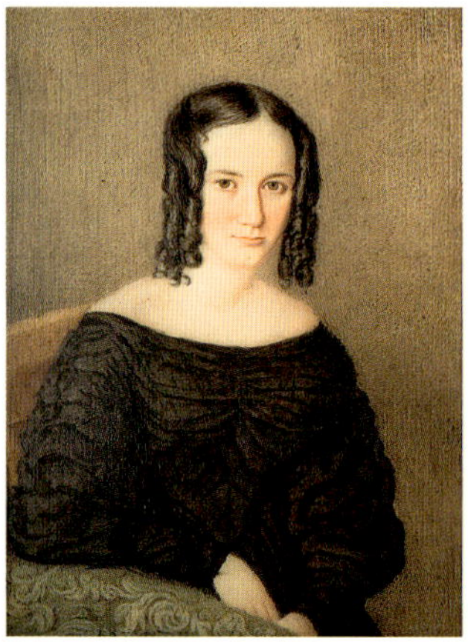

unknown artist
Portrait of an Unknown Female Member of the Pratt Family
oil on canvas 11 x 8.5
1991.FA.10

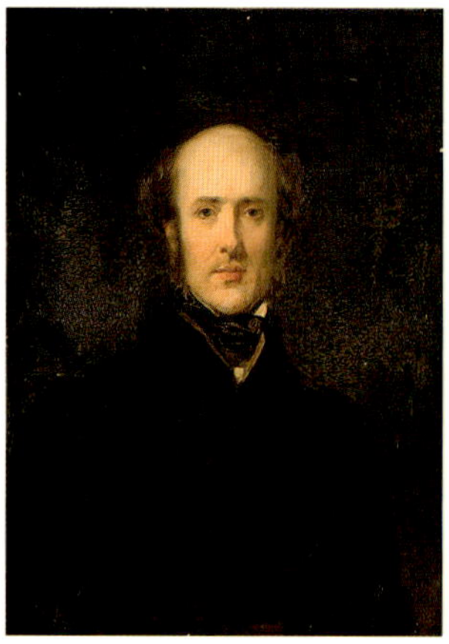

unknown artist
Portrait of an Unknown Male Member of the Mason Family
oil on canvas 76 x 63
1989.FA.18

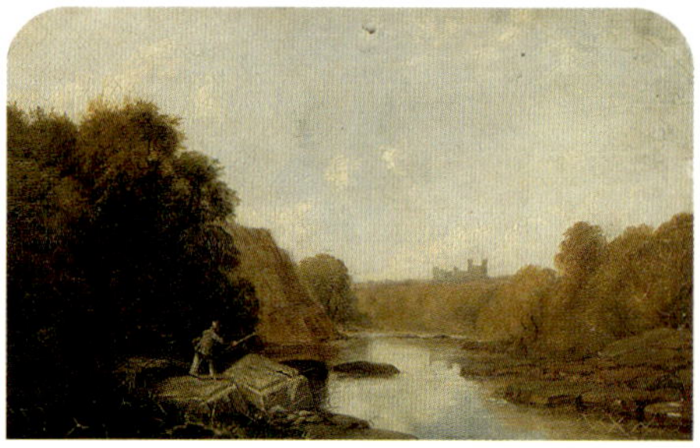

unknown artist
River Scene, Man Fishing
oil on canvas 30 x 44
1954.FA.131

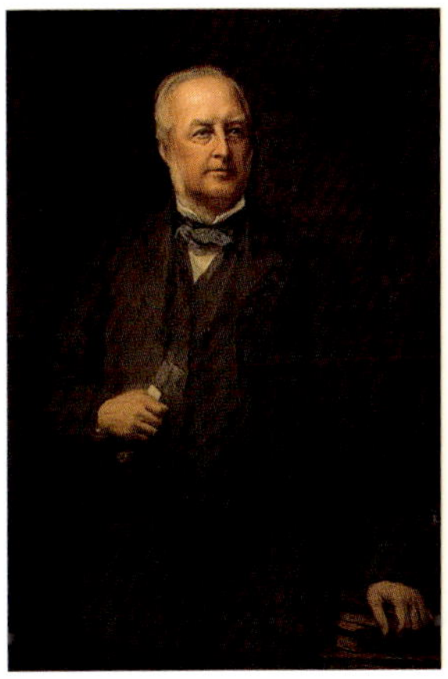

unknown artist
Robert Heath (1816–1893)
oil on canvas 140 x 100
PCF59

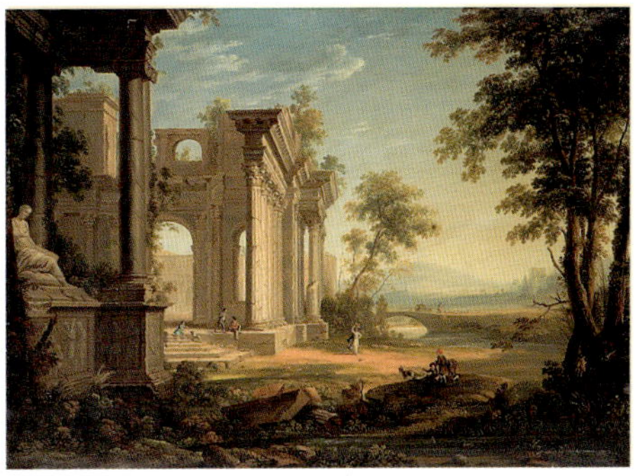

unknown artist
Ruined Classical Temple
oil on canvas 70 x 90
1950.FA.33

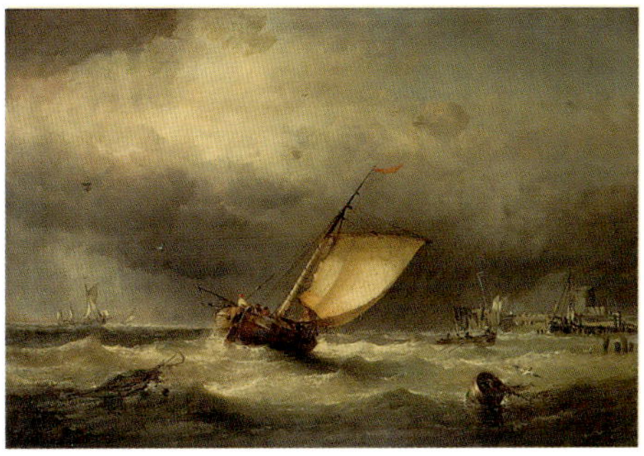

unknown artist
Seascape
oil on canvas 74.5 x 115.5
1946.FA.750

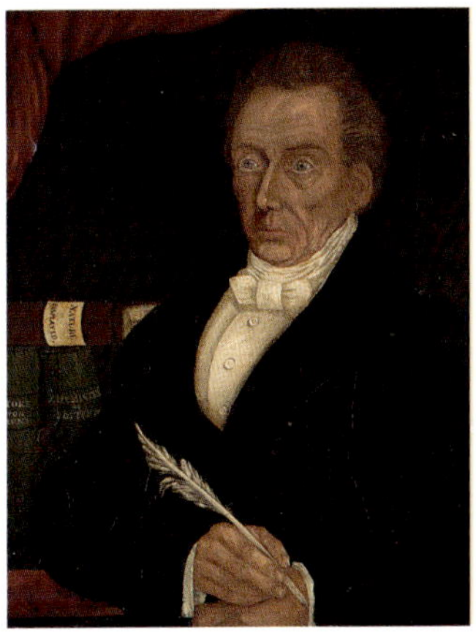

unknown artist
Simeon Shaw (1785–1859)
oil on canvas 70 x 52
1937.FA.287

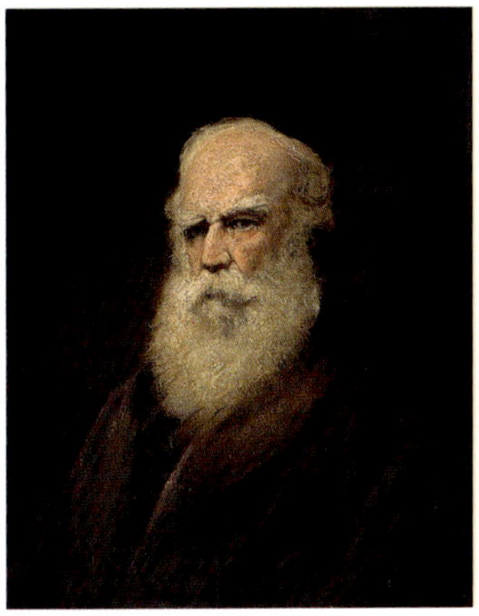

unknown artist
Sir Smith Child (1808–1896)
oil on canvas 125 x 100
1982.FA.3

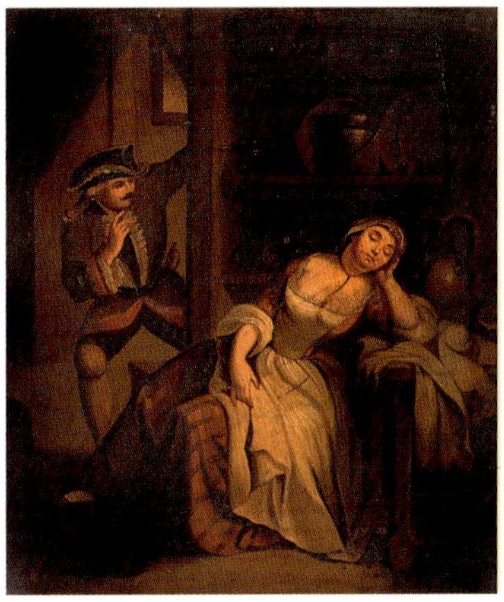

unknown artist
Soldier Disturbing a Sleeping Woman
oil on copper 24 x 20.5
1958.FA.56

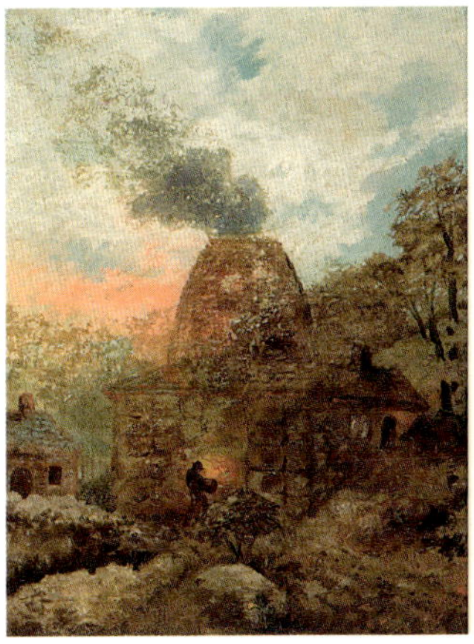

unknown artist
The Old Pottery Kiln, Bradwell Wood
oil on canvas 26 x 20
1954.FA.87

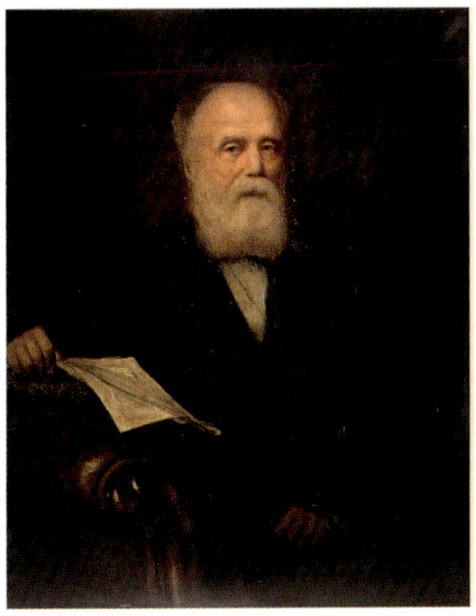

unknown artist
Thomas Peake (1798–1881)
oil on canvas 125 x 100
PCF60

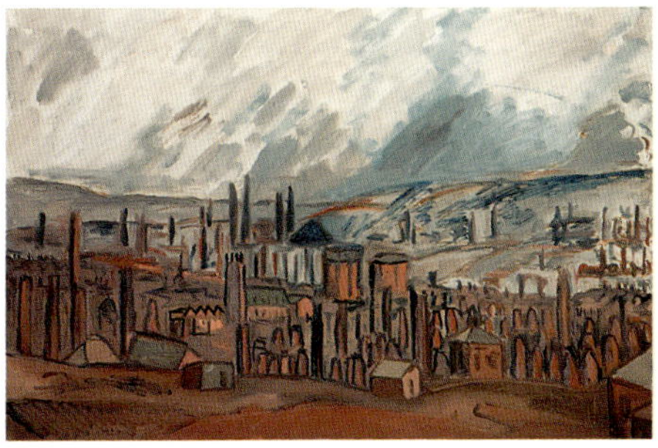

unknown artist
*Townscape**
oil on canvas 51 x 76
PCF61

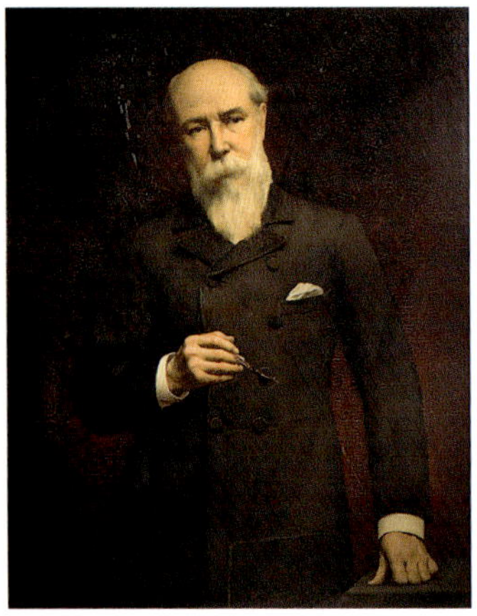

unknown artist
William Woodall, MP (1832–1901)
oil on canvas 111 x 86
1954.FA.110

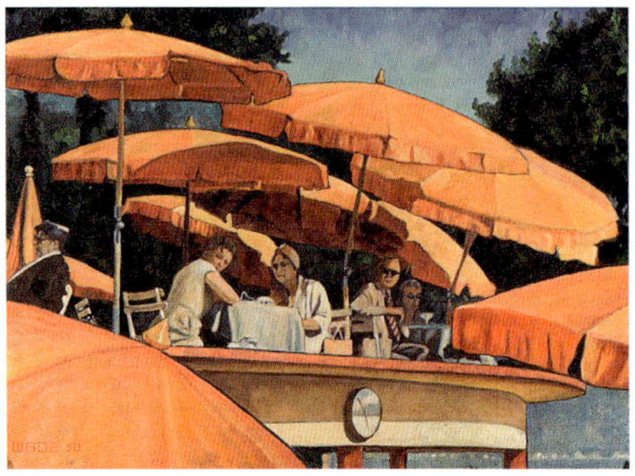

Wade, George A. active 1950–1960
Casino, Montreux 1958
oil on panel 68 x 89
1960.FA.112

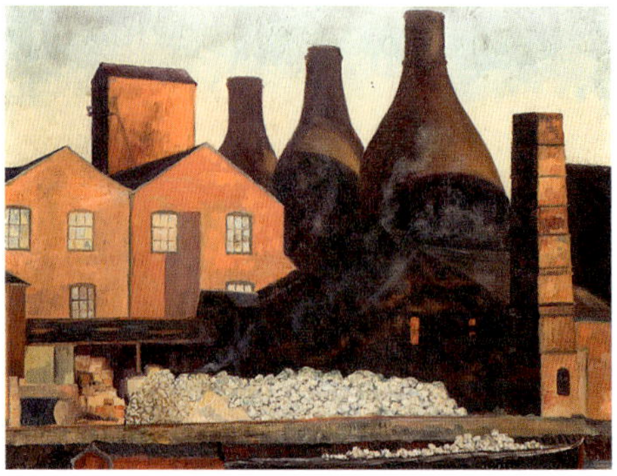

Wade, George A. active 1950–1960
Burgess and Leigh
oil on canvas 40 x 52
1950.FA.23

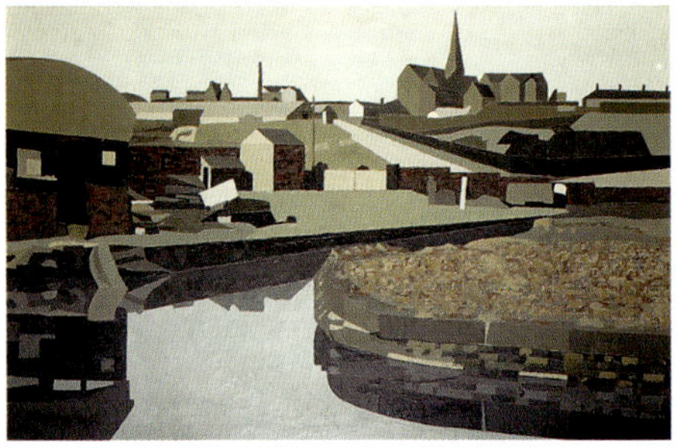

Wade, Maurice 1917–1991
Canal Wharf
oil on panel 60 x 90
1961.FA.63

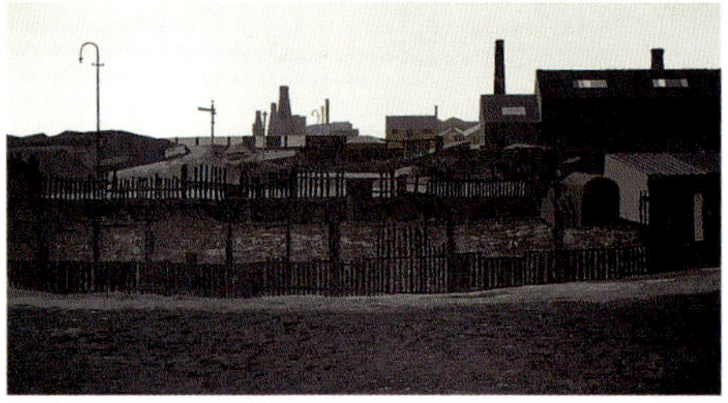

Wade, Maurice 1917–1991
Hen Runs at Sneyd
oil on panel 73.5 x 134
1962.FA.75

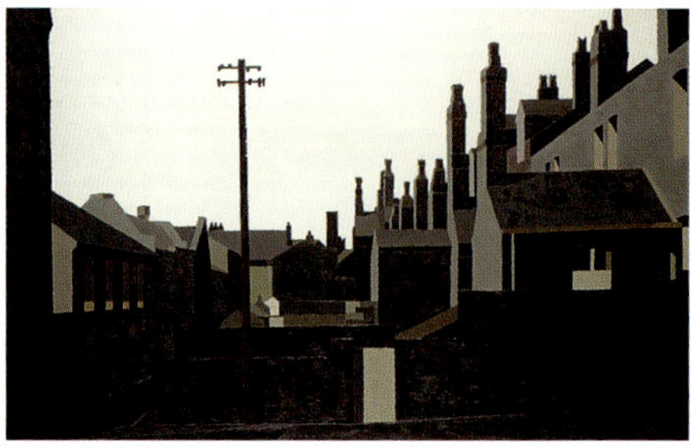

Wade, Maurice 1917–1991
Kitchen Chimneys
oil on panel 58 x 89
1964.FA.3A

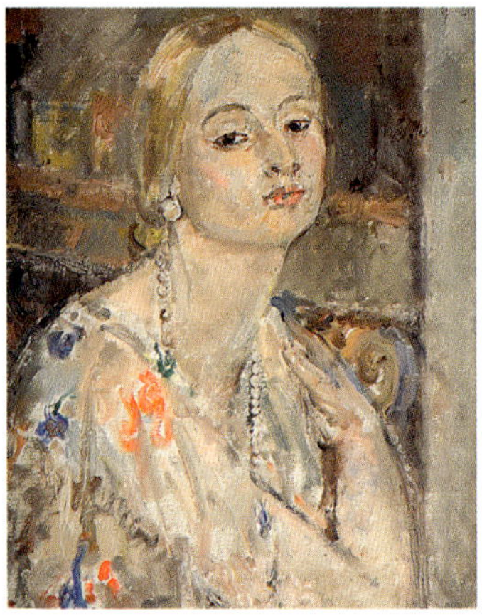

Walker, Ethel 1861–1951
The Young Sculptress
oil on canvas 49 x 38
1948.FA.877

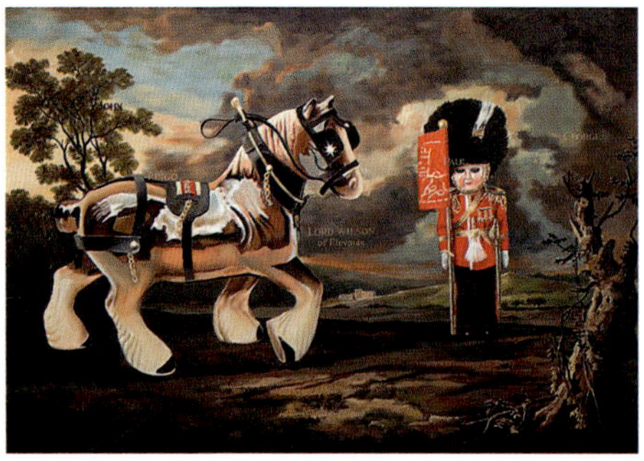

Wallinger, Mark b.1959
Lost Horizons
oil on canvas 152 x 214
1989.FA.21

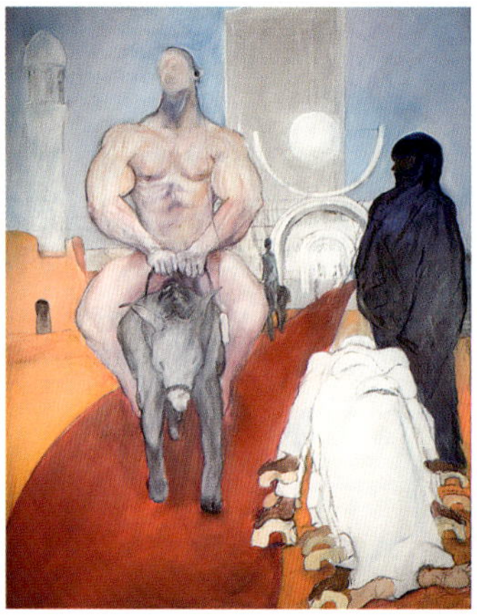

Wallis, Colin b.1937
Don Quixote in Lagos with Walkman
1983–1984
oil on canvas 205 x 156
1989.FA.20

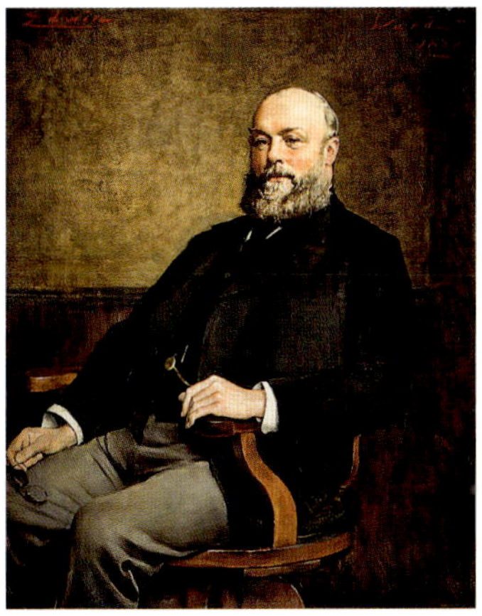

Ward, Edwin Arthur 1859–1933
James Meakin (b.c.1830)
oil on canvas 124 x 100
1992.FA.9

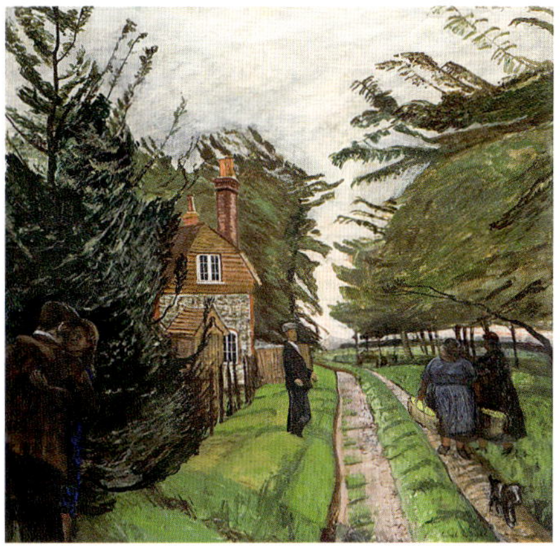

Weight, Carel Victor Morlais 1908–1997
The Pastoral Life 1958
oil on panel 121 x 121
1959.FA.60

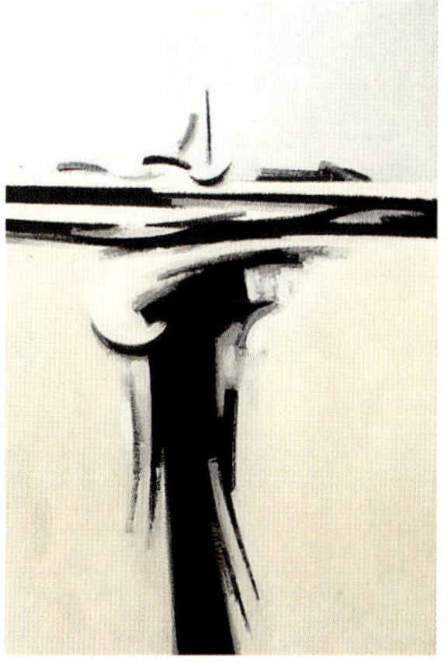

Wheeler, Geoffrey 1929–1995
Maritime Incident I
oil on board 87 x 59
1969.FA.8A

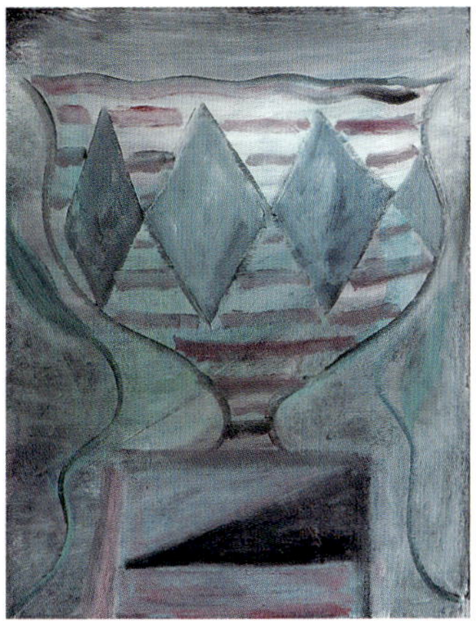

Wild, Tony b.1941
Vase with Diamond Shape 1982
acrylic on card 100 x 83
1983.FA.3

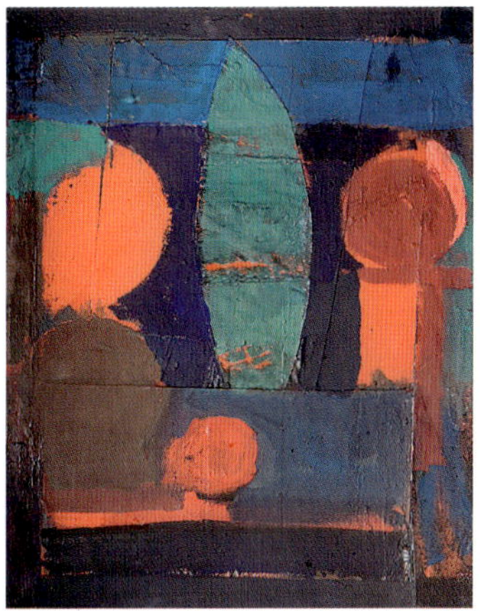

Wild, Tony b.1941
Terracotta Park II
acrylic on board 102 x 66
1986.FA.23

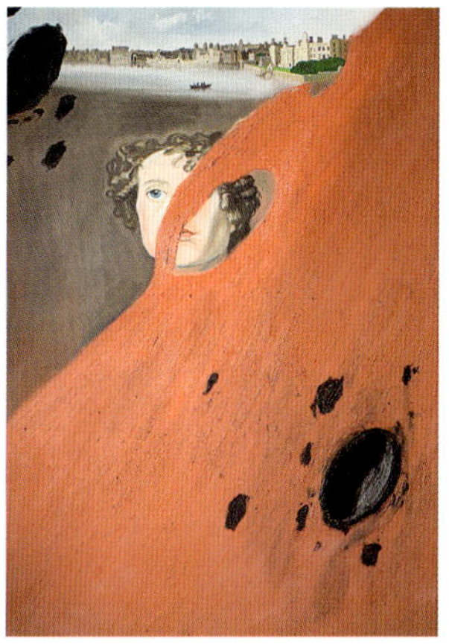

Williams, Alun b.1961
Official Portrait of the President of El Dorado
oil on canvas 173 x 120
1992.FA.8

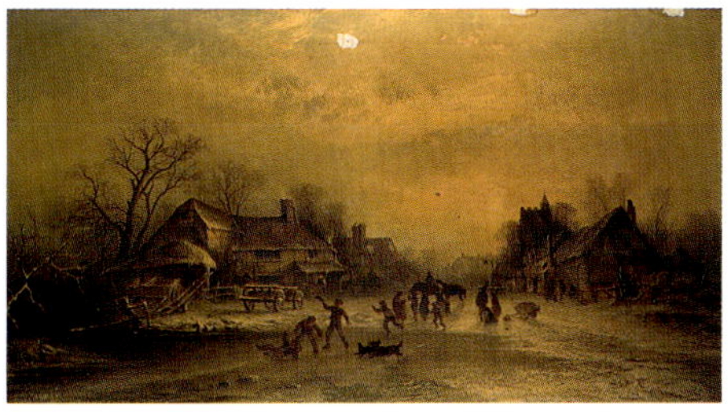

Williams, George Augustus 1814–1901
Frozen Mill Pond 1863
oil on canvas 59 x 123
1964.FA.1A

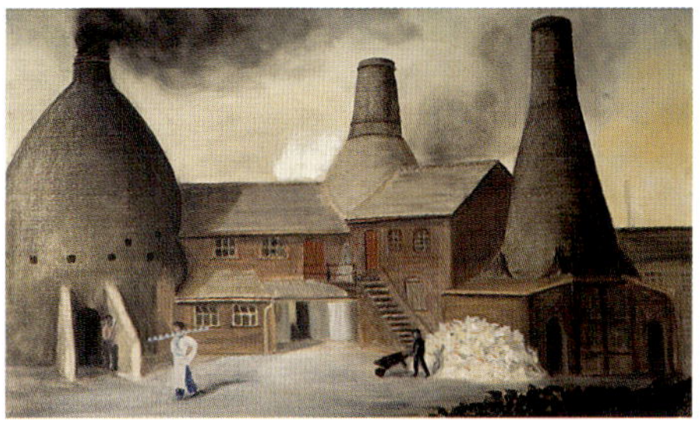

Wilson, Clive
The Master's Castle, Etruria 1949
oil on canvas 36.5 x 59
1950.FA.24

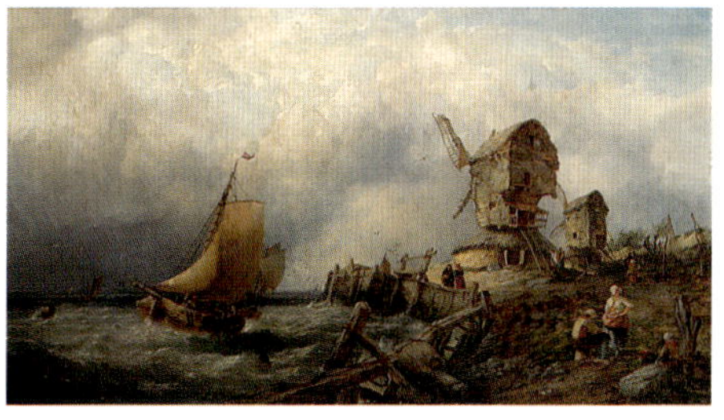

Wilson, John Glen 1774–1855
On the Scheldt
oil on canvas 64 x 112
1964.FA.2A

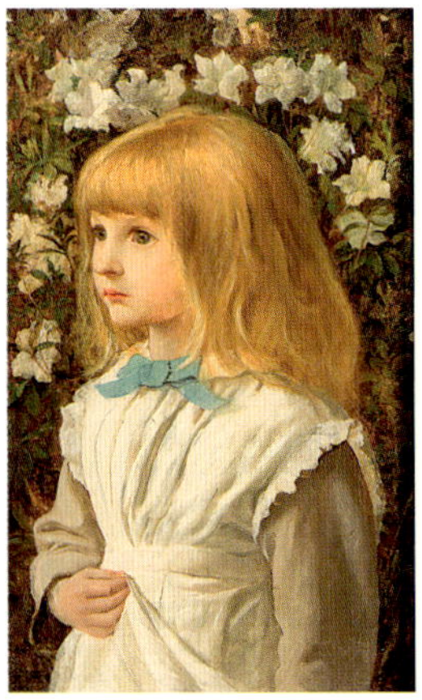

Wise, William
Childhood
oil on board 50 x 30
PCF62

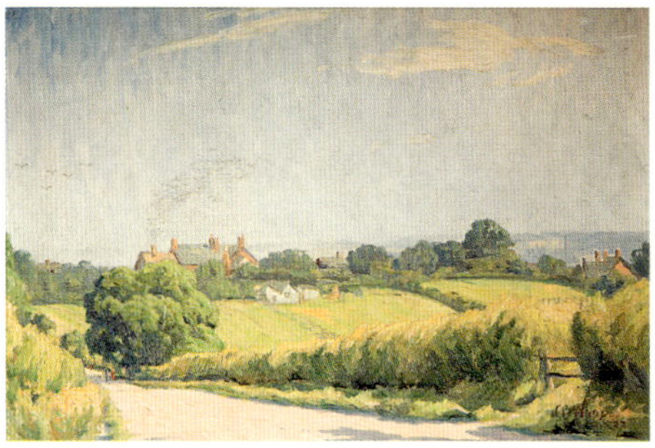

Wood, Charles Bernard b.1902
Leafy June, Hanchurch 1923
oil on board 34 x 49
1924.FA.1

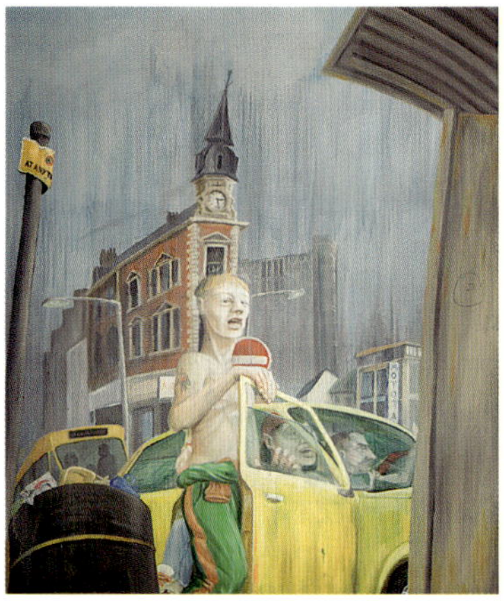

Wood, Mark b.1965
Joyriders 1991
acrylic on canvas 183 x 150
1992.FA.3

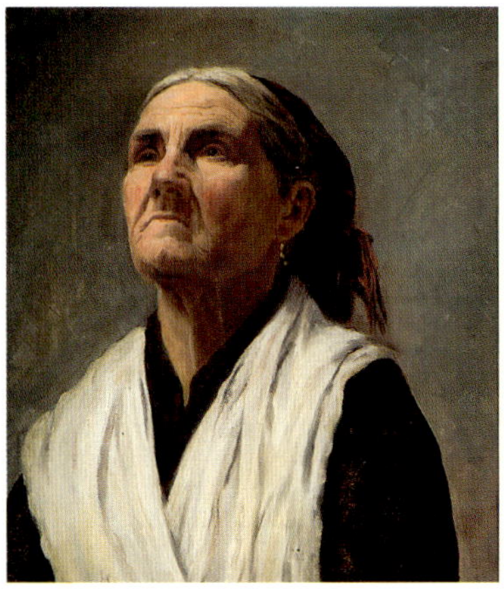

Wooldridge, Frederick Richard 1866–1952
Head of an Old Woman
oil on canvas 45 x 37
1950.FA.113

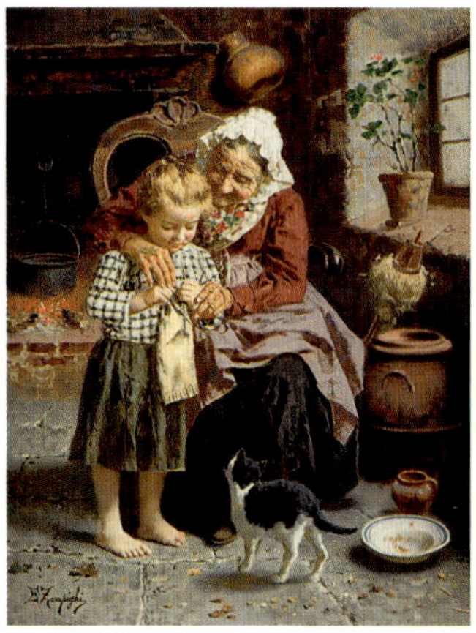

Zampighi, Eugenio 1859–1944
Her First Lesson
oil on canvas 58 x 44
1975.FA.11

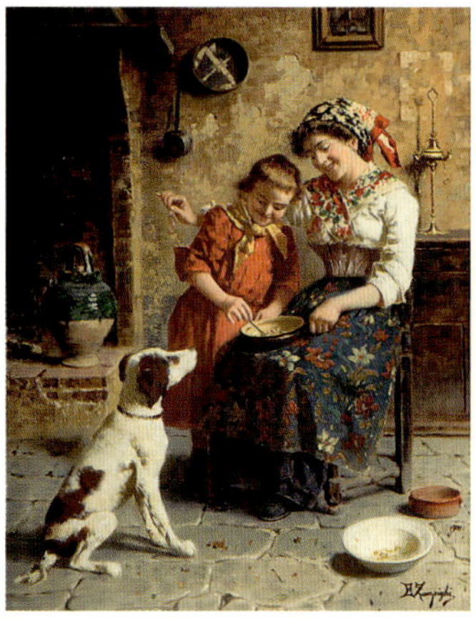

Zampighi, Eugenio 1859–1944
Tantalizing
oil on canvas 58 x 44
1975.FA.12

Wedgwood Museum

The Wedgwood Museum contains the world's greatest collection of Wedgwood ceramics and illustrates the living tradition of Wedgwood through three centuries. The Collection is of both national significance and international importance due to the survival of 75,000 manuscripts and pattern and shape records as well as an extensive ceramic collection. The idea for a Museum emanates from the concept of the founder, Josiah Wedgwood I, who set aside many of his own trials, experiments and finished ware for posterity. He was a potter, pioneer and philanthropist, whose interests embrace a very wide range of subjects in both the arts and sciences.

The Museum contains a unique collection of ceramics, fine art, artefacts, pattern books, manuscripts and mechanical objects and is one of the most comprehensive collections and complete studies of a single manufactory to survive. In total more than 8,000 rare ceramic items are held in the Trust by the Wedgwood Museum Trustees, together with a huge range of historically important manuscripts and correspondence about social, political and business life in the eighteenth and nineteenth centuries, including letters from Charles Darwin (Josiah I's grandson), Coleridge and many others.

The collections also contain a small but internationally significant fine art section, including paintings by George Stubbs, Sir Joshua Reynolds, Joseph Wright of Derby, George Romney and the American artist John Singer Sargent, as well as nineteenth and twentieth century watercolour design sketches by artists such as Lessore, Thomas Allen, Graham Sutherland and David Shepherd.

The museum galleries are closed to the public at the present time (2007) whilst major new galleries, a research area and educational facilities are constructed. This has been made possible through a Heritage Lottery Fund Grant of £5.85m towards the total cost. It is anticipated that the new Museum will reopen in Spring 2008.

Lynn Miller, Museum Information Officer & Nigel Spicer,
Learning and Access Manager

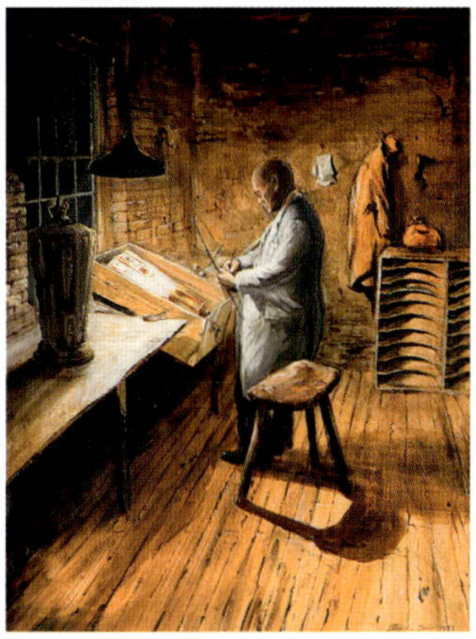

Barker, Charles
The Queen's Vase 1957
oil on board 77 x 59
PCF1

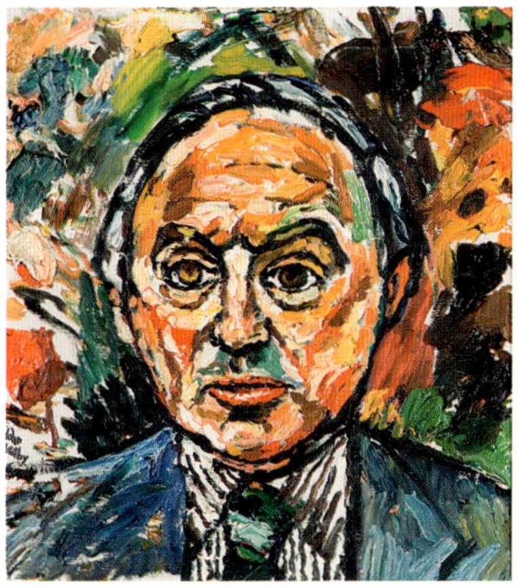

Bratby, John Randall 1928–1992
Sir Arthur Bryan (former Wedgwood Company Chairman & Wedgwood Museum Trust Chairman) 1980s
oil on canvas 40 x 35
PCF2

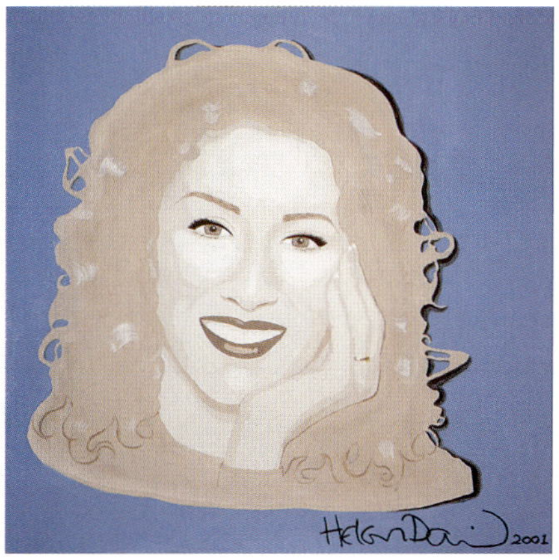

David, Helen
Wedgwood Me 2001
acrylic on canvas 76.5 x 76.5
PCF3 (P)

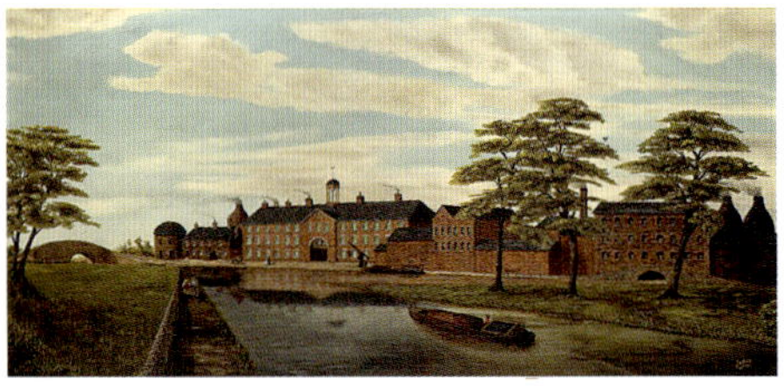

De Bod, E.
Etruria, Canal Front 1973
oil on canvas 50 x 100
9745

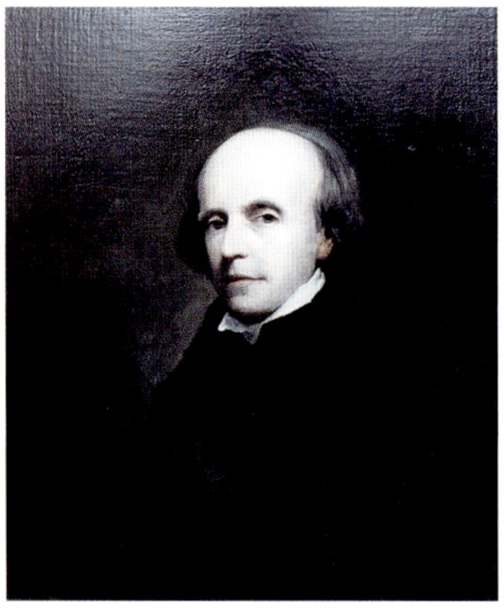

Jackson, John 1778–1831
John Flaxman (1755–1826)
oil on canvas 100 x 86
9900

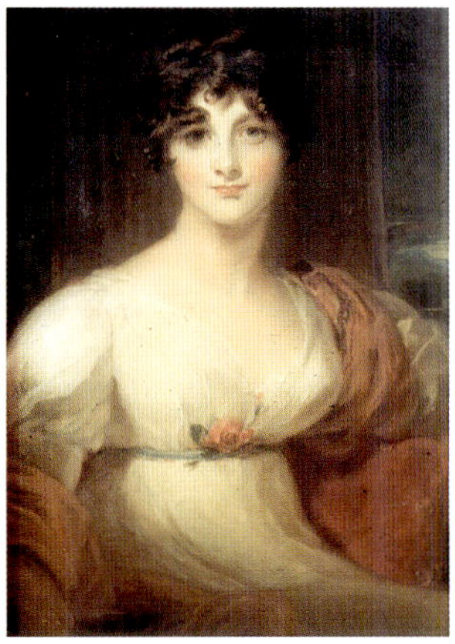

Lawrence, Thomas (copy of) 1769–1830
Louisa Jane Allen (Mrs John Wedgwood) (1771–1836)
oil on canvas 101 x 88
9249

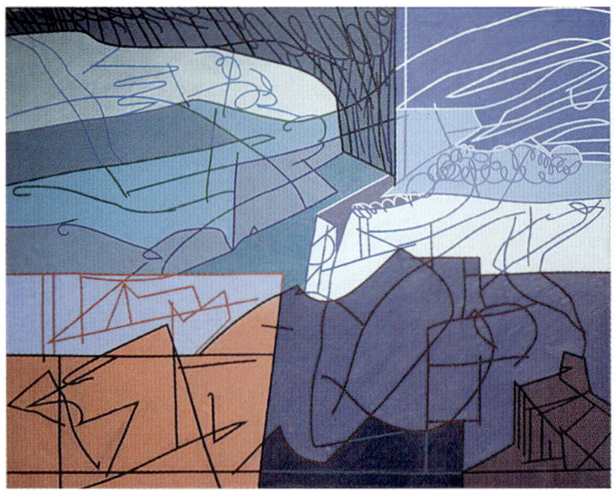

Lovatt, Enos b.1937
Abstract Potteries Landscape
acrylic on canvas 121 x 153
PCF4

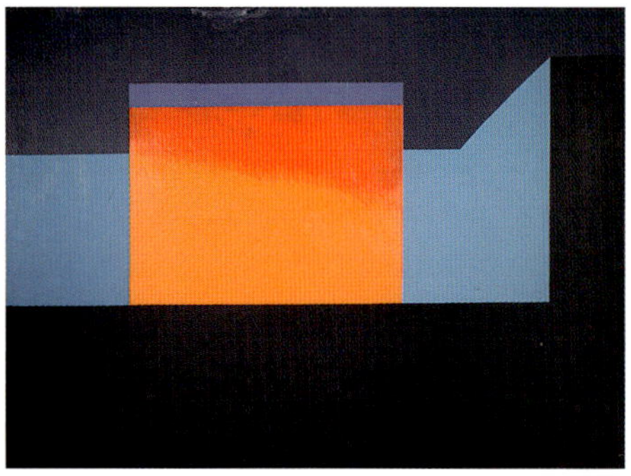

Lovatt, Enos b.1937
Geometric Shapes
acrylic on canvas 189 x 243
PCF5

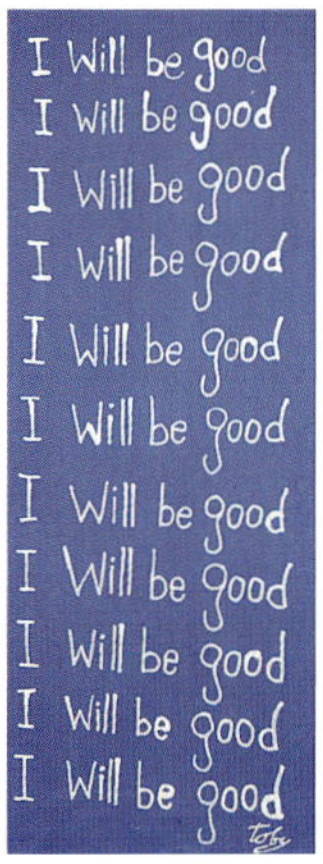

Mott, Toby
'I will be good' 2002
acrylic on canvas 80 x 30
PCF6 (P)

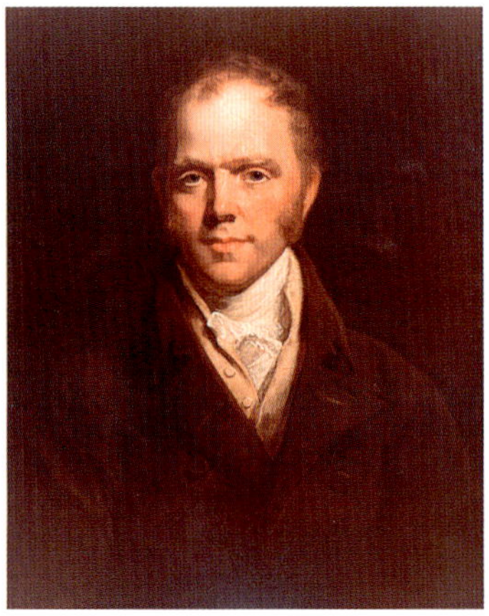

Owen, William 1769–1825
Josiah Wedgwood II (1769–1843)
oil on canvas 106.5 x 93
5615

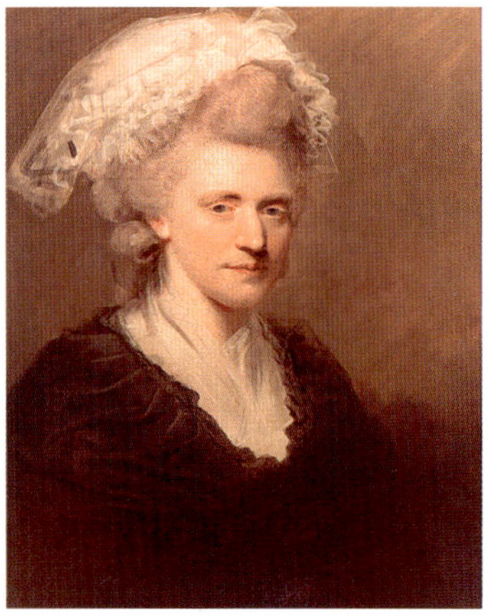

Reynolds, Joshua 1723–1792
Sarah Wedgwood (1734–1815) 1782
oil on canvas 109 x 95.5
5609

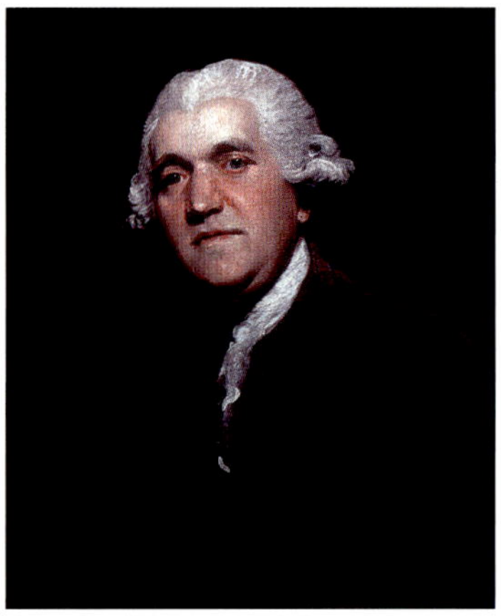

Reynolds, Joshua 1723–1792
Josiah Wedgwood I (1730–1795)
oil on canvas 108.5 x 96
5004

Facing page: Hoberman, Nicky, b.1967, *The Frog Princess* (detail), 1997, The New Art Gallery Walsall, (p. 207)

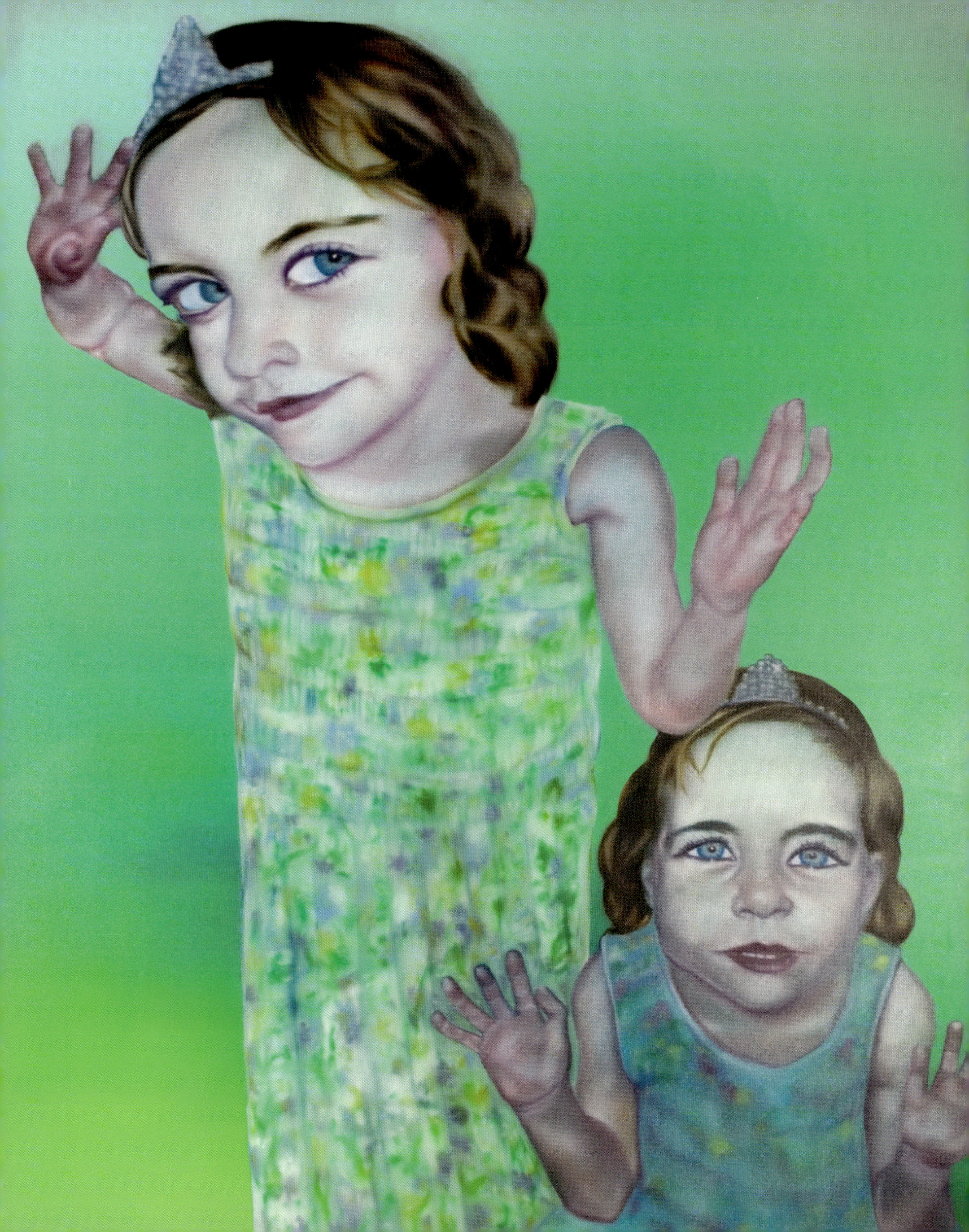

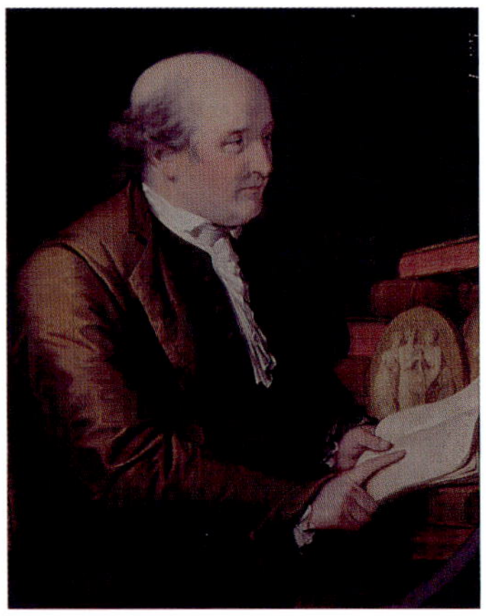

Rigaud, John Francis (attributed to)
1742–1810
Thomas Bentley (1731–1780) 1778
oil on canvas 117 x 96.5
5606

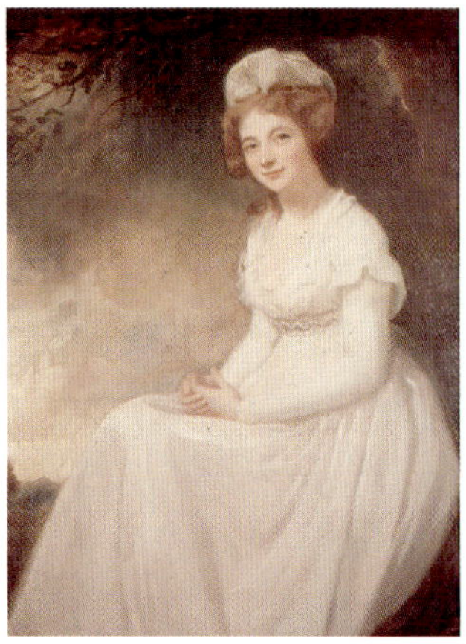

Romney, George 1734–1802
Elizabeth Allen (Mrs Josiah Wedgwood II) (1764–1846)
oil on canvas 158.5 x 129.5
5611

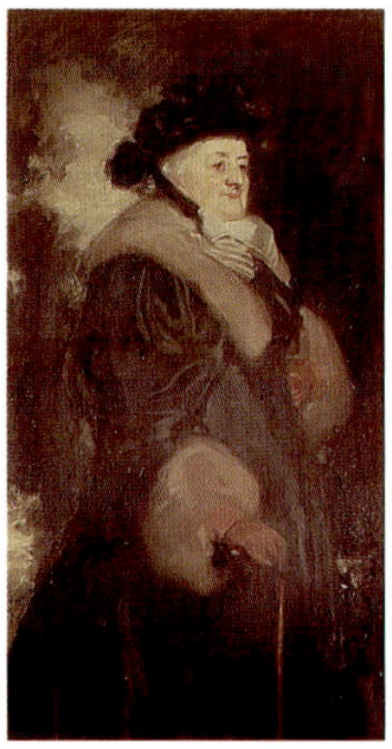

Sargent, John Singer 1856–1925
Mrs Robert Wedgwood (d.1906)
oil on canvas 142 x 72 (E)
5616

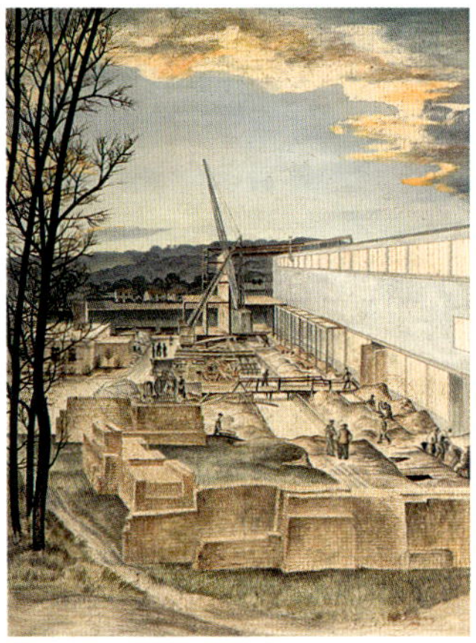

Skellern, Victor 1908–1966
Wedgwood Factory, Barlaston 1946
oil on board 64 x 46
PCF7

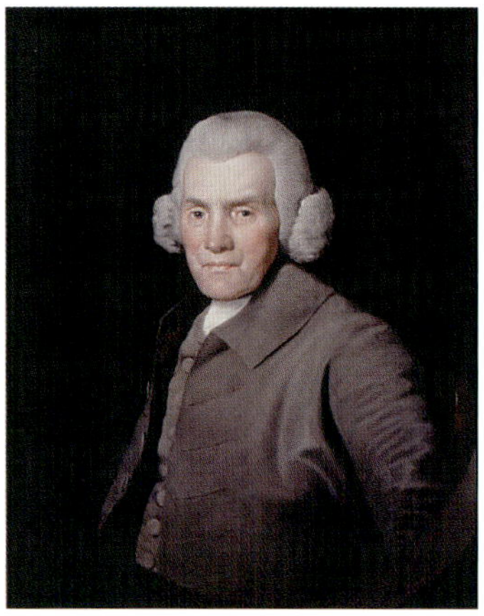

Stubbs, George 1724–1806
Richard Wedgwood (c.1701–1782) 1780
oil on wood panel 71 x 58.5
5612

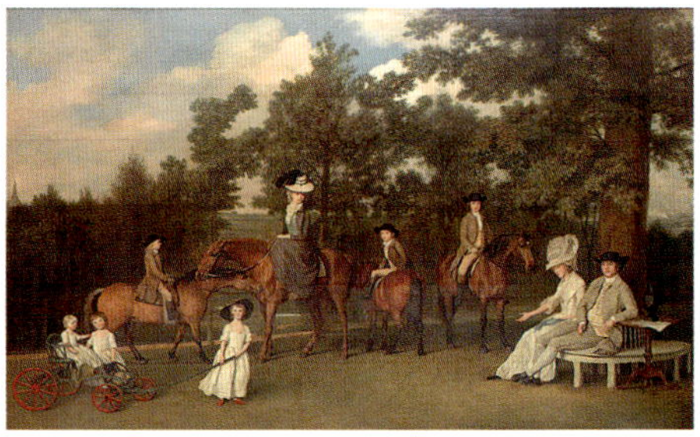

Stubbs, George 1724–1806
Wedgwood Family 1780
oil on wood panel 121.5 x 184
5703

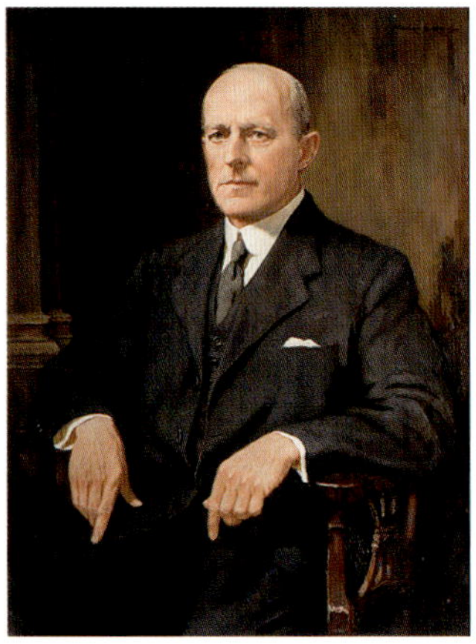

unknown artist
George Meakin (b.1864) 1950s
oil on canvas 120 x 95.5
PCF8

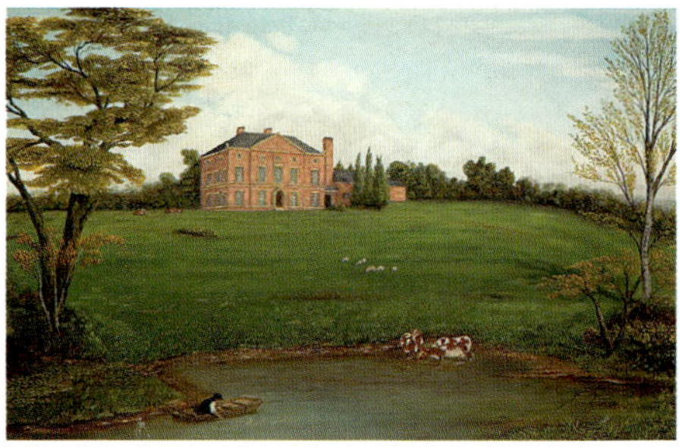

unknown artist late 20th C
Barlaston Hall
oil on canvas 49.5 x 75
PCF9

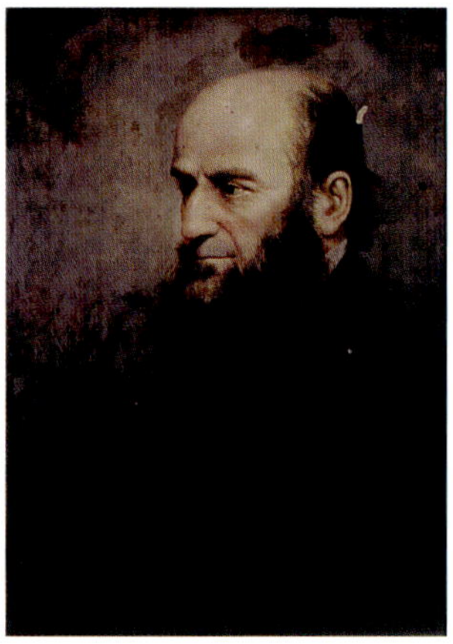

unknown artist
Francis Wedgwood (1800–1888)
oil on canvas 86.5 x 76
5569

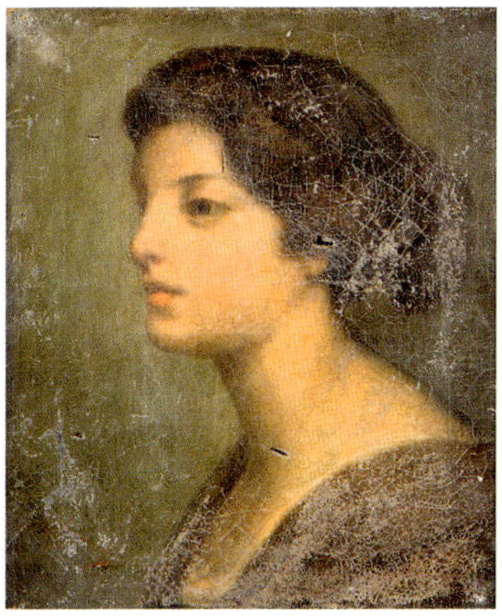

unknown artist
Portrait of a Lady
oil on canvas 41 x 33
PCF10

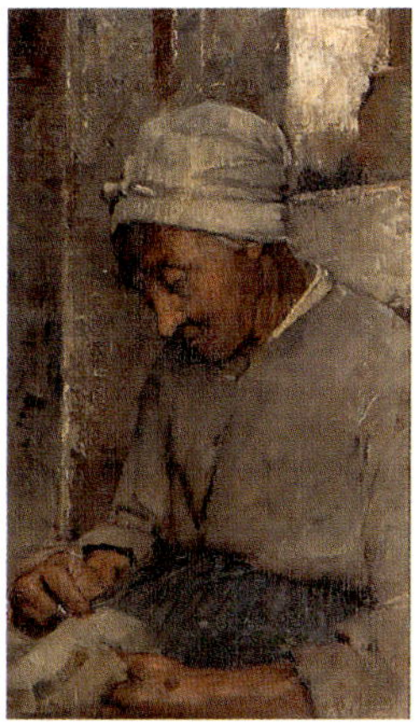

unknown artist
Woman Sewing
oil on canvas 26 x 15.5
PCF11

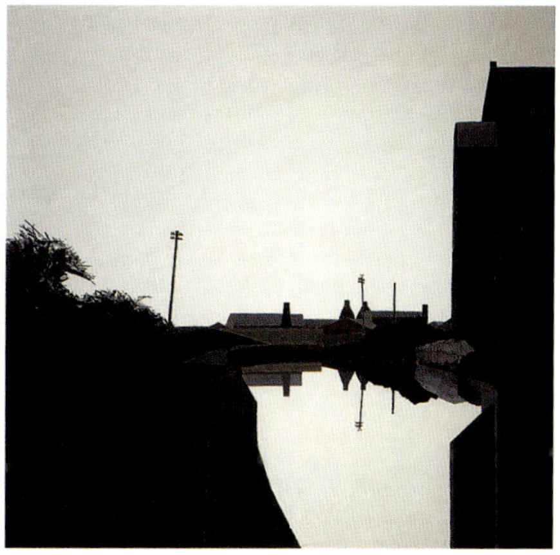

Wade, Maurice 1917–1991
Canal at Longport III 1970s
acrylic on board 90 x 90
PCF12

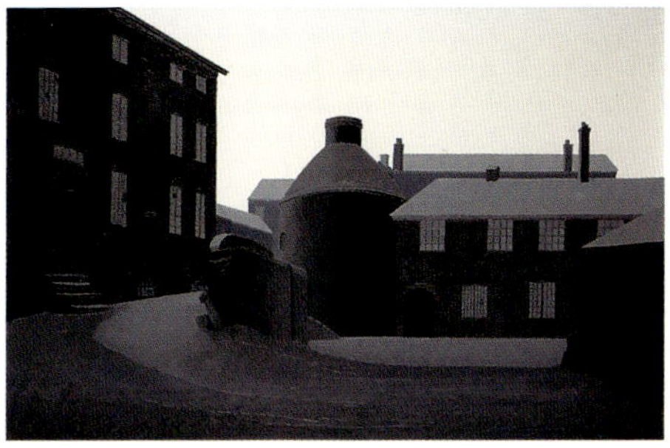

Wade, Maurice 1917–1991
North Round House and Bridge, Etruria 1970s
acrylic on board 53 x 80
203/75

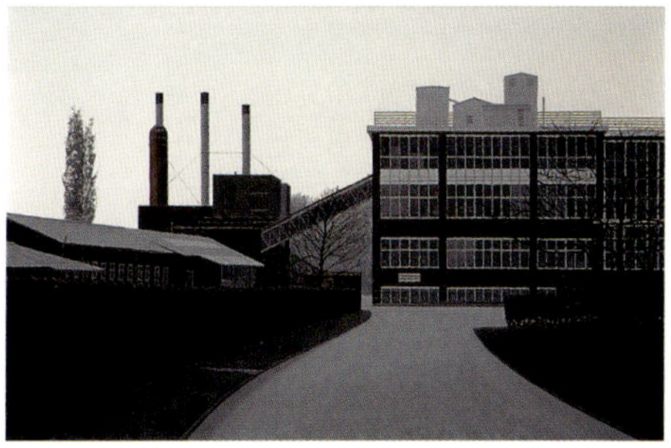

Wade, Maurice 1917–1991
Powerhouse and Workshop, Wedgwood 1970s
acrylic on board 53 x 76
PCF13

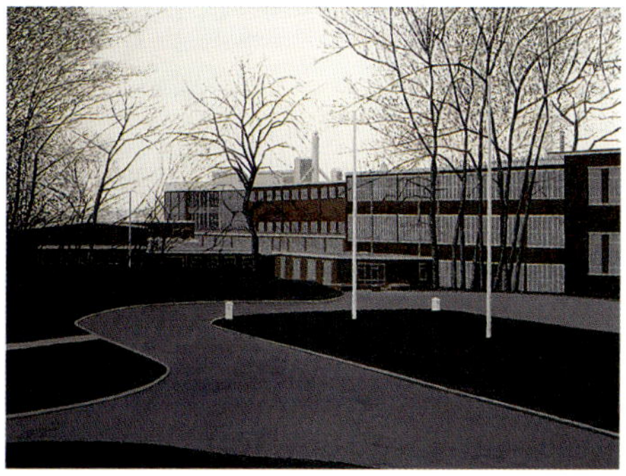

Wade, Maurice 1917–1991
South Facade, Wedgwood, Barlaston 1970s
acrylic on board 71 x 91
PCF14

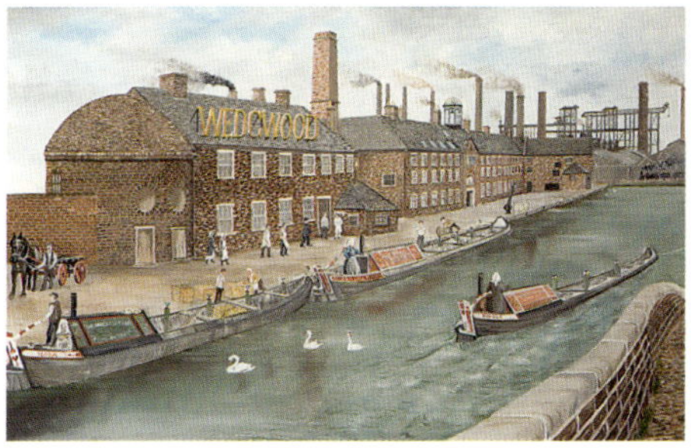

Wakefield, John
Wedgwood Factory, Etruria
acrylic on canvas 55 x 81
9270

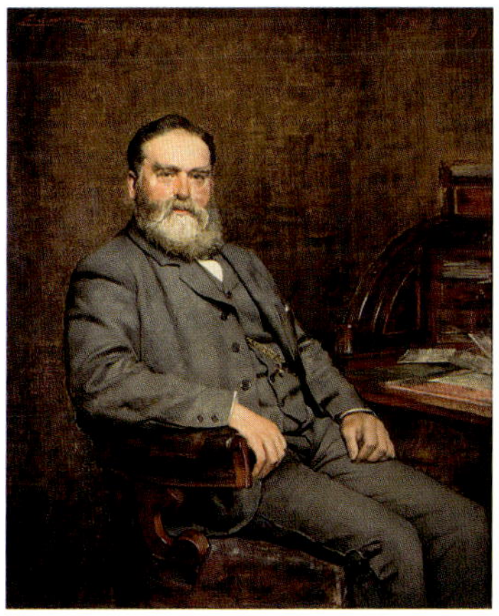

Ward, Edwin Arthur 1859–1933
George Meakin (1832–1891) 1889
oil on canvas 125 x 99
PCF15

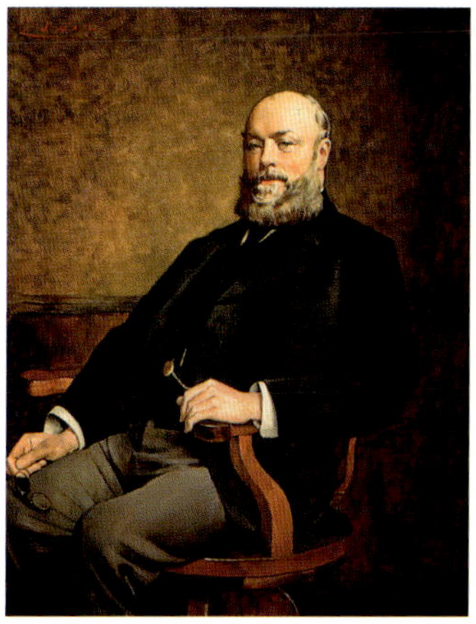

Ward, Edwin Arthur 1859–1933
James Meakin (1807–1852) 1889
oil on canvas 126 x 100
PCF16

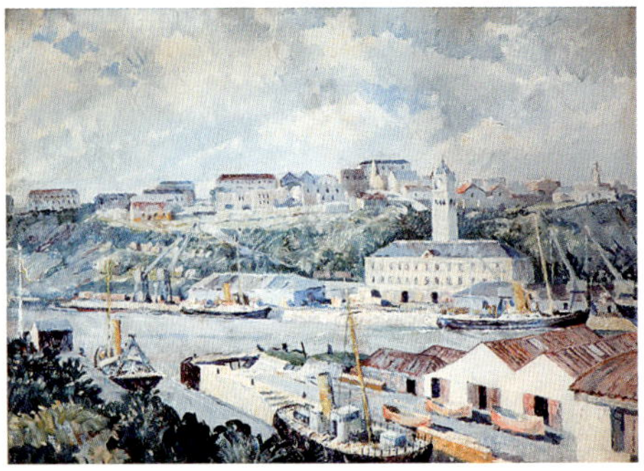

Wedgwood, Francis Charles Bowen
1898–1959
Buffalo Harbour, South Africa
oil on board 45 x 60
PCF17

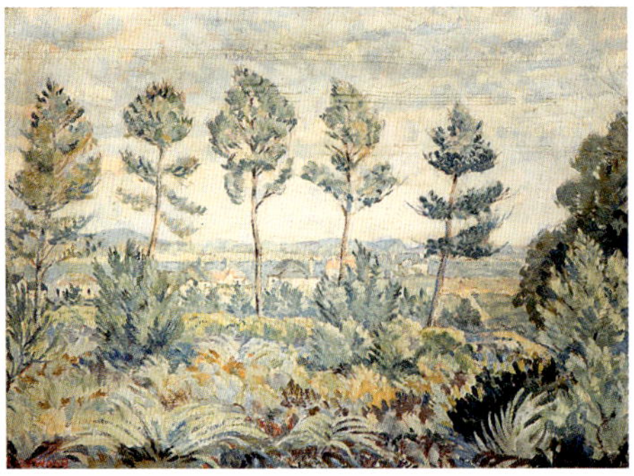

Wedgwood, Francis Charles Bowen
1898–1959
Five Sisters
oil on canvas 49 x 65
PCF18

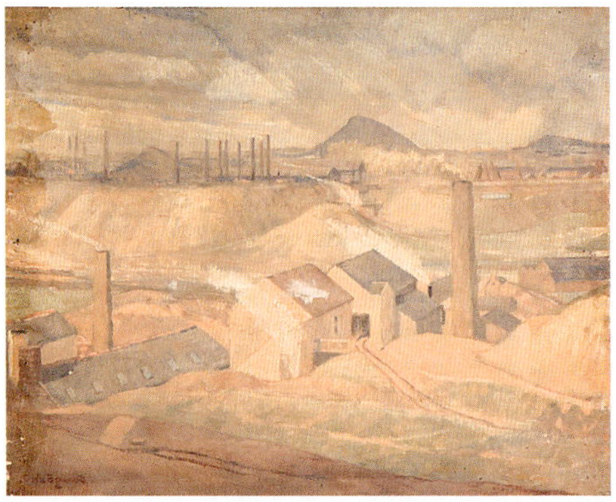

Wedgwood, Francis Charles Bowen
1898–1959
Wedgwood, Etruria
oil on canvas 51 x 61
PCF19

Tamworth Borough Council

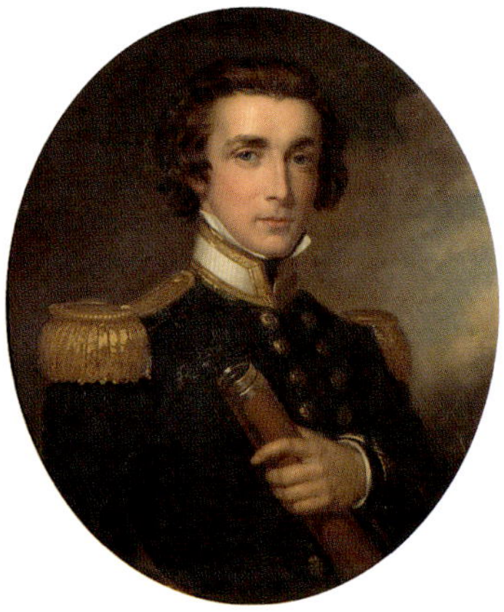

unknown artist
Captain Sir William Peel (1824–1858)
oil on canvas 75 x 60
PCF2

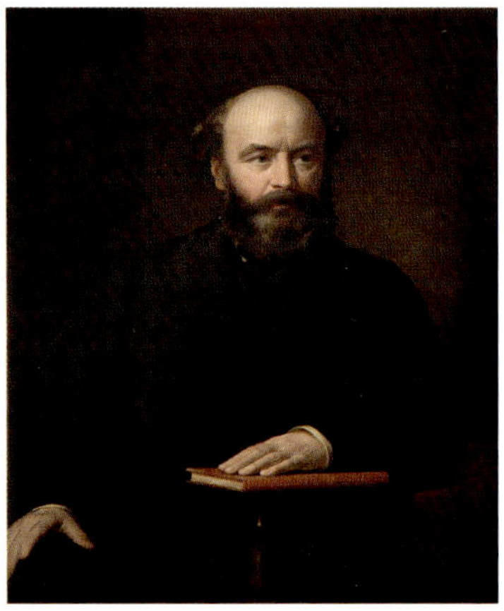

unknown artist
John Peel, MP for Tamworth (1804–1872)
oil on canvas 93 x 70
PCF7

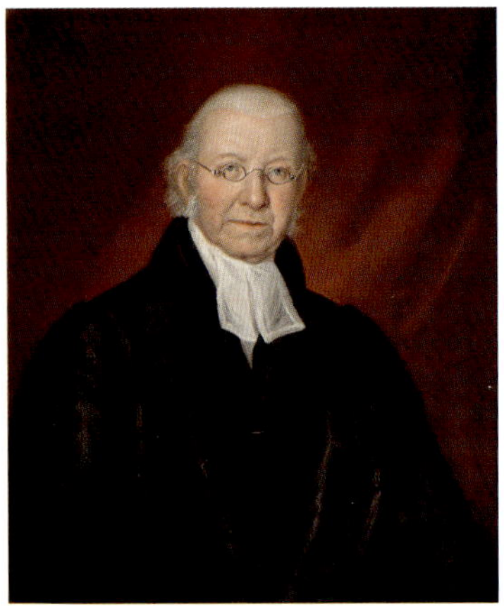

unknown artist
Reverend Francis Blick, MA
oil on canvas 75 x 60
PCF4

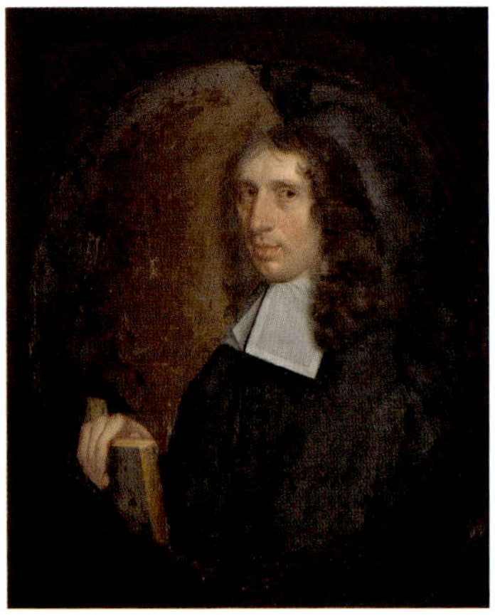

unknown artist
Reverend Rawlet
oil on canvas 90 x 70
PCF5

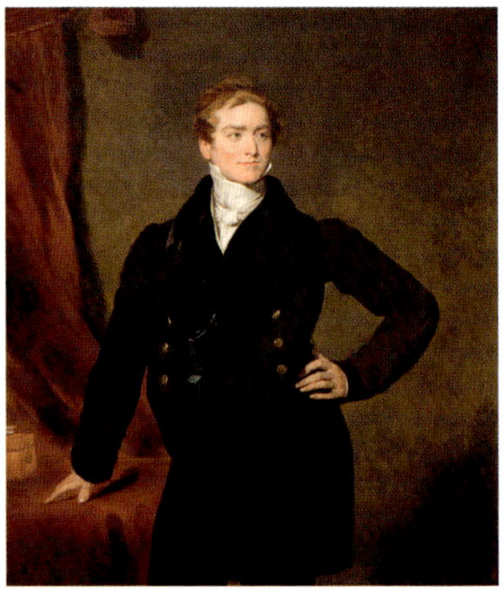

unknown artist
Sir Robert Peel (1788–1850)
oil on canvas 140 x 115
PCF1

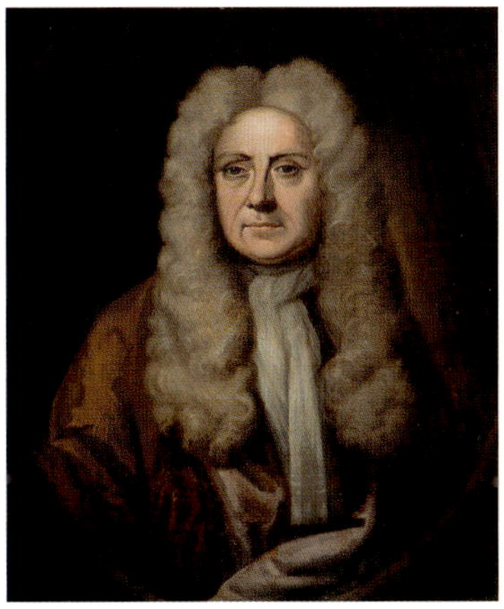

unknown artist
Thomas Guy (1644–1724)
oil on canvas 73 x 60
PCF3

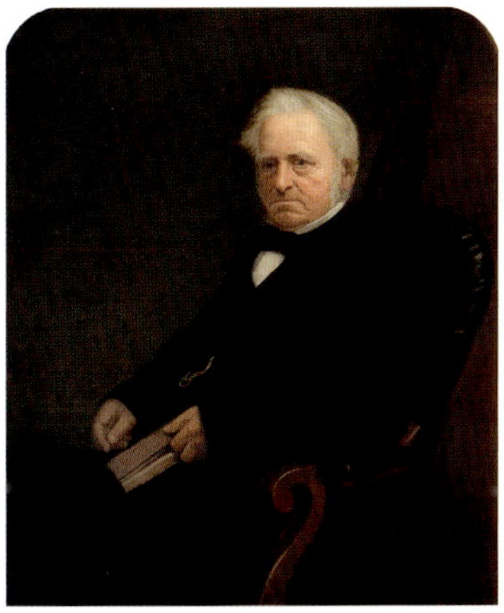

unknown artist
William Robinson, Mayor of Tamworth
oil on canvas 75 x 65
PCF6

Tamworth Castle

Tamworth Castle is situated in the town centre overlooking the confluence of the rivers Tame and Anker. An early wooden structure existed on the site in Anglo-Saxon times, when Queen Aethelfleda, daughter of King Alfred the Great, built defenses against the Danes. The Normans built the original motte and bailey castle on the man-made mound some time between 1070 and 1080. This was replaced in the 1180s by a polygonal stone shell keep.

The Castle has been owned by several families, all linked by marriage, and has been altered many times over the centuries. The oldest surviving section within the Shell Keep, is the north wing with its thirteenth century arched doorway, and there are examples of different periods of building through to the late eighteenth century. The most impressive room is the Great Hall with its oak-timbered tie beam roof that dates from the mid-fifteenth century.

The Castle is a heritage site and a museum, recreating how parts of the Castle would have been used during different periods of its history. Some of the Castle's collections are displayed in the room settings and an exhibition space, and include furniture, ceramics, costume and archaeological artefacts. The oil paintings in the collection include local views and portraits of some of the local gentry.

Sarah Williams, Collections Officer

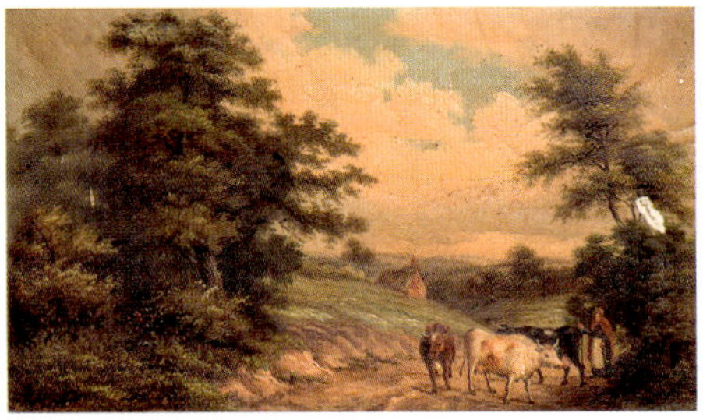

Baldwin, H.
Landscape
oil on canvas 29 x 50
1966.48

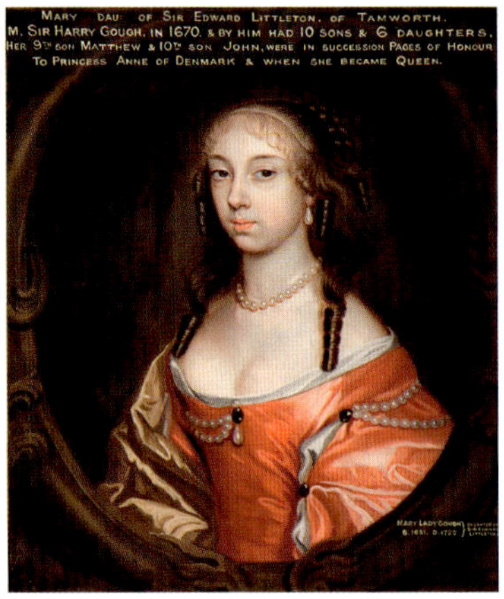

Beale, Mary (attributed to) 1633–1699
Lady Mary Gough (1657–1722) c.1670
oil on canvas 74 x 62
1989.1

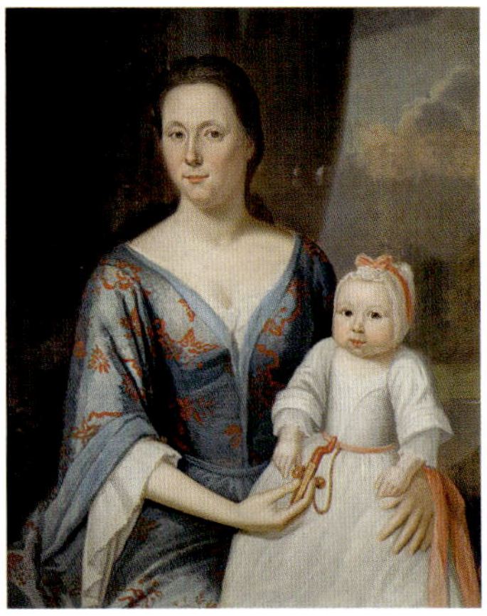

British (English) School early 18th C
Mrs Willington and Daughter
oil on canvas 90 x 68
1992.19

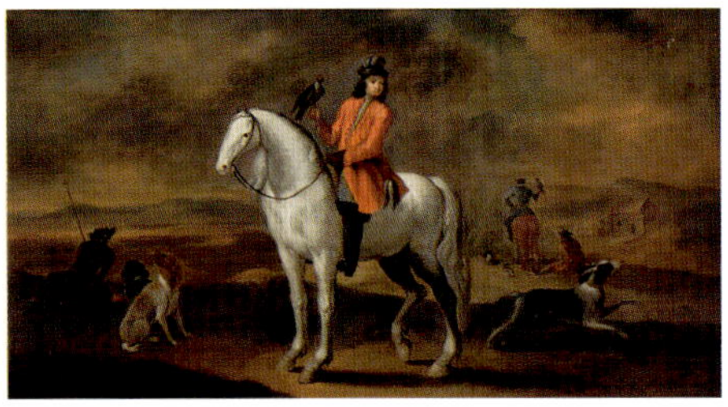

British (English) School mid-18th C
Hunting Scene (possibly Waldyue Willington, former Parliamentarian Governor of Tamworth Castle)
oil on canvas 85 x 143
1992.20

Brooke, Charlotte
Royalist
oil on canvas 28 x 22.5
1975.15

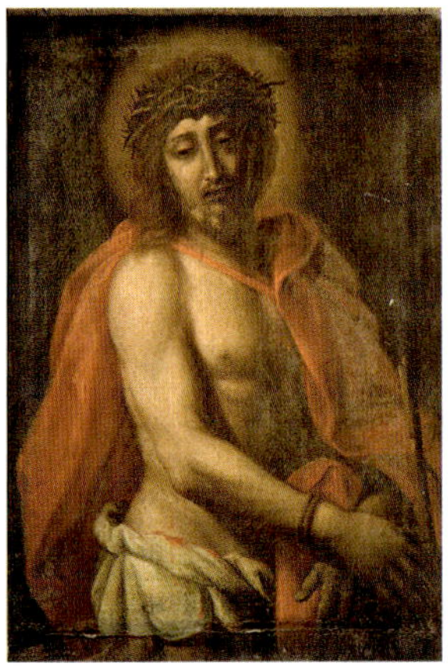

Dolci, Carlo 1616–1686
Ecce Homo
oil on canvas 66 x 49
1923.1.3

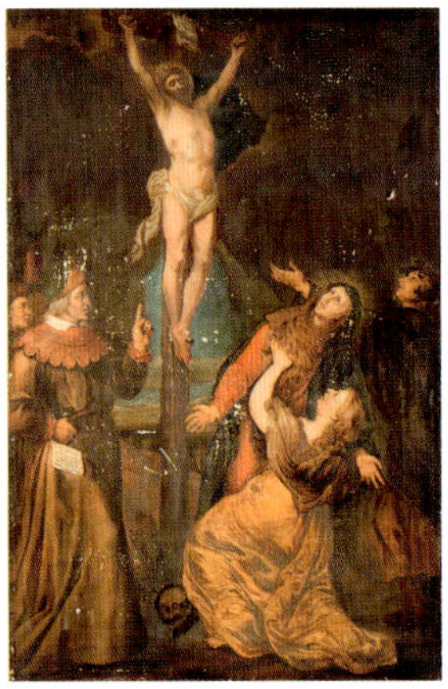

Dyck, Anthony van (after) 1599–1641
Crucifixion
oil on canvas 150 x 99
PCF1

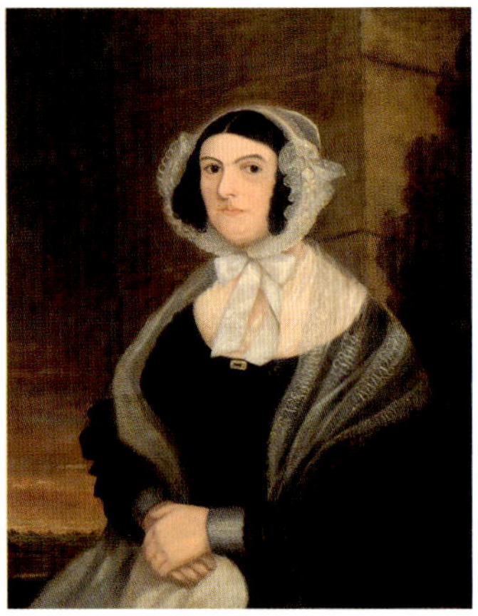

Elmore, R.
Maria Watton 1842
oil on canvas 90 x 70
1996.1

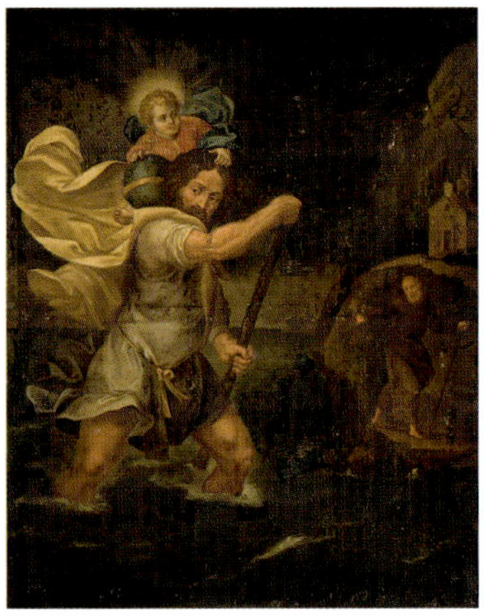

Elsheimer, Adam (after) 1578–1610
St Christopher, Carrying the Infant Christ across a Stream
oil on canvas 95 x 78
PCF2

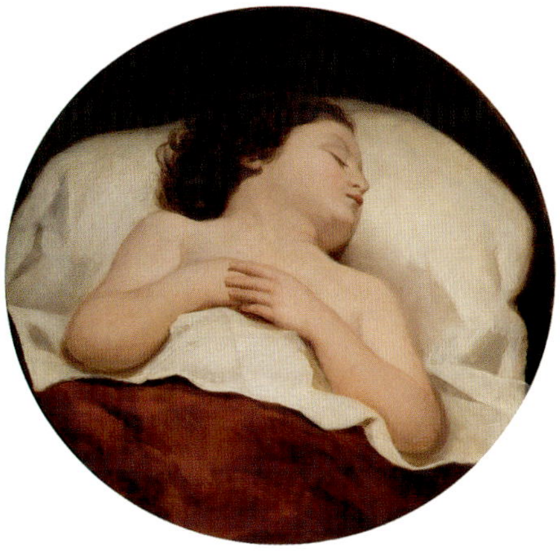

Etty, William 1787–1849
A Child Asleep
oil on canvas 52
1923.1.5

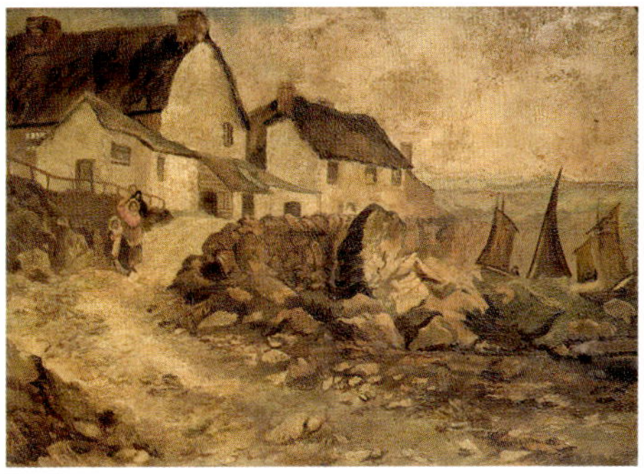

Finiger, H. A.
Cottages at the Seashore 1919
oil on canvas 37 x 50
1966.51

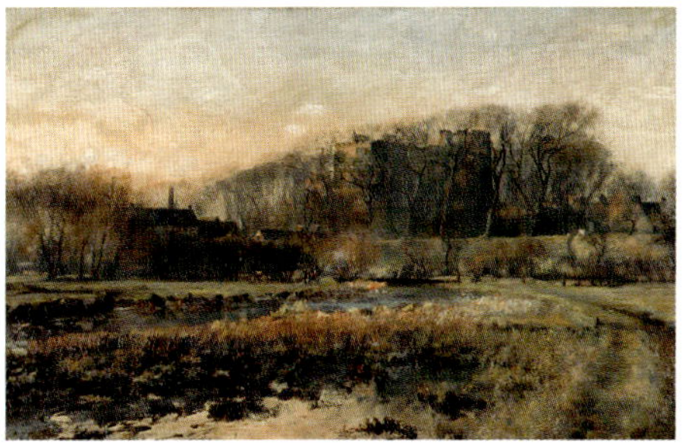

Fox, Charles James 1860–c.1937
Tamworth Castle 1899
oil on canvas 60 x 90
1966.51

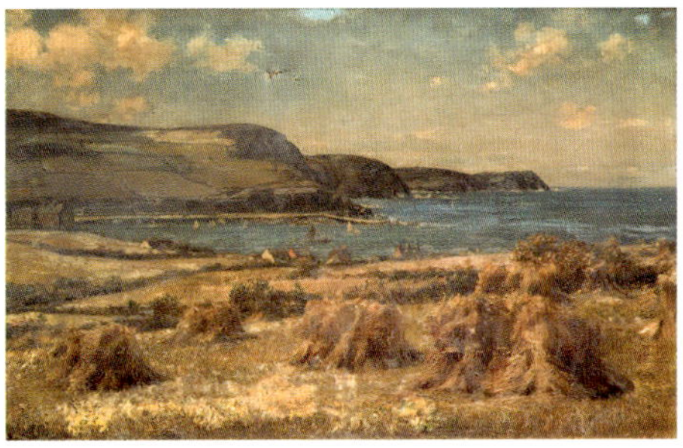

Fox, Charles James 1860–c.1937
Cornfield with Ricks
oil on canvas 60 x 90
1966.45.2

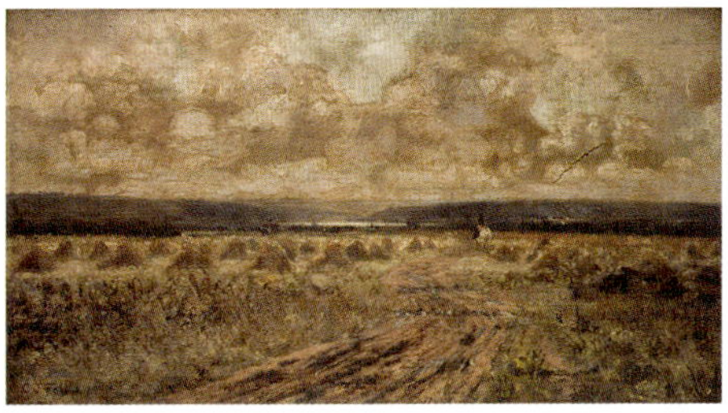

Fox, Charles James 1860–c.1937
Landscape with Horse and Rider (possibly Hampstead Heath)
oil on canvas 45 x 80
PCF3

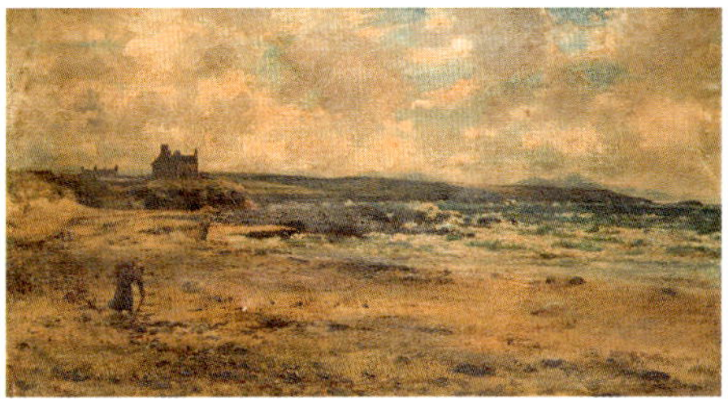

Fox, Charles James 1860–c.1937
Moorland Landscape
oil on canvas 44.5 x 80
1966.45.2

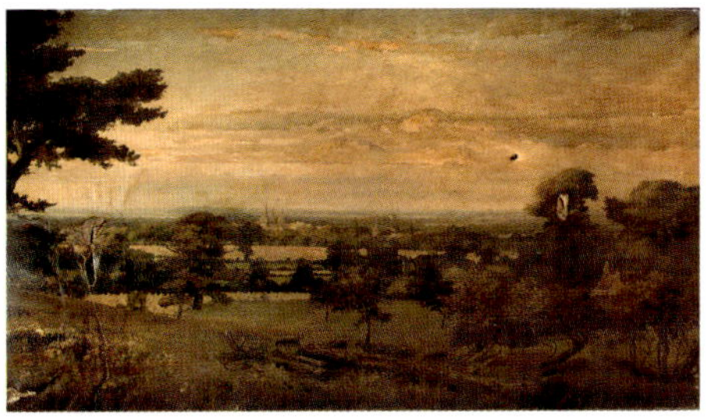

Fox, Charles James 1860–c.1937
View of Lichfield (detail)
oil on canvas 122 x 244
PCF4

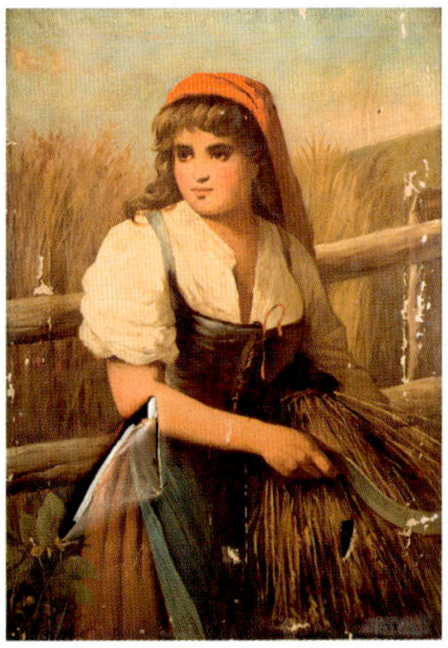

Italian School 19th C
Peasant Girl with Scythe
oil on canvas 114 x 76.5
PCF5

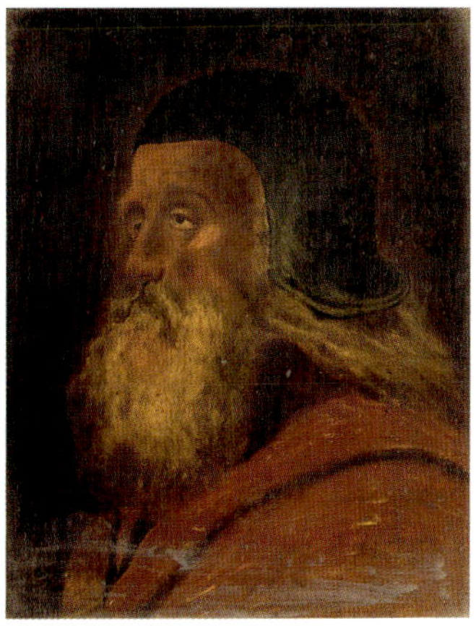

Italian School
Portrait of a Man
oil on board 24 x 19
837

Lawrence, Thomas (style of) 1769–1830
George Ferrers Townshend (d.1855), 3rd Marquis Townshend
oil on canvas 90 x 69
1991.185

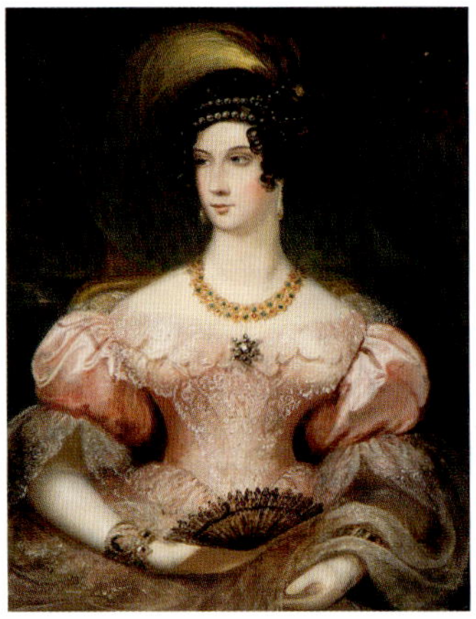

Lawrence, Thomas (style of) 1769–1830
Jane, Marchioness Townshend (wife of George Ferrers Townshend)
oil on canvas 89 x 68
1991.186

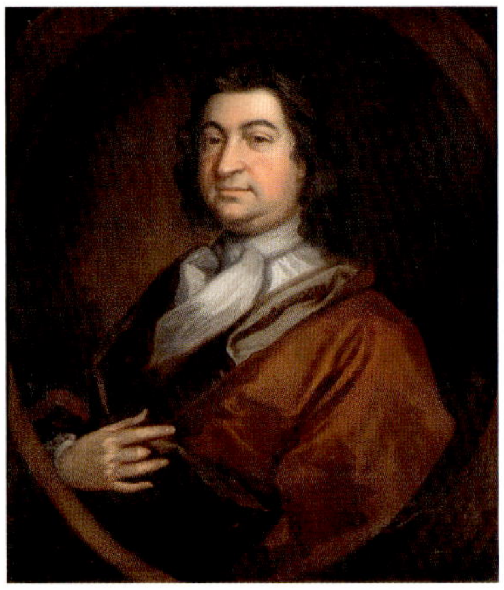

Lely, Peter (school of) 1618–1680
Dr Samuel Shaw (b. before 1710)
oil on canvas 75 x 62
L1969.35

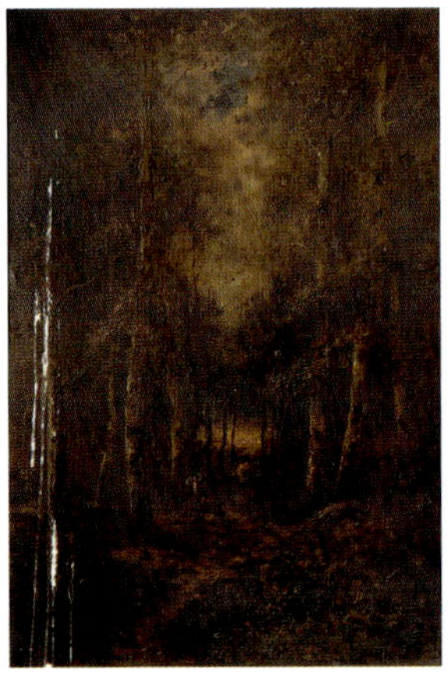

Manzoni, T.
Landscape, Forest Glade
oil on canvas 90 x 59
PCF6

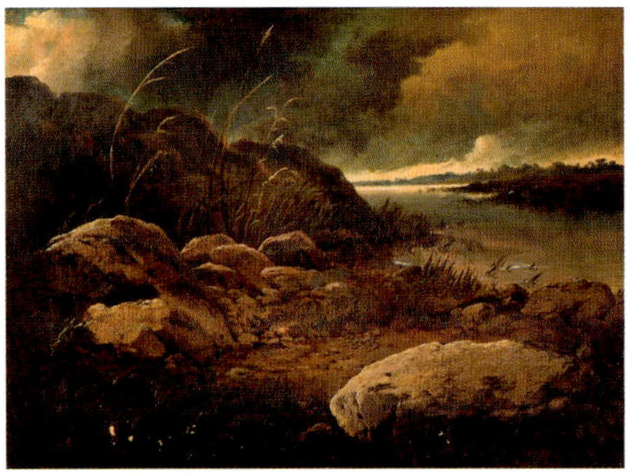

Niemann, Edmund John 1813–1876
The Coming Storm
oil on canvas 68 x 89
PCF7

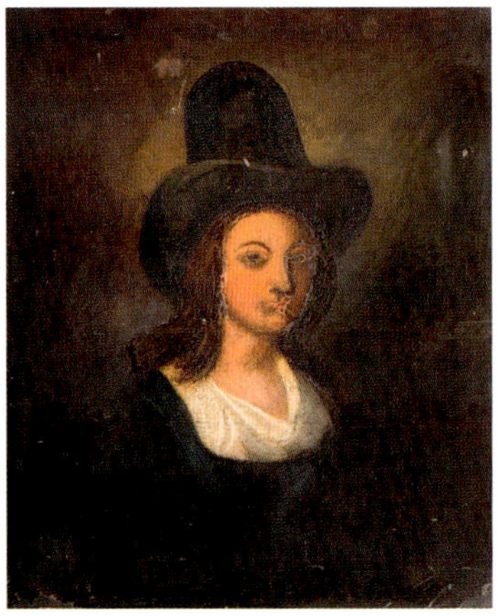

Opie, John 1761–1807
Welsh Lady
oil on canvas 76 x 62
1966.50

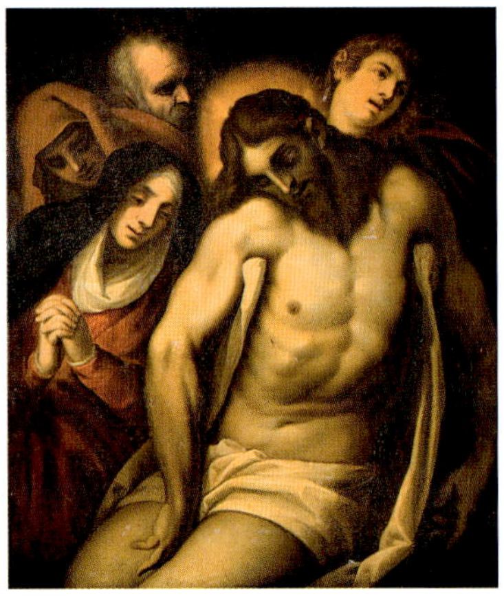

Palma, Jacopo il giovane 1544–1548–1628
Pietà
oil on canvas 112 x 93
1923.1.2

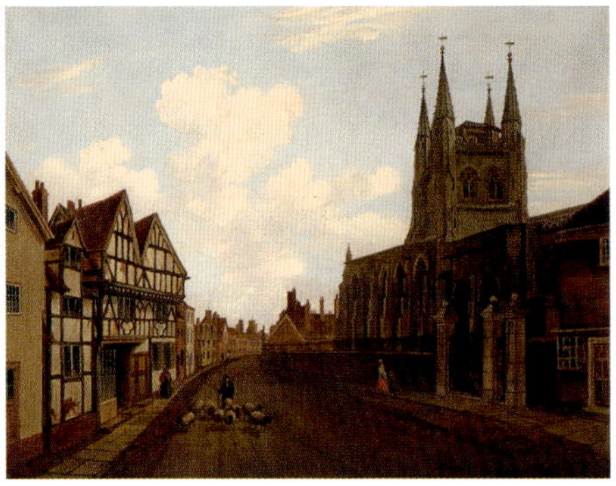

Pratt, Henry Lark I 1805–1873
St Editha's Church and the Old Paregoric Shop, Tamworth 1856
oil on canvas 42 x 58
2003.8.1

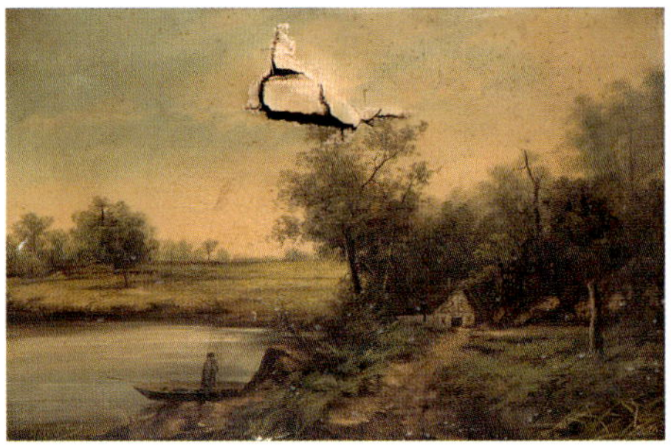

Preston, J.
Lake and Punt
oil on canvas 32 x 47.5
1966.49.2

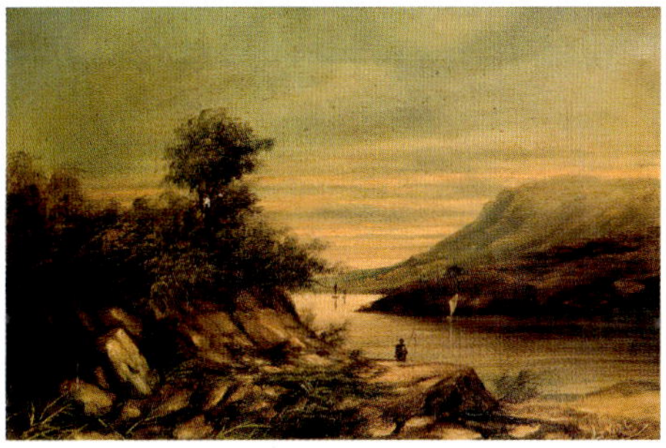

Preston, J.
Lake Landscape
oil on canvas 32 x 47
1966.49.1

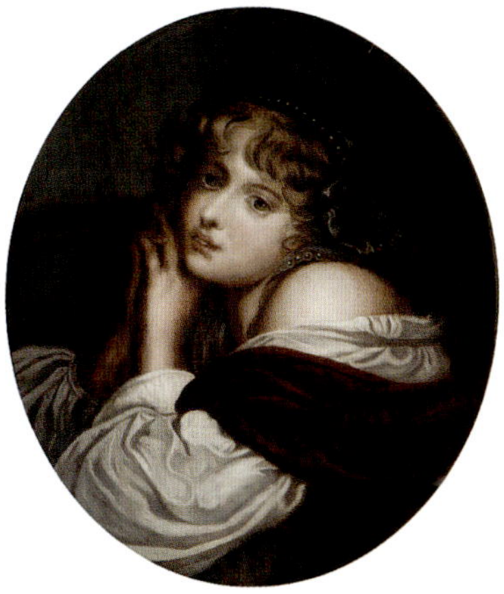

Sant, George active 1856–1877
Innocence
oil on canvas 60 x 49
1923.1.4

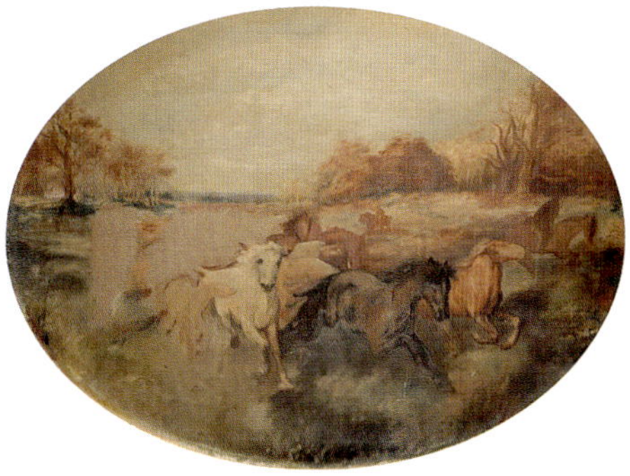

Stretton, Leon
Horses (unfinished)
oil on canvas 70 x 90
1938.2

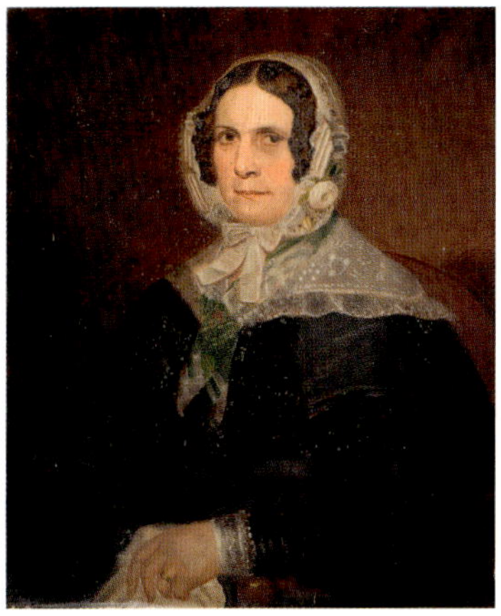

unknown artist
Mrs Tidy c.1865
oil on canvas 74 x 61
1967.51.2

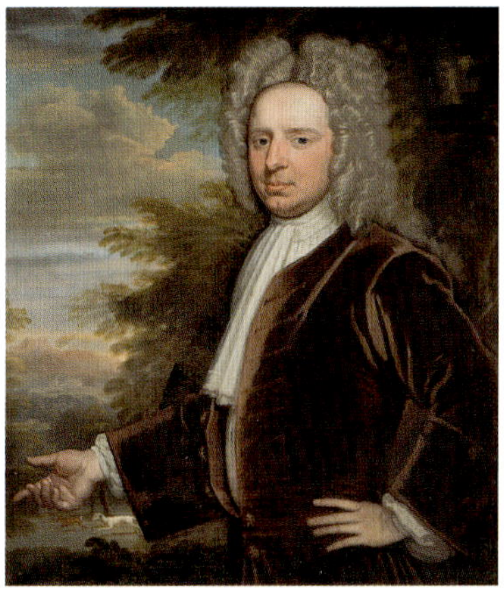

unknown artist
A Member of the Willington Family
oil on canvas 93 x 79
1992.17

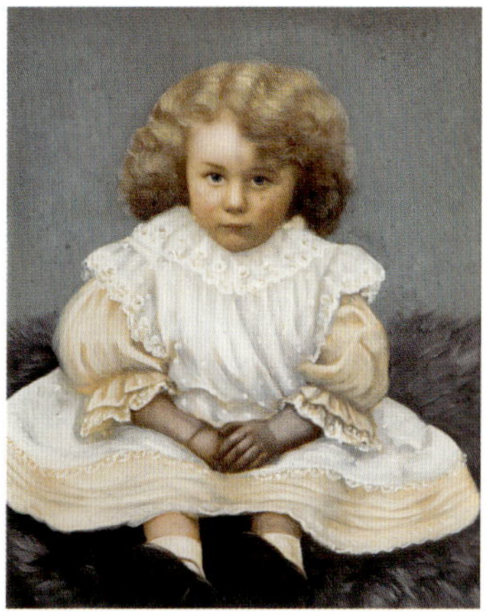

unknown artist
Child on an Animal Fur Rug
oil on canvas 46 x 37
PCF8

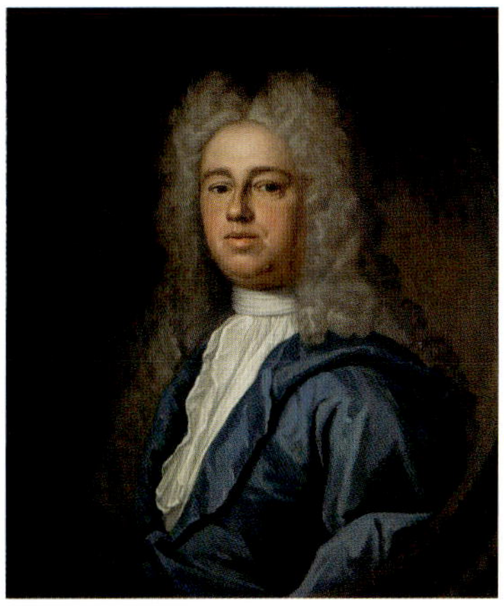

unknown artist
Mr Willington
oil on canvas 73 x 61
PCF9

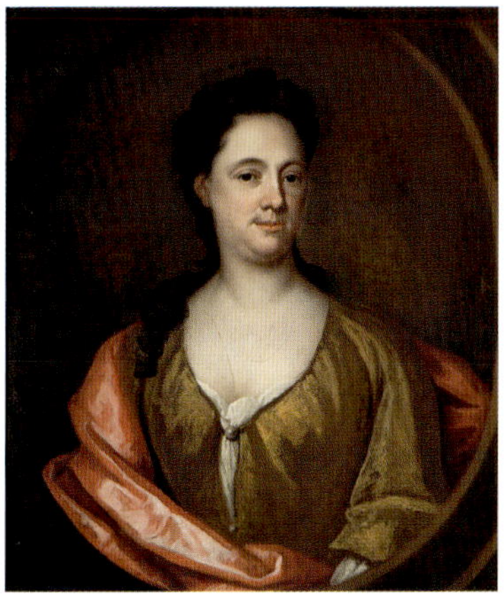

unknown artist
Martha Willington
oil on canvas 73 x 61
PCF10

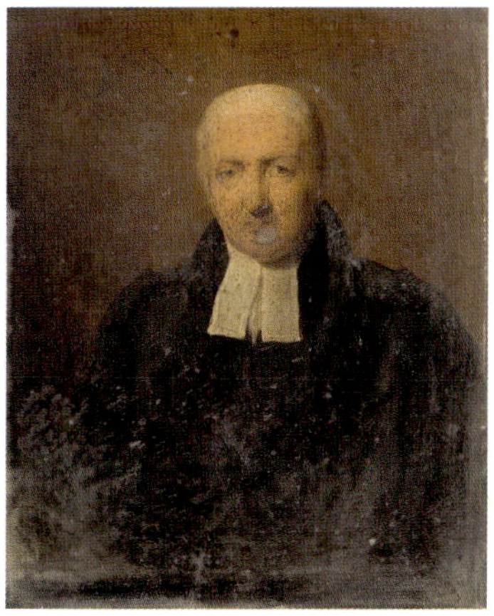

unknown artist
Methodist Minister
oil on canvas 24 x 19
838

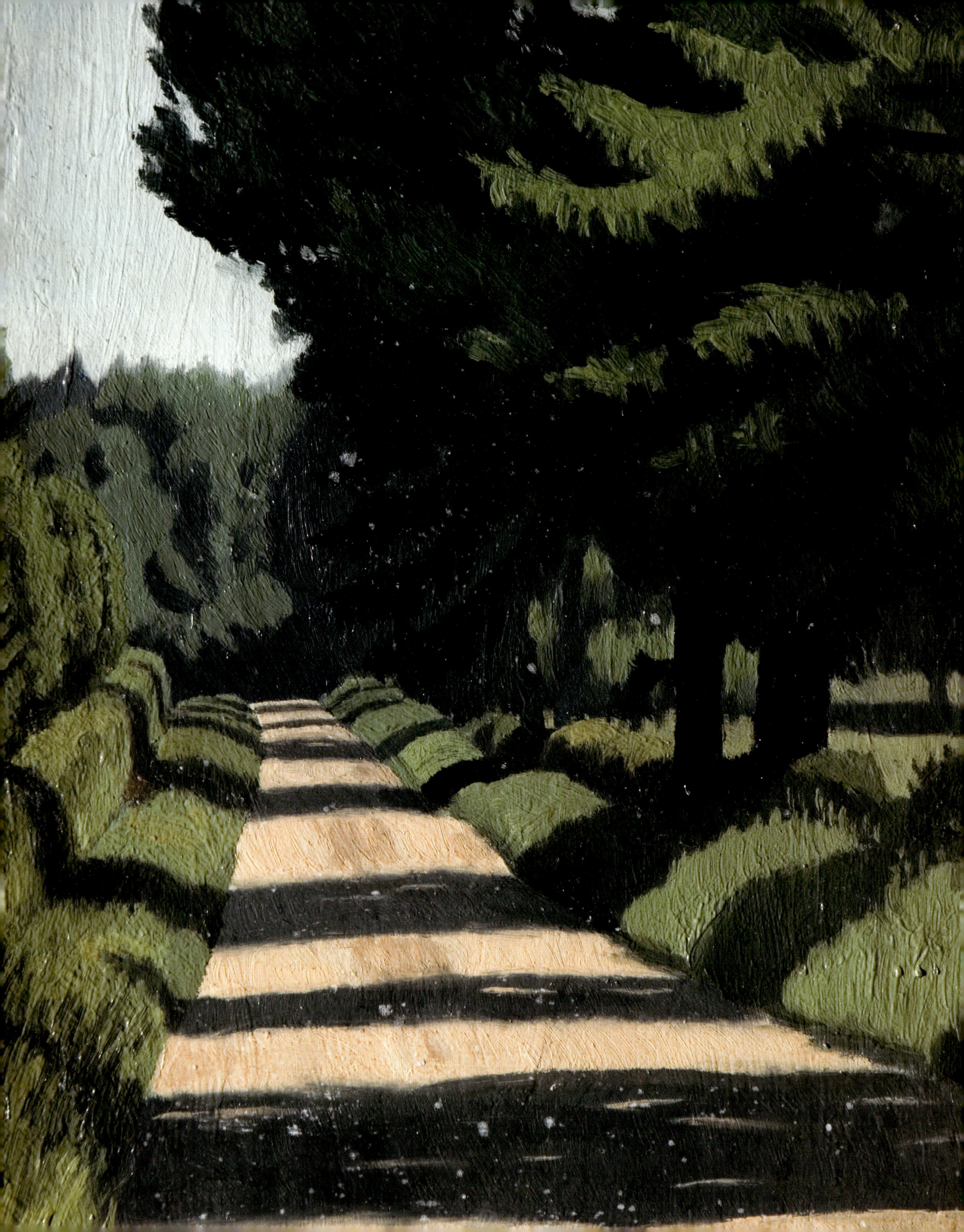

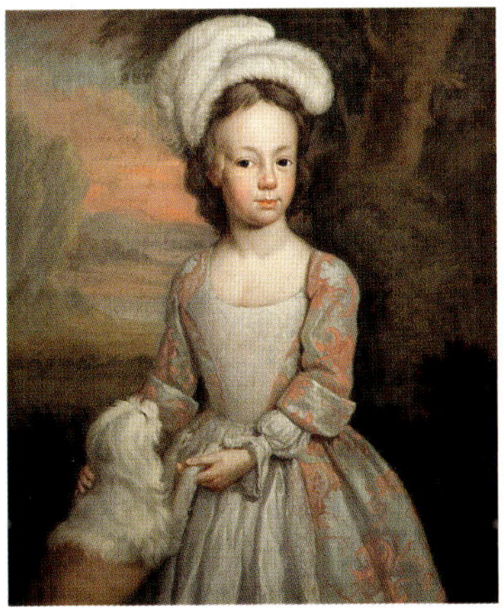

unknown artist
Miss Willington
oil on canvas 73 x 61
1992.18

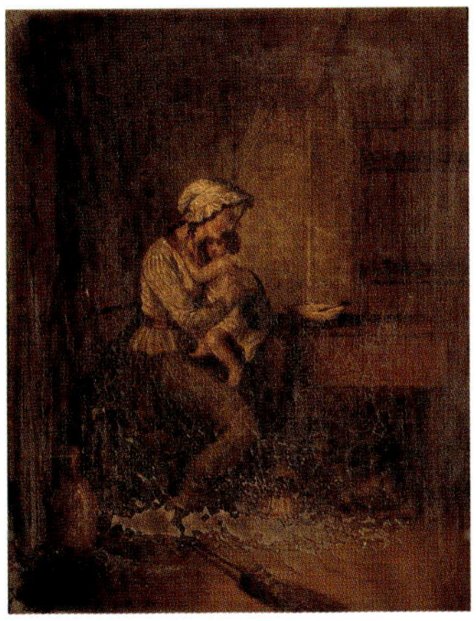

unknown artist
Mother and Child
oil on canvas 23 x 19
PCF11

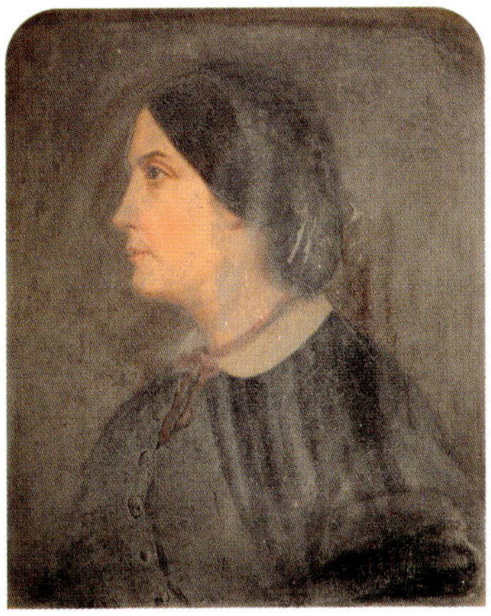

unknown artist
Portrait of a Lady
oil on canvas 44 x 36
PCF12

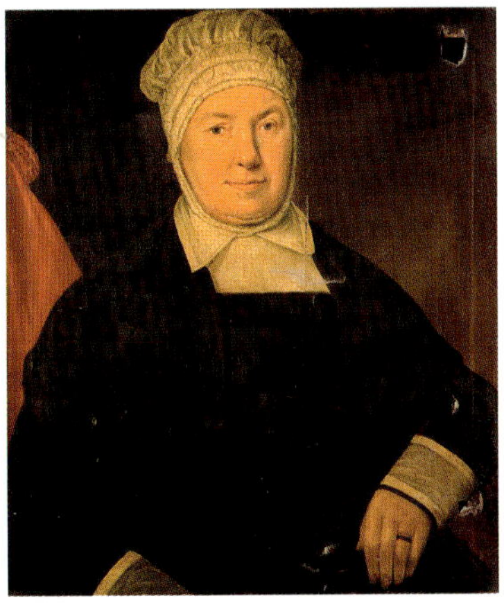

unknown artist
Portrait of a Lady
oil on canvas 75 x 63
PCF13

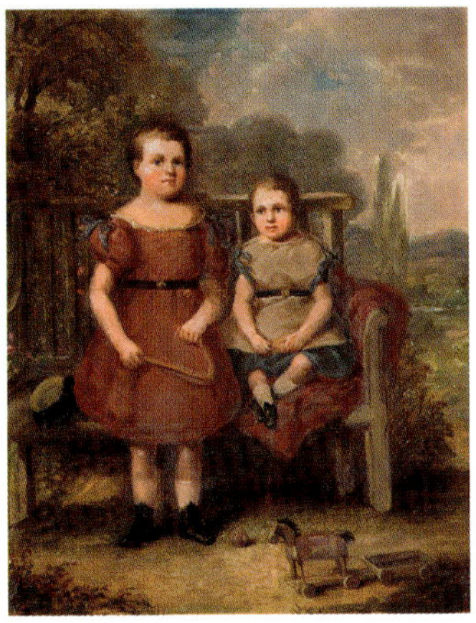

unknown artist
Portrait of Two Children
oil on canvas 51 x 41
1991.16

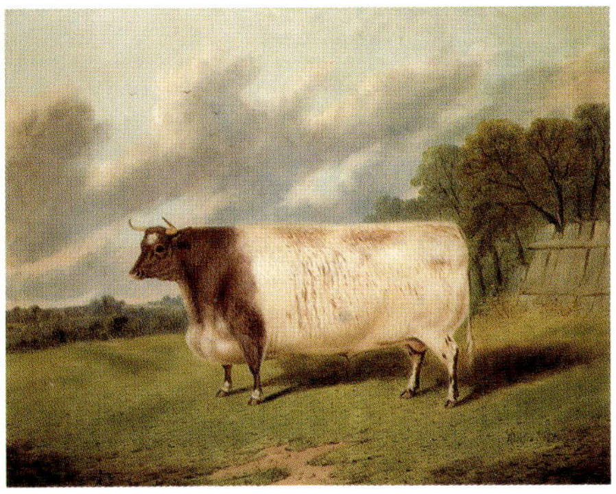

Whitford, Richard c.1821–1890
Bull, 'Champion' 1874
oil on canvas 61 x 73
1967.51.1

Tutbury Museum Trust

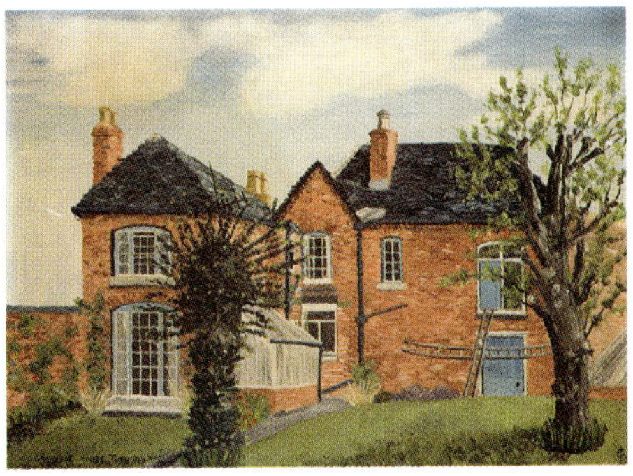

O. E. B.
Granville House, Tutbury
oil on board 35 x 45
VP98

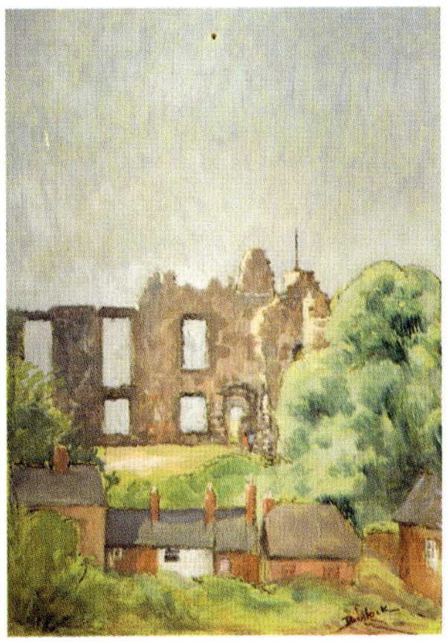

Bullock
Tutbury Castle
oil on board 51 x 35.5
CA13

Facing page: Chubb, Ralph Nicholas, 1892–1960, *The Country Lane* (detail), The Potteries Museum & Art Gallery (p. 113)

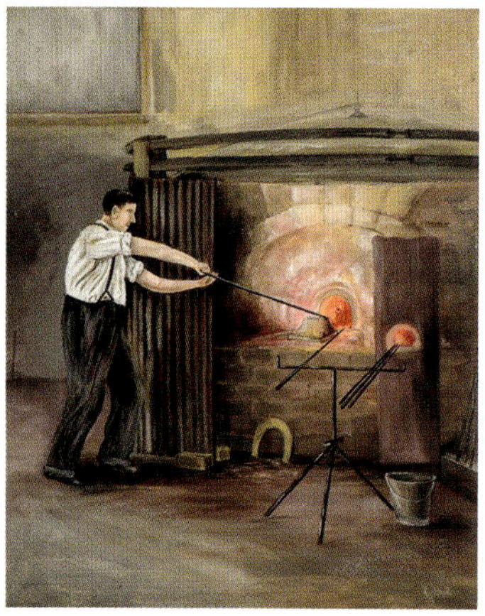

Hulme, Geoffrey
Glass Blowing, Harry Hassent and No.8 Pot
oil on board 44 x 35
GL100

Uttoxeter Heritage Centre

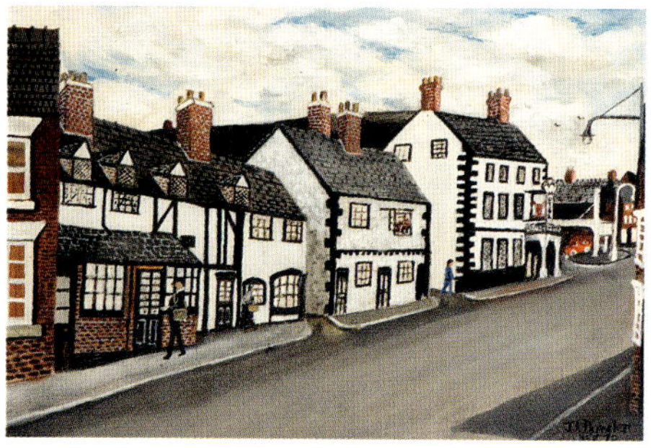

Hulme, Geoffrey
The White Hart Hotel, Carter Street, Uttoxeter 1978
oil on board 24 x 34
PCF1

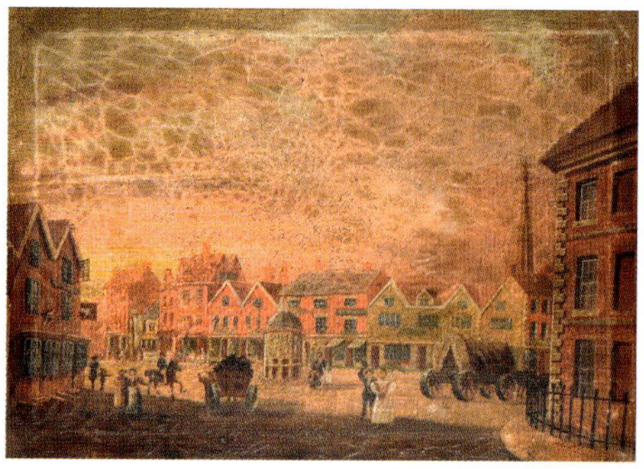

Redfern, Francis (attributed to)
Market Place, Uttoxeter c.1800
oil on canvas 44.5 x 60
PCF2

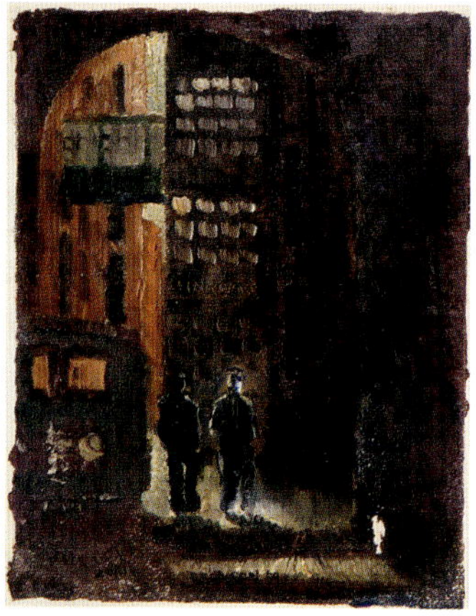

Wilson, Paul F. d.2000
'Clink Wharf', Southwark, London
oil on board 22.5 x 17.5
PCF4

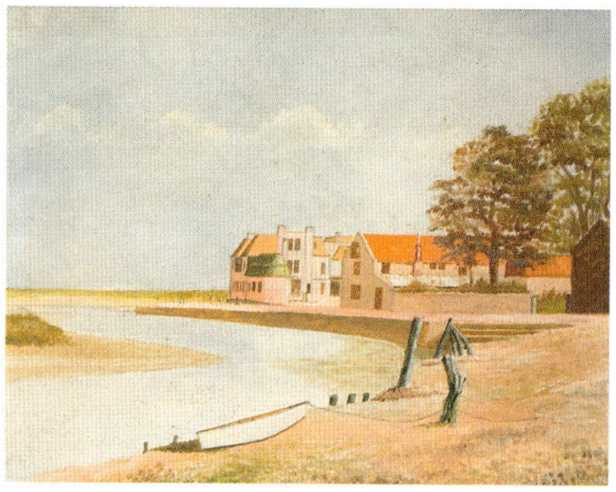

Wilson, Paul F. d.2000
River View
oil on board 40.5 x 51
PCF3

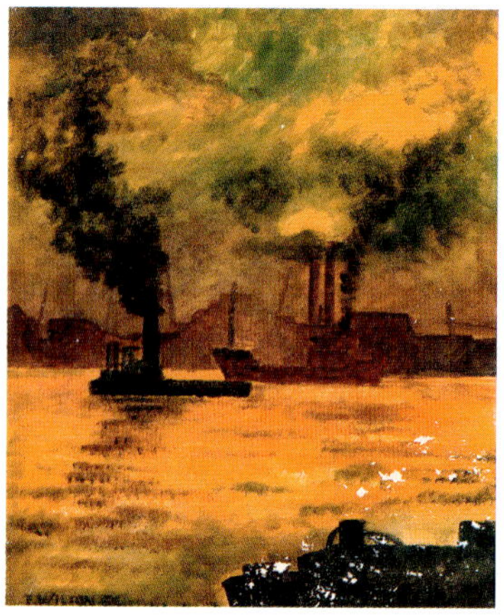

Wilson, Paul F. d.2000
Steam Ships
oil on board 44 x 35.5
PCF5

The New Art Gallery Walsall

The New Art Gallery Walsall is the home of the distinguished Garman Ryan Collection, which was donated to the Borough in 1972 by Lady Kathleen Epstein. It consists of 365 works of art, over a third of them being three-dimensional works from many different cultures and periods around the world including works from Africa, Oceania, China and South America. It also contains a wide-ranging body of the work of Sir Jacob Epstein and many significant works by European artists such as Van Gogh, Picasso, Monet, Turner, Corot, Renoir and Constable. The Collection contains many prints, sketches and drawings as well as paintings and sculptures, from fifteenth century medieval illuminated manuscripts to early paintings by Lucian Freud, who was Epstein's son-in-law.

Kathleen Epstein (née Garman) and her friend Sally Ryan were collecting during the 1950s and 1960s, purchasing works they liked and collecting work by friends and family. They added to an existing collection created by Jacob Epstein. Most of the Garman Ryan Collection is on long-term display with a related changing temporary exhibitions programme. Walsall has continued to collect works relating to the collection, adding in particular works by Sir Jacob Epstein and Lucian Freud, which have been purchased, bequeathed or donated. The full collection can be accessed through The New Art Gallery website www.artatwalsall.org.uk.

The permanent Art Collection consists of over 1,500 art works (264 of which are oils) collected since the foundation of Walsall Museum and Art Gallery in 1892. They are of many different media from the nineteenth and twentieth centuries, with some recently collected contemporary works from the twenty-first century. Nineteenth century artists represented in the collections include works by and attributed to Charles and William Shayer, Jozef Israëls, Frank Holl, Briton Riviere, Thomas Faed and Eugène Verboeckhoven. Twentieth century artists include Dod Procter, Cedric Morris and Lucian Freud. About one quarter of the collection comprises topographical works of the Borough of Walsall and its people from different periods. There are over 50 limited edition art prints by many artists from the 1960s onwards such as John Piper, Richard Hamilton and Peter Blake. Since the early 1970s, the Art Gallery has also collected contemporary art works in all media, many of which relate to the Garman Ryan Collection or by artists who have exhibited at the Gallery.

The New Art Gallery Walsall opened in February 2000, with £21 million funding from the Arts Lottery and the European Regional Development Fund. Designed by architects Caruso St John, the new building placed the Gallery in a unique position for a fresh approach to its collections.

The Contemporary Art Society Special Collections Scheme, which ran from 1998–2004 and was funded by the Arts Lottery, enabled Walsall to develop a strong collection of contemporary art works. The Special Collections Scheme at Walsall focused its collecting on works by international artists which demonstrated the diversity of contemporary art and which could be displayed dynamically and challengingly within the context of the unique architecture of the new purpose-built art gallery. Through this scheme, Walsall has been able to add key works to its collections by artists of international status including Gavin Turk, Hew Locke, Mike Nelson, Yoshihiro Suda, Dorothy Cross, Laura Ford, Darren Lago, Estelle Thompson, Richard Woods, Yinka Shonibare and

Rose Finn-Kelcey. The majority of works by these artists have been excluded from this catalogue as they are not oil based. These are part of the Permanent Collection and continue to strengthen the pre-existing contemporary works by artists such as Catherine Yass and Fiona Banner. The New Art Gallery Walsall continues to collect contemporary art works building upon the legacy of the Special Collections Scheme, both drawing upon the strengths of the existing collections and placing work within the context of the new gallery. A superb archive of material relating to the collections is also housed at The New Art Gallery Walsall, made accessible to the public through the specialist Art Library.

Jo Digger, Collections Curator

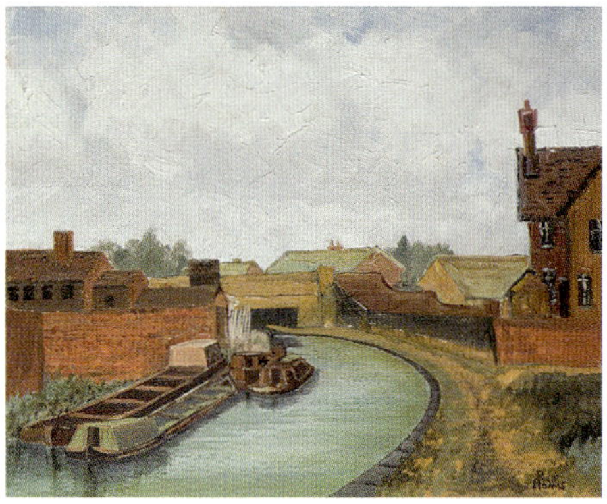

Adams, Philip b.1943
Canal at Pratts Bridge, Leamore, Walsall 1980
oil on board 31.5 x 37.5
P18/02

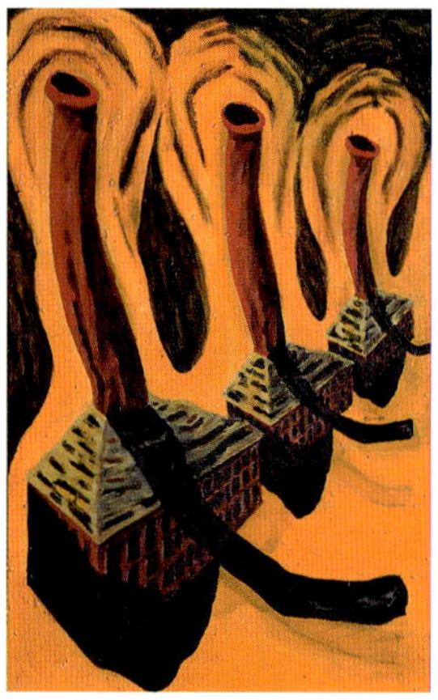

Allen, Robert b.1951
Out to Dry
acrylic on canvas 92 x 56
P23/93

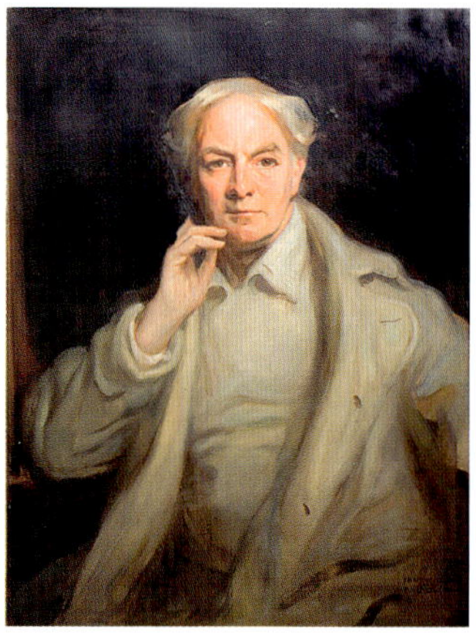

Amshewitz, John Henry 1882–1942
Jerome K. Jerome (1859–1927) (copy after Philip Alexius de László)
oil on canvas 90 x 69.5
P147/76

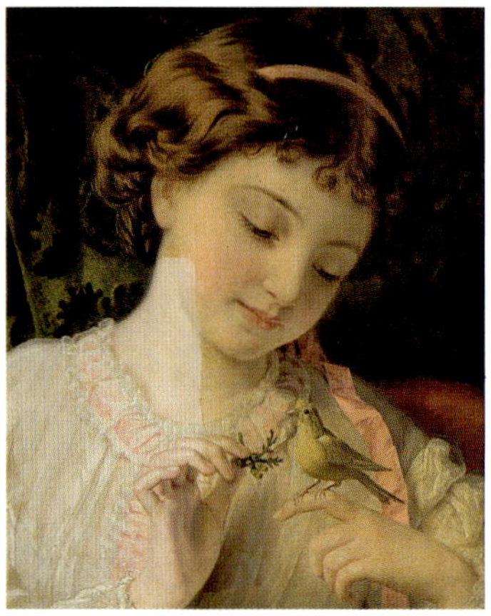

Anderson, Sophie 1823–1912
Pet Canary
oil on canvas 29 x 24
P49/76

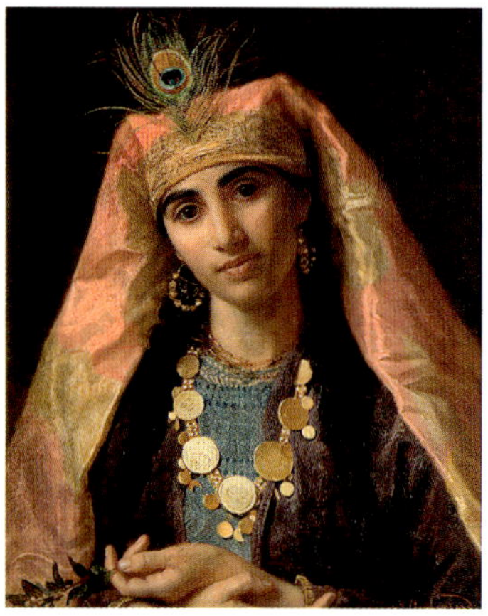

Anderson, Sophie 1823–1912
Scheherazade
oil on canvas 50 x 41
P69/76

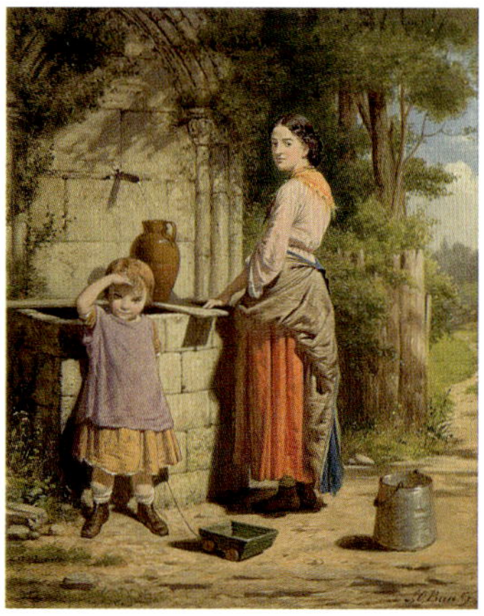

Banks, J. O. active 1856–1873
At the Fountain
oil on canvas 25 x 20
P206/76

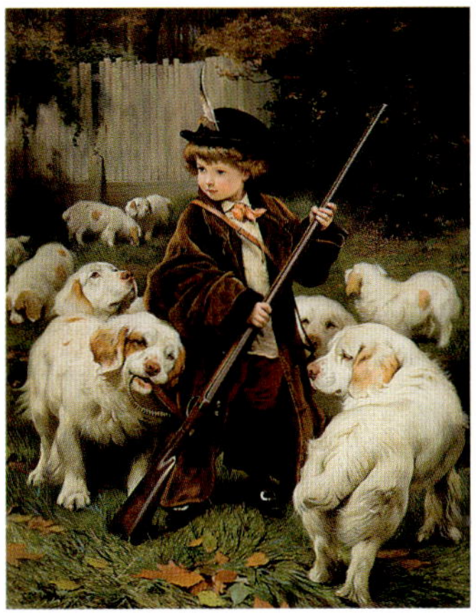

Barber, Charles Burton 1845–1894
The New Keeper 1888
oil on canvas 107 x 84
P327/76

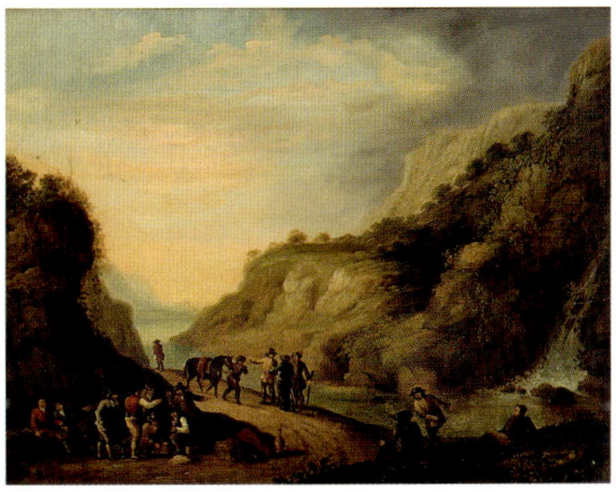

Barker, Thomas (attributed to) 1769–1847
The Smugglers' Rendezvous
oil on canvas 62 x 74
P9/76

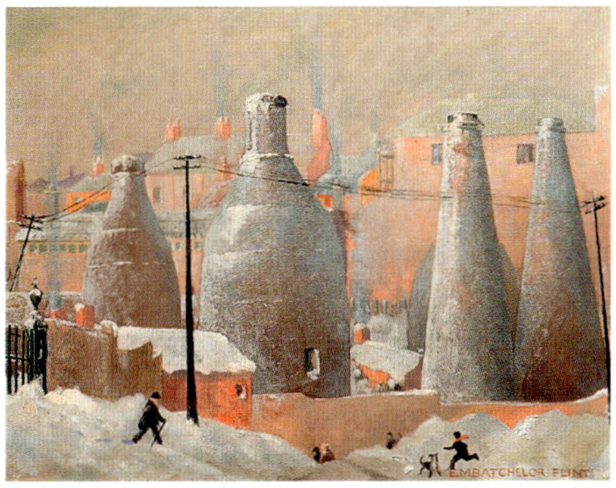

Batchelor-Flint, Emma 1857–1968
Bottle Kilns 1950
oil on canvas 40.5 x 51
P292/76

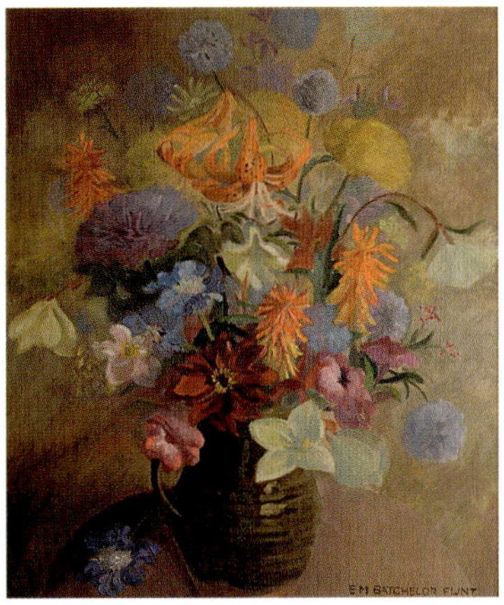

Batchelor-Flint, Emma 1857–1968
Early Autumn
oil on canvas 61 x 51
P230/76

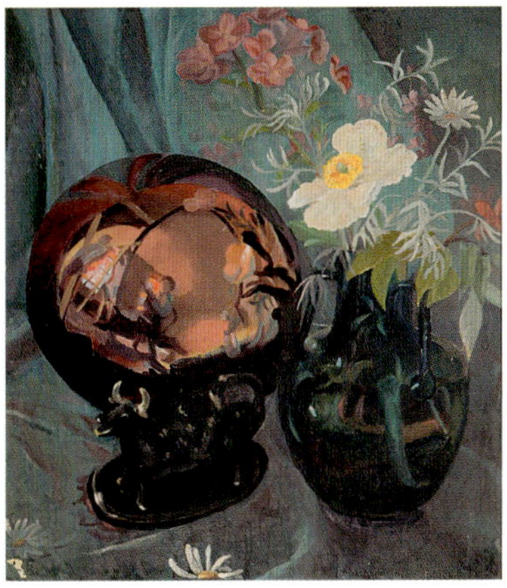

Batchelor-Flint, Emma 1857–1968
Red Witch Bowl
oil on canvas 60 x 51
P286/76

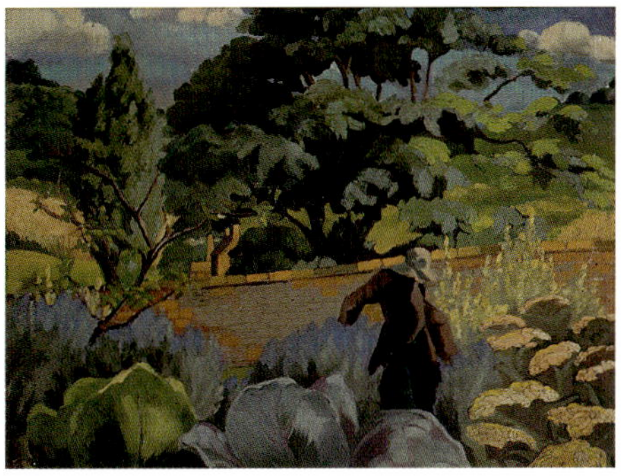

Batchelor-Flint, Emma 1857–1968
The Scarecrow
oil on canvas 48 x 63.5
P108/76

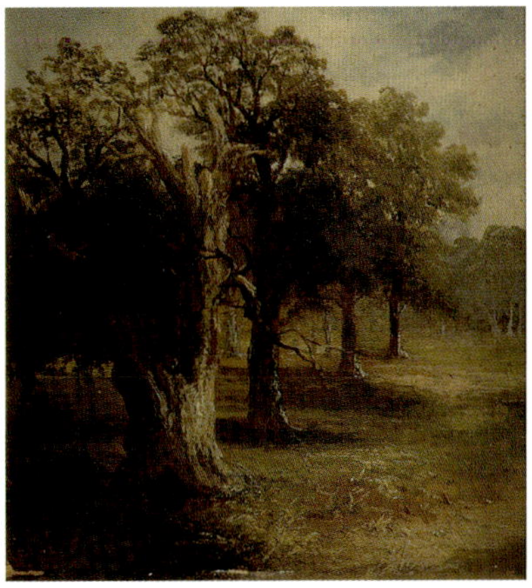

Bates, George active 1873–1893
Trees (Woodland Scene)
oil on board 28 x 25.5
P57/76

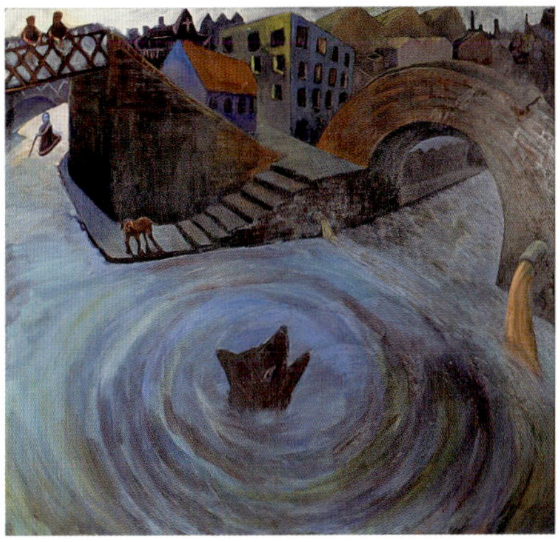

Bloomer, Paul b.1966
Soliloquy 1992
oil on canvas 148 x 152
P20/94

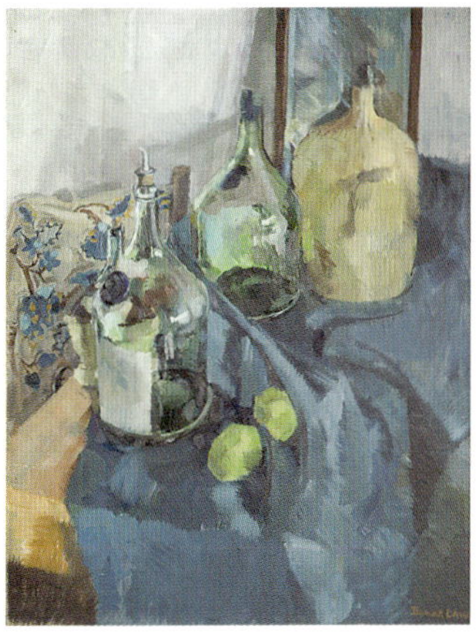

Bonar, Law
Still Life, Jar of Flowers and Fruit
oil on board 124.5 x 93.5
P4/80

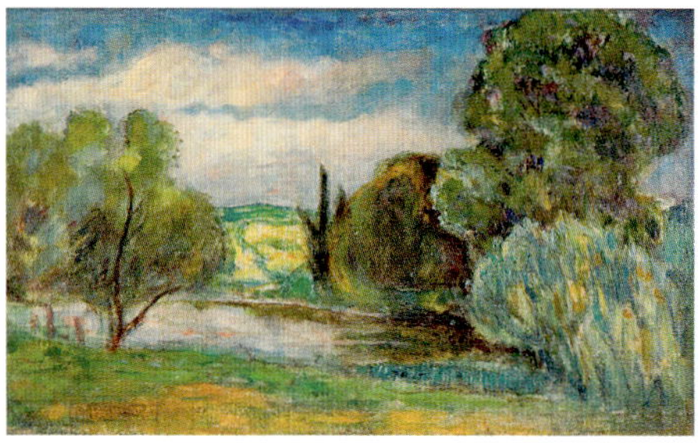

Bonnard, Pierre 1867–1947
La Seine à Vernon 1919
oil on canvas 38.5 x 62.5
GR.7

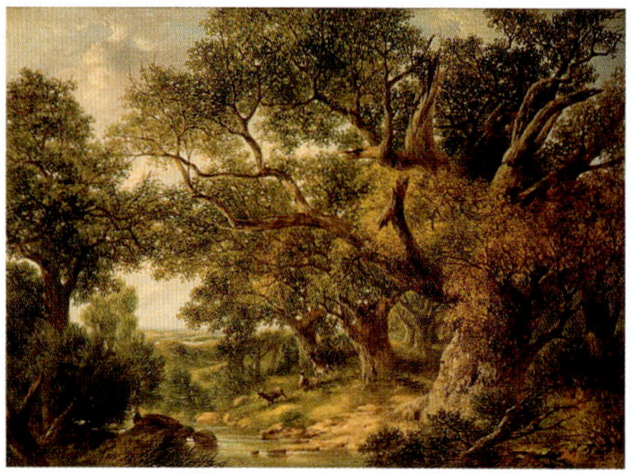

Bowley, Edward Orlando active 1840–1874
Landscape with Deer 1873
oil on canvas 88 x 122
P44/76

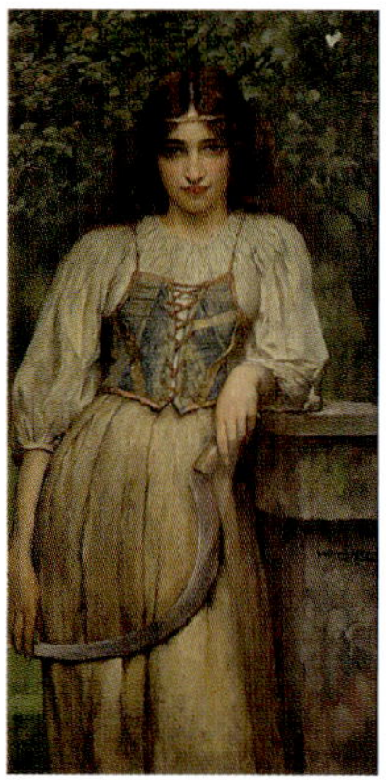

Breakspeare, William Arthur 1855–1914
Resting
oil on canvas 44.5 x 24
P22/76

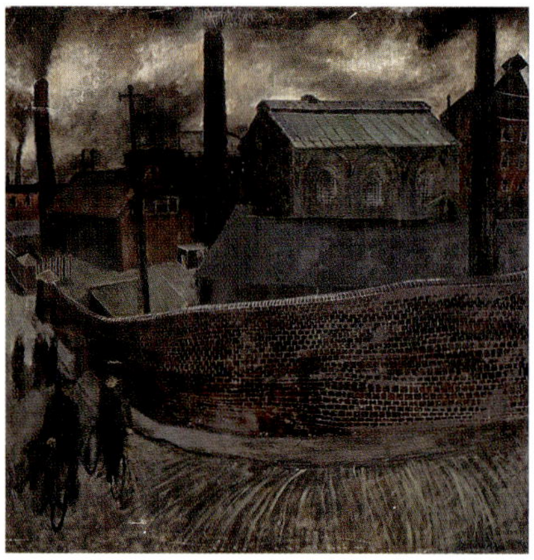

Bridgeman, Ann b.1934
Black Country 1960
oil on canvas 91.5 x 86.5
P211/76

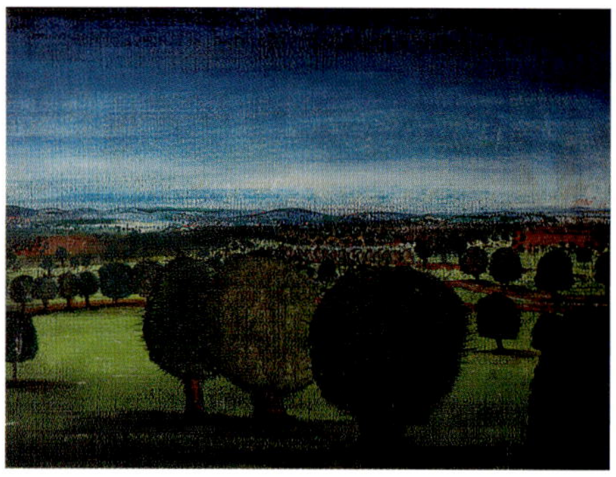

Bro, René 1930–1987
Landscape near Courgeron, Normandy 1962
oil on canvas 49.5 x 64
GR.10

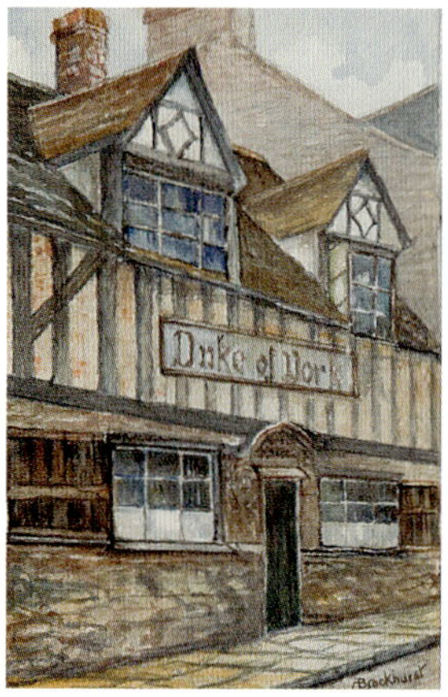

Brockhurst, A.
The 'Duke of York'
oil on canvas 28 x 25.5
P112/76

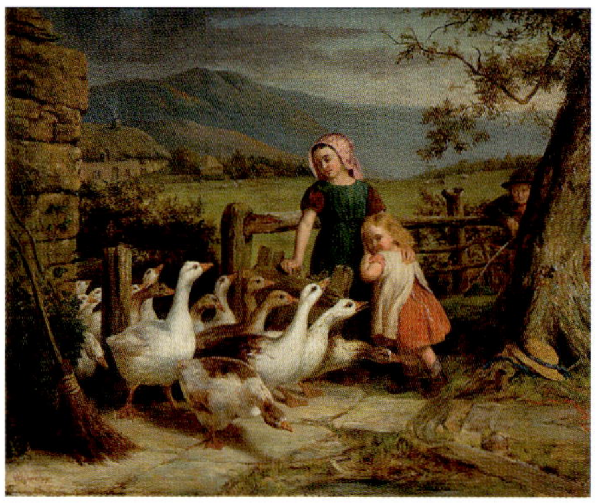

Bromley, William c.1818–1888
Preparing for Christmas
oil on canvas 62 x 75
P15/76

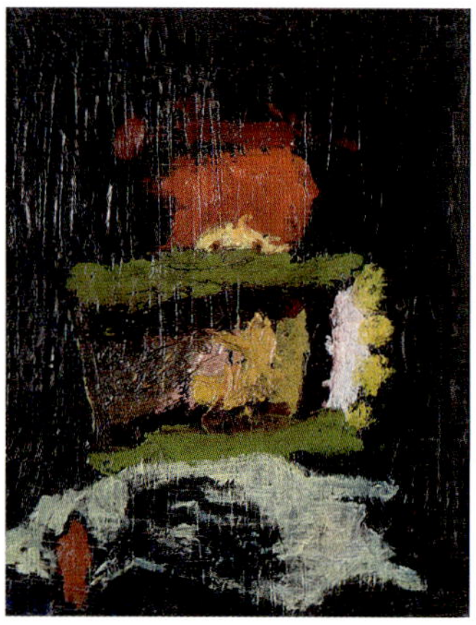

Buffet
Small Girl Reading Book
oil on canvas 30.5 x 24.5
GR.11

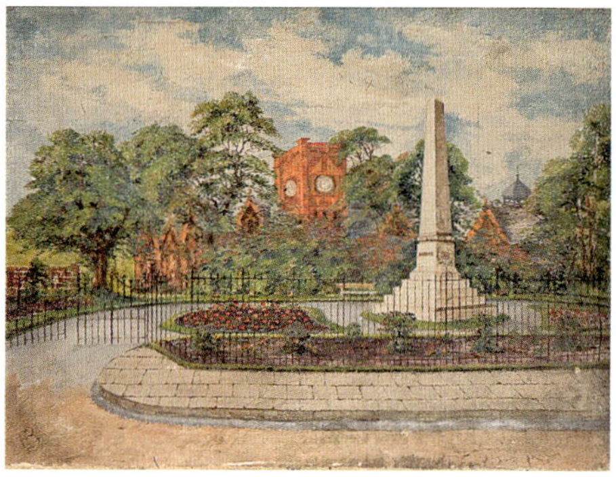

Burns, E.
Willenhall War Memorial
oil on board 23 x 43
P297/76

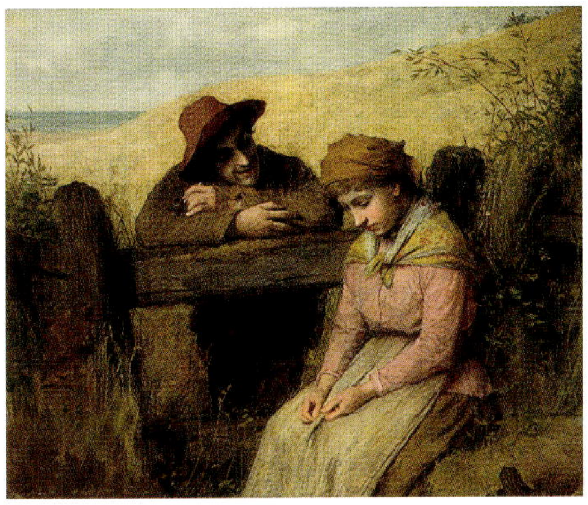

Burr, John 1831–1893
An Oft-Told Tale
oil on canvas 61 x 76
P324/76

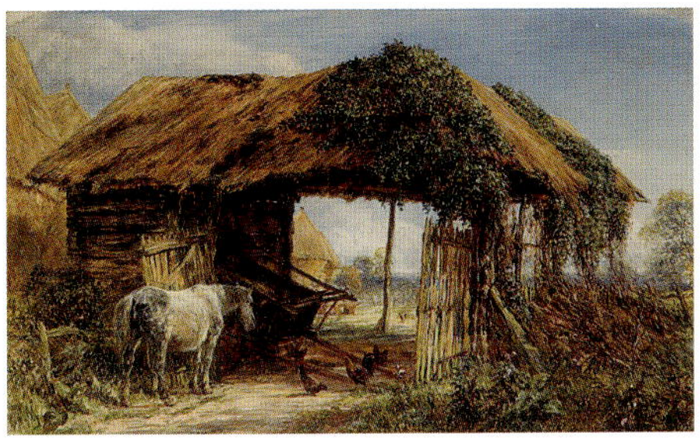

Burt, Charles Thomas 1823–1902
Farmyard Scene 1885–1895
oil on canvas 49 x 74.5
P6/85

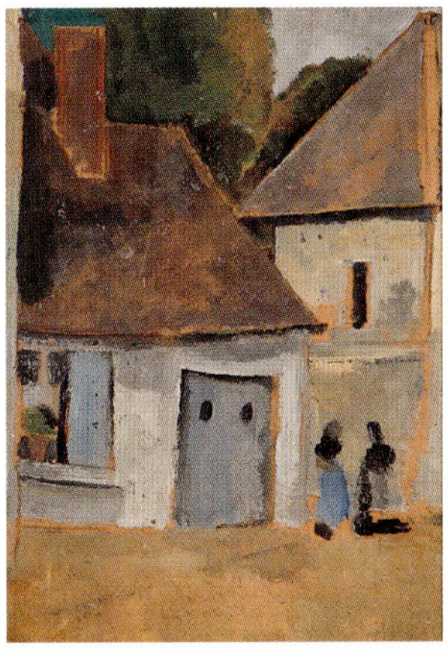

Cardew, Margaret 1899–1961
Normandy Village
oil on board 26.5 x 18.5
GR.359

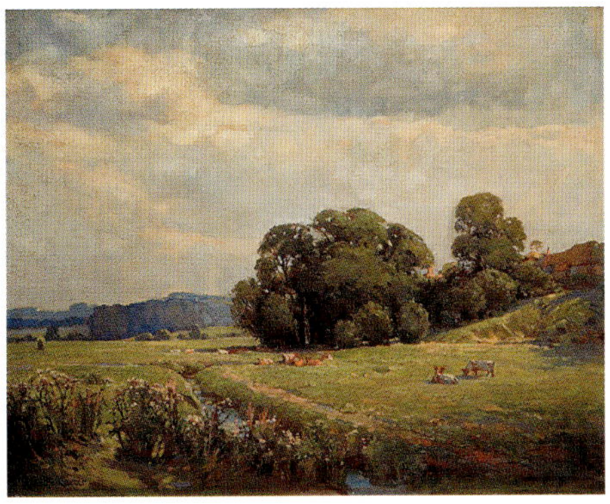

Carter, Robert Radcliffe b.1867
Water Meadows, Sussex
oil on canvas 63 x 75
P7/76

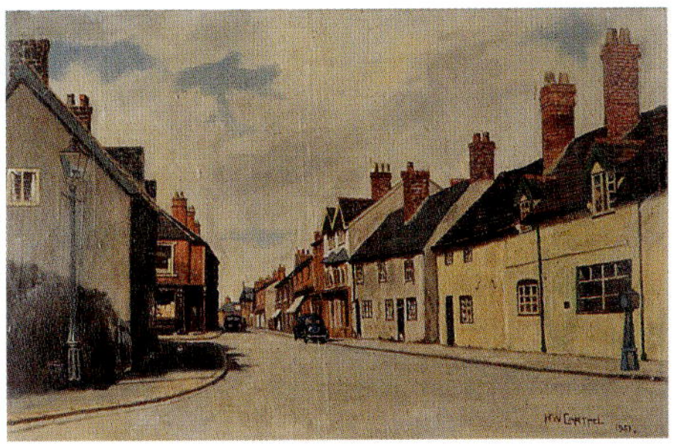

Cartmel, R. W. active 1951–1955
High Street, Aldridge 1951
oil on canvas 29 x 45.5
P5/84

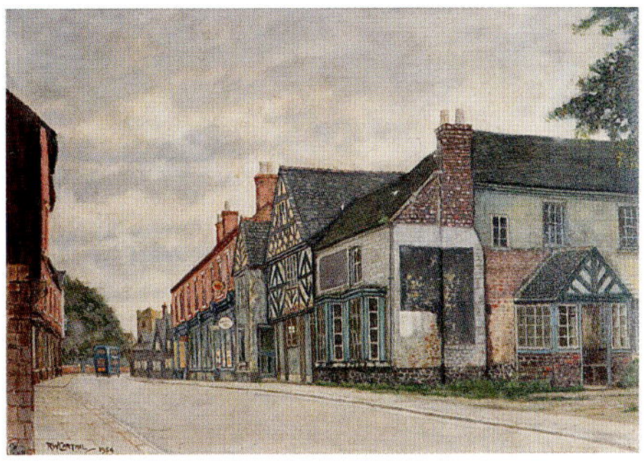

Cartmel, R. W. active 1951–1955
The Old Elms Hotel 1954
oil on canvas 43 x 60
P359/76

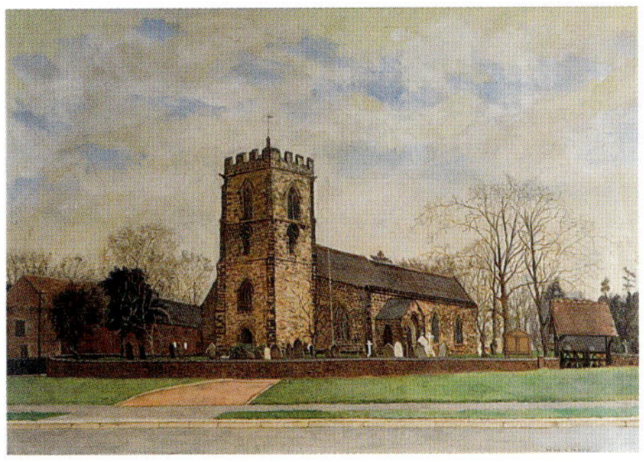

Cartmel, R. W. active 1951–1955
Aldridge Parish Church 1955
oil on canvas 43 x 60
P358/76

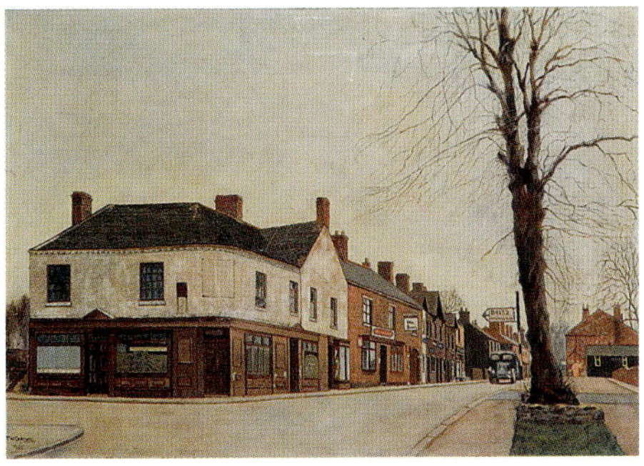

Cartmel, R. W. active 1951–1955
High Street, Aldridge 1955
oil on canvas 42 x 60
P357/76

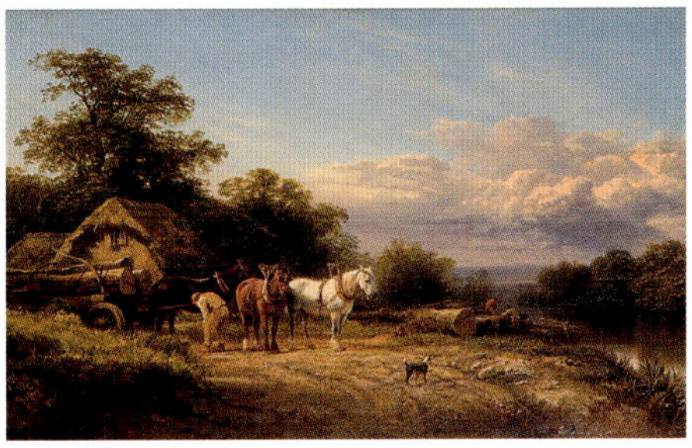

Cole, George 1810–1883
Horses with Timber Wagon 1880
oil on canvas 67 x 98
P17/76

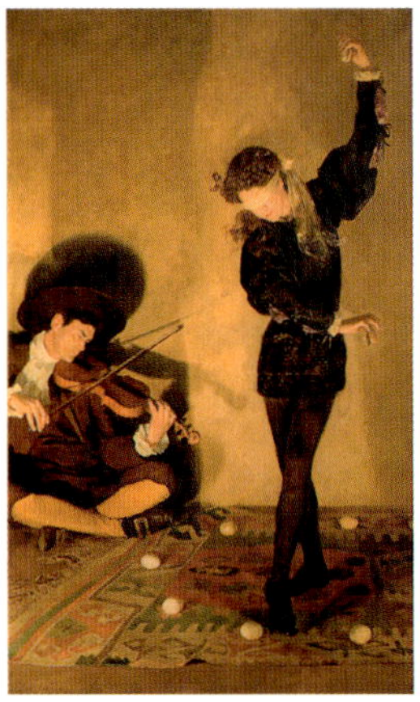

Collier, John 1850–1934
Egg Dance 1903
oil on canvas 171.5 x 105
P33/76

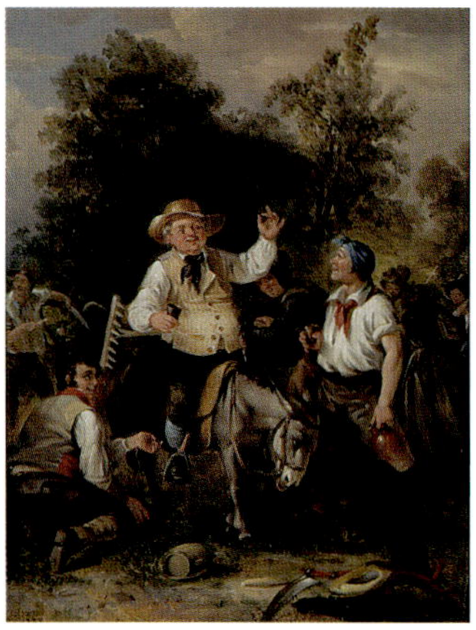

Colson, T.
The Jolly Farmer 1838
oil on canvas 31 x 24
P56/76

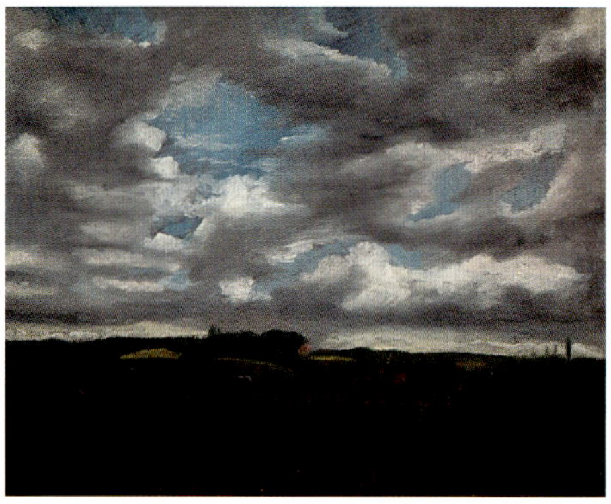

Constable, John 1776–1837
Landscape with Clouds 1820–1822
oil on paper on board 47 x 57
GR.23

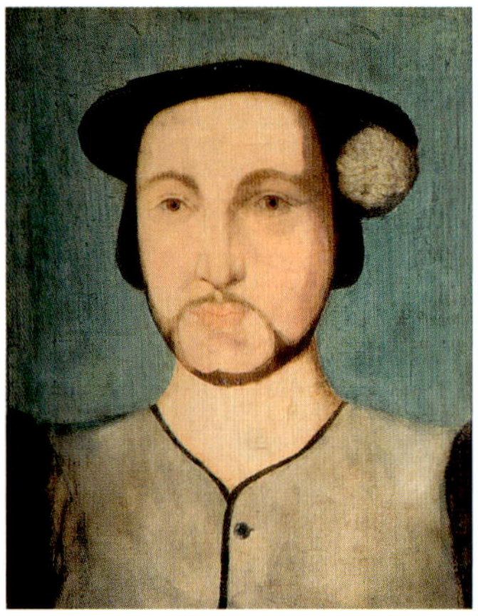

Corneille de Lyon, Claude (follower of)
1510–c.1574
Portrait of a Man 16th C
oil on panel 26.5 x 22
GR.21

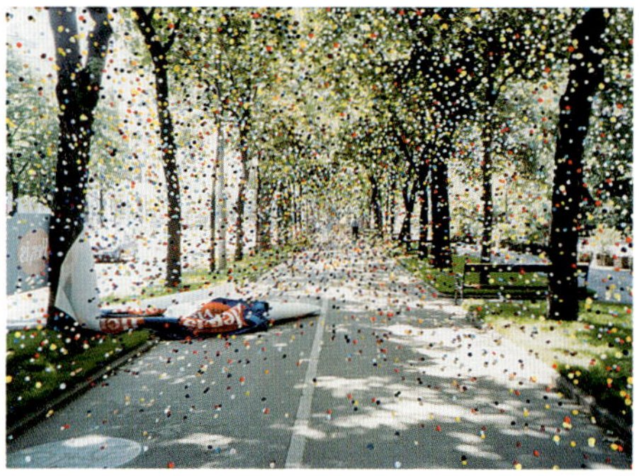

Cornet, May b.1975
After the Marathon 2003
oil on photograph mounted on
aluminium 30.5 x 40.5
GRE.1/05

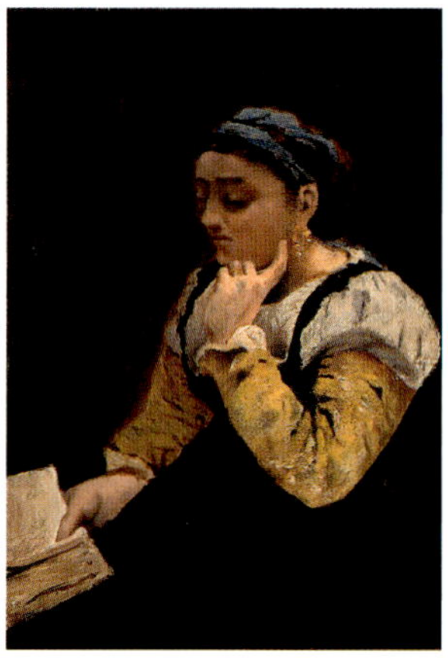

Corot, Jean-Baptiste-Camille (attributed to)
1796–1875
Woman Reading
oil on canvas 28 x 18.5
GR.27

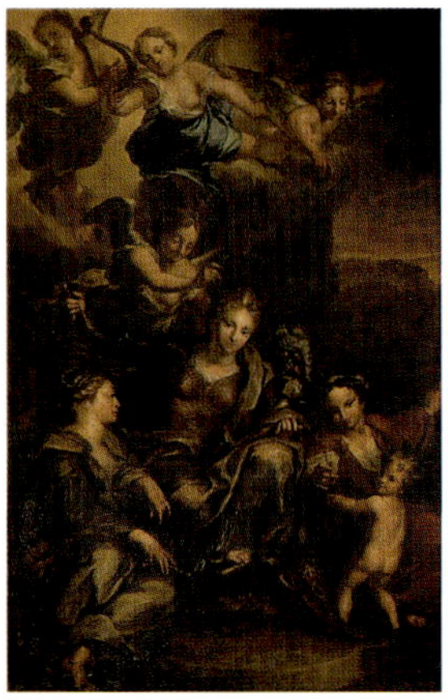

Correggio (after) c.1489–1534
Allegory of Virtue
oil on canvas 138 x 88
P11/76

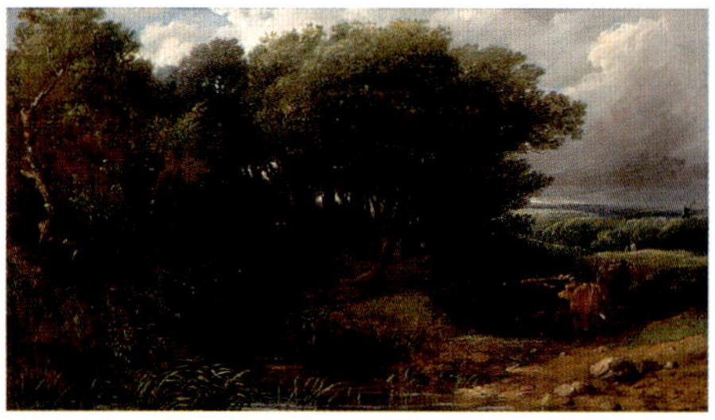

Cox, David the younger (attributed to)
1808–1885
Rural Scene
oil on canvas 36 x 63
P66/76

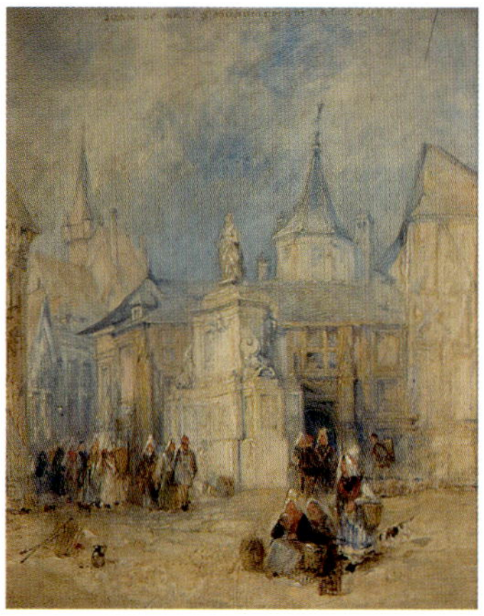

Creswick, Thomas 1811–1869
Monument to Joan of Arc at Rouen
oil on canvas 22 x 17
P220/76

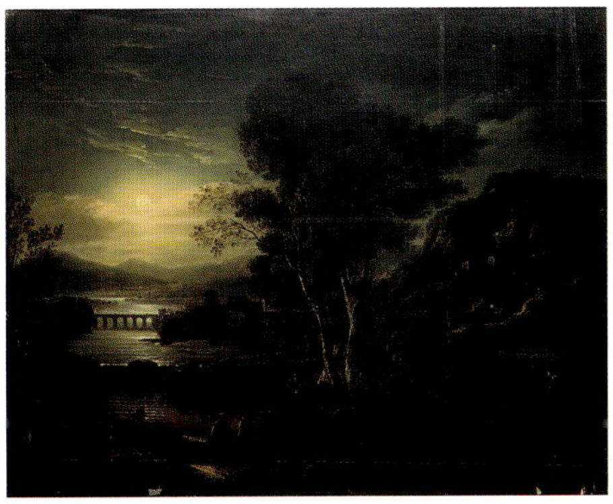

Crome, John (after) 1768–1821
Moonlight Scene 1821
oil on canvas 62 x 75
P25/76

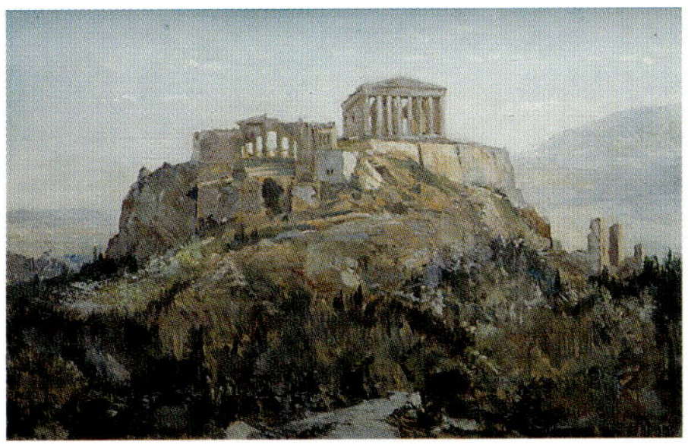

Cundall, Charles Ernest 1890–1971
The Acropolis
oil on canvas 30 x 46
P231/76

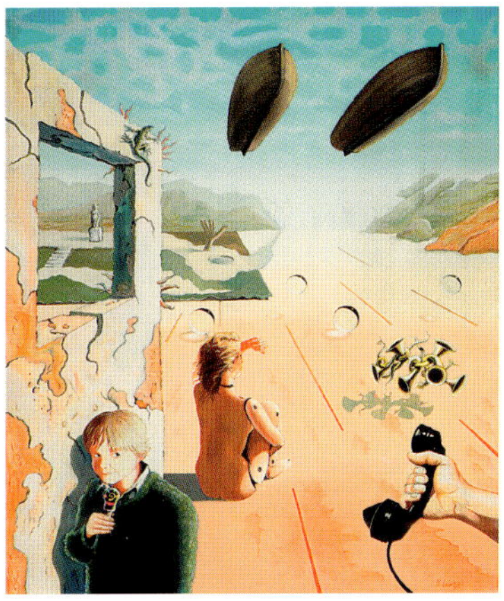

Cunha, Helio da
The Return of Ulysses
oil on canvas 81.5 x 65
P3/86

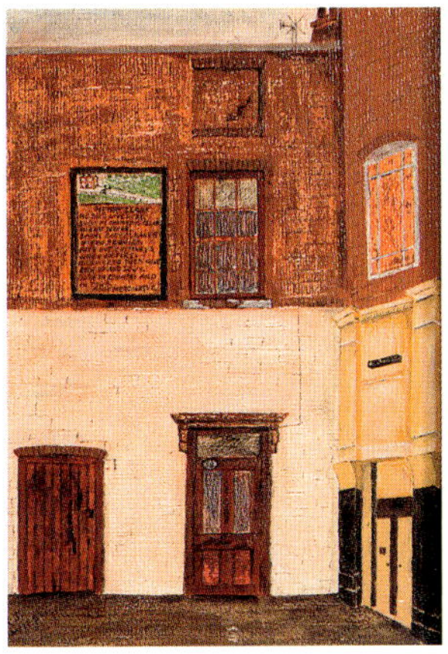

Davies, R. J.
Henry Clark's House, near Digbeth, Walsall
oil on canvas 30 x 20
P99/76

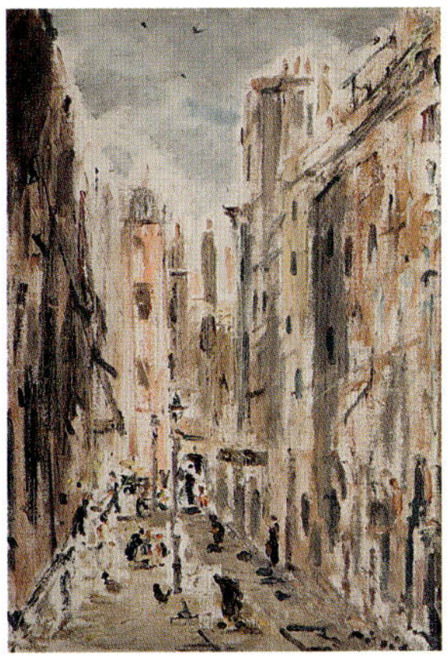

De Pisis, Filippo 1896–1956
Street Scene in Italy 1936
oil on canvas 47 x 32
GR.184

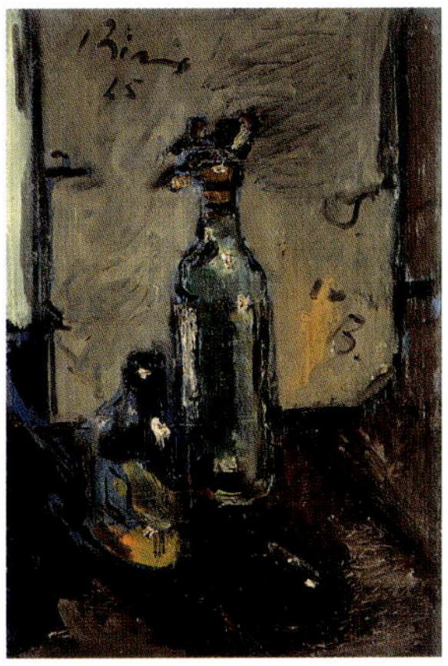

De Pisis, Filippo 1896–1956
Still Life with Bottles 1945
oil on canvas 50.5 x 34.5
GR.183

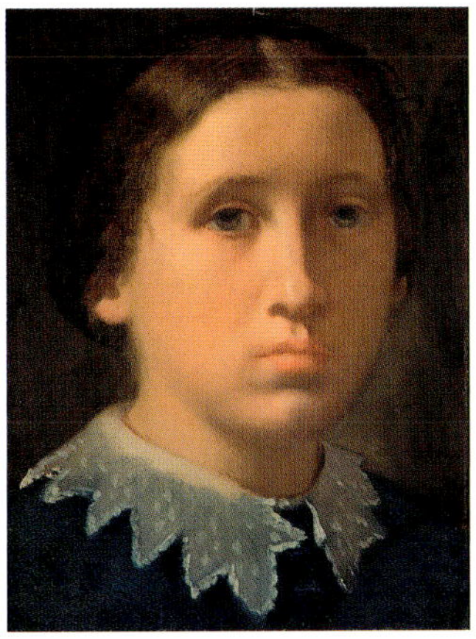

Degas, Edgar 1834–1917
Marguerite, soeur de l'artiste 1855–1857
oil on canvas 33 x 25
GR.33

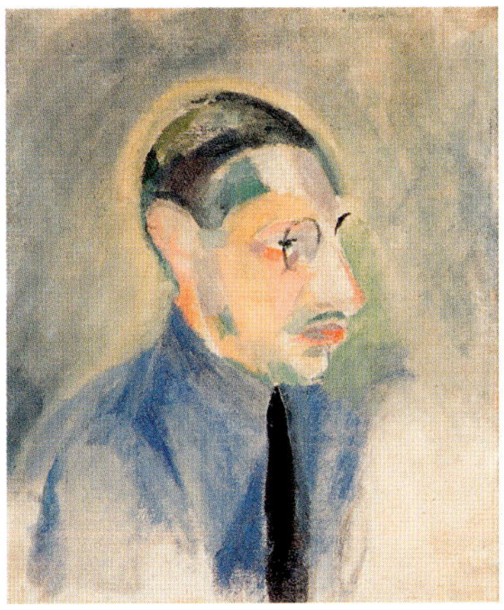

Delaunay, Robert 1885–1941
Igor Stravinsky (1882–1971) 1918
oil on canvas 63 x 52
GR.38

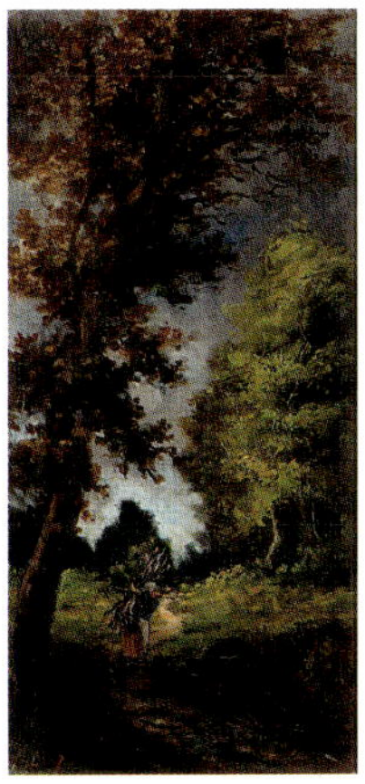

Diaz de la Peña, Narcisse Virgile 1808–1876
The Wood Gatherer
oil on canvas 44 x 20
GR.39

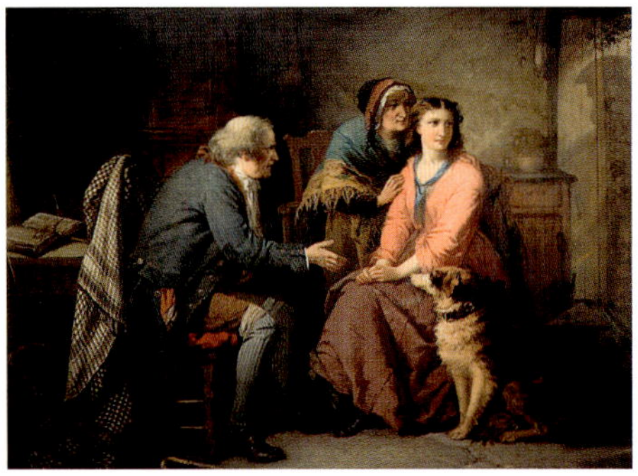

Drury, Edward Alfred Briscoe 1859–1944
Auld Robin Gray
oil on canvas 80 x 108
P221/76

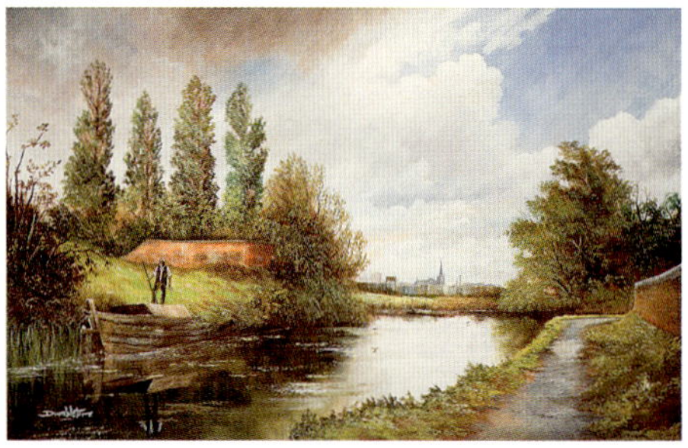

Dumbleton, Dennis b.1937
Walsall from the Birchills 1990
oil on canvas 60 x 90
P1/91

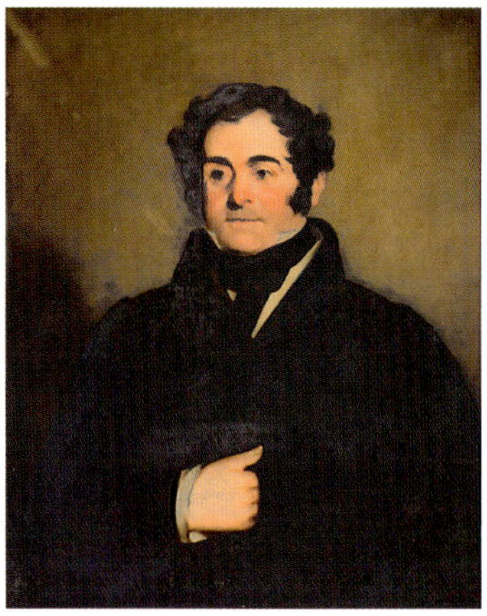

Dyer, E.
Richard Moore Fletcher 1865–1875
oil on canvas 91 x 70
P214/76

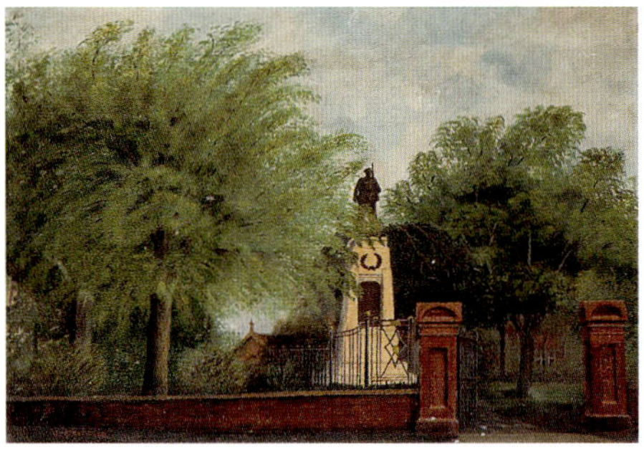

Eastwood, G.
Darlaston War Memorial
oil on canvas 38 x 51
P200/76

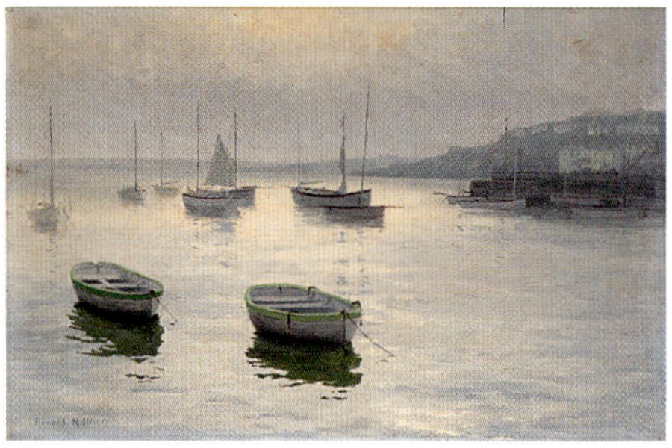

Elliott, Edith M. active 1889–1924
St Ives, Early Morning
oil on canvas 31.5 x 46
P236/76

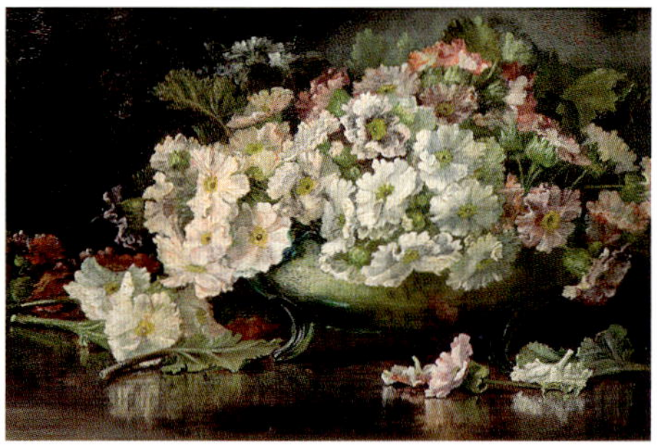

Elliott, Edith M. active 1889–1924
Still Life, Flowers in Bowl
oil on canvas 25.5 x 34
P167/76

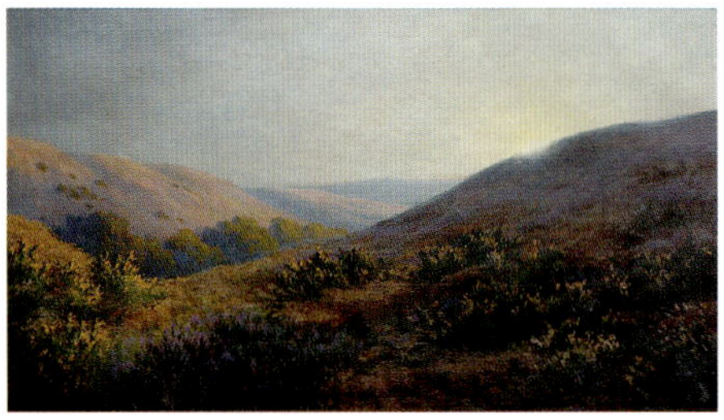

Elliott, Edward M. active 1898–1924
The Glory of the Dying Day
oil on canvas 34 x 60
P62/76

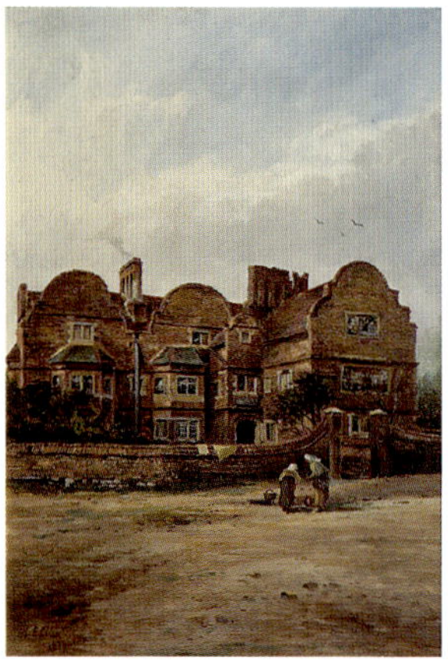

Ellis, Walter Erasmus active 1877–1899
White Hart Inn, Caldmore
oil on canvas 32 x 24
P168/76

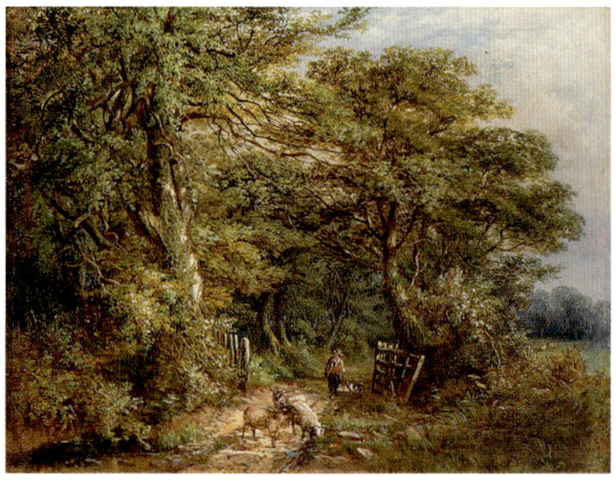

Ellis, William active 1858–1895
A Lane at Hamstead, Staffordshire
oil on canvas 49.5 x 63
GR.49

Facing page: Raeburn, Henry, 1756–1823, *William Fairlie of Fairlie (1754–1825)* (detail), Wolverhampton Art Gallery, (p. 316)

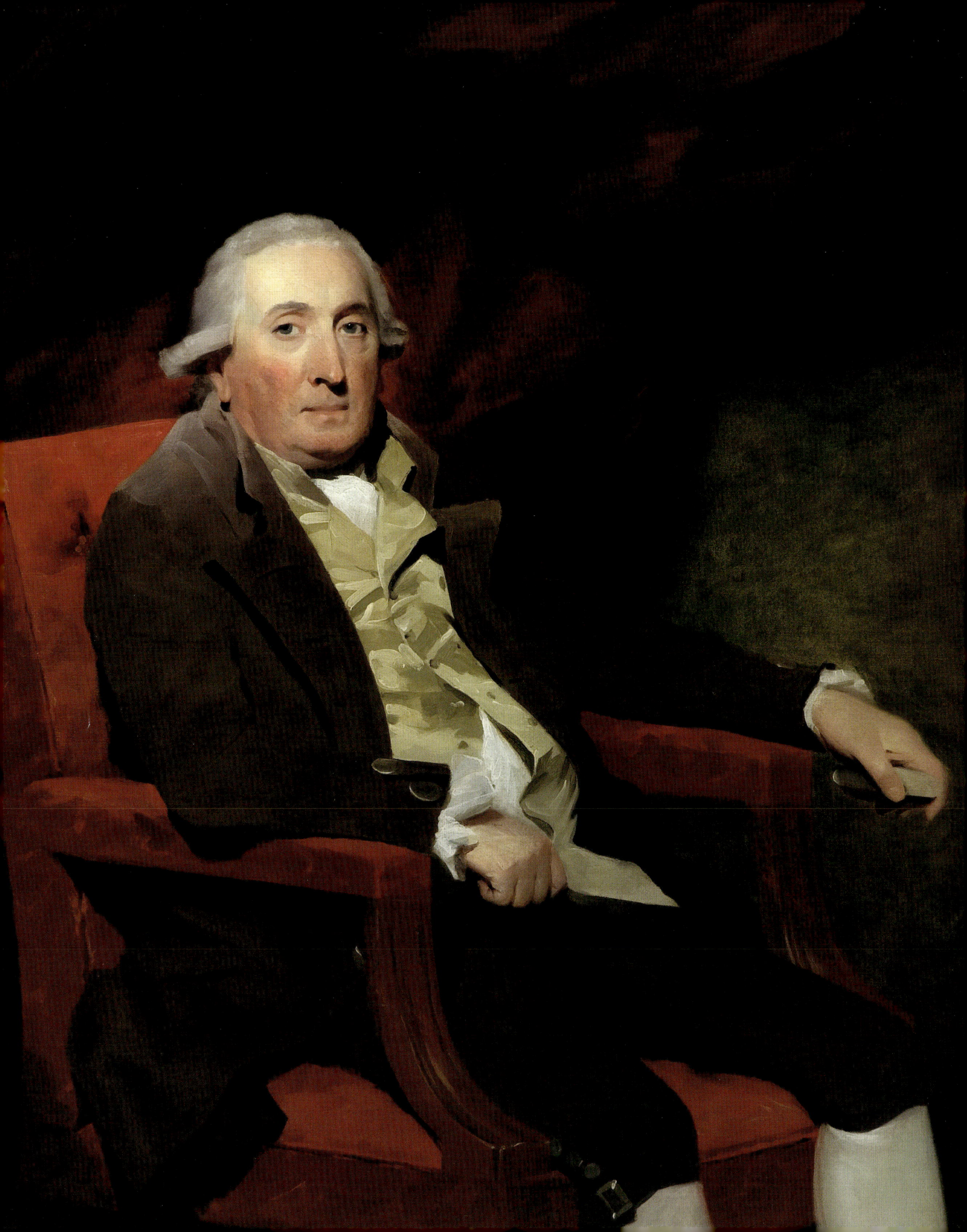

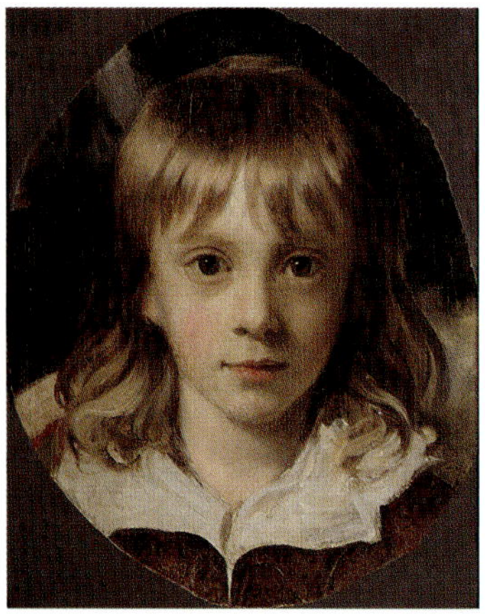

Elmore, Richard (attributed to) 1815–1881
Portrait of a Boy
oil on canvas 34 x 27
GR.50

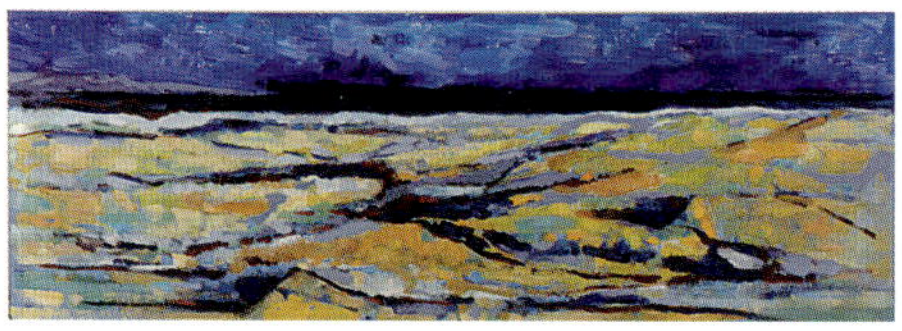

Emery, Louis 1918–1993
Seascape
oil on board 61 x 171

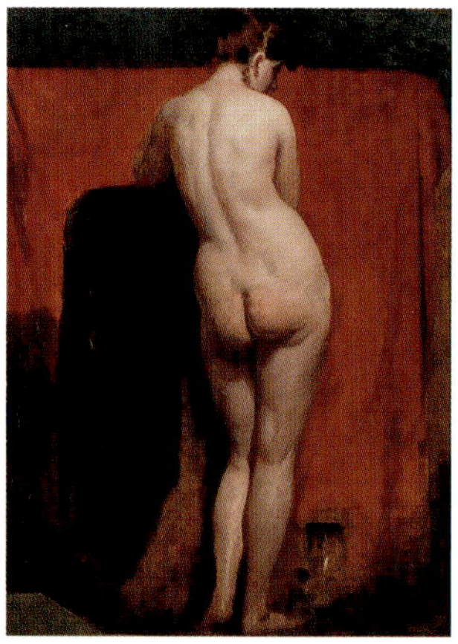

Etty, William 1787–1849
Standing Female Nude 1835–1840
oil on canvas 65.5 x 49
GR.92

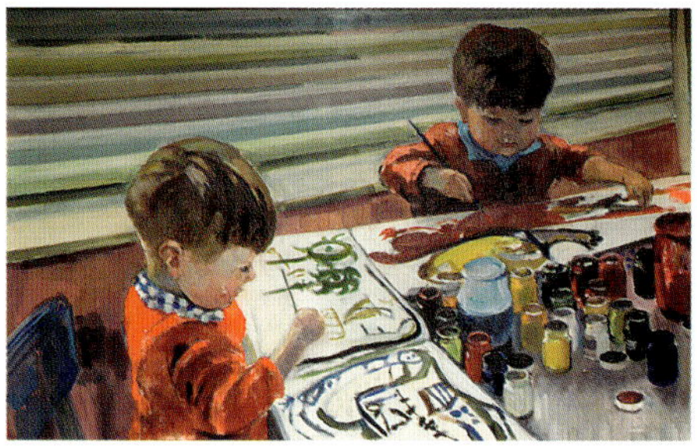

Everdon, J. R.
Two Young Artists 1960–1962
oil on canvas 55 x 85
P159/76

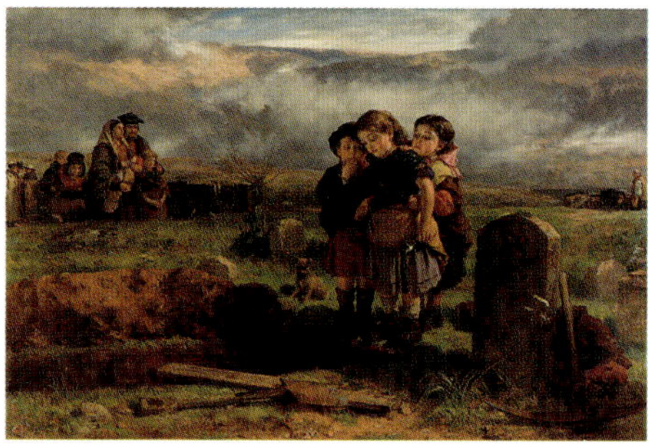

Faed, Thomas 1826–1900
God's Acre
oil on canvas 110 x 145
P326/76

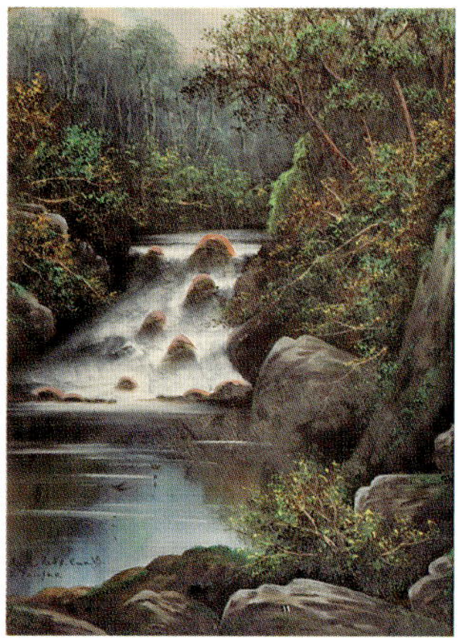

Fairfax, T.
Hawkfall, Cumberland
oil on canvas 51.5 x 36.5
P111/76

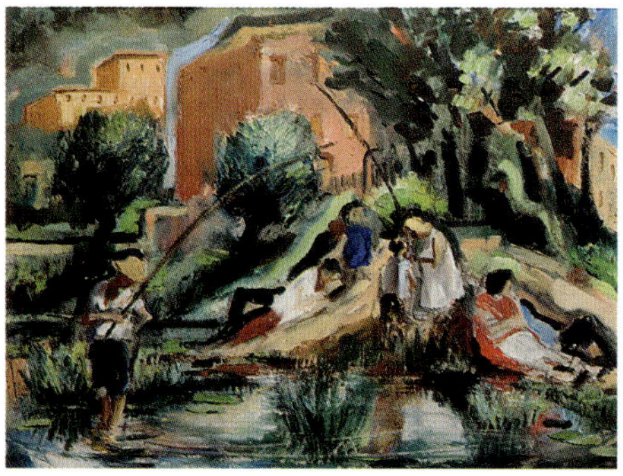

Faithful, Leila 1896–1994
Fishing on the Soane
oil on canvas 38 x 46
P153/76

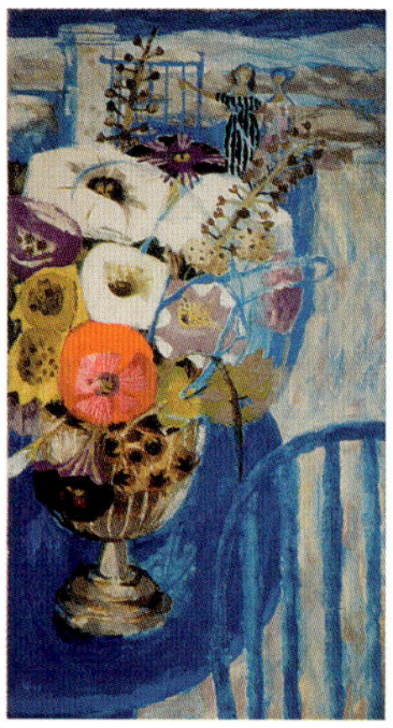

Fedden, Mary b.1915
Flowers in Tuscany
oil on canvas 76 x 40.5
P218/76

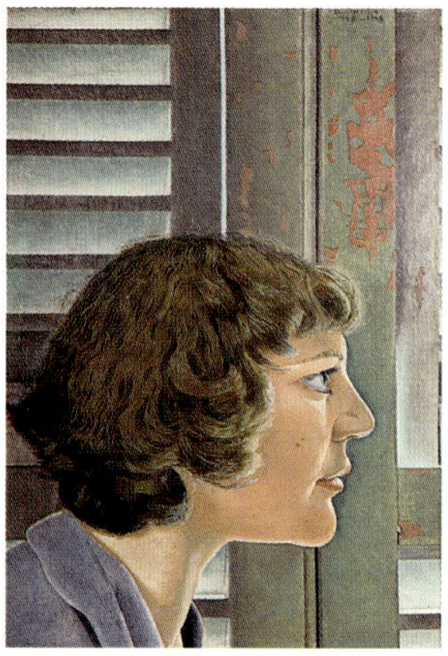

Freud, Lucian b.1922
Kitty 1948–1949
oil on board 35 x 24
GR.96

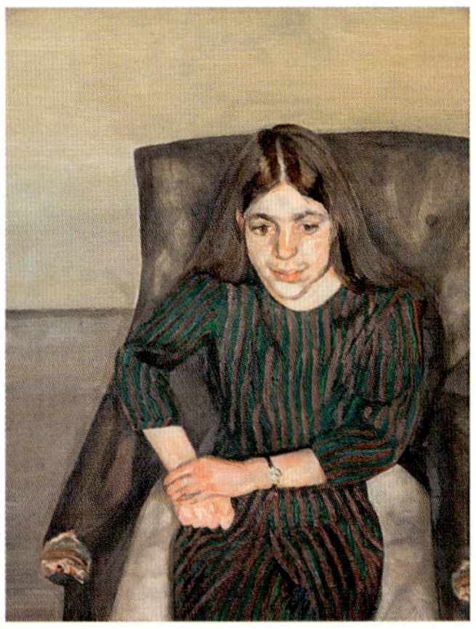

Freud, Lucian b.1922
Annabel 1967
oil on canvas 34.5 x 26.5
GR.97

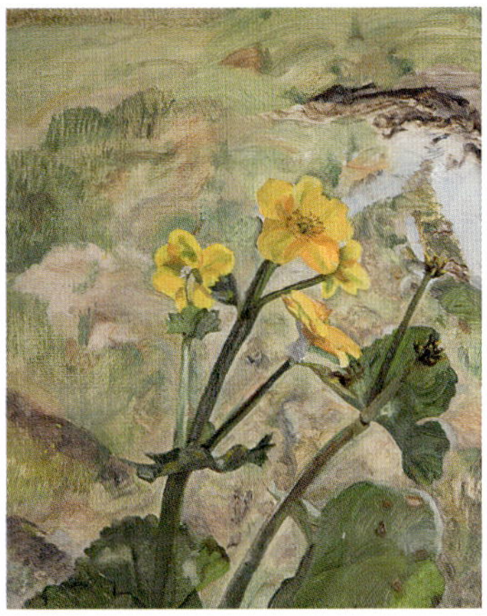

Freud, Lucian b.1922
Kingcups, Souvenir of Glen Artney 1967
oil on canvas 23 x 18.5
GR.98

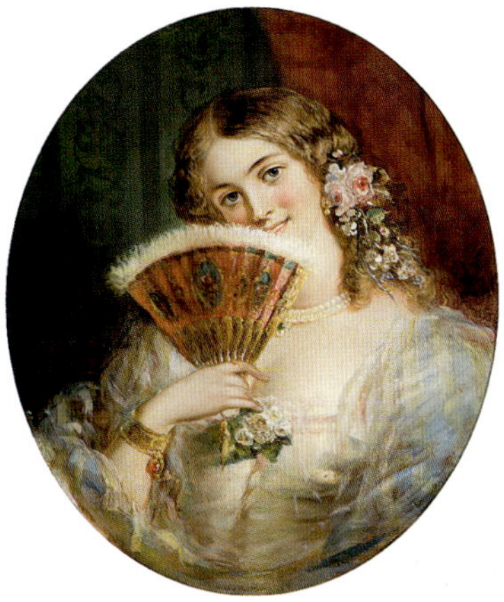

Frith, William Powell 1819–1909
Portrait of a Lady with a Fan 1885–1895
oil on canvas 76 x 63.5
P1/76

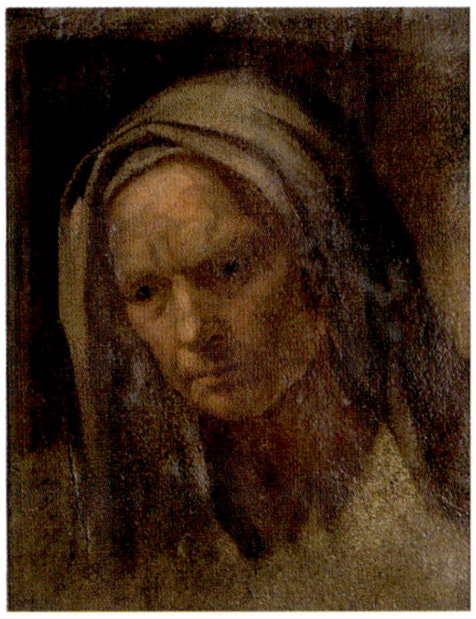

Fromentin, Eugène 1820–1876
Head of Old Woman
oil on board 16.5 x 13.5
GR.101

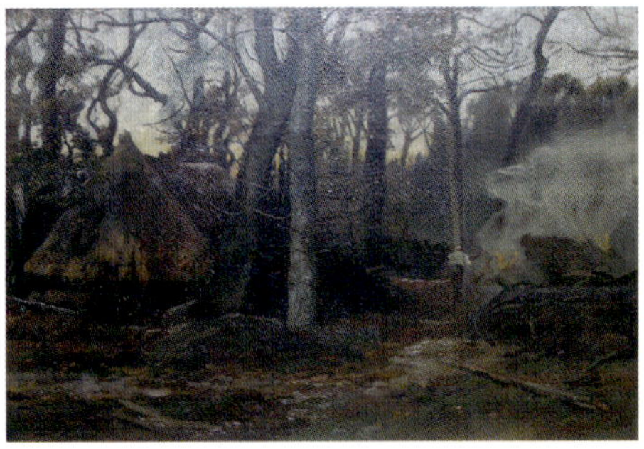

Fullwood, John 1854–1931
Charcoal Burners
oil on canvas 58 x 79
P28/76

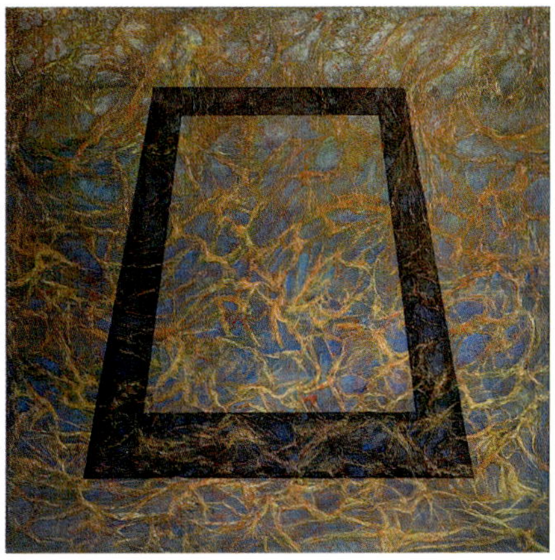

Gaete-Gwynne, Maria b.1947
Untitled 1995
oil & collage on paper 140 x 140
P17/96

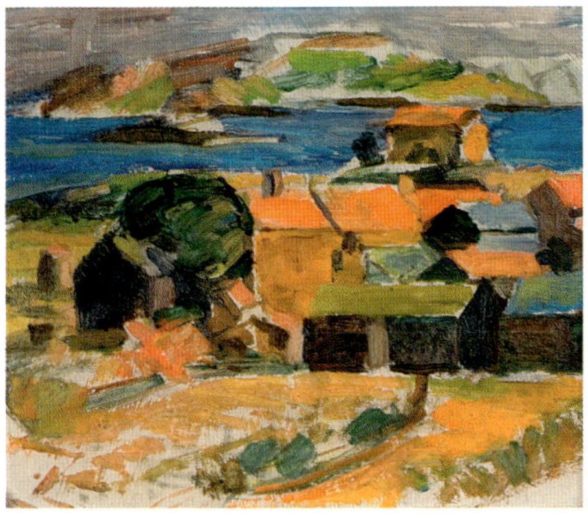

Gardiner, Clive 1891–1960
The Hamlet, Scilly Isles 1955
oil on board 11.5 x 14
GR.105

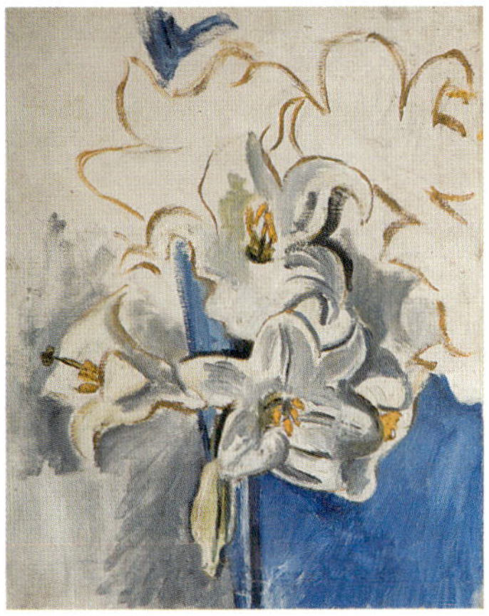

Garman, Theodore 1924–1954
Arum Lilies 1945–1954
oil on canvas 45 x 35
P7/88

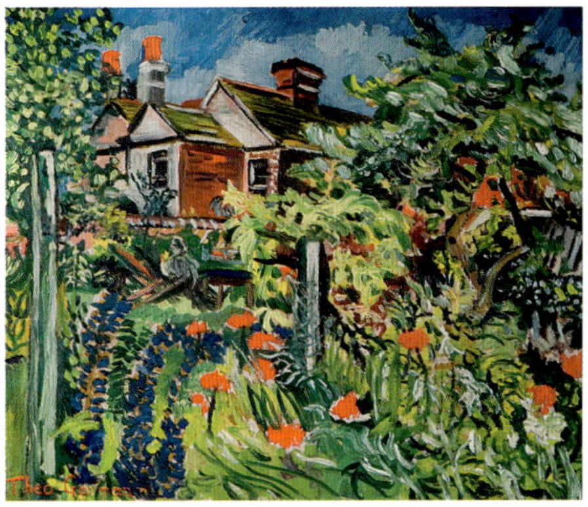

Garman, Theodore 1924–1954
Summer Garden, Harting 1947
oil on board 64 x 75
GR.108

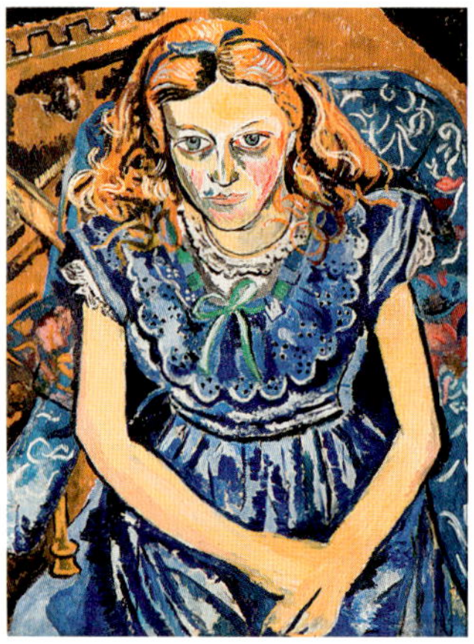

Garman, Theodore 1924–1954
The Blue Girl 1948
oil on canvas 121 x 90.5
GR.115

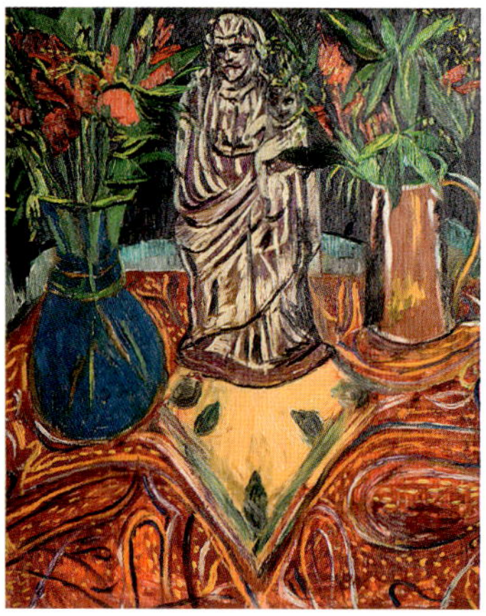

Garman, Theodore 1924–1954
Madonna with Flowers c.1948–1952
oil on canvas 125 x 99
PCF7

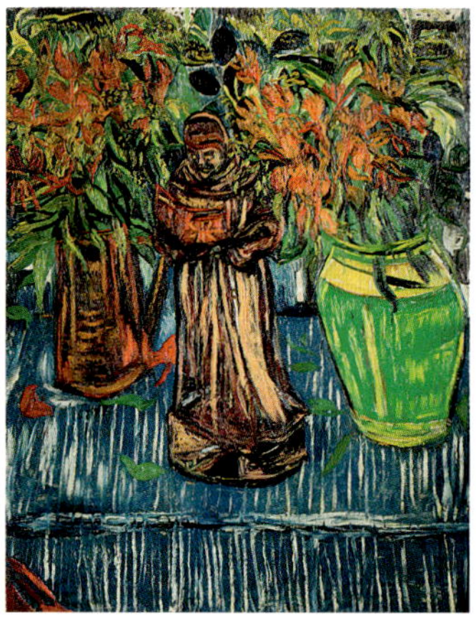

Garman, Theodore 1924–1954
The Wooden Monk c.1948–1952
oil on canvas 125 x 99
PCF8

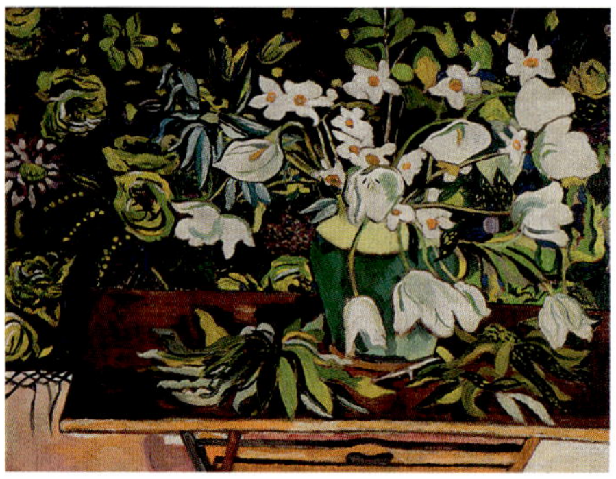

Garman, Theodore 1924–1954
Arum Lilies (Easter Flowers) 1949
oil on canvas 96 x 123
GR.109

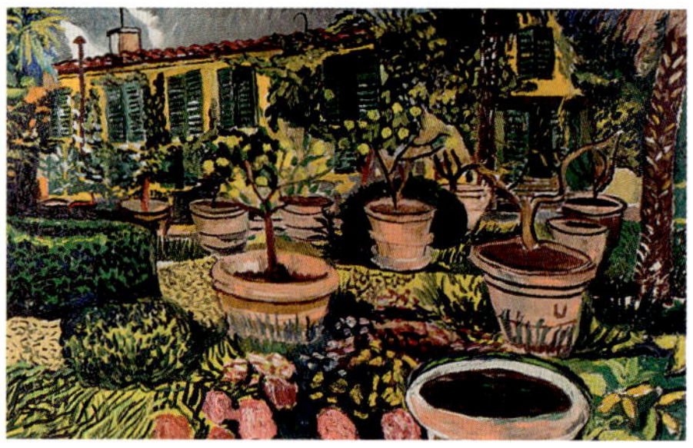

Garman, Theodore 1924–1954
Villa Solaia 1949
oil on canvas 88 x 139
GR.114

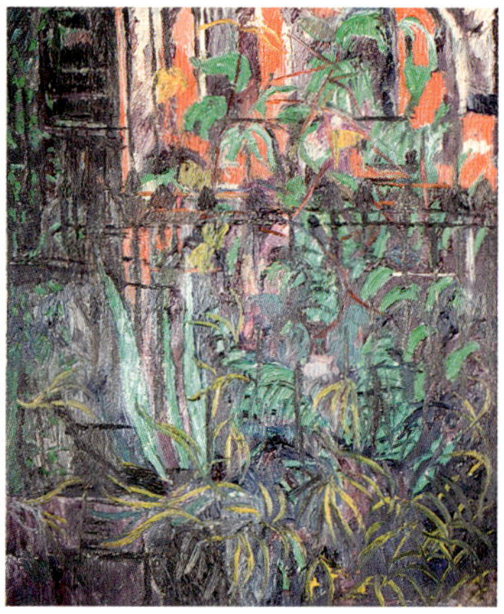

Garman, Theodore 1924–1954
Vegetation c.1950–1953
oil on canvas 91 x 71
PCF9

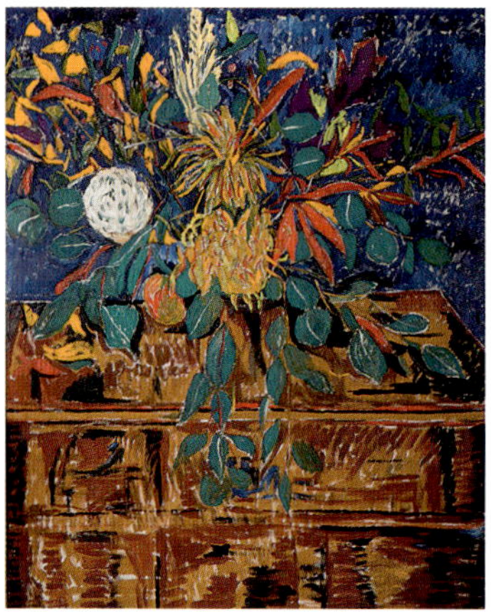

Garman, Theodore 1924–1954
Autumn Still Life c.1950–1954
oil on canvas 126 x 100
GR.116

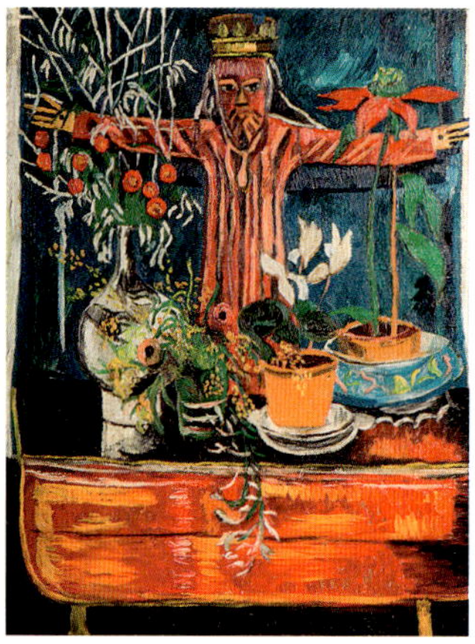

Garman, Theodore 1924–1954
Jesus Figure with Flowers 1951
oil on canvas 121 x 90
PCF10

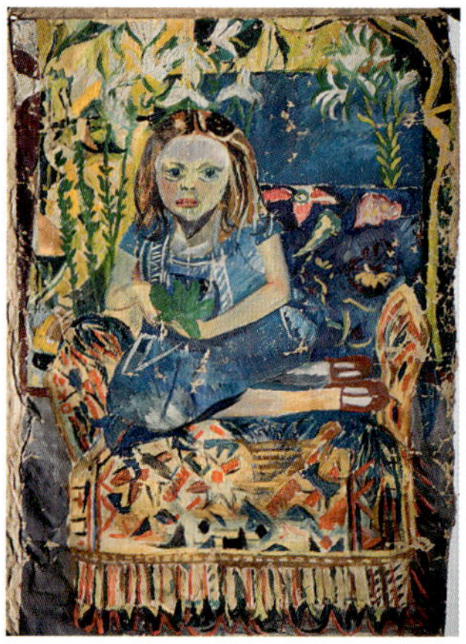

Garman, Theodore 1924–1954
Judith 1951
oil on canvas 150 x 102
PCF11

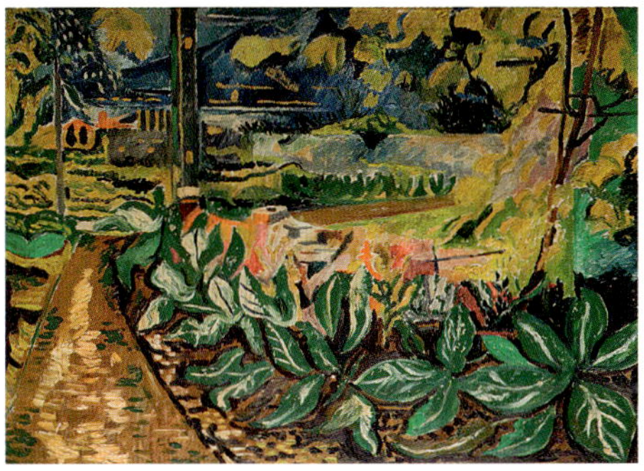

Garman, Theodore 1924–1954
Monte Gu 1951
oil on canvas 100 x 126
PCF12

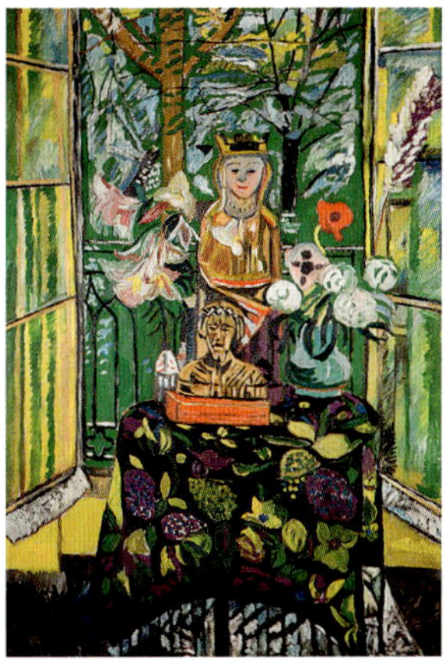

Garman, Theodore 1924–1954
Window Picture in June 1951
oil on canvas 179 x 119
GR.107

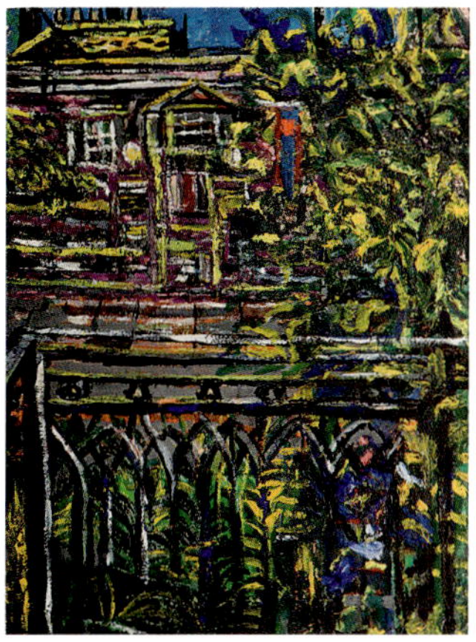

Garman, Theodore 1924–1954
Argyll House c.1951
acrylic & gouache on canvas 120 x 90
PCF13

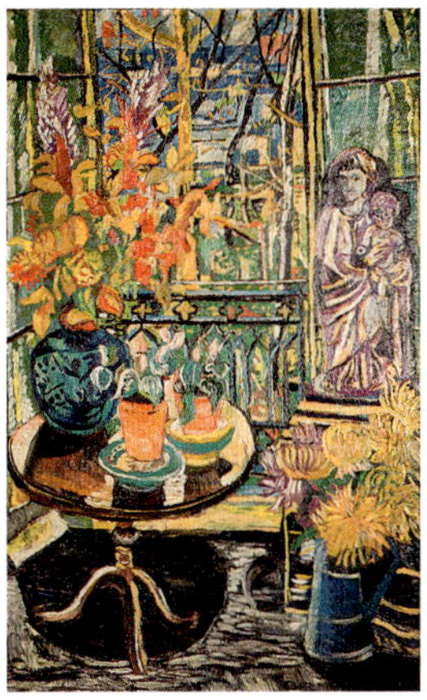

Garman, Theodore 1924–1954
Window Picture in November c.1951
oil on canvas 189 x 118
PCF14

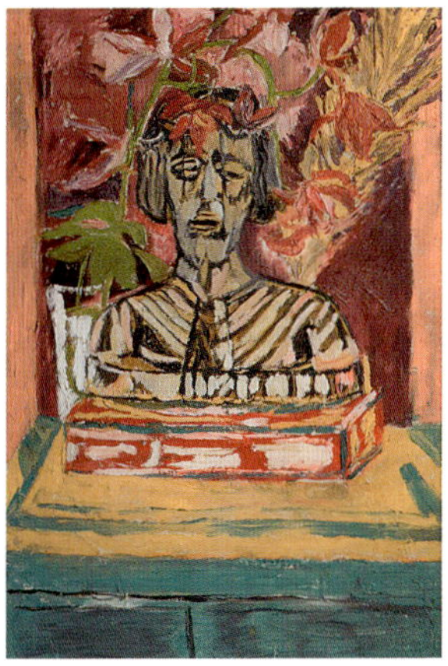

Garman, Theodore 1924–1954
Good Friday 1952
oil on canvas 77 x 52
GR.117

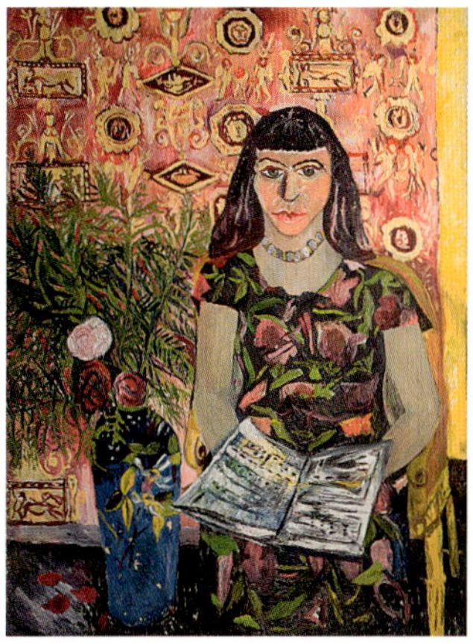

Garman, Theodore 1924–1954
Kathleen with Music 1952
oil on canvas 163 x 121
PCF15

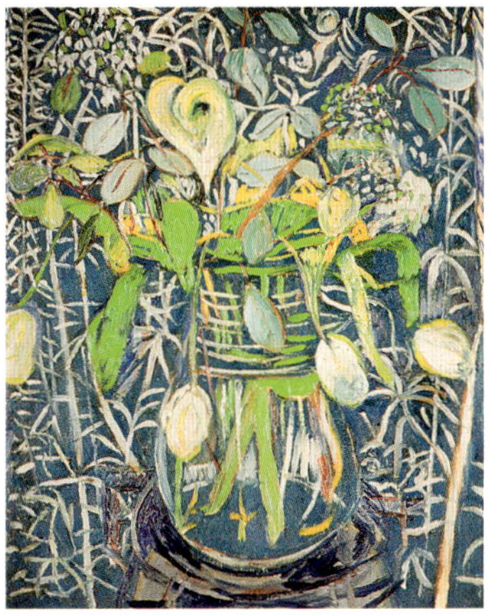

Garman, Theodore 1924–1954
Easter Flowers 1953
oil on canvas 89 x 69
PCF16

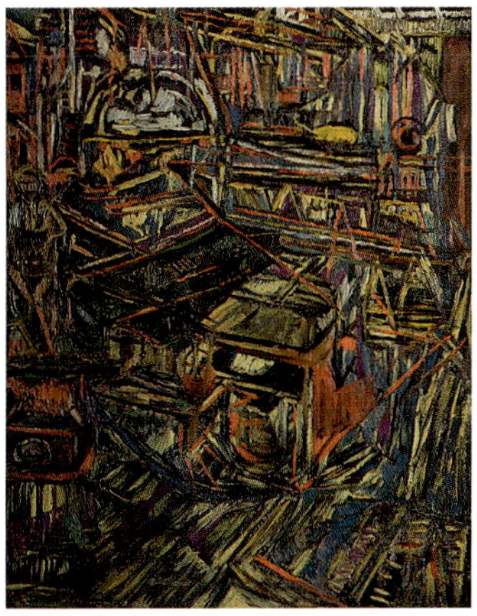

Garman, Theodore 1924–1954
The Old Forge, Chelsea 1953
oil on canvas 125 x 99
PCF18

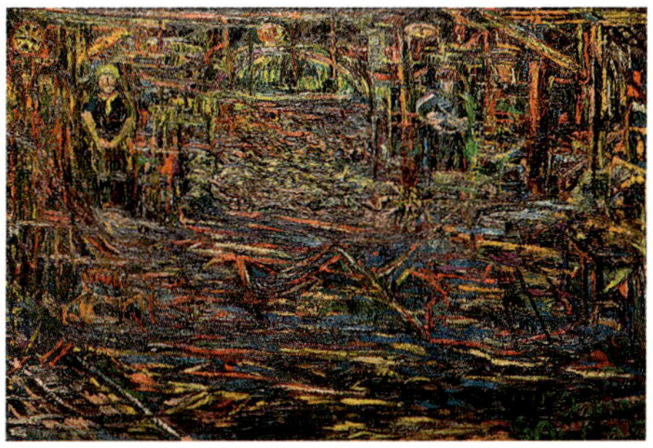

Garman, Theodore 1924–1954
The Old Forge, Chelsea (11) 1953
oil on canvas 118 x 161
PCF17

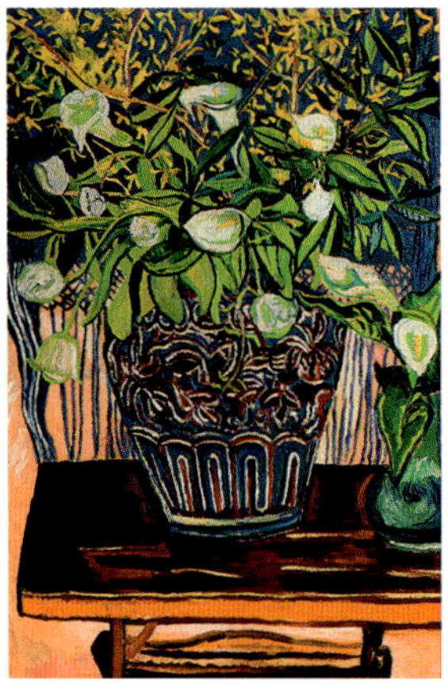

Garman, Theodore 1924–1954
Arum Lilies
oil on canvas 135 x 91
PCF19

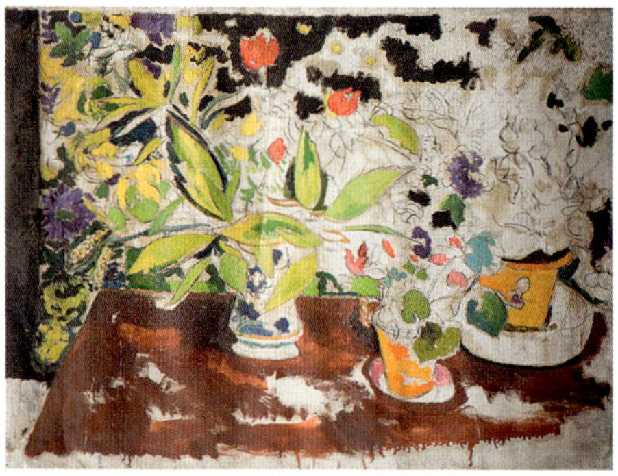

Garman, Theodore 1924–1954
Unfinished Canvas (1)
oil on canvas 98.5 x 127
PCF20

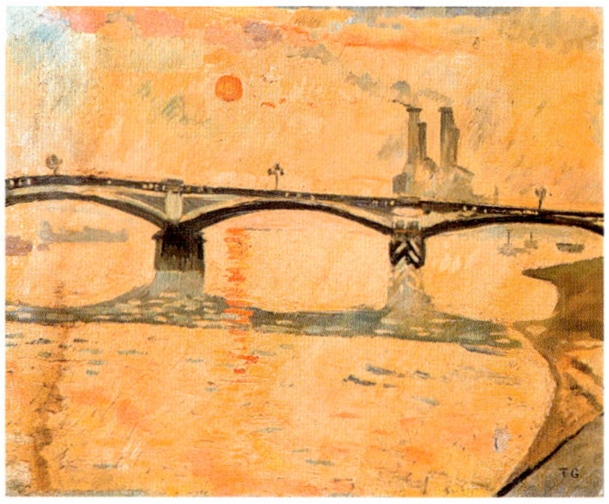

Garman, Theodore 1924–1954
Winter Sunset on the Thames
oil on canvas 51 x 61
PCF21

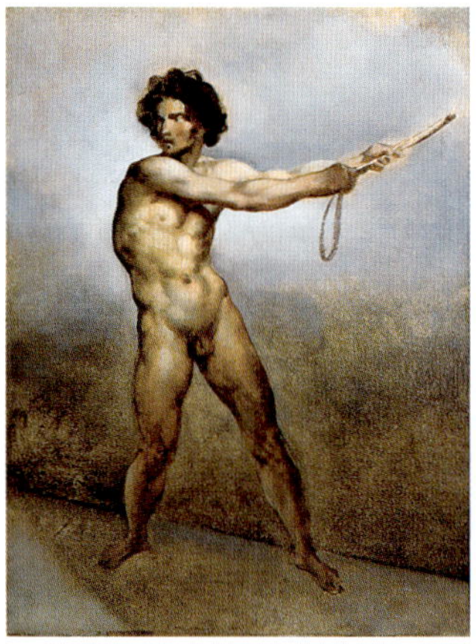

Géricault, Théodore 1791–1824
Etude d'un homme nu 1816–1818
oil on paper 28.5 x 21.5
GR.125

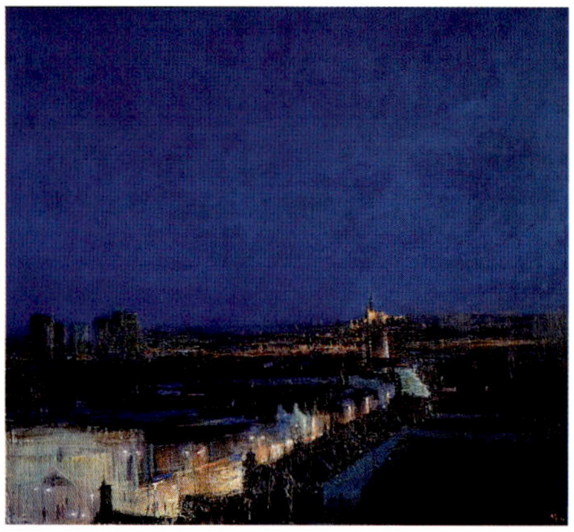

Gifford, Andrew b.1970
Walsall, Looking towards St Matthew's Church 1999
oil on canvas 110 x 120
P1/06

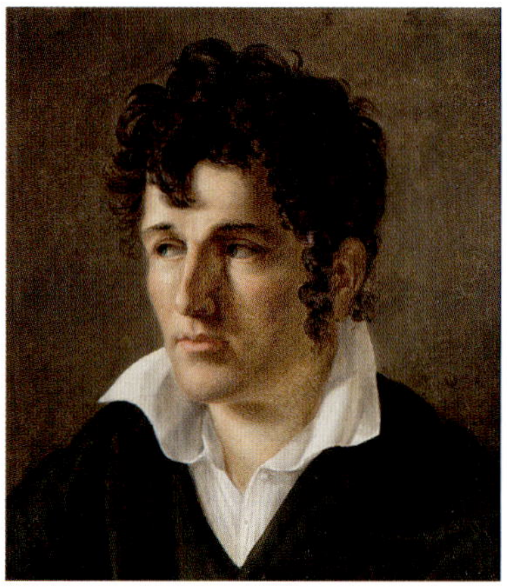

Girodet de Roucy-Trioson, Anne-Louis 1767–1824
François-René de Chateaubriand (1768–1848) 1791
oil on canvas 43 x 36
GR.127

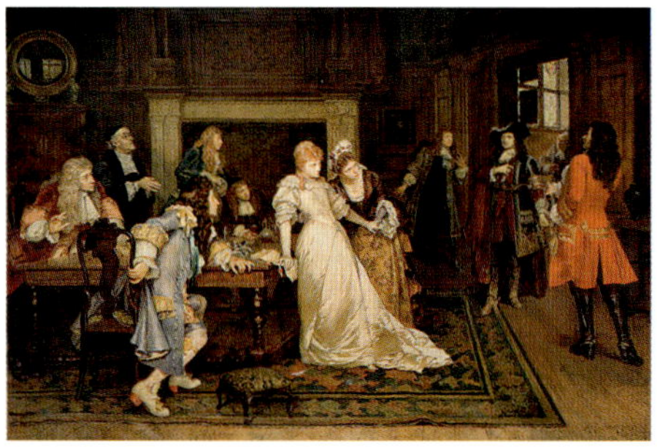

Glindoni, Henry Gillard 1852–1913
The Bride of Lammermoor 1885
oil on canvas 129.5 x 180
P43/76

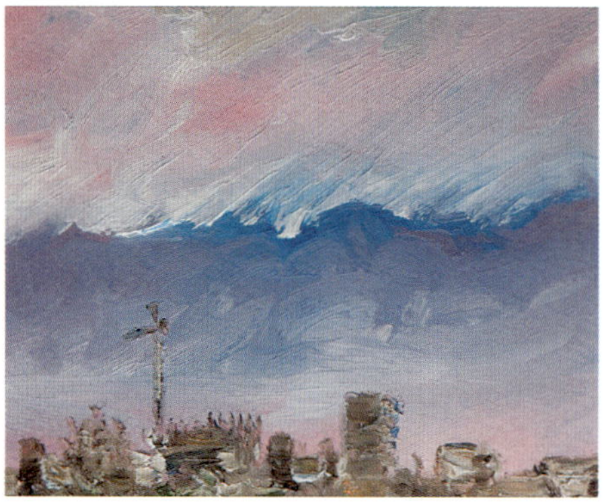

Gunning, David Edward b.1954
'On Site', Early Morning Construction 1997
oil on paper 13 x 15.5
P3/03

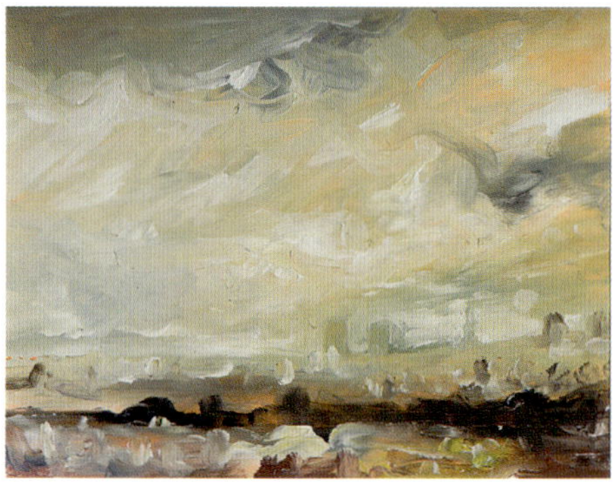

Gunning, David Edward b.1954
View of Walsall 1997
oil on board 21.5 x 27.5
P3/98

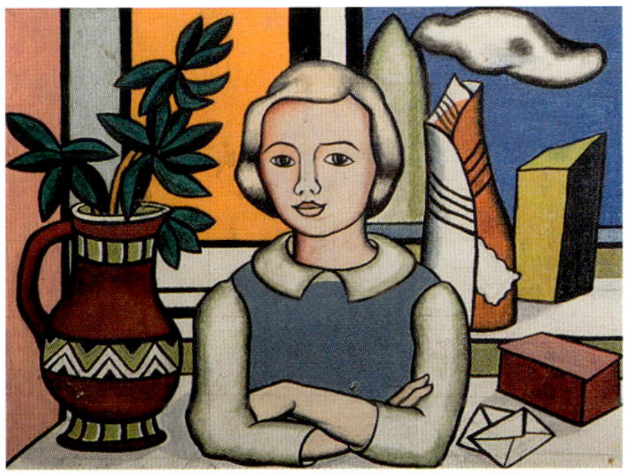

Hatt, Doris 1890–1969
Birthday
oil on canvas 34 x 44.5
P151/76

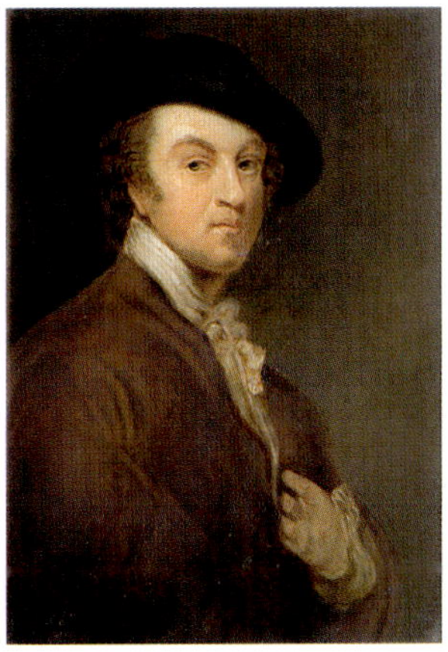

Haynes, A.
Portrait of a Man 1806
oil on canvas 29 x 22
P135/76

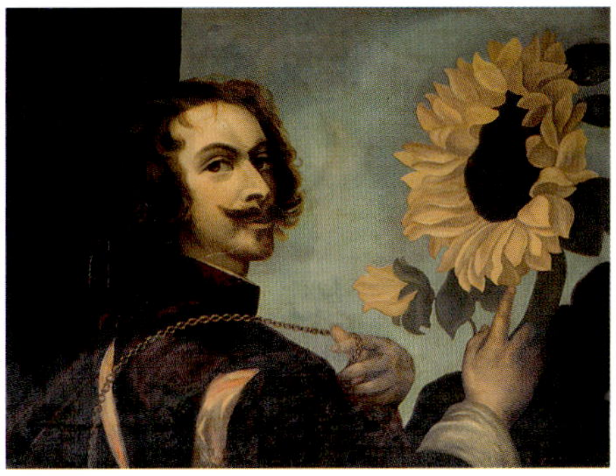

Haynes, B. active 1865–1890
Man with a Sunflower (after Anthony van Dyck) 1890
oil on canvas 62 x 74
P133/76

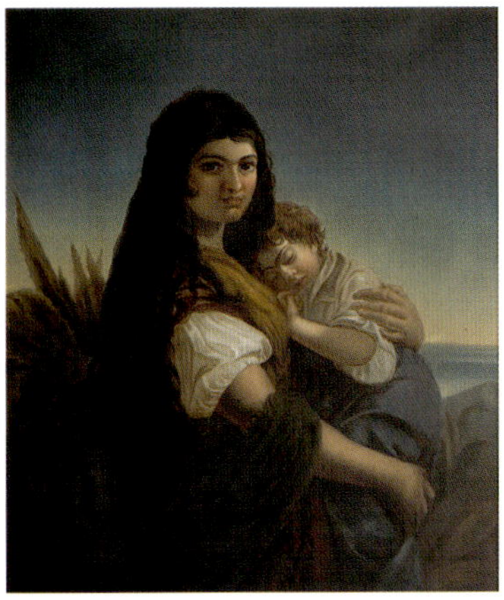

Haynes, B. active 1865–1890
Gypsy Love
oil on canvas 74 x 62
P132/76

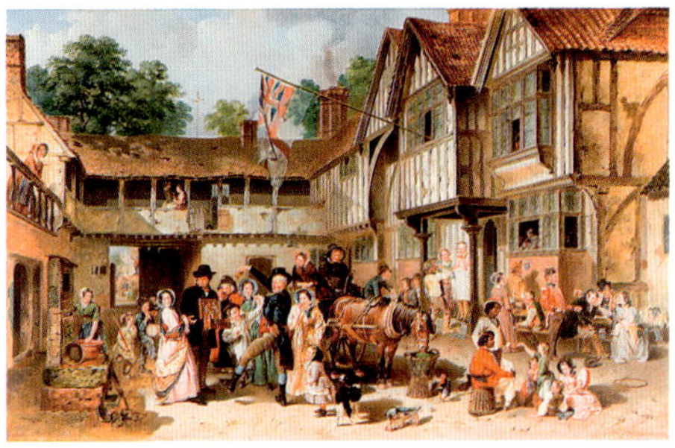

Henderson, W. S. P. active 1836–1874
Fair Day 1856
oil on panel 60 x 90
P31/76

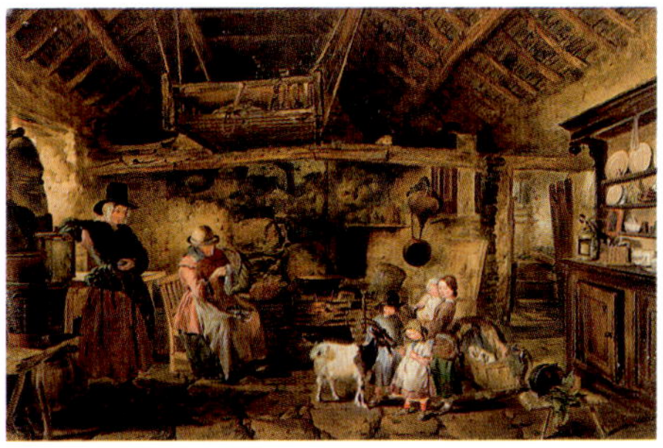

Henderson, W. S. P. active 1836–1874
Welsh Interior
oil on canvas 76 x 81
P131/76

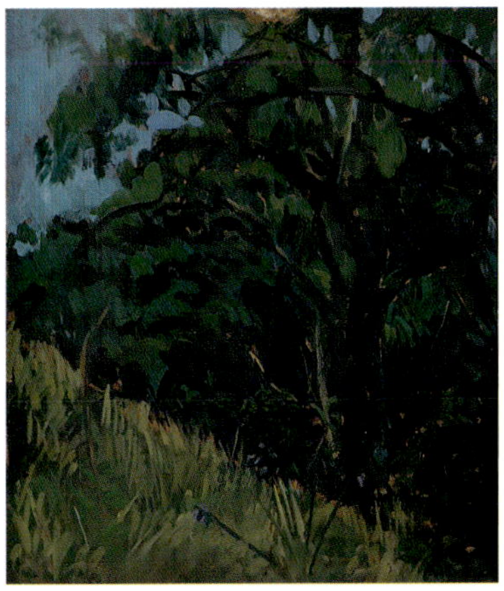

Hett, Charles b.1941
Landscape in Norfolk
acrylic on board 36 x 34
GR.139

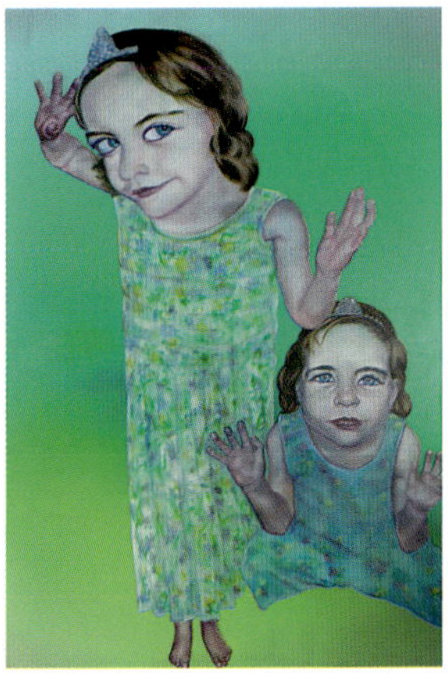

Hoberman, Nicky b.1967
The Frog Princess 1997
oil on canvas 244 x 152
P8/99

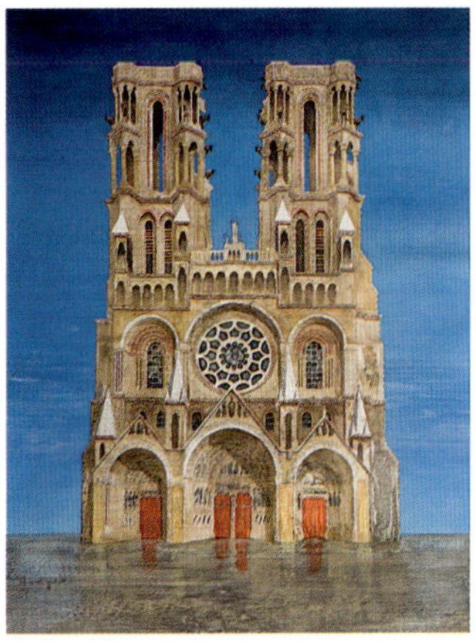

Hodges, Derek Ian 1921–2003
Laon Cathedral
oil on canvas 100 x 75
P3/06

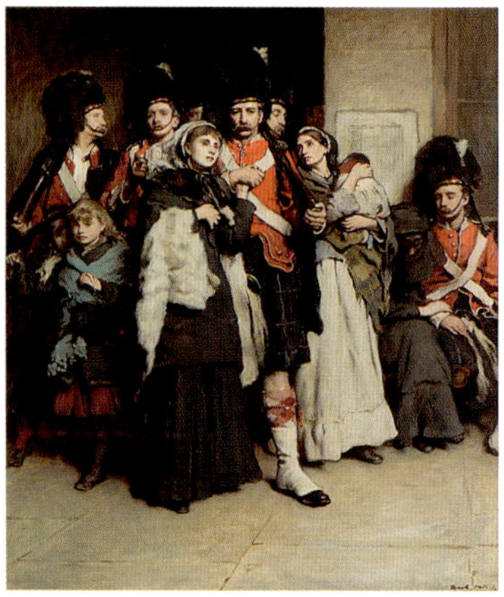

Holl, Frank 1845–1888
Ordered to the Front 1880
oil on canvas 75 x 64
P328/76

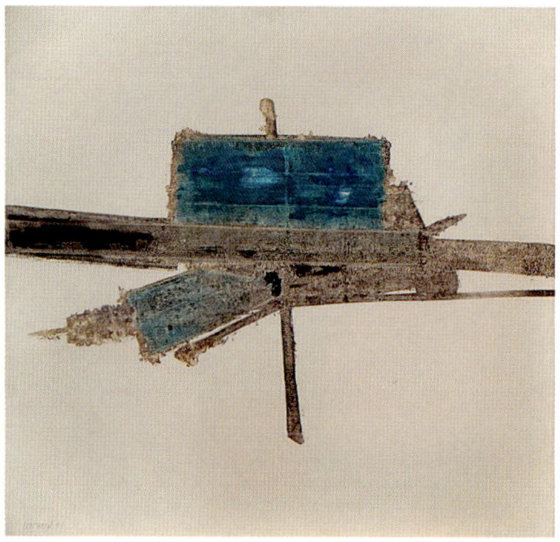

Ireland, Geoffrey b.1923
Untitled 1961
oil on canvas 76 x 76
GR.3.98

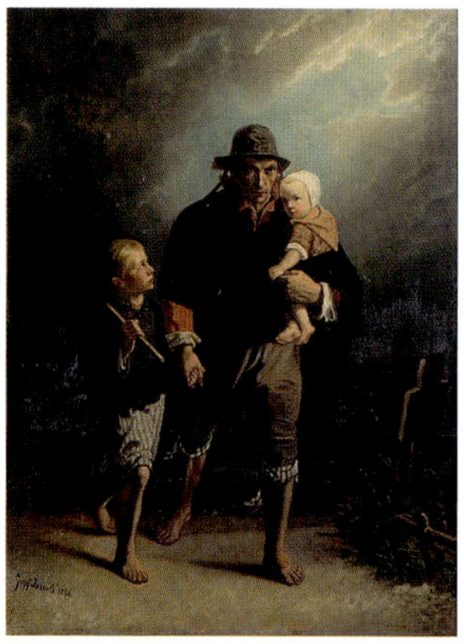

Israëls, Jozef (after) 1824–1911
The Widower, the Fisherman's Return 1854
oil on canvas 91 x 66
P30/76

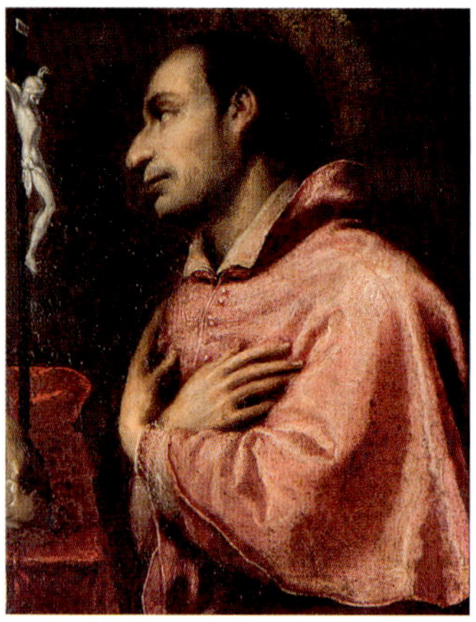

Italian (Lombard) School 17th C
San Carlo Boromeo in Adoration before a Crucifix
oil on copper 23 x 18
GR.241

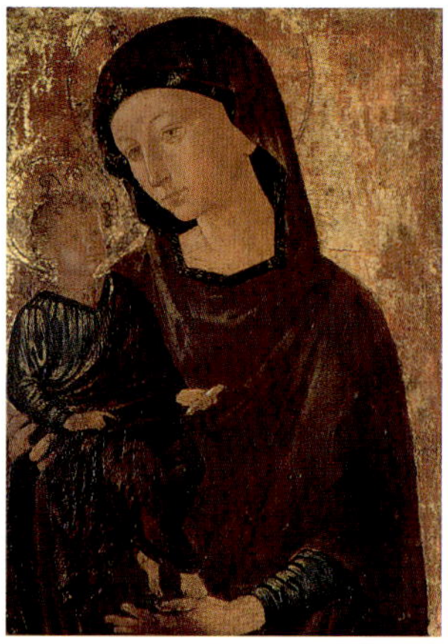

Italian School
The Madonna and Child c.1400
tempera, oil & gold on panel 43 x 31
GR.93

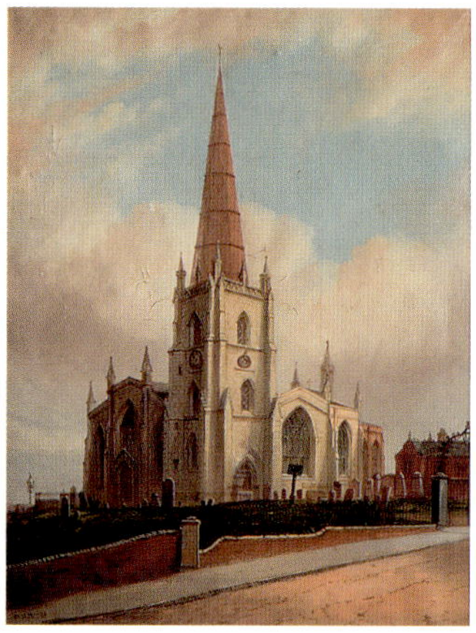

Jacobi, M. M. active 1882–1883
St Matthew's Church, Walsall
oil on canvas 48 x 35.5
P152/76

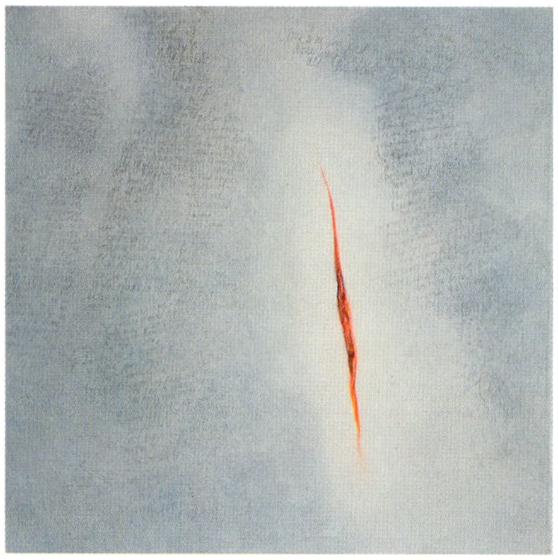

Johns, Myfanwy b.1958
Scission 1995
oil & pencil on canvas 55 x 55
P1/97

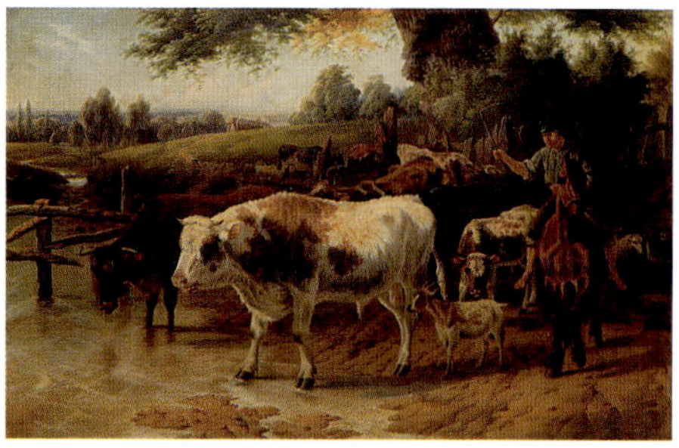

Jones, Charles 1836–1902
Cattle at a Stream 1869–1871
oil on canvas 61 x 89
P12/76

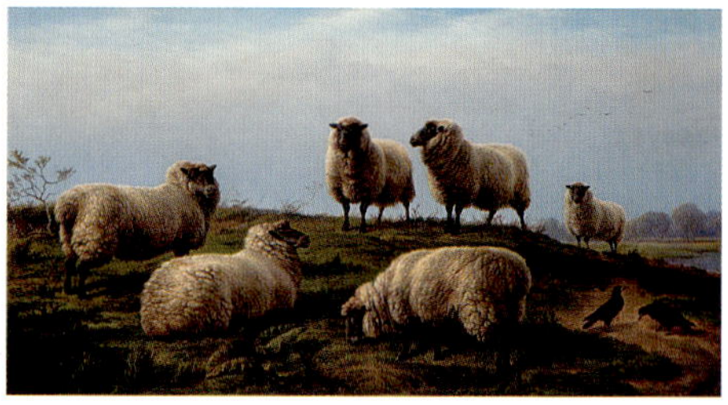

Jones, Charles 1836–1902
Sheep 1875
oil on canvas 34.3 x 50.2
P24/76

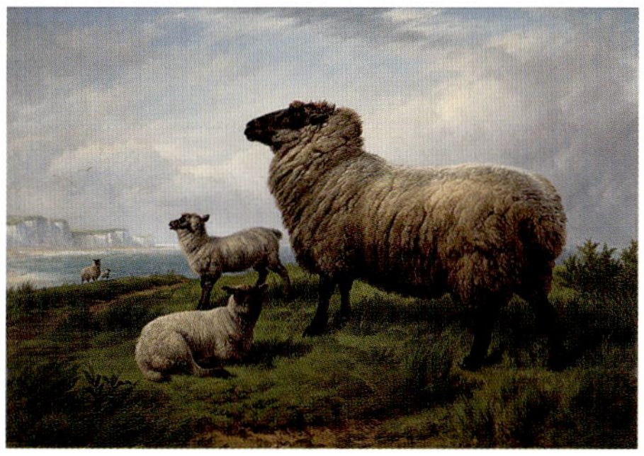

Jones, Charles 1836–1902
Sheep 1875
oil on canvas 85.5 x 112
P40/76

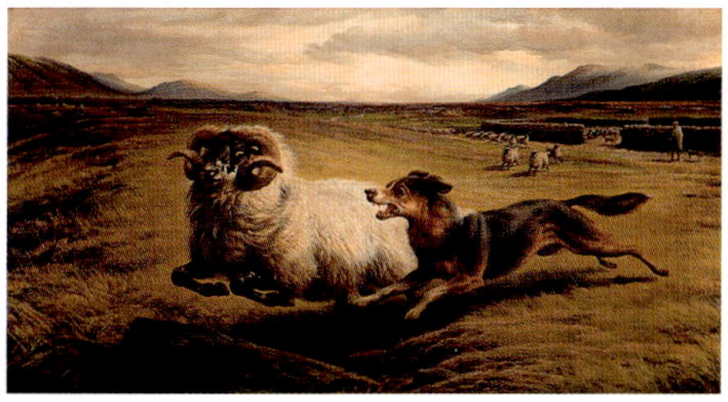

Jones, Charles 1836–1902
Hard Chase 1887
oil on canvas 121 x 212
P46/76

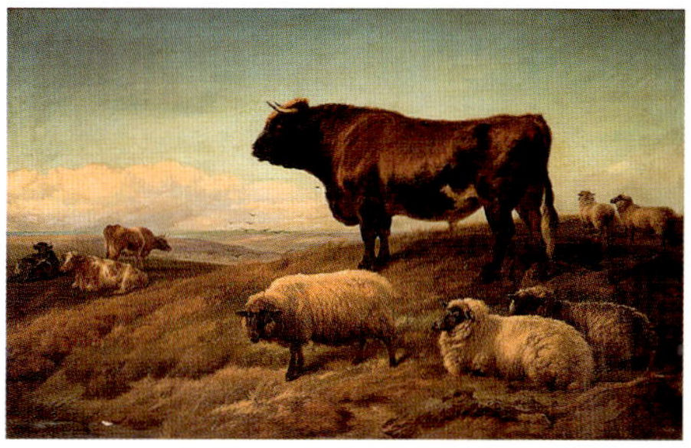

Jones, Charles 1836–1902
The Lord of the Downs
oil on canvas 119.5 x 180
P38/76

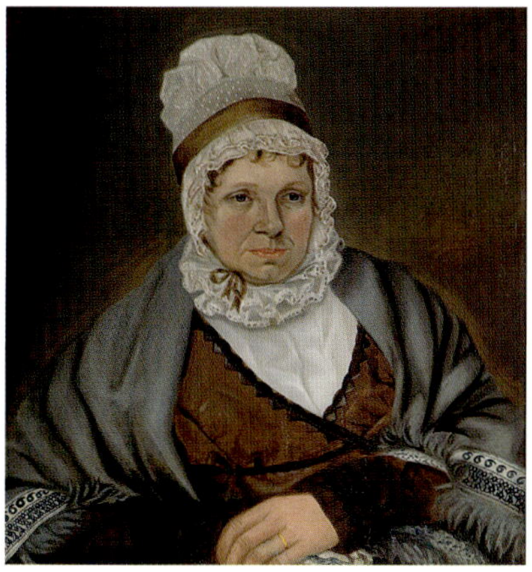

Keith, Alexander active 1808–1874
Dolly Eyland 1808
oil on canvas 68.5 x 62.5
P11/02

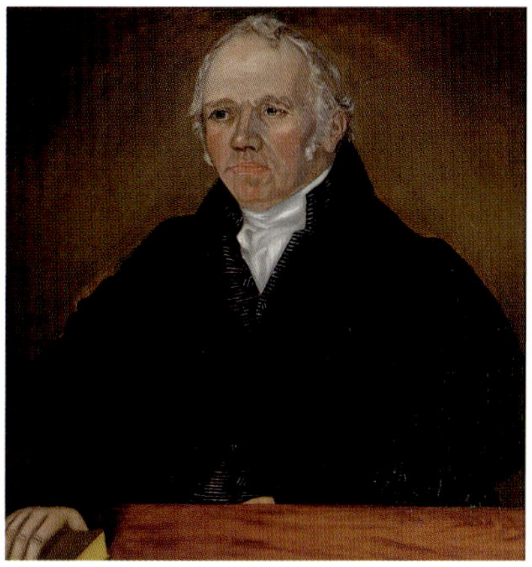

Keith, Alexander active 1808–1874
Moses Eyland 1808
oil on canvas 68.5 x 62.5
P12/02

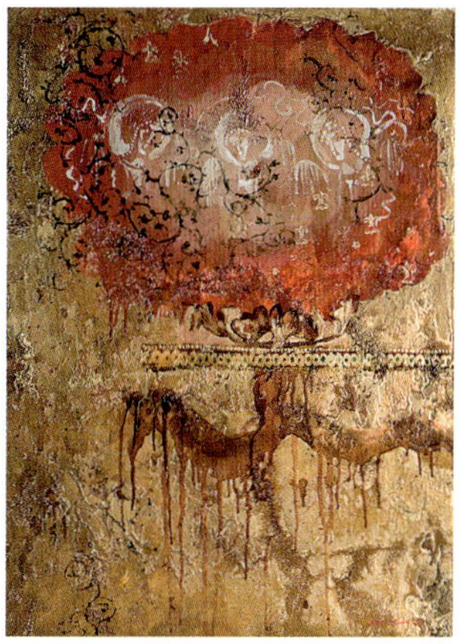

Kiat, Soh Siew
A Golden Ornament II 1992
oil on canvas 75 x 54.5
P24/93

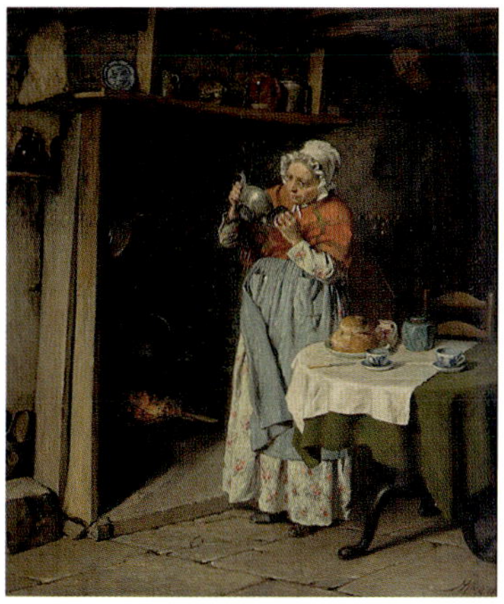

King, Haynes 1831–1904
An Old Friend Failing 1880
oil on canvas 60 x 50
P321/76

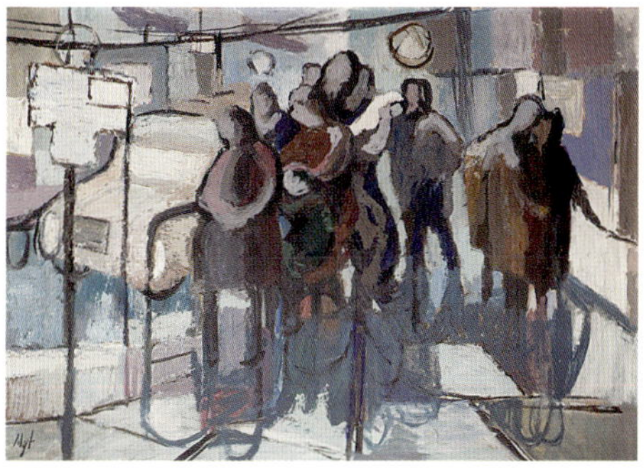

Kitchin, Myfanwy b.1917
At the Bus Stop 1969
oil on canvas 87 x 117
P275/76

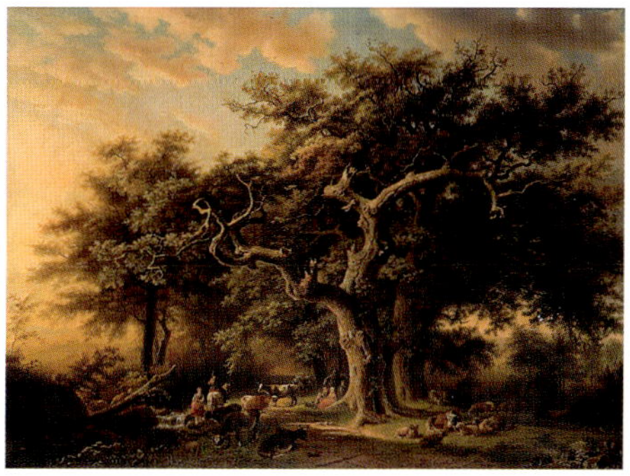

Koekkoek, Barend Cornelis 1803–1862
Woodland Scene
oil on canvas 96 x 119
P23/76

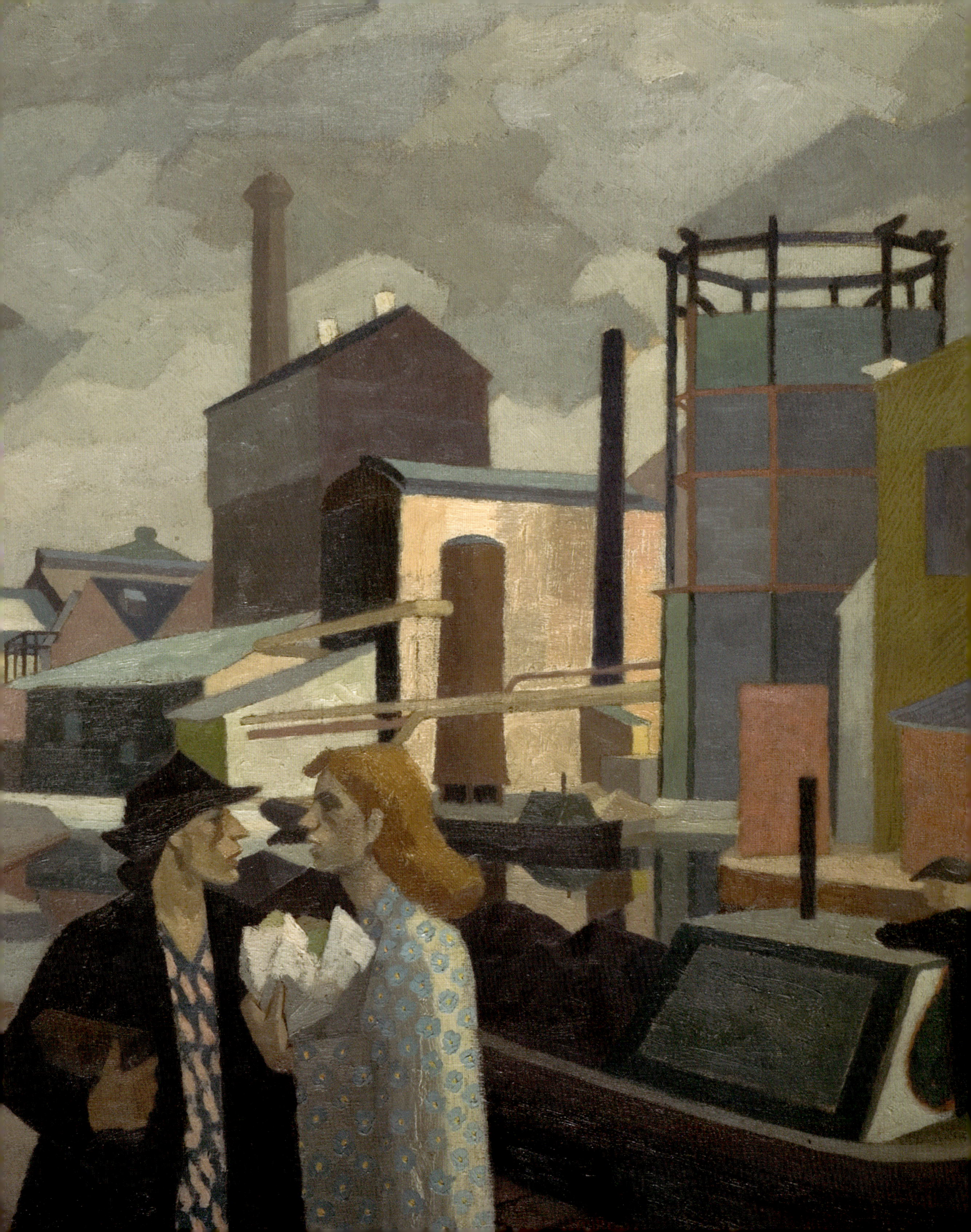

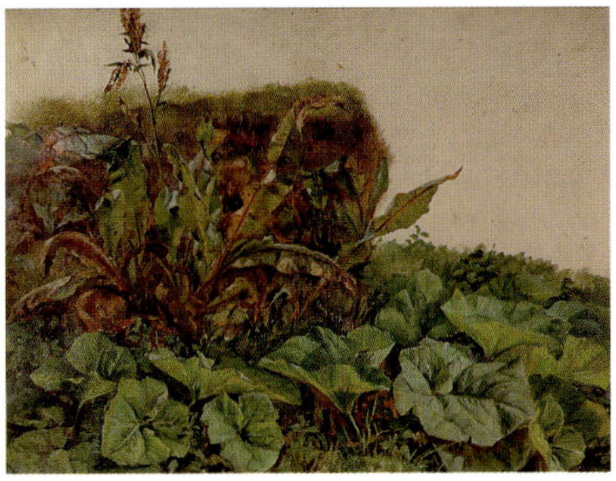

Landseer, Edwin Henry (attributed to)
1802–1873
Study of Wayside Plants 1866
oil on paper 26 x 33
GR.149

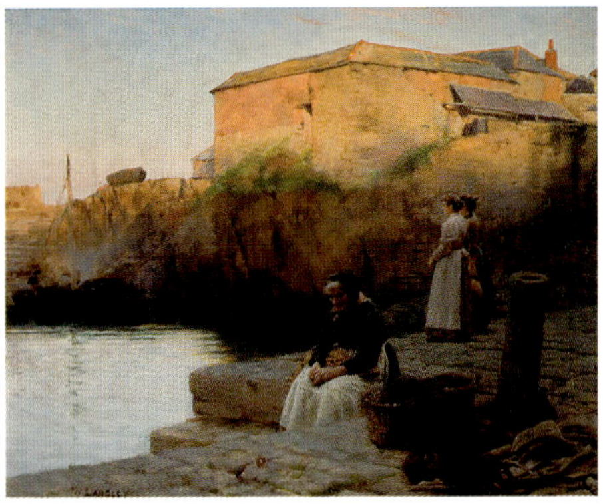

Langley, Walter 1852–1922
Evening at Coverack, Cornwall 1895
oil on canvas 49 x 60
P5/76

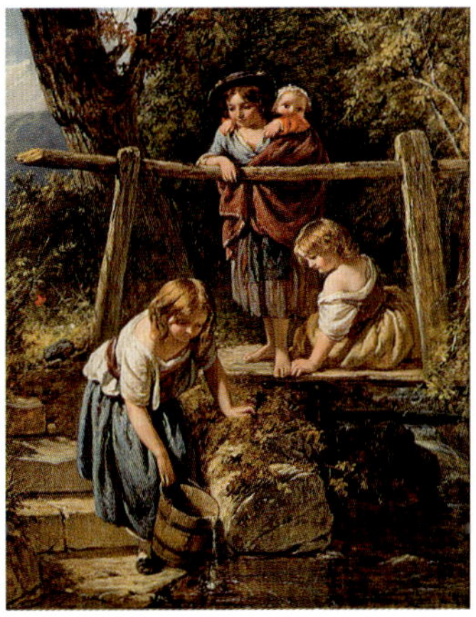

Le Jeune, Henry 1819–1904
Children at a Stream
oil on canvas 112 x 85
P35/76

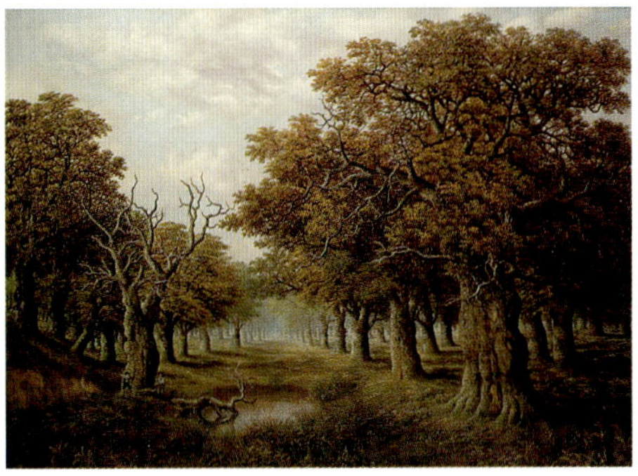

Leaver, Charles 1824–1888
In the New Forest 1885
oil on canvas 131 x 184
P226/76

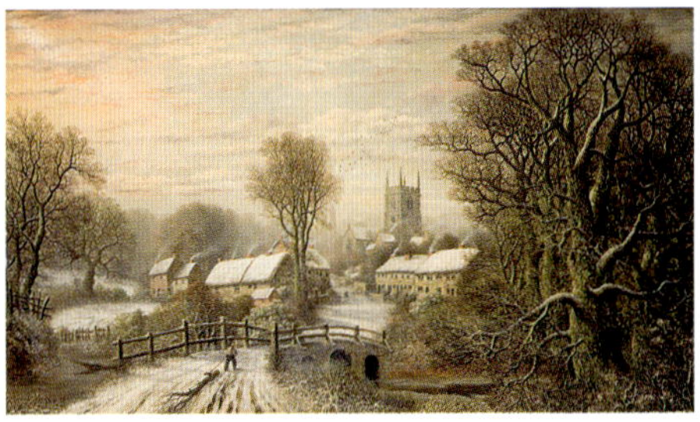

Leaver, Charles 1824–1888
Grendon Village, Northamptonshire
oil on canvas 84 x 141
P225/76

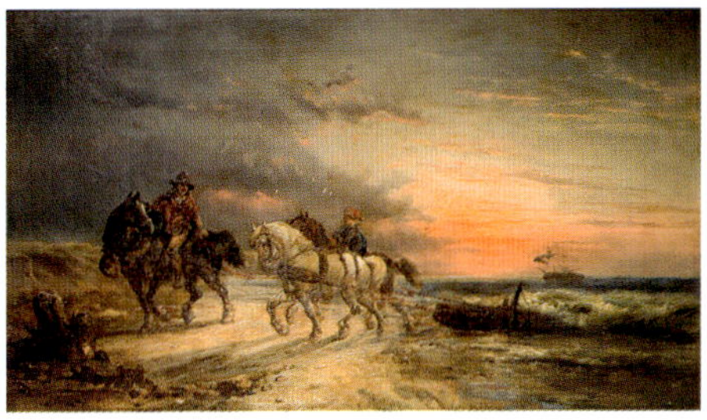

Leeuw, Alexis de active 1848–1887
The Wreckers
oil on canvas 74.5 x 125
P96/76

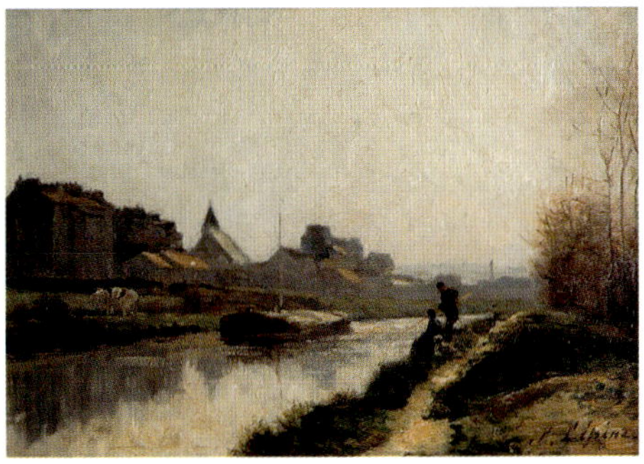

Lépine, Stanislas 1835–1892
Le canal
oil on canvas 20 x 28
GR.150

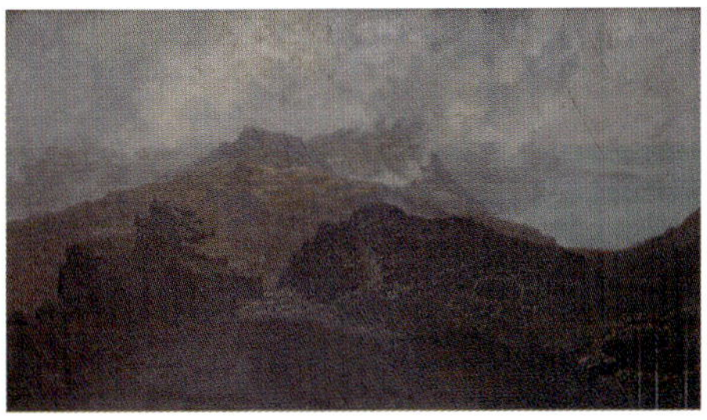

Lowe, G. E. active 1885
Tre'r Ceiri, Town of Fortresses
oil on canvas 73.5 x 124.5
P36/76

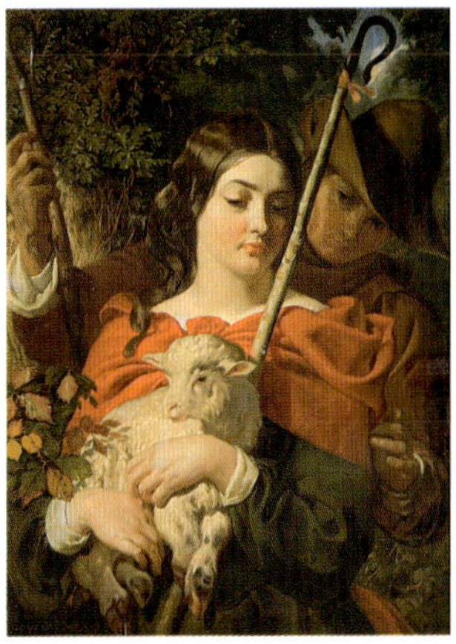

Maclise, Daniel 1806–1870
Phoebe and Silvius in the Forest of Arden, from Shakespeare's 'As You Like It' 1853
oil on canvas 59.5 x 44
P320/76

Facing page: Fereday, Joseph, 1917–2001, *Catchem's Corner, Bilston* (detail), Wolverhampton Art Gallery, (p. 271)

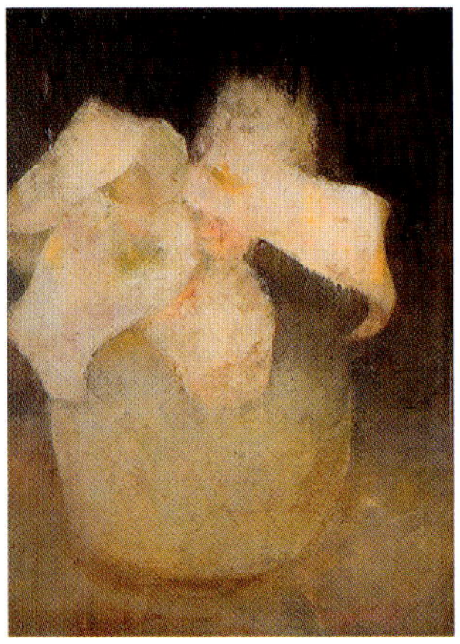

Mankes, Jan 1889–1920
White Orchid 1916
oil on board 22 x 16
GR.356

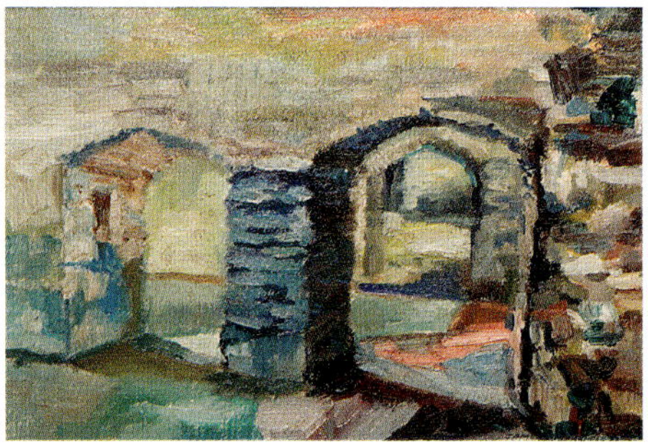

Marshall, James
The Crypt, Bishop's Palace, St David's
oil on board 24 x 34.5
PCF1 (P)

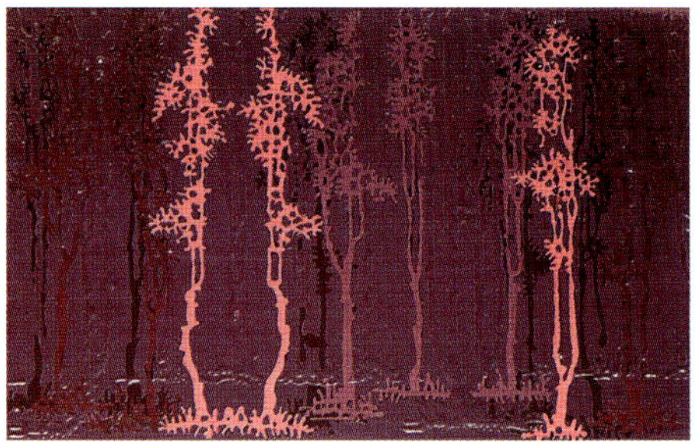

Maybank, Hannah b.1974
Hosts (II)
acrylic & latex on linen 28.5 x 38.5
P2/06

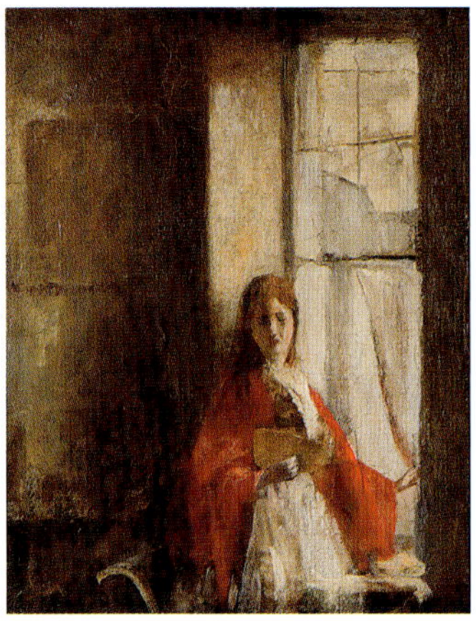

McEvoy, Ambrose 1878–1927
The Letter 1904–1906
oil on canvas 48.5 x 38.5
GR.159

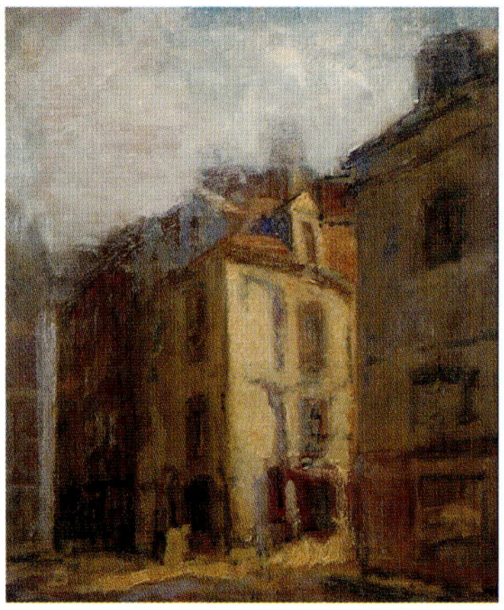

McEvoy, Ambrose 1878–1927
Dieppe Street Scene
oil on canvas 61 x 51
GR.158

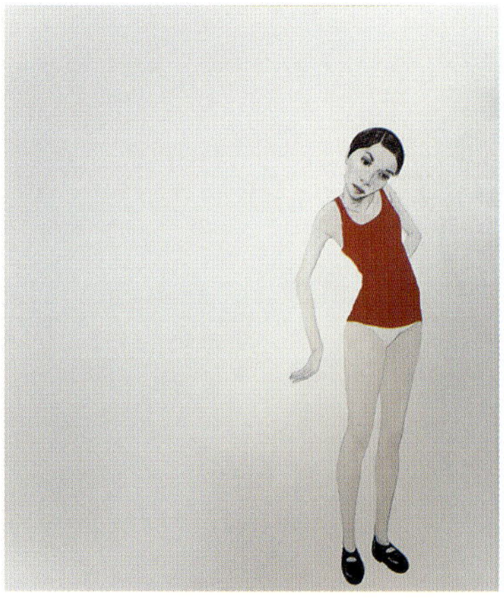

McLean, Ian 1973–2000
Sans amour 1996
oil on canvas 184 x 152
P75/01

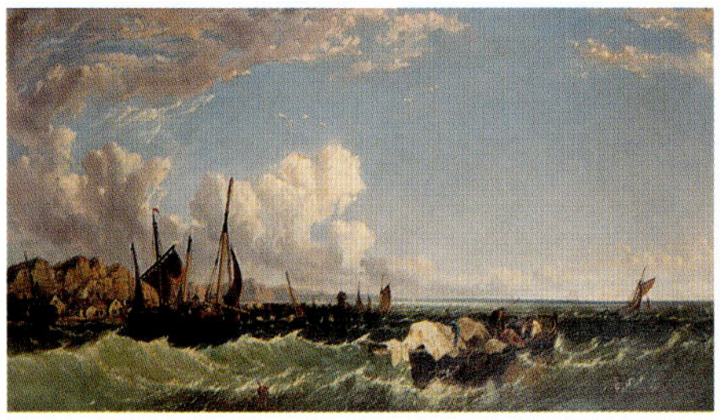

Meadows, Arthur Joseph 1843–1907
Ships in Choppy Sea
oil on canvas 72 x 124
P24/82

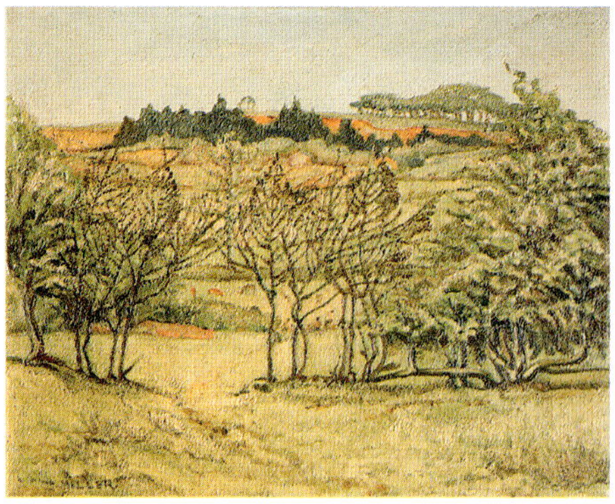

Miller
Barr Beacon
oil on canvas 48 x 56
PCF2

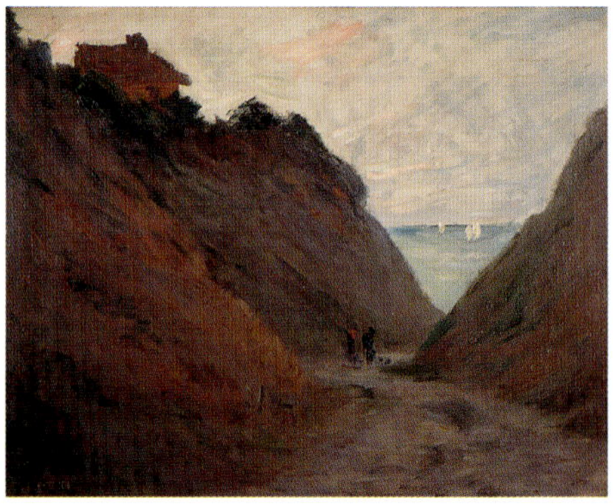

Monet, Claude 1840–1926
Le chemin creux dans la falaise à Varangeville 1882
oil on canvas 58 x 72
GR.171

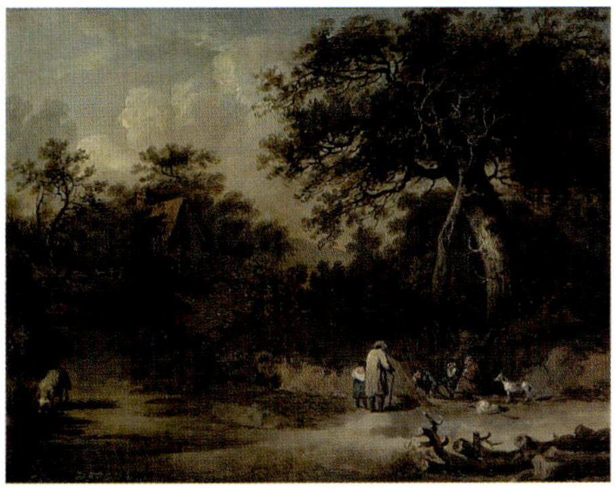

Morland, George 1763–1804
Rural Scene 1789
oil on board 30 x 37
P19/76

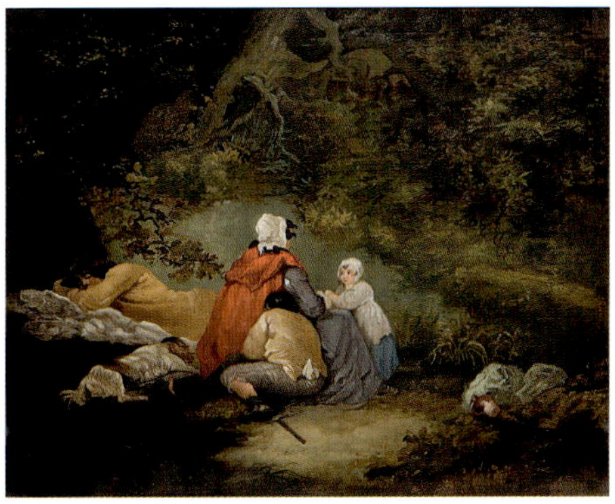

Morland, George 1763–1804
The Sleepers (Gypsy Scene)
oil on canvas 61 x 74
P41/76

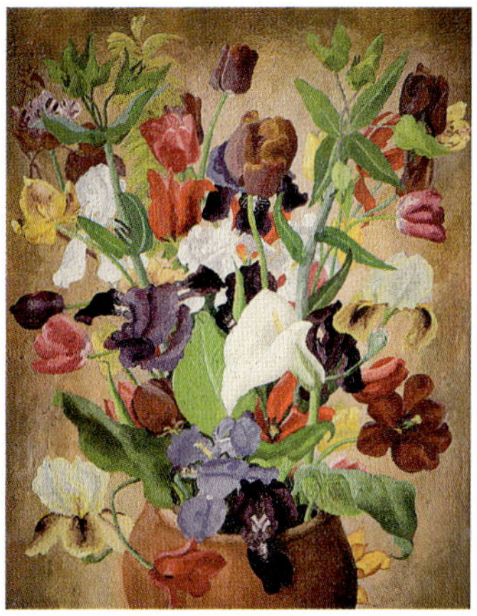

Morris, Cedric Lockwood 1889–1982
Irises and Tulips 1950s
oil on canvas 43 x 33
P216/76

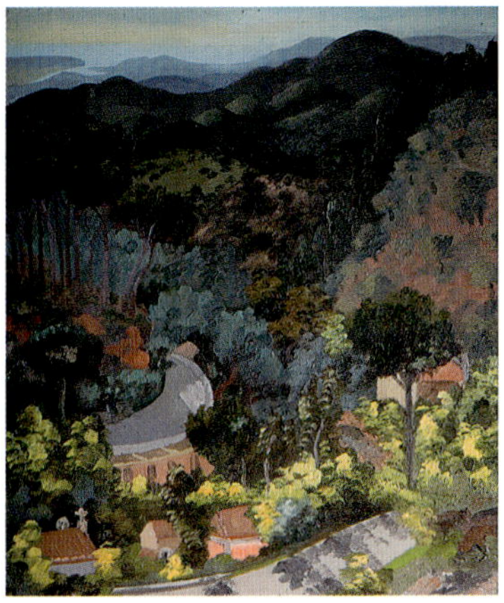

Morris, Cedric Lockwood 1889–1982
Monchique Foothills, Algarve
oil on canvas 58 x 48
P217/76

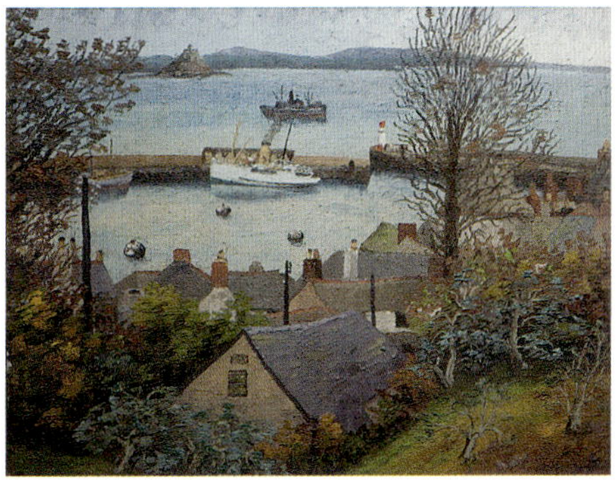

Morris, Cedric Lockwood 1889–1982
The Scilly Packet Boat
oil on canvas 63 x 79.5
P134/76

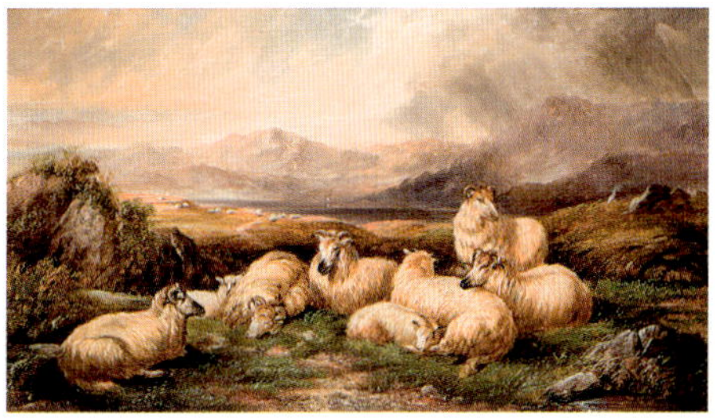

Morris, John Charles active 1851–1889
Sheep 1889
oil on canvas 76 x 127
P224/76

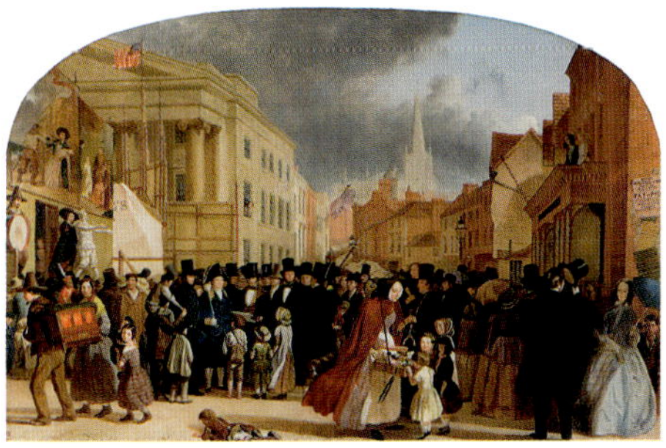

Mudge, Alfred active 1859–1885
Walking the Walsall Fair 1859
oil on canvas 59.5 x 90
P.LOAN 1/78

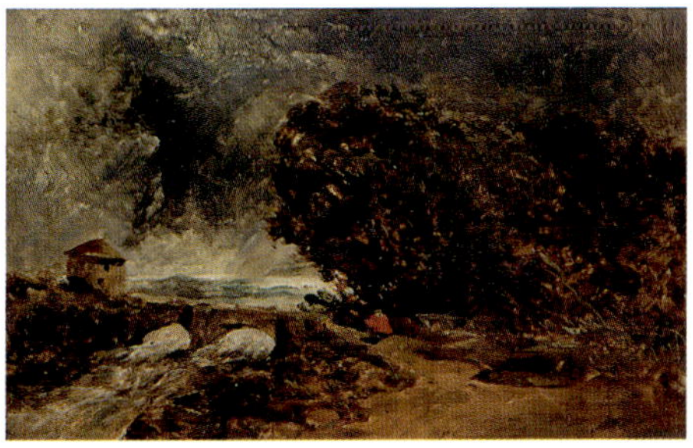

Müller, William James 1812–1845
The Approaching Storm
oil on canvas 20 x 32
P103/76

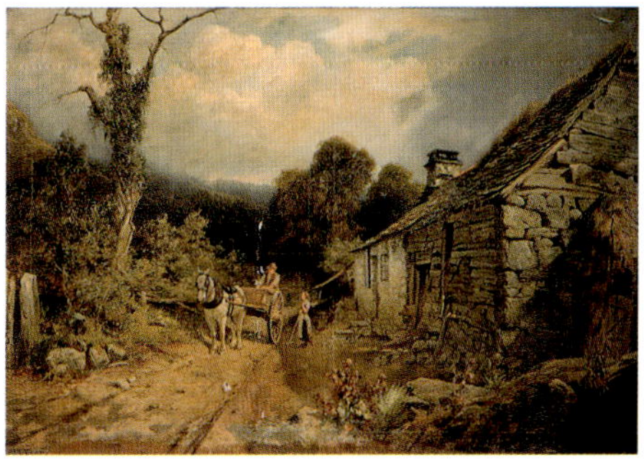

Munns, Henry Turner 1832–1898
Chat by the Way 1850–1878
oil on canvas 75 x 112
P34/76

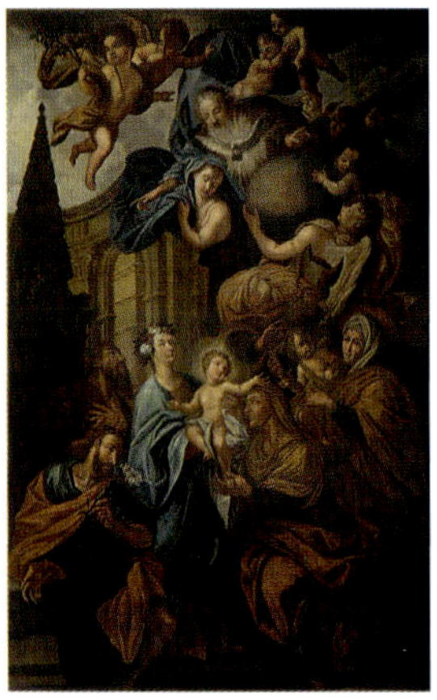

Murillo, Bartolomé Esteban (attributed to) 1618–1682
The Presentation in the Temple
oil on canvas 131 x 86.5
P45/76

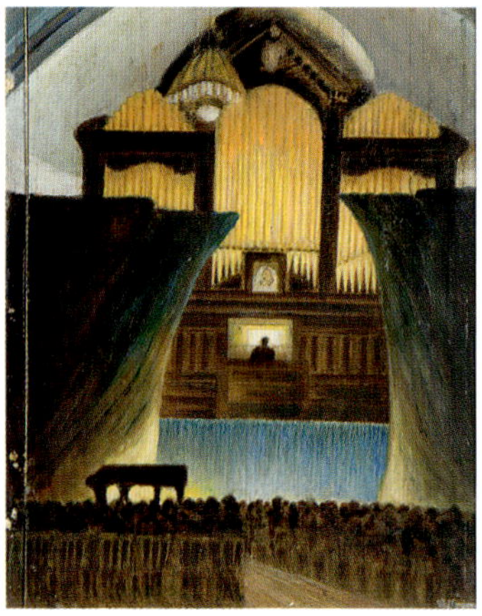

Murray, V. R.
T. W. North Giving an Organ Recital, Walsall Town Hall 1954
oil on canvas 38 x 31
P93/76

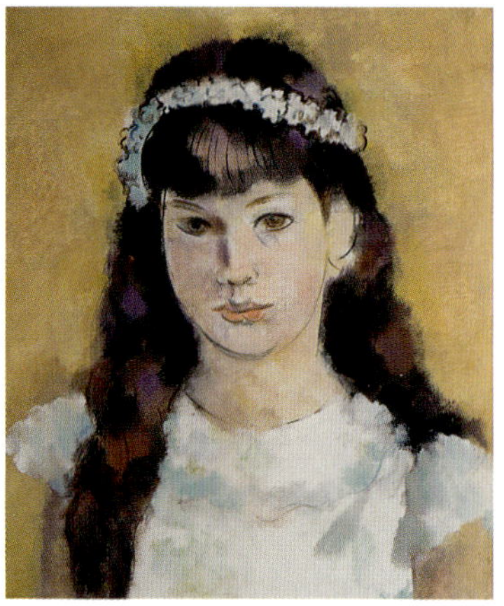

Müsham, Fritz 1881–1949
Esther 1934
oil on canvas 44 x 36
GR.174

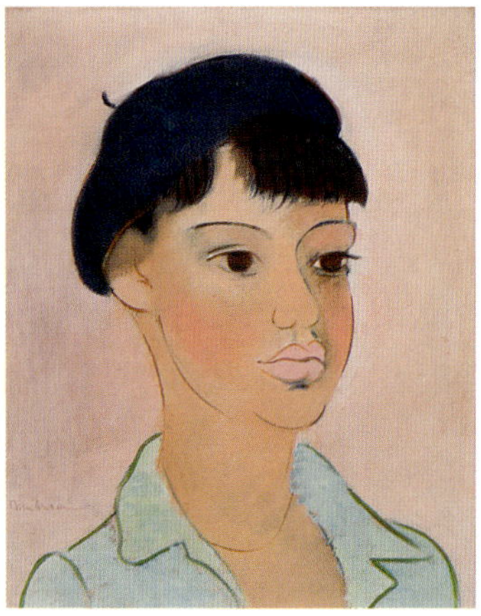

Müsham, Fritz 1881–1949
Theo 1934
oil on canvas 39.5 x 31
GR.175

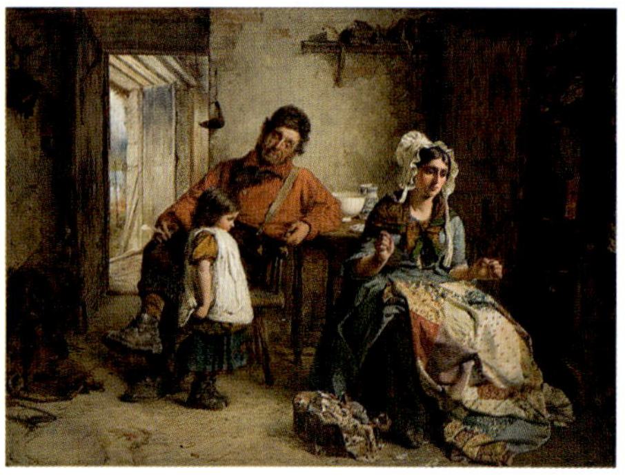

Nicol, Erskine 1825–1904
Kiss an' Make-It-Up 1867
oil on canvas 95 x 122
P37/76

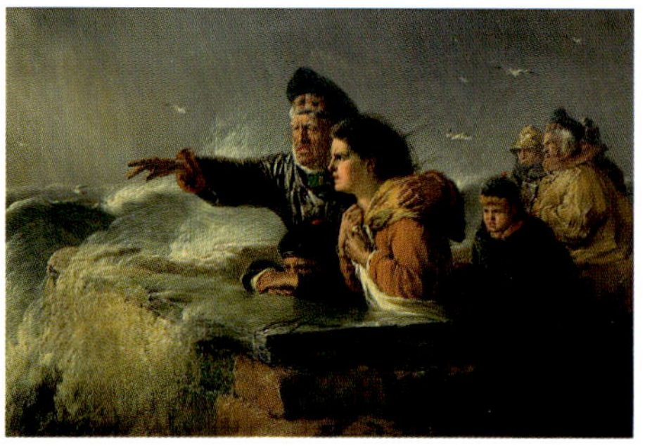

Nicol, Erskine 1825–1904
The Missing Boat 1877
oil on canvas 51 x 75
P322/76

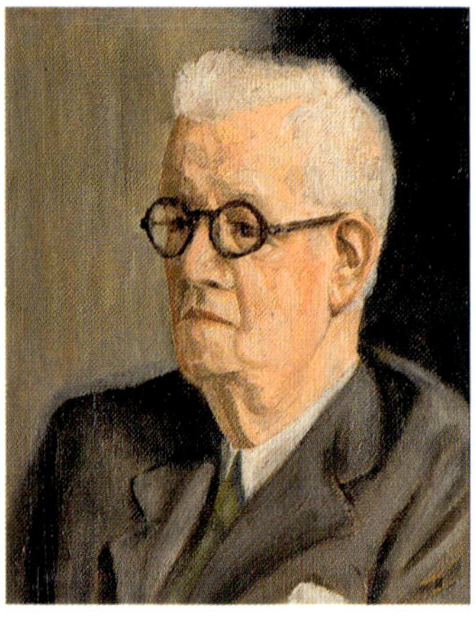

Orgill, Mollie
Portrait of the Artist's Father
oil on canvas 100 x 79
P7/95

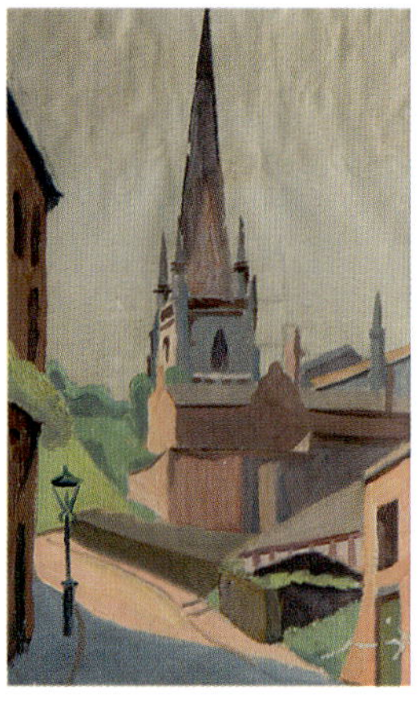

Orgill, Mollie
St Matthew's Church, Walsall
oil on board 31 x 18.5
P31/93

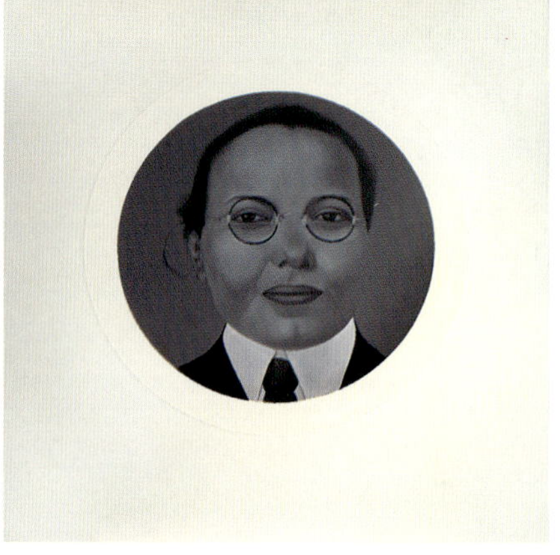

Palmer, Eugene b.1955
Sister Smith III
oil on canvas over board 84 x 82
P11/98

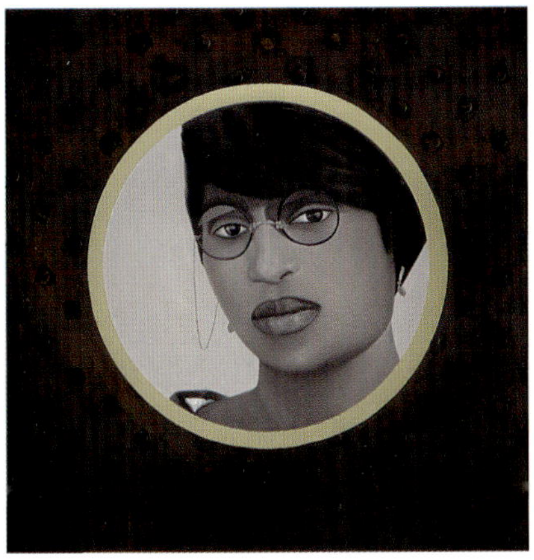

Palmer, Eugene b.1955
Wanting to Say I
oil on canvas over board 84 x 82
P10/98

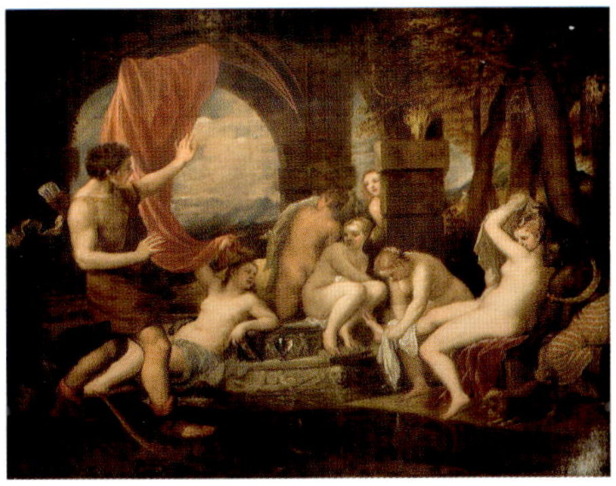

Phillip, John 1817–1867
Diana and Actaeon (after Titian)
oil on canvas 191 x 209
P223/76

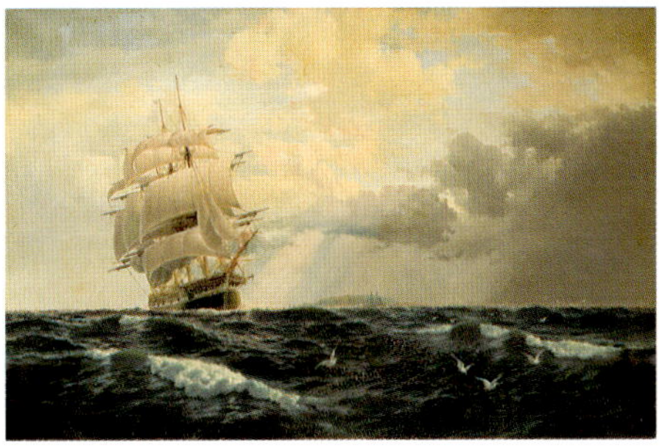

Preston, William F. active 1885–1889
Ship of the Line Going up the Solent
oil on canvas 90 x 125
P319/76

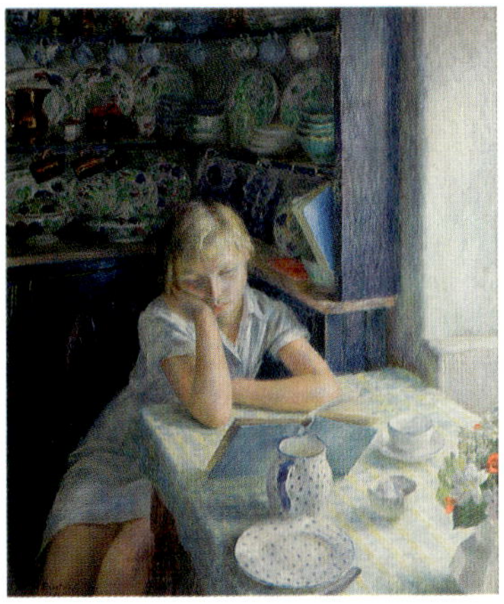

Procter, Dod 1892–1972
The Quiet Hour 1935
oil on canvas 76 x 63.5
P339/76

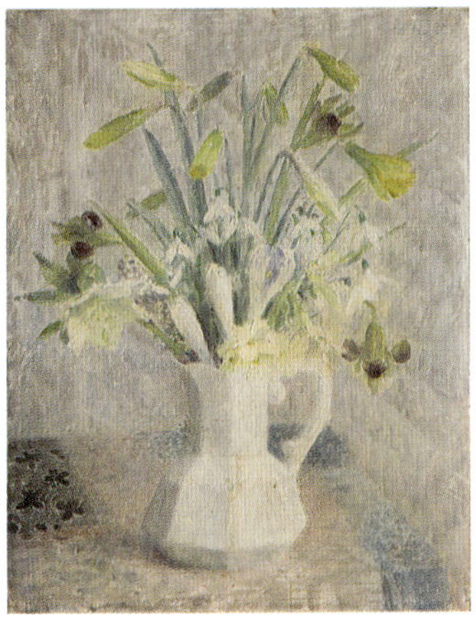

Procter, Dod 1892–1972
Spring Flowers
oil on canvas 47 x 35.5
P173/76

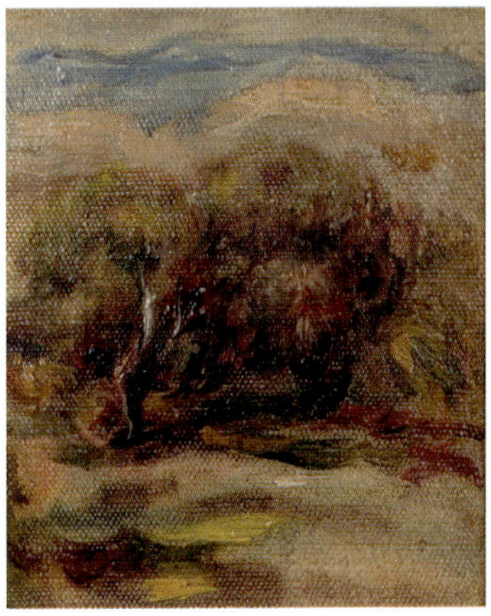

Renoir, Pierre-Auguste 1841–1919
Les oliviers à Cagnes-sur-Mer
oil on canvas 11 x 9.5
GR.199

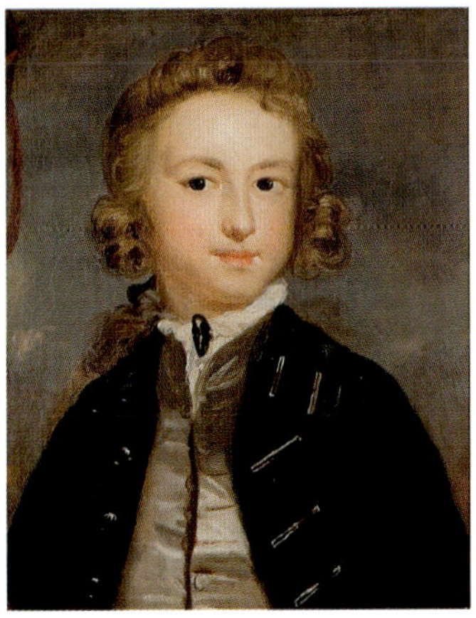

Reynolds, Joshua 1723–1792
Lieutenant Robert Haswell, RN (son of John Haswell of Tiverton, Devon) 1746–1747
oil on canvas 46 x 36
GR.200

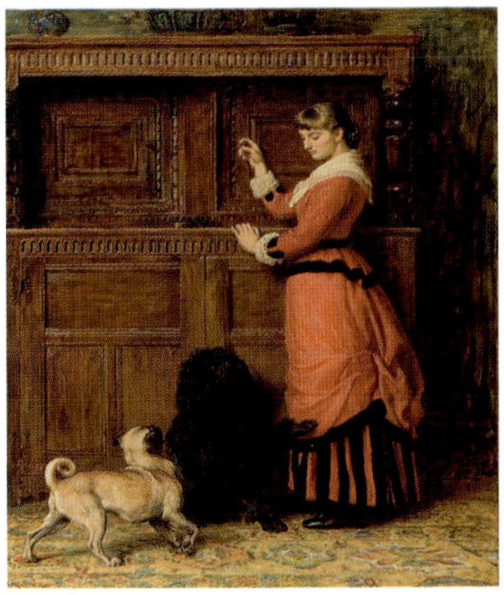

Riviere, Briton 1840–1920
Cupboard Love 1881
oil on canvas 143 x 112
P329/76

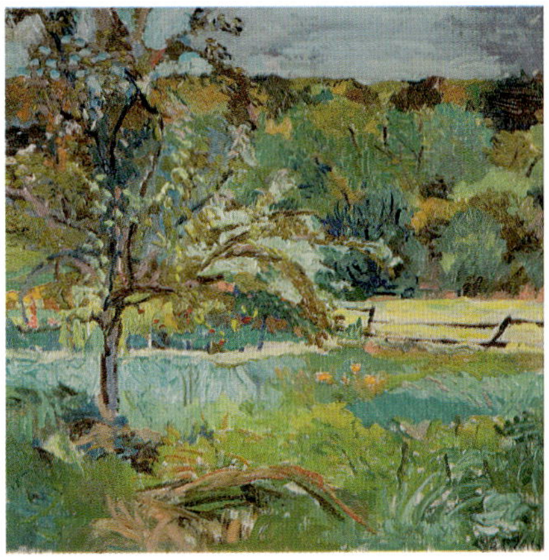

Ryan, Sally 1916–1968
The Cutting Garden, Connecticut 1960
oil on canvas 54.5 x 54.5
GR.219

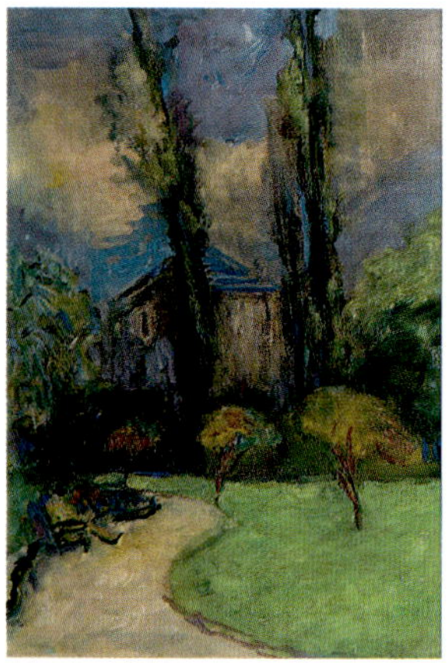

Ryan, Sally 1916–1968
Poplars at Dulwich 1965
oil on canvas 34 x 23.5
GR.218

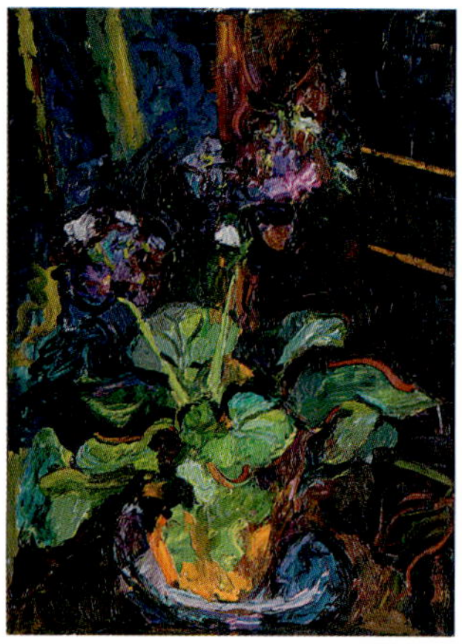

Ryan, Sally 1916–1968
Potted Plant 1966–1968
oil on canvas 60 x 44
GR.220

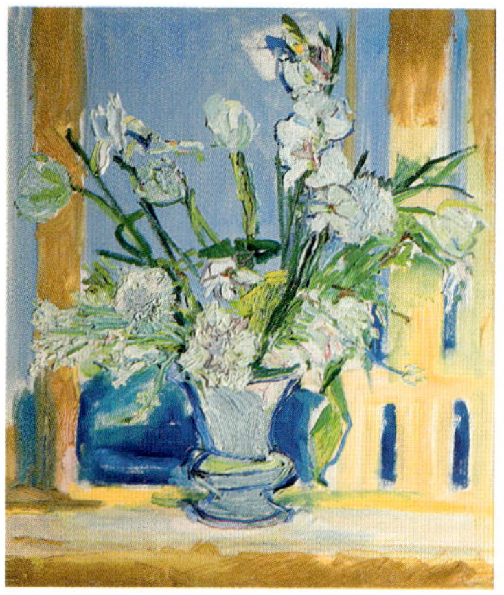

Ryan, Sally 1916–1968
Easter Flowers
oil on canvas 74 x 62
GRE.LOAN 27/02 (P)

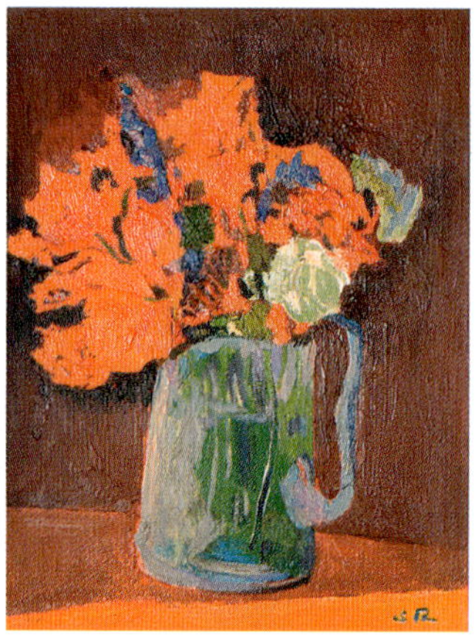

Ryan, Sally 1916–1968
Flower Painting (Nasturtiums)
oil on canvas 24 x 19
GR.216

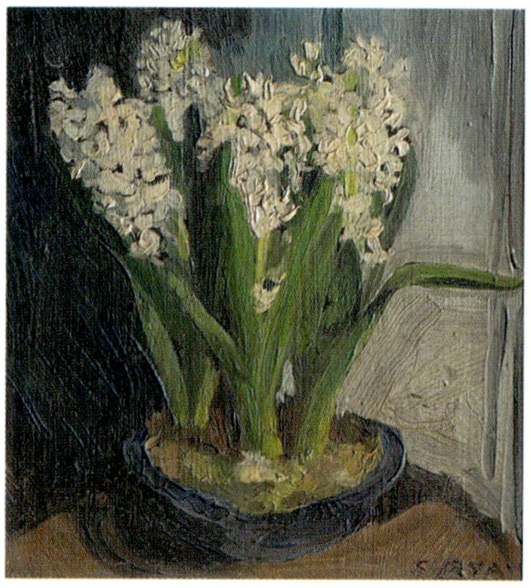

Ryan, Sally 1916–1968
Hyacinths
oil on canvas 12 x 11
GRE.LOAN 28/02 (P)

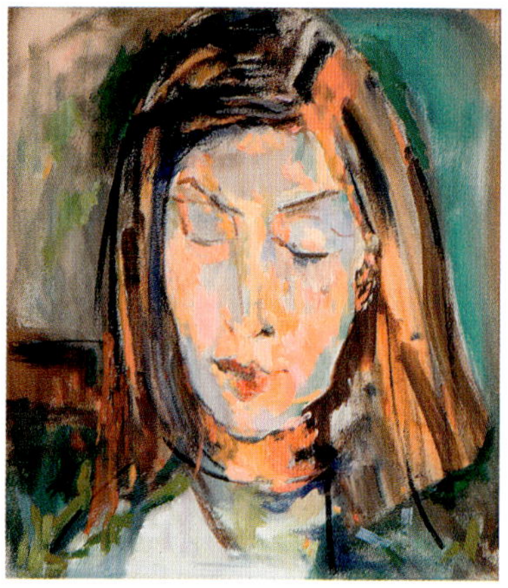

Ryan, Sally 1916–1968
Kathleen
oil on canvas 39.5 x 34
GR.217

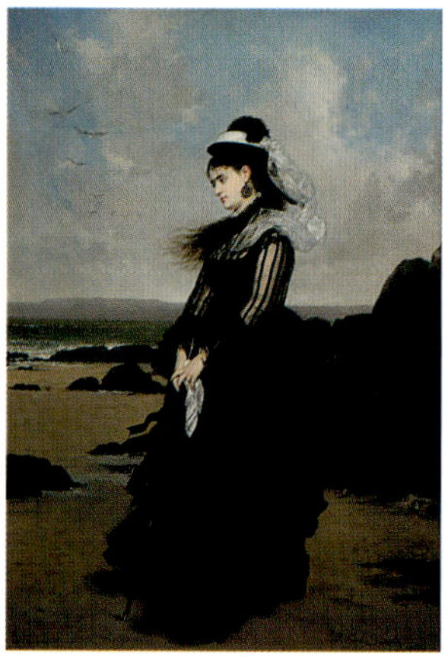

Saintin, Jules Émile 1829–1894
Woman in Black 1873
oil on canvas 86 x 61
P18/76

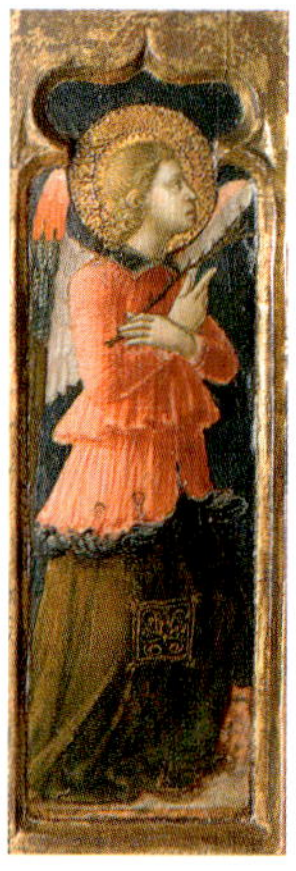

Salimbeni, Lorenzo (attributed to)
1374–c.1420
An Angel of the Annunciation
oil & gold on panel 42.5 x 17.5
GR.231

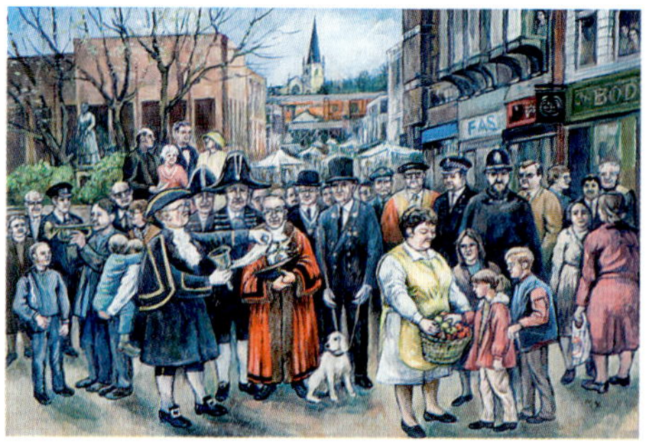

Sawbridge, Tony
Walking the Fair, Re-Enactment 1996
acrylic on board 56 x 90
P151/96

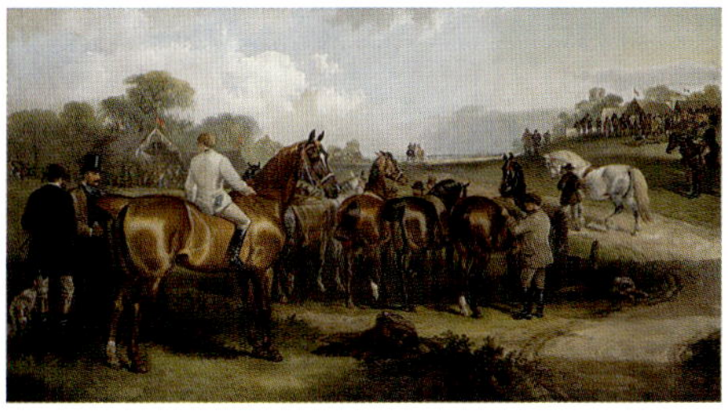

Shayer, Charles Waller 1826–1914
The Horse Fair 1870
oil on canvas 67.5 x 113
P27/76

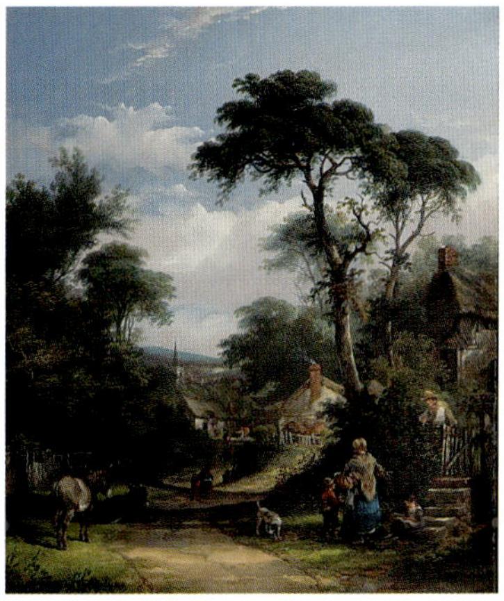

Shayer, Charles Waller 1826–1914
Landscape with Figures and Donkeys
oil on canvas 50 x 42.5
P20/76

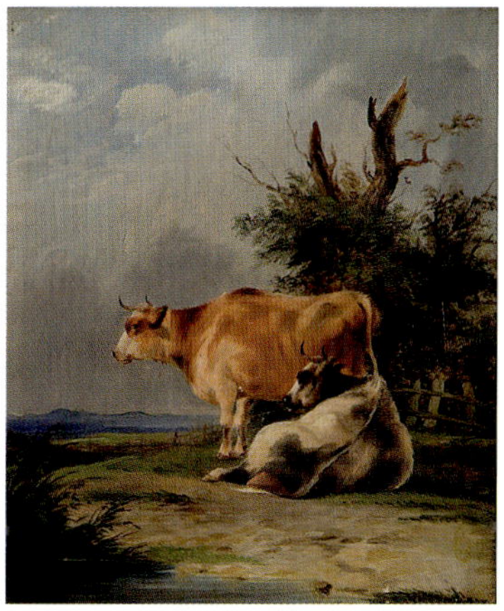

Shayer, Charles Waller (after) 1826–1914
Brown Cows Standing
oil on canvas 32 x 25
P21/76

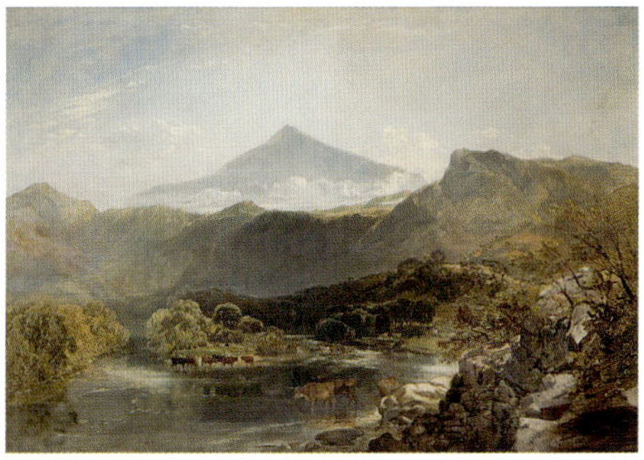

Shayer, William 1788–1879 & **Marshall, Charles** 1806–1890
Ben Nevis and Mountain Stream 1855
oil on canvas 99 x 138
P227/76

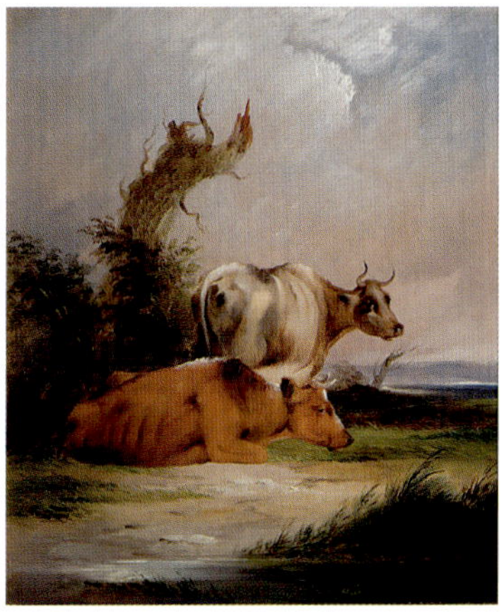

Shayer, William (after) 1788–1879
Cows, White Cow Standing
oil on canvas 29.5 x 24.5
P47/76

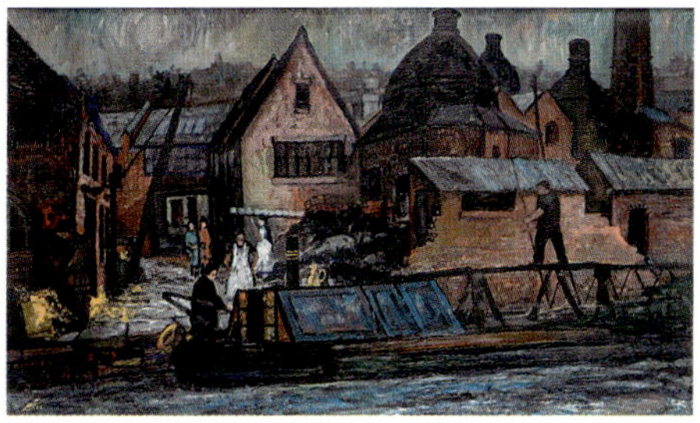

Smith, H. H.
Canal, Middleport
oil on canvas 60 x 90
P160/76

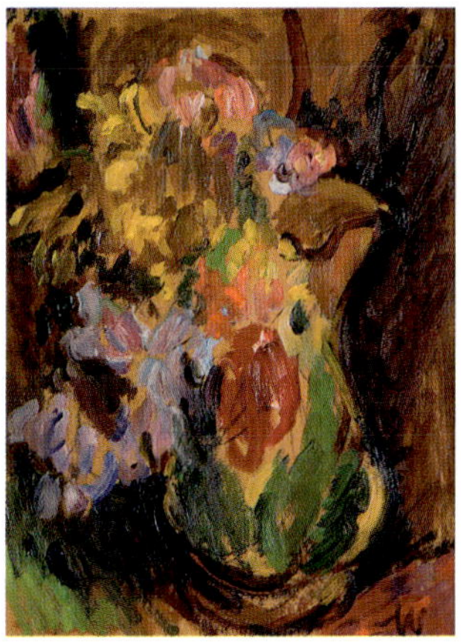

Smith, Matthew Arnold Bracy 1879–1959
Flower Piece 1952–1953
oil on board 49 x 39
GR.238

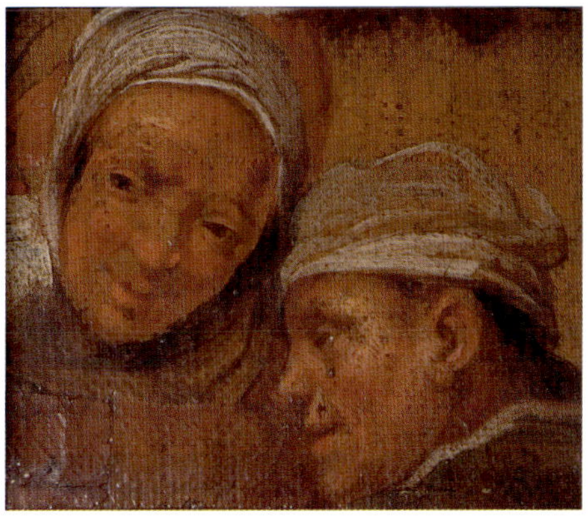

Sorgh, Hendrik Martensz. (follower of) c.1611–1670
Studies of Heads of Peasants
oil on canvas mounted on panel 7 x 8.5 (E)
GR.240a

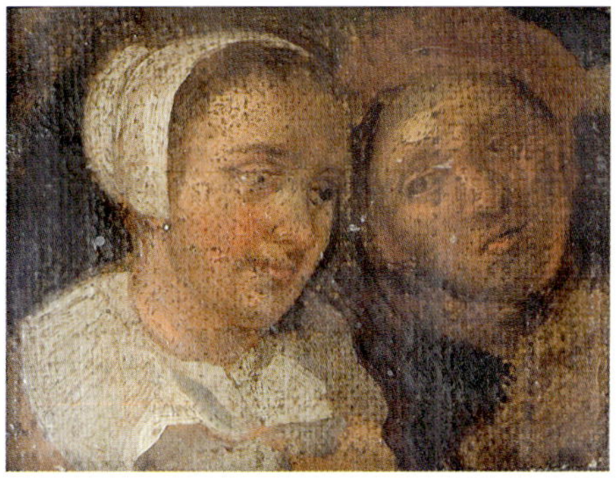

Sorgh, Hendrik Martensz. (follower of) c.1611–1670
Studies of Heads of Peasants
oil on canvas mounted on panel 7 x 8.5 (E)
GR.240b

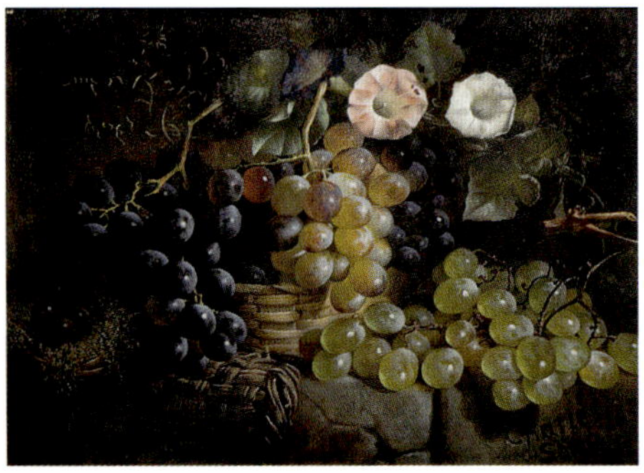

Stuart, Charles active 1854–1904
Study of Fruit
oil on canvas 34 x 44
P222/76

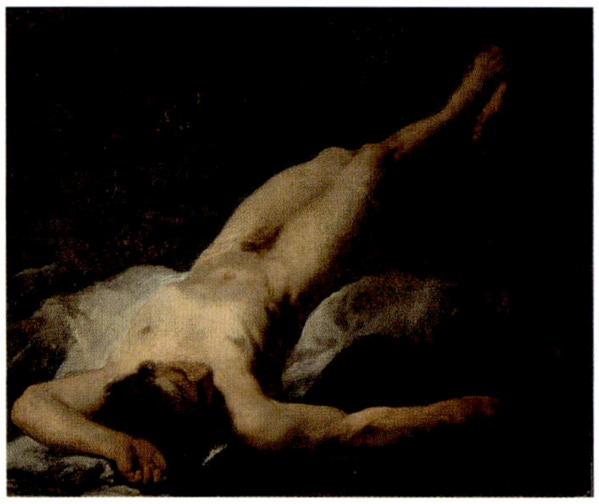

Subleyras, Pierre Hubert (follower of) 1699–1749
Hector Dragged through Troy
oil on canvas 60 x 72
GR.32

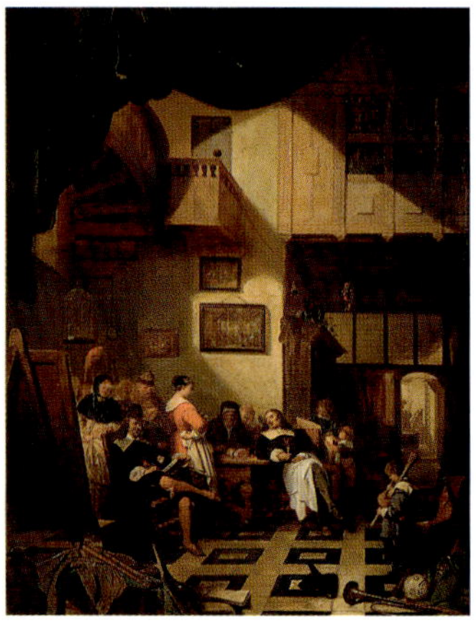

Tenkate, Herman 1822–1891
Van Dyck in the Studio of Van der Helst
oil on canvas 139 x 108
P42/76

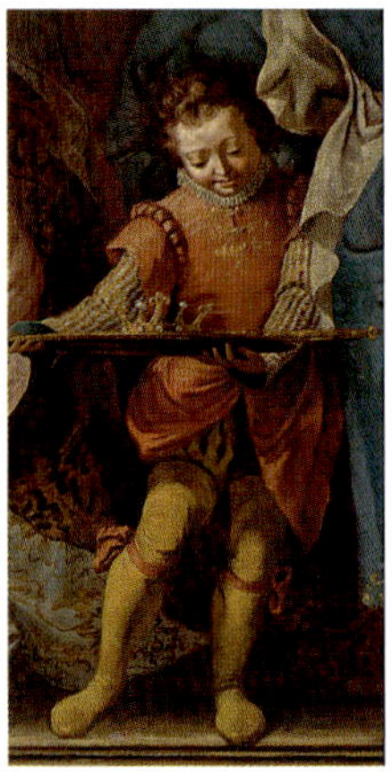

Tiepolo, Giovanni Battista (attributed to) 1696–1770
Page Boy c.1740–1750
oil on canvas 134 x 70
GR.247

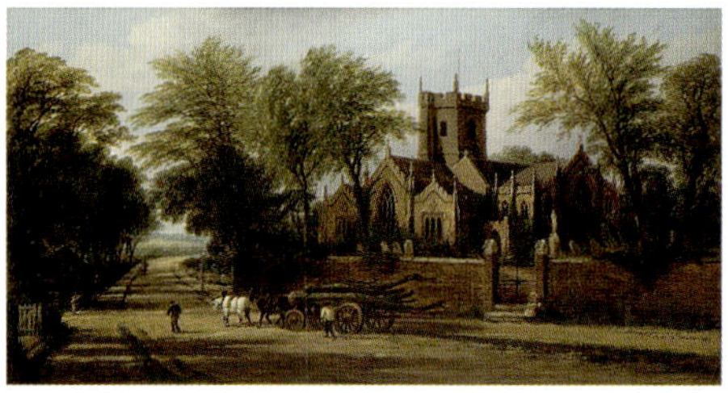

Thomas, Thomas active 1854–1896
Handsworth Church
oil on canvas 54.5 x 95.5
P2/76

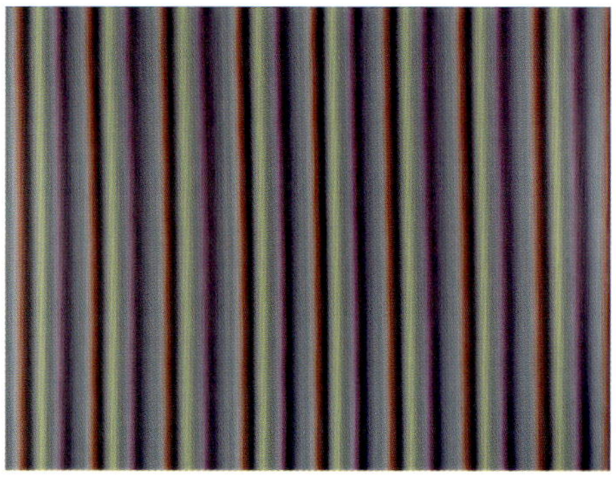

Thompson, Estelle b.1960
Fuse Painting, 7 'til 8 1998
oil on canvas 105 x 134
P3/00

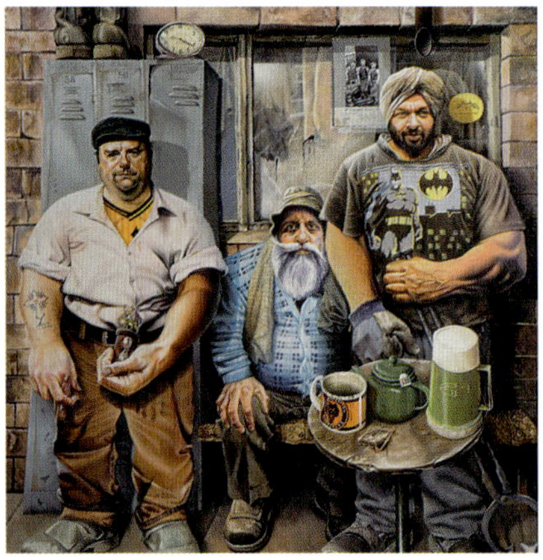

Tift, Andrew b.1968
The Black-Country Steelworkers 1992
acrylic on canvas 99 x 98
PCF3 (P)

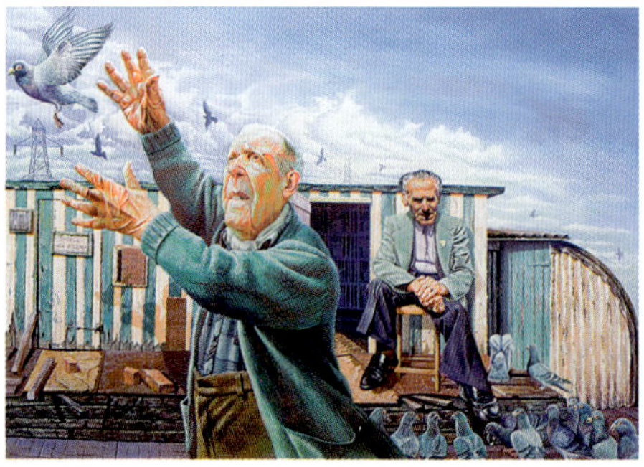

Tift, Andrew b.1968
Les and Ernie 1993
oil on board 75 x 102
P42/93

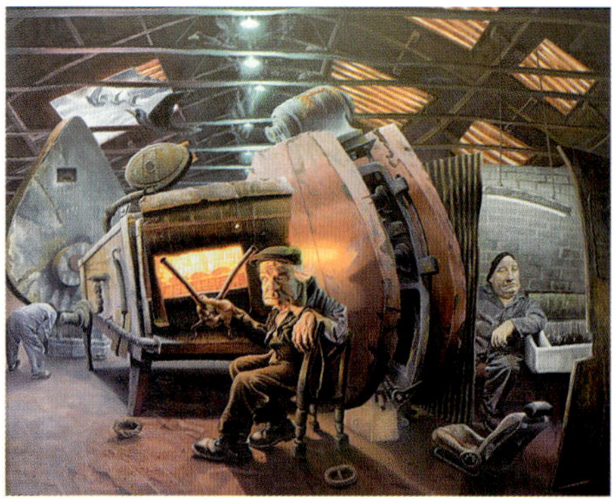

Tift, Andrew b.1968
'There are no longer any birds in last years' nests. Times change and we with them' 1993
acrylic on board 100 x 120
P19/94

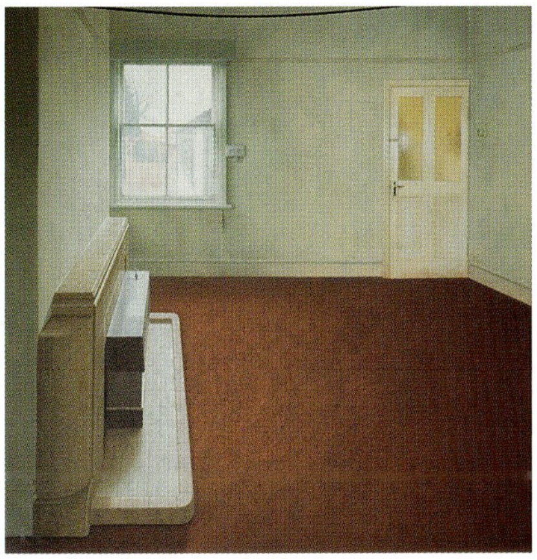

Tift, Andrew b.1968
Memorial Painting (left wing of diptych) 1997–1998
oil on board 99 x 94
P4/99

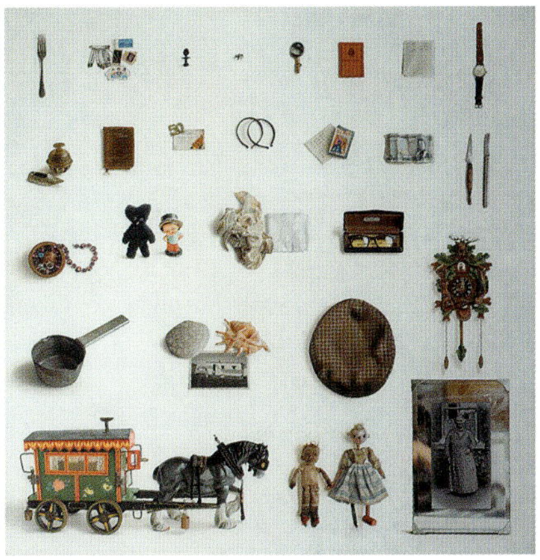

Tift, Andrew b.1968
Memorial Painting (right wing of diptych) 1997–1998
oil on board 99 x 94
P4/99

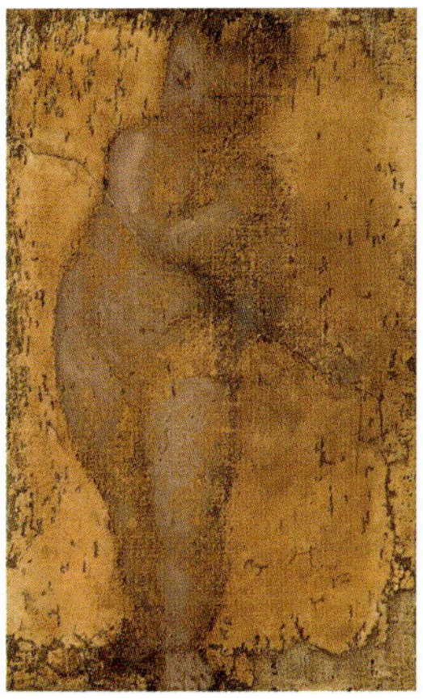

Titian (attributed to) c.1488–1576
Angel (Putto)
oil on paper mounted on canvas 41 x 24.5
GR.243

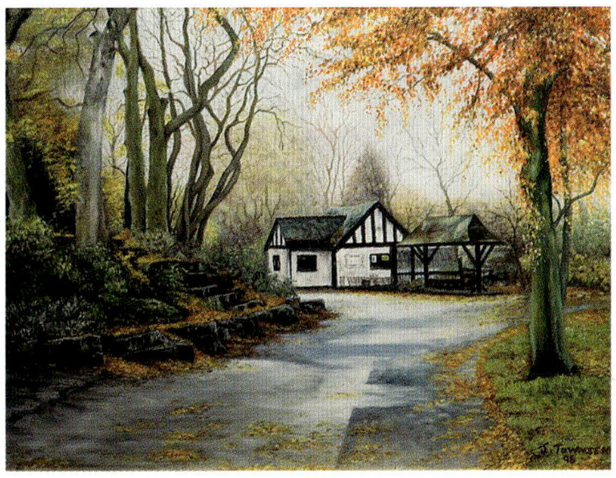

Townsend, June
The Arboretum, Walsall 1996
oil on canvas 38.5 x 50
P7/97

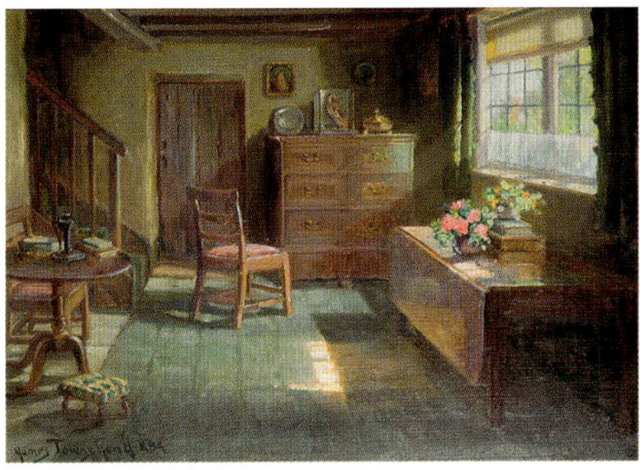

Townshend, James d.1949
Interior
oil on canvas 33 x 43
P234/76

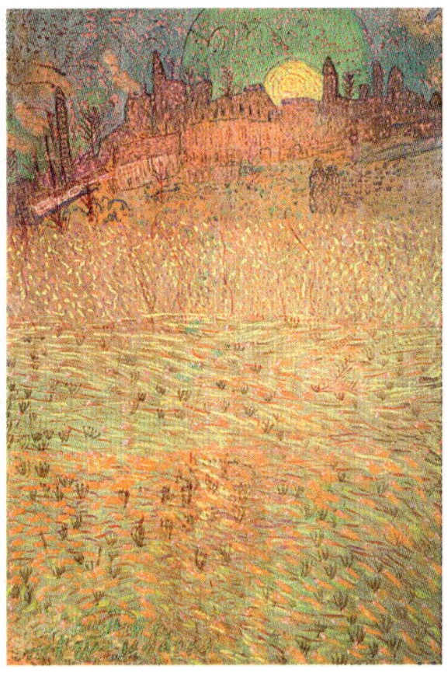

Uddin, Shafique b.1962
Two Friends Enjoying the Brilliant Sunshine and Magnificent Buildings 1989
oil on paper 150 x 100
P25/93

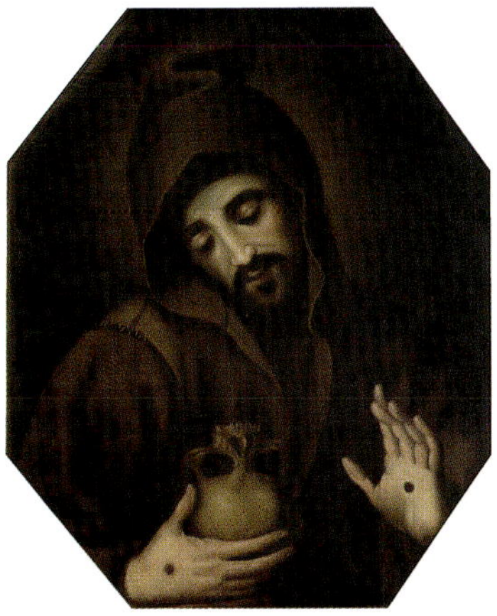

unknown artist 17th C
Man with Stigmata Holding a Skull
oil on canvas 66.5 x 53
P4/76

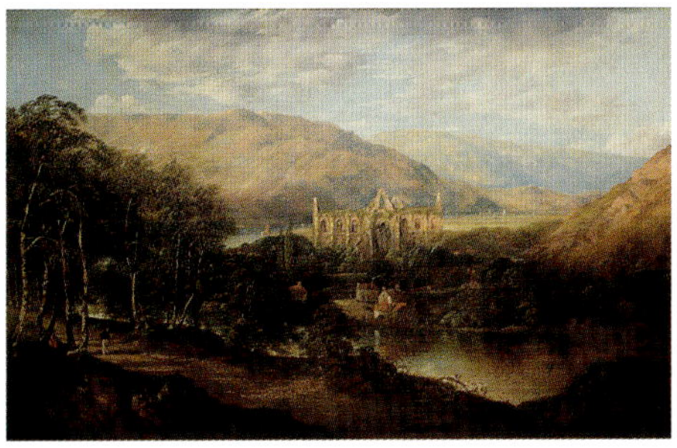

unknown artist
Tintern Abbey 1885–1895
oil on canvas 73 x 108
P8/85

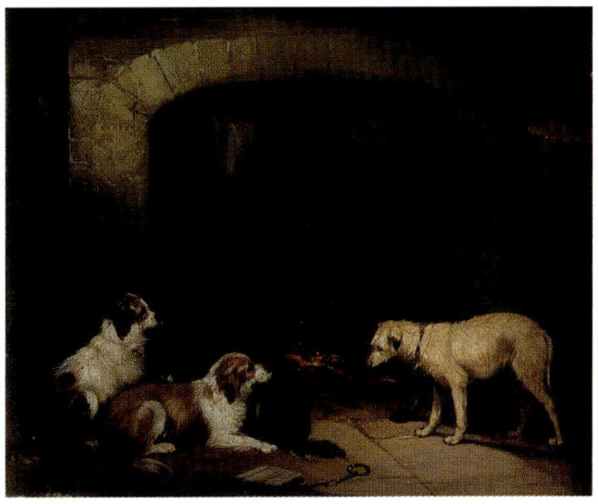

unknown artist 19th C
Four Dogs
oil on canvas 30.5 x 45.5
P171/76

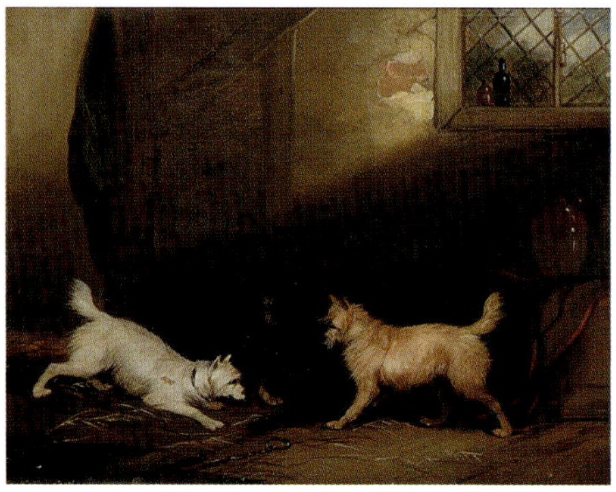

unknown artist 19th C
Two Dogs
oil on canvas 30.5 x 45.5
P172/76

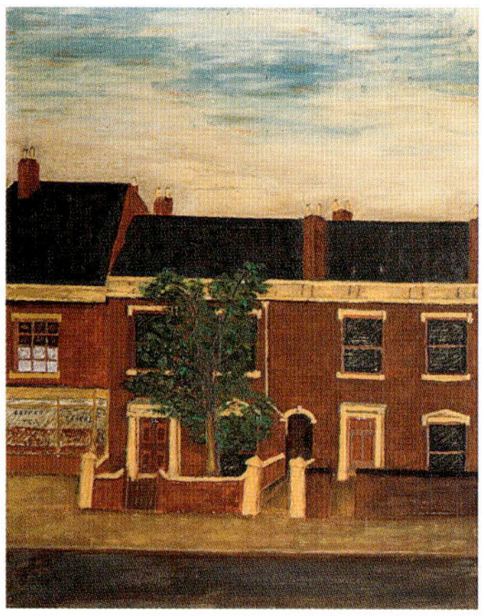

unknown artist
The Home of Miss E. M. Flint, now Demolished 1968
oil on board 37 x 28.5
PCF4

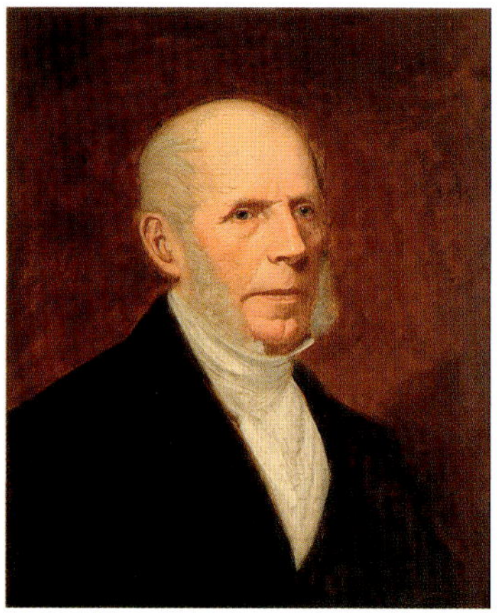

unknown artist
Alderman William Ward, JP
oil on canvas 59 x 49
P65/76

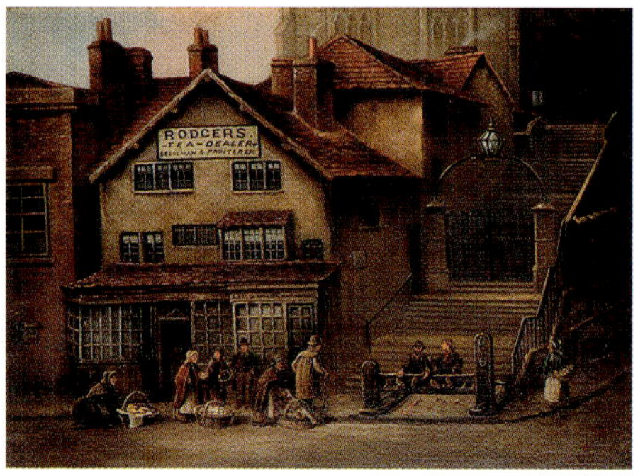

unknown artist
Bottom of St Matthew's Church Steps, Walsall
oil on canvas 31 x 40.5
P87/76

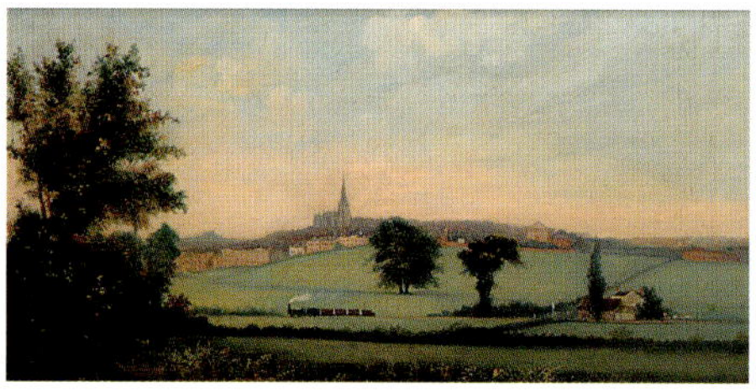

unknown artist
Bradford Street and Railway
oil on canvas 47 x 89
P266/76

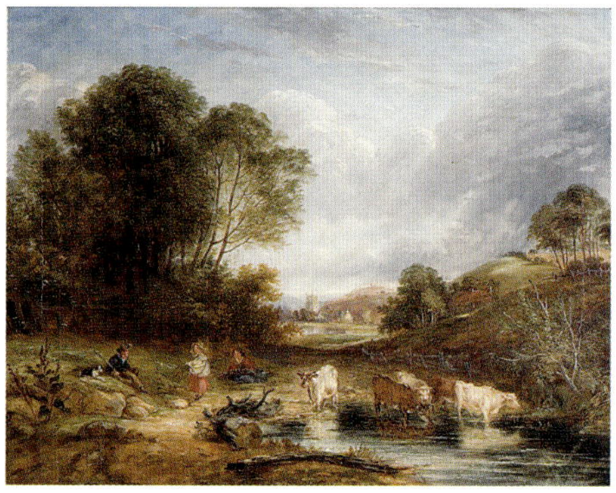

unknown artist
*Cattle at a Lake**
oil on canvas 61 x 74
PCF5

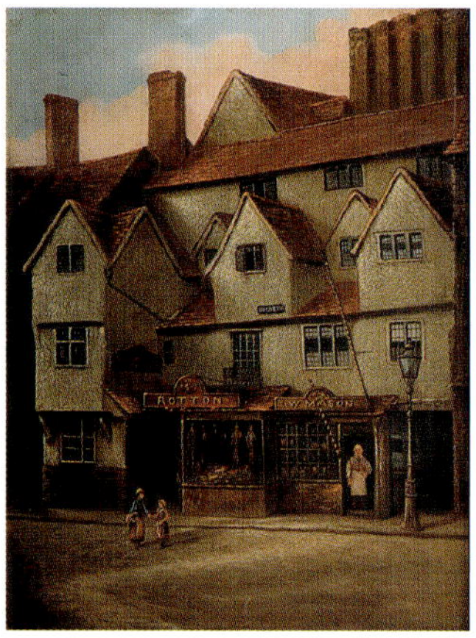

unknown artist
Digbeth
oil on canvas 39 x 29
P86/76

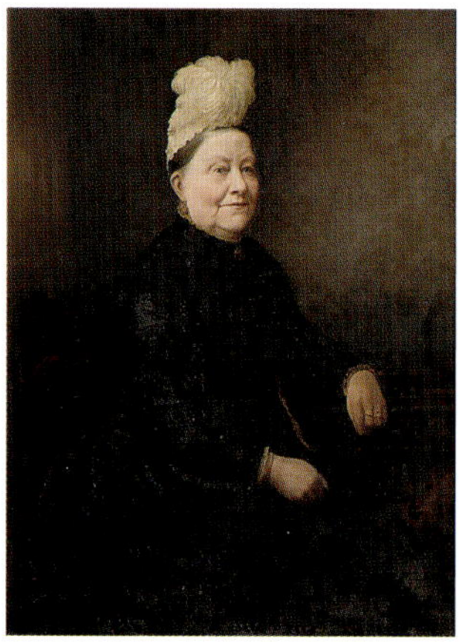

unknown artist
Eliza Wheway
oil on canvas 90 x 69
P149/76

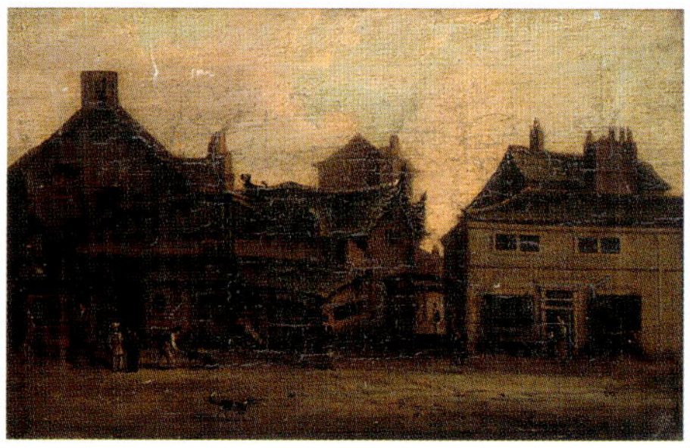

unknown artist
Houses, Men and Dog
oil on canvas 30.5 x 46
P293/76

Facing page: Burnett, June, b.1936, *Zoot 58* (detail), The Potteries Museum & Art Gallery (p. 106)

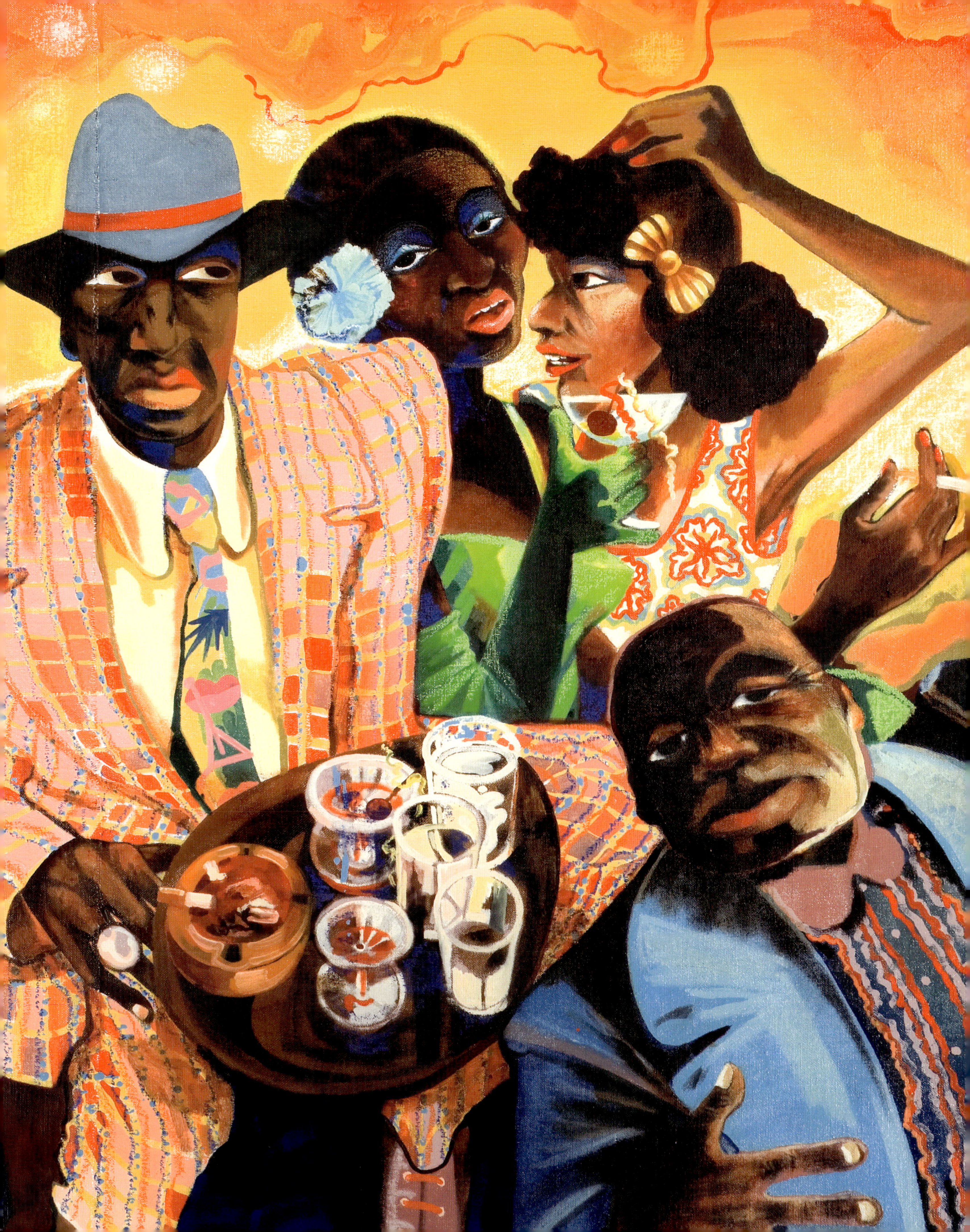

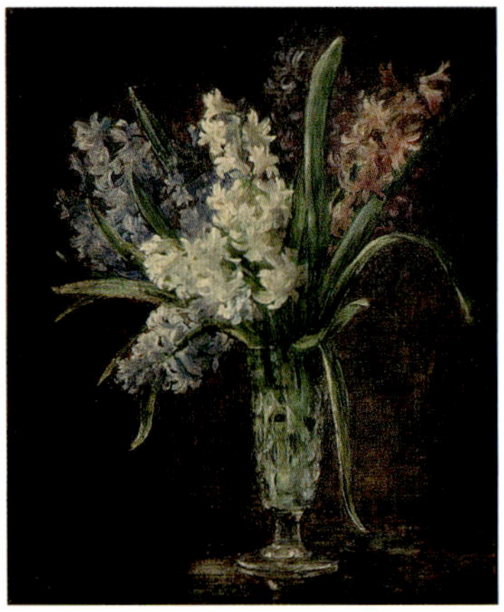

unknown artist
Hyacinths
oil on canvas 51.5 x 42
P235/76

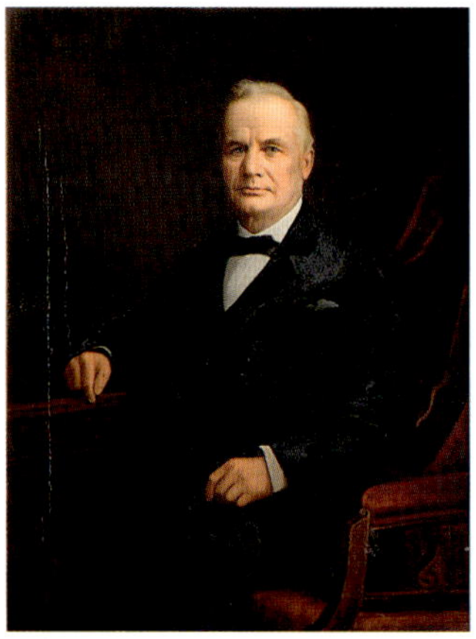

unknown artist
Job Wheway
oil on canvas 90 x 69
P148/76

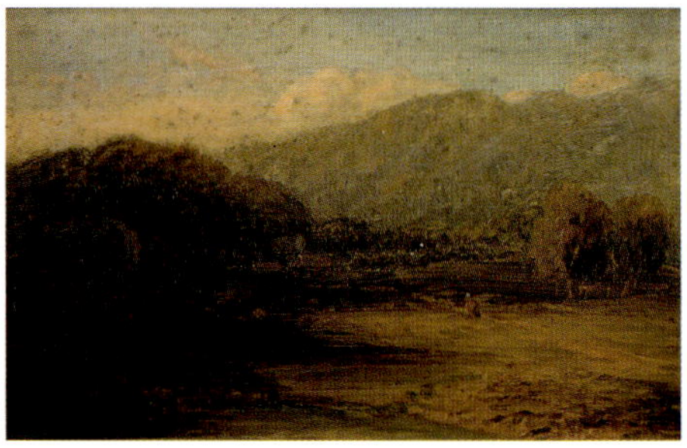

unknown artist
Landscape
oil on board 14 x 21
P100/76

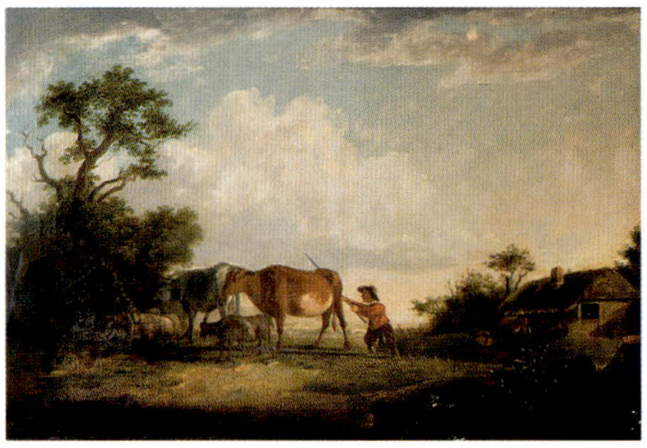

unknown artist
Landscape with Cattle and Cowherd
oil on canvas 49 x 71
P67/76

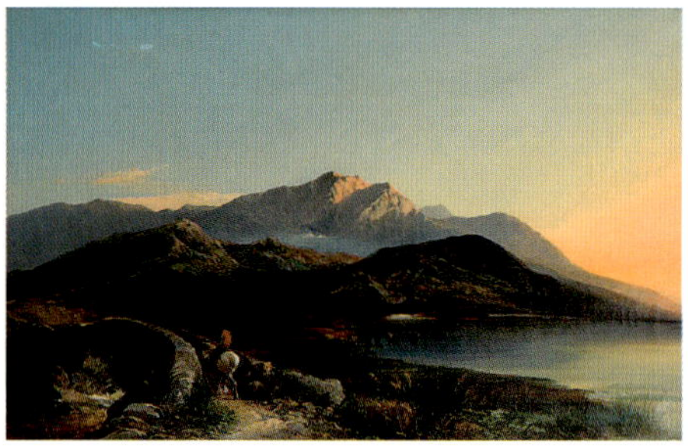

unknown artist
Mountain Scene
oil on canvas 49 x 74
P7/85

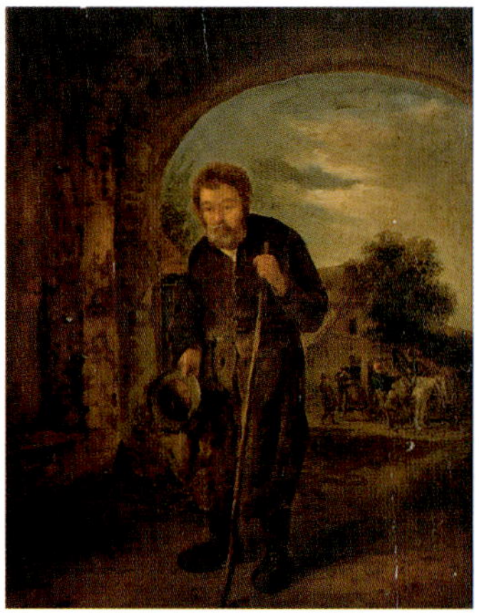

unknown artist
Old Man with a Stick (The Mendicant)
oil on canvas 31 x 23
P54/76

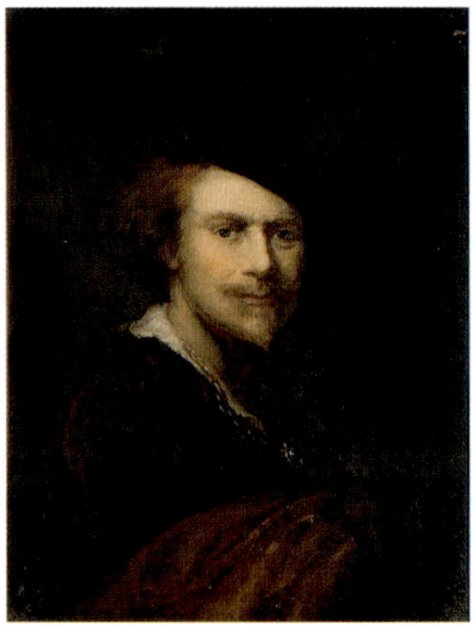

unknown artist
Portrait of a Man in Glengarry
oil on canvas 51 x 40.5
P138/76

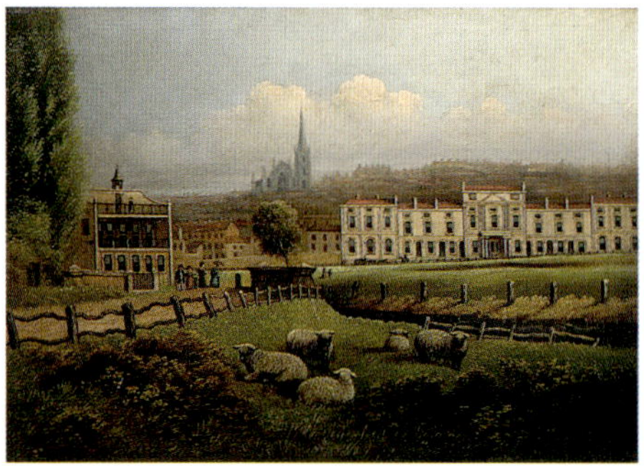

unknown artist
Racecourse, Bradford Street, Walsall
oil on canvas 30 x 40
P84/76

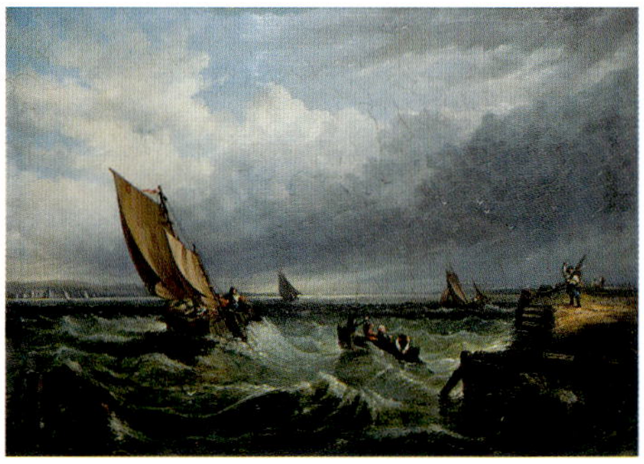

unknown artist
Seascape with Fishing Boats in a Stormy Sea
oil on canvas 48.5 x 67
P21/04

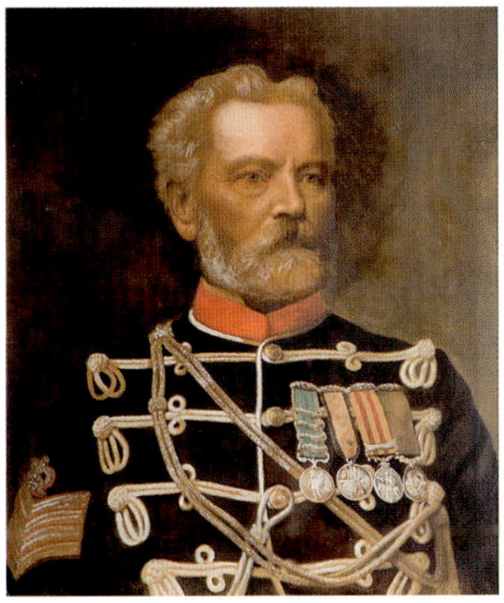

unknown artist
Sergeant Major William Purvis, Survivor of the Charge of the Light Brigade
oil on canvas 59 x 49
P337/76

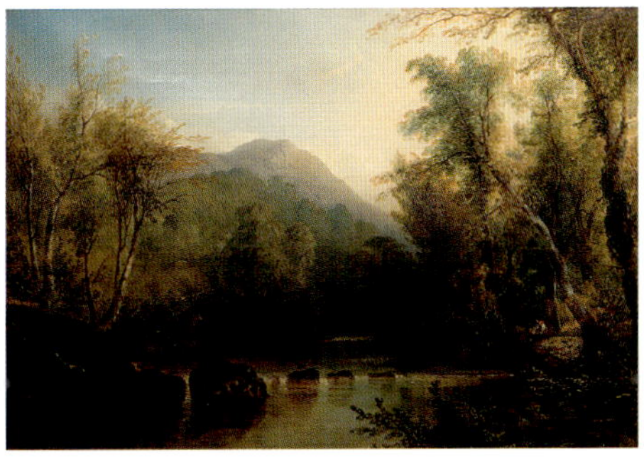

unknown artist
Stepping Stones
oil on canvas 37 x 51.5
PCF6

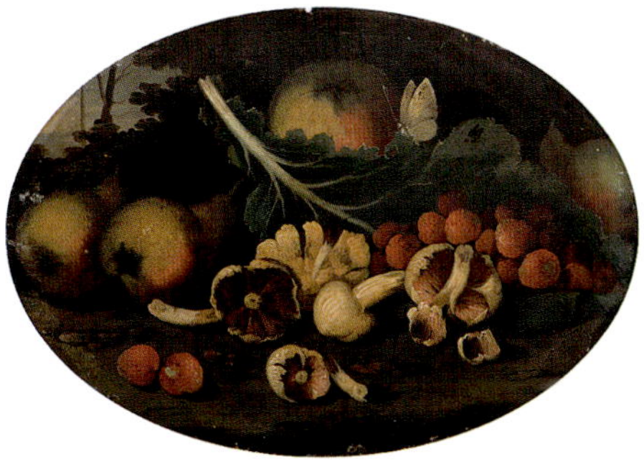

unknown artist
Still Life (Fruit and Vegetables)
oil on tin 26 x 35
P52/76

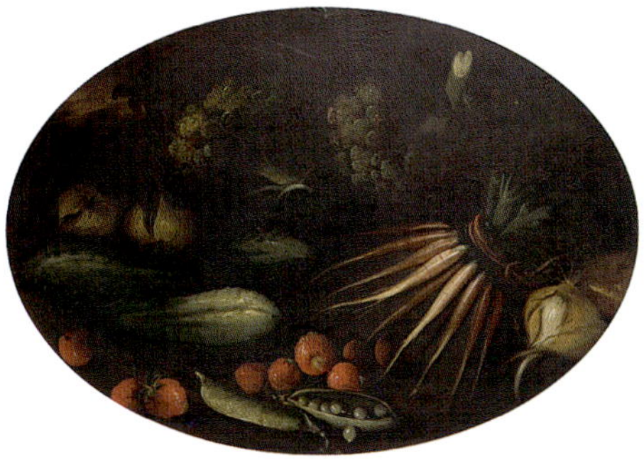

unknown artist
Still Life (Vegetables)
oil on tin 24 x 32
P51/76

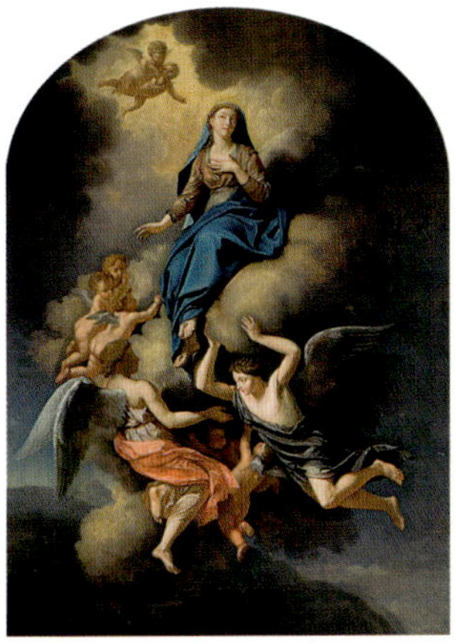

unknown artist
The Ascension of the Virgin into Heaven
oil on canvas 80 x 57
P8/76

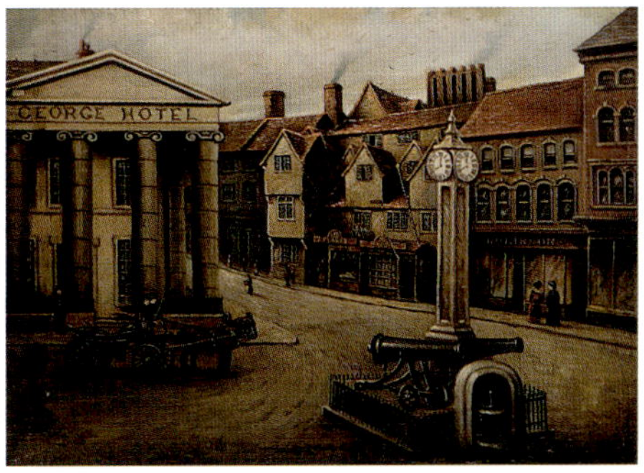

unknown artist
The George Hotel
oil on canvas 29 x 39
P89/76

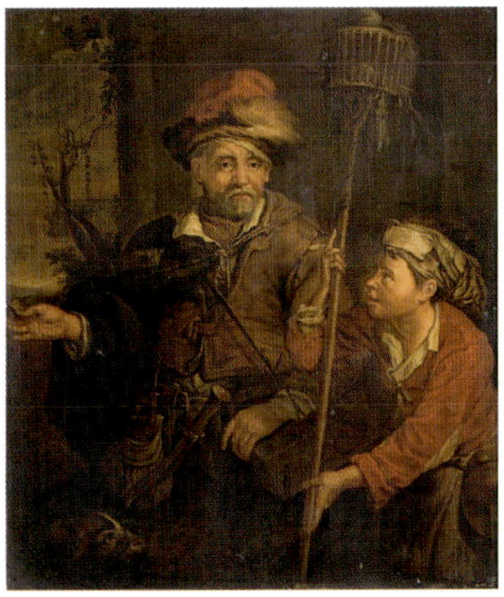

unknown artist
The Rat Catcher of Paris
oil on canvas 118.5 x 100
P55/76

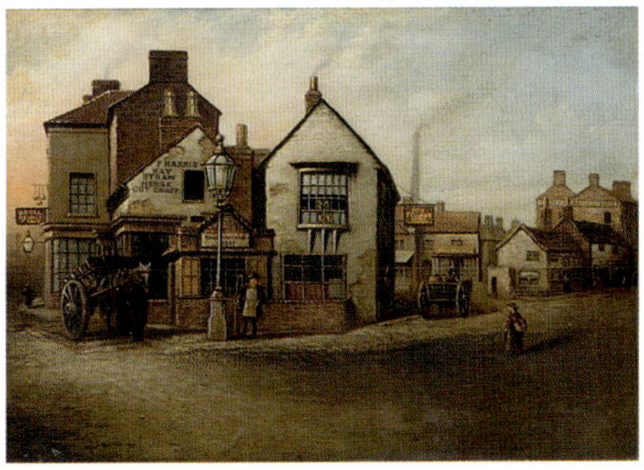

unknown artist
Town End Bank
oil on canvas 30.5 x 40.5
P85/76

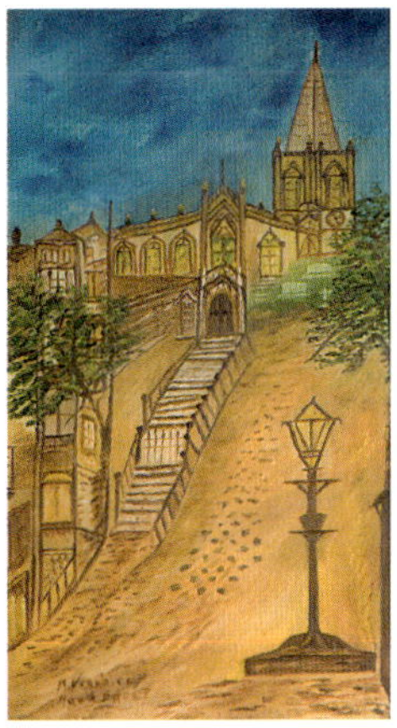

Venables, M.
St Matthew's Church Steps, Walsall
oil on canvas 48 x 25.5
P228/76

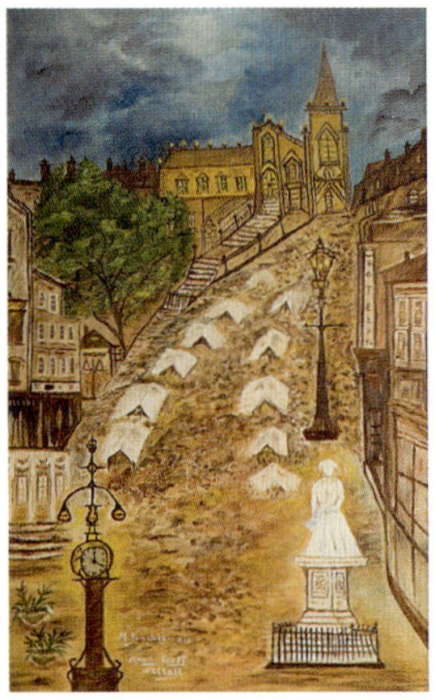

Venables, M.
The Market in the High Street, Walsall
oil on canvas 53 x 33
P229/76

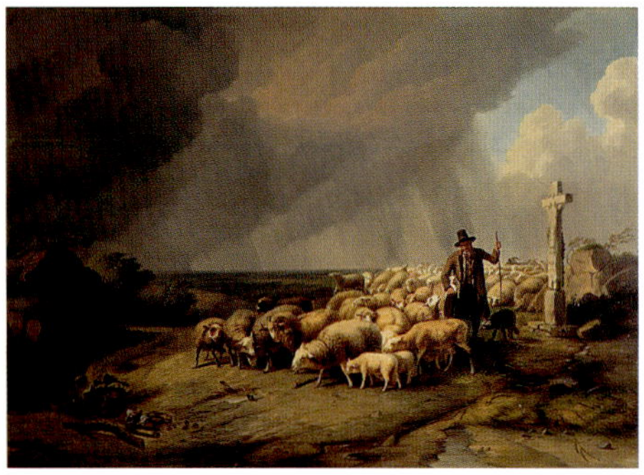

Verboeckhoven, Eugène 1799–1881
Gathering the Flock 1839
oil on canvas 40 x 55
P323/76

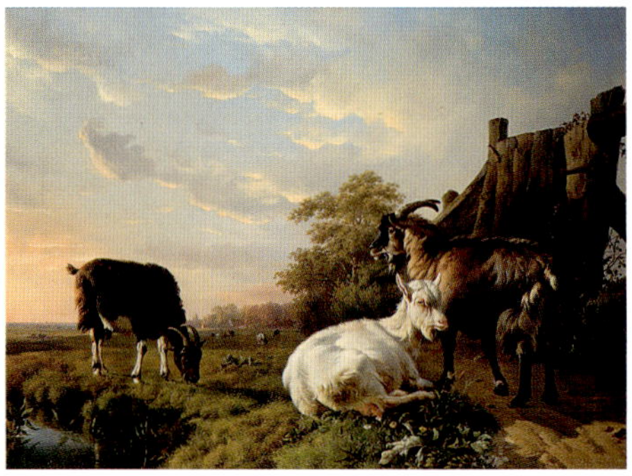

Verboeckhoven, Eugène 1799–1881
Goats 1840
oil on canvas 97 x 128.5
P32/76

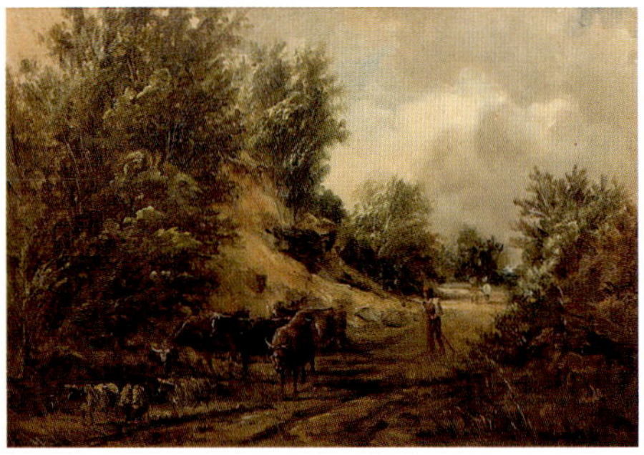

Vickers, Alfred 1786–1868
A Man Driving Cattle and Sheep 1866
oil on canvas 23 x 33
P344/76

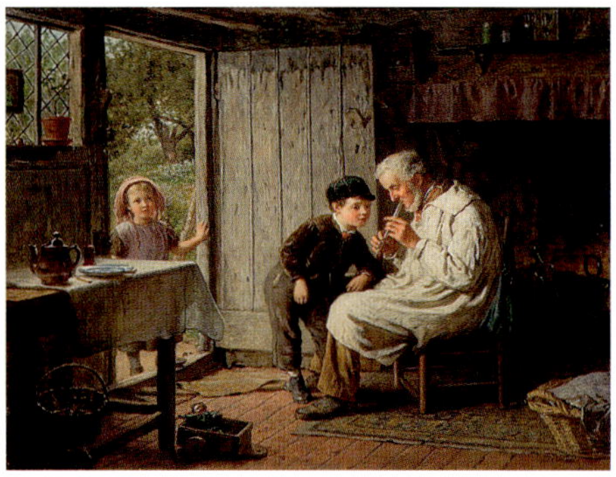

Waite, James Clarke 1832–1920
Penny Whistle 1863–1885
oil on canvas 51 x 61
P68/76

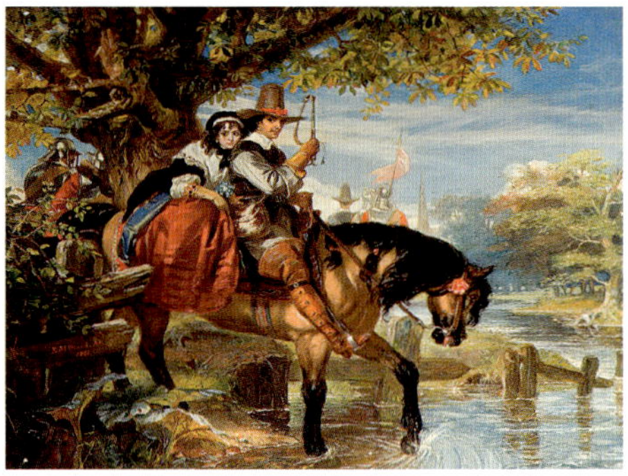

Ward, Edward Matthew 1816–1879
Charles II Assisted in His Escape by Jane Lane 1861
oil on canvas 31.5 x 46.5
P1/89

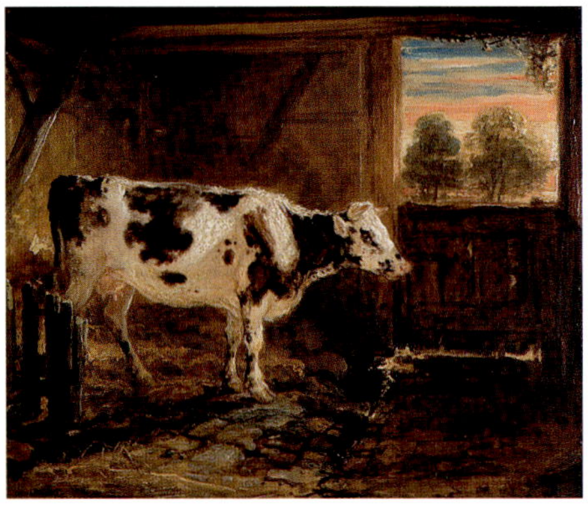

Ward, James 1769–1859
Cow in Barn
oil on panel 27 x 35
GR.250

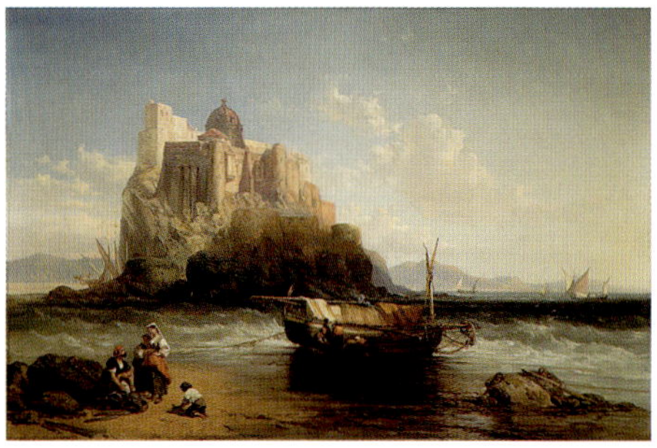

Webb, James c.1825–1895
The Castle of Ischia 1866
oil on canvas 104 x 150
P325/76

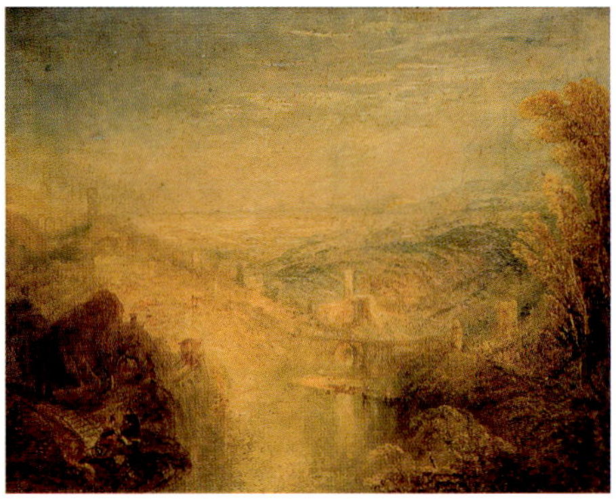

Webb, James (attributed to) c.1825–1895
Landscape
oil on canvas 60 x 74
P10/76

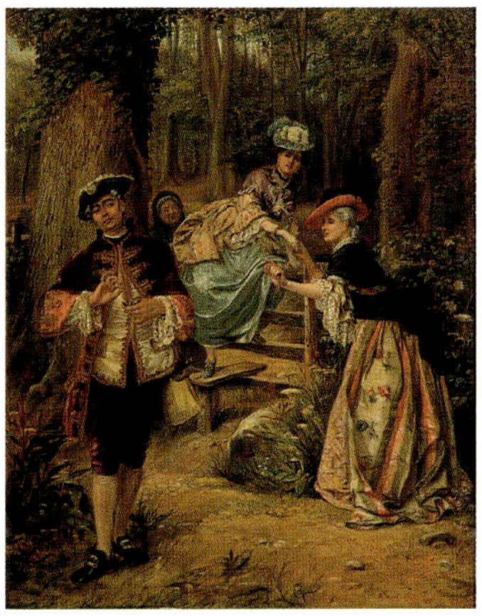

Weigall, Arthur Howes c.1836–1894
Before Marriage 1876
oil on canvas 89 x 68.5
P13/76

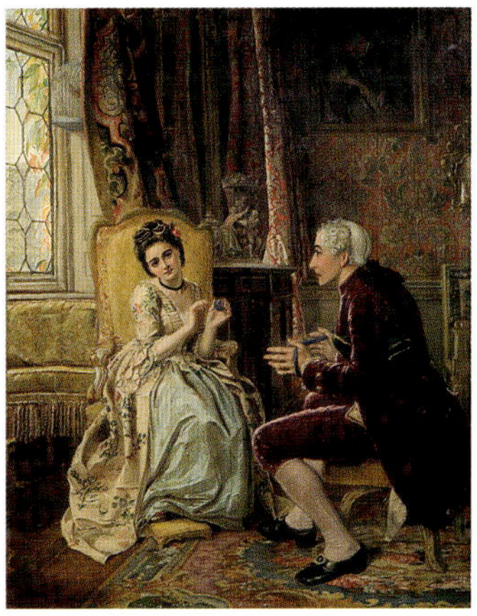

Weigall, Arthur Howes c.1836–1894
After Marriage 1881
oil on canvas 89 x 68.5
P29/76

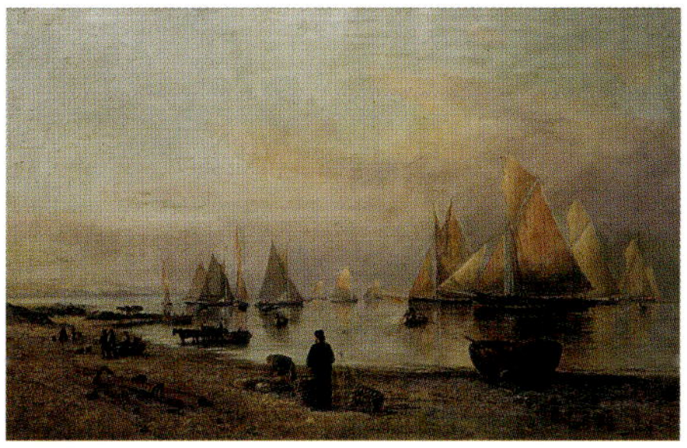

Williams, A.
Fishing Boats
oil on canvas 59 x 89
P16/76

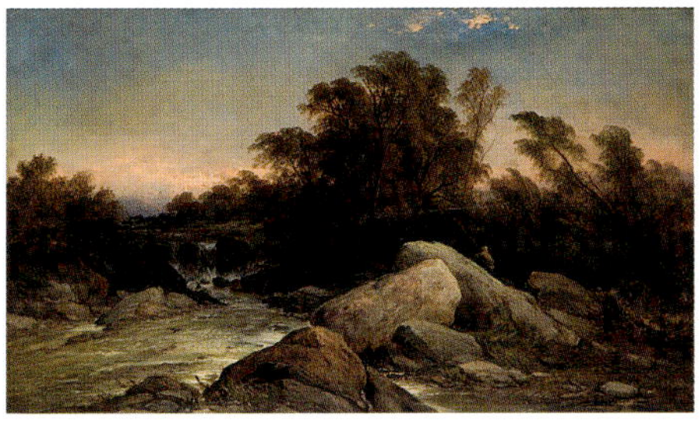

Williams, George Augustus 1814–1901
Near Dolgelly, North Wales
oil on canvas 38.5 x 65
P60/76

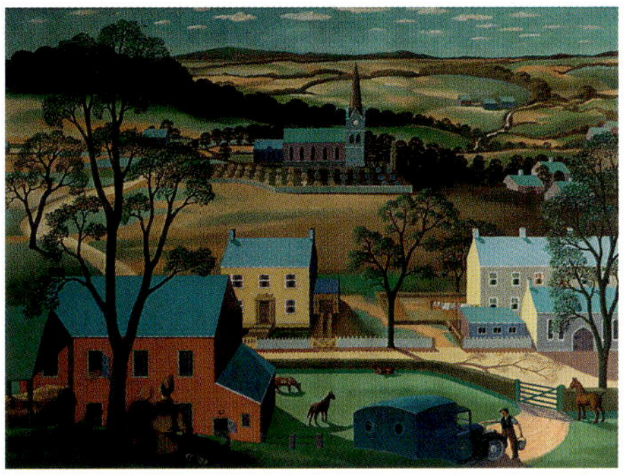

Willott, George
Sutton St James 1968
oil on canvas 63.5 x 81
P212/76

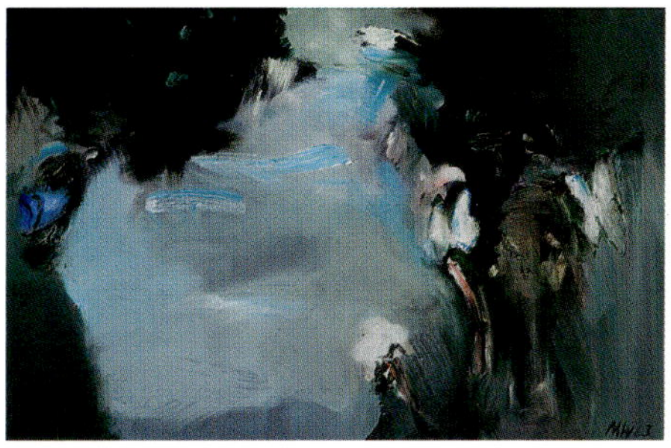

Wishart, Michael 1928–1996
Moths on a Blue Path 1963
oil on canvas 49.5 x 75
GR.260

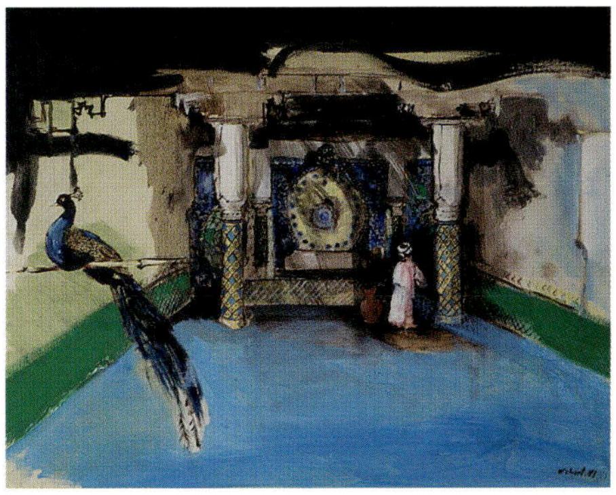

Wishart, Michael 1928–1996
Arab Courtyard, Fez 1971
oil on canvas 39 x 49
GR.259

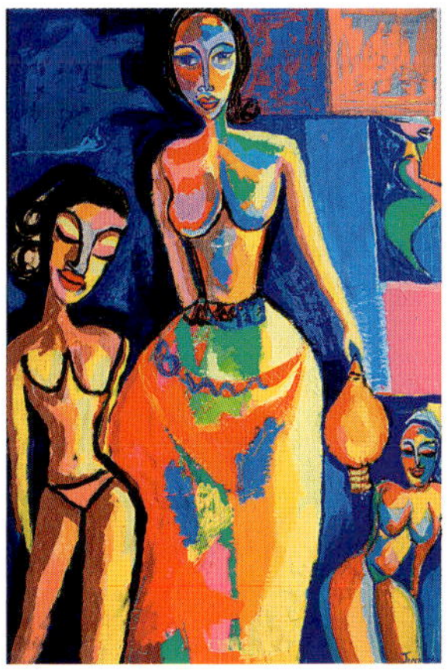

Wray, Jenny b.1967
Indian Goddess
acrylic on paper 112 x 79
P27/93

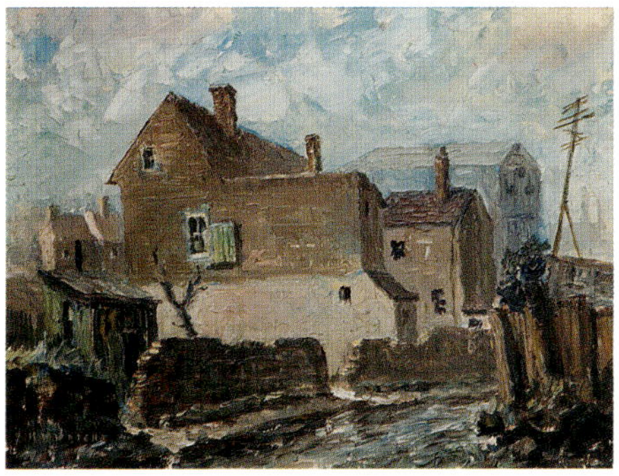

Wright, Herbert W. active 1945–1981
Hatherton, Walsall 1945
oil on canvas 34 x 45
P269/76

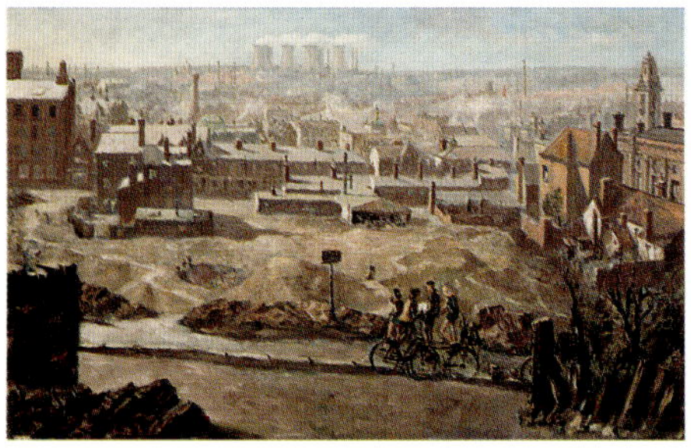

Wright, Herbert W. active 1945–1981
Walsall, as seen from Peal Street 1958
oil on board 60 x 89
P268/76

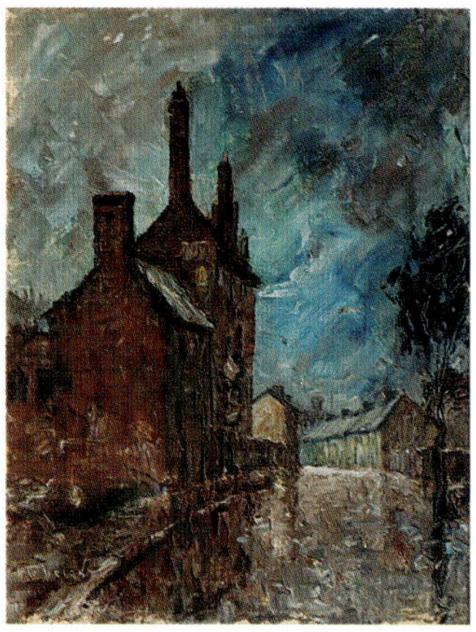

Wright, Herbert W. active 1945–1981
Back of Old Priory, Walsall 1968
oil on canvas 45 x 35
P270/76

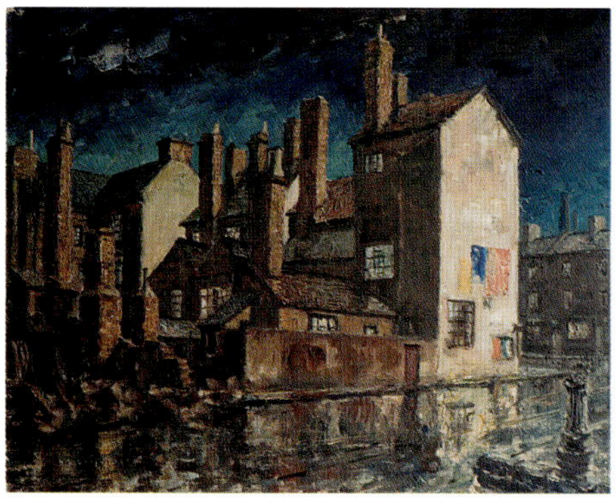

Wright, Herbert W. active 1945–1981
Birmingham Street, Walsall
oil on canvas 62 x 75
P271/76

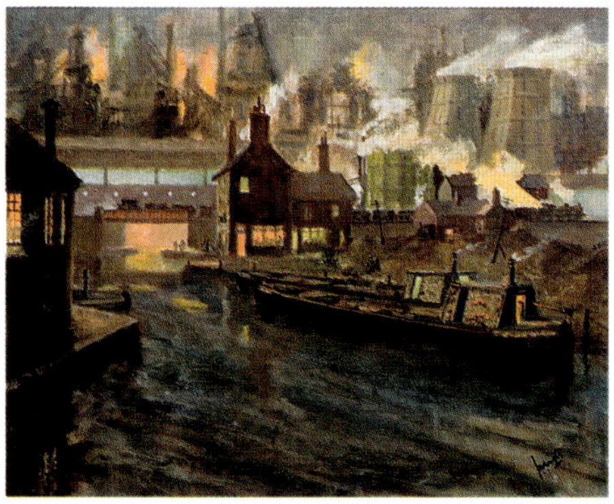

Wright, Herbert W. active 1945–1981
Midland Memories
oil on canvas 50 x 59
P13/81

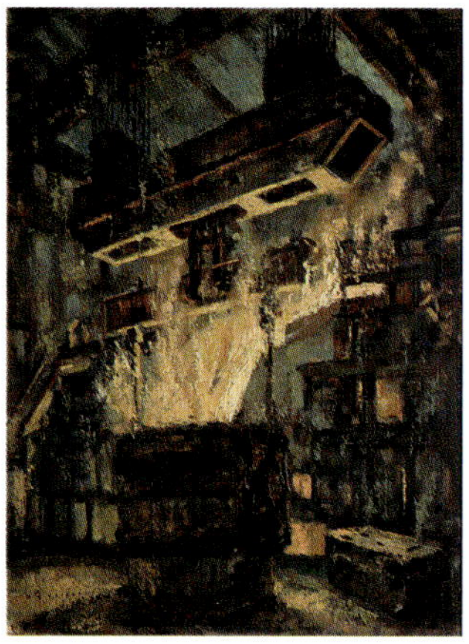

Wright, Herbert W. active 1945–1981
Tapping
oil on board 59.5 x 44
P306/76

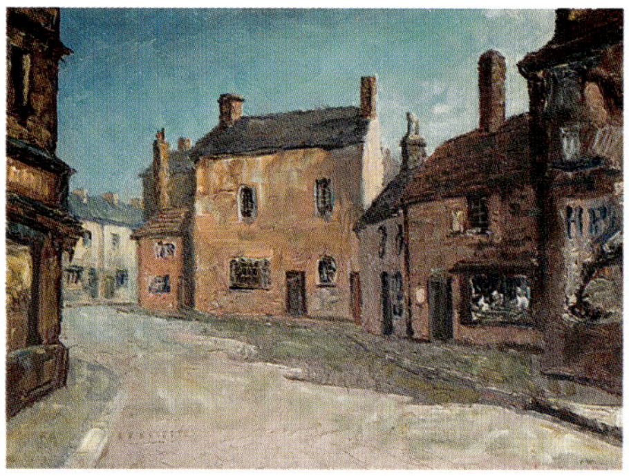

Wright, Herbert W. active 1945–1981
Wisemore, Walsall
oil on canvas 34 x 45
P267/76

New Cross Hospital

The majority of paintings in the collection at New Cross Hospital were originally hung in the now closed, Royal Hospital. The South Staffordshire General Hospital and Dispensary (later renamed The Royal Hospital) opened in 1849. It was funded by public contributions and the earliest portraits are of some of the wealthy patrons of the hospital, several of whom served on the Board of Management. The hospital continued as a publicly funded institution until the advent of the NHS.

By the 1880s some of the more senior members of the medical staff were commemorated by having their portraits hung in the hospital. This commemoration continued until the early 1950s. All the portraits were donated by the sitters to the hospital and were originally hung either in the Board Room, corridors or outside of appropriate wards and departments, some of which bore the names of the sitter.

New Cross Hospital opened in 1903 as the Wolverhampton Workhouse. It remained as such until the end of the workhouse system in 1930. It developed as a hospital from that date but still had a large accommodation for the elderly infirmed who could not look after themselves. It also had accommodation for the homeless, psychiatric patients and some maternity cases. Always the poor relation of the Royal, there was only one senior medical person who treated all medical and surgical patients. During the Second World War it served as a military hospital for Dutch troops serving in the area.

With the imminent closure of the Royal Hospital in 1997, the portraits were removed and taken to New Cross Hospital. Some of the portraits were cleaned and reframed before being hung at New Cross. The medical portraits were hung in the West Midlands Institute, those of Board members and the nursing staff in Hollybush House (now the Trust's administration offices).

Neil Fox, Chief Biomedical Scientist, Clinical Chemistry Department

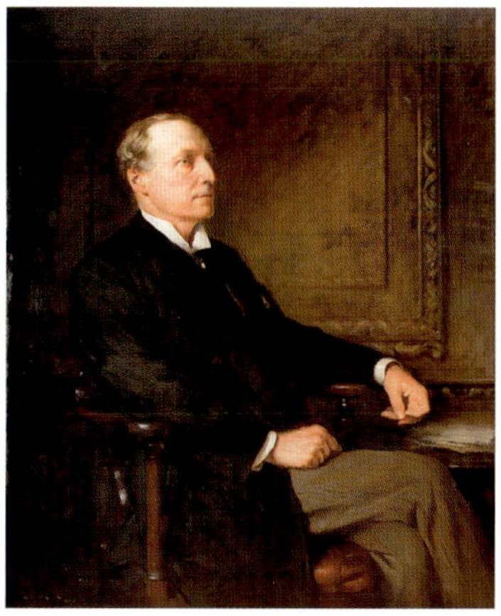

Calkin, Lance 1859–1936
T. Vincent Jackson (c.1836–1901), Surgeon, Mayor of Wolverhampton (1886–1887) 1902
oil on canvas 135 x 104
PCF1

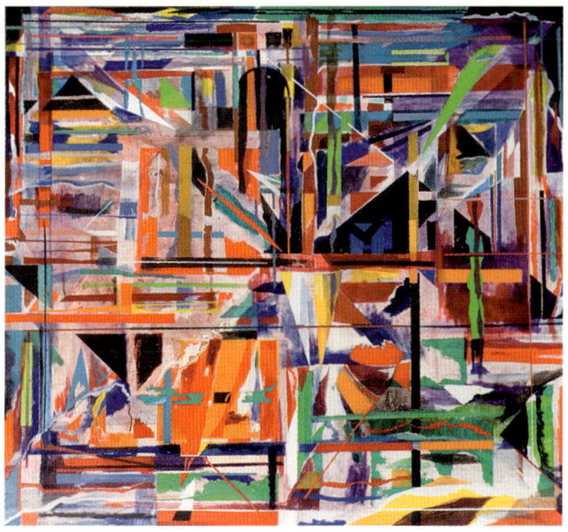

Chakraborty, Paresh C. b.1934
Festive Dance, 'Shankara' 1990s
oil on board 145 x 160
PCF31

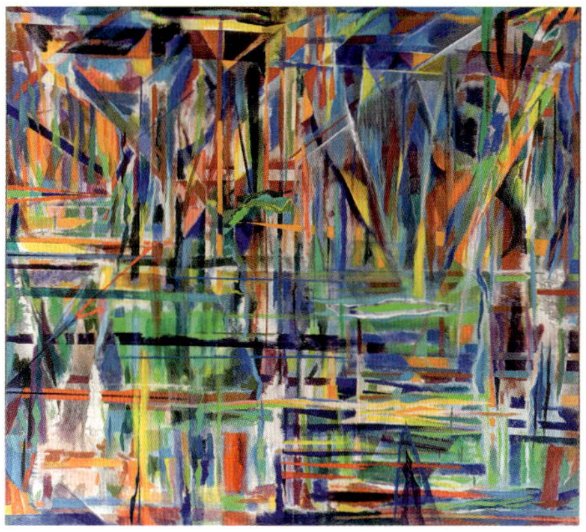

Chakraborty, Paresh C. b.1934
Monsoon Music (Rainy Season) 'Gauda Mallar' 1990s
oil on canvas 185 x 200
PCF32

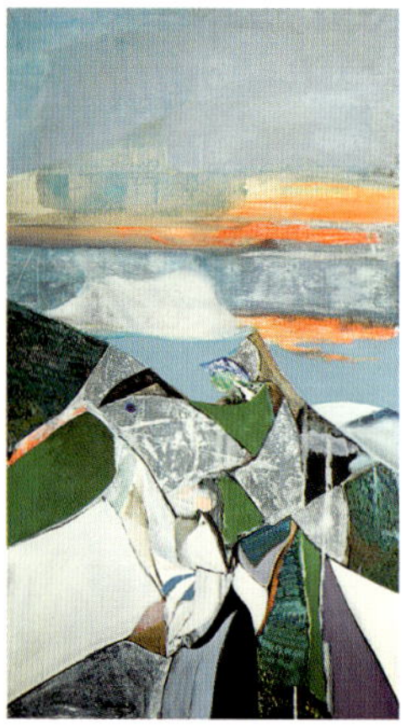

Grant, Keith b.1930
Triptych (left) 1967
oil on canvas 250 x 130
PCF30A

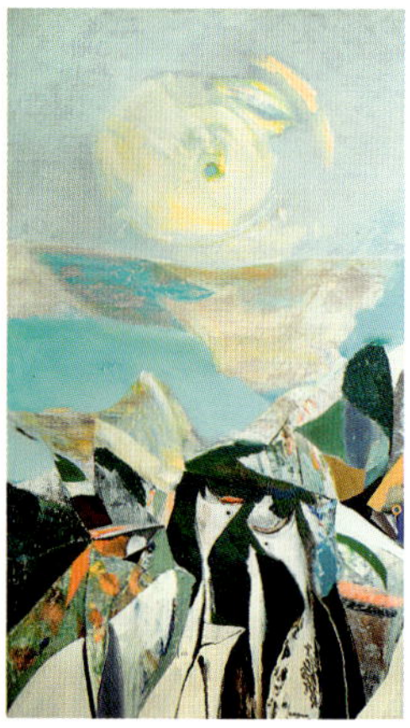

Grant, Keith b.1930
Triptych (centre) 1967
oil on canvas 250 x 130
PCF30B

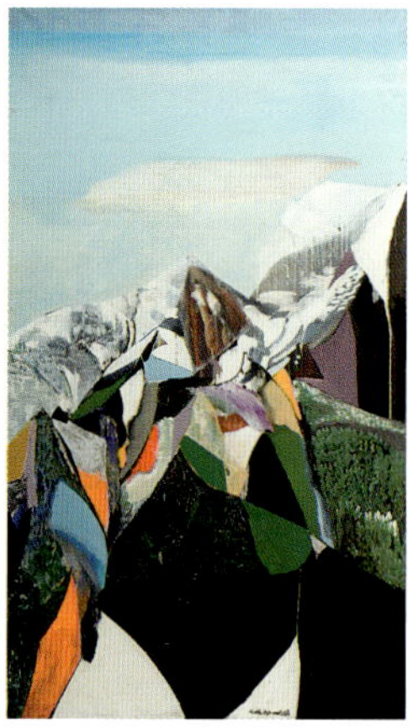

Grant, Keith b.1930
Triptych (right) 1967
oil on canvas 250 x 130
PCF30C

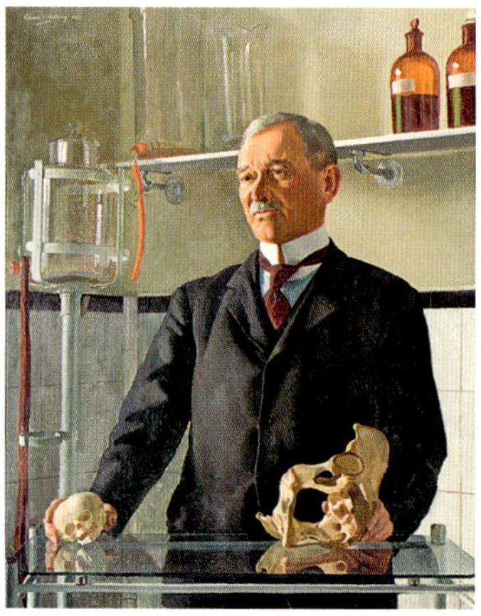

Halliday, Edward Irvine 1902–1984
Frederick Edge (1863–1937) 1931
oil on canvas 114 x 90
PCF2

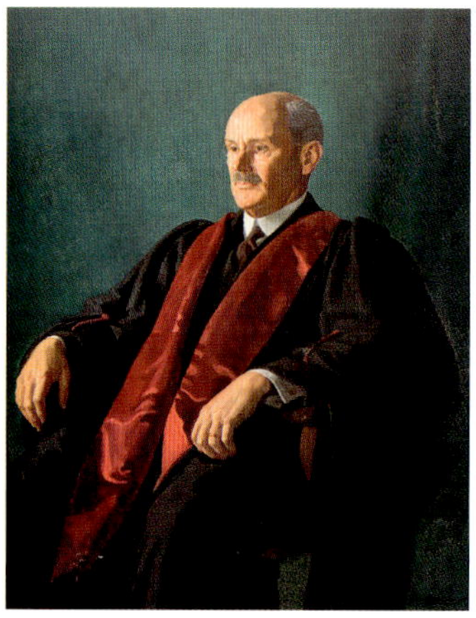

Halliday, Edward Irvine 1902–1984
W. F. Cholmeley, FRCS (1866–1949) 1931
oil on canvas 109 x 84
PCF3

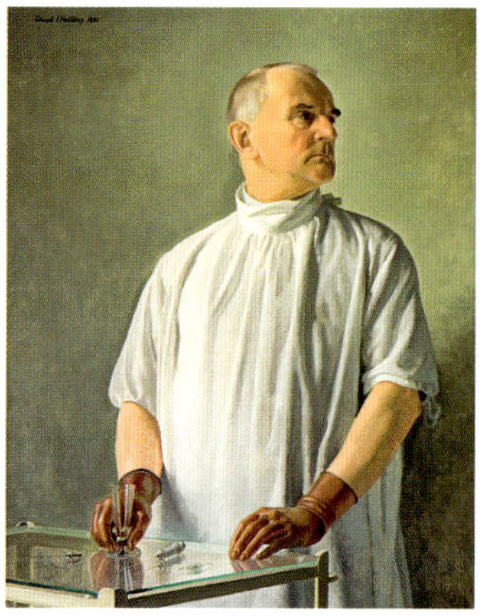

Halliday, Edward Irvine 1902–1984
Surgeon Edward Dranesly (1866–1948)
oil on canvas 112 x 86
PCF4

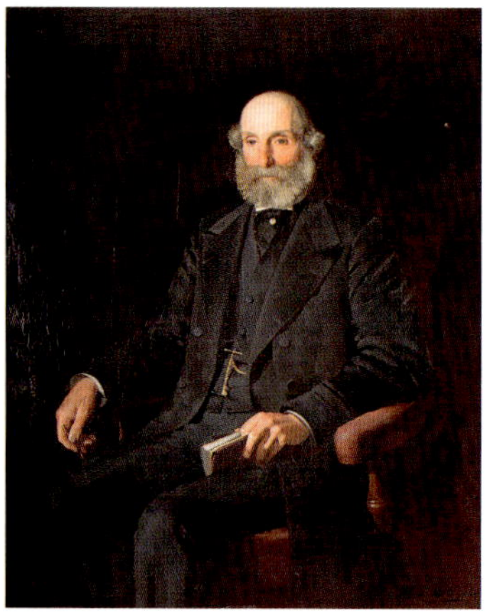

Hillwood, Thomas
William Millington (1821–1911)
oil on canvas 140 x 110
PCF5

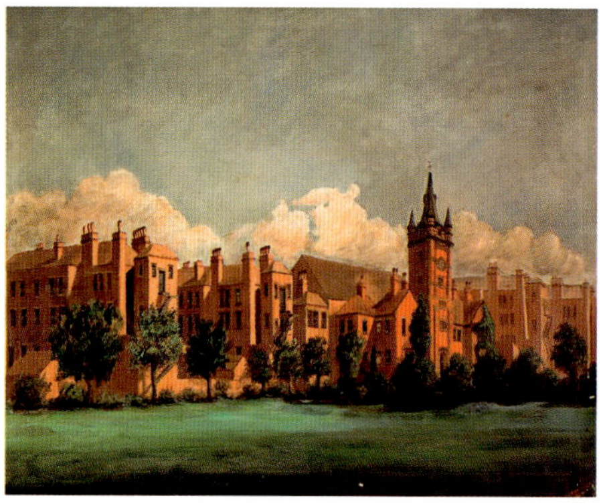

Morton, J.
New Cross 1924
oil on canvas 64 x 95
PCF6

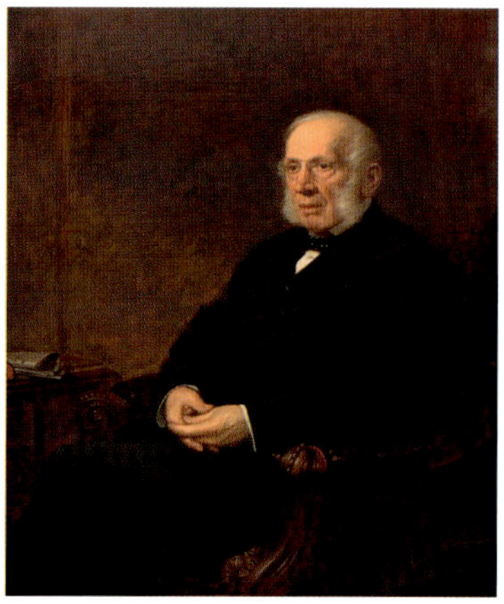

Munns, Henry Turner 1832–1898
Thomas Pinchard 1877
oil on canvas 127 x 102
PCF7

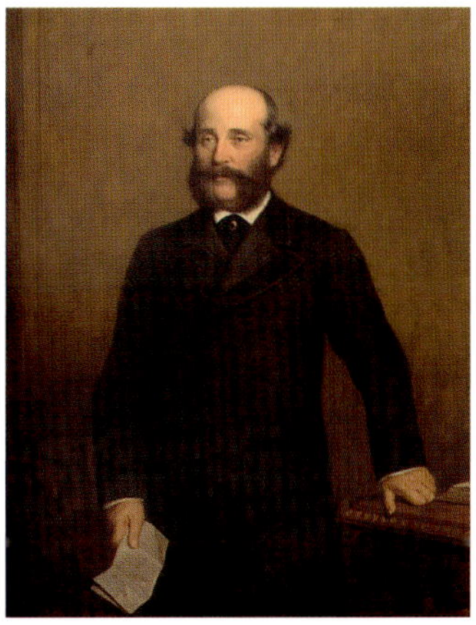

Munns, Henry Turner 1832–1898
Richard Briscoe 1880
oil on canvas 132 x 102
PCF8

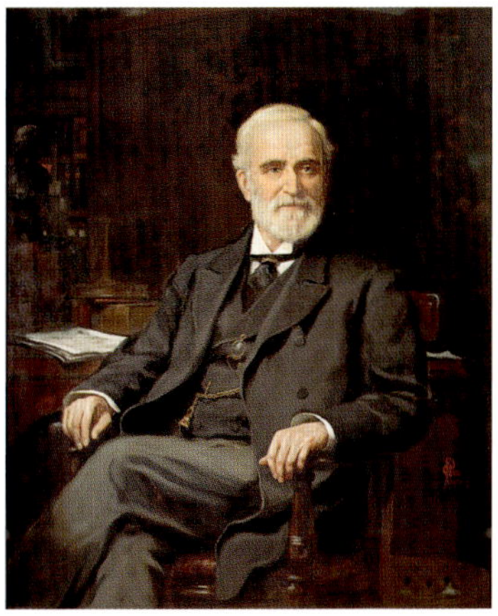

Phoenix, George 1863–1935
James Y. Totherick (d.1899) 1897
oil on canvas 142 x 112
PCF10

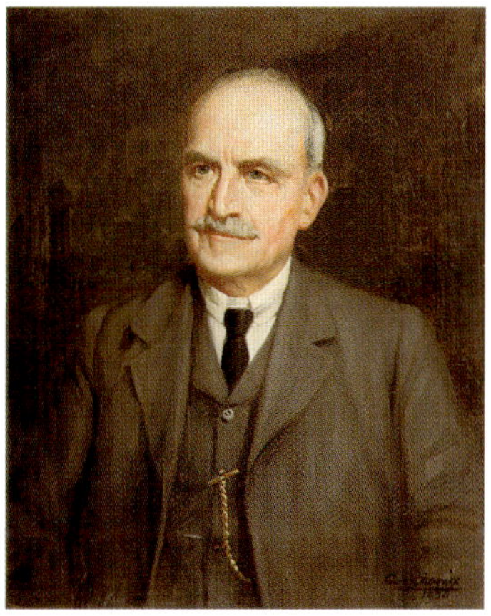

Phoenix, George 1863–1935
Henry Malet (1851–1924), MA, MD 1920
oil on canvas 65 x 55
PCF21

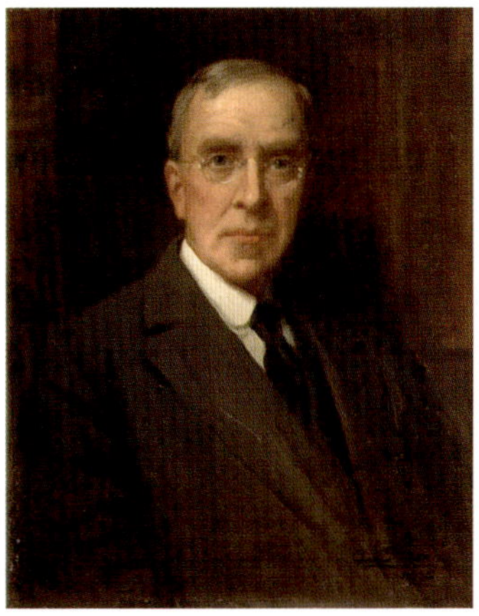

Phoenix, George 1863–1935
A. H. Carter (1873–1961) 1928
oil on canvas 66 x 53
PCF9

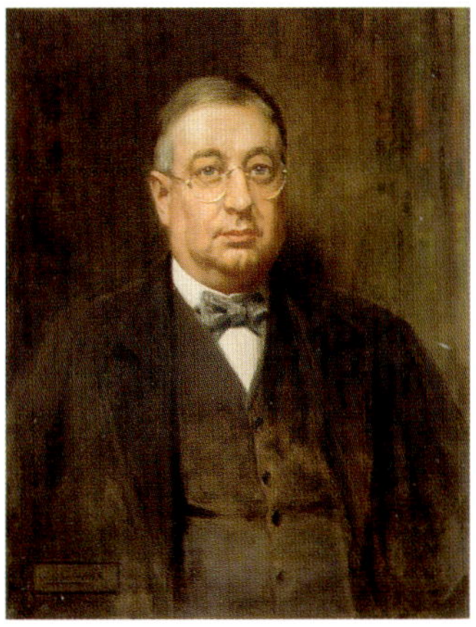

Phoenix, George 1863–1935
C. A. Stidson
oil on canvas 76 x 63.5
PCF13

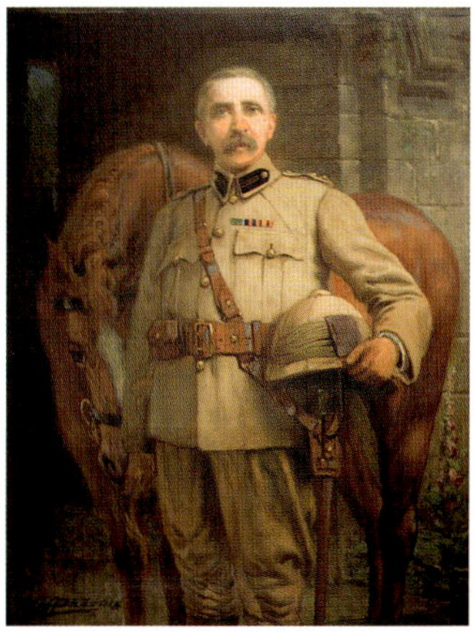

Phoenix, George 1863–1935
Charles Alexander MacMunn (1852–1911)
oil on canvas 145 x 107
PCF15

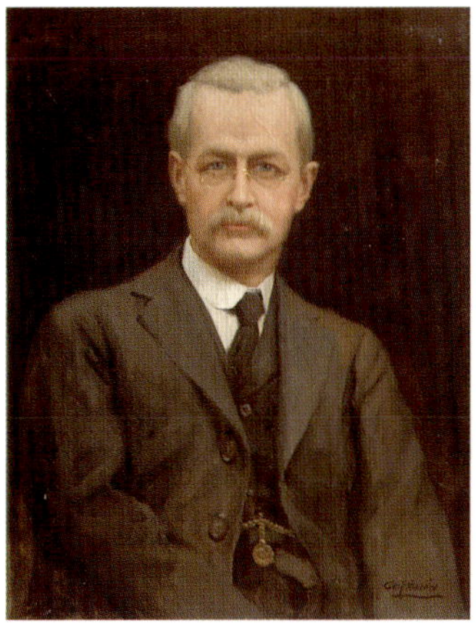

Phoenix, George 1863–1935
John Alfred Codd (c.1869–1920), MD
oil on canvas 65 x 55
PCF22

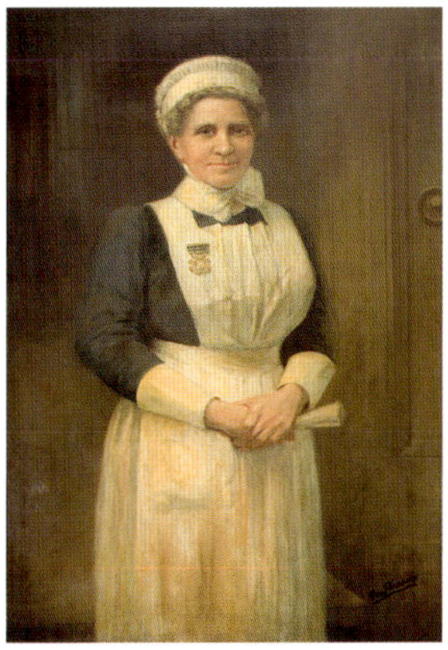

Phoenix, George 1863–1935
Sister Annie MacLaren (d.1912)
oil on canvas 135 x 84
PCF14

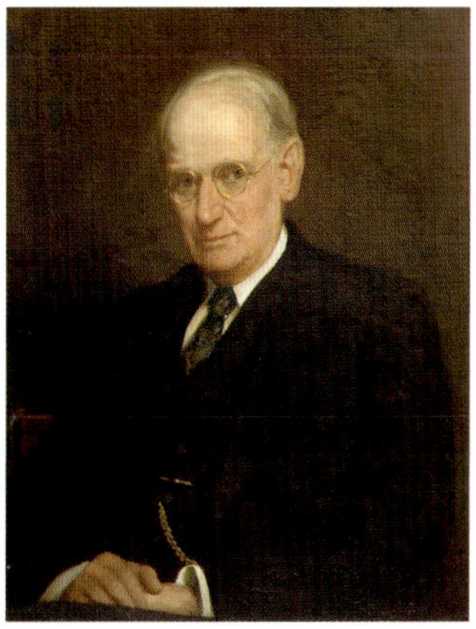

Phoenix, George 1863–1935
Thomas H. Glbraith (c.1862–1929)
oil on panel 71 x 58
PCF12

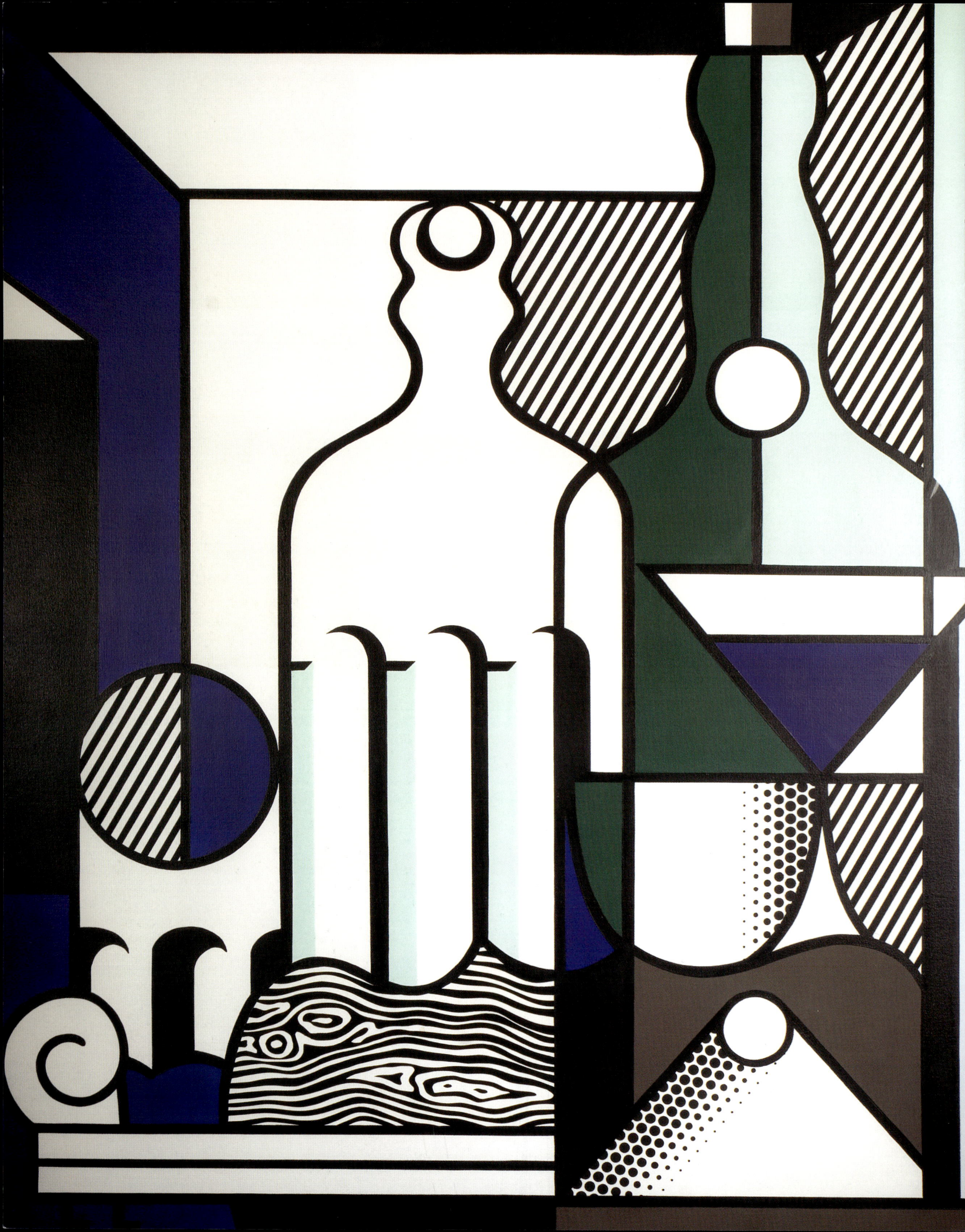

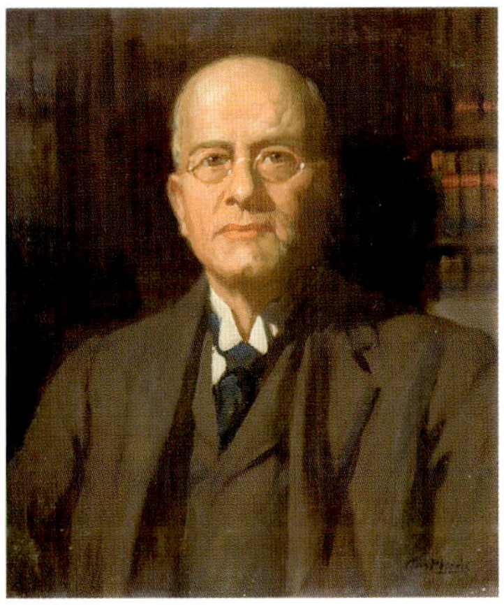

Phoenix, George 1863–1935
W. H. T. Winter (c.1855–1931)
oil on canvas 61 x 51
PCF11

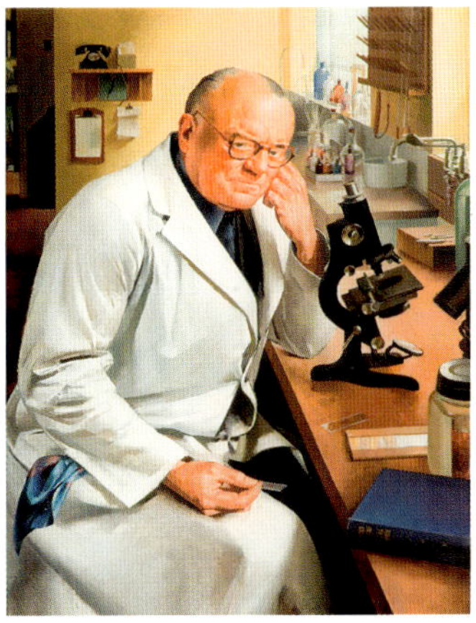

Turner, Harry b.1908
S. C. Dyke Seated in Laboratory (1886–1975)
1953
oil on canvas 91 x 66
PCF16

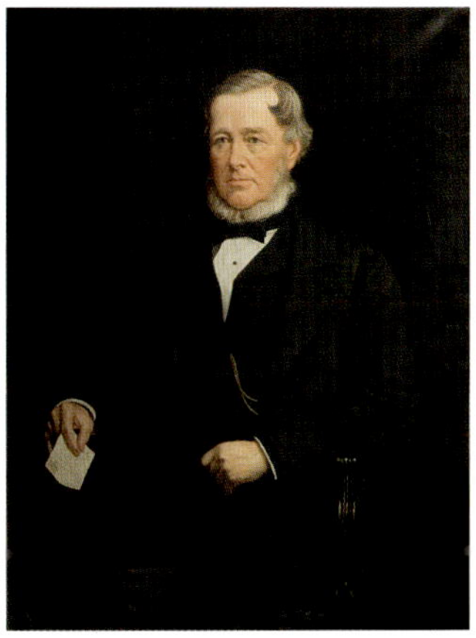

unknown artist
Edward Pugh 1882
oil on canvas 125 x 102
PCF17

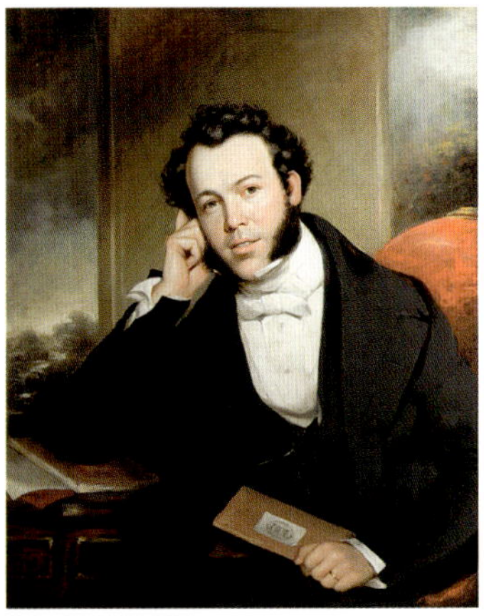

unknown artist
George Edwardes (d.1859), LSA, FRCS
oil on canvas 91 x 69
PCF20

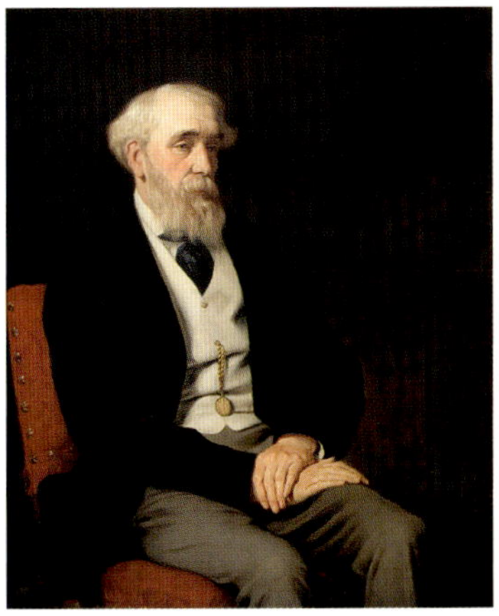

unknown artist
Henry Rogers
oil on canvas 127 x 102
PCF18

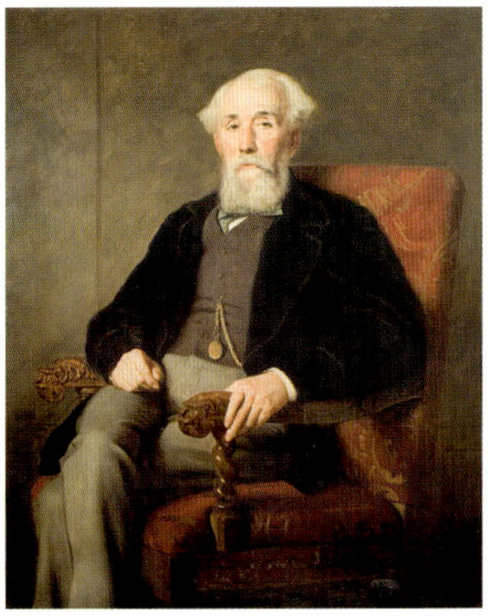

unknown artist
Henry Rogers
oil on canvas 127 x 102
PCF19

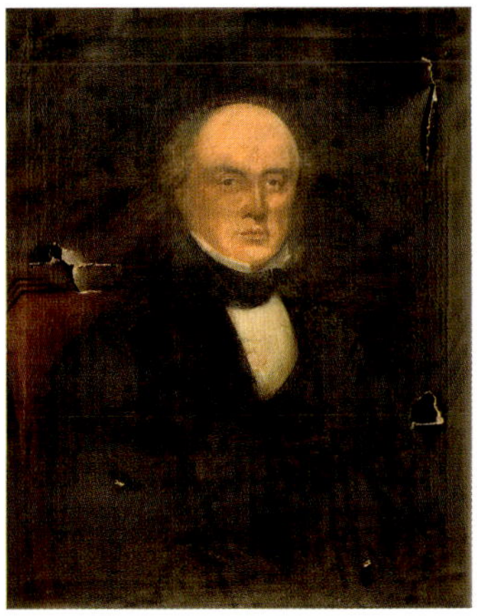

unknown artist
Portrait of a Gentleman
oil on canvas 75 x 61.5
PCF29

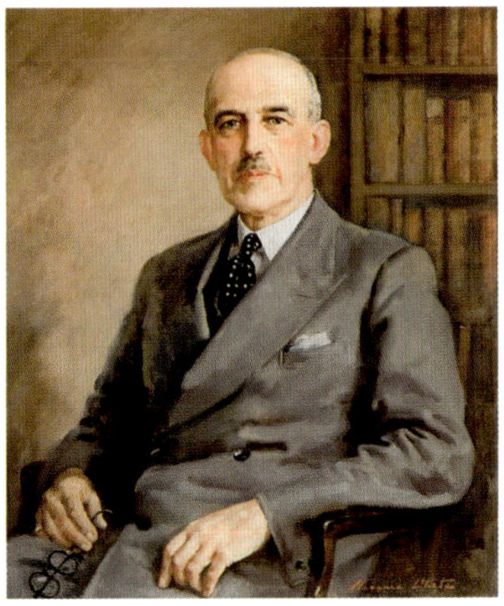

White, H.
H. H. C. Dent (1874–1972)
oil on canvas 86 x 68.5
PCF23

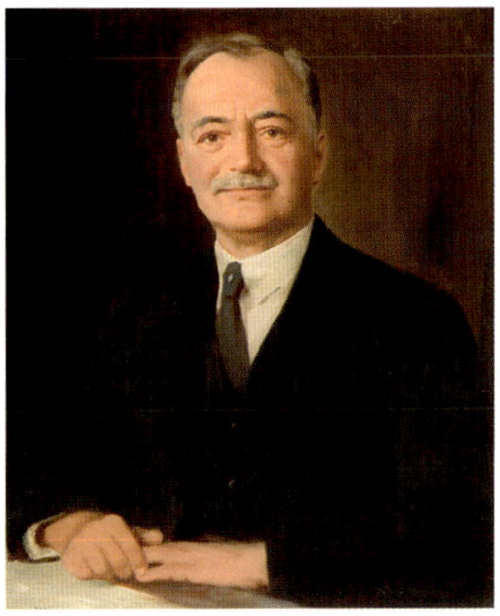

Wilson, Charles Heath 1809–1882
Edward Hayling Coleman
oil on canvas 76 x 63.5
PCF27

Facing page: Lichtenstein, Roy, 1923–1997, *Purist Painting with Bottles* (detail), 1975, Wolverhampton Art Gallery, (p. 295)

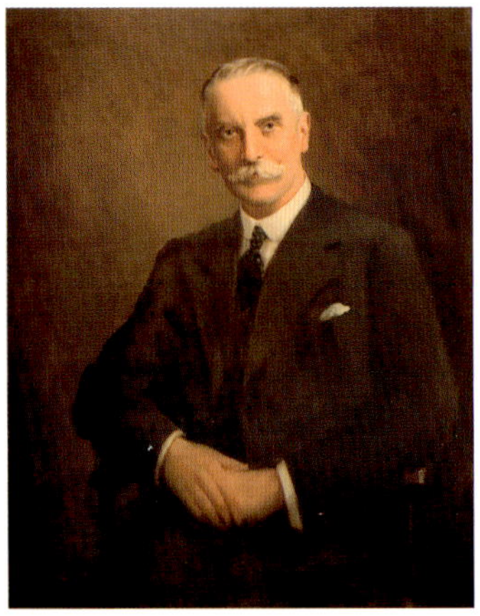

Wilson, Charles Heath 1809–1882
Lawley T. Smith
oil on canvas 107 x 84
PCF25

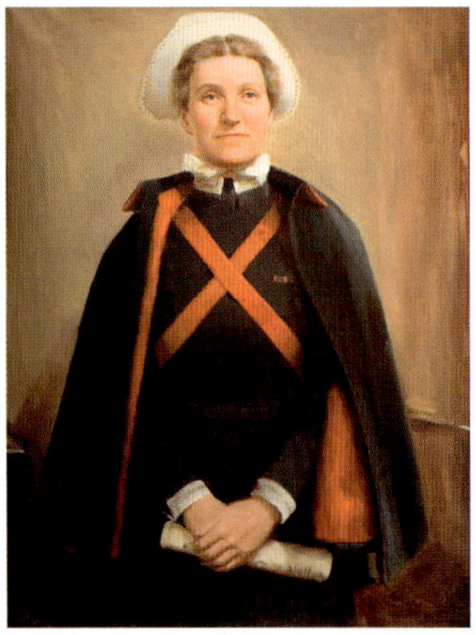

Wilson, Charles Heath 1809–1882
Matron Mary Millar
oil on canvas 102 x 76
PCF28

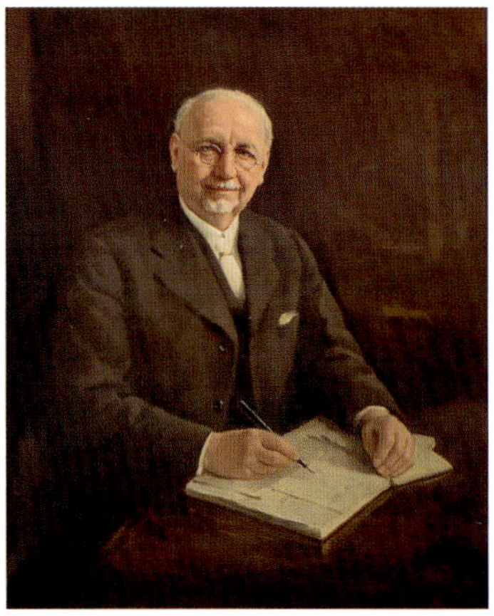

Wilson, Charles Heath 1809–1882
Tom Adams
oil on canvas 127 x 102
PCF26

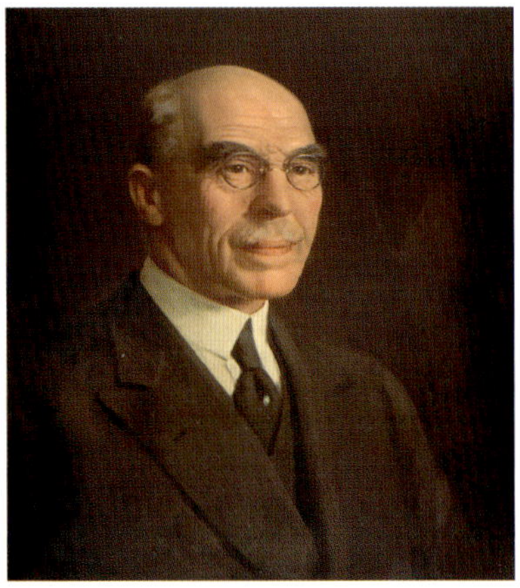

Wilson, Charles Heath 1809–1882
William Henry Harper
oil on canvas 60 x 50 (E)
PCF24

Wolverhampton Art Gallery

Wolverhampton Art Gallery opened to the public in 1884. It was built on land that was donated by the local council, with funding from a Wolverhampton building merchant, Philip Horsmann who also bequeathed paintings in 1886. Initially the gallery was designed as a showcase for fine arts and crafts, housing temporary exhibitions, but several large bequests in the late nineteenth century formed the basis of a permanent collection of art. The most significant of these was the donation of over 200 works, valued at £17,000, by wealthy tin-toy manufacturer Sidney Cartwright.

Cartwright was an avid collector of the Cranbrook Colony of artists, a group based in the pretty market town of Cranbrook in Kent. Their scenes of idyllic country life contained a combination of escapism and nostalgia that provided a welcome antidote to the horrors of industrialisation witnessed by the inhabitants of the rapidly expanding towns of the Midlands and North. For this reason, their paintings were especially popular adorning the drawing rooms of wealthy manufacturers. There are few regional collections that do not have at least a few examples of such a genre and Wolverhampton Art Gallery is particularly strong in this area.

In the 1960s, the first professional curator was appointed and a collecting policy was put in place. Priority was given to acquiring contemporary art and many controversial acquisitions were made of work by the leading artists of the time including Andy Warhol, Roy Lichtenstein, Richard Hamilton and Peter Blake. This foresight has enabled the gallery to amass a significant collection on Pop Art, unusual for a regional gallery of its size. One legacy of the Pop Art collection was the continued focus, throughout the 1970s and 1980s, on work that addressed the social and political landscape of modern Britain. By the late 1970s and early 1980s, this inevitably included art based on 'the troubles' in Northern Ireland and the foundation was laid for a unique collection of work relating to the struggle for power in Ulster.

In 2000–2005, the Gallery was part of a national scheme funded through the Arts Council Lottery and administered by the Contemporary Art Society. This scheme has enabled the art collection to expand further and again focuses on issue-based work by leading contemporary artists (some who paint in oils) including David Rayson, Tom Hunter, Richard Billingham, Rut Blees Luxembourg, Breda Beban and many others.

We are grateful to the Victoria & Albert Museum Purchase Grant Fund and the National Art Collections Fund for their financial support for acquisitions over the years. We have enjoyed a fruitful partnership with the Contemporary Art Society for a number of years and have benefited from their distribution scheme on many occasions. The Arts and Museums Service has an active Friends group who have played a vital role in finding those extra few pounds when all other funding possibilities have been exhausted. We continue to build on our collections and hope that they will be a valuable resource for visitors and researchers for years to come.

Marguerite Nugent, Head of Curatorial Services

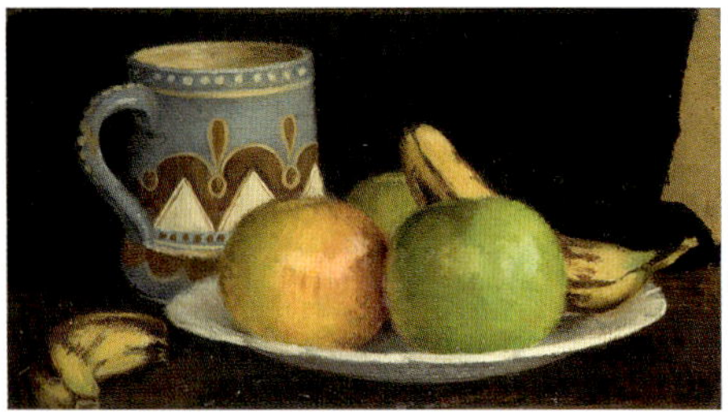

Addison, Alfred Henry
Still Life 1924
oil on board 18 x 28
OP147

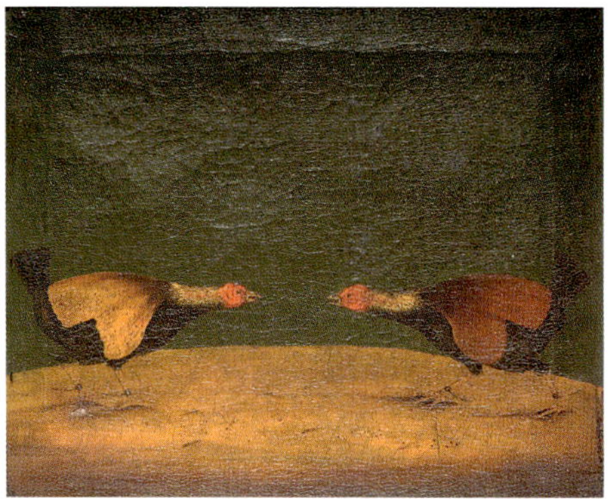

Alken, Henry Thomas (attributed to)
1785–1851
Cockfighting (two cocks face each other)
oil on canvas 30.5 x 35.5
OP155/1

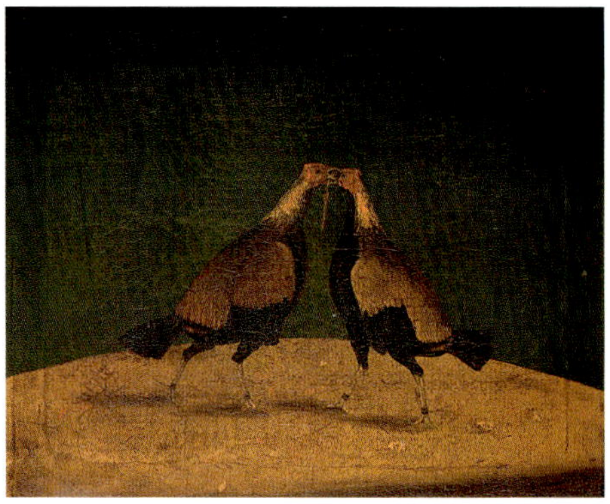

Alken, Henry Thomas (attributed to)
1785–1851
Cockfighting (two cocks attack each other)
oil on canvas 30.5 x 35.5
OP155/4

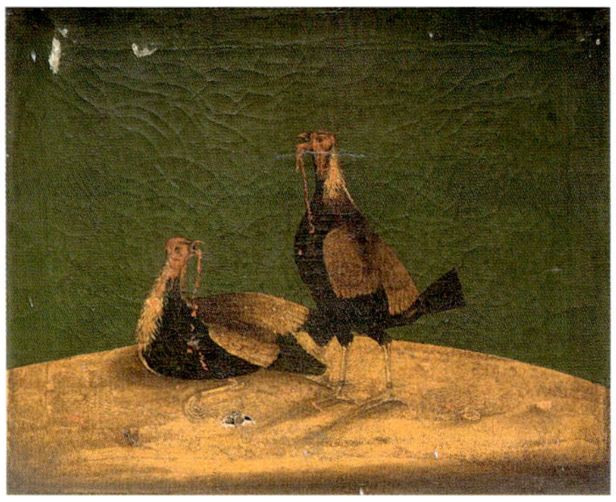

Alken, Henry Thomas (attributed to)
1785–1851
Cockfighting (both cocks bleeding from the mouth)
oil on canvas 30.5 x 35.5 (E)
OP155/3

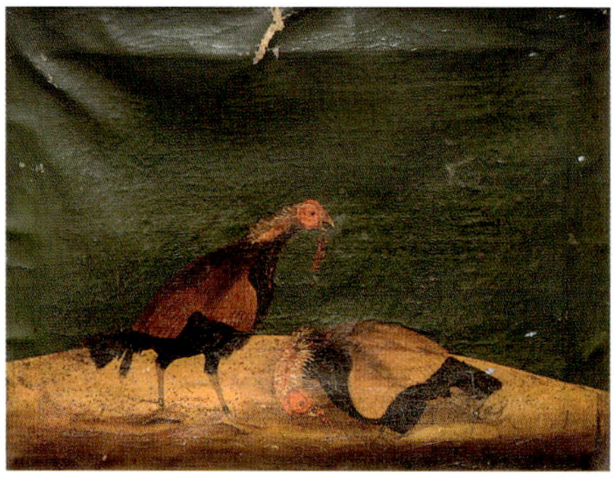

Alken, Henry Thomas (attributed to)
1785–1851
Cockfighting (one cock kills the other)
oil on canvas 30.5 x 35.5 (E)
OP155/2

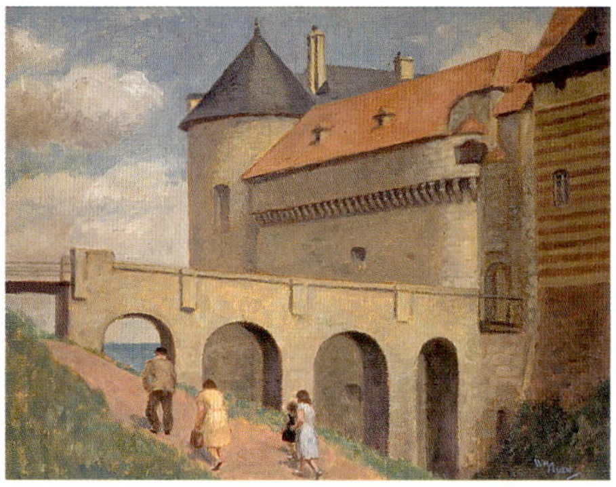

Allen, William Herbert 1863–1943
Château, Dieppe
oil on canvas 51 x 63
OP618

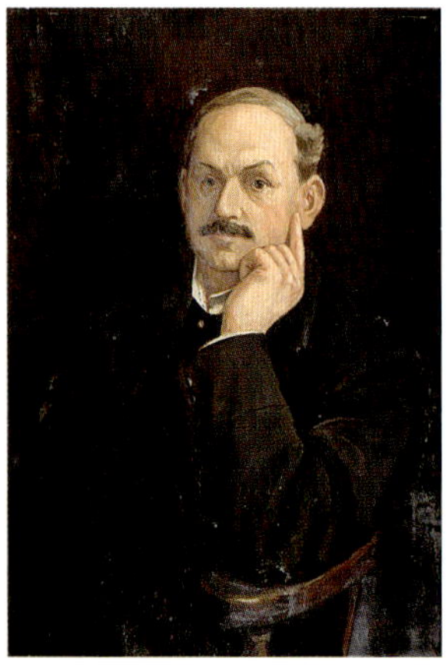

Allen, William Herbert 1863–1943
Mr Jordan
oil in panel 20.3 x 15.2
OP615

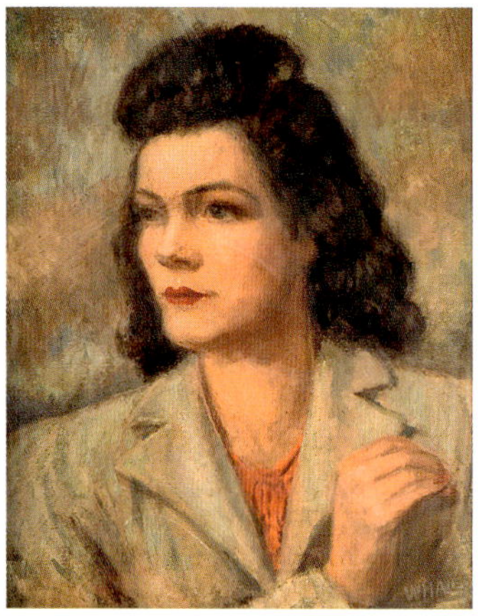

Allen, William Herbert 1863–1943
Portrait of a Woman (study)
oil on canvas 77 x 56
OP616

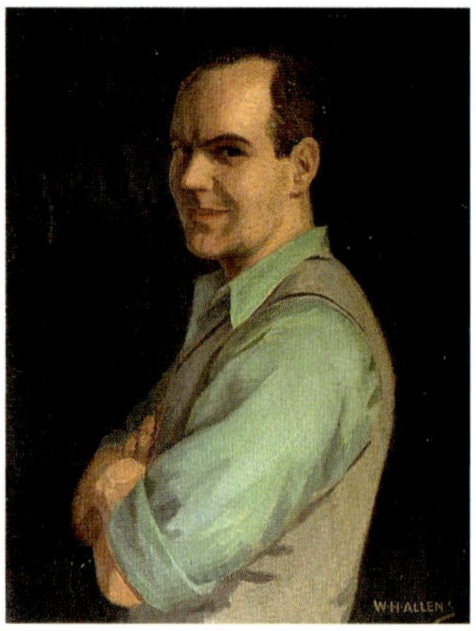

Allen, William Herbert 1863–1943
Self Portrait
oil on canvas 67 x 51
OP617

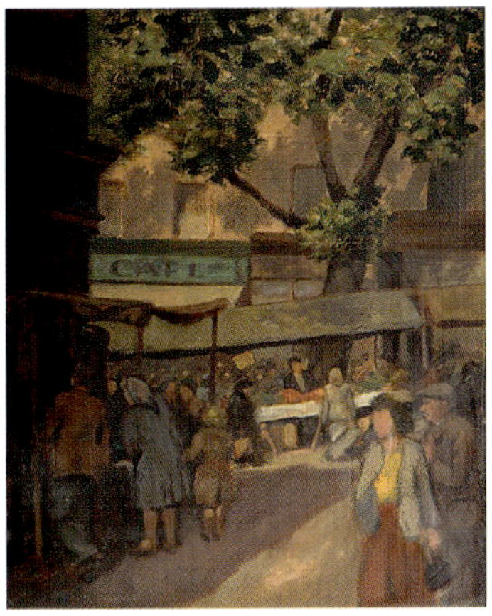

Allen, William Herbert 1863–1943
Street Market
oil on canvas 51 x 41.5
OP619

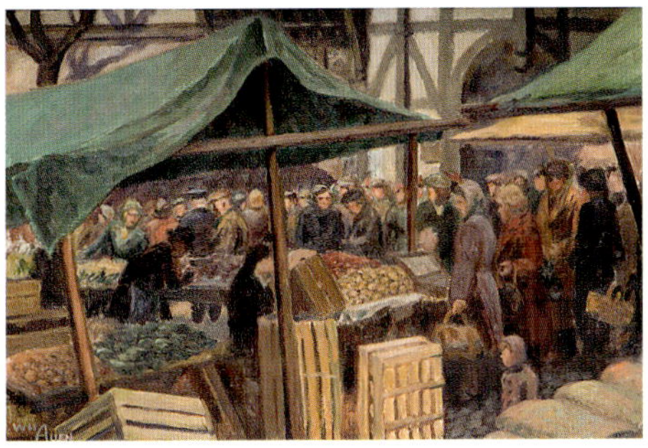

Allen, William Herbert 1863–1943
Street Market, Walsall
oil on canvas 51 x 64
OP621

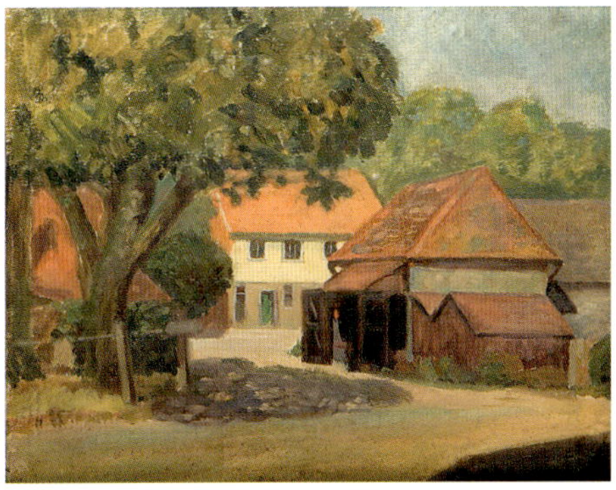

Allen, William Herbert 1863–1943
Sussex Farmyard
oil on canvas 32 x 40
OP620

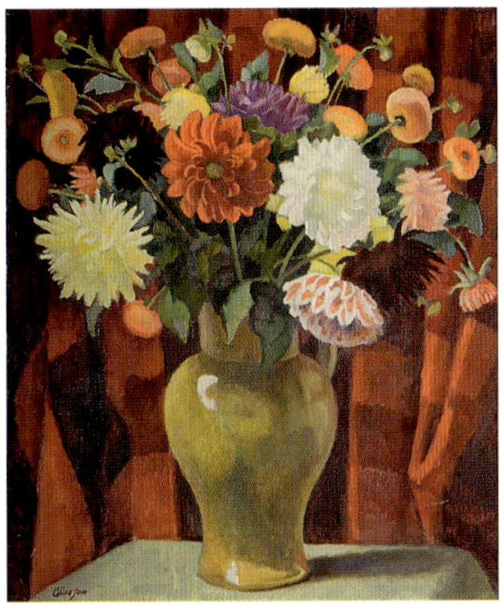

Allinson, Adrian Paul 1890–1959
Jug of Flowers
oil on canvas 68.5 x 56
OP290

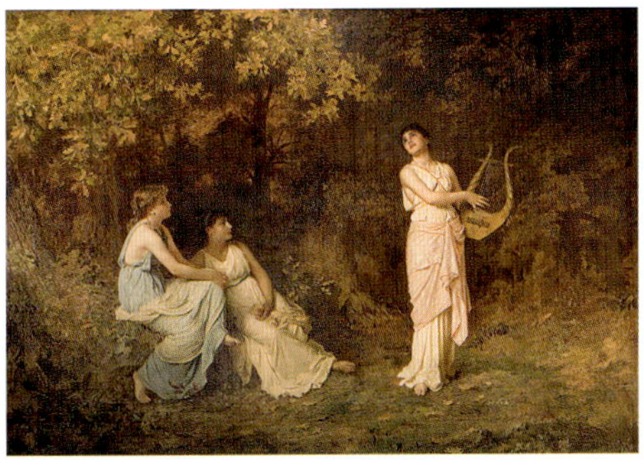

Anderson, Sophie 1823–1912
The Song 1881
oil on canvas 145 x 200.5
OP430

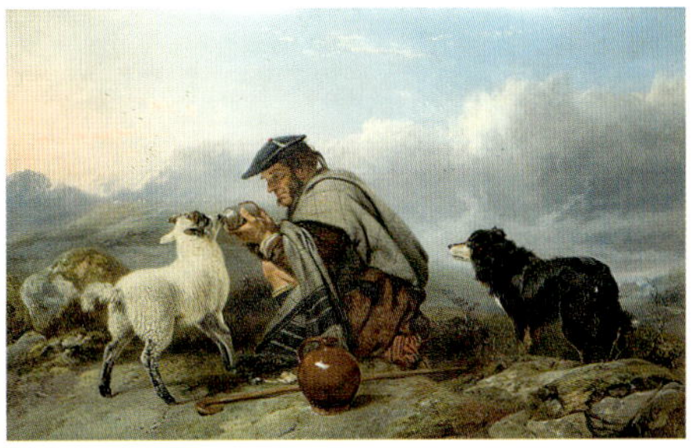

Ansdell, Richard 1815–1885
The Sick Lamb 1853
oil on canvas 61 x 94
OP397

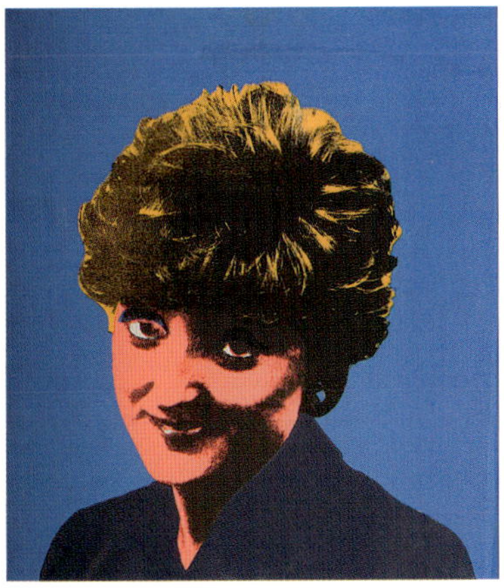

Anslow, Sonia
Princess Diana Look-a-Like 1990–1995
oil on canvas 68.5 x 56.5
OP894

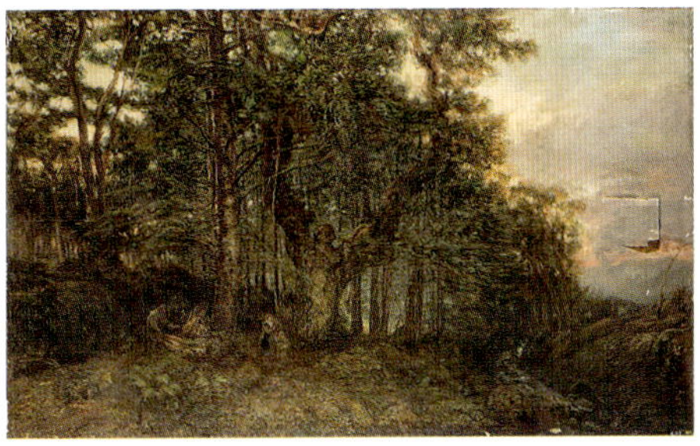

Anthony, Henry Mark 1817–1886
A Larch Forest
oil on canvas 116.8 x 185.4
OP441

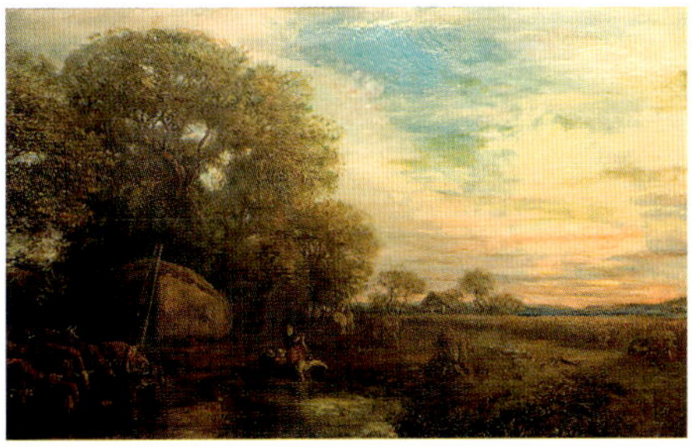

Anthony, Henry Mark 1817–1886
Autumn Evening
oil on canvas 78.5 x 104
OP123

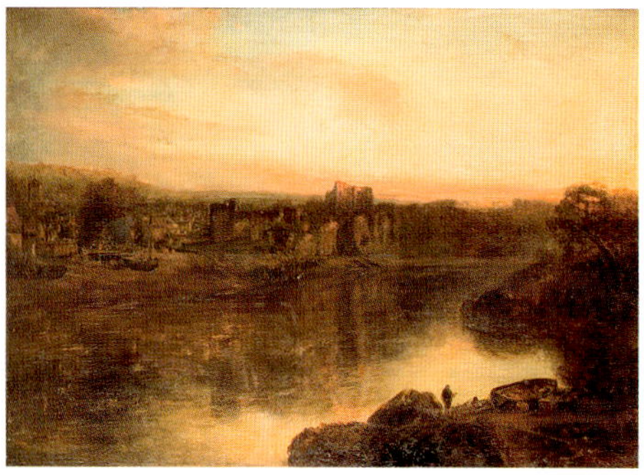

Anthony, Henry Mark 1817–1886
Chepstow Castle, Monmouthshire
oil on canvas 122 x 168
OP439

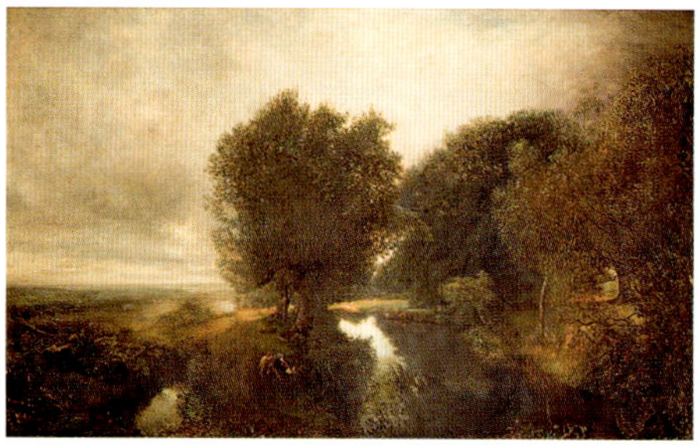

Anthony, Henry Mark 1817–1886
Nature's Mirror
oil on canvas 128 x 197
OP622

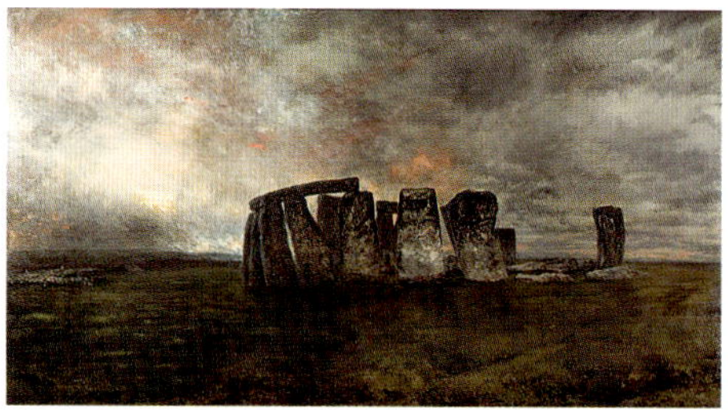

Anthony, Henry Mark 1817–1886
Stonehenge
oil on canvas 136 x 233
OP433

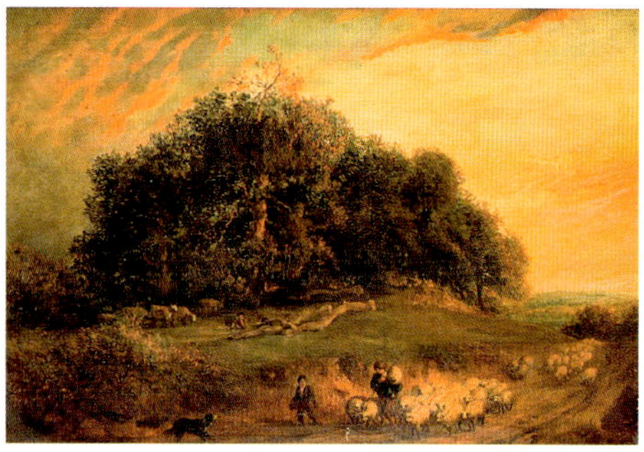

Anthony, Henry Mark 1817–1886
Sunset
oil on canvas 68.5 x 99
OP106

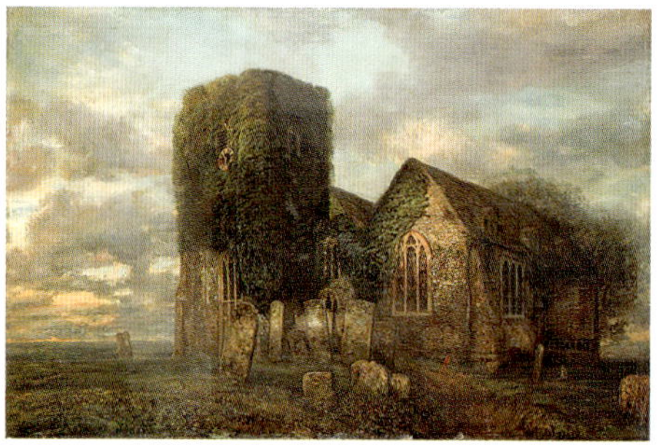

Anthony, Henry Mark 1817–1886
The Old Church
oil on canvas 132.1 x 188
OP440

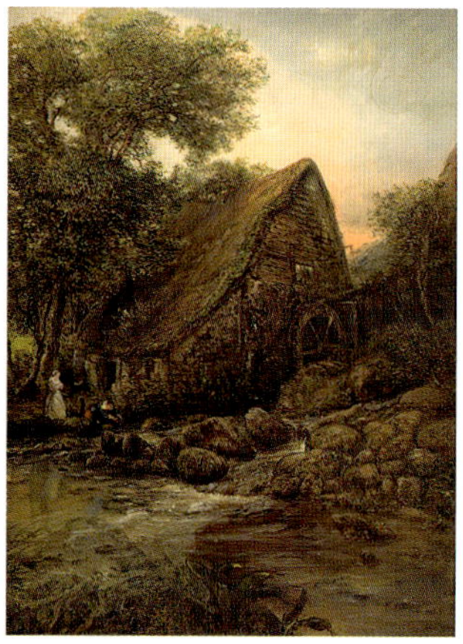

Anthony, Henry Mark 1817–1886
The Old Mill Wheel
oil on canvas 145 x 101.5
OP459

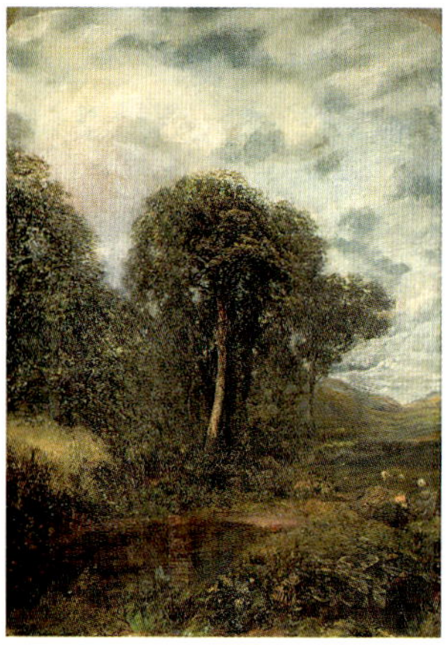

Anthony, Henry Mark 1817–1886
The Silver Spring
oil on canvas 154.9 x 106.7
OP453

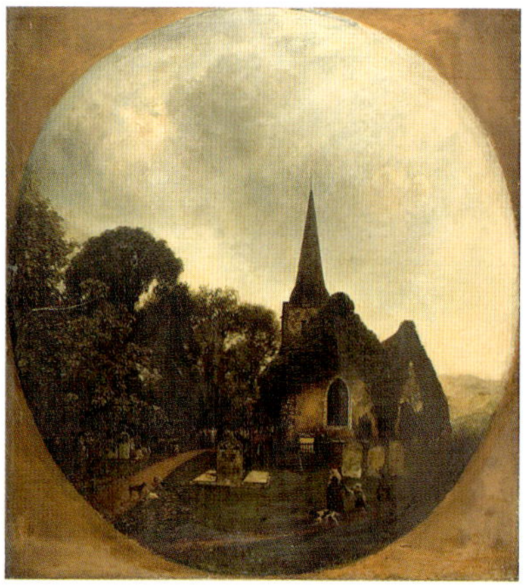

Anthony, Henry Mark 1817–1886
The Village Wedding
oil on canvas 203.2 x 201 (E)
OP432

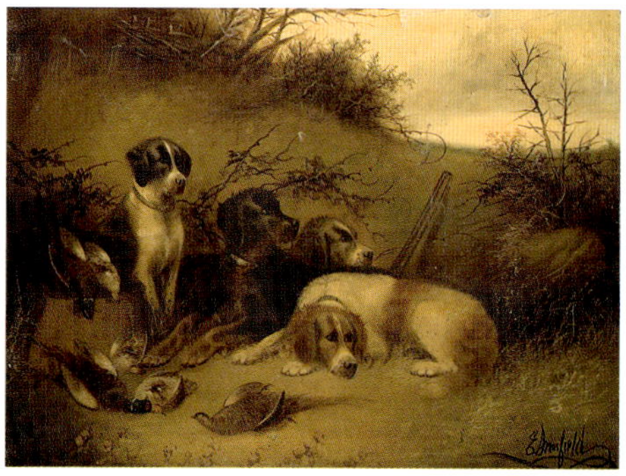

Armfield, Edward 1817–1896
Retrievers with Game
oil on canvas 71 x 91.5
OP600

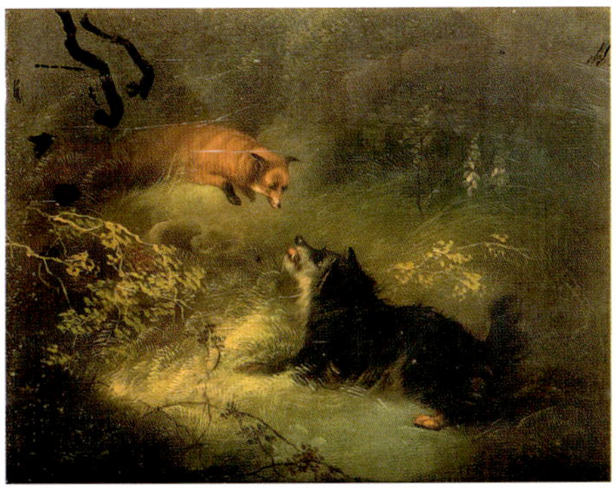

Armfield, George 1808–1893
Dog and Fox
oil on canvas 25.5 x 30.5
OP70

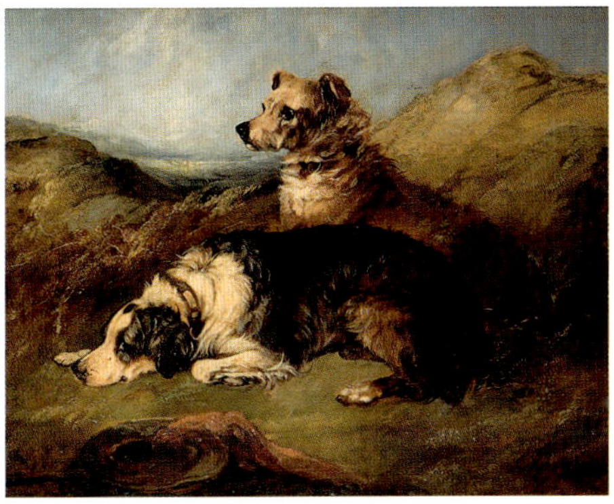

Armfield, George 1808–1893
Waiting
oil on canvas 51 x 61
OP367

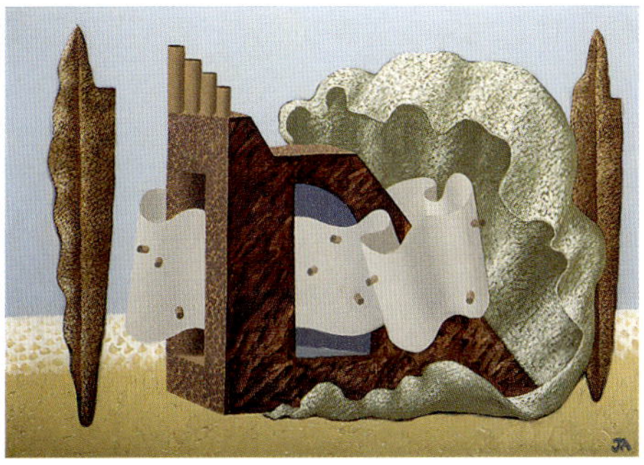

Armstrong, John 1893–1973
Organ Pipes 1929
oil on canvas 56 x 76
OP793

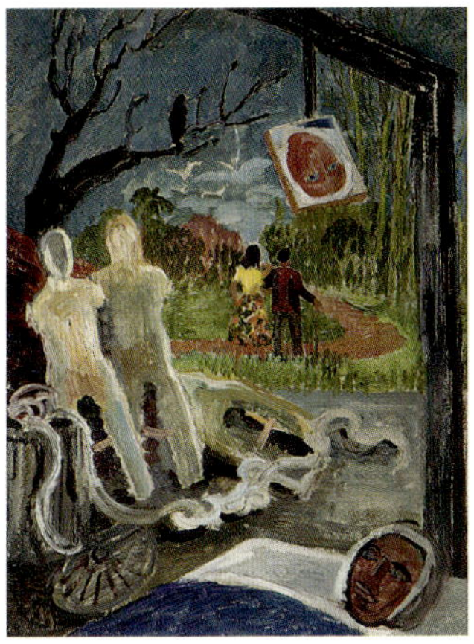

Arnett, Patricia
Walking away
oil on canvas 75 x 61
OP892

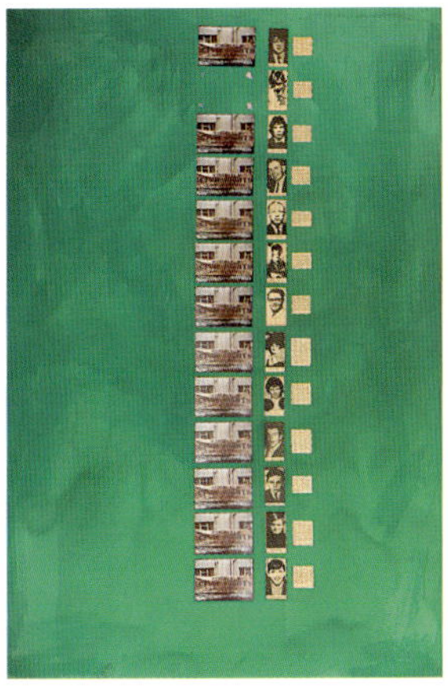

Atkinson, Conrad b.1940
Silver Liberties; A Souvenir of a Wonderful Anniversary Year (1 of 4) 1977
acrylic & mixed media on canvas 213 x 137
OP924i

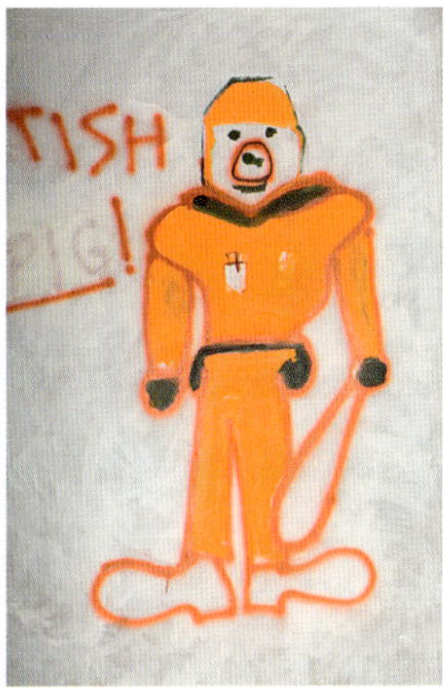

Atkinson, Conrad b.1940
Silver Liberties; A Souvenir of a Wonderful Anniversary Year (2 of 4) 1977
acrylic on canvas 213 x 137
OP924ii

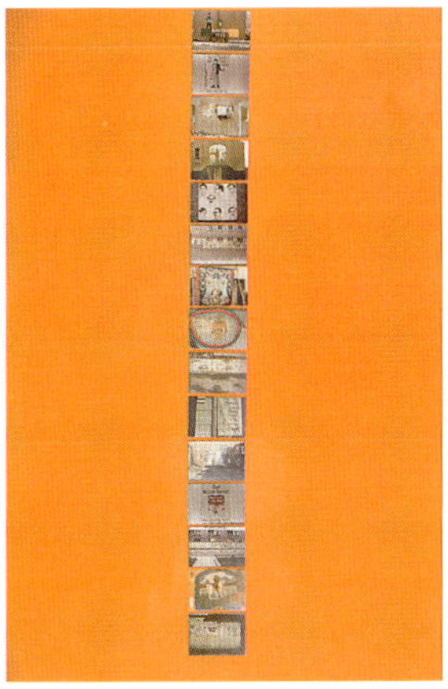

Atkinson, Conrad b.1940
Silver Liberties; A Souvenir of a Wonderful Anniversary Year (3 of 4) 1977
acrylic & mixed media on canvas 213 x 137
OP924iii

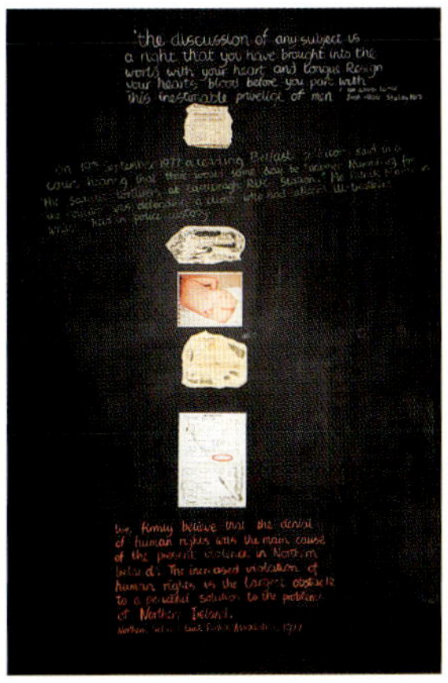

Atkinson, Conrad b.1940
Silver Liberties; A Souvenir of a Wonderful Anniversary Year (4 of 4) 1977
acrylic & mixed media on canvas 213 x 137
OP924iv

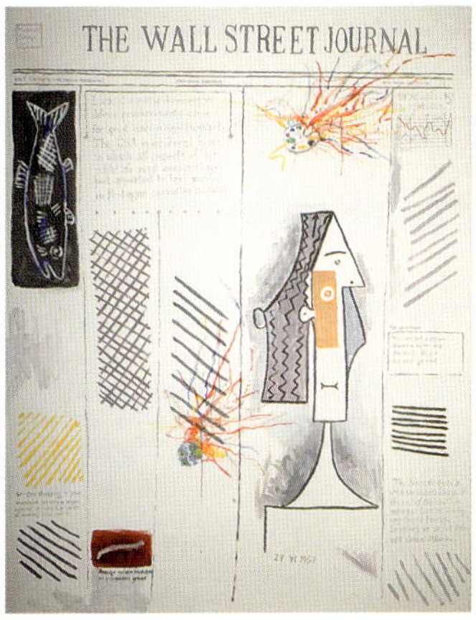

Atkinson, Conrad b.1940
Wall Street Journal 1986
oil on canvas 173 x 133
OP816

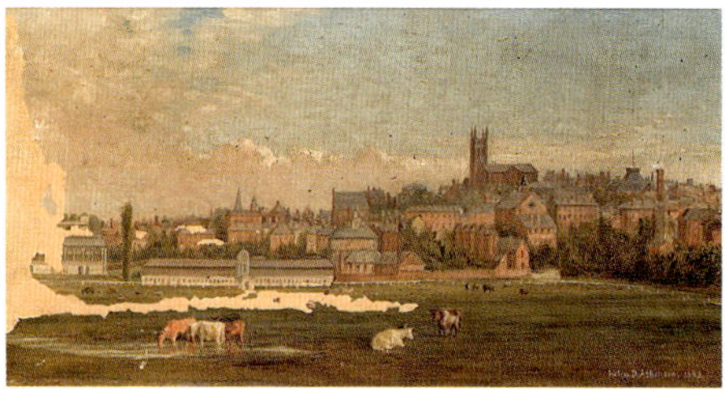

Atkinson, Helen D. active 1882–1884
Wolverhampton Racecourse 1882
oil on canvas 23 x 44
OP603

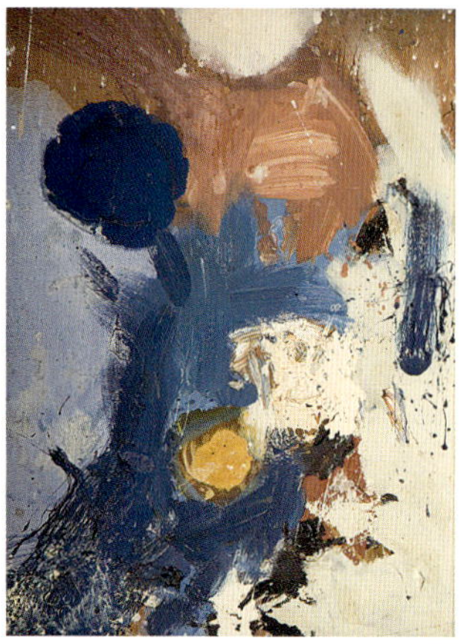

Ayres, Gillian b.1930
*Abstract**
oil on board 89 x 65
OP842

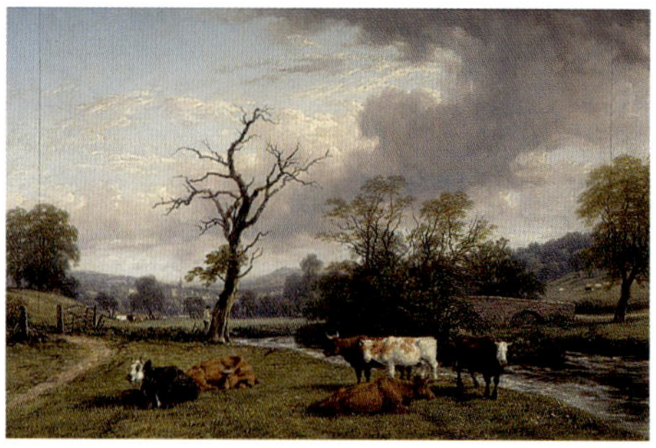

Baker, Thomas 1809–1869
Landscape and Cattle near Offchurch, Warwickshire 1848
oil on panel 26.5 x 31
OP55

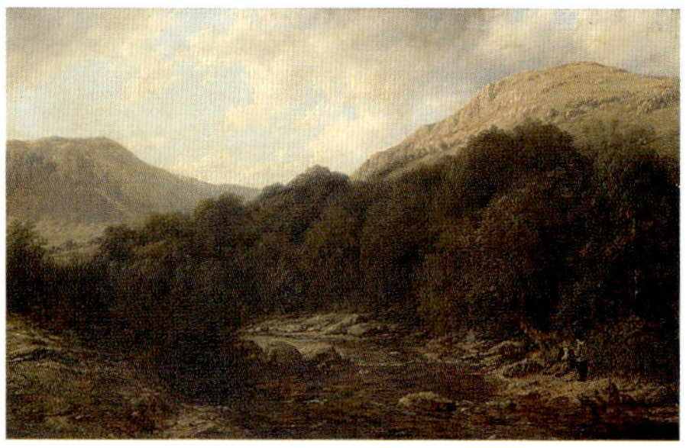

Baker, Thomas 1809–1869
River Scene
oil on canvas 50 x 77
OP821

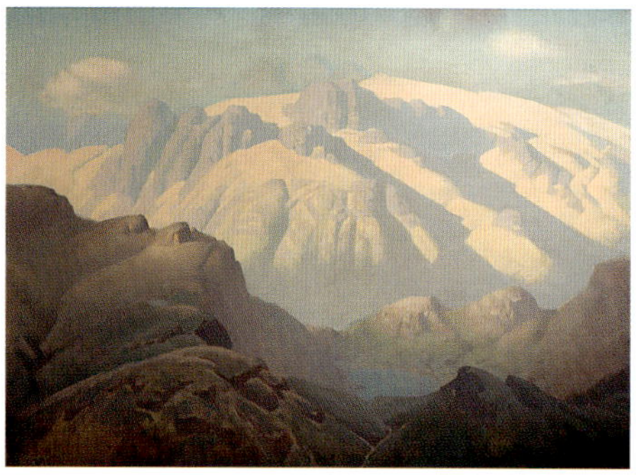

Banner, Delmar Harmond 1896–1983
September White Grass 1944–1945
oil on canvas 63.5 x 86.5
OP319

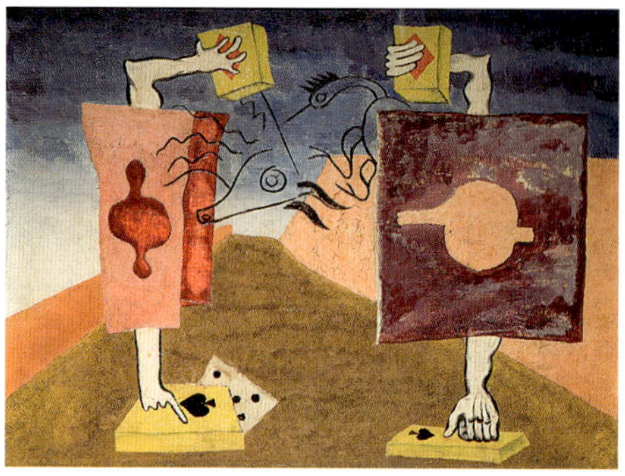

Banting, John 1902–1972
Card Players 1937
oil on board 43 x 57
OP798

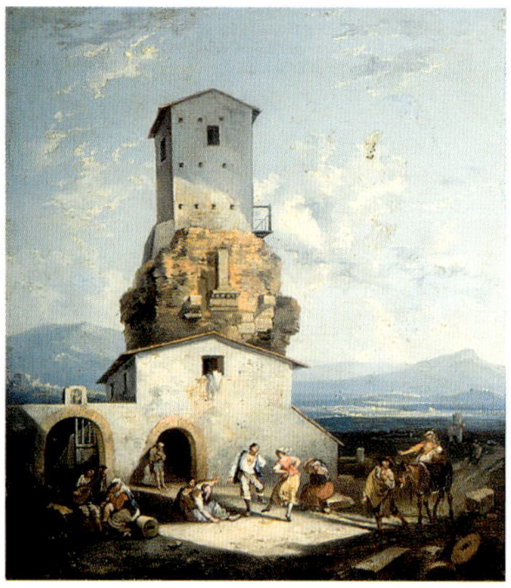

Barker, Thomas 1769–1847
Italian Landscape 1808
oil on canvas 36 x 32
OP200

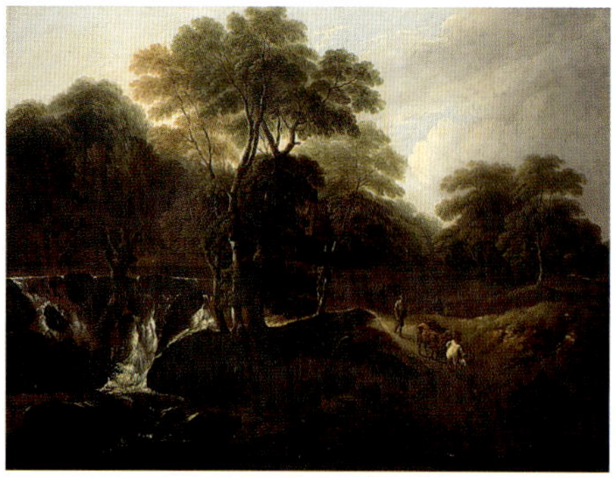

Barker, Thomas 1769–1847
Landscape with a Waterfall
oil on canvas 101.5 x 127
OP235

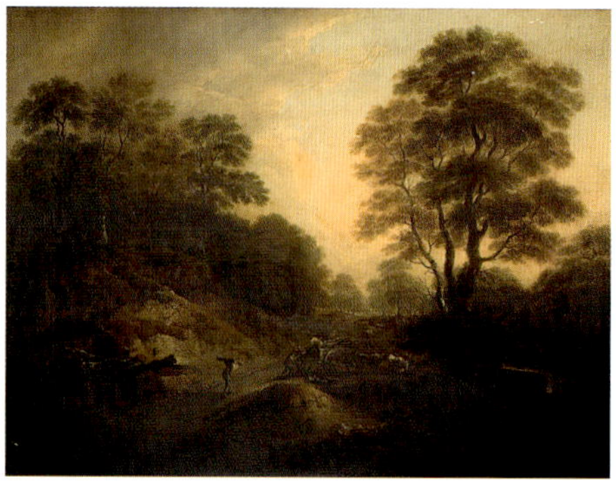

Barker, Thomas 1769–1847
Landscape with Cattle
oil on canvas 77.5 x 128.5
OP328

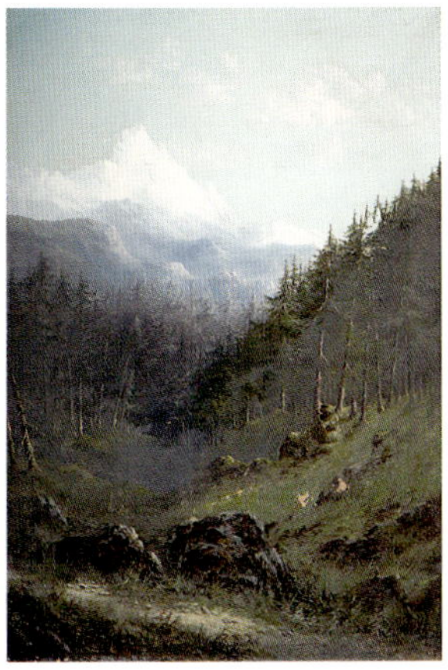

Barnes, Samuel John 1847–1901
In the Valley of the Rhône 1884–1886
oil on canvas 87.5 x 60 (E)
OP463

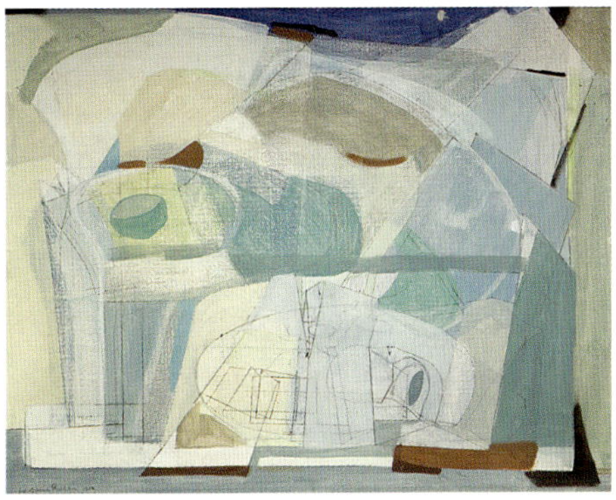

Barns-Graham, Wilhelmina 1912–2004
Glacier (Red and Blue) 1950
oil on canvas 62 x 75
OP841

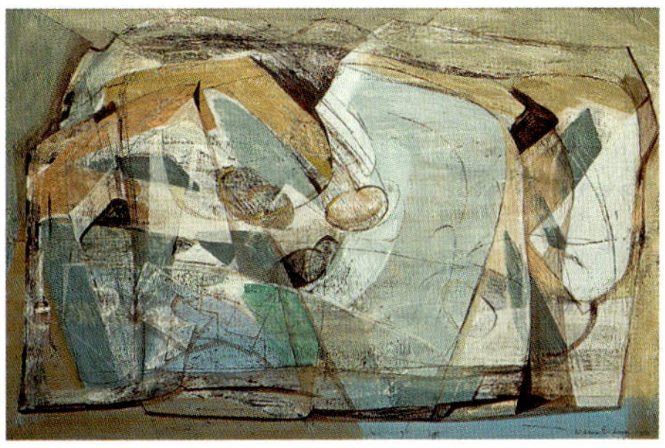

Barns-Graham, Wilhelmina 1912–2004
Glacier, Rock Forms 1950
oil on canvas 51 x 76
OP840

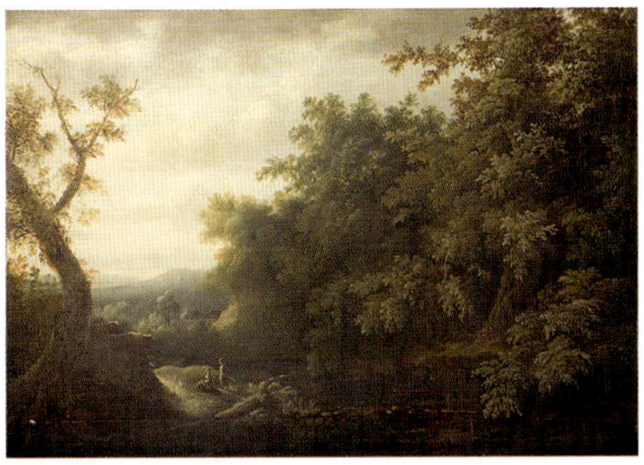

Barret, George (circle of) 1728/1732–1784
Landscape with Two Figures
oil on canvas 85 x 114.5
OP94

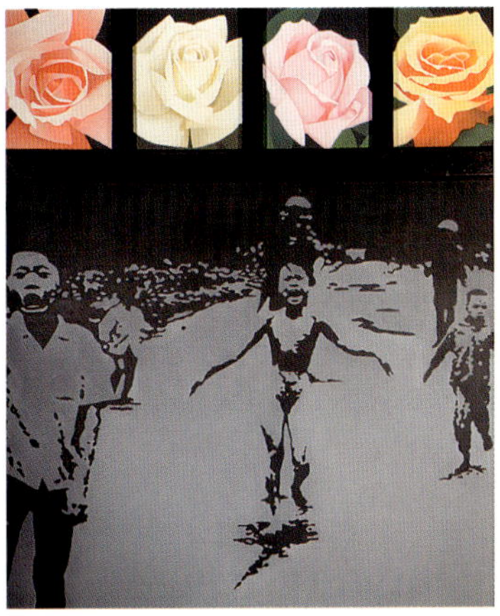

Barron, Bob b.1945
Suburban Summer Evenings 1984
acrylic on canvas 129 x 107
OP804

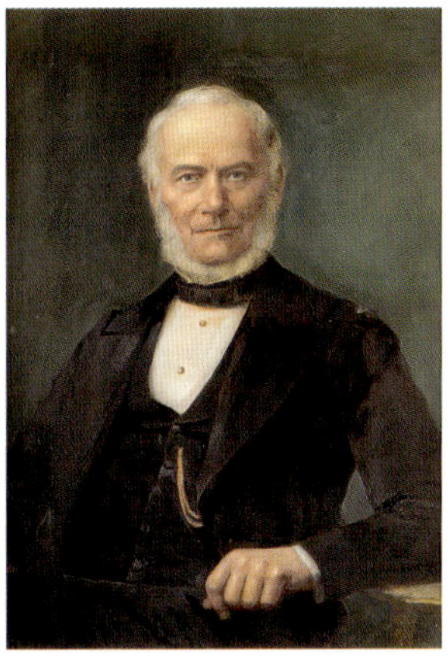

Bassett, William active 1850–1890
Richard Eldridge of the Bilston Township Committee
oil on canvas 66 x 47
OP623

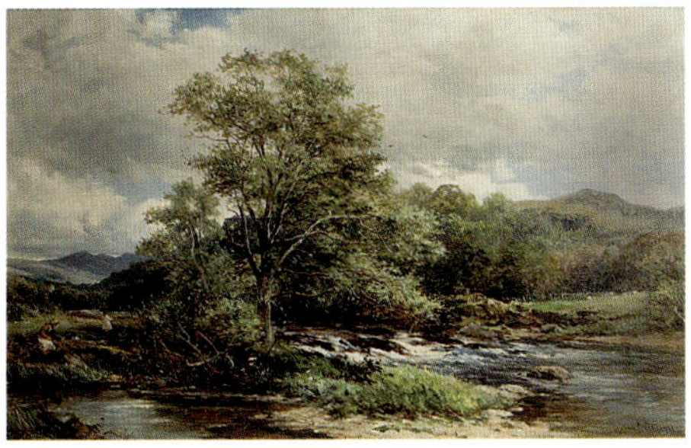

Bates, David c.1840–1921
The Banks of the Brathay, Ambleside, Westmoreland 1901
oil on canvas 61 x 91.5
OP111

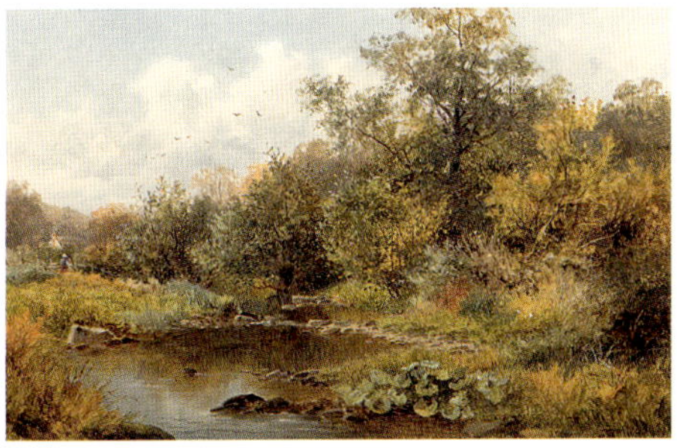

Bates, David c.1840–1921
Brook at Old Storridge, Worcestershire
oil on canvas 30 x 46.5
OP624

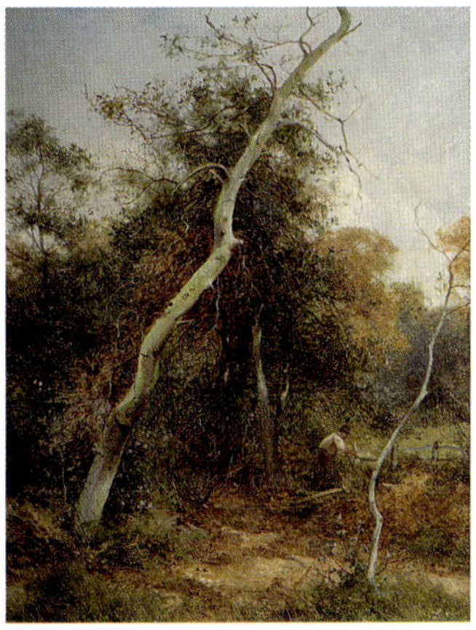

Bates, David c.1840–1921
Mending the Fence, Sutton Park
oil on canvas 46.5 x 36
OP627

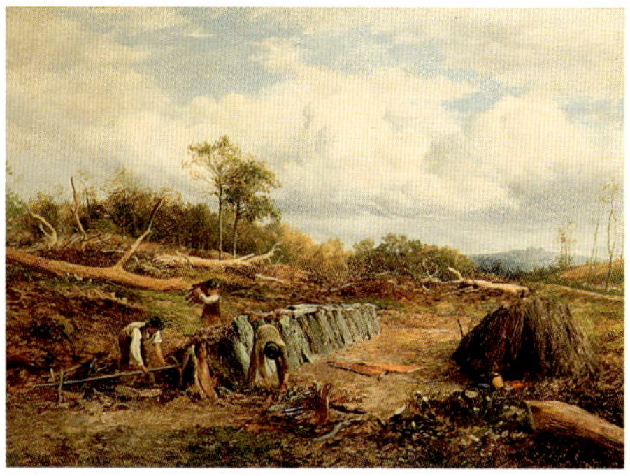

Bates, David c.1840–1921
Stacking the Oak Fence
oil on canvas 35.5 x 45.5
OP626

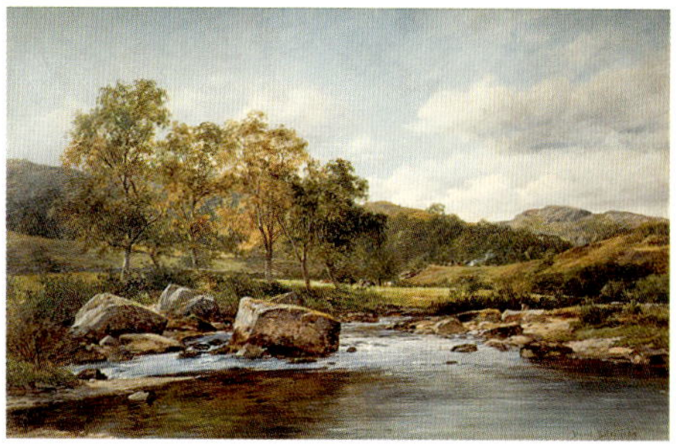

Bates, David c.1840–1921
Stepping Stones on the Llugwy
oil on canvas 61 x 92.5
OP625

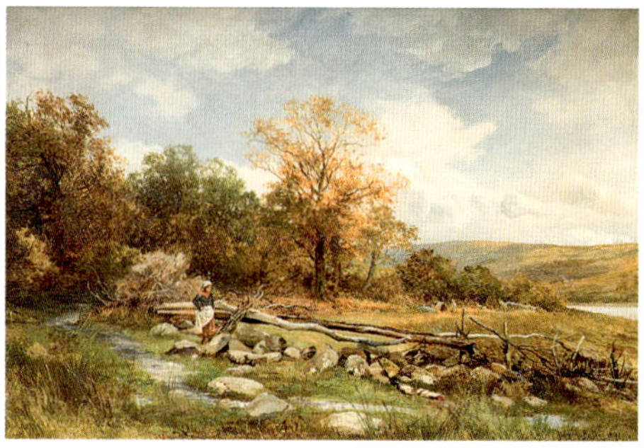

Bates, David c.1840–1921
Tidal Fence on the River Conway, Bachlediog
oil on canvas 61.5 x 75
OP628

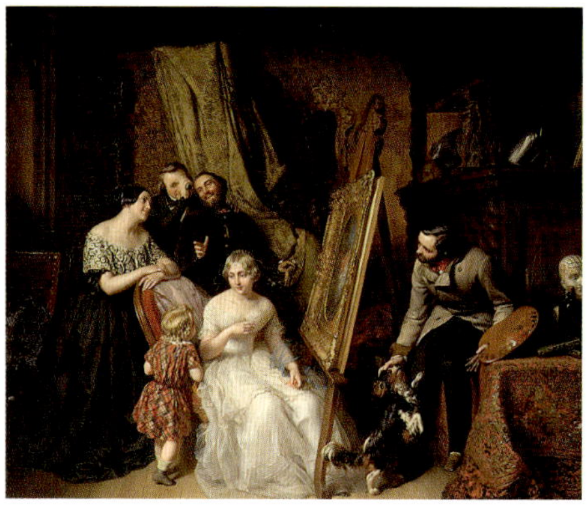

Baudin, Narcisse active 1850s–1880s
The Portrait
oil on panel 44.5 x 49.5
OP370

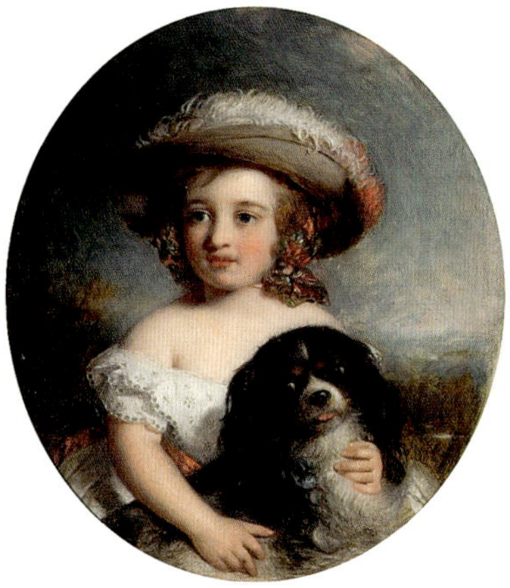

Baxter, Charles 1809–1878
'Love me, love my dog' 1853
oil on board 26 x 22
OP462

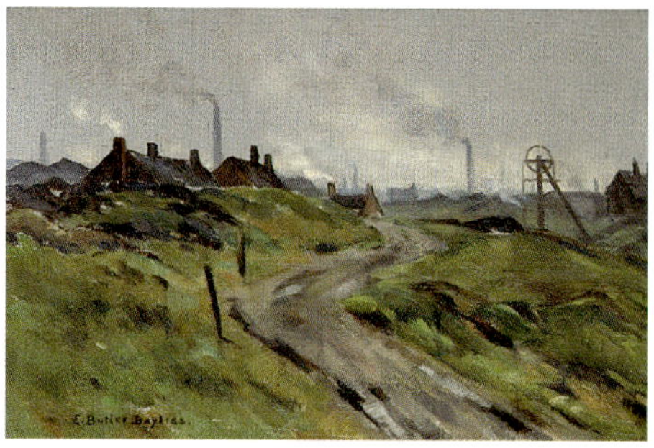

Bayliss, Edwin Butler 1874–1950
Black Country Landscape
oil on canvas 25.5 x 35
OP636

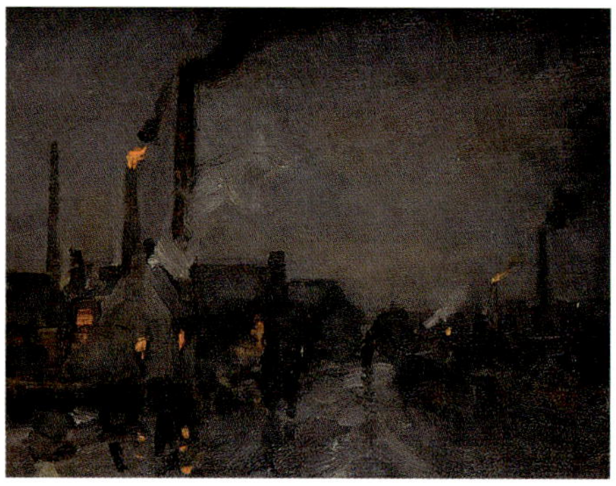

Bayliss, Edwin Butler 1874–1950
Black Country, Night, with Foundry
oil on canvas 35.5 x 46.5
OP631

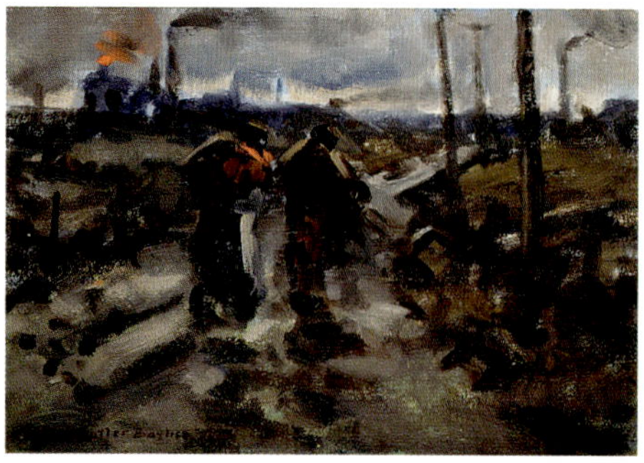

Bayliss, Edwin Butler 1874–1950
Black Country Scene
oil on board 25.5 x 36
OP631a

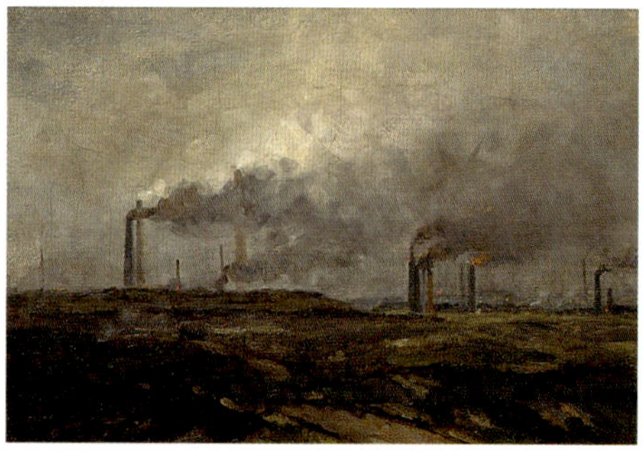

Bayliss, Edwin Butler 1874–1950
Black Country Skyline
oil on canvas 40.5 x 56.6
OP637

Facing page: Hill, Paul, b. 1959, *Whacky Backy* (detail), 2003, Staffordshire Arts and Museums Service (p.77)

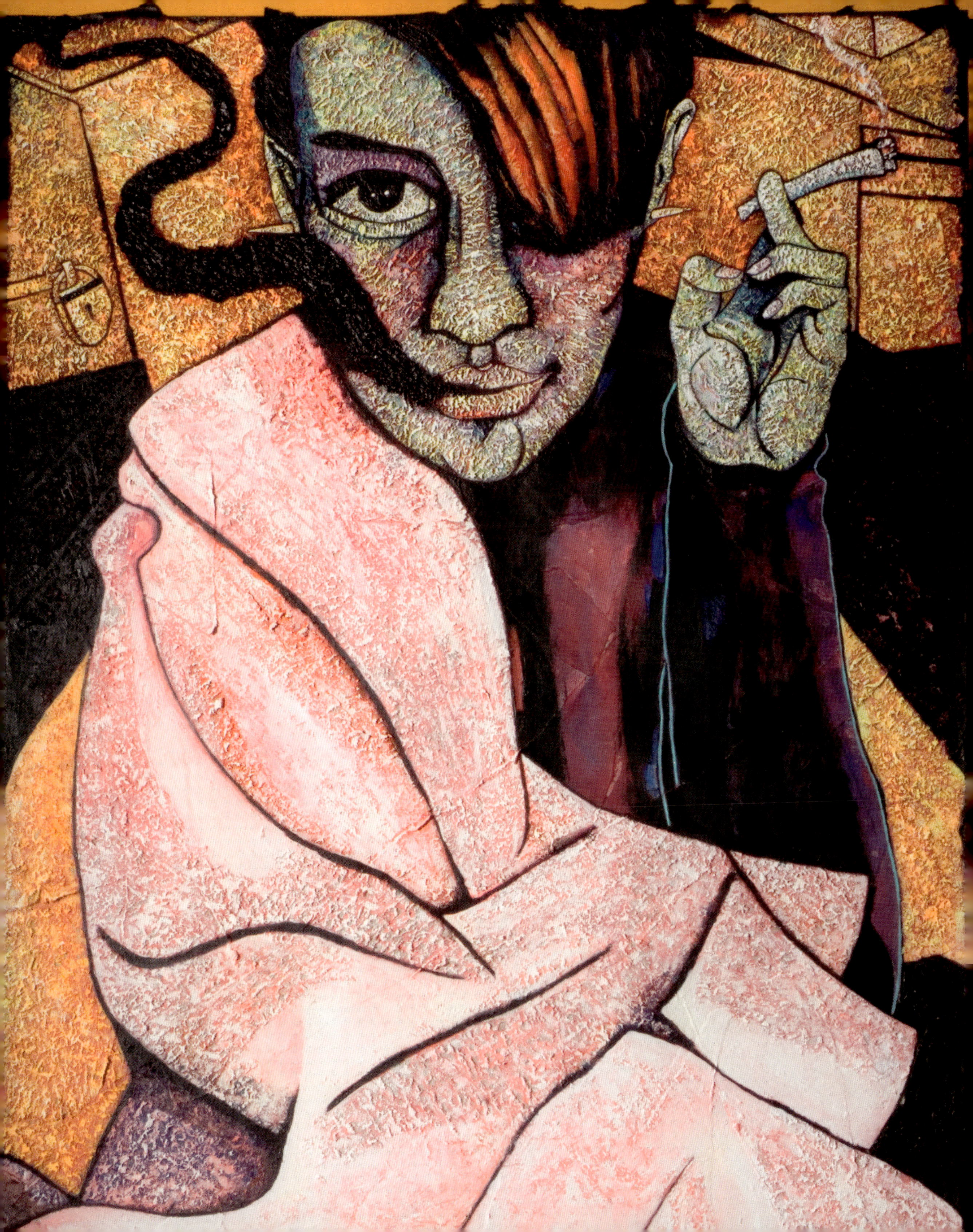

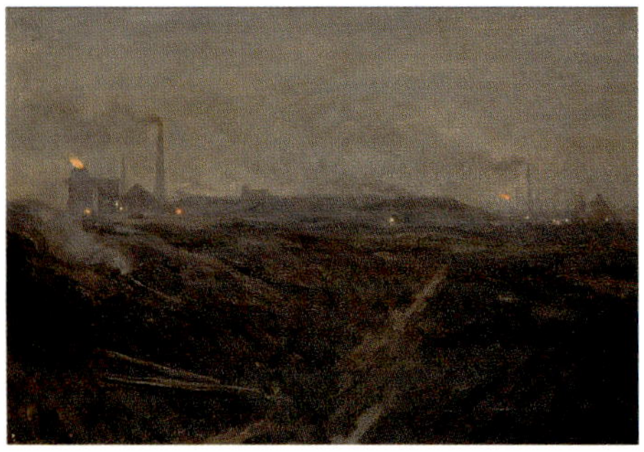

Bayliss, Edwin Butler 1874–1950
Blast Furnaces, Night
oil on canvas 39.5 x 54.5
OP629

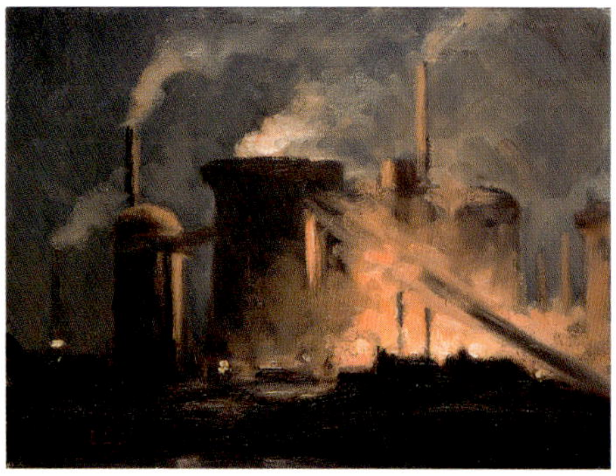

Bayliss, Edwin Butler 1874–1950
Blast Furnaces, Night
oil on board 21 x 27
OP629a

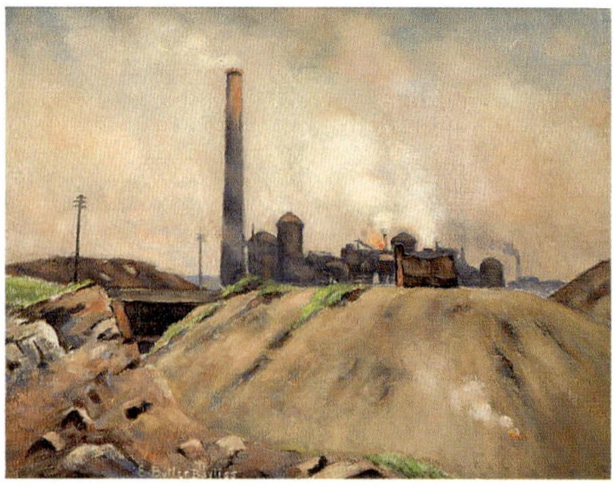

Bayliss, Edwin Butler 1874–1950
Capenfield Furnaces
oil on canvas 40 x 50
OP638

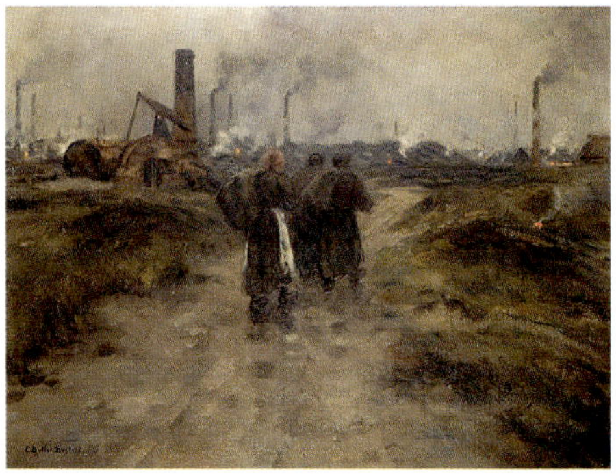

Bayliss, Edwin Butler 1874–1950
Evening in the Black Country
oil on canvas 71 x 92
OP630

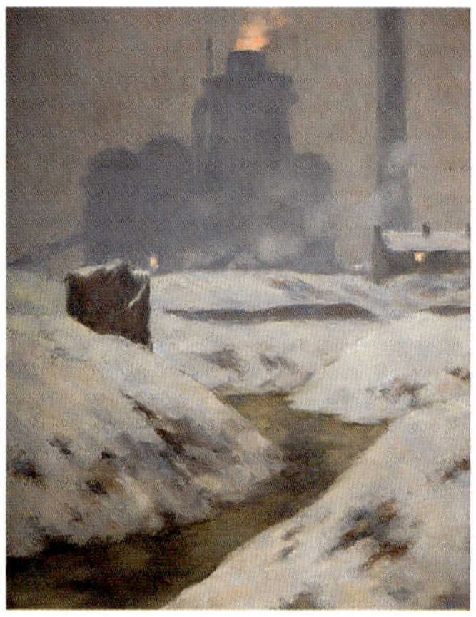

Bayliss, Edwin Butler 1874–1950
Furnace and Snow, Landscape
oil on canvas 54 x 43
OP634

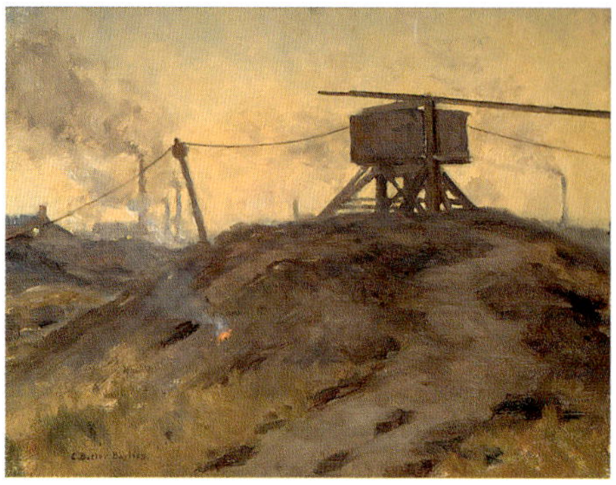

Bayliss, Edwin Butler 1874–1950
Gin Pit
oil on canvas 35 x 40
OP639

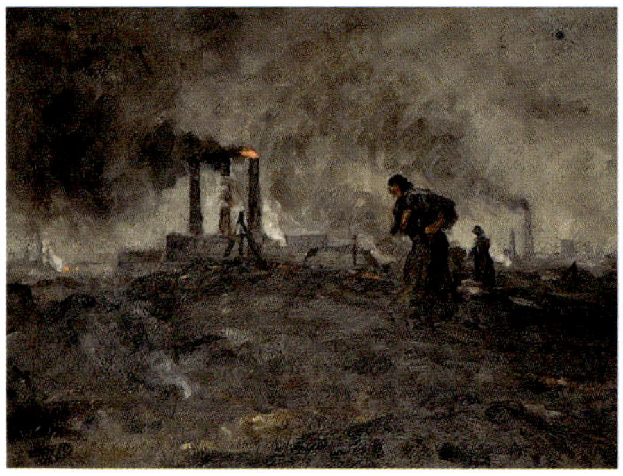

Bayliss, Edwin Butler 1874–1950
In the Black Country
oil on canvas 51 x 66
OP267

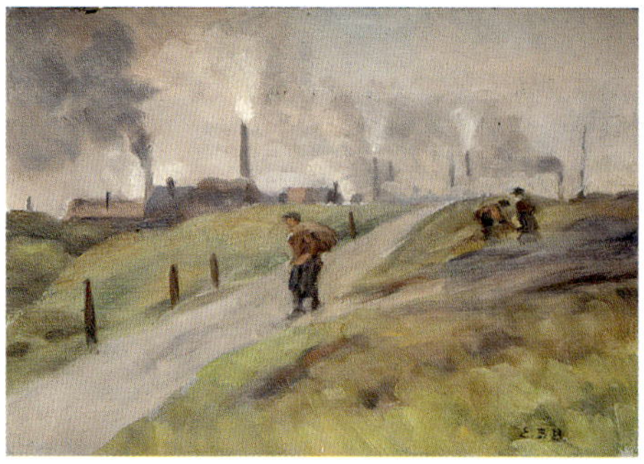

Bayliss, Edwin Butler 1874–1950
In the Black Country
oil on board 25.5 x 35.5
OP746

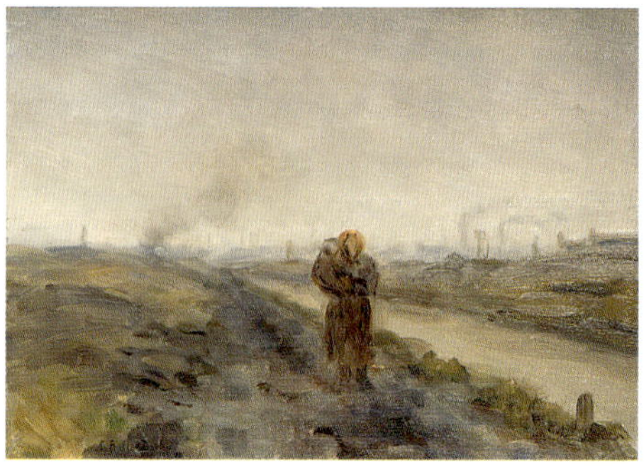

Bayliss, Edwin Butler 1874–1950
Mother and Child, Black Country Landscape
oil on canvas 25 x 34.5
OP635

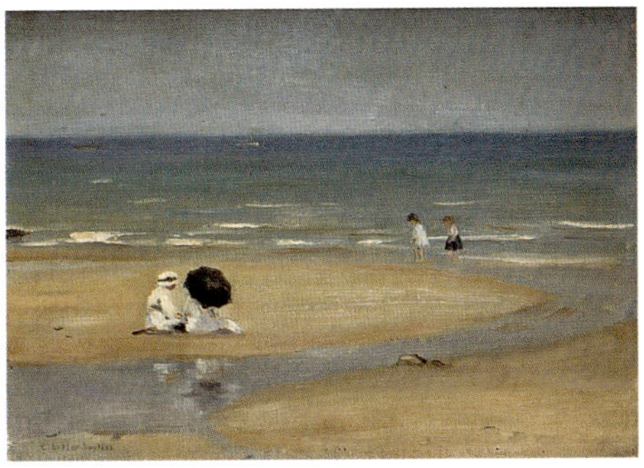

Bayliss, Edwin Butler 1874–1950
On the Beach
oil on board 25.5 x 35.5
OP748

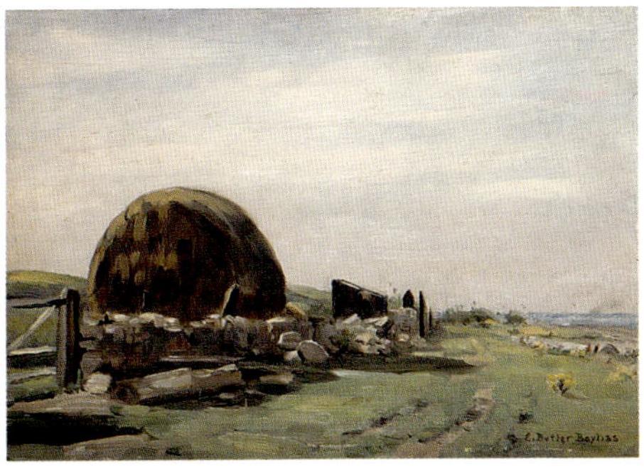

Bayliss, Edwin Butler 1874–1950
On the Shore
oil on board 25.5 x 35.5
OP745

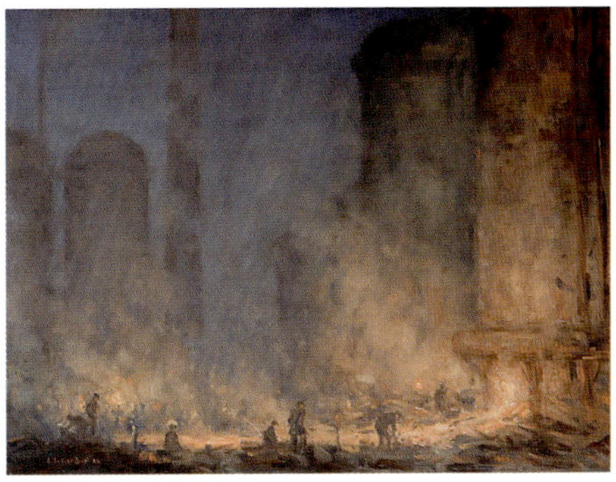

Bayliss, Edwin Butler 1874–1950
Pig Beds Tapping a Furnace
oil on canvas 40 x 54
OP632a

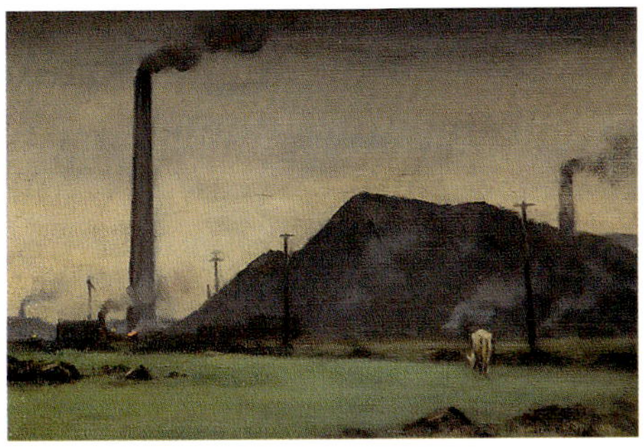

Bayliss, Edwin Butler 1874–1950
Spring Vale Furnaces
oil on canvas 39.5 x 54.5
OP632

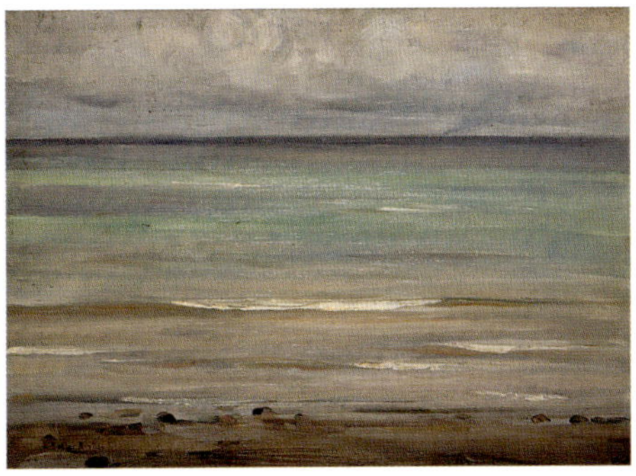

Bayliss, Edwin Butler 1874–1950
The Sea
oil on board 25.5 x 35.5
OP747

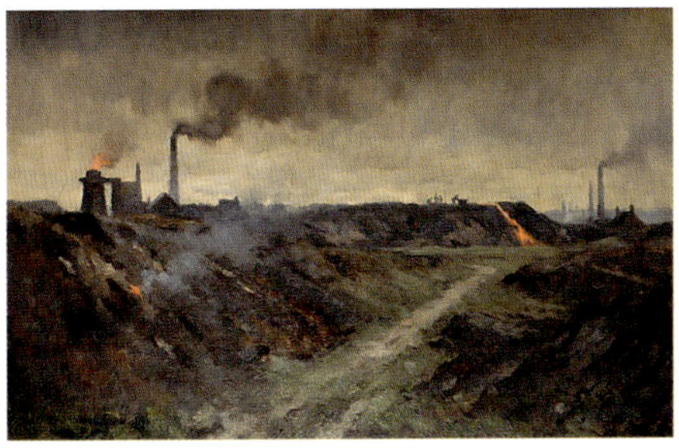

Bayliss, Edwin Butler 1874–1950
Tipping the Slag
oil on canvas 61 x 92
OP633

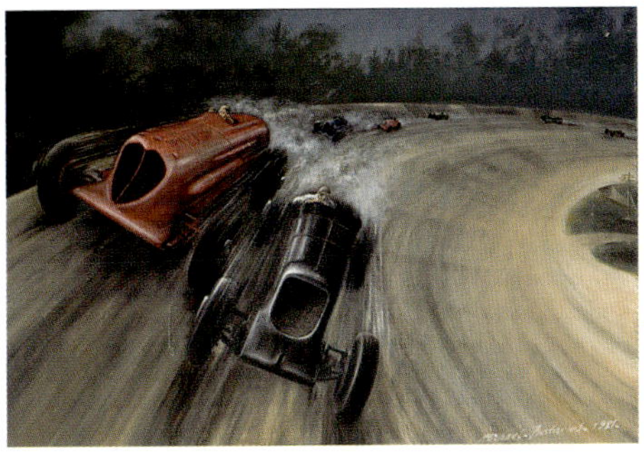

Beddows, Michael 1931–2005
The Golden Age of Brooklands' Monsters 1981
oil on canvas 39.5 x 55
OP896

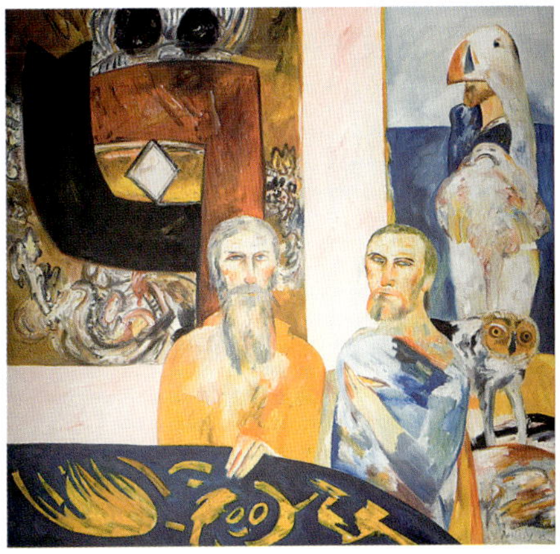

Bellany, John b.1942
Self Portrait with Alan Davie 1985
oil on canvas 172.5 x 172.5
OP801

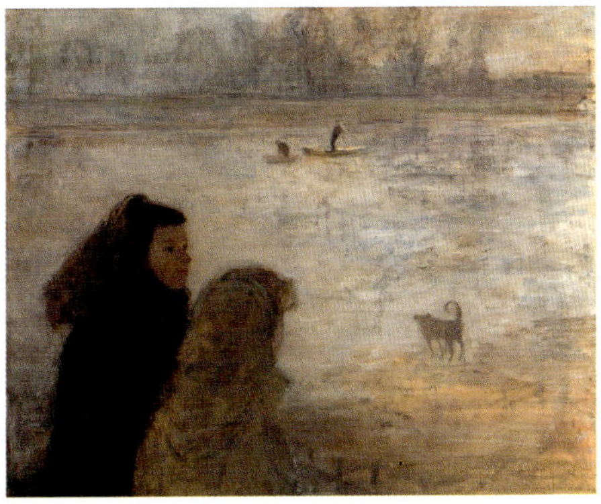

Bellingham-Smith, Elinor 1906–1988
Low Tide, Putney
oil on canvas 63.5 x 76
OP22

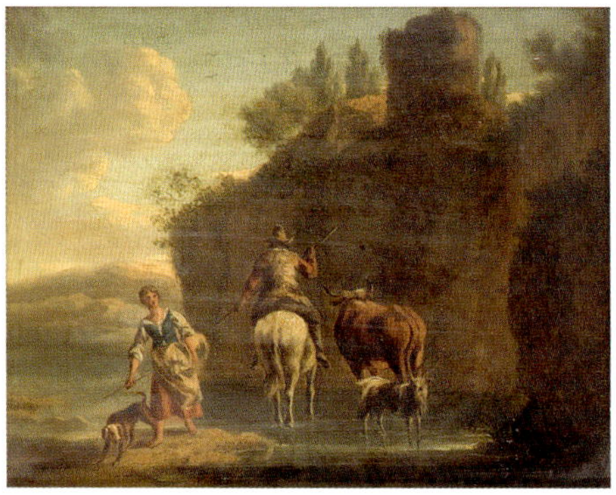

Berchem, Nicolaes (attributed to) 1620–1683
Landscape with Figures and Cattle
oil on canvas 25.5 x 30.5
OP31

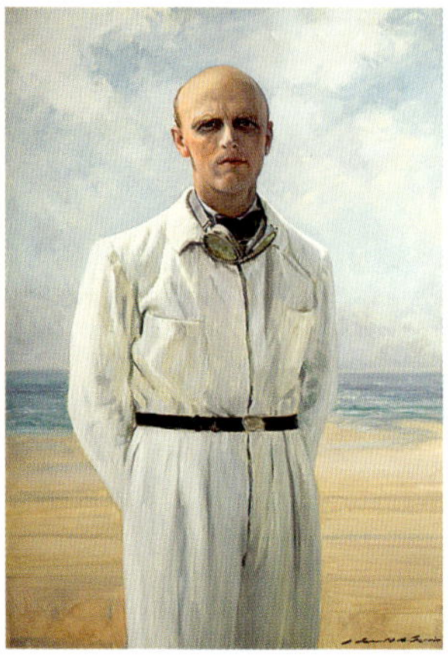

Berrie, John Archibald Alexander 1887–1962
Sir Henry Seagrave (1896–1930)
oil on canvas 127 x 86.5
OP511

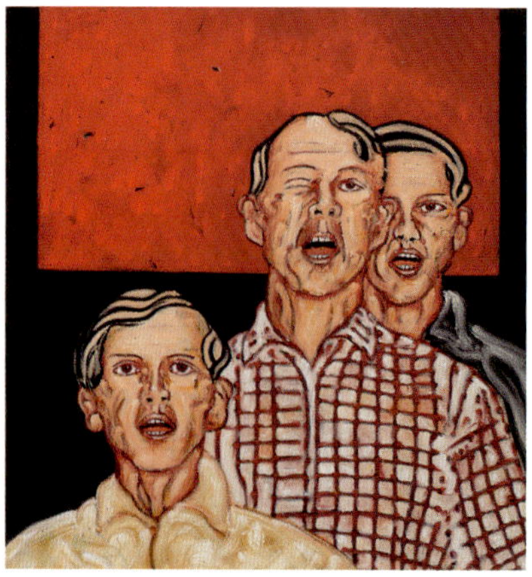

Bevan, Tony b.1951
The Meeting 1992
acrylic on canvas 90 x 81
OP868

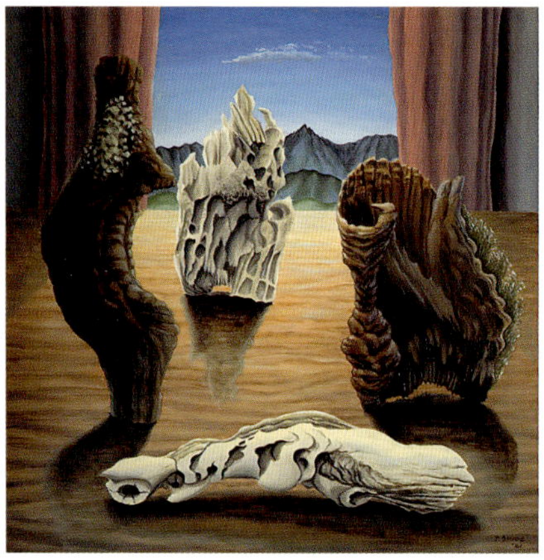

Bigge, John Selby 1892–1978
Wood Forms 1941
oil on board 51 x 49
OP794

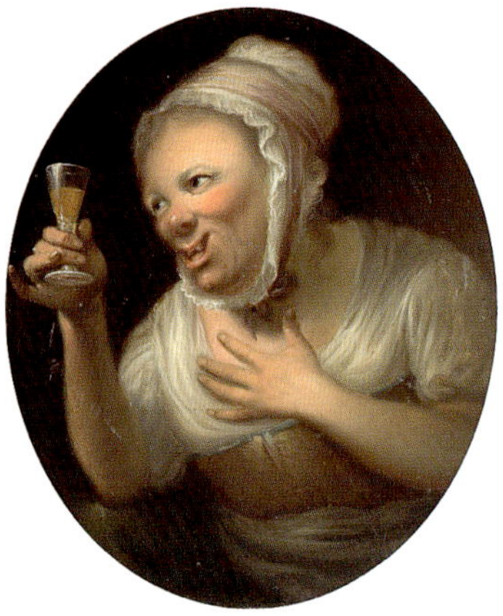

Bird, Edward 1772–1819
Intemperance 1795
oil on panel 15 x 12.5
OP915

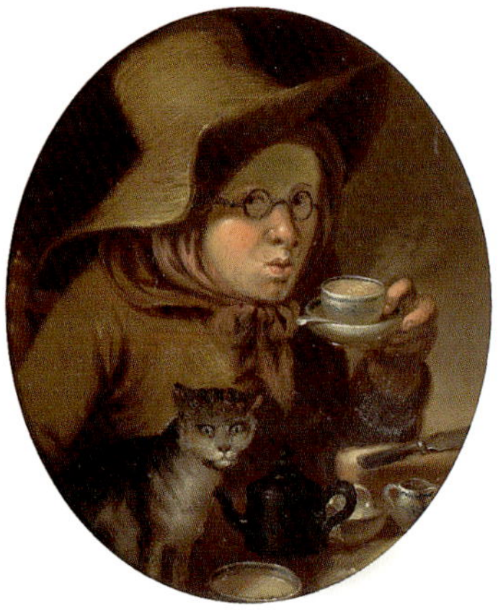

Bird, Edward 1772–1819
Teatotalism 1795
oil on panel 15 x 12.5
OP915

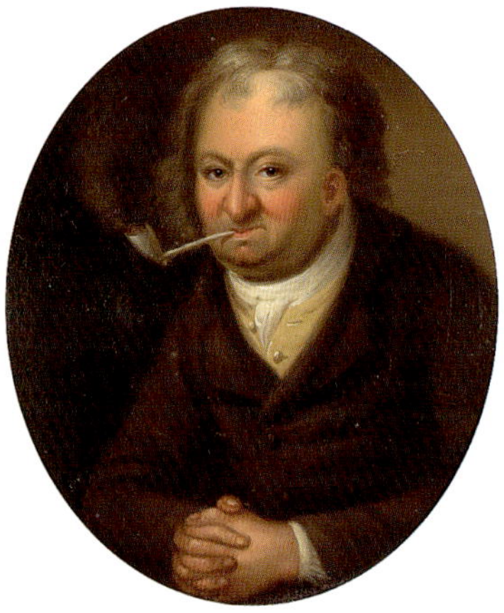

Bird, Edward 1772–1819
Temperance 1795
oil on panel 15 x 12.5
OP915

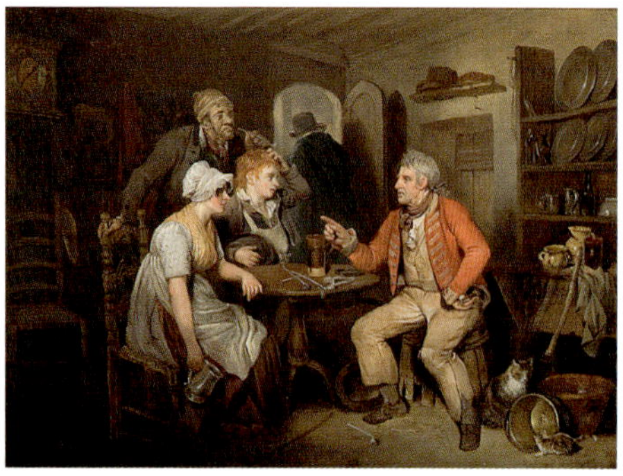

Bird, Edward 1772–1819
The Old Soldier's Story 1808
oil on canvas 163.5 x 206.5
OP926

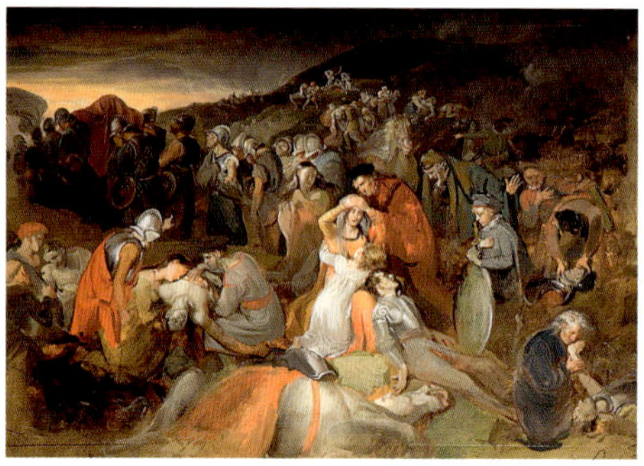

Bird, Edward 1772–1819
Study for 'The Day after the Battle of Chevy Chase' 1810–1812
oil on panel 67.5 x 94.5
OP85

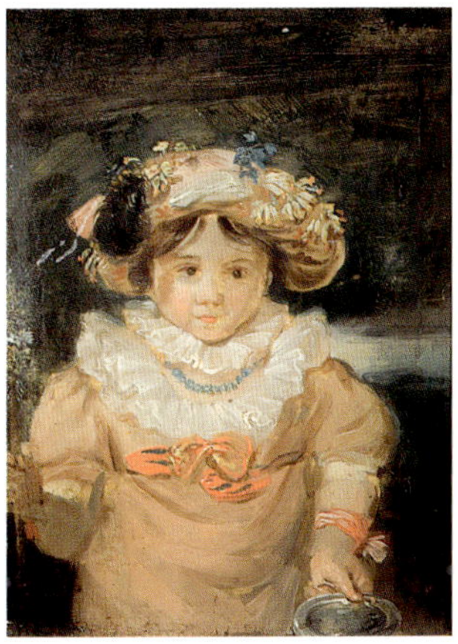

Bird, Edward 1772–1819
A Child with an Elaborate Headdress
oil on canvas 17 x 12
OP375

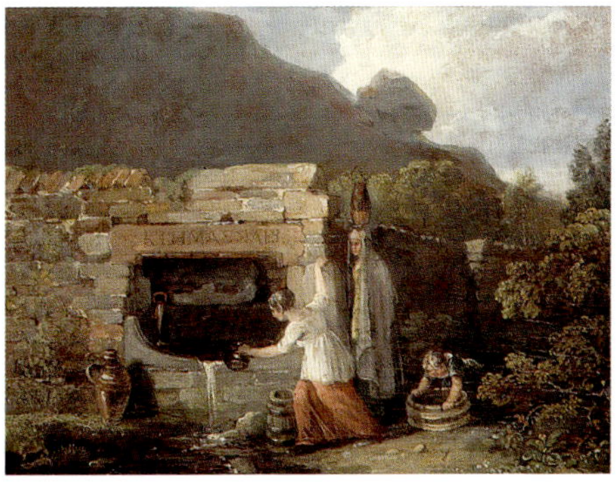

Bird, Edward 1772–1819
At the Well
oil on canvas 19 x 24
OP507

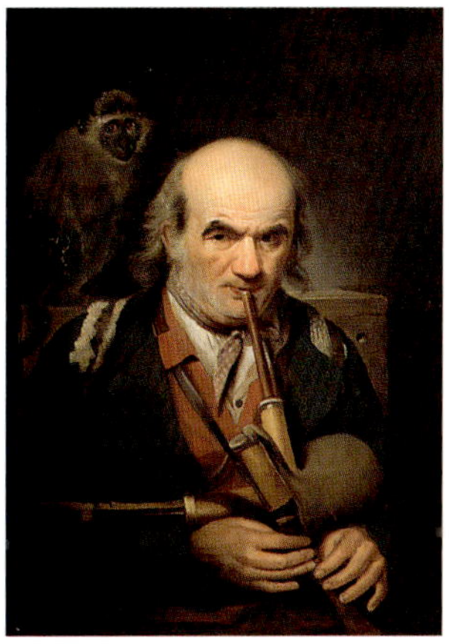

Bird, Edward 1772–1819
Italian Dancing-Dog Master
oil on canvas 91.5 x 63.5
OP766

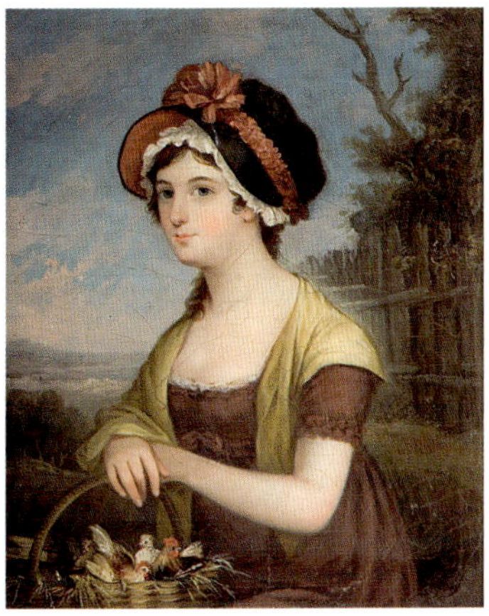

Bird, Edward 1772–1819
Ready for Market
oil on canvas 37 x 29
OP83

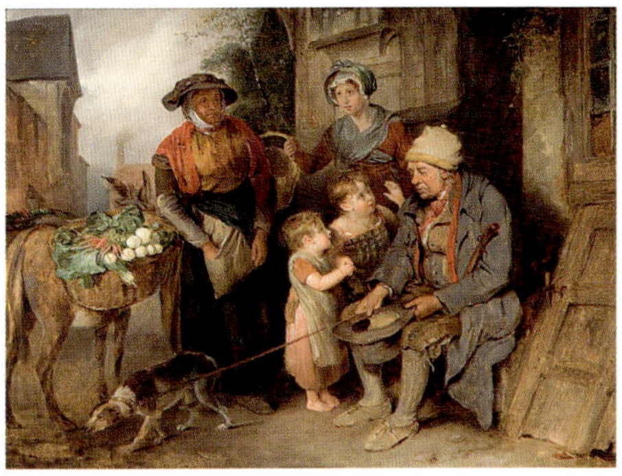

Bird, Edward 1772–1819
Setting off for Market
oil on board 79 x 97
OP927

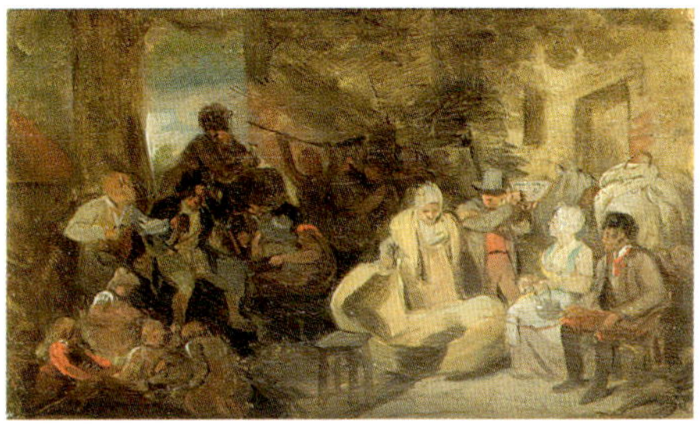

Bird, Edward 1772–1819
Study for 'The Country Auction'
oil on panel 7 x 11
OP504

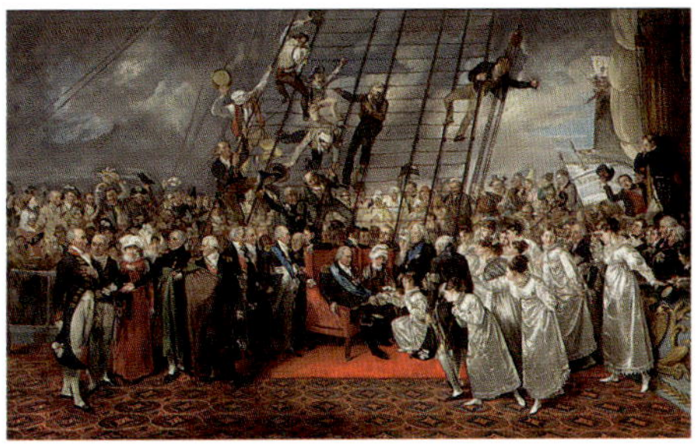

Bird, Edward 1772–1819
The Arrival of King Louis XVIII of France at Calais
oil on panel 110 x 174
OP121

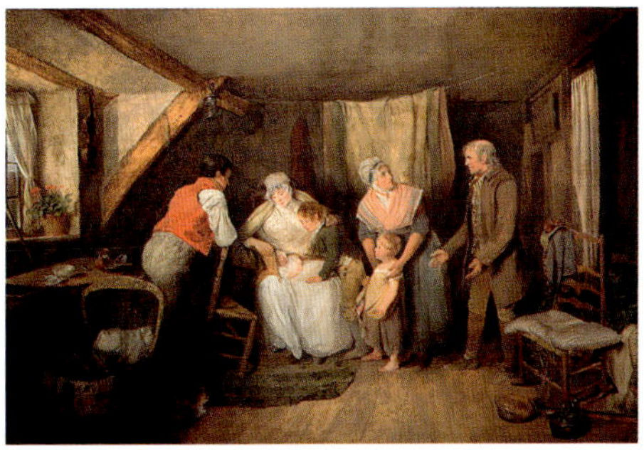

Bird, Edward 1772–1819
The Birth
oil on canvas 47.5 x 66
OP514

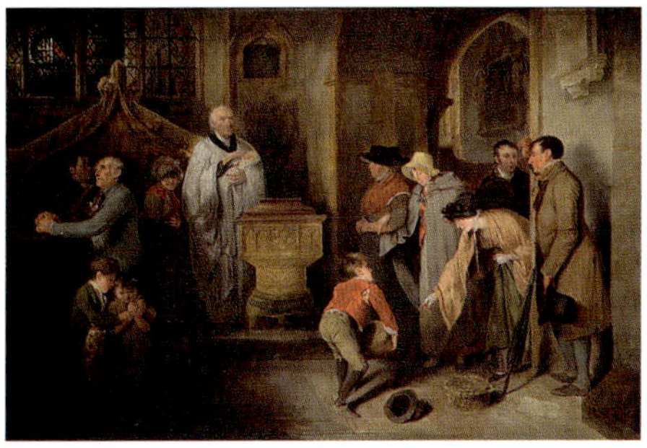

Bird, Edward 1772–1819
The Christening
oil on panel 47 x 65.5
OP81

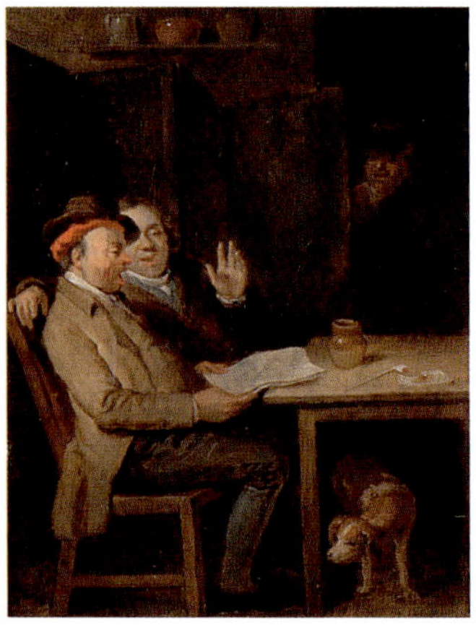

Bird, Edward 1772–1819
The Duet
oil on panel 22 x 17
OP149

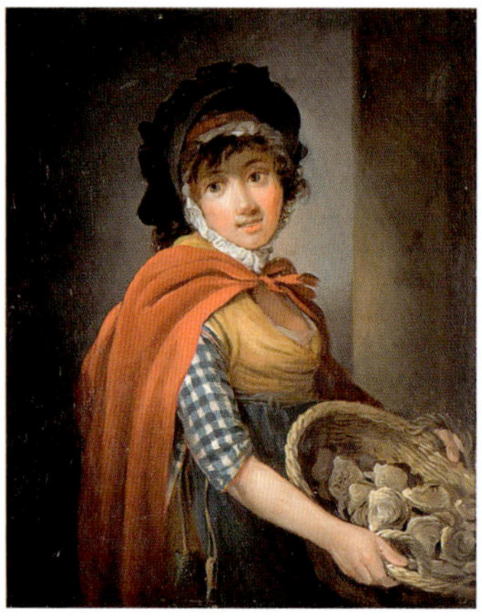

Bird, Edward 1772–1819
The Oyster Girl
oil on canvas 23.5 x 19.5
OP489

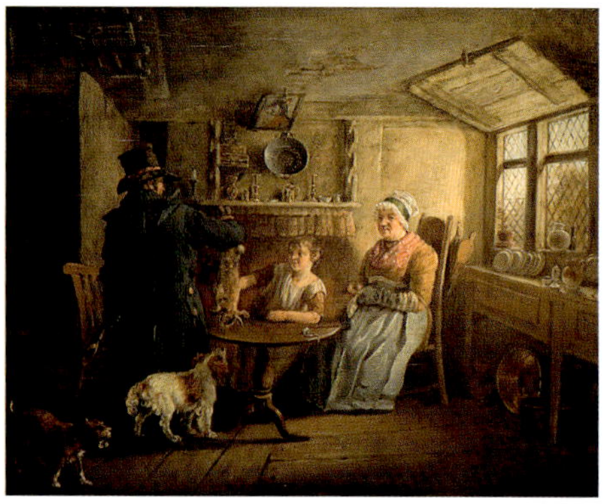

Bird, Edward 1772–1819
The Poacher's Return
oil on panel 37 x 43.5
OP237

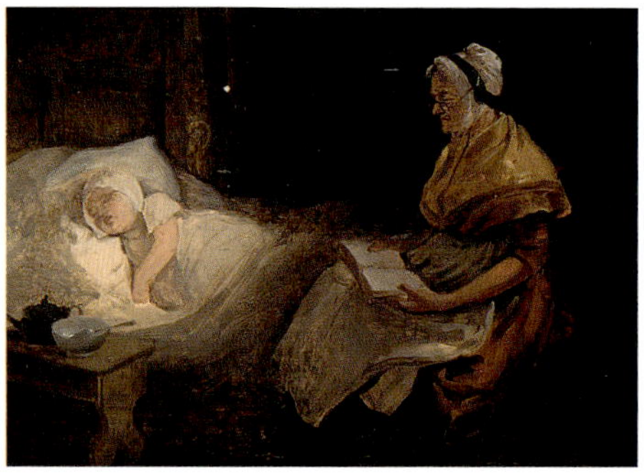

Bird, Edward 1772–1819
The Sick Child
oil on canvas 16.5 x 21.5
OP488

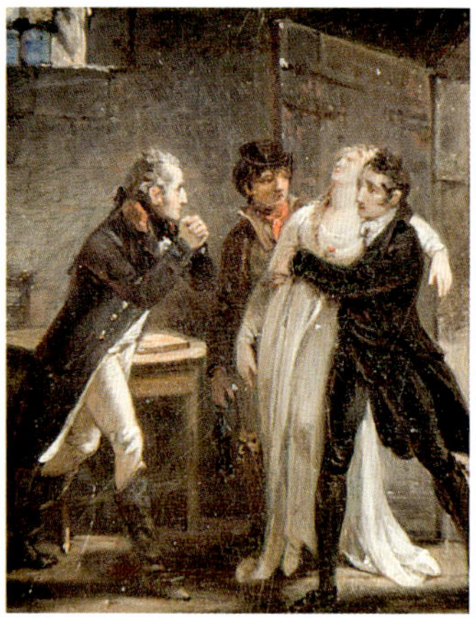

Bird, Edward 1772–1819
The Way to Get Married
oil on panel 16 x 14.5
OP606

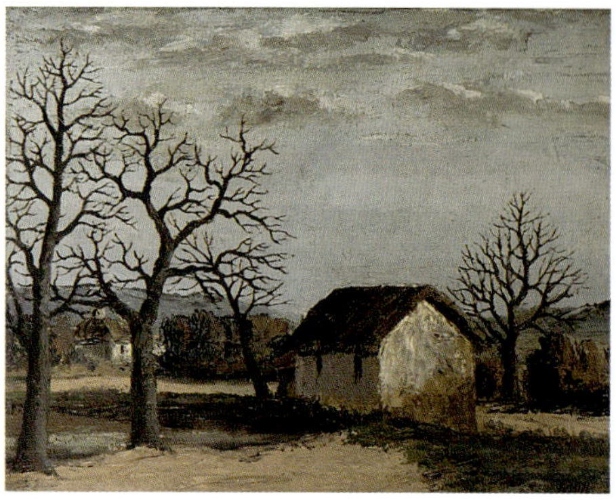

Bissill, George William 1896–1973
Shelbourne, Essex
oil on canvas 40.5 x 47
OP640

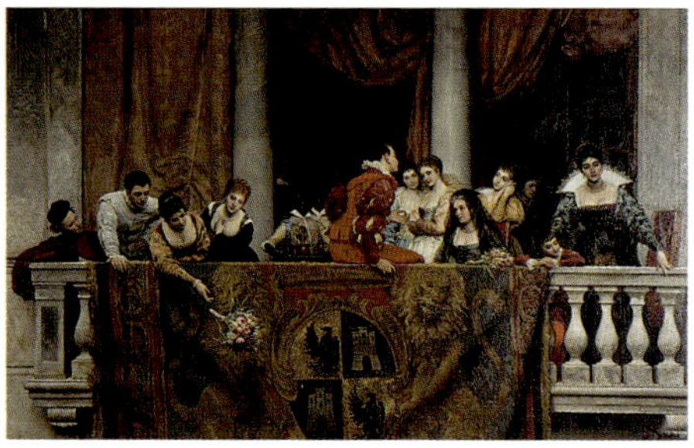

Blaas, Eugen von 1843–1931
At the Carnival 1870–1879
oil on canvas 155 x 236
OP140

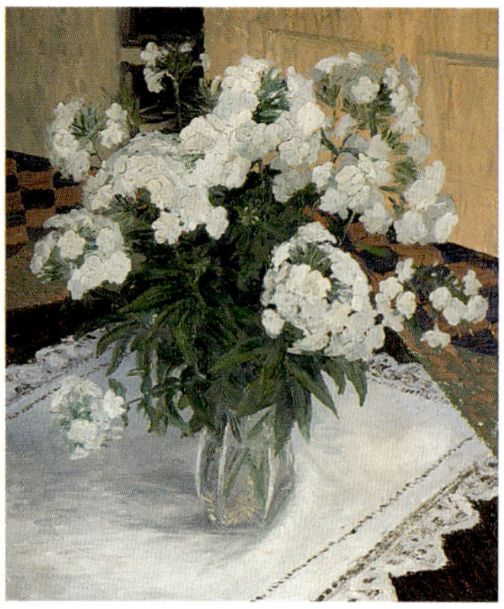

Bladen, Alfred active c.1925–1965
White Phlox on White Cloth
oil on canvas 61 x 51
OP291

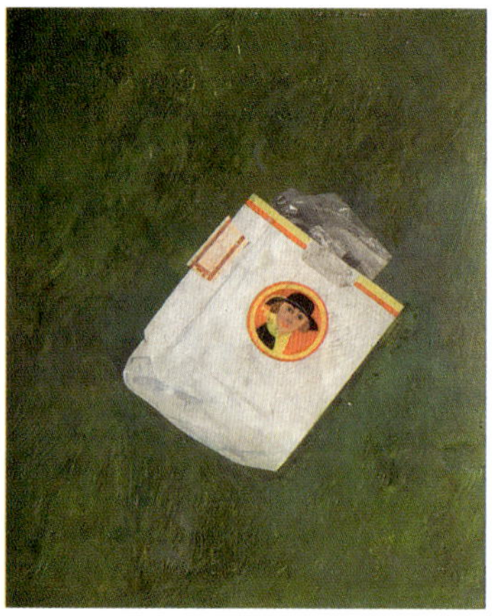

Blake, Peter b.1932
Cigarette Pack 1959–1960
oil on board 18.5 x 16
OP755

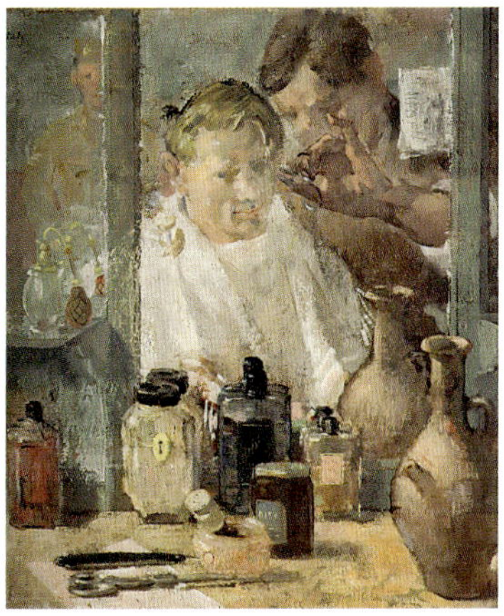

Blamey, Norman Charles 1914–1999
Camp Barber 1930–1947
oil on canvas 61 x 51
OP315

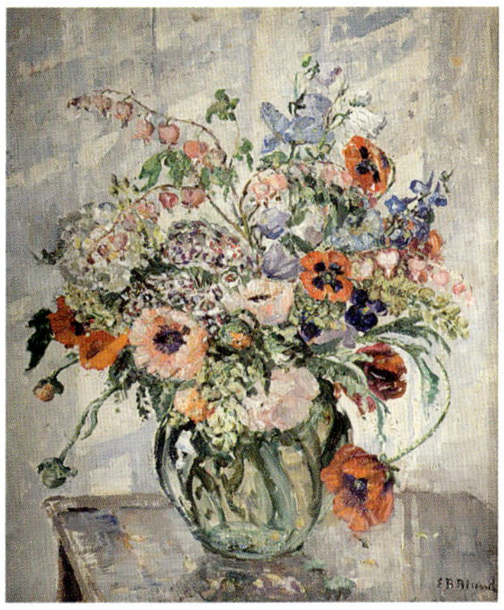

Bland, Emily Beatrice 1864–1951
Flower Piece
oil on canvas 61 x 50.5
OP269

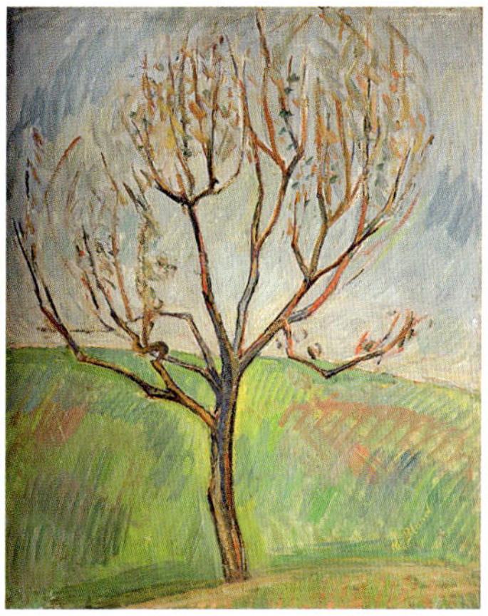

Blond, Maurice 1899–1974
A Tree
oil on board 91.5 x 71
OP321

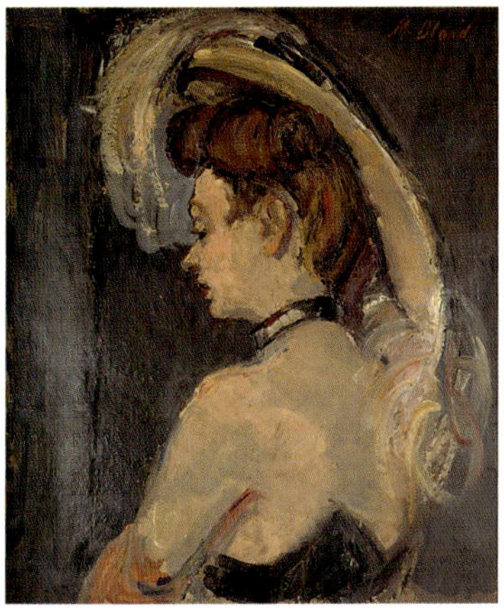

Blond, Maurice 1899–1974
Woman in a Hat
oil on canvas 51 x 40.5
OP312

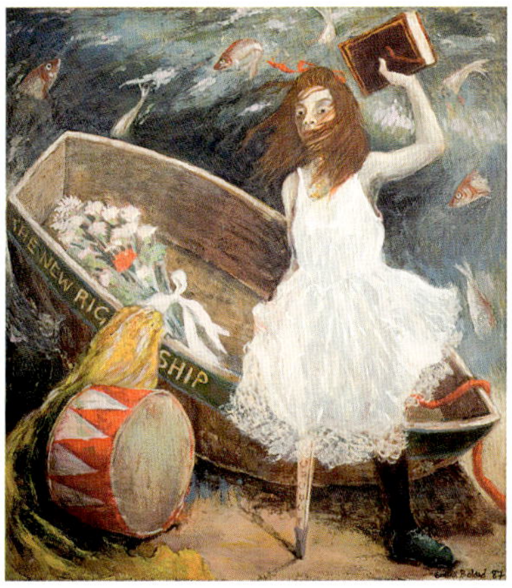

Bolland, Emma b.1962
A Declaration 1980–1988
oil on canvas 154.6 x 134
OP806

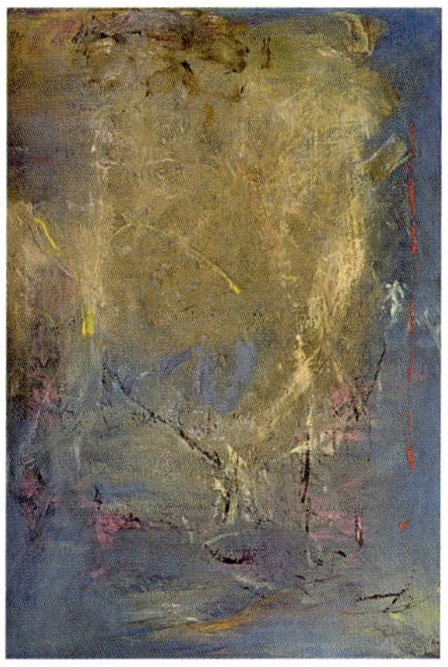

Bolton, Sylbert b.1959
Untitled 1980–1988
oil on canvas 135 x 69.5
OP812

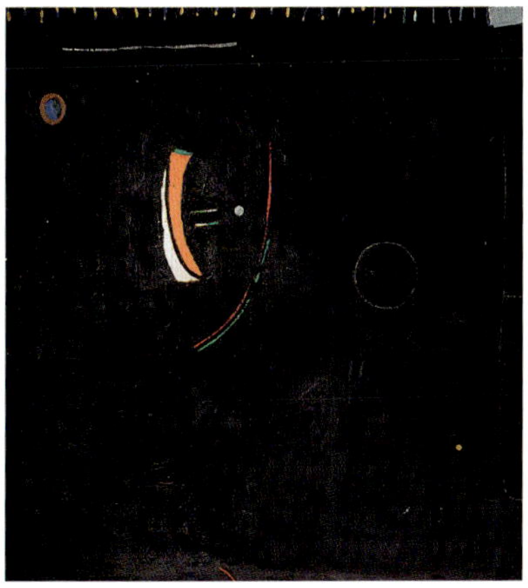

Bolton, Sylbert b.1959
Dark Dream
oil on canvas 122 x 122
OP764

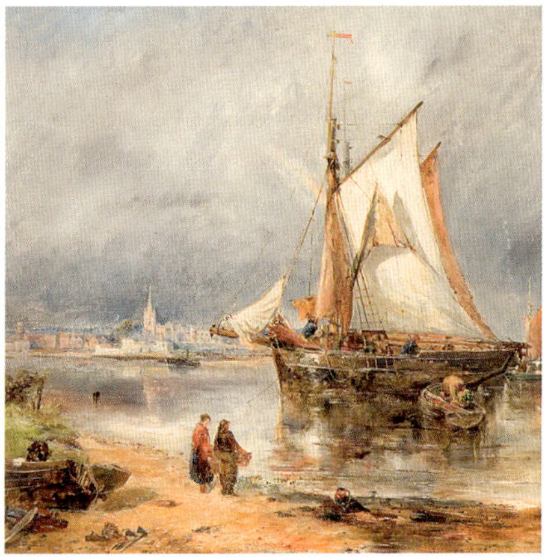

Bond, William Joseph Julius Caesar
1833–1926
Fishing Boats in an Estuary 1900–1914
oil on canvas 30.5 x 30.5
OP298

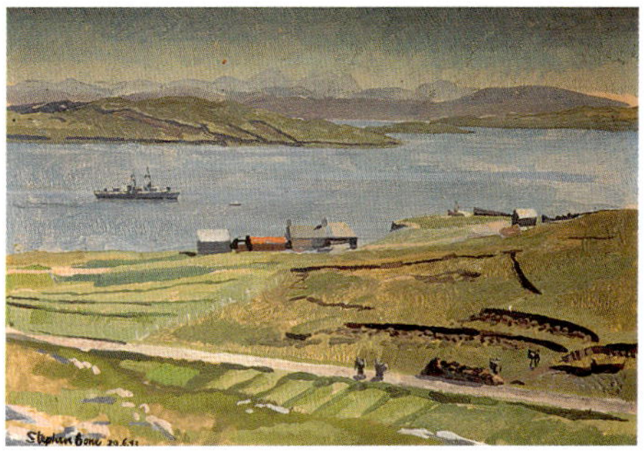

Bone, Stephen 1904–1958
Naval Rescue Launches in Loch Road, Isle of Lewis 1943
oil on board 25.5 x 35.5
OP347

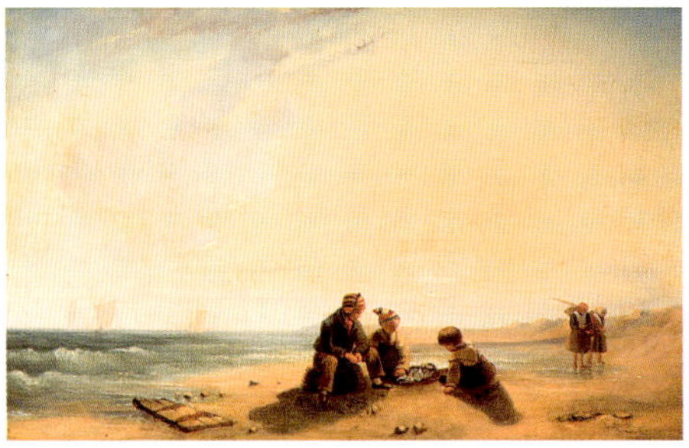

Bonington, Richard Parkes 1802–1828
French Coast Scene 1815–1828
oil on canvas 43.5 x 72.5
OP203

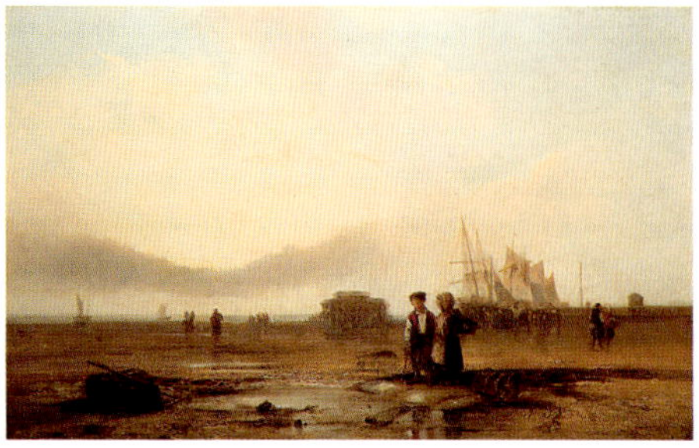

Bonington, Richard Parkes (attributed to)
1802–1828
Fort Rouge
oil on canvas 44 x 64
OP262

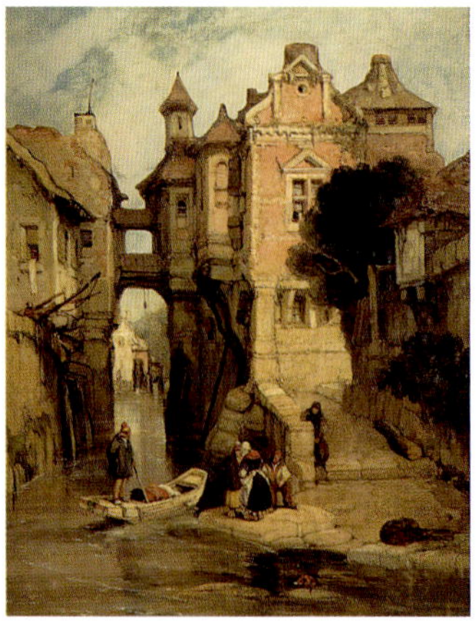

Bonington, Richard Parkes (attributed to)
1802–1828
Rouen
oil on canvas 61 x 45.5
OP232

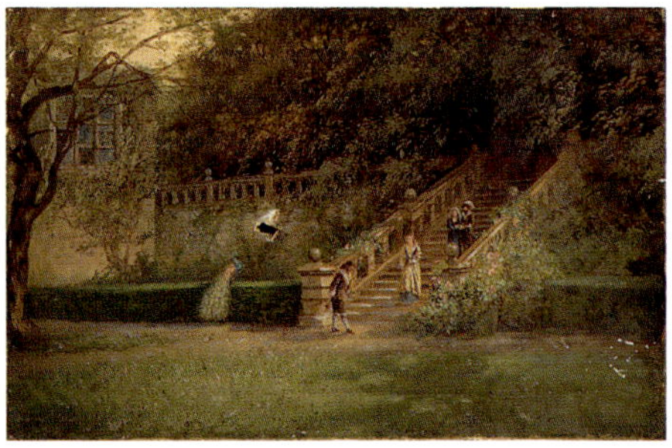

Booth, Samuel Lawson 1836–1928
Haddon Hall, Derbyshire
oil on canvas 40.6 x 61
OP641

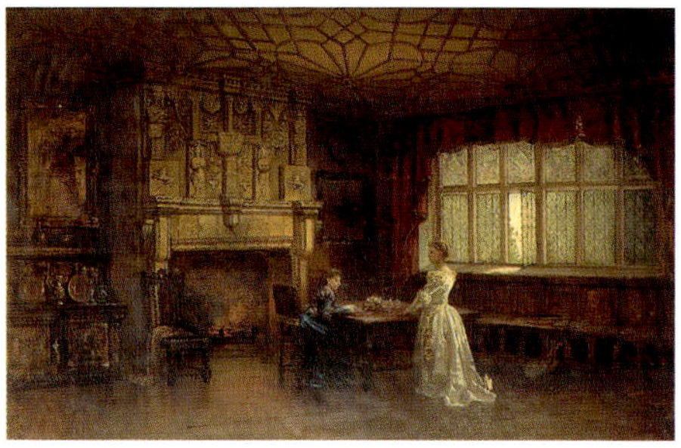

Booth, Samuel Lawson 1836–1928
Plas Mawr, Conway, in the Olden Days
oil on canvas 61 x 91.5
OP642

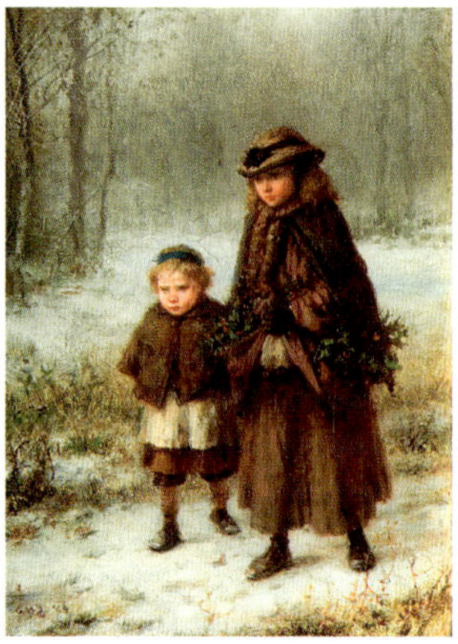

Boughton, George Henry 1833–1905
A Winter Morning's Walk 1864
oil on canvas 26 x 20.5
OP43

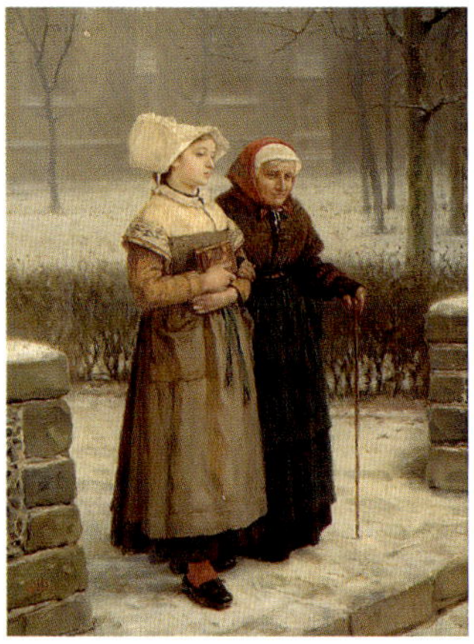

Boughton, George Henry 1833–1905
Returning from Mass, Brittany
oil on canvas 49.5 x 35.5
OP342

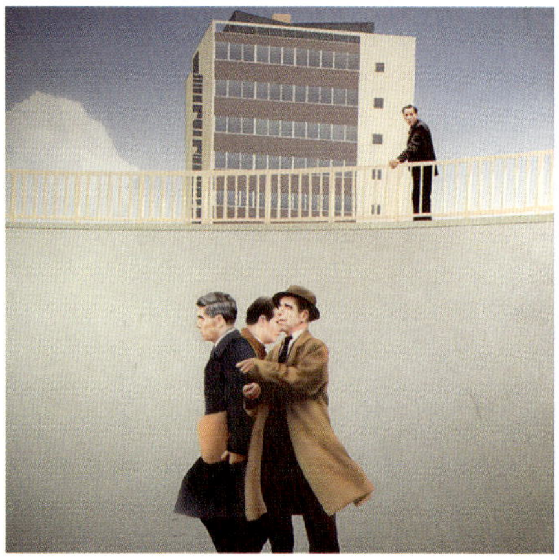

Boyd, Fionnuala b.1944 & **Evans, Leslie**
b.1945
Incident
acrylic on board 122 x 122
OP492

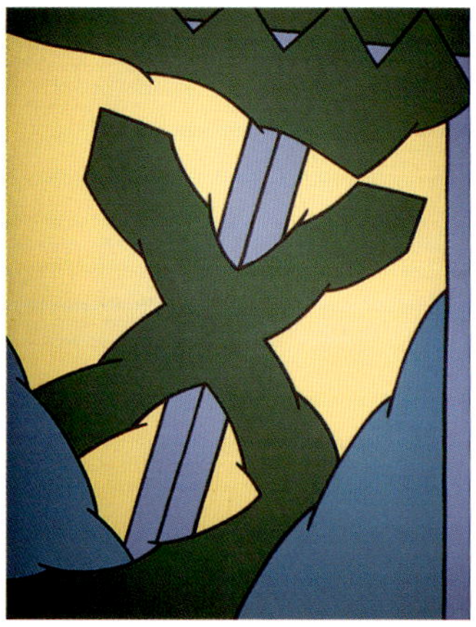

Brady, Carlene
Untitled 1968
acrylic on canvas 203 x 152.5
OP515

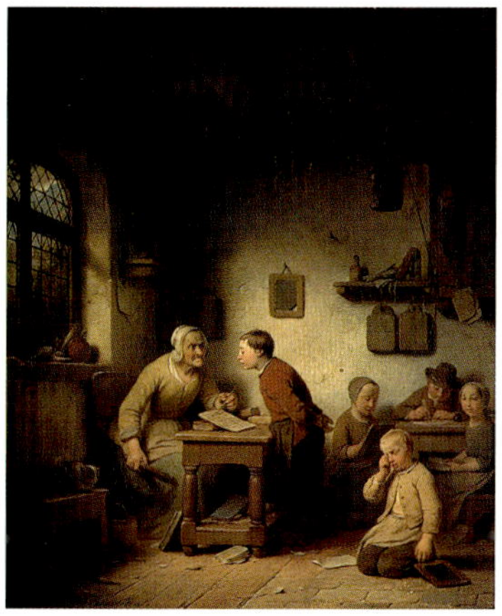

Braekeleer, Ferdinand de I 1792–1883
A Belgian School 1853
oil on panel 51.5 x 43
OP536

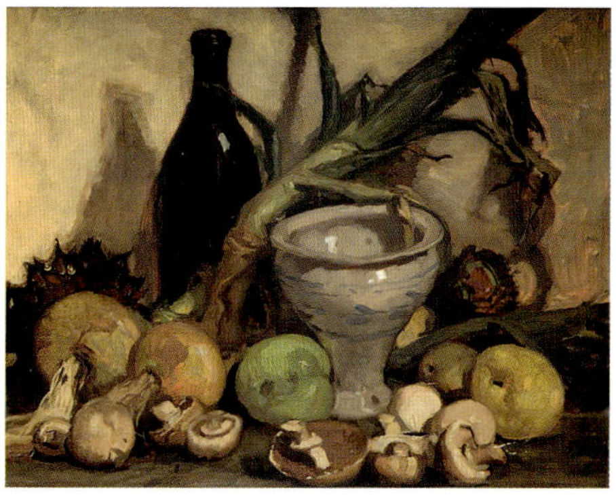

Brangwyn, Frank 1867–1956
Still Life 1924
oil on canvas 51 x 61
OP331

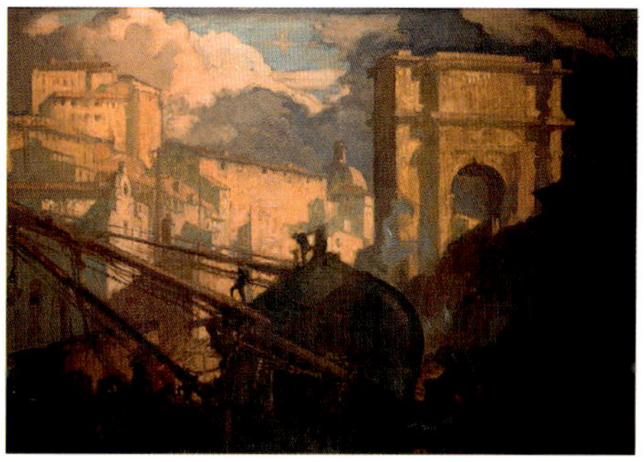

Brangwyn, Frank 1867–1956
Ancona
oil on canvas 104.1 x 142.2
OP335

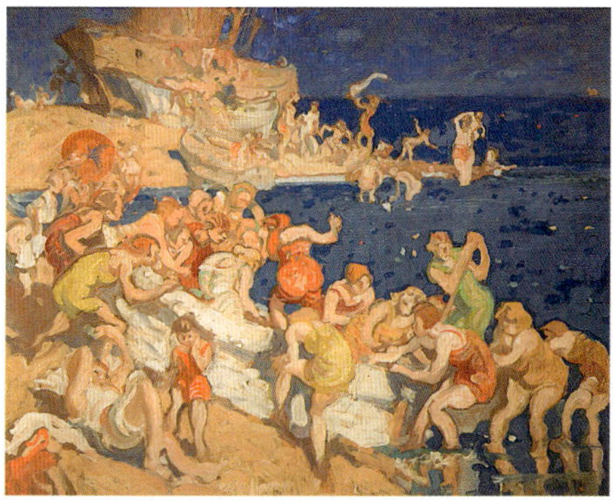

Brangwyn, Frank 1867–1956
Joy on the Beach
oil on board 63.5 x 76
OP105

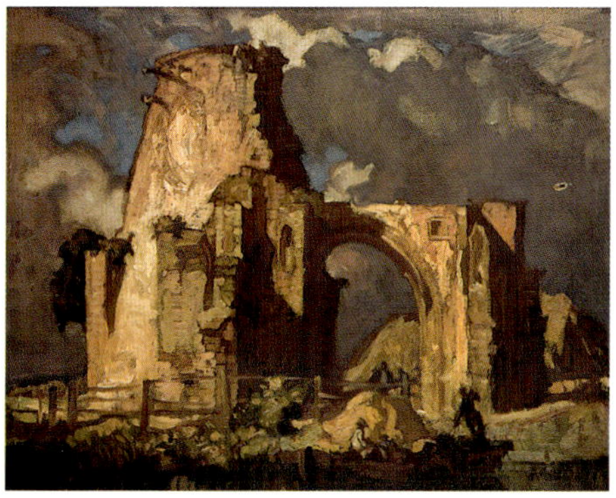

Brangwyn, Frank 1867–1956
St Benet's Abbey, Norfolk
oil on canvas 63.5 x 76
OP65

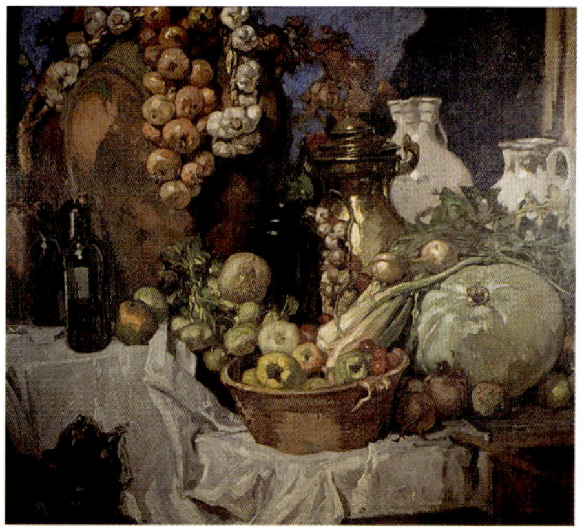

Brangwyn, Frank 1867–1956
The Brass Pot
oil on canvas 148 x 161.9
OP513

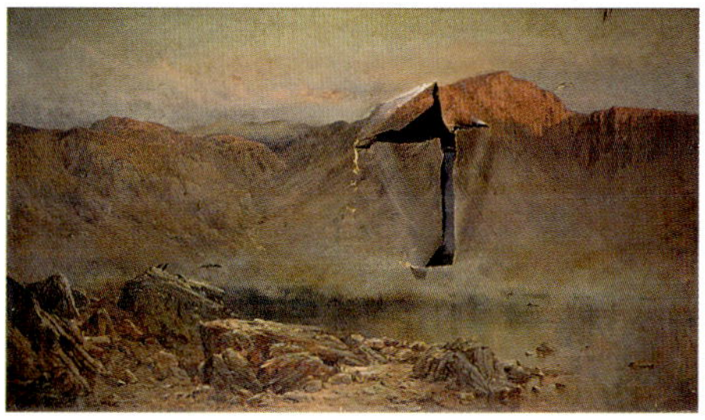

Breanski, Alfred de 1852–1928
Cader from Llyn Cader
oil on canvas 76 x 126
OP419

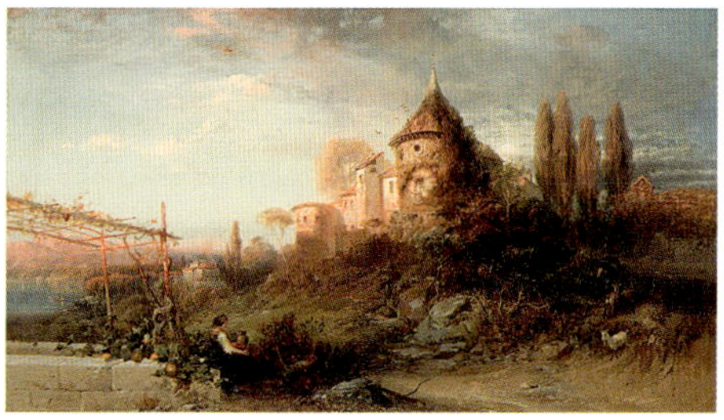

Bridell, Frederick Lee 1831–1863
The Vineyards at Meran, Tyrol
oil on canvas 49 x 78.5
OP643

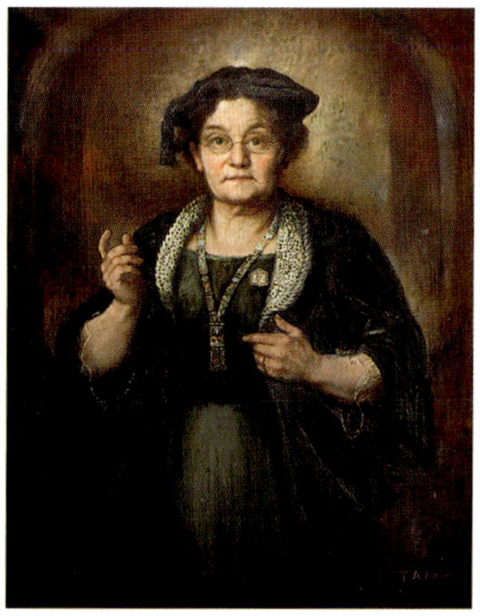

Bridson, Thomas Arthur 1860–1966
Councillor Emma Lloyd Sproson (d.1936), the First Woman Elected to the Wolverhampton Borough Council, 1 November 1921
oil on canvas 90 x 70
PCF1

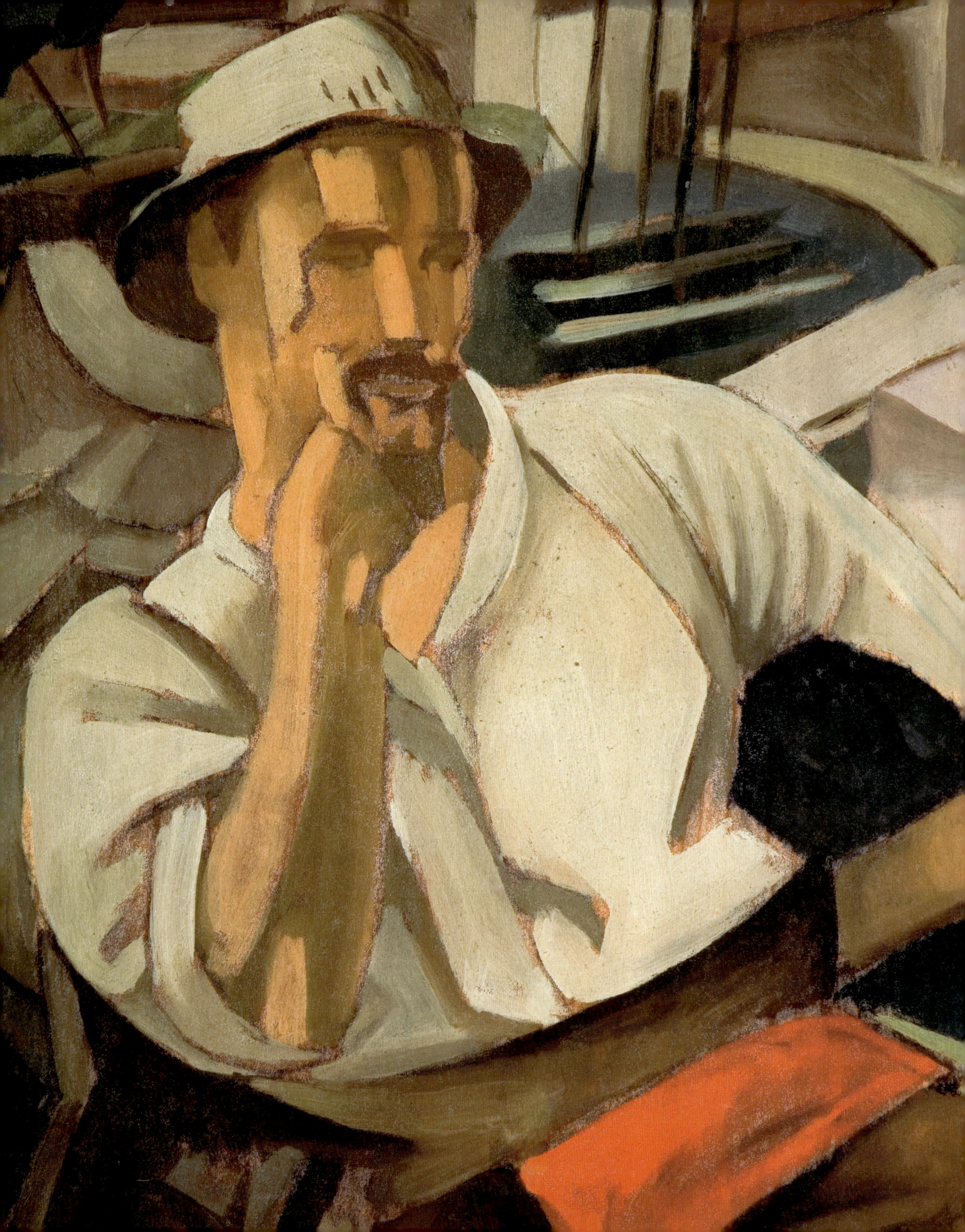

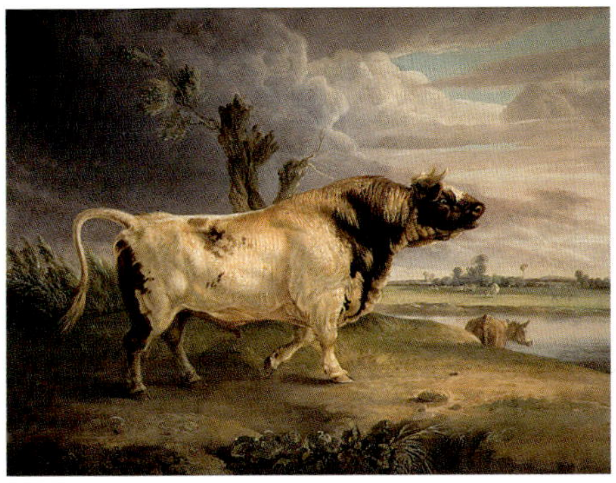

Bristow, Edmund 1787–1876
A Prize Bull
oil on canvas 61.5 x 77
OP225

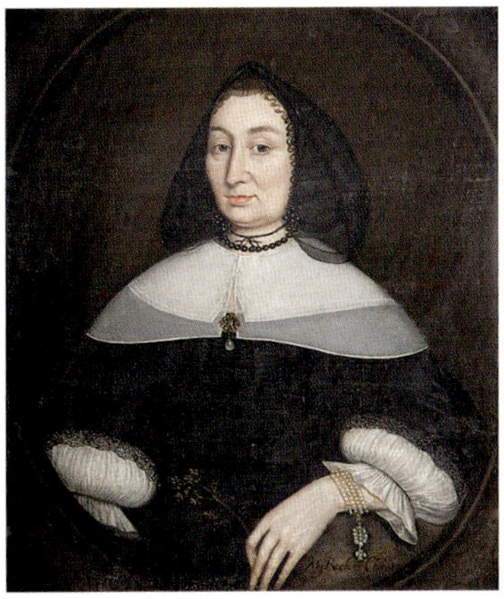

British (English) School 17th C
'My rock is Christ' (a Lady of the Bagot family)
oil on canvas 76 x 64
OP78

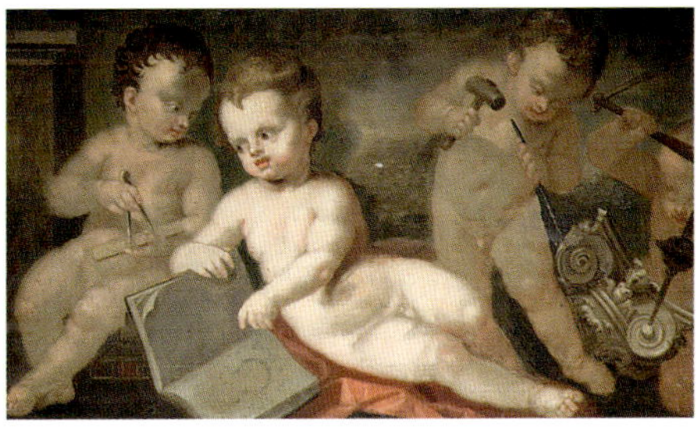

British (English) School early 18th C
Three Putti with Symbols of Architecture
oil on canvas 56 x 84.5
OP154

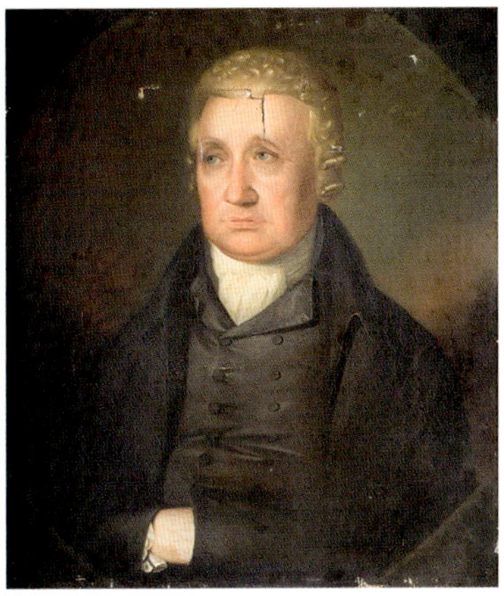

British (English) School 18th C
John Wilkinson
oil on canvas 78.5 x 66
OP300

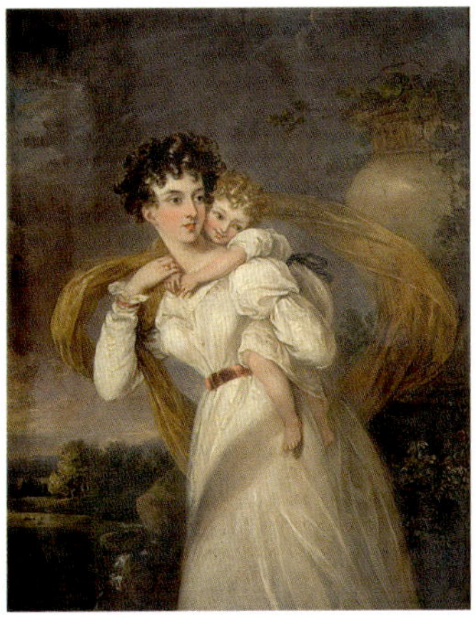

British (English) School 18th C
Woman and Child
oil on panel 48.5 x 38
OP339

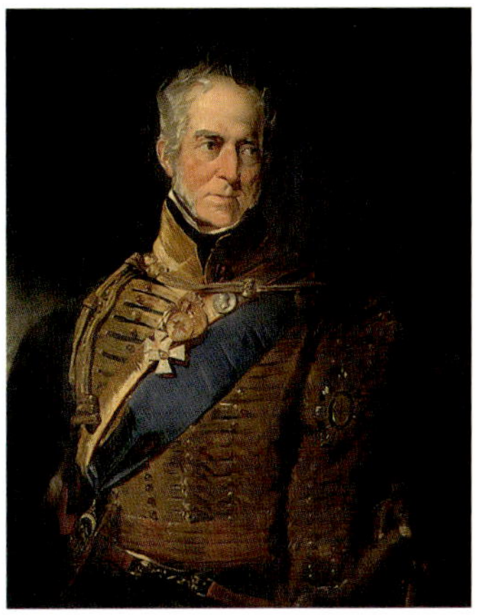

British (English) School 19th C
Henry William Paget (1768–1854), 1st Marquess of Anglesey
oil on canvas 97 x 76
OP77

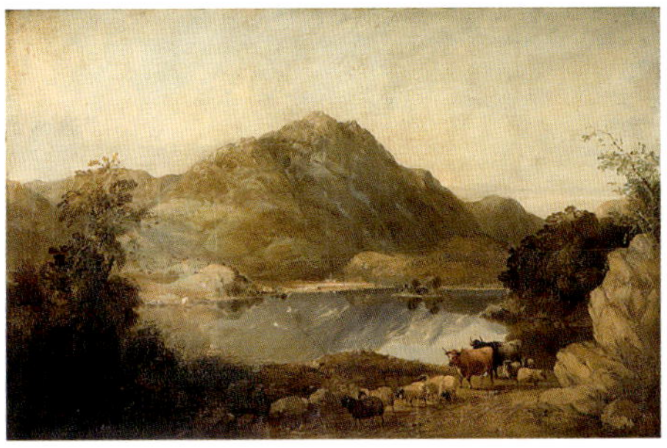

British (English) School 19th C
Landscape with Reflecting Lake
oil on canvas 75.5 x 113.5
OP601

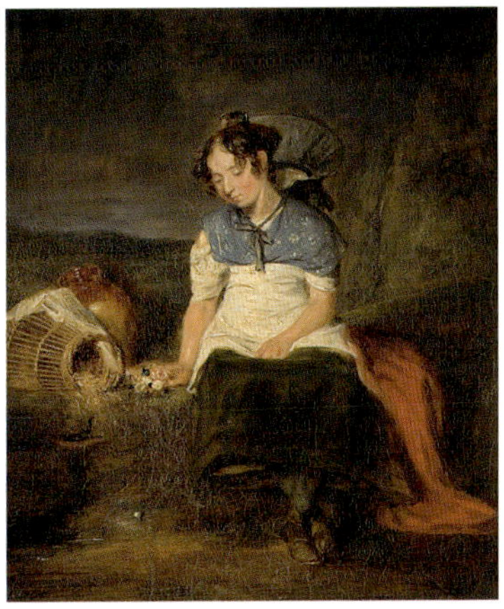

British (English) School 19th C
Lost in Thought
oil on canvas 28 x 21.5
OP361

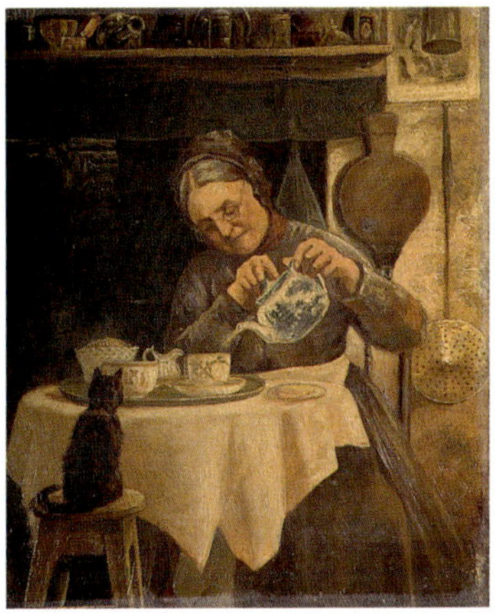

British (English) School 19th C
Old Woman Pouring Tea
oil on canvas 30.5 x 25.5
OP582

Facing page: Currie, John, 1883–1914, *Fisherman* (detail), The Potteries Museum & Art Gallery (p. 119)

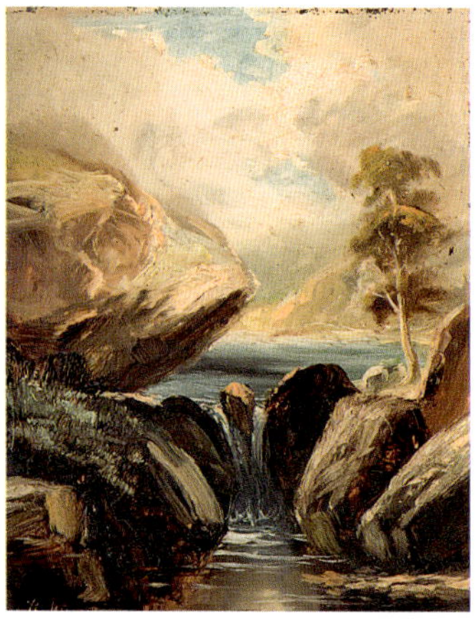

British (English) School 19th C
Waterfall
oil on board 25 x 20.5
OP148

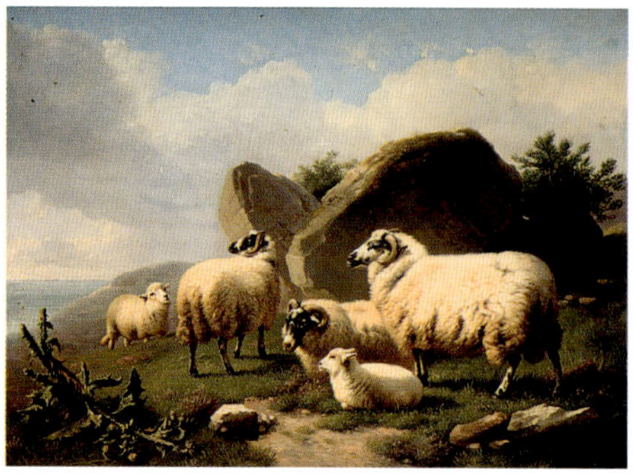

British (English) School
Landscape with Sheep
oil on panel 49 x 65
OP817

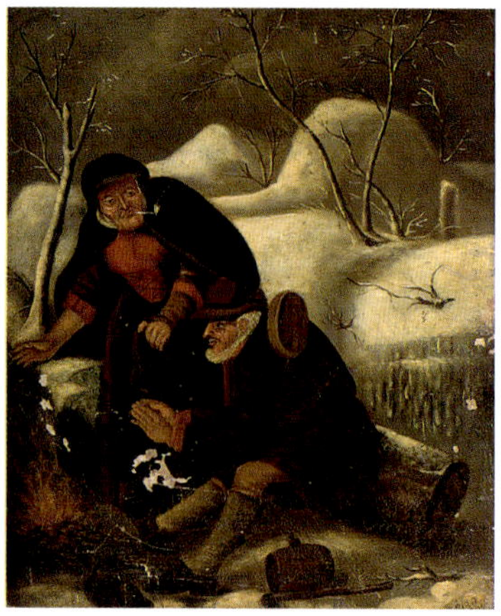

British School
Two Figures in a Winter Landscape 1792
oil on canvas 53.5 x 42.5
OP524

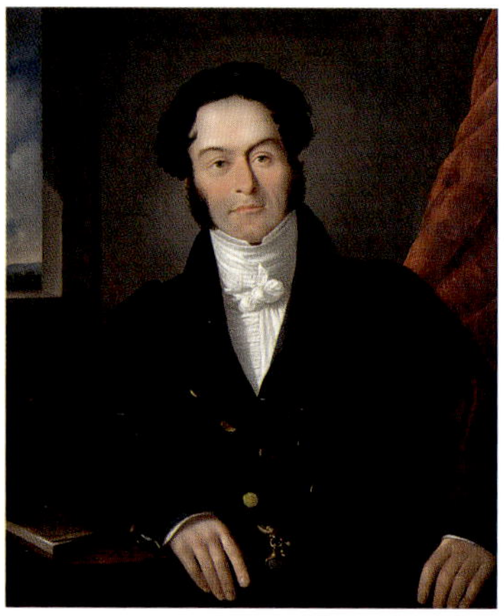

British School
Sidney Cartwright (1802–1883) 1820–1830
oil on canvas 76 x 63.5
OP364

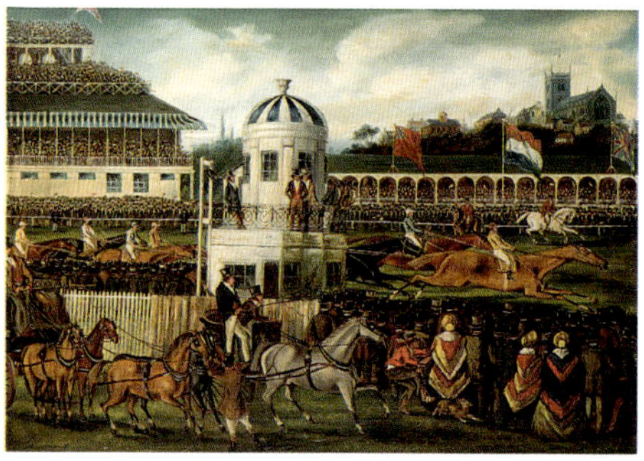

British School
The Race for Wolverhampton Stakes, 1839 1840
oil on canvas 52 x 70.6
OP484

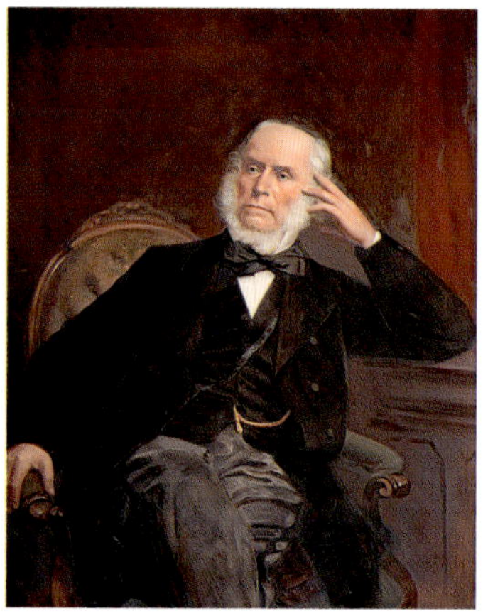

British School
Sidney Cartwright (1802–1883) 1870
oil on board 75.5 x 63.5
OP355

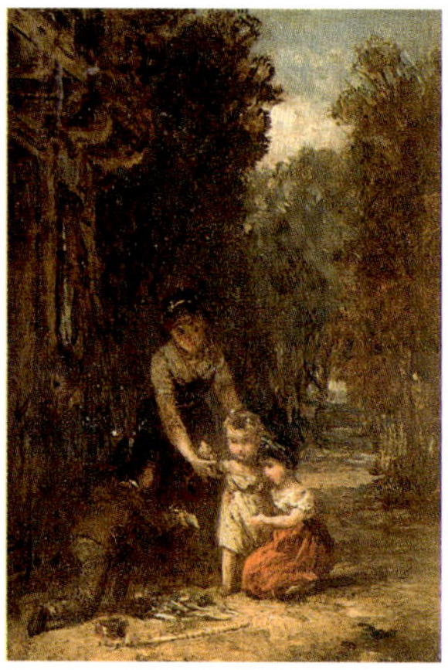

British School 19th C
A Great Catch
oil on panel 14 x 10
OP143

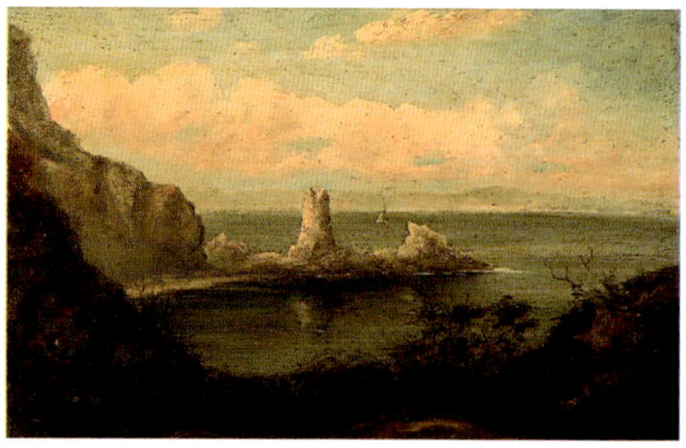

British School 19th C
Coast Scene
oil on canvas 30.5 x 45.5
OP466

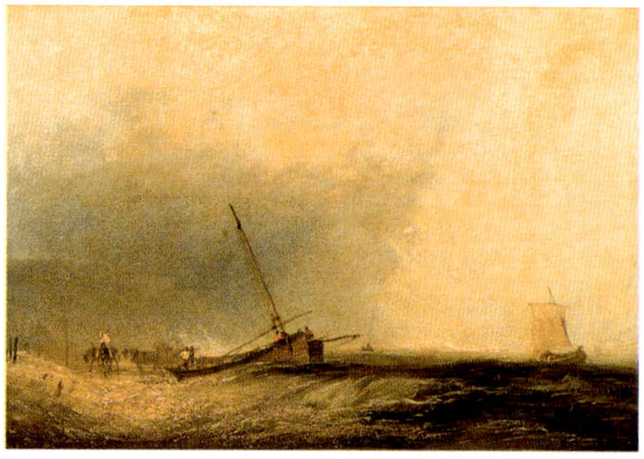

British School 19th C
Fishing Smack off the Coast
oil on canvas 38 x 53.5
OP160

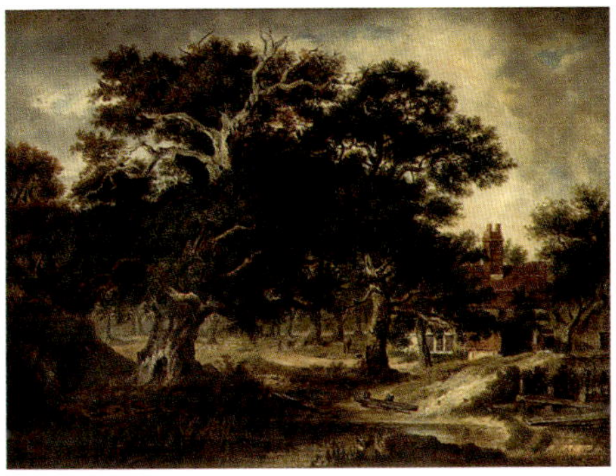

British School 19th C
Landscape
oil on canvas 43 x 63.5
OP127

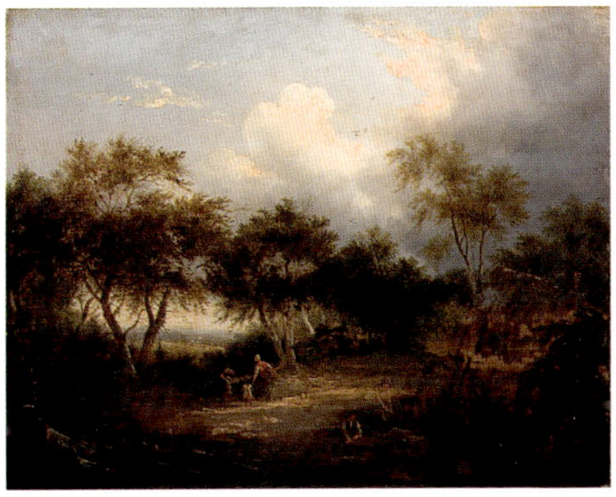

British School 19th C
Landscape with Fisherman (Wood Gatherers)
oil on panel 50 x 61
OP392

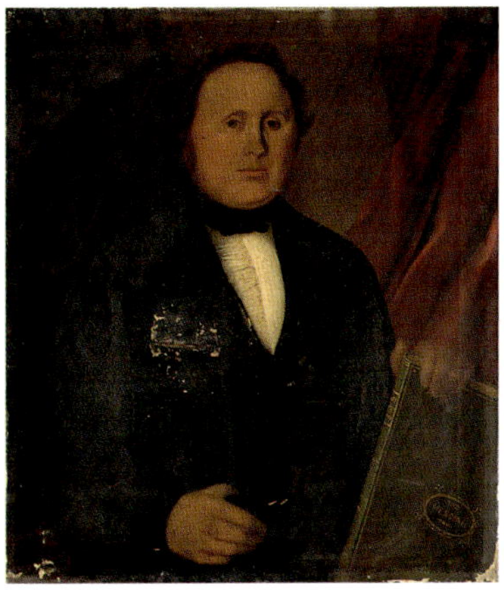

British School 19th C
Portrait of a Gentleman Holding a Copy of 'The Messiah'
oil on canvas 76.2 x 64.8
OP406

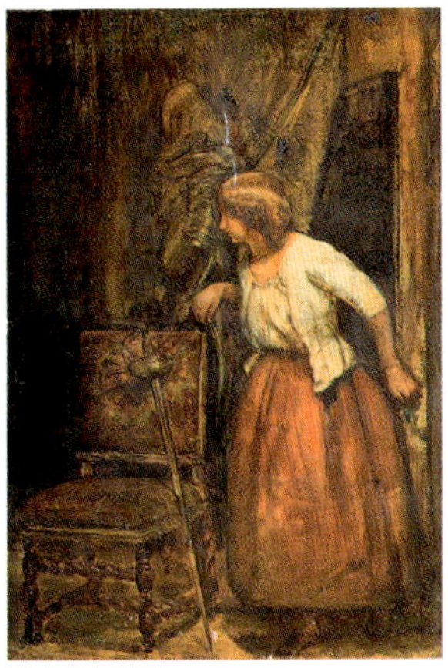

British School 19th C
Refuge
oil on canvas 61 x 40.5
OP153

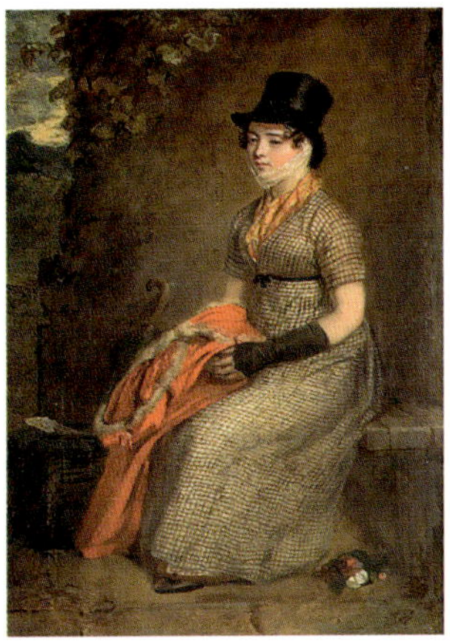

British School 19th C
Seated Lady (The Traveller)
oil on canvas 52.5 x 41
OP84

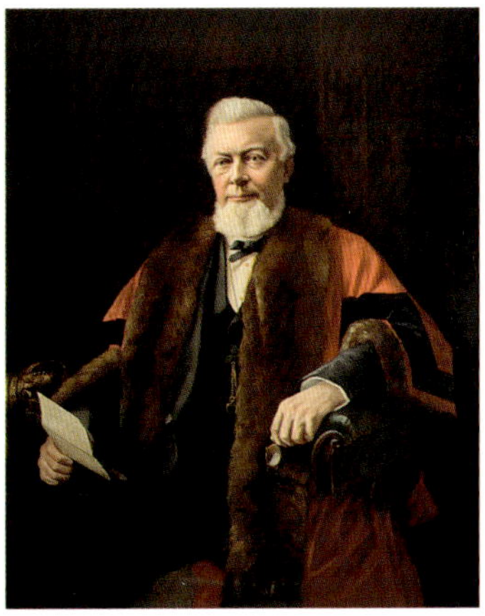

British School late 19th C
Thomas Bantock (1823–1895)
oil on canvas 133 x 105
OP893

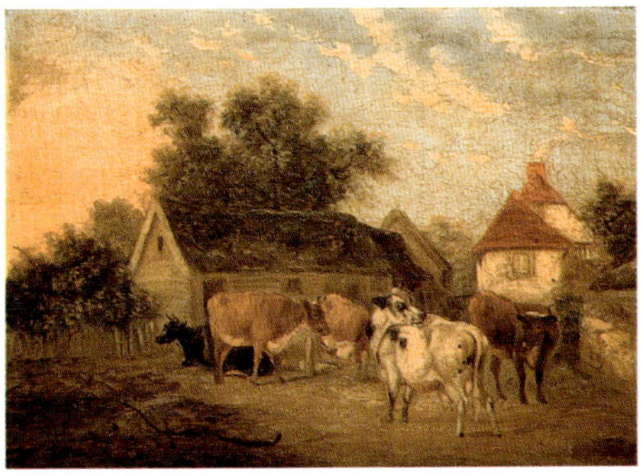

British School
Landscape of a Farmyard with Cows
oil on canvas 30.5 x 40.5
OP739

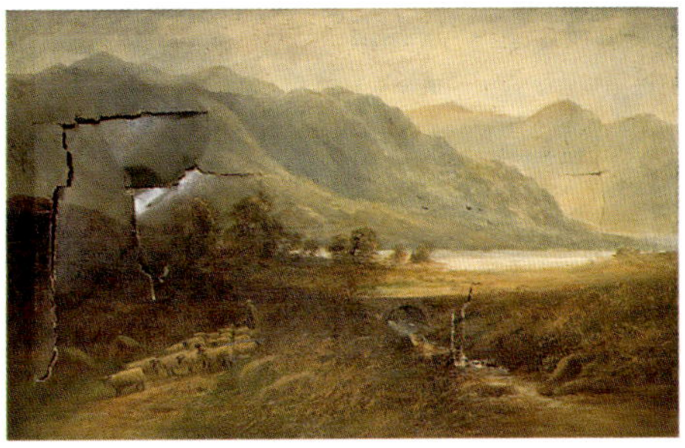

British School
Landscape with Sheep
oil on canvas 61 x 91.5
OP575

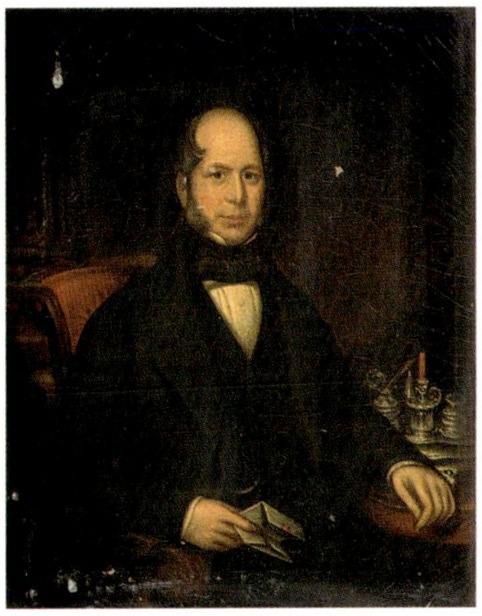

British School
Portrait of a Gentleman
oil on canvas 35 x 30.5
OP811

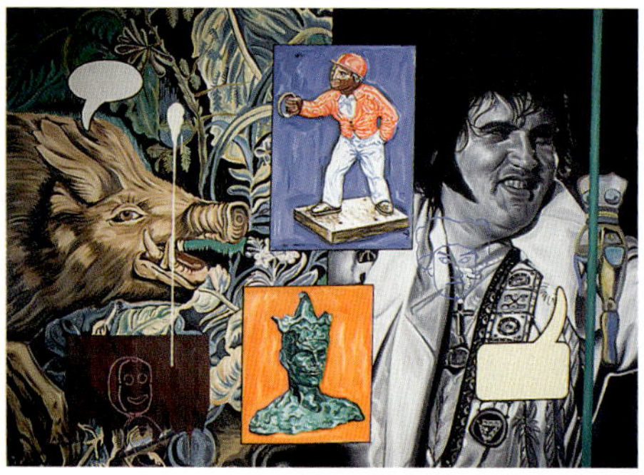

Brookes, Jason
Trojan 1992
oil on canvas 180 x 243
X3 (P)

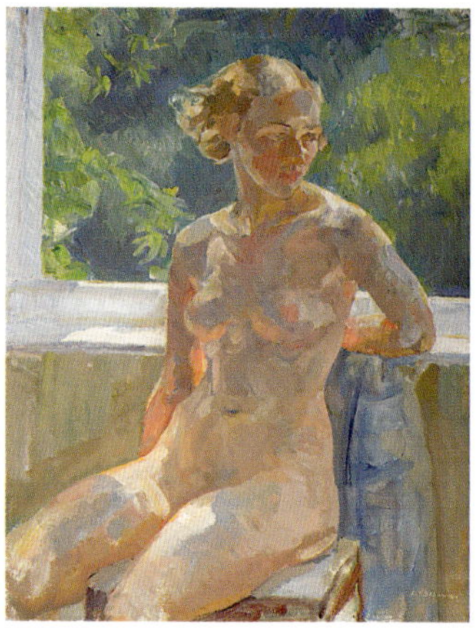

Browning, Amy Katherine 1881–1978
At the Window
oil on canvas 101.5 x 76
OP322

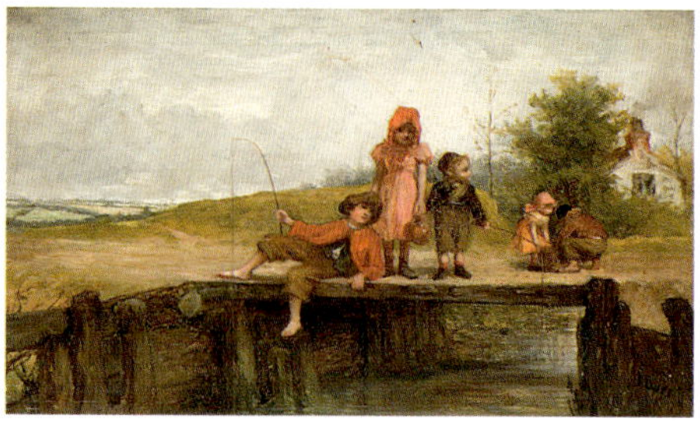

Burr, John 1831–1893
Little Fisher Folk
oil on canvas 20.5 x 30.5
OP46

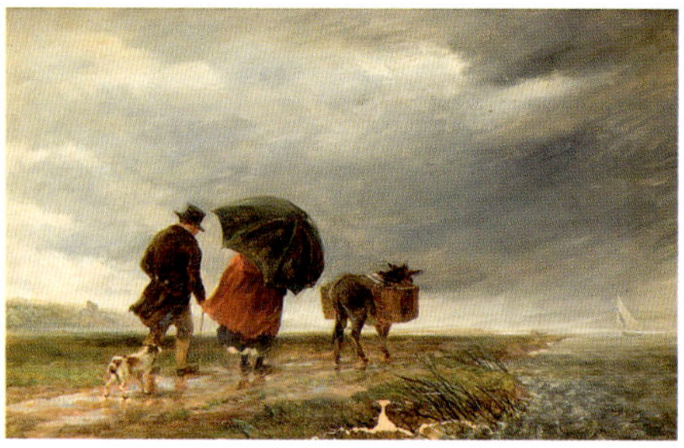

Burt, Charles Thomas 1823–1902
Going to the Ferry, Appledore, Devon; A Squally Day 1856
oil on canvas 40.5 x 61
OP356

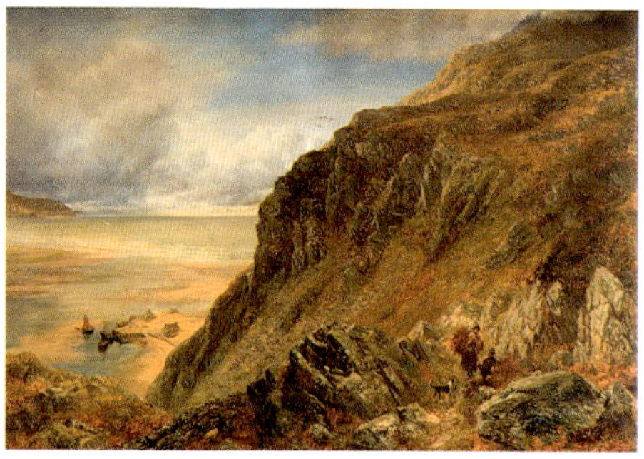

Burt, Charles Thomas 1823–1902
Near Barmouth
oil on panel 81 x 122
OP573

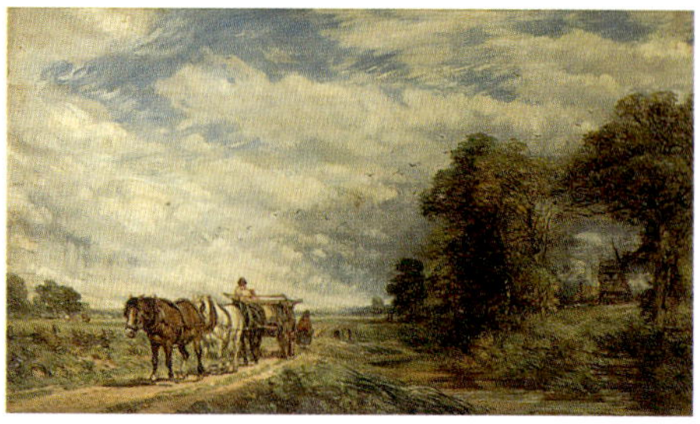

Burt, Charles Thomas 1823–1902
Team of Horses
oil on canvas 56 x 91
OP644

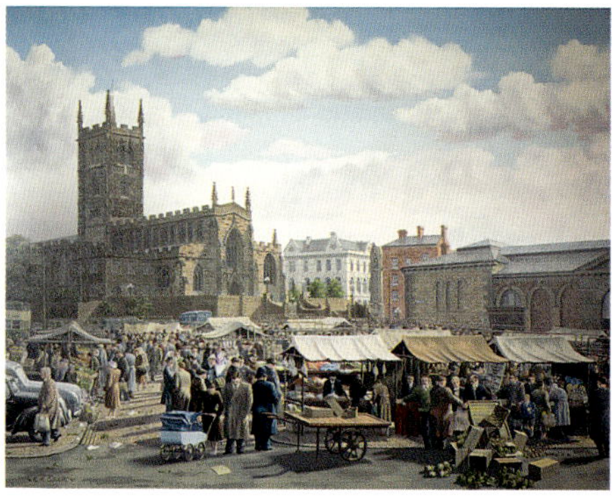

Calvert, R. K.
Wolverhampton Market
oil on canvas 100 x 124
PCF2

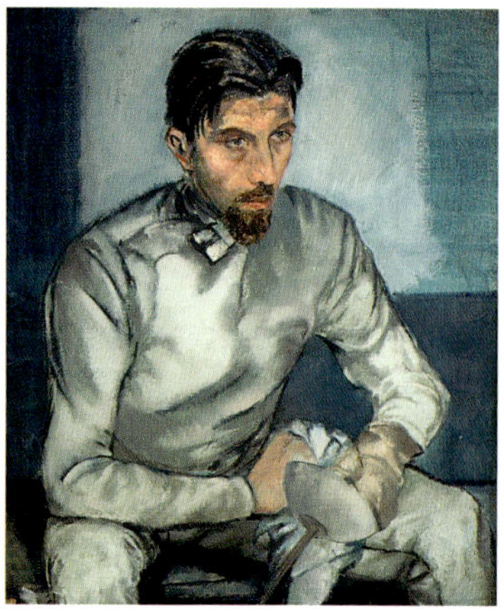

Campbell-Gray, Ian active 1933
The Fencer
oil on canvas 76 x 63.5
OP10

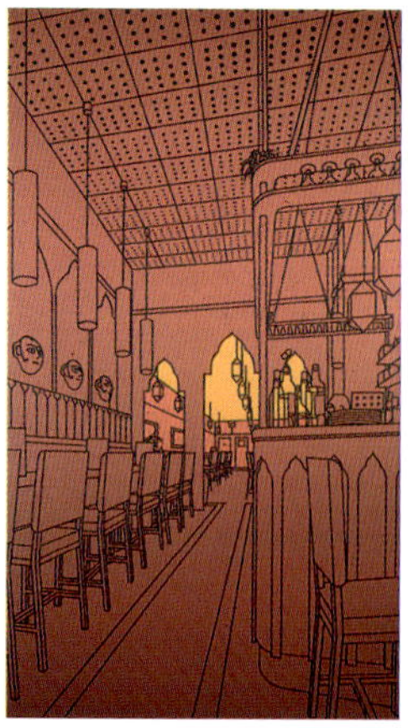

Caulfield, Patrick b.1936
Tandoori Restaurant 1971
acrylic on canvas 274 x 152.5
OP516

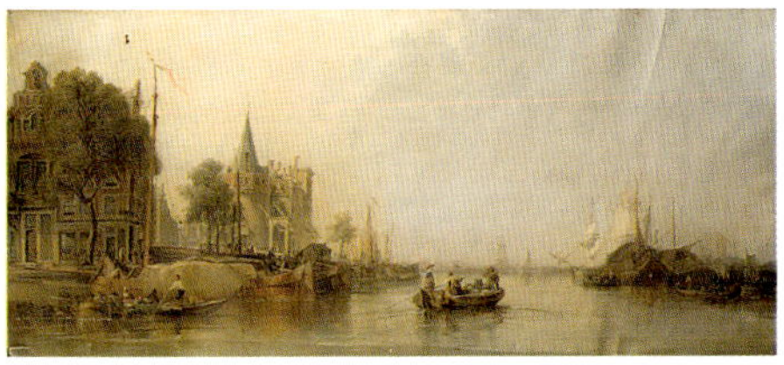

Chambers, George 1803–1840
Rotterdam
oil on canvas 56 x 122
OP540

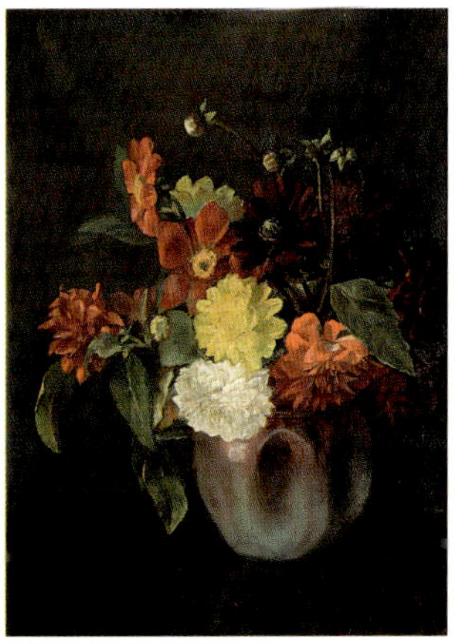

Chettle, Agnes Beatrice b.c.1900
Still Life, Flowers
oil on canvas 50.8 x 41.3
OP645

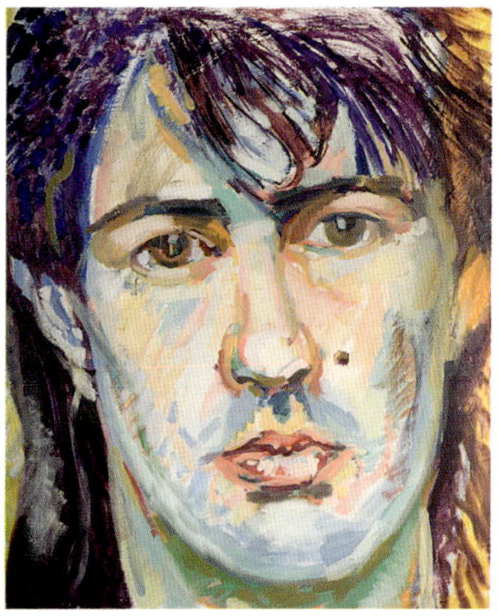

Clamp, Adrian b.1960
Self Portrait 1980s
oil on canvas 126 x 100
OP832

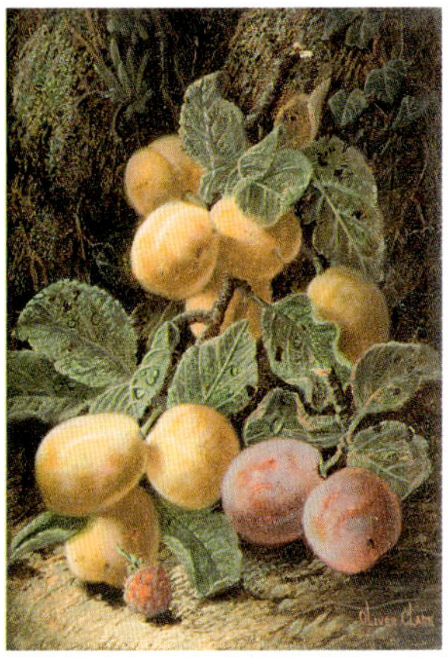

Clare, Oliver c.1853–1927
Still Life, Fruit
oil on canvas 23 x 18
OP646

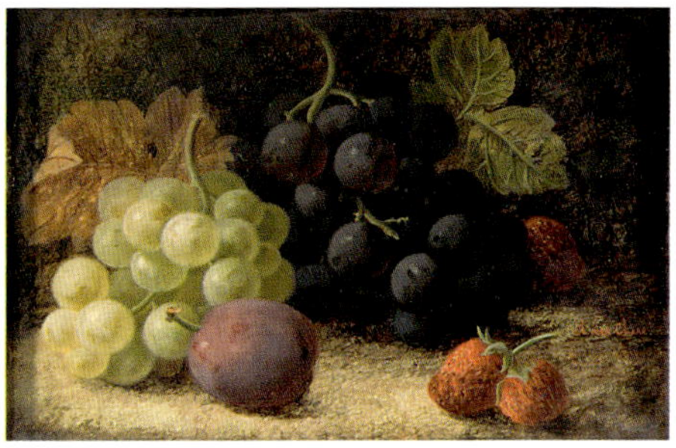

Clare, Oliver c.1853–1927
Still Life, Fruit
oil on panel 15 x 23
OP647

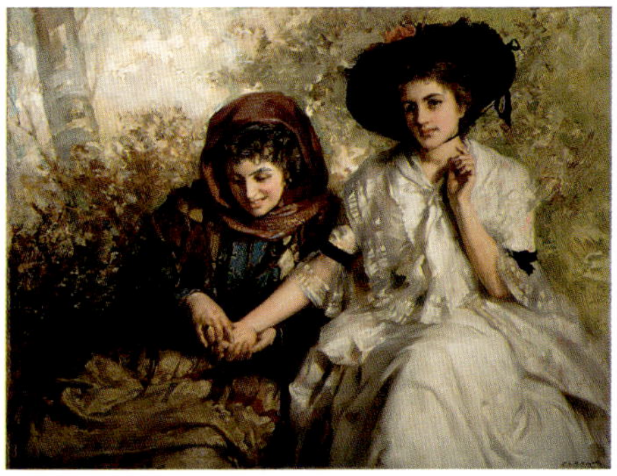

Clark, James 1858–1943
The Fortune Teller
oil on canvas 106.5 x 137
OP648

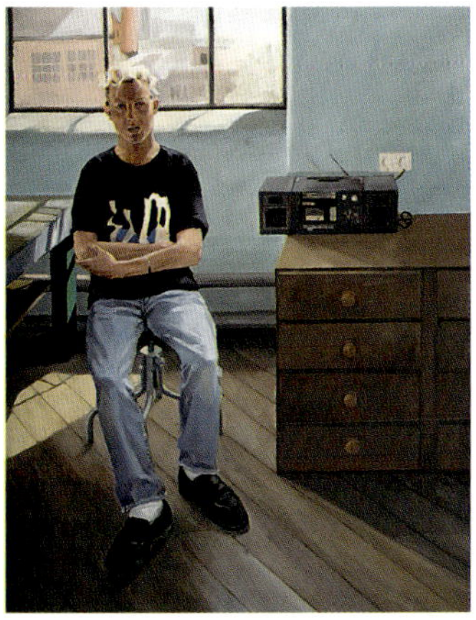

Clarke, Jacqueline
Josh 1990s
oil on canvas 92 x 70
OP860

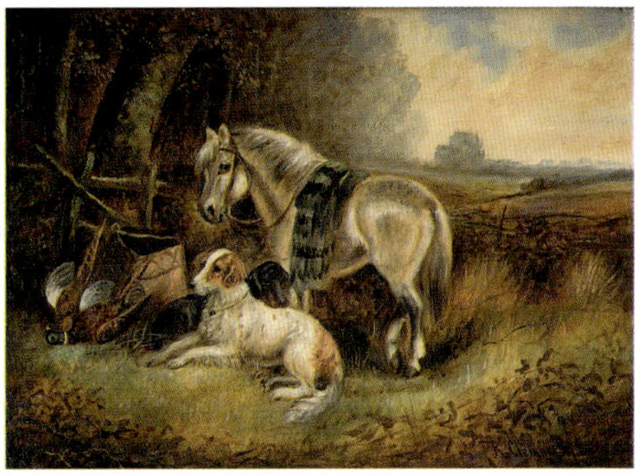

Cleminson, Robert active c.1864–c.1903
Game Dog
oil on canvas 39.1 x 58.4 (E)
OP874

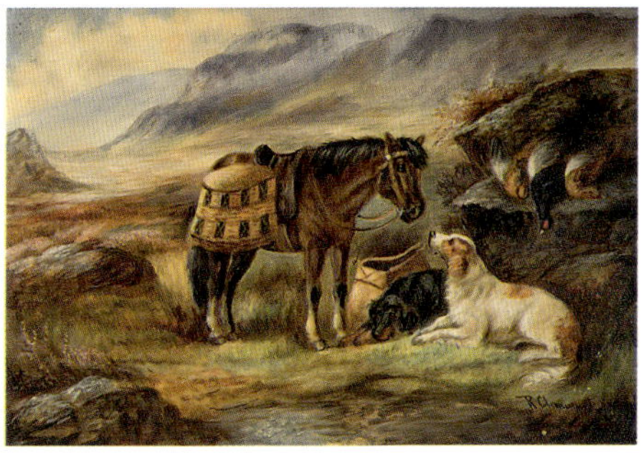

Cleminson, Robert active c.1864–c.1903
Pony
oil on canvas 40 x 60 (E)
OP873

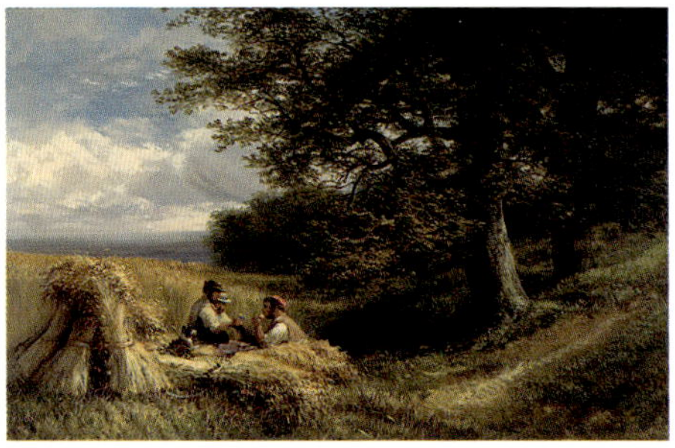

Cole, George Vicat 1833–1893
The Harvesters 1881
oil on canvas 52 x 76
OP117

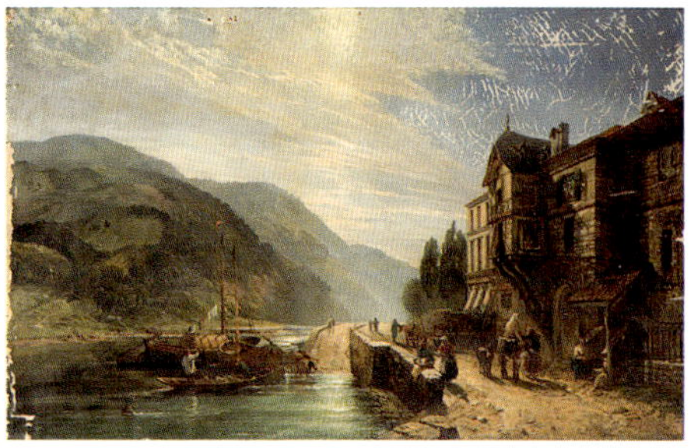

Cole, George Vicat 1833–1893
Konigswasser on the Rhine
oil on canvas 53.3 x 78.7
OP410

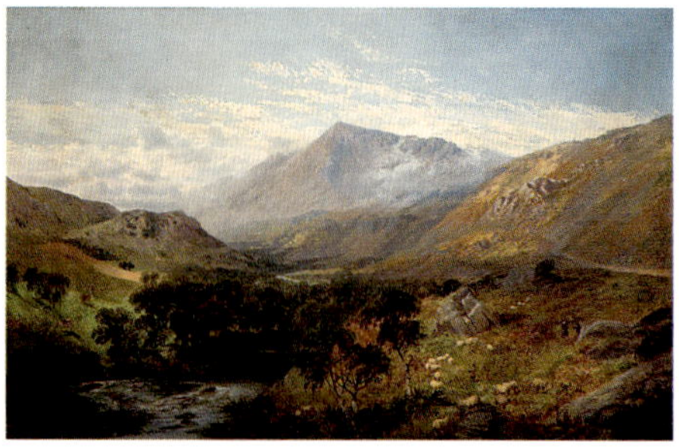

Cole, George Vicat 1833–1893
Near Borrowdale, Cumberland
oil on canvas 53.5 x 78.5
OP130

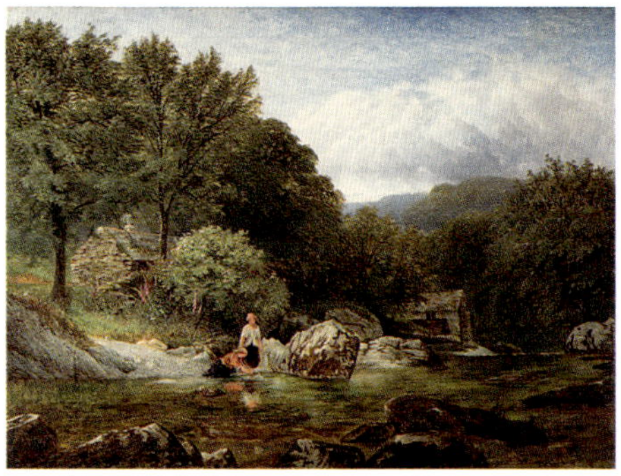

Cole, George Vicat 1833–1893
On the River Lledr, North Wales
oil on canvas 71 x 91.5
OP649

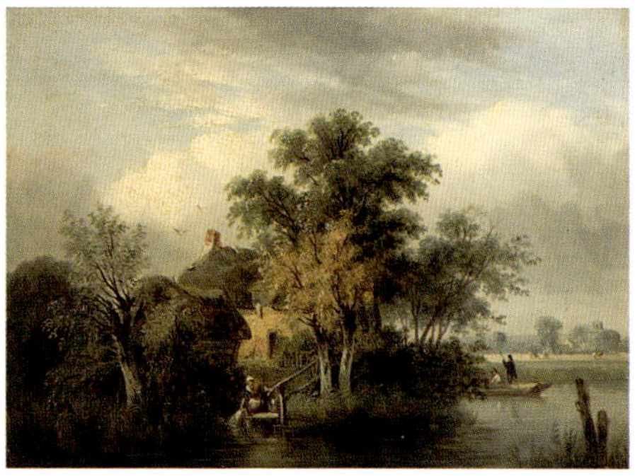

Colkett, Samuel David 1806–1863
The Trowse near Norwich 1849
oil on panel 20.5 x 26.5
OP36

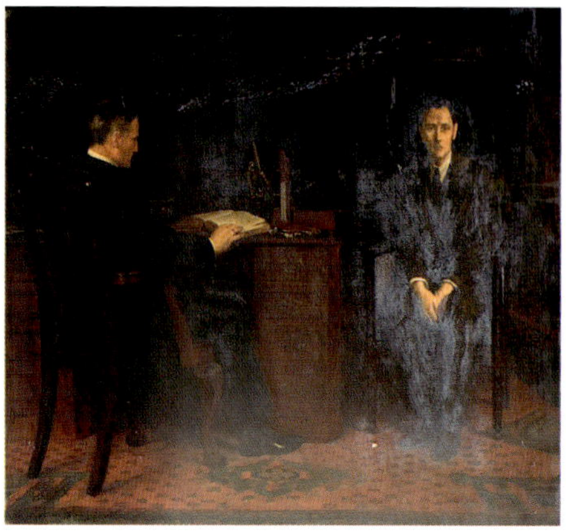

Collier, John 1850–1934
Sentence of Death
oil on canvas 132 x 162
OP445

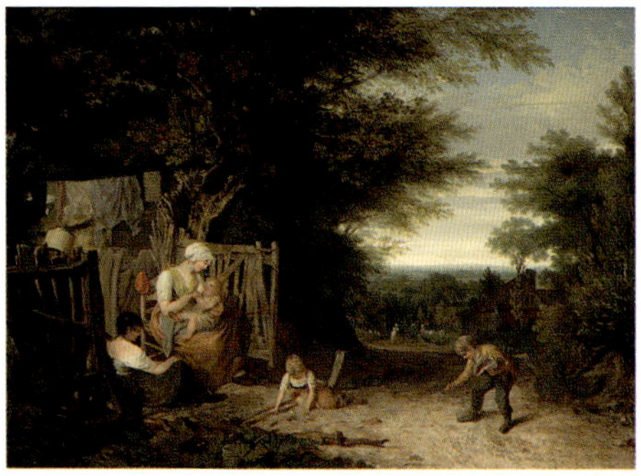

Collins, William 1788–1847
At the Cottage Gate
oil on panel 61 x 82.5
OP583

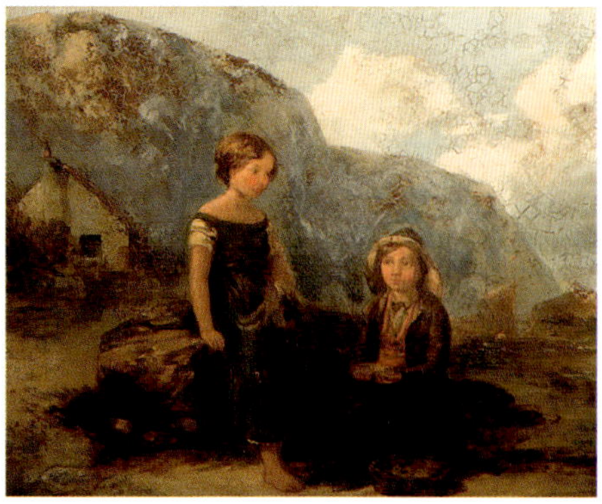

Collins, William 1788–1847
Children Gathering Seaweed
oil on canvas 30.5 x 35.5
OP47

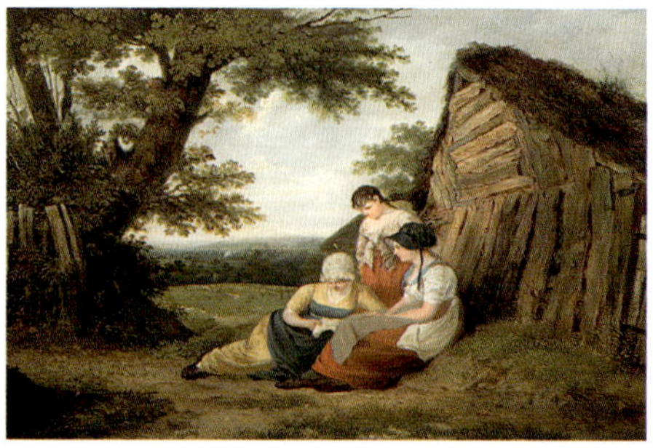

Collins, William 1788–1847
Landscape with Three Figures
oil on panel 45 x 51.5
OP207

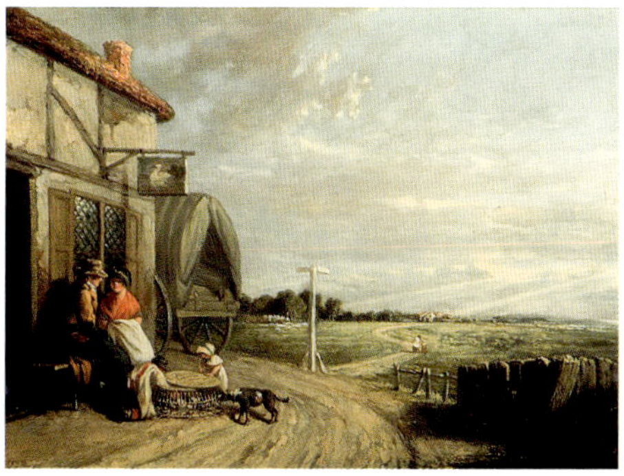

Collins, William 1788–1847
The Carrier's Resting Place
oil on canvas 27.5 x 34
OP214

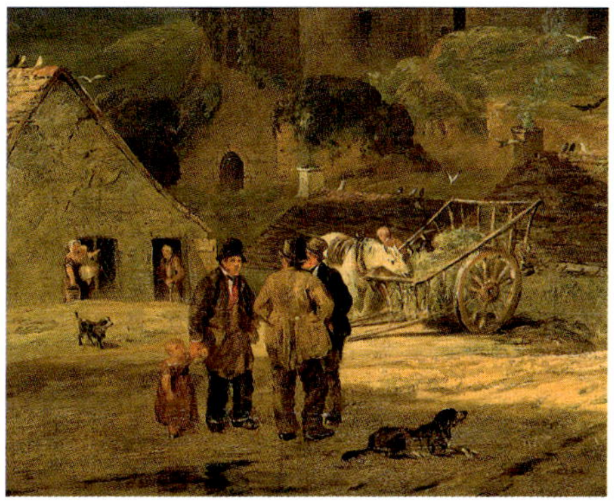

Collins, William 1788–1847
The Village Gossip
oil on canvas 48.5 x 58.5
OP174

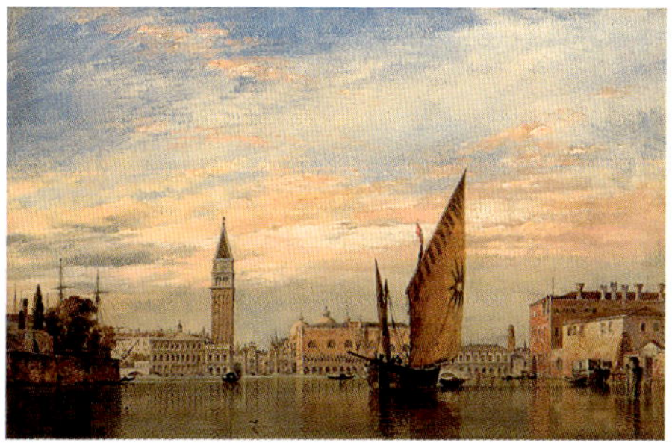

Cooke, Edward William 1811–1880
On the Bacino di San Marco, Venice 1851
oil on canvas 31 x 45
OP202

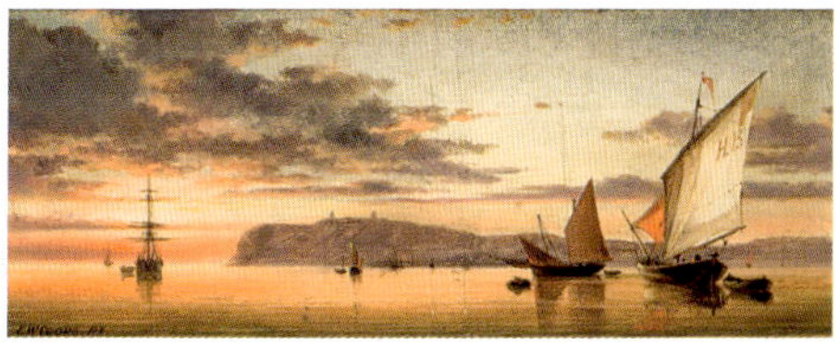

Cooke, Edward William 1811–1880
Sunset at Le Havre
oil on board 11.5 x 25
OP377

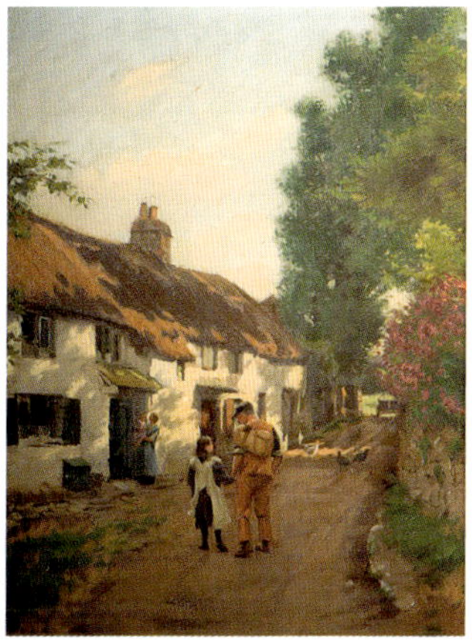

Cooke, John Percy active 1892–1939
Home Alone
oil on canvas 76 x 56
OP650

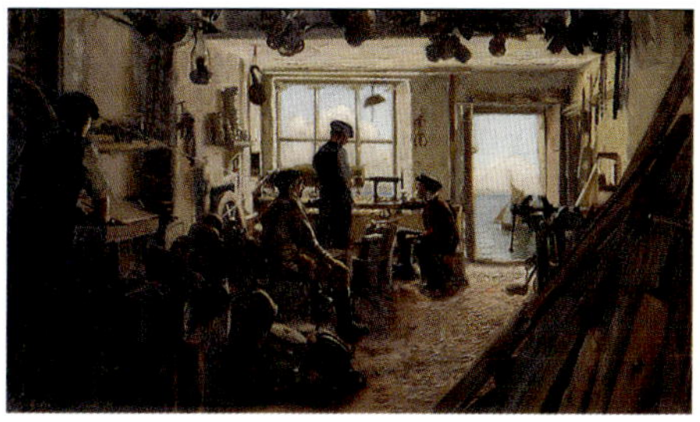

Cooke, John Percy active 1892–1939
The Blockmaker's Shop
oil on canvas 56 x 91.5
OP652

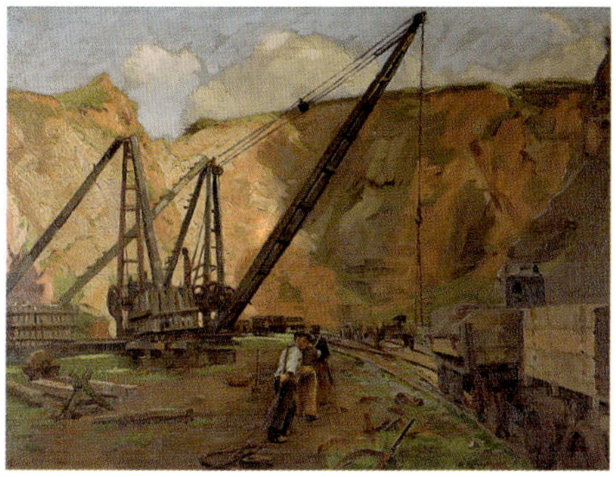

Cooke, John Percy active 1892–1939
The Quarry, Brixham, Devon
oil on canvas 71 x 91.5
OP651

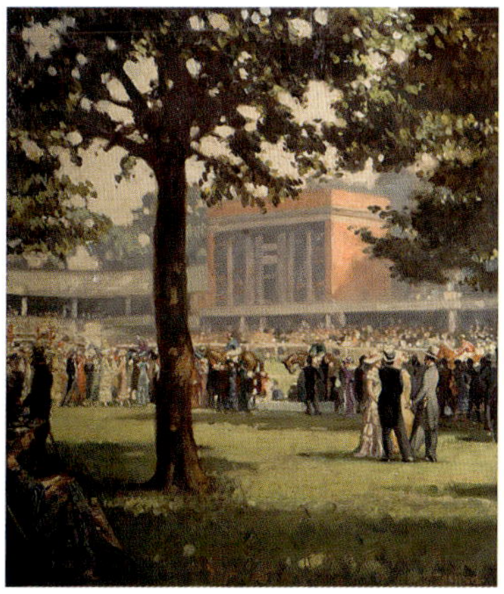

Cooper, Alfred Egerton 1883–1974
Ascot, the Paddock
oil on canvas 76 x 63.5
OP288

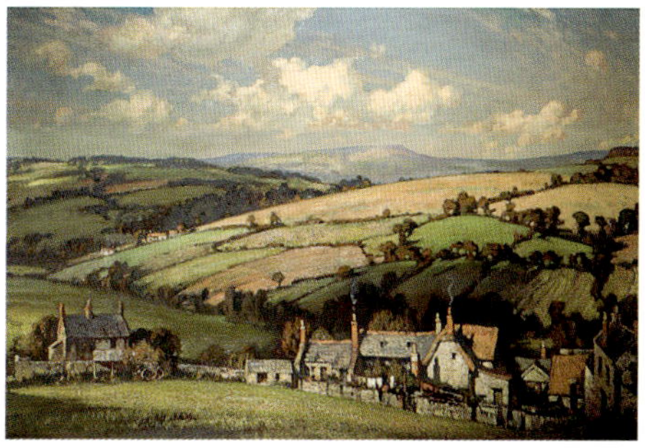

Cooper, Alfred Egerton 1883–1974
Dorset Landscape
oil on canvas 106.5 x 152.5
OP654

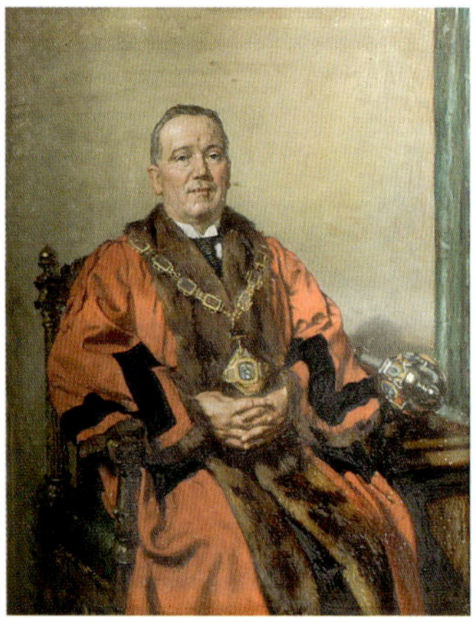

Cooper, Alfred Egerton 1883–1974
Herbert Beech
oil on canvas 127 x 101.5
OP658

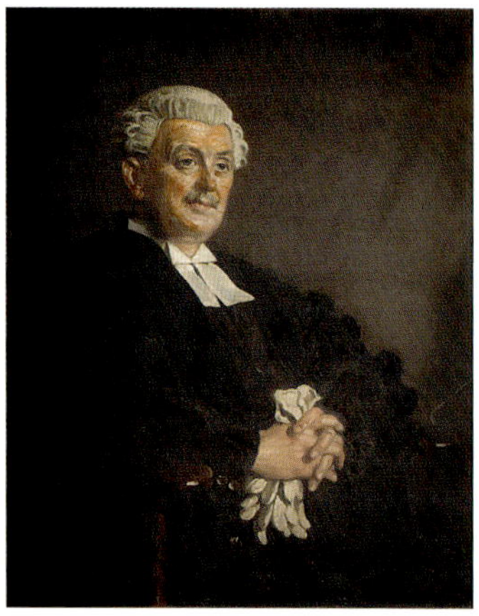

Cooper, Alfred Egerton 1883–1974
Joseph Arlidge
oil on canvas 91 x 71
OP657

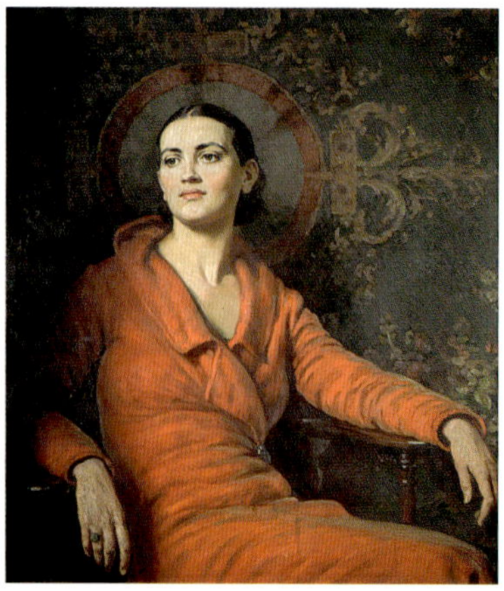

Cooper, Alfred Egerton 1883–1974
Lady in Red Velvet
oil on canvas 103 x 87
OP653

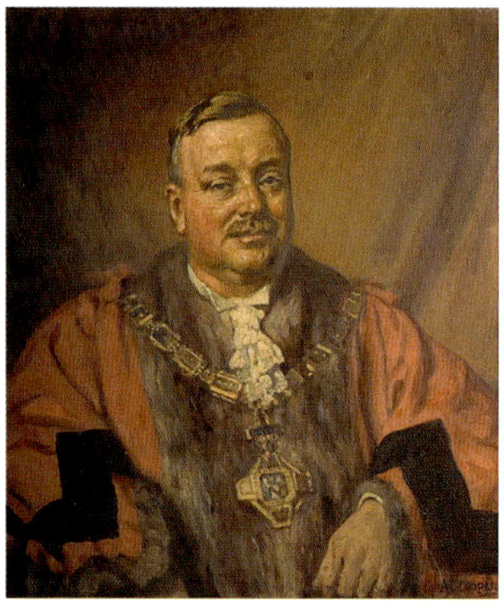

Cooper, Alfred Egerton 1883–1974
Martin Hughes
oil on canvas 76.5 x 64
OP656

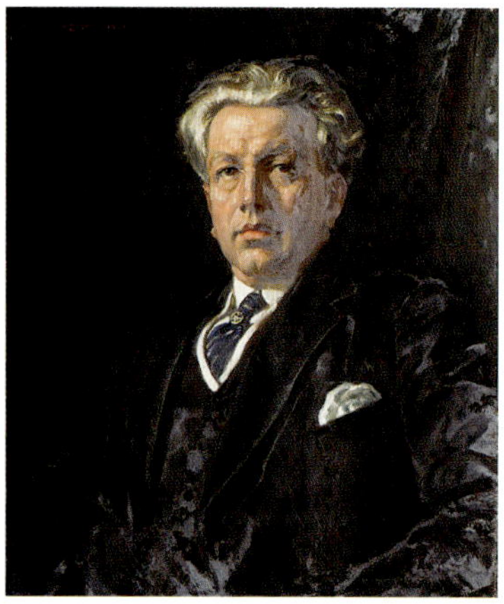

Cooper, Alfred Egerton 1883–1974
T. R. Wood
oil on canvas 76 x 63.5
OP655

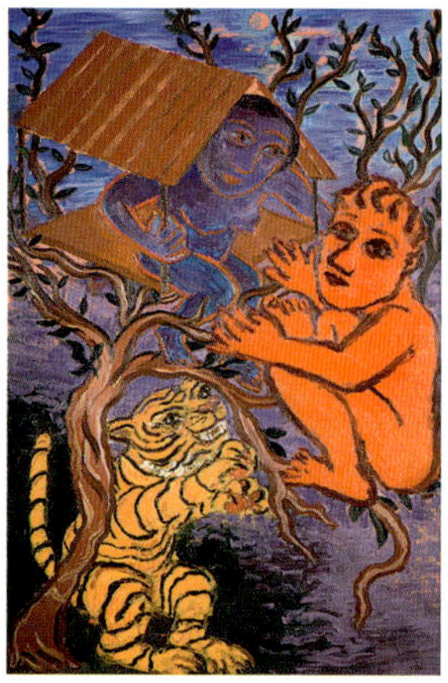

Cooper, Eileen b.1953
Tiger, Tiger 1985–1992
oil on canvas 168.5 x 126.5
OP856

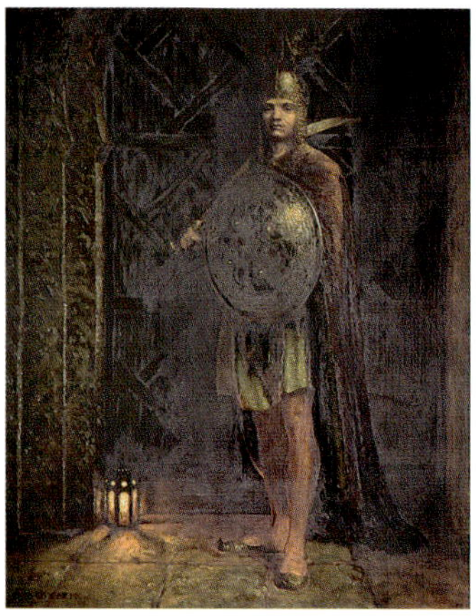

Cooper, Fred active 1906
Moorish Sentry
oil on canvas 66 x 51
OP659

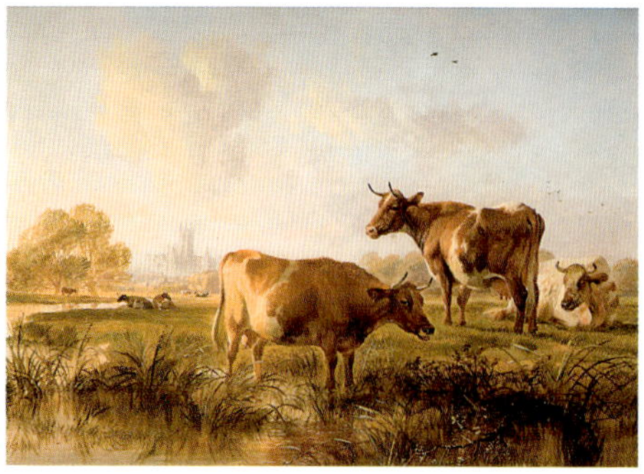

Cooper, Thomas Sidney 1803–1902
In the Canterbury Meadows 1863
oil on panel 23 x 30.5
OP359

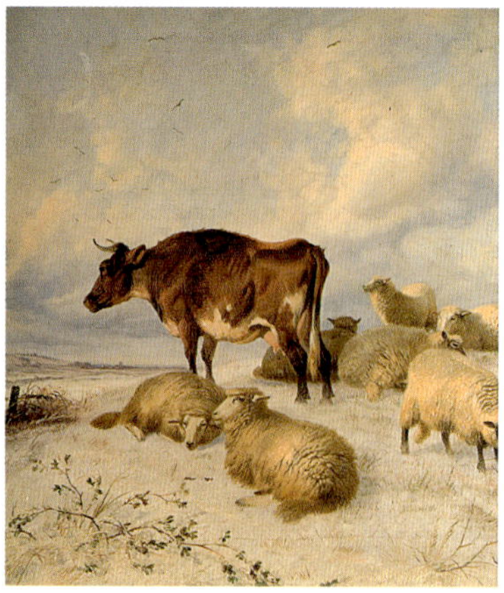

Cooper, Thomas Sidney 1803–1902
Cattle and Sheep in a Snowscape 1864
oil on canvas 35.5 x 30.5
OP38

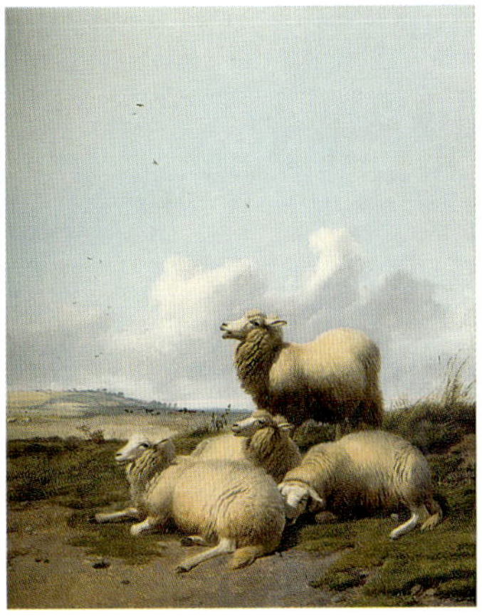

Cooper, Thomas Sidney 1803–1902
Four Sheep 1874
oil on panel 45 x 35
OP241

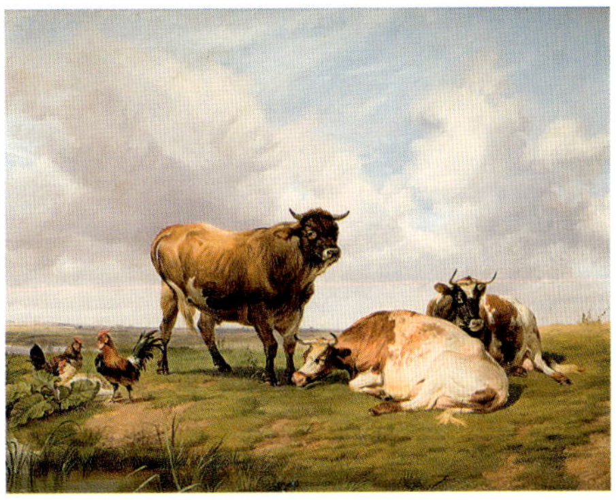

Cooper, Thomas Sidney 1803–1902
Landscape with Cattle and Fowl 1874
oil on canvas 42.5 x 53.5
OP173

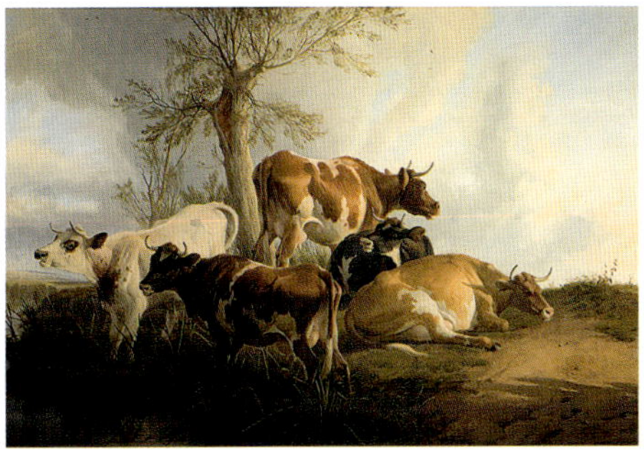

Cooper, Thomas Sidney 1803–1902
Cattle Scene 1876
oil on canvas 76 x 106.5
OP452

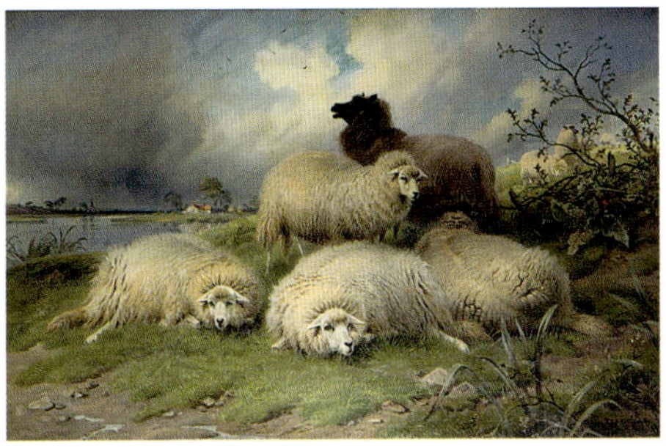

Cooper, Thomas Sidney 1803–1902
Canterbury Meadows 1899
oil on canvas 61 x 92
OP660

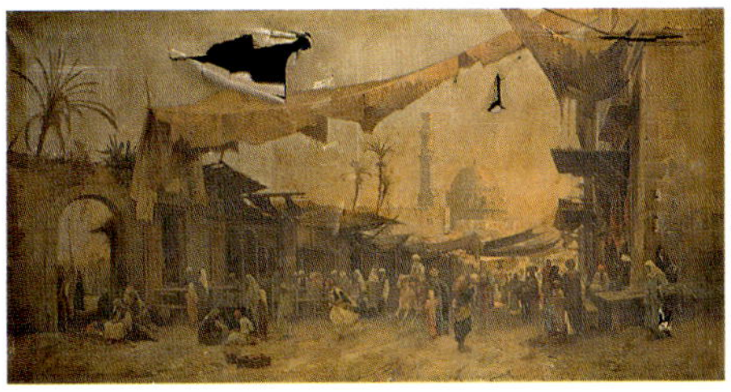

Corrodi, Hermann 1844–1905
View of Boulac, Cairo
oil on canvas 66 x 124.5
OP417

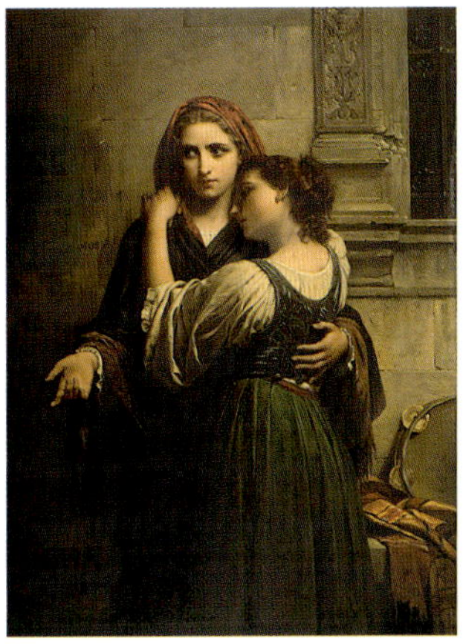

Cot, Pierre Auguste 1837–1883
Charity for My Sister
oil on canvas 145 x 104
OP661

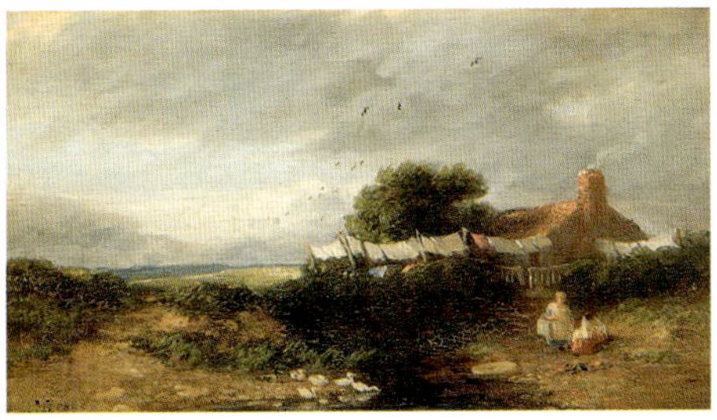

Cox, David the elder 1783–1859
Cottage on Dulwich Common, a Windy Day
1846
oil on canvas 22.6 x 35.5
OP204

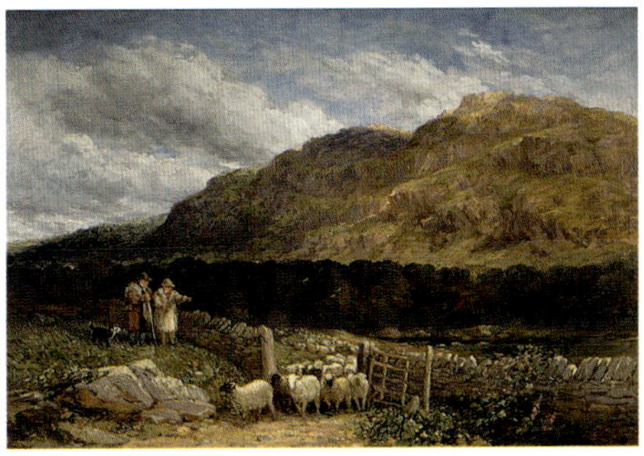

Cox, David the elder 1783–1859
Counting the Flock 1852
oil on canvas 61 x 86.5
OP211

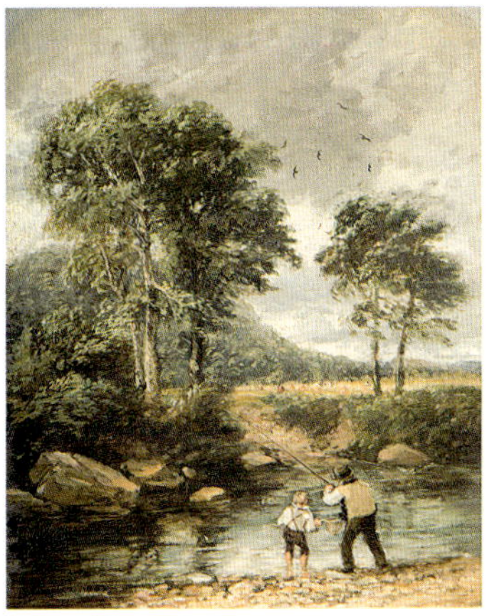

Cox, David the elder 1783–1859
On the Lledr, North Wales 1852
oil on canvas 45.5 x 35.5
OP373

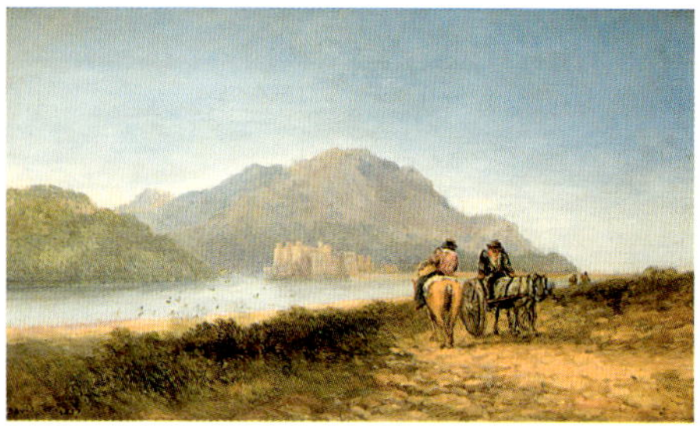

Cox, David the elder 1783–1859
Conway Castle, Caernarvonshire 1857
oil on canvas 43 x 69
OP19

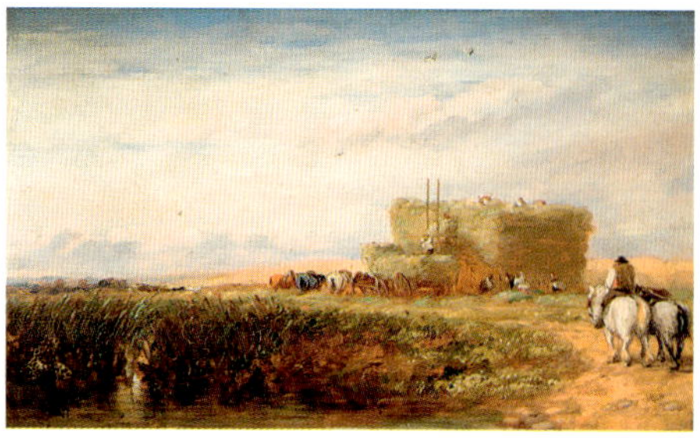

Cox, David the elder (circle of) 1783–1859
The Hayfield 1847
oil on canvas 22 x 35.5
OP186

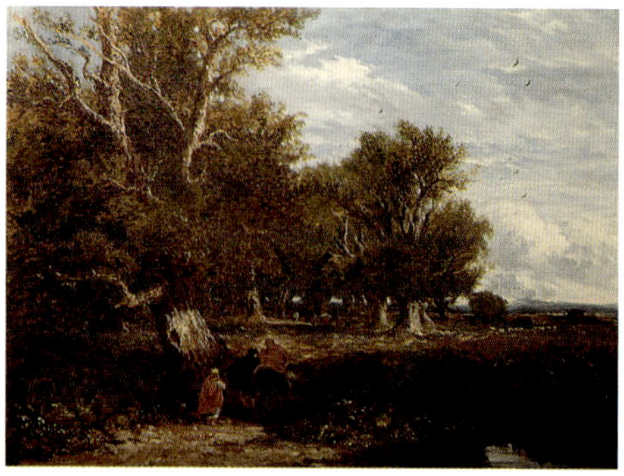

Cox, David the elder (circle of) 1783–1859
The Skirts of the Wood
oil on canvas 71 x 92
OP662

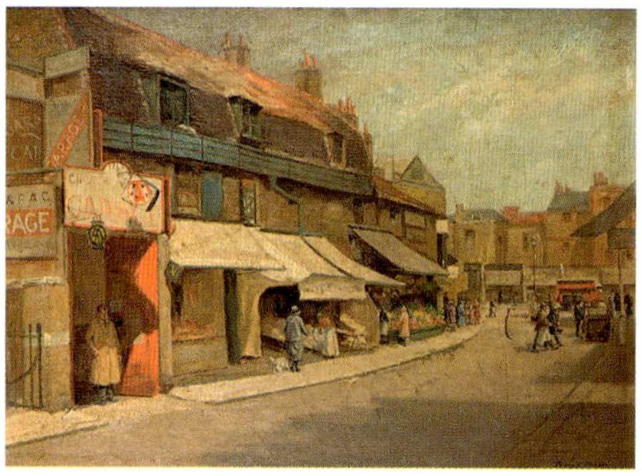

Craft, Percy Robert 1856–1934
Old Church Street, Chelsea
oil on canvas 51 x 66
OP317

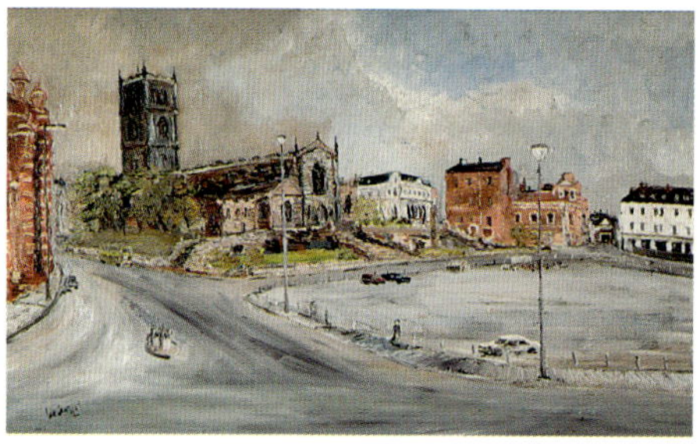

Craig
Wolverhampton 1989
oil on canvas 37 x 59
PCF3

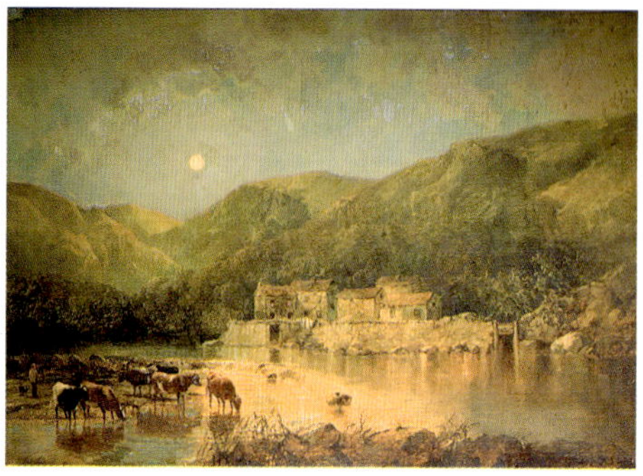

Creswick, Thomas 1811–1869
Landscape 1862
oil on canvas 91.5 x 122
OP125

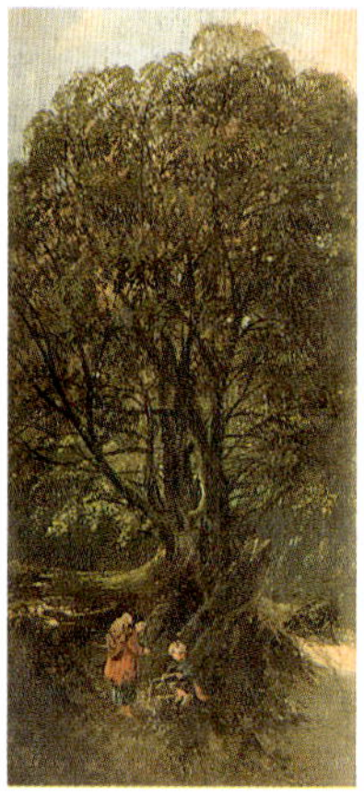

Creswick, Thomas 1811–1869
Landscape with Figures
oil on panel 28.5 x 14.5
OP26

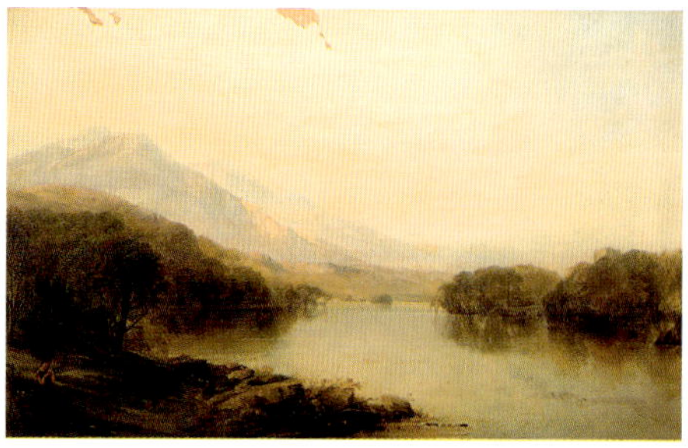

Creswick, Thomas 1811–1869
Loch Eck
oil on canvas 41.5 x 62
OP17

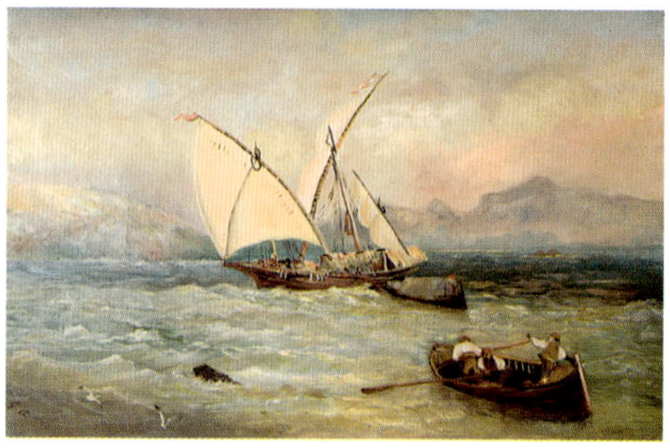

Creswick, Thomas 1811–1869
On the Tees
oil on canvas 26.5 x 36
OP183

Facing page: Batoni, Pompeo, 1708–1787, *John Chetwynd, 1st Earl Talbot (1750–1793)* (detail), 1773, Ingestre Hall Residential Arts Centre, (p. 5)

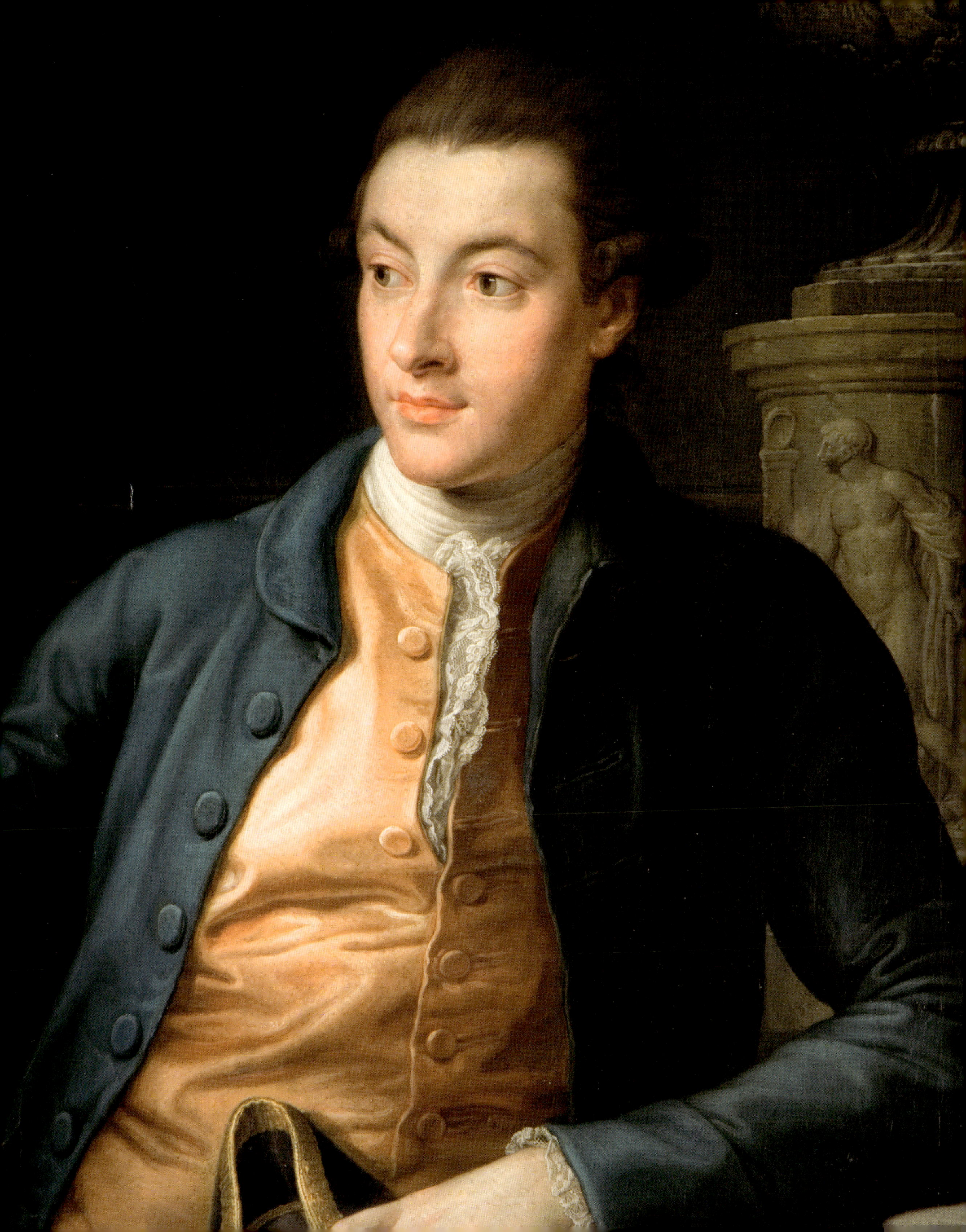

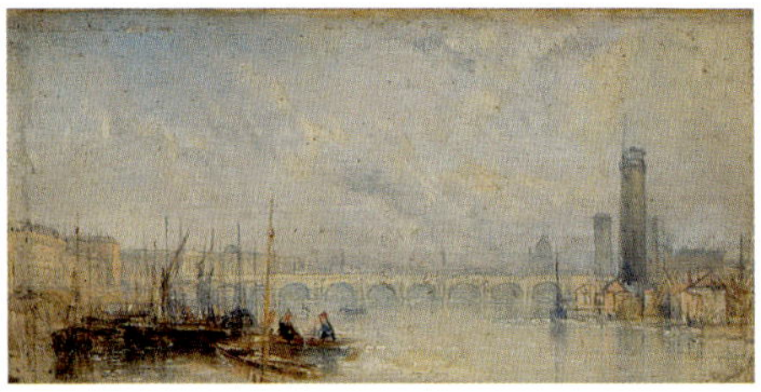

Creswick, Thomas 1811–1869
The Thames and the Shot Tower
oil on board 5 x 10
OP42

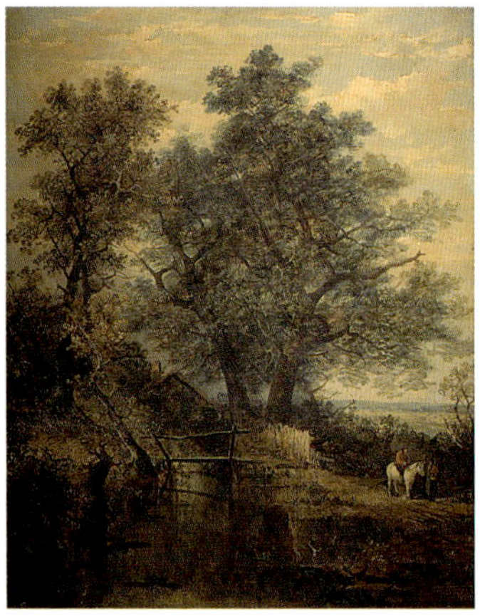

Crome, John 1768–1821
A Stream, Bridge, Trees and Two Figures in a Landscape
oil on canvas 112 x 85
OP663

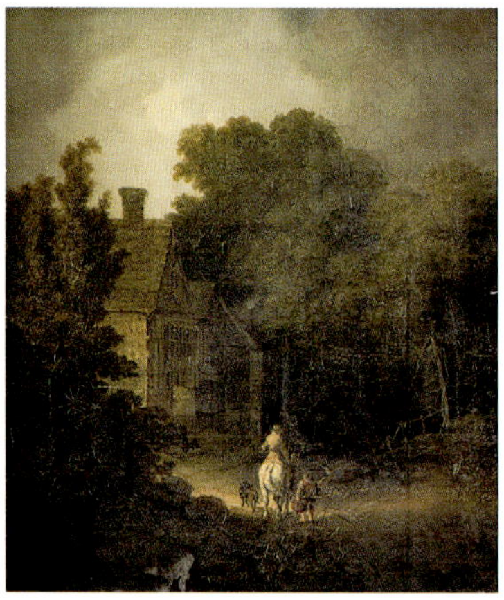

Crome, John 1768–1821
Landscape with Traveller
oil on canvas 76 x 63.5
OP247

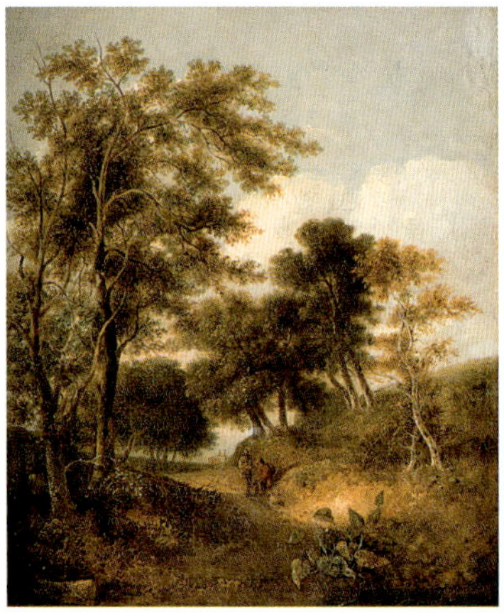

Crome, John 1768–1821
Lane near Norwich
oil on canvas 63.5 x 51
OP180

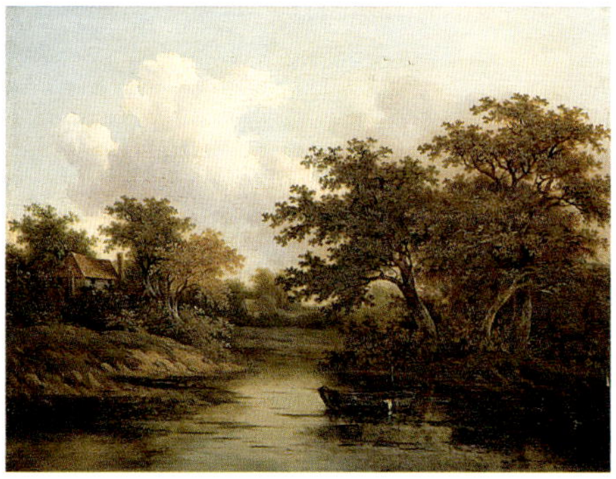

Crome, John 1768–1821
Solitude
oil on panel 44.5 x 55
OP227

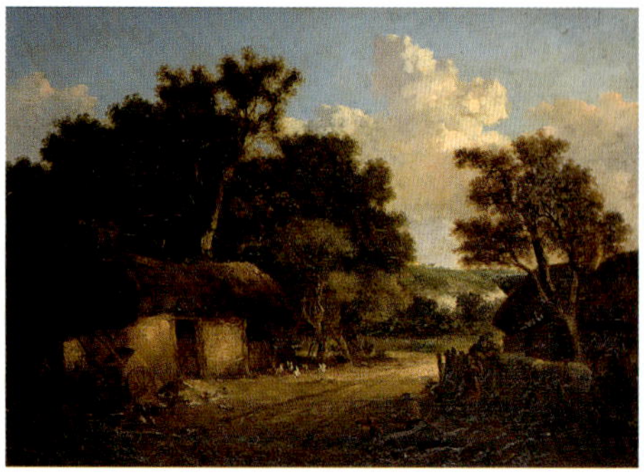

Crome, John (circle of) 1768–1821
Landscape with Cottage
oil on canvas 44.5 x 71
OP11

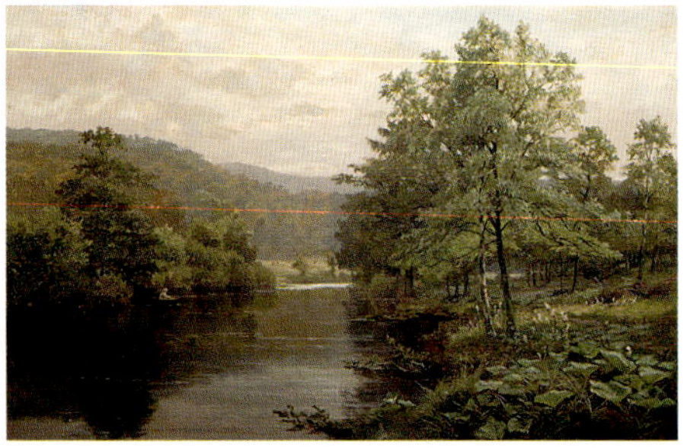

Cubley, Henry Hadfield 1848–1934
On the Derwent, Derbyshire 1886
oil on canvas 51.5 x 77
OP557

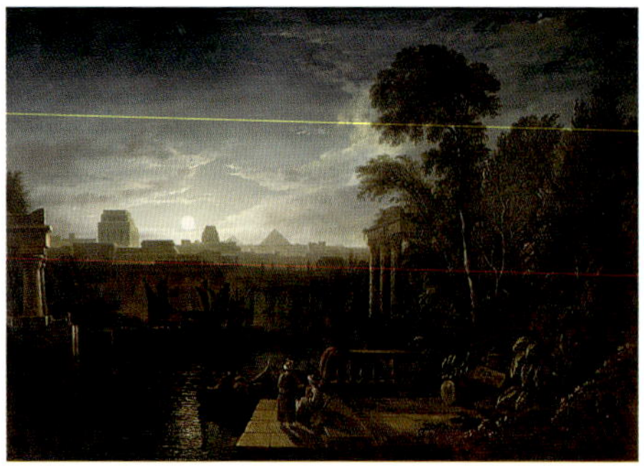

Danby, Francis 1793–1861
Moonlit View of an Eastern City 1859
oil on canvas 57 x 80.5
OP259

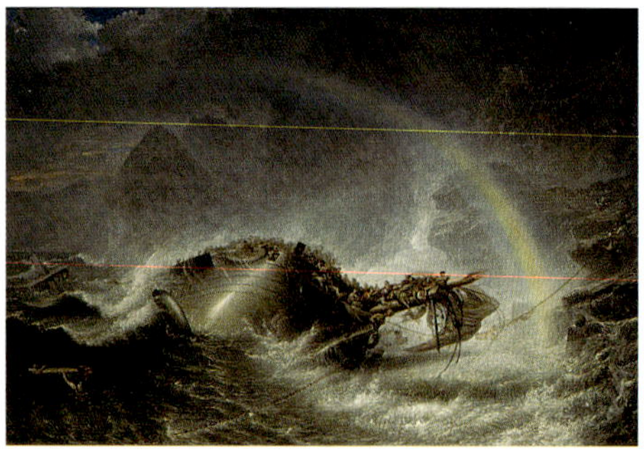

Danby, Francis 1793–1861
The Shipwreck 1859
oil on canvas 77.5 x 107.5
OP82

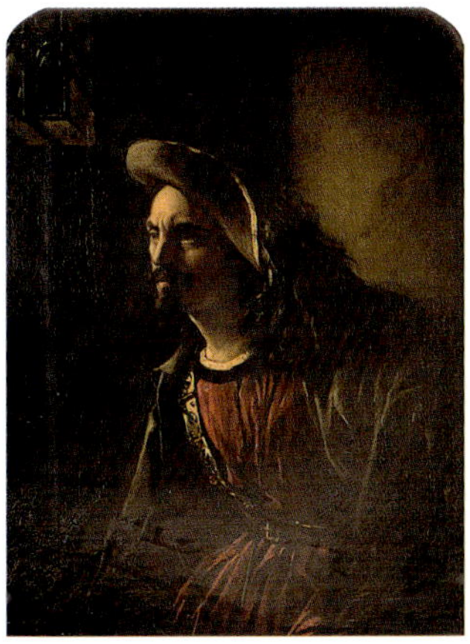

Daniels, William 1813–1880
Portrait of a Man in Plumed Hat
oil on canvas 43 x 33.5
OP548

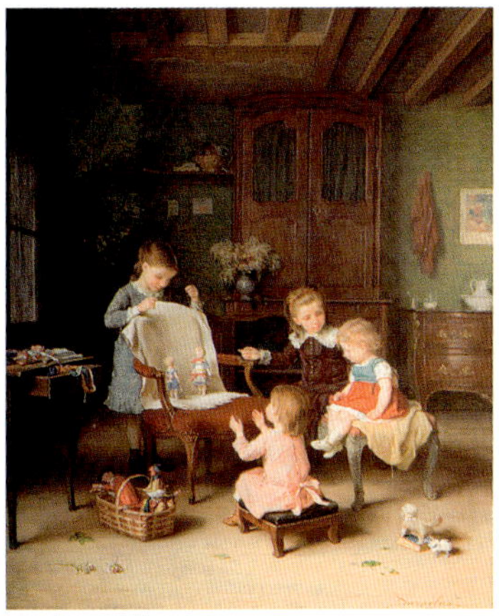

Dargelas, André-Henri 1828–1906
The Happy Family
oil on panel 47 x 37.5
OP482

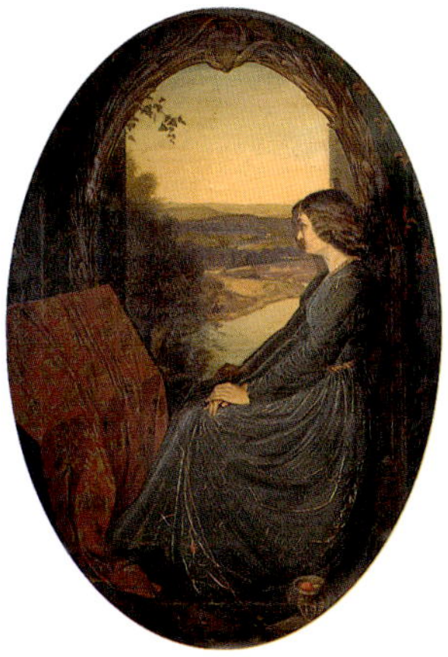

Darvall, Henry active 1848–1889
The Lady of Shalott 1848–1851
oil on canvas 86.5 x 61
OP351

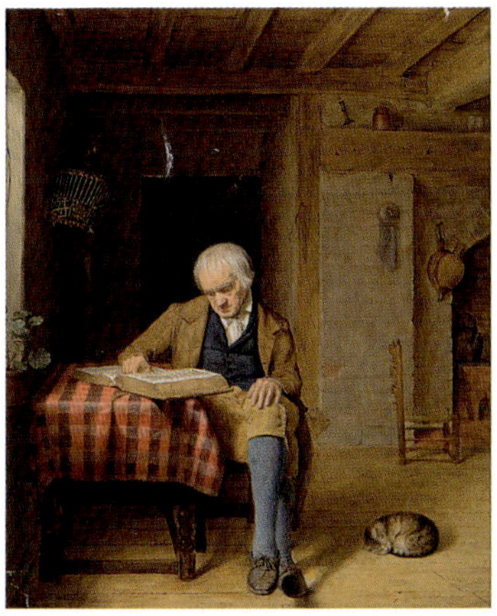

Davis, Edward Thompson 1833–1867
Sunday Afternoon 1853
oil on canvas 72.5 x 42
OP139

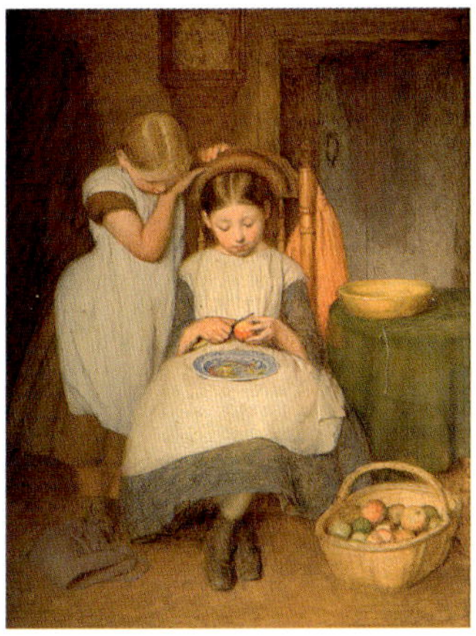

Davis, Edward Thompson 1833–1867
Preparing for Dinner
oil on panel 23 x 17
OP25

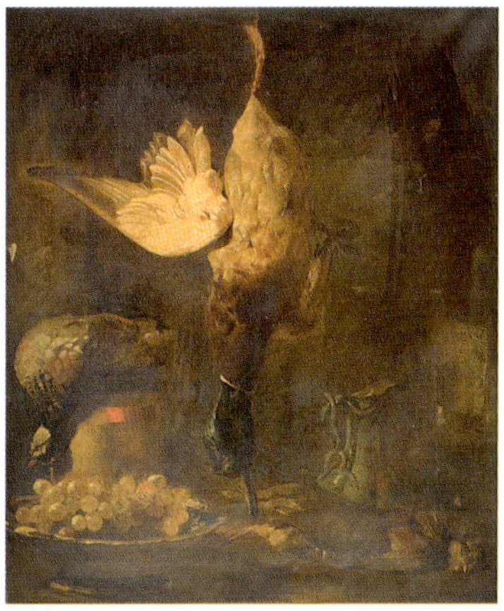

Davis, William 1812–1873
Still Life
oil on canvas 76 x 61.5
OP559

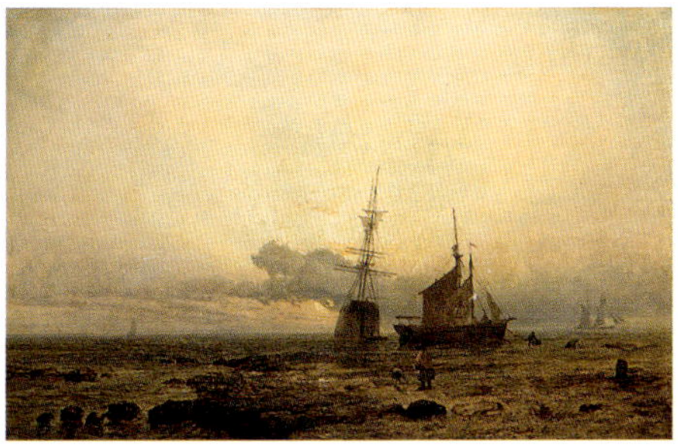

Dawson, Henry 1811–1878
Coast Scene, Evening 1853
oil on canvas 40.5 x 61
OP167

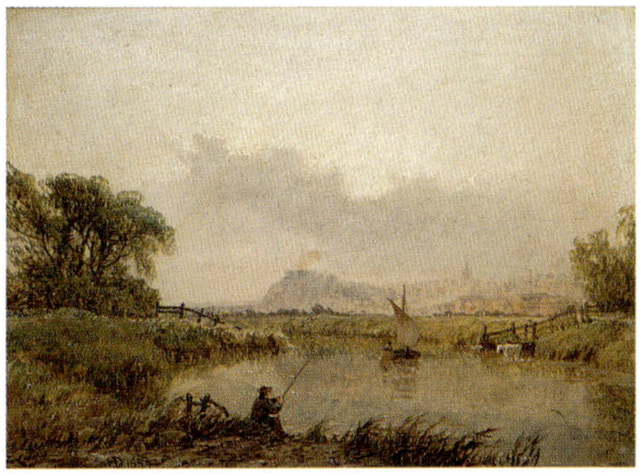

Dawson, Henry 1811–1878
Nottingham from the Trent 1853
oil on panel 15 x 20.5
OP48

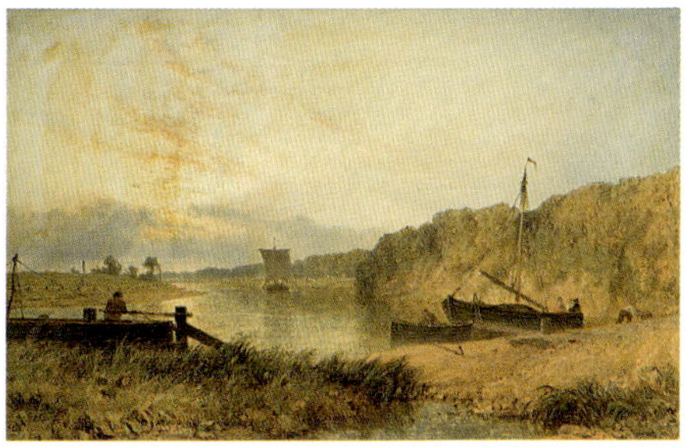

Dawson, Henry 1811–1878
On the Trent near Ratcliffe 1854
oil on canvas 51 x 76
OP365

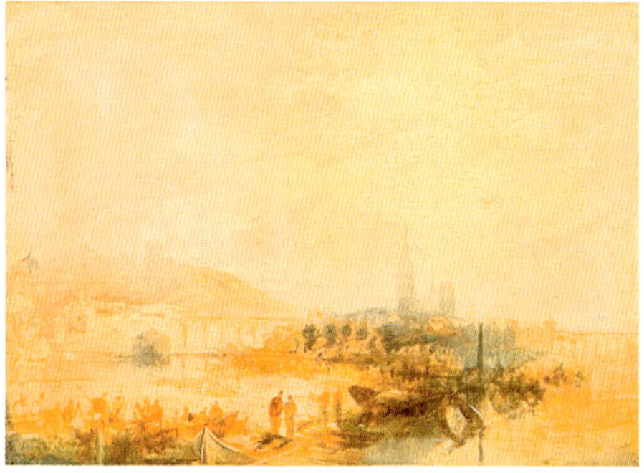

Dawson, Henry 1811–1878
A Study of Rouen
oil on panel 16 x 21.5
OP30

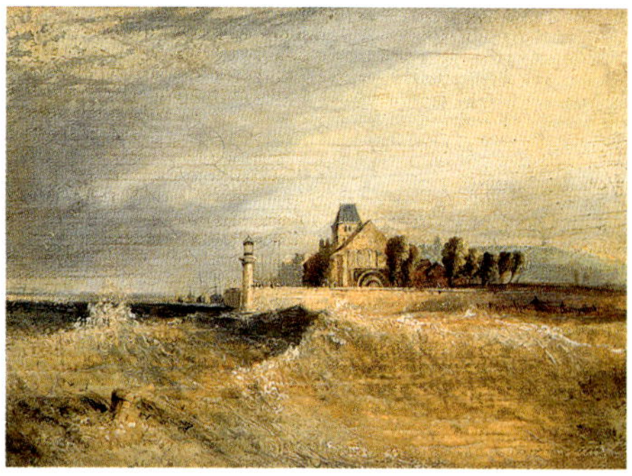

Dawson, Henry 1811–1878
Coast Scene with Pier
oil on board 19 x 25.5
OP34

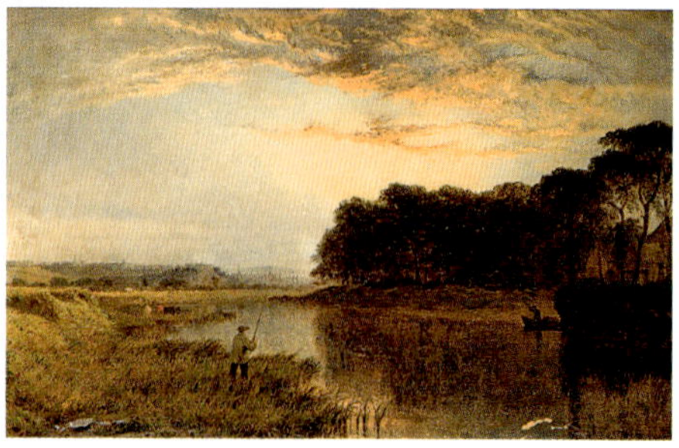

Dawson, Henry 1811–1878
On the Trent
oil on canvas 51 x 77
OP366

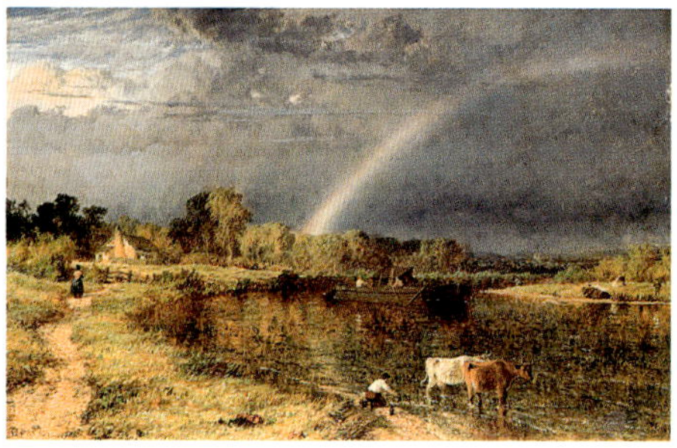

Dawson, Henry 1811–1878
The Rainbow
oil on canvas 38.5 x 56.6
OP665

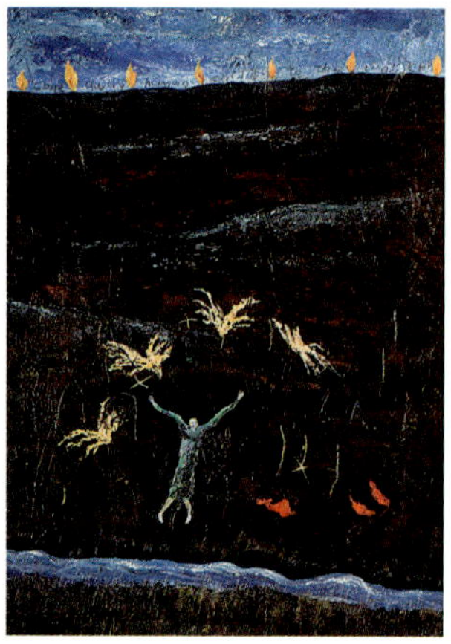

Deacy, Brendon b.1964
Stolen Woman
oil on board 81 x 65
OP861

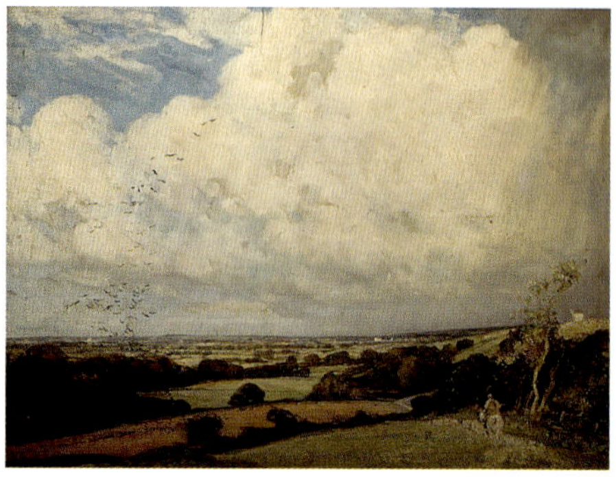

Deville, Joseph Vickers 1856–1925
View of Shropshire 1850
oil on canvas 72.5 x 91.5
OP485

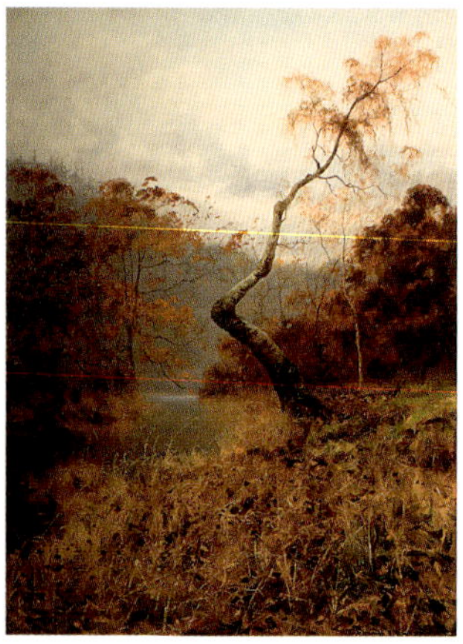

Deville, Joseph Vickers 1856–1925
The Silent Pool 1895
oil on canvas 127 x 91.5
OP416

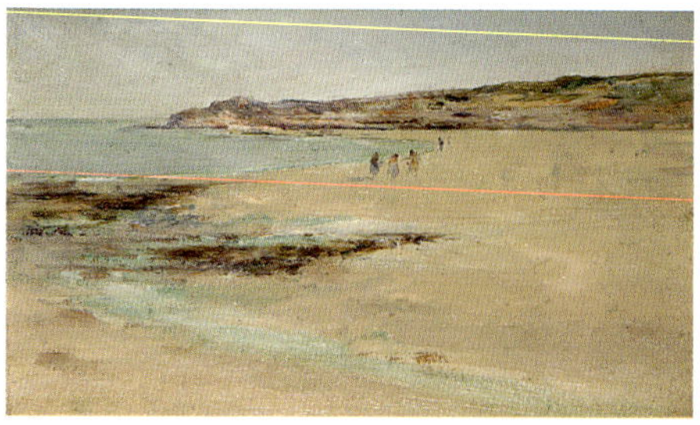

Deville, Joseph Vickers 1856–1925
Porthwen Bay, Angelsea 1905
oil on panel 15 x 23
OP297

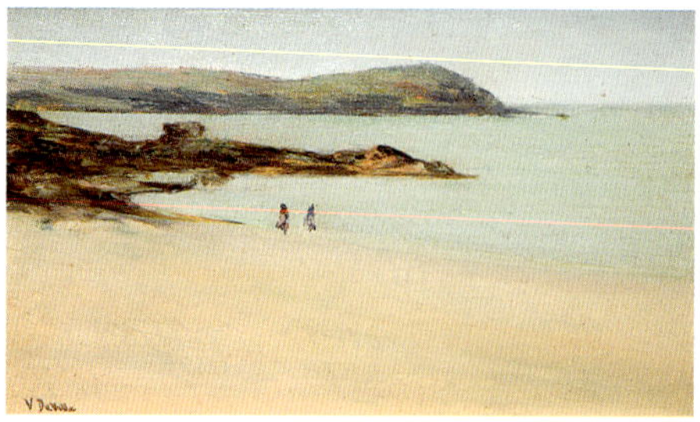

Deville, Joseph Vickers 1856–1925
Coast Scene
oil on canvas 14.6 x 23
OP156

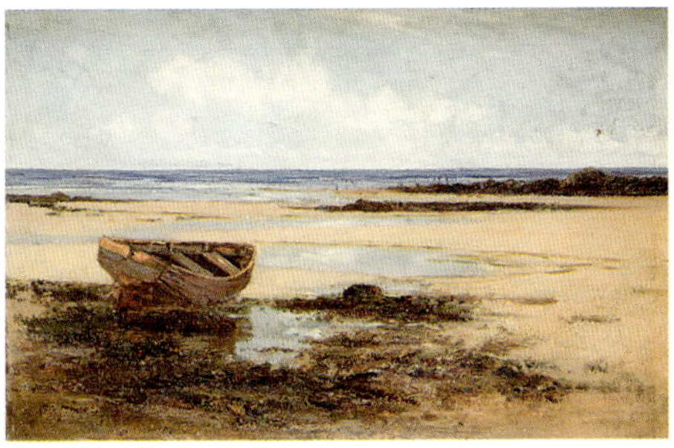

Deville, Joseph Vickers 1856–1925
Coast Scene
oil on canvas 40.5 x 61
OP302

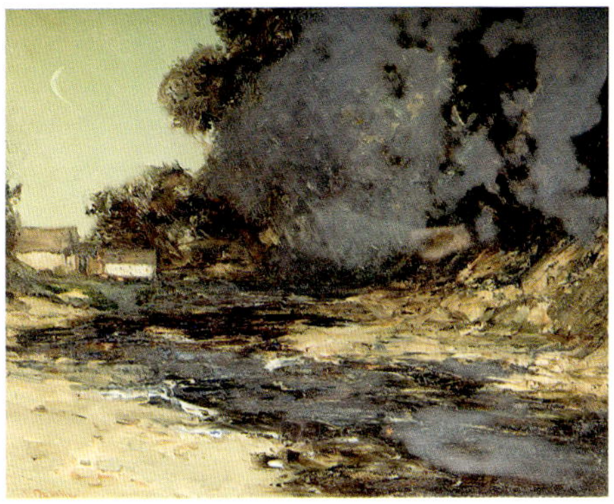

Deville, Joseph Vickers 1856–1925
Study for 'Trout Stream'
oil on canvas 29 x 35
OP591

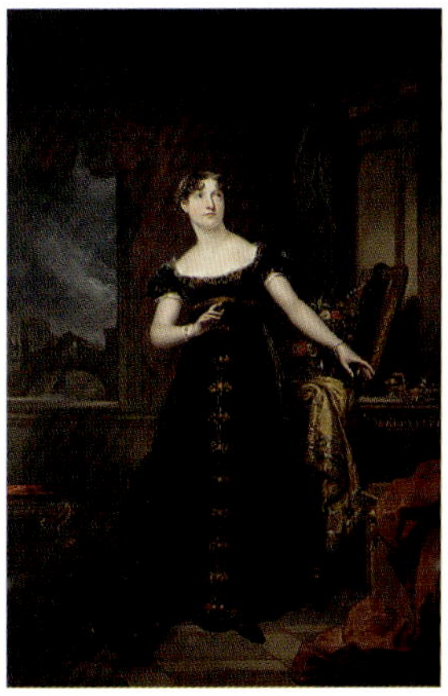

Devis, Arthur William 1762–1822
Miss Eliza O'Neill as Belvidera in Thomas Otway's 'Venice Preserved' 1816–1822
oil on canvas 254 x 160
OP86

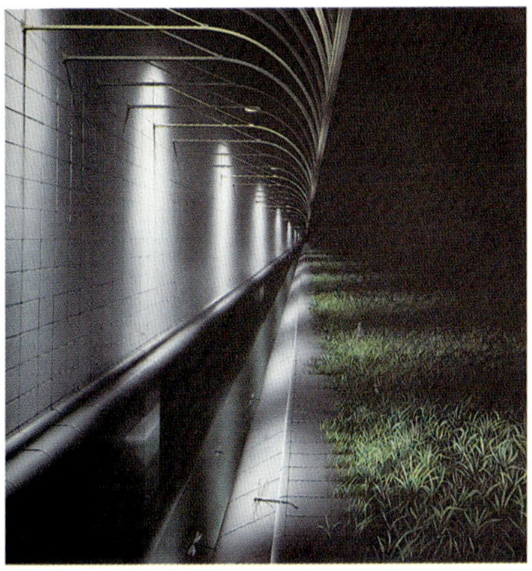

Dickinson, Timothy
Stadium, Night
oil on canvas 95.5 x 88.5
OP781

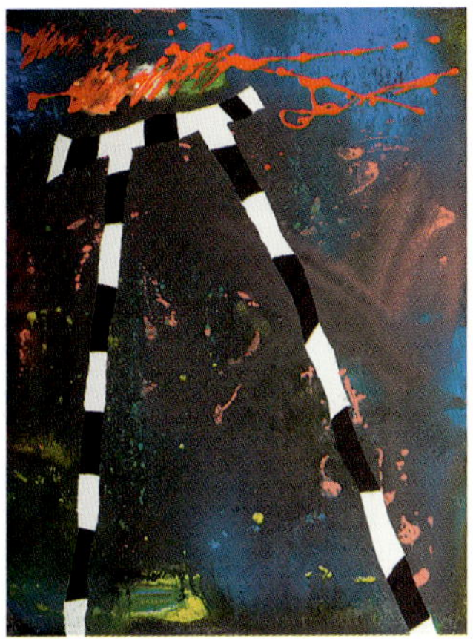

Dixon, Rex b.1939
16–18 April 1985 1985
oil on canvas 63 x 46
OP891

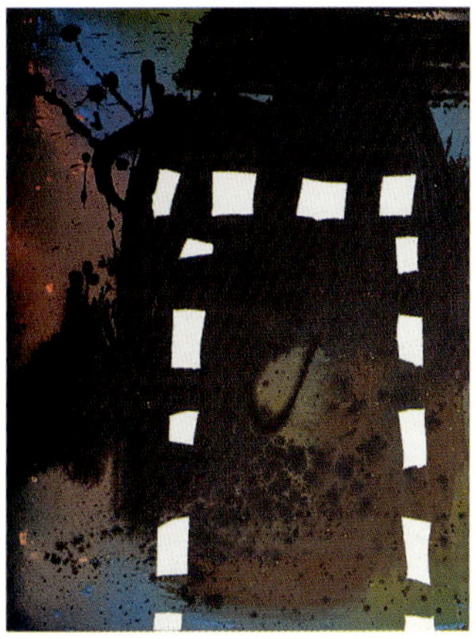

Dixon, Rex b.1939
16–18 April 1985 (Northern Ireland) 1985
oil on canvas 61 x 46
OP890

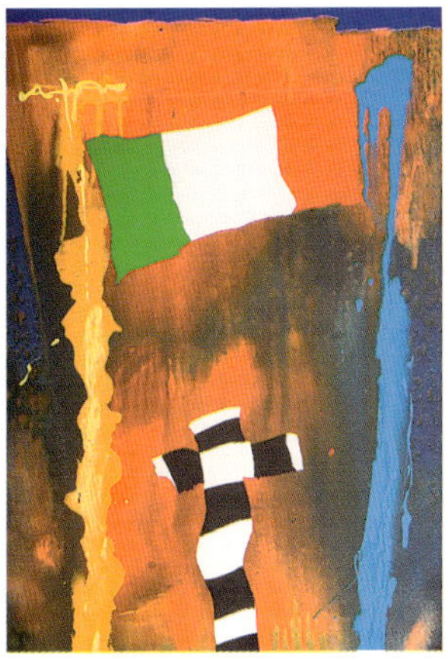

Dixon, Rex b.1939
Parade 29–4–85 to 1–5–85 1985
oil on canvas 76 x 51
OP895

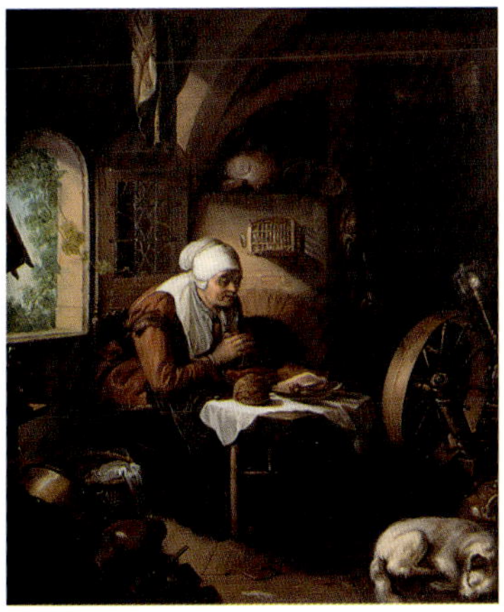

Dou, Gerrit 1613–1675
Grace before Meat
oil on panel 24.8 x 20.3
OP29

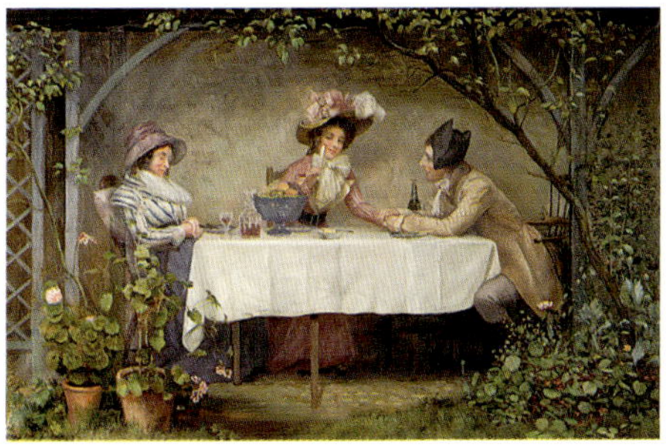

Downing, Delapoer active 1885–1902
Mother Has Fallen Asleep
oil on canvas 54.5 x 85
OP666

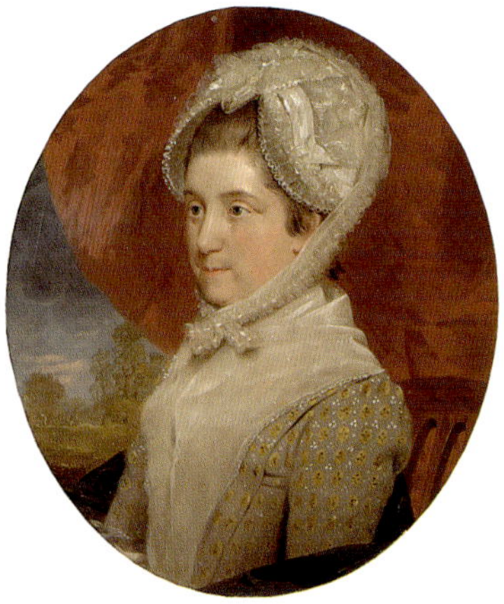

Downman, John 1750–1824
Portrait of a Lady 1778
oil on panel 25.5 x 20
OP757

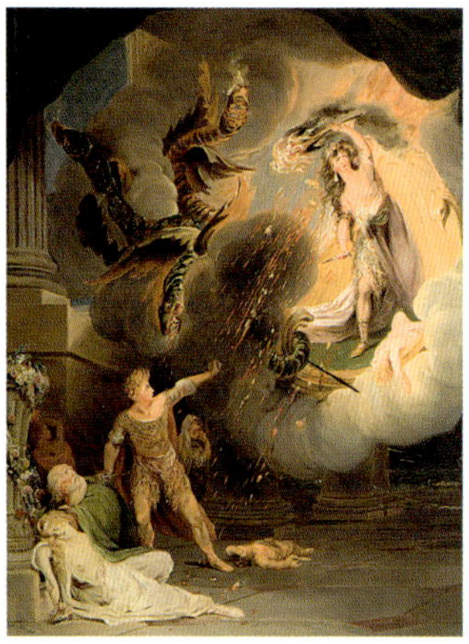

Downman, John 1750–1824
An Episode from the Story of Jason and Medea
oil on panel 59 x 44.5
OP480

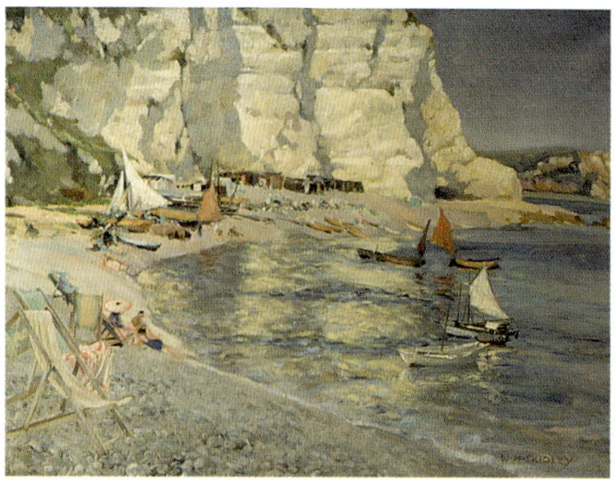

Dudley, William Harold 1890–1949
Beer, Devon
oil on canvas 56.6 x 70
OP676

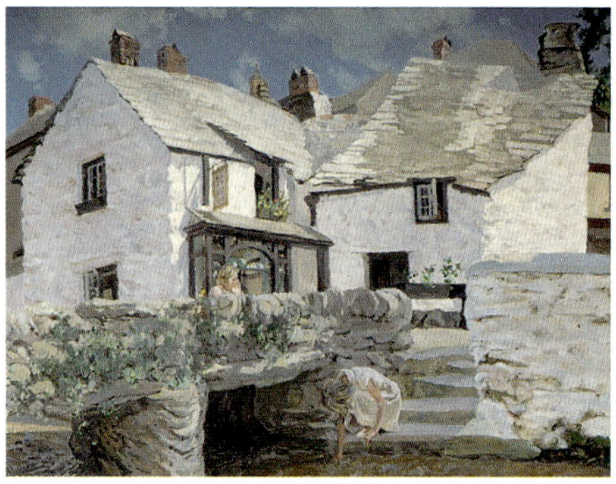

Dudley, William Harold 1890–1949
Couches's Cottage, Polperro
oil on canvas 51 x 61
OP673

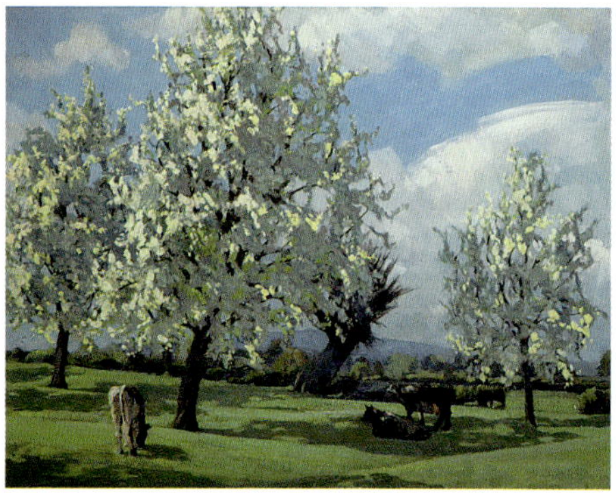

Dudley, William Harold 1890–1949
In the Cotswolds
oil on canvas 51 x 61.5
OP669

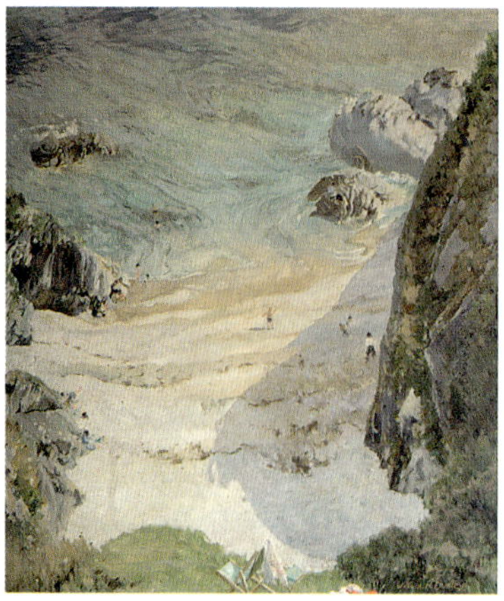

Dudley, William Harold 1890–1949
Lantivet Bay
oil on canvas 76 x 63.5
OP667

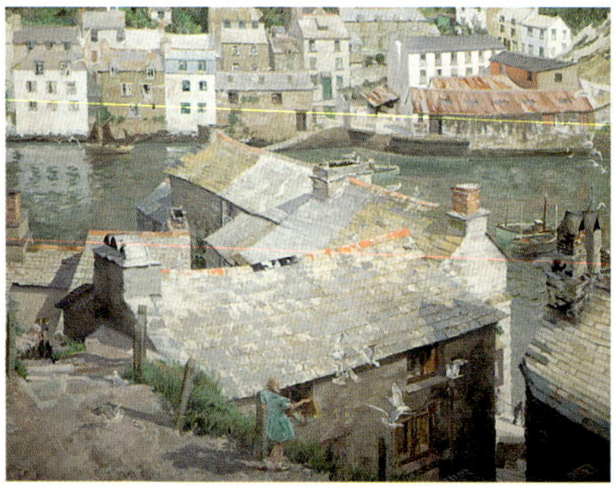

Dudley, William Harold 1890–1949
Old Polperro
oil on canvas 101.5 x 126.5
OP670

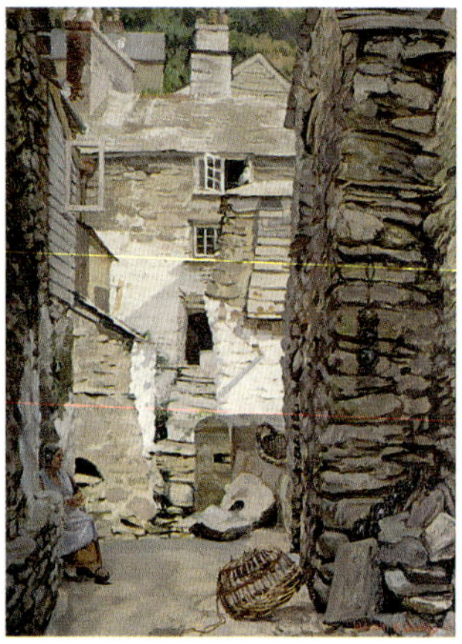

Dudley, William Harold 1890–1949
Polperro
oil on canvas 77 x 56
OP672

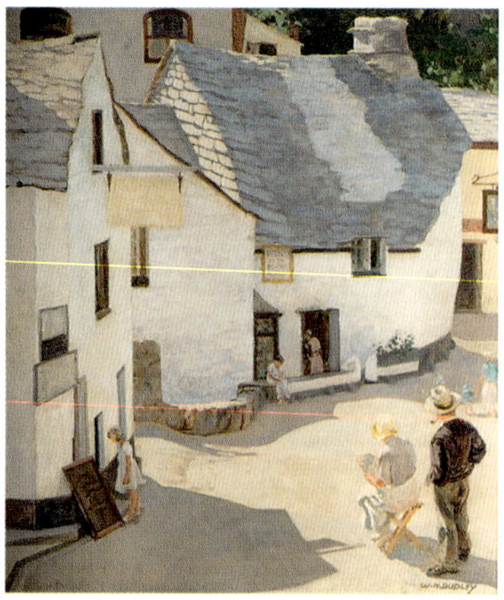

Dudley, William Harold 1890–1949
Polperro in Summertime
oil on board 60.5 x 51
OP671

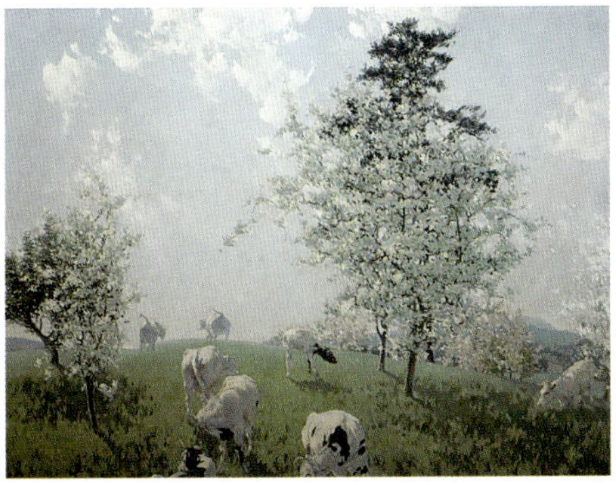

Dudley, William Harold 1890–1949
Silver, Blue and Green
oil on canvas 51 x 61
OP674

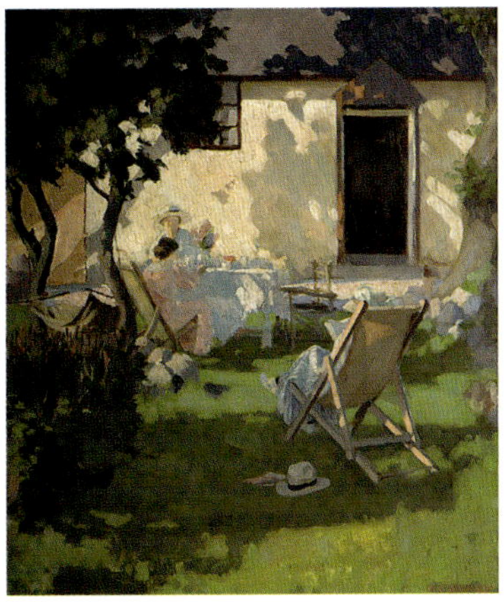

Dudley, William Harold 1890–1949
Summer Cottage
oil on canvas 62 x 52
OP679

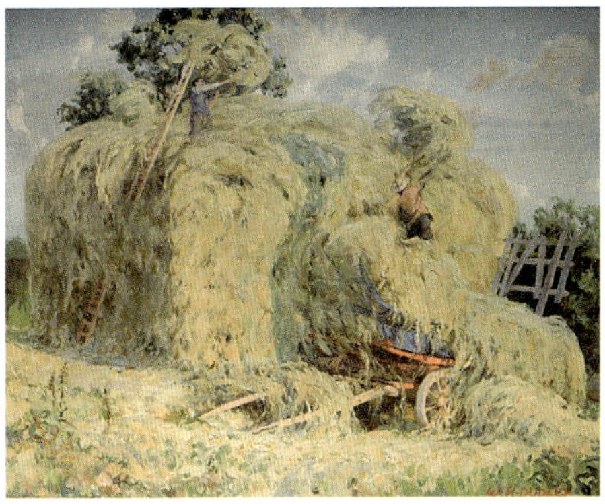

Dudley, William Harold 1890–1949
The New Rick
oil on canvas 51.5 x 61.5
OP675

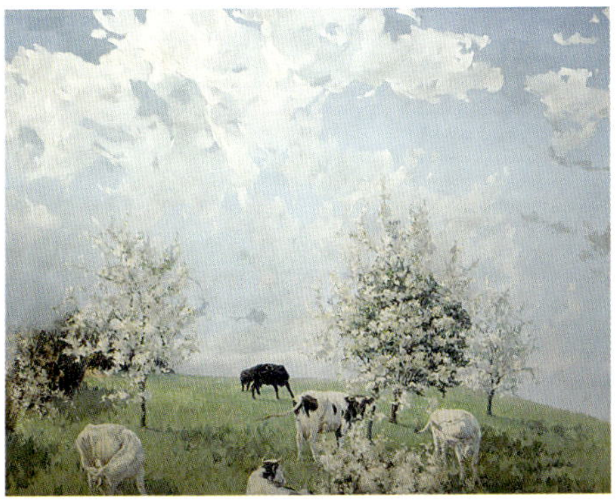

Dudley, William Harold 1890–1949
The Pear, the Sloe and Spring
oil on canvas 102 x 126.5
OP678

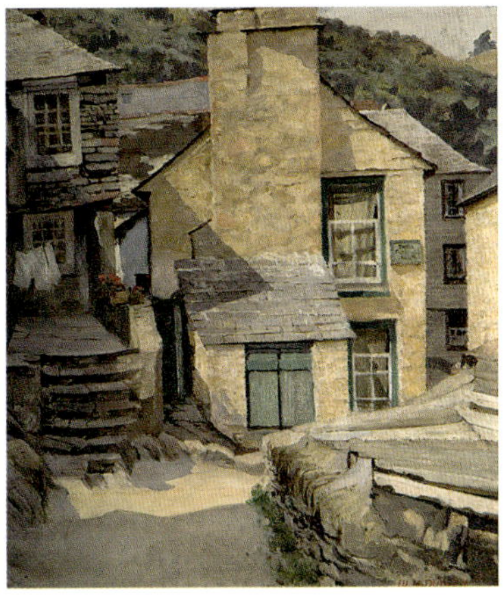

Dudley, William Harold 1890–1949
The 'Three Pilchards', Polperro
oil on canvas 56.5 x 51.5
OP677

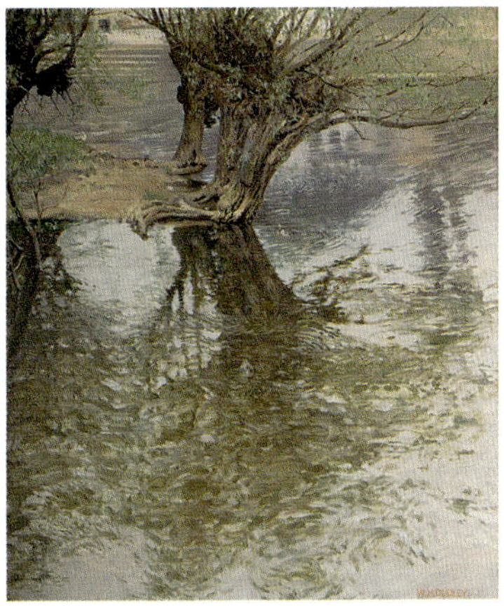

Dudley, William Harold 1890–1949
The Willows, Evesham
oil on canvas 76 x 64
OP668

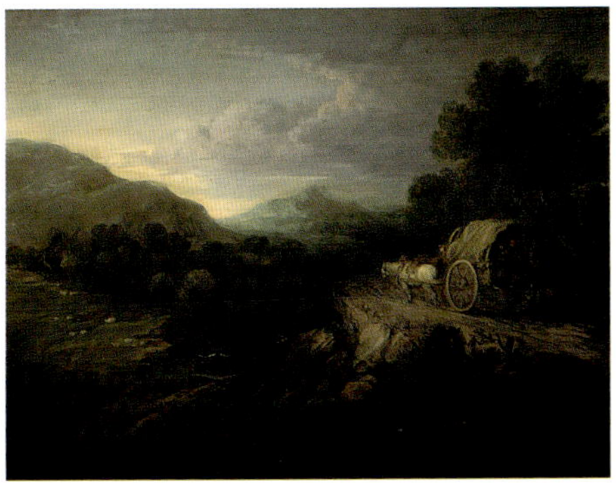

Dupont, Gainsborough 1754–1797
The Travellers
oil on canvas 63 x 76
OP87

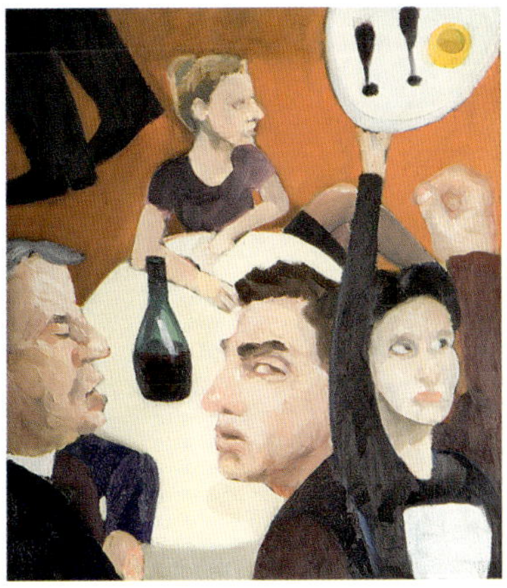

Durkin, Robert b.1966
Insufficient Units
oil on hessian 70 x 60
OP866

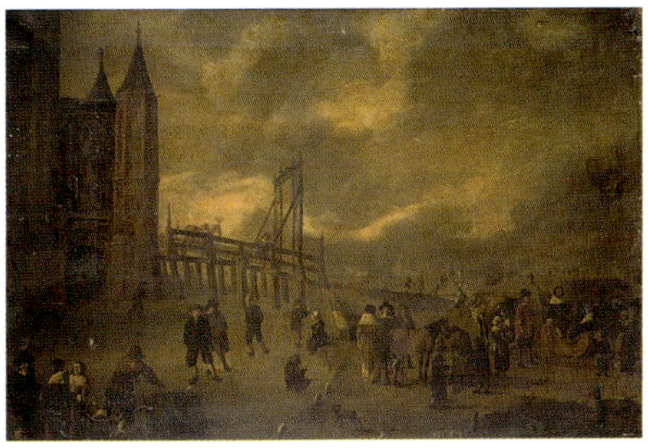

Dutch School 17th C
Skating on a Frozen River
oil on canvas 76 x 127
OP418

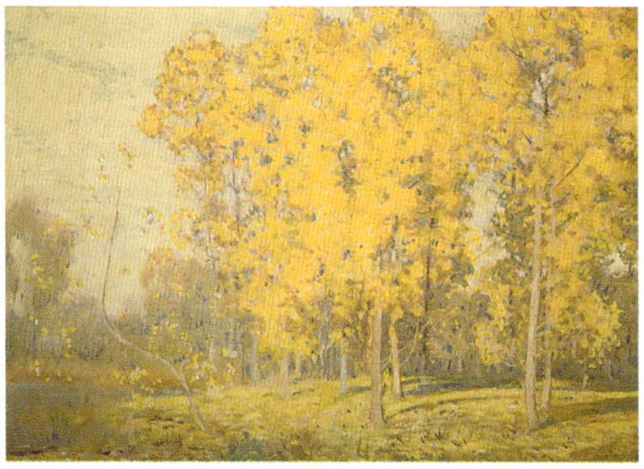

East, Alfred 1849–1913
Landscape with Trees, Autumn
oil on canvas 42.5 x 57
OP13

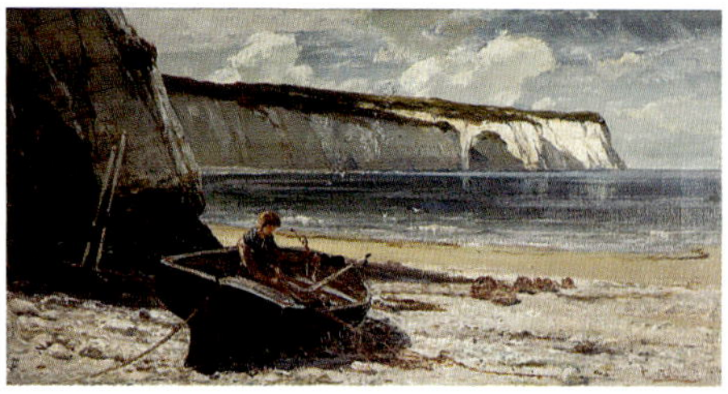

Ellis, Edwin 1841–1895
The Rainy Landing, Flamborough Head, Yorkshire
oil on canvas 45.5 x 84
OP478

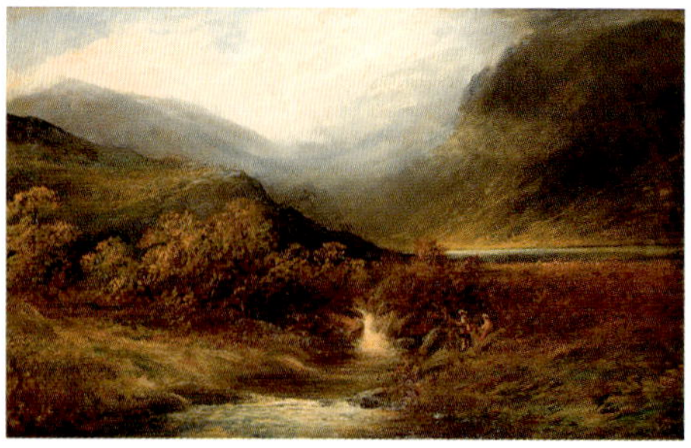

Ellis, Joseph active 1878
Mountain Stream with Sheep
oil on canvas 60.5 x 91.5
OP555

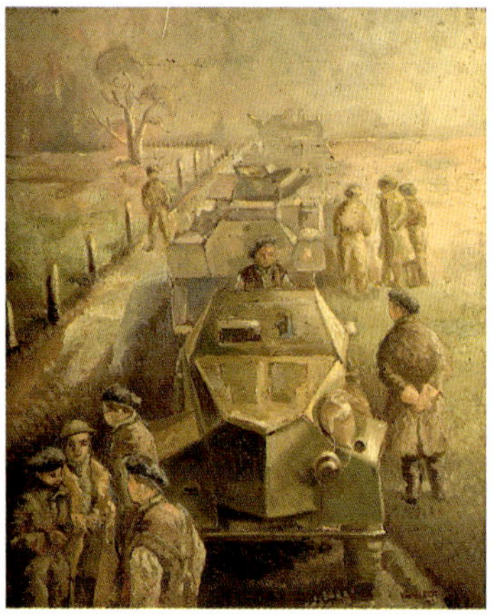

Elst, Willem van der
Wayside Halt 1943
oil on canvas 59 x 47
OP385

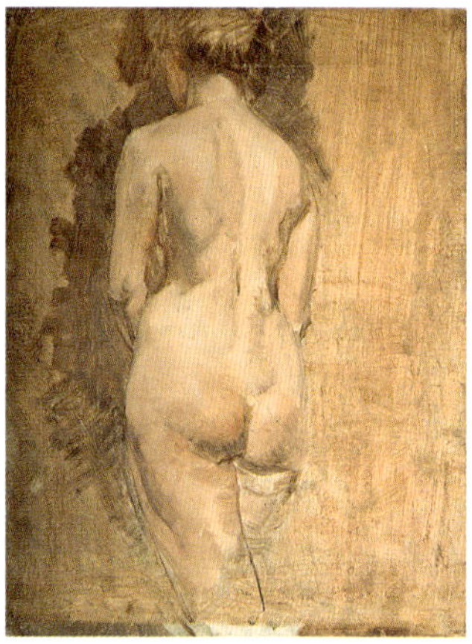

Emmerson, Robert Jackson 1878–1944
Life Study
oil on canvas 38 x 28
OP788

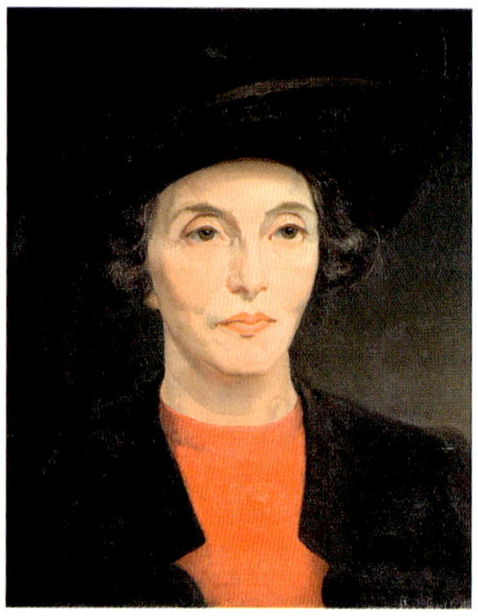

Emmerson, Robert Jackson 1878–1944
Mary Gibson (1888–1966)
oil on canvas 51 x 40.5
OP609

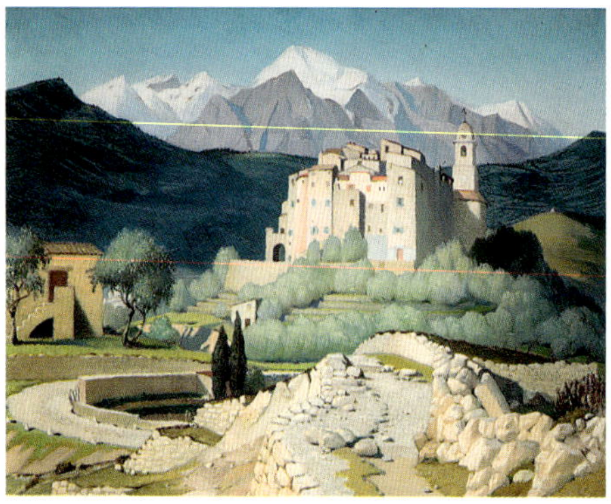

Emmerson, Robert Jackson 1878–1944
Sasso di Bordighera
oil on canvas 51 x 61
OP792

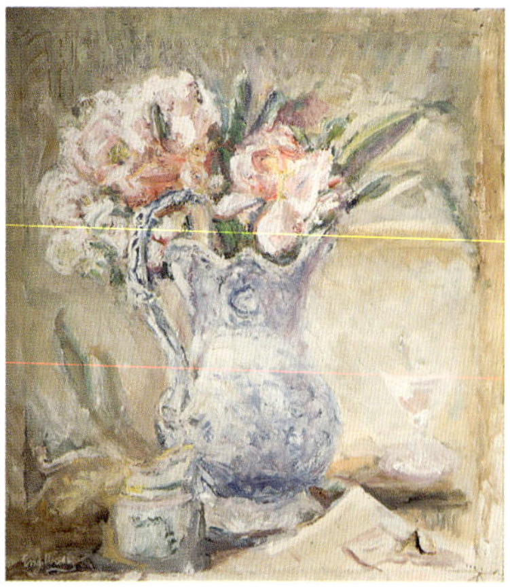

Engelbach, Florence 1872–1951
Peonies
oil on canvas 66 x 57
OP323

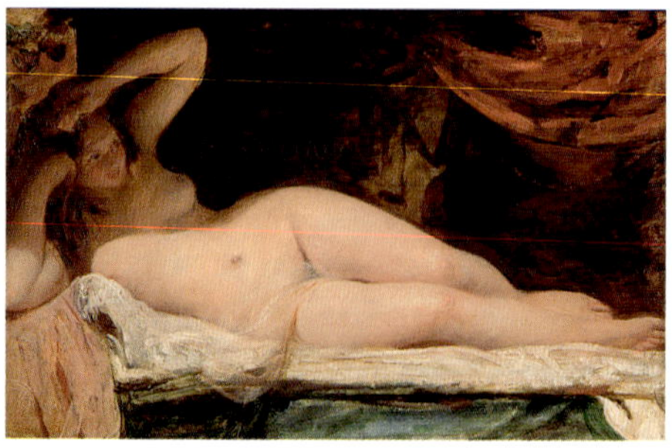

Etty, William 1787–1849
Reclining Nude
oil on card 31.5 x 47
OP67

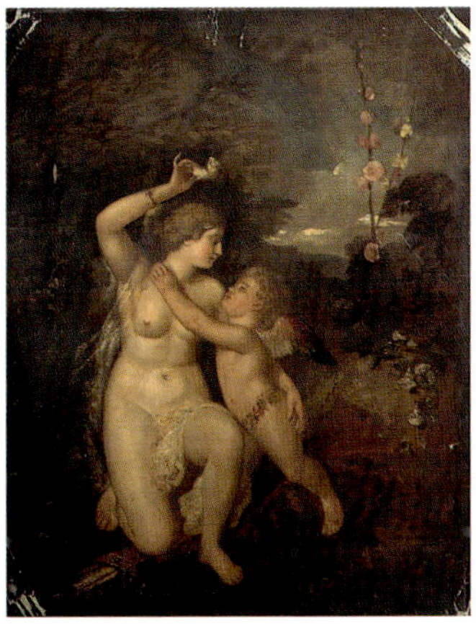

Etty, William 1787–1849
Venus and Cupid
oil on canvas 117 x 90
OP680

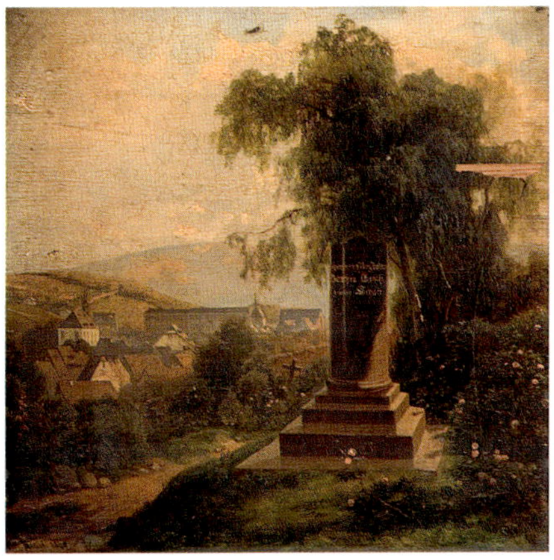

Facchi
Monument 1849
oil on panel 25.5 x 25.5
OP68

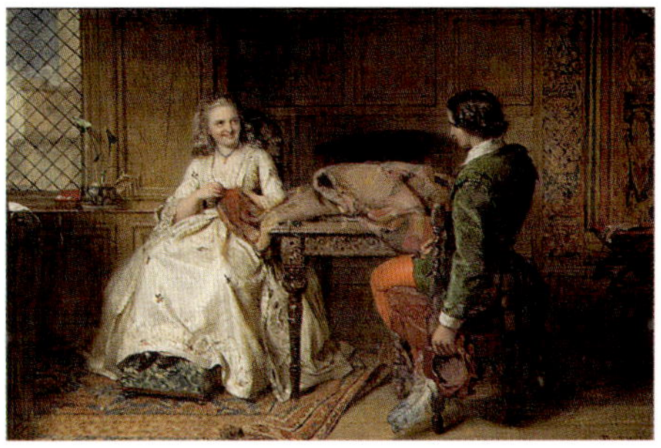

Faed, John 1820–1902
Catherine Seyton and Roland Graeme, from Sir Walter Scott's 'The Abbot' 1863
oil on board 21.5 x 32
OP170

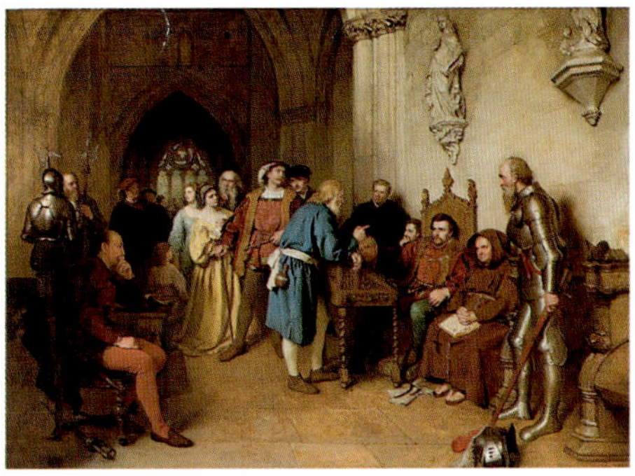

Faed, John 1820–1902
The Warning before Flodden 1874
oil on canvas 137 x 185
OP435

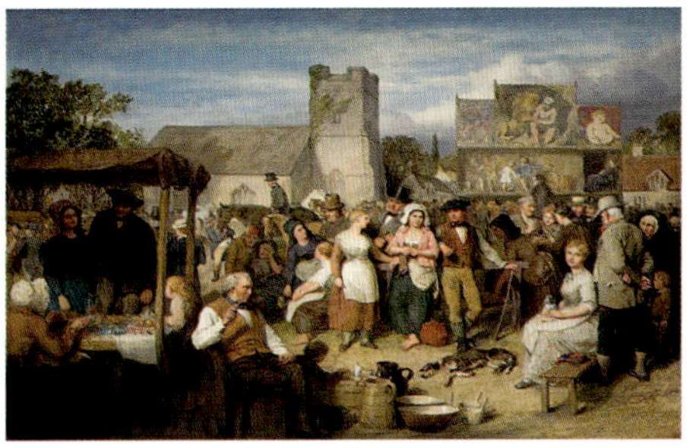

Faed, John 1820–1902
The Statute Fair
oil on board 41 x 58
OP215

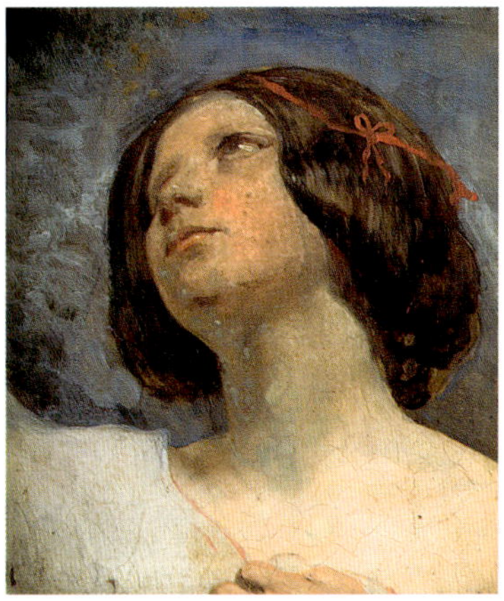

Faed, Thomas 1826–1900
Study of a Woman's Head
oil on canvas 13.5 x 11
OP40

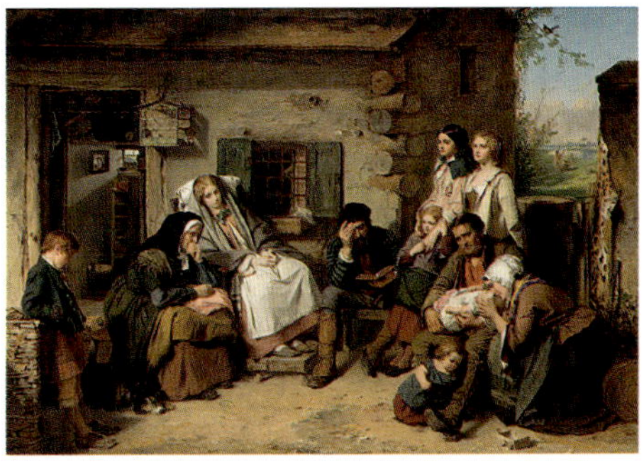

Faed, Thomas 1826–1900
Sunday in the Backwoods
oil on canvas 56 x 76
OP193

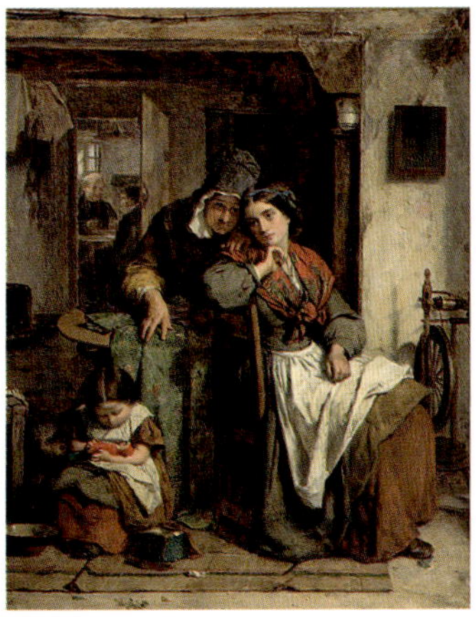

Faed, Thomas 1826–1900
The Silken Gown
oil on canvas 76 x 63.5
OP102

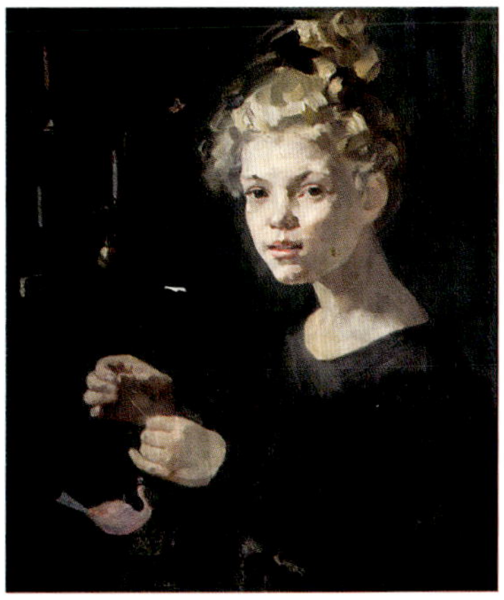

Fagan, Betty Maud Christian d.1932
Dressing the Christmas Tree
oil on canvas 61 x 51
OP295

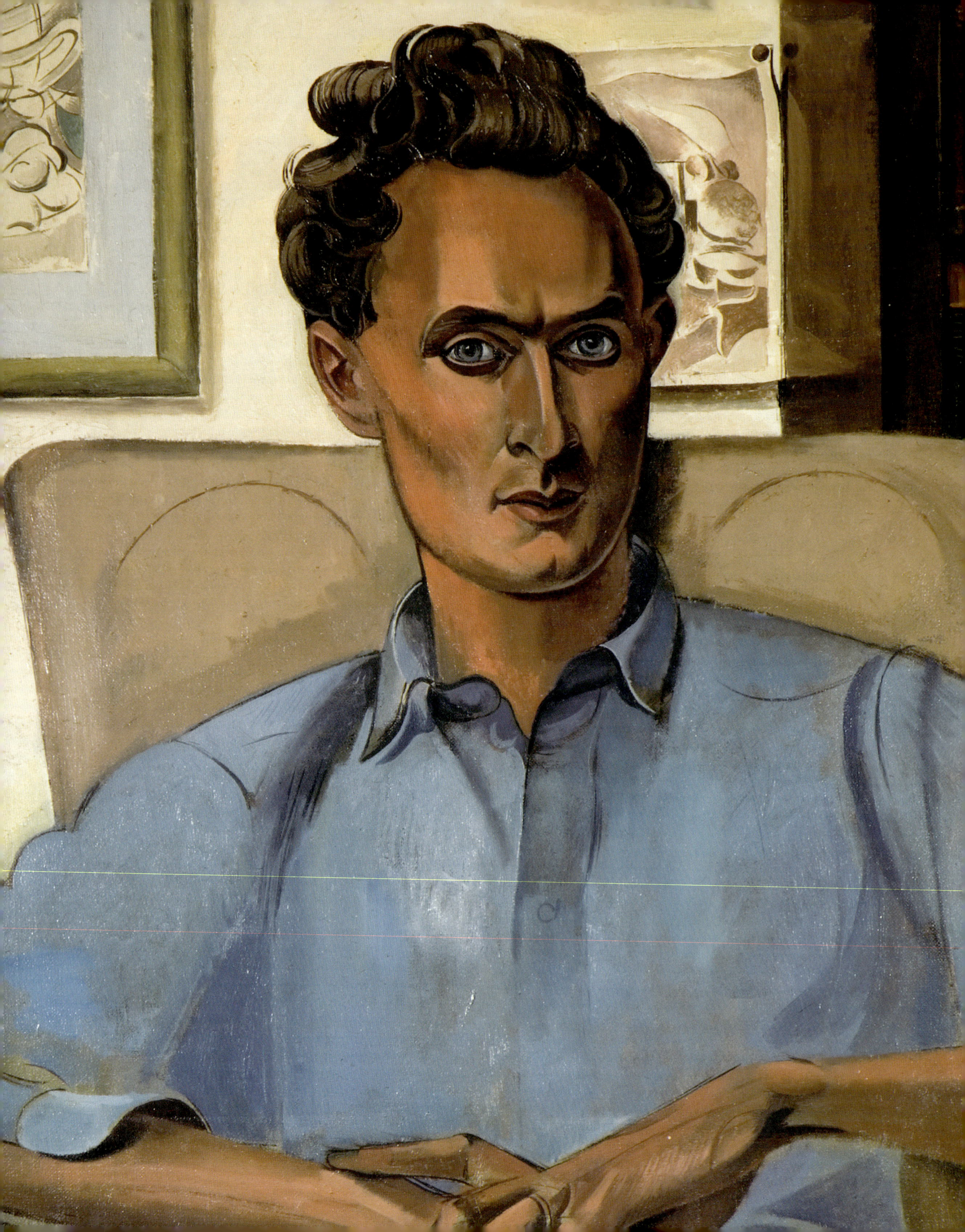

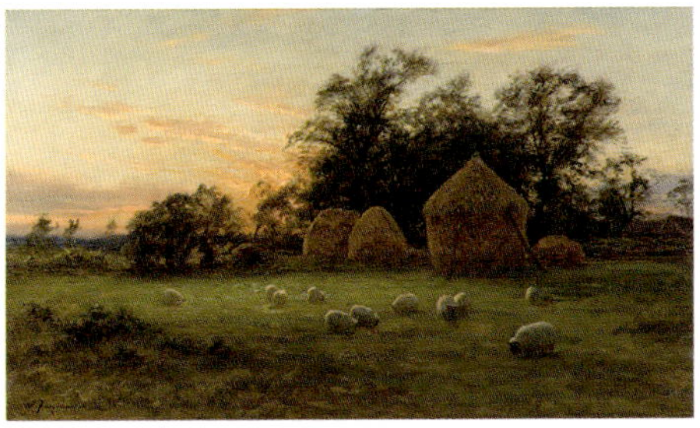

Farquharson, Joseph 1846–1935
Evening
oil on canvas 47 x 76
OP681

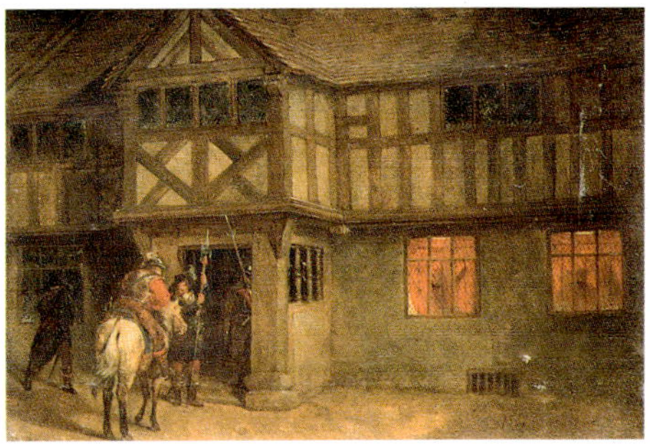

Farrier, Robert 1796–1879
The Courier
oil on canvas 25.5 x 32.5
OP150

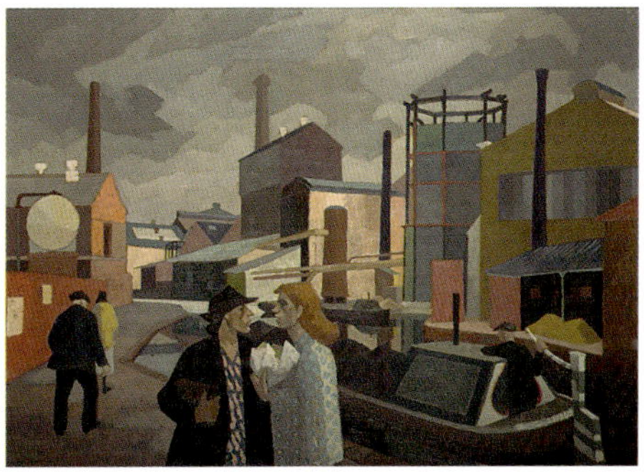

Fereday, Joseph 1917–2001
Catchem's Corner, Bilston
oil on canvas 56 x 76
OP682

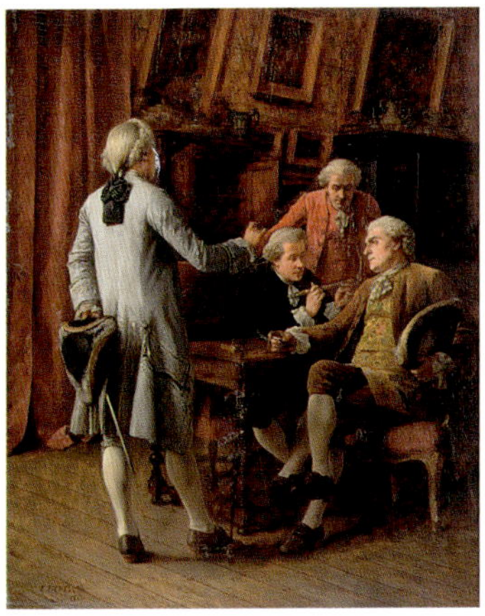

Fichel, Eugène 1826–1895
The Connoisseurs 1867
oil on canvas 28 x 21.5
OP283

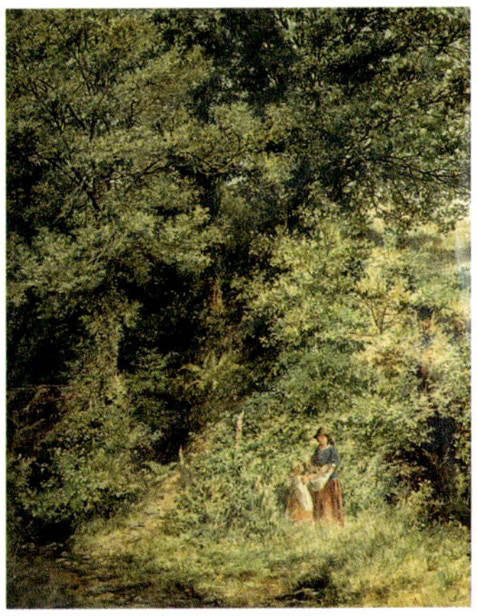

Finnie, John 1829–1907
Gathering Wild Flowers 1865
oil on canvas 56.6 x 44
OP578

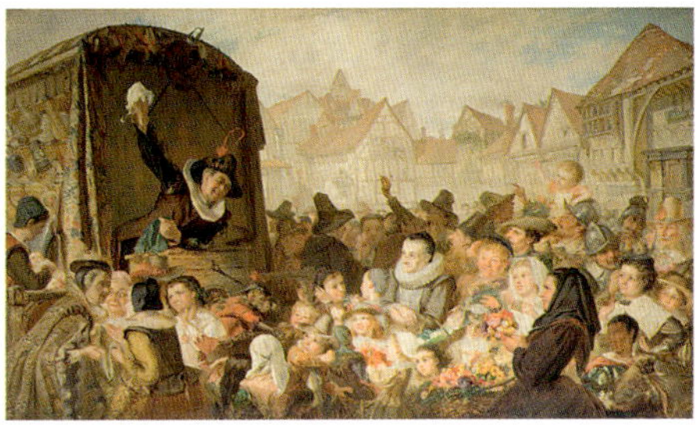

Fisk, William Henry 1827–1884
The Cheap-Jack
oil on canvas 73.5 x 119.5
OP451

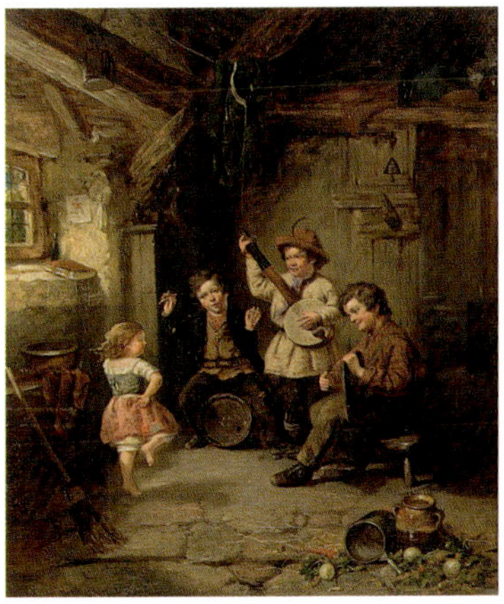

Fitzpatrick, Arthur active 1862–1870
Musical Union
oil on canvas 61.5 x 51.5
OP683

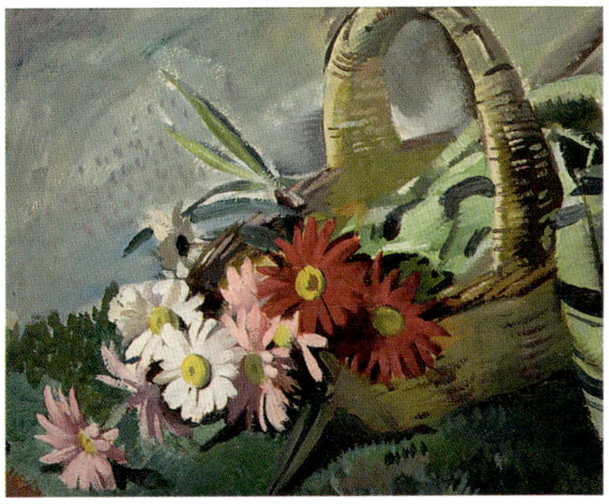

Fleetwood-Walker, Bernard 1893–1965
Still Life with Pyrethrums: Study for 'Amity'
1932–1935
oil on board 33.4 x 39.5
OP928

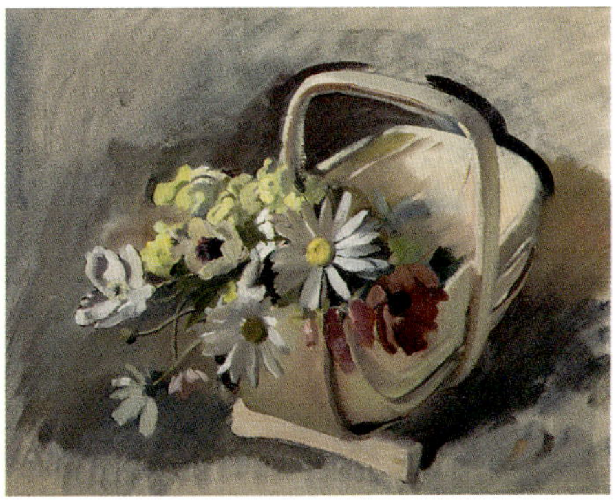

Fleetwood-Walker, Bernard 1893–1965
Trug with Dog Daisies: Study for 'Amity' 1932–1935
oil on board 37.5 x 44.8
OP929

Facing page: Lewis, Wyndham, 1882–1957, *Stephen Spender (1909–1995)* (detail), 1938, The Potteries Museum & Art Gallery (p. 137)

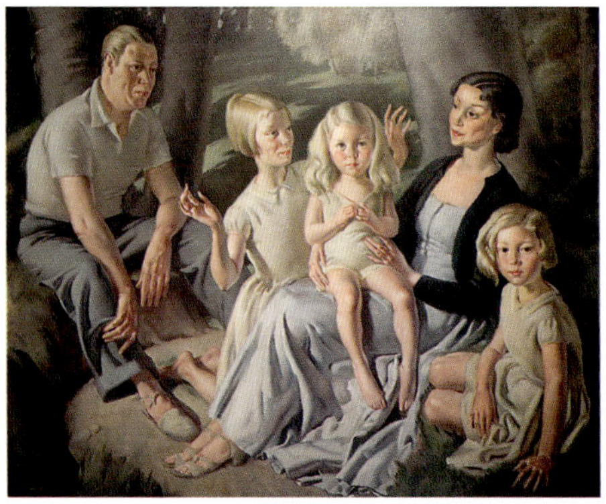

Fleetwood-Walker, Bernard 1893–1965
Mr and Mrs R. H. Butler and Their Daughters 1936
oil on canvas 127 x 152.5
OP903

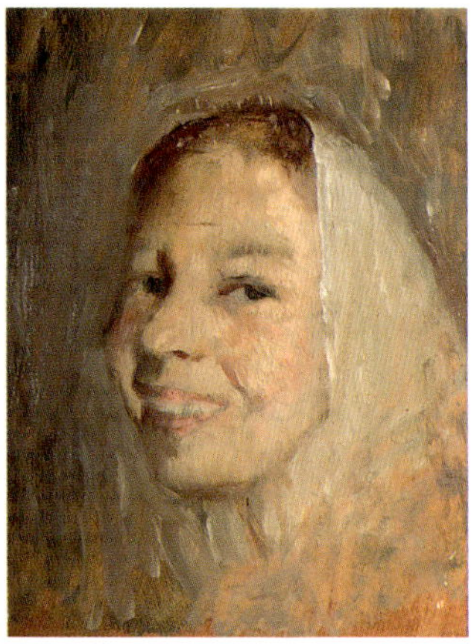

Fleetwood-Walker, Bernard 1893–1965
Smiling Girl 1962
oil on board 30.5 x 24
OP308

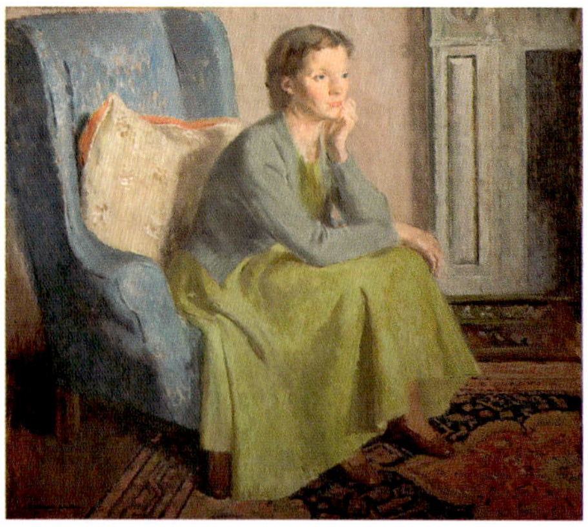

Fleetwood-Walker, Bernard 1893–1965
Christine
oil on board 91.5 x 101.5
OP597

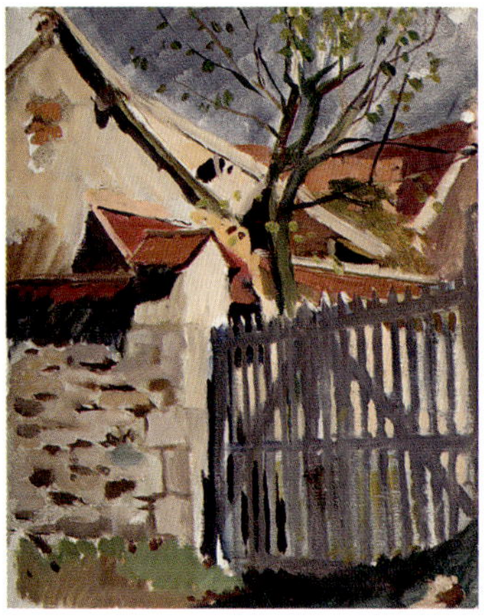

Fleetwood-Walker, Bernard 1893–1965
House and Gate
oil on board 45 x 35
OP930

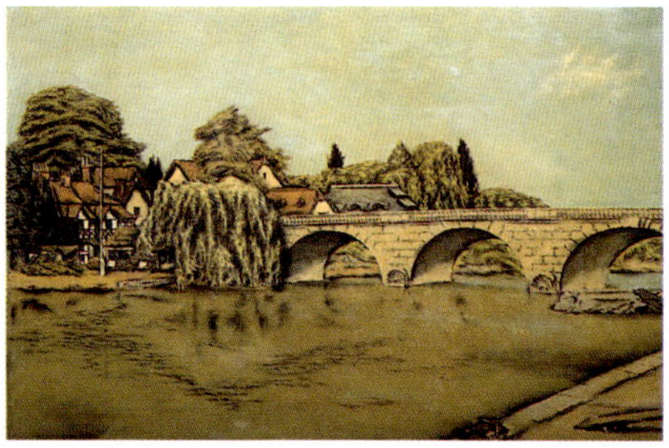

Fleiss, C.
Henley Bridge
oil on canvas 52.5 x 72.5
OP685

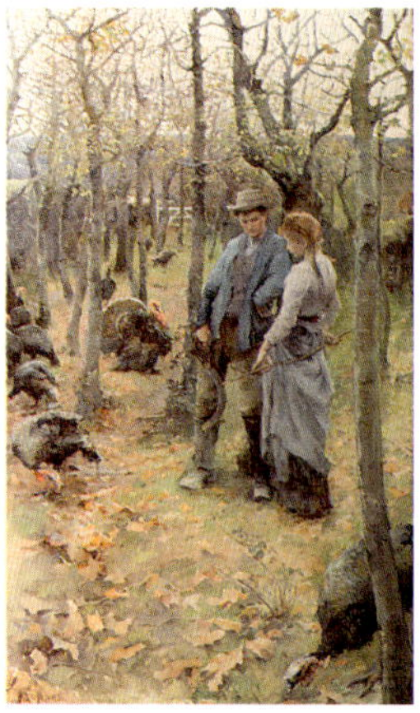

Forbes, Elizabeth Adela Stanhope 1859–1912
The Edge of the Woods 1894
oil on canvas 134.5 x 80
OP112

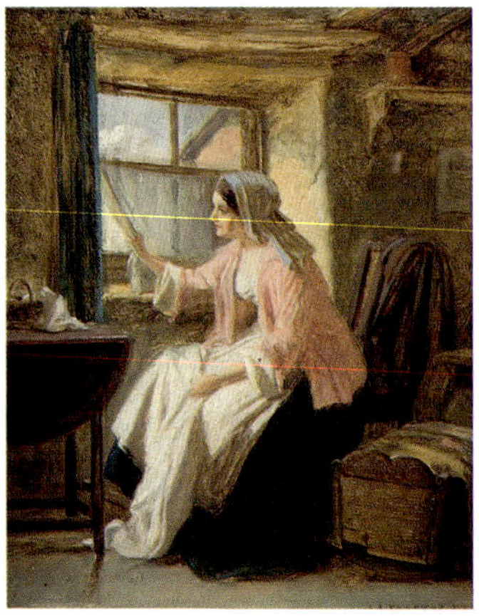

Freezor, George Augustus active 1861–1879
Expectation 1872
oil on canvas 25.5 x 20.5
OP254

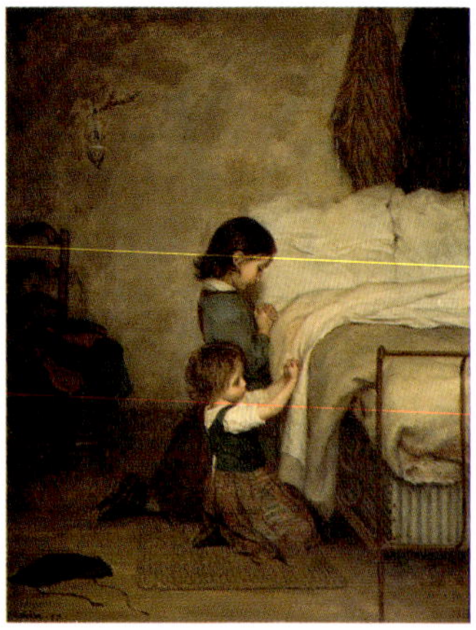

Frère, Pierre Edouard 1819–1886
The Prayer
oil on panel 38 x 30
OP6

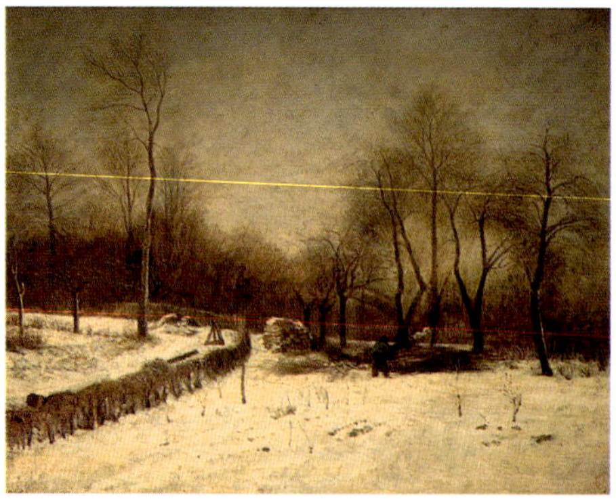

Frère, Pierre Edouard 1819–1886
Winter Scene
oil on panel 45.5 x 56
OP8

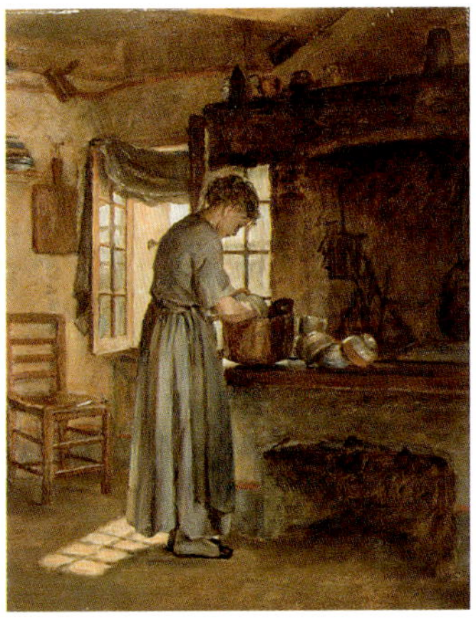

Frère, Pierre Edouard (circle of) 1819–1886
Cottage Interior mid-19th C
oil on canvas 56 x 45.5
OP152

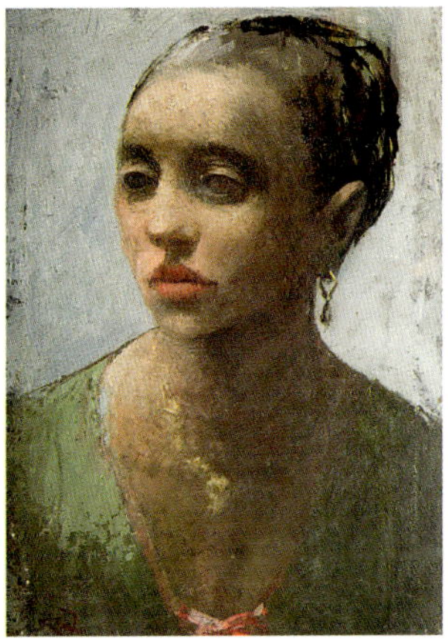

Frith, Clifford b.1924
Julie
oil on board 21 x 14.5
OP686

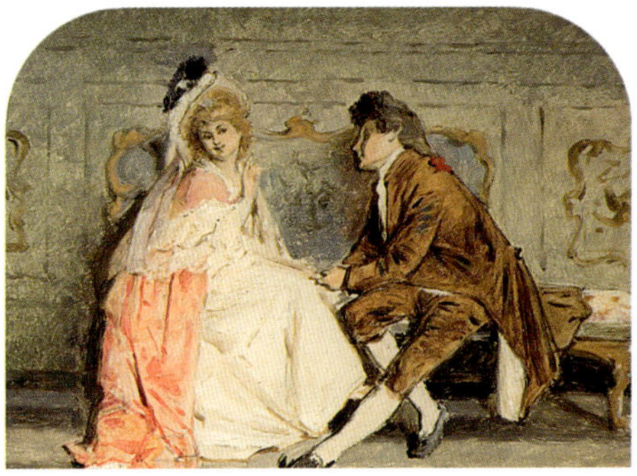

Frith, William Powell 1819–1909
Dolly Varden from Charles Dickens's 'Barnaby Rudge' (sketch) 1842
oil on board 17 x 23
OP253

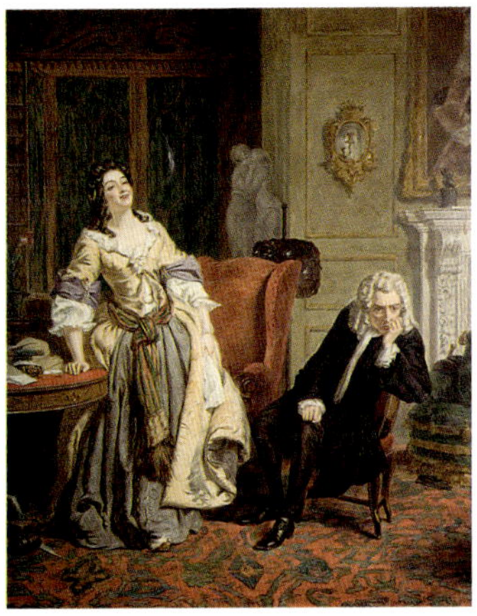

Frith, William Powell 1819–1909
The Rejected Poet 1863
oil on canvas 91.5 x 71
OP107

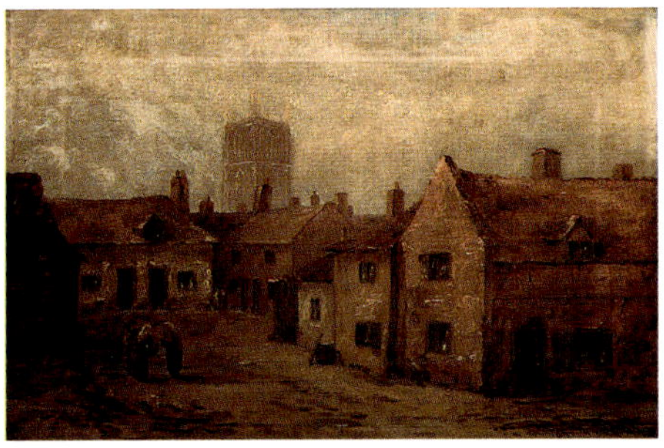

Fullwood, John 1854–1931
Bessie's Fold, North Street, Wolverhampton
oil on canvas 25.5 x 35.5
OP523

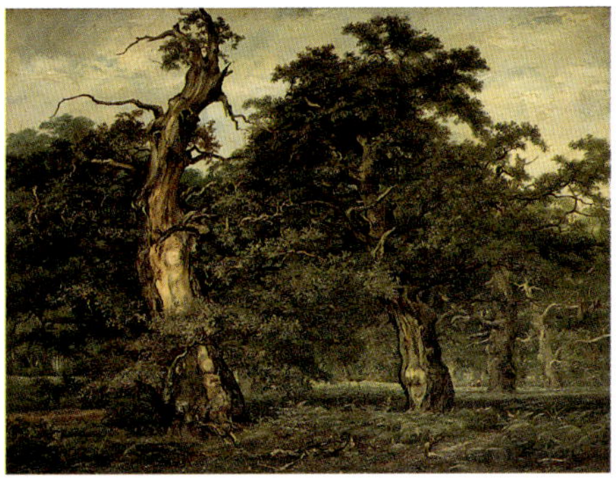

Fullwood, John 1854–1931
Forest Scene
oil on canvas 73.5 x 91.5
OP450

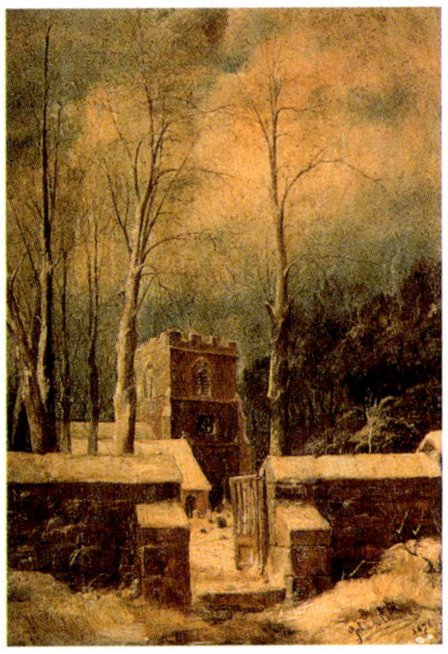

Fullwood, John 1854–1931
Tettenhall Church
oil on canvas 34.5 x 24.5
OP834

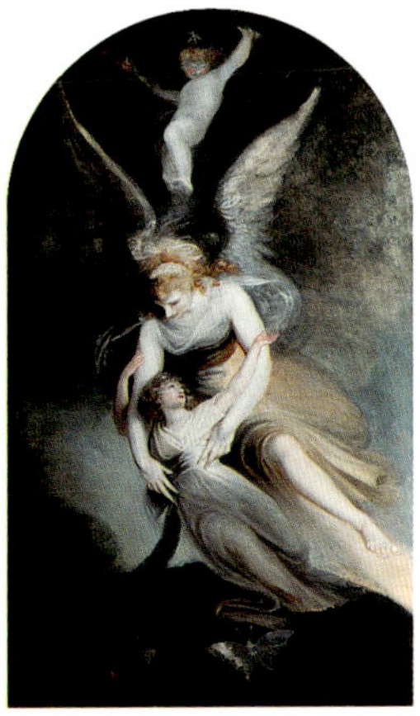

Fuseli, Henry 1747–1825
The Apothesis of Penelope Boothby 1792–1794
oil on canvas 213.5 x 121.5
OP79

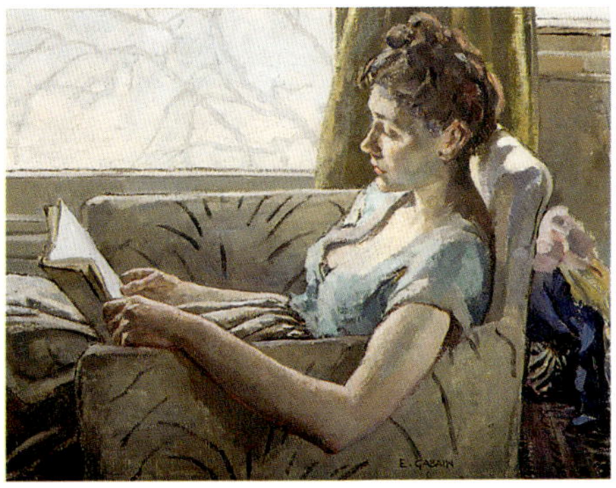

Gabain, Ethel 1883–1950
Reading
oil on canvas 40.5 x 51
OP287

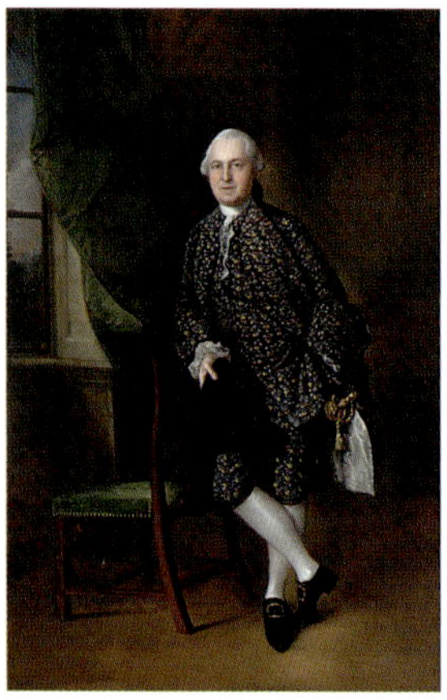

Gainsborough, Thomas 1727–1788
Sir Edward Turner, 2nd Bt of Ambrosden, Oxford (1719–1766) 1762
oil on canvas 229 x 147.5
OP491

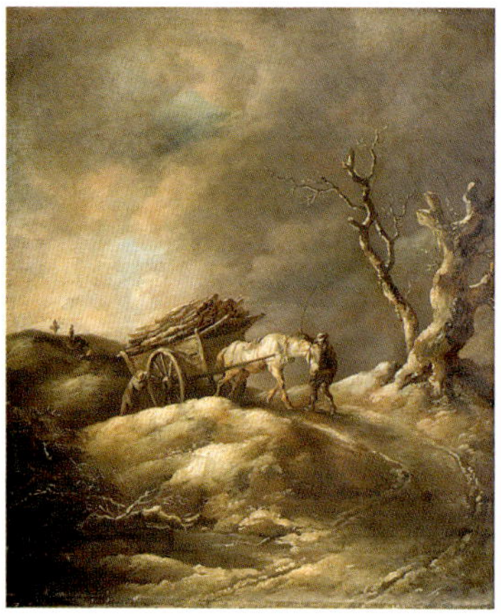

Gainsborough, Thomas (follower of)
1727–1788
Winter Scene with Horse and Cart late 18th C
oil on canvas 75 x 61
OP393

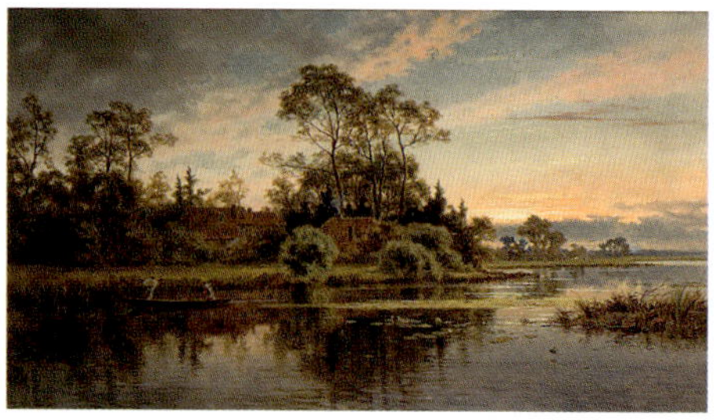

Gallon, Robert 1845–1925
Evening
oil on canvas 61 x 102
OP690

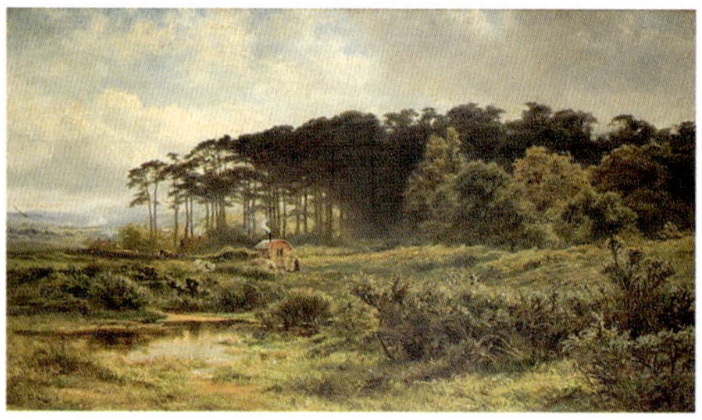

Gallon, Robert 1845–1925
Landscape with a Gypsy Caravan
oil on canvas 74.5 x 125
OP823

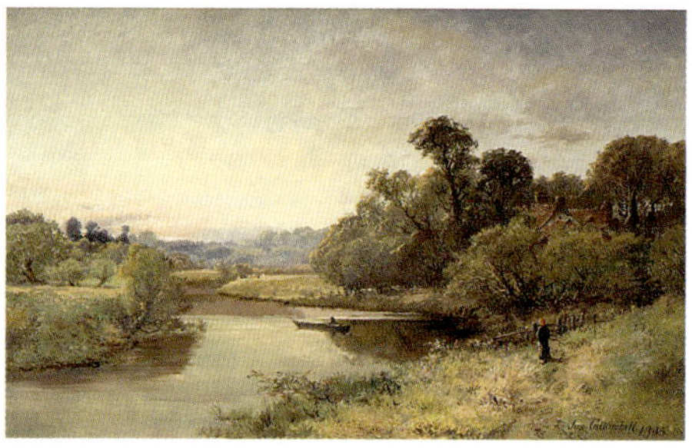

Gallowhill, James
The Avon near Stratford 1885
oil on canvas 30.5 x 45.5
OP286

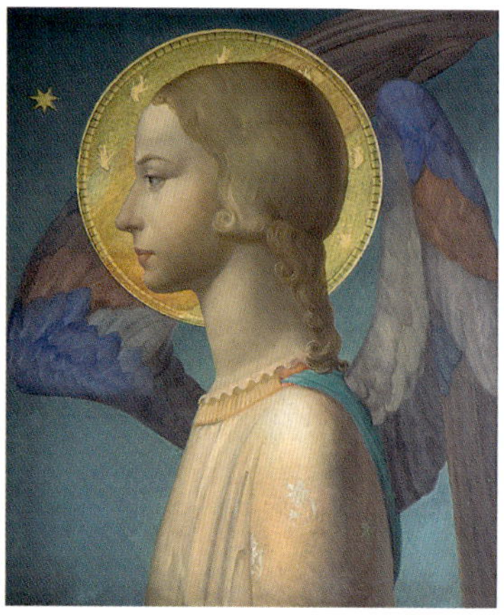

Gibson, Mary Gwenillan active 1927–1940
Angel
oil on slate 55 x 45
OP828

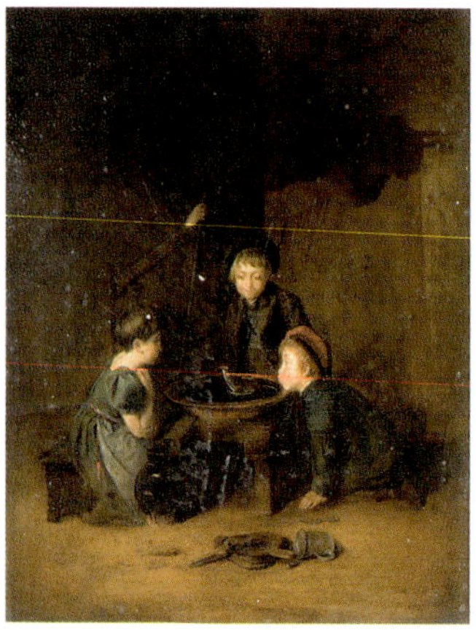

Gill, William active 1826–1869
The Toy Boat
oil on panel 36 x 30.5
OP551

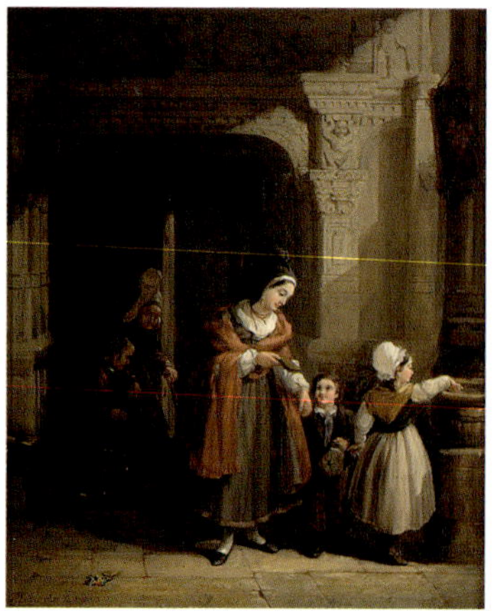

Goodall, Frederick 1822–1904
Entering a Church, Britanny 1840
oil on canvas 54 x 43
OP206

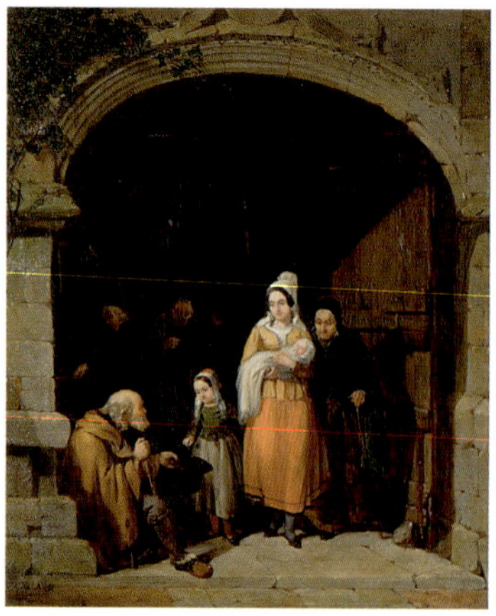

Goodall, Frederick 1822–1904
Leaving a Church, Brittany 1840
oil on canvas 53.5 x 43
OP188

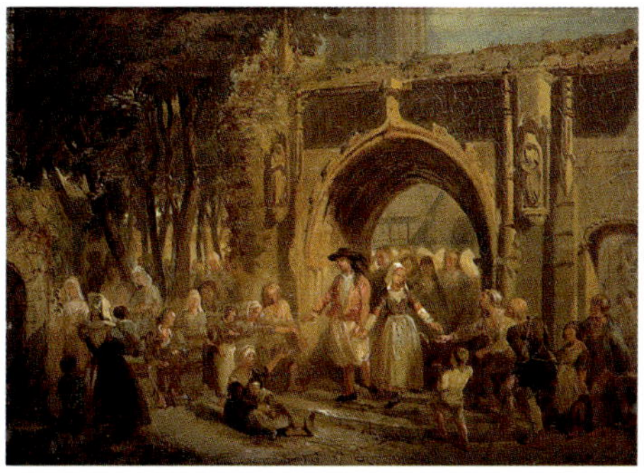

Goodall, Frederick 1822–1904
A Britanny Wedding 1840–1844
oil on board 32.5 x 40.5
OP467

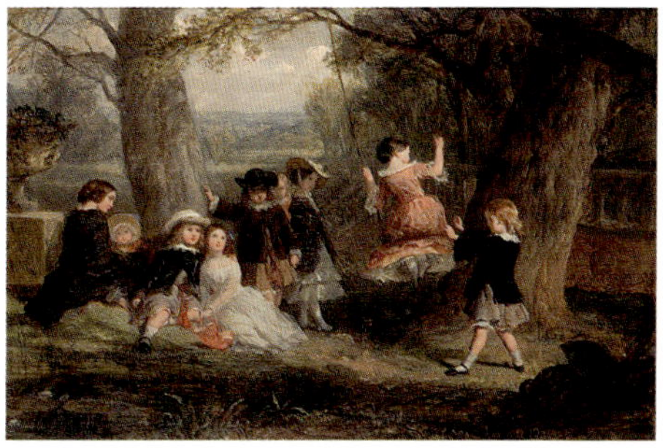

Goodall, Frederick 1822–1904
Study for 'The Swing' 1853
oil on canvas 18.5 x 25
OP205

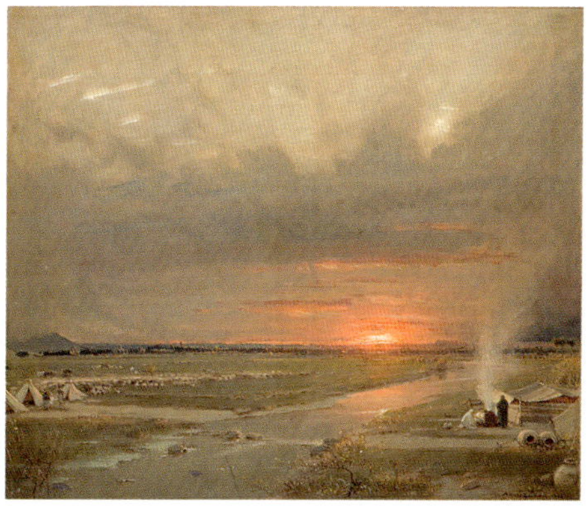

Goodwin, Albert 1845–1932
The City of Glittering Light 1905
oil on canvas 96.5 x 111.1
OP109

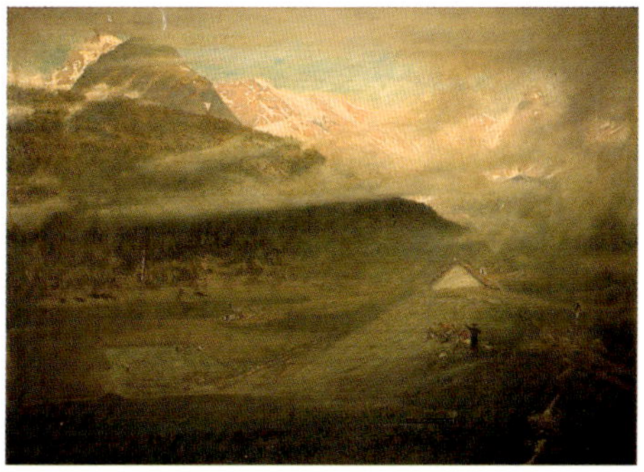

Goodwin, Albert 1845–1932
The Sermon in the Hayfield, Simplon
oil on canvas 81.5 x 112
OP110

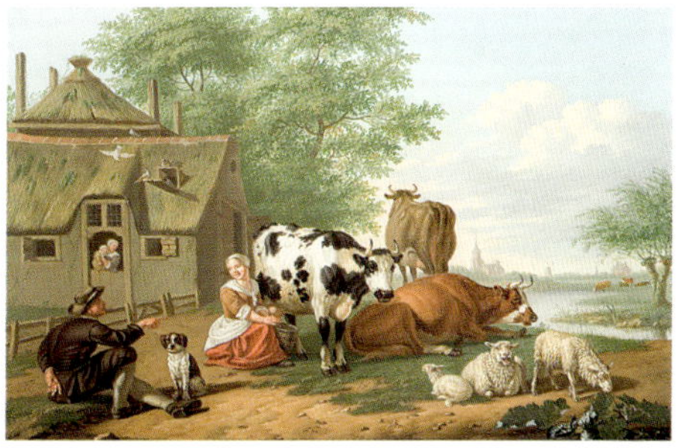

Gool, Jan van 1685–1763
Cattle in a Meadow
oil on panel 32 x 45 (E)
OP509

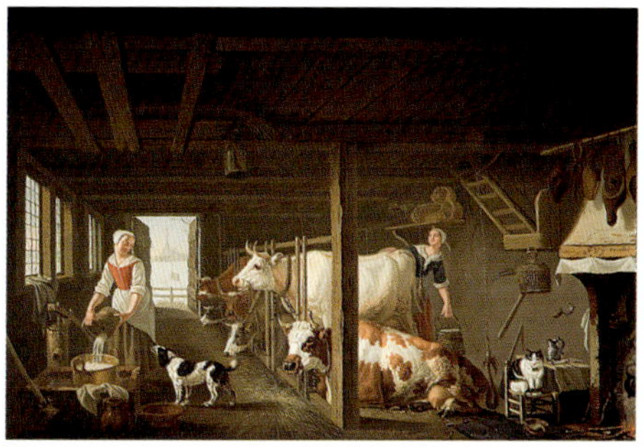

Gool, Jan van 1685–1763
Milking in Winter
oil on panel 32 x 45 (E)
OP508

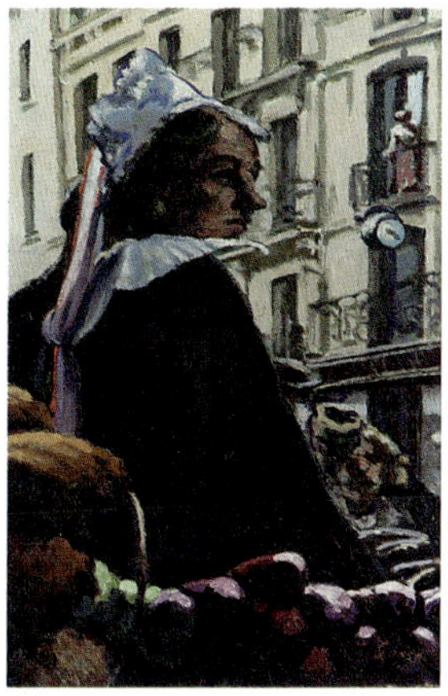

Gosse, Laura Sylvia 1881–1968
Breton Woman
oil on canvas 61 x 48.5
OP333

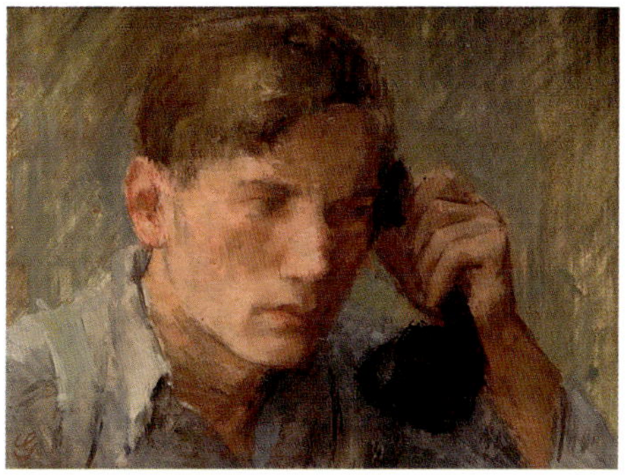

Gowing, Lawrence 1918–1991
On the Phone
oil on canvas 26.5 x 33.5
OP691

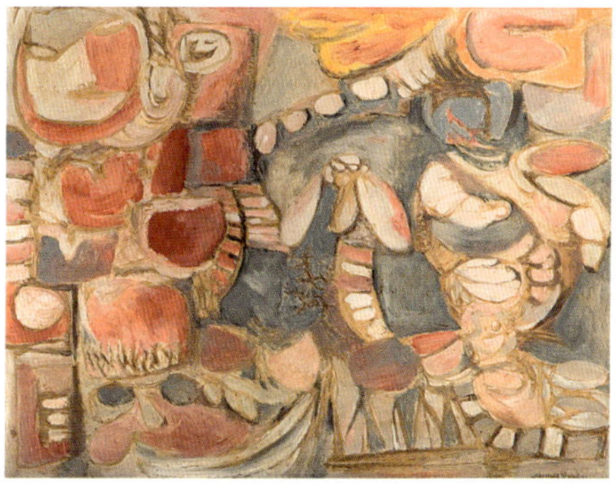

Grafton, Dennis b.1922
Composition 1990–1994
oil on board 59.5 x 75
OP871

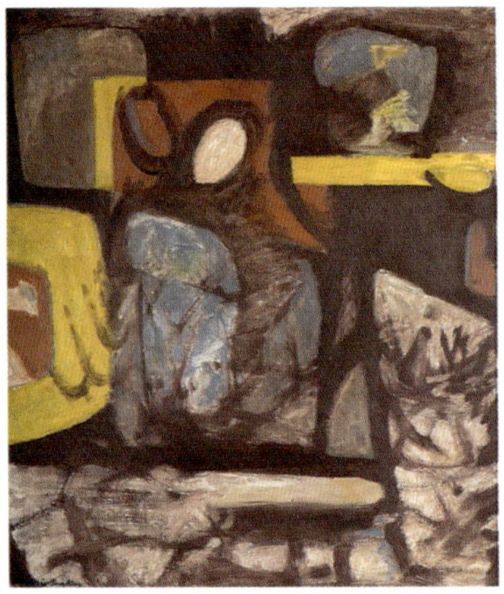

Grafton, Dennis b.1922
Reflections 1990–1994
oil on board 76.5 x 64
OP870

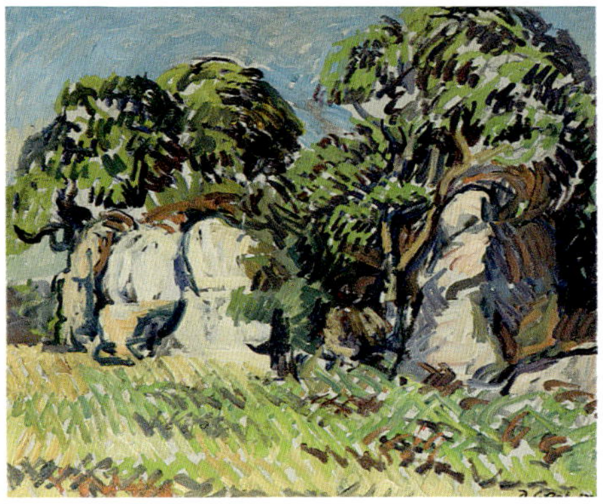

Grant, Duncan 1885–1978
Penns in the Rocks 1930
oil on board 45.5 x 54.5
OP795

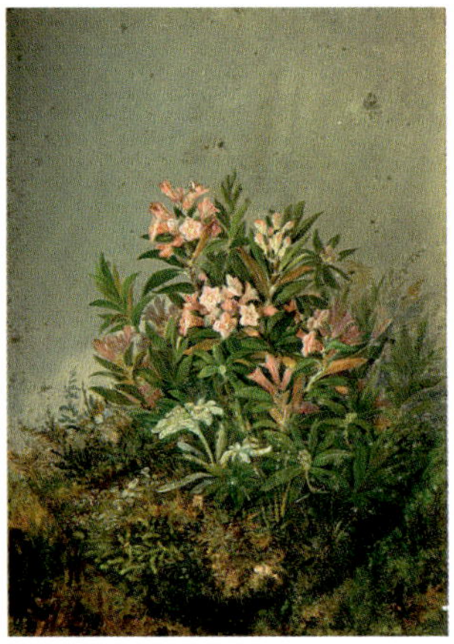

Hal, A.
Still Life, Flowers
oil on board 35 x 27.5
OP692

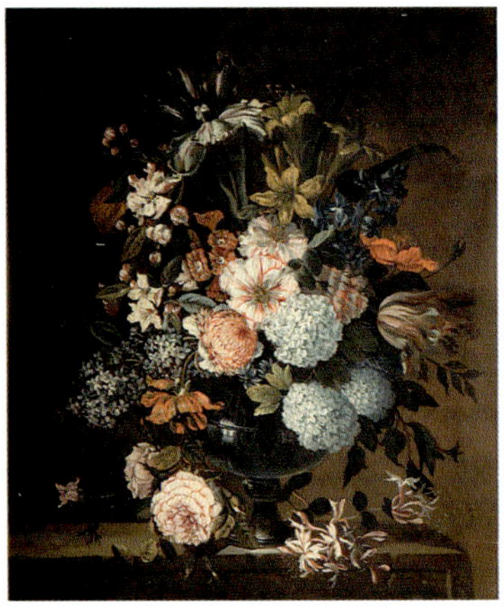

Hardimé, Pieter 1677/1678–1758
Vase of Flowers
oil on canvas 76 x 63.5
OP490

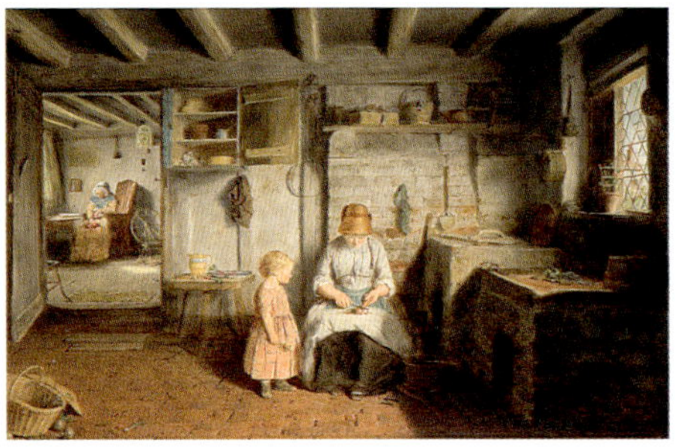

Hardy, Frederick Daniel 1827–1911
Preparing for Dinner 1854
oil on panel 23 x 33
OP231

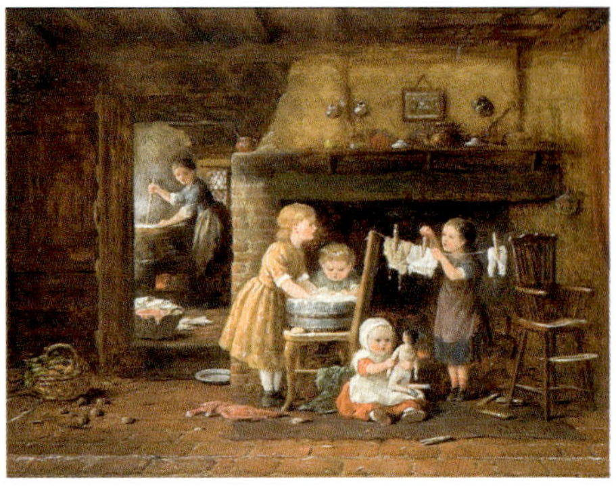

Hardy, Frederick Daniel 1827–1911
Washday 1860–1880
oil on panel 14 x 18
OP859

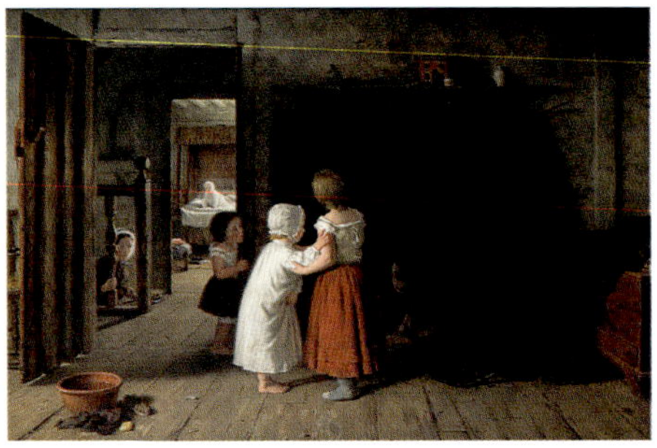

Hardy, Frederick Daniel 1827–1911
The Chimney Sweep 1866
oil on canvas 35.5 x 51.5
OP343

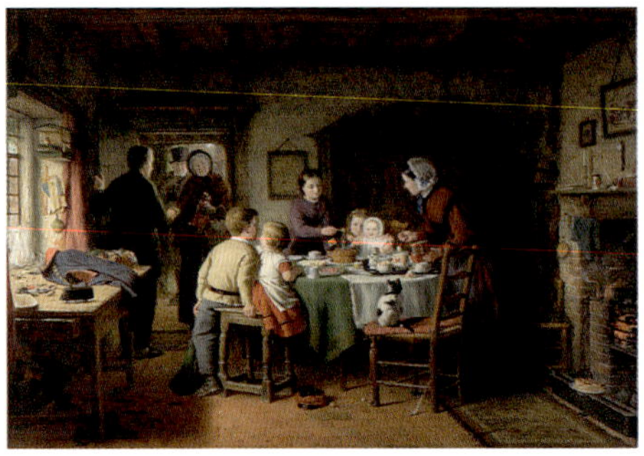

Hardy, Frederick Daniel 1827–1911
Baby's Birthday 1867
oil on canvas 66 x 91.5
OP371

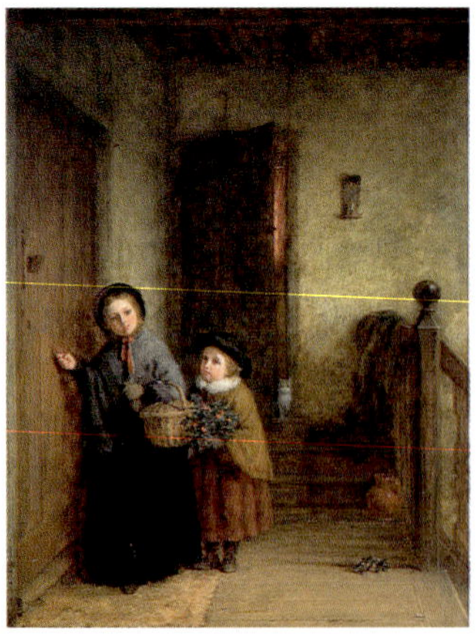

Hardy, Frederick Daniel 1827–1911
Christmas Visitors 1869
oil on canvas 61 x 45.5
OP337

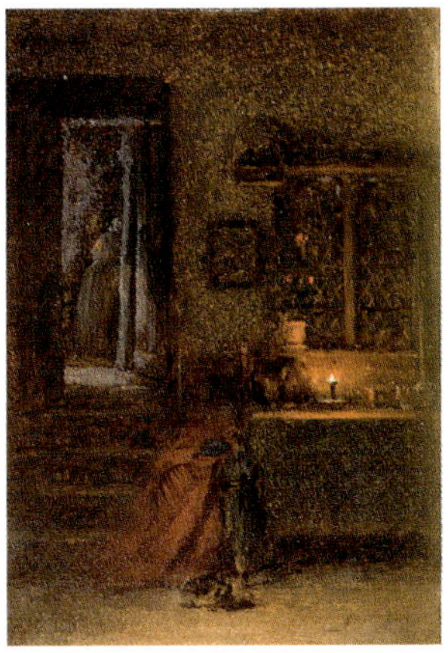

Hardy, Frederick Daniel 1827–1911
Study of an Interior 1871
oil on board 10 x 8
OP257

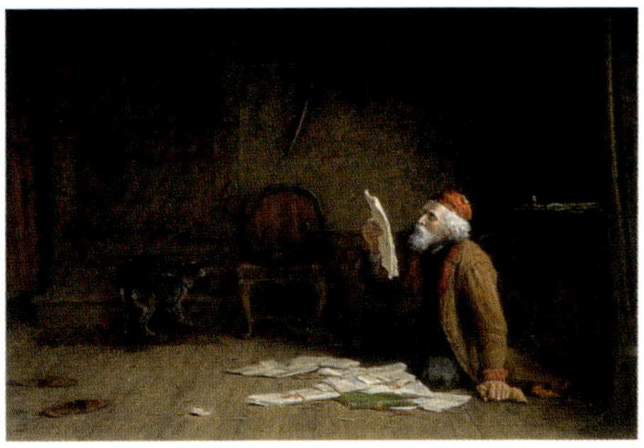

Hardy, Frederick Daniel 1827–1911
The Missing Deed 1871
oil on panel 33 x 41.5
OP353

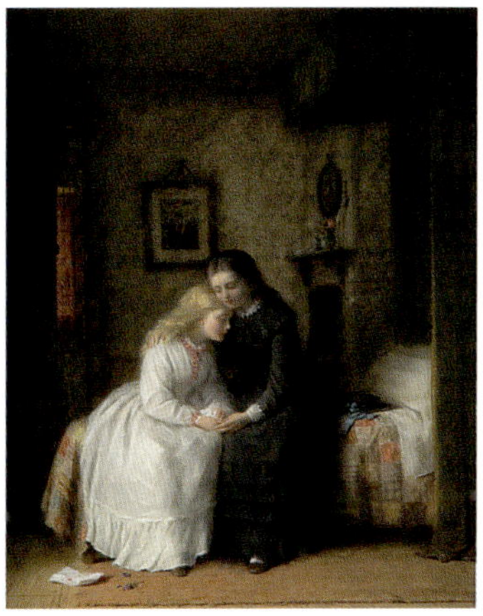

Hardy, Frederick Daniel 1827–1911
Sorrowful News 1872
oil on panel 33.5 x 26.5
OP224

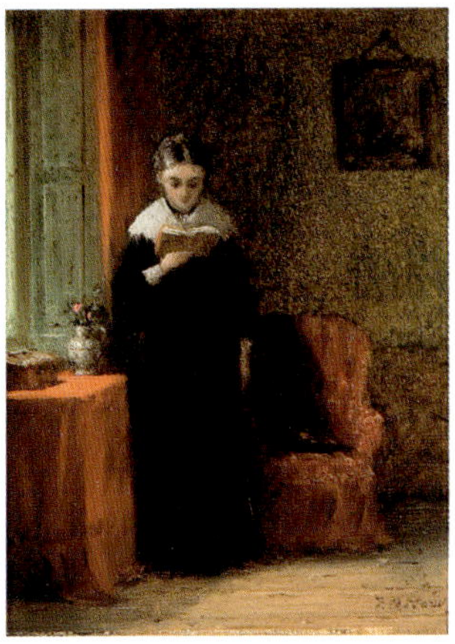

Hardy, Frederick Daniel 1827–1911
Study for 'Pleasant Pages' 1875
oil on board 10 x 8.5
OP256

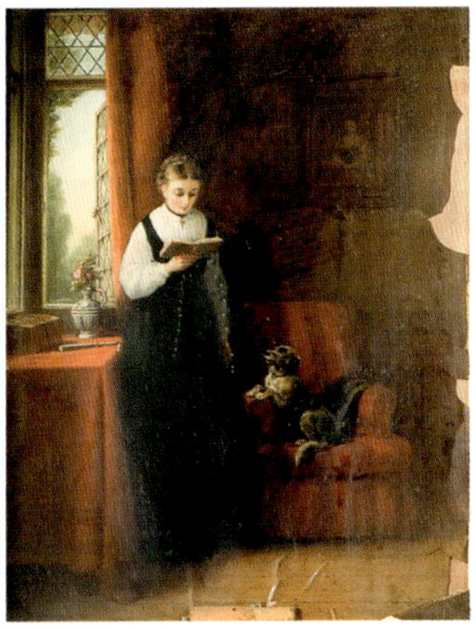

Hardy, Frederick Daniel 1827–1911
Pleasant Pages
oil on panel 62 x 45
OP552

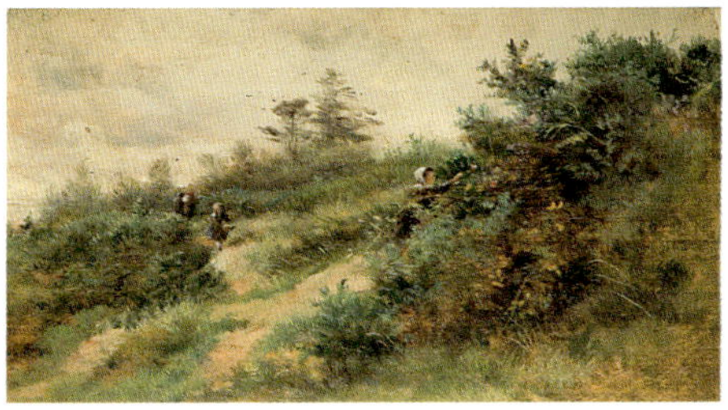

Hardy, Frederick Daniel 1827–1911
Near Windermere Lake 1878
oil on panel 12.5 x 21.5
OP54

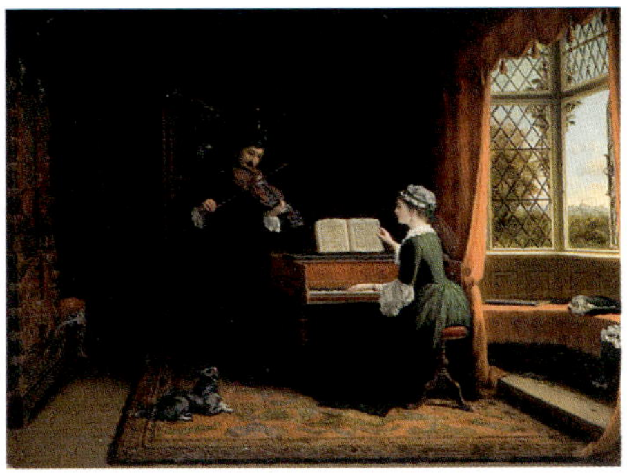

Hardy, Frederick Daniel 1827–1911
The Prelude 1878
oil on panel 35 x 45.5
OP7

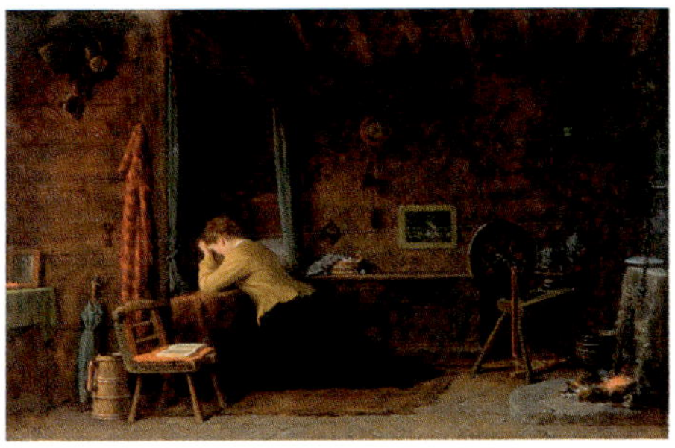

Hardy, Frederick Daniel 1827–1911
A Prayer for Those at Sea 1879
oil on board 25.5 x 43
OP348

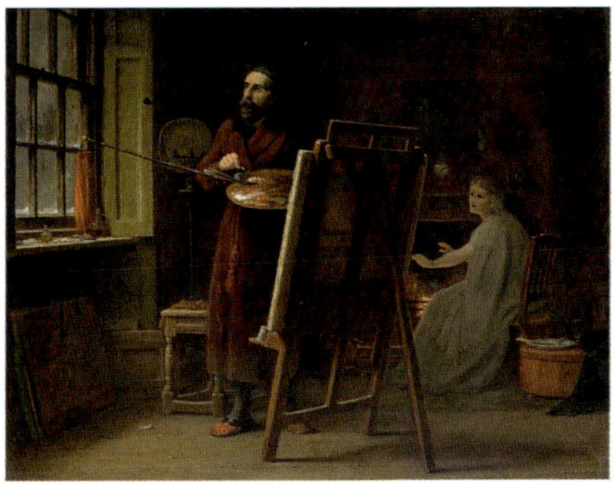

Hardy, Frederick Daniel 1827–1911
A Fog 1887
oil on canvas 61 x 82.5
OP59

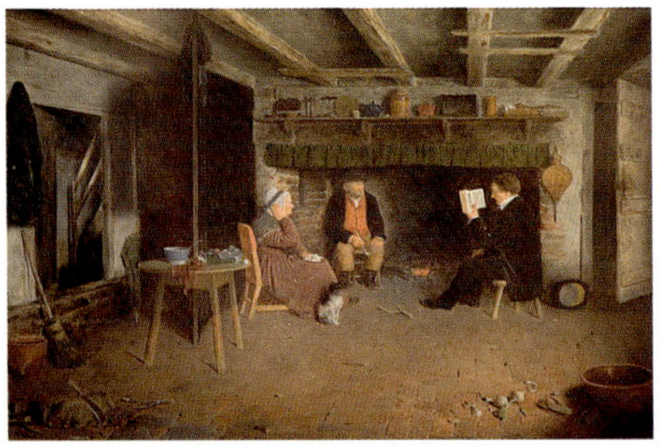

Hardy, Frederick Daniel 1827–1911
The Clergyman's Visit
oil on canvas 23 x 33
OP230

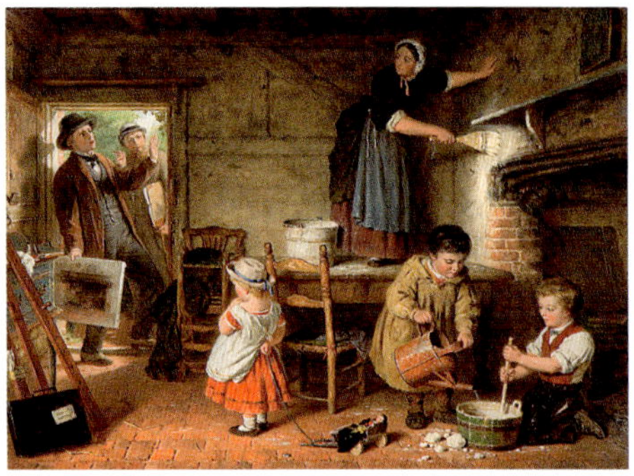

Hardy, Frederick Daniel 1827–1911
The Dismayed Artist
oil on canvas 45.5 x 61
OP194

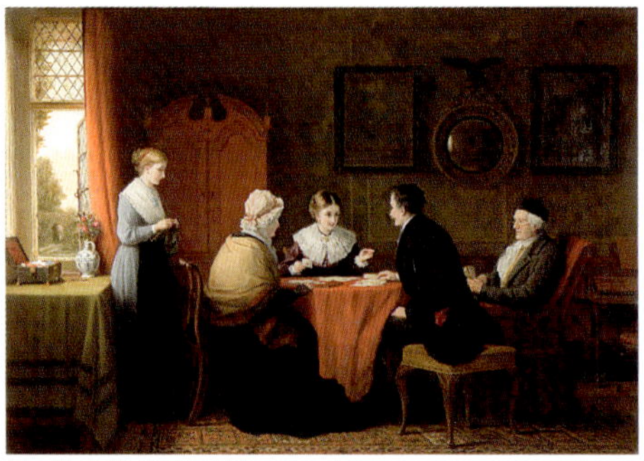

Hardy, Frederick Daniel 1827–1911
The Misdeal
oil on canvas 76 x 101.5
OP564

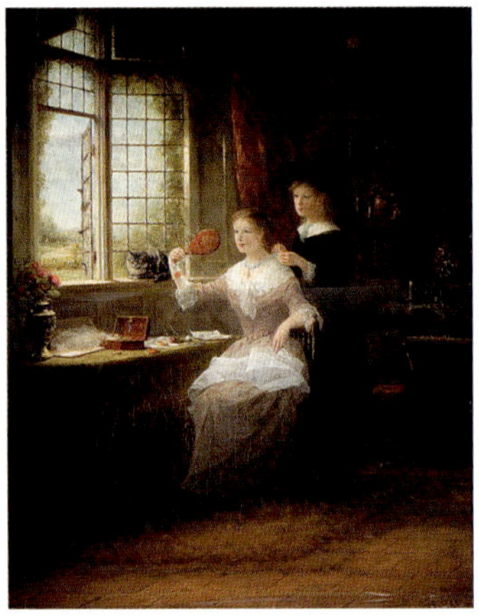

Hardy, Frederick Daniel 1827–1911
The Necklace
oil on canvas 67.5 x 52.5
OP822

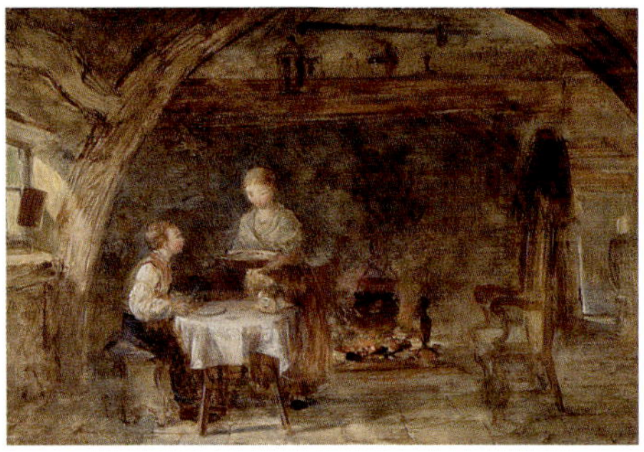

Hardy, Frederick Daniel 1827–1911
The Young Housekeeper
oil on panel 17 x 25
OP62

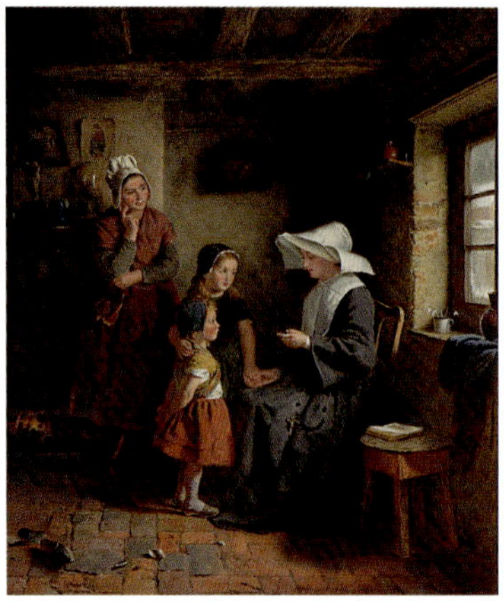

Hardy, George 1822–1909
Early Teaching
oil on panel 45.5 x 37.5
OP56

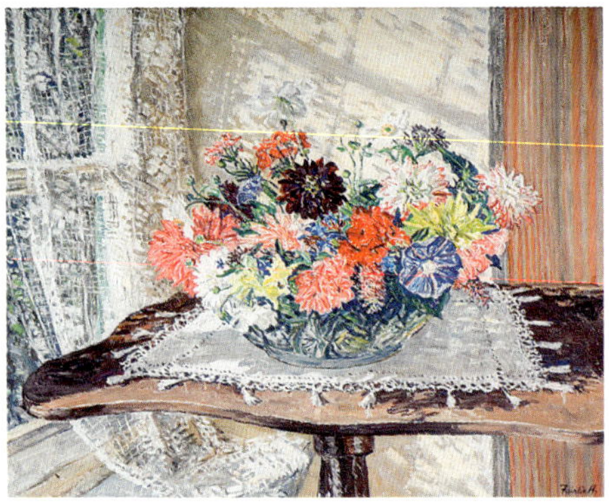

Harmar, Fairlie 1876–1945
Flowers
oil on canvas 51 x 61
OP313

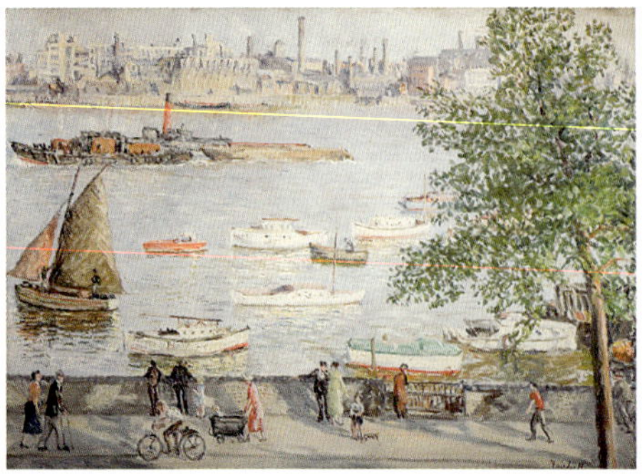

Harmar, Fairlie 1876–1945
Ships on the Thames
oil on canvas 66 x 86.5
OP594

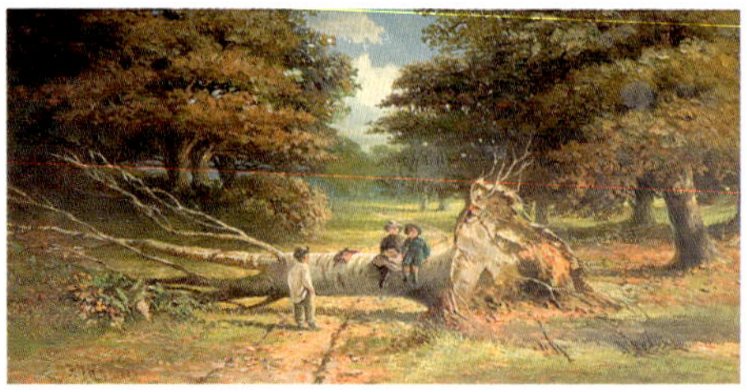

Harris, Frederick Henry Howard 1826–1901
The Babes in the Wood
oil on canvas 42 x 66
OP141

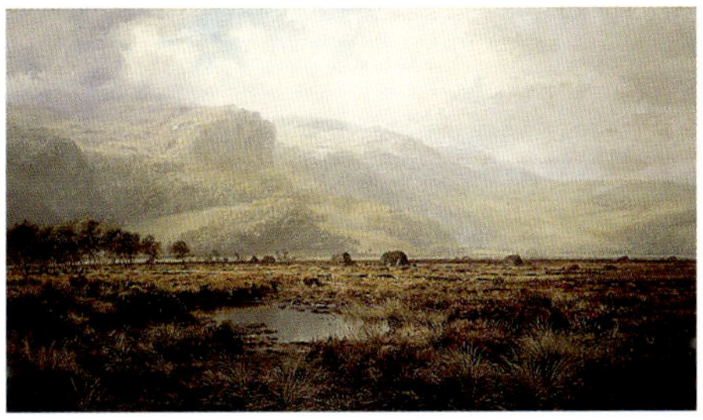

Hartland, Henry Albert 1840–1893
Near Barmouth 1881
oil on canvas 91.5 x 152.5
OP442

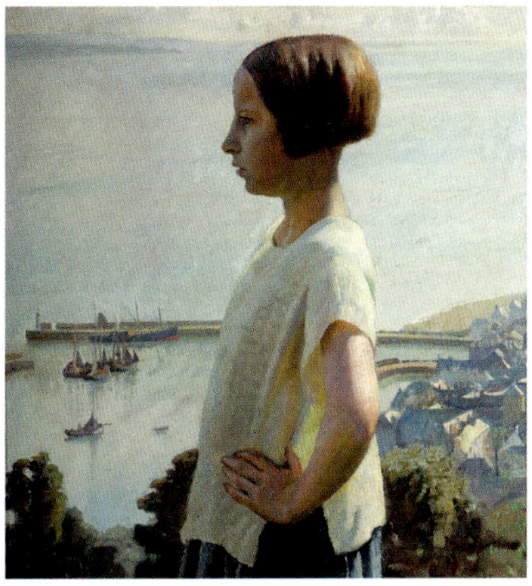

Harvey, Harold C. 1874–1941
The Little Maiden 1934
oil on canvas 50 x 45
OP294 ❋

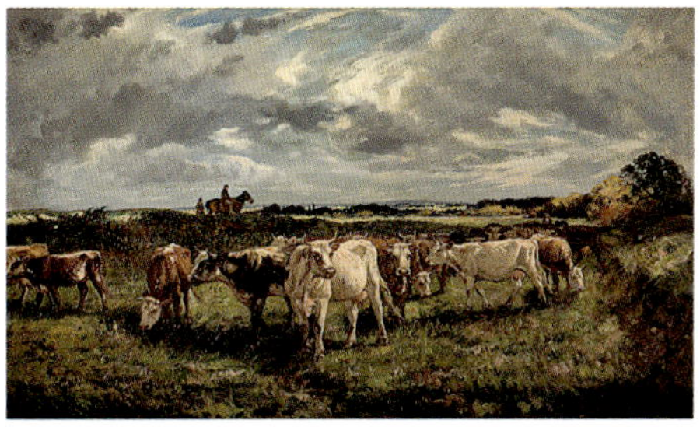

Harvey, John Rathbone 1862–1933
Changing Pastures
oil on canvas 87.5 x 138.5
OP693

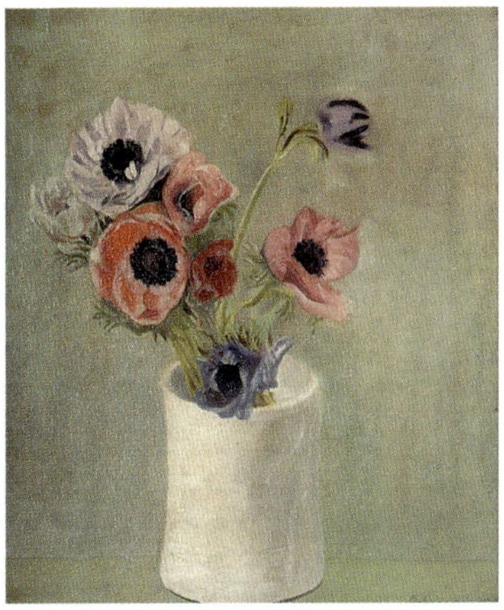

Hattemore, Archibald active 1926–1930
Anenomes
oil on canvas 30.5 x 25.5
OP296

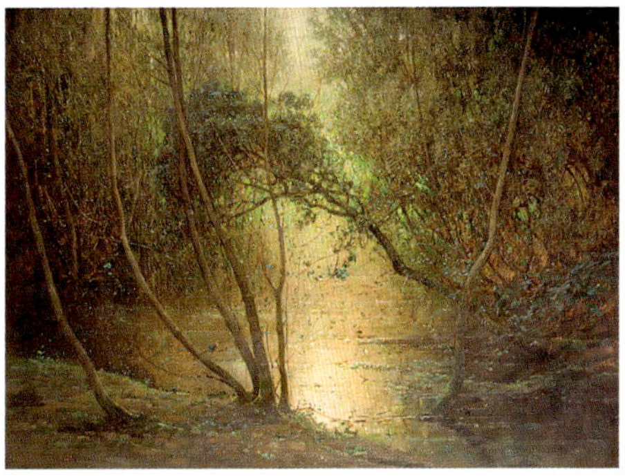

Haughton, Benjamin 1865–1924
Woodland Waters
oil on canvas 51 x 63.5
OP103

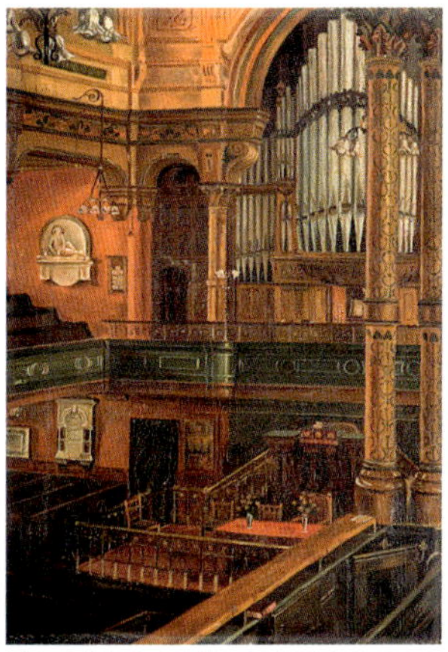

Hawkins, Grace Mary active 1910–1929
Interior of Queen Street Congregational Church
oil on canvas 40.5 x 28
OP689

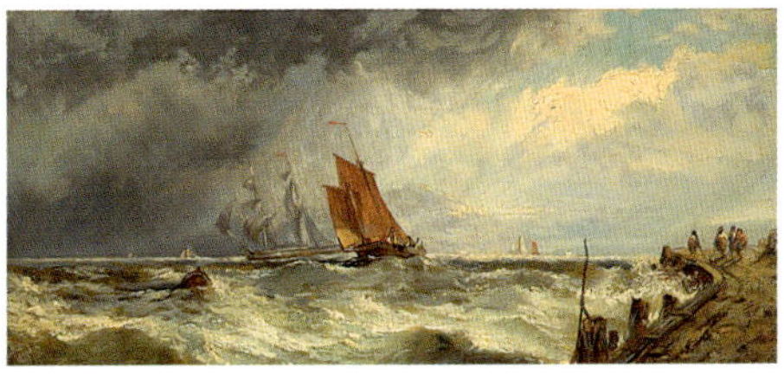

Hayes, Edwin 1819–1904
A Breezy Day
oil on canvas 20 x 40
OP360

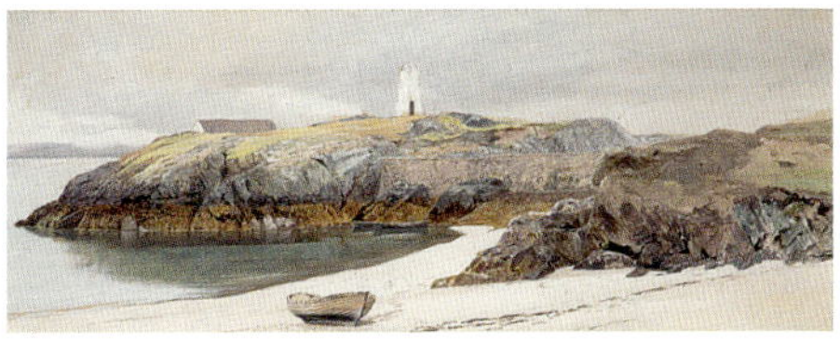

Hayes, Frederick William 1848–1918
The Lighthouse, Llanddwyn
oil on paper 24 x 59.5
OP567

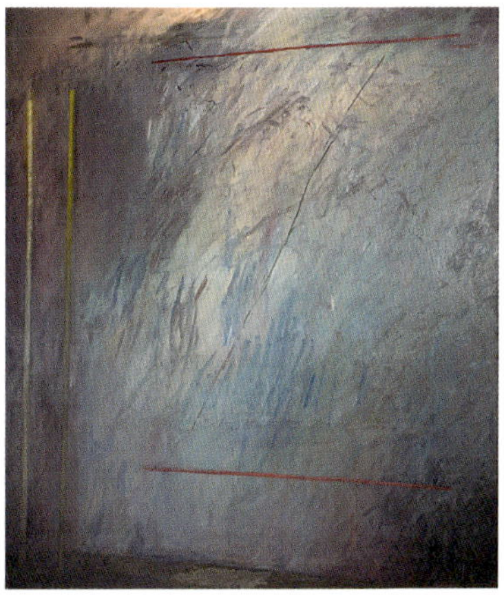

Hempton, Paul b.1946
Across a Ravine 1980–1988
oil on canvas 183 x 152.5
OP813

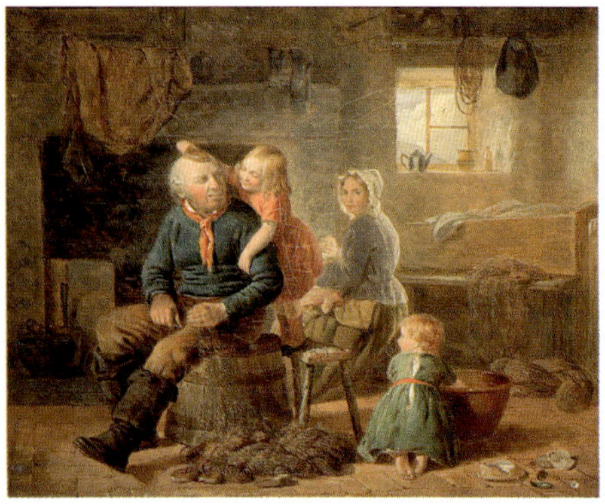

Hemsley, William 1819–1906
The Fisherman's Family 1858
oil on canvas 26 x 30.5
OP461

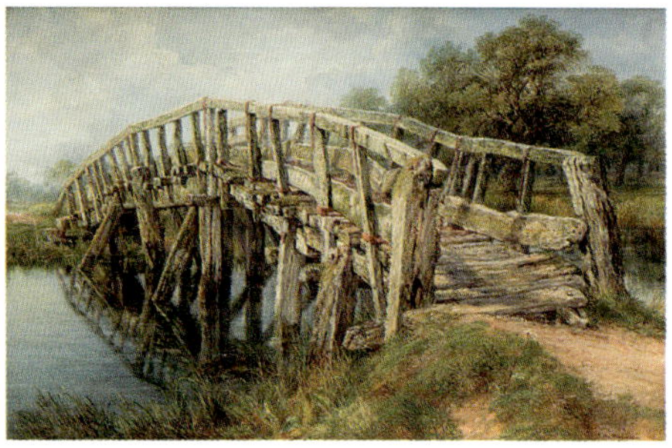

Henshaw, Frederick Henry 1807–1891
The Ladder Bridge, Weeping Cross, Staffordshire
oil on canvas 52 x 77.5
OP694

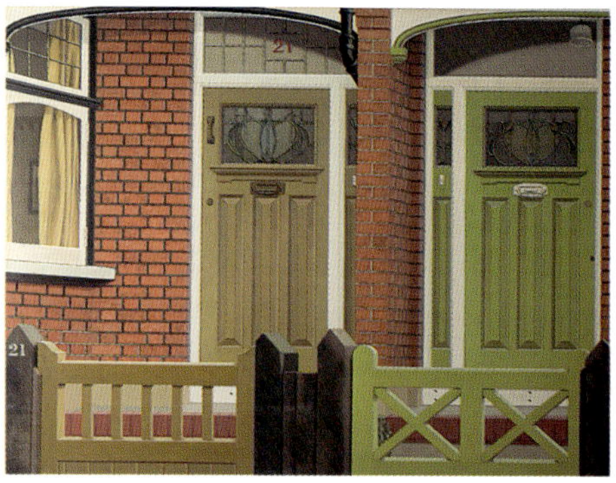

Hepher, David b.1935
Newly Redecorated Doors of Nos.21 and 22 1973
oil on canvas 193 x 243
OP592

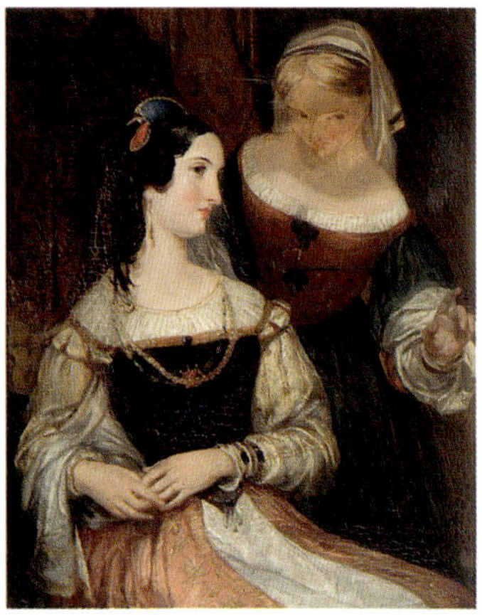

Herbert, John Rogers 1810–1890
Francesca
oil on panel 30.5 x 25.5
OP181

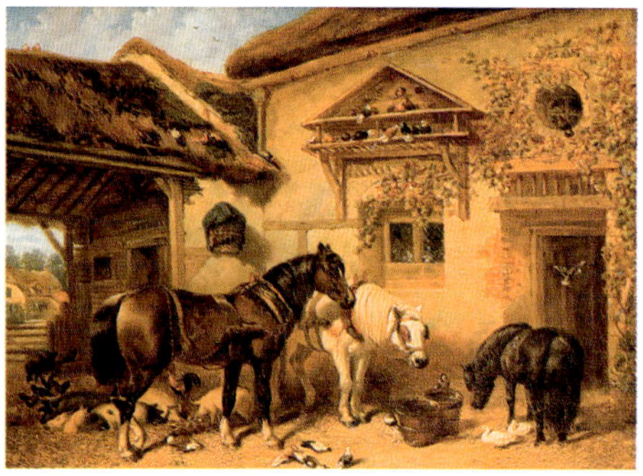

Herring, John Frederick I 1795–1865
Cottage Door and Farmstead 1843
oil on canvas 51 x 61
OP133

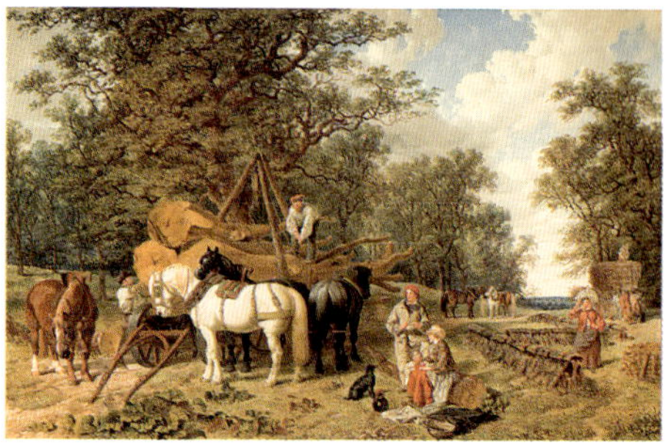

Herring, John Frederick I 1795–1865
The Timber Wagon 1858
oil on canvas 91.5 x 133.5
OP220

Hickin, George Arthur 1821–1885
Landscape and Cattle 1847
oil on canvas 56.2 x 82.6
OP476

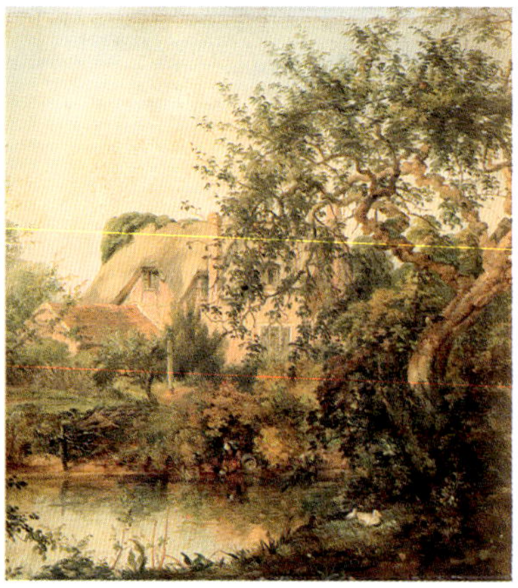

Hickin, George Arthur 1821–1885
The Cottager's Home 1847
oil on canvas 36 x 32
OP3

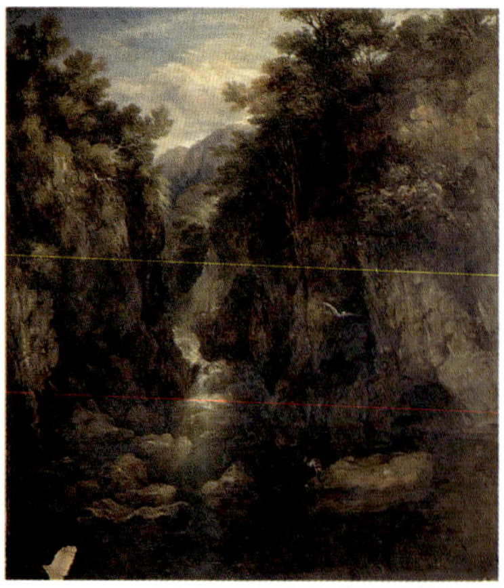

Hickin, George Arthur 1821–1885
Mountain Solitude, a Scene on the Conway 1848–1854
oil on canvas 66.5 x 56
OP168

Facing page: Halliday, Edward Irvine, 1902–1984, *Frederick Edge (1863–1937)* (detail), 1931, New Cross Hospital (p. 228)

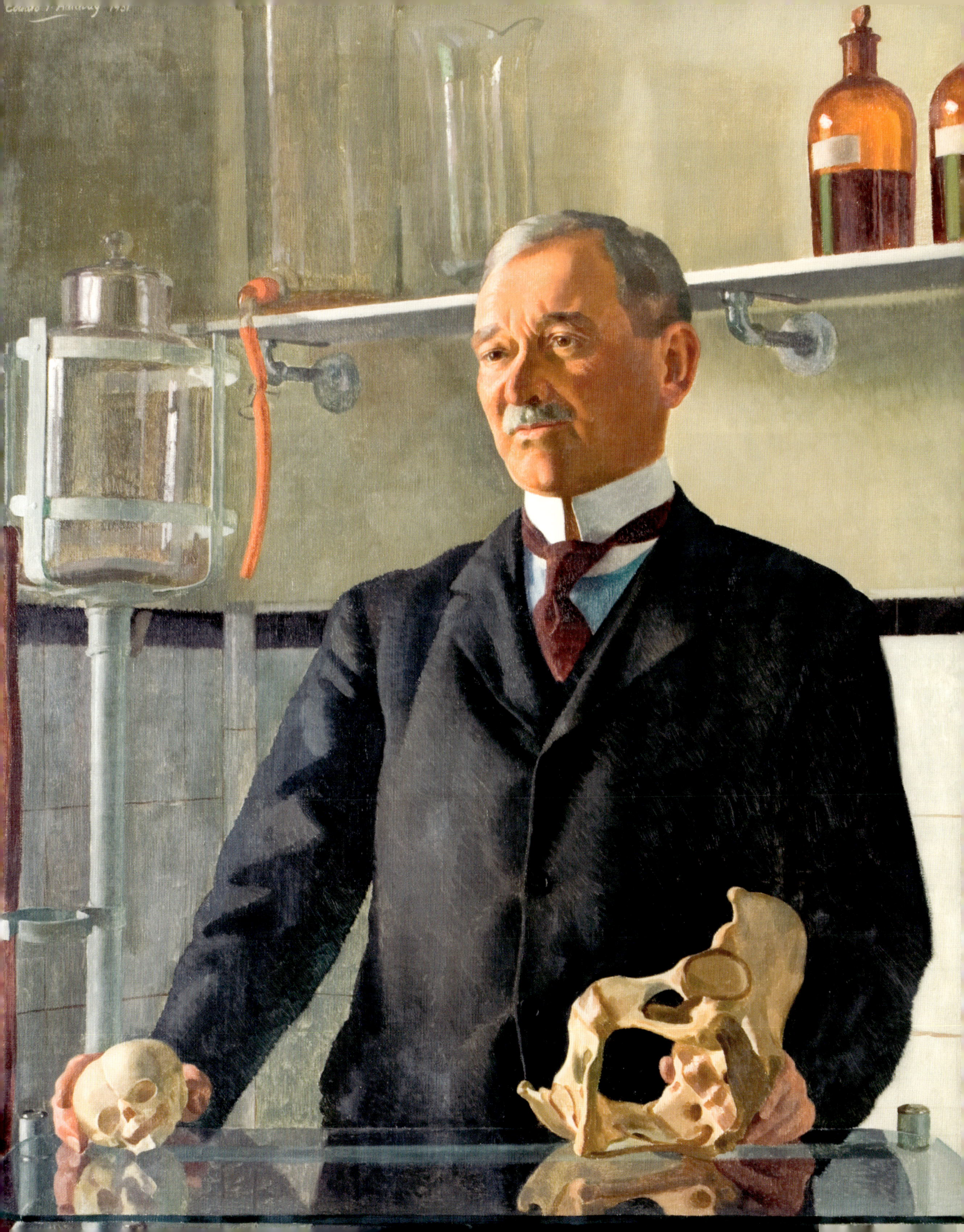

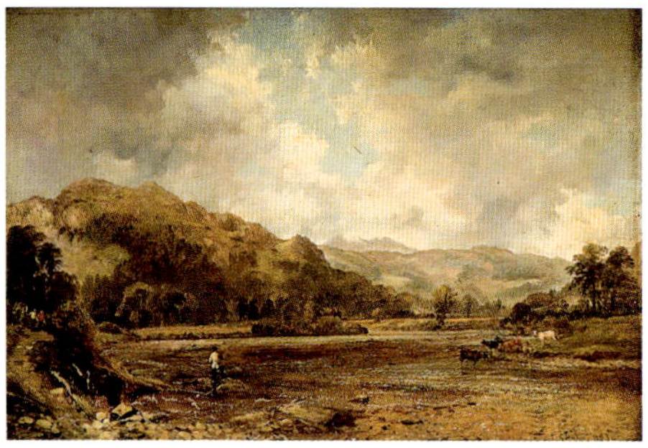

Hickin, George Arthur 1821–1885
On the Conway 1853
oil on canvas 36 x 51.5
OP547

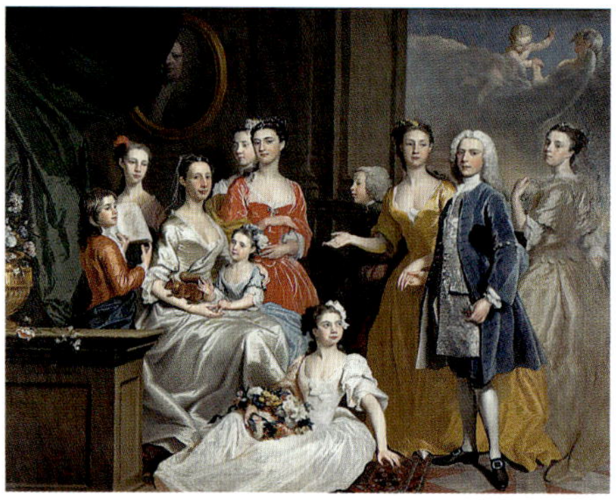

Highmore, Joseph 1692–1780
The Family of E. Lancelot Lee 1736
oil on canvas 237 x 290
OP784

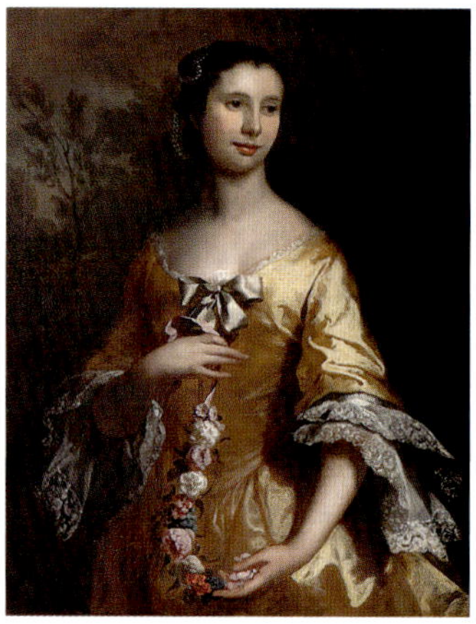

Highmore, Joseph 1692–1780
Elizabeth Lee (1729–1786), Wife of William Waller 1755
oil on canvas 89 x 68.5
OP876

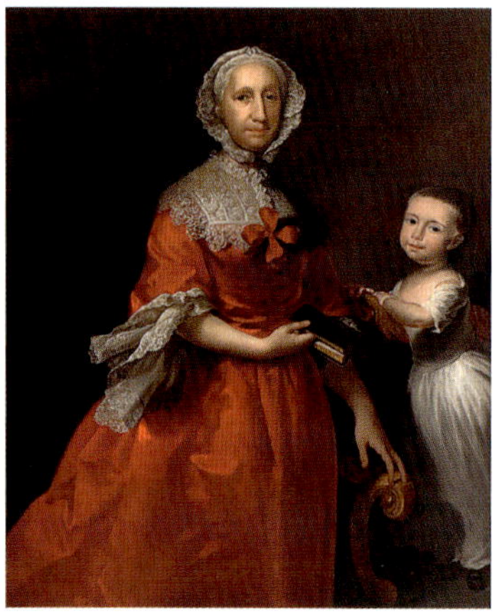

Highmore, Joseph 1692–1780
Isabella Lee and Her Grandson, William Waller 1759
oil on canvas 121.5 x 98
OP875

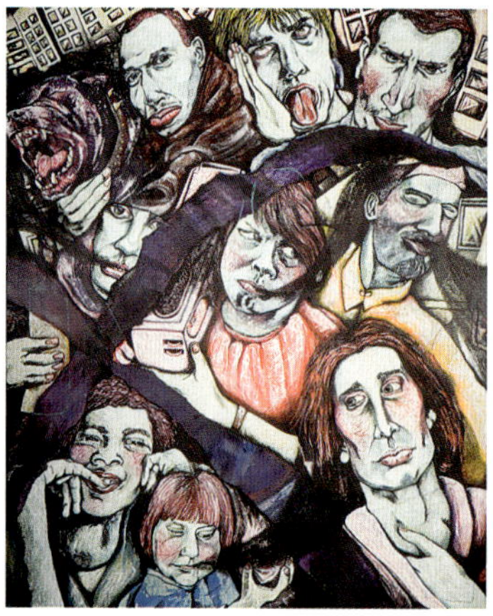

Hill, Paul b.1959
Bull Mastif 1989
oil on paper 118 x 93
OP901

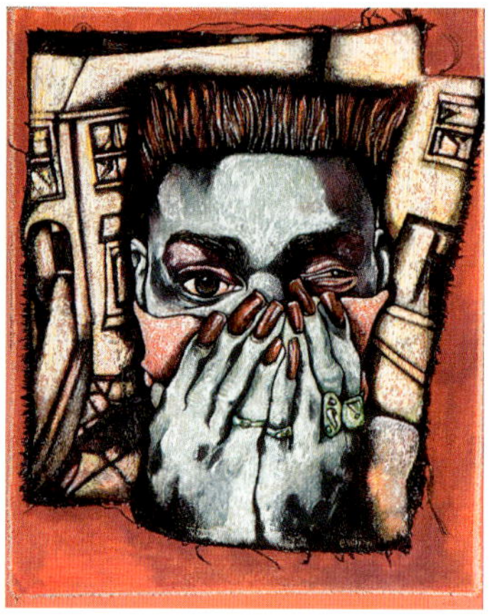

Hill, Paul b.1959
Four Rings 1990–1997
oil on canvas 48.5 x 38.5
OP885

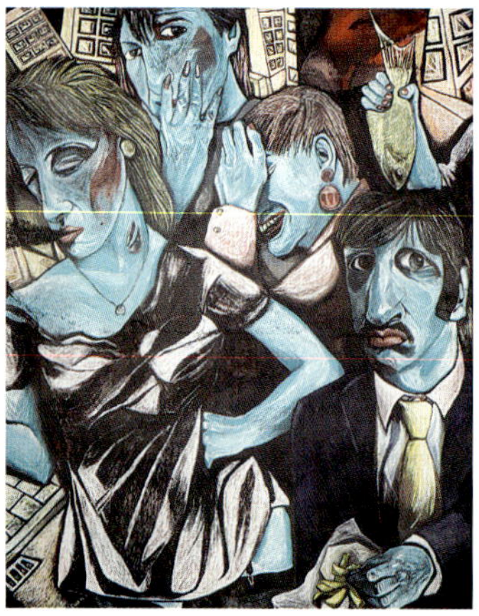

Hill, Paul b.1959
Don't Forget the Fish 1993
oil on paper 118 x 91
OP902

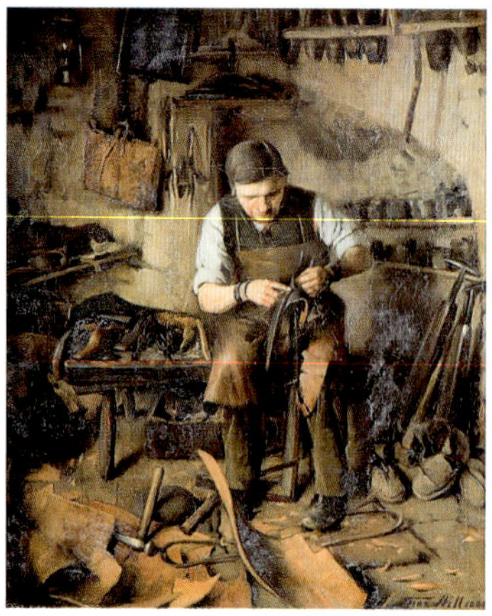

Hill, Thomas active 1878–1913
The Village Cobbler 1885
oil on canvas 49.3 x 39.4
OP178

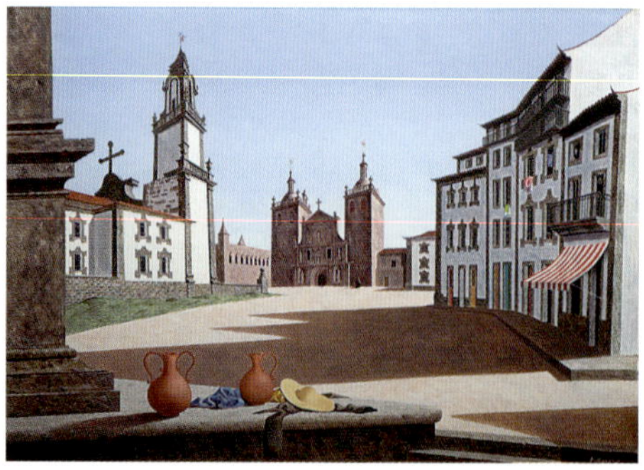

Hillier, Tristram Paul 1905–1983
Viseu, Portugal 1947
oil on linen 59.5 x 80
OP789

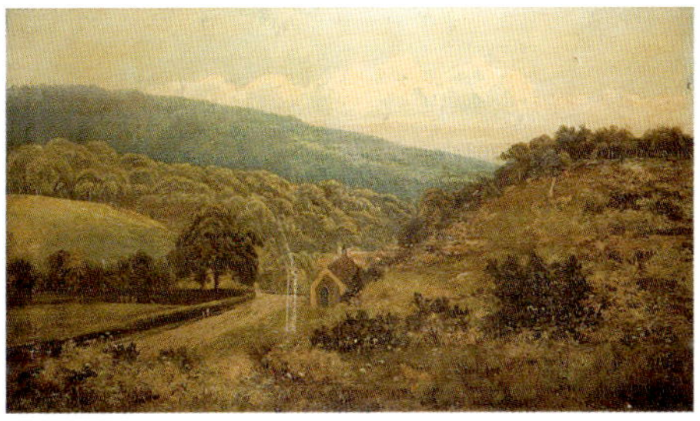

Hines, Theodore active 1876–1890
Landscape with a Church in a Valley
oil on canvas 76 x 127
OP413

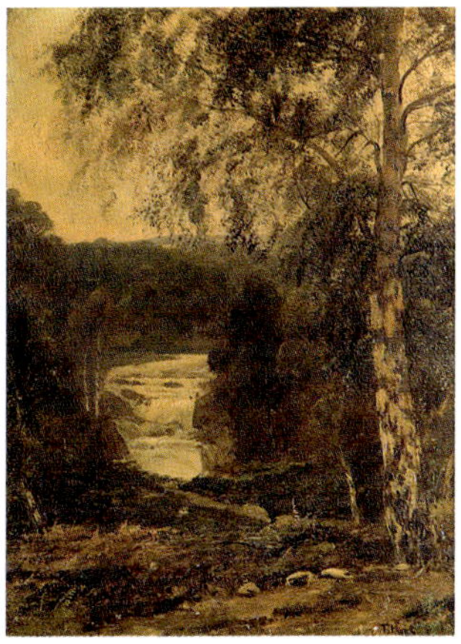

Hines, Theodore active 1876–1890
Mountain Scene with Waterfall
oil on canvas 35.5 x 25.5
OP546

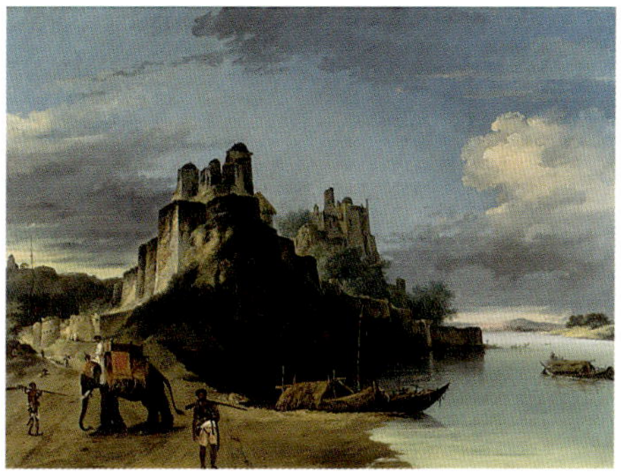

Hodges, William 1744–1797
South-West Face of Chunargarh Fortress
oil on canvas 122 x 160.5
OP613

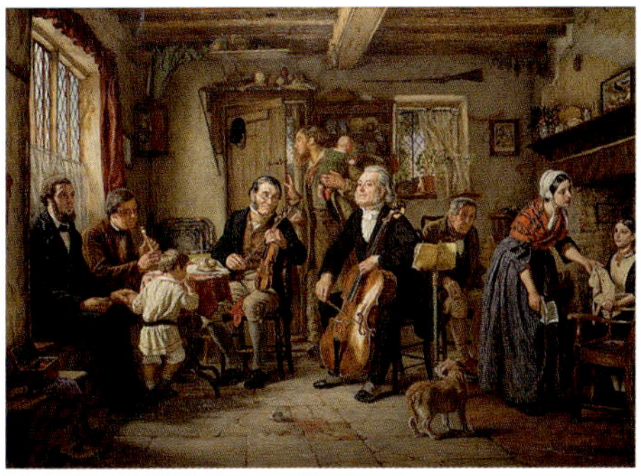

Hodgson, John Evan 1831–1895
A Philharmonic Rehearsal in a Farmhouse
1860
oil on canvas 86.5 x 112
OP91

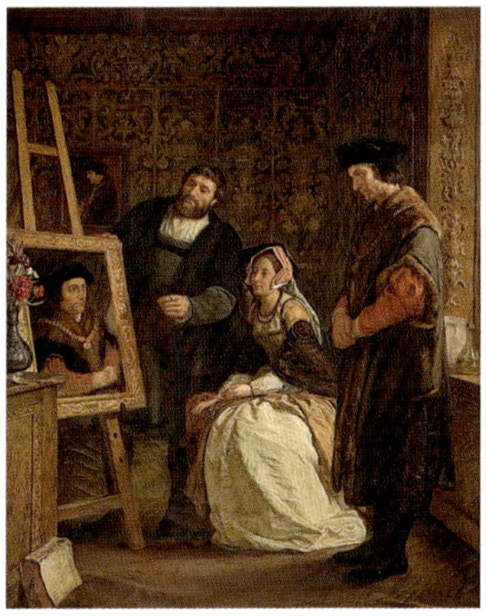

Hodgson, John Evan 1831–1895
Holbein's Studio 1861
oil on canvas 91.5 x 71
OP537

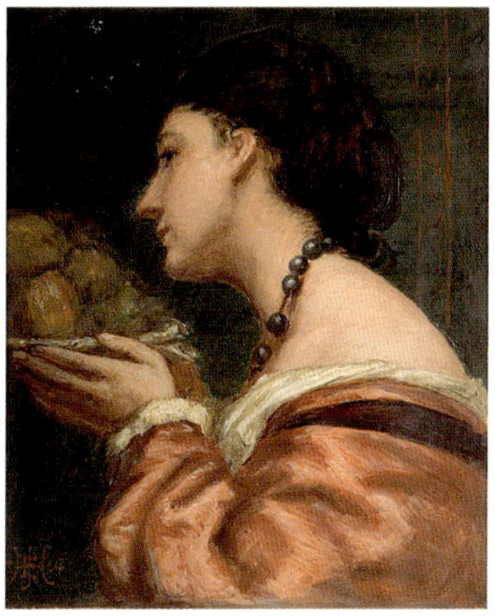

Hodgson, John Evan 1831–1895
The Fruit Bearer 1864
oil on canvas 23 x 19
OP379

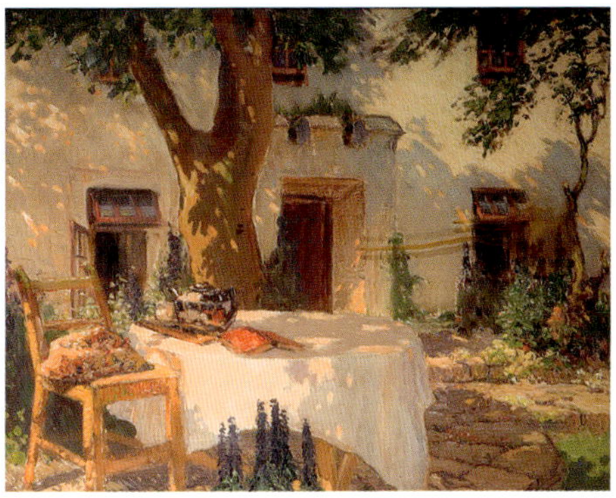

Hoggatt, William 1879–1961
Morning, the Artist's Cottage
oil on canvas 51 x 61
OP266

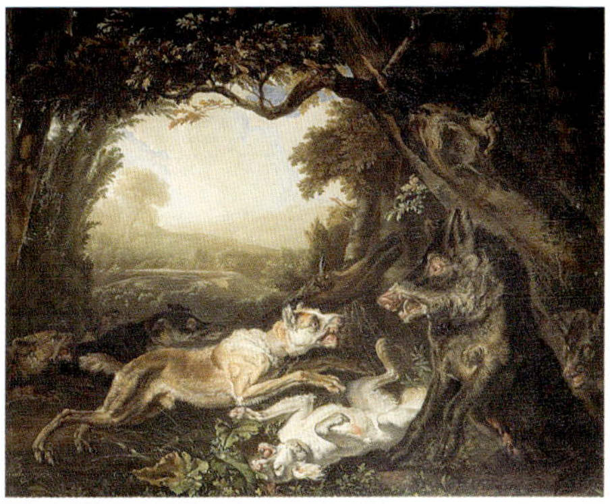

Hondius, Abraham c.1625–1691
A Boar Hunt
oil on canvas 70 x 81
OP517

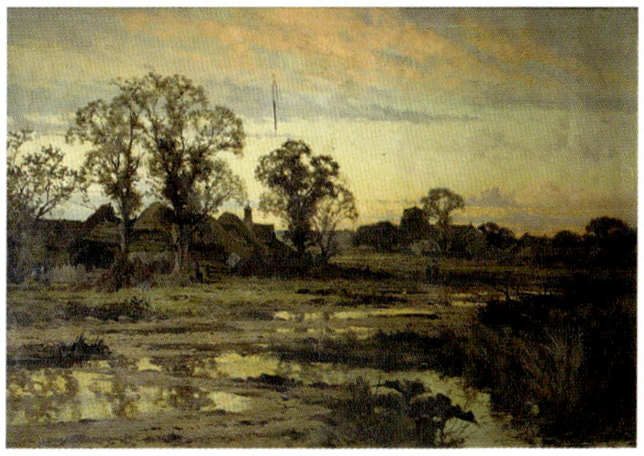

Hooper, John Horace c.1850–c.1899
Close of a Rainy Day
oil on canvas 86.5 x 122
OP695

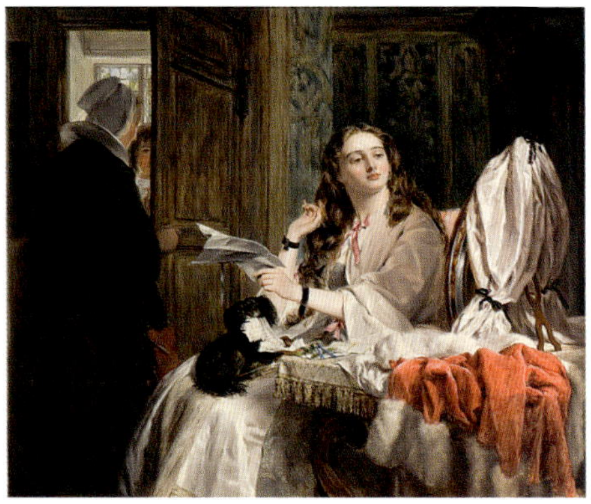

Horsley, John Calcott 1817–1903
St Valentine's Morning 1863
oil on canvas 59.5 x 71.5
OP169

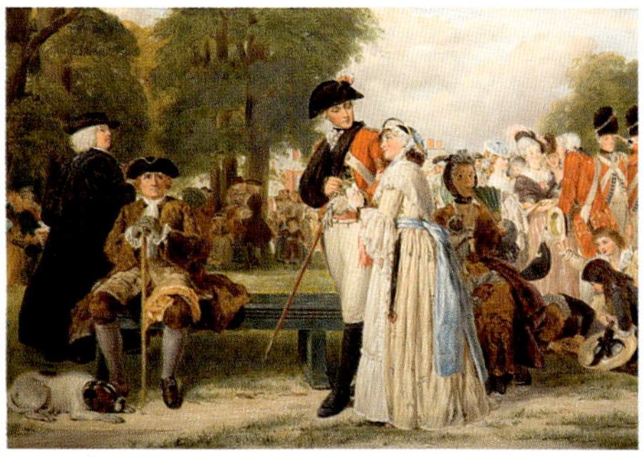

Horsley, John Calcott 1817–1903
The World Forgetting, by the World Forgot (Sunday Afternoon in Kensington Gardens) 1877
oil on canvas 26.5 x 37
OP199

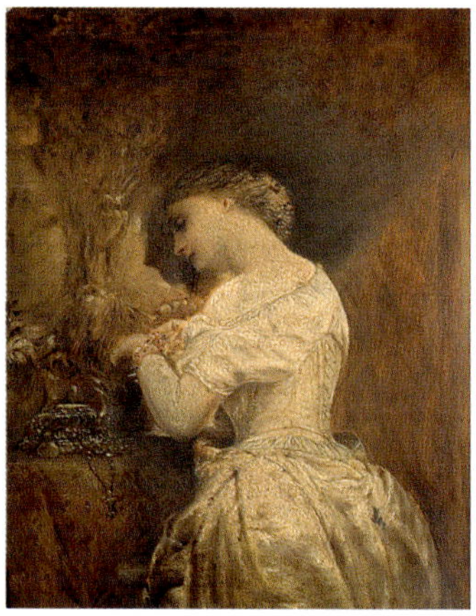

Horsley, John Calcott 1817–1903
A Lady with a Mirror
oil on board 25.5 x 20
OP897

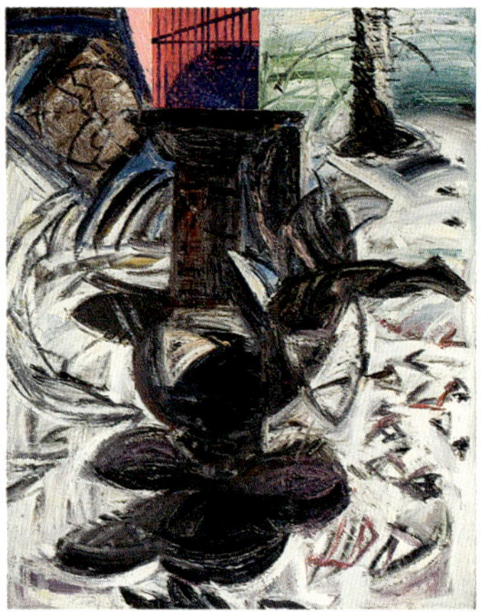

Hosking, Knighton Stephen b.1944
Himley Marker Series I 1981–1982
oil on canvas 183 x 152.5
OP802_I

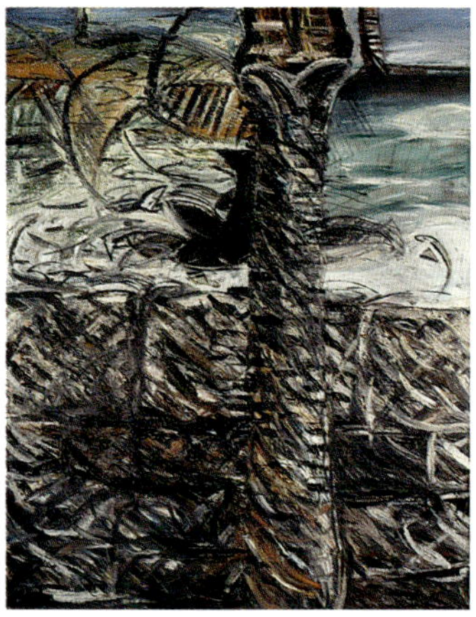

Hosking, Knighton Stephen b.1944
Himley Marker Series II 1981–1982
oil on canvas 183 x 152.5
OP802_II

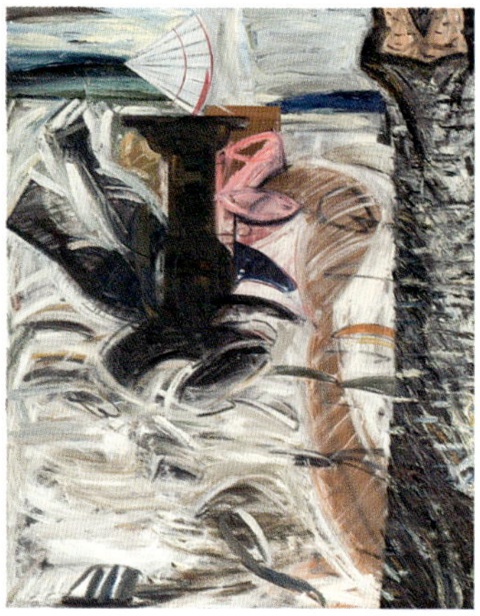

Hosking, Knighton Stephen b.1944
Himley Marker Series III 1981–1982
oil on canvas 183 x 152.5
OP802_III

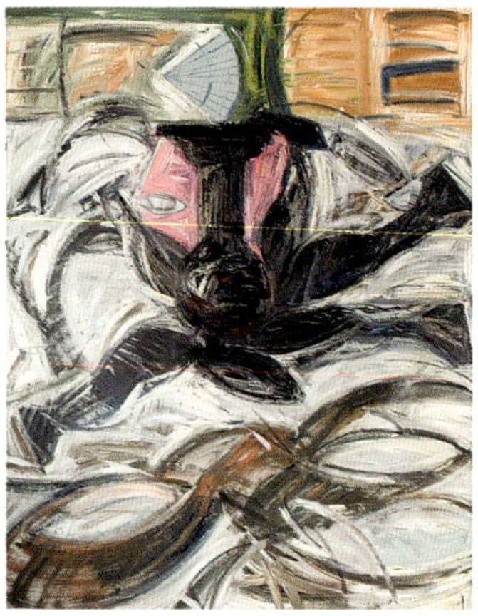

Hosking, Knighton Stephen b.1944
Himley Marker Series IV 1981–1982
oil on canvas 183 x 152.5
OP802_IV

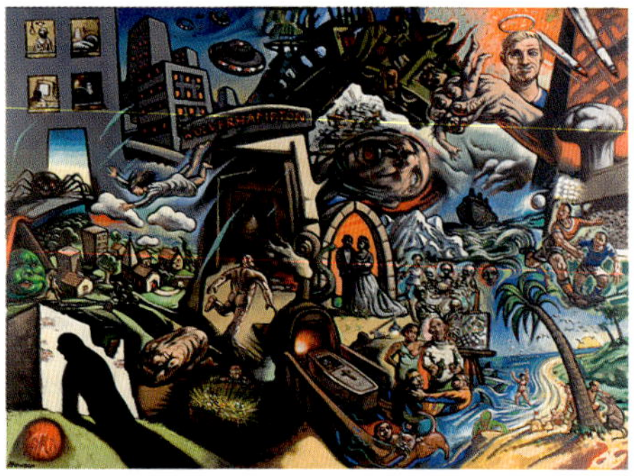

Howson, Peter b.1958
Wolverhampton Dream 2000
oil on canvas 183 x 244
OP907

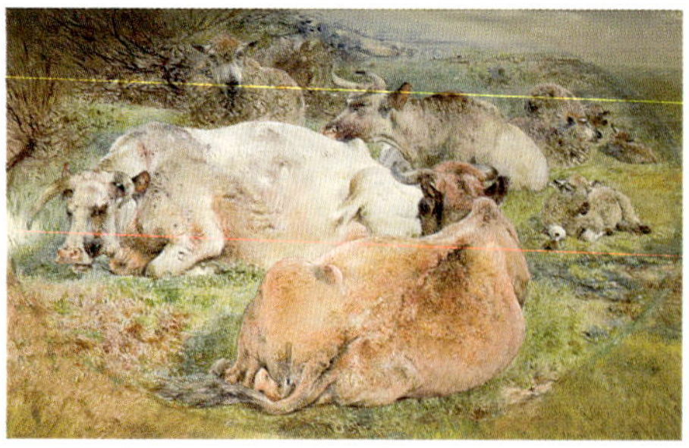

Huggins, William 1820–1884
Cattle and Sheep 1868
oil on board 34 x 49.5
OP581

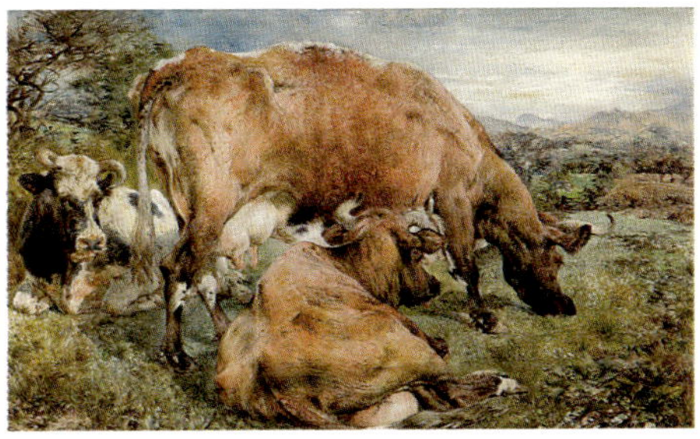

Huggins, William 1820–1884
Three Cows in a Field 1868
oil on board 31 x 46.5
OP135

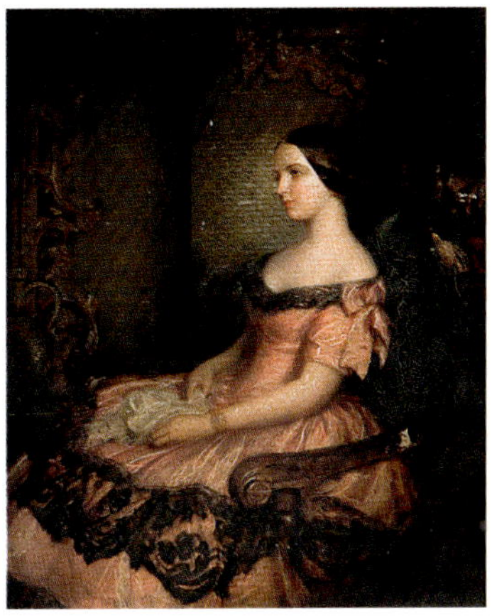

Hughes, Edward 1829–1908
Meditation
oil on panel 26 x 22
OP274

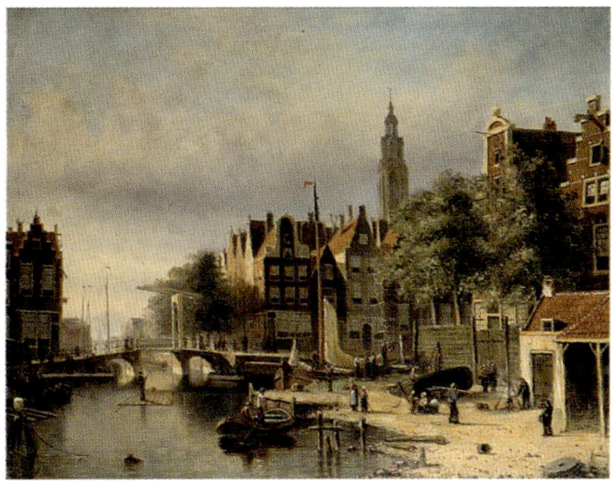

Hulk, Johannes Frederik 1829–1911
Rotterdam
oil on canvas 60 x 80
OP23

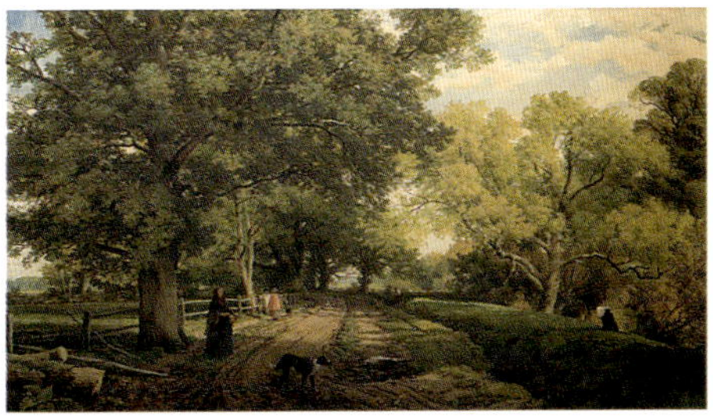

Hulme, Frederick William 1816–1884
A Warwickshire Landscape
oil on canvas 77 x 128.5
OP561

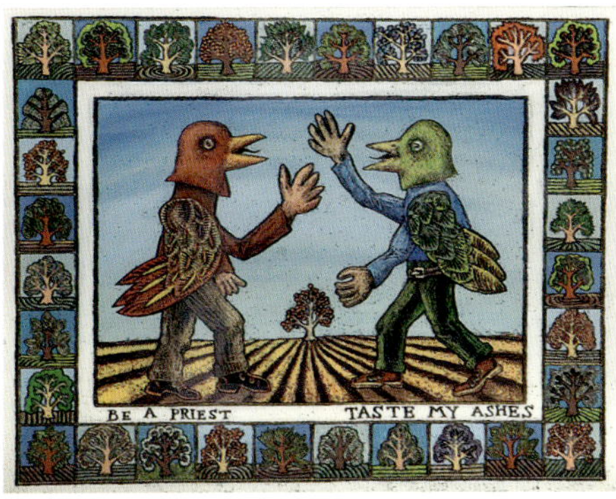

Humphreys, David b.1937
Be a Priest, Taste My Ashes
oil on plastic 33.5 x 41
OP831

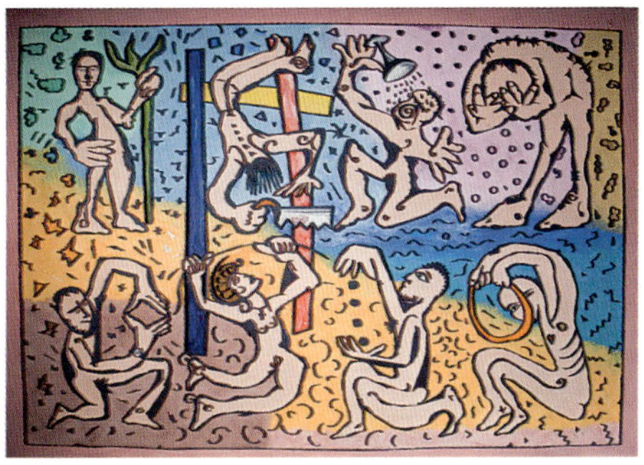

Humphreys, David b.1937
Eight Figures
oil on canvas 152.5 x 244
OP807

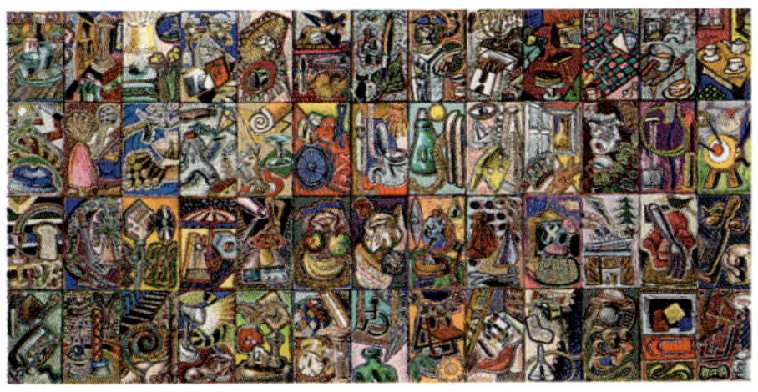

Humphreys, David b.1937
Pelfe, Cosy to Asphyxiating
enamel on paper 132 x 255.5
OP785

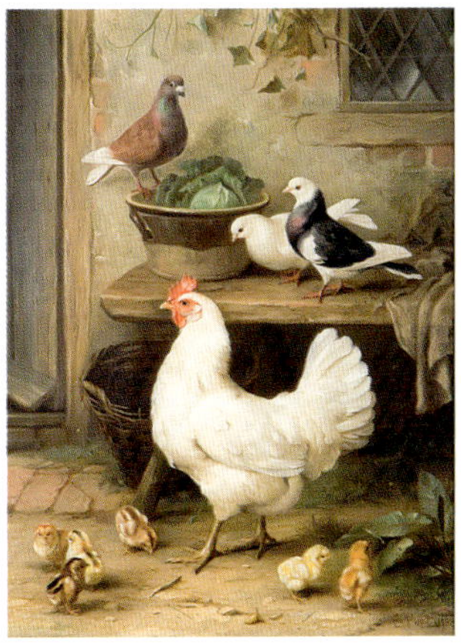

Hunt, Edgar 1876–1953
Waiting to Be Fed
oil on canvas 61 x 45.5
OP696

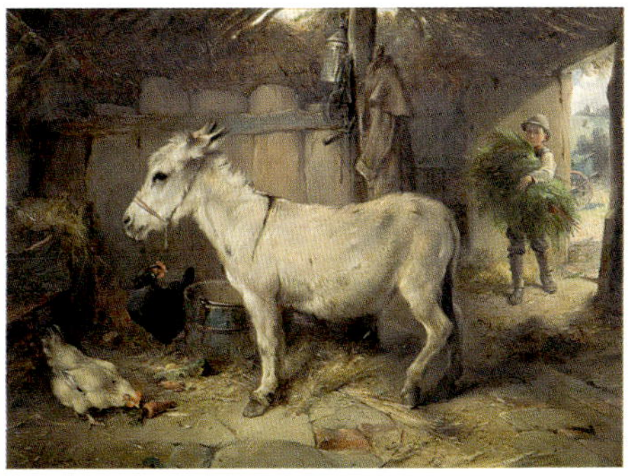

Hunt, Walter 1861–1941
The Donkey 1897
oil on canvas 30.5 x 40.5
OP45

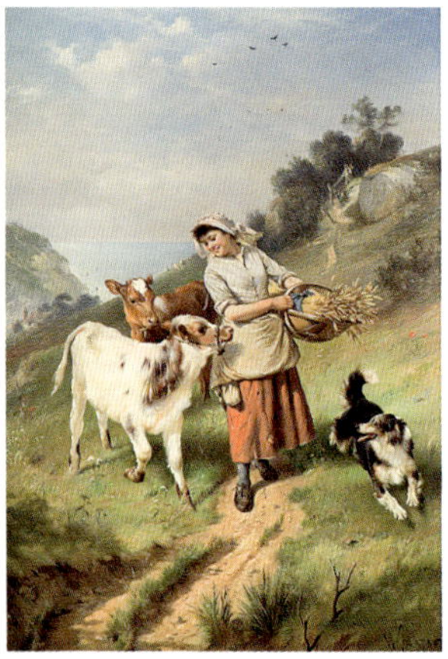

Hunt, Walter 1861–1941
A Girl with Two Calves
oil on canvas 114.5 x 77
OP697

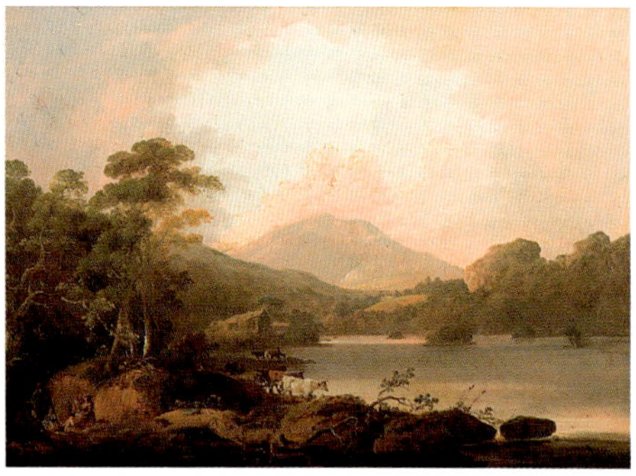

Ibbetson, Julius Caesar 1759–1817
Lakeside Landscape
oil on canvas 45.5 x 61
OP161

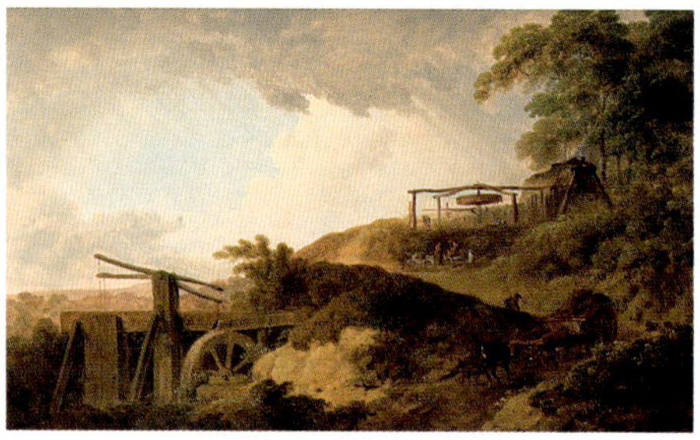

Ibbetson, Julius Caesar 1759–1817
The Watershot Wheel
oil on canvas 38 x 58.5
OP345

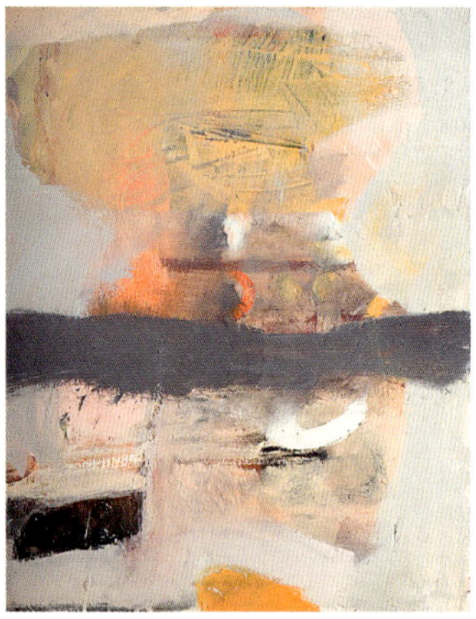

Irvin, Albert b.1922
Grey Streak
oil on canvas 101.5 x 76
OP251

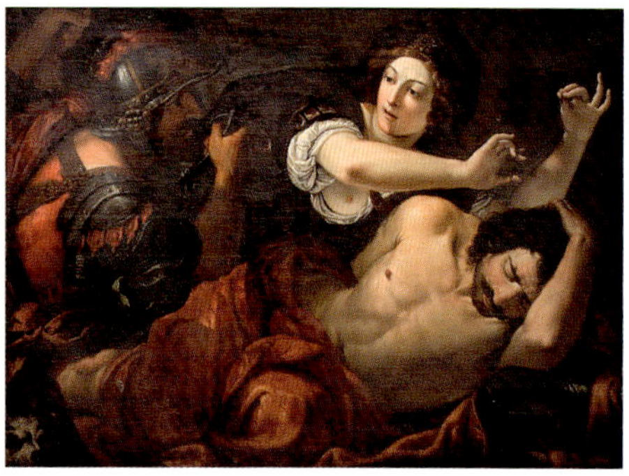

Italian School 17th C
Samson and Delilah
oil on canvas 116 x 151
OP427

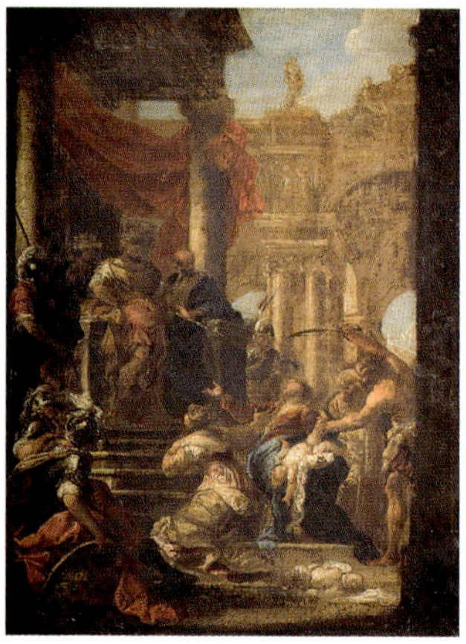

Italian School late 17th C
The Judgement of Solomon
oil on canvas 81 x 58.5
OP270

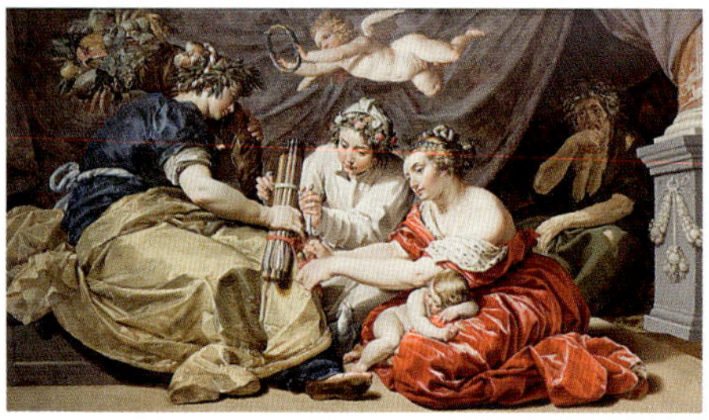

Janssens, Abraham c.1575–1632
Peace and Plenty 1614
oil on panel 217 x 264
OP580

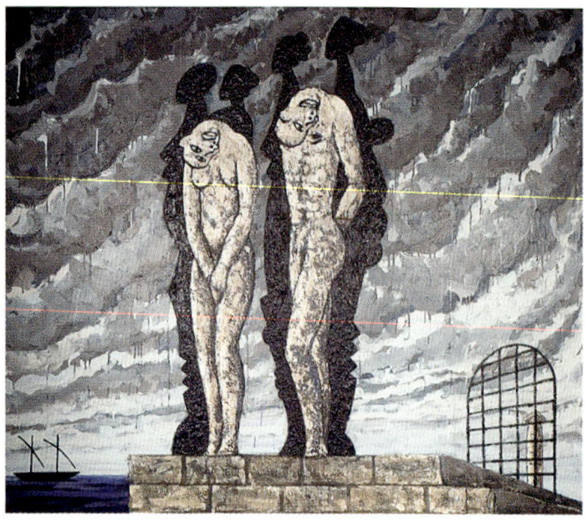

Jantjes, Gavin b.1948
No.6 from Korabra Series 1985
acrylic on canvas 180 x 200
OP805

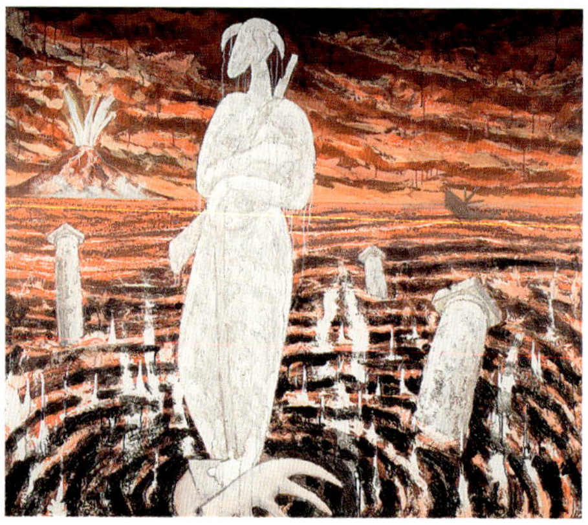

Jantjes, Gavin b.1948
No.6 from Korabra Series
acrylic on canvas 180 x 200
X2 (P)

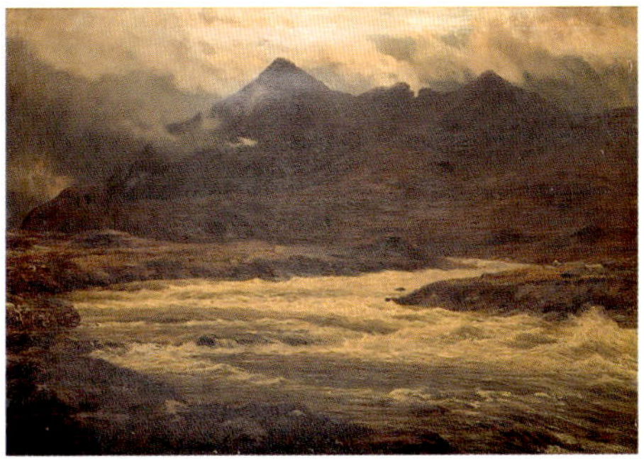

Johnson, Charles Edward 1832–1913
Mountain and Flood, Sgurr nan Gillean, Skye 1876
oil on canvas 86.5 x 122
OP412

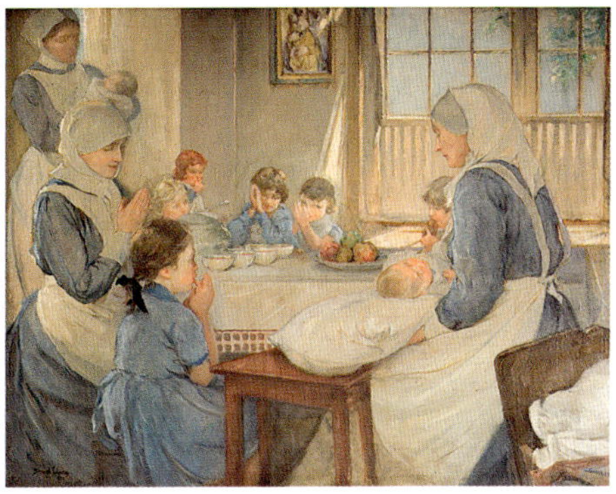

Johnson, Ernest Borough 1866–1949
Sisters and Brothers 1919
oil on canvas 101.5 x 127
OP131

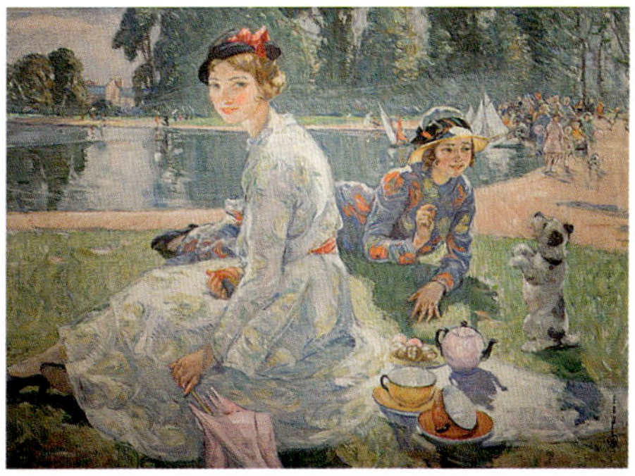

Johnson, Ernest Borough 1866–1949
The Round Pond 1934
oil on canvas 50.5 x 76
OP304

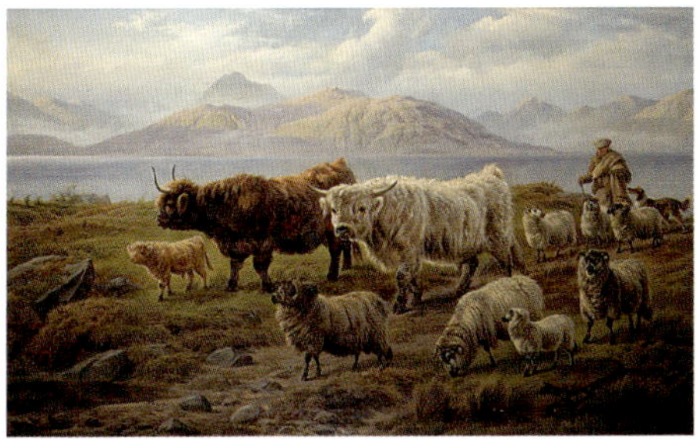

Jones, Charles 1836–1902
Autumn Afternoon, Loch Leven
oil on canvas 91.5 x 142
OP699

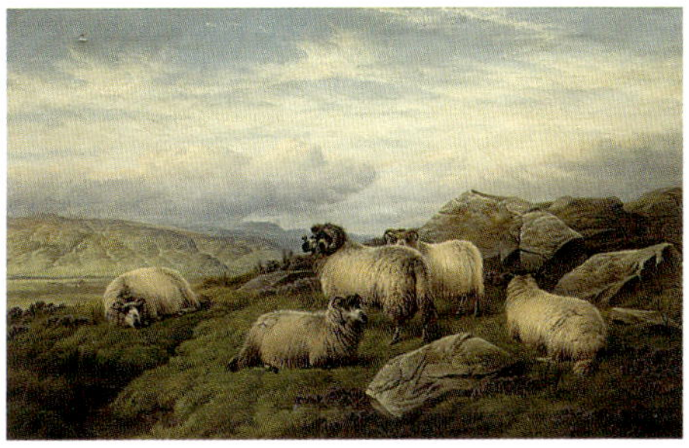

Jones, Charles 1836–1902
Sheep
oil on canvas 61 x 91.5
OP698

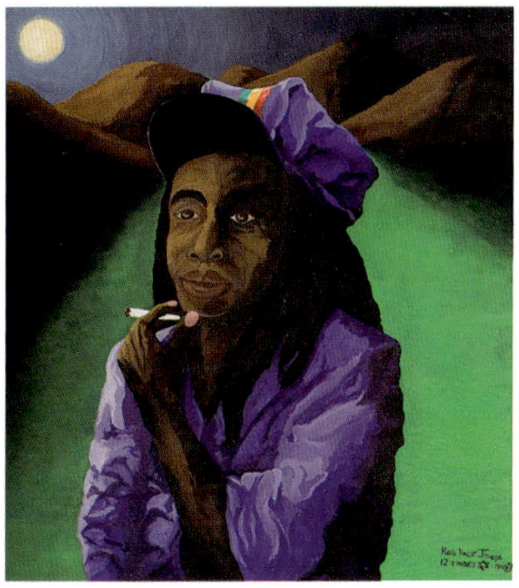

Joseph, Ras Vince active 1980s
Dread in Moonlight
oil on panel 60 x 39
OP809

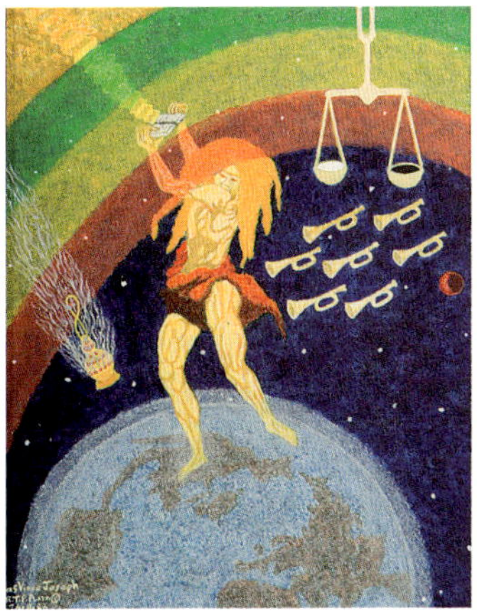

Joseph, Ras Vince active 1980s
Is Your Name Written There? 1980–1988
oil on canvas 24.5 x 19
OP810

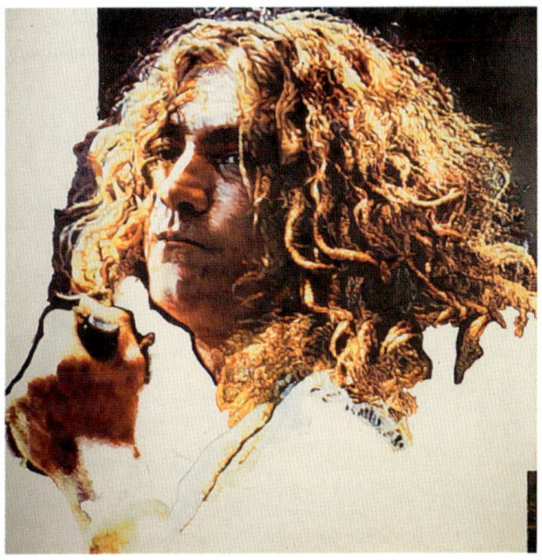

Judkins, John b.1951
Pop Star, '73 1973
oil on board 127 x 122 (E)
OP604

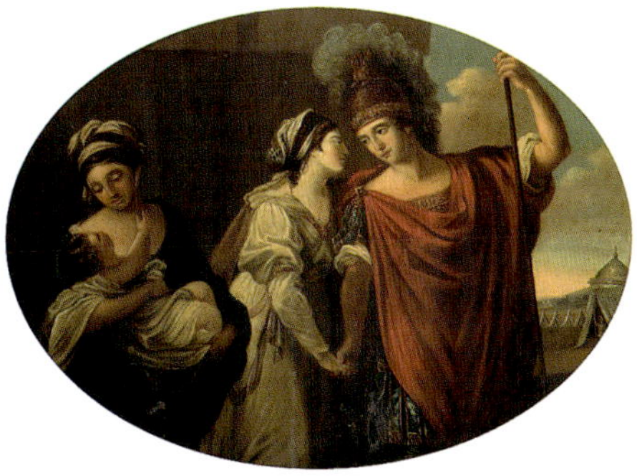

Kauffmann, Angelica 1741–1807
Decorative Panel
oil on copper 42 x 56
OP197

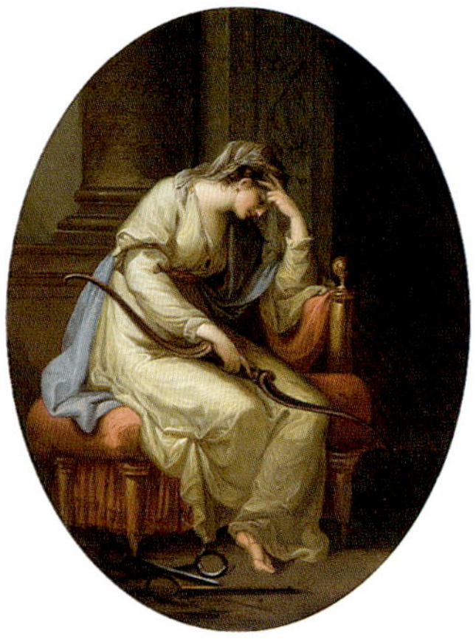

Kauffmann, Angelica 1741–1807
Penelope Weeping over the Bow of Ulysses
oil on copper 25.5 x 20
OP531

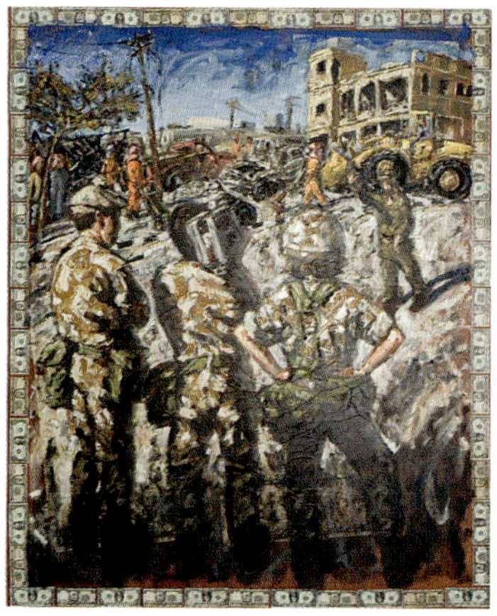

Keane, John b.1954
Freedom of the Press 1991
oil on canvas 213 x 169
OP862

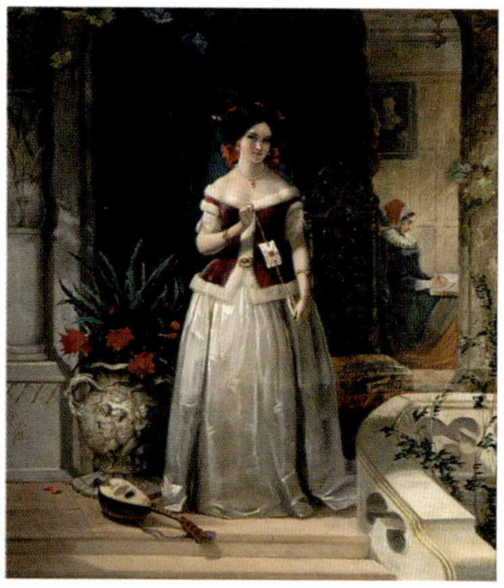

Keeling, William Knight 1807–1886
Love's Messenger 1856
oil on canvas 65 x 54.5
OP201

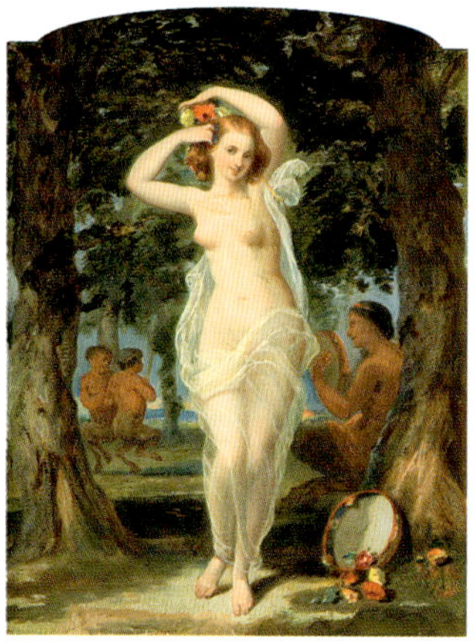

Keeling, William Knight 1807–1886
The Wood Nymph 1861
oil on canvas 40.5 x 30.5
OP164

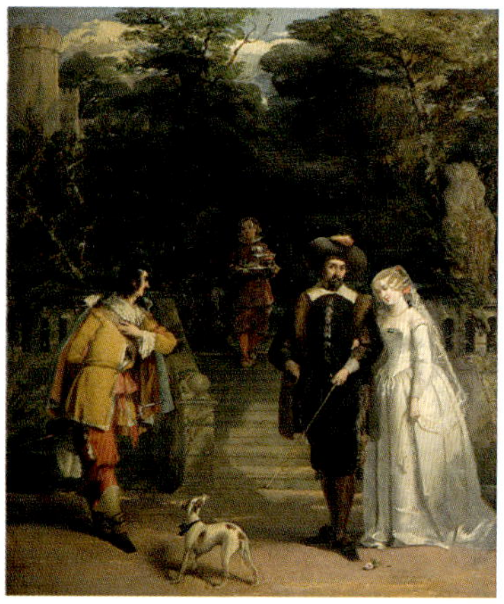

Keeling, William Knight 1807–1886
The Introduction 1862
oil on canvas 76 x 63.5
OP560

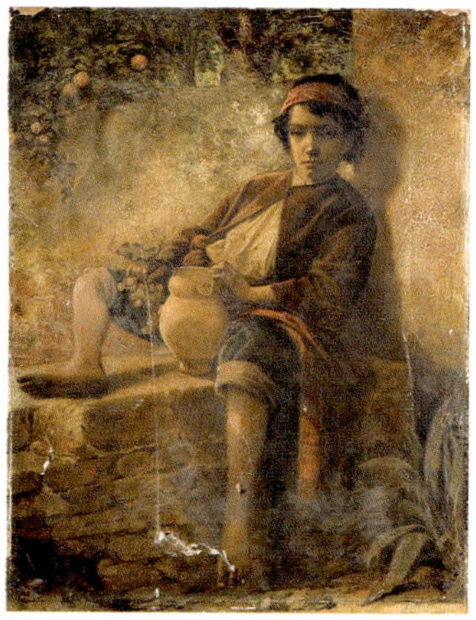

Keeling, William Knight 1807–1886
Midday Rest 1873
oil on canvas 61 x 45.7
OP473

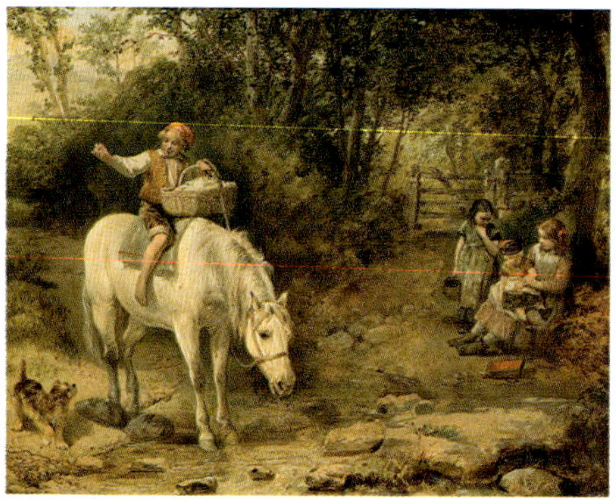

Keeling, William Knight 1807–1886
The Watering Place 1879
oil on canvas 48.5 x 58.5
OP568

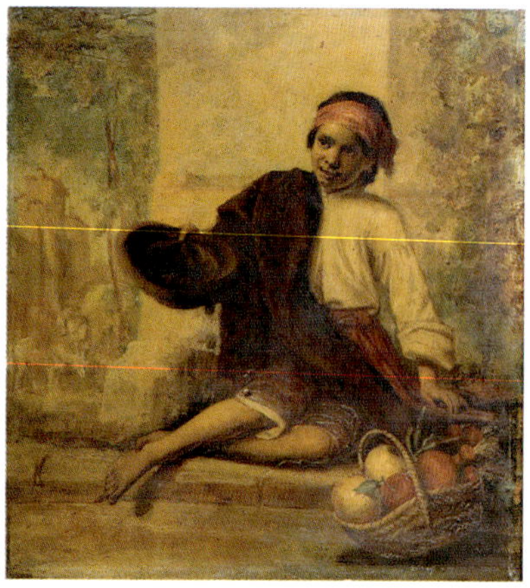

Keeling, William Knight 1807–1886
A Boy Selling Fruit 1880
oil on canvas 48.5 x 43
OP554

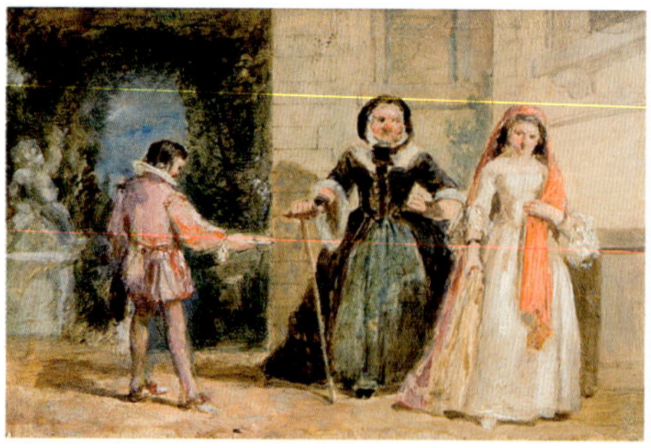

Keeling, William Knight 1807–1886
A Scene from Shakespeare
oil on panel 11.5 x 16
OP146

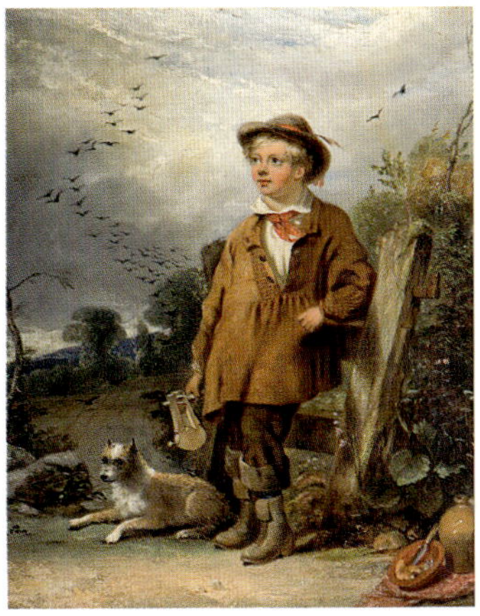

Keeling, William Knight 1807–1886
The Bird Scarer
oil on canvas 53.5 x 42
OP380

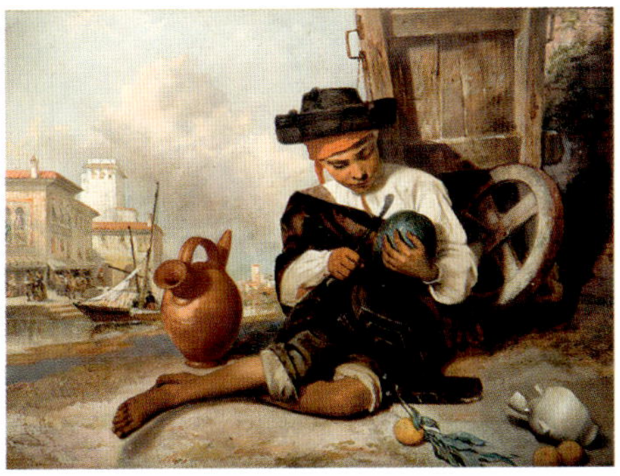

Keeling, William Knight 1807–1886
The Melon Seller
oil on canvas 37 x 48.5
OP24

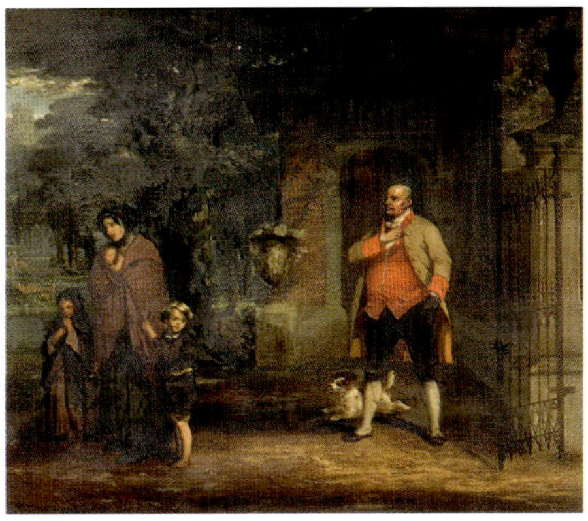

Keeling, William Knight 1807–1886
The Rejected Appeal
oil on canvas 59.5 x 68.5
OP579

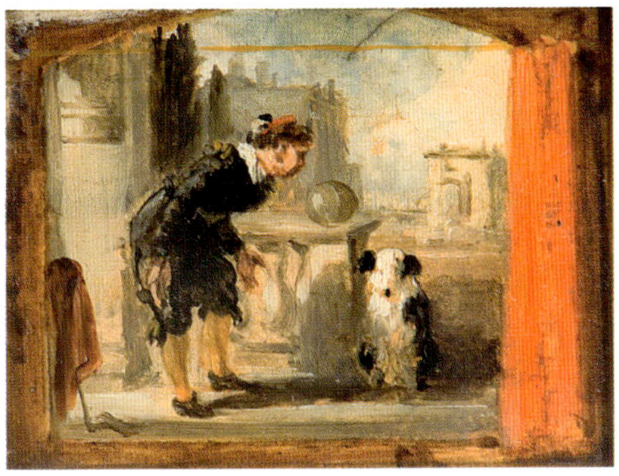

Keeling, William Knight 1807–1886
The Showman
oil on panel 9.6 x 12
OP376

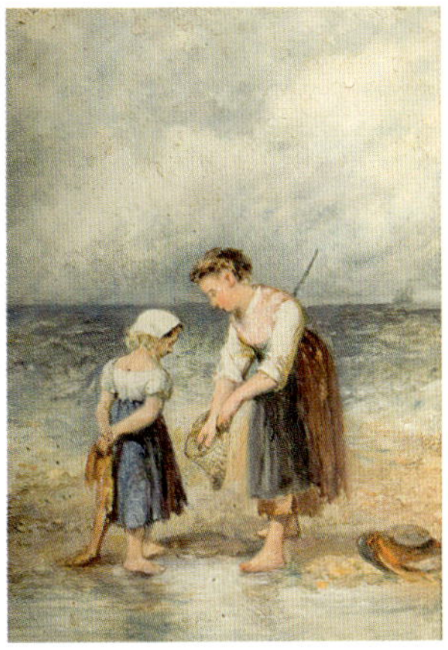

Keeling, William Knight 1807–1886
The Young Shrimpers
oil on board 18 x 12.5
OP144

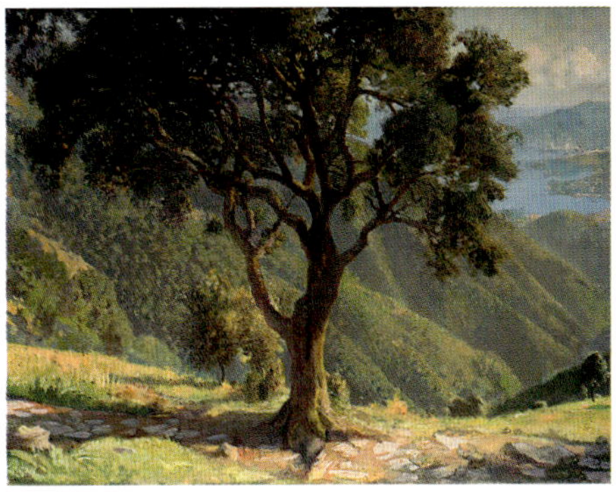

Kelly, Gerald Festus 1879–1972
The Ilex Tree 1933–1938
oil on canvas 66 x 81
OP330

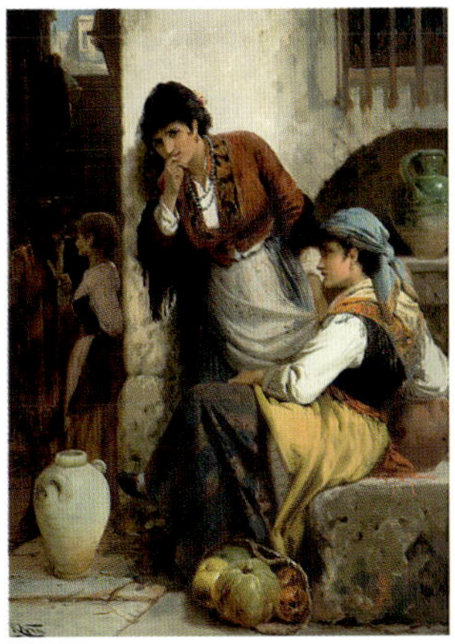

Kemm, Robert 1837–1895
Spanish Gypsies
oil on board 45.5 x 35.5
OP349

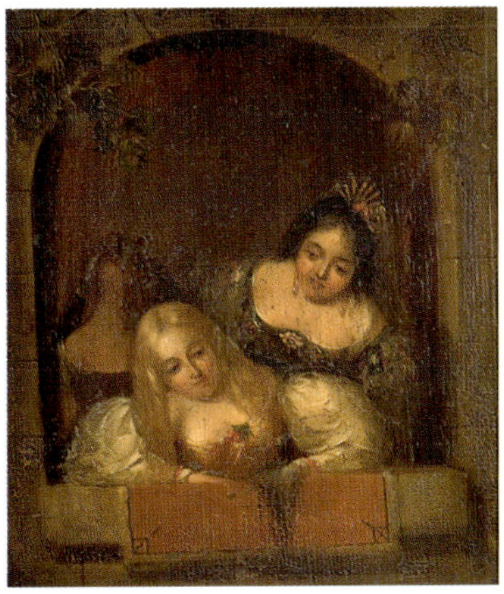

Kemm, Robert 1837–1895
Spanish Ladies
oil on panel 30.5 x 25.5
OP566

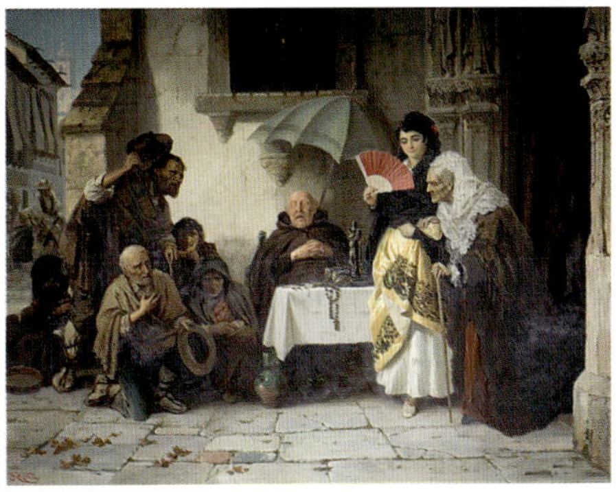

Kemm, Robert 1837–1895
The Beggars
oil on canvas 101.5 x 127
OP327

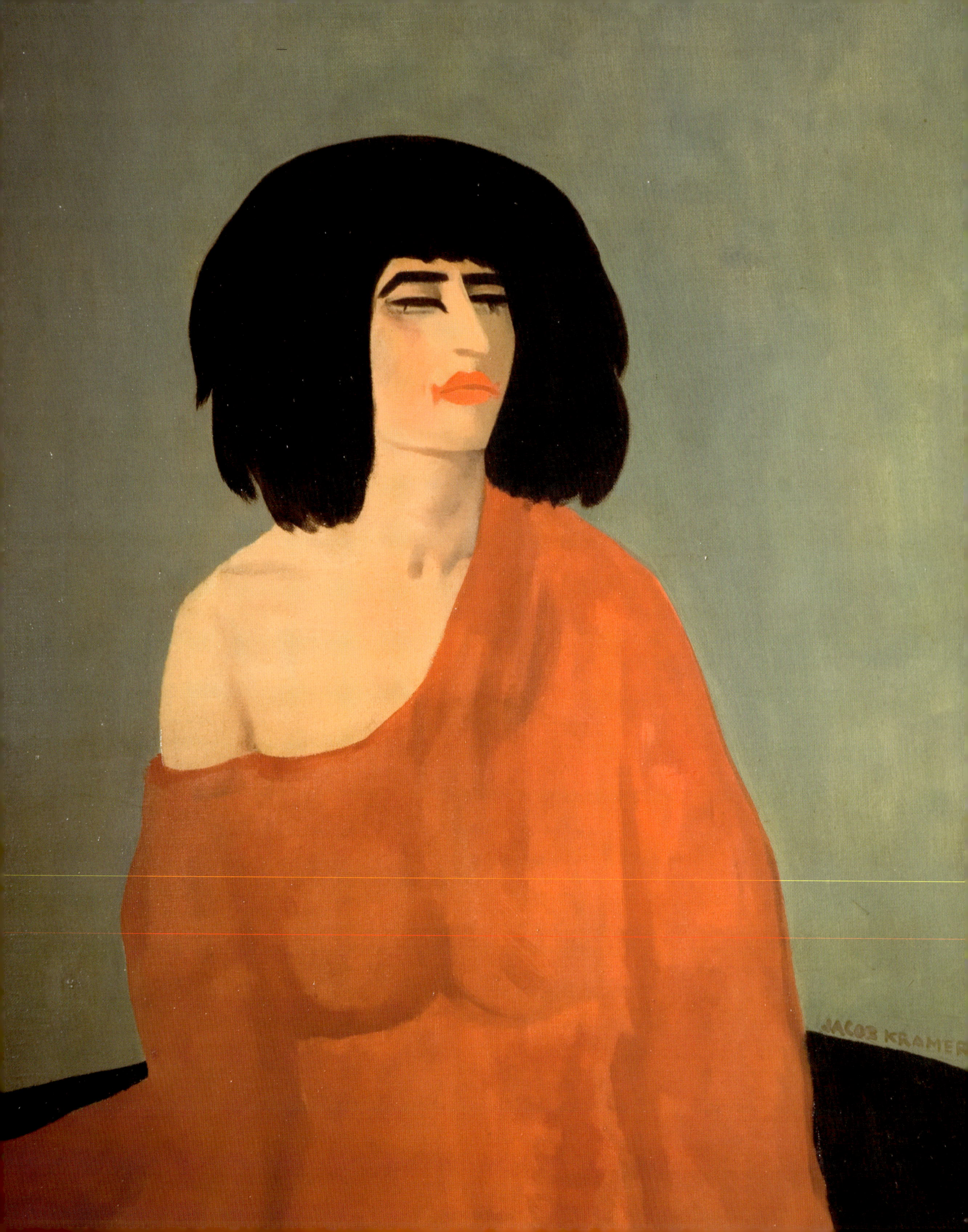
JACOB KRAMER

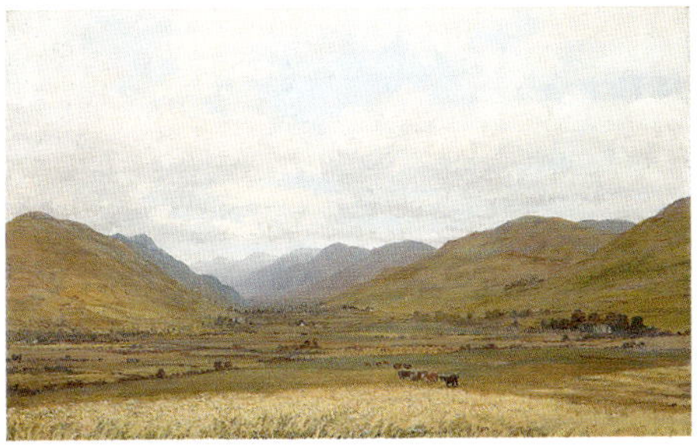

Kettle, Rupert Alfred 1817–1894
Near Abergwynant
oil on canvas 35.5 x 53.5
OP238

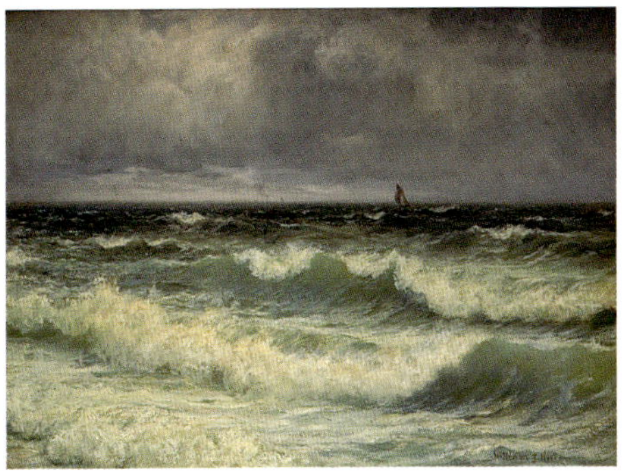

King, William Joseph 1857–after 1943
Stormy Anglesea
oil on canvas 35.5 x 46.5
OP700

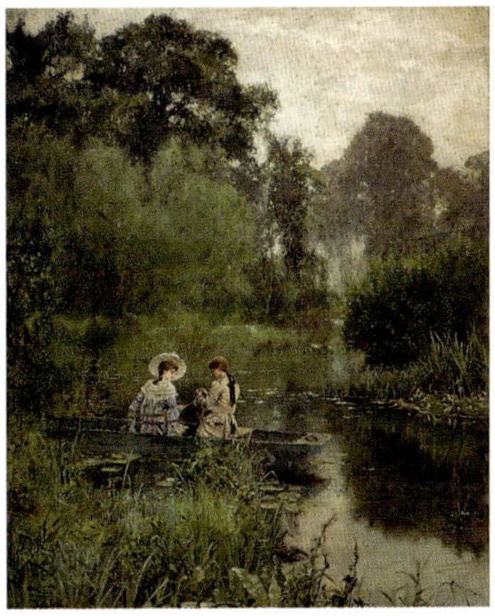

King, Yeend 1855–1924
Courtship
oil on canvas 101.5 x 81.5
OP701

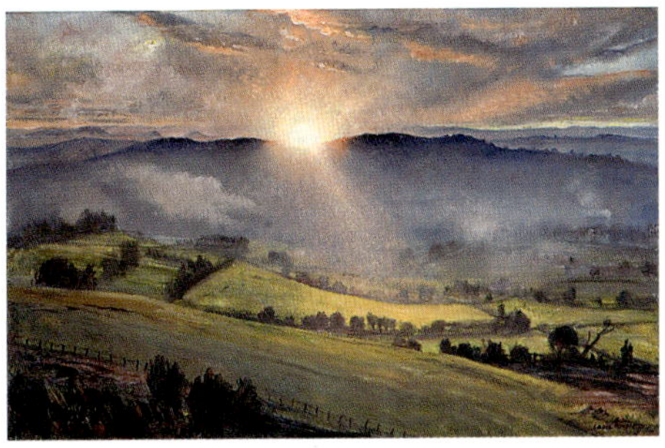

Knight, Laura 1877–1970
Sundown 1940–1947
oil on canvas 61 x 91.5
OP301

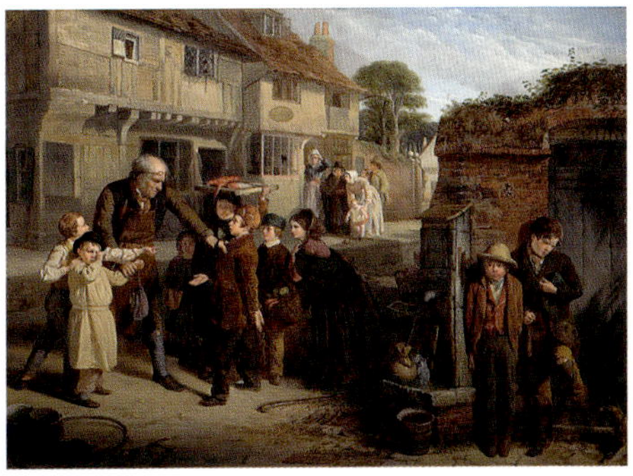

Knight, William Henry 1823–1863
The Broken Window 1855
oil on canvas 73.5 x 96.5
OP233

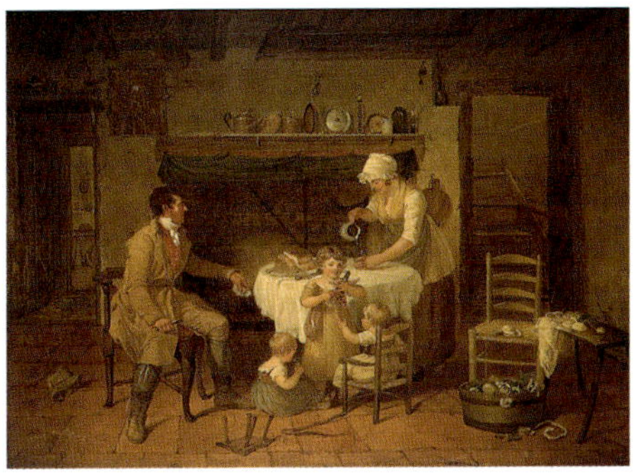

Knight, William Henry 1823–1863
Dinner Time
oil on canvas 45.5 x 61
OP213

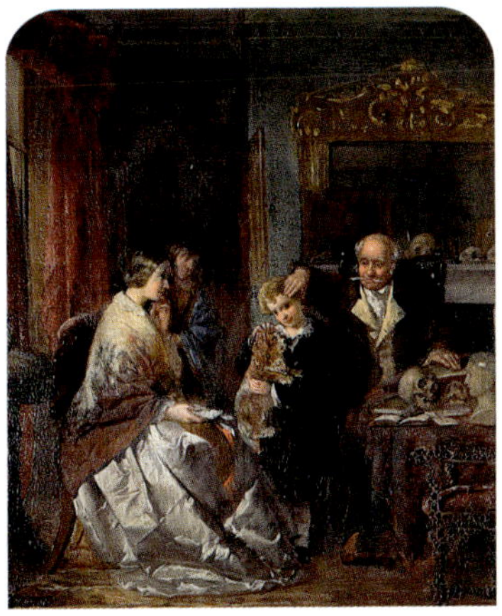

Knight, William Henry 1823–1863
Study for 'The Phrenologist'
oil on canvas 23.5 x 20.5
OP50

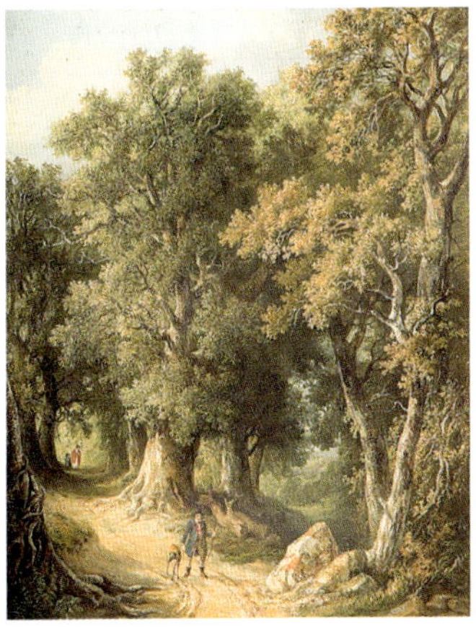

Ladbrooke, Robert 1770–1842
An Oak Glade
oil on canvas 66.5 x 51
OP92

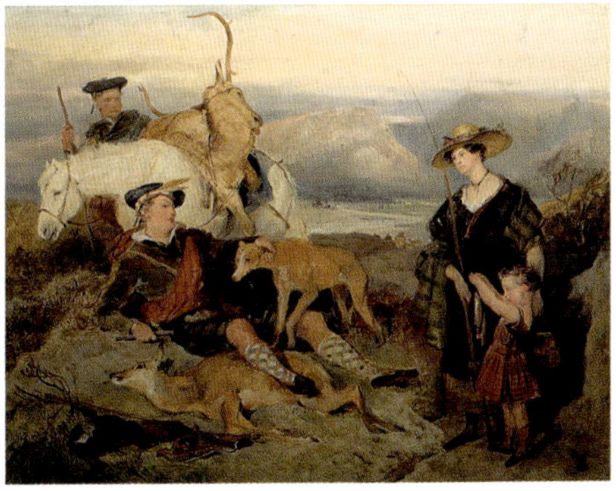

Landseer, Edwin Henry 1802–1873
Sketch for 'Deer-Stalking in the Highlands'
c.1828
oil on canvas 43 x 53.5
OP132

Facing page: Kramer, Jacob, 1892–1962, *Rohalla* (detail), University of Keele Art Collection, (p. 42)

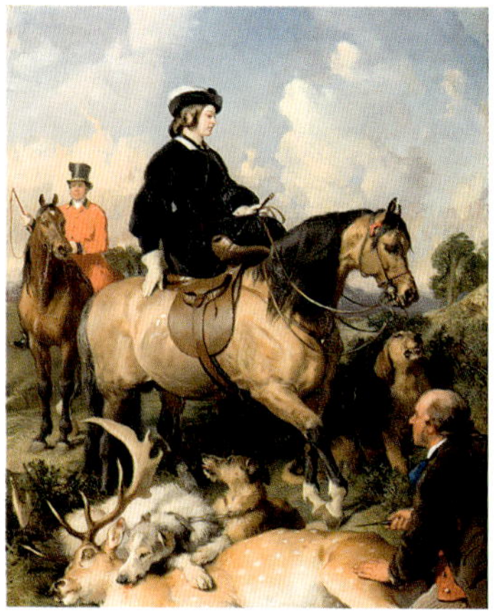

Landseer, Edwin Henry 1802–1873
Queen Victoria in Windsor Home Park 1865
oil on canvas 89.5 x 72.5
OP218

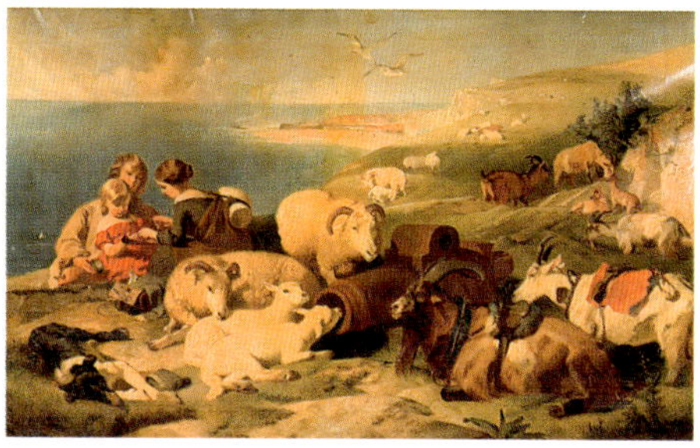

Landseer, Edwin Henry 1802–1873
On the Downs
oil on canvas 87 x 134.5
OP510

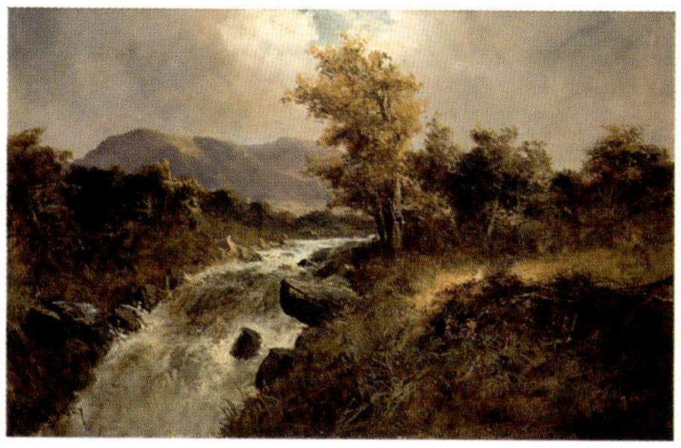

Langley, William active 1880–1920
Mountain Stream in Wales
oil on canvas 61 x 91.5
OP556

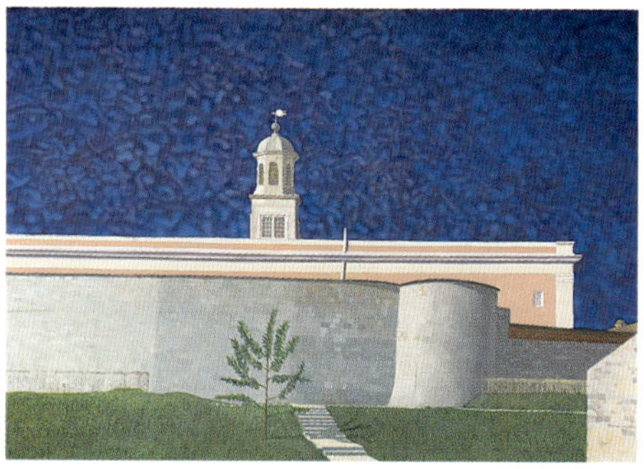

Langton, John b.1932
Debtors' Prison, York
oil on canvas 112 x 152.5
OP527

Latham, John 1921–2006
Troll Flower (from 'Review of Dictionary')
1968–1973
oil on canvas 92 x 56
OP918

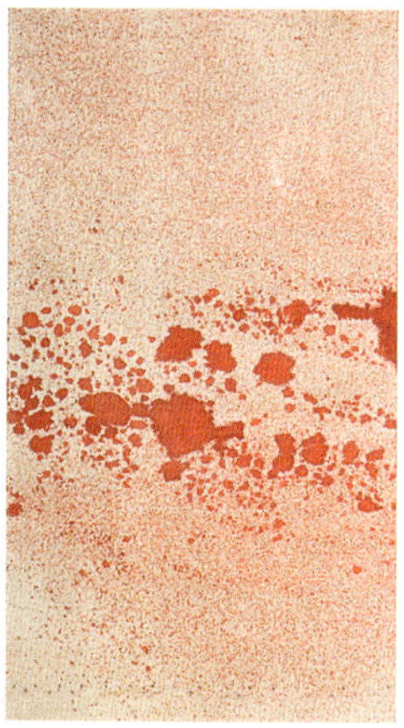

Latham, John 1921–2006
Cosmic Blood 1994
spray paint & acrylic on canvas 26.5 x 14
OP922

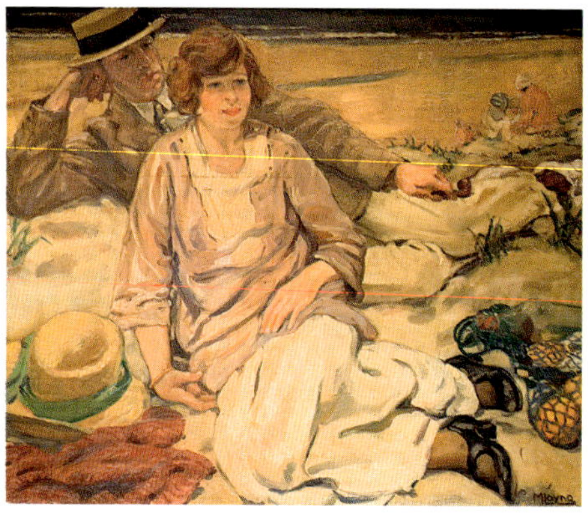

Layng, Mabel Frances 1881–1937
The Holidaymakers
oil on canvas 85 x 99
OP305

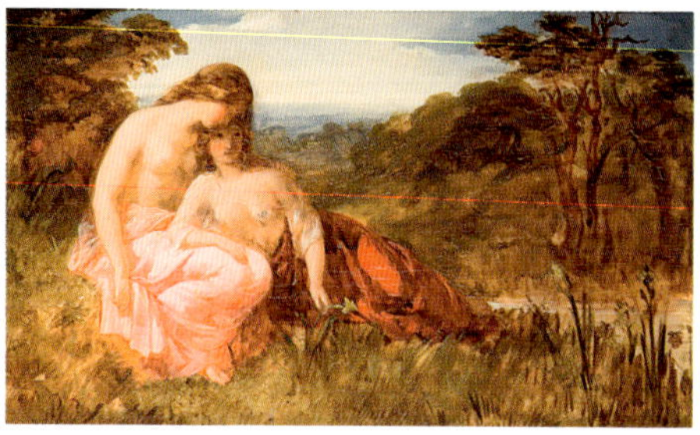

Le Jeune, Henry 1819–1904
Scene from Shakespeare's 'A Midsummer Night's Dream'
oil on canvas 30 x 45.5
OP179

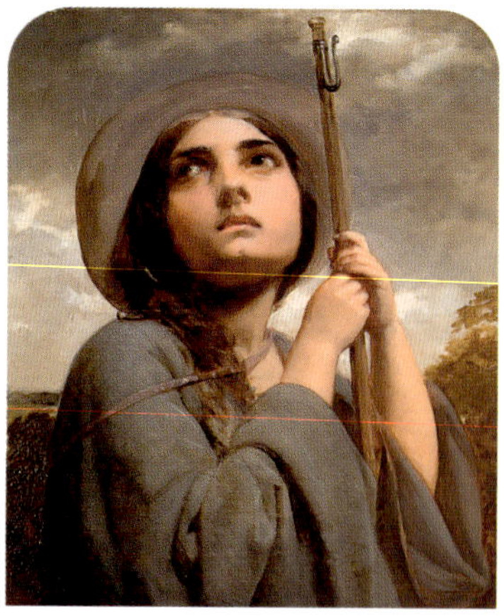

Le Jeune, Henry 1819–1904
The Pilgrim
oil on canvas 30.5 x 25.5
OP4

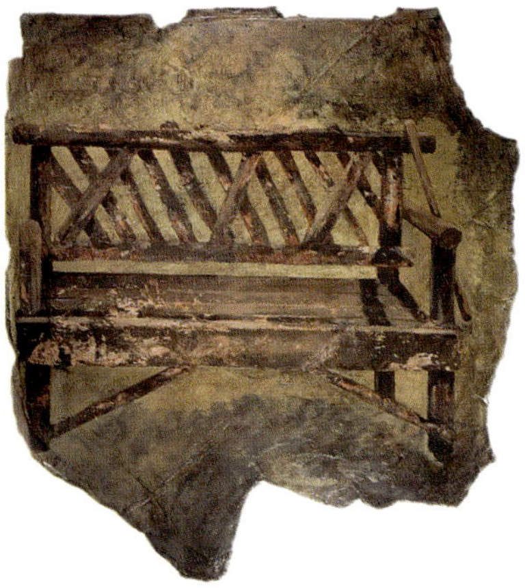

Leadbeater, Alexandra b.1956
Bench
mixed media & wax on paper 162 x 145
OP782

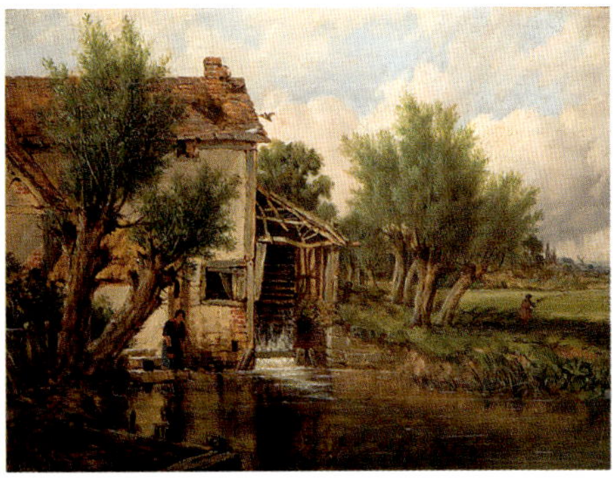

Leader, Benjamin Williams 1831–1923
An Old Mill, near Worcester 1880
oil on canvas 28 x 35.5
OP354

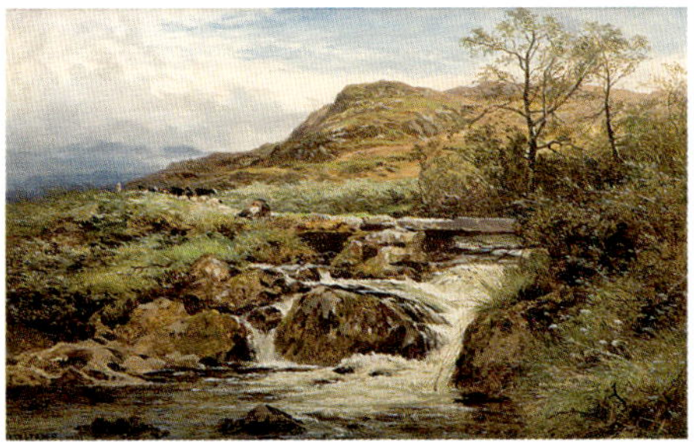

Leader, Benjamin Williams 1831–1923
On the Lledr, North Wales 1881
oil on canvas 40.5 x 61
OP184

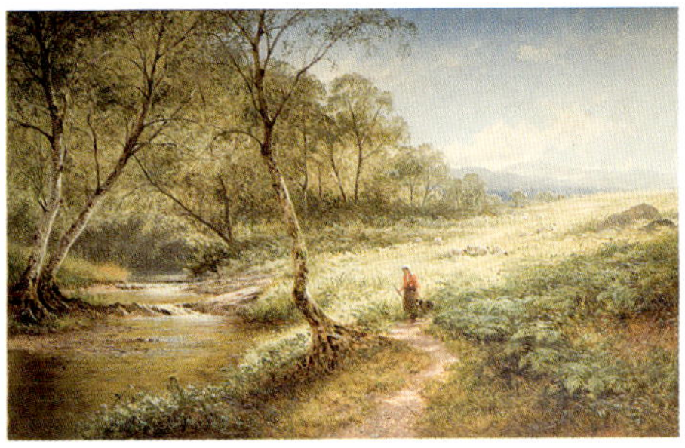

Leader, Benjamin Williams 1831–1923
Summertime, a Stream, near Dolgellau 1881
oil on canvas 71 x 106.5
OP142

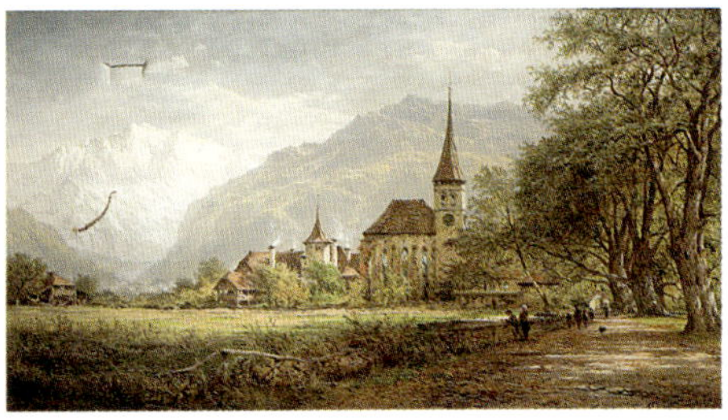

Leader, Benjamin Williams 1831–1923
Interlaken 1882
oil on canvas 50 x 130
OP97

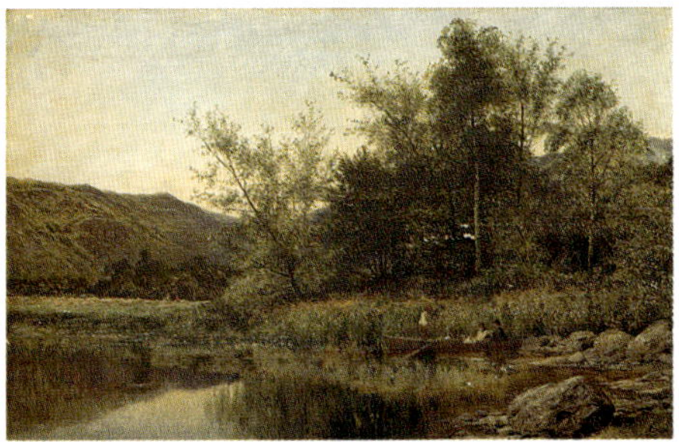

Leader, Benjamin Williams 1831–1923
Head of Ullswater, Summer
oil on panel 40 x 61
OP819

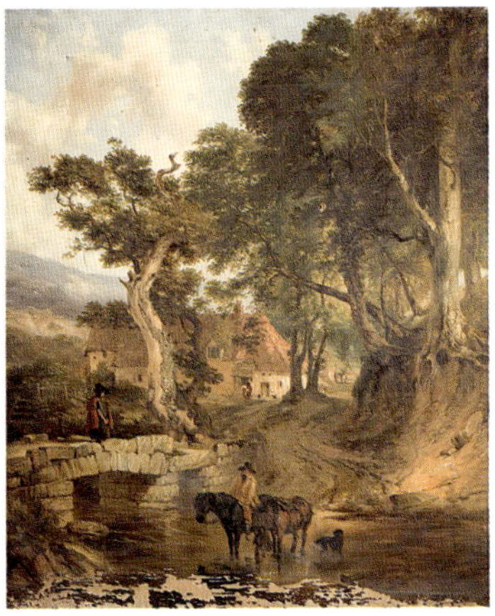

Lee, Frederick Richard 1798–1879
The Watering Place 1842
oil on canvas 127 x 101.5
OP396

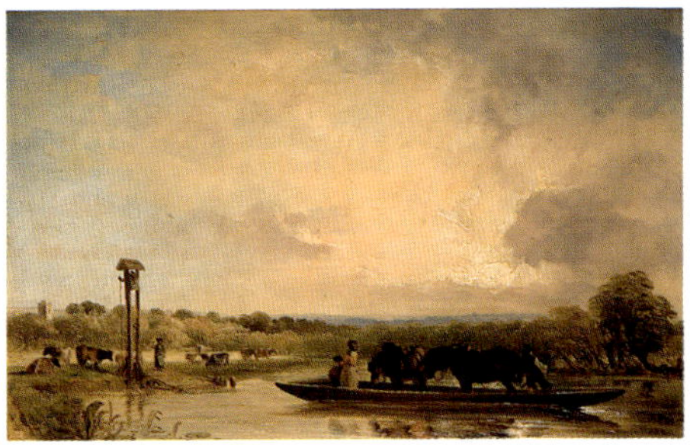

Lee, Frederick Richard 1798–1879
The Ferry Boat 1844
oil on board 30.5 x 45.5
OP369

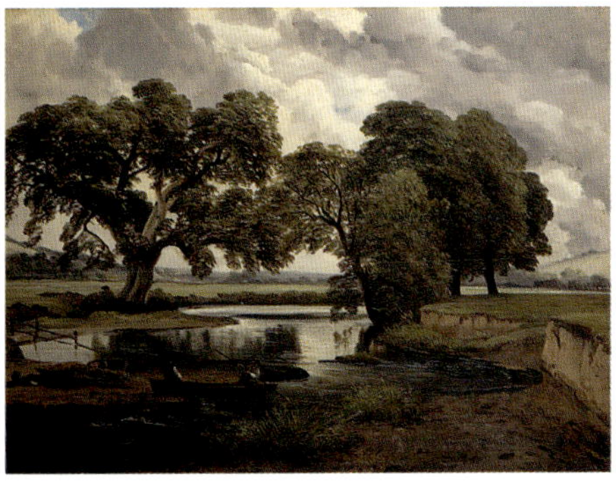

Lee, Frederick Richard 1798–1879
On the Trent 1861
oil on panel 35.5 x 45.5
OP14

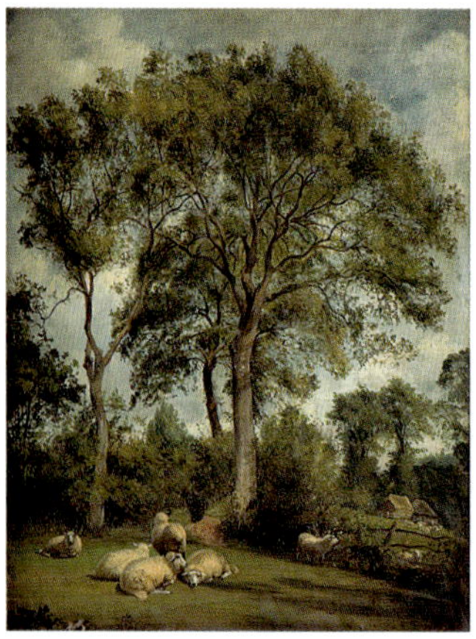

Lee, Frederick Richard 1798–1879
Landscape with Sheep
oil on canvas 59 x 45.5
OP16

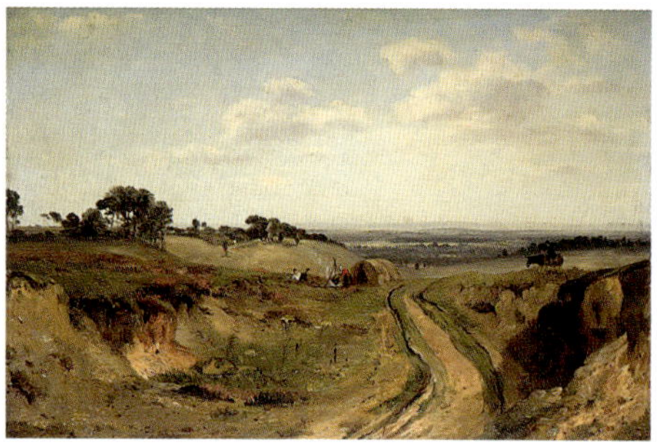

Lee, Frederick Richard 1798–1879
Near Oatlands
oil on card 35.5 x 40.5
OP64

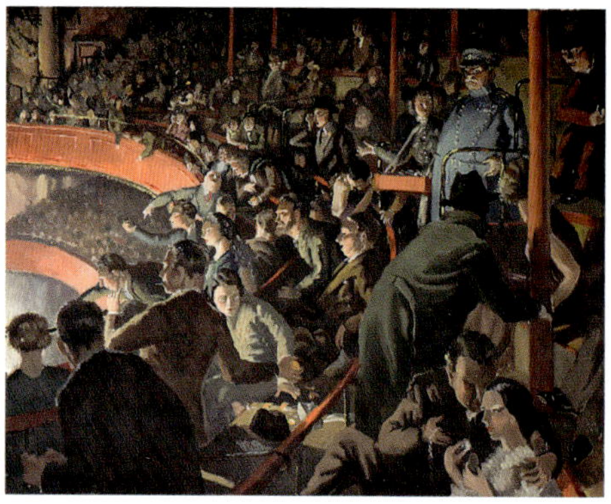

Leigh-Pemberton, John 1911–1997
The Gallery Objects 1925–1935
oil on canvas 63.5 x 76
OP318

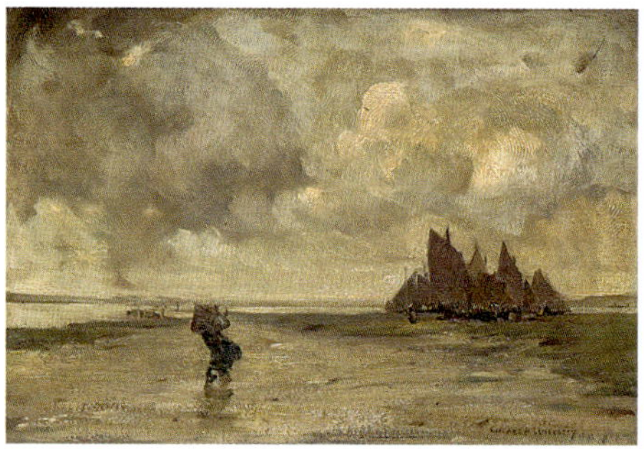

Lenfestey, Giffard Hocart 1872–1943
Beach Scene
oil on canvas 30.5 x 43
OP464

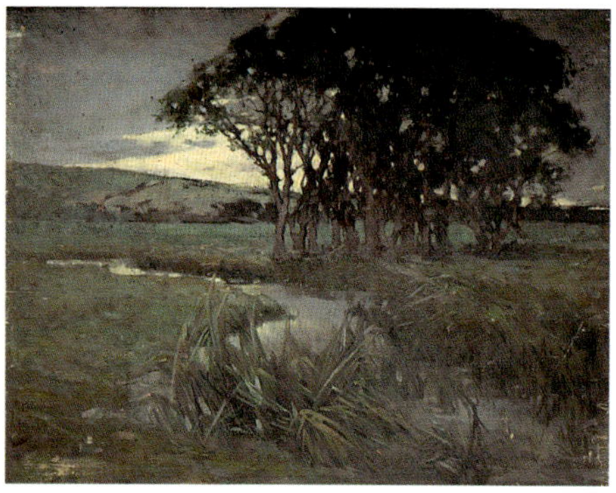

Lenfestey, Giffard Hocart 1872–1943
Evening, the Stream
oil on canvas 61 x 76.5
OP404

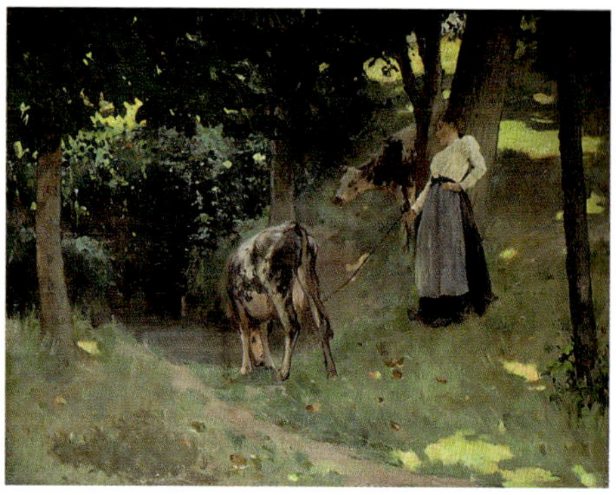

Lenfestey, Giffard Hocart 1872–1943
Girl with Two Cows
oil on canvas 61 x 76
OP403

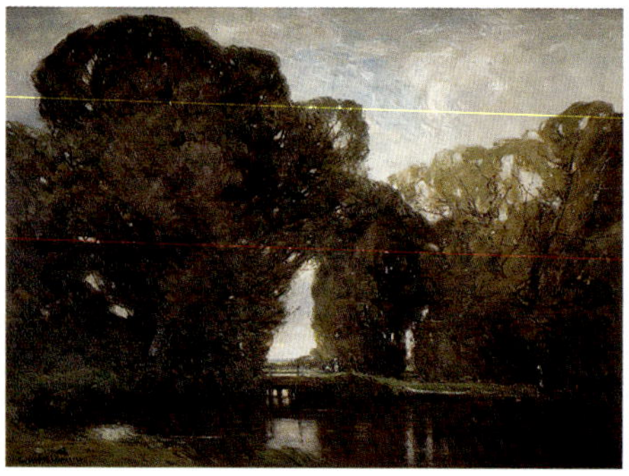

Lenfestey, Giffard Hocart 1872–1943
Solemn Stillness
oil on canvas 30.5 x 43
OP458

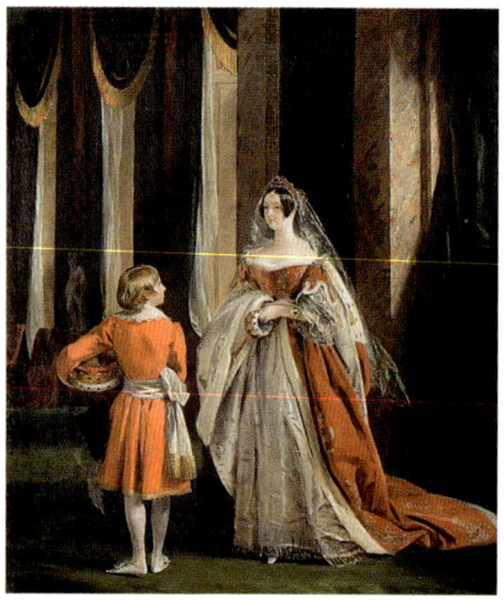

Leslie, Charles Robert 1794–1859
Harriet Elizabeth Georgiana Leveson-Gower, Duchess of Sutherland in Her Coronation Robes 1839
oil on canvas 82 x 68.5
OP192

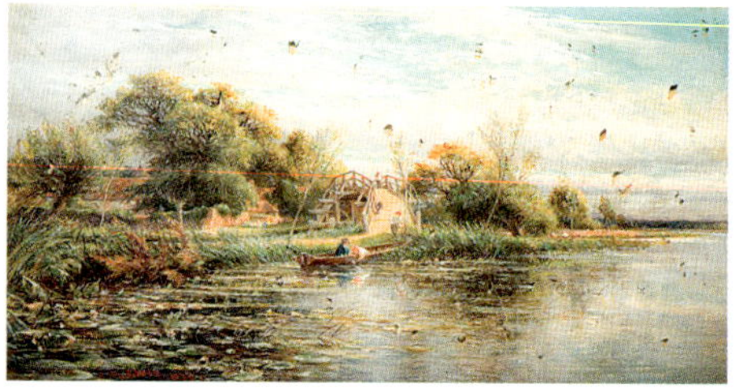

Lewis, Charles James 1830–1892
Hurley Bridge (a backwater on the Thames) 1875
oil on canvas 48.5 x 76
OP362

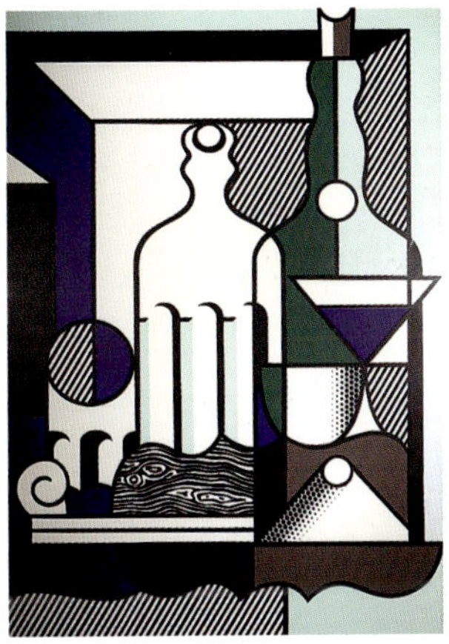

Lichtenstein, Roy 1923–1997
Purist Painting with Bottles 1975
oil on canvas 203 x 137
OP756

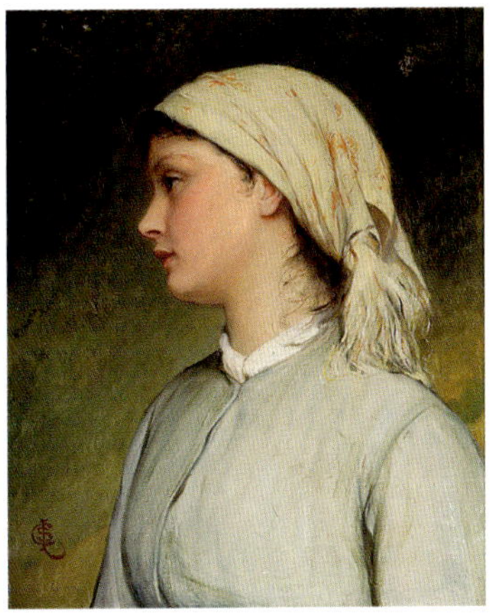

Lidderdale, Charles Sillem 1831–1895
Portrait Study
oil on canvas 51 x 40.5
OP341

Lin, Richard b.1933
Painted Relief 1965
oil on board 106.5 x 106.5
OP611

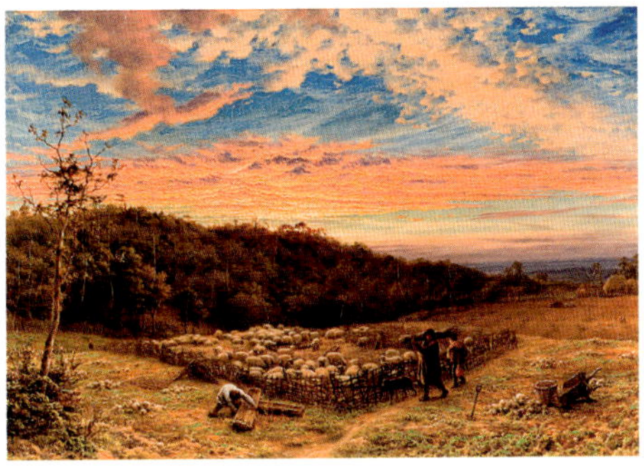

Linnell, James Thomas 1826–1905
The Sheepfold, Morning in Autumn
oil on canvas 61 x 84
OP350

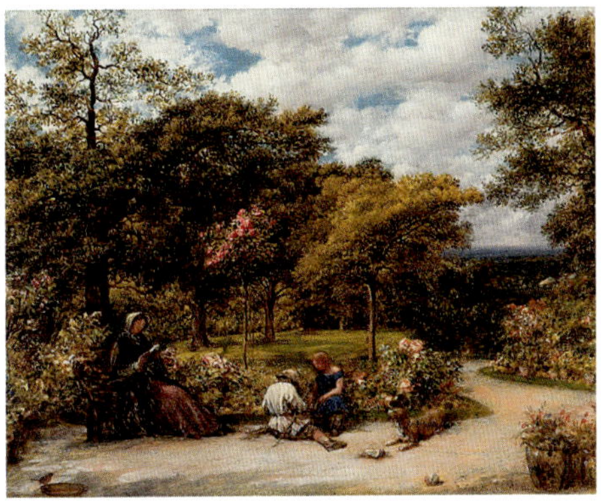

Linnell, John 1792–1882
My Garden at Redhill 1859
oil on canvas 63.5 x 76
OP122

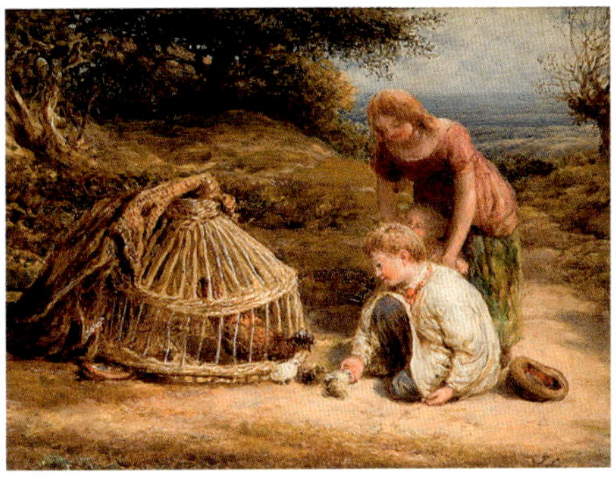

Linnell, John 1792–1882
Feeding the Chicks 1862
oil on canvas 26 x 32.5
OP229

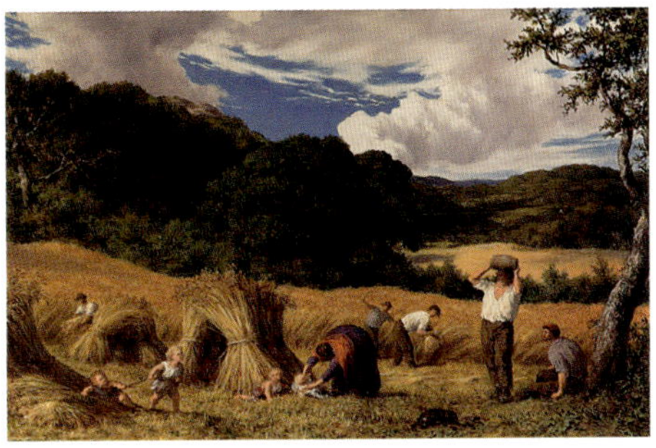

Linnell, William 1826–1906
Cornfield in Surrey 1860
oil on canvas 49.5 x 72.5
OP66

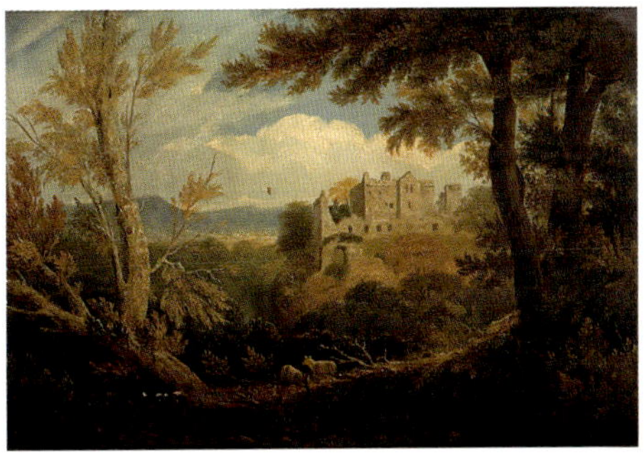

Linton, William 1791–1876
Castle Campbell
oil on canvas 44 x 59
OP9

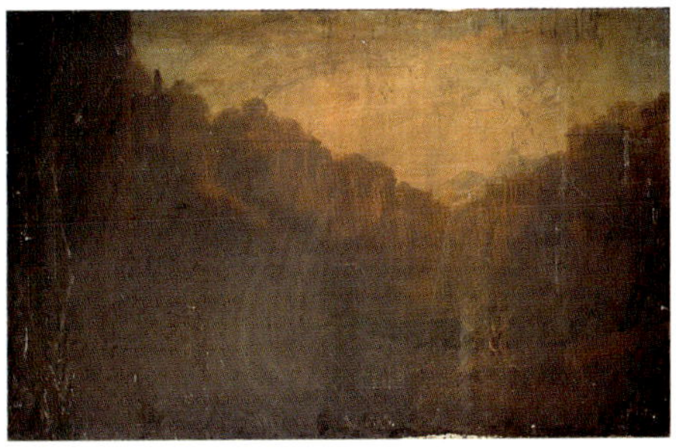

Linton, William 1791–1876
Delos, Greece
oil on canvas 121.9 x 185.4
OP429

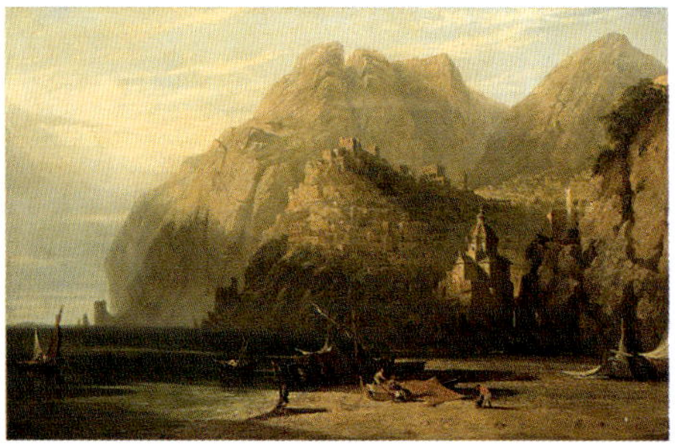

Linton, William 1791–1876
Positano and the Gulf of Salerno
oil on canvas 122 x 183
OP244

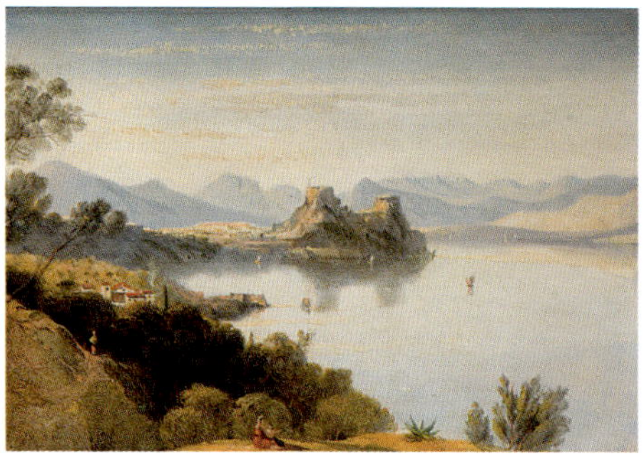

Linton, William 1791–1876
The Albanian Mountains with Corfu in the Distance
oil on canvas 28 x 38.5
OP32

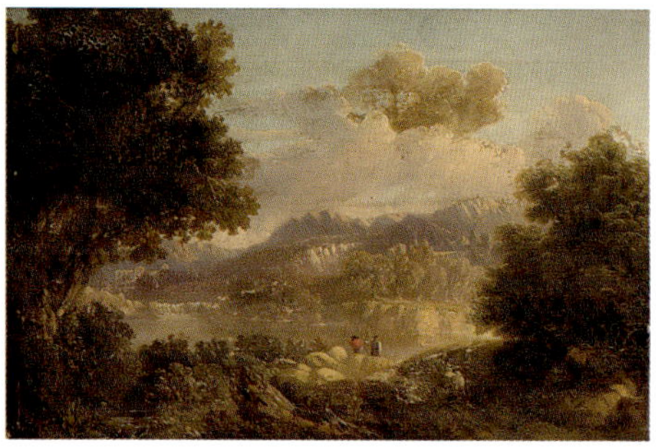

Linton, William (circle of) 1791–1876
Landscape with a Lake
oil on canvas 33 x 48.5
OP522

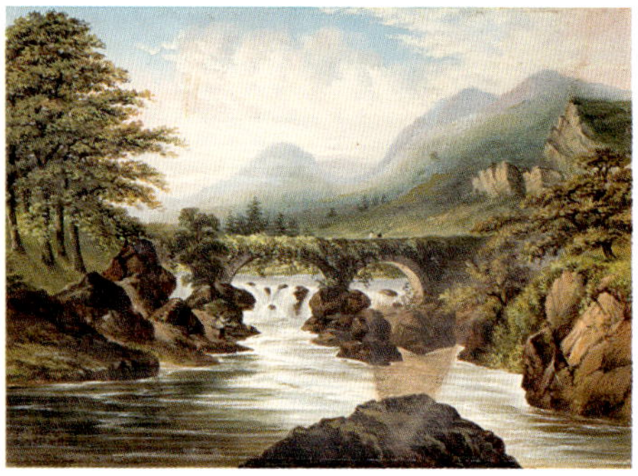

Lockley, Henry James active 1887–1920
Mountain Rapids with River
oil on canvas 24 x 30.5
OP521

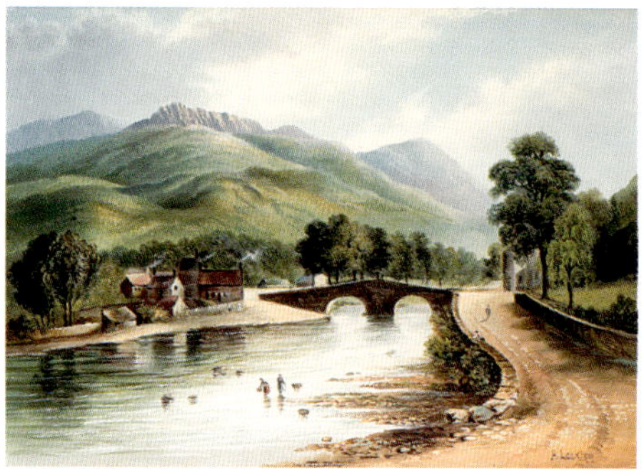

Lockley, Henry James active 1887–1920
Mountain Stream with Bridge
oil on canvas 24 x 30.5
OP529

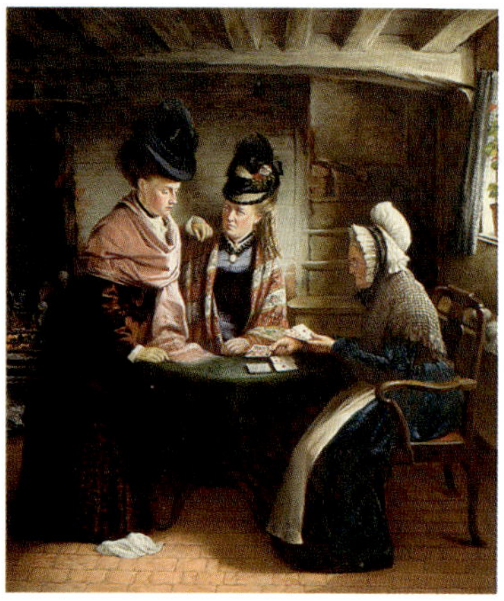

Lomas, John Lane active 1844–1884
The Fortune Teller
oil on canvas 76 x 63.5
OP702

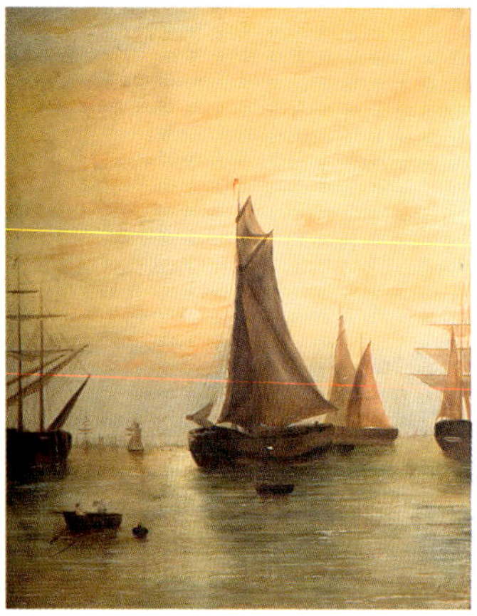

Loney, J. L.
Fishing Boats
oil on canvas 91.5 x 71
OP571

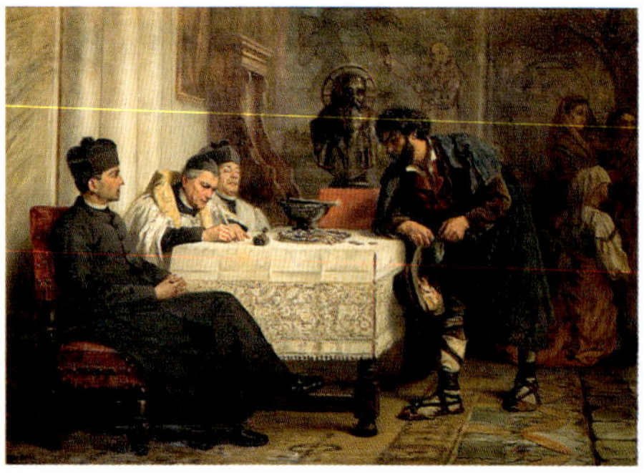

Long, Edwin 1829–1891
Peter's Pence 1867
oil on canvas 82.5 x 87.5
OP562

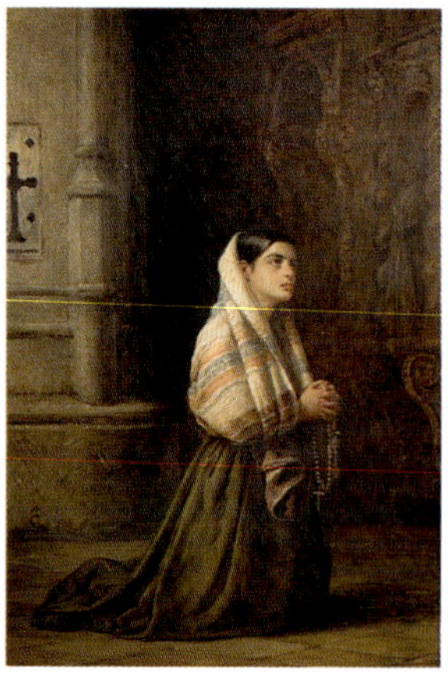

Long, Edwin 1829–1891
At Prayer
oil on canvas 127 x 86.5
OP454

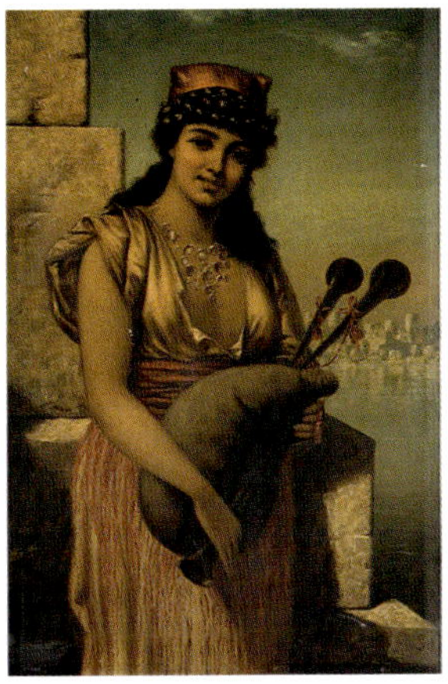

Long, Edwin 1829–1891
Girl with Bagpipes
oil on canvas 105.5 x 68.5
OP602

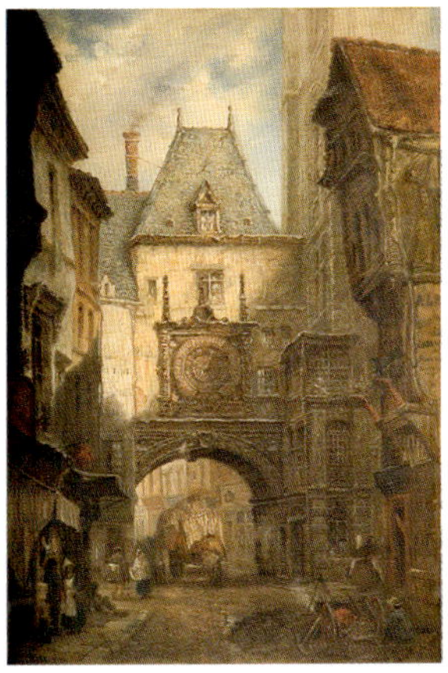

Lott, Frederick Tulley active 1852–1890
Rue de la Grosse Horloge, Rouen
oil on canvas 61 x 41.5
OP703

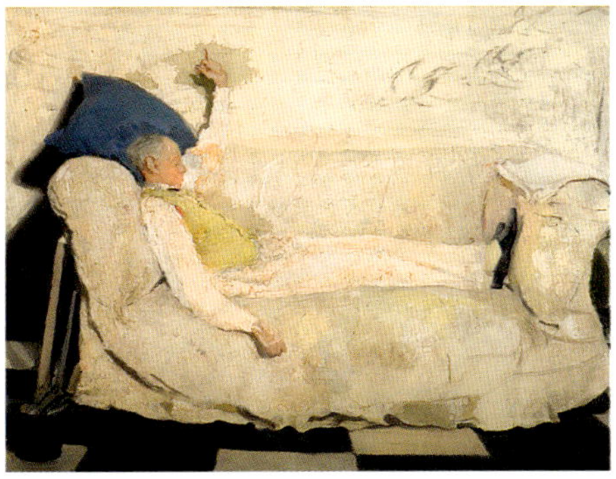

Low, Diana 1911–1975
Sir William Nicholson (1872–1949)
oil on canvas 52 x 67.5
OP163

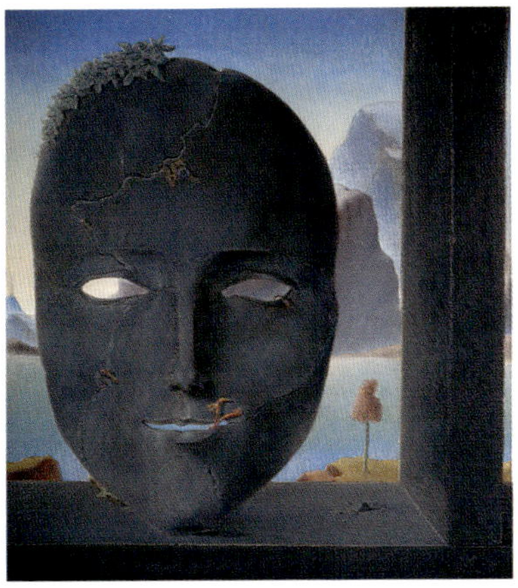

Lowinsky, Thomas Esmond 1892–1947
The Mask of Flora 1931
oil on canvas 31 x 27.5
OP53

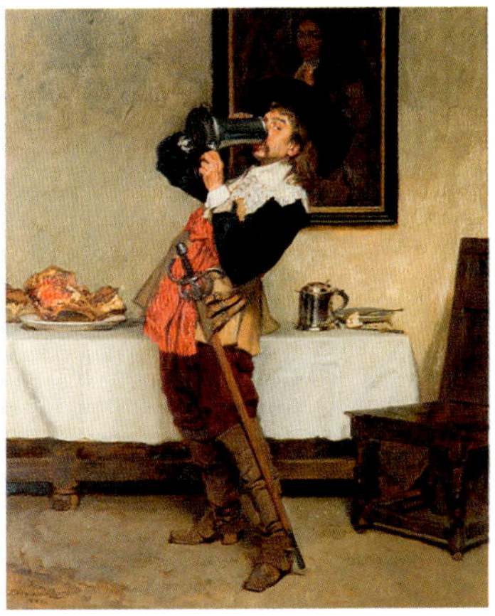

Lucas, Seymour 1849–1923
'Down to the Dregs' 1880
oil on canvas 56.6 x 45.5
OP57

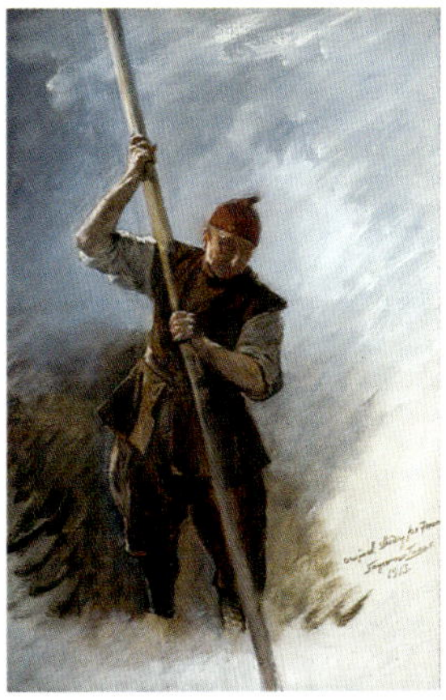

Lucas, Seymour 1849–1923
A Man with a Barge Pole (study for 'The Flight of the Five Members') 1913
oil on canvas 85 x 61
OP138/8

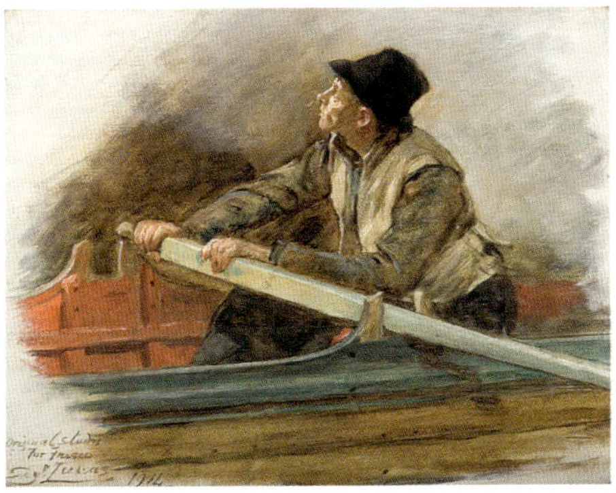

Lucas, Seymour 1849–1923
A Man Rowing (study for 'The Flight of the Five Members') 1914
oil on canvas 31.8 x 38.7
OP138/2

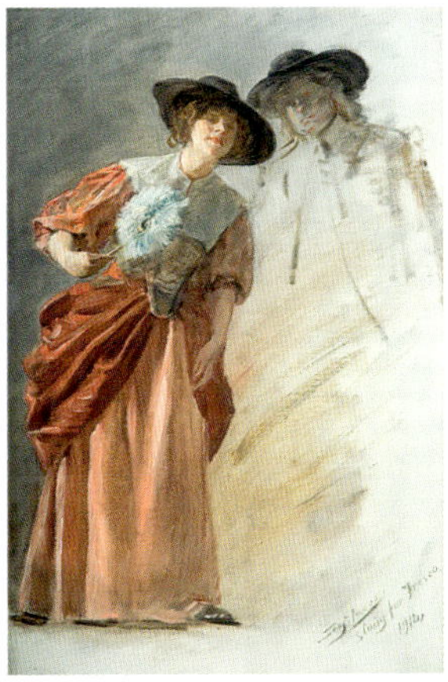

Lucas, Seymour 1849–1923
A Woman with a Fan, Head of a Man (study for 'The Flight of the Five Members') 1914
oil on canvas 54 x 35
OP138/6

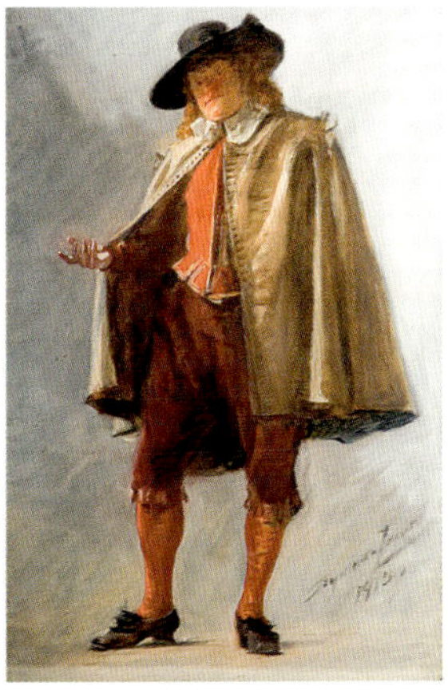

Lucas, Seymour 1849–1923
Standing Man (study for 'The Flight of the Five Members') 1914
oil on canvas 85 x 61
OP138/3

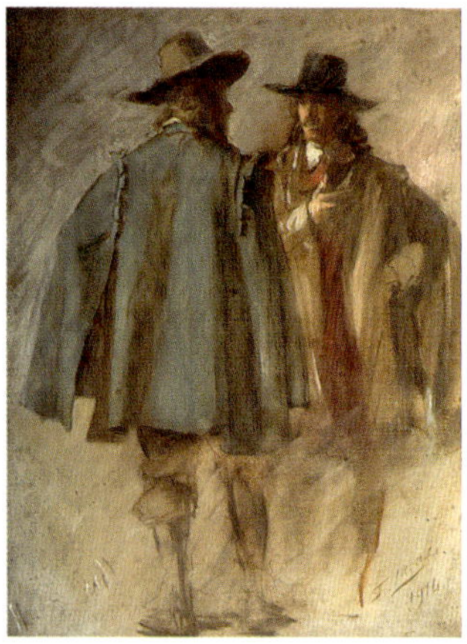

Lucas, Seymour 1849–1923
Two Standing Men (study for 'The Flight of the Five Members) 1914
oil on canvas 85 x 61
OP138/11

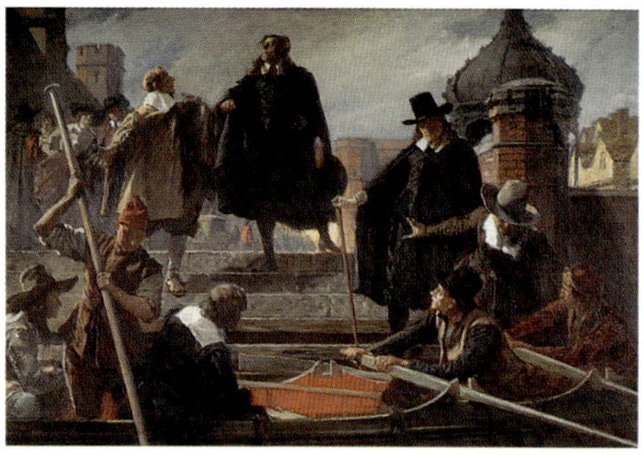

Lucas, Seymour 1849–1923
The Flight of the Five Members 1915
oil on canvas 60 x 84
OP138

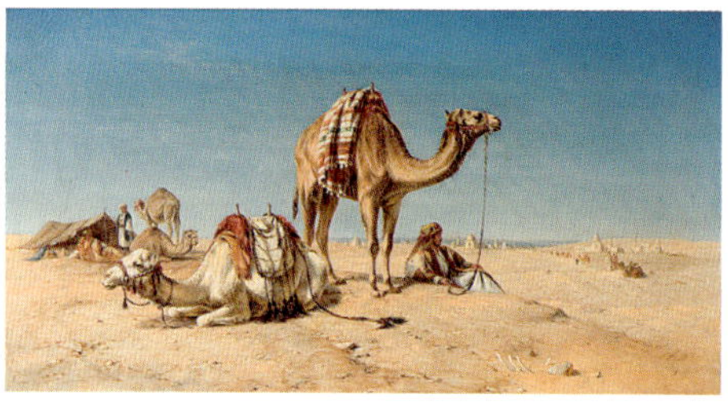

Luker, William c.1820–1892
A Halt in the Desert 1867
oil on board 40.5 x 76
OP260

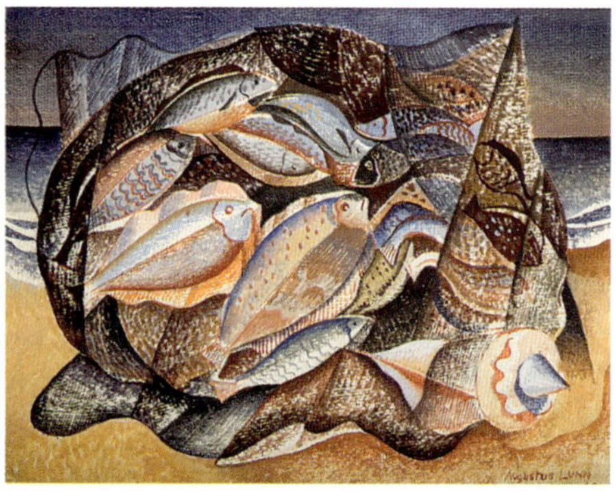

Lunn, Augustus 1905–1986
Fish 1940
oil on canvas 20.5 x 25.5
OP838

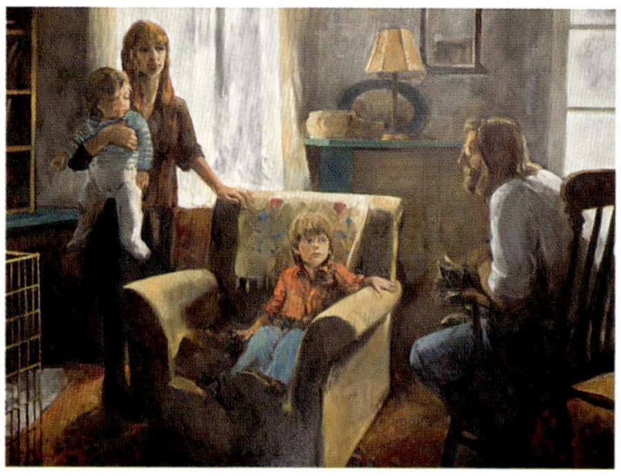

MacDonald, Bridget b.1943
Family Group 1980–1988
oil on canvas 138.5 x 182
OP815

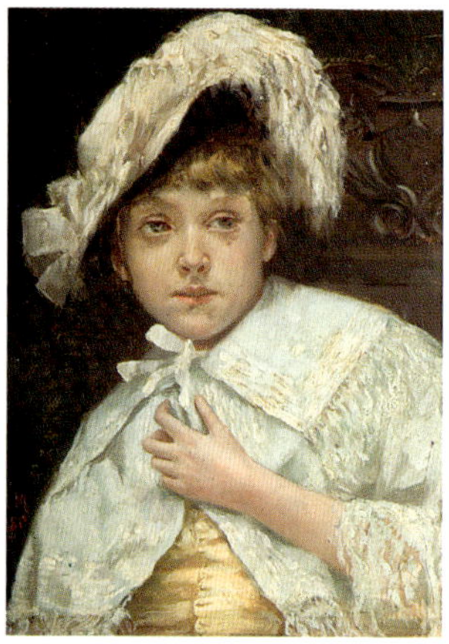

Machell, Reginald 1854–1927
Timidity 1880
oil on panel 25.5 x 18
OP72

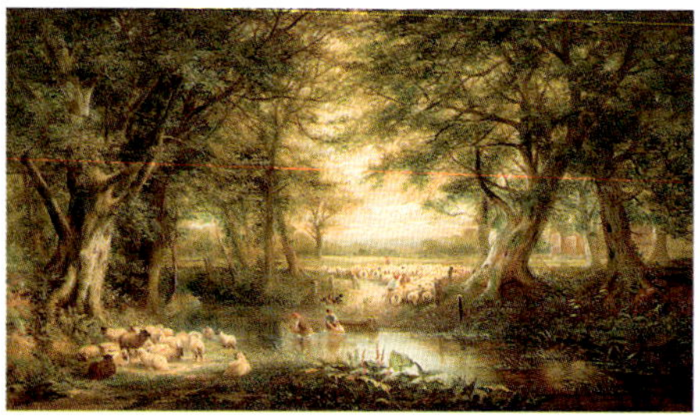

MacIntyre, Joseph Wrightson 1842–1897
Sheep Washing, Wellburn, Yorkshire 1869
oil on canvas 77.5 x 129.5
OP306

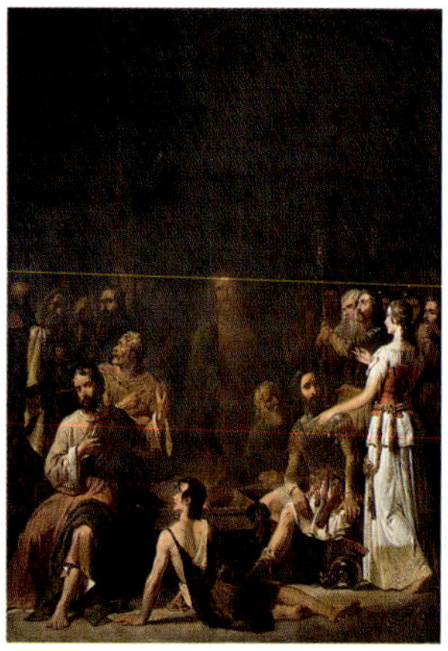

Maclise, Daniel 1806–1870
The Denial
oil on canvas 193 x 150
OP589

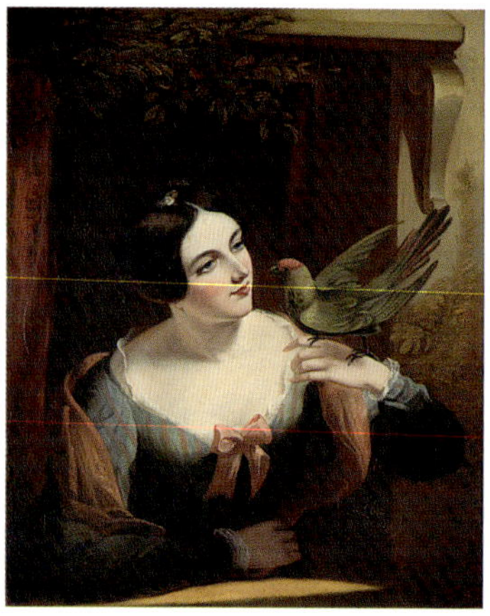

Maclise, Daniel 1806–1870
The Pet Bird
oil on canvas 92 x 70.6
OP217

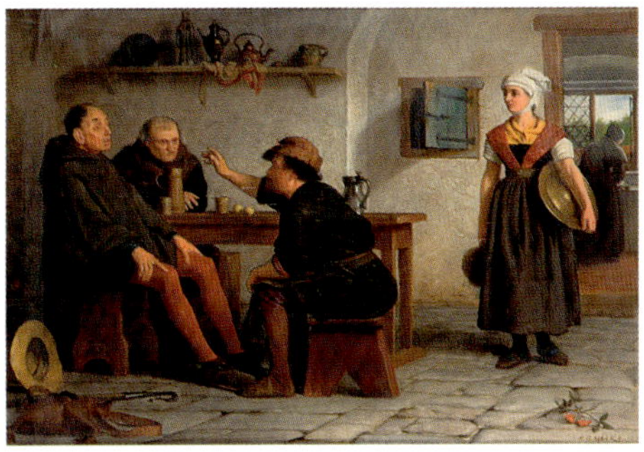

Marks, Henry Stacey 1829–1898
An Incredible Story
oil on canvas 47 x 61
OP172

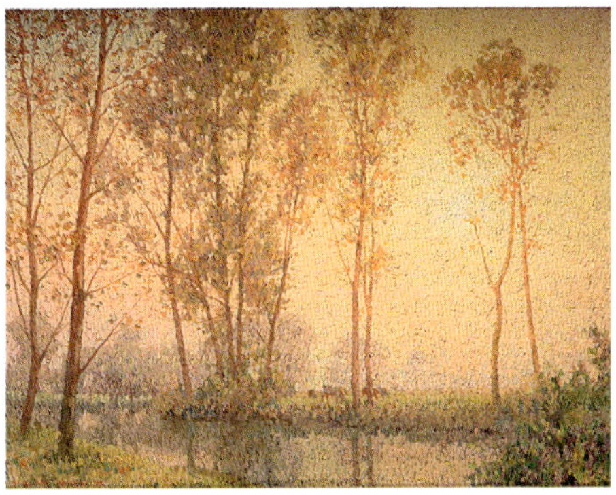

Marston, Reginald St Clair 1886–1943
Autumn Morning
oil on canvas 51 x 61
OP292

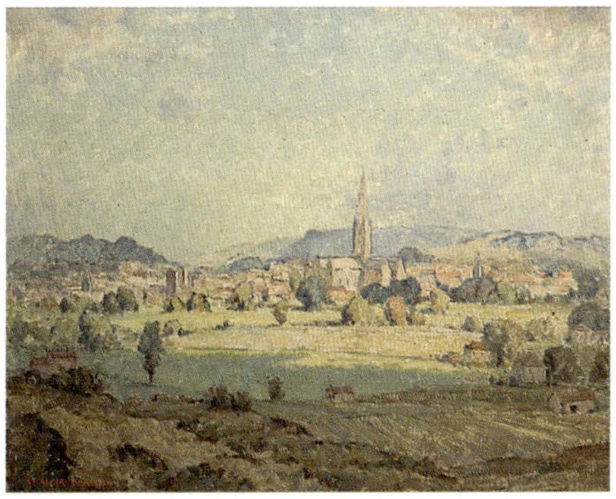

Marston, Reginald St Clair 1886–1943
Salisbury
oil on canvas 51 x 61
OP265

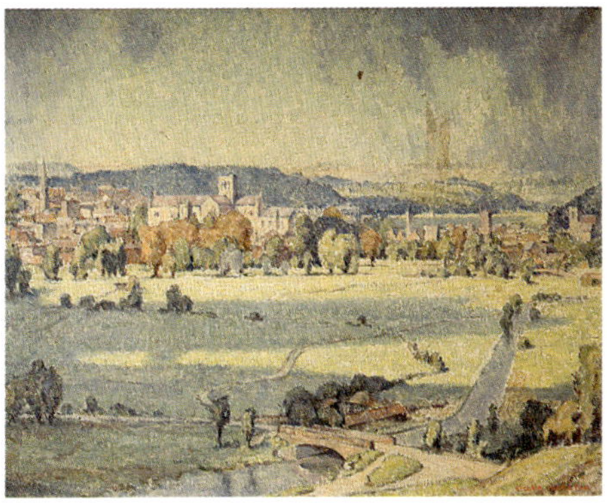

Marston, Reginald St Clair 1886–1943
Winchester
oil on canvas 51 x 61.5
OP595

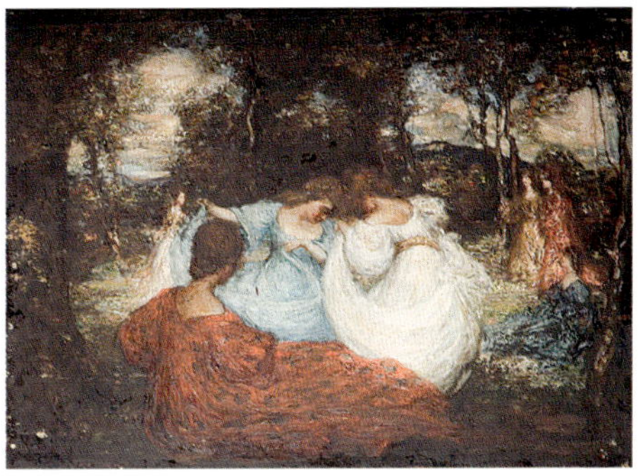

Martin, Anson A. active 1840–1872
A Sarabande
oil on panel 45.5 x 81.5
OP705

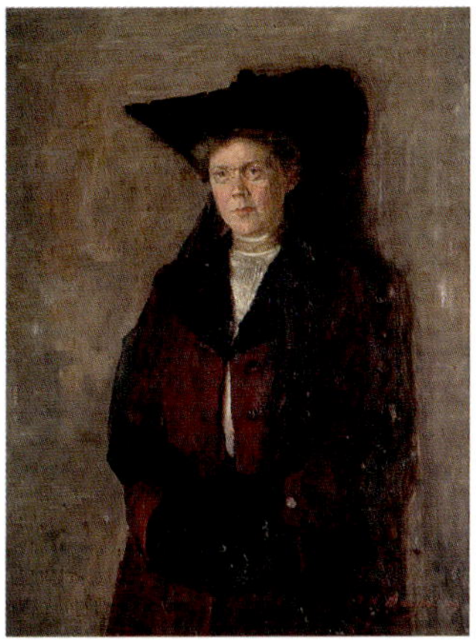

Mayer, Karl 1810–1876
Margaret Sparrow
oil on canvas 60 x 45
OP904

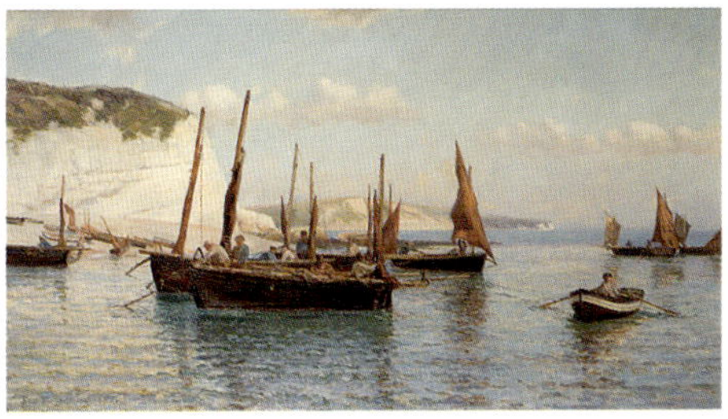

McCallum, Hamilton 1841–1896
Bell Trawlers Going out to Sea 1882
oil on canvas 45.5 x 81
OP704

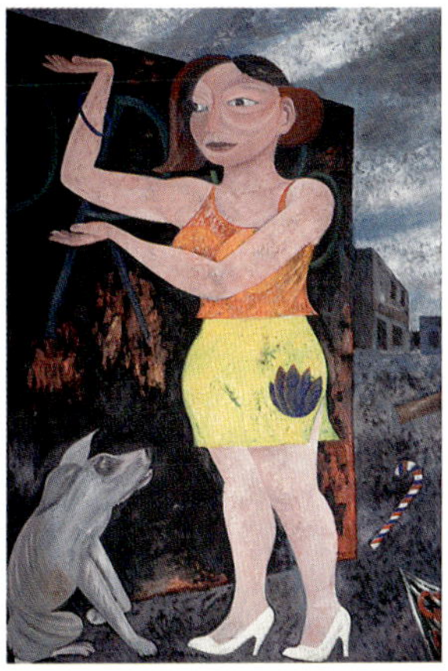

McFadyen, Jock b.1950
After the Parade 1984
oil on canvas 222 x 138
OP909

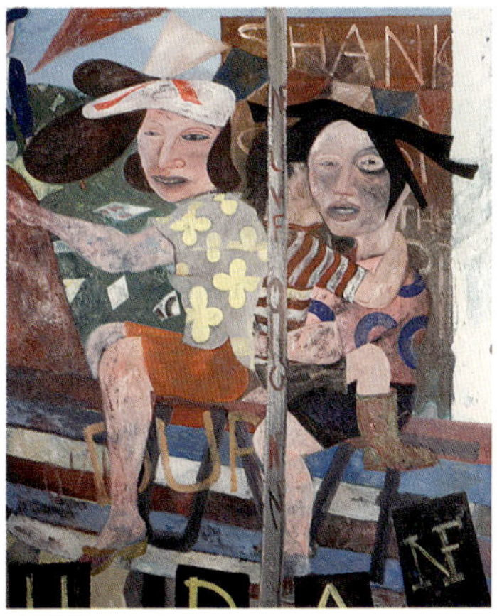

McFadyen, Jock b.1950
Shankill 1984
oil on canvas 215 x 160
OP908

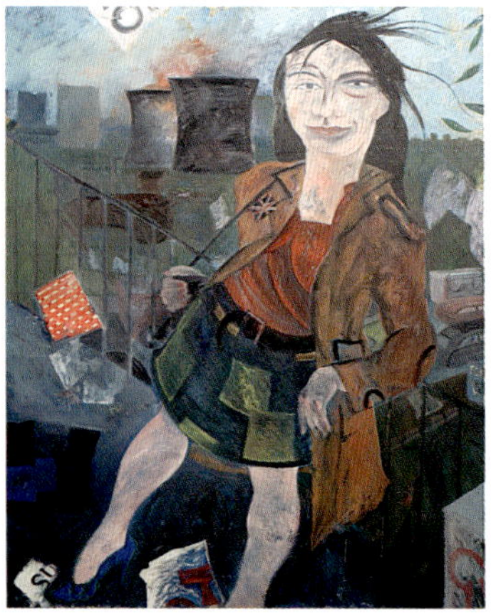

McFadyen, Jock b.1950
Coventry Girl, Motorway Bridge 1986–1987
oil on canvas 213 x 167
OP808

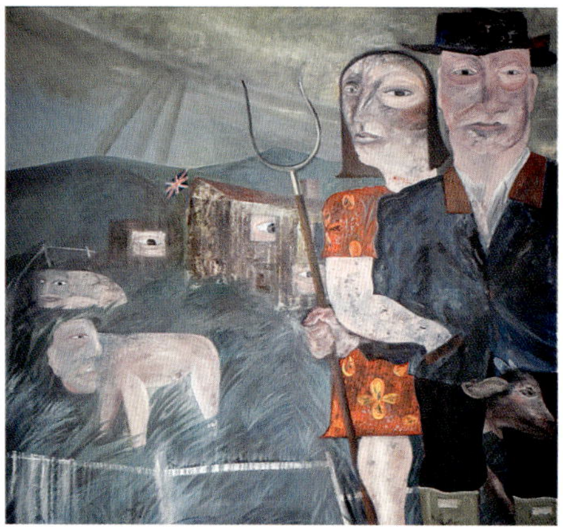

McFadyen, Jock b.1950
Irish Gothic 1986–1987
oil on canvas 207 x 212
OP879

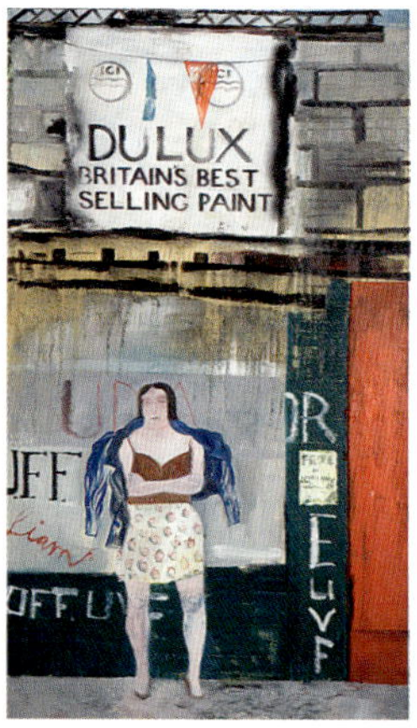

McFadyen, Jock b.1950
A Tinge of Yellow 1988
oil on canvas 178 x 101.5
OP910

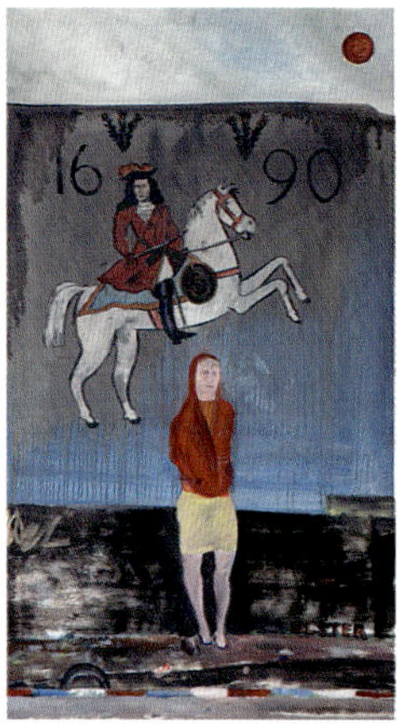

McFadyen, Jock b.1950
Prince of Orange 1988
oil on canvas 157.5 x 89
OP911

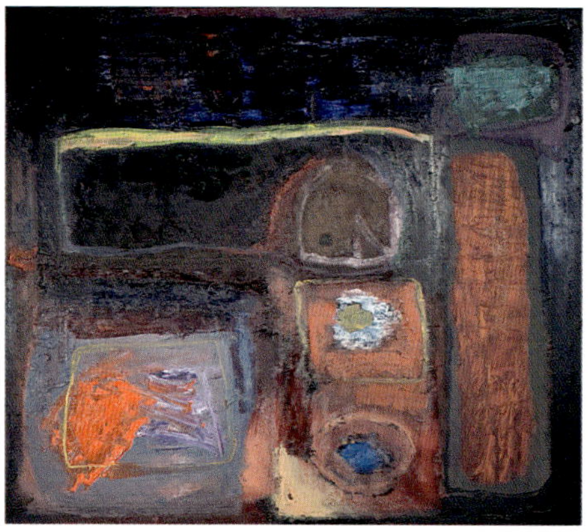

McKee, Cormac active 1980s–1990
Fill Aris (Full Circle) 1980s
oil on canvas 151 x 168.5
OP829

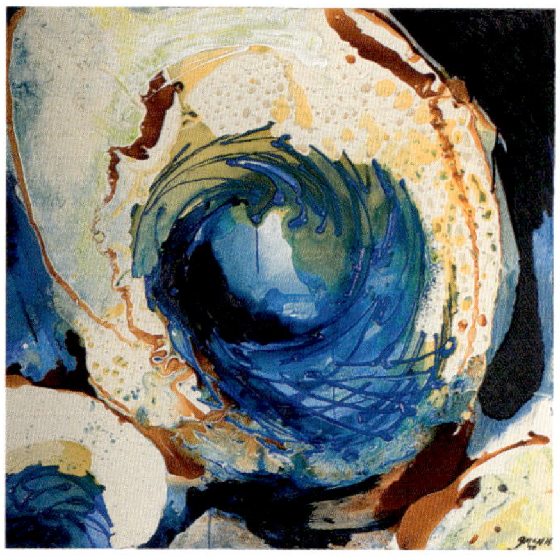

McNally-Hayes, Julie
Not Just a Girl Thing 1997
oil on canvas 91 x 91
OP887

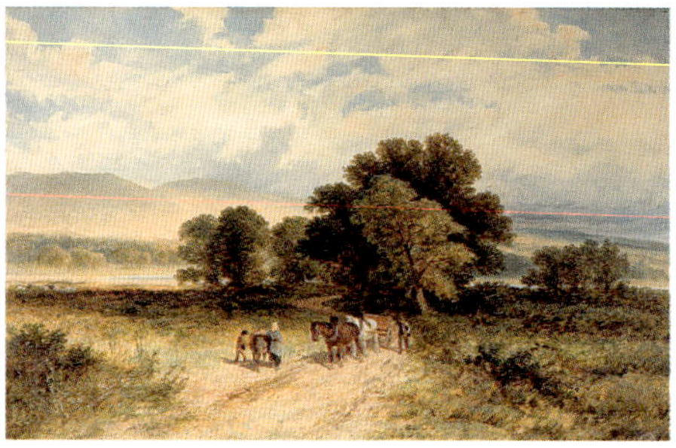

Meadows, James Edwin 1828–1888
Going Home 1875
oil on canvas 61 x 91.5 (E)
OP398

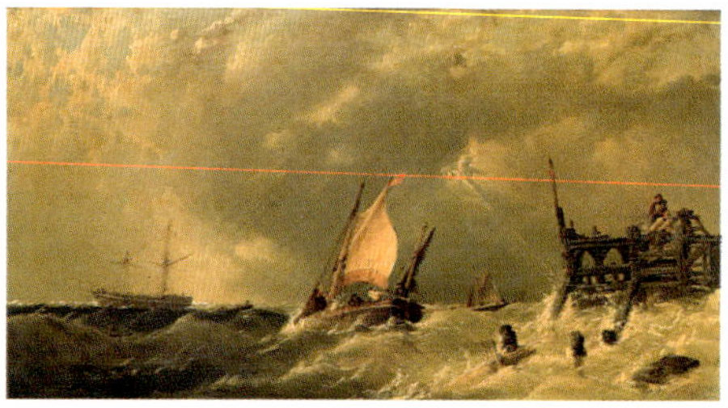

Meadows, James Edwin 1828–1888
The Storm 1885
oil on canvas 60.7 x 91.5 (E)
OP563

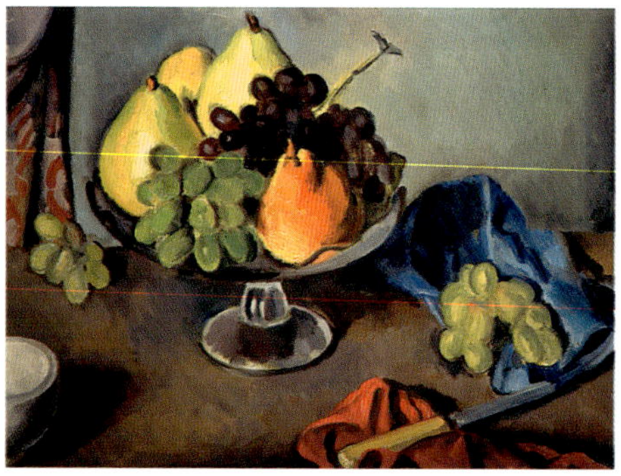

Meninsky, Bernard 1891–1950
Still Life
oil on canvas 46 x 61.5
OP706

Facing page: Procter, Dod, 1892–1972, *Clara* (detail), The Potteries Museum & Art Gallery (p. 151)

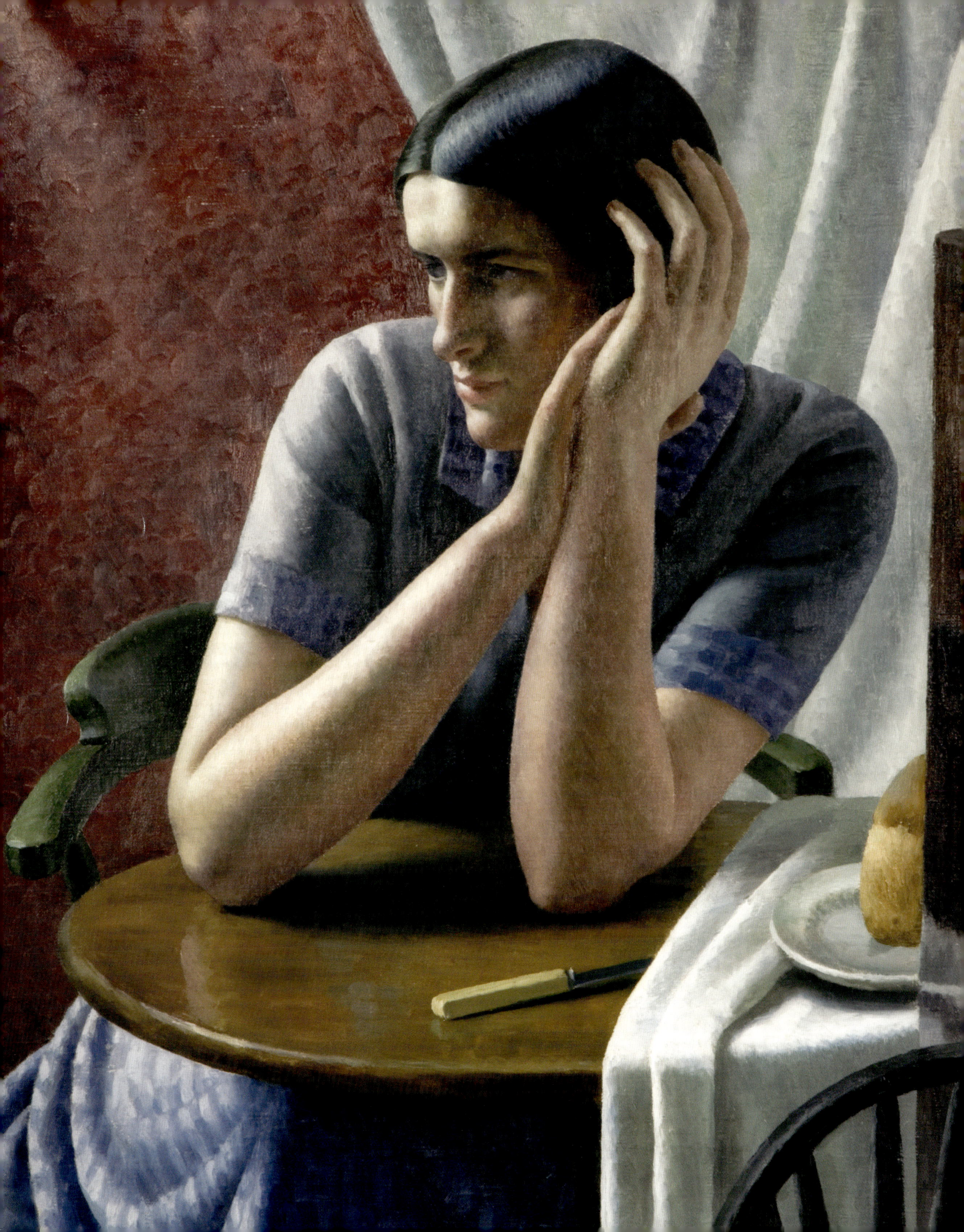

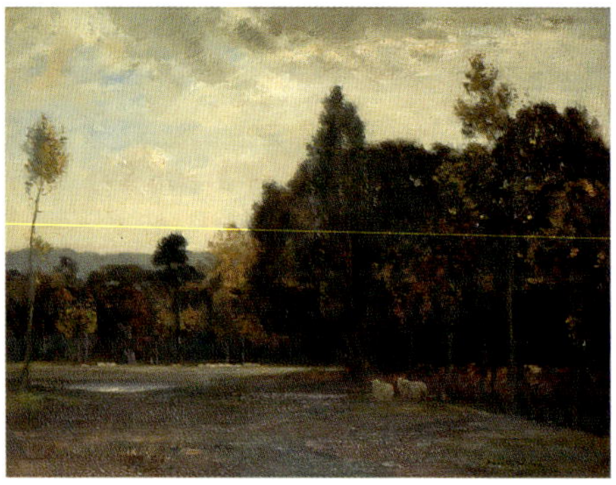

Michie, James Coutts 1861–1919
Autumn Landscape
oil on canvas 56 x 70
OP100

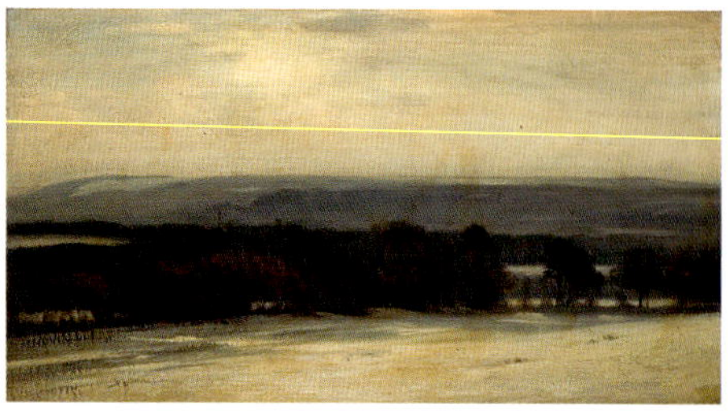

Michie, James Coutts 1861–1919
Winter Scene
oil on canvas 51 x 69
OP572

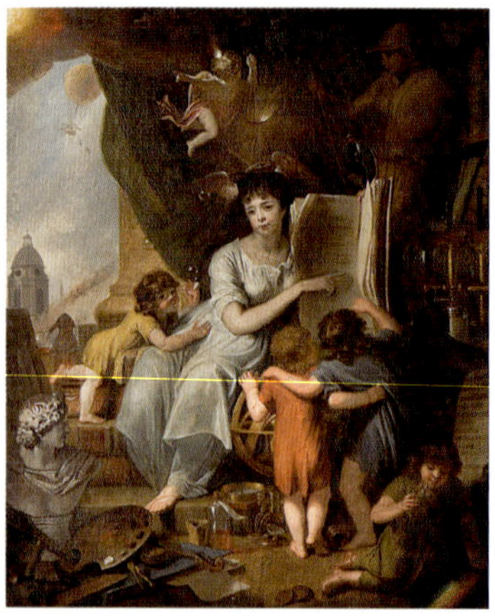

Millar, James 1735–1805
Allegory of Wisdom and Science (frontispiece for 'Encyclopaedia Brittannica') 1798
oil on canvas 125.5 x 101
OP120

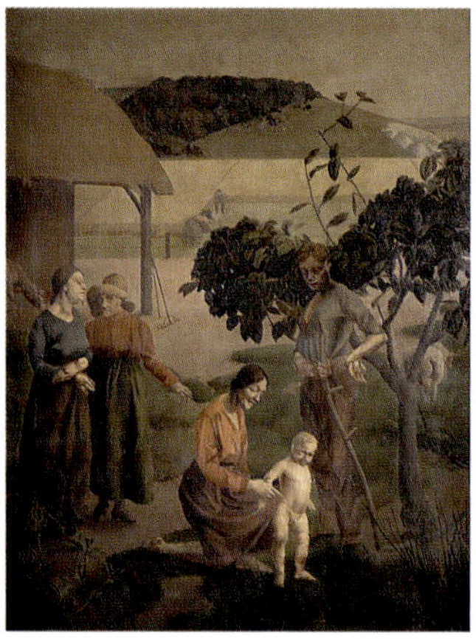

Monnington, Walter Thomas 1902–1976
The Farmstead
oil on canvas 122 x 91.5
OP325

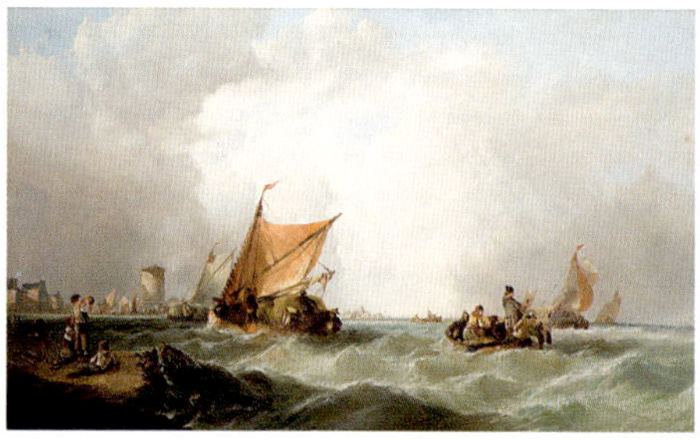

Montague, Alfred 1832–1883
Coast of Holland
oil on canvas 61.5 x 97
OP741

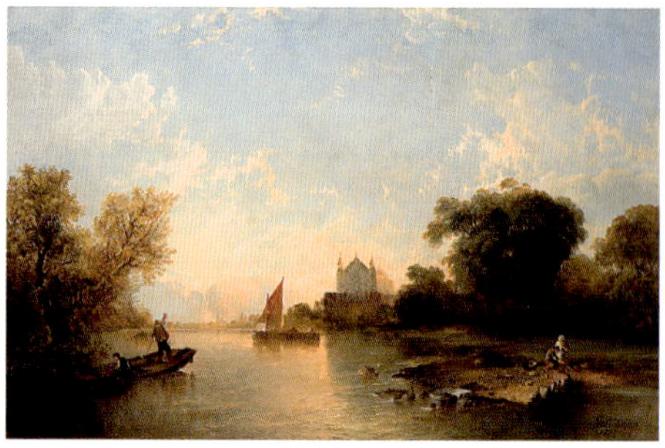

Montague, Alfred 1832–1883
Eton College from the River
oil on canvas 60 x 90
OP707

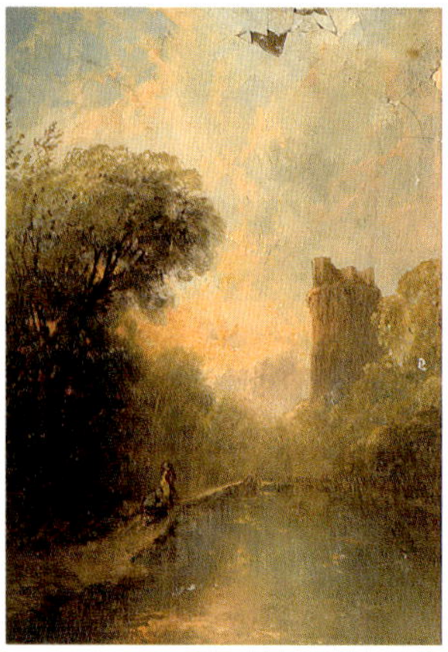

Montague, Alfred 1832–1883
Landscape with a Ruined Castle
oil on board 18.5 x 13.1
OP27

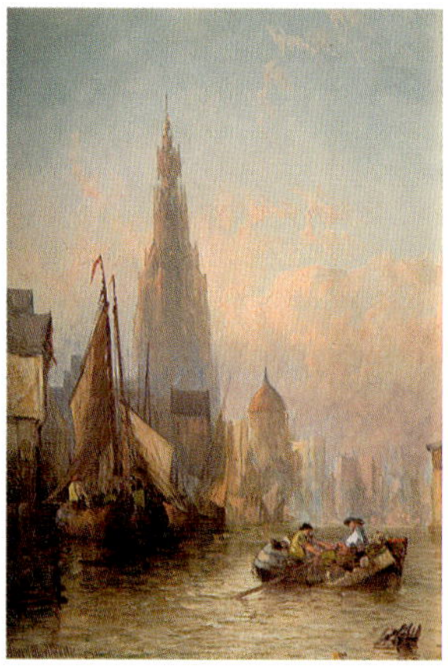

Montague, Alfred 1832–1883
On the Scheldt at Antwerp
oil on board 17 x 12
OP28

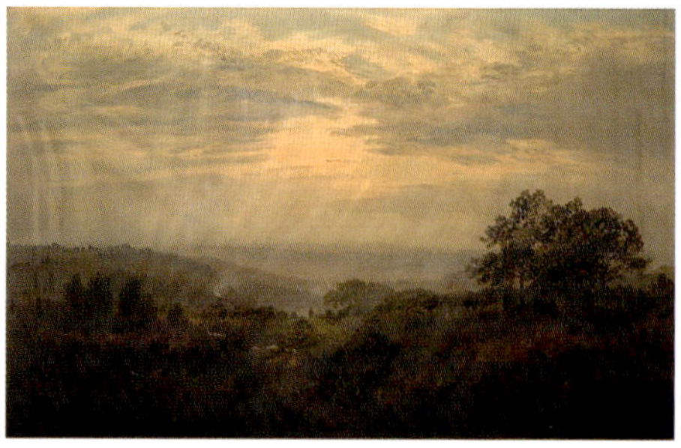

Moore, Henry 1831–1895
Southborough Common, near Tunbridge Wells 1869
oil on canvas 51 x 76
OP128

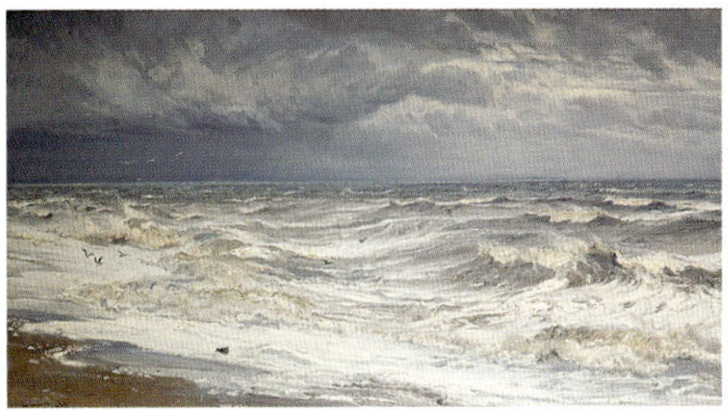

Moore, Henry 1831–1895
Winter Gale in the Channel 1872
oil on canvas 61 x 106.5
OP118

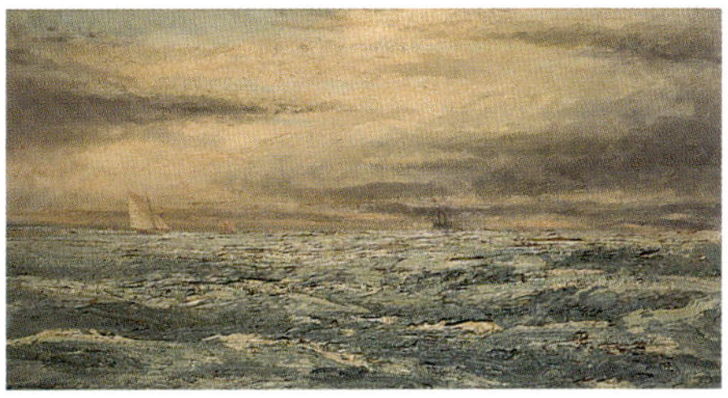

Moore, Henry 1831–1895
A Choppy Day in the Channel
oil on canvas 40.5 x 66
OP708

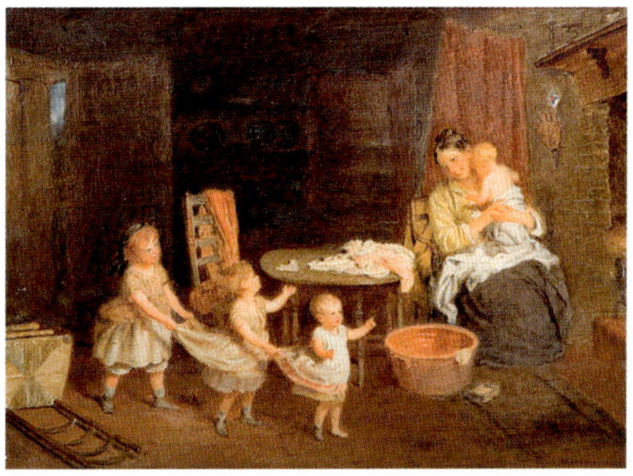

Morgan, John 1823–1886
The Bath
oil on canvas 38.5 x 45.5
OP15

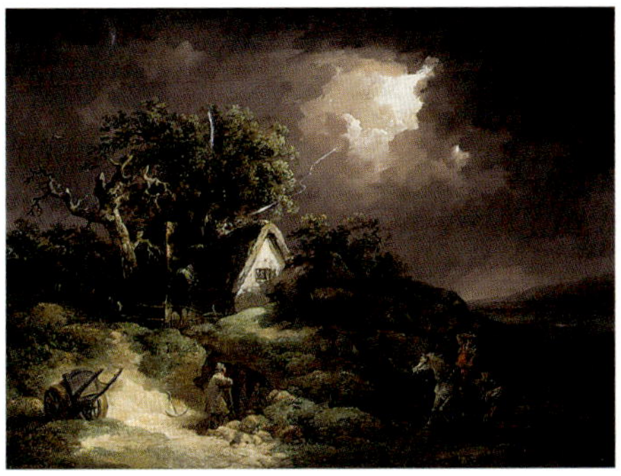

Morland, George 1763–1804
The Coming Storm, Isle of Wight 1789
oil on canvas 51 x 65.5
OP89

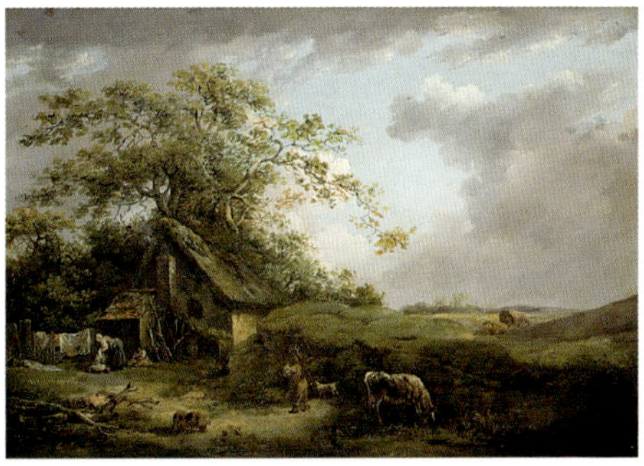

Morland, George 1763–1804
Landscape (Storm Cloud)
oil on canvas 85 x 115.5
OP90

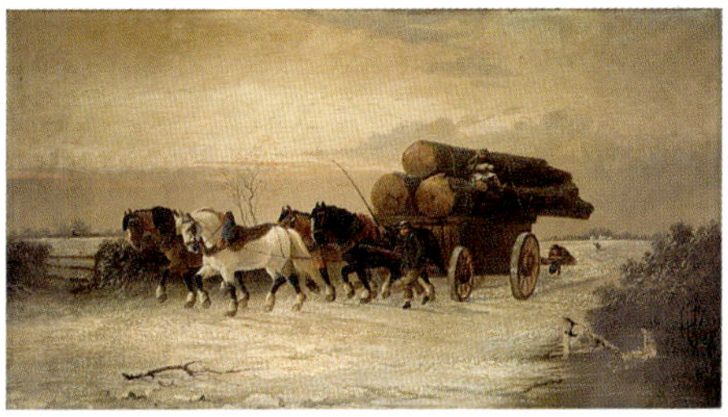

Morris, John Charles active 1851–1889
A Timber Wagon
oil on canvas 61 x 106.5
OP409

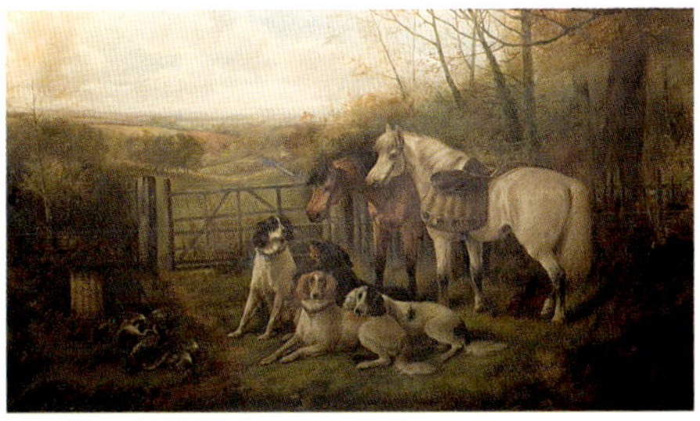

Morris, John Charles active 1851–1889
Close of a Day's Sport
oil on canvas 108 x 183
OP709

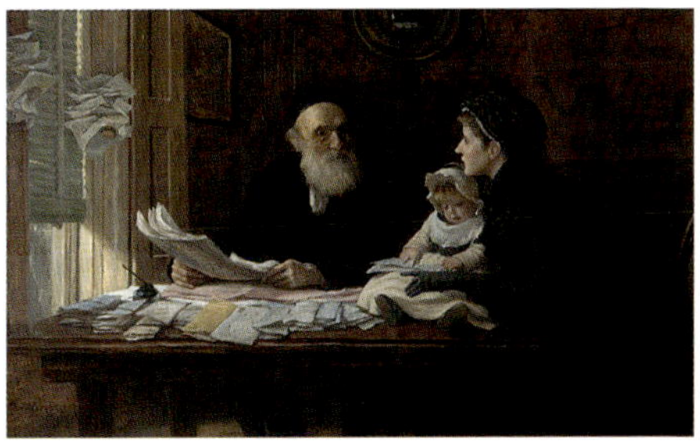

Morris, Phillip Richard 1838–1902
A Flaw in the Will
oil on canvas 92.5 x 139.5
OP99

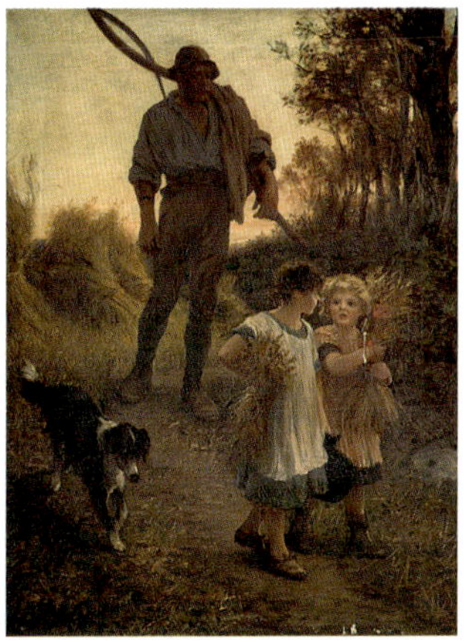

Morris, Phillip Richard 1838–1902
The Breadwinner
oil on canvas 91.4 x 66
OP399

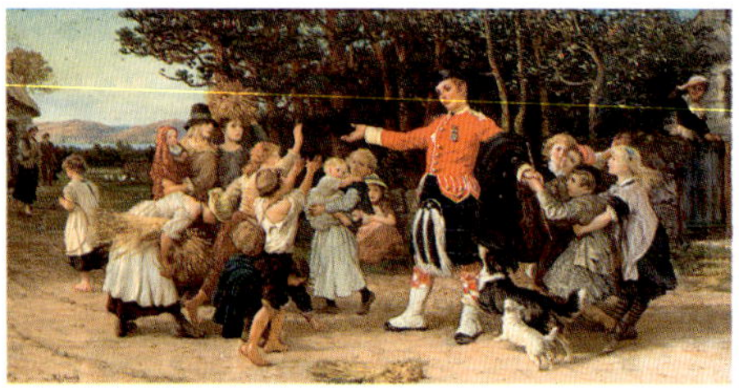

Morris, Phillip Richard 1838–1902
The Highland Laddies' Return
oil on canvas 119.5 x 223.5
OP431

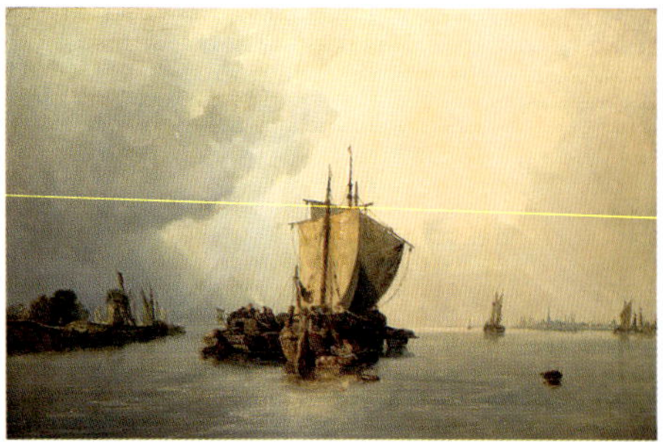

Müller, William James 1812–1845
The Mouth of the Scheldt 1836
oil on canvas 91.5 x 132
OP248

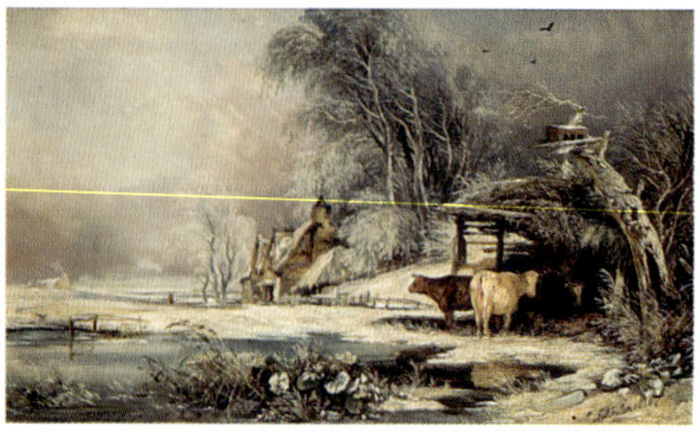

Müller, William James 1812–1845
A Lowering Day in Winter 1838
oil on canvas 38.5 x 63.5
OP60

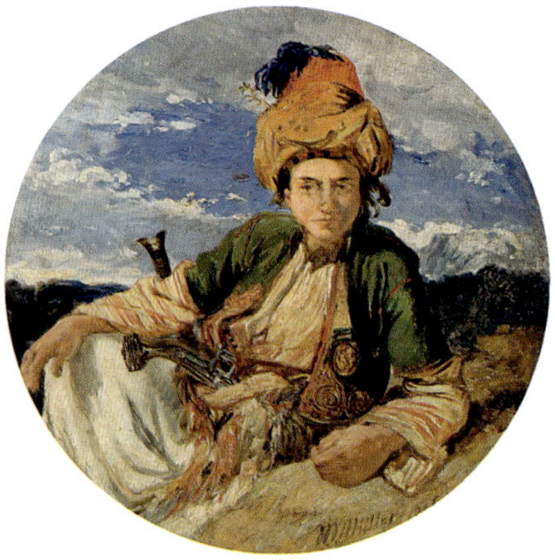

Müller, William James 1812–1845
Head of a Zingari, Xanthus 1845
oil on board 33
OP208

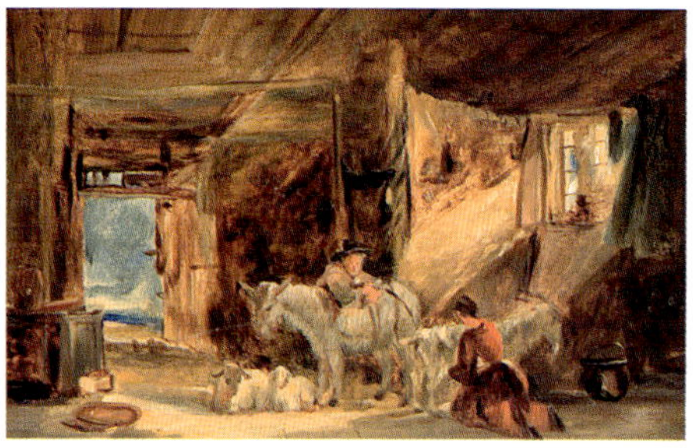

Müller, William James 1812–1845
Low Life
oil on panel 12.5 x 20.5
OP41

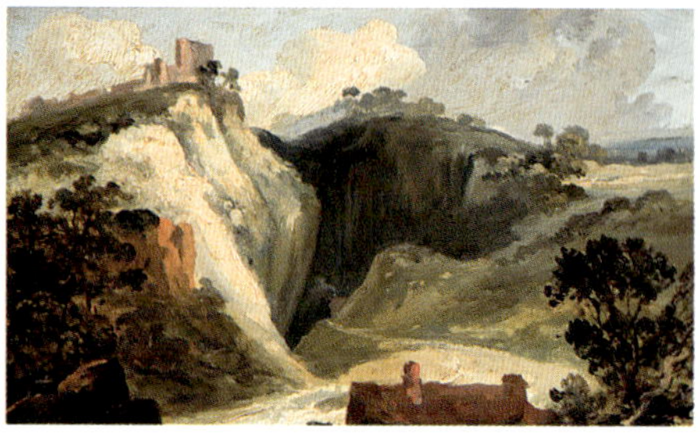

Müller, William James 1812–1845
The Peak Cavern, Derbyshire, Peveril Castle
oil on board 20.5 x 30.5
OP134

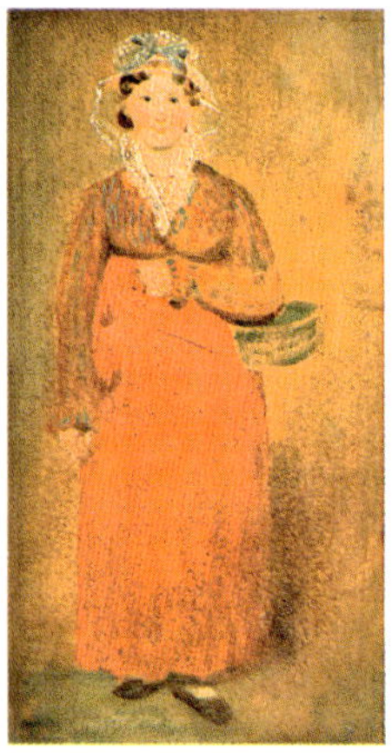

Mulready, William (attributed to)
1786–1863
A Market Girl
oil on card 18 x 10
OP258

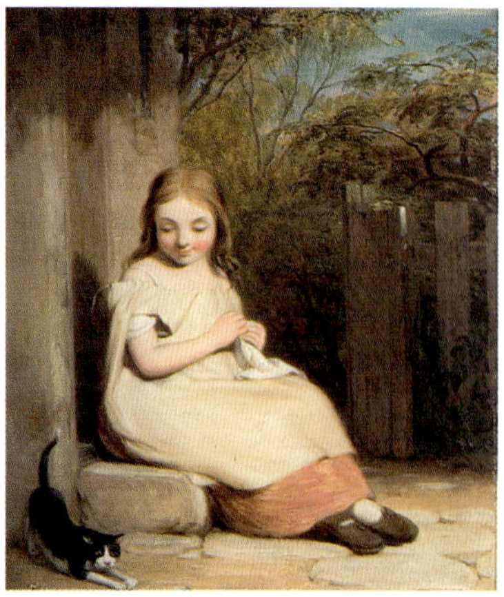

Mulready, William (attributed to)
1786–1863
Young Girl with a Kitten
oil on board 26.5 x 23
OP569

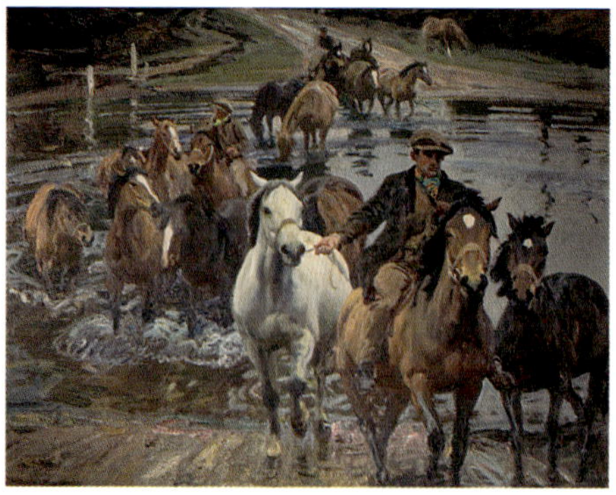

Munnings, Alfred James 1878–1959
The Ford
oil on canvas 138.5 x 165
OP284

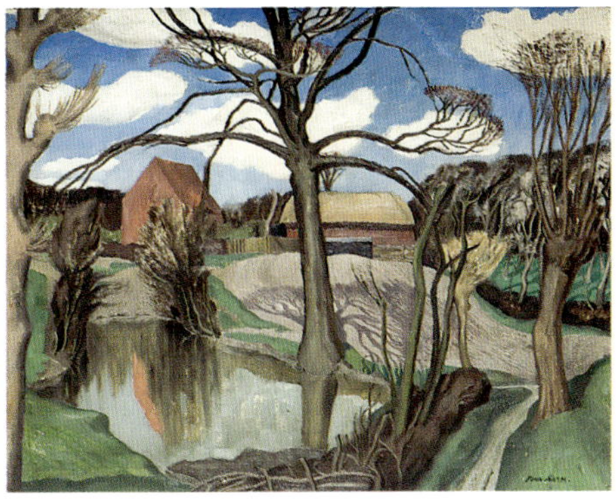

Nash, John Northcote 1893–1977
The Farm Pond 1940
oil on canvas 64.1 x 76.8
OP843

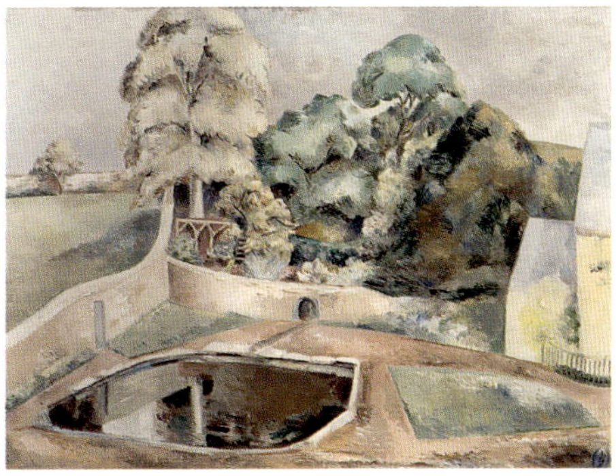

Nash, Paul 1889–1946
The Pond at Souldern 1926
oil on canvas 71 x 92
OP786

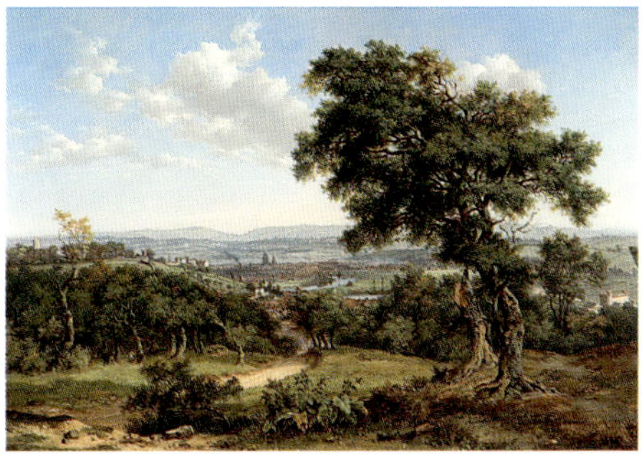

Nasmyth, Patrick 1787–1831
View of Bristol 1827
oil on canvas 72.5 x 102
OP88

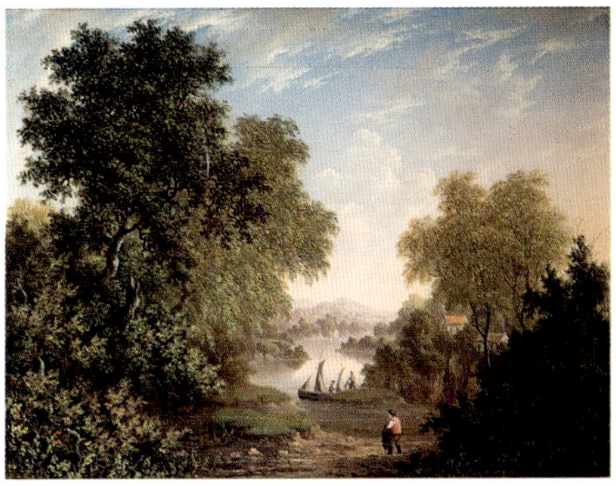

Nasmyth, Patrick 1787–1831
Lake Scene with Boats and Figures
oil on canvas 30.5 x 40.5
OP239

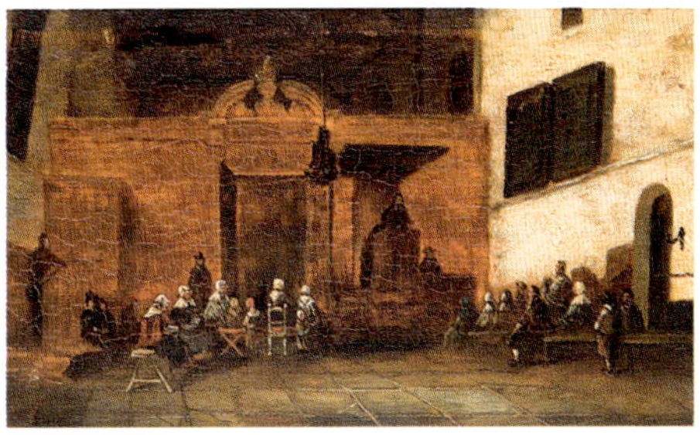

Neeffs, Peeter the younger 1620–1675 or
Neeffs, Peeter the elder c.1578–1656/1661
(attributed to)
At Worship
oil on panel 25.5 x 38
OP1

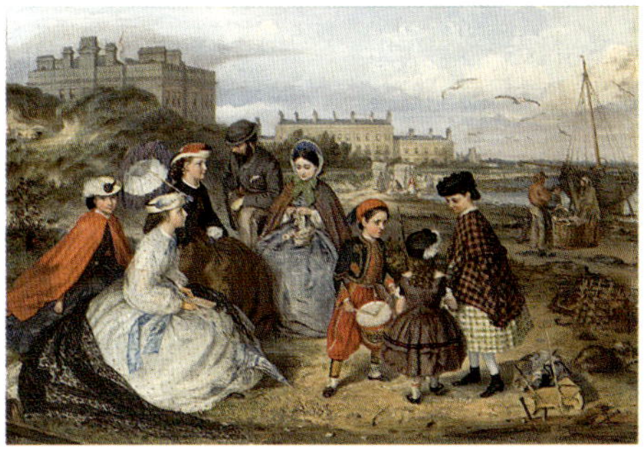

Nicholls, Charles Wynne 1831–1903
Queen Victoria and Her Family on Brighton Sands
oil on canvas 85.5 x 110
OP710

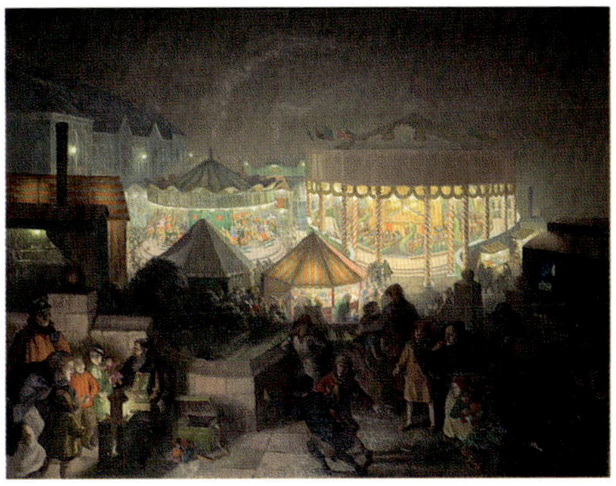

Nicholls, John
Wolverhampton Fair 1920–1925
oil on canvas 61 x 76
OP612

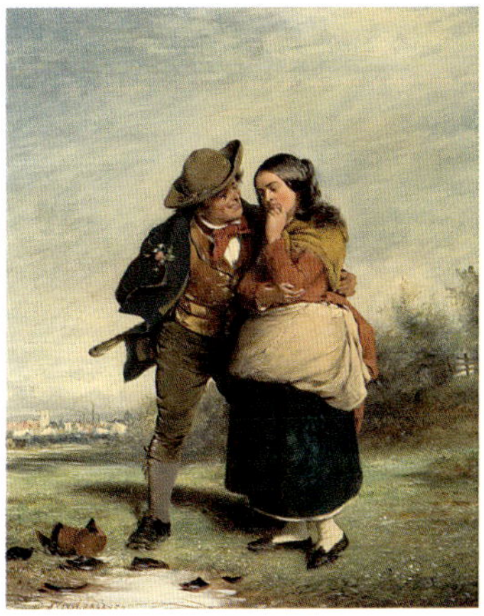

Nicol, Erskine 1825–1904
The Tale of an Irish Song 1857
oil on canvas 39.5 x 32
OP245

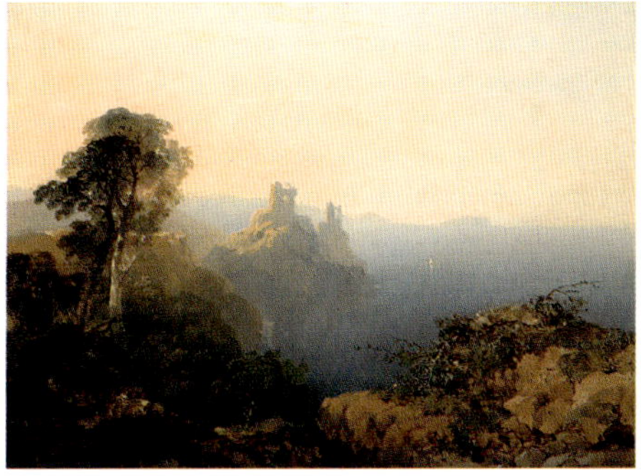

Niemann, Edmund John 1813–1876
Black Castle, Wicklow 1854
oil on canvas 35.5 x 45.5
OP189

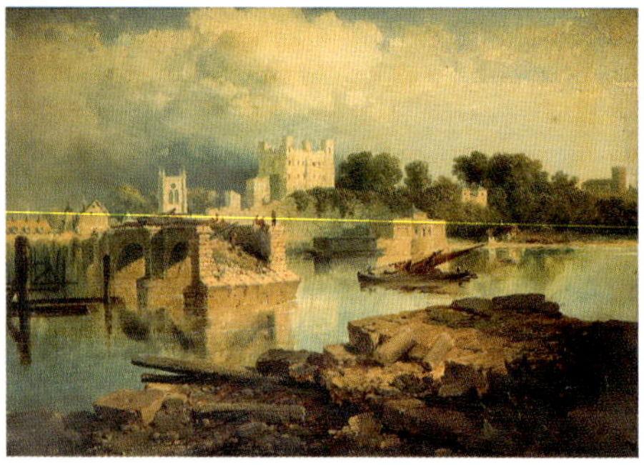

Niemann, Edmund John 1813–1876
Landscape near Rochester 1860
oil on board 36 x 46.5
OP544

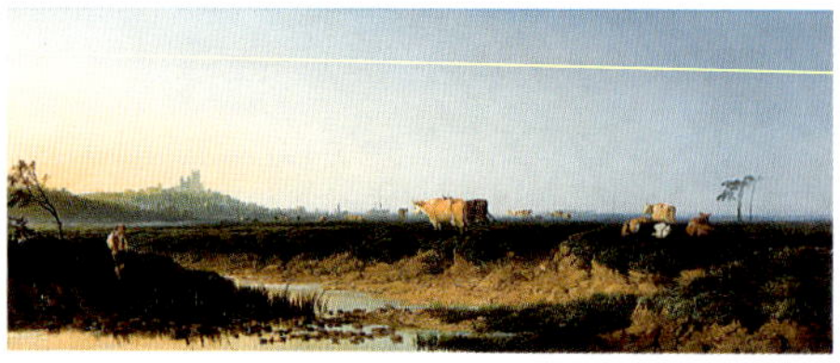

Niemann, Edmund John 1813–1876
A Distant View of Lincoln 1861
oil on canvas 39.5 x 91.5
OP162

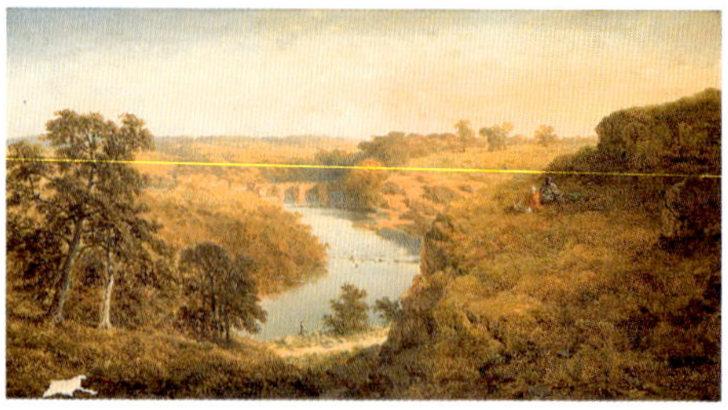

Niemann, Edmund John 1813–1876
On the Teme at Ludlow, Shropshire 1871
oil on canvas 45.5 x 81.5
OP58

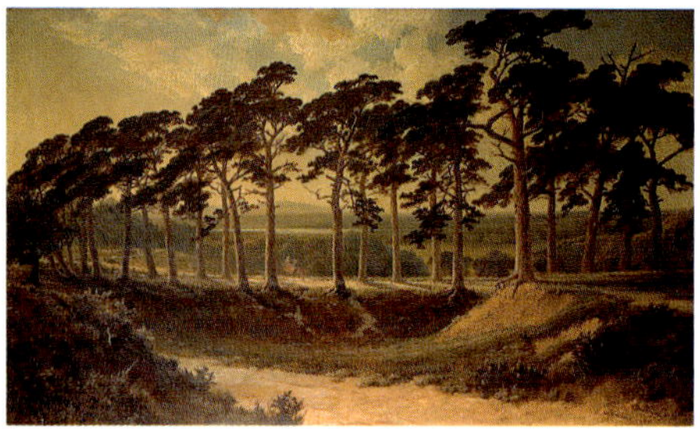

Niemann, Edmund John 1813–1876
Harrow from the Firs, Hampstead Heath 1875
oil on canvas 76 x 127
OP382

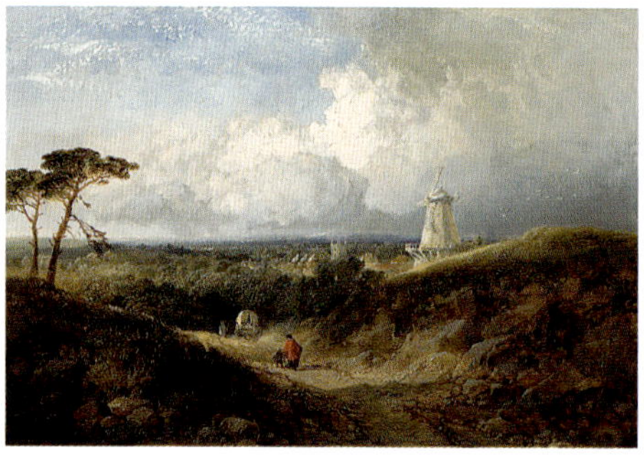

Niemann, Edmund John 1813–1876
Cranbrook, Kent
oil on canvas 35.5 x 51
OP299

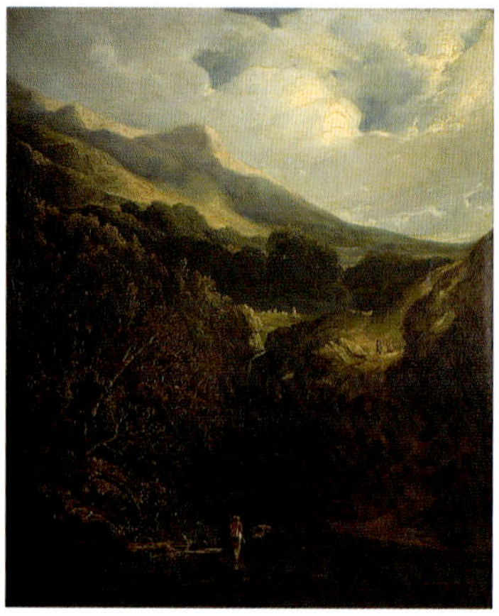

Niemann, Edmund John 1813–1876
Mountainous Landscape
oil on canvas 101.5 x 81
OP114

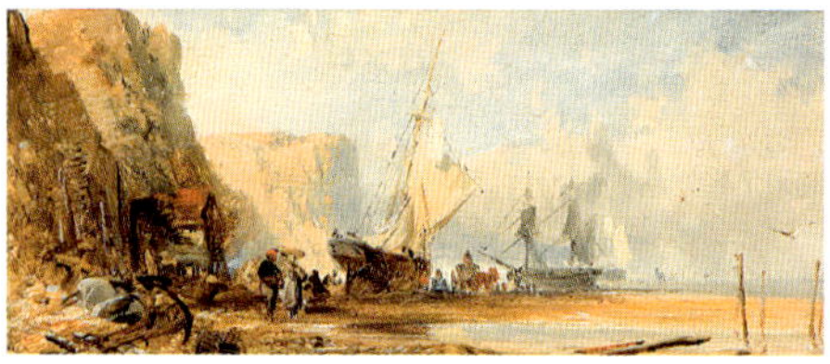

Niemann, Edmund John 1813–1876
On the East Coast
oil on card 13.5 x 30.5
OP71

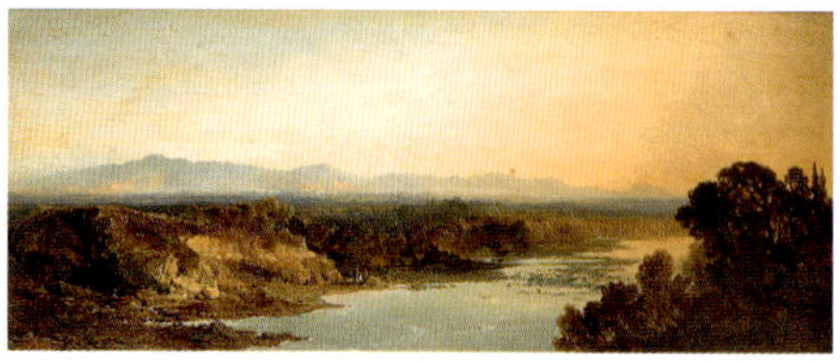

Niemann, Edmund John 1813–1876
On the Eden near Carlisle
oil on panel 35 x 49
OP12

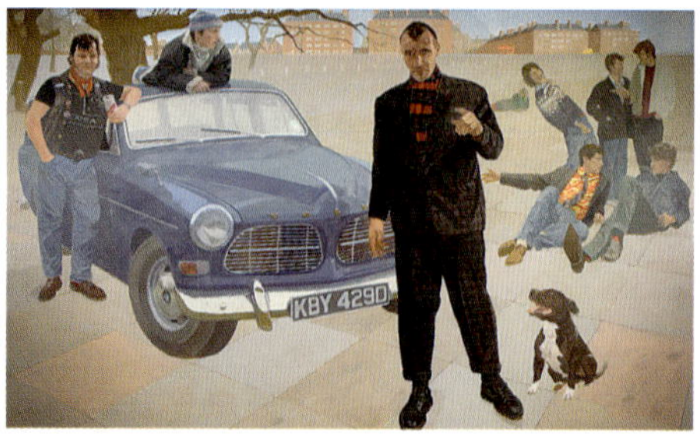

Ocean, Humphrey b.1951
Lord Volvo and His Estate 1982
acrylic on canvas 178 x 287.5
OP880

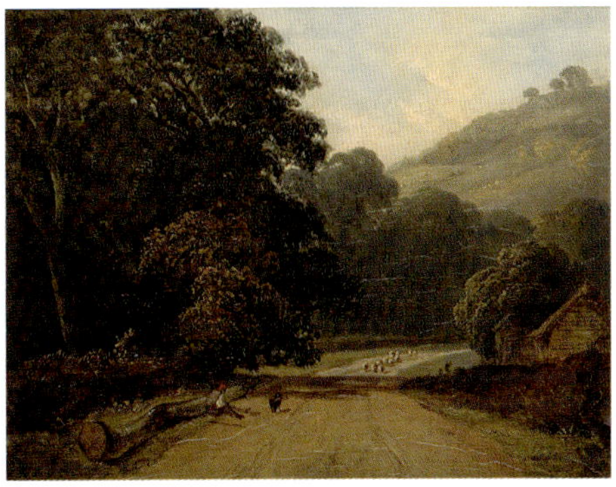

O'Connor, James Arthur 1791–1841
Landscape with Sheep
oil on canvas 21.5 x 27
OP33

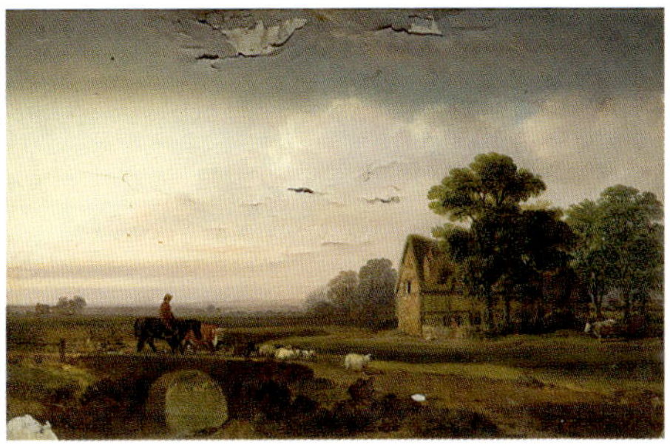

O'Connor, James Arthur 1791–1841
Landscape with Sheep and a Horseman
oil on panel 16.5 x 24
OP51

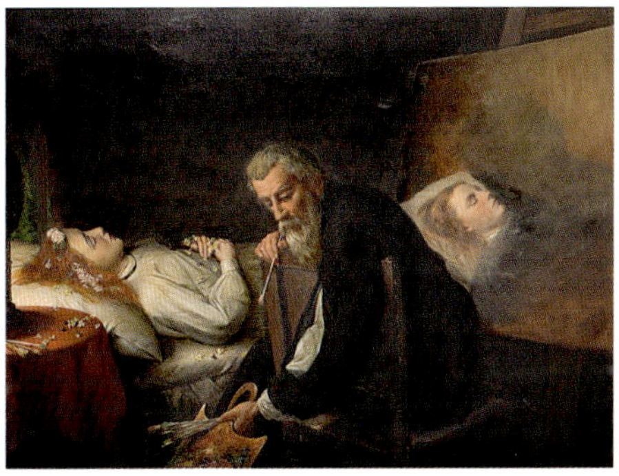

O'Neil, Henry Nelson 1817–1880
Tintoretto Painting His Dead Daughter 1873
oil on canvas 86.5 x 110
OP95

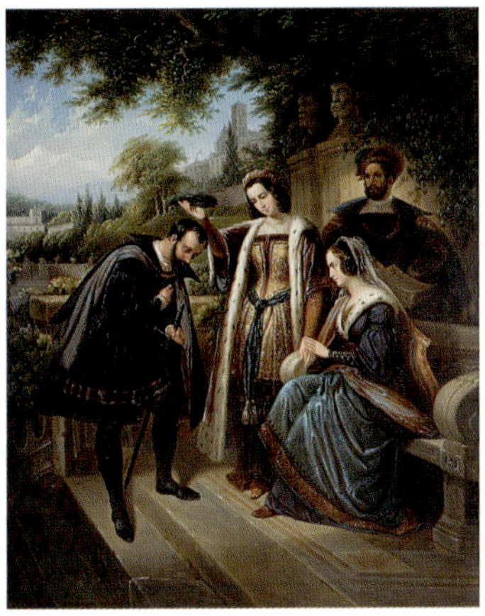

O'Neil, Henry Nelson 1817–1880
Queen Isabella and Columbus
oil on board 47.5 x 37.5
OP175

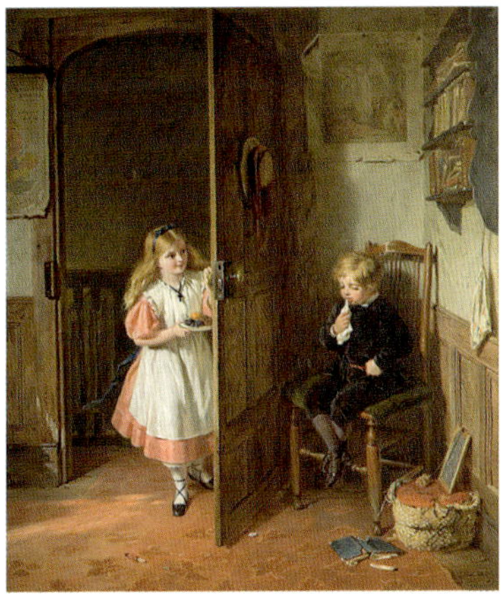

O'Neill, George Bernard 1828–1917
The Naughty Boy 1867
oil on canvas 46.5 x 38.5
OP39

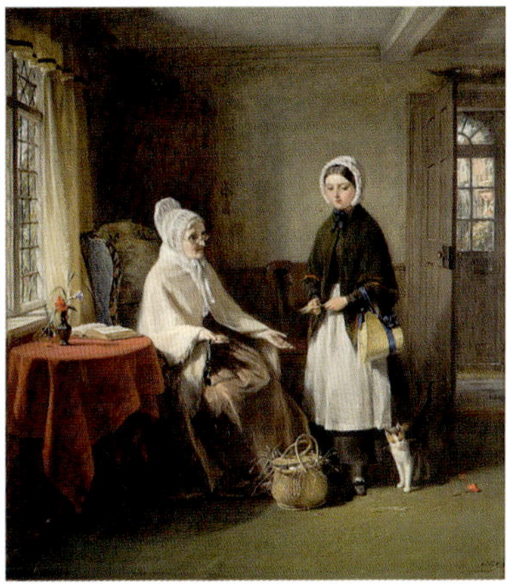

O'Neill, George Bernard 1828–1917
The Reproof 1867
oil on canvas 38 x 33
OP236

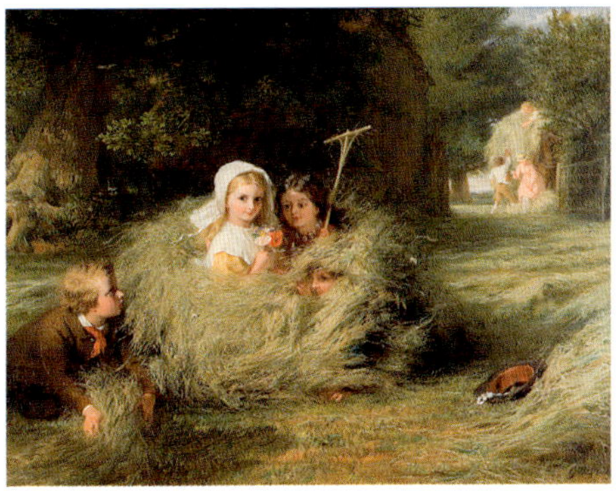

O'Neill, George Bernard 1828–1917
Nestlings 1870
oil on canvas 61 x 76
OP129

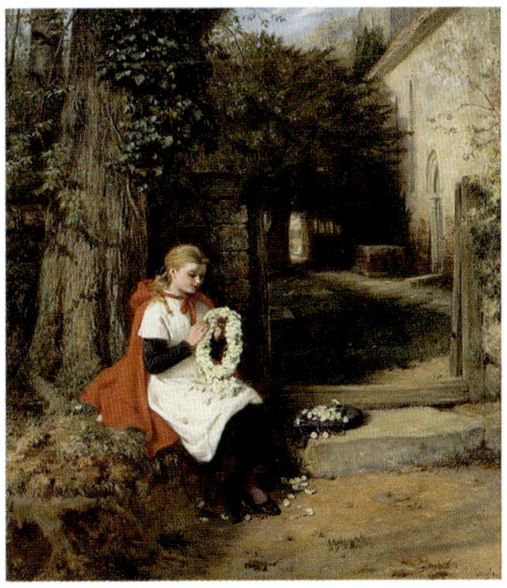

O'Neill, George Bernard 1828–1917
Not Forgotten 1882
oil on canvas 61 x 51
OP61

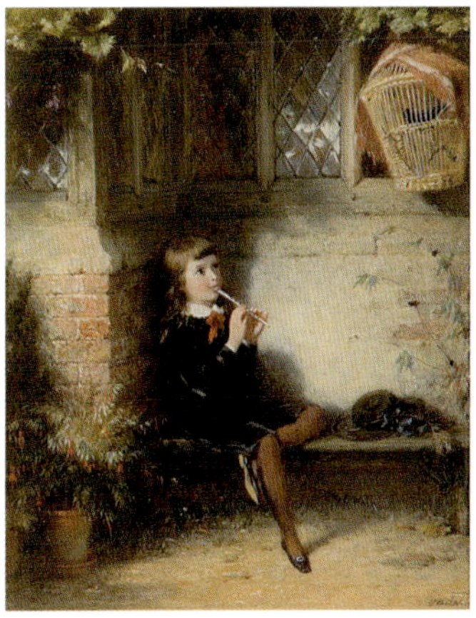

O'Neill, George Bernard 1828–1917
The Duet 1886
oil on canvas 25.5 x 19.5
OP171

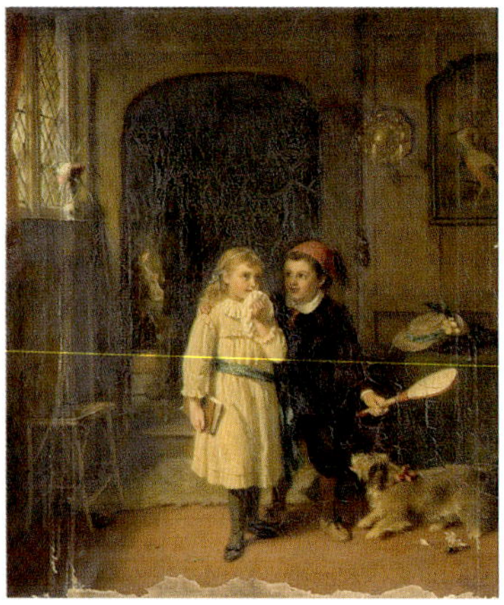

O'Neill, George Bernard 1828–1917
'Cheer up!'
oil on canvas 60 x 50
OP824

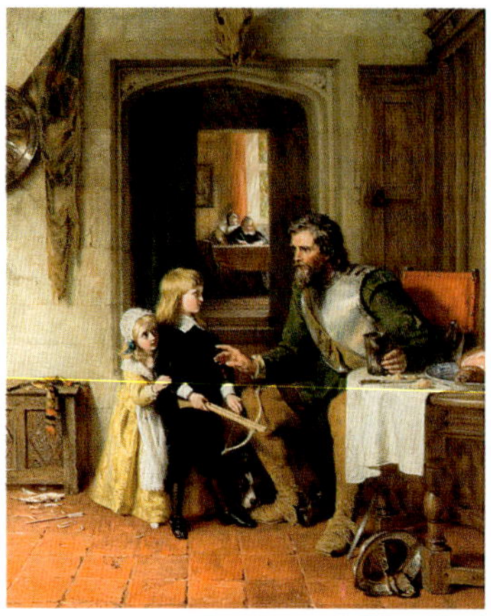

O'Neill, George Bernard 1828–1917
The Despatch
oil on canvas 78 x 61.5
OP565

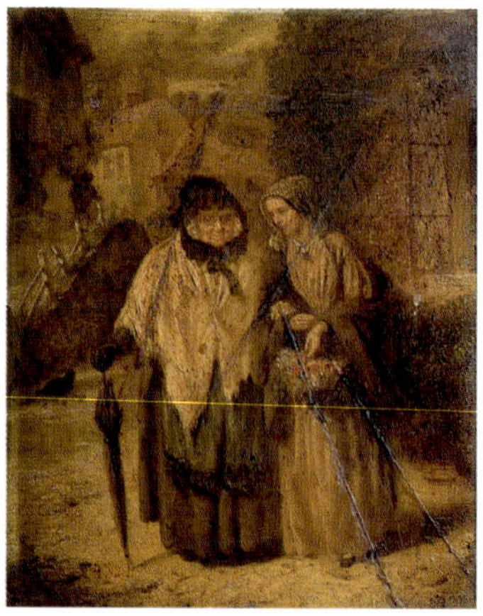

O'Neill, George Bernard 1828–1917
The Morning Walk
oil on panel 22 x 18
OP49

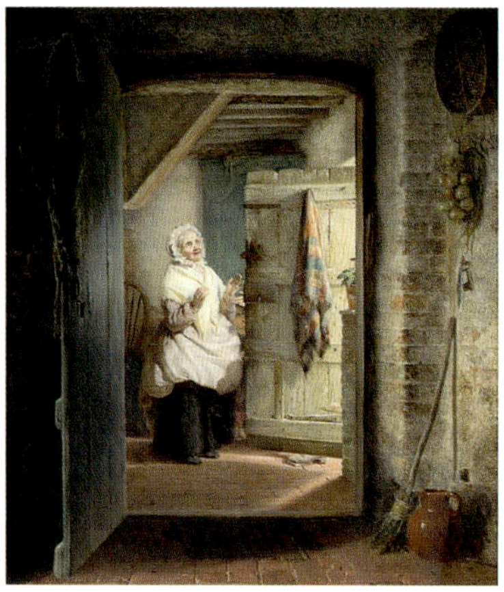

O'Neill, George Bernard 1828–1917
The Surprise
oil on board 35.5 x 30
OP187

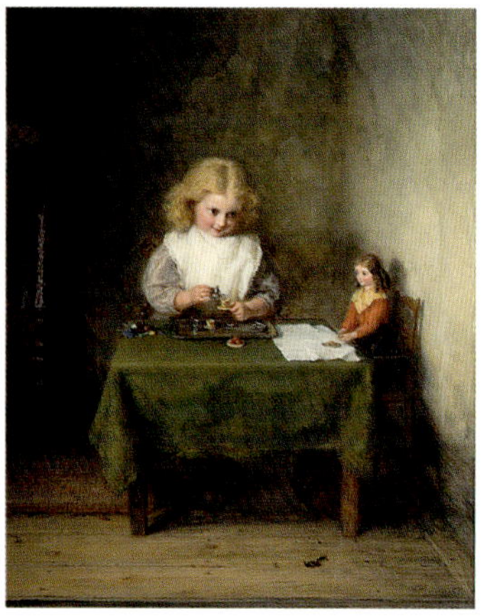

O'Neill, George Bernard 1828–1917
The Tête-à-Tête Tea
oil on canvas 51 x 40.5
OP340

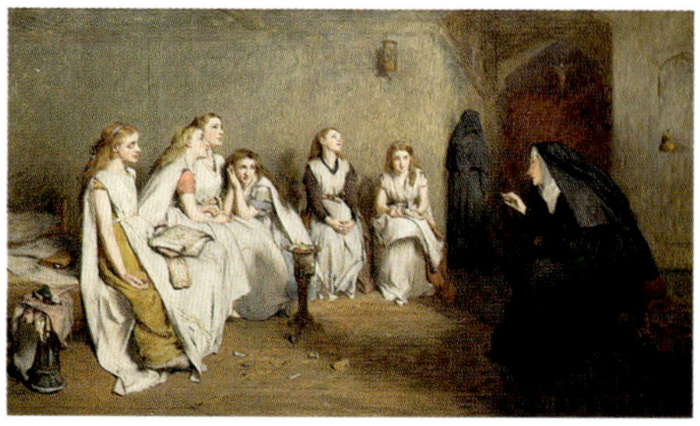

Orchardson, William Quiller 1832–1910
The Story of a Life
oil on canvas 58.5 x 94
OP108

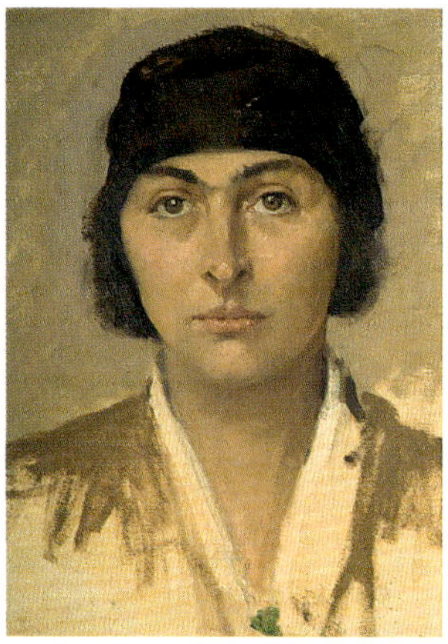

Outlaw, Dorette active 1920–1940
Self Portrait
oil on canvas 34 x 24
OP857

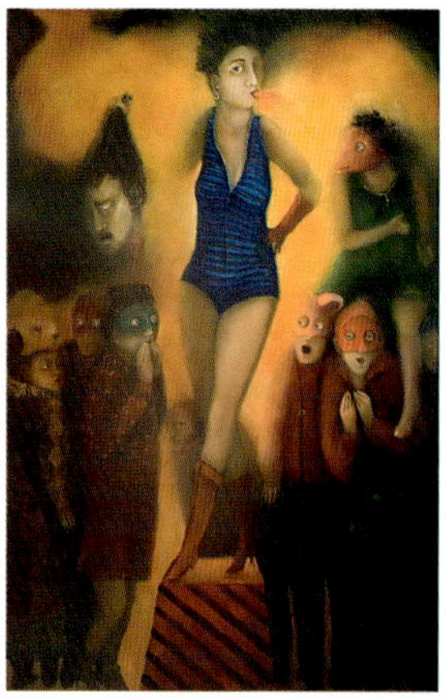

Pacheco, Ana Maria b.1943
Salome 1994–1995
oil on canvas 258 x 181
OP869

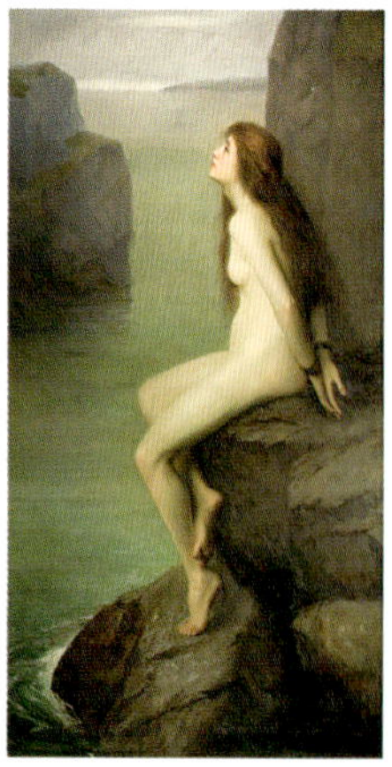

Page, Sarah active 1892–1935
Andromeda
oil on canvas 205 x 114
OP437

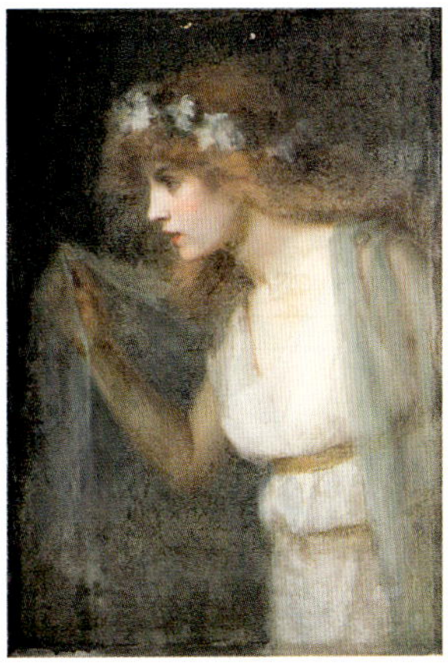

Page, Sarah active 1892–1935
Whisper of Spring
oil on canvas 205.5 x 114.5
OP610

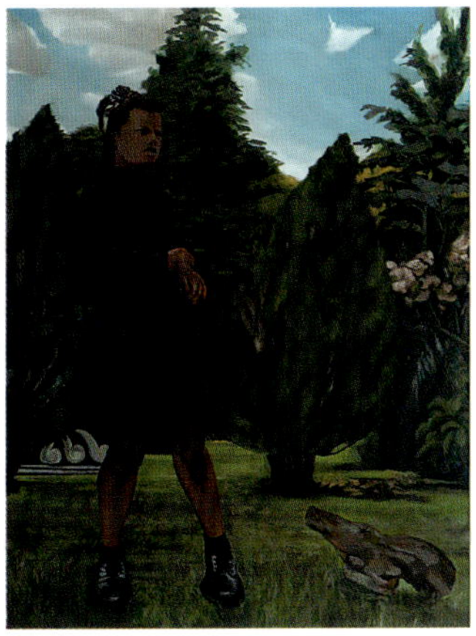

Palmer, Eugene b.1955
Duppy Shadow 1994
oil on canvas 210 x 155
OP881

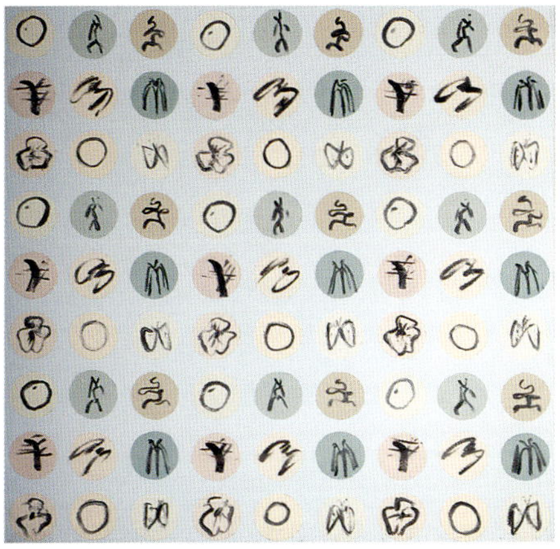

Parmar, Usha b.1968
Heiroglyph Triptych (left) 1990–1997
oil on canvas 79 x 77
OP884(i)

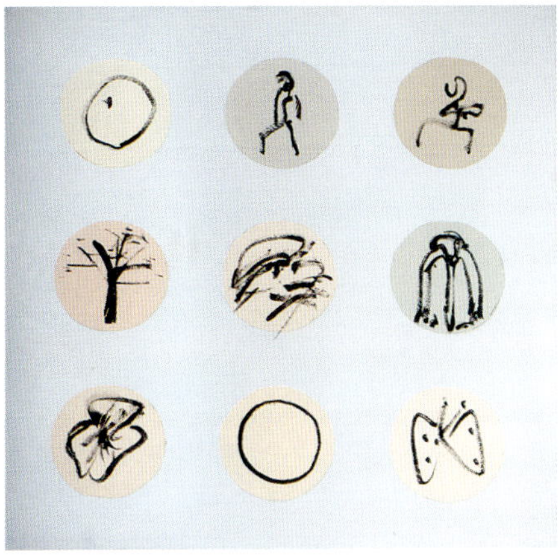

Parmar, Usha b.1968
Heiroglyph Triptych (centre) 1990–1997
oil on canvas 77 x 77
OP884(ii)

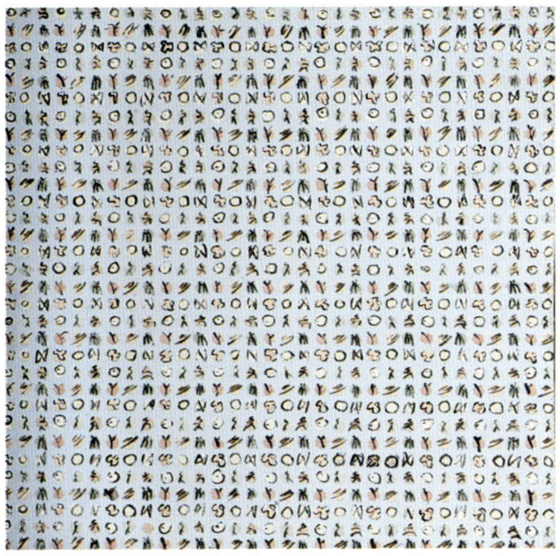

Parmar, Usha b.1968
Heiroglyph Triptych (right) 1990–1997
oil on canvas 32 x 32
OP884(iii)

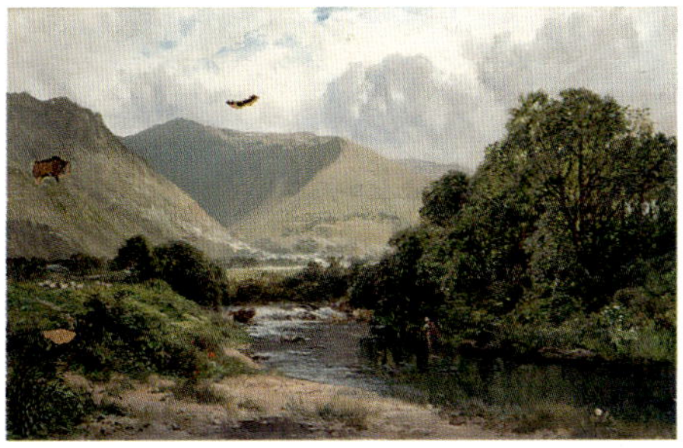

Peel, James 1811–1906
Near Rosthwaite
oil on canvas 30.5 x 45.5
OP18

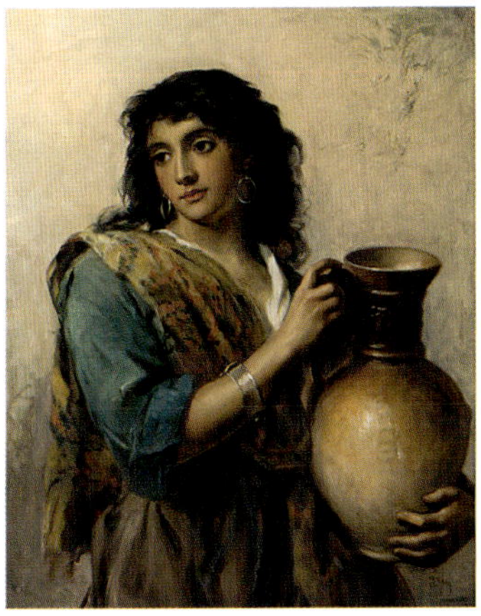

Pelham, Thomas Kent active 1860–1892
An Egyptian Beauty
oil on canvas 91.5 x 71
OP711

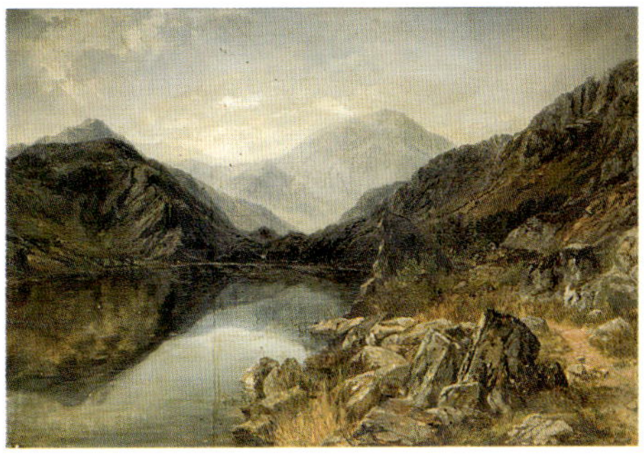

Percy, Sidney Richard (circle of) 1821–1886
View of Snowdon
oil on canvas 52 x 74
OP818

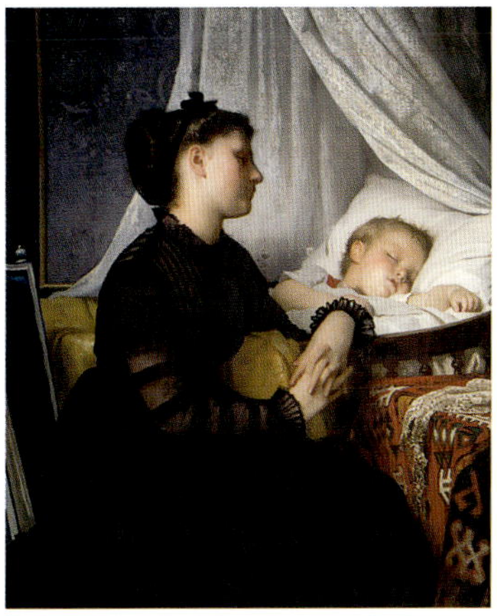

Perrault, Léon Bazile 1832–1908
Widowed and Fatherless 1874
oil on canvas 109 x 92.5
OP98

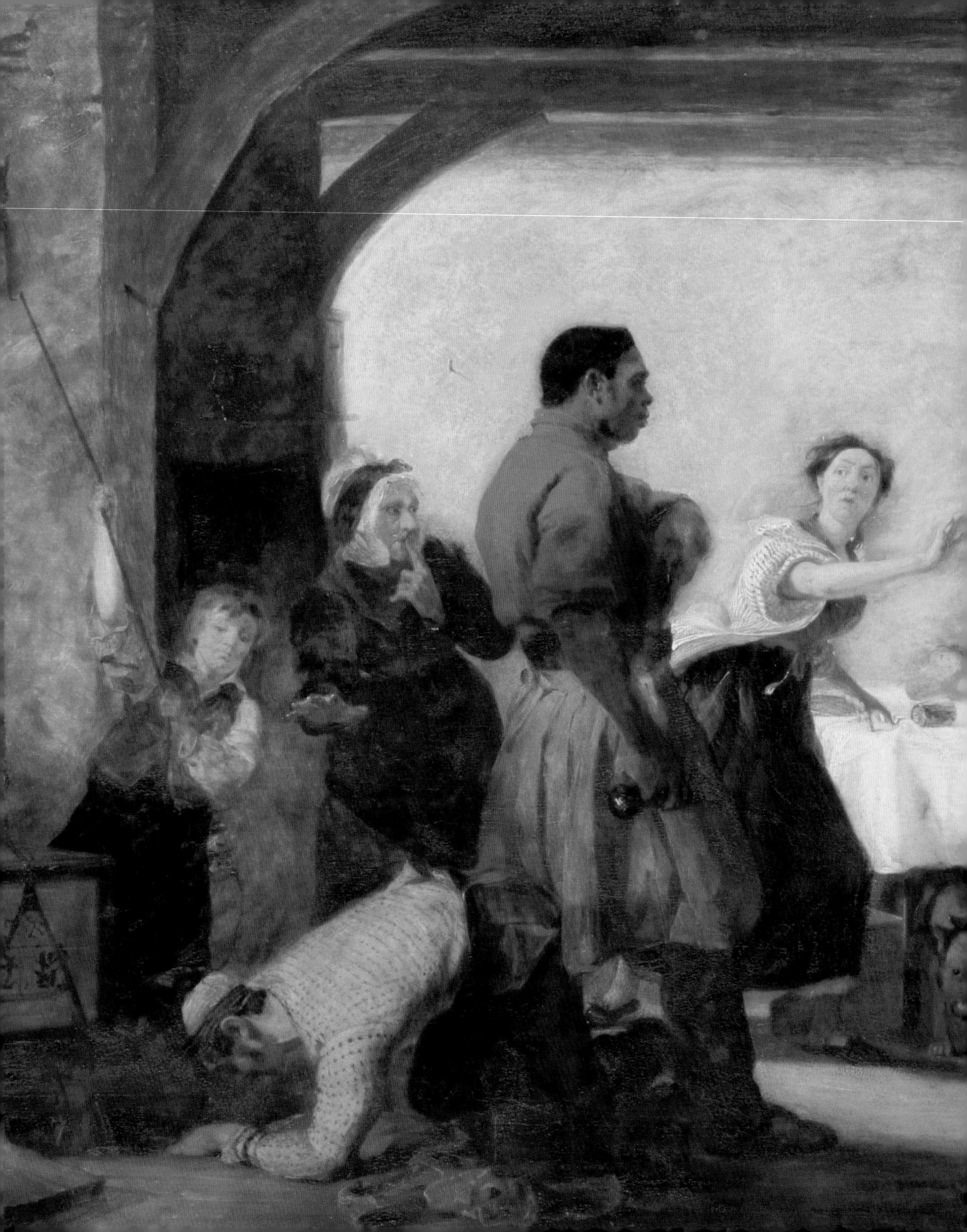

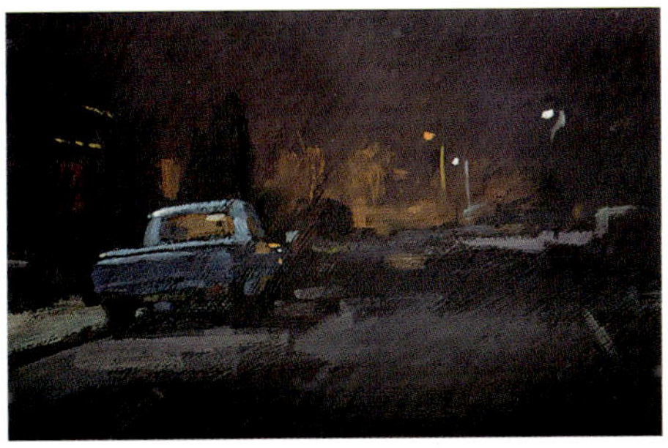

Perry, Robert b.1944
Blue Pickup, Brockmoor 1980s
oil on board 19.5 x 26.5
OP826

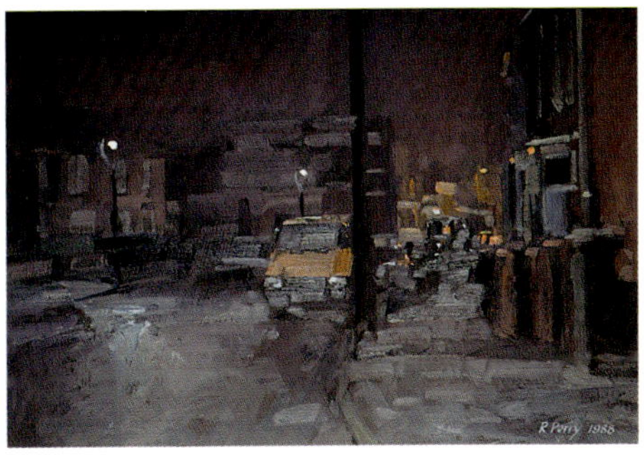

Perry, Robert b.1944
Transit, Wordsley 1980s
oil on board 41 x 58.5
OP827

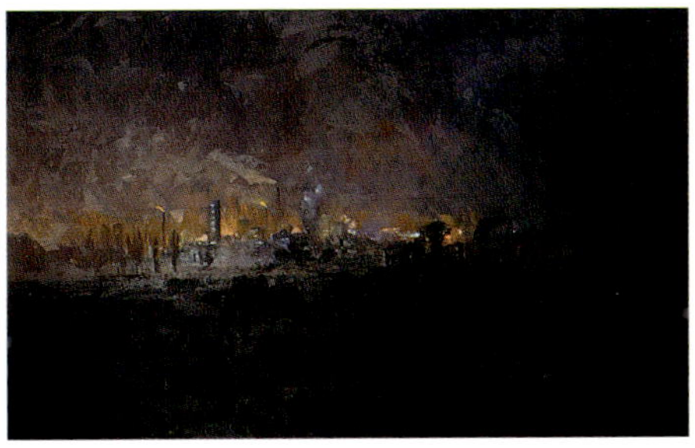

Perry, Robert b.1944
Synthetic Chemicals Factory 1989
oil on panel 121 x 190
OP825

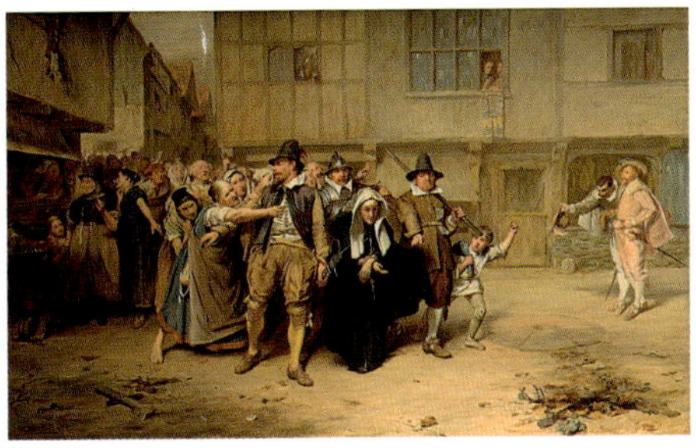

Pettie, John 1839–1893
An Arrest for Witchcraft in the Olden Time 1866
oil on canvas 61 x 94
OP456

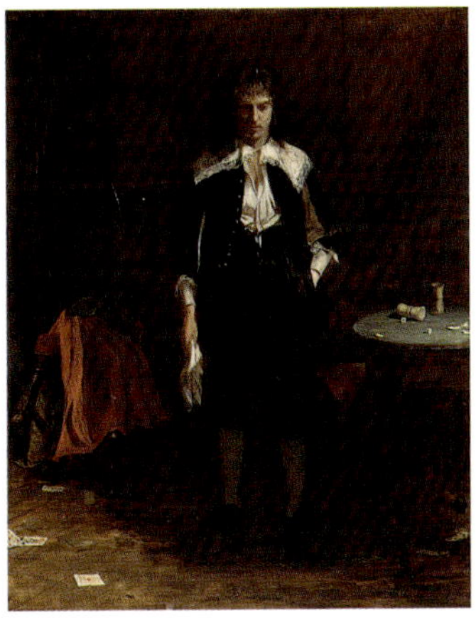

Pettie, John 1839–1893
Cleaned Out 1868
oil on canvas 72.5 x 54.5
OP75

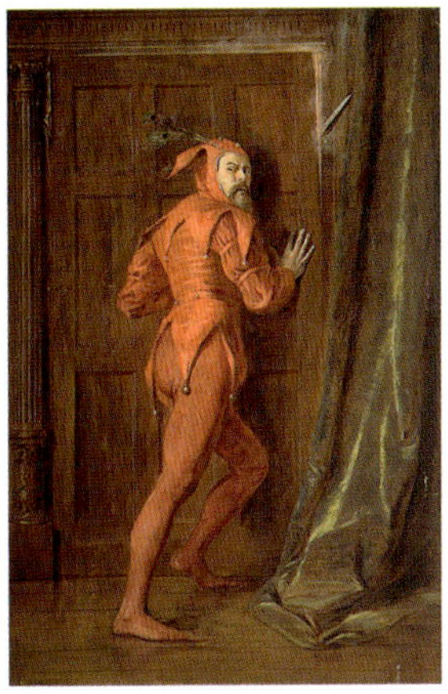

Pettie, John 1839–1893
Mephistopheles
oil on canvas 71 x 43.5
OP712

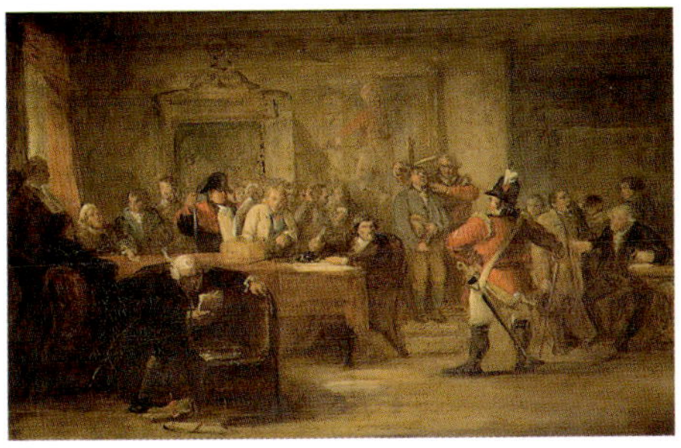

Phillip, John 1817–1867
The Recruit (sketch) 1849
oil on canvas 40.5 x 61
OP210

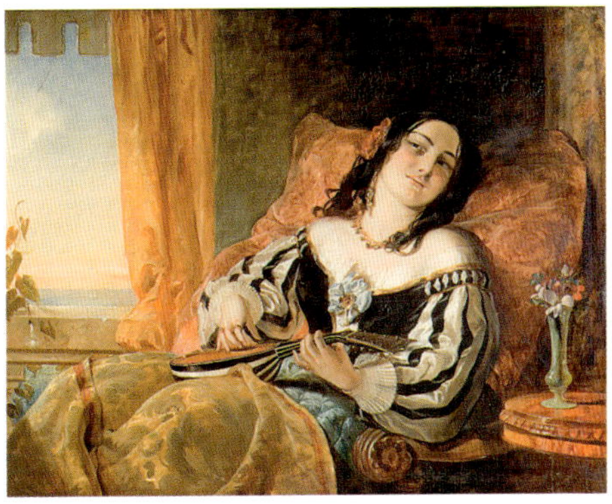

Phillip, John 1817–1867
A Lady Playing the Mandolin 1854
oil on canvas 51 x 61
OP219

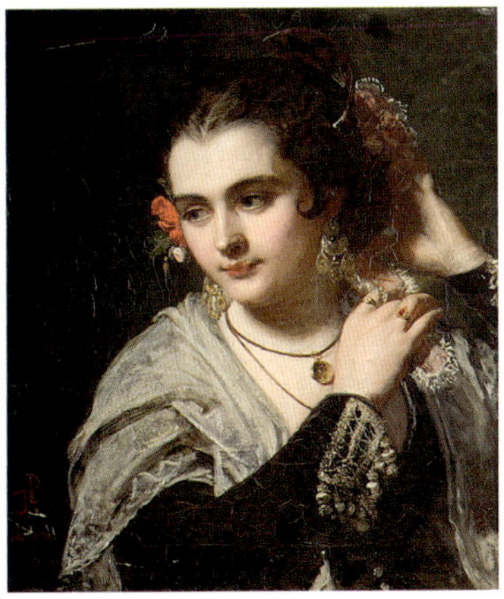

Phillip, John 1817–1867
La señorita, Cádiz 1858
oil on canvas 62 x 51.5
OP519

Facing page: Knight, John Prescott, 1803–1881, *Smugglers Alarmed* (detail), c.1830, Staffordshire Arts and Museums Service (p. 78)

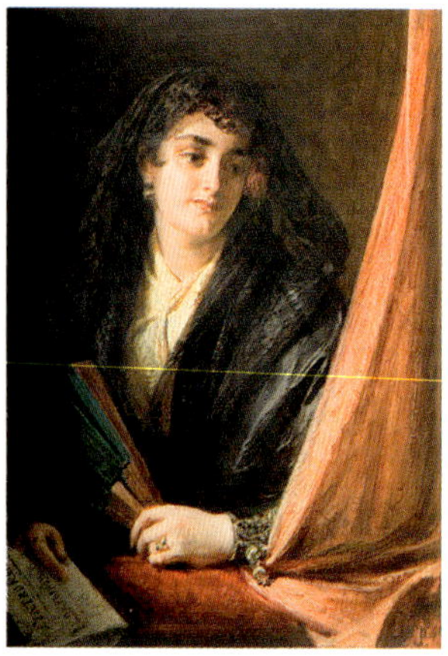

Phillip, John 1817–1867
At the Opera 1866
oil on board 61 x 46.5
OP368

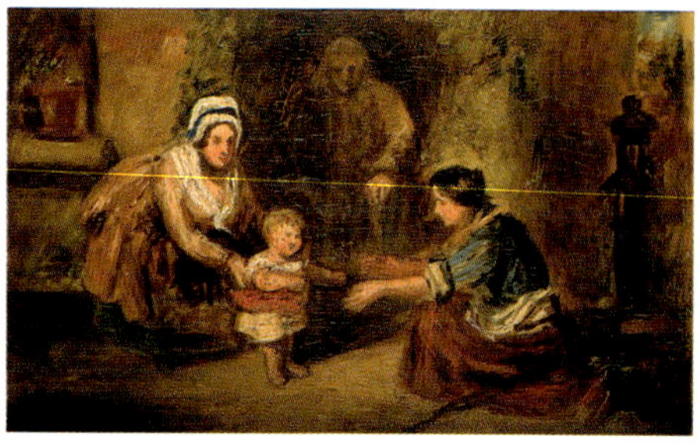

Phillip, John 1817–1867
First Steps
oil on canvas 52 x 63.5
OP182

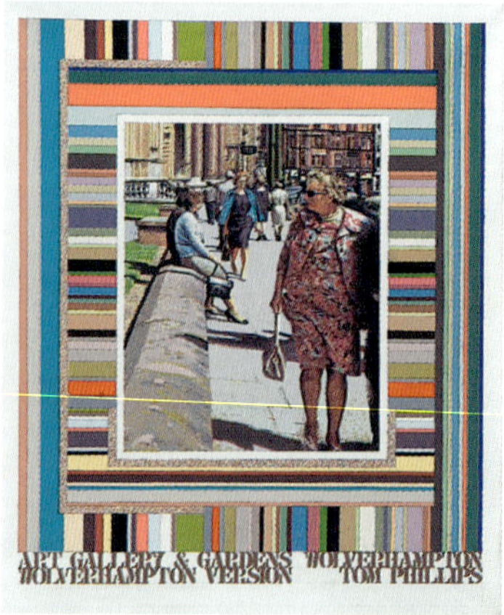

Phillips, Tom b.1937
Art Gallery and Gardens, Wolverhampton (left panel) 1970
oil on canvas 40.5 x 25.5
OP252

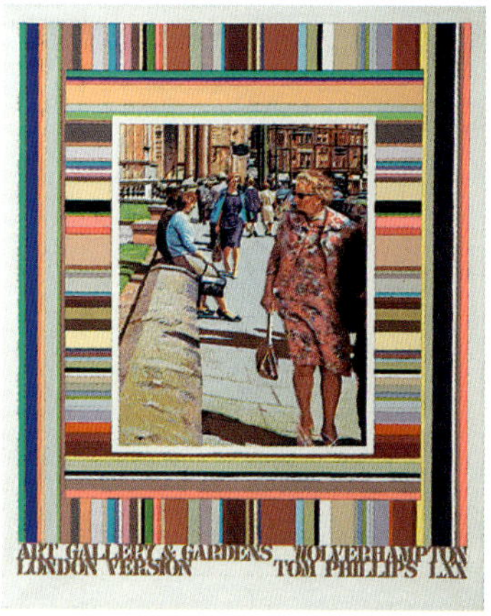

Phillips, Tom b.1937
Art Gallery and Gardens, Wolverhampton (right panel) 1970
oil on canvas 40.5 x 25.5
OP252

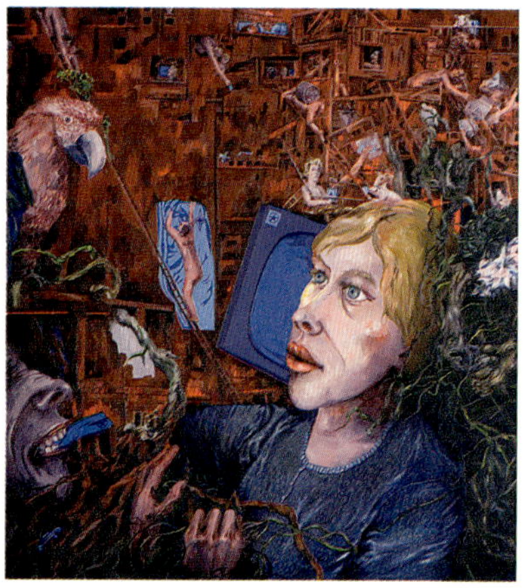

Phillips, Tony b.1952
Life Trap
oil on canvas 76.5 x 67.5
OP900

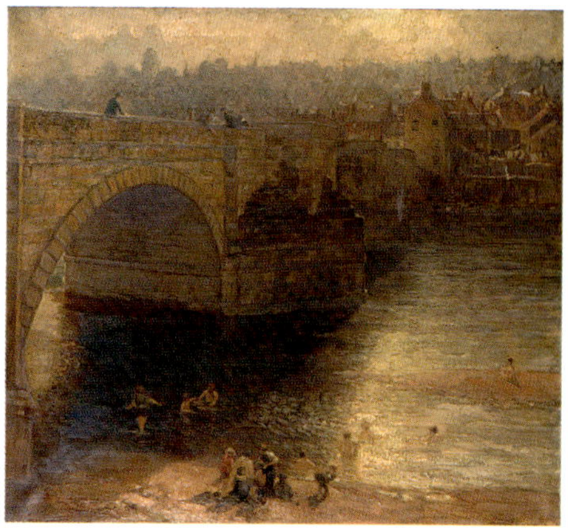

Phoenix, George 1863–1935
Bridgnorth, Shropshire
oil on canvas 94 x 101.5
OP477

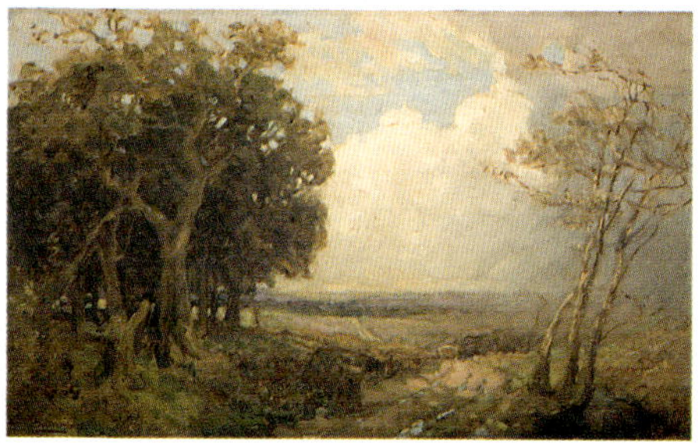

Phoenix, George 1863–1935
Corner of Cannock Chase
oil on canvas 40.5 x 61
OP714

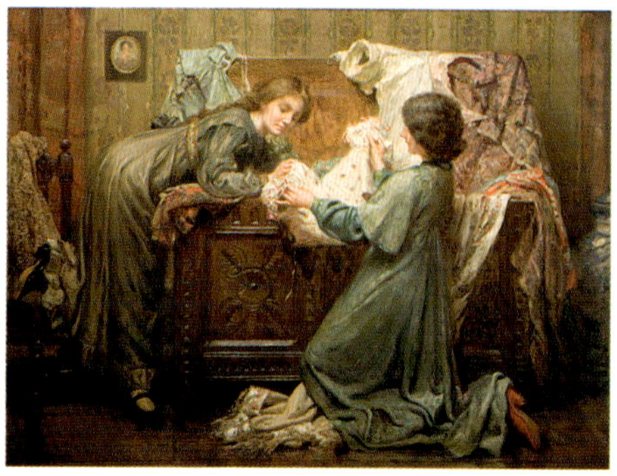

Phoenix, George 1863–1935
Grandmother's Wardrobe
oil on canvas 96.5 x 124.5
OP587

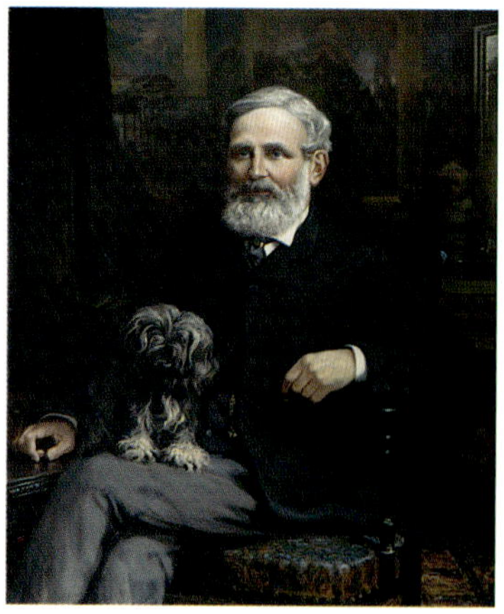

Phoenix, George 1863–1935
Philip Horsman, JP
oil on canvas 114.5 x 94
OP577

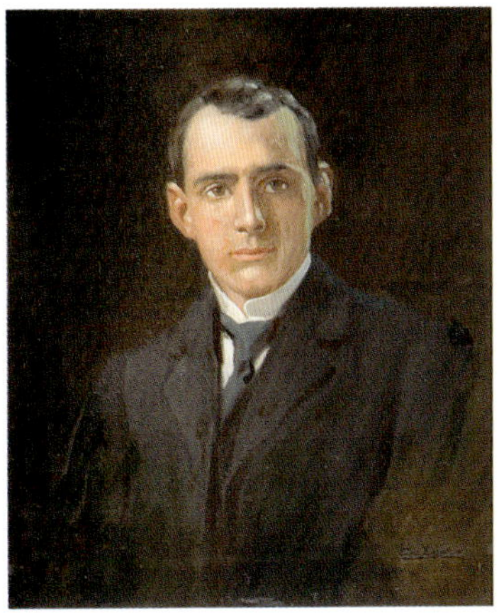

Phoenix, George 1863–1935
Reverend C. Carter
oil on canvas 82.5 x 68.5
OP906

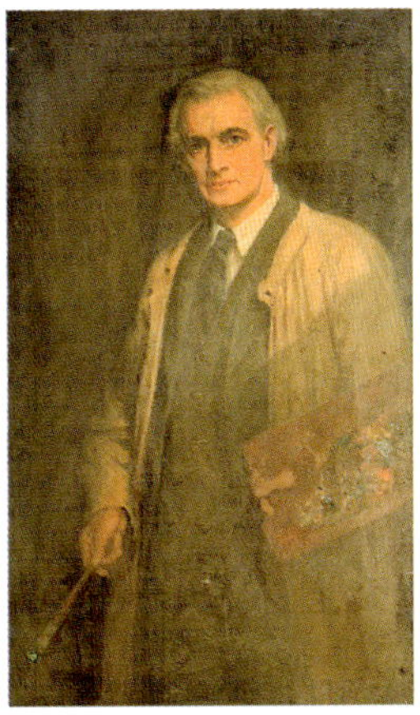

Phoenix, George 1863–1935
Self Portrait
oil on canvas 114.5 x 94
OP421

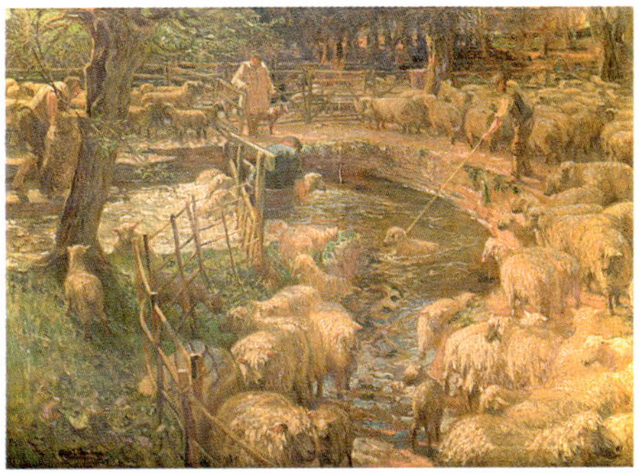

Phoenix, George 1863–1935
Sheep Washing
oil on canvas 96.5 x 124.5
OP411

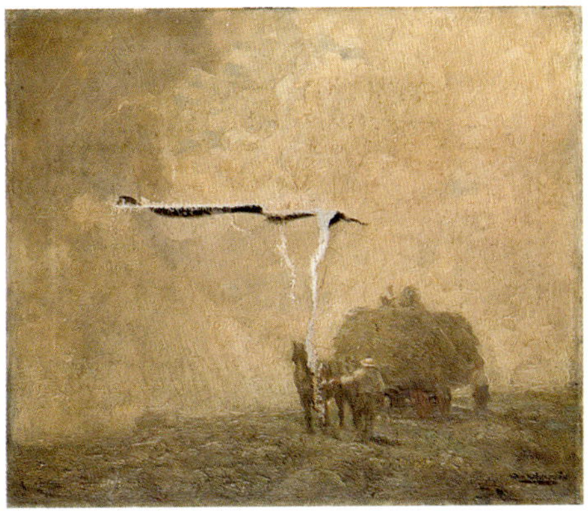

Phoenix, George 1863–1935
The Hayfield
oil on canvas 40.6 x 45.7
OP268

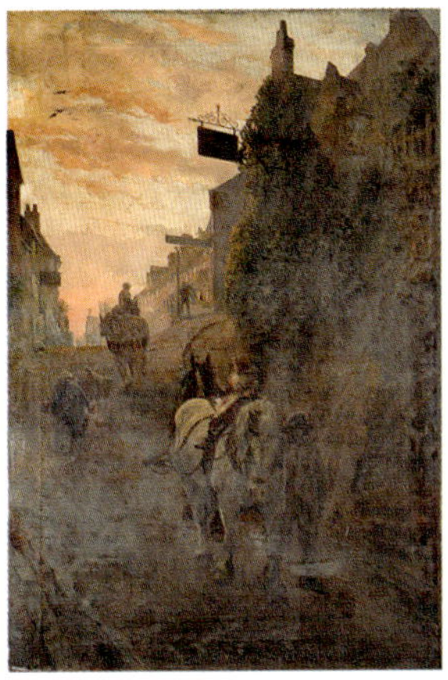

Phoenix, George 1863–1935
The Old Hill, Tettenhall
oil on canvas 167.6 x 106.7
OP423

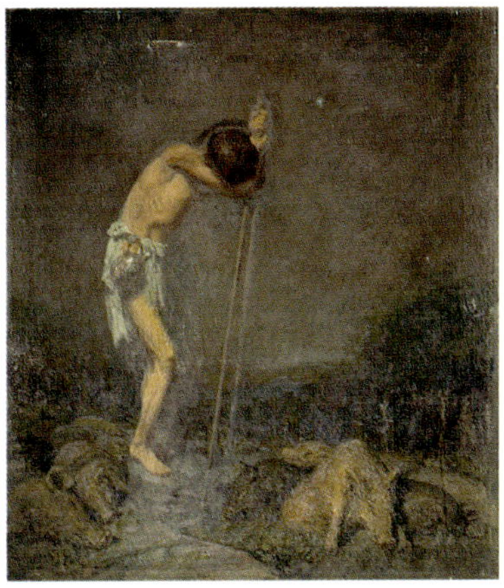

Phoenix, George 1863–1935
The Prodigal Son
oil on canvas 91.5 x 76
OP352

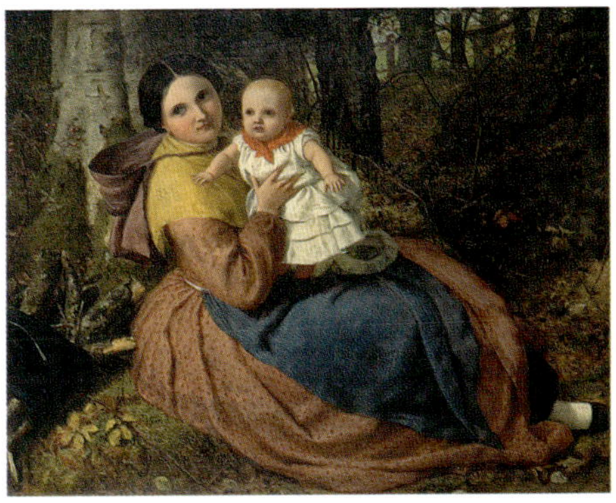

Pickersgill, Frederick Richard 1820–1900
The Artist's Son and Nurse 1863
oil on panel 38 x 45.5
OP541

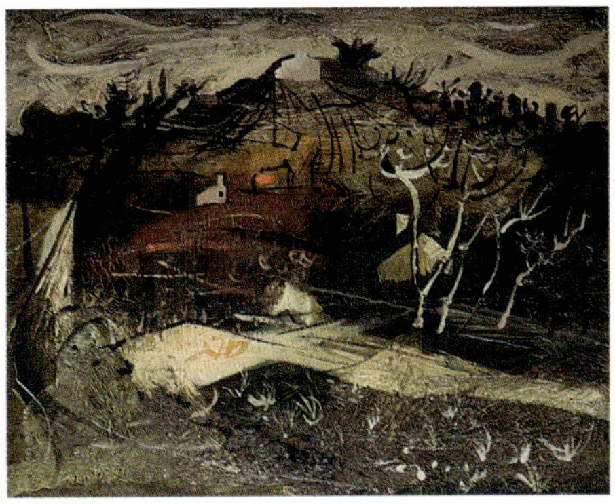

Piper, John 1903–1992
Welsh Landscape 1950
oil on canvas 51 x 61
OP835

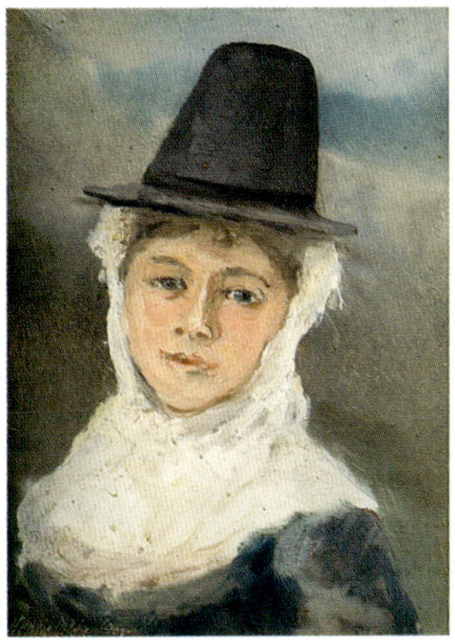

Pitcher, Henrie active c.1880–1904
Welshwoman 1902
oil on canvas 24 x 20
OP718

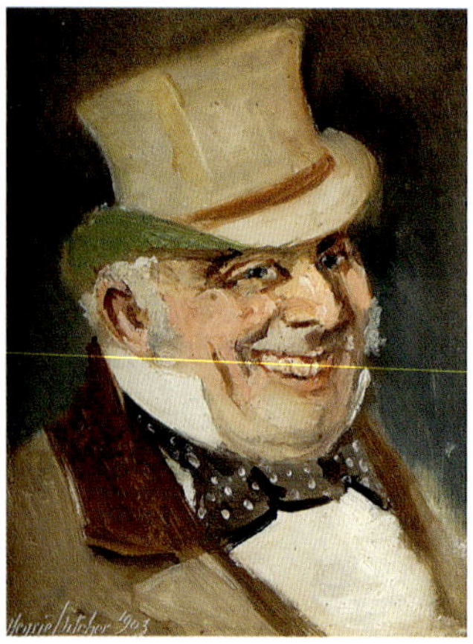

Pitcher, Henrie active c.1880–1904
Englishman 1903
oil on canvas 24 x 20
OP715

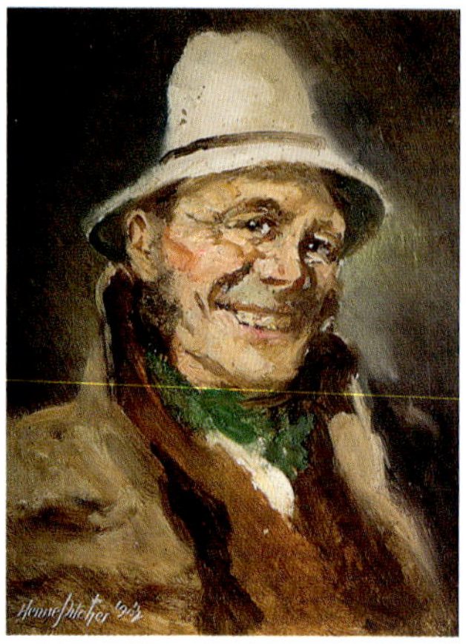

Pitcher, Henrie active c.1880–1904
Irishman 1903
oil on canvas 24 x 20
OP717

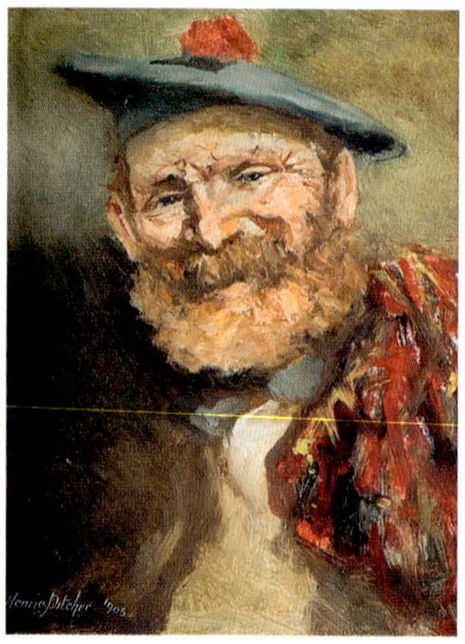

Pitcher, Henrie active c.1880–1904
Scotsman 1903
oil on canvas 24 x 20
OP716

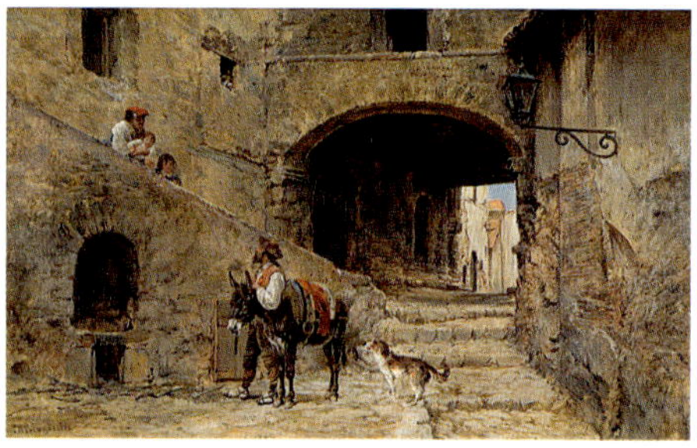

Poingdestre, Charles 1825–1905
Anticoli Corrado on the Sabine Mountains
oil on canvas 44 x 68
OP719

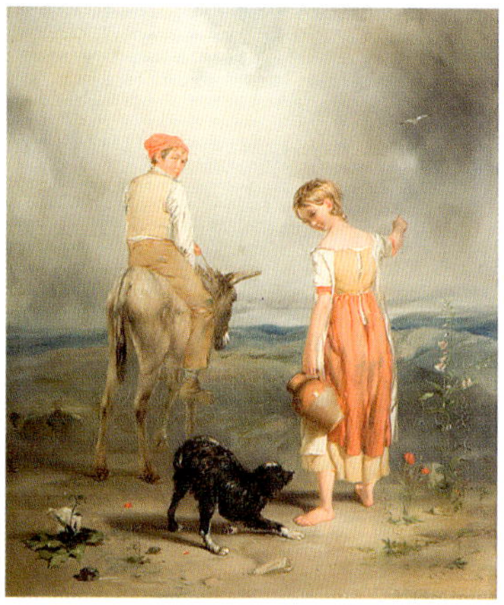

Poole, Paul Falconer 1807–1879
The Heath Belle 1831
oil on canvas 43 x 37
OP358

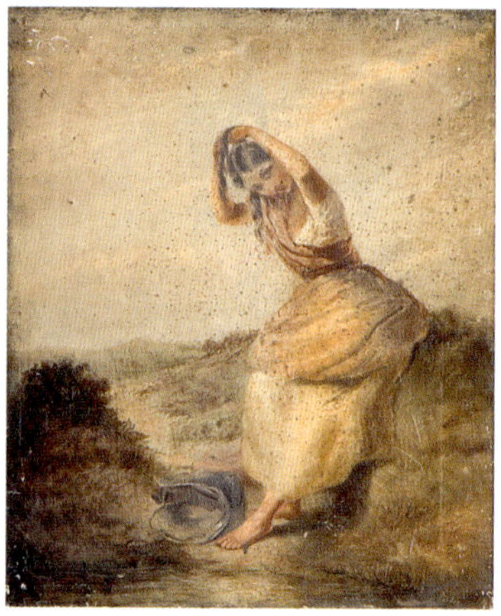

Poole, Paul Falconer 1807–1879
Peasant Girl in Moorland 1847
oil on canvas 50.8 x 40.6
OP386

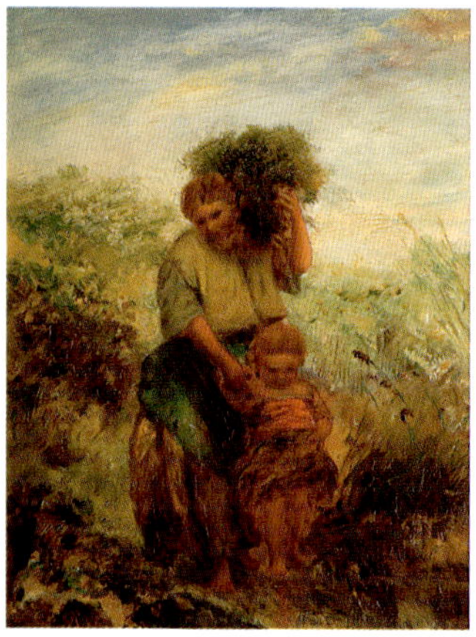

Poole, Paul Falconer 1807–1879
The Gorse Gatherer, Child Crossing Mountain Stream 1855
oil on panel 23 x 18
OP35

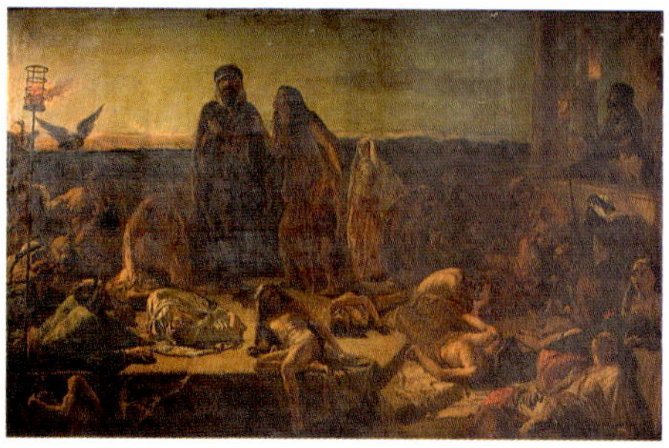

Poole, Paul Falconer 1807–1879
The Beleaguered City
oil on canvas 177.8 x 266.7
OP372

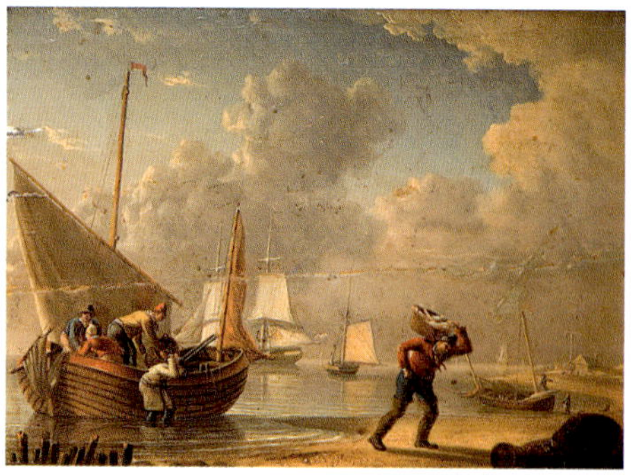

Powell, George
Fishing Smack Unloading
oil on panel 18 x 23
OP157

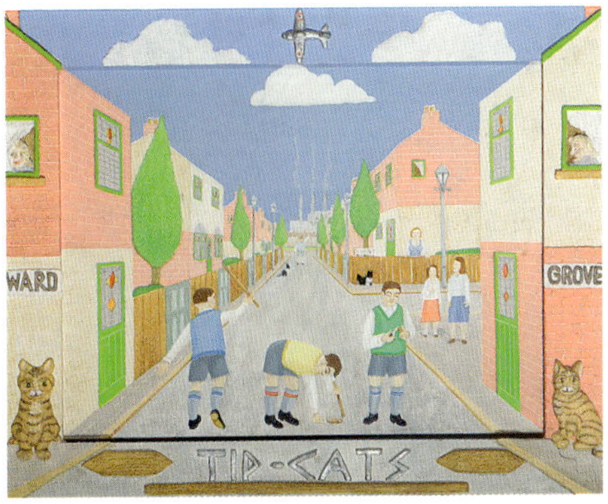

Powell, Michael James William b.1934
Tip Cats 1989–1995
oil on board 36 x 59
OP899

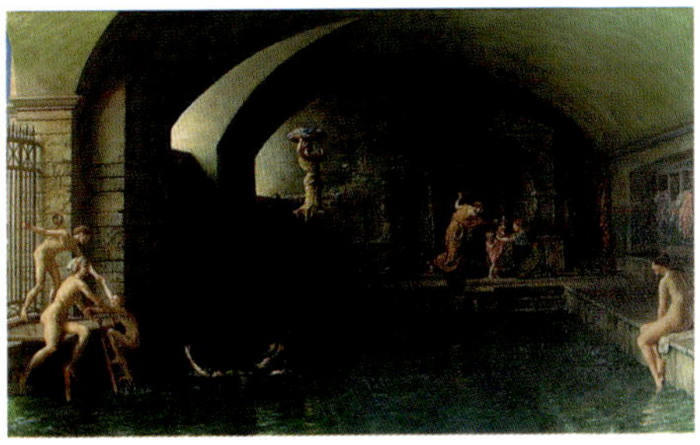

Poynter, Edward John 1836–1919
The Champion Swimmer 1914
oil on canvas 101.5 x 162.5
OP126

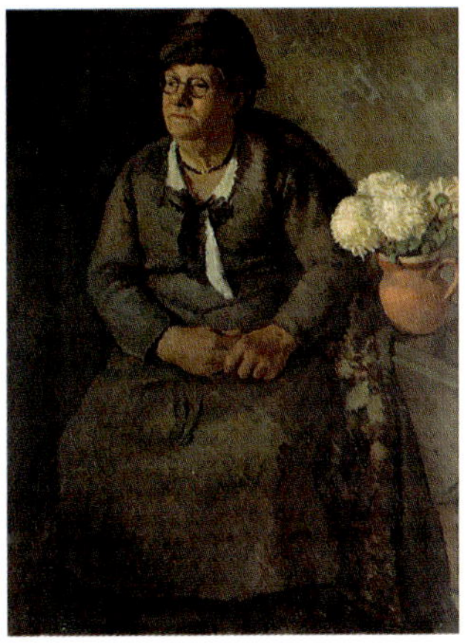

Preece, Patricia 1894–1966
The Visitor
oil on canvas 68.5 x 51
OP310

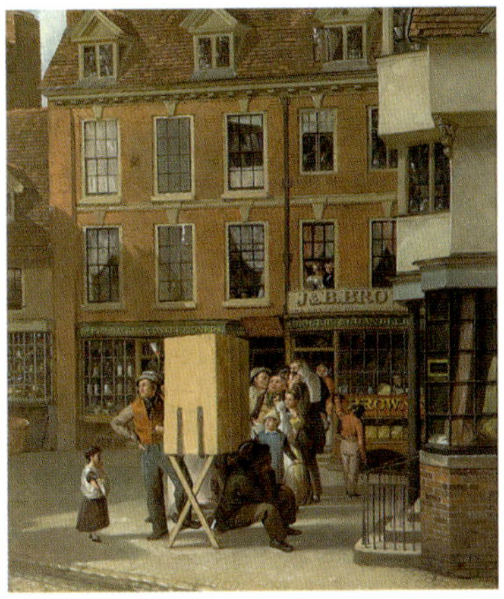

Pringle, William J. active c.1805–1860
High Green, Wolverhampton
oil on canvas 62 x 52
OP483

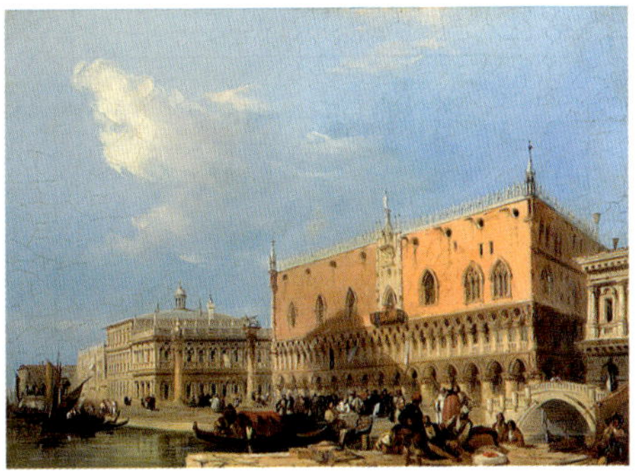

Pritchett, Edward active c.1828–1879
The Doge's Palace, Venice 1850–1864
oil on canvas 45.5 x 61.5
OP195

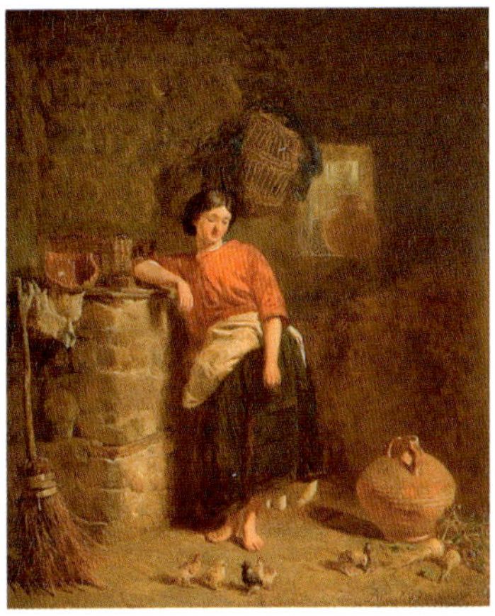

Provis, Alfred active 1843–1886
A Woman Watching Chickens 1860
oil on canvas 24 x 20.5
OP275

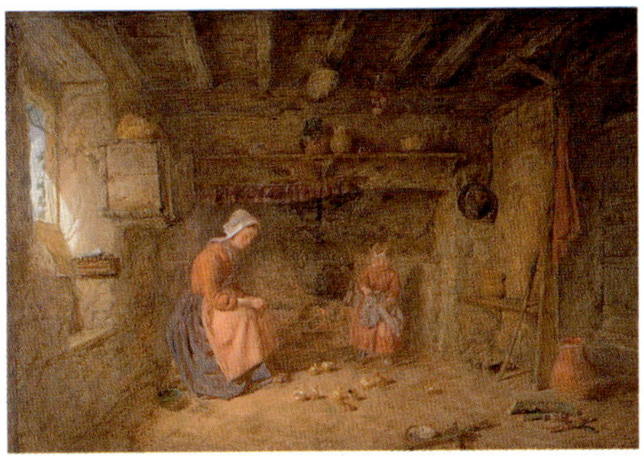

Provis, Alfred active 1843–1886
Feeding Time
oil on canvas 31 x 43
OP357

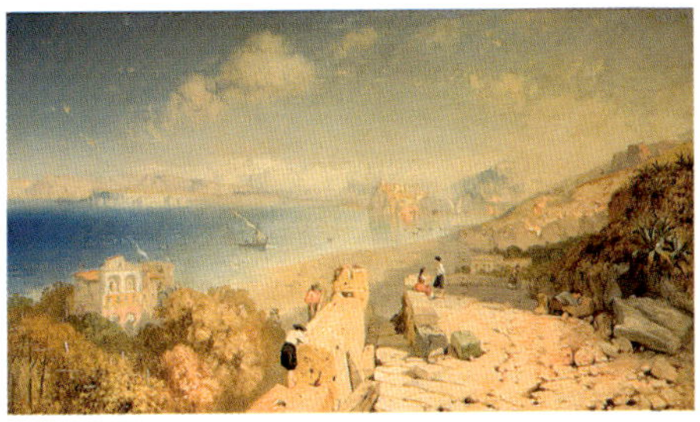

Pyne, James Baker 1800–1870
The Castle of Ischia and the Gulf Islands 1863
oil on canvas 54.5 x 90
OP246

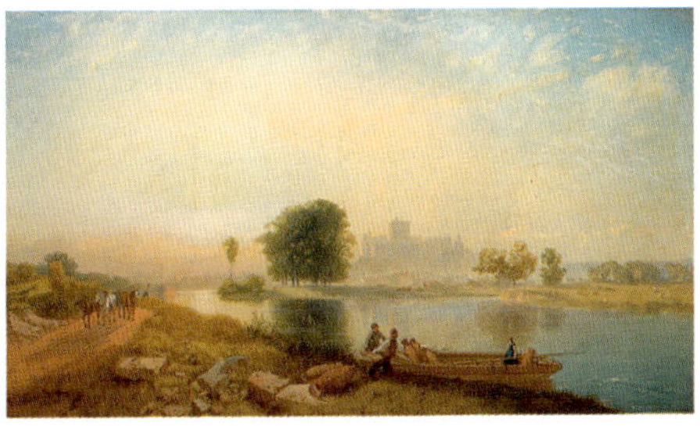

Pyne, James Baker 1800–1870
Windsor Castle, Morning 1869
oil on canvas 59 x 100
OP234

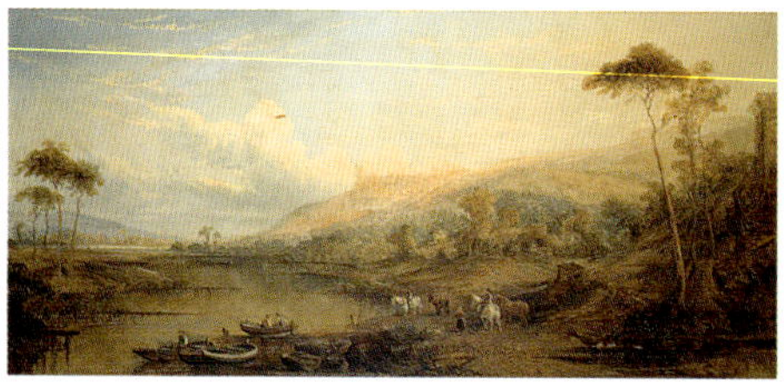

Pyne, James Baker 1800–1870
Evening, Arundel Castle, Sussex
oil on canvas 66 x 134.5
OP113

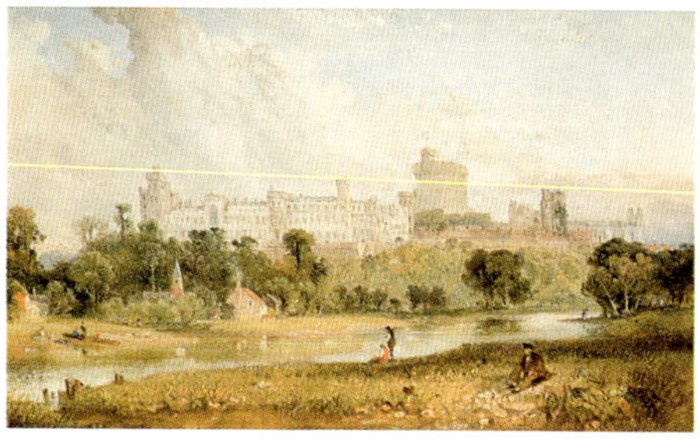

Pyne, James Baker 1800–1870
Windsor Castle
oil on canvas 23 x 35.5
OP216

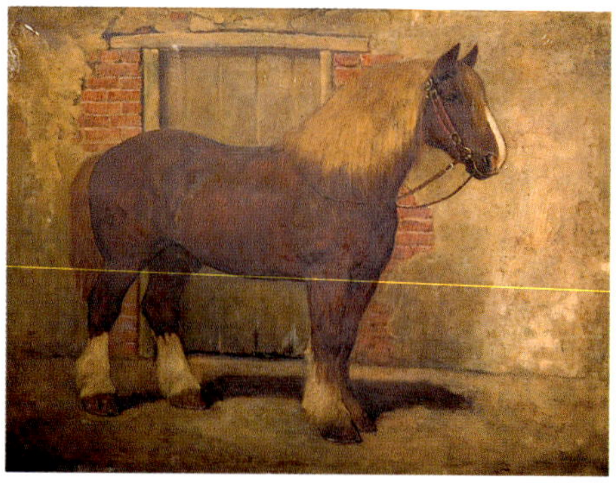

Quick, Richard active 1880–1889
Shire Horse
oil on canvas 59 x 73.5
OP872

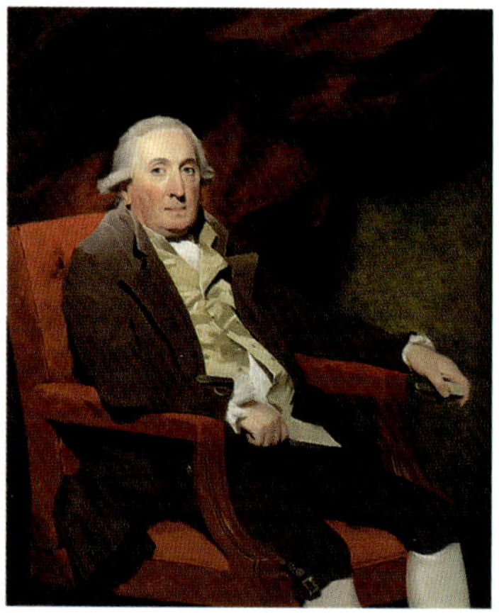

Raeburn, Henry 1756–1823
William Fairlie of Fairlie (1754–1825)
oil on canvas 123 x 100.5
OP533

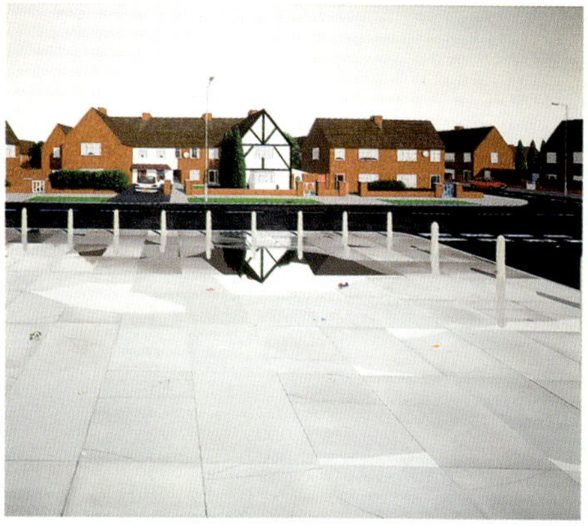

Rayson, David b.1966
Griffiths Drive 1999–2000
oil on canvas 110 x 121
OP905

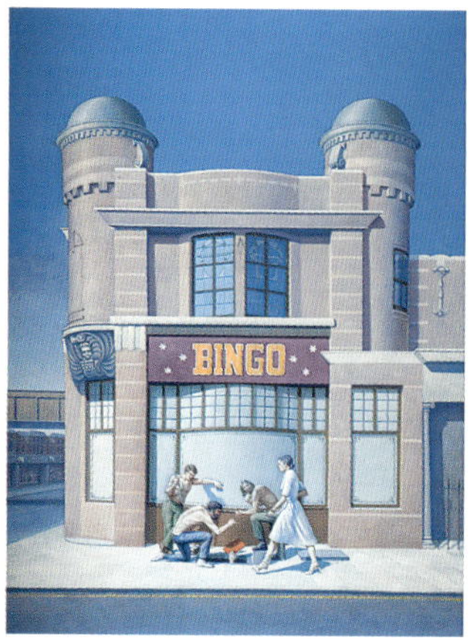

Redfern, David b.1947
Et in Arcadia, Bingo 1984
oil on canvas 162 x 114.5
OP791

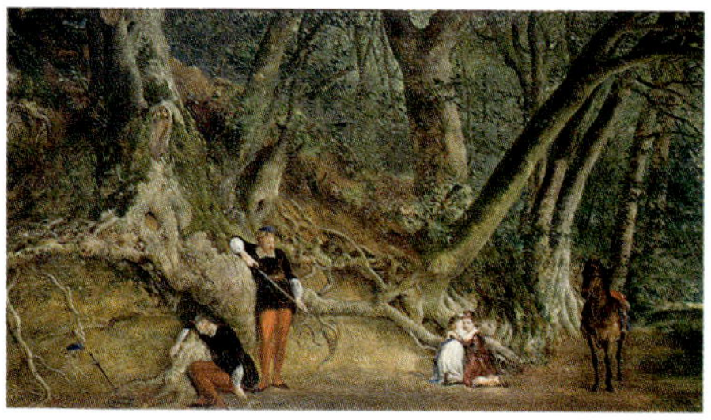

Redgrave, Richard 1804–1888
Babes in the Wood 1862
oil on canvas 35.5 x 61
OP166

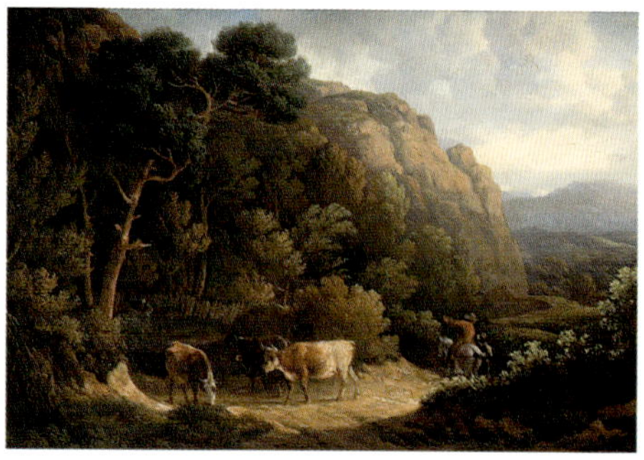

Reinagle, Philip 1749–1833
Landscape with Cows
oil on board 26.5 x 37.5
OP2

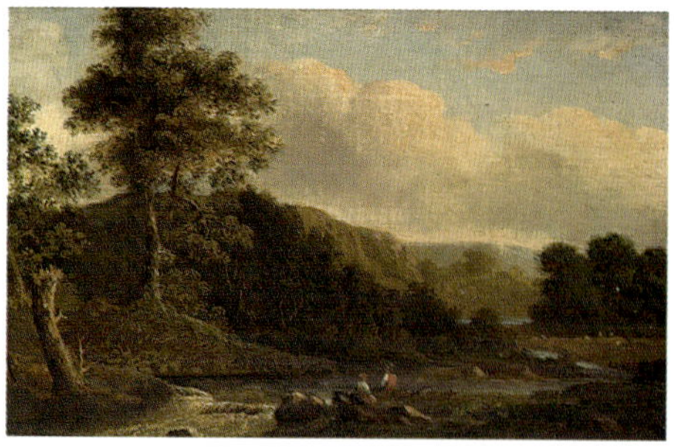

Reinagle, Philip (circle of) 1749–1833
River Scene with Figures
oil on canvas 25.5 x 35.5
OP73

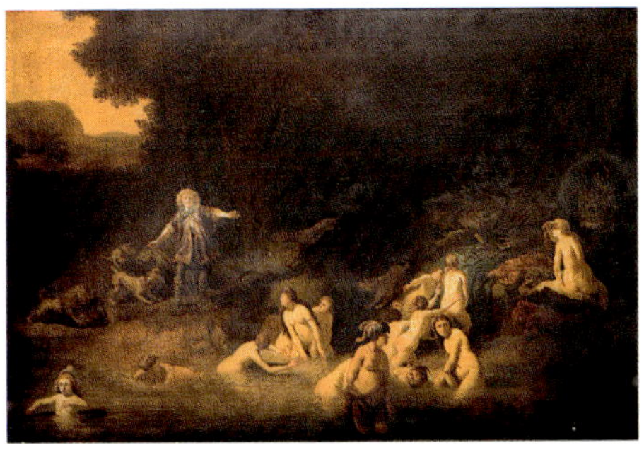

Rembrandt van Rijn (after) 1606–1669
Mythological Scene
oil on canvas 73.5 x 101.5
OP475

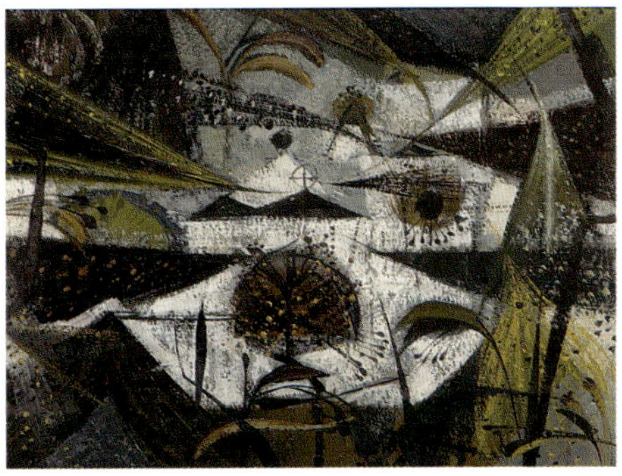

Reynolds, Alan b.1926
Polyphonic Autumn 1954
oil on canvas 30.5 x 39.5
OP837

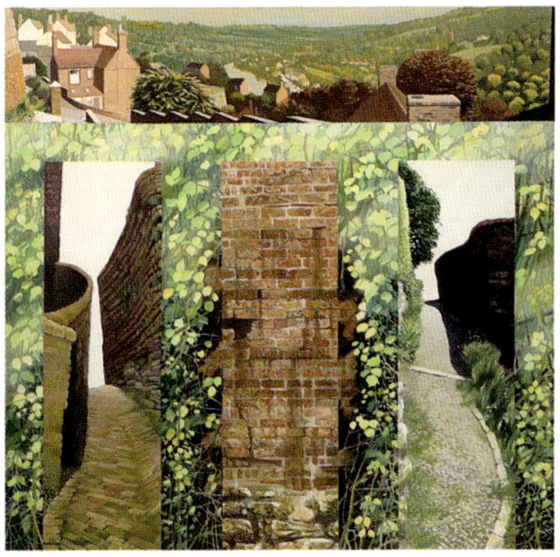

Rhodes, Bob b.1946
July (from the 'Ironbridge' series) 1982
acrylic on canvas 152.5 x 152.5
OP803

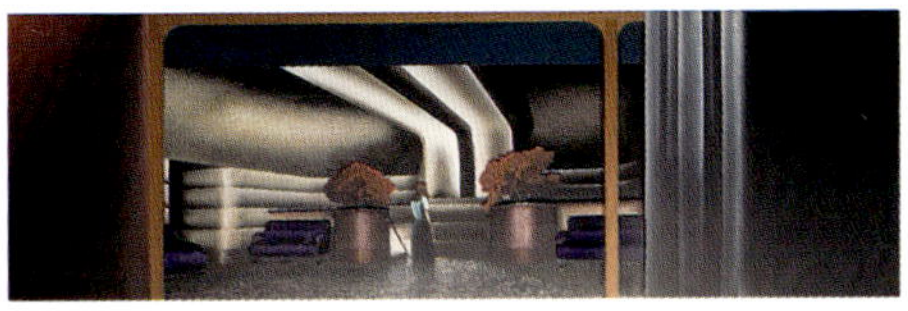

Rhodes, Bob b.1946
Odeon
mixed media on panel 61 x 183
OP590

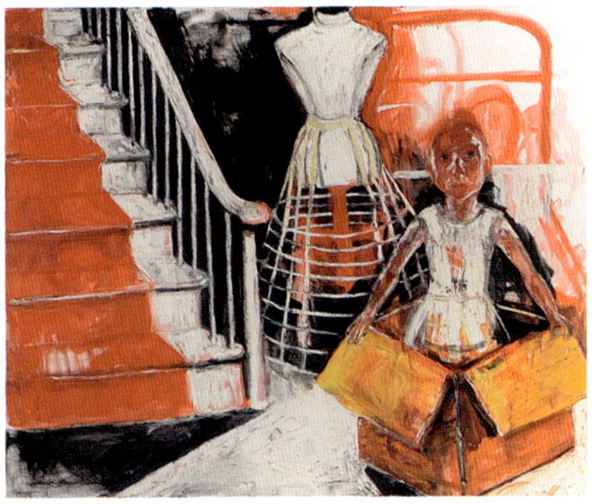

Rhys-James, Shani b.1953
Stairs II 1997
oil on canvas 180 x 210
OP898

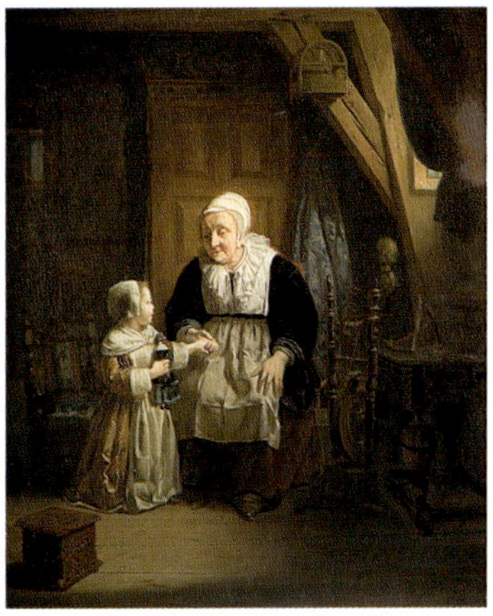

Ringeling, Hendrik 1812–1874
Woman and Child 1842
oil on canvas 41 x 33
OP281

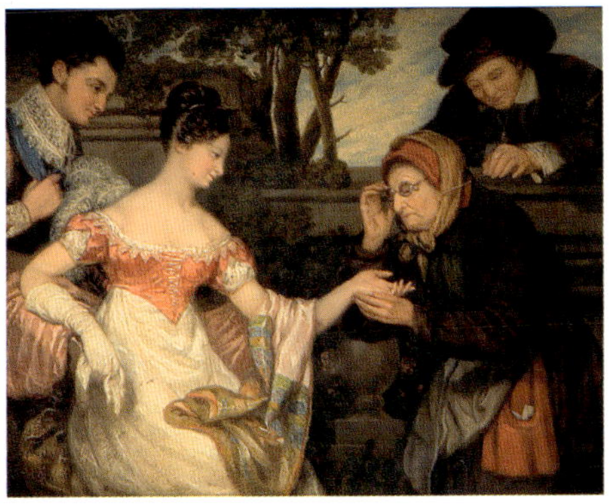

Rippingille, Edward Villiers 1798–1859
The Fortune Teller
oil on canvas 29 x 35.5
OP44

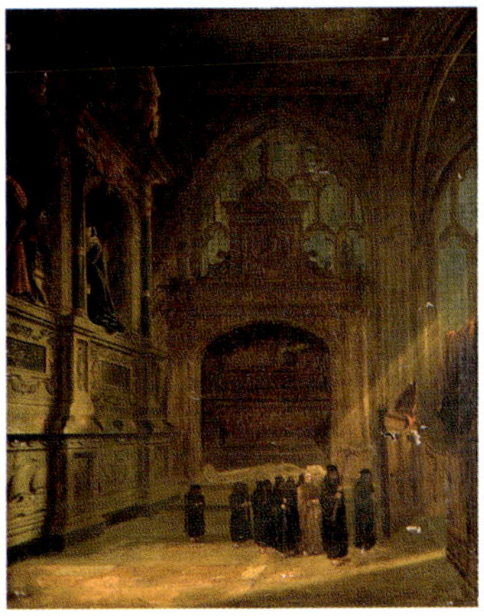

Roberts, David 1796–1864
Interior of Cologne Cathedral, with a Funeral
1838
oil on canvas 91.5 x 72
OP101

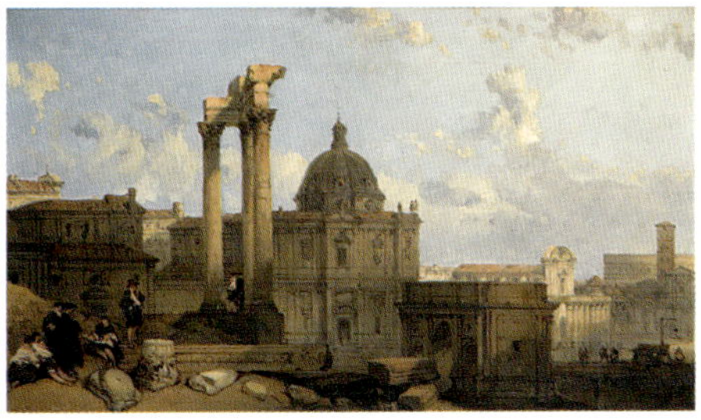

Roberts, David 1796–1864
Ruins of the Roman Forum 1859
oil on panel 38.5 x 62.5
OP212

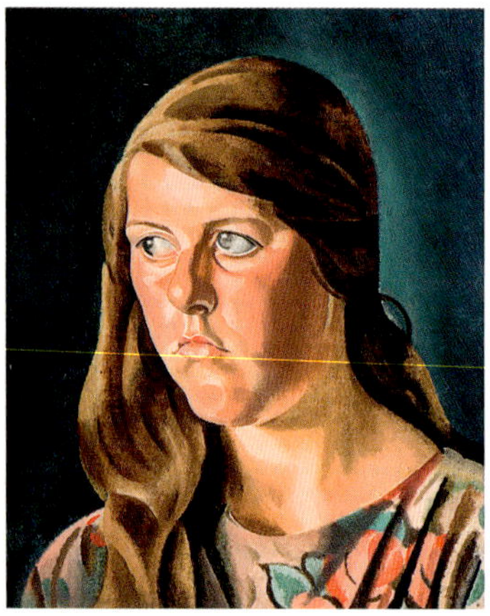

Roberts, William Patrick 1895–1980
Kit Roberts
oil on canvas 51 x 40.5
OP334

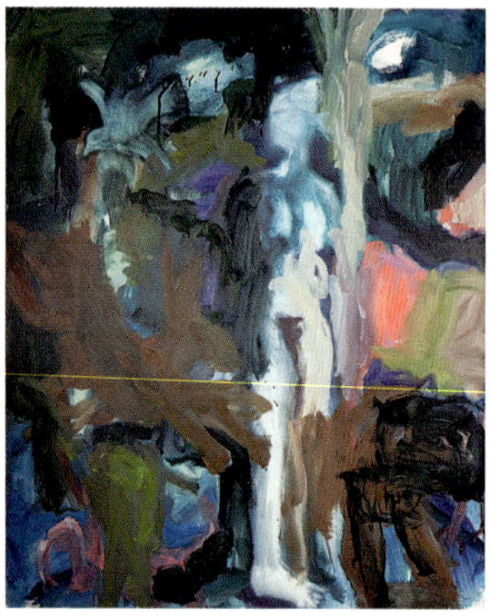

Ross, Arabella b.1959
The March Hare 1980–1988
oil on canvas 152 x 121
OP814

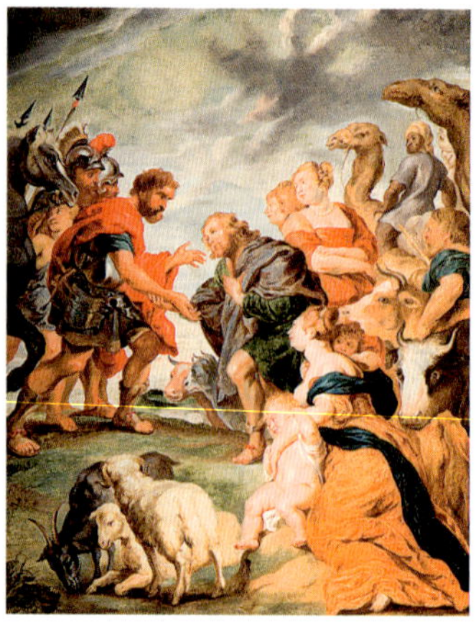

Rubens, Peter Paul (after) 1577–1640
The Meeting of Esau and Jacob 18th C
oil on panel 65.5 x 51.5
OP158

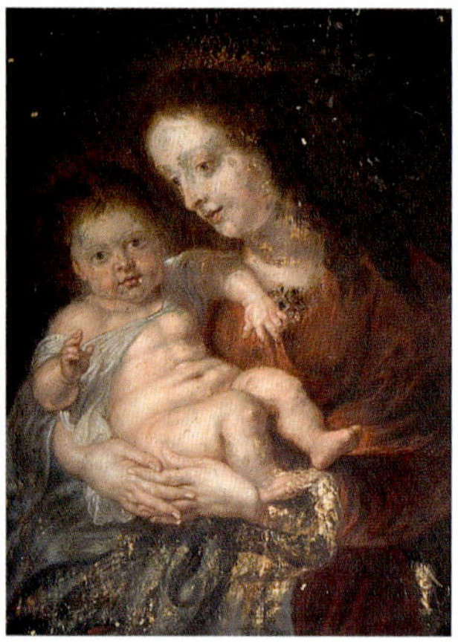

Rubens, Peter Paul (after) 1577–1640
Virgin and Child
oil on panel 44 x 32.5
OP276

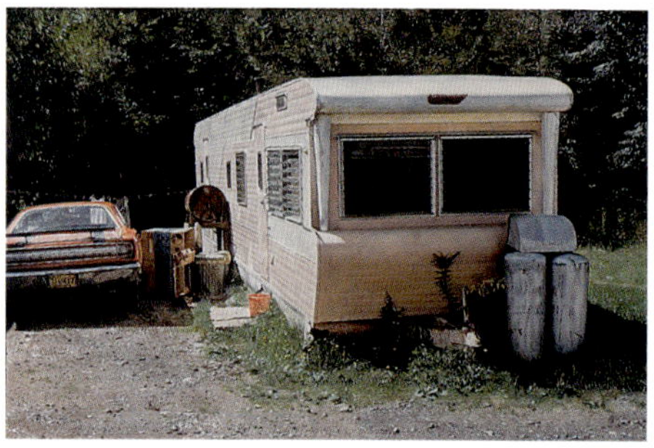

Salt, John b.1937
Pink Trailer with Plymouth 1974
oil on canvas 109 x 161.5
OP605

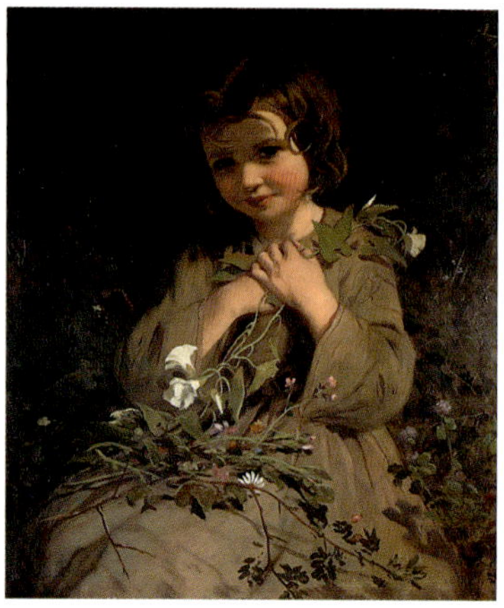

Sant, James 1820–1916
Wild Flowers
oil on canvas 76 x 63.5
OP402

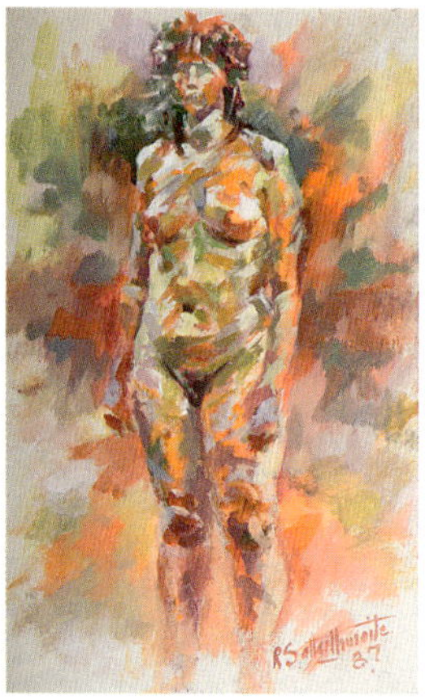

Satterthwaite, R.
Figure Study (front) 1987
oil on canvas 40 x 24.5
OP888

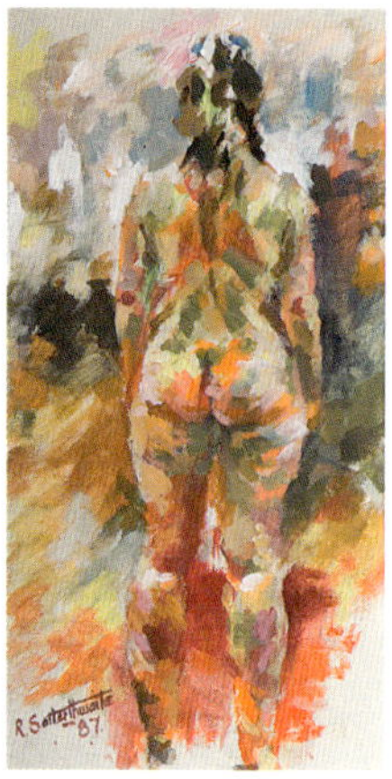

Satterthwaite, R.
Figure Study (back) 1987
oil on canvas 40 x 20
OP889

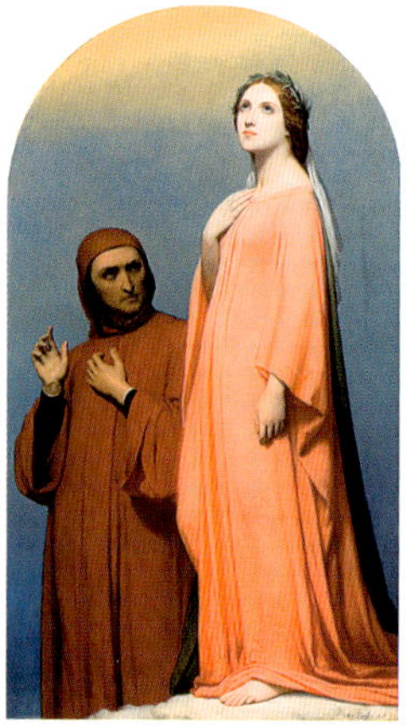

Scheffer, Ary 1795–1858
The Vision, Dante and Beatrice 1846
oil on canvas 200.5 x 109.5
OP249

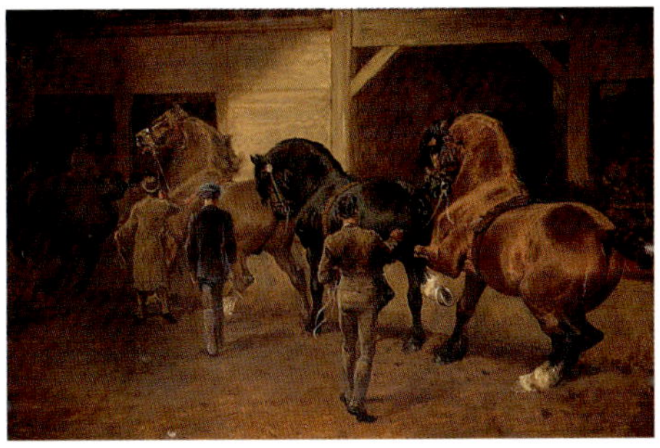

Shaillon, John
Carthorse Stallions
oil on canvas 86.5 x 128.5
OP414

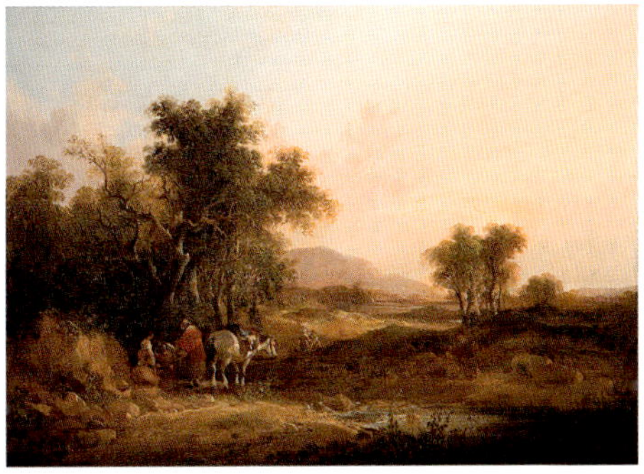

Shayer, William 1788–1879
Landscape
oil on canvas 45 x 61
OP209

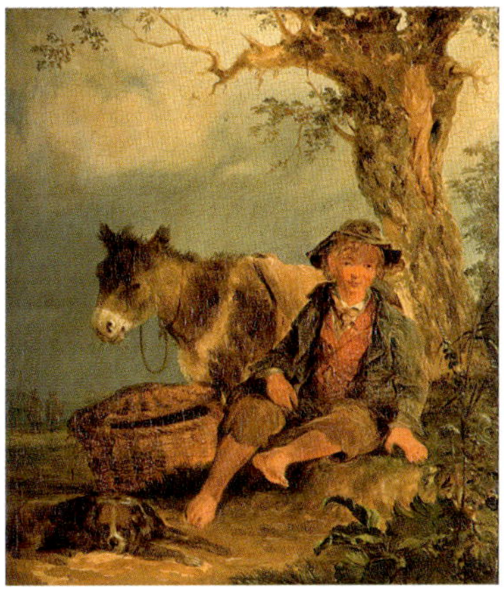

Shayer, William 1788–1879
Landscape with a Boy and Donkey
oil on board 35 x 30
OP185

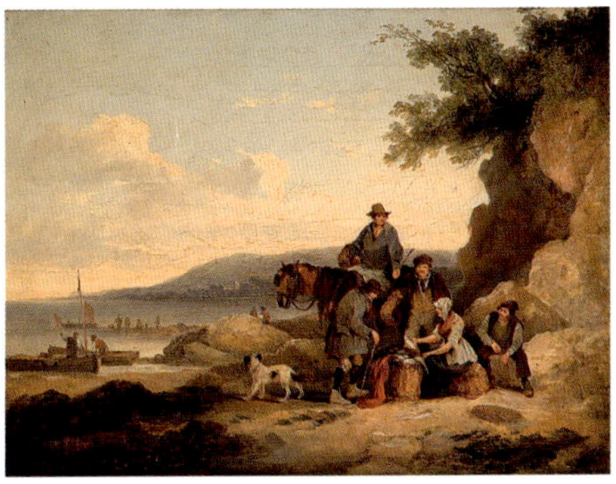

Shayer, William 1788–1879
On the Beach at Portishead
oil on canvas 35.5 x 45.5
OP196

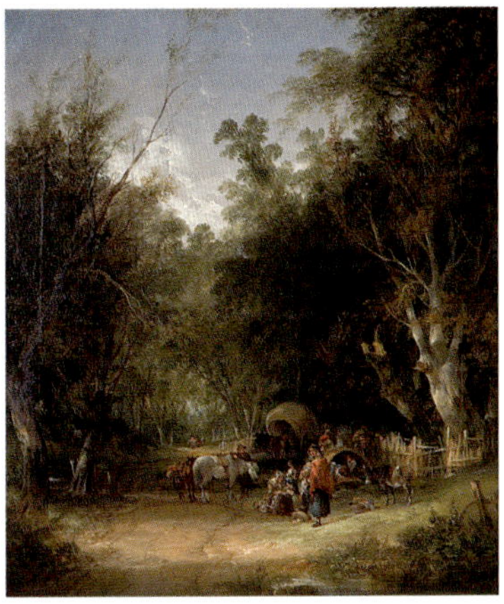

Shayer, William 1788–1879
The Gypsy Tent
oil on canvas 76 x 63.5
OP226

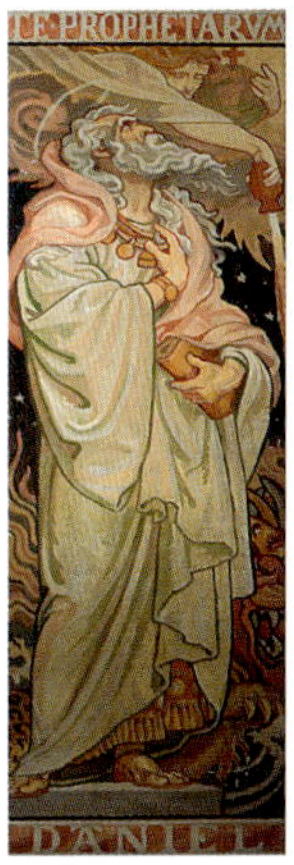

Shields, Frederick 1833–1911
Stained Glass Design, Daniel 1900–1910
oil on canvas 169 x 51
OP500

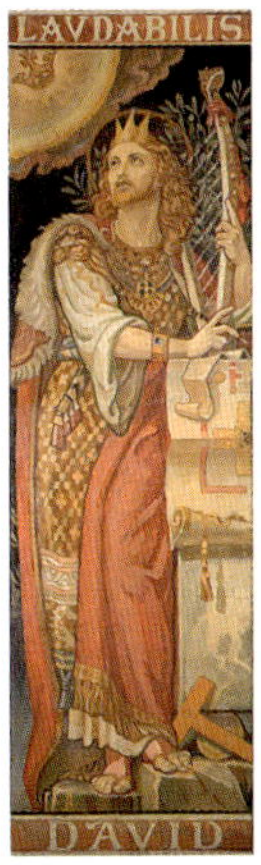

Shields, Frederick 1833–1911
Stained Glass Design, David 1900–1910
oil on canvas 171 x 50
OP503

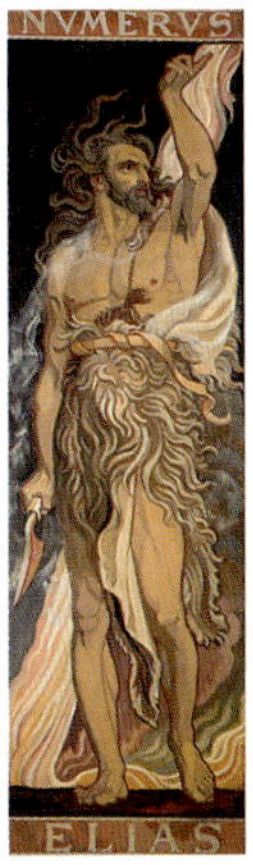

Shields, Frederick 1833–1911
Stained Glass Design, Elias 1900–1910
oil on canvas 170 x 50
OP496

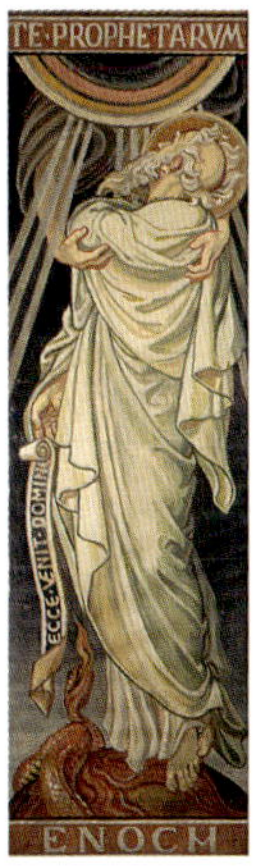

Shields, Frederick 1833–1911
Stained Glass Design, Enoch 1900–1910
oil on canvas 172.5 x 51
OP498

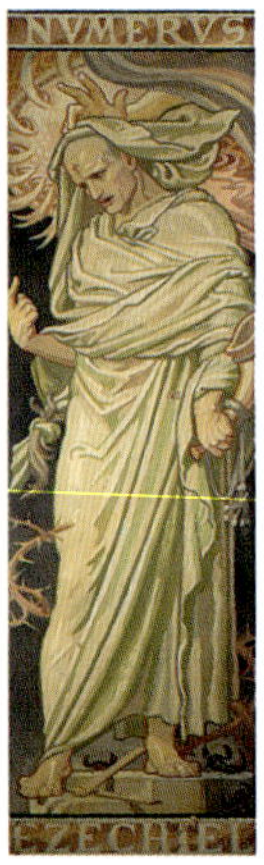

Shields, Frederick 1833–1911
Stained Glass Design, Ezekiel 1900–1910
oil on canvas 170 x 50
OP494

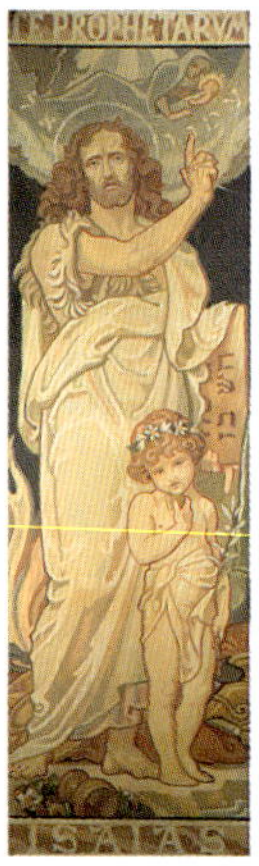

Shields, Frederick 1833–1911
Stained Glass Design, Isaiah 1900–1910
oil on canvas 171 x 49.5
OP501

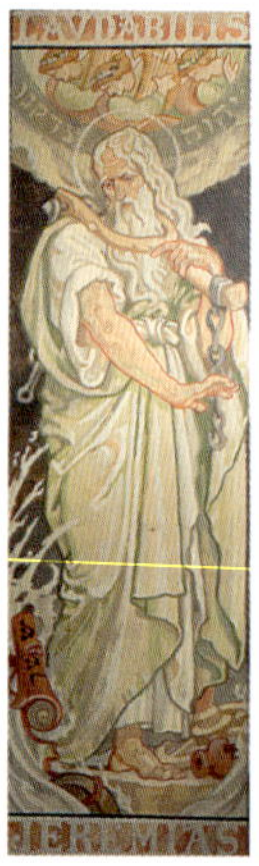

Shields, Frederick 1833–1911
Stained Glass Design, Jeremiah 1900–1910
oil on canvas 172.5 x 51
OP493

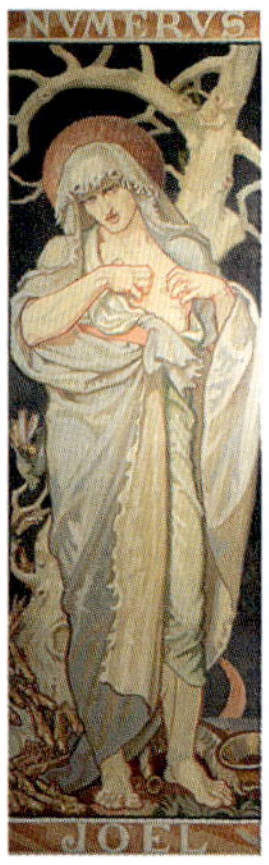

Shields, Frederick 1833–1911
Stained Glass Design, Joel 1900–1910
oil on canvas 170 x 50
OP495

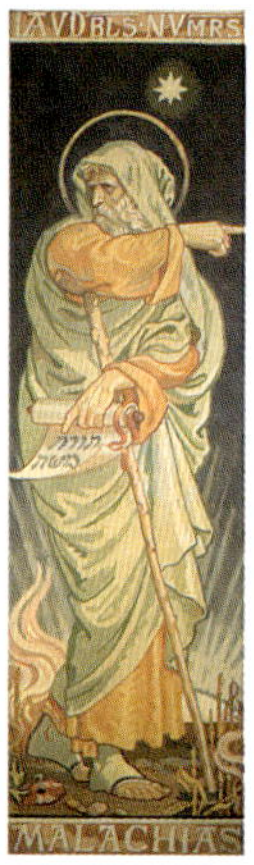

Shields, Frederick 1833–1911
Stained Glass Design, Malachi 1900–1910
oil on canvas 171 x 50
OP502

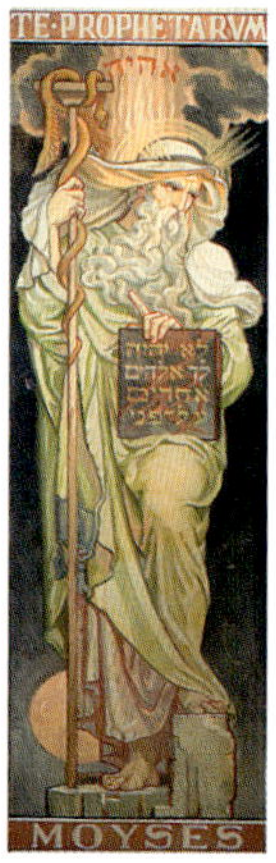

Shields, Frederick 1833–1911
Stained Glass Design, Moses 1900–1910
oil on canvas 171.5 x 50
OP499

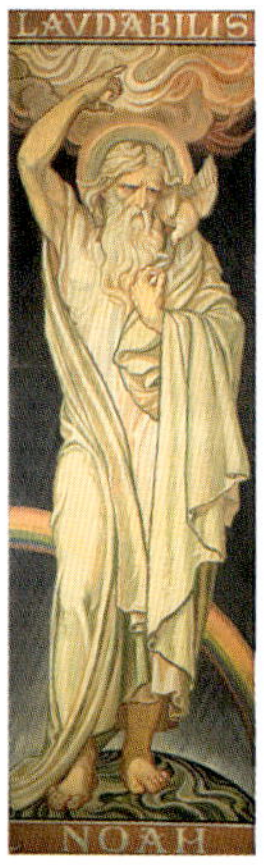

Shields, Frederick 1833–1911
Stained Glass Design, Noah 1900–1910
oil on canvas 170 x 49
OP497

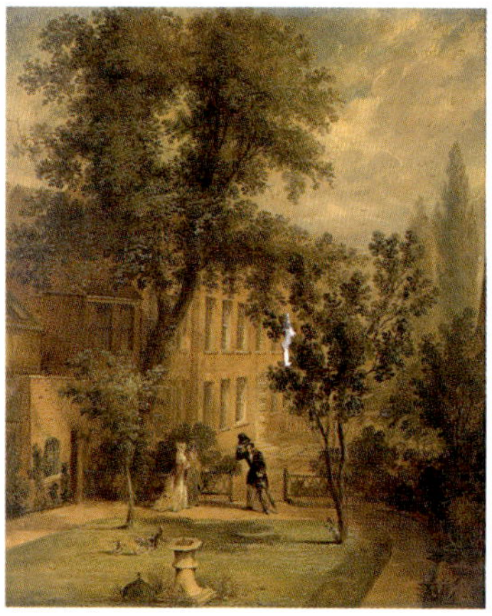

Shipham, Benjamin 1808–1872
Abel Chetwynd's Gift
oil on panel 38 x 35.5
OP608

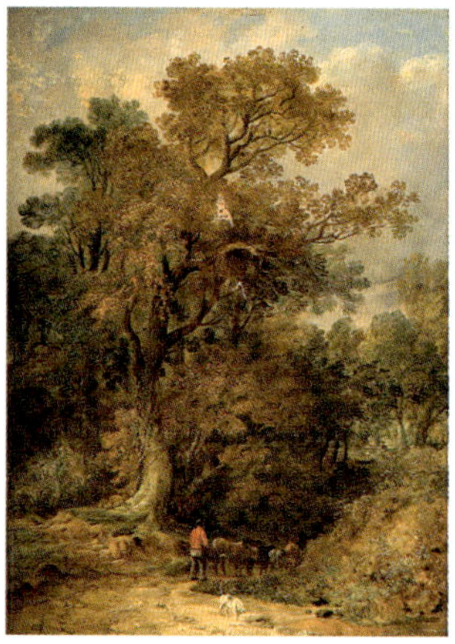

Shipham, Benjamin 1808–1872
In Epping Forest
oil on canvas 59 x 41
OP538

Facing page: Pemsel, Oliver, 1910–1989, *The Lock Gates* (detail), c.1935, The Potteries Museum & Art Gallery (p. 147)

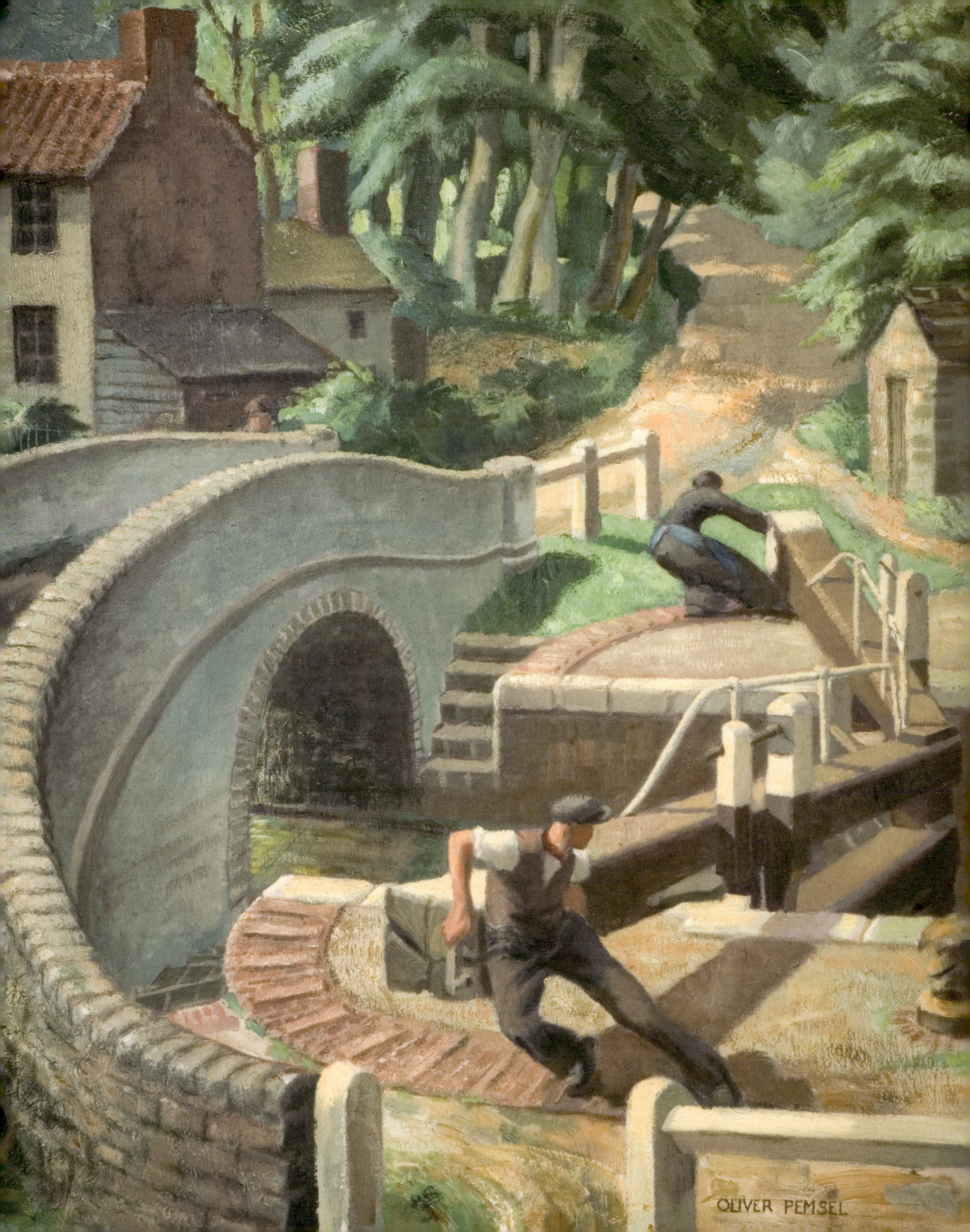
OLIVER PEMSEL

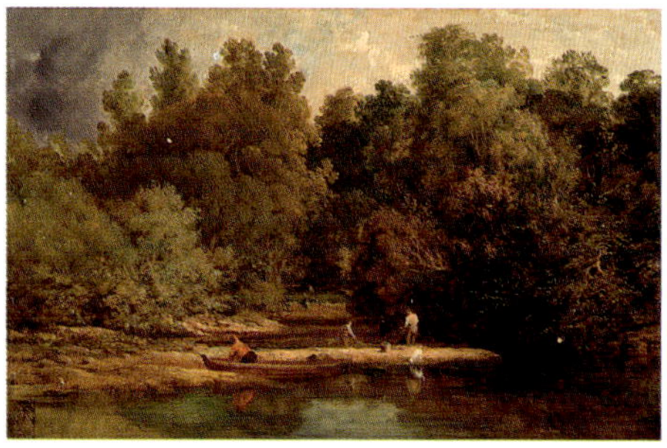

Shipham, Benjamin 1808–1872
On the Trent
oil on canvas 30.5 x 45.5
OP282

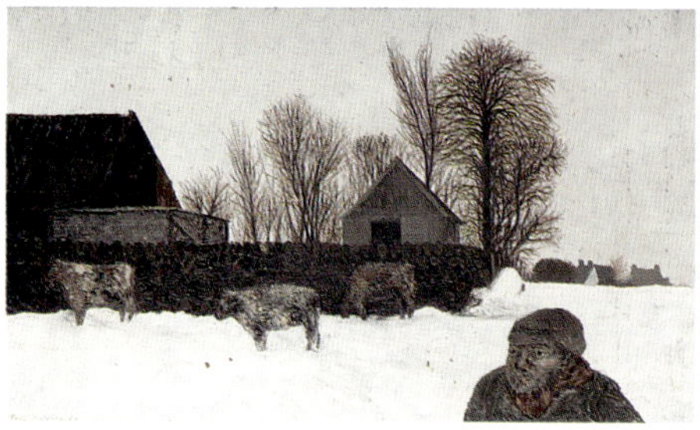

Simcock, Jack b.1929
Snowscape with Cows and Figures 1960
oil on hardboard 38 x 61
OP63

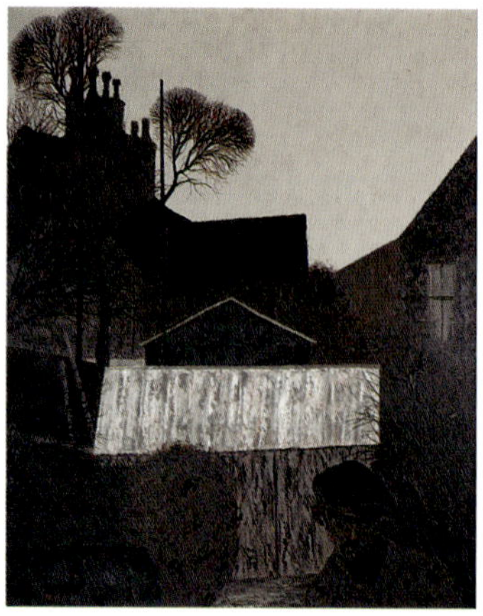

Simcock, Jack b.1929
Bourne Street, Mow Cop 1962
oil on hardboard 76 x 61
OP69

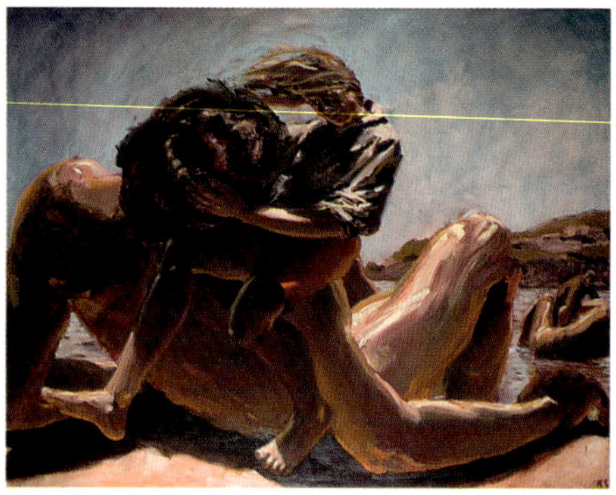

Sinnott, Kevin b.1947
Down to Earth 1990
oil on canvas 142 x 177
OP863

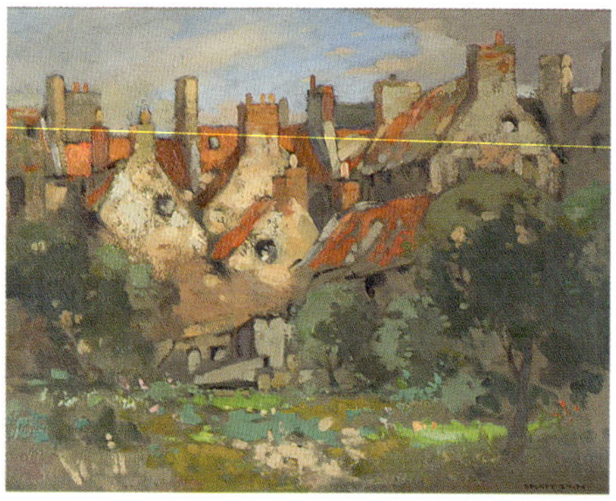

Smith, John Guthrie Spence 1880–1951
Red Roofs
oil on canvas 40.5 x 51
OP916

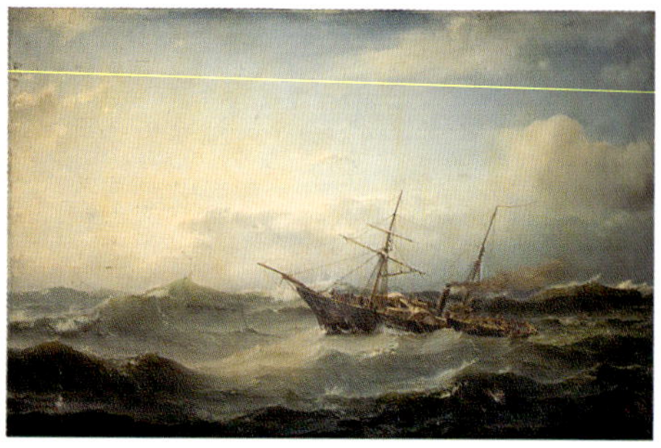

Sørensen, Carl Frederik 1818–1879
Storm in the North Sea
oil on canvas 118 x 173.5
OP425

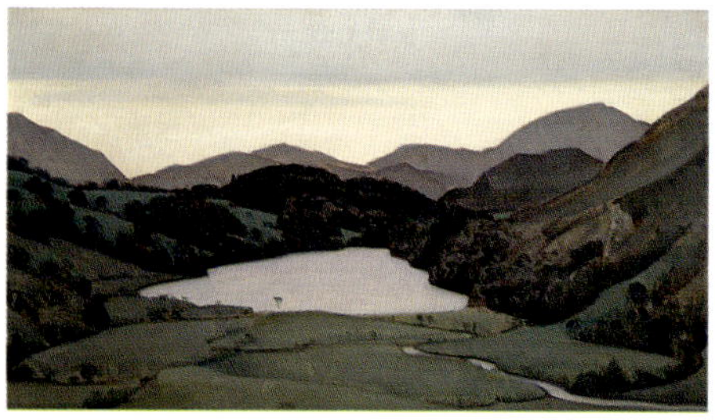

Speed, Harold 1872–1957
Llyn Gwynant after Rain
oil on canvas 40.5 x 68.5
OP104

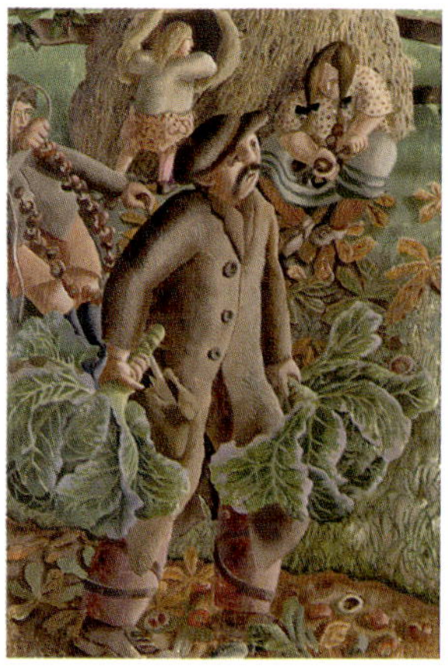

Spencer, Stanley 1891–1959
Chestnuts 1935–1945
oil on paper 39.5 x 25
OP787

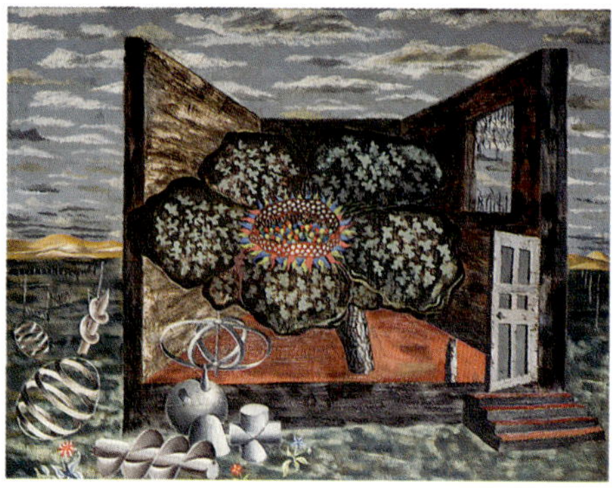

Spender, John Humphrey 1910–2005
Atomic Flower 1939–1940
oil on canvas 51 x 61
OP799

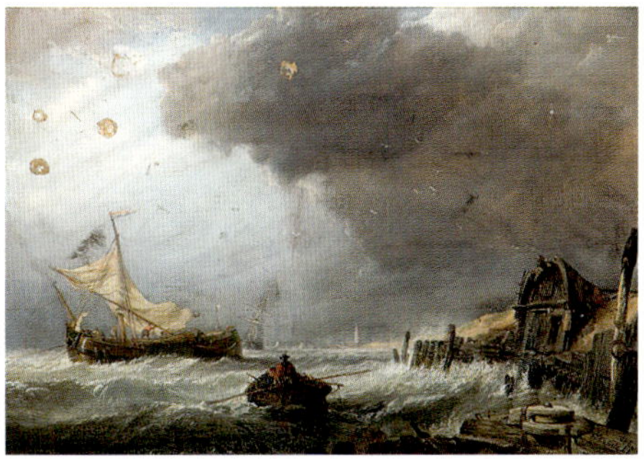

Stanfield, Clarkson 1793–1867
Off Calais 1856
oil on panel 41.5 x 57
OP280

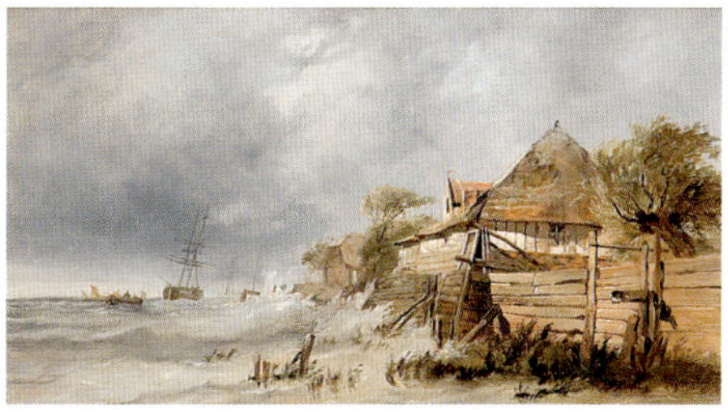

Stanfield, George Clarkson 1828–1878
Off the Dutch Coast
oil on canvas 38.5 x 66
OP136

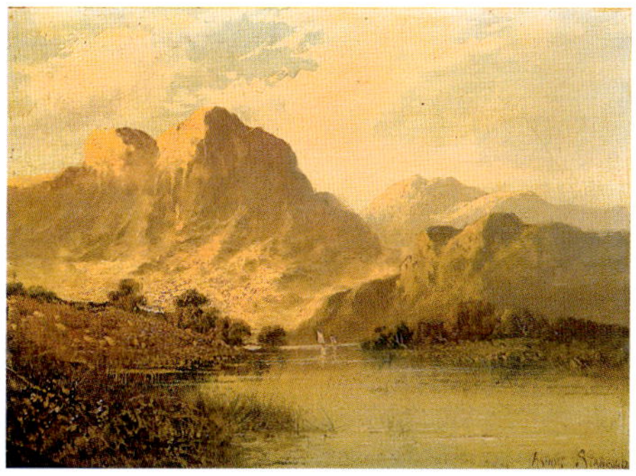

Stanford, Arthur
Mountain and Lake
oil on canvas 38 x 51
OP539

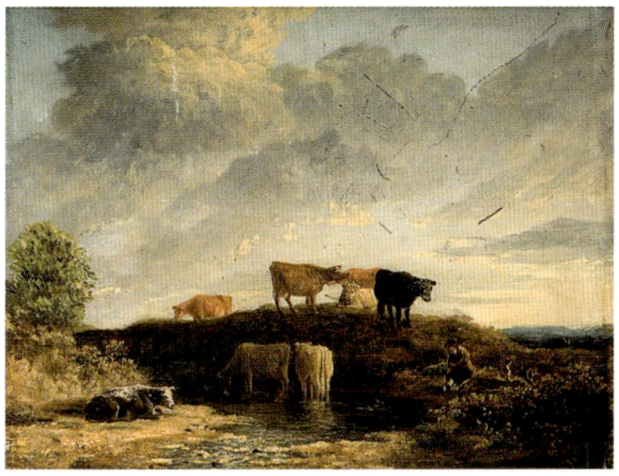

Stark, James 1794–1859
Cows at a Watering Place
oil on panel 35.5 x 44.5
OP278

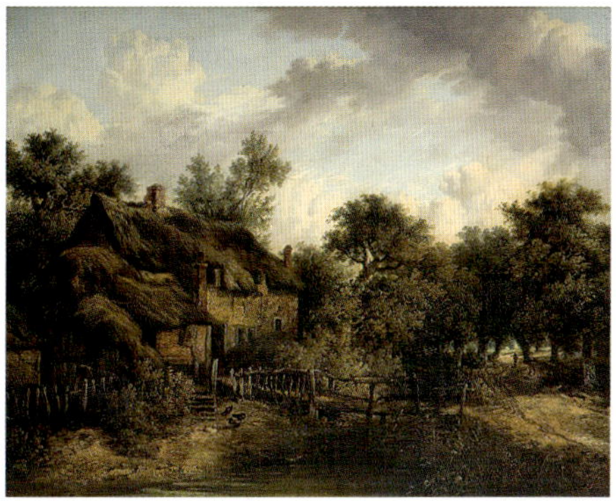

Stark, James 1794–1859
Landscape with a Cottage
oil on canvas 63.5 x 76
OP240

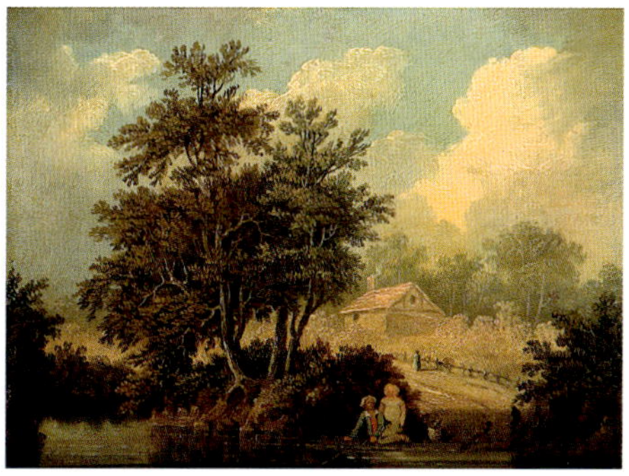

Stark, James 1794–1859
Landscape with Figures at a Stream
oil on canvas 23 x 28.5
OP243

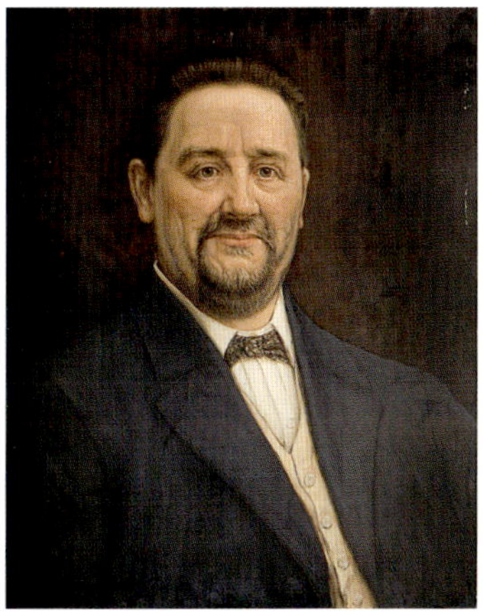

Steadman, J. T. active 1884–1911
Councillor Craddock
oil on board 38 x 32
OP721

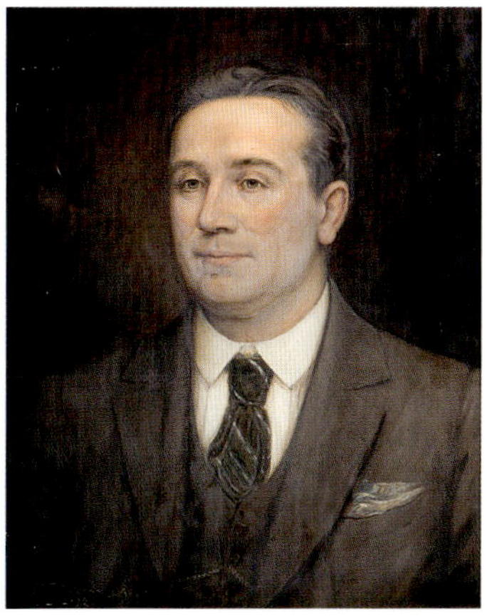

Steadman, J. T. active 1884–1911
H. Beach
oil on canvas 66.5 x 52
OP723

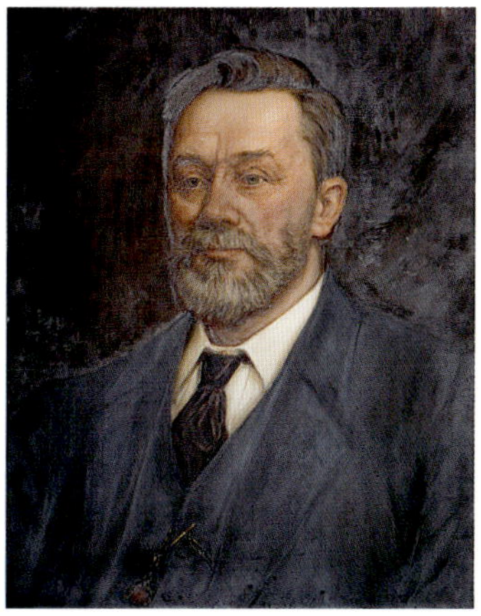

Steadman, J. T. active 1884–1911
W. Hughes
oil on canvas 66 x 51
OP722

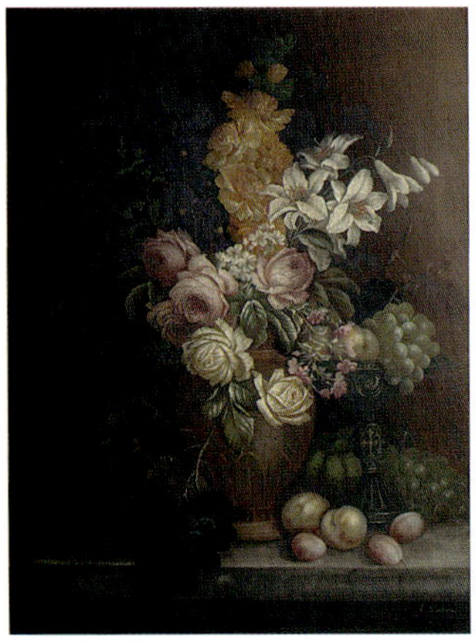

Steele, Edwin 1837–1898
Still Life, Flowers
oil on canvas 91.5 x 72.5
OP724

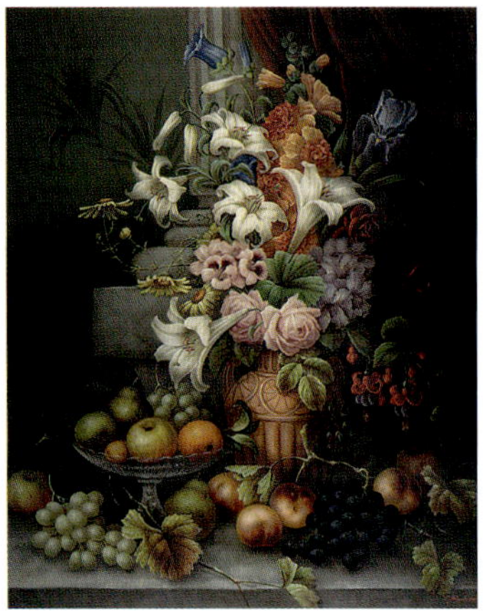

Steele, Edwin 1837–1898
Still Life, Flowers and Fruit
oil on canvas 100 x 77.5
OP725

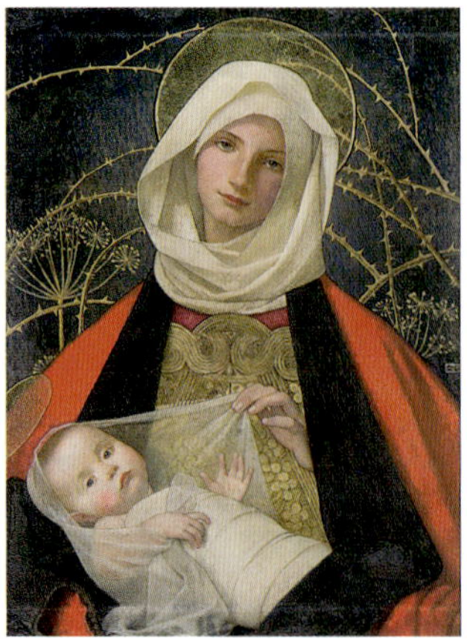

Stokes, Marianne 1855–1927
Madonna and Child
tempera on panel 81 x 61
OP272

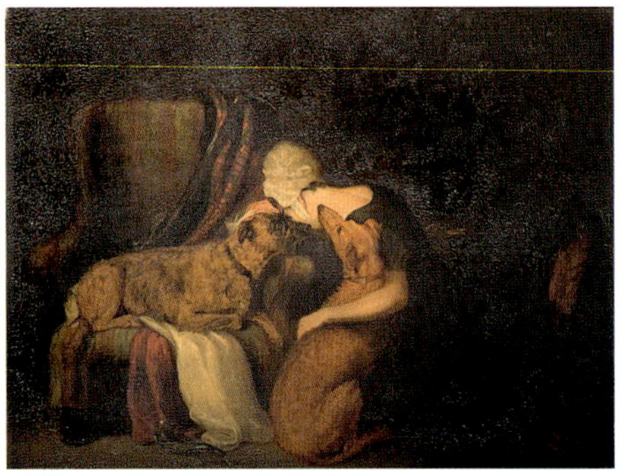

Stone, Frank 1800–1859
Sympathy
oil on panel 38 x 47
OP151

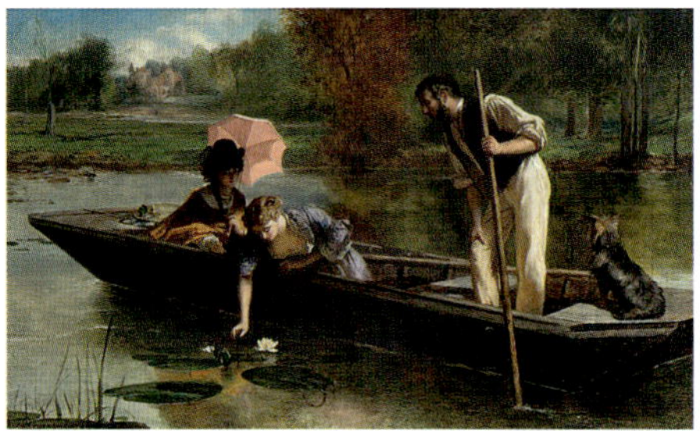

Stone, Marcus C. 1840–1921
A Pleasant Spot on the Thames 1863
oil on canvas 38 x 61
OP191

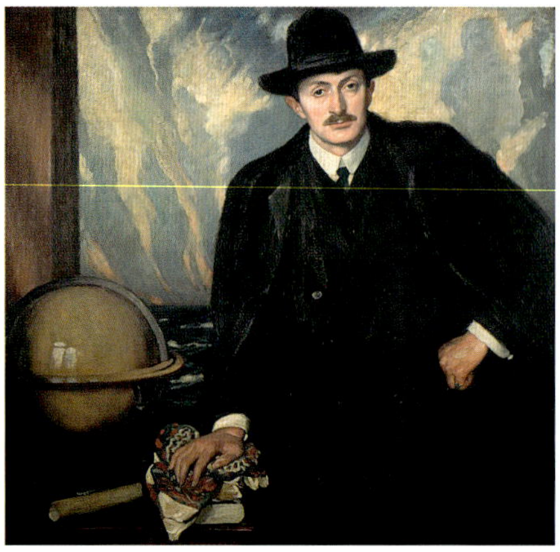

Strang, William 1859–1921
John Masefield (1878–1967) 1909
oil on canvas 122 x 122
OP336

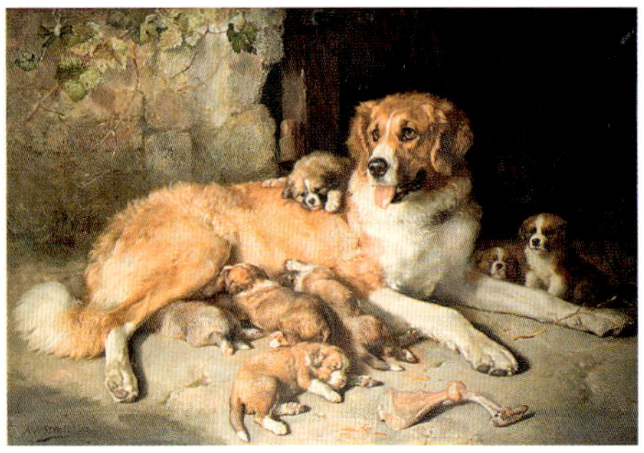

Strutt, Alfred William 1856–1924
Materfamilias 1870–1883
oil on canvas 114.5 x 159
OP326

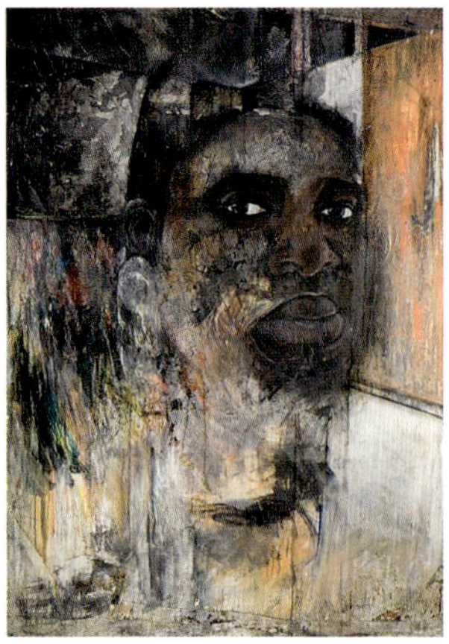

Suberu, Ade
Mirror Image I
mixed media on board 153 x 107
OP858

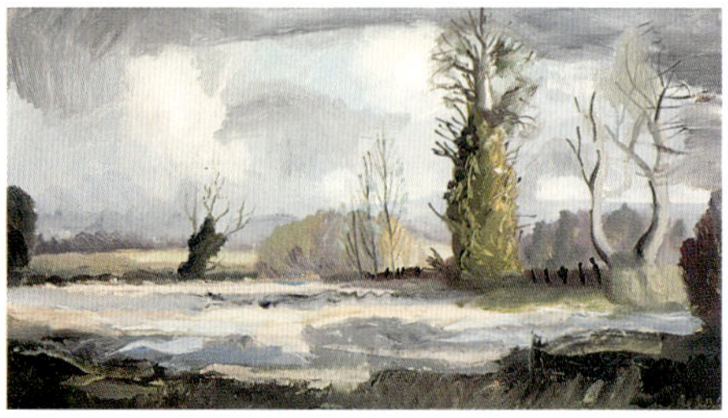

Suddaby, Rowland 1912–1972
Stour Valley, Suffolk
oil on board 35 x 48.5
OP726

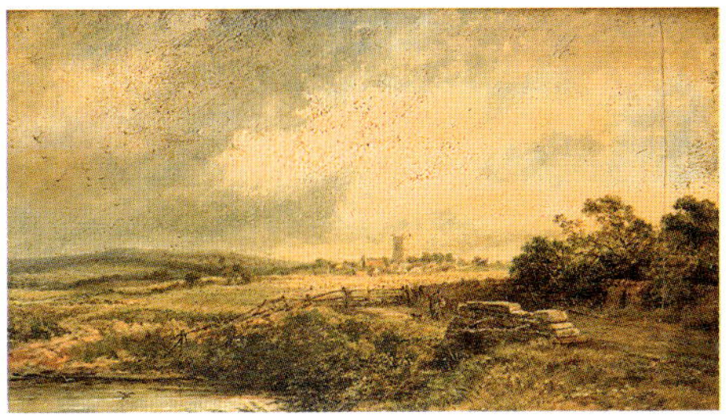

Syer, John 1815–1885
Country Landscape 1863
oil on panel 31.8 x 52.1
OP5

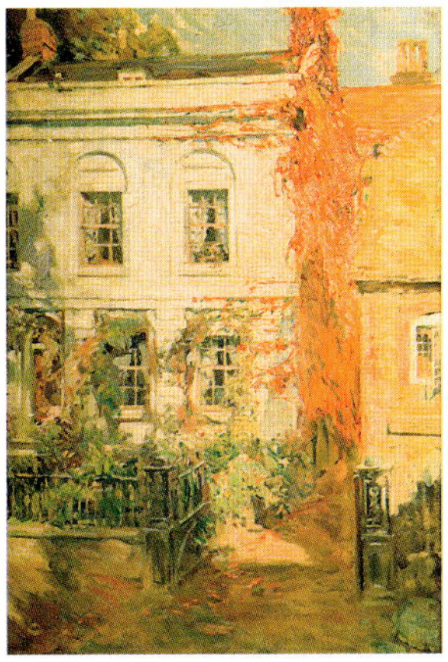

Symons, William Christian 1845–1911
The White House, Battle, Sussex
oil on canvas 74 x 49
OP303

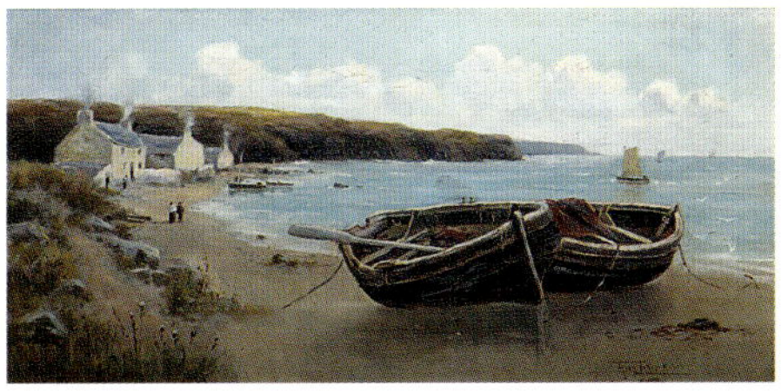

Tawson, Alex
On the Anglesey Coast
oil on canvas 31 x 59.5
OP771

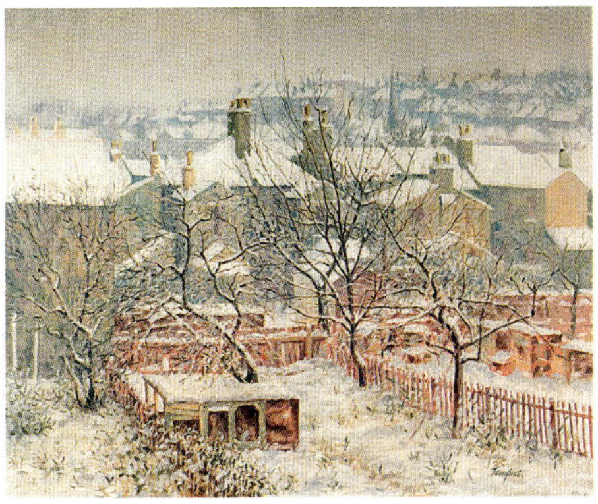

Tempest, Victor 1913–2003
Gardens in February 1935
oil on canvas 50.8 x 61
OP314

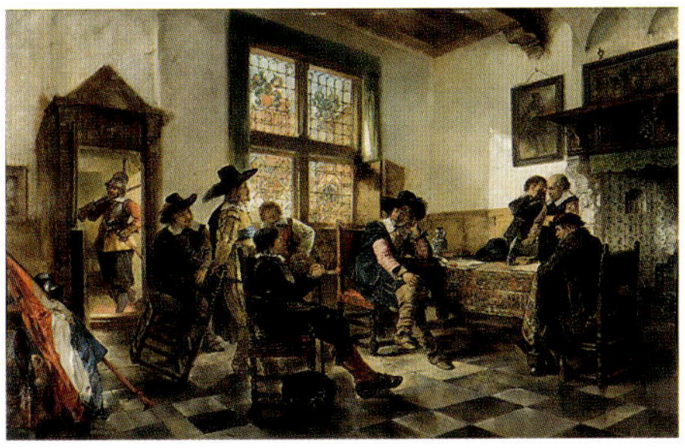

Tenkate, Herman 1822–1891
A Difference of Opinion as to a Treaty
oil on panel 61 x 94
OP455

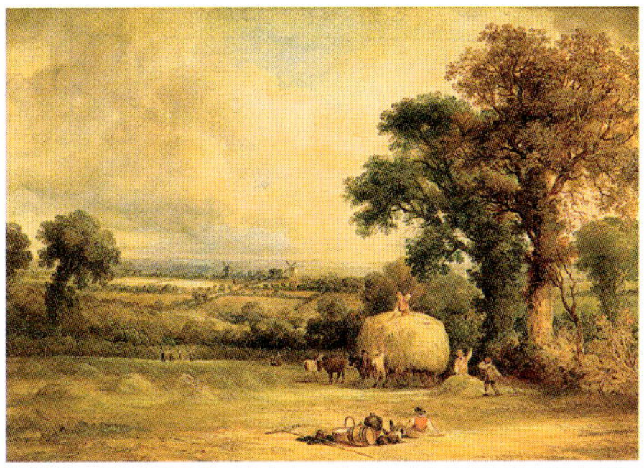

Tennant, John F. 1796–1872
Loading the Hay Wagon 1839
oil on canvas 55.9 x 76.2
OP115

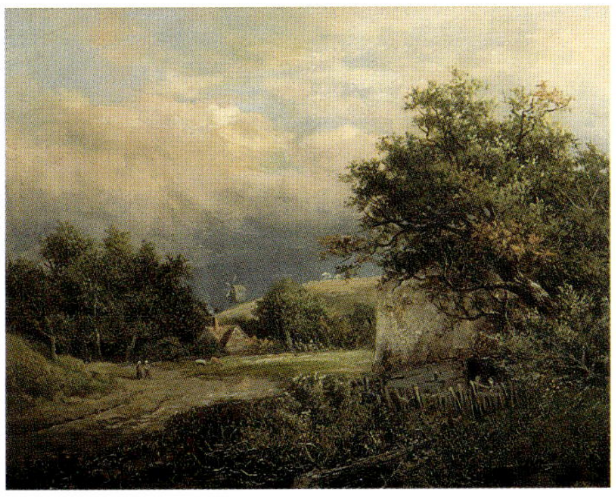

Thors, Joseph c.1834–1898
A Welsh Landscape
oil on board 25.5 x 30.5
OP223

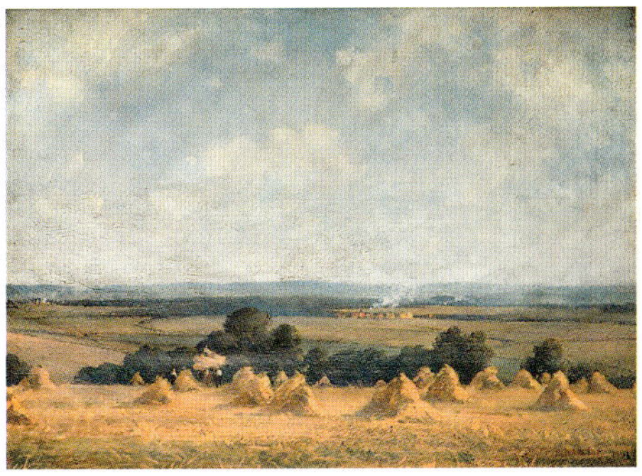

Toft, J. Alfonso 1866–1964
The Cornfield
oil on canvas 45.5 x 61
OP387

Toft, J. Alfonso 1866–1964
Windsor Castle
oil on canvas 51 x 61
OP391

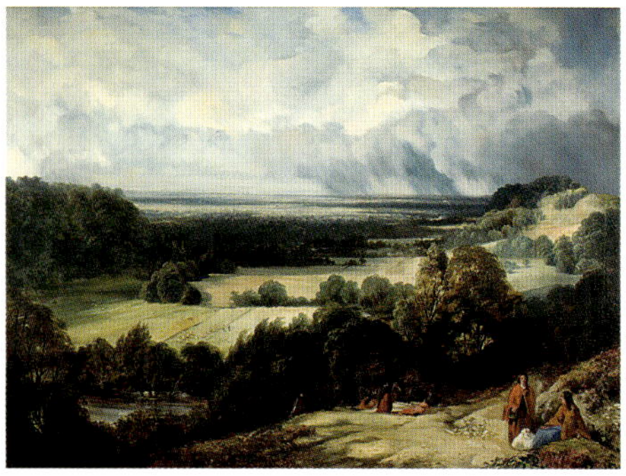

Tongue, Richard active 1835–1839
Landscape
oil on canvas 73.5 x 94
OP727

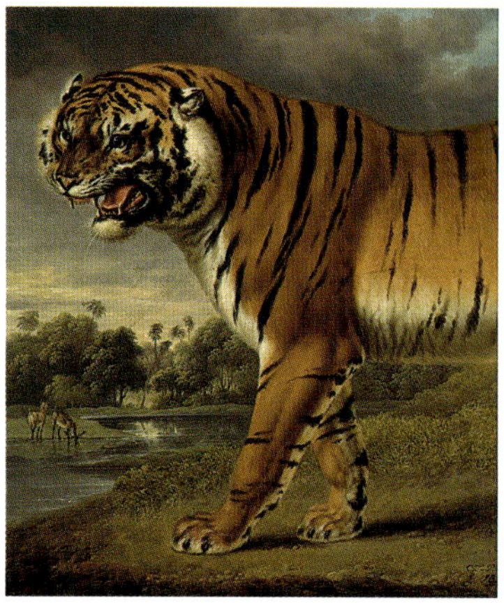

Towne, Charles 1781–1854
A Tiger 1818
oil on panel 33.5 x 22
OP338

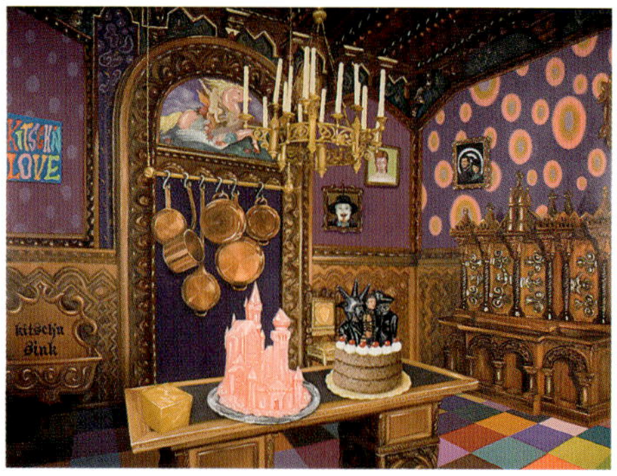

Treister, Suzanne b.1958
Entering the Kitchen 1995
oil on canvas 167.5 x 212
OP883

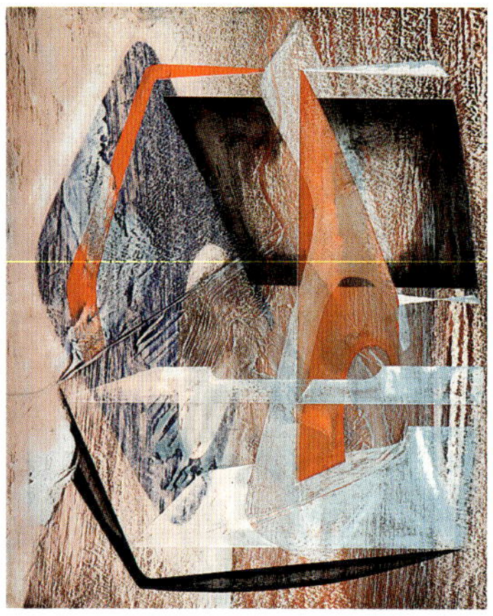

Tunnard, John 1900–1971
Pink Composition 1940s
oil on board 51 x 41.5
OP855

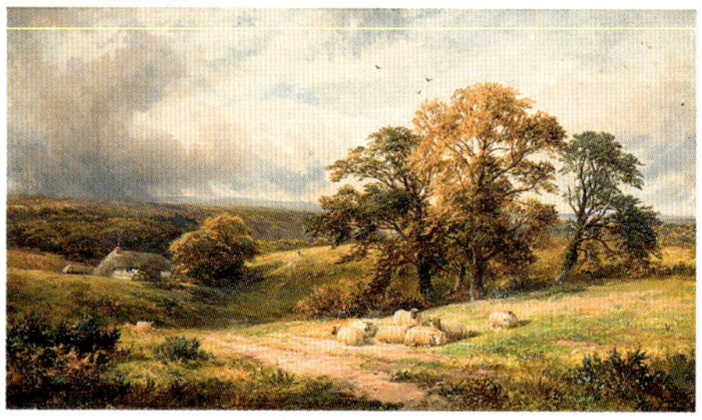

Turner, George II 1843–1910
A Quiet Scene in South Derbyshire 1885
oil on canvas 44 x 51
OP271

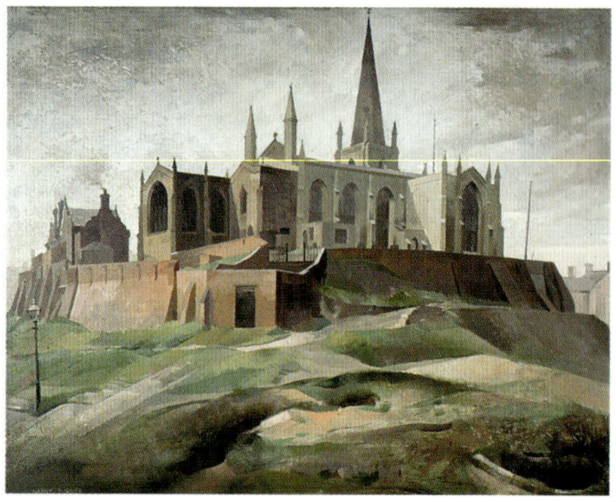

Turner, Harry M. 1912–1979
Walsall Church
oil on board 48 x 58
OP767

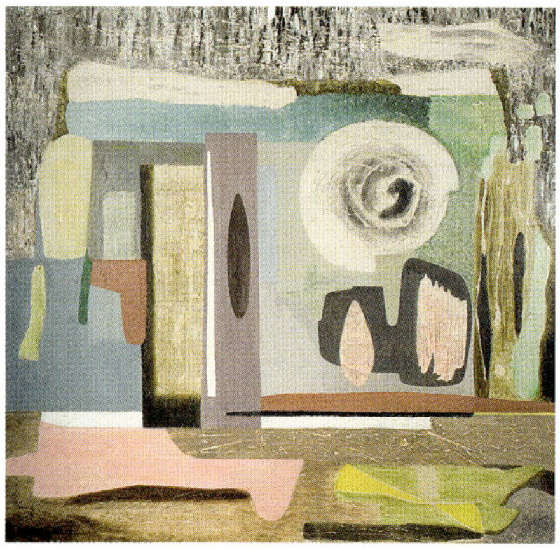

Twentyman, Anthony b.1906
Equinox
oil on board 119 x 122
OP765

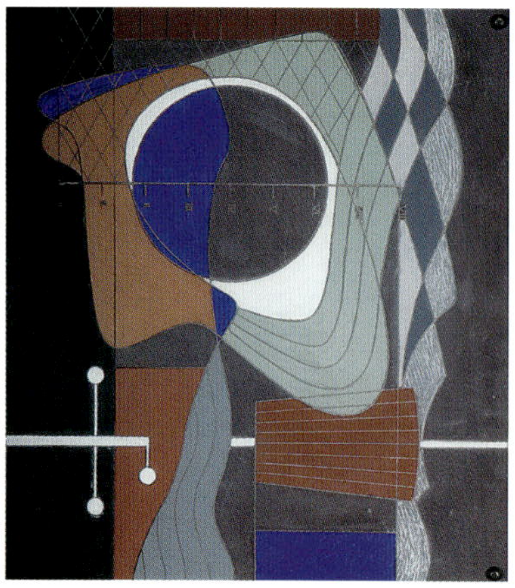

Twentyman, Anthony b.1906
Marine Image
oil on slate 35 x 30
OP830

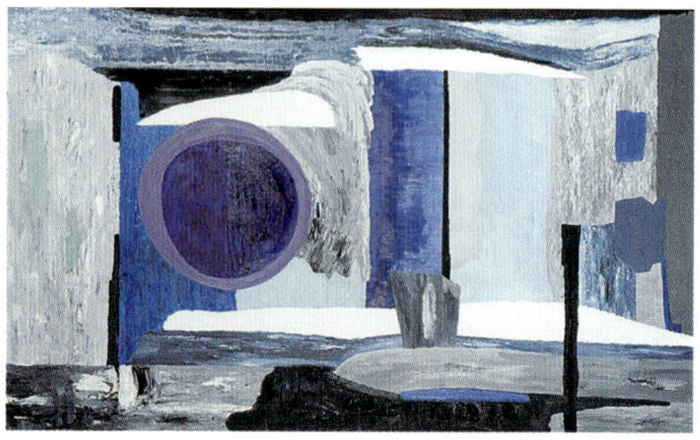

Twentyman, Anthony b.1906
Winter
oil on board 81.5 x 122
OP760

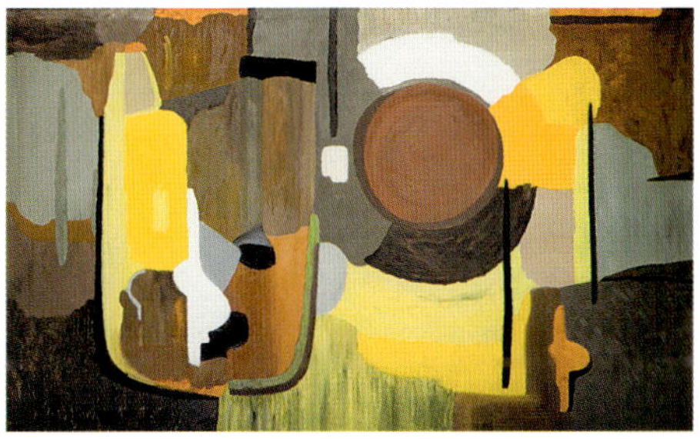

Twentyman, Anthony b.1906
Spring
oil on board 81 x 122
OP763

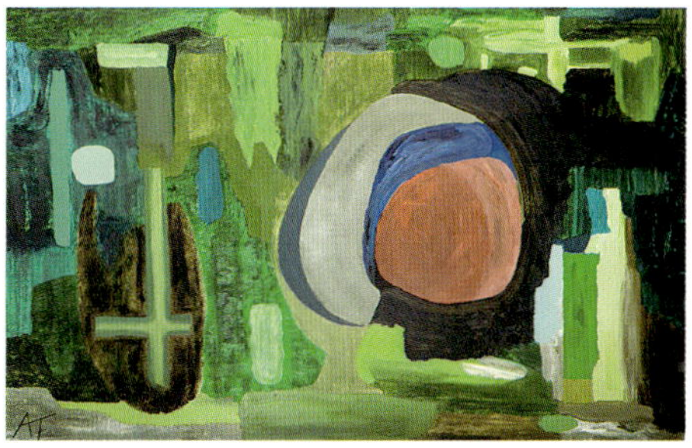

Twentyman, Anthony b.1906
Summer
oil on board 81.5 x 122
OP762

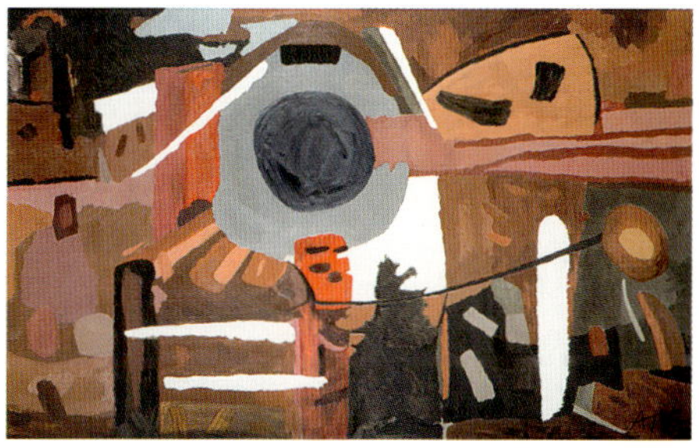

Twentyman, Anthony b.1906
Autumn
oil on canvas 81.5 x 122
OP761

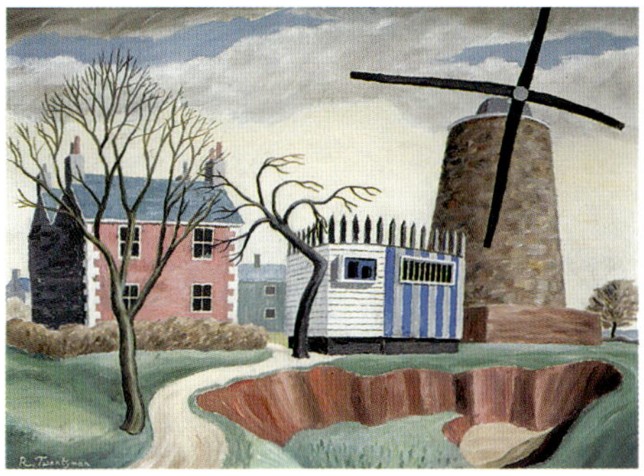

Twentyman, Richard 1903–1979
Pigeon Loft, Sedgley
oil on board 45 x 61
OP758

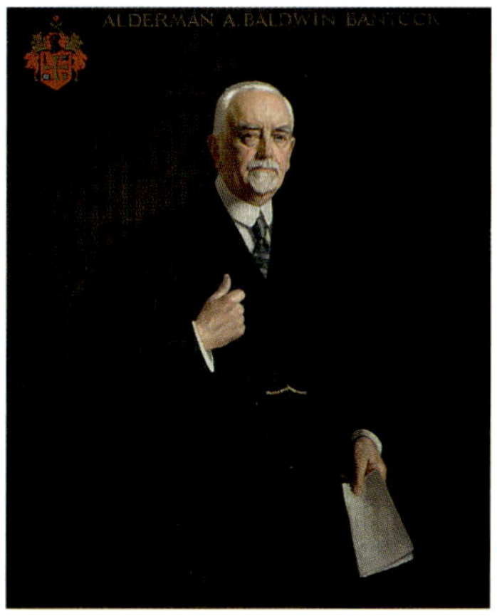

Underhill, William active 1848–1871
Alderman Albert Baldwin Bantock (1862–1938)
oil on canvas 129.5 x 103
OP487

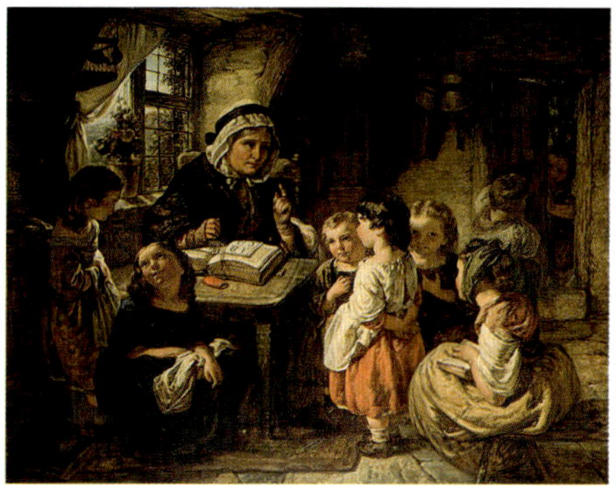

Underhill, William active 1848–1871
The Village School
oil on canvas 101.5 x 127
OP242

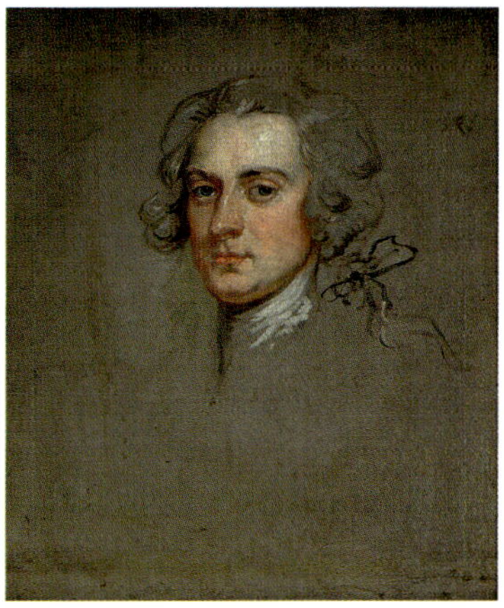

unknown artist
Portrait of a Gentleman 1740
oil on canvas 60.9 x 50.8
OP165

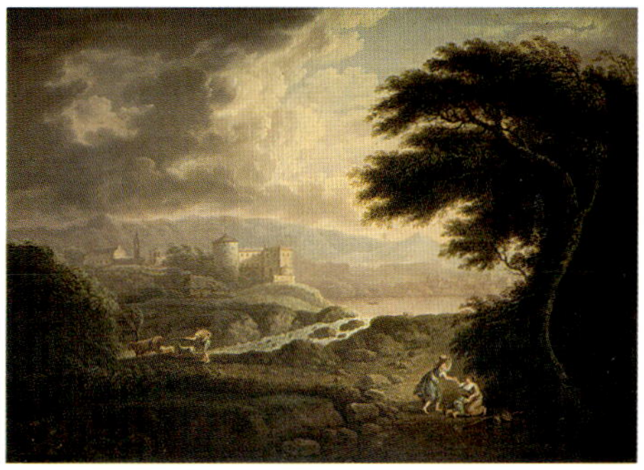

unknown artist 18th C
Italian Landscape
oil on canvas 58.5 x 78.5
OP116

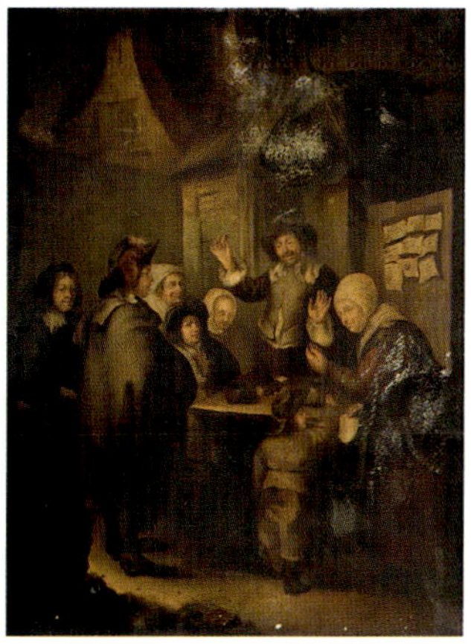

unknown artist late 18th C
The Card Sharper
oil on canvas 45.5 x 35.5
OP277

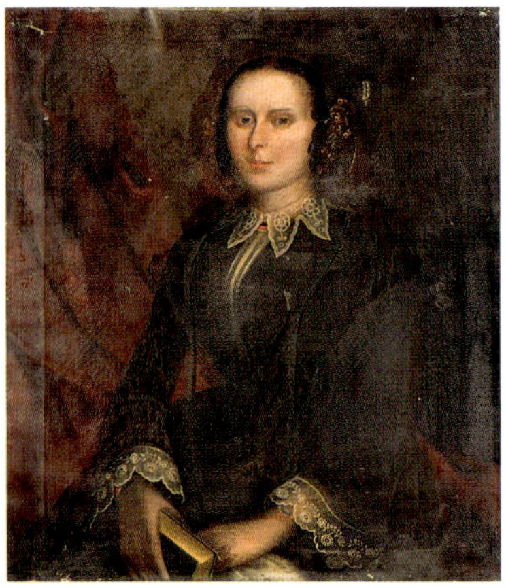

unknown artist
Portrait of a Lady 1850–1875
oil on canvas 76.2 x 63.5
OP400

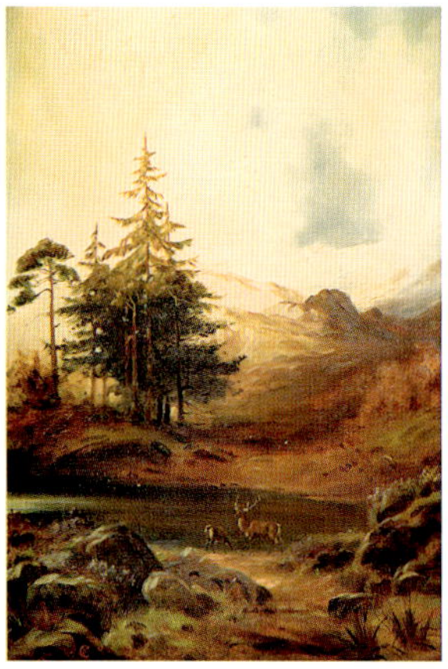

unknown artist 19th C
Highland Landscape with Two Stags
oil on canvas 61 x 40.5
OP688

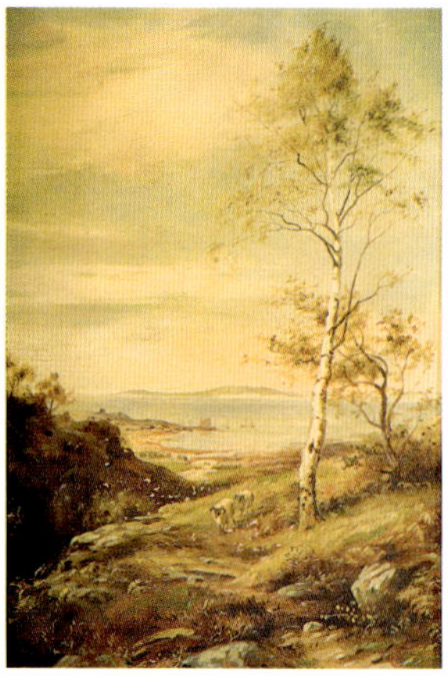

unknown artist 19th C
Landscape with Sheep, Sea and Boats
oil on canvas 61 x 40.5
OP687

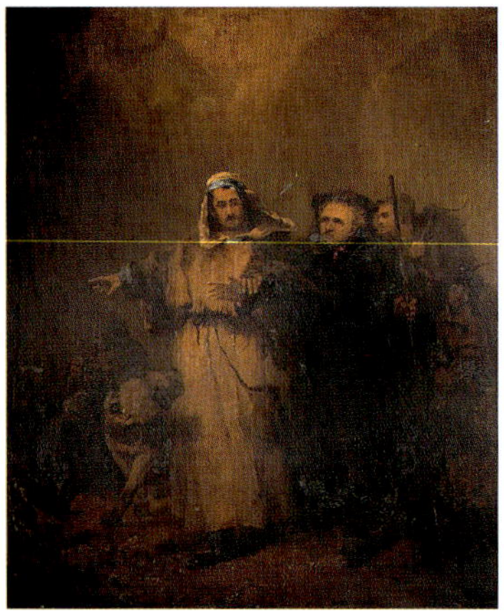

unknown artist 19th C
Monk, St Bernard Dog and Men in a Storm
oil on canvas 112 x 89
OP599

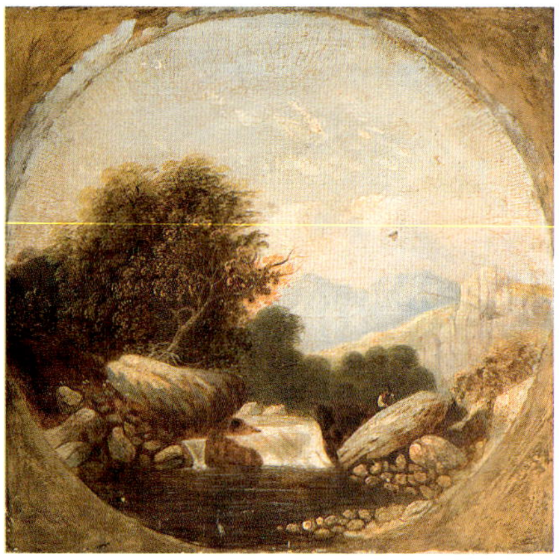

unknown artist 19th C
River Scene
oil on canvas 35.5 x 35.5
OP469

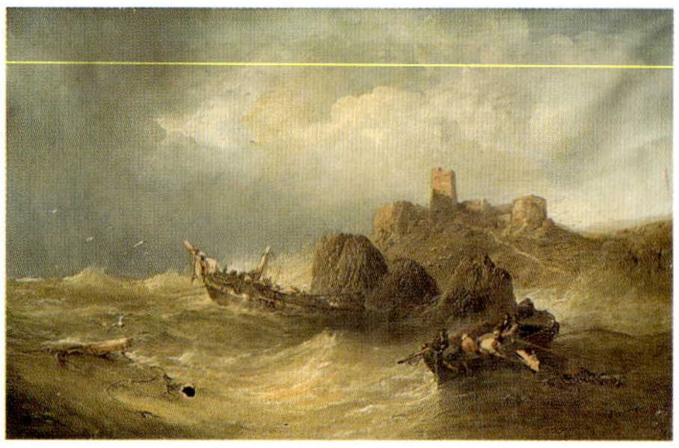

unknown artist 19th C
Shipwreck
oil on canvas 61 x 91.5
OP381

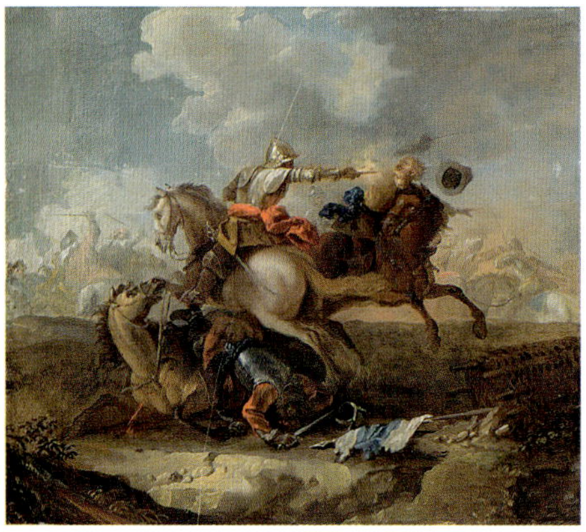

unknown artist
Battle Scene
oil on canvas 54.5 x 59.5
OP520

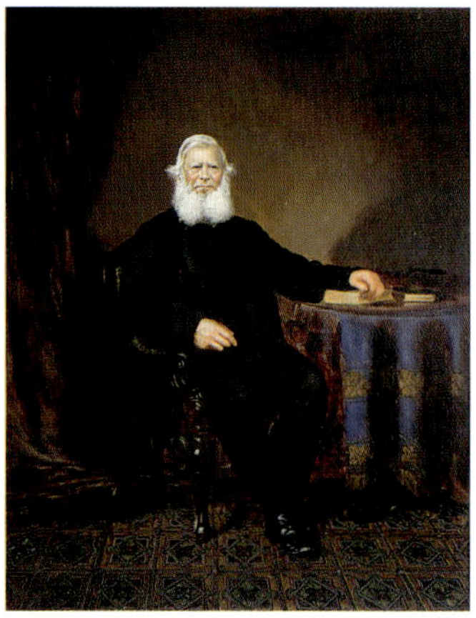

unknown artist
Benjamin Bantock
oil on canvas 36 x 28
PCF4

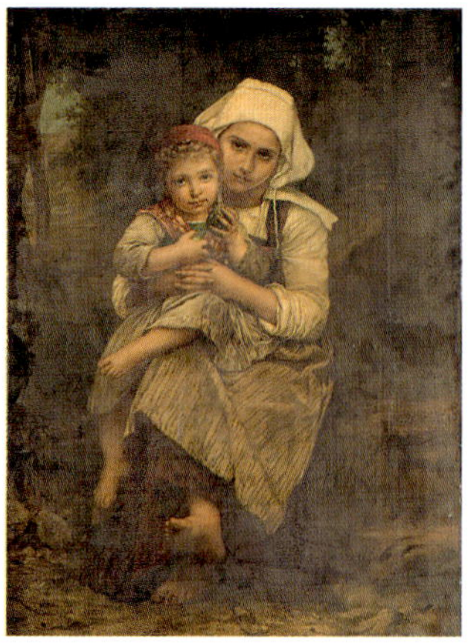

unknown artist
Breton Woman and Child
oil on canvas 129.5 x 92.7
OP779

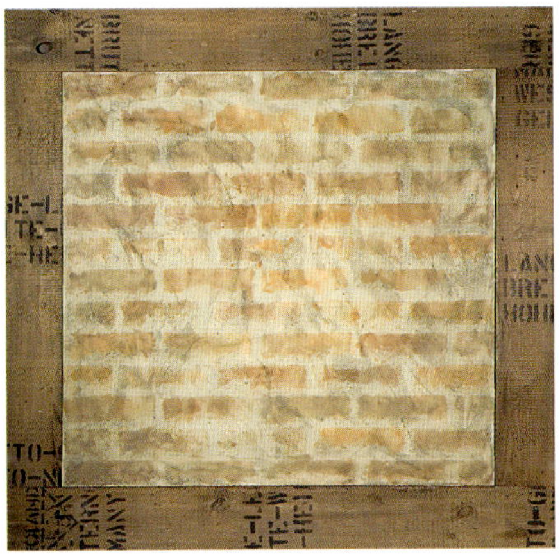

unknown artist
Brick Wall
oil on canvas & wood 128.5 x 128.5
PCF5

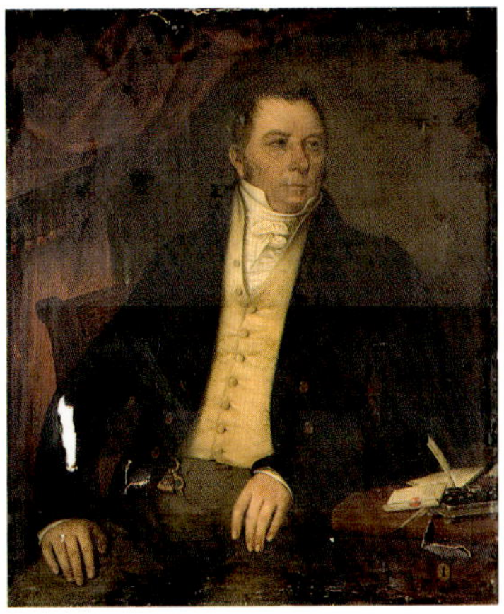

unknown artist
Edward Wooley
oil on canvas 108 x 87.6
OP751

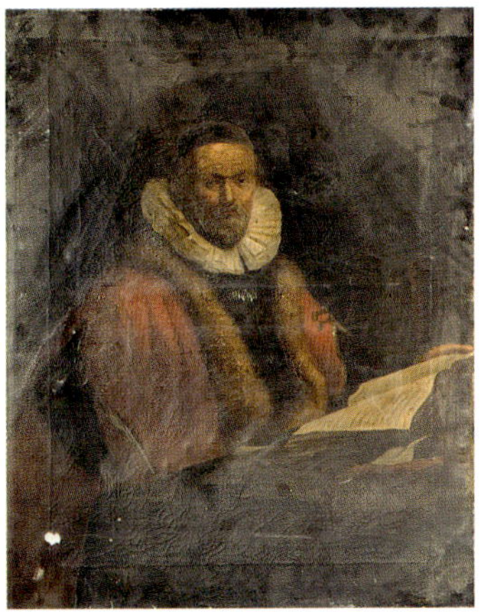

unknown artist
Gentleman with a Book, possibly Johannes Utenbogaert (1557–1644)
oil on canvas 116.8 x 91.4
OP778

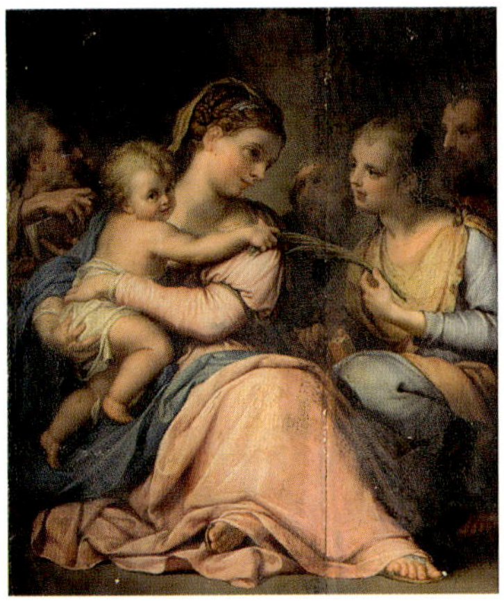

unknown artist
Holy Family
oil on panel 39.5 x 31.5
OP588

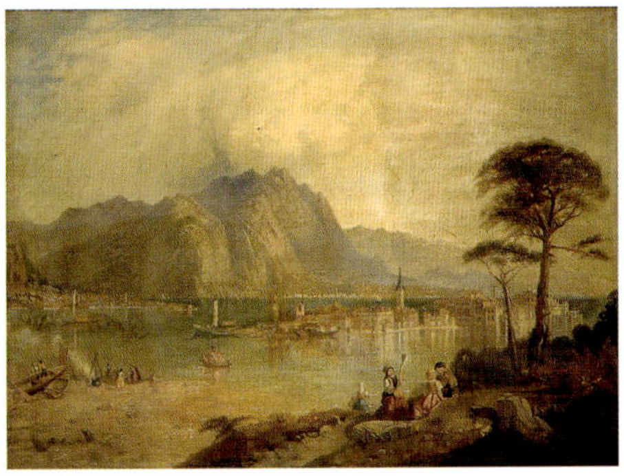

unknown artist
Italian Landscape with Lake
oil on canvas 71 x 91.5
OP780

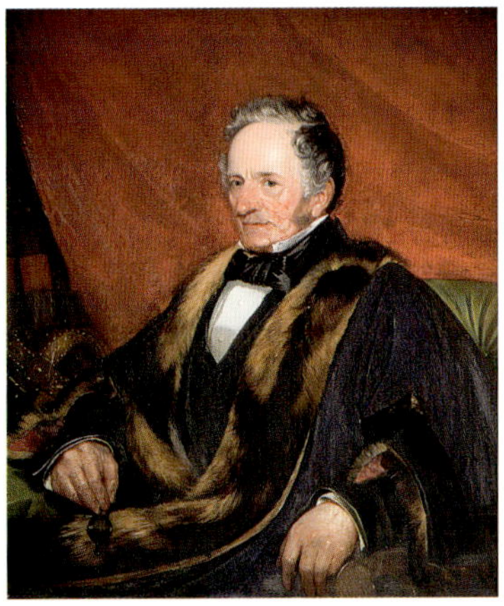

unknown artist
Jeremiah Wynne, Mayor of Wolverhampton (1852–1853)
oil on canvas 91 x 75
OP777

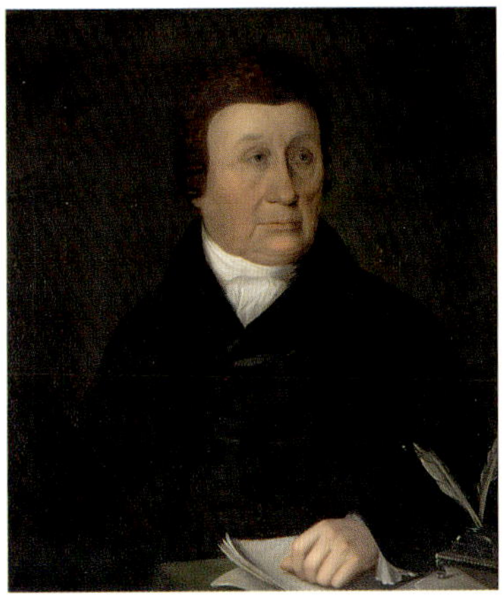

unknown artist
John Wilkinson (1728–1808)
oil on canvas 73.5 x 63.5
OP740

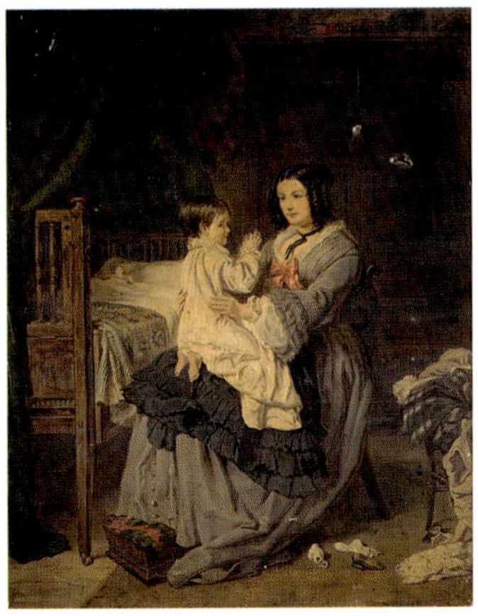

unknown artist
Mother and Child
oil on canvas 91.5 x 71
OP93

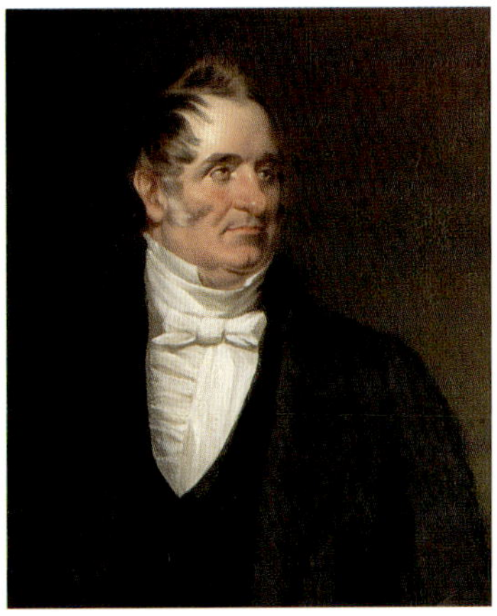

unknown artist
Mr George Benjamin Thorneycroft (1791–1851), First Mayor of Wolverhampton (1848–1849)
oil on canvas 75 x 60
PCF6

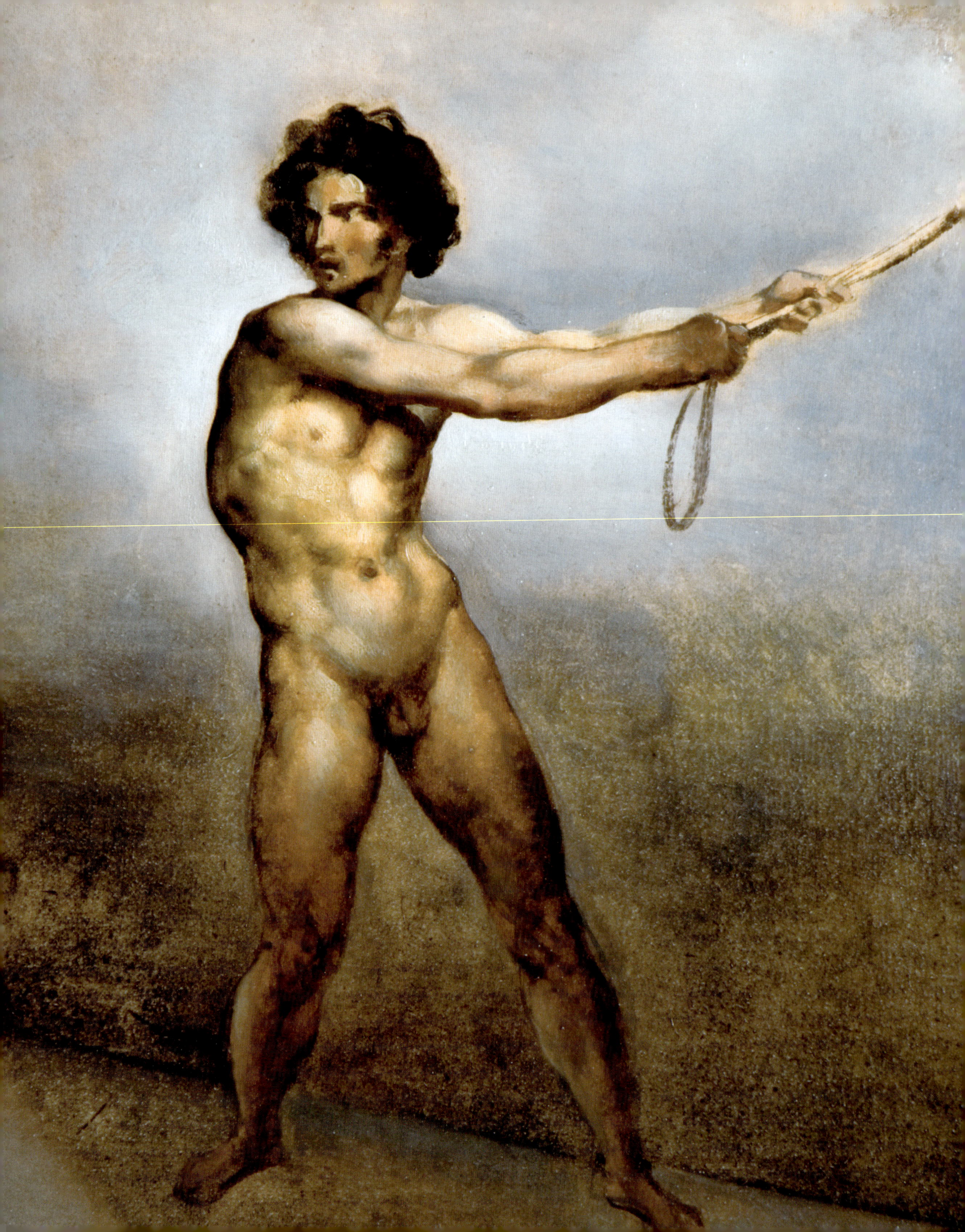

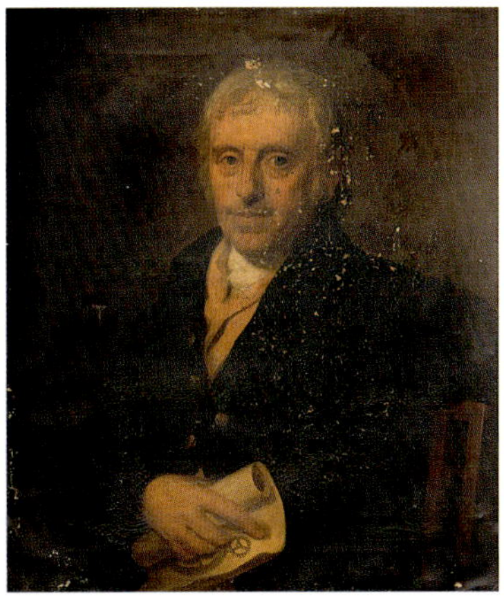

unknown artist
Portrait of a Gentleman
oil on canvas 75 x 60
OP740

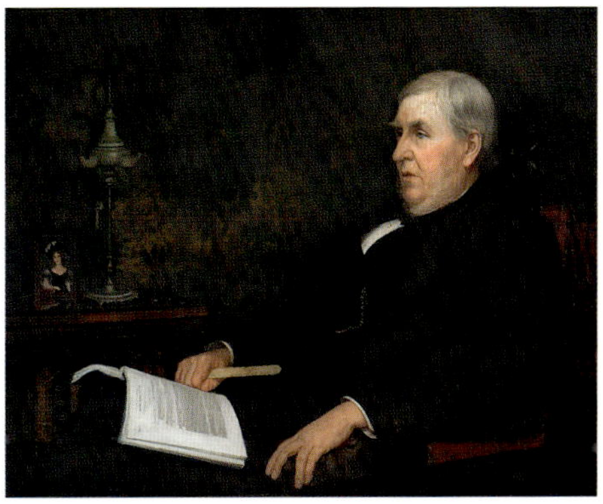

unknown artist
Portrait of a Gentleman with a Book
oil on canvas 92 x 115
PCF7

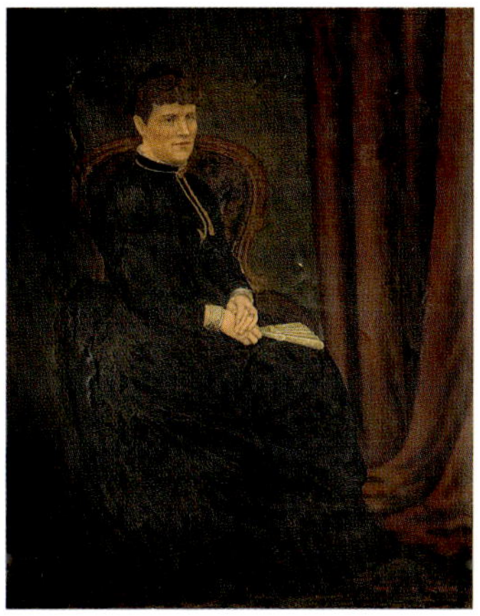

unknown artist
Portrait of a Lady with a Fan
oil on canvas 91.5 x 70.5
OP772

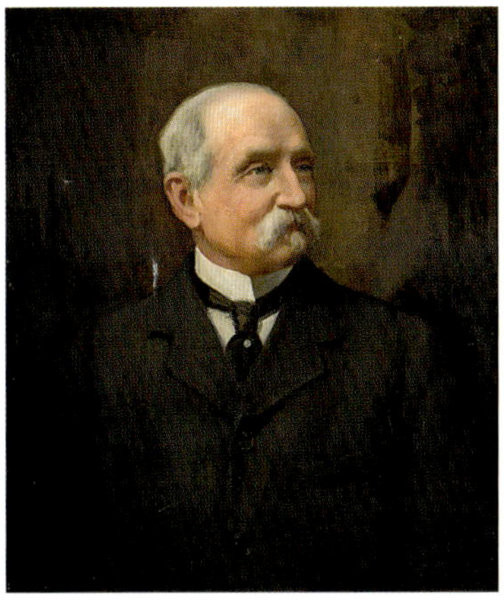

unknown artist
Portrait of a Man with a Moustache
oil on canvas 76 x 63.5
PCF8

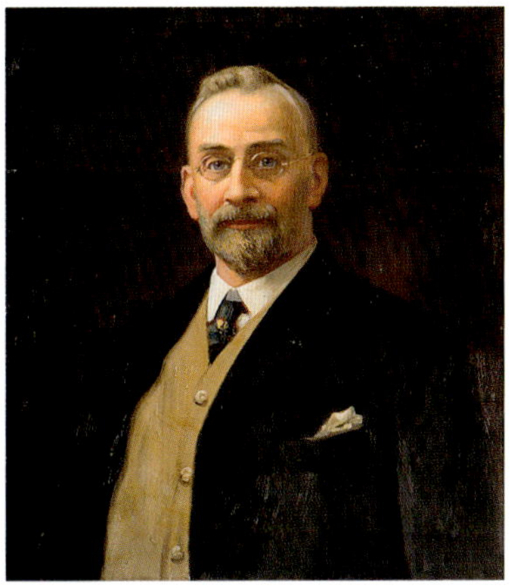

unknown artist
Portrait of a Man with Glasses
oil on canvas 71 x 61.5
PCF9

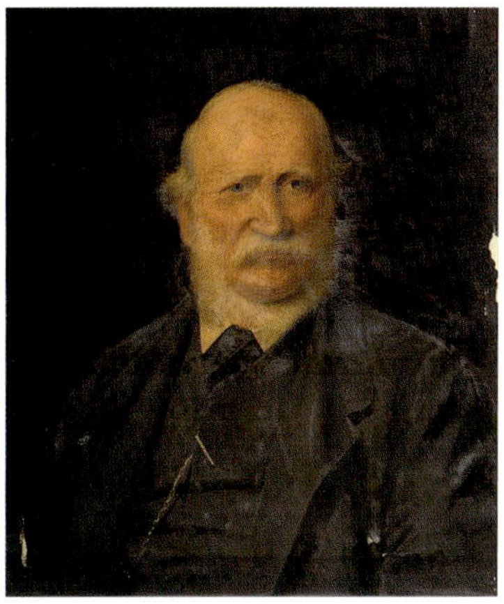

unknown artist
Portrait of an Unknown Gentleman
oil on canvas 61 x 51
OP774

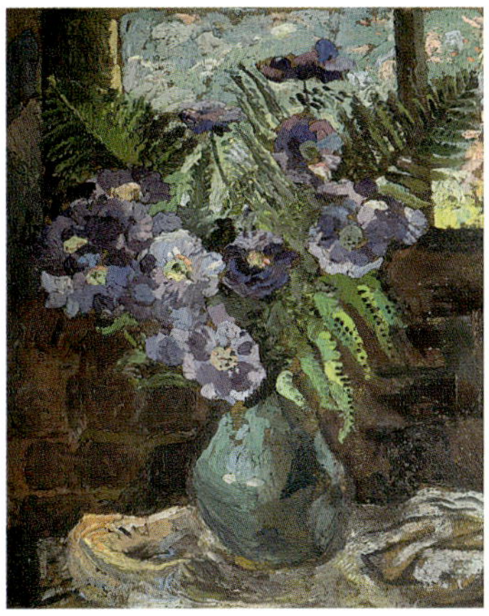

unknown artist
Still Life
oil on canvas 56 x 46
OP559a

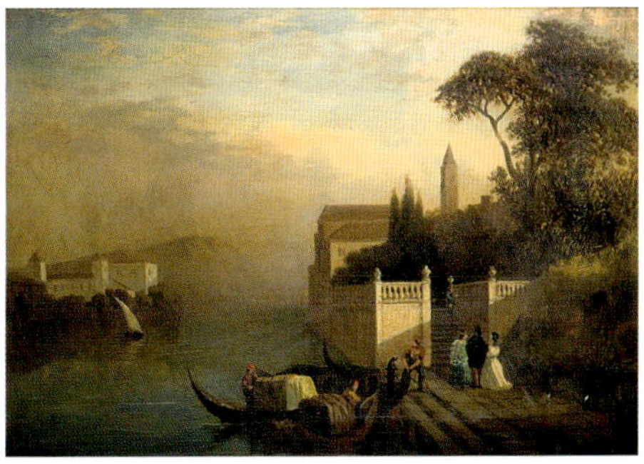

unknown artist
Venetian Scene
oil on canvas 25.5 x 35.5
OP596

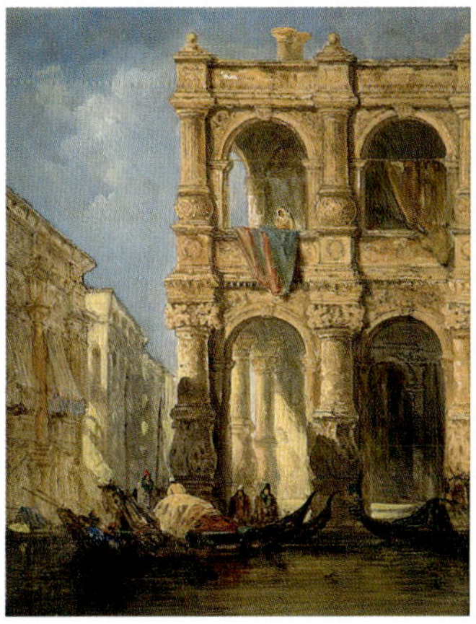

unknown artist
Venetian Scene
oil on canvas 45 x 34
PCF10

Facing page: Géricault, Théodore, 1791–1824, *Etude d'un homme nu* (detail), 1816–1818, The New Art Gallery Walsall, (p. 206)

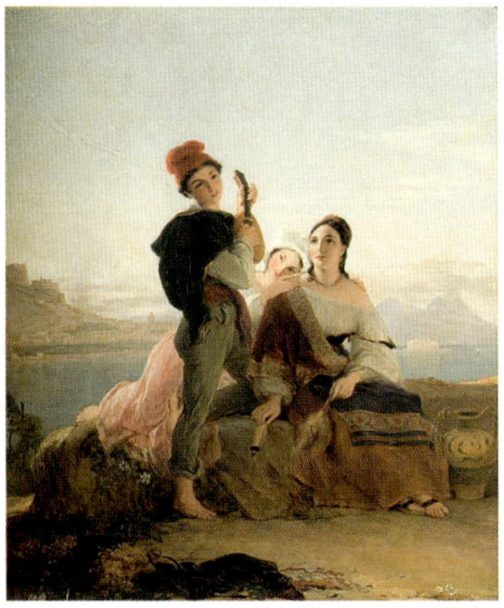

Unwins, Thomas 1782–1857
Neopolitan Peasants 1836
oil on board 89 x 72.5
OP80

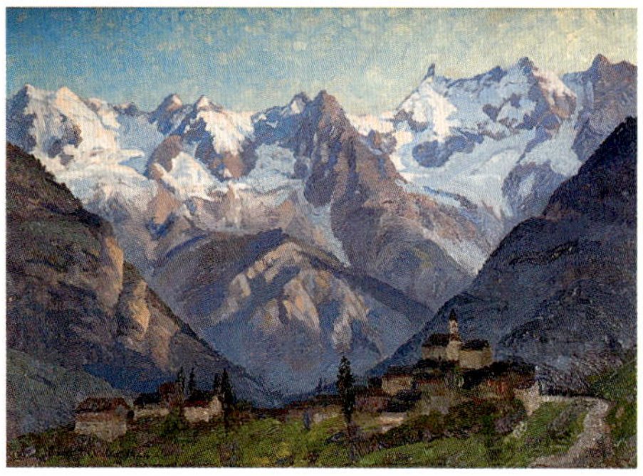

Vale, Enid Marjorie b.1890
The Mountain Barrier 1944
oil on board 49.5 x 65
OP311

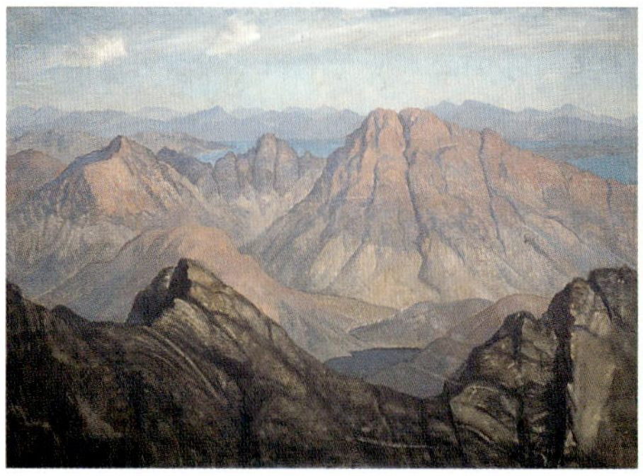

Vale, Enid Marjorie b.1890
The Mountain Range
oil on board 61 x 86.5
OP598

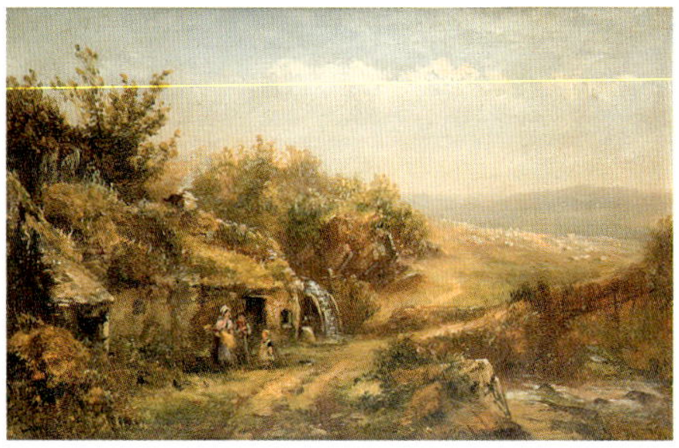

Vernon, William H. 1820–1909
Cottage and Mill Wheel
oil on canvas 30.5 x 45.5
OP550

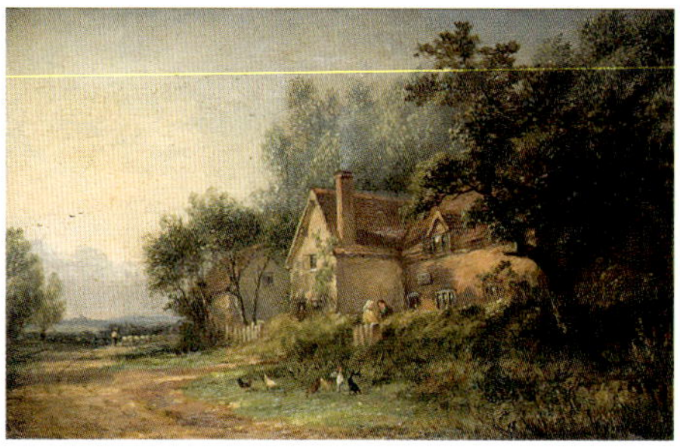

Vernon, William H. 1820–1909
Lane at Bridgnorth
oil on canvas 30 x 45
OP545

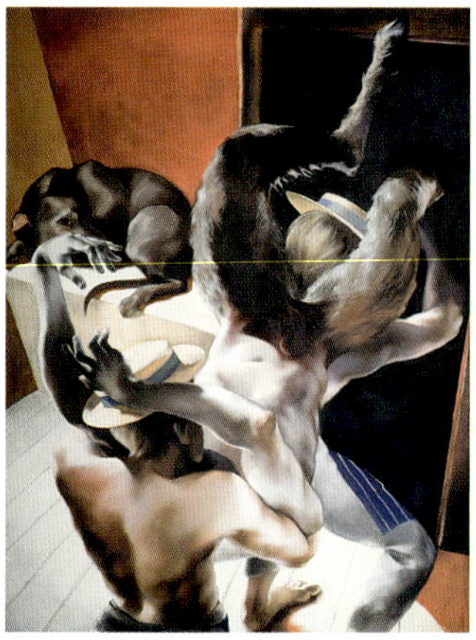

Vesely, Susan b.1953
The Leprochaun Has Died
oil on canvas 122 x 81.5
OP833

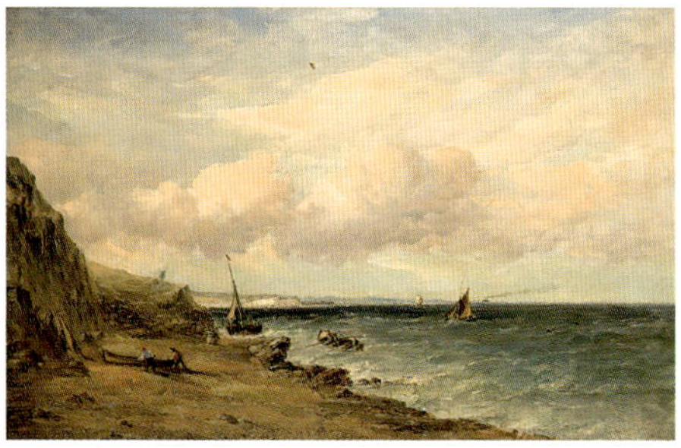

Vickers, Alfred 1786–1868
South Coast, Isle of Wight 1858
oil on canvas 40.5 x 61
OP21

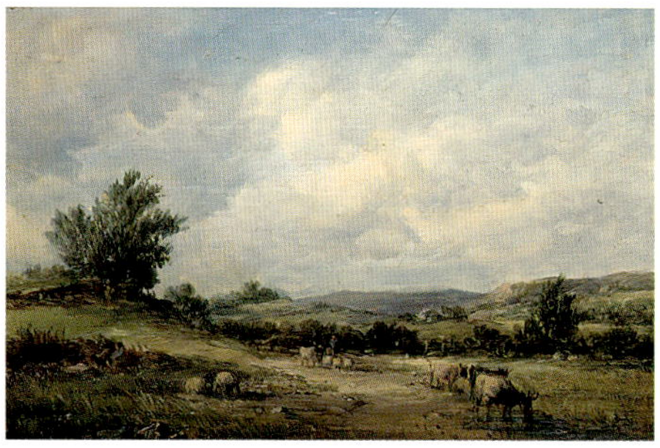

Vickers, Alfred 1786–1868
In the Vale of Neath
oil on panel 16.5 x 23.5
OP52

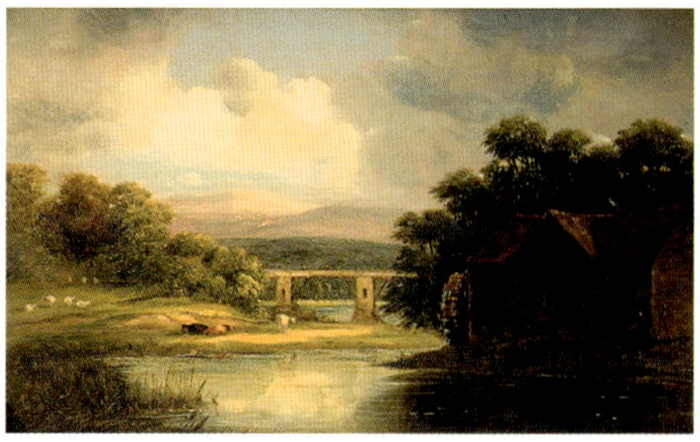

Vickers, Alfred 1786–1868
The Old Mill, Bath
oil on canvas 30.5 x 45.5
OP542

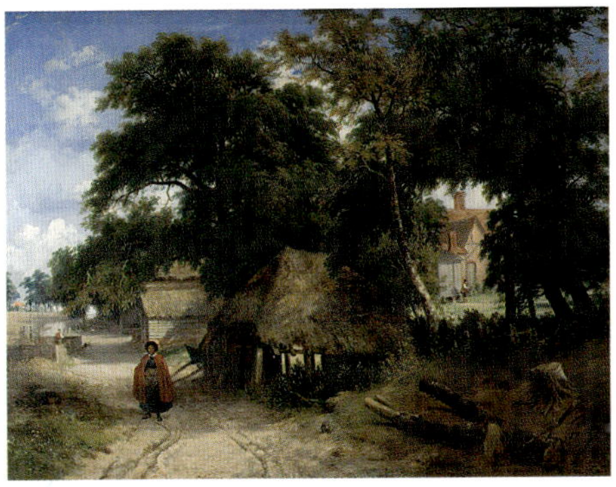

Vincent, George (attributed to) 1796–1831
An English Farmstead 1810–1831
oil on canvas 101.5 x 127
OP250

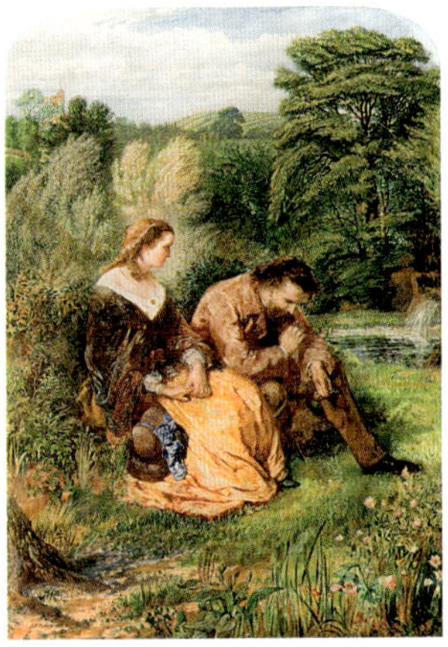

Vinter, John Alfred 1818–1905
The Miller's Daughter, from Tennyson 1859
oil on canvas 90.5 x 61
OP190

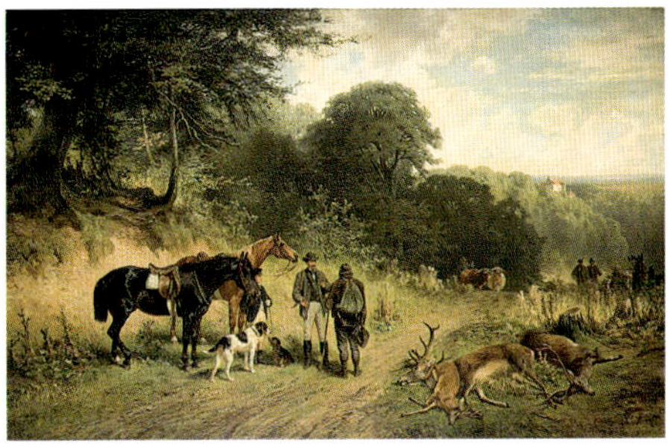

Voltz, Friedrich 1817–1886
A Good Day 1875
oil on canvas 80.5 x 124
OP415

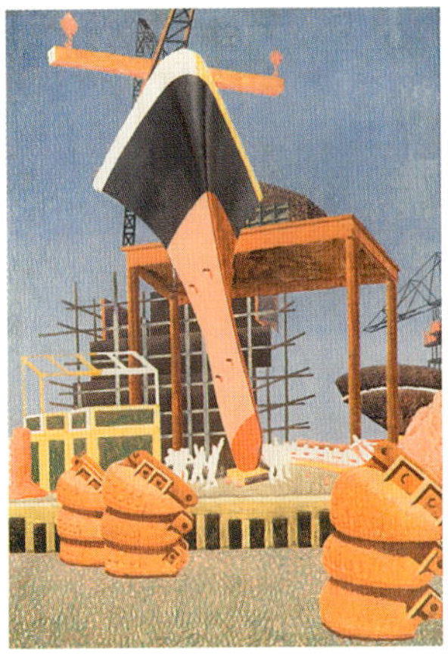

Wadsworth, Edward Alexander 1889–1949
Ship Building
oil on canvas 205.5 x 155
OP790

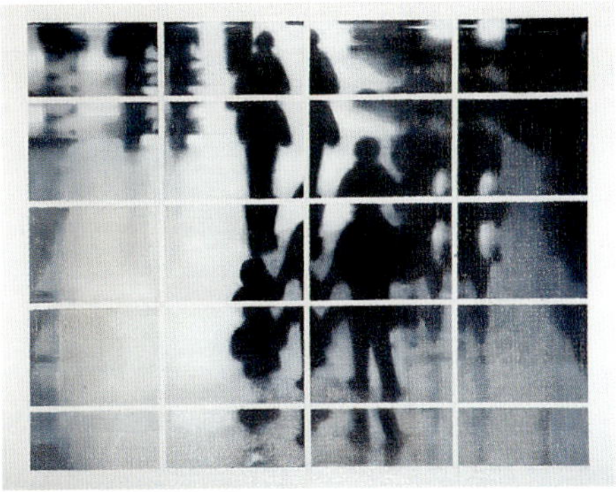

Wagg, Jamie b.1958
20/20 1993
oil on canvas 51 x 61
OP921

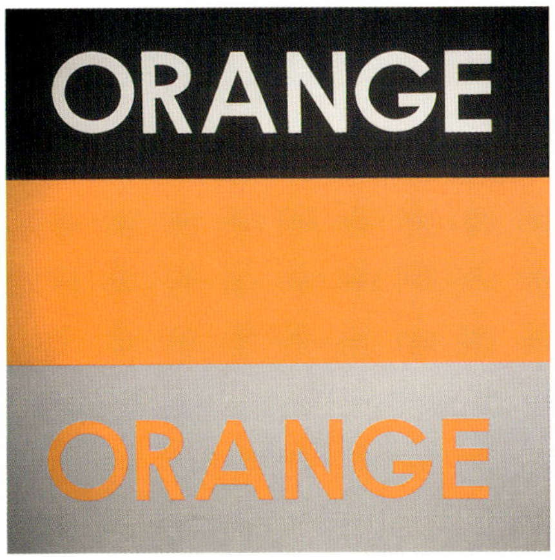

Walker, John b.1939
Marriage of the Verbal and the Visual 1975
acrylic on canvas 124 x 124
OP919

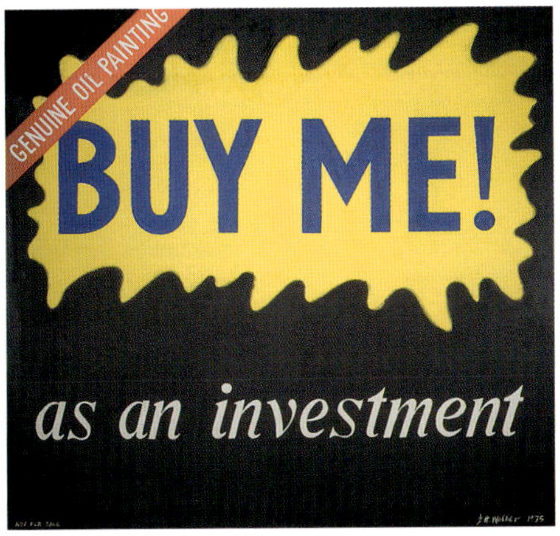

Walker, John b.1939
Not for Sale 1975
acrylic on canvas 124 x 124 (E)
OP920

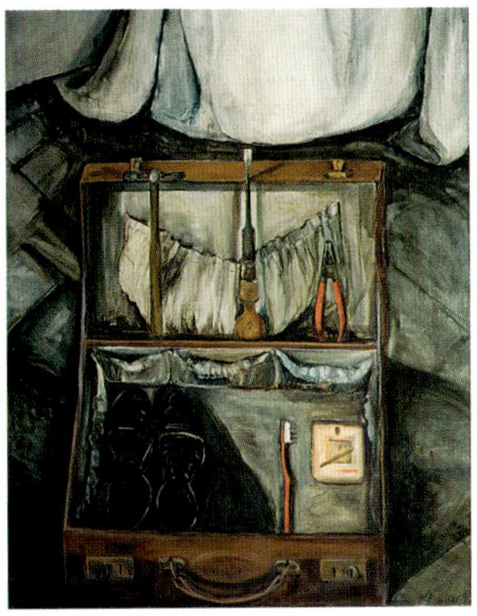

Walker, Maggie active 1980–1988
Suitcase
oil on canvas 107 x 81.5
OP867

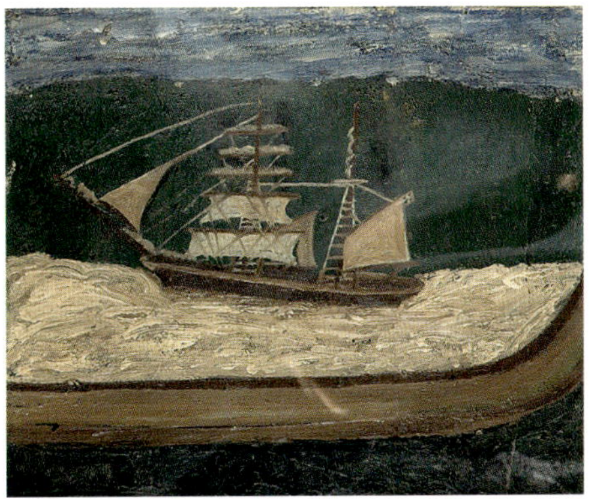

Wallis, Alfred 1855–1942
A Brig, Close to Shore 1930–1942
oil on board 24 x 28
OP854

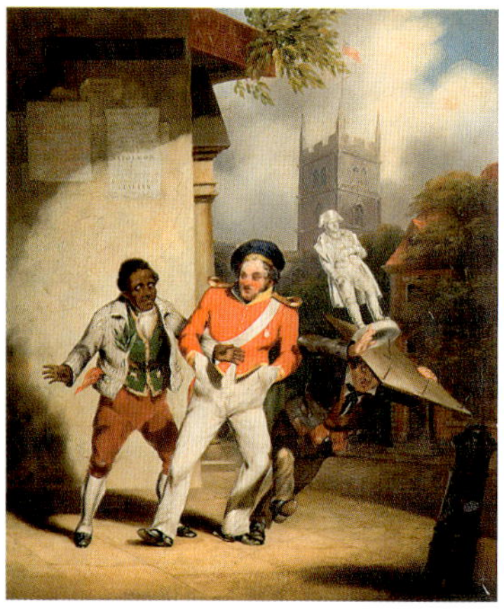

Wallis, George 1811–1891
The Fall of Napoleon 1836
oil on canvas 63.5 x 53
OP486

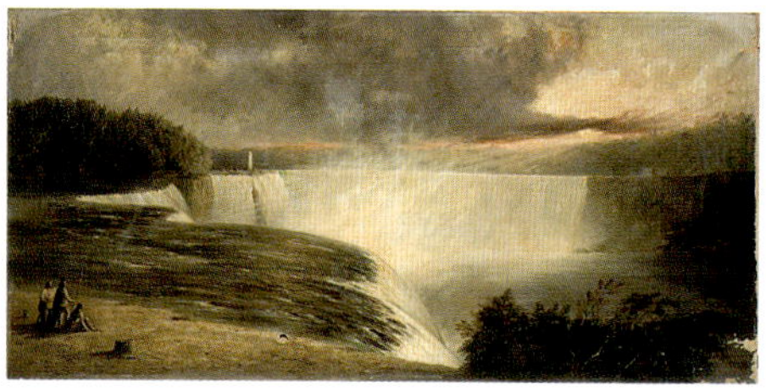

Wallis, George 1811–1891
The Falls of Niagara 1855
oil on canvas 78.7 x 165.1
OP424

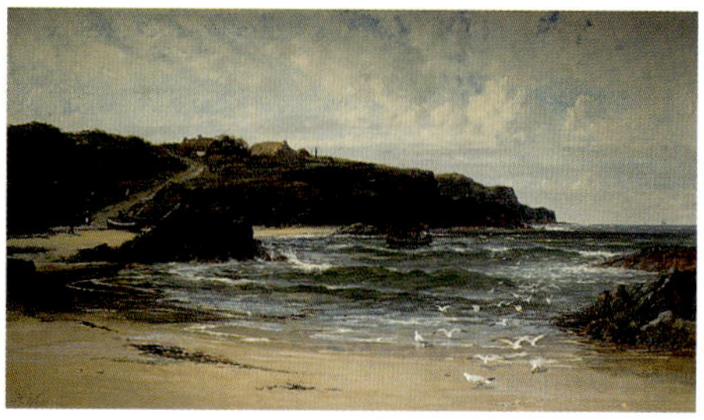

Wane, Richard 1852–1904
The Incoming Tide 1870–1890
oil on canvas 76 x 129.5
OP449

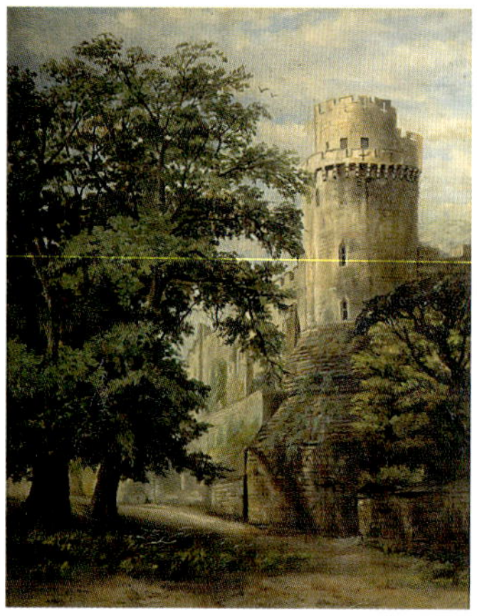

Ward, Amy Margaret b.1863
Castle and Trees
oil on canvas 45.5 x 36
OP728

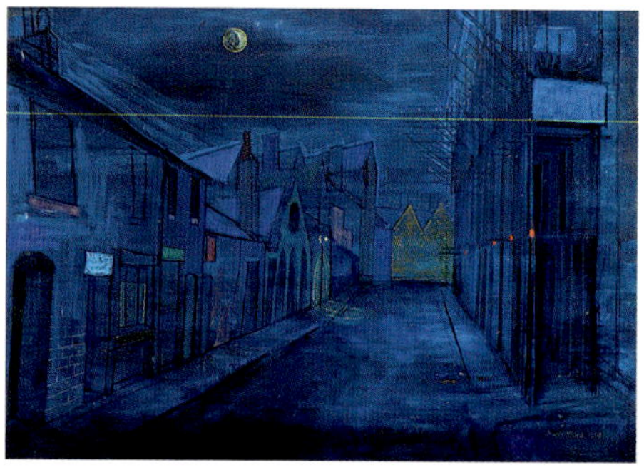

Ward, Frank Clifford 1914–1998
Street Scene, Wolverhampton 1958
oil on board 58.5 x 78.5
OP472

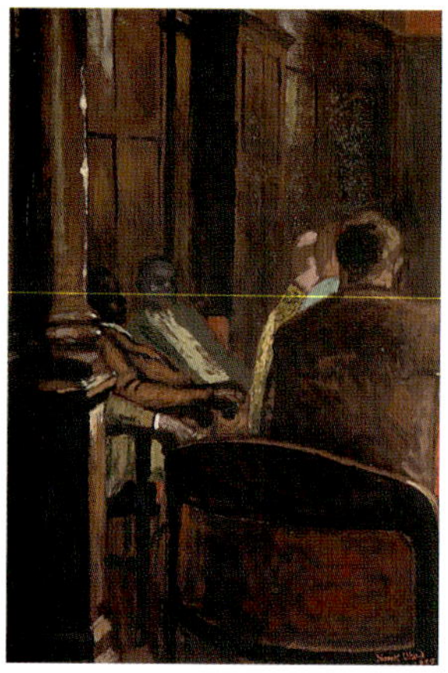

Ward, Frank Clifford 1914–1998
Interior with Figures (Shakespeare)
oil on board 61 x 42
OP593

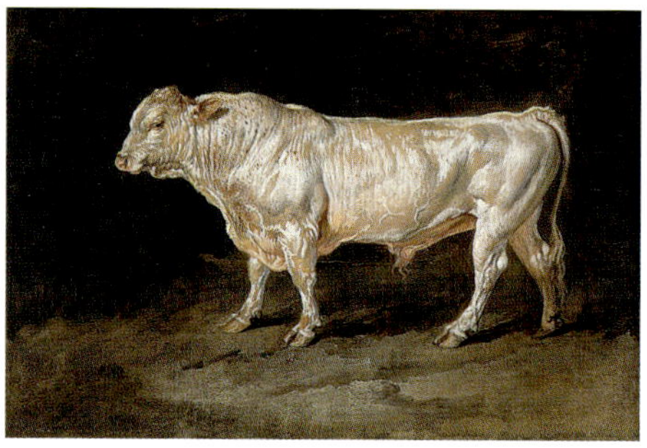

Ward, James 1769–1859
Study of a Prize Bull 1811–1815
oil on canvas 33 x 45.5
OP222

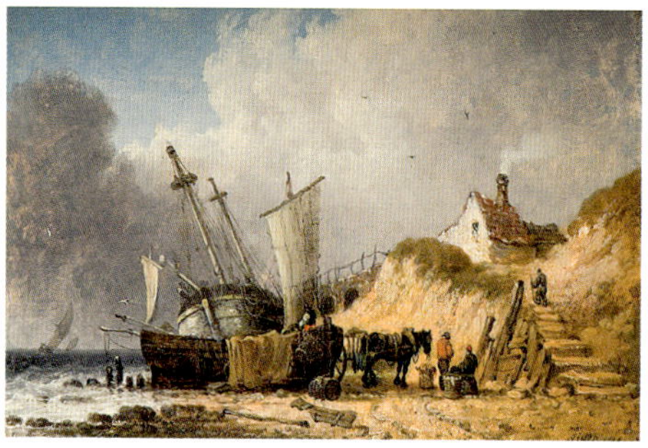

Ward, James (attributed to) 1769–1859
Coast Scene 1836
oil on panel 20.5 x 29
OP460

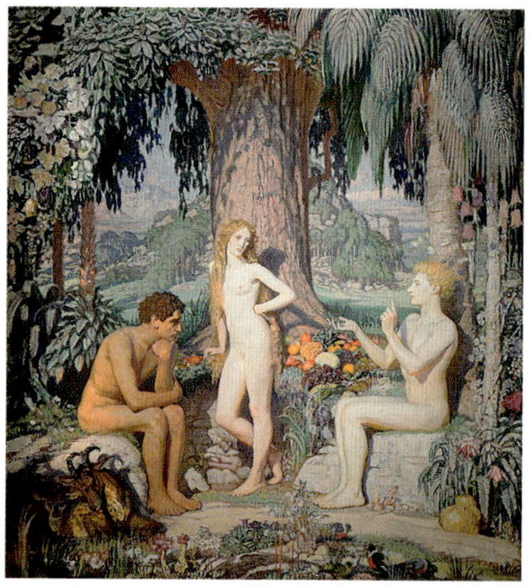

Watson, George Spencer 1869–1934
The Creation 1921
oil on canvas 162 x 142
OP76

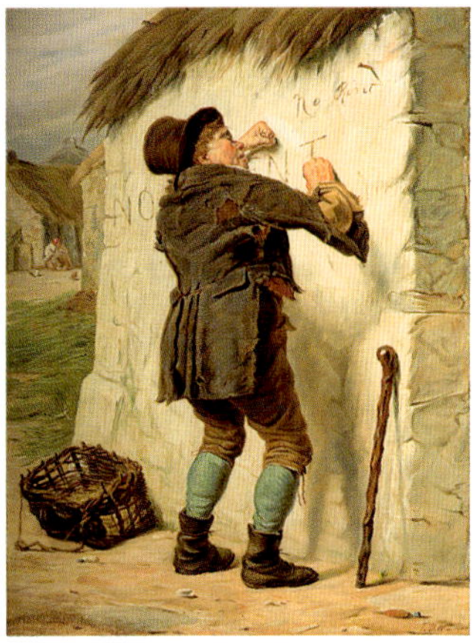

Watson, John Dawson 1832–1892
'No rint'
oil on canvas 61 x 46.5
OP729

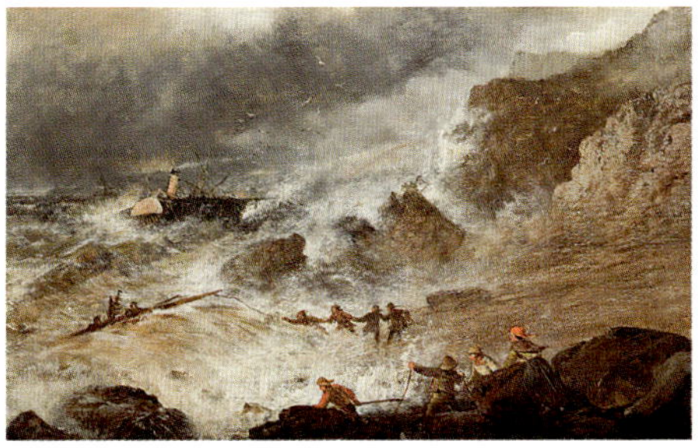

Webb, James c.1825–1895
After the Wreck (On the French Coast) 1870
oil on canvas 51 x 76.5
OP468

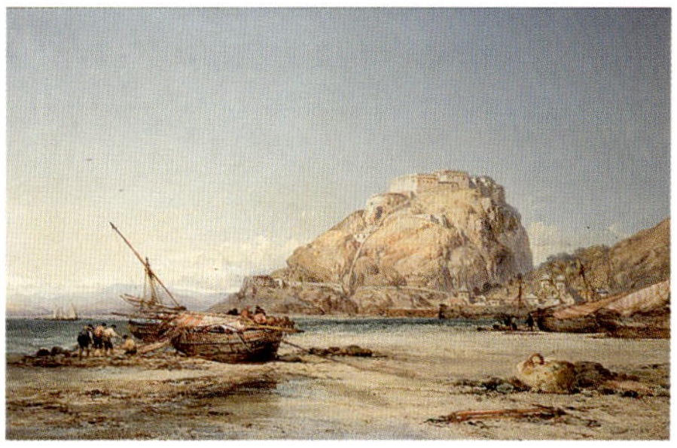

Webb, James c.1825–1895
San Sebastian 1874
oil on canvas 61 x 92
OP734

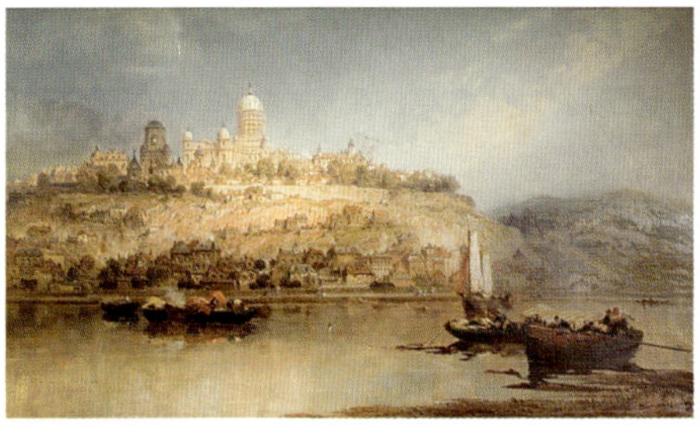

Webb, James c.1825–1895
Boulogne
oil on canvas 72.5 x 115.5
OP732

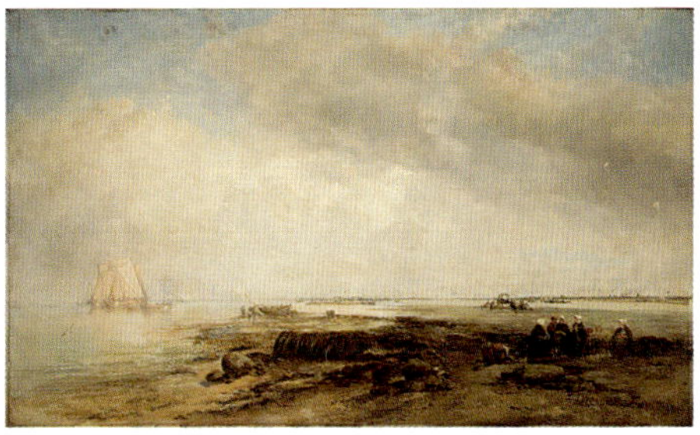

Webb, James c.1825–1895
Lowlands
oil on canvas 114.3 x 182.9
OP447

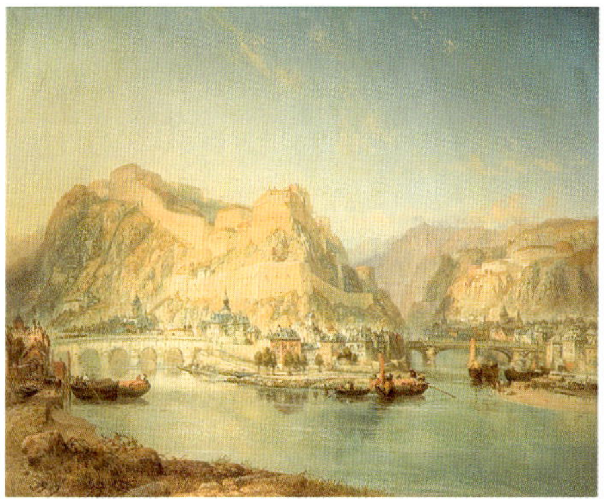

Webb, James c.1825–1895
Namur
oil on canvas 76 x 127
OP733

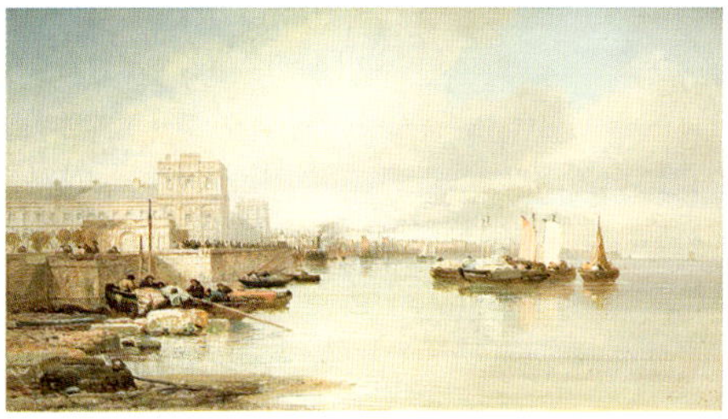

Webb, James c.1825–1895
Spanish Harbour
oil on canvas 61 x 92
OP730

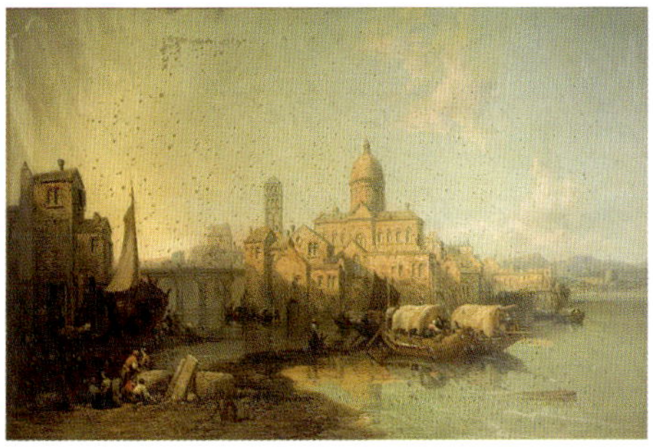

Webb, James c.1825–1895
Tangiers
oil on canvas 106.5 x 183
OP731

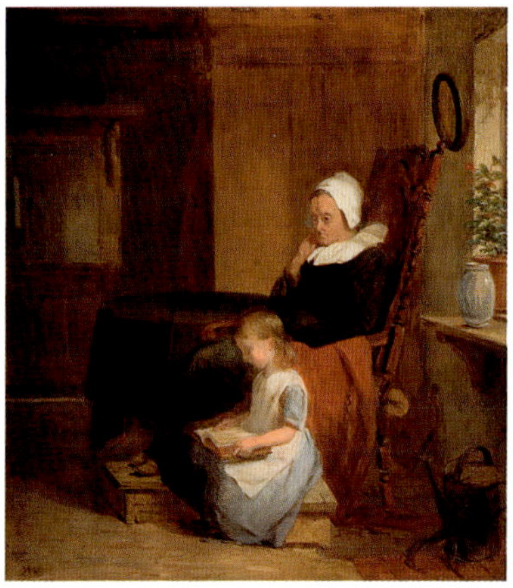

Webster, Thomas George 1800–1886
Sunday Afternoon
oil on panel 21.5 x 19
OP228

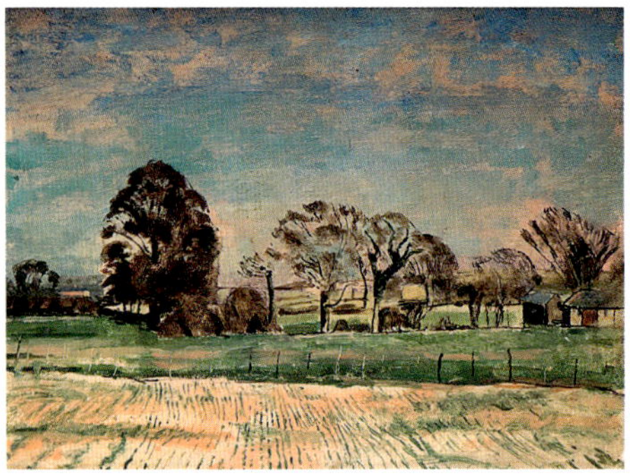

Weight, Carel Victor Morlais 1908–1997
Essex Landscape
oil on board 38 x 48
OP332

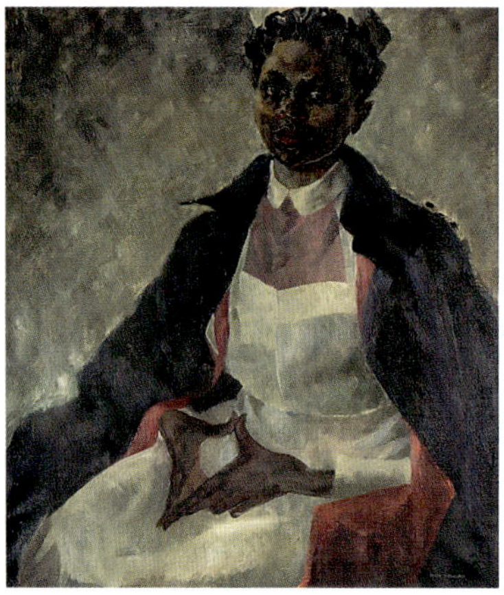

Welburn, Irene active 1936–1940
Nurse Brown
oil on canvas 66 x 56
OP316

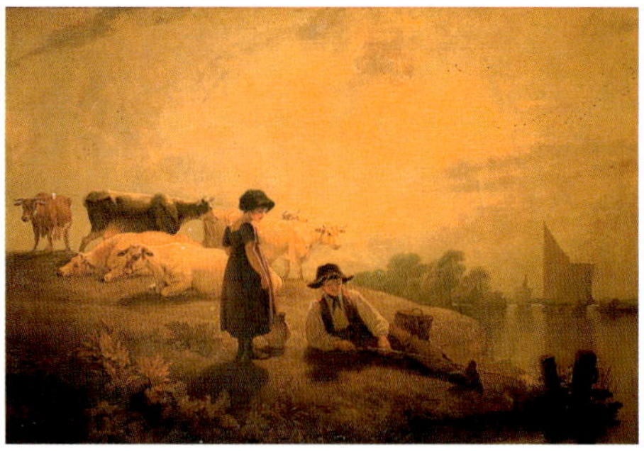

Westall, Richard 1765–1836
A Sunny Afternoon
oil on canvas 137 x 183
OP446

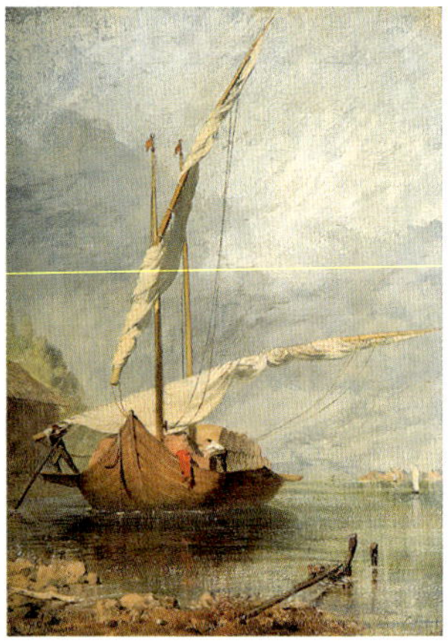

Whaite, Henry Clarence 1828–1912
Coast Scene 1851
oil on canvas 35.5 x 25.5
OP549

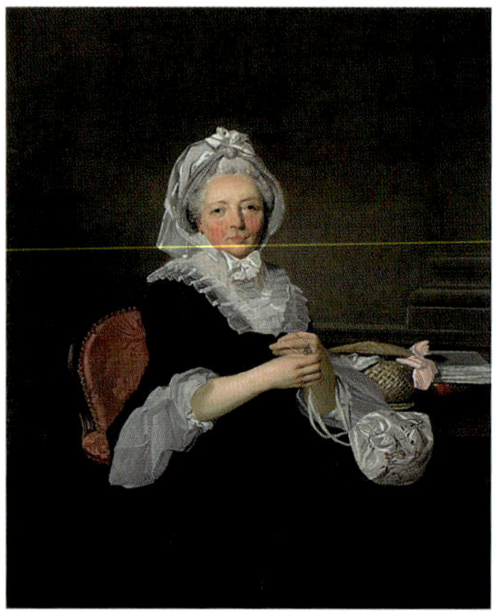

Wheatley, Francis 1747–1801
Mrs Pearce 1786
oil on canvas 134.5 x 109
OP759

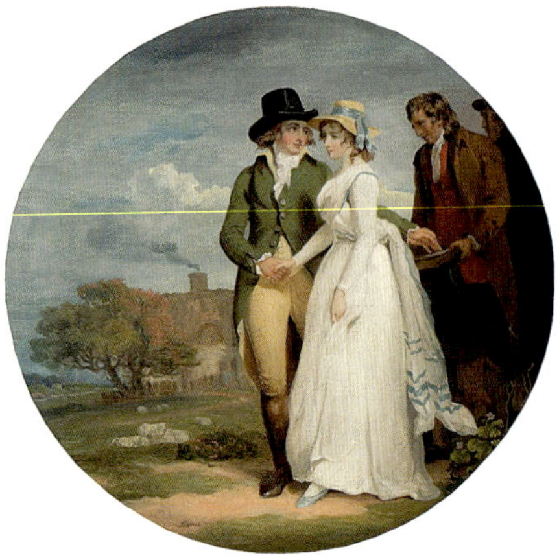

Wheatley, Francis 1747–1801
Love and Charity
oil on canvas 51
OP481

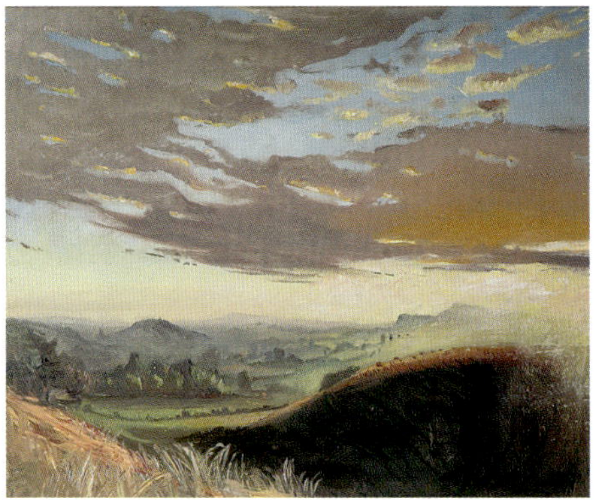

Wheeler, Charles 1892–1974
The Hollow in the Downs
oil on board 51 x 61
OP329

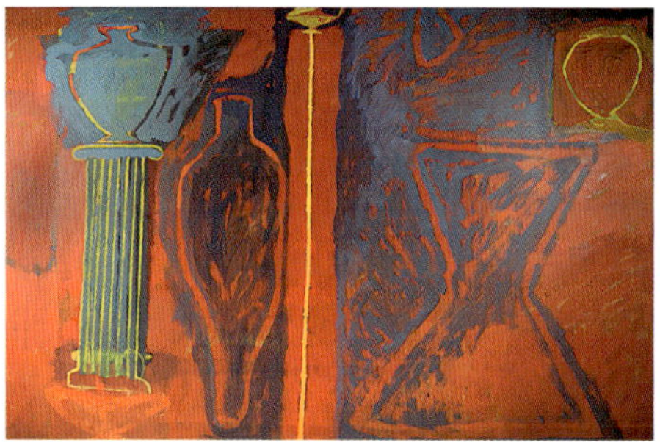

Whiteford, Kate b.1952
Pagan Painting I 1980–1986
oil on canvas 195 x 294
OP800

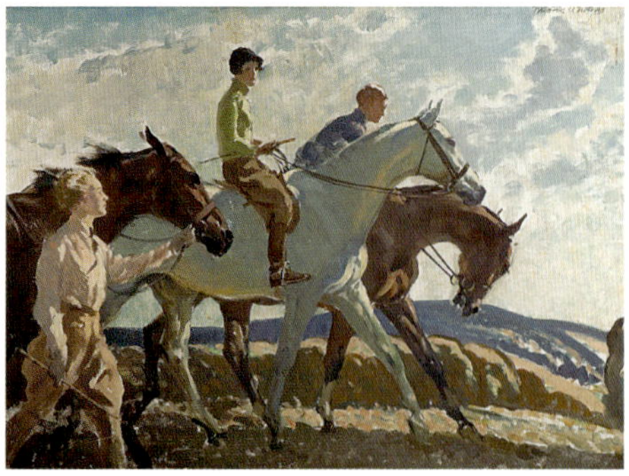

Whiting, Frederic 1874–1962
The Morning Ride
oil on canvas 71 x 91.5
OP289

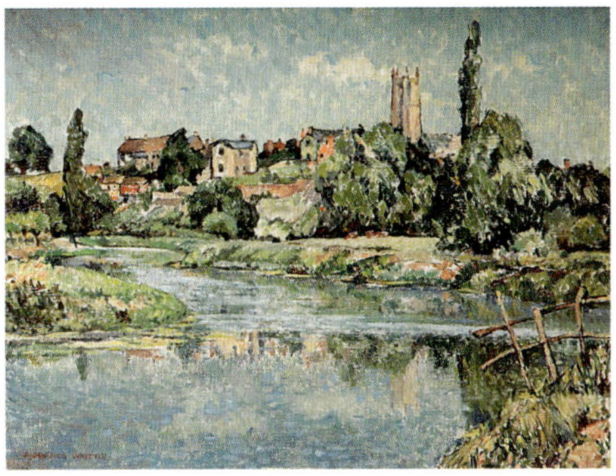

Whittle, Florence
Somerset Village
oil on canvas 40.5 x 51
OP285

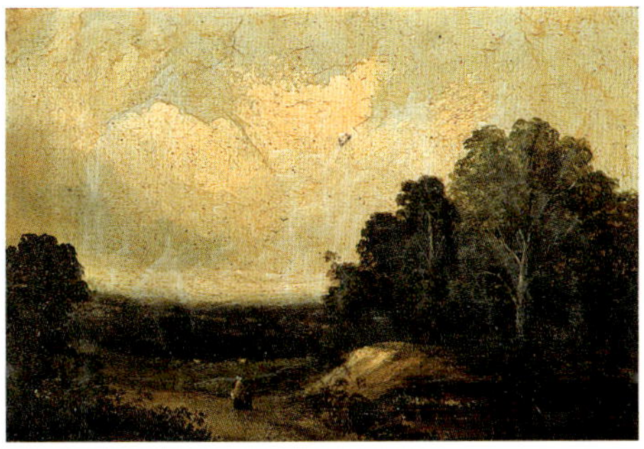

Whittle, Thomas active 1854–1896
Landscape
oil on canvas 30 x 40.5
OP735

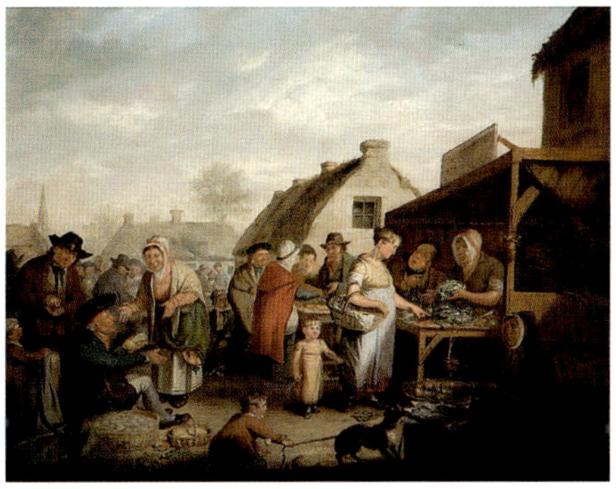

Wilkie, David (attributed to) 1785–1841
The Scottish Market Place 1818
oil on canvas 50 x 71
OP221

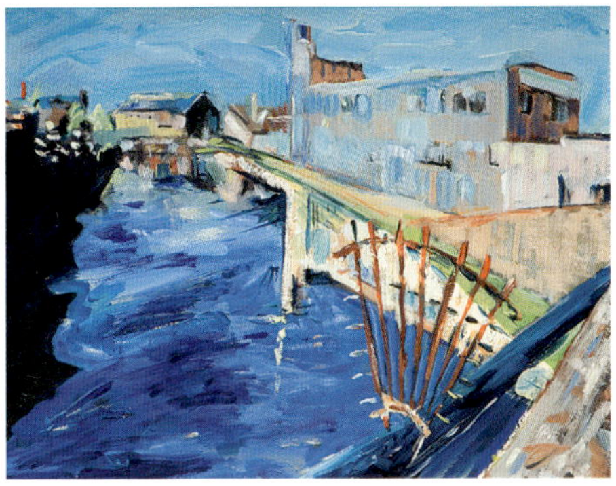

Willets, Gavin
Canal Junction
oil on canvas 30.5 x 40.5
OP844

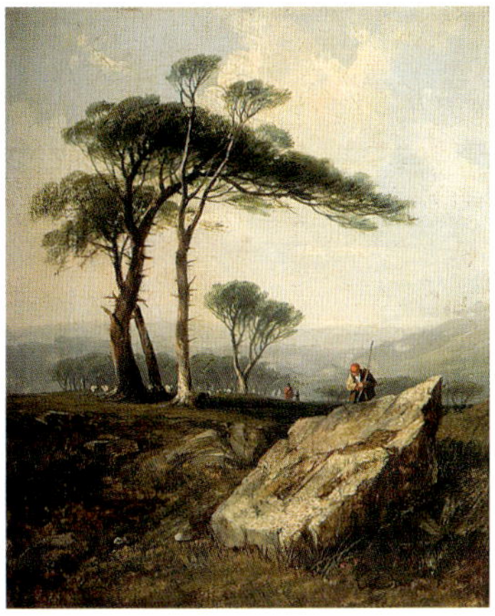

Williams, William 1808–1895
Claverton Downs 1844
oil on panel 28 x 23
OP378

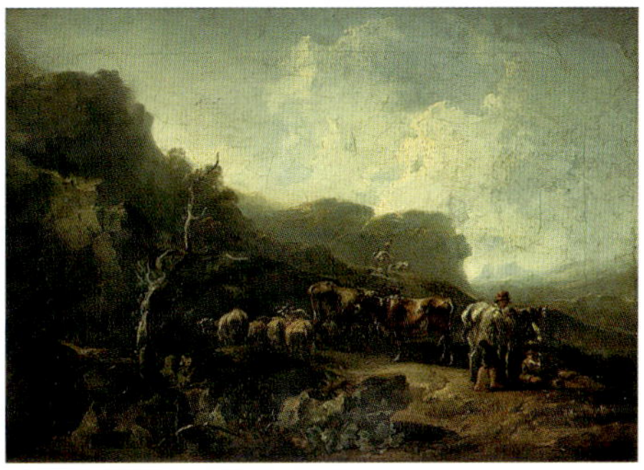

Williamson, Samuel 1792–1840
Landscape with Cattle
oil on canvas 46.5 x 63.5
OP363

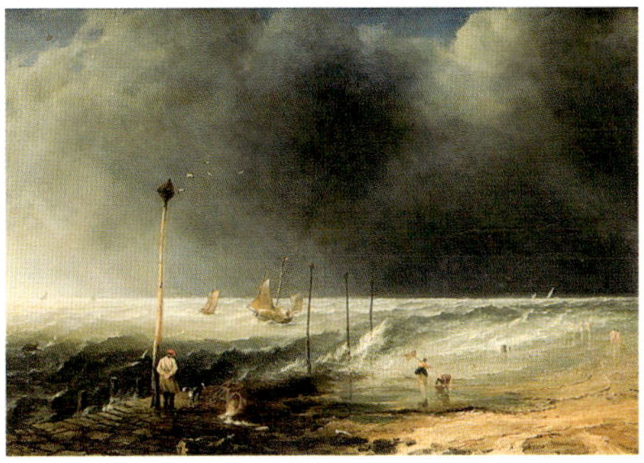

Wilson, John Glen 1774–1855
Approaching Storm, Entrance to the Firth of Forth
oil on canvas 76 x 106.5
OP119

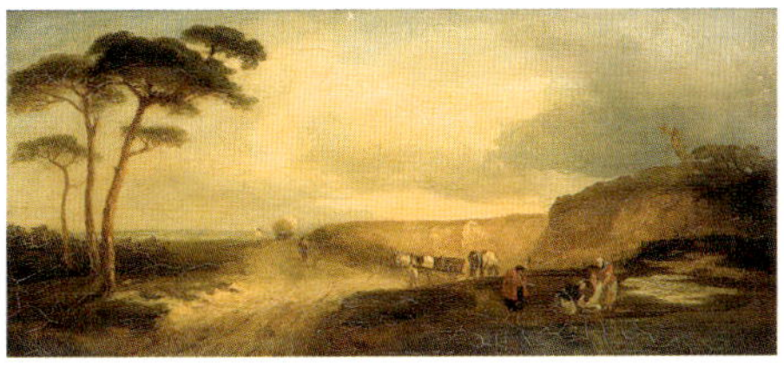

Wilson, John Glen 1774–1855
Landscape with Figures
oil on canvas 31 x 62
OP20

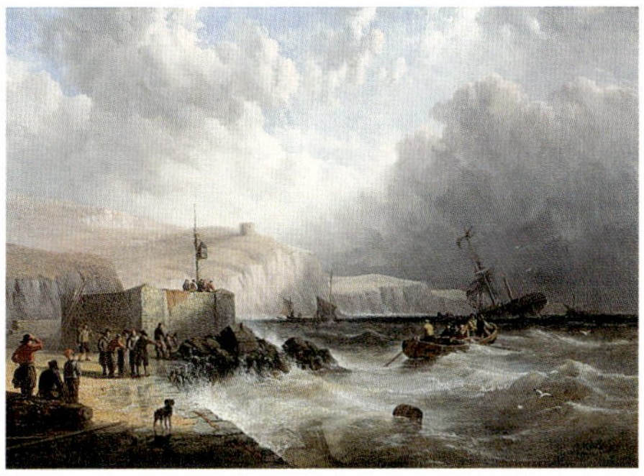

Wilson, John Glen 1774–1855
Wreck off Folkestone
oil on canvas 61 x 84
OP570

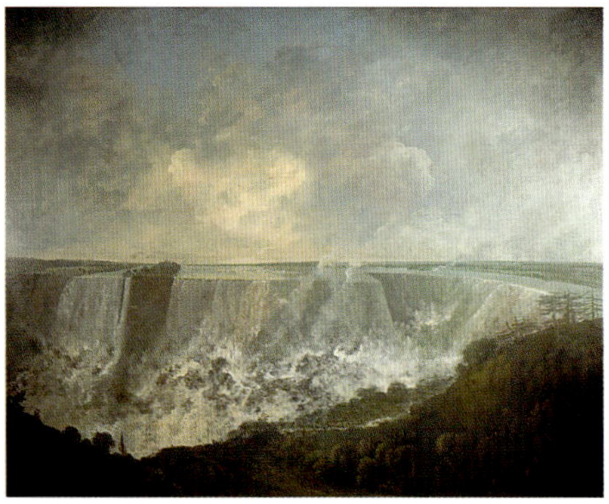

Wilson, Richard 1752–1802
Falls of Niagra 1770–1780
oil on canvas 154 x 185
OP96

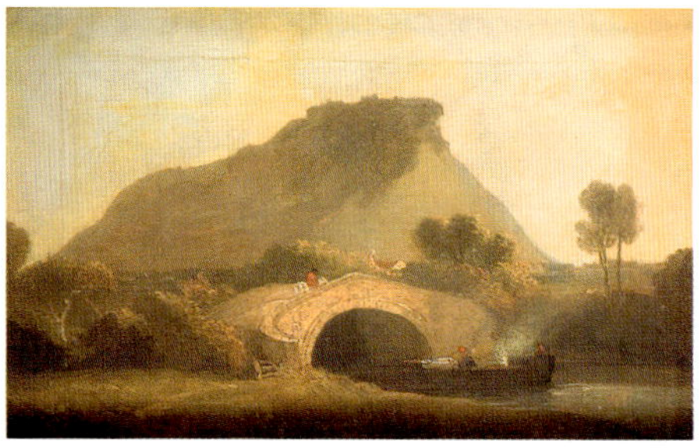

Wilson, Richard (circle of) 1752–1802
Canal Scene 19th C
oil on canvas 25.5 x 37.5
OP465

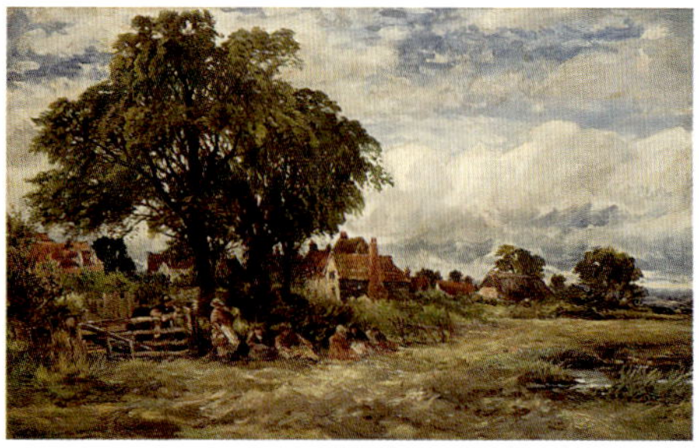

Wimperis, Edmund Morison 1835–1900
Farm near Brocklehurst 1890
oil on canvas 51 x 76
OP408

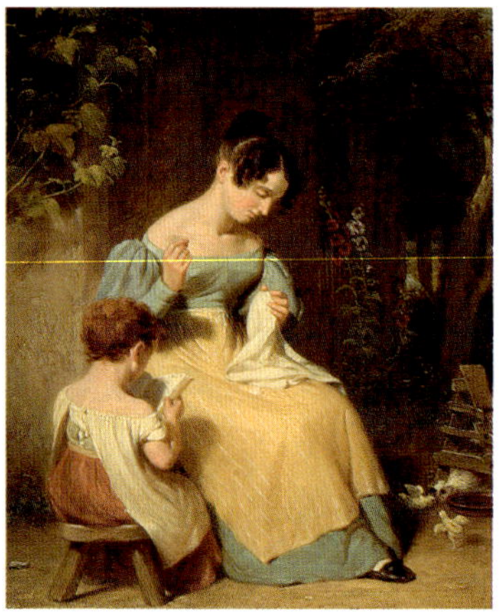

Witherington, William Frederick 1785–1865
The Lesson
oil on panel 28 x 25
OP474

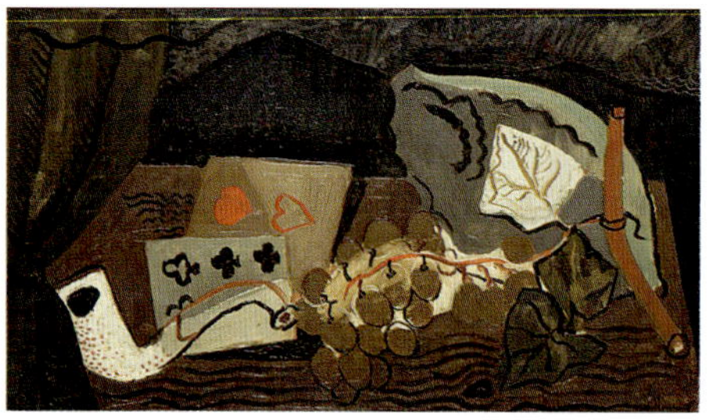

Wood, Christopher 1901–1930
Still Life with Cards and Pipe
oil on canvas 27 x 45.5
OP836

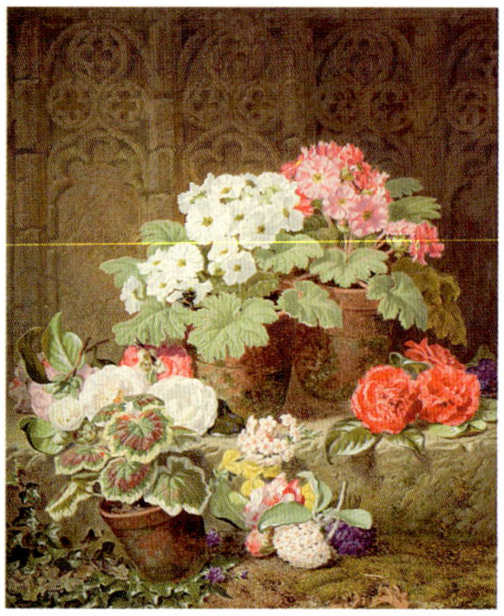

Worsey, Thomas 1829–1875
Still Life, Flowers
oil on canvas 81 x 67.3
OP736

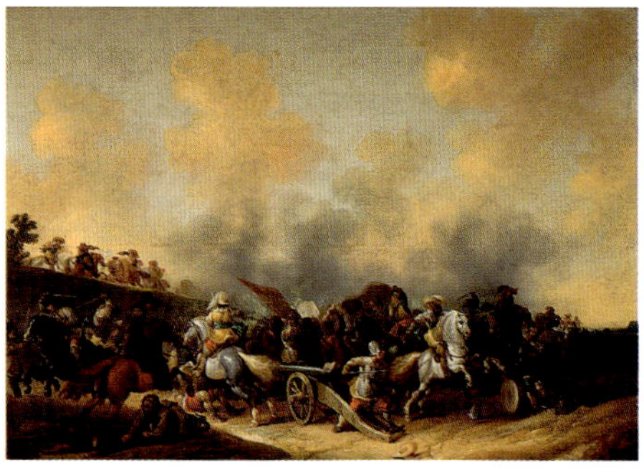

Wouwerman, Philips (attributed to) 1619–1668
Battle Scene
oil on panel 61 x 84
OP159

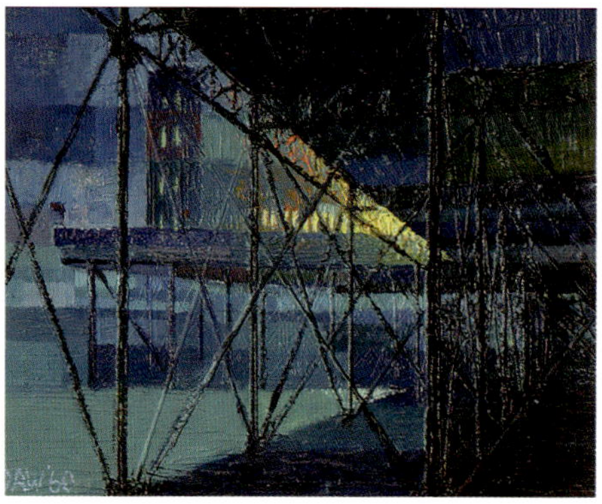

Wright, David b.1942
Blackpool Pier 1960
oil on canvas 45.5 x 62
OP309

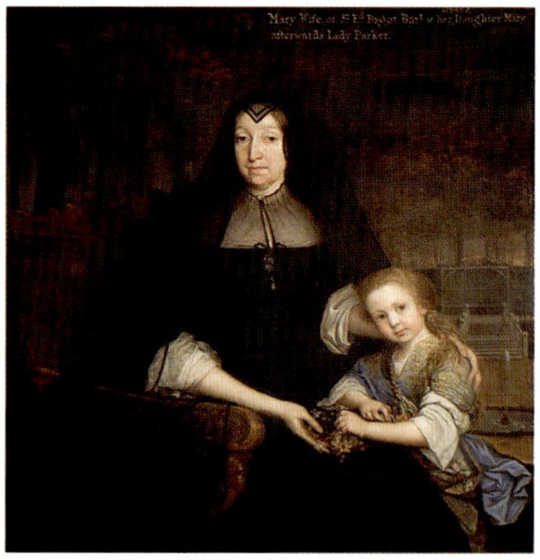

Wright, John Michael 1617–1694
Lady Mary Bagot and Granddaughter Mary, later Lady Parker
oil on canvas 118 x 125.5
OP512

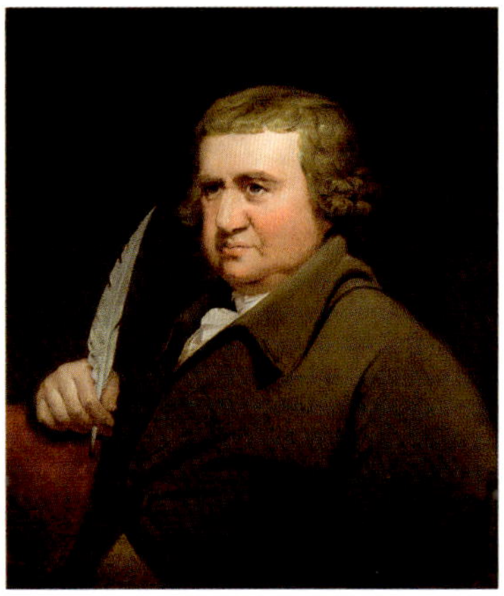

Wright, Joseph of Derby 1734–1797
Erasmus Darwin (1731–1802)
oil on canvas 76 x 63.5
OP528

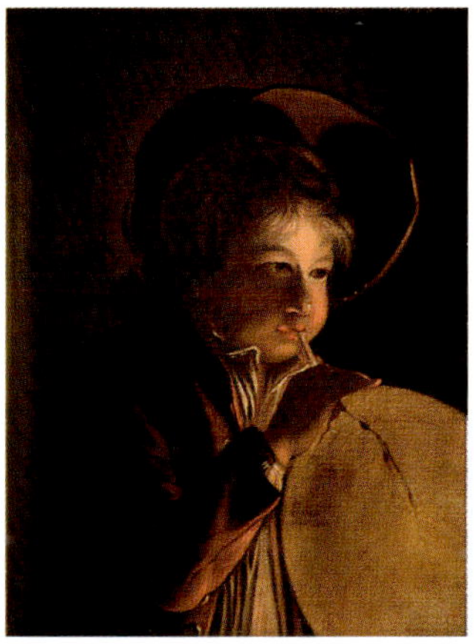

Wright, Joseph of Derby (after) 1734–1797
A Boy Blowing a Bladder in Candlelight
oil on canvas 54 x 42.5
OP261

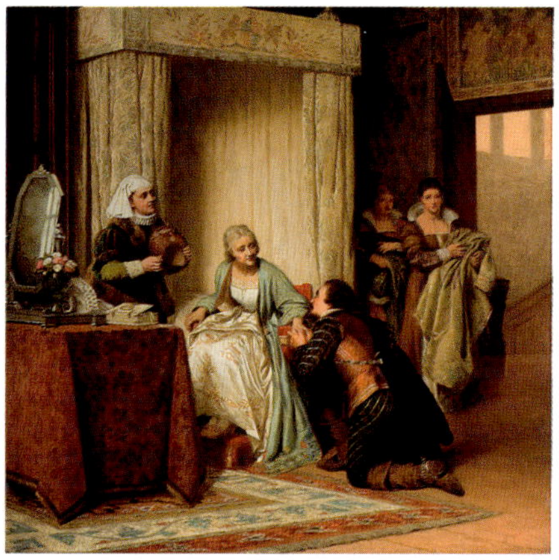

Wynfield, David Wilkie 1837–1887
An Incident in the Life of Queen Elizabeth I
oil on canvas 101.5 x 101.5
OP124

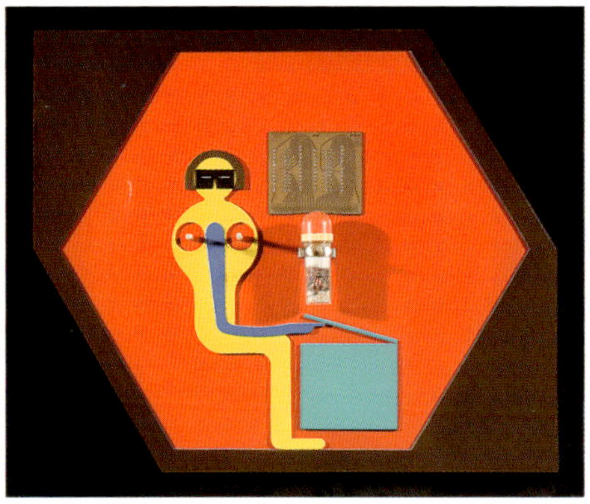

Yale, Brian b.1936
Pandora's Box 1968
enamel & plastic on board 70 x 80
OP912

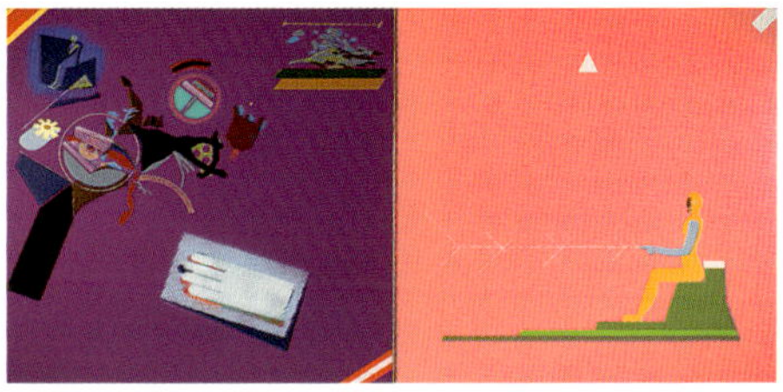

Yale, Brian b.1936
Hand of Destiny No.1 1969–1970
enamel on board 91 x 183
OP913

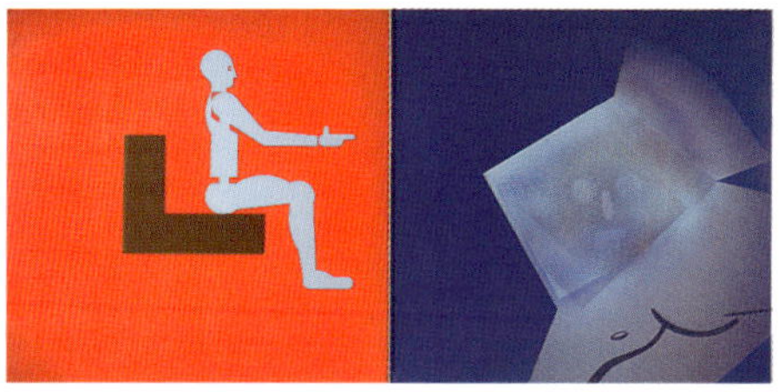

Yale, Brian b.1936
Hand of Destiny No.2 1969–1970
enamel on board 91 x 183
OP914

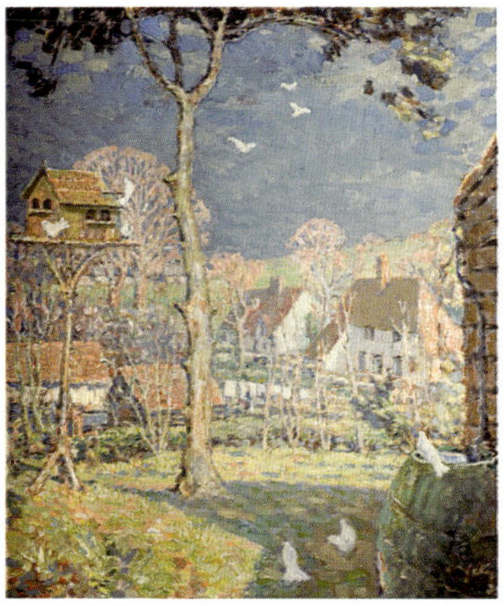

Yates, Thomas Brown b.1882
From My Garden 1900–1936
oil on canvas 76 x 63.5
OP320

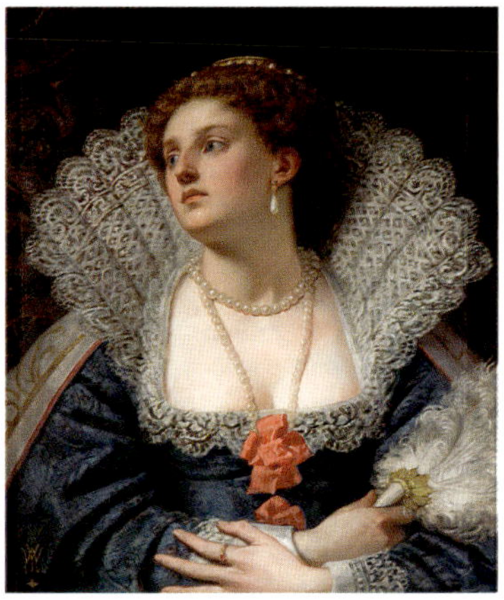

Yeames, William Frederick 1835–1918
Amy Robsart (1532–1560) 1884
oil on board 76 x 63.5
OP535

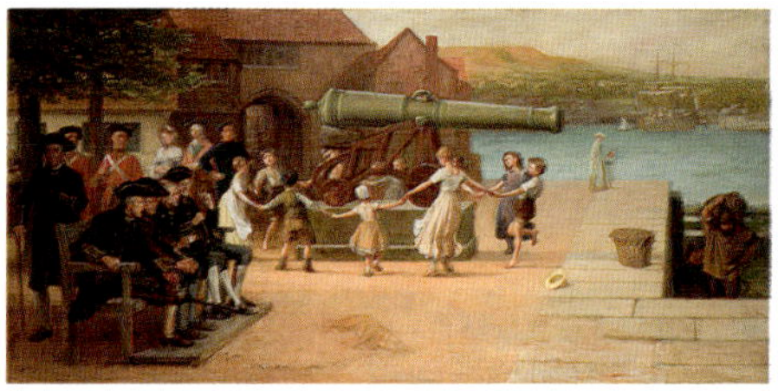

Yeames, William Frederick 1835–1918
Peace and War ('Here we go round the mulberry bush', from Besan and Rice's 'By Celia's Arbour')
oil on canvas 91.5 x 178
OP518

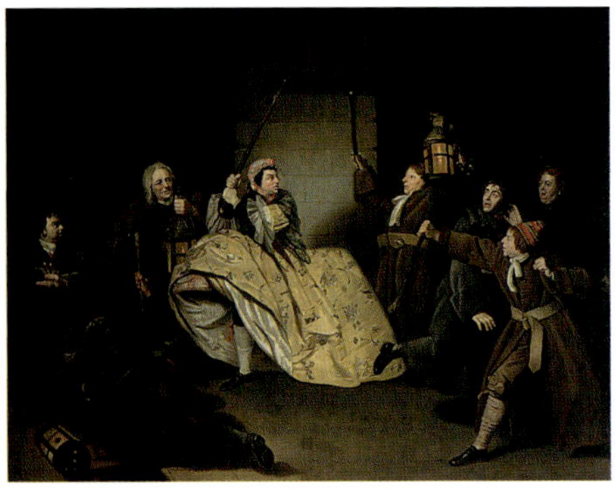

Zoffany, Johann 1733–1810
David Garrick as Sir John Brute in Vanbrugh's 'The Provoked Wife' 1763–1765
oil on canvas 99 x 124.5
OP607

Facing page: Allen, Harry Epworth, 1894–1958, *A Derbyshire Farmstead* (detail), The Potteries Museum & Art Gallery (p. 95)

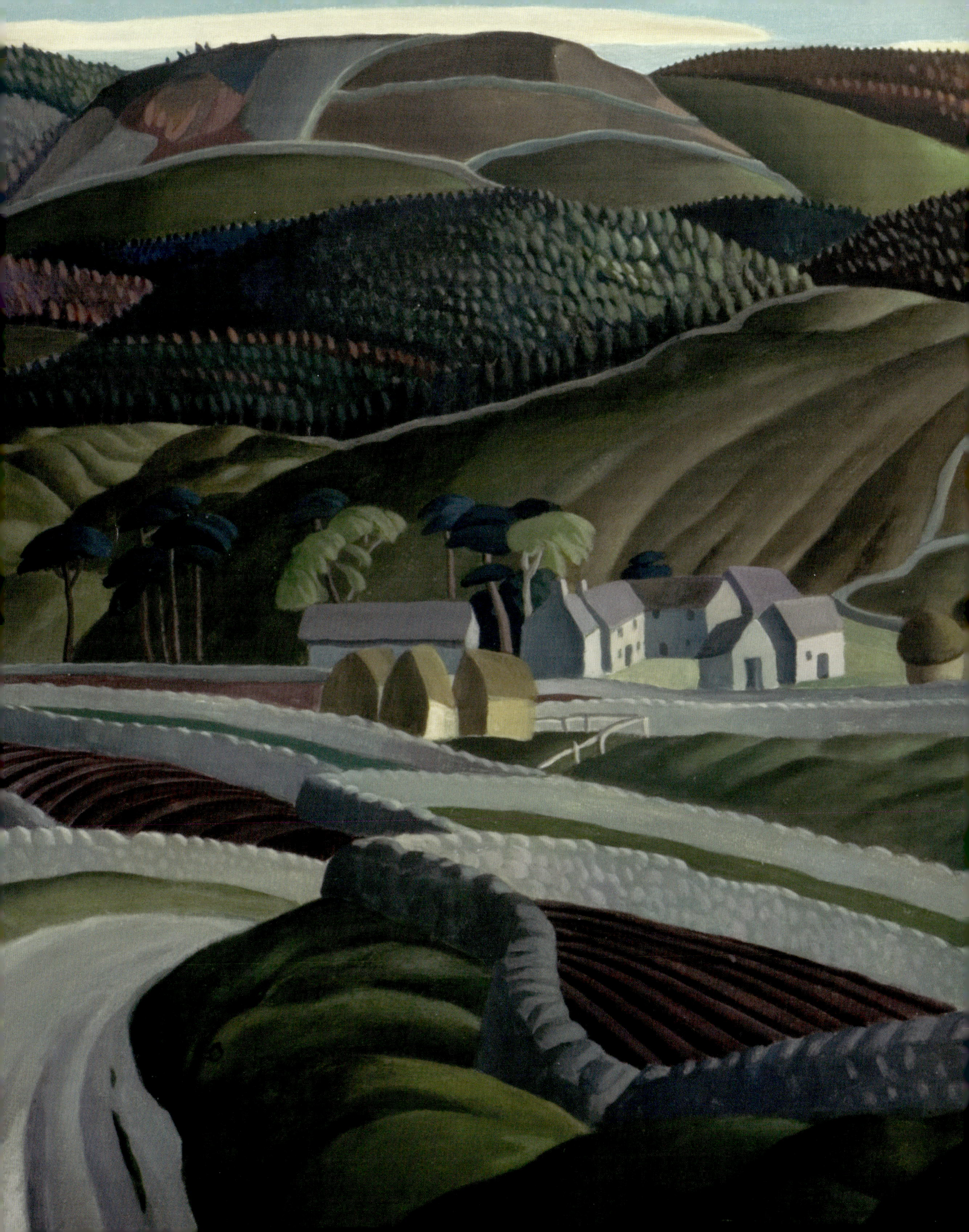

Paintings Without Reproductions

This section lists all the paintings that have not been included in the main pages of the catalogue. They were excluded as it was not possible to photograph them for this project. Additional information relating to acquisition credit lines or loan details is also included. For this reason the information below is not repeated in the Further Information section.

Biddulph Library

Simcock, Jack b.1929, *House on the Hill**, 46 x 61(E), oil on board, gift from the artist in memory of Mrs L. C. Johnson (1938–1959), not available at the time of photography

Samuel Johnson Birthplace Museum

unknown artist, *Two Gentlemen*, 47.5 x 60.5, oil on canvas, 2000.211, condition too fragmentary to be photographed

The Staffordshire Regiment Museum

Carroll, P., *Drummer of 64th Regiment*, oil on canvas, 5918, gift; on loan to Tidworth Barracks, Wiltshire at the time of photography

Cuneo, Terence Tenison, 1907–1996, *Baskeyfield*, oil on canvas, 4632, purchased; on loan to Tidworth Barracks, Wiltshire at the time of photography

Olivier, *Lieutenant General Sir Charles Tucker*, oil on canvas, 1629, gift; on loan to Tidworth Barracks, Wiltshire at the time of photography

unknown artist, *A. Burton, Private 203249*, oil on canvas, 8969, gift; on loan to Tidworth Barracks, Wiltshire at the time of photography

unknown artist, *Brigadier J. F. Beney, CMG, MBE*, oil on canvas, 6428, gift; on loan to Tidworth Barracks, Wiltshire at the time of photography

unknown artist, *Lieutenant General Sir Charles Tucker*, oil on canvas, 4401, on loan to Tidworth Barracks, Wiltshire at the time of photography

unknown artist, *Major General Alexander Leslie*, oil on canvas, 5919, gift; on loan to Tidworth Barracks, Wiltshire at the time of photography

unknown artist, *Sir John Campbell at Redan at Sebastopol, 1855*, oil on canvas, 4416, on loan to Tidworth Barracks, Wiltshire at the time of photography

unknown artist, *Wreck of Briton on Alderman Islands, 1844* , oil on canvas, 896, gift; on loan to Tidworth Barracks, Wiltshire at the time of photography

Sandwell Museums Service Collection

Bladon, T. Murray Bernard, b.1864, *Frederick Hackwood (1883–1923)*, 1909, 76.2 x 50.8, oil on canvas, P.96, transferred from Sandwell Metropolitan Borough Council Libraries, in conservation at time of photography

unknown artist, *Portrait of a Man at a Desk*, 127 x 101.5, oil on canvas, P.83, condition too fragmentary to be photographed

Staffordshire County Council

Bennett, Frank Moss, 1874 x 1953, *Study for a Portrait of Sir Gilbert Henry Claughton, Bt (1856–1921)*, 1922, oil on canvas, 30, gift from Roy Eustace Joy, before 1932, not available at the time of photography

Chorlton, J., *Portrait of a Lady*, 1915, 297 x 180, oil on canvas, 35, not available at the time of photography

Lockhart, William Ewart, 1846–1900, *William Heneage Legge, Lord Lewisham, 6th Earl of Dartmouth (1851–1936)*, 1887, oil on canvas, 31, gift from William Heneage Legge, not available at the time of photography

The Potteries Museum & Art Gallery

Shelley, Frederick, b.1865, *The Old Orchard, Shelton*, 69 x 48, oil on canvas, 1954.FA.98, old stock, acquired before the accession register and Stoke-on-Trent Museum were established, not available at the time of photography,

Wedgwood Museum

De Bod, E., *Etruria Hall*, 50 x 100, oil on canvas, 9746, gift from British Steel plc, 2000, in secure storage prior the to completion of the new Wedgwood Museum at the time of photography

Holmes, James, 1777–1860, *Josiah Wedgwood III (1795–1880)*, oil on canvas, 5614, transferred from Leith Hall Place, former residence of Ralph Vaughan Williams, in secure storage prior to completion of new Wedgwood Museum at time of photography

Wright, Joseph of Derby, 1734–1797, *A View of Dovedale*, 1793, 48.2 x 69.3, oil on canvas, not available at the time of photography

Wolverhampton Art Gallery

Anthony, Henry Mark, 1817–1886, *The City and Fortress of Lerida, Spain*, 104.1 x 203.2, oil on canvas, OP436, gift from Mr Philip Horsman, 1886, not available at the time of photography

Baker, Thomas, 1809–1869, *Landscape with Cattle*, 1849, 25.4 x 35.6, oil on canvas, OP177, gift, not available at the time of photography

Bird, Edward, 1772–1819, *Study for 'The Memorial to Lord Howe'*, 1790–1800, 29.8 x 24.1, oil on copper, OP505, gift, 1970, not available at the time of photography

Bird, Edward, 1772–1819, *Cupids Bathing*, 11.4 x 8.9, oil on copper, OP506, gift, 1887, not available at the time of photography

Dawson, Henry, 1811–1878, *In Dovedale*, 1853, 76.2 x 50.8, oil on canvas, OP614, gift from Mrs M. C. Cartwright, 1887, not available at the time of photography

Hodgson, John Evan, 1831–1895, *Queen Elizabeth Reviewing the Fleet*, 1864, 84 x 157.48, oil on canvas, OP263, gift; on loan to the Houses of Parliament at the time of photography

Hodgson, John Evan, 1831–1895, *The Return of Sir Francis Drake at Plymouth*, 84 x 157.9, oil on canvas, OP264, on loan to the Houses of Parliament at the time of photography

Keeling, William Knight, 1807–1886, *Seated Spaniard*, 1881, 55.3 x 38.1, oil on canvas, OP383, gift from Mrs M. C. Cartwright, 1887, in conservation at the time of photography

Lucas, Seymour, 1849–1923, *A Man in a Red Suit (Hazelrigg) (study for 'The Flight of Five Members')*, 1915, 85 x 61, oil on canvas, OP138/7, gift, 1916, not available at the time of photography

Lucas, Seymour, 1849–1923, *A Man on Steps (Earle) (study for 'The Flight of Five Members')*, 1915, 85 x 61, oil on canvas, OP138/5, gift, 1916, not available at the time of photography

Lucas, Seymour, 1849–1923, *A Man with a Staff (Hampden) (study for 'The Flight of Five Members')*, 1915, 85 x 61, oil on canvas, OP138/4, gift, 1916, not available at the time of photography

Lucas, Seymour, 1849–1923, *Puritan on Steps (Strode) (study for 'The Flight of Five Members')*, 1915, 85 x 61, oil on canvas, OP138/9, gift, 1916, not available at the time of photography

Lucas, Seymour, 1849–1923, *Seated Man in a Boat (Holles) (study for 'The Flight of Five Members')*, 1915, 85 x 61, oil on canvas, OP138/1, gift, 1916, not available at the time of photography

Lucas, Seymour, 1849–1923, *Seated Man in a Boat (Pym) (study for 'The Flight of Five Members')*, 1915, 85 x 61, oil on canvas, OP138/10, gift, 1916, not available at the time of photography

Müller, William James, (circle of), 1812–1845, *A Welsh Stream*, 1843, 48.3 x 69.5, oil on canvas, OP273, gift, 1948, not available at the time of photography

Phoenix, George, 1863–1935, *(R. A. Harper) J. W. Sankey*, 71.8 x 61.6, oil on canvas, OP713, gift, not available at the time of photography

Reinagle, Philip, 1749–1833, *Cattle in the Hartz District*, 26 x 38.1, oil on panel, OP37, gift from Mrs M. C. Cartwright, 1887, not available at the time of photography

Stark, James, 1794–1859, *Woody Landscape*, 104.1 x 142.2, oil on canvas, OP457, purchased, 1941, not available at the time of photography

unknown artist, 19th C, *Old Woman with an Apple*, 63.5 x 50.8, oil on canvas, OP558, gift, 1945, not available at the time of photography

unknown artist, 19th C, *Robert Bew*, oil on canvas, OP742, not available at the time of photography

unknown artist, *At the Cottage Door*, 14 x 10.1, oil on panel, OP255, gift from Mrs M. C. Cartwright, 1887, not available at the time of photography

unknown artist, *Canal Street, Wolverhampton*, 35.6 x 43.8, oil on canvas, OP279, not available at the time of photography

unknown artist, *Coast Scene with a Fisherman*, 50.8 x 76.2, oil on canvas, OP770, acquired, 1982, not available at the time of photography

unknown artist, *Country Cottage with a Family*, 50.8 x 61, oil on canvas, OP776, acquired, 1982, not available at the time of photography

unknown artist, *Landscape with a Lake*, 76.2 x 127, oil on canvas, OP773, gift, 1982, not available at the time of photography

unknown artist, *The Sacrifice of Iphigenia*, 137.2 x 88.9, oil on canvas, OP783, acquired, 1982, not available at the time of photography

Further Information

The paintings listed in this section have additional information relating to one or more of the five categories outlined below. This extra information is only provided where it is applicable and where it exists. Paintings listed in this section follow the same order as in the illustrated pages of the catalogue.

I	The full name of the artist if this was too long to display in the illustrated pages of the catalogue. Such cases are marked in the catalogue with a (…).
II	The full title of the painting if this was too long to display in the illustrated pages of the catalogue. Such cases are marked in the catalogue with a (…).
III	Acquisition information or acquisition credit lines as well as information about loans, copied from the records of the owner collection.
IV	Artist copyright credit lines where the copyright owner has been traced. Exhaustive efforts have been made to locate the copyright owners of all the images included within this catalogue and to meet their requirements. Any omissions or mistakes brought to our attention will be duly attended to and corrected in future publications.
V	The credit line of the lender of the transparency if the transparency has been borrowed. Bridgeman images are available subject to any relevant copyright approvals from the Bridgeman Art Library at www.bridgeman.co.uk

East Staffordshire Borough Council

Mason, Arnold 1885–1963, *Barges*, © the artist's estate
Stent, M. *Blue and Grey Squares**
Stent, M. *Blue Circles**
Sutton, Philip b.1928, *Landscape, June 1956*, © Philip Sutton RA
Townsend, E. *Evening*, gift from Councillor Miss M. Goodger, JP, 1936
Tuson, J. *Three Goblets*

Museum of Cannock Chase

Clare, Pat b.1938, *The Last Snapping*, gift from the artist, 2004, © the artist

Churnet Valley Railway

R. C. H. *Train at Cheddleton Station*
Simm, Richard b.1926, *Train at Cheddleton Station*, © the artist
Skidmore, Michael b.1943, *Class '4MT' Standard Tank 80136 at Cheddleton Station on the Churnet Valley Railway*, © the artist
unknown artist *F. A. L. Barnwell, Last General Manager of the North Staffordshire Railway Company (1919–1923)*

Ingestre Hall Residential Arts Centre

Bardwell, Thomas 1704–1767, *Catherine Talbot of Ingestre and Hillingdon (1722–1785)*, transferred to Sandwell Metropolitan Borough Council with the purchase of Ingestre Hall, 1959
Bardwell, Thomas 1704–1767, *The Honourable John Talbot, MP, of Lincoln's Inn Fields (1711–1756)*, transferred to Sandwell Metropolitan Borough Council with the purchase of Ingestre Hall, 1959
Batoni, Pompeo 1708–1787, *John Chetwynd, 1st Earl Talbot (1750–1793)*, transferred to Sandwell Metropolitan Borough Council with the purchase of Ingestre Hall, 1959
Beale, Mary 1633–1699, *The Honourable John Talbot, Younger Brother of Charles, Duke and 12th Earl of Shrewsbury (1664–1685/1686)*, transferred to Sandwell Metropolitan Borough Council with the purchase of Ingestre Hall, 1959
Beale, Mary (attributed to) 1633–1699, *Anna Maria, Countess of Shrewsbury (1642–1702)*, transferred to Sandwell Metropolitan Borough Council with the purchase of Ingestre Hall, 1959
British (English) School *Francis Talbot, 5th Earl of Shrewsbury, KG (1500–1560)*, transferred to Sandwell Metropolitan Borough Council with the purchase of Ingestre Hall, 1959
British (English) School *Elizabeth, Countess of Shrewsbury (c.1525–1608)*, transferred to Sandwell Metropolitan Borough Council with the purchase of Ingestre Hall, 1959
British (English) School *George Talbot, 6th Earl of Shrewsbury and Waterford (1528–1590)*, transferred to Sandwell Metropolitan Borough Council with the purchase of Ingestre Hall, 1959
British (English) School *Gilbert Talbot, 7th Earl of Shrewsbury (1552–1616)*, transferred to Sandwell Metropolitan Borough Council with the purchase of Ingestre Hall, 1959
British (English) School *Alathea Talbot, Countess of Arundel and Surrey (c.1590–1654)*, transferred to Sandwell Metropolitan Borough Council with the purchase of Ingestre Hall, 1959
British (English) School *John Talbot, 16th Earl of Shrewsbury and Waterford (1791–1852), and Charles Talbot*, transferred to Sandwell Metropolitan Borough Council with the purchase of Ingestre Hall, 1959
Cecill, Thomas (copy after) active 1625–1640, *Sir John Talbot, 1st Earl of Shrewsbury and Waterford (1383–1453)*, transferred to Sandwell Metropolitan Borough Council with the purchase of Ingestre Hall, 1959
Clifford, Edward 1844–1907, *Anna Theresa, Countess of Shrewsbury (1836–1912)*, transferred to Sandwell Metropolitan Borough Council with the purchase of Ingestre Hall, 1959
Clover, Joseph 1779–1853, *Lord James Beresford, 4th Son of Henry de la Poer (1816–1841)*, transferred to Sandwell Metropolitan Borough Council with the purchase of Ingestre Hall, 1959
Dahl, Michael I 1656/1659–1743, *Charles Talbot, Duke and 12th Earl of Shrewsbury (1660–1718)*, transferred to Sandwell Metropolitan Borough Council with the purchase of Ingestre Hall, 1959
Dutch School *A Country Scene*, transferred to Sandwell Metropolitan Borough Council with the purchase of Ingestre Hall, 1959
Dyck, Anthony van (school of) 1599–1641, *Sir Gilbert Talbot, Knight of Salwarp (1606–1695)*, transferred to Sandwell Metropolitan Borough Council with the purchase of Ingestre Hall, 1959
Grant, Henry active 1868–1895, *Ellen Mary, Countess of Shrewsbury*, transferred to Sandwell Metropolitan Borough Council with the purchase of Ingestre Hall, 1959
Hamburger, Johann Konrad 1809–1871, *John Talbot, 16th Earl of Shrewsbury and Waterford (1791–1852)*, transferred to Sandwell Metropolitan Borough Council with the purchase of Ingestre Hall, 1959
Hardy, Dorofield active 1882–1927, *Charles John Alton Chetwynd, Viscount Ingestre, MVO (1882–1915)*, transferred to Sandwell Metropolitan Borough Council with the purchase of Ingestre Hall, 1959
Herkomer, Hubert von 1849–1914, *Charles Henry John, 20th Earl of Shrewsbury and Waterford, KCVO (1877–1921)*, transferred to Sandwell Metropolitan Borough Council with the purchase of Ingestre Hall, 1959
Hoppner, John 1758–1810, *William Pitt, PC (1759–1806)*, transferred to Sandwell Metropolitan Borough Council with the purchase of Ingestre Hall, 1959
Jackson, John 1778–1831, *Henry John, Viscount Ingestre (1803–1868)*, transferred to Sandwell Metropolitan Borough Council with the purchase of Ingestre Hall, 1959
Janssens van Ceulen, Cornelis 1593–1661, *John Talbot of Grafton (1542–1611)*, transferred to Sandwell Metropolitan Borough Council with the purchase of Ingestre Hall, 1959
Janssens van Ceulen, Cornelis 1593–1661, *Margaret Talbot, Second Wife of John Talbot (d.1620)*, transferred to Sandwell Metropolitan Borough Council with the purchase of Ingestre Hall, 1959
Kneller, Godfrey (school of) 1646–1723, *Adelhida, Duchess of Shrewsbury (1665–1726)*, transferred to Sandwell Metropolitan Borough Council with the purchase of Ingestre Hall, 1959
Kneller, Godfrey (school of) 1646–1723, *Charles Talbot, Duke and 12th Earl of Shrewsbury (1660–1718)*, transferred to Sandwell Metropolitan Borough Council with the purchase of Ingestre Hall, 1959
Kneller, Godfrey (school of) 1646–1723, *Right Reverend William Talbot, Bishop of Durham (c.1658–*

1730), transferred to Sandwell Metropolitan Borough Council with the purchase of Ingestre Hall, 1959
Lely, Peter 1618–1680, *Sir Walter Chetwynd, MP of Ingestre (1634/1635–1693)*, transferred to Sandwell Metropolitan Borough Council with the purchase of Ingestre Hall, 1959
Medina, John Baptist de 1659–1710, *John Chetwynd, MP (d.1702)*, transferred to Sandwell Metropolitan Borough Council with the purchase of Ingestre Hall, 1959
Myn, Herman van der 1684–1781, *John Chetwynd, 2nd Viscount Chetwynd and Family*, transferred to Sandwell Metropolitan Borough Council with the purchase of Ingestre Hall, 1959
Orde, Cuthbert Julian 1888–1968, *John George Charles Henry Alton Alexander Chetwynd, 21st Earl of Shrewsbury and Waterford (1914–1980)*, transferred to Sandwell Metropolitan Borough Council with the purchase of Ingestre Hall, 1959
Phillips, Thomas 1770–1845, *The Children of the 2nd Earl Talbot*, transferred to Sandwell Metropolitan Borough Council with the purchase of Ingestre Hall, 1959
Phillips, Thomas 1770–1845, *The Children of the 2nd Earl Talbot*, transferred to Sandwell Metropolitan Borough Council with the purchase of Ingestre Hall, 1959
Phillips, Thomas 1770–1845, *Frances Thomasine, Countess Talbot, Wife of the 2nd Earl Talbot (1778–1819)*, transferred to Sandwell Metropolitan Borough Council with the purchase of Ingestre Hall, 1959
Prinsep, Valentine Cameron 1838–1904, *Theresa Susey Helen Talbot, Later Marchioness of Londonderry and Charles Henry John, Viscount Ingestre (1860–1921)*, transferred to Sandwell Metropolitan Borough Council with the purchase of Ingestre Hall, 1959
Reynolds, Joshua (copy after) 1723–1792, *Charlotte, Countess Talbot (1754–1804)*, transferred to Sandwell Metropolitan Borough Council with the purchase of Ingestre Hall, 1959
Reynolds, Joshua (copy of) 1723–1792, *Crossing the Brook*, transferred to Sandwell Metropolitan Borough Council with the purchase of Ingestre Hall, 1959
Russell, Theodore (attributed to) 1614–1689, *Sir Gilbert Talbot, Knight of Salwarp (1606–1695)*, transferred to Sandwell Metropolitan Borough Council with the purchase of Ingestre Hall, 1959
Slaughter, Stephen 1697–1765, *John Chetwynd, 2nd Viscount Chetwynd (c.1680–1767)*, transferred to Sandwell Metropolitan Borough Council with the purchase of Ingestre Hall, 1959
Solimena, Francesco (style of) 1657–1747, *The Virgin with the Infant Christ*, transferred to Sandwell Metropolitan Borough Council with the purchase of Ingestre Hall, 1959
Thompson, Thomas Clement c.1780–1857, *Charles Chetwynd, 2nd Earl Talbot (1777–1849)*, transferred to Sandwell Metropolitan Borough Council with the purchase of Ingestre Hall, 1959
unknown artist early 18th C, *Esther, Viscountess Chetwynd, Wife of John, 2nd Viscount Chetwynd, and Her Son, John Chetwynd (1699–1741)*, transferred to Sandwell Metropolitan Borough Council with the purchase of Ingestre Hall, 1959
unknown artist early 18th C, *The Honourable Mrs Mary Talbot, Wife of George Talbot of Heythrop (1698–1752)*, transferred to Sandwell Metropolitan Borough Council with the purchase of Ingestre Hall, 1959
unknown artist *A View of Beau Park*, transferred to Sandwell Metropolitan Borough Council with the purchase of Ingestre Hall, 1959
unknown artist early 19th C, *Charles John Chetwynd-Talbot, 19th Earl of Shrewsbury (1830–1877)*, transferred to Sandwell Metropolitan Borough Council with the purchase of Ingestre Hall, 1959
unknown artist early 19th C, *Maria Theresa, Countess of Shrewsbury (1795–1856)*, transferred to Sandwell Metropolitan Borough Council with the purchase of Ingestre Hall, 1959
unknown artist mid-19th C, *Captain Charles Arthur Talbot, Grandson of the 2nd Earl Talbot (1834–1869)*, transferred to Sandwell Metropolitan Borough Council with the purchase of Ingestre Hall, 1959
unknown artist *Alderman Reuben Farley, JP*, transferred to Sandwell Metropolitan Borough Council with the purchase of Ingestre Hall, 1959
unknown artist *Charles, 12th Earl & Duke of Shrewsbury, 1699*, transferred to Sandwell Metropolitan Borough Council with the purchase of Ingestre Hall, 1959
unknown artist *Charles John Chetwynd-Talbot, Viscount Ingestre (1830–1877)*, transferred to Sandwell Metropolitan Borough Council with the purchase of Ingestre Hall, 1959
unknown artist *Earl of Dartmouth*, transferred to Sandwell Metropolitan Borough Council with the purchase of Ingestre Hall, 1959
unknown artist *Edward Talbot, 8th Earl of Shrewsbury (1561–1618)*, transferred to Sandwell Metropolitan Borough Council with the purchase of Ingestre Hall, 1959
unknown artist *Esther, Mrs Chetwynd (1699–1741)*, transferred to Sandwell Metropolitan Borough Council with the purchase of Ingestre Hall, 1959
unknown artist *Honourable Mrs Catherine Talbot, Later Wife of Honourable John Talbot (1722–1785)*, transferred to Sandwell Metropolitan Borough Council with the purchase of Ingestre Hall, 1959
unknown artist *Portrait of a Lady*, transferred to Sandwell Metropolitan Borough Council with the purchase of Ingestre Hall, 1959
unknown artist *Sir Gilbert Talbot, Knight of Salwarp (1606–1695)*, transferred to Sandwell Metropolitan Borough Council with the purchase of Ingestre Hall, 1959
unknown artist *The Family of Captain Charles Arthur Talbot*, transferred to Sandwell Metropolitan Borough Council with the purchase of Ingestre Hall, 1959
Vanderbank, John c.1694–1739, *Charles Talbot, 1st Lord Talbot (1685–1737)*, transferred to Sandwell Metropolitan Borough Council with the purchase of Ingestre Hall, 1959
Vigée-LeBrun, Elisabeth Louise 1755–1842, *Charles Chetwynd, 2nd Earl Talbot (1777–1849)*, transferred to Sandwell Metropolitan Borough Council with the purchase of Ingestre Hall, 1959
Wortley, Archibald J. Stuart 1849–1905, *Sir Reginald Arthur James Talbot, KCB, 3rd Son of the 18th Earl of Shrewsbury (1841–1929)*, transferred to Sandwell Metropolitan Borough Council with the purchase of Ingestre Hall, 1959

Leek Town Council

Dawson, Robert 1926–1997, *Rain Storm over the Roaches*, gift from Mr Brown, 2005, © the artist's estate

Staffordshire Moorlands District Council

Bratby, John Randall 1928–1992, *Sunflowers*, gift from the artist, before 1992, © the artist's estate/www.bridgeman.co.uk
Breanski, Alfred de 1852–1928, *Silvery September*, gift from John Ward, 1956
Campling, H. R. active 1882–1904, *Rudyard Lake*, acquired, before 1994
Cubley, Henry Hadfield 1848–1934, *Morning Mists, Arrochar*, acquired, before 1994
Cubley, Henry Hadfield 1848–1934, *Leek from Ladderedge*, acquired, before 1994
Cubley, Henry Hadfield 1848–1934, *The Old Mill*, acquired, before 1994
England, Frederick John b.1939, *Rudyard Stream*, gift from the artist, 1970
Hammersley, W. *Mill Street, Leek*, acquired, before 1994
Hooper, John Horace c.1850–c.1899, *Near Guildford*, bequeathed from Mercy Moore, 1994
Jack, Richard 1866–1952, *The Swedish Dyehouse*, gift from Leek Amateur Operatic Society, 1895, © the artist's estate
Jack, Richard 1866–1952, *Loup Scar, Wharfedale*, gift from William Ryder, before 1994, © the artist's estate
Kean, William R. *Feeding the Calves*, gift from Arthur Littlewood, Leek Art College, 1981
Light, David b.1959, *Malaccan Beach*, acquired, before 1994, © the artist
Newey, Harry Foster 1858–1933, *Oxwich Moor*, acquired, before 1994
Nierinck, Dorothy M. *Welsh Coast*
O'Neill, A. *Newsboy*, acquired, before 1994
Oversby, M. D. *Brough Park and Nicholson Institute, Leek*
unknown artist *Arch of Titus, Rome*, gift from Mr Nicholson, 1949
unknown artist *Landscape Scene and Mountains*, acquired, before 1994
unknown artist *Landscape Scene at the Edge of the River*, acquired, before 1994
unknown artist *Market Square*, acquired, before 1994
Whistler, J. M. N. *Henley Regatta*, acquired, before 1994
Wyld, William 1806–1889, *Venice*, acquired, before 1994

Erasmus Darwin House

British (English) School early 19th C, *Reverend Chancellor James Thomas Law (1790–1876)*, on long-term loan from Lichfield District Council
British (English) School early 19th C, *William Green (?)*, on long-term loan from Lichfield District Council
Hoppner, John 1758–1810, *George Canning (1770–1827) (?)*, on long-term loan from Lichfield District Council
unknown artist early 19th C, *Dr Robert Levett of Lichfield (d.1782)*, on long-term loan from Lichfield District Council

Lichfield District Council

Bratby, John Randall 1928–1992, *Flowers of Summer*, on loan to Lichfield Cathedral, © the artist's estate/www.bridgeman.co.uk
British (English) School *Charles II (1630–1685)*, on loan to Lichfield Cathedral
Cotman, Frederick George 1850–1920, *The First Otter*
Paoletti, Antonio Ermolao 1834–1912, *Blind Man's Bluff*
Pickersgill, Henry William (style of) 1782–1875, *Canon Bailye (1783–1830)*, on loan to Lichfield Cathedral
Preston, William *Extensive Lake and Mountains*
Schmitt, Guido Philipp 1834–1922, *Reverend John Gylby Lonsdale (1818–1907)*, on loan to Lichfield Cathedral
Smith *Gulielmus Smyth, Bishop of Lincoln*, on loan to Lichfield Cathedral
unknown artist 19th C, *Reverend Chancellor Law*, on loan to Lichfield Cathedral
unknown artist mid-19th C, *Mr John Mott (1787–1869)*, on loan to Lichfield Cathedral
unknown artist mid-19th C, *Mrs Henrietta Mott*, on loan to Lichfield Cathedral
unknown artist *Biblical Figure*, on loan to Lichfield Cathedral
unknown artist *David Garrick (1717–1779)*, on loan to Lichfield Garrick Theatre

Lichfield Heritage Centre

Smith, H. J. b.1876, *View of Lichfield Cathedral*, gift from J. Wilson, 1987
Spence, Robert 1871–1964, *Woe to the Bloody City of Lichfield*, on loan from Lichfield City Council

Samuel Johnson Birthplace Museum

Buchanan, J. *Albert Sperrin (1903–1987)*, unknown provenance
Fulleylove, John 1845–1908, *Dr Johnson in Lichfield Cathedral*, transferred from Lichfield Museum and Free Library, 1970
Glover, John (circle of) 1767–1849, *Lichfield Cathedral from Sandford Street*, transferred from Lichfield Museum and Free Library, 1979
Holgate, W. J. (Reverend) c.1842–c.1920, *Johnson and Oliver Goldsmith Walking down Fleet Street, London*, gift from the artist, 1920
Holgate, W. J. (Reverend) c.1842–c.1920, *Lichfield Market Place during the Days of Dr Johnson*, gift from the artist, 1920
Millar, James 1735–1805, *Mrs Esther Day*, transferred from Lichfield Museum and Free

Library, 1934
Opie, John 1761–1807, *Reverend Dr John Taylor*, on loan from Mr J. A. N. Duff
Pether, William 1731–1819, *David Garrick (1717–1779)*, bequeathed by Mrs Frances Lomax, 1931
Pickering, Henry active 1740–c.1771, *Elizabeth Hunter, later Mrs Thomas Seward (d.1780)*, gift from Mr W. W. Worthington, 1924
Reynolds, Joshua (after) 1723–1792, *David Garrick between Tragedy and Comedy*, bequeathed by Colonel M. A. W. Swinfen Broun, 1948
Reynolds, Joshua (after) 1723–1792, *Samuel Johnson (1709–1784)*, gift from Mrs Lodor Symonds, 1924
Reynolds, Joshua (attributed to) 1723–1792, *Johnson as a Young Man (1709–1784)*, gift from Mr H. M. Luckock, 1909
Reynolds, Joshua (school of) 1723–1792, *Sir Thomas Mills (sometimes known as Major André) (d.1793)*, gift from Mr Michael Waterhouse, 1968
Sanders, John M. *Mrs Samuel Johnson (1689–1752)*, gift from Mr J. D. Austin, 1989
Sanders, John M. *Lichfield Market Square with Carriage*, unknown provenance
Smith, J. *Elias Ashmole (1617–1692) (after John Riley)*, transferred from Lichfield Museum and Free Library, 1970
unknown artist late 17th–early 18th C, *A Member of the Dyott Family*, transferred from Lichfield Museum and Free Library, 1934
unknown artist early 18th C, *Landscape in a Classical Manner*, transferred from Lichfield Museum and Art Gallery, 1968
unknown artist 18th C, *David Garrick (1717–1779) as a Young Man*, transferred from Lichfield Museum and Free Library, 1970
unknown artist late 18th–early 19th C, *Johnson's Willow*, bequeathed by Mrs Frances Lomax, 1931
unknown artist early 19th C, *Bishop Ryder (1777–1836)*
unknown artist 19th C, *Dr Johnson without His Wig (1709–1784)*, gift from Miss Gresley, 1934
unknown artist 19th C, *Johnson's Willow, St Chad's Church and Stowe House*, gift from A. Phillips, 1903
unknown artist *Samuel Johnson (1709–1784)*
unknown artist *South-West Prospect View of Lichfield*, gift from Mr Thomas Adie, 1856
Vandergucht, Benjamin (copy of) 1753–1794, *David Garrick in His Regalia as Steward of Stratford Jubilee, 1769*, transferred from Lichfield Museum and Free Library, 1970
Ward, Edward Matthew 1816–1879, *Johnson Reading the Manuscript of 'The Vicar of Wakefield'*, gift from Mrs E. J. Andrews, 1972
Willis-Pryce, George 1866–1949, *West Front of Lichfield Cathedral*, transferred from Lichfield Museum and Free Library, 1979
Wright, Joseph (after) 1756–1793, *Erasmus Darwin (1731–1802)*, transferred from Lichfield Museum and Art Gallery, 1970
Zoffany, Johann (attributed to) 1733–1810, *Bennet Langton Contemplating the Nolleken's Bust of Johnson*, purchased from the Selective Eye Gallery in Jersey, with the assistance of the Pilgrim Trust, Mr W. F. Wahrle, the Conduit Lands Trust, the Johnson Society of Lichfield and an anonymous donor, 1976

The Staffordshire Regiment Museum

Lancaster, J. *Lieutenant George Albert Cairns, VC (1913–1944), in Action in Burma (1944)*, gift
Lawson, Cecil active 1907–after 1944, *1st South Staffords on the March in Burma, 1944*
Lawson, Cecil active 1907–after 1944, *Capture of Ponte Grande, Syracuse, 1943*
Souter, John Balloch 1890–1972, *Lieutenant Colonel J. C. Chaytor*, gift
unknown artist *Officer of the 64th Foot*, purchased
unknown artist *QMS C. Laban, 5th South Staffords*, gift
unknown artist *A South Staffords Soldier*, purchased
unknown artist *Colonel Luke Lillingston*, gift
unknown artist *Lieutenant General Sir William Pringle*
unknown artist *Lieutenant General Thorne, Officer of the 80th Foot (1849–1850)*, gift
unknown artist *Lieutenant Thomas Quill*, gift

Borough Museum & Art Gallery

Borsky, Jiri b.1945, *Newcastle Market*, commissioned, 1999, © the artist
British (English) School *Nathaniel Beard (1696–1772), Mayor of Newcastle-under-Lyme*, acquired, before 1988
British (English) School *View of Newcastle from Keele Bank*, gift, 1995
British (English) School *Cattle by a Barn*, purchased, before 1988
British (English) School 19th C, *Figure by Cottage in Landscape*, acquired, before 1988
British (English) School 19th C, *Keele Church, Staffordshire*, acquired, before 1988
British (English) School 20th C, *Colonel Josiah Wedgwood (1872–1943)*, acquired before 1988, on loan to the Houses of Parliament Museum
British (English) School 20th C, *Longton Church*, acquired, before 1988
Brooks, Adriana J. *Newcastle, from Clayton Fields*, acquired, before 1988
Buss, Robert William 1804–1875, *The Mock Mayor*, bequeathed by Joseph Mayer, 1882
Buss, Robert William 1804–1875, *Cartoon for 'The Mock Mayor'*, bequeathed by Joseph Mayer, 1882
Castle, Fred 1912–1996, *Is this the Age of the Train?*, purchased, 1987, © the artist's estate
Castle, Fred 1912–1996, *Winter*, purchased, 1987, © the artist's estate
Castle, Fred 1912–1996, *Bosham*, purchased, 1988, © the artist's estate
Chester, Charlie *Lord Snowdon (b.1930)*, acquired, before 1988
Clarkson, Jack 1906–1986, *Sunset over Potteries Landscape*, purchased from the artist, 1963
Clarkson, Jack 1906–1986, *St Giles' Church*, purchased, before 1988
Clarkson, Jack 1906–1986, *Taylor's Stores*, purchased, before 1988
Clarkson, Jack 1906–1986, *Municipal Hall, Newcastle-under-Lyme*, purchased, before 1988
Clarkson, Jack 1906–1986, *Potteries View with Canal*, purchased from the artist, 1963
Clarkson, Jack 1906–1986, *Red Lion Square*, purchased, before 1988
Clarkson, Jack 1906–1986, *The Old Borough Treasurers, Nelson Place*, purchased from the artist, 1964
Colley, R. M. *Red Lion Square*, gift, 1948
Collinge, J. *Spring Lodge, Trentham*, gift from Mrs Lewis, 1993
Collinge, J. *Spring Valley, Trentham*, gift from Mrs Lewis, 1993
Cooper, Thomas Sidney 1803–1902, *Cattle and Sheep at Rest in a Meadow*, acquired, before 1988
Dawson, Dan *Roxy Cinema, Nelson Place*, gift, 1993
Everden, John *Canal Side Buildings, Middleport*, purchased, before 1988
Faulkner, Neil b.1952, *Parkwood Avenue*, purchased, 1992
Fletcher, Doreen b.1952, *View from Clayton Fields, Newcastle-under-Lyme*, purchased from the artist, c.1989, © the artist/www.bridgeman.co.uk
Fletcher, Doreen b.1952, *Salvation Army Building*, purchased, c.1985, © the artist/www.bridgeman.co.uk
Fryer, E. M. *Isle of Capri*, bequeathed, 1993
Griffiths, J. W. *Newcastle Market*, gift from the artist, before 1988
Harper, W. K. *Wood's Pottery, Longport*, purchased, before 1988
Harvey *Coal Miners*
Hinks, Thomas *Lodge House, Caverswall*, purchased from the artist, before 1988
Hinks, Thomas *Longport Bridge*, purchased, before 1988
Hinks, Thomas *The Dee Estuary*, purchased, before 1988
Hooper, John Horace c.1850–c.1899, *The Mill*, purchased, before 1988
Jacomb-Hood, George Percy 1857–1930, *Una*, bequeathed by John Gallimore, 1909
King, Yeend 1855–1924, *Figures by a Country Cottage*, purchased, before 1988
Lancaster, Gordon *Well Bank, Betley*, purchased from the artist with the assistance of the National Art Collections Fund, 1990
Lloyd, Tim b.1959, *A Town on Millennium's Eve*, commissioned, purchased from the artist, 1999, © the artist
Middleton, Jameson *Thirsty*, bequeathed by John Gallimore, 1909
Miller, Lesley b.1946, *View of Newcastle from Alsager's Bank*, commissioned, purchased from the artist, 1999, © the artist
Moore, David R. b.1941, *Lonnie and Sutch at the Frog Inn, Newcastle*, purchased, 1993, © the artist
Mottain *'La Roche'*
Munday, John active 1890–1903, *View of Maer Hall*, purchased, 1997
Munday, John active 1890–1903, *Clough Hall Lake, Kidsgrove*, acquired, before 1988
Munday, John active 1890–1903, *Mow Cop from Moss House Farm, near Hall Green*, purchased, before 1988
Mussill, William 1828–1906, *Study of Fruit and Nuts*, purchased, before 1988
Newlove, Margery G. *Bullerthorpe Farm*, purchased, 1976
Owen, Susan M. active 1974–1977 *The Pigeon Fancier*, purchased, 1988
Owen, Susan M. active 1974–1977 *Portrait of the School Caretaker*, purchased, before 1988
Owen, Susan M. active 1974–1977 *Unfinished Oil Sketch of a Young Woman's Face*, purchased, before 1988
Pratt, Henry Lark I 1805–1873, *Red Lion Square*, gift, before 1960
Pratt, Henry Lark I 1805–1873, *Looking West of St Luke's Church, Silverdale*, purchased, 2001
Pratt, Henry Lark I 1805–1873, *Old Farmstead in Trentham Road*, purchased, 2001
Pratt, Henry Lark I 1805–1873, *Trentham Hall*, bequeathed by John Gallimore, 1909
Pratt, Henry Lark I 1805–1873, *King Street, Newcastle-under-Lyme*, purchased, before 1988
Richardson, Jonathan the elder 1665–1745, *Elijah Fenton (1683–1730)*, gift, 1943
Ridgway, J. *Arnold Bennett (1867–1931)*, acquired, before 1988
Roe, Clarence 1850–1909, *Snowdonia*, purchased, 1964
Rose, Donald *Guildhall and Market Stalls*, acquired, before 1988
Scott, Alan *The Chapel in Silverdale Cemetery*, commissioned, purchased from the artist, 1999
Stanton, George Clark 1832–1894, *Shepherd Boys with their Flock*, gift, 1956
Stevenson, Stewart b.1935, *Betley Church*, commissioned, purchased from the artist, 1999, © the artist
Thirlwall, John b.1943, *After the Storm, St Giles*, commissioned, 1999, © the artist
Toft, J. Alfonso 1866–1964, *Cattle in Landscape, Trentham, Stoke-on-Trent*, acquired, before 1988
Tunstall, Eric 1897–1987, *The Advocate*, purchased, 1987
Turner, George II 1843–1910, *Country Lane with Cottage*, acquired, before 1988
unknown artist *Old Joe, the Newcastle Match Seller*, gift, 1973
Wade, George A. active 1950–1960, *Cloud Study*, acquired, before 1988
Whittle, Harry Armstrong active 1867–1876, *Fishing Boat in a Mountainous River Landscape with Cottages*, gift, 1949
Whittle, Harry Armstrong active 1867–1876, *Rowing Boat at the Bank*, gift, 1950
Wright, John Massey 1777–1866, *Claiming the Wichnor Flitch*, purchased, 1988

Keele University

Abrahams, Peter b.1958, *Carbon Horizon*, gift, 1988, © the artist
Atkinson, Amy B. 1859–1916, *Lady with a Dog*
Ayrton, Michael 1921–1975, *The White Jug*, gift from Dr Barnett Stross, 1962, © the artist's estate
Ayrton, Michael 1921–1975, *The Fortune Teller*, gift from Dr Barnett Stross, 1962, © the artist's estate
Ayrton, Michael 1921–1975, *Crayfish*, gift from Dr Barnett Stross, 1962, © the artist's estate
Borsky, Jiri b.1945, *The Auction*, purchased, 1983, © the artist
Brody, E. M. *Stripes and Circles*, acquired, 1960s
Clarke, Paul Montem b.1915, *Abstract Circles**, acquired, 1960s
Dai, Shi-he active 1989–1990, *Keele Hall*, purchased from the artist, 1990
Dai, Shi-he active 1989–1990, *Professor William Campbell Stewart*, purchased from the artist, 1990
Emery, Alston active 1973–c.1992, *Longton Ovens*, purchased from the artist, 1975
Folkes, Peter L. b.1923, *Still Life*, purchased from the artist, 1982, © the artist
Gleeson, David Paul b.1956, *Staffordshire Sheds, Castlefields*, purchased from the artist, 2002, © the artist

Gleeson, David Paul b.1956, *In the Victoria & Albert LIV*, purchased from the artist, 2002, © the artist
Goodwin, Robin L. H. *Lord Lindsay of Birker (1879–1952)*, purchased from the artist, 1953
Grant, Duncan 1885–1978, *The Wine Press*, gift from Dr Barnett Stross, 1961, © 1978 estate of Duncan Grant
Harding, Tony b.1946, *Squares**, acquired, 1976, © the artist
Held, Julie b.1958, *Stephanie Hurst*, © the artist
Held, Julie b.1958, *Woman with Swan I*, © the artist
Held, Julie b.1958, *Woman with Swan II*, © the artist
Held, Julie b.1958, *Ceyx*, purchased from the artist, 1993, © the artist
Held, Julie b.1958, *Anna and Bonnie*, purchased from the artist, 1993, © the artist
Henderson, Ian active 1966–1967, *Lancashire*, acquired, 1960s
Henderson, Ian active 1966–1967, *Professor Harold Taylor, Vice-Chancellor*, purchased from the artist, 1967
Ionschaev, Suulvan *Dr David Harrison, Vice-Chancellor*, purchased from the artist, 1991
Jones, J. *The Residence of Charles Meigh Esquire*, gift from E. J. D. Warrilow, 1988
King, Yeend 1855–1924, *Goose Girl*
King, Yeend 1855–1924, *Shepherd with His Flock*
Kramer, Jacob 1892–1962, *Child*, gift from Dr Barnett Stross, 1962, © William Roberts Society
Kramer, Jacob 1892–1962, *Rohalla*, gift from Dr Barnett Stross, 1962, © William Roberts Society
Kuhn, Andrzej b.1930, *Explorer*, purchased from the artist, 1980, © the artist
Leeson, Laurence b.1930, *Peninsula I*, purchased from the artist, 1962, © the artist
Leeson, Laurence b.1930, *Diminishing Circle*, purchased from the artist, 1963, © the artist
Leeson, Laurence b.1930, *Parts*, © the artist
Lovatt, Enos b.1937, *Landscape*, purchased, c.1960, © the artist
Lowry, Laurence Stephen 1887–1976, *The Mill Gates*, gift from Dr Barnett Stross, 1961, © courtesy of the estate of L. S. Lowry
Lyons, L. *Castle in a Landscape*
Naylor, Ian b.1964, *Dr Michael B. Akehurst*, commissioned by Keele University in honour of Dr Michael B. Akehurst, © the artist
Pass, Donald b.1930, *The Cedars*
Pass, Donald b.1930, *The Wave*
Pass, Donald b.1930, *White Landscape*
Pelham, Thomas Kent active 1860–1892, *At the Cottage Door*
Praag, Arnold van b.1926, *Susannah and the Elders I*, gift, 1998, © the artist
Reynolds, Joshua (attributed to) 1723–1792, *John Sneyd*
Simcock, Jack b.1929, *Trees and Houses*, gift from Joyce Wareham, 1980, © the artist
Simcock, Jack b.1929, *Farm*, purchased from the artist, 1970, © the artist
Simcock, Jack b.1929, *The Old House*, purchased from the artist, 1964, © the artist
Smart, Rowley 1887–1934, *The Four Witches*, gift from Dr Barnett Stross, 1962
Smart, Rowley 1887–1934, *Swedish Landscape*, gift from Dr Barnett Stross, 1962
Smart, Rowley 1887–1934, *Circus*, gift from Dr Barnett Stross, 1962
Smart, Rowley 1887–1934, *Giverny*, gift from Dr Barnett Stross, 1962
Smart, Rowley 1887–1934, *Mousehole*, gift from Dr Barnett Stross, 1962
Smart, Rowley 1887–1934, *Mousehole, the Harbour*, gift from Dr Barnett Stross, 1962
Smart, Rowley 1887–1934, *Nocturne*, gift from Dr Barnett Stross, 1962
Smyth, Leslie *Corfu*
Sneyd, Charlotte Augusta 1800–1882, *Colonel Walter Sneyd*, purchased as part of the Raymond Richards Collection, 1950s
Steele, Edwin 1803–1871, *Roses*
Trevelyan, Julian 1910–1989, *Italian Field*, gift from Keele University Students' Union, © the artist's estate
unknown artist *Le Play House, Belgrave Road, London*, gift from the Institute of Sociology, from the Le Play Collection, Special Collections and Archives, 1957
unknown artist *Circles**
unknown artist *Geometric Shapes**
unknown artist *Lord Lindsay of Birker (1879–1952)*
unknown artist *Portrait of a Girl*
Wild, Tony b.1941, *Gladioli*, © the artist

Sandwell Metropolitan Borough Council

Gibbs, J. *Daniel Hipkins*
Munns, John Bernard 1869–1942, *Thomas E. Saller, JP, CC*
unknown artist *Portrait of a Gentleman*
unknown artist *Joseph Hall (1789–1862)*, gift from the Misses Hall Best and Mr Robert Dudley Best
unknown artist *Portrait of a Gentleman*

Sandwell Museum Service Collection

Anthony, Henry Mark 1817–1886, *A Country Churchyard*, bequeathed by Mary Richards, 1891
Bagley, Samuel D. active 1886–1898, *Coming out of the Wood*
Bagley, Samuel D. active 1886–1898, *The Path through the Wood*
Baker, John L. b.1922, *Coal Mine*
Baker, Thomas 1809–1869, *River Avon, near Warwick*, bequeathed by Mary Richards, 1891
Baker, Thomas 1809–1869, *At the River's Brink*, bequeathed by Mary Richards, 1891
Barnfield, Fred b.1935, *Still Life*, gift, © the artist
Barnfield, Fred b.1935, *Woman*, gift, © the artist
Barnfield, Fred b.1935, *Domestic Interior*, gift, © the artist
Barnfield, Fred b.1935, *Domestic Interior*, gift, © the artist
Barnfield, Fred b.1935, *Standing Female*, gift, © the artist
Barnfield, Fred b.1935, *Still Life*, gift, © the artist
Bates, David c.1840–1921, *Joinville on the River Marne*, bequeathed by Mary Richards, 1891
Baxter, Charles 1809–1878, *The Sisters*, bequeathed by Mary Richards, 1891
Bayliss, Margaret E. active 1902–1938, *Mrs Issac Griffiths*, bequeathed by the sitter, c.1926
Biddle, Norman 1932–2000, *Pollution Pre-War*, purchased, 2005, © the artist's estate
Biddle, Norman 1932–2000, *Portrait*, purchased, © the artist's estate
Biddle, Norman 1932–2000, *Portrait of Two Faces*, purchased, © the artist's estate
Biddle, Norman 1932–2000, *Pouring Metal into Moulds*, purchased, © the artist's estate
Biddle, Norman 1932–2000, *Welding in Operation*, purchased, © the artist's estate
Billingsley, James active 1881–1932, *Landscape with Lake*
Billingsley, James active 1881–1932, *River Scene with Punt*
Bird, Edward (attributed to) 1772–1819, *Old Bearded Man*, bequeathed by Mary Richards, 1891
Burch, I. G. *Red Stripes on Green*, purchased from the Birmingham Artist Group, 1982
Cartwright, G. L. *Oak House*
Challis, Henry 1867–1962, *Self Portrait*, transferred from Smethwick Library, 1987
Challis, Henry 1867–1962, *Buckland Village*, transferred from Smethwick Library, 1987
Challis, Henry 1867–1962, *Shoeing the Horse*, transferred from Smethwick Library, 1987
Challis, Henry 1867–1962, *The Lodge, Warley Woods*, transferred from Smethwick Library, 1987
Challis, Henry 1867–1962, *The Old Church and Vicarage, Smethwick*, transferred from Smethwick Library, 1987
Challis Hodges, Ann *Henry Challis (1867–1962)*, transferred from Thimblemill Library, c.1976
Challis Hodges, Ann *Henry Challis (1867–1962), in His 95th Year*, transferred from Thimblemill Library, c.1976
Clarke, D. *Wednesbury Manor House*
Clemson, Joe *All Saints' Church, West Bromwich*, gift
Cockin, Alice active 1890–1900, *Brace of Pheasants*, gift
Cockin, Alice active 1890–1900, *Brace of Pheasants*, gift
Cole, George 1810–1883, *Windsor Castle from the Thames*, bequeathed by Mary Richards, 1891
Coleman, Edward 1795–1867, *Regency Gentleman*
Cotterill, Susan M. *Lighthouse*
Cox, Barry *Glassworks*
Creswick, Thomas 1811–1869, *Landscape with Harrow in the Distance*, bequeathed by Mary Richards, 1891
Crump, Joseph *Reverend J. H. Crump*
Dawson, Henry 1811–1878, *Seascape*, bequeathed by Mary Richards, 1891
Dawson, Henry 1811–1878, *Brent Knoll*, bequeathed
Dawson, Henry 1811–1878, *On the River Trent*, bequeathed by Mary Richards, 1891
Dupré, E. *Study of Dead Songbird (81)*, bequeathed by Mary Richards, 1891
Dupré, E. *Study of Dead Songbird (82)*, bequeathed by Mary Richards, 1891
Dupré, E. *Study of Dead Songbird (83)*, bequeathed by Mary Richards, 1891
Dupré, E. *Study of Dead Songbird (84)*, bequeathed by Mary Richards, 1891
Frazer, H. G. *The Old Oak House Museum, September 1912*
Gere, Charles March 1869–1957, *The Snowdon Range*
Gibbs, Joseph active 1852–1907, *Mary Ann Richards (1820–1894)*, bequeathed by Mary Richards, 1891
Gibbs, Joseph active 1852–1907, *Sir James Timmins Chance*, transferred from Smethwick Library, c.1987
Gibbs, Joseph active 1852–1907, *Alderman George Bowden, Mayor of Smethwick (1903–1905)*, transferred from Smethwick Library, c.1987
Gibbs, Joseph active 1852–1907, *Stepping Stones (The Nearest Way Home)*
Gibbs, Joseph active 1852–1907, *Frederick Talbot, Headmaster of Chance's School, Smethwick (1845–1892)*, transferred from Smethwick Library, c.1987
Gibbs, Joseph active 1852–1907, *Muriel Dorothy Windle*, gift
Gibot, E. *Wooded Landscape, Normandy*, bequeathed by Thomas Jones, 1922
Hargitt, Edward 1835–1895, *East Brent Church, Brent Knoll*, bequeathed by Mary Richards, 1891
Harper, John 1759–1841, *Dead Hare in Landscape*, bequeathed by Mary Richards, 1891
Harvey, George 1806–1876, *Interior, a Sad Scene*, bequeathed by Mary Richards, 1891
Hems *The Same Faith*
Hems *The Same Temptation*
Henshaw, Frederick Henry 1807–1891, *Windsor Castle from the Great Park (Morning)*, bequeathed by Mary Richards, 1891
Hodges, Merrett active c.1895–1961, *Alderman Arthur Thomas Morris, JP, Mayor of Smethwick (1927–1929)*, transferred from Smethwick Library, 1987
Hodges, Merrett active c.1895–1961, *Councillor George Henry Griffin, Mayor of Oldbury (1939–1940)*
Hodges, Merrett active c.1895–1961, *Lady in Black*
Horlor, George W. active 1849–1891, *A Corner of the Farmyard*, bequeathed by Mary Richards, 1891
Horlor, George W. active 1849–1891, *Calves Feeding*, bequeathed by Mary Richards, 1891
Hulme, Frederick William 1816–1884, *Waterfall*
Hulme, Frederick William 1816–1884, *A Surrey Landscape*, bequeathed
Irish, David *Abstract Spots on Dark Background*, purchased from the Birmingham Artist Group, 1982
Jansens, I. *Landscape with Cattle*, purchased from the trustees of Edward Smith, 1902
Jones, Frank Edwin 1919–1944, *Nude Study*, gift, 1999, © the artist's estate
Jones, Frank Edwin 1919–1944, *Portrait of a Boy*, gift, © the artist's estate
Koekkoek, Hermanus the elder 1815–1882, *Loading Boats*, bequeathed by Mary Richards, 1891
Leader, Benjamin Williams 1831–1923, *Near Line Park, Kent*, bequeathed by Mary Richards, 1891
Leader, Benjamin Williams 1831–1923, *Haymaking*, bequeathed by Mary Richards, 1891
Leaver, Charles 1824–1888, *On the Edge of the Forest*
Leidler, R. H. *The Reading Lesson*
Linnell, John 1792–1882, *Abraham's Vision*, bequeathed by Mary Richards, 1891
Lones, Thomas Sutton active 1889–1897, *Mrs Jabez Lones, First Mayoress of Smethwick (1899–1901)*
Lynton, Henry Stanton active 1886–1904, *Arabian Village Scene*
Lynton, Henry Stanton active 1886–1904, *Arabian Village Scene*
H. T. M. *Portrait of a Man with a Beard*
MacWhirter, John 1839–1911, *Cornfield with Figures*, bequeathed by Mary Richards, 1891
Millais, John Everett (attributed to) 1829–1896, *Hurdy Gurdy Boy*, purchased from Edwin Timmins, 1910

Miller, Philip Homan 1845–1928, *Alderman Wilson Lloyd, Mayor of the Wednesbury Corporation (1888–1890)*
Moore, Henry 1831–1895, *Grey Morning on the Beach*, bequeathed by Mary Richards, 1891
Morgan, Gary b.1962, *Richard Wattis (1912–1975)*, gift, 2004, © Gary Morgan
Morris, Stephen b.1935, *The Ruskin Connection*, gift, 2002, © the artist
Munns, Henry Turner 1832–1898, *Joseph Smith (d.1884)*, gift from British Steel plc, 1997
Norman, Horace *Street in Mombasa*
Oswald, John Henry active 1874–1899, *River Scene, Autumn on the Esk*, bequeathed by Mary Richards, 1891
Pettitt, Edwin Alfred 1840–1912, *Watermill, near Lynton, Devon*, bequeathed by Mary Richards, 1891
Pettitt, Edwin Alfred 1840–1912, *Idwal from Ben Glog*, bequeathed by Mary Richards, 1891
Pratt, Jonathan 1835–1911, *Interior, French Farmhouse*, bequeathed by Mr F. C. Guy, 1948
Richards, W. *Holy Trinity Church, Stratford-upon-Avon*
Rivers, Leopold 1852–1905, *O'er Hill and Dale*, transferred from Smethwick Library, 1987
Roberts, David 1796–1864, *St Mark's, Venice*, bequeathed by Thomas Jones, 1922
Roberts, David 1796–1864, *The Doge's Palace, Venice*, bequeathed by Thomas Jones, 1922
Roden, William Thomas 1817–1892, *A Wednesbury Cocker*, gift from Joshua Fellows, 1892
Salter, Edward active 1880–1888, *The Waterfall*
Smith, David Murray 1865–1952, *The Thames at Hammersmith*, gift from Miss Julia Lloyd, 1935
Smith, George 1829–1901, *Saying Grace, Cottage Interior*, bequeathed by Mary Richards, 1891
Stone, Marcus C. 1840–1921, *The Post Bag*, bequeathed by Mary Richards, 1891
Swain, Joseph 1859–1923, *Hereford Catherdral*, transferred from Smethwick Library, 1987
Swain, Joseph 1859–1923, *Warley Hall Farm*, transferred from Smethwick Library, 1997
Swain, Joseph 1859–1923, *Perry Hill Farm*, transferred from Smethwick Library, 1997
Syer, John 1815–1885, *Scene on the River Avon*, bequeathed by Mary Richards, 1891
Syer, John 1815–1885, *Estuary Scene*, bequeathed by Mary Richards, 1891
Syer, John 1815–1885, *River Scene, Rouen*, bequeathed by Mary Richards, 1891
Taylor, Edward Richard 1838–1912, *Galton Bridge*, transferred from Smethwick Library, 1987
Thomas, Frank *Warley Woods, Loading Timber*
Thors, Joseph c.1834–1898, *Punt Fishing*, bequeathed by Mary Richards, 1891
Thors, Joseph c.1834–1898, *The Homestead*, bequeathed by Mary Richards, 1891
Titian (copy after) c.1488–1576, *Laura De Dianti, Young Woman at Her Toilet*, purchased by the town clerk, 1917
unknown artist *Mary Rotton, Wife of Thomas Haden*, gift
unknown artist *Thomas Haden (1684–1756)*, gift
unknown artist 18th C, *Edward Fisher (1751–1810)*, transferred from Sandwell Metropolitan Borough Council Libraries, 1984
unknown artist 18th C, *Mary Bissell, (1751–1824), Wife of Edward Fisher*, transferred from Sandwell Metropolitan Borough Council Libraries, 1984
unknown artist *Smethwick Windmill*
unknown artist *John Whyman, JP*, transferred from Smethwick Library, 1987
unknown artist *Portrait of Gentleman with Glasses*
unknown artist *Alderman Henry Lloyd*
unknown artist *Alderman Iaian Oldbury, JP, Mayor (1896–1898 & 1902–1905)*
unknown artist *Alderman Issac Griffiths, JP, Wednesbury Corporation Mayor (1908–1909)*
unknown artist *Alderman John Ashley Kilvert, JP (1833–1920)*
unknown artist *Alderman K. H. Wilson, JP, Charter Mayor, Oldbury (1935–1936)*, transferred from Smethwick Library, 1987
unknown artist *Alfred Barrs, Frederick Barrs, Emmeline Barrs and Annie Elizabeth Haden*, gift, 1990
unknown artist *All Saints' Church, West Bromwich*
unknown artist *Barber Wilkes*, transferred from Sandwell Metropolitan Borough Council Libraries, 1984
unknown artist *C. D. Joynson, JP, Mayor of Wednesbury (1898–1900)*
unknown artist *Councillor John Knowles, JP, Mayor of Wednesbury (1894–1896)*
unknown artist *Cupid and Psyche*
unknown artist *George Collins, Chairman of Smethwick Library*, transferred from Smethwick Library, 1987
unknown artist *John James Russell*, gift from British Steel plc, 1997
unknown artist *Portrait of a Gentleman*
unknown artist *Portrait of a Gentleman (member of the Jesson family)*, transferred from West Bromwich Library, 1984
unknown artist *Portrait of a Gentleman with a Beard*
unknown artist *Portrait of a Man in Glasses with a Beard*
unknown artist *Portrait of a Man with a Wig*
unknown artist *Portrait of a Woman in a Bonnet*, transferred from Sandwell Metropolitan Borough Council Libraries, 1984
unknown artist *Portrait of a Young Cavalier*
unknown artist *Portrait of a Young Lady*
unknown artist *Portrait of a Young Woman*
unknown artist *Smethwick Windmill*, transferred from Smethwick Library, 1987
unknown artist *Still Life, Vase of Flowers*
unknown artist *The Night of Good Friday*, gift from L. A. Pritchard, MA, 1918
unknown artist *The Tipton Slasher*, transferred from Sandwell Metropolitan Borough Council Libraries, 2003
unknown artist *Wednesbury Alderman Mayor Hunt*
Verboeckhoven, Eugène 1799–1881, *Bull's Head*, bequeathed by Mary Richards, 1891
Vickers, Alfred 1786–1868, *Dutch Landscape*, bequeathed
Vickers, Alfred 1786–1868, *Windsor Castle from the Thames*, bequeathed by Mary Richards, 1891
Waldron West, E. *Kenneth Anthony and Gillian West*
Ward, James Charles active 1830–1878, *Angler's Nook*, bequeathed by Mary Richards, 1891
Ward, William H. active 1850–1899, *Pet Rabbits*, bequeathed by Mary Richards, 1891
Ward, William H. active 1850–1899, *Minding Baby*, bequeathed by Mary Richards, 1891
Watts, George Frederick 1817–1904, *The Wandering Minstrel*, purchased from Edwin Timmins, 1910
Webb, James c.1825–1895, *The Harbour, Amsterdam*, bequeathed by Mary Richards, 1891
Webb, James c.1825–1895, *Paris*, bequeathed by Mary Richards, 1891
Webb, James c.1825–1895, *A Quiet Evening*, bequeathed by Mary Richards, 1891
Webb, James c.1825–1895, *Naples*, bequeathed by Mary Richards, 1891
Webb, James c.1825–1895, *On the Dutch Coast*, bequeathed by Mrs Amy G. Cope, 1958
Wedgbury, David b.1937, *The Wedding*
White, J. A. *Oak House*, acquired, c.1986
Whitlock Brothers *Alderman Richard Williams (d.1909), JP, Honorary Freeman of the Borough of Wednesbury Corporation (1899)*
Williams, H. A. *Landscape*
Williams, H. A. *Landscape*
Willis-Pryce, George 1866–1949, *Old Church*, transferred from Smethwick Library, 1987
Willis-Pryce, George 1866–1949, *Old Chapel Farm*, transferred from Smethwick Library, 1987
Wivell, Abraham II (attributed to) active 1840–1865, *Edwin Richards*, bequeathed by Mary Richards, 1891

Museum of the Staffordshire Yeomanry

M. H. C. *John Stafford (1829–1932)*, transferred, c.1983
Sancha, Carlos Luis 1920–2001, *Officers of the Yeomanry at Dinner*, transferred, c.1969

Stafford Borough Council

Aris, Joyce active 1940s, *John Bradshaw, MP for Stafford (1602–1659) (after John Riley)*, gift from Sir Hugh Fraser, MP for Stafford, 1950s
Figueras, Tito *Sunset over the Sea*, gift from Tarragona Twinning Committee, 1990s
Torné, Tomás *Tarragona*, gift from Tarragona Twinning Committee, 1990s
unknown artist *Alderman Thomas Sidney (1805–1889)*, gift from Mr Thomas H. Sydney, JP, 1921
unknown artist *Matthew Craddock (1520–1592)*, purchased, c.1930s
unknown artist *Woodland Landscape*, gift from the Virginia, USA, Twinning Committee, 1990s

Staffordshire Arts and Museums Service

Arrowsmith, Thomas 1772–c.1829, *John Joule (1783–1858)*, gift from Miss Joule, 1974
Bardwell, Thomas 1704–1767, *A Member of the Whitby Family*, gift from Colonel E. Whitby, 1965
Barnardo, Eilidh 1911–1994, *On a Journey, 1968–1969*, gift from Mr F. Armour-Brown, 1998, © the artist's estate
Barnardo, Eilidh 1911–1994, *Ride into Khiva, Turkmenistan, Eastern USSR*, gift from Mr F. Armour-Brown, 1998, © the artist's estate
Barnardo, Eilidh 1911–1994, *Spoiling for a Fight*, gift from Mr F. Armour-Brown, 1998, © the artist's estate
Barnardo, Eilidh 1911–1994, *Crowded Pavement*, gift from Mr F. Armour-Brown, 1998, © the artist's estate
Barnardo, Eilidh 1911–1994, *Youthful Despair No.2*, gift from Mr F. Armour-Brown, 1998, © the artist's estate
Bracewell, J. H. *Greengate Street from the Bridge and the Old Pork Pie Shop*, purchased from Mrs Dale, 1956
Bracewell, J. H. *The Roebuck Inn, Stafford*, purchased from Mrs Dale, 1956
Bretland, Thomas W. 1802–1874, *Longhorn Cow*, purchased from Mr Shaw, 1975
Brown, Edward 1823–1877, *'Earl of Upton'*, acquired by the County Museum, 1977
Burnhill, Peter b.c.1930, *Wooden Bowl with Fruit*, purchased from the artist, 1992
Camm, Thomas William 1839–1912, *Christus Consolator*, purchased from the artist's family, 1965
Carter, Graham b.1975, *Lovely Big Hands*, commissioned as part of the 'Once Upon a Time' exhibition at the Blue Hall Gallery, 2005
Cartledge, William 1891–1976, *Shelton Bar and Messrs Josiah Wedgwood and Sons Ltd*, purchased from the artist, 1951
Chandler, John Westbrooke 1764–1804/1805, *William Horton (1750–1832)*, purchased from Miss E. L. Knight, before 1974
Charlton, John 1849–1917, *Florence Parker-Jervis (d.1938)*, gift from Mr G. Parker-Jervis, 1966
Clewlow, Harry active 1919–1939, *Roll of Honour for W. H. Dorman, 1914–1918*, gift from Mr D. Clancey, 2002, © Staffordshire Arts and Museums Service
Cooper, Lucien b.c.1960, *Primary*, purchased from the artist, 1991
Dahl, Michael I 1656/1659–1743, *Thomas Whitby*, gift from Colonel E. Whitby, 1965
Dahl, Michael I 1656/1659–1743, *Thomas Whitby's Sister*, gift from Colonel E. Whitby, 1965
Davies, E. J. *St Thomas's Farm, near Stafford*, gift from artist, before 1961
Drummond, Julian 1824–1906, *Cottage Interior*, acquired, before 1961
Dutton, John Frederick Harrison active 1890–1918, *Mr E. R. Twemlow*, gift from the county architects, 1968
Dutton, Martin J. *Stafford Landscape*, purchased from the artist, c.1955
Gauci, A. M. active 1848–1884, *'Sir Arthur'*, purchased from Iona Antiques, 1988
Gleeson, David Paul b.1956, *Feathers and Sugared Almonds*, purchased from the artist, 1994, © the artist
Gregory, G. active 1836–1848, *'Conqueror'*, acquired by the County Museum, 1977
Halliday, Edward Irvine 1902–1984, *Lord Justice Wrottesley*, acquired, before 1961, © the artist's estate
Held, Julie b.1958, *Portrait of a Man*, gift from the artist, 1997, © the artist
Hickman, F. W. *Fox and George, Eastgate Street, Stafford, Demolished 1904*, purchased from Mrs Dale, 1956
Hill, Paul b.1959, *Whacky Backy*, purchased from the artist, 2004, © the artist

Hudson, Thomas 1701–1779, *Mrs R. Whitby*, gift from Colonel E. Whitby, 1965; on loan to the Ancient High House, Stafford
Hudson, Thomas 1701–1779, *Richard Whitby*, gift from Colonel E. Whitby, 1965
Jones, Horace Overton active 1894–1924, *Dale's Shop, Stafford*, acquired from Mrs Price, 1956
Jones, T. W. *The Noah's Ark Inn, Crabbery Street, Stafford*, acquired, before 1961
Jones, T. W. *The Noah's Ark Inn, Crabbery Street, Stafford*, purchased from Mrs Price, 1956
Keeling, Michael 1750–1820, *Daniel Chisenhale of Arley (1725–1798)*, purchased at the auction of the contents of Gaynes Park, 1976
Keeling, Michael 1750–1820, *Hannah Longworth (1721–1780)*, purchased at the auction of the contents of Gaynes Park, 1976
Keeling, Michael 1750–1820, *William Horton (1750–1832)*, purchased from Miss E. L. Knight, before 1974
Knight, John Prescott 1803–1881, *Clarissa Isabella Hague (1798/1799–1869)*, purchased from Mr L. D. de la Riviere, 1972
Knight, John Prescott 1803–1881, *Self Portrait in a Brown Study*, purchased from Mr L. D. de la Riviere, 1965
Knight, John Prescott 1803–1881, *Smugglers Alarmed*, purchased from Mr M. L. Armitage, before 1961
Knight, John Prescott 1803–1881, *Mrs John Prescott Knight and Her Children*, purchased from Mr L. D. de la Riviere, 1965
Knight, John Prescott 1803–1881, *Portrait of a Lady*, purchased from Mr L. D. de la Riviere, 1965
Knight, John Prescott 1803–1881, *Clarissa Isabella Knight (1798/1799–1869)*, purchased from Mr L. D. de la Riviere, 1972
Knight, John Prescott 1803–1881, *Self Portrait*, purchased from Mr L. D. de la Riviere, 1965
Knight, John Prescott 1803–1881, *Miles Julian Prescott Knight (1835–1871)*, purchased from Mr L. D. de la Riviere, 1965
Knight, John Prescott 1803–1881, *A. S. Prescott (1832–1917)*, purchased from King and Chasemore Auctioneers, 1971
Knight, John Prescott 1803–1881, *Clare (Miss Clara) (1838–1869)*, purchased from Mr L. D. de la Riviere, 1965
Lawton, G. *Izaak Walton's Birthplace, Stafford*, purchased from Mrs Dale, 1956
Layng, Mabel Frances 1881–1937, *The Omnibus*, gift from Miss A. C. Layng, 1938
Lippett, Mark b.1975, *Spring Sun*, purchased from the artist, 2004
Lord, Tessa *Jug and Cushions*, purchased from the artist, 1992
Markey, Peter b.1930, *Black-Faced Sheep*, purchased from the artist, 1991, © the artist
Milroy, Lisa b.1959, *Lotus 'Career Girl' Shoe*, purchased from the artist, 2002, © the artist
Milroy, Lisa b.1959, *Lotus 'Career Girl' Shoe*, purchased from the artist, 2002, © the artist
Milroy, Lisa b.1959, *Lotus 'Career Girl' Shoe*, purchased from the artist, 2002, © the artist
Milroy, Lisa b.1959, *Lotus 'Career Girl' Shoe*, purchased from the artist, 2002, © the artist
Milroy, Lisa b.1959, *Lotus 'Career Girl' Shoe*, purchased from the artist, 2002, © the artist
Milroy, Lisa b.1959, *Lotus Shoe*, purchased from the artist, 2002, © the artist
Milroy, Lisa b.1959, *Lotus Shoe*, purchased from the artist, 2002, © the artist
Milroy, Lisa b.1959, *Lotus Shoe*, purchased from the artist, 2002, © the artist
Milroy, Lisa b.1959, *Lotus Shoe*, purchased from the artist, 2002, © the artist
Neiland, Brendan b.1941, *Awning*, gift from Lucy and Naomi Neiland, 1993, © the artist
Neiland, Brendan b.1941, *Shire Hall*, purchased from the artist, 1993, © the artist
Neiland, Brendan b.1941, *Shire Hall Atrium*, purchased from the artist, 1993, © the artist
Nuttall, M. P. *Fishing Lodge, Beresford Dale*, acquired, before 1961
O'Neil, Henry Nelson (attributed to) 1817–1880, *The Recruiting Sergeant (The King's Shilling)*, acquired, before 1961
Owen, William 1769–1825, *John Sparrow (1736–1821), Chairman of Quarter Sessions (1792–1816)*, acquired, before 1991
Phillips, Tony b.1952, *Homes*, purchased from the artist, 2004
Reed, Graeme John Robert b.1964, *Elephant*, purchased from the artist, 1993
Scott, John 1802–1885, *Mary Anne Jervis, Lady Forester (c.1803–1893)*, gift from Mr G. Parker-Jervis, 1966
Shaw, David Carson b.1942, *Walking in the Heat*, purchased from the artist, 1989
Simpson, W. Graham active 1880–1898, *Hubert de Gotham Parker-Jervis (1859–1894)*, gift from Mr G. Parker-Jervis, 1966
Speed, Harold 1872–1957, *Sir Walter Essex (1857–1941)*, gift from the executors of the estate of Sir Walter Essex, before 1962
Thors, Joseph c.1834–1898, *Road near Warwick*, acquired, before 1961
unknown artist *George Granville, 2nd Marquis of Stafford, 1st Duke of Sutherland (1758–1833)*, acquired, before 1991
unknown artist *St Mary's Church, Stafford*, gift from Councillor L. Dobson, before 1961
unknown artist *The Pretty Pigs*, bequeathed by Mr J. Astbury, 2006
unknown artist *Elizabethan House, Gaolgate, Stafford*, purchased from Mrs Dale, c.1961
unknown artist early 19th C, *Francis Joule, Maltster (1755–1837)*, gift from Miss Joule, 1974
unknown artist early 19th C, *Mary Joule (d.1828)*, gift from Miss Joule, 1974
unknown artist early 19th C, *Mrs Smith, Mother of Mary Joule*, gift from Miss Joule, 1974
unknown artist early 19th C, *Sarah Joule (d.1828)*, gift from Miss Joule, 1974
unknown artist mid-19th C, *John Smith Joule (1806–1879)*, gift from Miss Joule, 1974
unknown artist 19th C, *Daniel and the Lions*, gift from Mr C. Bagnall, 1964
unknown artist 19th C, *Portrait of a Young Man in a Toga*, acquired, before 1961
unknown artist *Dale's Shop, Stafford*, purchased from Mrs Dale, c.1961
unknown artist early 20th C, *Bust of Izaak Walton*, acquired, before 1961
Weake, D. B. *Farmyard, Shirley*, purchased from the artist, c.1960
Wilson, Douglas b.1936, *High Offley*, purchased from Abbot & Holder, 1995, © the artist
Wood, Thomas Peploe 1817–1845, *The Bridge at Ilam*, acquired, before 1961
Wood, Thomas Peploe 1817–1845, *Ilam Hall*, acquired, before 1961
Wood, Thomas Peploe 1817–1845, *Cattle Piece*, gift from the Cuthbert family, c.1920–1940
Wood, Thomas Peploe 1817–1845, *Gypsy Scene*, gift from the Cuthbert family, c.1920–1940

Staffordshire County Council

Bennett, Frank Moss 1874–1952, *Thomas Francis Anson, Baron Soberton, Viscount Anson of Shugborough and Orgreave, Earl of Lichfield (1856–1918)*, purchased by public subscription, c.1919, © the artist's estate
Bennett, Frank Moss 1874–1952, *Frank James, DL, JP (1821–1924)*, purchased by public subscription, 1921, © the artist's estate
Bennett, Frank Moss 1874–1952, *Sir Gilbert Henry Claughton, Bt (1856–1921)*, purchased by public subscription, 1921, © the artist's estate
Bennett, Frank Moss 1874–1952, *Lieutenant-Colonel William Edward Harrison (d.1937), OBE*, purchased by public subscription, 1933, © the artist's estate
Birley, Oswald Hornby Joseph 1880–1952, *Lieutenant-Colonel George Augustus Anson (b.1857), CBE*, purchased by public subscription, 1929, © the artist's estate
Birley, Oswald Hornby Joseph 1880–1952, *Sir John Edwin Mitchell (1863–1931), OBE*, gift, 1930–1931, © the artist's estate
Birley, Oswald Hornby Joseph 1880–1952, *Roy Eustace Joy, MA*, purchased by public subscription, before 1940, © the artist's estate
British (English) School *Sir Richard Bagot (c.1530–1597)*, purchased from the Bagot family, 1946
British (English) School *Mary Saunders (d.1608), Lady Bagot*, purchased from the Bagot family, 1946
British (English) School *Sir Walter Aston of Tixall (1584–1639)*, purchased from the Picture Fund, 1945
British (English) School *Sir Julian Osborn Whitehouse (d.1942), JP for Staffordshire (1926–1942)*
Campion, Oliver 1928–2000, *F. A. Cholerton, CBE, M Univ (Keele) (d.2004), Chairman of Staffordshire County Council (1981–1989)*, © the artist's estate
Collier, John 1850–1934, *Edward George Percy Littleton, 3rd Baron Hatherton (1842–1930)*, purchased by public subscription, 1913
Collings, Keturah b.1862, *Robert George Paterson, OBE*, purchased from the Picture Fund, 1946
Dicksee, Frank 1853–1928, *Godfrey Rathbone Benson, Baron Charnwood (1864–1945)*, gift from Lady Charnwood, 1938
Dodd, Francis 1874–1949, *Colonel Sir William John Kent, CBE, TD, DL, JR*, commissioned via the Picture Fund, after 1945, © the artist's estate
Harper, Edward Steel II 1878–1951, *Lieutenant-Colonel Joseph Henry Wilkinson, DL, JP, VD (1845–1931)*, commissioned via the Picture Fund, 1921
Herkomer, Hubert von 1849–1914, *Dudley Francis Stuart Ryder, 4th Baron Harrowby, Viscount Sandon, 4rd Earl of Harrowby (1831–1900)*, purchased by public subscription,1900
Hudson, Thomas 1701–1779, *Jeremiah Smith of Brewood, High Sheriff of Staffordshire*, gift from Mrs Beatrice Agar, 1938
Hudson, Thomas (attributed to) 1701–1779, *John Leveson Gower, 2nd Baron and 1st Earl Gower, Viscount Trentham (1694–1754)*, acquired, c.1975
Llewellyn, William Samuel Henry 1858–1941, *Sir Reginald Hardy, 2nd Bt, of Dunstall Park (1848–1938)*, purchased by public subscription
Ouless, Walter William 1848–1933, *Thomas Fletcher Twemlow of Betley (1816–1894)*, acquired, c.1932
Owen, William 1769–1825, *Charlotte Sparrow*, gift from Miss P. Chetwynd
Owen, William 1769–1825, *Elizabeth Sparrow of Bishton Hall*, gift from Miss P. Chetwynd
Owen, William 1769–1825, *John Sparrow of Bishton Hall (1736–1821)*, purchased by public subscription, before 1932
Owen, William 1769–1825, *Lady Hannah Chetwynd*, gift from Miss P. Chetwynd
Owen, William (attributed to) 1769–1825, *Sir George Chetwynd, 2nd Bt, of Grendon and Brocton (1783–1850)*, gift from Miss P. Chetwynd
Palin, William Mainwaring 1862–1947, *Francis Elliott Kitchener, MA, JP (1838–1915)*, bequeathed, c.1915
Palin, William Mainwaring 1862–1947, *John Wilcox Edge (1844–1923)*, gift from John Wilcox Edge or his son
Smith, Vivian Brett *Portrait of a Gentleman*
Trent, Irene E. *John T. Homer, CBE, DL*, gift from Dr F. A. Homer, 1934
Watt, George Fiddes 1873–1960, *William Heneage Legge, 6th Earl and 8th Baron of Dartmouth (1851–1936)*, purchased by public subscription, before 1932

Staffordshire Police Museum

Sheldon, Chris William b.1948, *Longton Police Station*, gift from the artist, © the artist
Sheldon, Chris William b.1948, *Stoke Police Station*, gift from the artist, © the artist
Sheldon, Chris William b.1948, *Lichfield Police Station*, gift from the artist, © the artist
Sheldon, Chris William b.1948, *Rugeley Police Station*, gift from the artist, © the artist
Sheldon, Chris William b.1948, *Burton-on-Trent Police Station*, gift from the artist, © the artist
Sheldon, Chris William b.1948, *Burslem Police Station*, gift from the artist, © the artist
Sheldon, Chris William b.1948, *Kidsgrove Police Station*, gift from the artist, © the artist
Sheldon, Chris William b.1948, *Tamworth Police Station*, gift from the artist, © the artist
Sheldon, Chris William b.1948, *Baswich House, Stafford*, gift from the artist, © the artist
Sheldon, Chris William b.1948, *Uttoxeter Police Station*, gift from the artist, © the artist
Sheldon, Chris William b.1948, *Leek Police Station*, gift from the artist, © the artist
Sheldon, Chris William b.1948, *Stafford Police Station*, gift from the artist, 1998, © the artist
unknown artist *Portrait of a Staffordshire Policeman*, purchased from Wallis & Wallis, 1998
unknown artist *Portrait of a Staffordshire Policeman's Wife*, purchased from Wallis & Wallis, 1998

Spode Museum Trust

Holdway, Harold 1913–2002, *William Wendel, Chairman of Carborundum International*, gift, c.1995, © the artist's estate
Jones, Horace Overton active 1894–1924, *At Rhosneigr, Anglesey*, gift
Jones, Horace Overton (attributed to) active 1984–1924, *Hunting with Hounds*, gift
unknown artist *The Right Worshipful W. T. Copeland (1797–1868), Alderman, President*, purchased from the Royal Hospital of Bridewell and Bethlem, 1960s

The Potteries Museum & Art Gallery

Abbotts, T. G. *Steel Town*, purchased from the Society of Staffordshire Artists, 1967
Agar, Eileen 1899–1991, *The New Planet*, purchased, 1999
Allen, Harry Epworth 1894–1958, *A Derbyshire Farmstead*, purchased from the Royal Academy of Arts, 1934
Allinson, Adrian Paul 1890–1959, *Ibiza*, purchased from Spurr, Bradford, West Yorkshire, 1937
Allinson, Adrian Paul 1890–1959, *Ibizan Orchard*, purchased from Miss Molly Mitchell-Smith, 1962
Allinson, Adrian Paul 1890–1959, *The Fig Tree*, bequeathed by Miss Peggy Mitchell-Smith, 1986
Allinson, Adrian Paul 1890–1959, *The Goat Farm*, gift from Miss Molly Mitchell-Smith, 1967
Annan, Dorothy 1908–1983, *Still Life with Flowers*, gift from Dudley Tennant, 1947
Arandale, J. M. *St Peter's Church, Stoke-on-Trent*, gift from Ridgway's, Stoke-on-Trent, 1961
Ashbaugh, Dennis John b.1946, *It Looks Grim*, gift from the Contemporary Art Society, 1983, © the artist
Ashton, James 1859–1935, *Mount Kandy, Colombo*, gift from Mrs I. Holland, 1961
Ashwell, B. C. *James Clover*
Aumonier, James 1832–1911, *At Barking*, bequeathed by William Woodall, 1954
Ayrton, Michael 1921–1975, *The Tip, Hanley*, purchased from the Christopher Hull Gallery, 1982, © the artist's estate
Bajo, D. Y. *Smoke and Snow*, gift from Percy Cooper, 1950
Ball, J. Pat *Composition*, gift from the Friends of the Art Gallery, 1967
Ball, J. Pat *Wet Afternoon*, gift from the Friends of the Museum and Art Gallery, 1969
Bas, Edward le 1904–1966, *Café Royale*, purchased from the Royal Academy, 1949
Bennett, Charles Howson active 1912–1913, *Sweetpeas in an Earthenware Bowl*, gift from Miss Julia Kearns, 1958
Bennett, Charles Howson active 1912–1913, *Roses in a Glass Vase*, gift from Miss Julia Kearns, 1958
Bennett, Charles Howson active 1912–1913, *Bronze Wallflowers in a Glass Vase*, gift from Miss Julia Kearns, 1958
Bennett, Charles Howson active 1912–1913, *Pink, Yellow and Red Roses*, gift from Miss Julia Kearns, 1958
Bevan, Robert Polhill 1865–1925, *The Ash Tree*, purchased from Sotheby's, 1953
Birch, Samuel John Lamorna 1869–1955, *Fresh Winds on a May Day, Isla River, Aberdeenshire*, purchased from the artist, 1931, © the artist's estate
Birchall, Harold H. *Reflections, Etruria Vale*, purchased, 1960
Birley, Oswald Hornby Joseph 1880–1952, *Bernard Moore (1850–1935)*, © the artist's estate
Birley, Oswald Hornby Joseph 1880–1952, *A. P. Llewellyn*, © the artist's estate
Blake, Rosa K. active 1926–1962, *Wetton Quarry*, bequeathed by the artist, 1962
Blake, Rosa K. active 1926–1962, *Ludchurch*, gift from the artist, 1960
Blake, Rosa K. active 1926–1962, *Alton Castle*, bequeathed by the artist, 1962
Bodley, Josselin 1893–1974, *Frost*, bequeathed by Dr W. D. Wilkins, 1964
Boote, R., Mollart D., Mountford J. & Stewart A. *Potteries*, gift from Manor Engineering & Co. and J. Knox Ltd, 1960
Borsky, Jiri b.1945, *Actors in a Dressing Room*, purchased from the artist, 1980, © the artist
Boullemier, Antonin c.1840–1900, *Infant Bacchantes*, old stock, acquired before the accession register and Stoke-on-Trent Museum were established
Boullemier, Antonin c.1840–1900, *Infant Bacchantes*, old stock, acquired before the accession register and Stoke-on-Trent Museum were established
Boullemier, Antonin c.1840–1900, *Infant Bacchantes Drinking*, old stock, acquired before the accession register and Stoke-on-Trent Museum were established
Boullemier, Antonin c.1840–1900, *Putti with Flowers*, old stock, acquired before the accession register and Stoke-on-Trent Museum were established
Boullemier, Antonin c.1840–1900, *The Late Mrs. W. Sherratt of Handle House, Stoke-on-Trent*, gift from Harold M. Sherratt, 1961
Boullemier, Lucien 1877–1948, *George Howson (1818–1896)*, gift from Armitage Shanks Ltd, 1986
Bowers, Kelvin b.1946, *Swimming Pool (Coat Hooks and Crescent Moon)*, purchased from the artist, 1991
Bowyer, William b.1926, *Short Back and Sides*, purchased, 1958
Boyd, Stephen b.1959, *The Tempest (after Giorgione)*, purchased from the artist, 1990, © the artist
Bradley, William 1801–1857, *Portrait of a Seated Woman Sleeping*, gift from Mrs R. Moxon, 1946
Brangwyn, Frank 1867–1956, *Rome*, purchased from Mr N. B. Walker, 1937, © the artist's etate/www.bridgeman.co.uk
Brangwyn, Frank 1867–1956, *San Giorgio, Venice*, acquired, 1963, © the artist's etate/www.bridgeman.co.uk
Bridgeman, Ann b.1934, *Pimlico*, purchased from the artist, 1958, © the artist
Brockhurst, Gerald Leslie 1890–1978, *Ballynakill, Connemara*, purchased from R. H. Spurr, Southport, 1947
Brooker, Peter Alfred 1900–1965, *The Dead Christ*, gift from the Duveen Paintings Fund, 1962
Brown, Charles William 1882–1961, *Flowers in a Vase*, bequeathed by the artist, 1961
Brown, Charles William 1882–1961, *The Solent from Portsdown Hill*, bequeathed by the artist, 1961
Brown, Charles William 1882–1961, *Alton Towers*, bequeathed by the artist, 1961
Brown, Charles William 1882–1961, *Back Gardens*, bequeathed by the artist, 1961
Brown, Charles William 1882–1961, *Clovelly, Devon*, bequeathed by the artist, 1961
Brown, Charles William 1882–1961, *Garden*, bequeathed by the artist, 1961
Brown, Charles William 1882–1961, *Puppy*, bequeathed by the artist, 1961
Brown, Charles William 1882–1961, *Demolition*, bequeathed by the artist, 1961
Brown, Charles William 1882–1961, *Flowers in a Jug*, bequeathed by the artist, 1961
Brown, Charles William 1882–1961, *'Owd Harry'*, bequeathed by the artist, 1961
Brown, Charles William 1882–1961, *Tapping a Blast Furnace*, bequeathed by the artist, 1961
Brown, Charles William 1882–1961, *Interior*, bequeathed by the artist, 1961
Brown, Charles William 1882–1961, *Interior*, bequeathed by the artist, 1961
Brown, Charles William 1882–1961, *Me, 76*, bequeathed by the artist, 1961
Brown, Charles William 1882–1961, *Mixed Industry, Shelton*, bequeathed by the artist, 1961
Brown, Charles William 1882–1961, *Night Watch*, bequeathed by the artist, 1961
Brown, Charles William 1882–1961, *Port-Down Hill, Portsmouth*, bequeathed by the artist, 1961
Brown, Charles William 1882–1961, *Rocks and Sea*, bequeathed by the artist, 1961
Brown, Charles William 1882–1961, *Self Portrait*, bequeathed by the artist, 1961
Brown, Charles William 1882–1961, *View of Portsmouth Harbour*, bequeathed by the artist, 1961
Brown, Charles William 1882–1961, *Alton Towers*, bequeathed by the artist, 1961
Brown, Charles William 1882–1961, *Anemones*, bequeathed by the artist, 1961
Brown, Charles William 1882–1961, *Anemones*, bequeathed by the artist, 1961
Brown, Charles William 1882–1961, *Boating*, bequeathed by the artist, 1961
Brown, Charles William 1882–1961, *Cliffs, Sea and Gulls*, bequeathed by the artist, 1961
Brown, Charles William 1882–1961, *Cliffs, Sea and Gulls*, bequeathed by the artist, 1961
Brown, Charles William 1882–1961, *Desolation*, bequeathed by the artist, 1961
Brown, Charles William 1882–1961, *Garden*, bequeathed by the artist, 1961
Brown, Charles William 1882–1961, *Garden*, bequeathed by the artist, 1961
Brown, Charles William 1882–1961, *Industrial Scene*, bequeathed by the artist, 1961
Brown, Charles William 1882–1961, *My Father*, bequeathed by the artist, 1961
Brown, Charles William 1882–1961, *North Staffordshire Landscape*, bequeathed by the artist, 1961
Brown, Charles William 1882–1961, *Shelton*, bequeathed by the artist, 1961
Brown, Charles William 1882–1961, *Tower*, bequeathed by the artist, 1961
Brown, Charles William 1882–1961, *Trentham*, bequeathed by the artist, 1961
Brown, Charles William 1882–1961, *Walking in the Park*, bequeathed by the artist, 1961
Brown, Charles William 1882–1961, *Winworth Dale, Tean*, bequeathed by the artist, 1961
Brown, Charles William 1882–1961, *Woman and Child*, gift, 1989
Brown, Robert b.1927, *King's Cross*, purchased from the Royal Academy, 1956
Browning, Amy Katherine 1881–1978, *Early Morning*, purchased from Spurr, Southport, 1945, © Joanna Dunham
Buckley *The Vicar of Sneyd*, gift from Reverend W. B. Sandberg, c.1954
Budd, Herbert Ashwin 1881–1950, *View on the Churnet*, old stock, acquired before the accession register and Stoke-on-Trent Museum were established
Budd, Herbert Ashwin 1881–1950, *The Chess Board*, purchased from Mrs H. A. Budd, 1951
Budd, Herbert Ashwin 1881–1950, *Interior*, purchased from Mrs H. A. Budd, 1951
Burnett, June b.1936, *Zoot 58*, purchased from the artist, 1990, © the artist
Burnley, Heather b.1937, *Portrait*, purchased from the artist, 1962, © the artist
Burrows, Roy b.1922, *Abstraction from Log*, purchased from the artist, 1968
Burrows, Roy b.1922, *Cowlyd Hafod*, purchased from the Pentagon Gallery, Stoke-on-Trent, 1973
Butler, Charles J. *The Vagabond, Beare Green Common*
Buttle, George Allen 1870–1925, *The Three Bays*, old stock, acquired before the accession register and Stoke-on-Trent Museum were established
Cadell, Francis Campbell Boileau 1883–1937, *Blue and Orange*, purchased from R. H. Spurr, Southport, 1958, © Cadell estate, courtesy of Portland Gallery
Cameron, David Young 1865–1945, *Caudebec*, purchased from R. H. Spurr, Southport, 1945, © the artist's estate
Cameron, David Young 1865–1945, *Dunstaffnage*, bequeathed by Dr John Russell, 1947, © the artist's estate
Cameron, David Young 1865–1945, *Over the Hills, near Glasgow*, bequeathed by Mr H. F. Wood, 1963, © the artist's estate
Capey, John *Tunstall Manor Court Leet*, gift from the artist, 1909
Caravaggio, Michelangelo Merisi da (after) 1571–1610, *St Anthony Abbot*, old stock, acquired before the accession register and Stoke-on-Trent Museum were established
Carr, Henry Marvell 1894–1970, *B. R. Hill, HH, First Battalion, KRRC, 6852209, RFN (Soldier Cleaning His Rifle)*, gift from the War Artists Advisory Committee, 1947
Cartledge, William 1891–1976, *Ridgways, Bedford Works, Shelton*, gift from the Friends of the Art Gallery, 1950
Cartlidge, George 1868–1961, *Portrait of a Lady*, gift from Mrs Doris Melland, 1963
Cartlidge, George 1868–1961, *Study of a Dead Chaffinch*, gift from Mrs Doris Melland, 1963
Cartlidge, George 1868–1961, *Miss Mary Cartlidge*, gift from Mrs Doris Melland, 1963
Cartlidge, George 1868–1961, *Still Life, Chrysanthemums*, gift from Mrs Doris Melland, 1963
Cartlidge, George 1868–1961, *Marguerites*, gift from Mrs Doris Melland, 1963
Cartlidge, George 1868–1961, *Roses*, gift from Mrs Doris Melland, 1963
Cartlidge, George 1868–1961,

Farmyard Evening, Hale House, Horton, gift from Mrs Doris Melland, 1963
Cartlidge, George 1868–1961, *Landscape with a Tree at Sunset*, gift from Mrs Doris Melland, 1963
Cartlidge, George 1868–1961, *Self Portrait*, gift from Mrs Doris Melland, 1963
Cartlidge, George 1868–1961, *Woodland Scene*, gift from Mrs Doris Melland, 1963
Cartlidge, George 1868–1961, *Miss Mary Cartlidge*, gift from Mrs Doris Melland, 1963
Cartlidge, George 1868–1961, *Miss Annie Sneyd Falkner (Mrs Willets)*, gift from Mrs Doris Melland, 1963
Cartlidge, George 1868–1961, *Mrs Alfred Leese, Aunt to George Cartlidge*, gift from Mrs Doris Melland, 1963
Cartlidge, George 1868–1961, *Bluebells, Cliff Park, Rudyard*, gift from Mrs Doris Melland, 1963
Cartlidge, George 1868–1961, *Geeson Hill, Rudyard*, gift from Mrs Doris Melland, 1963
Cartlidge, George 1868–1961, *The Cart Road*, gift from Mrs Doris Melland, 1963
Cartlidge, George 1868–1961, *Winter Sunshine, Cliff Park, Rudyard*, gift from Mrs Doris Melland, 1963
Cartlidge, George 1868–1961, *Boot Hall, Horton, from the Brook*, gift from Mrs Doris Melland, 1963
Cartlidge, George 1868–1961, *Boy in Red*, gift from Mrs Doris Melland, 1963
Cartlidge, George 1868–1961, *Oat Kivers, Horton*, gift from Mrs Doris Melland, 1963
Cartlidge, George 1868–1961, *Springtime, Haracles Hall Field, Rudyard*, gift from Mrs Doris Melland, 1963
Cartlidge, George 1868–1961, *Burning Autumn Leaves*, gift from Mrs Doris Melland, 1963
Cartlidge, George 1868–1961, *Borth-y-Gest, North Wales*, gift from Mrs Doris Melland, 1963
Cartlidge, George 1868–1961, *Moorland Landscape*, gift from Mrs Doris Melland, 1963
Cartlidge, George 1868–1961, *In September, a Staffordshire Hilltop*, gift from Mrs Doris Melland, 1963
Cartlidge, George 1868–1961, *A Cherry Tree in May, New House in Horton*, gift from Mrs Doris Melland, 1963
Cartlidge, George 1868–1961, *Alhambra Tile Works, Newport, Kentucky, USA*, gift from Mrs Doris Melland, 1963
Cartlidge, George 1868–1961, *Ohio River, Newport, Kentucky, USA*, gift from Mrs Doris Melland, 1963
Cartlidge, George 1868–1961, *Point Pleasant, Ohio, USA*, gift from Mrs Doris Melland, 1963
Cartlidge, George 1868–1961, *Field to Daisy House, Horton*, gift from Mrs Doris Melland, 1963
Cartlidge, George 1868–1961, *A Model from Art School (Portrait of an Old Man)*, gift from Mrs Doris Melland, 1963
Cartlidge, George 1868–1961, *A Moorland Road, Bradshaw*, gift from Mrs Doris Melland, 1963
Cartlidge, George 1868–1961, *George Falkner Cartlidge*, gift from Mrs Doris Melland, 1963
Cartlidge, George 1868–1961, *Landscape, Silver Birch Trees and Rocks*, gift from Mrs Doris Melland, 1963
Cartlidge, George 1868–1961, *Lewis George Cartlidge*, gift from Mrs Doris Melland, 1963
Cartlidge, George 1868–1961, *Moon Rising over a Field of Corn Stooks*, gift from Mrs Doris Melland, 1963
Cartlidge, George 1868–1961, *Moon through Fir Trees, Rudyard*, gift from Mrs Doris Melland, 1963
Cartlidge, George 1868–1961, *N. Benjamin Beaumont Barlow*, gift from Mrs Doris Melland, 1963
Cartlidge, George 1868–1961, *Study of a Male Nude with Javelin*, gift from Mrs Doris Melland, 1963
Cartlidge, George 1868–1961, *Two Goats in a Field by a Tree*, gift from Mrs Doris Melland, 1963
Cartlidge, George 1868–1961, *Winter Scene, Heath House Road, Rudyard*, gift from Mrs Doris Melland, 1963
Chapman, Anthea b.1933, *Flowers on the Table*, purchased from the Royal Academy Summer Exhibition, 1967, © the artist
Chubb, Ralph Nicholas 1892–1960, *The Red Farm*, gift from the artist, 1959
Chubb, Ralph Nicholas 1892–1960, *The Country Lane*, gift from the artist, 1959
Clark, Cosmo 1897–1967, *Evening Light in a Spanish Garden*, purchased from the artist at the Royal Academy, 1966
Clarke, Paul Montem b.1915, *The Merry Wives*, purchased from the artist, 1957
Clarke, Paul Montem b.1915, *Portrait of a Malay Girl, Mary*, purchased from the artist, 1958
Clarke, Paul Montem b.1915, *In the Bottle Oven*, gift from the Friends of the Art Gallery, 1960
Clarkson, Jack 1906–1986, *Century Street, Hanley*, purchased from Mrs Fielding, 1986
Clarkson, Jack 1906–1986, *Market Inn*, gift from the Friends of the Art Gallery, 1950
Clarkson, Jack 1906–1986, *View of Hanley*, purchased from Mrs Fielding, 1986
Clausen, George 1852–1944, *Normandy Peasant*, gift from Mrs J. B. Ashwell, 1949, © Clausen estate
Clausen, George 1852–1944, *Rickyard, Morning*, bequeathed by Dr John Russell, 1947, © Clausen estate
Clay, A. P. *Canal Scene, House and Narrowboat*, bequeathed by Mrs F. L. Clay, 1973
Clay, A. P. *Rural Scene*, bequeathed by Mrs F. L. Clay, 1973
Cohen, Bernard b.1933, *Somersault*, gift from the Contemporary Art Society, 1979, © the artist
Coldstream, William Menzies 1908–1987, *At the Zoo*, gift from the Contemporary Art Society, 1931, © the artist's estate/www.bridgeman.co.uk
Coldstream, William Menzies 1908–1987, *Mrs Auden*, gift from Sir Kenneth Clark, the Contemporary Art Society, 1947, © the artist's estate/www.bridgeman.co.uk
Collier, John 1708–1786, *Tim Bobbin and His Wife*, gift from Mrs Doris Melland, 1963
Collier, John 1850–1934, *Brotherhood of Man*, gift from Mrs Collier, 1936
Connard, Philip 1875–1958, *The Lilac Dress*, purchased, 1926
Constable, John 1776–1837, *Trentham Hall*, purchased from Sotheby's, 1984
Cooke, John b.1929, *Lathkill Dale*, purchased from the Pentagon Gallery, Stoke-on-Trent, 1973, © the artist
Cooper, Eileen b.1953, *Out of the Wild*, gift from the Contemporary Art Society, 1989, © Eileen Cooper 2007. All rights reserved, DACS
Cooper, Gerald 1898–1975, *Winter*, purchased from the Royal Academy, 1935
Cope, J. *Guildford*, bequeathed by William Woodall, 1954
Cope, Norman d.1943, *Nude Old Man*, gift from Stanley Cope, 1972
Cope, Norman d.1943, *Portrait of an Old Man*, gift from Stanley Cope, 1972
Coverley, Tracey b.1970, *From Charlie's Point*, purchased from the artist, 1991
Coxon, Raymond James 1896–1997, *Hebden Bridge, Yorkshire*, gift from the Contemporary Art Society, 1940, © the artist's estate
Coxon, Raymond James 1896–1997, *Kitchen Garden*, gift from the Contemporary Art Society, 1940, © the artist's estate
Coxon, Raymond James 1896–1997, *Portmadoc*, purchased from the artist, 1987, © the artist's estate
Cubley, Henry Hadfield 1848–1934, *The Incoming Tide*, purchased from Louis Taylor, 1950
Cubley, Henry Hadfield 1848–1934, *Farmyard*
Cubley, Henry Hadfield 1848–1934, *Highland Castle*
Cubley, Henry Hadfield 1848–1934, *Landscape with Pier and Lake*
Cubley, Henry Hadfield 1848–1934, *Landscape with Sheep*
Cubley, Henry Hadfield 1848–1934, *Mountain and Lake*
Currie, John 1883–1914, *Self Portrait*, purchased from Elizabeth Diamond, 1998
Currie, John 1883–1914, *The Glad Eye, Dressed for Promenade*, purchased from Mr T. Ratcliff, 1963
Currie, John 1883–1914, *Some Later Primitives and Madame Tisceron*, purchased from Dr H. A. Lyth, 1957
Currie, John 1883–1914, *The Supper*, purchased from Dr H. A. Lyth, 1945
Currie, John 1883–1914, *Mark Gertler (1891–1939)*, purchased from Dr H. A. Lyth, 1935
Currie, John 1883–1914, *The Red Necklace*, gift from Sir Edward Marsh, the Contemporary Art Society, 1957
Currie, John 1883–1914, *The Witch*, purchased from Jackson's Pictures Ltd, 1953
Currie, John 1883–1914, *Normandy Landscape*, purchased from Miss Pickering, 1952
Currie, John 1883–1914, *The Procession*, purchased from Mrs E. Poole, 1958
Currie, John 1883–1914, *Study for 'Woman's Pay'*, purchased from Mrs E. Poole, 1958
Currie, John 1883–1914, *The House*, purchased from Mrs E. Poole, 1958
Currie, John 1883–1914, *A Girl from Afar*, gift from Mr A. Margulies, 1963
Currie, John 1883–1914, *Breton Woman with Apples*, purchased from Mrs E. Poole, 1958
Currie, John 1883–1914, *Dartmouth*, purchased from Dr H. A. Lyth, 1952
Currie, John 1883–1914, *Female Portrait*, purchased from Jackson's Pictures Ltd, 1952
Currie, John 1883–1914, *Fisherman*, purchased from Mrs E. Poole, 1958
Currie, John 1883–1914, *Head of a Girl*, purchased from Jackson's Pictures Ltd, Manchester, 1953
Currie, John 1883–1914, *Newlyn, Looking towards Mousehole*, purchased from Dr H. A. Lyth, 1952
Currie, John 1883–1914, *Penkhull*, gift from Arnold Bennett, 1950
Currie, John 1883–1914, *The Procession*, purchased from Mrs E. Poole, 1958
Darwin, Robin 1910–1974, *Nude*, gift from the Contemporary Art Society, 1947
Dawbarn, Joseph Yelverton 1856–1943, *Fishing Village on the Zuider Zee*, bequeathed by Mr H. F. Wood, 1963
De Wint, Peter 1784–1849, *Cliveden-on-Thames*, gift from the National Art Collections Fund, 1940
Dessau, Paul Lucien 1909–1999, *Invasion*, purchased from the Fireman Artists' Exhibition, 1942
Donne, Walter J. 1867–1930, *Temple of the Sun*, gift from the artist, 1935
Donne, Walter J. 1867–1930, *Onecote*, gift from Reverend Grindley Johnson, 1952
Donne, Walter J. 1867–1930, *A Moorland Landscape, Staffordshire*, gift from Reverend Grindley Johnson, 1952
Dunlop, Ronald Ossory 1894–1973, *Eileen*, purchased from the Redfern Gallery, 1933
Dunlop, Ronald Ossory 1894–1973, *C. R. W. Nevinson (1889–1946)*, purchased from R. H. Spurr, Southport, 1946
Dunlop, Ronald Ossory 1894–1973, *The Poet*, gift from the Contemporary Art Society, 1933
Ellis, Edwin 1841–1895, *House and Gardens*, gift from Lord Howard de Walden, the Contemporary Arts Society, 1929
Emery, Alston active 1973–c.1992, *Bethesda Chapel*, gift from Mrs Alston Emery, 1995
Emery, John 1777–1822, *Boy with Rabbit*, bequeathed by Miss F. M. Rees, 1991
Emery, John 1777–1822, *Marianne and Anne*
Emery, John 1777–1822, *Marianne in Confirmation Dress*
Emery, John 1777–1822, *Portrait of a Young Lady*
Emery, John 1777–1822, *Portrait of the Artist's Daughters*
Emery, John 1777–1822, *Self Portrait*
Emery, John 1777–1822, *Self Portrait*
Emery, John 1777–1822, *Susannah Toft*
Emery, John (after) 1777–1822, *Self Portrait*, bequeathed by Miss F. M. Rees, 1991
Emery, John (after) 1777–1822, *Susannah Toft*, bequeathed by Miss F. M. Rees, 1991
England, Frederick John b.1939, *Joseph Rosenstock at Lewisham Station*, purchased from the Society of Staffordshire Artists, 1967
England, Frederick John b.1939, *Below Five Clouds, the Roaches*, purchased from the artist at the Freedom from Hunger Exhibition, 1963
Errill, Frederick F. *April Moonrise*, bequeathed by Dr W. D. Wilkins, 1964
Etty, William 1787–1849, *A Greek Slave*, old stock, acquired before the accession register and Stoke-on-Trent Museum were established
Evans, E. J. B. active c.1900–1920, *Etruria*
Eves, Reginald Grenville 1876–1941, *Colonel Henry Edward Medlicott (1882–1948)*, gift from Her Majesty's Government, 1947
Farquharson, David 1839–1907, *Forest of Meikleour, Perthshire*, purchased from R. H. Spurr, Southport, 1972
Ferguson, V. active 1940s, *Food Production, Jamaica*, gift from the War Artists Advisory Committee, 1947
Fidler, Harry 1856–1935, *Clearing the Potato Field*, gift from C. J.

Eardley, 1935
Fidler, Harry 1856–1935, *The Last Journey*, gift from Dr J. J. R. Abcarius, 1935
Findler, L. *Cheddleton*, gift from Mr Guy Moore, 1954
Fisher, Mark 1841–1923, *Cows Grazing*, purchased from Jackson's, Nantwich, 1955
Fleetwood-Walker, Bernard 1893–1965, *The Family*, purchased from the Royal Academy, 1932, © the artist's estate
Fletcher, Doreen b.1952, *Beats Grocers*, gift from the Friends of the Museum and Art Gallery, 1982, © the artist/www.bridgeman.co.uk
Forsyth, Gordon Mitchell 1879–1952, *Jim Mason (1879–1952)*, bequeathed by Mrs Mason, 1957
Forsyth, Gordon Mitchell 1879–1952, *Market Drayton, Shropshire*, purchased from the artist, 1941
Forsyth, Gordon Mitchell 1879–1952, *Old Houses, St Ives*, acquired, 1924
Forsyth, Gordon Mitchell 1879–1952, *The Sytch, Burslem*, old stock, acquired before the accession register and Stoke-on-Trent Museum were established
Forsyth, Gordon Mitchell 1879–1952, *The Yellow Lamp*, purchased from Mrs C. Heath, 1972
Forsyth, Moira 1905–1991, *Trees at Sellack, Wye Valley*, bequeathed by Dr W. D. Wilkins, 1964
Frost, Terry 1915–2003, *Yellow and Ochre*, gift from the Contemporary Art Society, 1986, © the artist's estate
Fry, Roger Eliot 1866–1934, *Immortelles*, purchased from Jackson's Pictures Ltd, 1953
Gabain, Ethel 1883–1950, *Miss Edith Evans in a Restoration Comedy*, purchased from the artist, 1935
Gertler, Mark 1892–1939, *Head of a Basque Shepherdess*, gift from the Contemporary Arts Society, 1935, © by permission of Luke Gertler
Gibson, William Alfred 1866–1931, *On the Riviera*, bequeathed by Dr John Russell, 1947
Giles, Anthony E. b.1925, *Tinscape*, purchased from the artist at the Royal Academy, 1966
Gilman, Harold 1876–1919, *Interior with a Girl by a Mantelpiece*, purchased from Thomas Agnew and Sons Ltd, London, 1979
Ginner, Charles 1878–1952, *Salisbury Cathedral*, purchased from Spurr, Bradford, West Yorkshire, 1937
Gleaves, Percy 1882–1944, *Three Trees*, gift from Mrs Gleaves, 1970
Gleaves, Percy 1882–1944, *Coastal Scene*, gift from Mrs Gleaves, 1970
Gleaves, Percy 1882–1944, *Japanese Anemones and Zinnias in a Glass Vase*, gift from Mrs Gleaves, 1970
Gleaves, Percy 1882–1944, *Portrait of an Old Man*, gift from Mrs Gleaves, 1970
Gleaves, Percy 1882–1944, *Still Life of Leeks against a Basket*, gift from Mrs Gleaves, 1970
Gleaves, Percy 1882–1944, *Still Life of Oranges in front of a Mirror*, gift from Mrs Gleaves, 1970
Gleaves, Percy 1882–1944, *Study of Foxgloves*, gift from Mrs Gleaves, 1970
Gleaves, Percy 1882–1944, *Study of Gladioli*, gift from Mrs Gleaves, 1970
Gleaves, Percy 1882–1944, *Study of Thistles*, gift from Mrs Gleaves, 1970
Gleaves, Percy 1882–1944, *Sweet Peas in a Green Vase*, gift from Mrs Gleaves, 1970
Gleaves, Percy 1882–1944, *The Origin of the Milky Way (after Jacopo Tintoretto)*
Gogin, Charles 1844–1931, *A Sussex Lane*, gift, 1945
Gore, Spencer 1878–1914, *Harrington Square from No.2 Houghton Place*, purchased from the Anthony D'Offay Gallery, London, 1983
Gosling, Paul *Medicine*, purchased from the artist, 1991
Gosse, Laura Sylvia 1881–1968, *St Rémy*, purchased from Connell Galleries, 1934, © the artist's estate/www.bridgeman.co.uk
Grant, Duncan 1885–1978, *Flatford-on-Avon*, purchased from R. H. Spurr, Southport, 1948, © 1978 estate of Duncan Grant
Greaves, Walter 1846–1930, *The Haymarket*, purchased from Richard Hancock, 1953
Greaves, Walter 1846–1930, *The Street Singer*, purchased from Spurr, Bradford, West Yorkshire, 1938
Green, Aaron 1820–1898, *Epsom Downs, 1863*, gift from Miss G. Gurney, 1958
Green, Aaron 1820–1898, *Girl with a Lamb*, gift from Miss G. Gurney, 1958
Green, Frank Harold *Spencer Green (1839–1903)*, gift from Charles Green, 2001
Greenwood, Orlando 1892–1989, *The Card*, purchased from Jackson's Pictures Ltd, 1957
Grundy, Robert B. *New Industry*, purchased from the Changing Face of the Potteries Exhibition, 1960
Gunn, Herbert James 1893–1964, *Michie*, purchased from Spurr, Bradford, West Yorkshire, 1942, © estate of the artist
Gwynne-Jones, Allan 1892–1982, *Honeysuckle*, purchased from Abbott and Holder, London, 1953, © the artist's estate/www.bridgeman.co.uk
Hall, Oliver 1869–1957, *Marshland on the Norfolk Coast*, purchased from the Royal Academy, 1932
Hargitt, Edward 1835–1895, *Landscape with Cattle and Women Feeding Hens*, old stock, acquired before the accession register and Stoke-on-Trent Museum were established
Hart, Anna active 1944–1945, *Mr Eric Young*, gift from the artist, 1945
Hastling, Annie E. b.1845, *Still Life*, bequeathed by William Woodall, 1954
Haughton, Benjamin 1865–1924, *A Cornish Homestead*, gift from Mrs Haughton, 1937
Heath, Nancy Lilian 1922–1995, *Cottages, Old Fishguard*, purchased from the artist, 1959, © the artist's estate
Heath, Nancy Lilian 1922–1995, *Sheila*, gift from Dr E. Isaacson, 1968, © the artist's estate
Hepple, Norman 1908–1994, *Mother and Child*, purchased from the Royal Academy, 1950, © the artist's estate/www.bridgeman.co.uk
Herald, Albert b.1925, *Mother and Child*, purchased from the artist, 1960
Herkomer, Hubert von 1849–1914, *Head of an Old Man*, purchased from W. C. Allman, 1958
Hilditch, Tom 1933–1985, *Walking Man*, purchased from Reverend G. Whitty, 1988
Hilditch, Tom 1933–1985, *Seated Man*, purchased from Reverend G. Whitty, 1988
Hinks, Thomas *Sutherland Road, Longton*, purchased from the artist, 1962
Hitchens, Ivon 1893–1979, *House with Blue Door, among Trees*, purchased from Mr A. Freer, 1988, © Ivon Hitchens' estate/Jonathan Clark & Co.
Holland, James 1800–1870, *Flowers from Nature*, purchased from V. Joseph, 1950
Holland, James 1800–1870, *The Fish Market*, old stock, acquired before the accession register and Stoke-on-Trent Museum were established
Holland, James 1800–1870, *Venice*, purchased from the Pallser Galleries, 1939
Holland, James 1800–1870, *North Door, Notre Dame, Paris*, purchased from Abbott and Holder, London, 1954
Holland, James 1800–1870, *Countrymen with a White Horse*, purchased from Stanley W. Fisher, 1965
Holland, James 1800–1870, *Venice*, purchased from R. H. Spurr, Southport, 1951
Holland, James 1800–1870, *Anglers by a Cottage on a River Bank*, purchased from R. H. Spurr, Southport, 1946
Holland, James 1800–1870, *Bridge and Trees*, purchased from Humphrey Longden, 1949
Holland, James 1800–1870, *Bridge and Waterfall Scene*, purchased from Humphrey Longden, 1949
Holland, James 1800–1870, *Canal Scene, Venice*, bequeathed by Mr H. F. Wood, 1963
Holland, James 1800–1870, *Catching the Pig at Boston Fair*, purchased from Mrs J. B. Ashwell, 1949
Holland, James 1800–1870, *Distant View of Birmingham*, purchased from R. H. Spurr, Southport, 1948
Holland, James 1800–1870, *Grand Canal, Venice*, old stock, acquired before the accession register and Stoke-on-Trent Museum were established
Holland, James 1800–1870, *Lake and Castle Scene*, purchased from C. W. Kilby, 1948
Holland, James 1800–1870, *Llangollen*, gift from B. Roth, 1946
Holland, James 1800–1870, *On the Rhône*
Holland, James 1800–1870, *The Wheelwright's Shop*, purchased from R. H. Spurr, Southport, 1956
Holland, James 1800–1870, *Venice*, purchased from Jackson's, Manchester, 1949
Holland, James 1800–1870, *Venice, Narrow Canal*, purchased from Mrs Fletcher, 1949
Holland, James 1800–1870, *Windmill*, purchased from C. W. Kilby, 1948
Holland, James 1800–1870, *Windmill and the Sea*, purchased from Humphrey Longden, 1949
Holland, James 1800–1870, *Yacht Scene*, purchased from Jackson's, Manchester, 1951
Holmes, Charles John 1868–1936, *Bude Canal*, bequeathed by Dr John Russell, 1947
Holmes, Charles John 1868–1936, *The Eden, near Lazonby*, purchased from Colnaghi, 1928
Houston, George 1869–1947, *Killin*, bequeathed by Dr John Russell, 1926
Houthuesen, Albert Anthony 1903–1979, *The Supper at Emmaus*, gift from the Duveen Paintings Fund, 1962, © reproduced by permission of the Trustees of the Albert Houthuesen Trust
How, Julia Beatrice 1867–1932, *Etude, le perroquet*, purchased from the Art Exhibitions Bureau, 1936
Hunt, Cecil Arthur 1873–1965, *Atlas Mountains, near Constantine*, purchased from the Royal Academy, 1933
Hunter, George Leslie 1877–1931, *Still Life*, purchased from T. and R. Annan, 1946
Isherwood, James Lawrence 1917–1988, *Head of a Nigerian*, purchased from the artist, 1958
Jackson, G. *View of a Cobbled Street with Peasants*, purchased from Mrs A. S. Dawson, 1957
Jackson, Gerald Goddard b.1878, *William Douglas-Phillips*
Johnson, Charles G. 1902–1983, *The Green, Kennington Road*, purchased from the artist at the Royal Academy Exhibition, 1961
Kelman, A. *Street Scene*, purchased from Jackson's, Nantwich, 1957
Kennerley, George b.1912, *Industrial Landscape*, purchased from the artist, 1959
King, Jeremy b.1933, *La Forêt, Fouesnant*, purchased from the Royal Academy, 1967
King, Yeend 1855–1924, *On the Upper Thames*, bequeathed by William Woodall, 1954
Kirk, Eve 1900–1969, *The Red Chimney: A Bombed Part of London*, purchased from Abbott and Holder, London, 1956
Klinghoffer, Clara 1900–1970, *The Oriental Necklace*, purchased from Spurr, Bradford, West Yorkshire, 1938
Knight, John William Buxton 1842/1843–1908, *Near Harwich*, purchased from Jackson's, Nantwich, 1955
Knight, John William Buxton 1842/1843–1908, *Moorland Landscape*, acquired, 1947
Knight, Laura 1877–1970, *The Rehearsal*, purchased from R. H. Spurr, Southport, 1967, © the estate of Dame Laura Knight 2007. All rights reserved, DACS
Knight, Laura 1877–1970, *The Rosinbacks*, purchased, 1932, © the estate of Dame Laura Knight 2007. All rights reserved, DACS
Kortright, Reginald Guy b.1877, *The Priest's Walk*, purchased from the Royal Academy, 1933
Kramer, Jacob 1892–1962, *Dolores*, purchased from the artist, 1934, © William Roberts Society
La Thangue, Henry Herbert 1859–1929, *Nude Study*, gift, 1944
Lamb, Henry 1883–1960, *Fatigue, Canadian Forces*, gift from the War Artists Advisory Committee, 1947, © estate of Henry Lamb
Layng, Mabel Frances 1881–1937, *The Sewing Girl*, gift from Miss A. C. Layng, 1938
Leapman, David b.1959, *Treeman*, gift from the Contemporary Art Society, 1992, © the artist
Lees, Derwent 1885–1931, *Arenig Fawr*, gift from the Contemporary Art Society, 1924
Leeson, Laurence b.1930, *The Orchard No.2*, purchased, 1974
Lessore, Jules 1849–1892, *Notre Dame de Paris*, gift from the Sickert Trust, 1947
Lessore, Thérèse 1884–1945, *The Pump Room, Bath*, purchased from Holden, London, 1945, © the artist's estate
Lewis, Wyndham 1882–1957, *Stephen Spender (1909–1995)*, purchased from Spurr, Bradford, West Yorkshire, 1939, © the artist's estate
Livesay, Richard 1750–c.1826, *Rear Admiral Clement Sneyd (1773–1854)*, purchased from Humphrey Longden, 1952
Lovatt, James Alfred 1873–1952, *The Barge Builder's Yard, Stone*, purchased from the Society of Staffordshire Artists Exhibition, 1945
Low, Diana 1911–1975, *Sunderland Bowl with Flowers*, purchased from the Royal Academy, 1949

Lowry, Laurence Stephen 1887–1976, *The Empty House*, purchased from Mrs Berry, 1942, © courtesy of the estate of L. S. Lowry
Lowry, Laurence Stephen 1887–1976, *The Courtyard*, gift from Harold Marks, 1989, © courtesy of the estate of L. S. Lowry
Macbryde, Robert 1913–1966, *The Supper at Emmaus*, gift from the Contemporary Art Society, 1980
Maclaren, Helen b.1898, *Old Barn in Hertfordshire*, purchased from Willoughby Art Gallery, London, 1937
Maddox, Conroy 1912–2005, *The Late Sleeper*, purchased from the artist, 1995, © the artist's estate
Makinson, Trevor b.1926, *Camden Town Street*, purchased from the artist, 1948
Malkin, John *Astbury Church*, gift from Mrs Awty, 1960
Malkin, John *Trentham Hall*, gift, 1944
Marks, Margret 1899–1990, *Quarry, Cauldon Low*, gift from Harold Marks, 1997, © the artist's estate
Marks, Margret 1899–1990, *Yellow Field, Earlsterndale, Derbyshire*, gift from Harold Marks, 1997, © the artist's estate
Marriott, Frederick 1860–1941, *Frank Clayton Bennett*, gift from Mr Richard Bennett, 1967
Mason, Arnold 1885–1963, *Job Nixon (1891–1938)*, purchased from the artist, © the artist's estate
Mason, George Heming 1818–1872, *Evening, near Southport*, purchased from Simon Reynolds, 1994
Mason, George Heming 1818–1872, *Sketch for 'Girls Dancing, a Pastoral Symphony'*, purchased from Christie's, 1935
Mason, George Heming 1818–1872, *Goatherd of the Campagna*, old stock, acquired before the accession register and Stoke-on-Trent Museum were established
Mason, George Heming 1818–1872, *Roman Ox (Lying down)*, purchased from Dr R. M. Lodge, 1992
Mason, George Heming 1818–1872, *Roman Ox (Standing)*, purchased from Dr R. M. Lodge, 1992
Mason, George Heming 1818–1872, *Threshing Corn*, purchased from Christie's, 1935
Mason, George Heming (attributed to) 1818–1872, *Cottage Interior*, gift from the Friends of the Museum and Art Gallery, 1955
McCall, William b.c.1786, *Josiah Spode II (1754–1827)*, gift, 1954
McEvoy, Ambrose 1878–1927, *Mrs Lydia Russell*, purchased from Jackson's Pictures Ltd, 1961
McGregor, Robert 1848–1922, *Crab Fishers*, bequeathed by William Woodall, 1954
McKinnon, Sine 1901–1996, *Ponte Vecchio, Florence*, purchased from Alex Reid and Lefevre Ltd, 1935
Meninsky, Bernard 1891–1950, *Lady in Red*, gift from the Contemporary Art Society, 1952, © the artist's estate
Meninsky, Bernard 1891–1950, *Seated Nude*, gift from the Contemporary Art Society, 1947, © the artist's estate
Milward, Frith 1906–1982, *Hindlow, Derbyshire*, gift from the Friends of the Museum and Art Gallery, 1969
Moira, Gerald 1867–1959, *On the Edge of Dartmoor*, gift from the artist, 1942
Monnoyer, Jean-Baptiste 1636–1699, *Still Life of Flowers*, bequeathed by Miss I. Slater, 1980
Moreau, Luc-Albert 1882–1948, *Head of a Woman*, old stock, acquired before the accession register and Stoke-on-Trent Museum were established
Mostyn, Thomas Edward 1864–1930, *The Cardinal's Garden*
Muirhead, David 1867–1930, *The Bridge at Aylesford*, purchased from Colnaghi, 1928
Munnings, Alfred James 1878–1959, *Tagg's Island*, bequeathed by Dr John Russell, 1927, © the artist's estate
Munnings, Alfred James 1878–1959, *A Piper*, bequeathed by Dr John Russell, 1927, © the artist's estate
Munnings, Alfred James 1878–1959, *Point-to-Point*, bequeathed by Dr John Russell; on loan to the Sir Alfred Munnings Art Museum, Essex, 1927, © the artist's estate
Murray, David 1849–1933, *Windsor Castle*, gift from the artist, 1933
Murray, David 1849–1933, *Study*, purchased from Christie's, 1935
Mussill, Wenzel d.1906, *Portrait of the Artist's Housekeeper*, gift from A. T. Wood, 1935
Mussill, William 1828–1906, *Still Life of Fruit with Blue Tit*
Naviasky, Philip 1894–1982, *Flower Piece*, purchased from the artist, 1935, © the artist's estate
Nelson, Geoffrey C. active 1914–1931, *The South of France*, gift from the Duveen Paintings Fund, 1962
Nevinson, Christopher 1889–1946, *Sandy Path*, purchased from Holden, London, 1945, © the artist's estate/www.bridgeman.co.uk
Newey, Harry Foster 1858–1933, *Harvesting Scene*, acquired, 1954
Newey, Harry Foster 1858–1933, *In an Old Orchard*, old stock, acquired before the accession register and Stoke-on-Trent Museum were established
Nicholson, William 1872–1949, *Flower Piece with Books*, purchased from the Beaux Arts Gallery, London, 1928, © Elizabeth Banks
Nierinck, Dorothy M. *The Mermaid Pool*, purchased from the artist, 1967
Ninnes, Bernard 1899–1971, *In for Repairs*, purchased from the St Ives Society of Artists, 1932
Nixon, Job 1891–1938, *Near Lamorna*, purchased from the Job Nixon Memorial Exhibition, 1946
Nixon, Job 1891–1938, *Portrait of a Man*
Nixon, Job 1891–1938, *Rochester*, gift from Mrs Nixon, 1942
Northcote, James 1746–1831, *Elijah Mayer (1765–1813)*, old stock, acquired before the accession register and Stoke-on-Trent Museum were established
Northcote, James 1746–1831, *Mrs Mayer*, old stock, acquired before the accession register and Stoke-on-Trent Museum were established
O'Connor, John 1830–1899, *View from the National Gallery*, old stock, acquired before the accession register and Stoke-on-Trent Museum were established
O'Connor, John 1830–1899, *Edinburgh from St Anthony's Chapel*, bequeathed by William Woodall, 1954
O'Connor, John 1830–1899, *Rome, The Bridge of Sant'Angelo*
O'Connor, John 1830–1899, *St Paul's from Ludgate Hill*, bequeathed by William Woodall, 1954
O'Connor, John 1830–1899, *The Town Hall of Vicenza*, gift from William Woodall
O'Connor, John 1830–1899, *Venetian Scene*
O'Conor, Roderic 1860–1940, *Interior*, purchased from Jackson's, Nantwich, 1956
Ormrod, Frank 1897–1988, *Garden and Pond*, purchased from the Royal Academy, 1949
Orpen, William 1878–1931, *St Patrick*, purchased from the Beaux Arts Gallery, London, 1936
Orpen, William 1878–1931, *The New Bonnet*, purchased from R. H. Spurr, Southport, 1967
Padwick, Philip Hugh 1876–1958, *Landscape with Trees*, purchased from Bourlet and Co., London, 1959
Palin, William Mainwaring 1862–1947, *William Millett Edge*, gift from Mrs M. E. Dene, 1954
Palin, William Mainwaring 1862–1947, *Thomas Hulme, JP (1830–1905)*, gift, 1954
Palin, William Mainwaring 1862–1947, *The Temple of Fame*, gift from the artist, 1935
Palin, William Mainwaring 1862–1947, *The Temple of Minerva*, gift from the artist, 1935
Palin, William Mainwaring 1862–1947, *John Alcock, JP*, old stock, acquired before the accession register and Stoke-on-Trent Museum were established
Palin, William Mainwaring 1862–1947, *William Woodall, MP (1832–1901)*, old stock, acquired before the accession register and Stoke-on-Trent Museum were established
Parry, David Henry 1793–1826, *The Misses Heywoods*, purchased from R. H. Spurr, Southport, 1972
Parsons, Alfred William 1847–1920, *The Swede Harvest*, bequeathed by Mr H. F. Wood, 1963
Parsons, Francis d.1804, *James Brindley (1716–1772)*, old stock, acquired before the accession register and Stoke-on-Trent Museum were established
Pass, Donald b.1930, *Nude Study*, purchased from the artist, 1954
Paterson, James 1854–1932, *Still Life: Persian, Japanese, Dutch*, purchased from R. H. Spurr, Southport, 1947
Peake, John Nash 1837–1905, *Sir Smith Child (1808–1896)*, gift from Miss Teresa Child, 1982
Peake, John Nash 1837–1905, *Fishing Fleet, Tenby*, old stock, acquired before the accession register and Stoke-on-Trent Museum were established
Peake, John Nash 1837–1905, *The Isle of Arran*, gift from J. B. Allman, 1960
Peake, John Nash 1837–1905, *The Matterhorn*, old stock, acquired before the accession register and Stoke-on-Trent Museum were established
Peake, John Nash 1837–1905, *The Last Load*, old stock, acquired before the accession register and Stoke-on-Trent Museum were established
Pemsel, Oliver 1910–1989, *The Lock Gates*, purchased from the Royal Academy, 1935
Penson, Frederick Thomas 1866–1951, *Cornish Miner*, gift from Mrs J. B. Ashwell, 1949
Peploe, Samuel John 1871–1935, *Still Life*, purchased from R. H. Spurr, Southport, 1960
Peppercorn, Arthur Douglas 1847–1926, *Quiet Waters*, purchased from R. H. Spurr, Southport, 1972
Phillips, Norman 1920–1988, *Borer and Mate*, gift from Mrs Phillips, 1994
Phipps, J. active 1838–1861, *York Racecourse*, gift from Mrs Dawson, 1954
Pickering, W. E. *Five Women Working by a Table*, purchased from Mr Tilletson Hyde, 1953
Pickering, W. E. *Spanish Scene*, purchased from Mr Tilletson Hyde, 1953
Plant, Simon b.1954, *The Tare*, purchased from the artist, 1990
Pollock, Fred b.1937, *Firefly Summer*, acquired, 1996, © the artist
Potter, Frank Huddlestone 1845–1887, *Morning Tea*, purchased, 1958
Pourbus, Frans the younger 1569–1622, *Woman in a White Cap*, gift from Dr W. D. Wilkins, 1957
Pratt, Henry Lark I 1805–1873, *Trent Vale from Penkhull*, old stock, acquired before the accession register and Stoke-on-Trent Museum were established
Pratt, Henry Lark I 1805–1873, *Boothen Mill, Stoke*, purchased from Mr J. Myatt, 1908
Pratt, Henry Lark I 1805–1873, *Etruria Hall*, old stock, acquired before the accession register and Stoke-on-Trent Museum were established
Pratt, Henry Lark I 1805–1873, *Local Landscape*, old stock, acquired before the accession register and Stoke-on-Trent Museum were established
Pratt, Henry Lark I 1805–1873, *Local Landscape*, old stock, acquired before the accession register and Stoke-on-Trent Museum were established
Pratt, Henry Lark I 1805–1873, *Local Landscape*, old stock, acquired before the accession register and Stoke-on-Trent Museum were established
Pratt, Henry Lark I 1805–1873, *Potteries Landscape*
Pratt, Henry Lark I 1805–1873, *Strongford Mill, near Trentham*, purchased, 1954
Pratt, Henry Lark I 1805–1873, *View from Basford Bank*, old stock, acquired before the accession register and Stoke-on-Trent Museum were established
Pratt, Henry Lark I 1805–1873, *View of Stoke from Penkhull*, gift, 1985
Pratt, Henry Lark I (attributed to) 1805–1873, *View of Stoke from Penkhull*, gift from Mr W. Rees-Jones, 1925
Procter, Dod 1892–1972, *Clara*, purchased, 1928, © the artist's estate/www.bridgeman.co.uk
Procter, Dod 1892–1972, *Girl in White*, purchased from the artist, 1926, © the artist's estate/www.bridgeman.co.uk
Proudfoot, James 1908–1971, *Dark Girl*, purchased from R. H. Spurr, Southport, 1937
Prout, Margaret Fisher 1875–1963, *La patronne*, purchased from the Royal Academy, 1963
Raay, G. W. *Rynsburg Arnhem Vor, 1944*
Rapp, Ginette 1928–1998, *Yport*, purchased from the artist, 1956
Reed, Graeme John Robert b.1964, *Looking Closely at the Flowers*, purchased from the artist at the 7th Stoke Open Exhibition, 1993
Richter, Herbert Davis 1874–1955, *Diana*, purchased from the Royal Academy, 1932
Richter, Herbert Davis 1874–1955, *The Flower Show*
Roberts, Ellis William 1860–1930, *Sir Henry Doulton (1820–1897)*, old stock, acquired before the accession register and Stoke-on-Trent Museum were established
Roberts, Ellis William 1860–1930, *George Bennion*
Roberts, William Patrick 1895–1980, *Portrait of a Negress*, gift from the Contemporary Art Society, 1923, © William Roberts Society
Robertson, Constance 1895–1964,

Scabious, gift from Alderman A. C. Harvey, 1935
Robinson, John Charles 1824–1913, *Still Life with Fruit*, purchased from J. Ashton, 1945
Roisi, A. M. *Rest by the Sea*, old stock, acquired before the accession register and Stoke-on-Trent Museum were established
Roldan, Eduardo b.1926, *La Giralda, Seville*
Rush *Wooded Scene with Two Figures and a Horse*, old stock, acquired before the accession register and Stoke-on-Trent Museum were established
Russell, Walter Westley 1867–1949, *Boulogne Sands*, purchased from Jackson's, Manchester, 1950
Russell, Walter Westley 1867–1949, *Lydia*, purchased from Jackson's, Manchester, 1950
Ryan, Adrian 1920–1998, *Dawn, Newlyn, Cornwall*, gift from the Contemporary Art Society, 1959, © the estate of Adrian Ryan
Ryles, Frederick Rieland 1831–1908, *Self Portrait*, gift from Mrs Mary Keys, 1985
Ryles, Frederick Rieland 1831–1908, *Simeon Shaw (1785–1859)*, gift from Mrs Mary Keys, 1985
Ryles, Frederick Rieland 1831–1908, *Thomas Pinder (d.1867)*, old stock, acquired before the accession register and Stoke-on-Trent Museum were established
Ryles, Thomas 1825–1903, *Job Ridgway (1759–1814)*, old stock, acquired before the accession register and Stoke-on-Trent Museum were established
Ryles, Thomas (attributed to) 1825–1903, *William Hackwood (d.1849)*, purchased from W. B. Cooper, 1951
Sambrook, Elliott *Alderman William Bratt, JP, Electoral Mayor of Burslem, November 1898*, gift from A. E. Bennett, 1964
Schwarz-Abrys, Léon 1905–1990, *Porte de Montreuil, Paris*, purchased from Mrs E. Poole, 1958
Seabrooke, Elliott 1886–1950, *The Blue Cloth*, purchased from Abbott and Holder, London, 1958
Shannon, Charles Haslewood 1863–1937, *Lady in Grey Fur*, old stock, acquired before the accession register and Stoke-on-Trent Museum were established
Sharp, Dorothea 1874–1955, *The Market, Cassis*, purchased from R. H. Spurr, Southport, 1973
Shave, Terry b.1952, *Fire Ring Series No.15*, purchased from Midlands Contemporary Art, 1990, © the artist
Shayer, William 1788–1879, *The Blue Ball, North Devon*, old stock, acquired before the accession register and Stoke-on-Trent Museum were established
Shelton, John b.1923, *Clown Resting*, gift from Mrs Lovatt, 1987
Shelton, John b.1923, *Cat on a Table*, purchased from the Mayor Gallery, London, 1989
Sickert, Walter Richard 1860–1942, *Maurice Asselin (1882–1947)*, purchased from Spurr, Bradford, West Yorkshire, 1941, © estate of Walter R. Sickert/DACS 2007
Sickert, Walter Richard 1860–1942, *Don Juan and Haidee (Idyll) (after Gilbert)*, gift from the Contemporary Art Society, 1965, © estate of Walter R. Sickert/ DACS 2007
Sickert, Walter Richard 1860–1942, *The Wave*, purchased from Jackson's, 1956, © estate of Walter R. Sickert/ DACS 2007
Simcock, Jack b.1929, *From a Back Lane*, gift from the Friends of the Museum and Art Gallery, 1950, © the artist
Simcock, Jack b.1929, *The Rose and Crown*, purchased from the artist, 1957, © the artist
Simcock, Jack b.1929, *Biddulph Moor*, purchased from the artist, 1957, © the artist
Simcock, Jack b.1929, *Two Figures*, bequeathed by Reginald George Haggar, 1987, © the artist
Simcock, Jack b.1929, *Manor Farm*, purchased from the artist, 1960, © the artist
Simcock, Jack b.1929, *Houses*, gift from Reginald George Haggar, 1977, © the artist
Simcock, Jack b.1929, *Cottages and Head*, gift from the Contemporary Art Society, 1973, © the artist
Simcock, Jack b.1929, *Landscape*, gift from Reginald George Haggar, 1977, © the artist
Sims, Charles 1873–1928, *Country Scene, Forest Trees*, bequeathed by Dr John Russell, 1927
Skinner, John b.1953, *Ernest James Dalzell Warrillow, MBE, FSA, Photographer and Historian (1909–2000)*, gift from the Ironmarket Press, 1978
Smart, Rowley 1887–1934, *Self Portrait*, purchased from Abbott and Holder, London, 1956
Smith, Matthew Arnold Bracy 1879–1959, *Seated Nude*, purchased from Browse and Darby, London, 1979, © by permission of the copyright holder
Smith, T. *View of Pottery, Fareham*, purchased from Grenville Clarke, 1942
Somerville, Howard 1873–1952, *Norah*, gift from the Misses Adamson, 1965
Spear, Ruskin 1911–1990, *Spring in Hammersmith*, gift from the Contemporary Art Society, 1949, © the artist's estate/www.bridgeman.co.uk
Spencer, Gilbert 1893–1979, *Self Portrait*, gift from the Contemporary Art Society, 1952, © the artist's estate/www.bridgeman.co.uk
Spencer, Noël 1900–1986, *Landscape with Lock Gates*, gift from the artist, 1980
Spencer, Noël 1900–1986, *Landscape with Lock Gates*, gift from the artist, 1980
Spencer, Noël 1900–1986, *Landscape with Lock Gates and Building*, gift from the artist, 1980
Spencer, Noël 1900–1986, *Middleport Pottery*, gift from the artist, 1980
Spencer, Noël 1900–1986, *Mow Cop from Kent Green*, gift from the artist, 1980
Spencer, Noël 1900–1986, *Wood's Pottery, Longport*, gift from the artist, 1980
Spurrier, Steven 1878–1961, *The Card Game*, purchased from the Royal Academy, 1948
Stanley, Jacqueline b.1928, *Warrington Square, Dublin*, gift from the Friends of the Museum and Art Gallery, 1969, © the artist
Stanyer, Peter b.1952, *Lenny Hackett*, gift from the artist, 1979
Stanyer, Peter b.1952, *The Chapel of Rest, the Death of My Father*, gift from the artist, 1979
Steele, Edwin 1837–1898, *Still Life of Flowers and Fruit*, gift from Mr H. Bagnall, 1950
Steele, Edwin 1837–1898, *Still Life of Flowers and Fruit*, gift from Mr H. Bagnall, 1950
Steele, Edwin 1837–1898, *Still Life of Flowers and Fruit*, gift from Mrs S. Morris, 1962
Steele, Edwin 1837–1898, *Still Life of Fruit*, gift from Mrs S. Morris, 1962
Steele, Edwin 1837–1898, *Still Life of Fruit*, gift from Mrs S. Morris, 1962
Steele, Edwin 1837–1898, *Still Life of Flowers and Fruit*, purchased from Timothy Churchill, 1958
Steele, Edwin 1837–1898, *Still Life of Flowers and Bird's Nest*, gift from Mr H. Bagnall, 1950
Steele, Edwin 1837–1898, *Still Life of Flowers and Fruit*, gift from Mr H. Bagnall, 1950
Steele, Edwin 1837–1898, *Still Life of Grapes and Vine*, old stock, acquired before the accession register and Stoke-on-Trent Museum were established
Steer, Philip Wilson 1860–1942, *Freshwater Bay*, purchased from Jackson's, Manchester, 1950, © Tate, London 2007
Steggles, Walter James 1908–1997, *Three Trees*, gift from the Contemporary Art Society, 1945
Strang, William 1859–1921, *Supper Time*, purchased from T. and R. Annan, 1928
Strange, A. Victor *A Thorn amidst Roses*
Strange, A. Victor *Classical Scene*
Strange, A. Victor *St Roch Curing the Plague (after Jacopo Tintoretto)*
Sutherland, Graham Vivian 1903–1980, *Foundry, Ladle Feeding Furnace*, gift from the War Artists Advisory Committee, 1947, © estate of Graham Sutherland
Sutton, Philip b.1928, *'Shall I compare thee to a summer's day?'*, © Philip Sutton RA
Tait, Jessie b.1928, *Home and Factory*, gift from the Friends of the Art Gallery, 1950
Talmage, Algernon Mayow 1871–1939, *Break in the Storm*, purchased from the Draycott House sale, 1938
Taylor, James Spence b.1921, *Les toits*, purchased from Marlborough Fine Art Company, 1956
Theaker, Harry George 1873–1954, *Minstrel*
Thompson, Philip *Bayswater*, purchased, 1956
Thorogood, Stanley 1873–1953, *Breakfast Is Ready*, bequeathed by Mrs Joy Margaret Dewey, 1993
Tickner, H. *Dr Spunton*
Tittensor, Harry 1887–1942, *Alderman John Hughes*, purchased, 1950
Tittensor, Harry 1887–1942, *Man on a Horse*
Tittensor, Harry 1887–1942, *Place des Alpes*, purchased from the artist, 1941
Tittensor, Harry 1887–1942, *Polperro*, gift from Mrs M. Ridout, 1963
Tittensor, Harry 1887–1942, *Rue de la Paix, Lisieux*, purchased from Mrs Tittensor, 1942
Toft, Charles 1831–1909, *Self Portrait*, gift from Mrs G. Tregaskis, 1959
Toft, Charles 1831–1909, *Still Life, Dead Game*, gift from Mrs E. M. Tregaskis, 1961
Toft, J. Alfonso 1866–1964, *Finchale Priory*, gift from Mrs P. R. Richardson, 1967
Toft, J. Alfonso 1866–1964, *A Castle Gate and Wall*, gift from Mrs P. R. Richardson, 1967
Toft, J. Alfonso 1866–1964, *Alnwick Castle*, gift from Mrs P. R. Richardson, 1964
Toft, J. Alfonso 1866–1964, *Alnwick Castle*, gift from Mrs P. R. Richardson, 1967
Toft, J. Alfonso 1866–1964, *Alnwick Castle*, gift from Mrs P. R. Richardson, 1967
Toft, J. Alfonso 1866–1964, *Alnwick Castle*, gift from Mrs P. R. Richardson, 1967
Toft, J. Alfonso 1866–1964, *Alton Towers*, gift from Mrs P. R. Richardson, 1967
Toft, J. Alfonso 1866–1964, *Bamburgh Castle*, gift from Mrs P. R. Richardson, 1967
Toft, J. Alfonso 1866–1964, *Bamburgh Castle*, gift from Mrs P. R. Richardson, 1967
Toft, J. Alfonso 1866–1964, *Caernarvon Castle*, gift from Mrs P. R. Richardson, 1967
Toft, J. Alfonso 1866–1964, *Caernarvon Castle from Twit Hill*, gift from Mrs P. R. Richardson, 1967
Toft, J. Alfonso 1866–1964, *Castle on a Hill*, gift from Mrs P. R. Richardson, 1967
Toft, J. Alfonso 1866–1964, *Castle, River and Viaduct*, gift from Mrs P. R. Richardson, 1967
Toft, J. Alfonso 1866–1964, *Castle Ruins in Mist*, gift from Mrs P. R. Richardson, 1967
Toft, J. Alfonso 1866–1964, *Castle Ruins on a Mound*, gift from Mrs P. R. Richardson, 1967
Toft, J. Alfonso 1866–1964, *Castle Ruins on a Mound (possibly Wigmore Castle)*, gift from Mrs P. R. Richardson, 1967
Toft, J. Alfonso 1866–1964, *Castle Scene*, gift from Mrs P. R. Richardson, 1967
Toft, J. Alfonso 1866–1964, *Castle with Yellow Sky*, gift from Mrs P. R. Richardson, 1967
Toft, J. Alfonso 1866–1964, *Country Lane*, gift from Mrs P. Richardson, 1964
Toft, J. Alfonso 1866–1964, *Dolbadarn Castle*, gift from Mrs P. R. Richardson, 1967
Toft, J. Alfonso 1866–1964, *Dolbadarn Castle and Lake*, gift from Mrs P. R. Richardson, 1967
Toft, J. Alfonso 1866–1964, *Dolbadarn Castle and Lake*, gift from Mrs P. R. Richardson, 1967
Toft, J. Alfonso 1866–1964, *Dunstanburgh Castle*, gift from Mrs P. R. Richardson, 1967
Toft, J. Alfonso 1866–1964, *Ellesborough, Buckinghamshire*, gift from Mrs P. R. Richardson, 1967
Toft, J. Alfonso 1866–1964, *Haughton Castle*, gift from Mrs P. R. Richardson, 1967
Toft, J. Alfonso 1866–1964, *Holy Island*, gift from Mrs P. R. Richardson, 1967
Toft, J. Alfonso 1866–1964, *Hornby, near Lancaster*, gift from Mrs P. R. Richardson, 1967
Toft, J. Alfonso 1866–1964, *Hornby Castle, near Lancaster*, gift from Mrs P. R. Richardson, 1967
Toft, J. Alfonso 1866–1964, *Hylton Castle, near Durham*, gift from Mrs P. R. Richardson, 1967
Toft, J. Alfonso 1866–1964, *Keep on a Mound, with River and Cows*, gift from Mrs P. R. Richardson, 1967
Toft, J. Alfonso 1866–1964, *Kenilworth Castle*, gift from Mrs P. R. Richardson, 1967
Toft, J. Alfonso 1866–1964, *Kenilworth Castle*, gift from Mrs P. R. Richardson, 1967
Toft, J. Alfonso 1866–1964, *Kenilworth Castle*, gift from Mrs P. R. Richardson, 1967
Toft, J. Alfonso 1866–1964, *Lancaster from the Aqueduct over River Lune*, gift from Mrs P. R. Richardson, 1967
Toft, J. Alfonso 1866–1964, *Langley Castle*, gift from Mrs P. R. Richardson, 1967
Toft, J. Alfonso 1866–1964, *Langley Castle, North Tyne*, gift from Mrs P. R. Richardson, 1967
Toft, J. Alfonso 1866–1964, *Ludlow Castle*, gift from Mrs P. R. Richardson, 1967
Toft, J. Alfonso 1866–1964, *Ludlow Castle*, gift from Mrs P. R. Richardson, 1967
Toft, J. Alfonso 1866–1964, *Ludlow Castle*, gift from Mrs P. R. Richardson, 1967

Toft, J. Alfonso 1866–1964, *Middleham Castle*, gift from Mrs P. R. Richardson, 1967
Toft, J. Alfonso 1866–1964, *Neidpath Castle*, gift from Mrs P. R. Richardson, 1967
Toft, J. Alfonso 1866–1964, *Norham Castle*, gift from Mrs P. R. Richardson, 1967
Toft, J. Alfonso 1866–1964, *Norham Castle*, gift from Mrs P. R. Richardson, 1967
Toft, J. Alfonso 1866–1964, *Powis Castle*, gift from Mrs P. R. Richardson, 1967
Toft, J. Alfonso 1866–1964, *Stokesay Castle*, gift from Mrs P. R. Richardson, 1967
Toft, J. Alfonso 1866–1964, *Stokesay Castle*, gift from Mrs P. R. Richardson, 1967
Toft, J. Alfonso 1866–1964, *Turzel Castle*, gift from Mrs P. R. Richardson, 1967
Toft, J. Alfonso 1866–1964, *Warkworth Castle*, gift from Mrs P. R. Richardson, 1967
Toft, J. Alfonso 1866–1964, *Warkworth Castle*, gift from Mrs P. R. Richardson, 1967
Toft, J. Alfonso 1866–1964, *Warkworth Castle*, gift from Mrs P. R. Richardson, 1967
Toft, J. Alfonso 1866–1964, *Warkworth Castle*, gift from Mrs P. R. Richardson, 1967
Toft, J. Alfonso 1866–1964, *Wigmore Castle*, gift from Mrs P. R. Richardson, 1967
Tolansky, Ottilie 1912–1977, *Self Portrait*, purchased from the artist, 1964
Tomlinson, Reginald R. 1885–1978, *The Old Mug*, purchased from the artist at the Society of Staffordshire Artists Exhibition, 1935
Tomlinson, Reginald R. 1885–1978, *John Adams, Potter*, purchased from the artist, 1962
Toren, Amikam b.1945, *Untitled: Armchair Painting*, purchased from the Contemporary Art Society, 2006. © the artist
Tunstall, Eric 1897–1987, *Mabel Gardening*, purchased from the artist, 1958
Tunstall, Eric 1897–1987, *The Dancer*, purchased from the artist, 1959
unknown artist *Portrait of a Woman*, gift from Miss Pearson, 1953
unknown artist *Woman Wearing White Cap, Black Dress and Holding a Book*, gift from Miss Pearson, 1953
unknown artist *William Allen of Stoke in Full Dress Uniform of the Life Guards*, gift from J. T. Morrall, 1958
unknown artist *Lady of Keele*, gift from Mrs Mary Oates, 1942
unknown artist *William Cooper, Mayor of Longton*, gift from Miss Cooper, 1960
unknown artist *Alderman George Ridgway (1822–1899)*
unknown artist *Study of a Head*
unknown artist *Council Chambers, Hanley Town Hall*
unknown artist *Alderman Francis Thomas Wood*, gift from Mr C. P. Wood, 1982
unknown artist *Aphrodite Victorious**
unknown artist *Boat and Cottage*, old stock, acquired before the accession register and Stoke-on-Trent Museum were established
unknown artist *Boy Seated beside a Goat*, gift from Mr W. Barnett, 1963
unknown artist *Elizabeth Heming (Mrs George Miles Mason)*, gift from Rosalind Billingham, 1989
unknown artist *Enoch Wood (1759–1840)*, old stock, acquired before the accession register and Stoke-on-Trent Museum were established
unknown artist *Mrs Enoch Wood (1758–1841)*, old stock, acquired before the accession register and Stoke-on-Trent Museum were established
unknown artist *Field Marshall the Right Honourable Lord Roberts, VC, GCB, CGSI*
unknown artist *Fishing Boats*, purchased by Mrs N. Bainbridge, 1961
unknown artist *Fishing Boats*, purchased by Mrs N. Bainbridge, 1961
unknown artist *Fishing Boats**
unknown artist *Fishing Boats and a Group of Women*, purchased by Mrs N. Bainbridge, 1961
unknown artist *Fishing Boats in a Bay with a Group of Fishermen*, purchased by Mrs N. Bainbridge, 1961
unknown artist *Forest Scene**
unknown artist *J. A. Kirkham, Mayor of Stoke*
unknown artist *John Davenport (1765–1848)*, old stock, acquired before the accession register and Stoke-on-Trent Museum were established
unknown artist *John Wood II (1778–1848)*, gift from Captain Michael Lumsden, 1966
unknown artist *Josiah Spode II (1755–1827) in Hunting Costume*, old stock, acquired before the accession register and Stoke-on-Trent Museum were established
unknown artist *Josiah Wedgwood's Old Mill on the Jenkins*, gift from Mrs Prendergast, 1952
unknown artist *Landscape with Castle Ruins*
unknown artist *Madonna and Child*, bequeathed by Dr M. A. Chamberlain, 1975
unknown artist *Mary Baddely, née Wedgwood (1764–1824)*, gift from Captain Michael Lumsden, 1966
unknown artist *Mary Wood, née Price, of Brownhills (1742–1825)*, gift from Captain Michael Lumsden, 1966
unknown artist *Meeting in Venice**
unknown artist *Miles Mason (1752–1822), Potter*, gift from Rosalind Billingham, 1989
unknown artist *Portrait of a Gentleman**
unknown artist *Portrait of a Gentleman**
unknown artist *Portrait of a Gentleman**
unknown artist *Portrait of a Gentleman**
unknown artist *Portrait of a Gentleman**
unknown artist *Portrait of a Gentleman**
unknown artist *Portrait of a Gentleman**
unknown artist *Portrait of a Lady**
unknown artist *Portrait of a Reverend**
unknown artist *Portrait of an Unknown Female Member of the Pratt Family*, bequeathed by Miss Kate Howson, 1991
unknown artist *Portrait of an Unknown Male Member of the Mason Family*, gift from Rosalind Billingham, 1989
unknown artist *River Scene, Man Fishing*, old stock, acquired before the accession register and Stoke-on-Trent Museum were established
unknown artist *Robert Heath (1816–1893)*
unknown artist *Ruined Classical Temple*, purchased from Tildesly's Ltd, Stoke-on-Trent, 1950
unknown artist *Seascape*, gift from Mrs R. Moxon, 1946
unknown artist *Simeon Shaw (1785–1859)*, gift from Mr C. B. Foxall, 1937
unknown artist *Sir Smith Child (1808–1896)*, acquired, 1982
unknown artist *Soldier Disturbing a Sleeping Woman*, gift from Reverend H. S. B. Corn, 1958
unknown artist *The Old Pottery Kiln, Bradwell Wood*, old stock, acquired before the accession register and Stoke-on-Trent Museum were established
unknown artist *Thomas Peake (1798–1881)*
unknown artist *Townscape**
unknown artist *William Woodall, MP (1832–1901)*, old stock, acquired before the accession register and Stoke-on-Trent Museum were established
Wade, George A. active 1950–1960, *Casino, Montreux*, gift from the artist, 1960
Wade, George A. active 1950–1960, *Burgess and Leigh*, gift from the artist, 1950
Wade, Maurice 1917–1991, *Canal Wharf*, purchased from the artist, 1961, © the artist's estate
Wade, Maurice 1917–1991, *Hen Runs at Sneyd*, purchased from the artist, 1962, © the artist's estate
Wade, Maurice 1917–1991, *Kitchen Chimneys*, purchased, 1964, © the artist's estate
Walker, Ethel 1861–1951, *The Young Sculptress*, purchased from Jackson's, 1948, © the artist's estate/www.bridgeman.co.uk
Wallinger, Mark b.1959, *Lost Horizons*, gift from the Contemporary Art Society, 1989
Wallis, Colin b.1937, *Don Quixote in Lagos with Walkman*, gift from the artist, 1989
Ward, Edwin Arthur 1859–1933, *James Meakin (b.c.1830)*, gift from Andrew Meakin, 1992
Weight, Carel Victor Morlais 1908–1997, *The Pastoral Life*, purchased from the artist, 1959, © the estate of the artist
Wheeler, Geoffrey 1929–1995, *Maritime Incident I*, gift from the Friends of the Museum and Art Gallery, 1969
Wild, Tony b.1941, *Vase with Diamond Shape*, purchased from Midland View Two Exhibition, 1983, © the artist
Wild, Tony b.1941, *Terracotta Park II*, gift from West Midlands Arts Association, 1986, © the artist
Williams, Alun b.1961, *Official Portrait of the President of El Dorado*, gift from the artist, © the artist
Williams, George Augustus 1814–1901, *Frozen Mill Pond*, gift from Miss J. M. Southam, 1964
Wilson, Clive *The Master's Castle, Etruria*, gift from Mr S. J. Looker, 1950
Wilson, John Glen 1774–1855, *On the Scheldt*, gift from Maurice A. Wade, 1964
Wise, William *Childhood*
Wood, Charles Bernard b.1902, *Leafy June, Hanchurch*, acquired, 1924
Wood, Mark b.1965, *Joyriders*, purchased from the artist, 1991, © the artist
Wooldridge, Frederick Richard 1866–1952, *Head of an Old Woman*, gift from the artist, 1950
Zampighi, Eugenio 1859–1944, *Her First Lesson*, gift from Mrs M. Titley, 1975
Zampighi, Eugenio 1859–1944, *Tantalizing*, gift from Mrs M. Titley, 1975

Wedgwood Museum

Barker, Charles *The Queen's Vase*, transferred from Mason's Ironstone Factory Museum, c.1999
Bratby, John Randall 1928–1992, *Sir Arthur Bryan (former Wedgwood Company Chairman & Wedgwood Museum Trust Chairman)*, donated by Sir Arthur Bryan, c.1985, © the artist's estate/www.bridgeman.co.uk
David, Helen *Wedgwood Me*, on long-term loan from the artist, © the artist
De Bod, E. *Etruria, Canal Front*, gift from British Steel plc, 2000
Jackson, John 1778–1831, *John Flaxman (1755–1826)*, acquired from Nicholas Bagshawe of Edury Galleries, London, purchased with the assistance of the National Art Collections Fund and the Resource/Victoria & Albert Museum Purchase Grant Fund, photo credit: Wedgwood Museum Trust
Lawrence, Thomas (copy of) 1769–1830, *Louisa Jane Allen (Mrs John Wedgwood) (1771–1836)*, purchased from Leith Hill Place, Surrey, photo credit: Wedgwood Museum Trust
Lovatt, Enos b.1937, *Abstract Potteries Landscape*, gift from the Wedgwood Company, c.1990, © the artist
Lovatt, Enos b.1937, *Geometric Shapes*, gift from the Wedgwood Company, c.1990, © the artist
Mott, Toby *'I will be good'*, on long-term loan from the artist
Owen, William 1769–1825, *Josiah Wedgwood II (1769–1843)*, gift from the Wedgwood Company, previously held at Leith Hill Place, Surrey, photo credit: Wedgwood Museum Trust
Reynolds, Joshua 1723–1792, *Sarah Wedgwood (1734–1815)*, gift from the Wedgwood Company, previously held at Leith Hill Place, Surrey, photo credit: Wedgwood Museum Trust
Reynolds, Joshua 1723–1792, *Josiah Wedgwood I (1730–1795)*, purchased from Mrs Koppel, London, 1939, photo credit: Wedgwood Museum Trust
Rigaud, John Francis (attributed to) 1742–1810, *Thomas Bentley (1731–1780)*, gift from the Wedgwood Company, previously held at Leith Hill Place, Surrey, photo credit: Wedgwood Museum Trust
Romney, George 1734–1802, *Elizabeth Allen (Mrs Josiah Wedgwood II) (1764–1846)*, gift from the Wedgwood Company, previously held at Leith Hill Place, Surrey, photo credit: Wedgwood Museum Trust
Sargent, John Singer 1856–1925, *Mrs Robert Wedgwood (d.1906)*, donated by Mrs Wedgwood's daughter, Eliza, 1960s, photo credit: Wedgwood Museum Trust
Skellern, Victor 1908–1966, *Wedgwood Factory, Barlaston*
Stubbs, George 1724–1806, *Richard Wedgwood (c.1701–1782)*, bequeathed by Dr Ralph Vaughan Williams, 1944, gift from the Wedgwood Company, previously held at Leith Hill Place, Surrey, photo credit: Wedgwood Museum Trust
Stubbs, George 1724–1806, *Wedgwood Family*, gift from Miss Phoebe Wedgwood, 1968; on loan to Tate Britain, photo credit: Wedgwood Museum Trust
unknown artist *George Meakin (b.1864)*, transferred from the Johnson Bros Factory, c.1984
unknown artist late 20th C, *Barlaston Hall*
unknown artist *Francis Wedgwood (1800–1888)*, gift from Miss B. Brownsword, London, 1962, photo

credit: Wedgwood Museum Trust
unknown artist *Portrait of a Lady*
unknown artist *Woman Sewing*
Wade, Maurice 1917–1991, *Canal at Longport III*, gift from the Wedgwood Company, c.1990, © the artist's estate
Wade, Maurice 1917–1991, *North Round House and Bridge, Etruria*, gift from the Wedgwood Company, c.1990, © the artist's estate
Wade, Maurice 1917–1991, *Powerhouse and Workshop, Wedgwood*, gift from the Wedgwood Company, c.1990, © the artist's estate
Wade, Maurice 1917–1991, *South Facade, Wedgwood, Barlaston*, gift from the Wedgwood Company, c.1990, © the artist's estate
Wakefield, John *Wedgwood Factory, Etruria*, gift from Ann Hulme, 1999
Ward, Edwin Arthur 1859–1933, *George Meakin (1832–1891)*, transferred from the Johnson Bros Factory, c.1984
Ward, Edwin Arthur 1859–1933, *James Meakin (1807–1852)*, transferred from the Johnson Bros Factory, c.1984
Wedgwood, Francis Charles Bowen 1898–1959, *Buffalo Harbour, South Africa*
Wedgwood, Francis Charles Bowen 1898–1959, *Five Sisters*
Wedgwood, Francis Charles Bowen 1898–1959, *Wedgwood, Etruria*

Tamworth Borough Council

unknown artist *Captain Sir William Peel (1824–1858)*
unknown artist *John Peel, MP for Tamworth (1804–1872)*
unknown artist *Reverend Francis Blick, MA*, gift from Llewelyn Lloyd, 1858
unknown artist *Reverend Rawlet*
unknown artist *Sir Robert Peel (1788–1850)*
unknown artist *Thomas Guy (1644–1724)*, gift from Sir Charles Mansfield Clarke, 1852
unknown artist *William Robinson, Mayor of Tamworth*, gift from Edward Robinson, 1875

Tamworth Castle

Baldwin, H. *Landscape*
Beale, Mary (attributed to) 1633–1699, *Lady Mary Gough (1657–1722)*, purchased, 1989
British (English) School early 18th C, *Mrs Willington and Daughter*, acquired via the Wakefield Bequest
British (English) School mid-18th C, *Hunting Scene (possibly Waldyue Willington, former Parliamentarian Governor of Tamworth Castle)*, acquired via the Wakefield Bequest
Brooke, Charlotte *Royalist*, gift, 1975
Dolci, Carlo 1616–1686, *Ecce Homo*, gift, 1923
Dyck, Anthony van (after) 1599–1641, *Crucifixion*
Elmore, R. *Maria Watton*, acquired via the Watton Bequest
Elsheimer, Adam (after) 1578–1610, *St Christopher, Carrying the Infant Christ across a Stream*, acquired, c.1923
Etty, William 1787–1849, *A Child Asleep*, gift, 1923
Finiger, H. A. *Cottages at the Seashore*
Fox, Charles James 1860–c.1937, *Tamworth Castle*, gift from the artist, 1906
Fox, Charles James 1860–c.1937, *Cornfield with Ricks*, gift from the artist, 1906
Fox, Charles James 1860–c.1937, *Landscape with Horse and Rider (possibly Hampstead Heath)*, gift from the artist, 1906
Fox, Charles James 1860–c.1937, *Moorland Landscape*, gift from the artist, 1906
Fox, Charles James 1860–c.1937, *View of Lichfield (detail)*, gift from the artist, 1906
Italian School 19th C, *Peasant Girl with Scythe*
Italian School *Portrait of a Man*
Lawrence, Thomas (style of) 1769–1830, *George Ferrers Townshend (d.1855), 3rd Marquis Townshend*, reaccessioned, 1991
Lawrence, Thomas (style of) 1769–1830, *Jane, Marchioness Townshend (wife of George Ferrers Townshend)*, reaccessioned, 1991
Lely, Peter (school of) 1618–1680, *Dr Samuel Shaw (b. before 1710)*, on loan from Tamworth Grammar School
Manzoni, T. *Landscape, Forest Glade*
Niemann, Edmund John 1813–1876, *The Coming Storm*
Opie, John 1761–1807, *Welsh Lady*
Palma, Jacopo il giovane 1544–1548–1628, *Pietà*, gift from John Alkin's widow, 1923
Pratt, Henry Lark I 1805–1873, *St Editha's Church and the Old Paregoric Shop, Tamworth*, purchased with the assistance of the Friends of Tamworth Castle, 2003
Preston, J. *Lake and Punt*
Preston, J. *Lake Landscape*
Sant, George active 1856–1877, *Innocence*, gift from John Alkin's widow, 1923
Stretton, Leon *Horses (unfinished)*, gift, 1938
unknown artist *Mrs Tidy*, gift from Mr Arthur Tidy, 1967
unknown artist *A Member of the Willington Family*, acquired via the Wakefield Bequest, 1992
unknown artist *Child on an Animal Fur Rug*
unknown artist *Martha Willington*, acquired via the Wakefield Bequest, after 1992
unknown artist *Mr Willington*, acquired via the Wakefield Bequest, after 1992
unknown artist *Methodist Minister*
unknown artist *Miss Willington*, acquired via the Wakefield Bequest
unknown artist *Mother and Child*
unknown artist *Portrait of a Lady*
unknown artist *Portrait of a Lady*
unknown artist *Portrait of Two Children*, purchased, 1991
Whitford, Richard c.1821–1890, *Bull, 'Champion'*, gift from Mr Arthur Tidy, 1967

Tutbury Museum Trust

O. E. B. *Granville House, Tutbury*, donated, before 2002
Bullock *Tutbury Castle*, donated, before 2002
Hulme, Geoffrey *Glass Blowing, Harry Hassent and No.8 Pot*, donated, 1993

Uttoxeter Heritage Centre

Hulme, Geoffrey *The White Hart Hotel, Carter Street, Uttoxeter*, donated, c.1986
Redfern, Francis (attributed to) *Market Place, Uttoxeter*, acquired by the Town Council before the opening of the Museum
Wilson, Paul F. d.2000, *'Clink Wharf', Southwark, London*, bequeathed by the artist, 2000
Wilson, Paul F. d.2000, *River View*, bequeathed by the artist, 2000
Wilson, Paul F. d.2000, *Steam Ships*, bequeathed by the artist, 2000

The New Art Gallery Walsall

Adams, Philip b.1943, *Canal at Pratts Bridge, Leamore, Walsall*, gift from the artist, 2002, © the New Art Gallery Walsall
Allen, Robert b.1951, *Out to Dry*, purchased from the artist, 1993, © the artist
Amshewitz, John Henry 1882–1942, *Jerome K. Jerome (1859–1927) (copy after Philip Alexius de László)*, on loan to the Jerome K. Jerome Museum, Walsall
Anderson, Sophie 1823–1912, *Pet Canary*, gift from H. J. Thrustan, 1930
Anderson, Sophie 1823–1912, *Scheherazade*, gift from H. J. Thrustan, 1932
Banks, J. O. active 1856–1873, *At the Fountain*, gift from H. J. Thrustan, 1930
Barber, Charles Burton 1845–1894, *The New Keeper*, purchased from the Frederick Lonsdale estate, 1954
Barker, Thomas (attributed to) 1769–1847, *The Smugglers' Rendezvous*, gift from Alderman C. C. Walker, 1929
Batchelor-Flint, Emma 1857–1968, *Bottle Kilns*, acquired, 1976
Batchelor-Flint, Emma 1857–1968, *Early Autumn*
Batchelor-Flint, Emma 1857–1968, *Red Witch Bowl*, acquired, 1976
Batchelor-Flint, Emma 1857–1968, *The Scarecrow*, on loan to Walsall Metropolitan Borough Council
Bates, George active 1873–1893, *Trees (Woodland Scene)*, gift from Alderman C. C. Walker, 1929
Bloomer, Paul b.1966, *Soliloquy*, purchased from the artist, 1994, © the artist
Bonar, Law *Still Life, Jar of Flowers and Fruit*, gift from Mrs D. M. Wynne, 1980
Bonnard, Pierre 1867–1947, *La Seine à Vernon*, gift from Kathleen Epstein, 1973, © ADAGP, Paris and DACS, London 2007
Bowley, Edward Orlando active 1840–1874, *Landscape with Deer*, gift from Alderman C. C. Walker, 1929
Breakspeare, William Arthur 1855–1914, *Resting*, gift from W. H. Moore, c.1899
Bridgeman, Ann b.1934, *Black Country*, purchased from the Society of Staffordshire Artists, 1976, © the artist
Bro, René 1930–1987, *Landscape near Courgeron, Normandy*, gift from Kathleen Epstein, 1973
Brockhurst, A. *The 'Duke of York'*, gift from Mrs A. Brockhurst
Bromley, William c.1818–1888, *Preparing for Christmas*, gift from Councillor Williams, 1897
Buffet *Small Girl Reading Book*, gift from Kathleen Epstein, 1973
Burns, E. *Willenhall War Memorial*
Burr, John 1831–1893, *An Oft-Told Tale*, purchased from the Frederick Lonsdale estate, 1954
Burt, Charles Thomas 1823–1902, *Farmyard Scene*, transferred from the Town Hall, acquired, c.1985
Cardew, Margaret 1899–1961, *Normandy Village*, gift from Kathleen Epstein, 1973
Carter, Robert Radcliffe b.1867, *Water Meadows, Sussex*, gift from G. J. Wiggin, 1976
Cartmel, R. W. active 1951–1955, *High Street, Aldridge*, transferred from the Architects Department, Walsall, acquired, 1984, on loan to Aldridge Library
Cartmel, R. W. active 1951–1955, *The Old Elms Hotel*, acquired from Aldridge Council House, 1976, on loan to Aldridge Library
Cartmel, R. W. active 1951–1955, *Aldridge Parish Church*, acquired from Aldridge Council House, 1976, on loan to Aldridge Library
Cartmel, R. W. active 1951–1955, *High Street, Aldridge*, acquired from Aldridge Council House, 1976, on loan to Aldridge Library
Cole, George 1810–1883, *Horses with Timber Wagon*, gift from H. J. Thrustan, 1932
Collier, John 1850–1934, *Egg Dance*, gift from J. E. Guest, 1976
Colson, T. *The Jolly Farmer*, gift from Alderman C. C. Walker, 1929; on loan to the Jerome K. Jerome Museum, Walsall
Constable, John 1776–1837, *Landscape with Clouds*, gift from Kathleen Epstein, 1973
Corneille de Lyon, Claude (follower of) 1510–c.1574, *Portrait of a Man*, gift from Kathleen Epstein, 1973
Cornet, May b.1975, *After the Marathon*, purchased, 2005, © the artist
Corot, Jean-Baptiste-Camille (attributed to) 1796–1875, *Woman Reading*, gift from Kathleen Epstein, 1973
Correggio (after) c.1489–1534, *Allegory of Virtue*, gift from Professor Archibald Stanton Whitfield
Cox, David the younger (attributed to) 1808–1885, *Rural Scene*, gift from Alderman C. C. Walker, 1929
Creswick, Thomas 1811–1869, *Monument to Joan of Arc at Rouen*, gift from Councillor Mrs W. Hughes, 1897
Crome, John (after) 1768–1821, *Moonlight Scene*, gift from Alderman C. C. Walker, 1929
Cundall, Charles Ernest 1890–1971, *The Acropolis*, purchased from the Royal West of England Academy, 1967, © courtesy of the artist's estate/www.bridgeman.co.uk
Cunha, Helio da *The Return of Ulysses*
Davies, R. J. *Henry Clark's House, near Digbeth, Walsall*, gift from the artist, 1976
De Pisis, Filippo 1896–1956, *Street Scene in Italy*, gift from Kathleen Epstein, 1973
De Pisis, Filippo 1896–1956, *Still Life with Bottles*, gift from Kathleen Epstein, 1973
Degas, Edgar 1834–1917, *Marguerite, soeur de l'artiste*, gift from Kathleen Epstein, 1973
Delaunay, Robert 1885–1941, *Igor Stravinsky (1882–1971)*, gift from Kathleen Epstein, 1973
Diaz de la Peña, Narcisse Virgile 1808–1876, *The Wood Gatherer*, gift from Kathleen Epstein, 1973
Drury, Edward Alfred Briscoe 1859–1944, *Auld Robin Gray*, gift from Alderman C. C. Walker, 1929
Dumbleton, Dennis b.1937, *Walsall from the Birchills*, purchased from the artist, 1991
Dyer, E. *Richard Moore Fletcher*
Eastwood, G. *Darlaston War Memorial*
Elliott, Edith M. active 1889–1924, *St Ives, Early Morning*, gift from Miss Mary Jean Elliot, 1967; on loan to Walsall Registry Office
Elliott, Edith M. active 1889–1924, *Still Life, Flowers in Bowl*, gift from Lady Holden, 1913
Elliott, Edward M. active 1898–1924, *The Glory of the Dying Day*, gift from Lady Holden
Ellis, Walter Erasmus active 1877–1899, *White Hart Inn, Caldmore*,

gift from John J. P. Scott, 1913
Ellis, William active 1858–1895, *A Lane at Hamstead, Staffordshire*, gift from Kathleen Epstein, 1973
Elmore, Richard (attributed to) 1815–1881, *Portrait of a Boy*, gift from Kathleen Epstein, 1973
Emery, Louis 1918–1993, *Seascape*, donated by the estate of the artist, 1994
Etty, William 1787–1849, *Standing Female Nude*, gift from Kathleen Epstein, 1973
Everdon, J. R. *Two Young Artists*, purchased, 1962
Faed, Thomas 1826–1900, *God's Acre*, purchased from the Frederick Lonsdale estate, 1954; on loan to Walsall Metropolitan Borough Council, Mayor's Parlour
Fairfax, T. *Hawkfall, Cumberland*
Faithful, Leila 1896–1994, *Fishing on the Soane*, purchased, 1951
Fedden, Mary b.1915, *Flowers in Tuscany*, purchased from Miss A. Stone, before 1976, © the artist
Freud, Lucian b.1922, *Kitty*, gift from Kathleen Epstein, 1973, © Lucian Freud
Freud, Lucian b.1922, *Annabel*, gift from Kathleen Epstein, 1973, © Lucian Freud
Freud, Lucian b.1922, *Kingcups, Souvenir of Glen Artney*, gift from Kathleen Epstein, 1973, © Lucian Freud
Frith, William Powell 1819–1909, *Portrait of a Lady with a Fan*, gift from Alderman C. C. Walker, 1929
Fromentin, Eugène 1820–1876, *Head of Old Woman*, gift from Kathleen Epstein, 1973
Fullwood, John 1854–1931, *Charcoal Burners*, gift from E. J. Shaw, 1902
Gaete-Gwynne, Maria b.1947, *Untitled*, purchased from the artist, © the artist
Gardiner, Clive 1891–1960, *The Hamlet, Scilly Isles*, gift from Kathleen Epstein, 1973
Garman, Theodore 1924–1954, *Arum Lilies*, gift from Michael Fraser, 1988, © the artist's estate
Garman, Theodore 1924–1954, *Summer Garden, Harting*, gift from Kathleen Epstein, 1973, © the artist's estate
Garman, Theodore 1924–1954, *The Blue Girl*, gift from Kathleen Epstein, 1973, © the artist's estate
Garman, Theodore 1924–1954, *Madonna with Flowers*, purchased from the estate of Beth Lipkin with the assistance of the Victoria & Albert Museum Purchase Grant Fund, © the artist's estate
Garman, Theodore 1924–1954, *The Wooden Monk*, purchased from the estate of Beth Lipkin with the assistance of the Victoria & Albert Museum Purchase Grant Fund, © the artist's estate
Garman, Theodore 1924–1954, *Arum Lilies (Easter Flowers)*, gift from Kathleen Epstein, 1973, © the artist's estate
Garman, Theodore 1924–1954, *Villa Solaia*, gift from Kathleen Epstein, 1973, © the artist's estate
Garman, Theodore 1924–1954, *Vegetation*, purchased from the estate of Beth Lipkin with the assistance of the Victoria & Albert Museum Purchase Grant Fund, © the artist's estate
Garman, Theodore 1924–1954, *Autumn Still Life*, gift from Kathleen Epstein, 1973, © the artist's estate
Garman, Theodore 1924–1954, *Jesus Figure with Flowers*, purchased from the estate of Beth Lipkin with the assistance of the Victoria & Albert Museum Purchase Grant Fund, © the artist's estate
Garman, Theodore 1924–1954, *Judith*, purchased from the estate of Beth Lipkin with the assistance of the Victoria & Albert Museum Purchase Grant Fund, © the artist's estate
Garman, Theodore 1924–1954, *Monte Gu*, purchased from the estate of Beth Lipkin with the assistance of the Victoria & Albert Museum Purchase Grant Fund, © the artist's estate
Garman, Theodore 1924–1954, *Window Picture in June*, gift from Kathleen Epstein, 1973, © the artist's estate
Garman, Theodore 1924–1954, *Argyll House*, purchased from the estate of Beth Lipkin with the assistance of the Victoria & Albert Museum Purchase Grant Fund, 2007, © the artist's estate
Garman, Theodore 1924–1954, *Window Picture in November*, purchased from the estate of Beth Lipkin with the assistance of the Victoria & Albert Museum Purchase Grant Fund, © the artist's estate
Garman, Theodore 1924–1954, *Good Friday*, gift from Kathleen Epstein, 1973, © the artist's estate
Garman, Theodore 1924–1954, *Kathleen with Music*, purchased from the estate of Beth Lipkin with the assistance of the Victoria & Albert Museum Purchase Grant Fund, © the artist's estate
Garman, Theodore 1924–1954, *Easter Flowers*, purchased from the estate of Beth Lipkin with the assistance of the Victoria & Albert Museum Purchase Grant Fund, 2007, © the artist's estate
Garman, Theodore 1924–1954, *The Old Forge, Chelsea*, purchased from the estate of Beth Lipkin with the assistance of the Victoria & Albert Museum Purchase Grant Fund, © the artist's estate
Garman, Theodore 1924–1954, *The Old Forge, Chelsea (11)*, purchased from the estate of Beth Lipkin with the assistance of the Victoria & Albert Museum Purchase Grant Fund, © the artist's estate
Garman, Theodore 1924–1954, *Arum Lilies*, purchased from the estate of Beth Lipkin with the assistance of the Victoria & Albert Museum Purchase Grant Fund, © the artist's estate
Garman, Theodore 1924–1954, *Unfinished Canvas (1)*, purchased from the estate of Beth Lipkin with the assistance of the Victoria & Albert Museum Purchase Grant Fund, © the artist's estate
Garman, Theodore 1924–1954, *Winter Sunset on the Thames*, purchased from the estate of Beth Lipkin with the assistance of the Victoria & Albert Museum Purchase Grant Fund, © the artist's estate
Géricault, Théodore 1791–1824, *Etude d'un homme nu*, gift from Kathleen Epstein, 1973
Gifford, Andrew b.1970, *Walsall, Looking towards St Matthew's Church*, puchased from the artist, 2006
Girodet de Roucy-Trioson, Anne-Louis 1767–1824, *François-René de Chateaubriand (1768–1848)*, gift from Kathleen Epstein, 1973
Glindoni, Henry Gillard 1852–1913, *The Bride of Lammermoor*, gift from Alderman E. T. Holden
Gunning, David Edward b.1954, *'On Site', Early Morning Construction*, gift from McAlpines, 2003, © the artist
Gunning, David Edward b.1954, *View of Walsall*, purchased from the artist, 1998, © the artist
Hatt, Doris 1890–1969, *Birthday*
Haynes, A. *Portrait of a Man*
Haynes, B. active 1865–1890, *Man with a Sunflower (after Anthony van Dyck)*
Haynes, B. active 1865–1890, *Gypsy Love*, gift from H. H. Tucker, JP, 1936
Henderson, W. S. P. active 1836–1874, *Fair Day*, gift from H. J. Thrustan, 1930; on loan to Walsall Registry Office
Henderson, W. S. P. active 1836–1874, *Welsh Interior*, gift from H. J. Thrustan, 1930
Hett, Charles b.1941, *Landscape in Norfolk*, gift from Kathleen Epstein, 1973, © the artist
Hoberman, Nicky b.1967, *The Frog Princess*, purchased by the Contemporary Art Society through the Special Collections Scheme with the assistance of the Arts Council, 1999, © courtesy of the artist and Kinz, Tillou & Feigen, NY
Hodges, Derek Ian 1921–2003, *Laon Cathedral*, donated by Katherine Hodges, 2006, © the artist's estate
Holl, Frank 1845–1888, *Ordered to the Front*, purchased from the Frederick Lonsdale estate, 1954; on loan to Walsall Metropolitan Borough Council, Mayor's Parlour
Ireland, Geoffrey b.1923, *Untitled*, gift from the artist, 1998
Israëls, Jozef (after) 1824–1911, *The Widower, the Fisherman's Return*, gift from Alderman C. C. Walker, 1929
Italian (Lombard) School 17th C, *San Carlo Boromeo in Adoration before a Crucifix*, gift from Kathleen Epstein, 1973
Italian School *The Madonna and Child*, gift from Kathleen Epstein, 1973
Jacobi, M. M. active 1882–1883, *St Matthew's Church, Walsall*, gift from the Misses Sammons, 1962
Johns, Myfanwy b.1958, *Scission*, purchased from the artist, 1997, © the artist
Jones, Charles 1836–1902, *Cattle at a Stream*, gift from Alderman C. C. Walker, 1929
Jones, Charles 1836–1902, *Sheep*, gift from M. J. Billingsley, 1956
Jones, Charles 1836–1902, *Sheep*, gift from H. J. Thrustan, 1930
Jones, Charles 1836–1902, *Hard Chase*, gift from Thomas Gameson
Jones, Charles 1836–1902, *The Lord of the Downs*, gift from George Skidmore, 1931
Keith, Alexander active 1808–1874, *Dolly Eyland*, gift from Dorothy Sollis, 2002
Keith, Alexander active 1808–1874, *Moses Eyland*, gift from Dorothy Sollis, 2002
Kiat, Soh Siew *A Golden Ornament II*, purchased from the artist, 1993
King, Haynes 1831–1904, *An Old Friend Failing*, purchased from the Frederick Lonsdale estate, 1954
Kitchin, Myfanwy b.1917, *At the Bus Stop*, purchased, 1976
Koekkoek, Barend Cornelis 1803–1862, *Woodland Scene*, gift from Alderman C. C. Walker, 1929
Landseer, Edwin Henry (attributed to) 1802–1873, *Study of Wayside Plants*, gift from Kathleen Epstein, 1973
Langley, Walter 1852–1922, *Evening at Coverack, Cornwall*, purchased from Walter R. Langley, 1898
Le Jeune, Henry 1819–1904, *Children at a Stream*
Leaver, Charles 1824–1888, *In the New Forest*
Leaver, Charles 1824–1888, *Grendon Village, Northamptonshire*
Leeuw, Alexis de active 1848–1887, *The Wreckers*, gift from Mrs E. A. Holmes, 1961
Lépine, Stanislas 1835–1892, *Le canal*, gift from Kathleen Epstein, 1973
Lowe, G. E. active 1885, *Tre'r Ceiri, Town of Fortresses*, gift from Alderman E. T. Holden
Maclise, Daniel 1806–1870, *Phoebe and Silvius in the Forest of Arden, from Shakespeare's 'As You Like It'*, purchased from the Frederick Lonsdale estate, 1954
Mankes, Jan 1889–1920, *White Orchid*, gift from Kathleen Epstein, 1973
Marshall, James *The Crypt, Bishop's Palace, St David's*, on loan
Maybank, Hannah b.1974, *Hosts (II)*, purchased from the artist, 2006, © the artist
McEvoy, Ambrose 1878–1927, *The Letter*, gift from Kathleen Epstein, 1973
McEvoy, Ambrose 1878–1927, *Dieppe Street Scene*, gift from Kathleen Epstein, 1973
McLean, Ian 1973–2000, *Sans amour*, gift from the Saatchi Collection distributed by the National Art Collections Fund, 2001
Meadows, Arthur Joseph 1843–1907, *Ships in Choppy Sea*, transferred from Walsall Town Hall, 1982
Miller *Barr Beacon*
Monet, Claude 1840–1926, *Le chemin creux dans la falaise à Varangeville*, gift from Kathleen Epstein, 1973
Morland, George 1763–1804, *Rural Scene*, purchased; on loan to the Jerome K. Jerome Museum, Walsall
Morland, George 1763–1804, *The Sleepers (Gypsy Scene)*, gift from Alderman C. C. Walker, 1929
Morris, Cedric Lockwood 1889–1982, *Irises and Tulips*, purchased from the artist, 1953, © trustees of the Cedric Lockwood Morris Estate/Foundation
Morris, Cedric Lockwood 1889–1982, *Monchique Foothills, Algarve*, purchased from the artist, 1953, © trustees of the Cedric Lockwood Morris Estate/Foundation
Morris, Cedric Lockwood 1889–1982, *The Scilly Packet Boat*, purchased, 1953, © trustees of the Cedric Lockwood Morris Estate/ Foundation
Morris, John Charles active 1851–1889, *Sheep*
Mudge, Alfred active 1859–1885, *Walking the Walsall Fair*, on loan from Wolverhampton Art Gallery
Müller, William James 1812–1845, *The Approaching Storm*
Munns, Henry Turner 1832–1898, *Chat by the Way*, gift from W. M. Bayliss
Murillo, Bartolomé Esteban (attributed to) 1618–1682, *The Presentation in the Temple*, gift from Alderman Llewellyn, 1937
Murray, V. R. *T. W. North Giving an Organ Recital, Walsall Town Hall*
Müsham, Fritz 1881–1949, *Esther*, gift from Kathleen Epstein, 1973
Müsham, Fritz 1881–1949, *Theo*, gift from Kathleen Epstein, 1973
Nicol, Erskine 1825–1904, *Kiss an' Make-It-Up*, gift from Mrs T. A. Hill
Nicol, Erskine 1825–1904, *The Missing Boat*, purchased from the Frederick Lonsdale estate, 1954
Orgill, Mollie *Portrait of the Artist's Father*, gift from R. L. Simpson, 1995
Orgill, Mollie *St Matthew's Church, Walsall*, gift from St Matthew's Church, Walsall, 1993
Palmer, Eugene b.1955, *Sister Smith III*, purchased from the artist, 1998
Palmer, Eugene b.1955, *Wanting to*

Say I, purchased from the artist, 1998
Phillip, John 1817–1867, *Diana and Actaeon (after Titian)*, gift from Alderman C. C. Walker, 1915
Preston, William F. active 1885–1889, *Ship of the Line Going up the Solent*, gift from Mr G. C. Preston, 1969
Procter, Dod 1892–1972, *The Quiet Hour*, purchased, 1953, © the artist's estate/www.bridgeman.co.uk
Procter, Dod 1892–1972, *Spring Flowers*, purchased, © the artist's estate/www.bridgeman.co.uk
Renoir, Pierre-Auguste 1841–1919, *Les oliviers à Cagnes-sur-Mer*, gift from Kathleen Epstein, 1973
Reynolds, Joshua 1723–1792, *Lieutenant Robert Haswell, RN (son of John Haswell of Tiverton, Devon)*, gift from Kathleen Epstein, 1973
Riviere, Briton 1840–1920, *Cupboard Love*, purchased from the Frederick Lonsdale estate, 1954; on loan to Walsall Metropolitan Borough Council, Mayor's Parlour
Ryan, Sally 1916–1968, *The Cutting Garden, Connecticut*, gift from Kathleen Epstein, 1973
Ryan, Sally 1916–1968, *Poplars at Dulwich*, gift from Kathleen Epstein, 1973
Ryan, Sally 1916–1968, *Potted Plant*, gift from Kathleen Epstein, 1973
Ryan, Sally 1916–1968, *Easter Flowers*, purchased from the estate of Beth Lipkin with the assistance of the Victoria & Albert Museum Purchase Grant Fund
Ryan, Sally 1916–1968, *Flower Painting (Nasturtiums)*, gift from Kathleen Epstein, 1973
Ryan, Sally 1916–1968, *Hyacinths*, purchased from the estate of Beth Lipkin with the assistance of the Victoria & Albert Museum Purchase Grant Fund
Ryan, Sally 1916–1968, *Kathleen*, gift from Kathleen Epstein, 1973
Saintin, Jules Émile 1829–1894, *Woman in Black*
Salimbeni, Lorenzo (attributed to) 1374–c.1420, *An Angel of the Annunciation*, gift from Kathleen Epstein, 1973
Sawbridge, Tony *Walking the Fair, Re-Enactment*
Shayer, Charles Waller 1826–1914, *The Horse Fair*, gift from William Christie, 1899
Shayer, Charles Waller 1826–1914, *Landscape with Figures and Donkeys*, gift from Samuel Drew, 1922
Shayer, Charles Waller (after) 1826–1914, *Brown Cows Standing*, gift from H. J. Thrustan, 1932; on loan to the Jerome K. Jerome Museum, Walsall
Shayer, William 1788–1879 & **Marshall, Charles** 1806–1890 *Ben Nevis and Mountain Stream*, gift from Alderman C. C. Walker, 1929
Shayer, William (after) 1788–1879, *Cows, White Cow Standing*, gift from H. J. Thrustan
Smith, H. H. *Canal, Middleport*, purchased, 1962
Smith, Matthew Arnold Bracy 1879–1959, *Flower Piece*, gift from Kathleen Epstein, 1973, © by permission of the copyright holder
Sorgh, Hendrik Martensz. (follower of) c.1611–1670, *Studies of Heads of Peasants*, gift from Kathleen Epstein, 1973
Sorgh, Hendrik Martensz. (follower of) c.1611–1670, *Studies of Heads of Peasants*, gift from Kathleen Epstein, 1973
Stuart, Charles active 1854–1904, *Study of Fruit*
Subleyras, Pierre Hubert (follower of) 1699–1749, *Hector Dragged through Troy*, gift from Kathleen Epstein, 1973
Tenkate, Herman 1822–1891, *Van Dyck in the Studio of Van der Helst*, gift from Alderman C. C. Walker, 1929
Tiepolo, Giovanni Battista (attributed to) 1696–1770, *Page Boy*, gift from Kathleen Epstein, 1973
Thomas, Thomas active 1854–1896, *Handsworth Church*, purchased, 1915
Thompson, Estelle b.1960, *Fuse Painting, 7 'til 8*, purchased with the CAS Special Collections Scheme from the Purdy Hicks Gallery, 2000, © the artist
Tift, Andrew b.1968, *The Black-Country Steelworkers*, on loan from the artist, © the artist
Tift, Andrew b.1968, *Les and Ernie*, purchased from the artist, 1993, on loan to the Town Hall of Walsall Metropolitan Borough Council, © the artist
Tift, Andrew b.1968, *'There are no longer any birds in last years' nests. Times change and we with them'*, purchased from the artist, 1994, on loan to Walsall Metropolitan Borough Council, © the artist
Tift, Andrew b.1968, *Memorial Painting (left wing of diptych)*, purchased from the artist, 1998, © the artist
Tift, Andrew b.1968, *Memorial Painting (right wing of diptych)*, purchased from the artist, 1998, © the artist
Titian (attributed to) c.1488–1576, *Angel (Putto)*, gift from Kathleen Epstein, 1973
Townsend, June *The Arboretum, Walsall*, purchased from Walsall Society of Artists, 1997
Townshend, James d.1949, *Interior*, gift from Miss Mary Jean Elliot, 1967
Uddin, Shafique b.1962, *Two Friends Enjoying the Brilliant Sunshine and Magnificent Buildings*, purchased from the Ikon Gallery, Birmingham, 1990
unknown artist 17th C, *Man with Stigmata Holding a Skull*, gift from Ernest Beebee
unknown artist *Tintern Abbey*, transferred from Walsall Town Hall, 1985
unknown artist 19th C, *Four Dogs*
unknown artist 19th C, *Two Dogs*
unknown artist *The Home of Miss E. M. Flint, now Demolished*
unknown artist *Alderman William Ward, JP*, gift from S. A. Grundy Newman, 1913
unknown artist *Bottom of St Matthew's Church Steps, Walsall*, gift from Mrs Thornhill, 1939
unknown artist *Bradford Street and Railway*
unknown artist *Cattle at a Lake**, on loan
unknown artist *Digbeth*, gift from Mrs Thornhill, 1939
unknown artist *Eliza Wheway*, gift from Ada Wheway, 1891
unknown artist *Houses, Men and Dog*
unknown artist *Hyacinths*, gift from Miss Mary Jean Elliot, 1967
unknown artist *Job Wheway*, gift from Ada Wheway, 1891
unknown artist *Landscape*
unknown artist *Landscape with Cattle and Cowherd*, on loan to the Jerome K. Jerome Museum, Walsall
unknown artist *Mountain Scene*, on loan to Walsall Registry Office
unknown artist *Old Man with a Stick (The Mendicant)*, gift from Alderman C. C. Walker, 1929
unknown artist *Portrait of a Man in Glengarry*
unknown artist *Racecourse, Bradford Street, Walsall*, gift from Mrs Thornhill, 1949
unknown artist *Seascape with Fishing Boats in a Stormy Sea*, transferred from Walsall Town Hall, 2004
unknown artist *Sergeant Major William Purvis, Survivor of the Charge of the Light Brigade*
unknown artist *Stepping Stones*
unknown artist *Still Life (Fruit and Vegetables)*
unknown artist *Still Life (Vegetables)*
unknown artist *The Ascension of the Virgin into Heaven*, gift from T. W. Nind, 1976
unknown artist *The George Hotel*, gift from Mrs Stevenson
unknown artist *The Rat Catcher of Paris*, gift from Miss Brace
unknown artist *Town End Bank*, gift from Mrs Thornhill, 1939
Venables, M. *St Matthew's Church Steps, Walsall*, gift from Mr Meers, 1974
Venables, M. *The Market in the High Street, Walsall*
Verboeckhoven, Eugène 1799–1881, *Gathering the Flock*, purchased from the Frederick Lonsdale estate, 1954; on loan to Walsall Metropolitan Borough Council, Mayor's Parlour
Verboeckhoven, Eugène 1799–1881, *Goats*, gift from Alderman C. C. Walker, 1929
Vickers, Alfred 1786–1868, *A Man Driving Cattle and Sheep*
Waite, James Clarke 1832–1920, *Penny Whistle*, gift from H. J. Thrustan, 1930
Ward, Edward Matthew 1816–1879, *Charles II Assisted in His Escape by Jane Lane*, purchased with the assistance of the Victoria & Albert Museum Purchase Grant Fund, 1989
Ward, James 1769–1859, *Cow in Barn*, gift from Kathleen Epstein, 1973
Webb, James c.1825–1895, *The Castle of Ischia*, gift from George Skidmore, 1956
Webb, James (attributed to) c.1825–1895, *Landscape*, gift from Alderman C. C. Walker, 1929
Weigall, Arthur Howes c.1836–1894, *Before Marriage*, gift from Mrs A. E. Hirst
Weigall, Arthur Howes c.1836–1894, *After Marriage*, gift from M. Hirst
Williams, A. *Fishing Boats*, gift from Alderman C. C. Walker, 1929
Williams, George Augustus 1814–1901, *Near Dolgelly, North Wales*, gift from Alderman C. C. Walker, 1929
Willott, George *Sutton St James*, purchased
Wishart, Michael 1928–1996, *Moths on a Blue Path*, gift from the National Art Collections Fund, © the artist's estate
Wishart, Michael 1928–1996, *Arab Courtyard, Fez*, gift from Kathleen Epstein, 1973, © the artist's estate
Wray, Jenny b.1967, *Indian Goddess*, purchased from the artist, 1993
Wright, Herbert W. active 1945–1981, *Hatherton, Walsall*, gift from the artist, 1976
Wright, Herbert W. active 1945–1981, *Walsall, as seen from Peal Street*
Wright, Herbert W. active 1945–1981, *Back of Old Priory, Walsall*, gift from the artist, 1976
Wright, Herbert W. active 1945–1981, *Birmingham Street, Walsall*, gift from the artist, 1976
Wright, Herbert W. active 1945–1981, *Midland Memories*, gift from the artist, 1981
Wright, Herbert W. active 1945–1981, *Tapping*, gift from the artist
Wright, Herbert W. active 1945–1981, *Wisemore, Walsall*

New Cross Hospital

Calkin, Lance 1859–1936, *T. Vincent Jackson (c.1836–1901), Surgeon, Mayor of Wolverhampton (1886–1887)*
Chakraborty, Paresh C. b.1934, *Festive Dance, 'Shankara'*, gift from the artist, c.1996, © the artist
Chakraborty, Paresh C. b.1934, *Monsoon Music (Rainy Season) 'Gauda Mallar'*, gift from the artist, c.1996, © the artist
Grant, Keith b.1930, *Triptych (left)*, © the artist
Grant, Keith b.1930, *Triptych (centre)*, © the artist
Grant, Keith b.1930, *Triptych (right)*, © the artist
Halliday, Edward Irvine 1902–1984, *Frederick Edge (1863–1937)*, acquired, 1931, © the artist's estate
Halliday, Edward Irvine 1902–1984, *W. F. Cholmeley, FRCS (1866–1949)*, acquired, 1931, © the artist's estate
Halliday, Edward Irvine 1902–1984, *Surgeon Edward Dranesly (1866–1948)*, © the artist's estate
Hillwood, Thomas *William Millington (1821–1911)*
Morton, J. *New Cross*, acquired, 1924
Munns, Henry Turner 1832–1898, *Thomas Pinchard*, acquired, 1877
Munns, Henry Turner 1832–1898, *Richard Briscoe*
Phoenix, George 1863–1935, *James Y. Totherick (d.1899)*
Phoenix, George 1863–1935, *Henry Malet (1851–1924), MA, MD*
Phoenix, George 1863–1935, *A. H. Carter (1873–1961)*
Phoenix, George 1863–1935, *C. A. Stidson*
Phoenix, George 1863–1935, *Charles Alexander MacMunn (1852–1911)*
Phoenix, George 1863–1935, *John Alfred Codd (c.1869–1920), MD*
Phoenix, George 1863–1935, *Sister Annie MacLaren (d.1912)*
Phoenix, George 1863–1935, *Thomas H. Glbraith (c.1862–1929)*
Phoenix, George 1863–1935, *W. H. T. Winter (c.1855–1931)*
Turner, Harry b.1908, *S. C. Dyke Seated in Laboratory (1886–1975)*, acquired, 1953
unknown artist *Edward Pugh*
unknown artist *George Edwardes (d.1859), LSA, FRCS*
unknown artist *Henry Rogers*
unknown artist *Henry Rogers*, gift from Lichfield Diocesan Council, 2005
unknown artist *Portrait of a Gentleman*
White, H. *H. H. C. Dent (1874–1972)*
Wilson, Charles Heath 1809–1882, *Edward Hayling Coleman*
Wilson, Charles Heath 1809–1882, *Lawley T. Smith*
Wilson, Charles Heath 1809–1882, *Matron Mary Millar*
Wilson, Charles Heath 1809–1882, *Tom Adams*
Wilson, Charles Heath 1809–1882, *William Henry Harper*

Wolverhampton Art Gallery

Addison, Alfred Henry *Still Life*, gift from the Contemporary Art Society, 1963
Alken, Henry Thomas (attributed to) 1785–1851, *Cockfighting (two cocks face each other)*, purchased, 1940
Alken, Henry Thomas (attributed to) 1785–1851, *Cockfighting (two*

cocks attack each other), purchased, 1940

Alken, Henry Thomas (attributed to) 1785–1851, *Cockfighting (both cocks bleeding from the mouth)*, purchased, 1940

Alken, Henry Thomas (attributed to) 1785–1851, *Cockfighting (one cock kills the other)*, purchased, 1940

Allen, William Herbert 1863–1943, *Château, Dieppe*, gift, 1921, © the artist's estate

Allen, William Herbert 1863–1943, *Mr Jordan*, gift from Mrs M. C. Cartwright, 1887, © the artist's estate

Allen, William Herbert 1863–1943, *Portrait of a Woman (study)*, gift, 1921, © the artist's estate

Allen, William Herbert 1863–1943, *Self Portrait*, gift, 1921, © the artist's estate

Allen, William Herbert 1863–1943, *Street Market*, gift, 1921, © the artist's estate

Allen, William Herbert 1863–1943, *Street Market, Walsall*, gift, 1921, © the artist's estate

Allen, William Herbert 1863–1943, *Sussex Farmyard*, gift, 1921, © the artist's estate

Allinson, Adrian Paul 1890–1959, *Jug of Flowers*, gift, 1963

Anderson, Sophie 1823–1912, *The Song*, purchased, 1886

Ansdell, Richard 1815–1885, *The Sick Lamb*, gift from Mr Philip Horsman, 1886

Anslow, Sonia *Princess Diana Look-a-Like*, purchased, 1998

Anthony, Henry Mark 1817–1886, *A Larch Forest*, gift from Mr Philip Horsman, 1886

Anthony, Henry Mark 1817–1886, *Autumn Evening*, gift from Mr Philip Horsman, 1886

Anthony, Henry Mark 1817–1886, *Chepstow Castle, Monmouthshire*, gift from Mr Philip Horsman, 1886

Anthony, Henry Mark 1817–1886, *Nature's Mirror*, gift from Mr William Thompson, 1937

Anthony, Henry Mark 1817–1886, *Stonehenge*, gift, 1884

Anthony, Henry Mark 1817–1886, *Sunset*, bequeathed by Mr Paul Lutz, 1899

Anthony, Henry Mark 1817–1886, *The Old Church*, gift from Mr Philip Horsman, 1886

Anthony, Henry Mark 1817–1886, *The Old Mill Wheel*, gift from Mr Philip Horsman, 1886

Anthony, Henry Mark 1817–1886, *The Silver Spring*, gift from Mr Philip Horsman, 1886

Anthony, Henry Mark 1817–1886, *The Village Wedding*, gift, 1884

Armfield, Edward 1817–1896, *Retrievers with Game*, acquired, 1974

Armfield, George 1808–1893, *Dog and Fox*, gift, 1956

Armfield, George 1808–1893, *Waiting*, gift from Mr Philip Horsman, 1886

Armstrong, John 1893–1973, *Organ Pipes*, purchased with the assistance of the Victoria & Albert Museum Purchase Grant Fund, 1984, © the artist's estate

Arnett, Patricia *Walking away*, purchased, 1998

Atkinson, Conrad b.1940, *Silver Liberties; A Souvenir of a Wonderful Anniversary Year (1 of 4)*, purchased, 2005, © the artist

Atkinson, Conrad b.1940, *Silver Liberties; A Souvenir of a Wonderful Anniversary Year (2 of 4)*, purchased, 2005, © the artist

Atkinson, Conrad b.1940, *Silver Liberties; A Souvenir of a Wonderful Anniversary Year (3 of 4)*, purchased, 2005, © the artist

Atkinson, Conrad b.1940, *Silver Liberties; A Souvenir of a Wonderful Anniversary Year (4 of 4)*, purchased, 2005, © the artist

Atkinson, Conrad b.1940, *Wall Street Journal*, purchased with the assistance of the Museums & Galleries Commission/Victoria & Albert Museum Purchase Grant Fund, 1988, © the artist

Atkinson, Helen D. active 1882–1884, *Wolverhampton Racecourse*, acquired, 1974

Ayres, Gillian b.1930, *Abstract**, gift from Anthony Twentyman, 1991, © the artist

Baker, Thomas 1809–1869, *Landscape and Cattle near Offchurch, Warwickshire*, gift from Mrs M. C. Cartwright, 1887

Baker, Thomas 1809–1869, *River Scene*, gift, 1989

Banner, Delmar Harmond 1896–1983, *September White Grass*, gift, 1949

Banting, John 1902–1972, *Card Players*, purchased with the assistance of the Museums & Galleries Commission/Victoria & Albert Museum Purchase Grant Fund, 1986

Barker, Thomas 1769–1847, *Italian Landscape*, gift, 1884

Barker, Thomas 1769–1847, *Landscape with a Waterfall*, gift, 1884

Barker, Thomas 1769–1847, *Landscape with Cattle*, gift, 1884

Barnes, Samuel John 1847–1901, *In the Valley of the Rhône*, gift, 1884

Barns-Graham, Wilhelmina 1912–2004, *Glacier (Red and Blue)*, gift from Anthony Twentyman, 1991, © by courtesy of the Barns-Graham Charitable Trust

Barns-Graham, Wilhelmina 1912–2004, *Glacier, Rock Forms*, gift from Anthony Twentyman, 1991, © by courtesy of the Barns-Graham Charitable Trust

Barret, George (circle of) 1728/1732–1784, *Landscape with Two Figures*

Barron, Bob b.1945, *Suburban Summer Evenings*, gift, 1986, © the artist

Bassett, William active 1850–1890, *Richard Eldridge of the Bilston Township Committee*

Bates, David c.1840–1921, *The Banks of the Brathay, Ambleside, Westmoreland*, acquired, 1970

Bates, David c.1840–1921, *Brook at Old Storridge, Worcestershire*, gift from Mr William Thompson, 1937

Bates, David c.1840–1921, *Mending the Fence, Sutton Park*, gift from Mr William Thompson, 1937

Bates, David c.1840–1921, *Stacking the Oak Fence*, gift from Mr William Thompson, 1937

Bates, David c.1840–1921, *Stepping Stones on the Llugwy*, gift from Mr William Thompson, 1937

Bates, David c.1840–1921, *Tidal Fence on the River Conway, Bachlediog*, gift from Mr William Thompson, 1937

Baudin, Narcisse active 1850s–1880s, *The Portrait*, gift from Mrs M. C. Cartwright, 1887

Baxter, Charles 1809–1878, *'Love me, love my dog'*, gift from Mrs M. C. Cartwright, 1887

Bayliss, Edwin Butler 1874–1950, *Black Country Landscape*

Bayliss, Edwin Butler 1874–1950, *Black Country, Night, with Foundry*

Bayliss, Edwin Butler 1874–1950, *Black Country Scene*

Bayliss, Edwin Butler 1874–1950, *Black Country Skyline*

Bayliss, Edwin Butler 1874–1950, *Blast Furnaces, Night*

Bayliss, Edwin Butler 1874–1950, *Blast Furnaces, Night*

Bayliss, Edwin Butler 1874–1950, *Capenfield Furnaces*

Bayliss, Edwin Butler 1874–1950, *Evening in the Black Country*

Bayliss, Edwin Butler 1874–1950, *Furnace and Snow, Landscape*

Bayliss, Edwin Butler 1874–1950, *Gin Pit*

Bayliss, Edwin Butler 1874–1950, *In the Black Country*, purchased, 1936

Bayliss, Edwin Butler 1874–1950, *In the Black Country*

Bayliss, Edwin Butler 1874–1950, *Mother and Child, Black Country Landscape*

Bayliss, Edwin Butler 1874–1950, *On the Beach*, gift

Bayliss, Edwin Butler 1874–1950, *On the Shore*

Bayliss, Edwin Butler 1874–1950, *Pig Beds Tapping a Furnace*

Bayliss, Edwin Butler 1874–1950, *Spring Vale Furnaces*

Bayliss, Edwin Butler 1874–1950, *The Sea*

Bayliss, Edwin Butler 1874–1950, *Tipping the Slag*

Beddows, Michael 1931–2005, *The Golden Age of Brooklands' Monsters*, gift

Bellany, John b.1942, *Self Portrait with Alan Davie*, purchased with the assistance of the Museums & Galleries Commission/Victoria & Albert Museum Purchase Grant Fund, 1986, © the artist/www.bridgeman.co.uk

Bellingham-Smith, Elinor 1906–1988, *Low Tide, Putney*, gift from the Contemporary Art Society. 1950, © the artist's estate

Berchem, Nicolaes (attributed to) 1620–1683, *Landscape with Figures and Cattle*, gift from Mrs M. C. Cartwright, 1887

Berrie, John Archibald Alexander 1887–1962, *Sir Henry Seagrave (1896–1930)*, gift, 1932

Bevan, Tony b.1951, *The Meeting*, purchased with the assistance of the Museums & Galleries Commission/Victoria & Albert Museum Purchase Grant Fund, 1995, © the artist

Bigge, John Selby 1892–1978, *Wood Forms*, purchased with the assistance of the Museums & Galleries Commission/Victoria & Albert Museum Purchase Grant Fund, 1985, © the artist's estate

Bird, Edward 1772–1819, *Intemperance*, purchased, 2003

Bird, Edward 1772–1819, *Teatotalism*, purchased, 2003

Bird, Edward 1772–1819, *Temperance*, purchased, 2003

Bird, Edward 1772–1819, *The Old Soldier's Story*, purchased, 2006

Bird, Edward 1772–1819, *Study for 'The Day after the Battle of Chevy Chase'*, bequeathed by Mr Paul Lutz, 1899

Bird, Edward 1772–1819, *A Child with an Elaborate Headdress*, gift, 1939

Bird, Edward 1772–1819, *At the Well*, purchased, 1910

Bird, Edward 1772–1819, *Italian Dancing-Dog Master*, purchased with the assistance of the Victoria & Albert Museum Purchase Grant Fund, 1981

Bird, Edward 1772–1819, *Ready for Market*, gift from Mrs M. C. Cartwright, 1887

Bird, Edward 1772–1819, *Setting off for Market*, purchased, 2006

Bird, Edward 1772–1819, *Study for 'The Country Auction'*, purchased, 1972

Bird, Edward 1772–1819, *The Arrival of King Louis XVIII of France at Calais*, purchased, 1935

Bird, Edward 1772–1819, *The Birth*, gift, 1884

Bird, Edward 1772–1819, *The Christening*, gift, 1884

Bird, Edward 1772–1819, *The Duet*, gift, 1907

Bird, Edward 1772–1819, *The Oyster Girl*, purchased, 1912

Bird, Edward 1772–1819, *The Poacher's Return*, purchased from Mr Paul Lutz, 1908

Bird, Edward 1772–1819, *The Sick Child*, gift from Mrs M. C. Cartwright, 1887

Bird, Edward 1772–1819, *The Way to Get Married*, gift from the Friends of the Art Gallery, 1976

Bissill, George William 1896–1973, *Shelbourne, Essex*, gift from the Contemporary Art Society, 1952

Blaas, Eugen von 1843–1931, *At the Carnival*, gift, 1884

Bladen, Alfred active c.1925–1965, *White Phlox on White Cloth*, purchased, 1948

Blake, Peter b.1932, *Cigarette Pack*, purchased with the assistance of the Victoria & Albert Museum Purchase Grant Fund, 1980, © Peter Blake 2007

Blamey, Norman Charles 1914–1999, *Camp Barber*, gift from Mr Gerald P. Mander, 1949, © estate of Norman Blamey /Licensed by DACS 2007

Bland, Emily Beatrice 1864–1951, *Flower Piece*, gift from Mr Gerald P. Mander, 1934

Blond, Maurice 1899–1974, *A Tree*, gift, 1954

Blond, Maurice 1899–1974, *Woman in a Hat*, purchased, 1955

Bolland, Emma b.1962, *A Declaration*, purchased, 1988, © the artist

Bolton, Sylbert b.1959, *Untitled*, purchased, 1988, © the artist

Bolton, Sylbert b.1959, *Dark Dream*, purchased, 1981, © the artist

Bond, William Joseph Julius Caesar 1833–1926, *Fishing Boats in an Estuary*, gift, 1914

Bone, Stephen 1904–1958, *Naval Rescue Launches in Loch Road, Isle of Lewis*, gift, 1949

Bonington, Richard Parkes 1802–1828, *French Coast Scene*, gift from Mrs M. C. Cartwright, 1887

Bonington, Richard Parkes (attributed to) 1802–1828, *Fort Rouge*, gift from Mrs M. C. Cartwright, 1887

Bonington, Richard Parkes (attributed to) 1802–1828, *Rouen*, purchased, 1954

Booth, Samuel Lawson 1836–1928, *Haddon Hall, Derbyshire*, gift from William Thompson, 1937

Booth, Samuel Lawson 1836–1928, *Plas Mawr, Conway, in the Olden Days*, gift from Mr William Thompson, 1937

Boughton, George Henry 1833–1905, *A Winter Morning's Walk*, gift from Mrs M. C. Cartwright, 1887

Boughton, George Henry 1833–1905, *Returning from Mass, Brittany*, gift from Mrs M. C. Cartwright, 1887

Boyd, Fionnuala b.1944 & **Evans, Leslie** b.1945 *Incident*, purchased, 1973, © the artists

Brady, Carlene *Untitled*, gift from the Contemporary Art Society, 1972

Braekeleer, Ferdinand de I 1792–1883, *A Belgian School*, bequeathed by Mr Paul Lutz, 1899

Brangwyn, Frank 1867–1956, *Still Life*, gift from the artist, 1950, © the artist's estate/www.bridgeman.co.uk

Brangwyn, Frank 1867–1956, *Ancona*, gift from the artist, 1950, © the artist's estate/www.bridgeman.co.uk

Brangwyn, Frank 1867–1956, *Joy on the Beach*, gift from the artist, 1950, © the artist's estate/www.bridgeman.co.uk

Brangwyn, Frank 1867–1956, *St Benet's Abbey, Norfolk*, gift from the

artist, 1956, © the artist's estate/www.bridgeman.co.uk
Brangwyn, Frank 1867–1956, *The Brass Pot*, purchased, 1933, © the artist's estate/www.bridgeman.co.uk
Breanski, Alfred de 1852–1928, *Cader from Llyn Cader*, gift from a private collection, 1885
Bridell, Frederick Lee 1831–1863, *The Vineyards at Meran, Tyrol*
Bridson, Thomas Arthur 1860–1966, *Councillor Emma Lloyd Sproson (d.1936), the First Woman Elected to the Wolverhampton Borough Council, 1 November 1921*, on display at Wolverhampton Civic Centre
Bristow, Edmund 1787–1876, *A Prize Bull*, gift, 1910
British (English) School 17th C, *'My rock is Christ' (a Lady of the Bagot family)*, gift from Mr Gerald P. Mander, 1950**British (English) School** early 18th C, *Three Putti with Symbols of Architecture*, acquired, 1970
British (English) School 18th C, *John Wilkinson*, acquired, 1970
British (English) School 18th C, *Woman and Child*, bequeathed by Mr Paul Lutz, 1899
British (English) School 19th C, *Henry William Paget (1768–1854), 1st Marquess of Anglesey*, gift from Wolverhampton Town Hall, 1900
British (English) School 19th C, *Landscape with Reflecting Lake*, acquired, 1974
British (English) School 19th C, *Lost in Thought*, gift from Mr Philip Horsman, 1886
British (English) School 19th C, *Old Woman Pouring Tea*, acquired, 1970
British (English) School 19th C, *Waterfall*
British (English) School *Landscape with Sheep*, purchased, 1989
British School *Two Figures in a Winter Landscape*, acquired, 1970
British School *Sidney Cartwright (1802–1883)*, gift from Mrs M. C. Cartwright, 1887
British School *The Race for Wolverhampton Stakes, 1839*, acquired, 1970
British School *Sidney Cartwright (1802–1883)*, gift from Mrs M. C. Cartwright, 1887
British School 19th C, *A Great Catch*, gift from Mrs M. C. Cartwright, 1887
British School 19th C, *Coast Scene*, acquired, 1970
British School 19th C, *Fishing Smack off the Coast*, acquired, 1970
British School 19th C, *Landscape*, gift from Mrs M. C. Cartwright, 1887
British School 19th C, *Landscape with Fisherman (Wood Gatherers)*, acquired, 1970
British School 19th C, *Portrait of a Gentleman Holding a Copy of 'The Messiah'*, gift, 1970
British School 19th C, *Refuge*, gift from Mr Philip Horsman, 1886
British School 19th C, *Seated Lady (The Traveller)*, gift from Mrs M. C. Cartwright, 1887
British School late 19th C, *Thomas Bantock (1823–1895)*, gift, 1998
British School *Landscape of a Farmyard with Cows*
British School *Landscape with Sheep*, acquired, 1970
British School *Portrait of a Gentleman*
Brookes, Jason *Trojan*, on loan from Chris Booton
Browning, Amy Katherine 1881–1978, *At the Window*, purchased, 1934, © Joanna Dunham
Burr, John 1831–1893, *Little Fisher Folk*, gift from Mr Philip Horsman, 1886
Burt, Charles Thomas 1823–1902, *Going to the Ferry, Appledore, Devon; A Squally Day*, gift from Mrs M. C. Cartwright, 1887
Burt, Charles Thomas 1823–1902, *Near Barmouth*, purchased, 1886
Burt, Charles Thomas 1823–1902, *Team of Horses*, gift from Mr William Thompson, 1937
Calvert, R. K. *Wolverhampton Market*
Campbell-Gray, Ian active 1933, *The Fencer*, gift from the Contemporary Art Society, 1963
Caulfield, Patrick b.1936, *Tandoori Restaurant*, purchased with the assistance of the Victoria & Albert Museum Purchase Grant Fund, 1972, © Patrick Caulfied 2007. All rights reserved, DACS
Chambers, George 1803–1840, *Rotterdam*, gift, 1886
Chettle, Agnes Beatrice b.c.1900, *Still Life, Flowers*, gift from Mr William Thompson, 1937
Clamp, Adrian b.1960, *Self Portrait*, purchased, 1990, © the artist
Clare, Oliver c.1853–1927, *Still Life, Fruit*, gift from Mr William Thompson, 1937
Clare, Oliver c.1853–1927, *Still Life, Fruit*, gift from Mr William Thompson, 1937
Clark, James 1858–1943, *The Fortune Teller*, gift from Mr William Thompson, 1937, © the artist's estate/www.bridgeman.co.uk
Clarke, Jacqueline *Josh*, purchased, 1992
Cleminson, Robert active c.1864–c.1903, *Game Dog*, gift, 1994
Cleminson, Robert active c.1864–c.1903, *Pony*, gift, 1994
Cole, George Vicat 1833–1893, *The Harvesters*, gift, 1886
Cole, George Vicat 1833–1893, *Konigswasser on the Rhine*, gift from Mr Philip Horsman, 1886
Cole, George Vicat 1833–1893, *Near Borrowdale, Cumberland*, gift from Mr Philip Horsman, 1886
Cole, George Vicat 1833–1893, *On the River Lledr, North Wales*, gift from Mr William Thompson, 1937
Colkett, Samuel David 1806–1863, *The Trowse near Norwich*, gift from Mrs M. C. Cartwright, 1887
Collier, John 1850–1934, *Sentence of Death*, gift, 1934
Collins, William 1788–1847, *At the Cottage Gate*, gift from Mrs M. C. Cartwright, 1887
Collins, William 1788–1847, *Children Gathering Seaweed*, gift from Mrs M. C. Cartwright, 1887
Collins, William 1788–1847, *Landscape with Three Figures*, bequeathed by Mr Paul Lutz, 1899
Collins, William 1788–1847, *The Carrier's Resting Place*, gift from Mrs M. C. Cartwright, 1887
Collins, William 1788–1847, *The Village Gossip*, gift from Mr Philip Horsman, 1886
Cooke, Edward William 1811–1880, *On the Bacino di San Marco, Venice*, gift from Mrs M. C. Cartwright, 1887
Cooke, Edward William 1811–1880, *Sunset at Le Havre*, bequeathed by Mr Paul Lutz, 1899
Cooke, John Percy active 1892–1939, *Home Alone*
Cooke, John Percy active 1892–1939, *The Blockmaker's Shop*, gift, 1942
Cooke, John Percy active 1892–1939, *The Quarry, Brixham, Devon*, gift, 1942
Cooper, Alfred Egerton 1883–1974, *Ascot, the Paddock*, purchased, 1945
Cooper, Alfred Egerton 1883–1974, *Dorset Landscape*, gift, 1937
Cooper, Alfred Egerton 1883–1974, *Herbert Beech*, gift from a private collection
Cooper, Alfred Egerton 1883–1974, *Joseph Arlidge*, gift from a private collection
Cooper, Alfred Egerton 1883–1974, *Lady in Red Velvet*, gift, 1937
Cooper, Alfred Egerton 1883–1974, *Martin Hughes*, gift from a private collection
Cooper, Alfred Egerton 1883–1974, *T. R. Wood*, gift from a private collection
Cooper, Eileen b.1953, *Tiger, Tiger*, gift from the Contemporary Art Society, 1992, © Eileen Cooper 2007. All rights reserved, DACS
Cooper, Fred active 1906, *Moorish Sentry*, gift, 1951
Cooper, Thomas Sidney 1803–1902, *In the Canterbury Meadows*, gift from Mrs M. C. Cartwright, 1887
Cooper, Thomas Sidney 1803–1902, *Cattle and Sheep in a Snowscape*, gift from Mrs M. C. Cartwright, 1887
Cooper, Thomas Sidney 1803–1902, *Four Sheep*, gift from Mr Philip Horsman, 1886
Cooper, Thomas Sidney 1803–1902, *Landscape with Cattle and Fowl*, gift from Mrs M. C. Cartwright, 1887
Cooper, Thomas Sidney 1803–1902, *Cattle Scene*, gift from Mr Philip Horsman, 1886
Cooper, Thomas Sidney 1803–1902, *Canterbury Meadows*
Corrodi, Hermann 1844–1905, *View of Boulac, Cairo*, gift, 1909
Cot, Pierre Auguste 1837–1883, *Charity for My Sister*, gift from Mr William Thompson, 1937
Cox, David the elder 1783–1859, *Cottage on Dulwich Common, a Windy Day*, gift from Mrs M. C. Cartwright, 1887
Cox, David the elder 1783–1859, *Counting the Flock*, purchased, 1954
Cox, David the elder 1783–1859, *On the Lledr, North Wales*, gift from Mrs M. C. Cartwright, 1887
Cox, David the elder 1783–1859, *Conway Castle, Caernarvonshire*, bequeathed by Mr Paul Lutz, 1899
Cox, David the elder (circle of) 1783–1859, *The Hayfield*, gift from Mrs M. C. Cartwright, 1887
Cox, David the elder (circle of) 1783–1859, *The Skirts of the Wood*, gift from Mr William Thompson, 1937
Craft, Percy Robert 1856–1934, *Old Church Street, Chelsea*, gift, 1935
Craig *Wolverhampton*
Creswick, Thomas 1811–1869, *Landscape*, gift, 1936
Creswick, Thomas 1811–1869, *Landscape with Figures*, gift from Mrs M. C. Cartwright, 1887
Creswick, Thomas 1811–1869, *Loch Eck*, gift from Mrs M. C. Cartwright, 1887
Creswick, Thomas 1811–1869, *On the Tees*, bequeathed by Mr Paul Lutz, 1899
Creswick, Thomas 1811–1869, *The Thames and the Shot Tower*, gift from Mrs M. C. Cartwright, 1887
Crome, John 1768–1821, *A Stream, Bridge, Trees and Two Figures in a Landscape*, gift, 1937
Crome, John 1768–1821, *Landscape with Traveller*, bequeathed by Mr Paul Lutz, 1899
Crome, John 1768–1821, *Lane near Norwich*, gift from Mrs M. C. Cartwright, 1887
Crome, John 1768–1821, *Solitude*, originally part of the Gaskell Collection, purchased, 1954
Crome, John (circle of) 1768–1821, *Landscape with Cottage*, gift from Mrs M. C. Cartwright, 1887
Cubley, Henry Hadfield 1848–1934, *On the Derwent, Derbyshire*, purchased, 1886
Danby, Francis 1793–1861, *Moonlit View of an Eastern City*, gift from Mr Philip Horsman, 1886
Danby, Francis 1793–1861, *The Shipwreck*, gift, 1935
Daniels, William 1813–1880, *Portrait of a Man in Plumed Hat*, gift, 1914
Dargelas, André-Henri 1828–1906, *The Happy Family*, gift from Mr Philip Horsman, 1886
Darvall, Henry active 1848–1889, *The Lady of Shalott*, acquired, 1970
Davis, Edward Thompson 1833–1867, *Sunday Afternoon*, gift from Mrs M. C. Cartwright, 1887
Davis, Edward Thompson 1833–1867, *Preparing for Dinner*, gift from Mrs M. C. Cartwright, 1887
Davis, William 1812–1873, *Still Life*, gift, 1914
Dawson, Henry 1811–1878, *Coast Scene, Evening*, gift from Mrs M. C. Cartwright, 1887
Dawson, Henry 1811–1878, *Nottingham from the Trent*, gift from Mrs M. C. Cartwright, 1887
Dawson, Henry 1811–1878, *On the Trent near Ratcliffe*, gift from Mrs M. C. Cartwright, 1887
Dawson, Henry 1811–1878, *A Study of Rouen*, gift from Mrs M. C. Cartwright, 1887
Dawson, Henry 1811–1878, *Coast Scene with Pier*, gift from Mrs M. C. Cartwright, 1887
Dawson, Henry 1811–1878, *On the Trent*, gift from Mrs M. C. Cartwright, 1887
Dawson, Henry 1811–1878, *The Rainbow*, gift from Mr William Thompson, 1937
Deacy, Brendon b.1964, *Stolen Woman*, purchased, © the artist
Deville, Joseph Vickers 1856–1925, *View of Shropshire*, gift, 1923
Deville, Joseph Vickers 1856–1925, *The Silent Pool*, gift, 1886
Deville, Joseph Vickers 1856–1925, *Porthwen Bay, Angelsea*, gift, 1928
Deville, Joseph Vickers 1856–1925, *Coast Scene*, gift, 1928
Deville, Joseph Vickers 1856–1925, *Coast Scene*, gift, 1928
Deville, Joseph Vickers 1856–1925, *Study for 'Trout Stream'*, gift from the Friends of Wolverhampton Art Gallery, 1974
Devis, Arthur William 1762–1822, *Miss Eliza O'Neill as Belvidera in Thomas Otway's 'Venice Preserved'*, purchased, 1970
Dickinson, Timothy *Stadium, Night*, gift from the Contemporary Art Society, 1983
Dixon, Rex b.1939, *16–18 April 1985*, purchased
Dixon, Rex b.1939, *16–18 April 1985 (Northern Ireland)*, purchased
Dixon, Rex b.1939, *Parade 29–4–85 to 1–5–85*, gift
Dou, Gerrit 1613–1675, *Grace before Meat*, gift from Mrs M. C. Cartwright, 1887; on loan to the Geffrye Museum, London
Downing, Delapoer active 1885–1902, *Mother Has Fallen Asleep*, gift from Mr William Thompson, 1937
Downman, John 1750–1824, *Portrait of a Lady*, purchased with the assistance of the Victoria & Albert Museum Purchase Grant Fund and the Friends of Wolverhampton Art Gallery, 1979
Downman, John 1750–1824, *An Episode from the Story of Jason and Medea*, purchased with the assistance of the Victoria & Albert Museum Purchase Grant Fund, 1972
Dudley, William Harold 1890–1949, *Beer, Devon*, gift, 1954
Dudley, William Harold 1890–1949, *Couches's Cottage, Polperro*,

gift, 1954
Dudley, William Harold 1890–1949, *In the Cotswolds*, gift, 1954
Dudley, William Harold 1890–1949, *Lantivet Bay*, gift, 1954
Dudley, William Harold 1890–1949, *Old Polperro*, gift, 1937
Dudley, William Harold 1890–1949, *Polperro*, gift, 1954
Dudley, William Harold 1890–1949, *Polperro in Summertime*, gift, 1954
Dudley, William Harold 1890–1949, *Silver, Blue and Green*, gift, 1954
Dudley, William Harold 1890–1949, *Summer Cottage*, gift, 1954
Dudley, William Harold 1890–1949, *The New Rick*, gift, 1954
Dudley, William Harold 1890–1949, *The Pear, the Sloe and Spring*, gift, 1954
Dudley, William Harold 1890–1949, *The 'Three Pilchards', Polperro*, gift, 1954
Dudley, William Harold 1890–1949, *The Willows, Evesham*, gift, 1954
Dupont, Gainsborough 1754–1797, *The Travellers*, gift from Mrs M. C. Cartwright, 1887
Durkin, Robert b.1966, *Insufficient Units*, gift, 1994
Dutch School 17th C, *Skating on a Frozen River*, gift from a private collection, 1944
East, Alfred 1849–1913, *Landscape with Trees, Autumn*, gift, 1915
Ellis, Edwin 1841–1895, *The Rainy Landing, Flamborough Head, Yorkshire*, gift from Mr Philip Horsman, 1886
Ellis, Joseph active 1878, *Mountain Stream with Sheep*, acquired, 1970
Elst, Willem van der *Wayside Halt*, acquired, 1970
Emmerson, Robert Jackson 1878–1944, *Life Study*, gift, 1984
Emmerson, Robert Jackson 1878–1944, *Mary Gibson (1888–1966)*, gift, 1976
Emmerson, Robert Jackson 1878–1944, *Sasso di Bordighera*, gift, 1984
Engelbach, Florence 1872–1951, *Peonies*, purchased, 1936
Etty, William 1787–1849, *Reclining Nude*, gift from Mrs M. C. Cartwright, 1887
Etty, William 1787–1849, *Venus and Cupid*, gift, 1937
Facchi *Monument*, acquired, 1970
Faed, John 1820–1902, *Catherine Seyton and Roland Graeme, from Sir Walter Scott's 'The Abbot'*, gift from Mrs M. C. Cartwright, 1887
Faed, John 1820–1902, *The Warning before Flodden*, gift from Mr Philip Horsman, 1886
Faed, John 1820–1902, *The Statute Fair*, gift from Mr Philip Horsman, 1886
Faed, Thomas 1826–1900, *Study of a Woman's Head*, gift from Mrs M. C. Cartwright, 1887
Faed, Thomas 1826–1900, *Sunday in the Backwoods*, gift from Mrs M. C. Cartwright, 1887
Faed, Thomas 1826–1900, *The Silken Gown*, gift from Mrs M. C. Cartwright, 1887
Fagan, Betty Maud Christian d.1932, *Dressing the Christmas Tree*, gift, 1954
Farquharson, Joseph 1846–1935, *Evening*, gift from Mr William Thompson, 1937
Farrier, Robert 1796–1879, *The Courier*, bequeathed by Mr Paul Lutz, 1899
Fereday, Joseph 1917–2001, *Catchem's Corner, Bilston*, purchased, 1952
Fichel, Eugène 1826–1895, *The Connoisseurs*, gift from Mrs M. C. Cartwright, 1887
Finnie, John 1829–1907, *Gathering Wild Flowers*, gift, 1923
Fisk, William Henry 1827–1884, *The Cheap-Jack*, gift from Mr Philip Horsman, 1886
Fitzpatrick, Arthur active 1862–1870, *Musical Union*, gift from Mr William Thompson, 1937
Fleetwood-Walker, Bernard 1893–1965, *Still Life with Pyrethrums: Study for 'Amity'*, purchased, 2005, © the estate of Mrs P. Fleetwood-Walker
Fleetwood-Walker, Bernard 1893–1965, *Trug with Dog Daisies: Study for 'Amity'*, purchased, 2005, © the estate of Mrs P. Fleetwood-Walker
Fleetwood-Walker, Bernard 1893–1965, *Mr and Mrs R. H. Butler and Their Daughters*, purchased, 1999, © the estate of Mrs P. Fleetwood-Walker
Fleetwood-Walker, Bernard 1893–1965, *Smiling Girl*, purchased, 1966, © the estate of Mrs P. Fleetwood-Walker
Fleetwood-Walker, Bernard 1893–1965, *Christine*, purchased, 1966, © the estate of Mrs P. Fleetwood-Walker
Fleetwood-Walker, Bernard 1893–1965, *House and Gate*, gift, 2005, © the estate of Mrs P. Fleetwood-Walker
Fleiss, C. *Henley Bridge*, gift, 1957
Forbes, Elizabeth Adela Stanhope 1859–1912, *The Edge of the Woods*, gift, 1917
Freezor, George Augustus active 1861–1879, *Expectation*, gift from Mrs M. C. Cartwright, 1887
Frère, Pierre Edouard 1819–1886, *The Prayer*, gift from Mrs M. C. Cartwright, 1887
Frère, Pierre Edouard 1819–1886, *Winter Scene*, gift from Mrs M. C. Cartwright, 1887
Frère, Pierre Edouard (circle of) 1819–1886, *Cottage Interior*, gift from Mr Philip Horsman, 1886
Frith, Clifford b.1924, *Julie*, gift, © the artist
Frith, William Powell 1819–1909, *Dolly Varden from Charles Dickens's 'Barnaby Rudge' (sketch)*, gift from Mrs M. C. Cartwright, 1887
Frith, William Powell 1819–1909, *The Rejected Poet*, gift from Mrs M. C. Cartwright, 1887
Fullwood, John 1854–1931, *Bessie's Fold, North Street, Wolverhampton*, gift, 1920
Fullwood, John 1854–1931, *Forest Scene*, gift, 1941
Fullwood, John 1854–1931, *Tettenhall Church*, purchased, 1990
Fuseli, Henry 1747–1825, *The Apothesis of Penelope Boothby*, gift, 1927
Gabain, Ethel 1883–1950, *Reading*, gift from Mr Gerald P. Mander, 1946
Gainsborough, Thomas 1727–1788, *Sir Edward Turner, 2nd Bt of Ambrosden, Oxford (1719–1766)*, purchased with the assistance of the Victoria & Albert Museum Purchase Grant Fund, 1971
Gainsborough, Thomas (follower of) 1727–1788, *Winter Scene with Horse and Cart*, gift, 1908
Gallon, Robert 1845–1925, *Evening*, gift from Mr William Thompson, 1937
Gallon, Robert 1845–1925, *Landscape with a Gypsy Caravan*, gift, 1989
Gallowhill, James *The Avon near Stratford*, gift from Mr Philip Horsman, 1886
Gibson, Mary Gwenillan active 1927–1940, *Angel*, purchased, 1990
Gill, William active 1826–1869, *The Toy Boat*, gift, 1884
Goodall, Frederick 1822–1904, *Entering a Church, Britanny*, bequeathed by Mr Paul Lutz, 1899
Goodall, Frederick 1822–1904, *Leaving a Church, Brittany*, bequeathed by Mr Paul Lutz, 1899
Goodall, Frederick 1822–1904, *A Britanny Wedding*, gift from Mr Philip Horsman, 1886
Goodall, Frederick 1822–1904, *Study for 'The Swing'*, gift from Mrs M. C. Cartwright, 1887
Goodwin, Albert 1845–1932, *The City of Glittering Light*, purchased from Christie's, 1928
Goodwin, Albert 1845–1932, *The Sermon in the Hayfield, Simplon*, gift, 1928
Gool, Jan van 1685–1763, *Cattle in a Meadow*, gift from Mrs M. C. Cartwright, 1887
Gool, Jan van 1685–1763, *Milking in Winter*, gift from Mrs M. C. Cartwright, 1887
Gosse, Laura Sylvia 1881–1968, *Breton Woman*, gift from the Contemporary Art Society, 1952, © the artist's estate/www.bridgeman.co.uk
Gowing, Lawrence 1918–1991, *On the Phone*, gift, © the artist's estate
Grafton, Dennis b.1922, *Composition*, gift, 1994
Grafton, Dennis b.1922, *Reflections*, gift, 1994
Grant, Duncan 1885–1978, *Penns in the Rocks*, purchased with the assistance of the Museums & Galleries Commission/Victoria & Albert Museum Purchase Grant Fund, 1985, © 1978 estate of Duncan Grant
Hal, A. *Still Life, Flowers*, gift from Mr William Thompson, 1937
Hardimé, Pieter 1677/1678–1758, *Vase of Flowers*, gift, 1955
Hardy, Frederick Daniel 1827–1911, *Preparing for Dinner*, gift from Mrs M. C. Cartwright, 1887
Hardy, Frederick Daniel 1827–1911, *Washday*, purchased with the assistance of the Museums & Galleries Commission/Victoria & Albert Museum Purchase Grant Fund, 1992
Hardy, Frederick Daniel 1827–1911, *The Chimney Sweep*, gift from Mrs M. C. Cartwright, 1887
Hardy, Frederick Daniel 1827–1911, *Baby's Birthday*, gift from Mrs M. C. Cartwright, 1887
Hardy, Frederick Daniel 1827–1911, *Christmas Visitors*, gift from Mrs M. C. Cartwright, 1887
Hardy, Frederick Daniel 1827–1911, *Study of an Interior*, gift from Mrs M. C. Cartwright, 1887
Hardy, Frederick Daniel 1827–1911, *The Missing Deed*, gift from Mrs M. C. Cartwright, 1887
Hardy, Frederick Daniel 1827–1911, *Sorrowful News*, gift from Mrs M. C. Cartwright, 1887
Hardy, Frederick Daniel 1827–1911, *Study for 'Pleasant Pages'*, gift from Mrs M. C. Cartwright, 1887
Hardy, Frederick Daniel 1827–1911, *Pleasant Pages*, gift from Mrs M. C. Cartwright, 1887
Hardy, Frederick Daniel 1827–1911, *Near Windermere Lake*, gift from Mrs M. C. Cartwright, 1887
Hardy, Frederick Daniel 1827–1911, *The Prelude*, gift from Mrs M. C. Cartwright, 1887
Hardy, Frederick Daniel 1827–1911, *A Prayer for Those at Sea*, gift from Mrs M. C. Cartwright, 1887
Hardy, Frederick Daniel 1827–1911, *A Fog*, gift from Mrs M. C. Cartwright, 1887
Hardy, Frederick Daniel 1827–1911, *The Clergyman's Visit*, gift from Mrs M. C. Cartwright, 1887
Hardy, Frederick Daniel 1827–1911, *The Dismayed Artist*, gift from Mrs M. C. Cartwright, 1887
Hardy, Frederick Daniel 1827–1911, *The Misdeal*, gift from Mrs M. C. Cartwright, 1887
Hardy, Frederick Daniel 1827–1911, *The Necklace*, gift, 1989
Hardy, Frederick Daniel 1827–1911, *The Young Housekeeper*, gift from Mr Philip Horsman, 1886
Hardy, George 1822–1909, *Early Teaching*, gift from Mrs M. C. Cartwright, 1887
Harmar, Fairlie 1876–1945, *Flowers*, gift, 1943
Harmar, Fairlie 1876–1945, *Ships on the Thames*, purchased, 1939
Harris, Frederick Henry Howard 1826–1901, *The Babes in the Wood*, acquired, 1910
Hartland, Henry Albert 1840–1893, *Near Barmouth*, gift, 1886
Harvey, Harold C. 1874–1941, *The Little Maiden*, gift, 1935, © the artist's estate/www.bridgeman.co.uk
Harvey, John Rathbone 1862–1933, *Changing Pastures*
Hattemore, Archibald active 1926–1930, *Anenomes*, gift from the Contemporary Art Society, 1956
Haughton, Benjamin 1865–1924, *Woodland Waters*, gift, 1937
Hawkins, Grace Mary active 1910–1929, *Interior of Queen Street Congregational Church*
Hayes, Edwin 1819–1904, *A Breezy Day*, gift from Mr Philip Horsman, 1886
Hayes, Frederick William 1848–1918, *The Lighthouse, Llanddwyn*, gift, 1921
Hempton, Paul b.1946, *Across a Ravine*, purchased, 1988
Hemsley, William 1819–1906, *The Fisherman's Family*, gift, 1885
Henshaw, Frederick Henry 1807–1891, *The Ladder Bridge, Weeping Cross, Staffordshire*, gift from Mr William Thompson, 1937
Hepher, David b.1935, *Newly Redecorated Doors of Nos.21 and 22*, purchased with the assistance of the Victoria & Albert Museum Purchase Grant Fund, 1974, © the artist
Herbert, John Rogers 1810–1890, *Francesca*, gift from Mr Philip Horsman, 1886
Herring, John Frederick I 1795–1865, *Cottage Door and Farmstead*, gift from Mr Philip Horsman, 1886
Herring, John Frederick I 1795–1865, *The Timber Wagon*, gift from Mr Philip Horsman, 1886
Hickin, George Arthur 1821–1885, *Landscape and Cattle*, gift from Mrs M. C. Cartwright, 1887
Hickin, George Arthur 1821–1885, *The Cottager's Home*, gift from Mrs M. C. Cartwright, 1887
Hickin, George Arthur 1821–1885, *Mountain Solitude, a Scene on the Conway*, gift from Mrs M. C. Cartwright, 1887
Hickin, George Arthur 1821–1885, *On the Conway*, gift from Mrs M. C. Cartwright, 1887
Highmore, Joseph 1692–1780, *The Family of E. Lancelot Lee*, purchased with the assistance of the Victoria & Albert Museum Purchase Grant Fund and the National Art Collections Fund, 1984
Highmore, Joseph 1692–1780, *Elizabeth Lee (1729–1786), Wife of William Waller*, purchased with the assistance of the Museums & Galleries Commission/Victoria & Albert Museum Purchase Grant Fund, the Pilgrim Trust and the Friends of Wolverhampton Art Gallery, 1995
Highmore, Joseph 1692–1780, *Isabella Lee and Her Grandson, William Waller*, purchased with the assistance of the Museums & Galleries Commission/Victoria & Albert Museum Purchase Grant Fund, the Pilgrim Trust and the Friends of Wolverhampton Art Gallery, 1995
Hill, Paul b.1959, *Bull Mastif*, purchased

Hill, Paul b.1959, *Four Rings*, purchased, 1997
Hill, Paul b.1959, *Don't Forget the Fish*, purchased
Hill, Thomas active 1878–1913, *The Village Cobbler*, gift from Mr Philip Horsman, 1886
Hillier, Tristram Paul 1905–1983, *Viseu, Portugal*, purchased with the assistance of the Victoria & Albert Museum Purchase Grant Fund, 1984, © the artist's estate
Hines, Theodore active 1876–1890, *Landscape with a Church in a Valley*, acquired, 1970
Hines, Theodore active 1876–1890, *Mountain Scene with Waterfall*, acquired, 1970
Hodges, William 1744–1797, *South-West Face of Chunargarh Fortress*, gift, 1937
Hodgson, John Evan 1831–1895, *A Philharmonic Rehearsal in a Farmhouse*, gift from Mrs M. C. Cartwright, 1887
Hodgson, John Evan 1831–1895, *Holbein's Studio*, gift, 1951
Hodgson, John Evan 1831–1895, *The Fruit Bearer*, gift from Mrs M. C. Cartwright, 1887
Hoggatt, William 1879–1961, *Morning, the Artist's Cottage*, purchased, 1943
Hondius, Abraham c.1625–1691, *A Boar Hunt*, gift, 1885
Hooper, John Horace c.1850–c.1899, *Close of a Rainy Day*, gift from Mr William Thompson, 1937
Horsley, John Calcott 1817–1903, *St Valentine's Morning*, gift from Mrs M. C. Cartwright, 1887
Horsley, John Calcott 1817–1903, *The World Forgetting, by the World Forgot (Sunday Afternoon in Kensington Gardens)*, gift from Mrs M. C. Cartwright, 1887
Horsley, John Calcott 1817–1903, *A Lady with a Mirror*, gift, 1998
Hosking, Knighton Stephen b.1944, *Himley Marker Series I*, purchased with the assistance of the Museums & Galleries Commission/Victoria & Albert Museum Purchase Grant Fund, 1986, © the artist
Hosking, Knighton Stephen b.1944, *Himley Marker Series II*, purchased with the assistance of the Museums & Galleries Commission/Victoria & Albert Museum Purchase Grant Fund, 1986, © the artist
Hosking, Knighton Stephen b.1944, *Himley Marker Series III*, purchased with the assistance of the Museums & Galleries Commission/Victoria & Albert Museum Purchase Grant Fund, 1986, © the artist
Hosking, Knighton Stephen b.1944, *Himley Marker Series IV*, purchased with the assistance of the Museums & Galleries Commission/Victoria & Albert Museum Purchase Grant Fund, 1986, © the artist
Howson, Peter b.1958, *Wolverhampton Dream*, purchased, 2000, © the artist
Huggins, William 1820–1884, *Cattle and Sheep*, gift, 1914
Huggins, William 1820–1884, *Three Cows in a Field*, gift, 1914
Hughes, Edward 1829–1908, *Meditation*, gift from Mrs M. C. Cartwright, 1887
Hulk, Johannes Frederik 1829–1911, *Rotterdam*, gift from Mrs M. C. Cartwright, 1887
Hulme, Frederick William 1816–1884, *A Warwickshire Landscape*, gift from Mrs M. C. Cartwright, 1887
Humphreys, David b.1937, *Be a Priest, Taste My Ashes*, purchased, 1990, © the artist
Humphreys, David b.1937, *Eight Figures*, purchased, 1988, © the artist
Humphreys, David b.1937, *Pelfe, Cosy to Asphyxiating*, purchased, 1983, © the artist
Hunt, Edgar 1876–1953, *Waiting to Be Fed*, gift from Mr William Thompson, 1937
Hunt, Walter 1861–1941, *The Donkey*, gift from Mrs Kate P. Bantock, 1950
Hunt, Walter 1861–1941, *A Girl with Two Calves*, gift from Mr William Thompson, 1937
Ibbetson, Julius Caesar 1759–1817, *Lakeside Landscape*, bequeathed by Mr Paul Lutz, 1899
Ibbetson, Julius Caesar 1759–1817, *The Watershot Wheel*, bequeathed by Mr Paul Lutz, 1899
Irvin, Albert b.1922, *Grey Streak*, gift from the Contemporary Art Society, 1964, © the artist
Italian School 17th C, *Samson and Delilah*, acquired, 1970
Italian School late 17th C, *The Judgement of Solomon*, gift from Mr Philip Horsman, 1886
Janssens, Abraham c.1575–1632, *Peace and Plenty*, purchased, 1885
Jantjes, Gavin b.1948, *No.6 from Korabra Series*, purchased with the assistance of the Museums & Galleries Commission/Victoria & Albert Museum Purchase Grant Fund, 1987, © the artist
Jantjes, Gavin b.1948, *No.6 from Korabra Series*, on loan from the artist, © the artist
Johnson, Charles Edward 1832–1913, *Mountain and Flood, Sgurr nan Gillean, Skye*, purchased, 1885
Johnson, Ernest Borough 1866–1949, *Sisters and Brothers*, gift, 1947
Johnson, Ernest Borough 1866–1949, *The Round Pond*, gift, 1947
Jones, Charles 1836–1902, *Autumn Afternoon, Loch Leven*, gift from Mr William Thompson, 1937
Jones, Charles 1836–1902, *Sheep*, gift from Mr William Thompson, 1937
Joseph, Ras Vince active 1980s, *Dread in Moonlight*, gift, 1988
Joseph, Ras Vince active 1980s, *Is Your Name Written There?*, purchased, 1988
Judkins, John b.1951, *Pop Star, '73*, gift from the Contemporary Art Society, 1975
Kauffmann, Angelica 1741–1807, *Decorative Panel*, purchased, 1941
Kauffmann, Angelica 1741–1807, *Penelope Weeping over the Bow of Ulysses*, gift from Mrs M. C. Cartwright, 1887
Keane, John b.1954, *Freedom of the Press*, purchased with the assistance of the Museums & Galleries Commission/Victoria & Albert Museum Purchase Grant Fund and the Contemporary Art Society Scheme, 1993, © the artist
Keeling, William Knight 1807–1886, *Love's Messenger*, gift from Mrs M. C. Cartwright, 1887
Keeling, William Knight 1807–1886, *The Wood Nymph*, gift from Mrs M. C. Cartwright, 1887
Keeling, William Knight 1807–1886, *The Introduction*, gift from Mrs M. C. Cartwright, 1887
Keeling, William Knight 1807–1886, *Midday Rest*, gift from Mrs M. C. Cartwright, 1887
Keeling, William Knight 1807–1886, *The Watering Place*, gift from Mrs M. C. Cartwright, 1887
Keeling, William Knight 1807–1886, *A Boy Selling Fruit*, gift from Mrs M. C. Cartwright, 1887
Keeling, William Knight 1807–1886, *A Scene from Shakespeare*, gift from Mrs M. C. Cartwright, 1887
Keeling, William Knight 1807–1886, *The Bird Scarer*, gift from Mrs M. C. Cartwright, 1887
Keeling, William Knight 1807–1886, *The Melon Seller*, gift from Mrs M. C. Cartwright, 1887
Keeling, William Knight 1807–1886, *The Rejected Appeal*, gift from Mrs M. C. Cartwright, 1887
Keeling, William Knight 1807–1886, *The Showman*, gift from Mrs M. C. Cartwright, 1887
Keeling, William Knight 1807–1886, *The Young Shrimpers*, gift from Mrs M. C. Cartwright, 1887
Kelly, Gerald Festus 1879–1972, *The Ilex Tree*, purchased, 1946
Kemm, Robert 1837–1895, *Spanish Gypsies*, gift, 1949
Kemm, Robert 1837–1895, *Spanish Ladies*, gift, 1949
Kemm, Robert 1837–1895, *The Beggars*, gift, 1949
Kettle, Rupert Alfred 1817–1894, *Near Abergwynant*, gift from Mr Philip Horsman, 1886
King, William Joseph 1857–after 1943, *Stormy Anglesea*, gift from Mr William Thompson, 1937
King, Yeend 1855–1924, *Courtship*, gift from Mr William Thompson, 1937
Knight, Laura 1877–1970, *Sundown*, purchased, 1947, © the estate of Dame Laura Knight 2007. All rights reserved, DACS
Knight, William Henry 1823–1863, *The Broken Window*, gift from Mrs M. C. Cartwright, 1887
Knight, William Henry 1823–1863, *Dinner Time*, gift from Mr Philip Horsman, 1886
Knight, William Henry 1823–1863, *Study for 'The Phrenologist'*, gift from Mrs M. C. Cartwright, 1887
Ladbrooke, Robert 1770–1842, *An Oak Glade*, gift from Mrs M. C. Cartwright, 1887
Landseer, Edwin Henry 1802–1873, *Sketch for 'Deer-Stalking in the Highlands'*, bequeathed by Mr Paul Lutz, 1899
Landseer, Edwin Henry 1802–1873, *Queen Victoria in Windsor Home Park*, gift from Mrs M. C. Cartwright, 1887
Landseer, Edwin Henry 1802–1873, *On the Downs*, gift from Mrs Kate P. Bantock, 1950
Langley, William active 1880–1920, *Mountain Stream in Wales*, acquired, 1970
Langton, John b.1932, *Debtors' Prison, York*, purchased, 1972, © the artist
Latham, John 1921–2006, *Troll Flower (from 'Review of Dictionary')*, gift, 2002
Latham, John 1921–2006, *Cosmic Blood*, gift, 2002
Layng, Mabel Frances 1881–1937, *The Holidaymakers*, gift, 1938
Le Jeune, Henry 1819–1904, *Scene from Shakespeare's 'A Midsummer Night's Dream'*, acquired, 1886
Le Jeune, Henry 1819–1904, *The Pilgrim*, gift from Mrs M. C. Cartwright, 1887
Leadbeater, Alexandra b.1956, *Bench*, gift from the Contemporary Art Society, 1983, © the artist
Leader, Benjamin Williams 1831–1923, *An Old Mill, near Worcester*, gift from Mrs M. C. Cartwright, 1887
Leader, Benjamin Williams 1831–1923, *On the Lledr, North Wales*, gift from Mr Philip Horsman, 1886
Leader, Benjamin Williams 1831–1923, *Summertime, a Stream, near Dolgellau*, gift from Mr Philip Horsman, 1886
Leader, Benjamin Williams 1831–1923, *Interlaken*, gift, 1949
Leader, Benjamin Williams 1831–1923, *Head of Ullswater, Summer*, purchased, 1989
Lee, Frederick Richard 1798–1879, *The Watering Place*, gift, 1886
Lee, Frederick Richard 1798–1879, *The Ferry Boat*, gift from Mrs M. C. Cartwright, 1887
Lee, Frederick Richard 1798–1879, *On the Trent*, gift from Mrs M. C. Cartwright, 1887
Lee, Frederick Richard 1798–1879, *Landscape with Sheep*, gift from Mrs M. C. Cartwright, 1887
Lee, Frederick Richard 1798–1879, *Near Oatlands*, gift from Mrs M. C. Cartwright, 1887
Leigh-Pemberton, John 1911–1997, *The Gallery Objects*, gift from Mr Gerald P. Mander, 1935
Lenfestey, Giffard Hocart 1872–1943, *Beach Scene*, gift, 1944
Lenfestey, Giffard Hocart 1872–1943, *Evening, the Stream*, gift from a private collection
Lenfestey, Giffard Hocart 1872–1943, *Girl with Two Cows*, gift, 1950
Lenfestey, Giffard Hocart 1872–1943, *Solemn Stillness*, gift, 1944
Leslie, Charles Robert 1794–1859, *Harriet Elizabeth Georgiana Leveson-Gower, Duchess of Sutherland in Her Coronation Robes*, gift from Mrs M. C. Cartwright, 1887
Lewis, Charles James 1830–1892, *Hurley Bridge (a backwater on the Thames)*, gift, 1949
Lichtenstein, Roy 1923–1997, *Purist Painting with Bottles*, purchased with the assistance of the Victoria & Albert Museum Purchase Grant Fund, 1979
Lidderdale, Charles Sillem 1831–1895, *Portrait Study*, gift, 1934
Lin, Richard b.1933, *Painted Relief*, gift, 1977
Linnell, James Thomas 1826–1905, *The Sheepfold, Morning in Autumn*, gift from Mrs M. C. Cartwright, 1887
Linnell, John 1792–1882, *My Garden at Redhill*, gift from Mrs M. C. Cartwright, 1887
Linnell, John 1792–1882, *Feeding the Chicks*, gift from Mrs M. C. Cartwright, 1887
Linnell, William 1826–1906, *Cornfield in Surrey*, gift from Mrs M. C. Cartwright, 1887
Linton, William 1791–1876, *Castle Campbell*, gift, 1884
Linton, William 1791–1876, *Delos, Greece*, gift, 1918
Linton, William 1791–1876, *Positano and the Gulf of Salerno*, gift, 1884
Linton, William 1791–1876, *The Albanian Mountains with Corfu in the Distance*, gift from Mrs M. C. Cartwright, 1887
Linton, William (circle of) 1791–1876, *Landscape with a Lake*, acquired, 1922
Lockley, Henry James active 1887–1920, *Mountain Rapids with River*
Lockley, Henry James active 1887–1920, *Mountain Stream with Bridge*, acquired, 1970
Lomas, John Lane active 1844–1884, *The Fortune Teller*
Loney, J. L. *Fishing Boats*, acquired, 1970
Long, Edwin 1829–1891, *Peter's Pence*, gift, 1886
Long, Edwin 1829–1891, *At Prayer*, gift from Mr Philip Horsman, 1886
Long, Edwin 1829–1891, *Girl with Bagpipes*, acquired, 1974
Lott, Frederick Tulley active 1852–1890, *Rue de la Grosse Horloge, Rouen*, gift from Mr William Thompson, 1937
Low, Diana 1911–1975, *Sir William Nicholson (1872–1949)*, gift from Mr Gerald P. Mander, 1936
Lowinsky, Thomas Esmond 1892–1947, *The Mask of Flora*, gift from the Contemporary Art Society, 1946
Lucas, Seymour 1849–1923, *'Down*

to the Dregs', gift from Mr Philip Horsman, 1886
Lucas, Seymour 1849–1923, *A Man with a Barge Pole (study for 'The Flight of the Five Members')*, gift from Mr Philip Horsman, 1886
Lucas, Seymour 1849–1923, *A Man Rowing (study for 'The Flight of the Five Members')*, gift, 1916
Lucas, Seymour 1849–1923, *A Woman with a Fan, Head of a Man (study for 'The Flight of the Five Members')*, gift, 1916
Lucas, Seymour 1849–1923, *Standing Man (study for 'The Flight of the Five Members')*, gift, 1916
Lucas, Seymour 1849–1923, *Two Standing Men (study for 'The Flight of the Five Members')*, gift, 1916
Lucas, Seymour 1849–1923, *The Flight of the Five Members*, gift
Luker, William c.1820–1892, *A Halt in the Desert*, gift from Mrs M. C. Cartwright, 1887
Lunn, Augustus 1905–1986, *Fish*, gift from the trustees of the artist, 1991
MacDonald, Bridget b.1943, *Family Group*, purchased, 1988, © the artist
Machell, Reginald 1854–1927, *Timidity*, acquired, 1970
MacIntyre, Joseph Wrightson 1842–1897, *Sheep Washing, Wellburn, Yorkshire*, acquired, 1970
Maclise, Daniel 1806–1870, *The Denial*, acquired, 1970
Maclise, Daniel 1806–1870, *The Pet Bird*, gift, 1886
Marks, Henry Stacey 1829–1898, *An Incredible Story*, gift from Mrs M. C. Cartwright, 1887
Marston, Reginald St Clair 1886–1943, *Autumn Morning*, purchased, 1935
Marston, Reginald St Clair 1886–1943, *Salisbury*, gift, 1949
Marston, Reginald St Clair 1886–1943, *Winchester*, acquired, 1974
Martin, Anson A. active 1840–1872, *A Sarabande*, gift from Mr William Thompson, 1937
Mayer, Karl 1810–1876, *Margaret Sparrow*, gift, 2000
McCallum, Hamilton 1841–1896, *Bell Trawlers Going out to Sea*, gift from Mr William Thompson, 1937
McFadyen, Jock b.1950, *After the Parade*, gift, 2000, © the artist
McFadyen, Jock b.1950, *Shankill*, purchased, 2000, © the artist
McFadyen, Jock b.1950, *Coventry Girl, Motorway Bridge*, purchased with the assistance of the Museums & Galleries Commission/Victoria & Albert Museum Purchase Grant Fund, 1988, © the artist
McFadyen, Jock b.1950, *Irish Gothic*, purchased with the assistance of the Museums & Galleries Commission/Victoria & Albert Museum Purchase Grant Fund and the National Art Collections Fund, 1996, © the artist
McFadyen, Jock b.1950, *A Tinge of Yellow*, gift, 2001, © the artist
McFadyen, Jock b.1950, *Prince of Orange*, gift, 2001, © the artist
McKee, Cormac active 1980s–1990, *Fill Aris (Full Circle)*, purchased from the artist, 1990
McNally-Hayes, Julie *Not Just a Girl Thing*, purchased, 1998
Meadows, James Edwin 1828–1888, *Going Home*, gift from Mr Philip Horsman, 1886
Meadows, James Edwin 1828–1888, *The Storm*, gift from Mr Philip Horsman, 1886
Meninsky, Bernard 1891–1950, *Still Life*, gift, © the artist's estate
Michie, James Coutts 1861–1919, *Autumn Landscape*, gift, 1924
Michie, James Coutts 1861–1919, *Winter Scene*, gift, 1924
Millar, James 1735–1805, *Allegory of Wisdom and Science (frontispiece for 'Encyclopaedia Brittannica')*, acquired, 1970
Monnington, Walter Thomas 1902–1976, *The Farmstead*, gift from the Contemporary Art Society, 1944, © the artist's estate
Montague, Alfred 1832–1883, *Coast of Holland*, gift from Mr William Thompson, 1937
Montague, Alfred 1832–1883, *Eton College from the River*
Montague, Alfred 1832–1883, *Landscape with a Ruined Castle*, gift from Mr Philip Horsman, 1886
Montague, Alfred 1832–1883, *On the Scheldt at Antwerp*, gift from Mr Philip Horsman, 1886
Moore, Henry 1831–1895, *Southborough Common, near Tunbridge Wells*, gift, 1885
Moore, Henry 1831–1895, *Winter Gale in the Channel*, gift, 1886
Moore, Henry 1831–1895, *A Choppy Day in the Channel*, gift from Mr William Thompson, 1937
Morgan, John 1823–1886, *The Bath*, gift from Mr Philip Horsman, 1886
Morland, George 1763–1804, *The Coming Storm, Isle of Wight*, gift from Mrs M. C. Cartwright, 1887
Morland, George 1763–1804, *Landscape (Storm Cloud)*, gift from Mrs M. C. Cartwright, 1887
Morris, John Charles active 1851–1889, *A Timber Wagon*, purchased, 1970
Morris, John Charles active 1851–1889, *Close of a Day's Sport*, gift from Mr William Thompson, 1937
Morris, Phillip Richard 1838–1902, *A Flaw in the Will*, gift, 1886
Morris, Phillip Richard 1838–1902, *The Breadwinner*, gift, 1885
Morris, Phillip Richard 1838–1902, *The Highland Laddies' Return*, gift, 1886
Müller, William James 1812–1845, *The Mouth of the Scheldt*, gift from Mrs M. C. Cartwright, 1887
Müller, William James 1812–1845, *A Lowering Day in Winter*, gift from Mr Philip Horsman, 1886
Müller, William James 1812–1845, *Head of a Zingari, Xanthus*, gift from Mrs M. C. Cartwright, 1887
Müller, William James 1812–1845, *Low Life*, gift from Mrs M. C. Cartwright, 1887
Müller, William James 1812–1845, *The Peak Cavern, Derbyshire, Peveril Castle*, gift from Mrs M. C. Cartwright, 1887
Mulready, William (attributed to) 1786–1863, *A Market Girl*, gift from Mrs M. C. Cartwright, 1887
Mulready, William (attributed to) 1786–1863, *Young Girl with a Kitten*, acquired, 1970
Munnings, Alfred James 1878–1959, *The Ford*, purchased, 1956, © the artist's estate
Nash, John Northcote 1893–1977, *The Farm Pond*, gift from the trustees of the artist, 1991, © artistic trustee of the estate of John Nash
Nash, Paul 1889–1946, *The Pond at Souldern*, purchased with the assistance of the Victoria & Albert Museum Purchase Grant Fund and the Paul Nash Trust, 1983, © Tate, London 2007
Nasmyth, Patrick 1787–1831, *View of Bristol*, gift from Mrs M. C. Cartwright, 1887
Nasmyth, Patrick 1787–1831, *Lake Scene with Boats and Figures*, purchased, 1941
Neeffs, Peeter the younger 1620–1675 or **Neeffs, Peeter the elder** c.1578–1656/1661 **(attributed to)** *At Worship*, gift from Mr Philip Horsman, 1886
Nicholls, Charles Wynne 1831–1903, *Queen Victoria and Her Family on Brighton Sands*, gift from Mr William Thompson, 1937
Nicholls, John *Wolverhampton Fair*, gift, 1977
Nicol, Erskine 1825–1904, *The Tale of an Irish Song*, bequeathed by Mr Paul Lutz, 1899
Niemann, Edmund John 1813–1876, *Black Castle, Wicklow*, gift from Mrs M. C. Cartwright, 1887
Niemann, Edmund John 1813–1876, *Landscape near Rochester*, gift from Mrs M. C. Cartwright, 1887
Niemann, Edmund John 1813–1876, *A Distant View of Lincoln*, gift from Mr Philip Horsman, 1886
Niemann, Edmund John 1813–1876, *On the Teme at Ludlow, Shropshire*, gift from Mrs M. C. Cartwright, 1887
Niemann, Edmund John 1813–1876, *Harrow from the Firs, Hampstead Heath*, gift, 1887
Niemann, Edmund John 1813–1876, *Cranbrook, Kent*, gift from Mrs M. C. Cartwright, 1887
Niemann, Edmund John 1813–1876, *Mountainous Landscape*, gift from Mrs M. C. Cartwright, 1887
Niemann, Edmund John 1813–1876, *On the East Coast*, gift from Mrs M. C. Cartwright, 1887
Niemann, Edmund John 1813–1876, *On the Eden near Carlisle*, gift from Mrs M. C. Cartwright, 1887
Ocean, Humphrey b.1951, *Lord Volvo and His Estate*, purchased with the assistance of the Museums & Galleries Commission/Victoria & Albert Museum Purchase Grant Fund and the Pilgrim Trust, 1996, © DACS 2007
O'Connor, James Arthur 1791–1841, *Landscape with Sheep*, gift from Mrs M. C. Cartwright, 1887
O'Connor, James Arthur 1791–1841, *Landscape with Sheep and a Horseman*, gift from Mrs M. C. Cartwright, 1887
O'Neil, Henry Nelson 1817–1880, *Tintoretto Painting His Dead Daughter*, gift from Mr Philip Horsman, 1886
O'Neil, Henry Nelson 1817–1880, *Queen Isabella and Columbus*, bequeathed by Mr Paul Lutz, 1899
O'Neill, George Bernard 1828–1917, *The Naughty Boy*, gift, 1887
O'Neill, George Bernard 1828–1917, *The Reproof*, gift from Mrs M. C. Cartwright, 1887
O'Neill, George Bernard 1828–1917, *Nestlings*, gift from Mrs M. C. Cartwright, 1887
O'Neill, George Bernard 1828–1917, *Not Forgotten*, gift from Mr Philip Horsman, 1886
O'Neill, George Bernard 1828–1917, *The Duet*, gift from Mr Philip Horsman, 1886
O'Neill, George Bernard 1828–1917, *'Cheer up!'*, gift, 1989
O'Neill, George Bernard 1828–1917, *The Despatch*, gift from Mrs M. C. Cartwright, 1887
O'Neill, George Bernard 1828–1917, *The Morning Walk*, gift from Mrs M. C. Cartwright, 1887
O'Neill, George Bernard 1828–1917, *The Surprise*, gift from Mrs M. C. Cartwright, 1887
O'Neill, George Bernard 1828–1917, *The Tête-à-Tête Tea*, gift from Mrs M. C. Cartwright, 1887
Orchardson, William Quiller 1832–1910, *The Story of a Life*, gift from Mrs M. C. Cartwright, 1887
Outlaw, Dorette active 1920–1940, *Self Portrait*, gift, 1992
Pacheco, Ana Maria b.1943, *Salome*, purchased with the assistance of the Museums & Galleries Commission/Victoria & Albert Museum Purchase Grant Fund, 1995, © Ana Maria Pacheco, courtesy of Pratt Contemporary Art
Page, Sarah active 1892–1935, *Andromeda*, gift from the artist, 1926
Page, Sarah active 1892–1935, *Whisper of Spring*, gift, 1977
Palmer, Eugene b.1955, *Duppy Shadow*, purchased with the assistance of the Museums & Galleries Commission/Victoria & Albert Museum Purchase Grant Fund, 1996
Parmar, Usha b.1968, *Heiroglyph Triptych (left)*, purchased, 1997, © the artist
Parmar, Usha b.1968, *Heiroglyph Triptych (centre)*, purchased, 1997, © the artist
Parmar, Usha b.1968, *Heiroglyph Triptych (right)*, purchased, 1997, © the artist
Peel, James 1811–1906, *Near Rosthwaite*, gift from Mr Philip Horsman, 1886
Pelham, Thomas Kent active 1860–1892, *An Egyptian Beauty*, gift from Mr William Thompson, 1937
Percy, Sidney Richard (circle of) 1821–1886, *View of Snowdon*, purchased, 1989
Perrault, Léon Bazile 1832–1908, *Widowed and Fatherless*, gift, 1900
Perry, Robert b.1944, *Blue Pickup, Brockmoor*, © the artist
Perry, Robert b.1944, *Transit, Wordsley*, purchased, 1989, © the artist
Perry, Robert b.1944, *Synthetic Chemicals Factory*, purchased, 1990, © the artist
Pettie, John 1839–1893, *An Arrest for Witchcraft in the Olden Time*, gift from Mrs M. C. Cartwright, 1887
Pettie, John 1839–1893, *Cleaned Out*, gift from Mr Philip Horsman, 1886
Pettie, John 1839–1893, *Mephistopheles*, gift from Mr William Thompson, 1937
Phillip, John 1817–1867, *The Recruit (sketch)*, gift from Mr Philip Horsman, 1886
Phillip, John 1817–1867, *A Lady Playing the Mandolin*, gift from Mrs M. C. Cartwright, 1887
Phillip, John 1817–1867, *La señorita, Cádiz*, gift from Mrs M. C. Cartwright, 1887
Phillip, John 1817–1867, *At the Opera*, gift from Mrs M. C. Cartwright, 1887
Phillip, John 1817–1867, *First Steps*, gift from Mr Philip Horsman, 1886
Phillips, Tom b.1937, *Art Gallery and Gardens, Wolverhampton (left panel)*, purchased with the assistance of the Victoria & Albert Museum Purchase Grant Fund, 1970, © DACS 2007
Phillips, Tom b.1937, *Art Gallery and Gardens, Wolverhampton (right panel)*, purchased with the assistance of the Victoria & Albert Museum Purchase Grant Fund, 1970, © DACS 2007
Phillips, Tony b.1952, *Life Trap*, © the artist
Phoenix, George 1863–1935, *Bridgnorth, Shropshire*, gift from the artist, 1922
Phoenix, George 1863–1935, *Corner of Cannock Chase*, gift from Mr William Thompson, 1937
Phoenix, George 1863–1935, *Grandmother's Wardrobe*, gift, 1922
Phoenix, George 1863–1935, *Philip Horsman, JP*, purchased, 1900
Phoenix, George 1863–1935, *Reverend C. Carter*, gift, 2000
Phoenix, George 1863–1935, *Self Portrait*, gift from the artist, 1922
Phoenix, George 1863–1935, *Sheep Washing*, gift from the artist, 1922
Phoenix, George 1863–1935, *The Hayfield*, gift, 1922

Phoenix, George 1863–1935, *The Old Hill, Tettenhall*, gift from the artist, 1922
Phoenix, George 1863–1935, *The Prodigal Son*, gift, 1936
Pickersgill, Frederick Richard 1820–1900, *The Artist's Son and Nurse*, gift from Mrs M. C. Cartwright, 1887
Piper, John 1903–1992, *Welsh Landscape*, gift from the trustees of the artist, 1991, © the artist's estate
Pitcher, Henrie active c.1880–1904, *Welshwoman*, gift from Mr William Thompson, 1937
Pitcher, Henrie active c.1880–1904, *Englishman*, gift from Mr William Thompson, 1937
Pitcher, Henrie active c.1880–1904, *Irishman*, gift from Mr William Thompson, 1937
Pitcher, Henrie active c.1880–1904, *Scotsman*, gift from Mr William Thompson, 1937
Poingdestre, Charles 1825–1905, *Anticoli Corrado on the Sabine Mountains*, gift from Mr William Thompson, 1937
Poole, Paul Falconer 1807–1879, *The Heath Belle*, bequeathed by Mr Paul Lutz, 1899
Poole, Paul Falconer 1807–1879, *Peasant Girl in Moorland*, gift, 1915
Poole, Paul Falconer 1807–1879, *The Gorse Gatherer, Child Crossing Mountain Stream*, gift, 1915
Poole, Paul Falconer 1807–1879, *The Beleaguered City*, gift, 1884
Powell, George *Fishing Smack Unloading*, gift from Mrs M. C. Cartwright, 1887
Powell, Michael James William b.1934, *Tip Cats*, purchased by the Friends of the Art Gallery, 1994, © Michael James William Powell
Poynter, Edward John 1836–1919, *The Champion Swimmer*, gift, 1919
Preece, Patricia 1894–1966, *The Visitor*, gift from the Contemporary Art Society, 1946, © 2007. All rights reserved, DACS
Pringle, William J. active c.1805–1860, *High Green, Wolverhampton*, gift, 1953
Pritchett, Edward active c.1828–1879, *The Doge's Palace, Venice*, gift from Mrs M. C. Cartwright, 1887
Provis, Alfred active 1843–1886, *A Woman Watching Chickens*, gift from Mr Philip Horsman, 1886
Provis, Alfred active 1843–1886, *Feeding Time*, gift from Mr Philip Horsman, 1886
Pyne, James Baker 1800–1870, *The Castle of Ischia and the Gulf Islands*, gift, 1886
Pyne, James Baker 1800–1870, *Windsor Castle, Morning*, gift from Mr Philip Horsman, 1886
Pyne, James Baker 1800–1870, *Evening, Arundel Castle, Sussex*, gift, 1920
Pyne, James Baker 1800–1870, *Windsor Castle*, bequeathed by Mr Paul Lutz, 1899
Quick, Richard active 1880–1889, *Shire Horse*, gift, 1994
Raeburn, Henry 1756–1823, *William Fairlie of Fairlie (1754–1825)*, purchased with the assistance of the Victoria & Albert Museum Purchase Grant Fund, 1973
Rayson, David b.1966, *Griffiths Drive*, purchased through the Contemporary Art Society Special Collections Scheme with funds from the Arts Council Lottery Fund, 2000, © the artist
Redfern, David b.1947, *Et in Arcadia, Bingo*, purchased with the assistance of the Victoria & Albert Museum Purchase Grant Fund, 1984, © the artist
Redgrave, Richard 1804–1888, *Babes in the Wood*, purchased from Mr Philip Horsman, 1886
Reinagle, Philip 1749–1833, *Landscape with Cows*, gift from Mrs M. C. Cartwright, 1887
Reinagle, Philip (circle of) 1749–1833, *River Scene with Figures*, gift, 1968
Rembrandt van Rijn (after) 1606–1669, *Mythological Scene*, gift from Mrs M. C. Cartwright, 1887
Reynolds, Alan b.1926, *Polyphonic Autumn*, gift from the trustees of the artist, 1991, © the artist
Rhodes, Bob b.1946, *July (from the 'Ironbridge' series)*, purchased with the assistance of the Museums & Galleries Commission/Victoria & Albert Museum Purchase Grant Fund, 1986
Rhodes, Bob b.1946, *Odeon*, gift, 1974
Rhys-James, Shani b.1953, *Stairs II*, purchased with the assistance of the Museums & Galleries Commission/Victoria & Albert Museum Purchase Grant Fund, 1999, © the artist
Ringeling, Hendrik 1812–1874, *Woman and Child*, gift from Mrs M. C. Cartwright, 1887
Rippingille, Edward Villiers 1798–1859, *The Fortune Teller*, gift from Mrs Kate P. Bantock, 1950
Roberts, David 1796–1864, *Interior of Cologne Cathedral, with a Funeral*, gift from Mr Philip Horsman, 1886
Roberts, David 1796–1864, *Ruins of the Roman Forum*, gift from Mrs M. C. Cartwright, 1887
Roberts, William Patrick 1895–1980, *Kit Roberts*, gift, 1959, © William Roberts Society
Ross, Arabella b.1959, *The March Hare*, purchased, 1988
Rubens, Peter Paul (after) 1577–1640, *The Meeting of Esau and Jacob*, gift from Mrs M. C. Cartwright, 1887
Rubens, Peter Paul (after) 1577–1640, *Virgin and Child*, acquired, 1900
Salt, John b.1937, *Pink Trailer with Plymouth*, purchased with the assistance of the Victoria & Albert Museum Purchase Grant Fund, 1975, © the artist
Sant, James 1820–1916, *Wild Flowers*, gift from Mr Philip Horsman, 1886
Satterthwaite, R. *Figure Study (front)*, purchased, 1997
Satterthwaite, R. *Figure Study (back)*, purchased, 1997
Scheffer, Ary 1795–1858, *The Vision, Dante and Beatrice*, gift, 1938
Shaillon, John *Carthorse Stallions*
Shayer, William 1788–1879, *Landscape*, purchased, 1954
Shayer, William 1788–1879, *Landscape with a Boy and Donkey*, bequeathed by Mr Paul Lutz, 1899
Shayer, William 1788–1879, *On the Beach at Portishead*, gift, 1945
Shayer, William 1788–1879, *The Gypsy Tent*, gift from Mr Philip Horsman, 1886
Shields, Frederick 1833–1911, *Stained Glass Design, Daniel*, gift from Frank Brangwyn, 1950
Shields, Frederick 1833–1911, *Stained Glass Design, David*, gift from Frank Brangwyn, 1950
Shields, Frederick 1833–1911, *Stained Glass Design, Elias*, gift from Frank Brangwyn, 1950
Shields, Frederick 1833–1911, *Stained Glass Design, Enoch*, gift from Frank Brangwyn, 1950
Shields, Frederick 1833–1911, *Stained Glass Design, Ezekiel*, gift from Frank Brangwyn, 1950
Shields, Frederick 1833–1911, *Stained Glass Design, Isaiah*, gift from Frank Brangwyn, 1950
Shields, Frederick 1833–1911, *Stained Glass Design, Jeremiah*, gift from Frank Brangwyn, 1950
Shields, Frederick 1833–1911, *Stained Glass Design, Joel*, gift from Frank Brangwyn, 1950
Shields, Frederick 1833–1911, *Stained Glass Design, Malachi*, gift from Frank Brangwyn, 1950
Shields, Frederick 1833–1911, *Stained Glass Design, Moses*, gift from Frank Brangwyn, 1950
Shields, Frederick 1833–1911, *Stained Glass Design, Noah*, gift from Frank Brangwyn, 1950
Shipham, Benjamin 1808–1872, *Abel Chetwynd's Gift*, gift from Mrs M. C. Cartwright, 1887
Shipham, Benjamin 1808–1872, *In Epping Forest*, gift from Mrs M. C. Cartwright, 1887
Shipham, Benjamin 1808–1872, *On the Trent*, gift from Mrs M. C. Cartwright, 1887
Simcock, Jack b.1929, *Snowscape with Cows and Figures*, acquired, 1965, © the artist
Simcock, Jack b.1929, *Bourne Street, Mow Cop*, gift, 1965, © the artist
Sinnott, Kevin b.1947, *Down to Earth*, gift, 1992
Smith, John Guthrie Spence 1880–1951, *Red Roofs*, gift, 2003
Sørensen, Carl Frederik 1818–1879, *Storm in the North Sea*, acquired, 1970
Speed, Harold 1872–1957, *Llyn Gwynant after Rain*, purchased, 1939
Spencer, Stanley 1891–1959, *Chestnuts*, purchased with the assistance of the Victoria & Albert Museum Purchase Grant Fund and the Friends of the Art Gallery, 1983, © estate of Stanley Spencer 2007. All rights reserved, DACS
Spender, John Humphrey 1910–2005, *Atomic Flower*, purchased with the assistance of the Museums & Galleries Commission/Victoria & Albert Museum Purchase Grant Fund, 1986, © the Humphrey Spender Archive
Stanfield, Clarkson 1793–1867, *Off Calais*, gift from Mrs M. C. Cartwright, 1887
Stanfield, George Clarkson 1828–1878, *Off the Dutch Coast*, gift from Mrs M. C. Cartwright, 1887
Stanford, Arthur *Mountain and Lake*, gift, 1915
Stark, James 1794–1859, *Cows at a Watering Place*, gift from Mr Philip Horsman, 1886
Stark, James 1794–1859, *Landscape with a Cottage*, gift from Mrs M. C. Cartwright, 1887
Stark, James 1794–1859, *Landscape with Figures at a Stream*, purchased, 1941
Steadman, J. T. active 1884–1911, *Councillor Craddock*
Steadman, J. T. active 1884–1911, *H. Beach*
Steadman, J. T. active 1884–1911, *W. Hughes*
Steele, Edwin 1837–1898, *Still Life, Flowers*
Steele, Edwin 1837–1898, *Still Life, Flowers and Fruit*
Stokes, Marianne 1855–1927, *Madonna and Child*, gift from Mr Gerald P. Mander, 1930
Stone, Frank 1800–1859, *Sympathy*, gift from Mrs M. C. Cartwright, 1887
Stone, Marcus C. 1840–1921, *A Pleasant Spot on the Thames*, gift from Mrs M. C. Cartwright, 1887
Strang, William 1859–1921, *John Masefield (1878–1967)*, gift, 1929
Strutt, Alfred William 1856–1924, *Materfamilias*, gift, 1884
Suberu, Ade *Mirror Image I*, purchased, 1992
Suddaby, Rowland 1912–1972, *Stour Valley, Suffolk*, © the artist's estate
Syer, John 1815–1885, *Country Landscape*, gift from Mr William Thompson, 1937
Symons, William Christian 1845–1911, *The White House, Battle, Sussex*, purchased, 1913
Tawson, Alex *On the Anglesey Coast*, purchased, 1982
Tempest, Victor 1913–2003, *Gardens in February*, purchased, 1947
Tenkate, Herman 1822–1891, *A Difference of Opinion as to a Treaty*, gift, 1886
Tennant, John F. 1796–1872, *Loading the Hay Wagon*, gift from Mrs M. C. Cartwright, 1887
Thors, Joseph c.1834–1898, *A Welsh Landscape*, gift from Mr Philip Horsman, 1886
Toft, J. Alfonso 1866–1964, *The Cornfield*, gift, 1964
Toft, J. Alfonso 1866–1964, *Windsor Castle*, gift, 1964
Tongue, Richard active 1835–1839, *Landscape*, gift, 1937
Towne, Charles 1781–1854, *A Tiger*, gift, 1914
Treister, Suzanne b.1958, *Entering the Kitchen*, purchased with the assistance of the Museums & Galleries Commission/Victoria & Albert Museum Purchase Grant Fund and the Contemporary Art Society Scheme, 1996, © the artist
Tunnard, John 1900–1971, *Pink Composition*, purchased with the assistance of the Museums & Galleries Commission/Victoria & Albert Museum Purchase Grant Fund, 1992
Turner, George II 1843–1910, *A Quiet Scene in South Derbyshire*, acquired, 1970
Turner, Harry M. 1912–1979, *Walsall Church*, gift, 1981
Twentyman, Anthony b.1906, *Equinox*, gift from the trustees of the artist, 1981
Twentyman, Anthony b.1906, *Marine Image*, gift from the trustees of the artist, 1990
Twentyman, Anthony b.1906, *Winter*, gift from the trustees of the artist, 1981
Twentyman, Anthony b.1906, *Spring*, gift from the trustees of the artist, 1981
Twentyman, Anthony b.1906, *Summer*, gift from the trustees of the artist, 1981
Twentyman, Anthony b.1906, *Autumn*, gift from the trustees of the artist, 1981
Twentyman, Richard 1903–1979, *Pigeon Loft, Sedgley*, gift from the trustees of the artist, 1980
Underhill, William active 1848–1871, *Alderman Albert Baldwin Bantock (1862–1938)*, transferred, 1950
Underhill, William active 1848–1871, *The Village School*, gift from Mrs M. C. Cartwright, 1887
unknown artist *Portrait of a Gentleman*, gift from Mrs M. C. Cartwright, 1887
unknown artist 18th C, *Italian Landscape*, purchased, 1941
unknown artist late 18th C, *The Card Sharper*, acquired, 1900
unknown artist *Portrait of a Lady*, gift, 1970
unknown artist 19th C, *Highland Landscape with Two Stags*
unknown artist 19th C, *Landscape with Sheep, Sea and Boats*
unknown artist 19th C, *Monk, St Bernard Dog and Men in a Storm*, acquired, 1974
unknown artist 19th C, *River Scene*, acquired, 1910
unknown artist 19th C, *Shipwreck*, acquired, 1970
unknown artist *Battle Scene*, gift, 1940
unknown artist *Benjamin Bantock*
unknown artist *Breton Woman and Child*, acquired, 1982

unknown artist *Brick Wall*
unknown artist *Edward Wooley*, purchased, 1959
unknown artist *Gentleman with a Book, possibly Johannes Utenbogaert (1557–1644)*, acquired, 1982
unknown artist *Holy Family*, gift from Mrs M. C. Cartwright, 1887
unknown artist *Italian Landscape with Lake*, acquired, 1982
unknown artist *Jeremiah Wynne, Mayor of Wolverhampton (1852–1853)*
unknown artist *John Wilkinson (1728–1808)*
unknown artist *Mother and Child*
unknown artist *Mr George Benjamin Thorneycroft (1791–1851), First Mayor of Wolverhampton (1848–1849)*, on display at Wolverhampton Civic Centre
unknown artist *Portrait of a Gentleman*
unknown artist *Portrait of a Gentleman with a Book*
unknown artist *Portrait of a Lady with a Fan*, acquired, 1982
unknown artist *Portrait of a Man with a Moustache*
unknown artist *Portrait of a Man with Glasses*
unknown artist *Portrait of an Unknown Gentleman*, gift, 1982
unknown artist *Still Life*, gift, 1914
unknown artist *Venetian Scene*, acquired, 1974
unknown artist *Venetian Scene*
Unwins, Thomas 1782–1857, *Neopolitan Peasants*, gift from Mrs M. C. Cartwright, 1887
Vale, Enid Marjorie b.1890, *The Mountain Barrier*, purchased, 1945
Vale, Enid Marjorie b.1890, *The Mountain Range*, acquired, 1974
Vernon, William H. 1820–1909, *Cottage and Mill Wheel*, gift, 1907
Vernon, William H. 1820–1909, *Lane at Bridgnorth*, gift, 1907
Vesely, Susan b.1953, *The Leprochaun Has Died*, purchased, 1990, © the artist
Vickers, Alfred 1786–1868, *South Coast, Isle of Wight*, bequeathed by Mr Paul Lutz, 1899
Vickers, Alfred 1786–1868, *In the Vale of Neath*
Vickers, Alfred 1786–1868, *The Old Mill, Bath*, gift from Mrs M. C. Cartwright, 1887
Vincent, George (attributed to) 1796–1831, *An English Farmstead*, gift from Mr Philip Horsman, 1886
Vinter, John Alfred 1818–1905, *The Miller's Daughter, from Tennyson*, gift from Mr Philip Horsman, 1886
Voltz, Friedrich 1817–1886, *A Good Day*, gift from Mr Philip Horsman, 1886
Wadsworth, Edward Alexander 1889–1949, *Ship Building*, purchased with the assistance of the Victoria & Albert Museum Purchase Grant Fund, 1984, © estate of Edward Wadsworth 2007. All rights reserved, DACS
Wagg, Jamie b.1958, *20/20*, gift, 2002
Walker, John b.1939, *Marriage of the Verbal and the Visual*, gift, 2002, © the artist
Walker, John b.1939, *Not for Sale*, gift, 2002, © the artist
Walker, Maggie active 1980–1988, *Suitcase*, purchased, 1988
Wallis, Alfred 1855–1942, *A Brig, Close to Shore*, purchased with the assistance of the Museums & Galleries Commission/Victoria & Albert Museum Purchase Grant Fund, 1992
Wallis, George 1811–1891, *The Fall of Napoleon*, gift, 1937
Wallis, George 1811–1891, *The Falls of Niagara*, gift, 1892
Wane, Richard 1852–1904, *The Incoming Tide*, gift, 1890
Ward, Amy Margaret b.1863, *Castle and Trees*
Ward, Frank Clifford 1914–1998, *Street Scene, Wolverhampton*, purchased, 1959
Ward, Frank Clifford 1914–1998, *Interior with Figures (Shakespeare)*, acquired, 1974
Ward, James 1769–1859, *Study of a Prize Bull*, gift from Mrs M. C. Cartwright, 1887
Ward, James (attributed to) 1769–1859, *Coast Scene*, gift from Mrs M. C. Cartwright, 1887
Watson, George Spencer 1869–1934, *The Creation*, purchased from the Friends of the Art Gallery, 1934
Watson, John Dawson 1832–1892, *'No rint'*, gift from Mr William Thompson, 1937
Webb, James c.1825–1895, *After the Wreck (On the French Coast)*, purchased, 1886
Webb, James c.1825–1895, *San Sebastian*, gift from Mr William Thompson, 1937
Webb, James c.1825–1895, *Boulogne*, gift from Mr William Thompson, 1937
Webb, James c.1825–1895, *Lowlands*, gift, 1910
Webb, James c.1825–1895, *Namur*, gift from Mr William Thompson, 1937
Webb, James c.1825–1895, *Spanish Harbour*, gift from Mr William Thompson, 1937
Webb, James c.1825–1895, *Tangiers*, gift from Mr William Thompson, 1937
Webster, Thomas George 1800–1886, *Sunday Afternoon*, bequeathed by Mr Paul Lutz, 1899
Weight, Carel Victor Morlais 1908–1997, *Essex Landscape*, gift from the Contemporary Art Society, 1954, © the estate of the artist
Welburn, Irene active 1936–1940, *Nurse Brown*, gift, 1968
Westall, Richard 1765–1836, *A Sunny Afternoon*, gift from Mrs M. C. Cartwright, 1887
Whaite, Henry Clarence 1828–1912, *Coast Scene*, gift, 1887
Wheatley, Francis 1747–1801, *Mrs Pearce*, purchased with the assistance of the Victoria & Albert Museum Purchase Grant Fund and the National Art Collections Fund, 1981
Wheatley, Francis 1747–1801, *Love and Charity*, purchased with the assistance of the Victoria & Albert Museum Purchase Grant Fund, 1972
Wheeler, Charles 1892–1974, *The Hollow in the Downs*, gift from the trustees of the A. B. Thompson Memorial Fund, 1958
Whiteford, Kate b.1952, *Pagan Painting I*, gift from the Contemporary Art Society, 1986
Whiting, Frederic 1874–1962, *The Morning Ride*, gift, 1935
Whittle, Florence *Somerset Village*, purchased, 1944
Whittle, Thomas active 1854–1896, *Landscape*
Wilkie, David (attributed to) 1785–1841, *The Scottish Market Place*, gift from Mrs M. C. Cartwright, 1887
Willets, Gavin *Canal Junction*, purchased, 1991
Williams, William 1808–1895, *Claverton Downs*, gift from Mr Philip Horsman, 1886
Williamson, Samuel 1792–1840, *Landscape with Cattle*, gift, 1914
Wilson, John Glen 1774–1855, *Approaching Storm, Entrance to the Firth of Forth*, gift, 1886
Wilson, John Glen 1774–1855, *Landscape with Figures*, gift from Mr Philip Horsman, 1886
Wilson, John Glen 1774–1855, *Wreck off Folkestone*, bequeathed by Mr Paul Lutz, 1899
Wilson, Richard 1752–1802, *Falls of Niagra*, gift, 1884
Wilson, Richard (circle of) 1752–1802, *Canal Scene*, gift from Mr Philip Horsman, 1886
Wimperis, Edmund Morison 1835–1900, *Farm near Brocklehurst*, gift, 1932
Witherington, William Frederick 1785–1865, *The Lesson*, gift from Mrs M. C. Cartwright, 1887
Wood, Christopher 1901–1930, *Still Life with Cards and Pipe*, gift from the trustees of the artist, 1991
Worsey, Thomas 1829–1875, *Still Life, Flowers*, gift from Mr William Thompson, 1937
Wouwerman, Philips (attributed to) 1619–1668, *Battle Scene*, gift from Mrs M. C. Cartwright, 1887
Wright, David b.1942, *Blackpool Pier*, purchased, 1961
Wright, John Michael 1617–1694, *Lady Mary Bagot and Granddaughter Mary, later Lady Parker*, gift from Mr Gerald P. Mander, 1950
Wright, Joseph of Derby 1734–1797, *Erasmus Darwin (1731–1802)*, purchased, 1972
Wright, Joseph of Derby (after) 1734–1797, *A Boy Blowing a Bladder in Candlelight*, gift, 1884
Wynfield, David Wilkie 1837–1887, *An Incident in the Life of Queen Elizabeth I*, gift, 1884
Yale, Brian b.1936, *Pandora's Box*, gift, 2001, © courtesy of the artist/www.bridgeman.co.uk
Yale, Brian b.1936, *Hand of Destiny No.1*, gift, 2001, © courtesy of the artist/www.bridgeman.co.uk
Yale, Brian b.1936, *Hand of Destiny No.2*, gift, 2001, © courtesy of the artist/www.bridgeman.co.uk
Yates, Thomas Brown b.1882, *From My Garden*, purchased, 1936
Yeames, William Frederick 1835–1918, *Amy Robsart (1532–1560)*, gift from Mrs M. C. Cartwright, 1887
Yeames, William Frederick 1835–1918, *Peace and War ('Here we go round the mulberry bush', from Besan and Rice's 'By Celia's Arbour')*, gift, 1886
Zoffany, Johann 1733–1810, *David Garrick as Sir John Brute in Vanbrugh's 'The Provoked Wife'*, purchased with the assistance of the Victoria & Albert Museum Purchase Grant Fund, 1976

Facing page: Spencer, Gilbert, 1893–1979, *Self Portrait* (detail), 1914, The Potteries Museum & Art Gallery (p. 156)

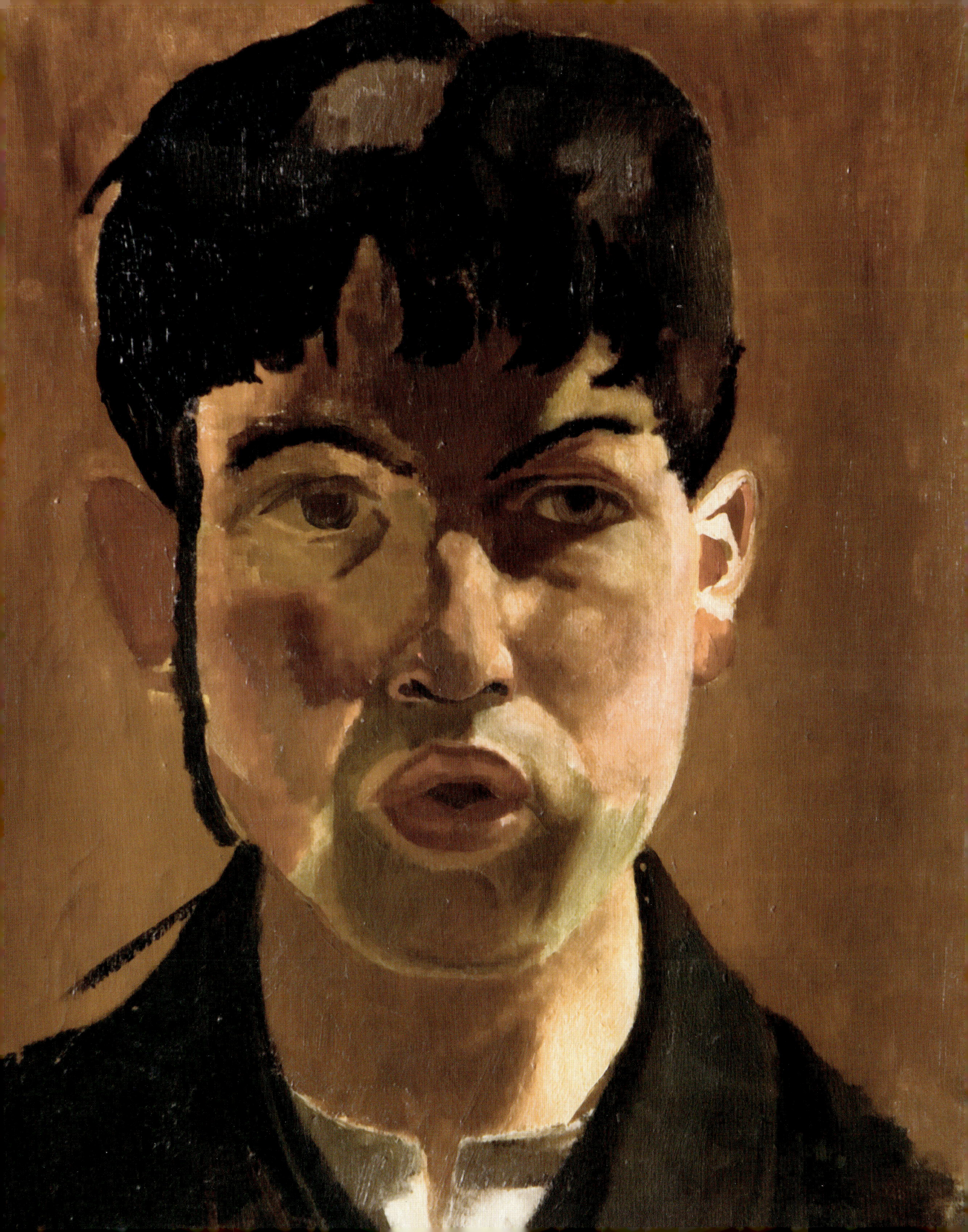

Collection Addresses

Biddulph

Biddulph Library
Tunstall Road, Biddulph ST8 6HH
Telephone 01782 512103

Burton-upon-Trent

East Staffordshire Borough Council:

Midland Grain Warehouse
Derby Street, Burton-upon-Trent DE14 2JJ
Telephone 01283 508000

The Brewhouse Arts Centre
Union Street, Burton-upon-Trent DE14 1EB
Telephone 01283 508350

Cannock

Museum of Cannock Chase
Valley Road, Hednesford, Cannock WS12 1TD
Telephone 01543 877666

Cheddleton

Churnet Valley Railway
Cheddleton Station, Station Road, Cheddleton ST13 7EE
Telephone 01538 360522

Ingestre

Ingestre Hall Residential Arts Centre
Ingestre ST18 0RF
Telephone 01889 270225

Leek

Leek Town Council
15 Stockwell Street, Leek ST13 6DH
Telephone 01538 381271

Staffordshire Moorlands District Council
Moorlands House, Stockwell Street, Leek ST13 6HQ
Telephone 01538 483483

Lichfield

Erasmus Darwin House
Beacon Street, Lichfield WS13 7AD
Telephone 01543 306260

Lichfield District Council:

Lichfield Cathedral
The Close, Lichfield WS13 7LD
Telephone 01543 306100

Lichfield District Council House
District Council House
Frog Lane, Lichfield WS13 6YY
Telephone 01543 308999

Lichfield Garrick Theatre
Castle Dyke, Lichfield WS13 6HR
Telephone 01543 308999

Lichfield Heritage Centre
Market Square, Lichfield WS13 6LG
Telephone 01543 256611

Samuel Johnson Birthplace Museum
Breadmarket Street, Lichfield WS13 6LG
Telephone 01543 264972

The Staffordshire Regiment Museum
Whittington Barracks, Lichfield WS14 9PY
Telephone 01543 434394

Newcastle-under-Lyme

Borough Museum & Art Gallery
Brampton Park, Newcastle-under-Lyme ST5 0QP
Telephone 01782 619705

Keele University
Keele, Newcastle-under-Lyme ST5 5BG
Telephone 01782 583376

Sandwell

Sandwell Metropolitan Borough Council:

Sandwell Metropolitan Borough Council
Sandwell Council House
Freeth Street, PO Box 2374, Oldbury B69 3DE
Telephone 0845 3597501

Tipton Carnegie Centre
Victoria Road, Tipton DY4 8SR
Telephone 0121 530 5258

Sandwell Museum Service Collection:

Sandwell Museum Service
Sandwell Metropolitan Borough Council
Cultural Services, PO Box 42
Environment House, Lombard Street
West Bromwich B70 8RU
Telephone 0121 569 8203

Bishop Asbury's Cottage
Newton Road, Great Barr B43 6HN
Telephone 0121 553 0759

Galton Valley Canal Heritage Centre
Brasshouse Lane, Smethwick B66 1BA
Telephone 0121 558 8195

Haden Hill House
Halesowen Road, Cradley Heath B64 7JU
Telephone 01384 569444

Oak House
Oak Road, West Bromwich B70 8HJ
Telephone 0121 553 0759

Sandwell Council House
Oldbury, West Midlands B69 3DE
Telephone 0845 358 2200

Tipton Heritage Centre
Tipton Library, Unit 19, Tipton Shopping Centre,
Owen Street, Tipton, West Midlands DY4 8QE
Telephone 0121 557 1796

Wednesbury Museum & Art Gallery
Holyhead Road, Wednesbury WS10 7DF
Telephone 0121 5560683

Stafford

Museum of the Staffordshire Yeomanry
The Ancient High House, Greengate Street
Stafford ST16 2JA
Telephone 01785 619131

Stafford Borough Council:

Stafford Borough Council Civic Centre
Civic Centre, Riverside, Stafford ST16 3AQ
Telephone 01785 619000

The Ancient High House
Greengate Street, Stafford ST16 2JA
Telephone 01785 619131

Staffordshire Arts and Museums Service:

Staffordshire Arts and Museums Service
Shugborough, Milford near Stafford ST17 0XB
Telephone 01889 881388

Staffordshire County Museum
Shugborough, Milford near Stafford ST17 0XB
Telephone 01889 881388

The Shire Hall Gallery
Market Square, Stafford ST16 2LD
Telephone 01785 278345

Staffordshire County Council
St Chad's Place
Stafford ST16 2LR
Telephone 01785 223121

Staffordshire Police Museum
c/o Staffordshire Arts and Museums Service
Staffordshire County Museum
Shugborough, Milford, Stafford ST17 0XB
Telephone 01889 881388

Stoke-on-Trent

Spode Museum Trust
Church Street, Stoke-on-Trent ST4 1BX
Telephone 01782 744011

The Potteries Museum & Art Gallery:

Hanley Town Hall
Albion Street, Hanley, Stoke-on-Trent ST1 1XP
Telephone 01782 235389

Stoke-on-Trent City Council
Civic Centre, Glebe Street
Stoke-on-Trent ST4 1RN
Telephone 01782 234567

The Potteries Museum & Art Gallery
Bethesda Street, Hanley
Stoke-on-Trent ST1 3DW
Telephone 01782 232323

Wedgwood Museum
Barlaston, Stoke-on-Trent ST12 9ES
Telephone 01782 282818

Tamworth

Tamworth Borough Council
Marmion House, Lichfield Street, Tamworth B79 7BZ
Telephone 01827 709709

Tamworth Castle
The Holloway, Tamworth B79 7NA
Telephone 01827 709629

Tutbury

Tutbury Museum Trust
Charity House, Duke Street, Tutbury
near Burton-upon-Trent DE13 9NE
Telephone 01283 814191

Uttoxeter

Uttoxeter Heritage Centre:

Uttoxeter Heritage Centre
34–36 Carter Street, Uttoxeter ST14 8EU
Telephone 01889 568426

Uttoxeter Town Council
Town Hall, High Street, Uttoxeter ST14 7HN
Telephone 01889 564085

Walsall

The New Art Gallery Walsall:

Aldridge Library
Rookery Lane, Aldridge, Walsall WS9 8NN
Telephone 01922 743601

Jerome K. Jerome Birthplace Museum
Belsize House, Bradford Street Walsall WS1 1PN
Telephone 01922 653116

The New Art Gallery Walsall
Gallery Square, Walsall WS2 8LG
Telephone 01922 654400

Walsall Metropolitan Borough Council
Civic Centre
The Civic Centre, Walsall WS1 1TP
Telephone 01922 650000

Walsall Register Office
Walsall Council, Civic Centre
Hatherton Road, Walsall WS1 1TN
Telephone 01922 652267

Wolverhampton

New Cross Hospital
Wednesfield Road, Wolverhampton WV10 0QP
Telephone 01902 307999

Wolverhampton Art Gallery:

Bantock House
Finchfield Road, Wolverhampton WV3 9LQ
Telephone 01902 552195

Wolverhampton Art Gallery
Lichfield Street, Wolverhampton WV1 1DU
Telephone 01902 552055

Wolverhampton City Council Civic Centre
Civic Centre, St Peter's Square
Wolverhampton WV1 1SH
Telephone 01902 551155

Wolverhampton Combined Court Centre
Pipers Row, Wolverhampton WV1 3LQ
Telephone 01902 481000

Index of Artists

In this catalogue, artists' names and the spelling of their names follow the preferred presentation of the name in the Getty Union List of Artist Names (ULAN) as of February 2004, if the artist is listed in ULAN.

The page numbers next to each artist's name below direct readers to paintings that are by the artist; are attributed to the artist; or, in a few cases, are more loosely related to the artist being, for example, 'after', 'the circle of' or copies of a painting by the artist. The precise relationship between the artist and the painting is listed in the catalogue.

Supporters of the Public Catalogue Foundation

Master Patrons

The Public Catalogue Foundation is greatly indebted to the following Master Patrons who have helped it in the past or are currently working with it to raise funds for the publication of their county catalogues. All of them have given freely of their time and have made an enormous contribution to the work of the Foundation.

Peter Andreae *(Hampshire)*
Sir Henry Aubrey-Fletcher, Bt, Lord Lieutenant of Buckinghamshire *(Berkshire and Buckinghamshire)*
Sir Nicholas Bacon, DL, High Sheriff of Norfolk *(Norfolk)*
Peter Bretherton *(West Yorkshire: Leeds)*
Richard Compton *(North Yorkshire)*
George Courtauld, DL, Vice Lord Lieutenant of Essex *(Essex)*
The Marquess of Downshire *(North Yorkshire)*
Jenny Farr, Vice Lord Lieutenant of Nottinghamshire *(Nottinghamshire)*
Mark Fisher, MP *(Staffordshire)*
Patricia Grayburn, MBE DL *(Surrey)*
The Lady Mary Holborow, Lord Lieutenant of Cornwall *(Cornwall)*
Tommy Jowitt *(West Yorkshire)*
Sir Michael Lickiss *(Cornwall)*
Lord Marlesford, DL *(Suffolk)*
The Most Hon. The Marquess of Salisbury, PC, DL *(Hertfordshire)*
Phyllida Stewart-Roberts, OBE, Lord Lieutenant of East Sussex *(East Sussex)*
Leslie Weller, DL *(West Sussex)*

Financial Support

The Public Catalogue Foundation is particularly grateful to the following organisations and individuals who have given it generous financial support since the project started in 2003.

National Sponsor

Christie's

Benefactors (£10,000–£50,000)

City of Bradford Metropolitan District Council
Deborah Loeb Brice Foundation
The Bulldog Trust
A. & S. Burton 1960 Charitable Trust
The John S. Cohen Foundation
Christie's
Mr Lloyd Dorfman
The Foyle Foundation
Hampshire County Council
Peter Harrison Foundation
Hiscox plc
ICAP plc
Kent County Council
The Linbury Trust
The Manifold Trust
Robert Warren Miller
The Monument Trust
Miles Morland
National Gallery Trust
Stavros S. Niarchos Foundation
Norfolk County Council
Provident Financial
P. F. Charitable Trust
The Pilgrim Trust
RAB Capital plc
Renaissance West Midlands
Saga Group Ltd
The Bernard Sunley Charitable Foundation
University College, London
University of Leeds
Garfield Weston Foundation

Series Patrons
(Minimum donation of £2,500)

Philip Athill
Harry Bott
Janey Buchan
Dr Peter Cannon-Brookes
Mrs Greta Fenston
Glasgow Museums
Patricia Grayburn, MBE DL
G. Laurence Harbottle
Paul & Fiona Hart
Paul & Kathrine Haworth
Neil Honebon
Michael Jacobson
The Keatley Trust
John Kendall, Esq.
Michael A. Lambert, CBE
David & Amanda Leathers
Richard & Amicia Oldfield
Miles Morland
Adam Sedgwick
Sir Harry & Lady Soloman
Stuart M. Southall
University of Surrey
Chloe Teacher
David & Cissy Walker
Ken Willis
Mr & Mrs Jo Windsor
Mr & Mrs Charles Wyvill

Catalogue Patrons
(£1,000–£10,000)

ACE Study Tours
Adams & Remers
Marcus & Kate Agius
The AIM Foundation
John Alston, CBE
Amberley Castle
Chairman of Cornwall County Council, Mrs Doris Anson, OBE JP
Archant Ltd
G. F. Armitage Family Charitable Trust
Mr Ian Askew
Aurelius Charitable Trust
The Bacon Charitable Trust
Basingstoke and Deane Borough Council
Barlow Robbins LLP
Mr James & Lady Emma Barnard
Sir Christopher Bland
The Charlotte Bonham-Carter Charitable Trust
H. R. Pratt Boorman Family Foundation
The Bowerman Charitable Trust
Viscountess Boyd Charitable Trust
Bramdean Asset Management LLP
Peter Bretherton
Mrs T. Brotherton-Ratcliffe
Mr & Mrs Patrick Burgess
Mr & Mrs Mark Burrell
Arnold J. Burton Charitable Trust
C. J. R. & Mrs C. L. Calderwood
Chichester District Council
The Timothy Colman Charitable Trust
Cornwall County Council
Mr S. J. D. Corsan
Graeme Cottam & Gloriana Marks de Chabris
Coutts Charitable Trust
Elaine Craven, Earl Street Employment Consultants Ltd
Harriett Cullen
Mr Robert Dean
Deborah Gage (Works of Art) Ltd
De La Rue Charitable Trust
The Duke of Devonshire's Charitable Trust
Sir Harry Djanogly, CBE
Professor Patrick & Dr Grace Dowling
Marquess of Douro
East Sussex County Council
Eastbourne Borough Council
EEMLAC, through the Association for Suffolk Museums
Lord & Lady Egremont
Sir John & Lady Elliott
Andrew & Lucy Ellis
Essex County Council
Marc Fitch Fund
Elizabeth & Val Fleming
The Friends of Historic Essex
The Friends of the Royal Pavilion, Art Gallery & Museums, Brighton
The Friends of Southampton's Museums, Archives and Galleries
The Friends of York Art Gallery (E. J. Swift Bequest)
Christopher & Catherine Foyle
Lewis & Jacqueline Golden
Gorringes
Charles Gregson
The Gulland Family

David Gurney
Philip Gwyn
The Hartnett Charitable Trust
Hazlitt, Gooden & Fox Ltd
Heartwood Wealth Management Ltd
Lady Hind Trust
Hobart Charitable Trust
David & Prue Hopkinson
Isle of Wight Council
The J. and S. B. Charitable Trust
Alan and Penny Jerome
Tommy Jowitt
The Keatley Trust
Kent Messenger Group
Garrett Kirk, Jr
Lord Lea of Crondall OBE
The Leche Trust
Leeds Art Collections Fund
Leeds City Council
Leeds Philosophical and Literary Society
Tom Lugg & the Lane Family
Mark & Sophie Lewisohn
Maidstone Borough Council
The Marlay Group
The Piet Mendels Foundation
The Mercers' Company
MLA East of England
Mr. Paul Myners
Rupert Nabarro
Newcastle City Council
Oakmoor Trust
The Orr Mackintosh Foundation
Sir Idris Pearce
The Pennycress Trust
Portsmouth City Council
Mr John Rank
Rathbone Investment Management Ltd
The Hans and Märit Rausing Charitable Trust
Roger & Jane Reed
Renaissance North East
Renaissance South East
Renaissance South West
Michael Renshall, CBE MA FCA
Sir Miles & Lady Rivett-Carnac
Rothschild Foundation
Royal Cornwall Museum
Russell New
Scarfe Charitable Trust
Shaftesbury PLC
The Shears Foundation
Smith & Williamson
South West of England Regional Development Agency
Caroline M. Southall
Stuart M. Southall
Southampton City Council
Mrs Andrew Stewart-Roberts, OBE
Mr Peter Stormonth Darling
Strutt and Parker
Suffolk County Council, through the Association for Suffolk Museums
Surrey County Council
The John Swire 1989 Charitable Trust
The Tanner Trust
The Thistle Trust
Trusthouse Charitable Foundation
University College Falmouth
University of Essex
The Walland Trust Fund
John Wates Charitable Trust
Leslie Weller, DL
West Sussex County Council
Wilkin & Sons Ltd
Peter Wolton Charitable Trust
Michael J. Woodhall, FRICS